HAROLD MACMILLAN: WAR DIARIES

other books by Harold Macmillan

Winds of Change 1914–1939
The Blast of War 1939–1945
Tides of Fortune 1945–1955
Riding the Storm 1956–1959
Pointing the Way 1959–1961
At the End of the Day 1961–1963
The Past Masters

War Diaries

POLITICS AND WAR IN THE MEDITERRANEAN

January 1943–May 1945

HAROLD MACMILLAN

MACMILLAN

ISBN 0 333 37198 4

First published 1984 by
Macmillan London Limited
London and Basingstoke

Associated companies in Auckland, Dallas,
Delhi, Dublin, Hong Kong, Johannesburg,
Lagos, Manzini, Melbourne, Nairobi,
NewYork, Singapore, Tokyo, Washington
and Zaria

Phototypeset by Wyvern Typesetting Limited, Bristol
Printed in Hong Kong

TO
THE MEMORY OF
John Wyndham

TO

THE MEMORY OF

John Wyndham

List of Illustrations

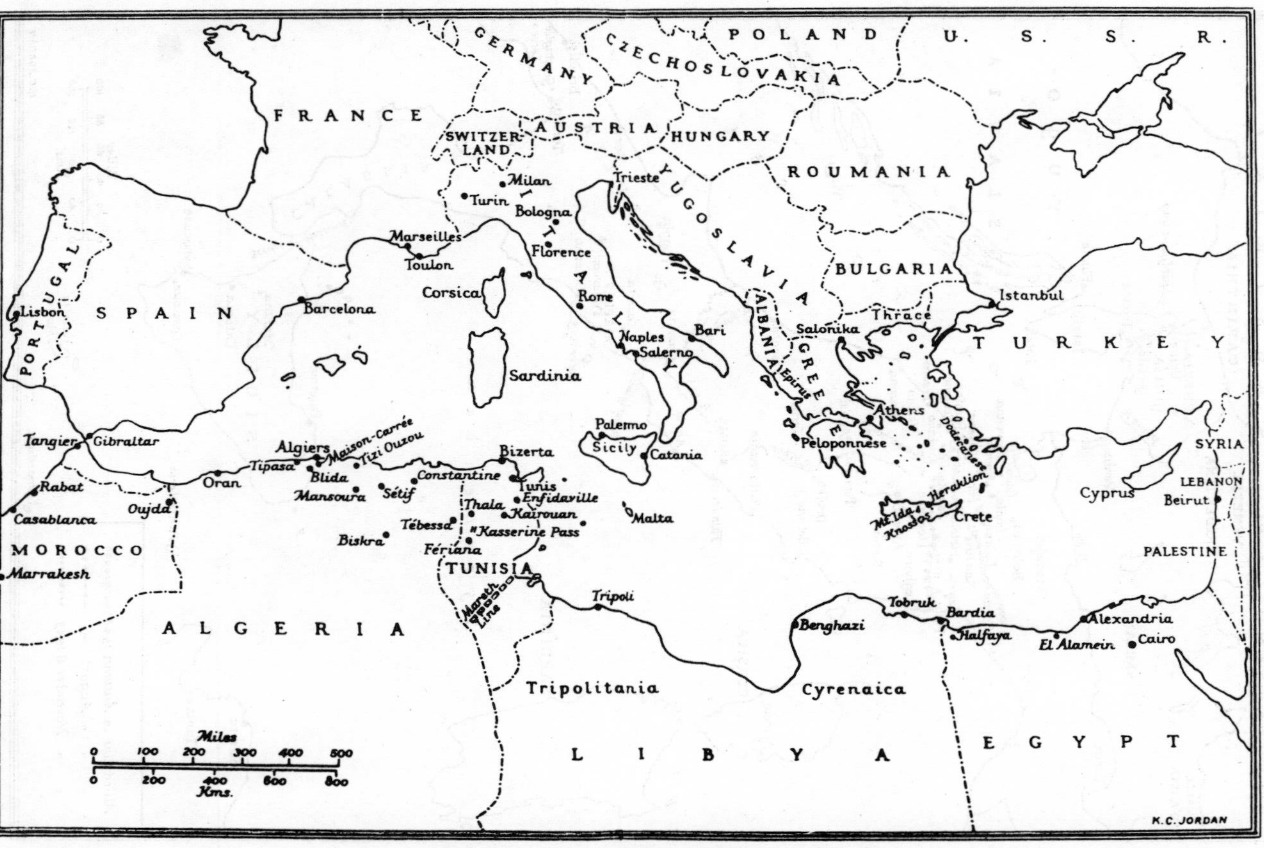

North Africa and the Mediterranean

SWITZERLAND
AUSTRIA
VENEZIA TRIDENTINA
CARINTHIA
VALLE D'AOSTA
VENEZIA GIULIA
Udine
Ljubljana Gap
Gorizia
Isonzo R.
Piave R.
Trieste
MILAN
Venice
Turin
R. Po
Istria
Fiume
YUGOSLAVIA
Modena
Pola
Quarnarolo Is.
Genoa
Bologna
Lugo
Ravenna
Imola
Faenza
La Spezia
Loiano
Forli
Cesena
APENNINES
Futa Pass
Rimini
Lucca
Pistoia
Riccione
San Marino
Pisa
R. Arno
Coriano
Pesaro
Florence
Urbino
Leghorn
Marecchia R.
Ancona
Arezzo
Siena
ADRIATIC SEA
Perugia
Assisi
Vis
Orvieto
L. Bolsena
R. Tiber
Terni
Ajaccio
CORSICA
Pescara
Civitavecchia
R. Sangro
ROME
Fiumicino
R. Liri
Anzio
Cassino
Foggia
APULIA
Caserta
Bari
R. Garigliano
NAPLES
Vesuvius
Sorrento
Salerno
Brindisi
Taranto
Grottaglie
Lecce
SARDINIA
Tyrrhenian Sea
CALABRIA
Strait of Messina
Palermo
Mt. Etna
SICILY
Catania
Bizerta
Tunis
Pantelleria
Syracuse
Cassibile
Valletta
Malta
Lampedusa
Allied Line in Autumn 1944
" " " August "
" " November 6 1943
Miles
0 20 40 60 80 100
0 40 80 120 160
Kms.
K.C. JORDAN

Italy

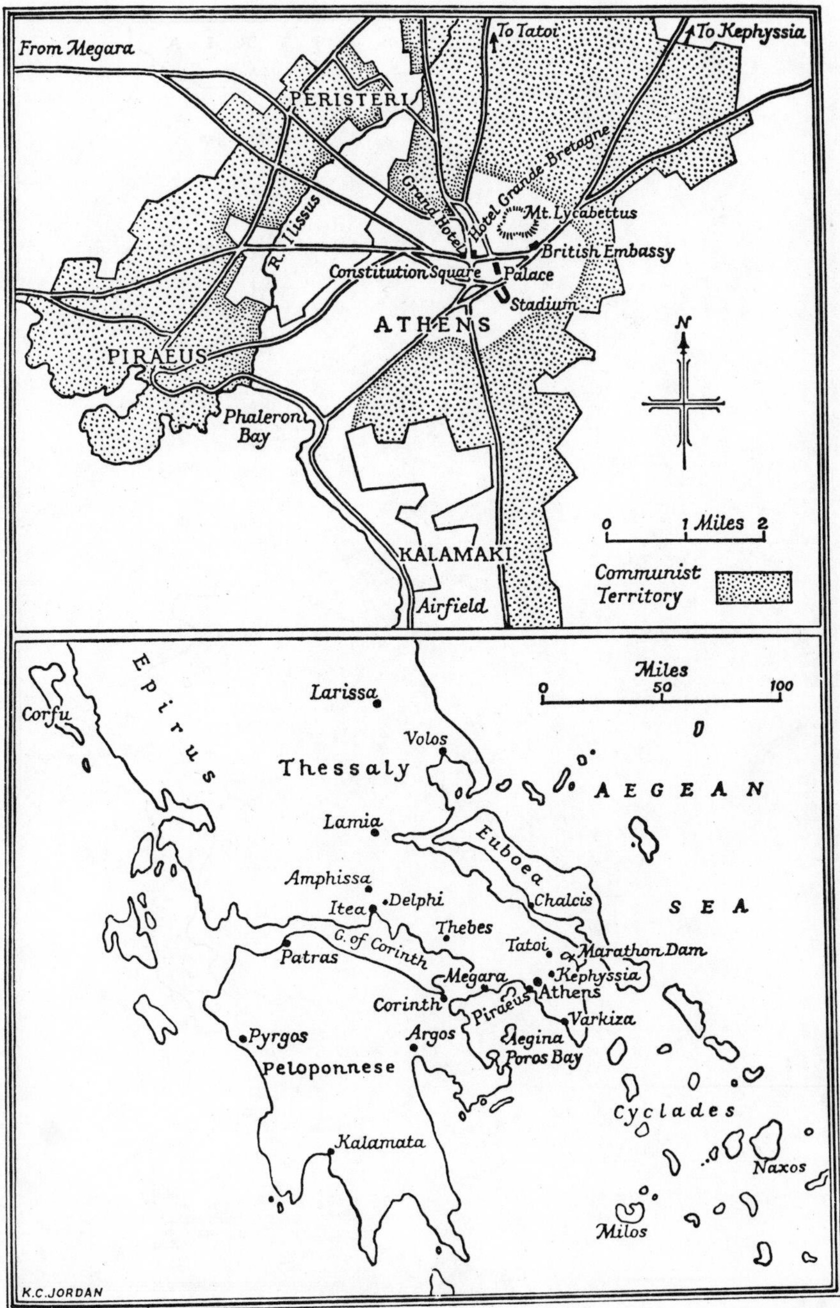

Athens and Greece

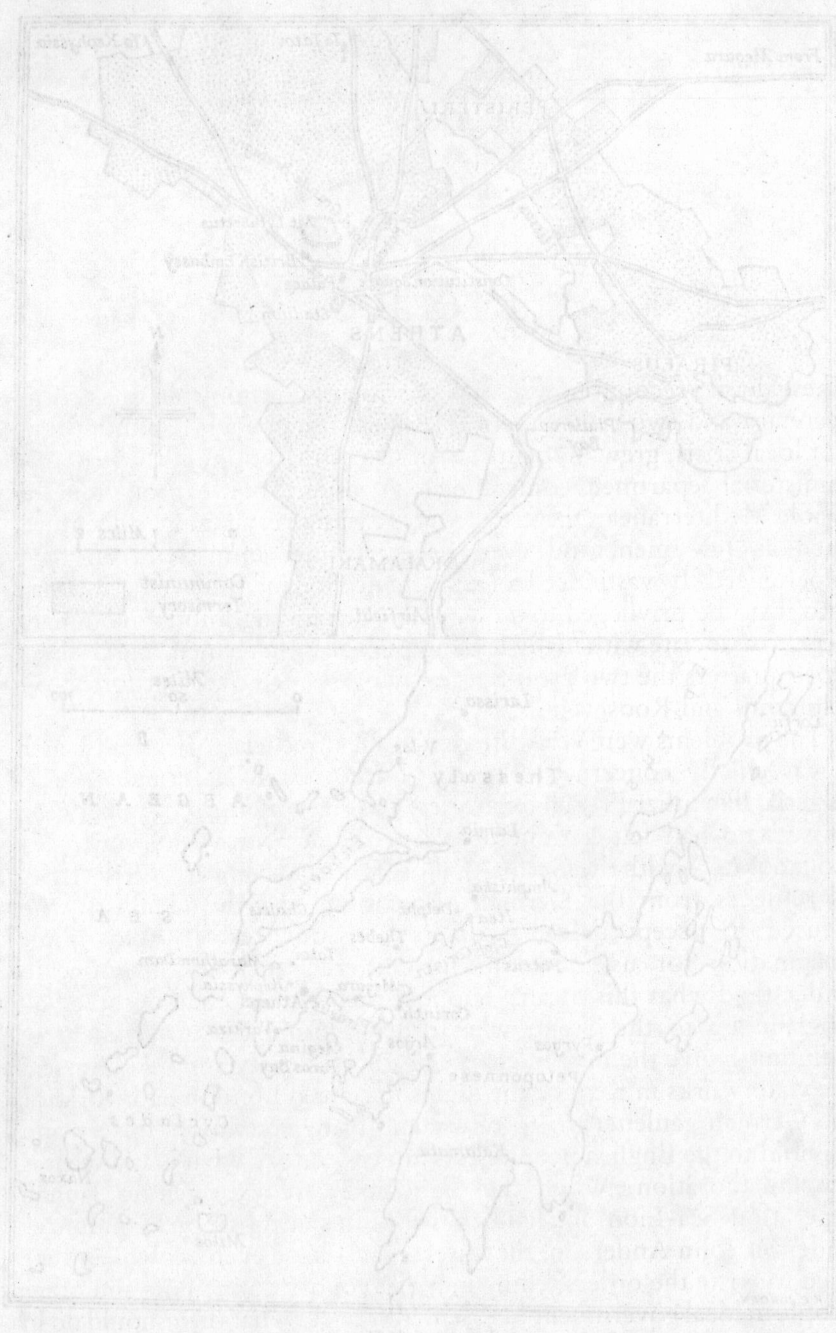

Preface

These diaries recount how a small mission of one minister, one private secretary and two typists, sent to Algiers to cope with an immediate but local crisis, grew, not entirely of its own volition, into a full-scale ministerial department controlling many aspects of life throughout the whole Mediterranean theatre of war. It was a very strange adventure, such as few men, and even fewer cabinet ministers, can have experienced. It was indeed a lucky chance for me to have been thrust into it, to be privileged to work with outstanding military commanders, to associate with many leading European statesmen, and to see at close quarters the two great figures who presided over our fortunes – Churchill and Roosevelt.

The problems were very different in the three territories with which I was chiefly concerned: French North Africa, Italy and Greece. Algeria, like other French territories, was riven by the schism between those who had felt it right to accept the armistice and work – or 'collaborate' – with the Germans, those who had come to North Africa as refugees from the German occupation, and the Gaullists who refused to accept defeat – or its consequences. It needs some imagination for us, never having suffered such an invasion, to understand what this means. Suppose the Germans had occupied all England up to the Trent, what orders should the government in Edinburgh give the man in charge of the electricity supply in Sussex, the waterworks in Kent or the drains in central London – to work for the German gauleiter, or to refuse and bring starvation, misery and typhoid to the English people? It is not easy to say what is and what is not collaboration. When the Germans were expected to launch Operation 'Sea-Lion' and land on the south coast, I sat on a committee under Sir John Anderson, the wisest man I have ever known, and we tried to write the orders telling mayors, county councillors and other people in local government or essential services what they should do in case of invasion. After about a week's work we gave it up. It was impossible. Any orders would appear to be purely collaborationist – or else purely anarchical.

As soon as I arrived in Algiers I began to realise that the problems presented to us were far more complex than they had seemed at home. The British people regarded Operation 'Torch', the Anglo-American expedition to North Africa, as largely for the purpose of liberating French people under Hitler's rule and re-establishing free and democratic government. But its real purpose was to set up a base from which our armies, having just landed, could move towards the British Army under Alexander and Montgomery, coming from Cairo, so that they could make a juncture at Tunis or Bizerta and then sweep all the German forces out of North Africa. This was a difficult operation because the lines of communication were so long. The main American base was at Casablanca, some eight hundred miles west of the headquarters at Algiers. The troops of the First (British) Army and the Americans fighting with them were spread out to the east, through four hundred miles of very difficult country, where the lines of communication ran through mountain tunnels and over culverts and bridges that provided an easy target for irregular forces raised from the already discontented North African population. It was therefore very important to maintain in power the great French colonial system to keep order throughout the country, even if this meant confirming in power, at least for the time being, governors who were thought to be Vichyites. Only slowly, after the union between Vichyites and Gaullists became firmer, and de Gaulle began to take over the reins, could we afford to remove these governors and trust to the firm and efficient basis of the French colonial system.

Meanwhile I had to meet a press in Algiers which was chiefly concerned with such things as the Pétainist and even Nazi laws which had been introduced, especially against the Jews. It was a difficult balance, but I decided that the campaign must take first place. We would do all we could to heal the wounds of the French schism between the Gaullists and the Giraudists and to remove legislation obnoxious to all liberal-minded people, but above all we must support General Eisenhower and his forces. And we did so not for a matter of weeks, but of months, before the battle of Tunis ensured complete victory.

The problem in Italy was quite different. Nobody there could be found who had served Mussolini, nobody admitted to having been a Fascist; and yet it was equally difficult to find anyone who was an active anti-Fascist. With the universal charm of that people they accepted the invaders, sometimes with delight and sometimes with resignation. Whatever we were, we were a new *combinazione*, and there was no question of anything but working with us. A few people we found who had outlived the twenty years of Mussolini's rule. They were very old, nearly eighty, politicians of the cabinet he had replaced, intellectuals, a philosopher or two, such as Benedetto Croce, but they were not the stuff of which to make useful executive officers to govern those parts of Italy which we gradually conquered. On the other hand, the official machinery of Allied Military Government seemed to be far too unwieldy, and when I became head of the Allied Control Commission I soon found myself removing superfluous British and American officers and giving more and more authority to any Italians who could be found to exercise it.

In Greece I found something that I had hardly realised the existence of before: the bitter animosities, lasting for generations, which divided the political world, the *politikos kosmos*, as it was called. Ever since the First World War the battle between the King and Venizelos had raged. The two parties, the Venizelist – or Liberal – party and the Royalist party were both essentially bourgeois; on the whole the Royalists commanded the support of the peasants, the Venizelists that of the towns. It was a situation not dissimilar to the normal division in British politics in the middle of the last century. But the hatreds and the animosities were undying. When the political situation became intolerable a 'tyrant', in the true Greek sense of the word, was appointed. Often he would govern better than anybody else, improve the economic situation, build roads, and so on – and then, of course, be overthrown. So the cycle began again: democracy, the breakdown of democracy; liberalism, the breakdown of liberalism; coalition; the breakdown of coalition; and then another tyrant. The Greeks seemed determined to stick to the Aristotelian cycle.

When we arrived the King was in exile, having left when the Germans occupied the country, and there was still great hostility to him and his brother, as well as a strong feeling among the Venizelists that they should take power. While this argument continued, it looked as if a quite new force might take over – the democratic resistance movement, ELAS, which had been operating in the hills supported by British supplies and money. It soon formed itself into an irregular army, better armed, better trained, more determined than any of the other, unorganised, Greek forces. We therefore had first to fight a battle to restore to the Greek people the opportunity to make their own decisions. That was the story of the Greek rebellion.

I was often asked why, in the absence of the King or any alternative recognised head of government, I had recommended Archbishop Damaskinos as Regent. It was simple. Two bourgeois – or respectable – parties were at loggerheads. One wished to abolish the monarchy, the other to retain it. I thought that with this very popular archbishop as Regent we might manage to combine the two forces and preserve the principles of Royalty without having a King.

I have already described these thirty months in *The Blast of War*, in which I have frequently quoted from the text of the Diaries. But here, on reading the Diaries as I wrote them, the reader will find something different. In my autobiography I tried to provide an orderly exposition of the great political and military issues and a chronicle of the events as they occurred. Passages of relevance to these issues were selected to illustrate the particular theme upon which I was writing, the French schism, the Italian surrender, the Greek rebellion, and so on. Each crisis was described in its turn. But the Diaries reveal that these events did not happen in an orderly sequence. All too often several crises were going on at the same time, and I was having to make continual journeys, from Algiers to Brindisi, later Caserta or Naples or Rome, and then to Athens. Indeed at one time I was almost commuting between Italy and Greece. Fortunately by then I no longer had to suffer the excruciating discomfort of much of the air travel of that time, having been given an aeroplane of my own by an American general.

The Diaries were written on odd pieces of paper, notepaper or scribbling paper, whatever was available, in aeroplanes, in waiting rooms, in my own bedroom at night, and occasionally in tents, caravans or huts where I was a guest of one of the commanders. They are necessarily somewhat confused and repetitive. They began as letters to my wife, but soon became a regular daily journal, which I continued to write even when she was able to come out and visit me. I used to send them home to her in the diplomatic bag every two or three weeks, whenever one was available. She preserved them carefully. They were copied out, so far as the typist could read my handwriting. Mistakes, mainly in the names of people and places, have been corrected wherever they have been noticed, but I am conscious that a number must still remain. Otherwise the Diaries are printed as written, with nothing omitted apart from some gratuitous repetitions, some family matters that would be largely incomprehensible to the general reader, and a very few remarks that might cause needless pain to living people. Nothing whatever of historical relevance to the military or political scene has been altered or omitted from the Diaries. Meanwhile the complete archive remains under the scrutiny of my official biographer, Mr Alistair Horne.

There have, on the other hand, been a number of additions. For instance, sometimes, rather than transcribe the record of a conversation, perhaps with General de Gaulle or some other leader, into the text of my diary, I merely sent home a copy of the record itself, which I had made for my own benefit, in order to send back to the Foreign Office. A selection from the more interesting documents of this kind has been included. There were also occasions, such as during the preparations for the invasion of Sicily or the first Italian approaches for an armistice, when events were too sensitive and secret for me to mention them in the Diaries; I therefore wrote up a fuller account of the episode when it was all over. These too have been drawn upon to augment the narrative. A few explanatory insertions have been added together with a number of footnotes. I am grateful to Mr Peter James for compiling the material for the latter.

I hope that this more informal account of the actual life of our small mission, where high drama alternated with lighter moments, and tedium and austerity with action and excitement, may prove entertaining as well as providing material for the historian.

The campaigns and the political issues of forty years ago are now a matter for historians, and history will not forget them. But the details of the lives that we, the participants, led are already almost forgotten, and may for that reason be of interest to the reader today.

Introduction

In the autumn of 1942 the Allies began their campaign to clear the Axis forces out of the whole of North Africa. In Egypt the battle of El Alamein was won by 3 November, and Montgomery's forces were ready to pursue the enemy out of Egypt and attack their main base in the Italian colony of Libya. Further west lay Tunisia, Algeria and French Morocco, all of which were under the suzerainty of Vichy France.

It was to occupy these French territories that Operation 'Torch' was mounted. While British and Commonwealth troops had fought and won in the Western Desert, the new assault was to be a joint operation under the command of an American general, Eisenhower, and supported by the American marines. Britain had broken with Vichy France in 1940, but the United States had retained an ambassador there, in the person of Admiral Leahy, a close friend of President Roosevelt, and a man who, though unable to converse in intelligible French, was believed by his countrymen to be a supreme exponent of the French mentality. American businessmen had been active in French North Africa, and America still believed that she was beloved by the French while Britain was not.

There were therefore some grounds for hoping that the French forces and administration in North Africa might be persuaded not only to acquiesce in our landings, but actively to co-operate with our armies. It was a vital part of Allied policy to rally to our side as much of the French empire, and of the French fighting forces as we could. At the fall of France General de Gaulle had established the Free French Forces in London, and kept the flame of French resistance alive. Much of the French overseas empire had rallied to him, but the attempt by British and Free French Forces to take over the important West African base of Dakar had been a disaster, with Frenchmen fighting against Frenchmen. Our experience in Syria, which was then a French Mandate, had been somewhat similar. The French Vice-President and Foreign Minister, Admiral Darlan, had readily acquiesced when German and Italian Air Forces had set up bases there, and British and

Free French forces were obliged to take over the country – but not without bitter resistance on the part of the Vichy French. With these unhappy experiences in mind, and with their predisposition, or even prejudice, in favour of the Vichy French, the Americans were determined that de Gaulle and the Free French should have no part in Operation 'Torch' or even be told of it beforehand. With these wishes Churchill perforce complied.

But if the French rulers of North Africa were not to accept de Gaulle as their lawful authority – whom would they accept? Here it is necessary to understand something of the mentality of the officers of the French Army. Unlike Britain, where the authority of the Crown has been virtually unquestioned since the Glorious Revolution of 1688, France has had many changes of régime since 1789, at each of which the question arose, to whom did a serving officer owe his allegiance? This dilemma provoked a legalistic answer, but one deeply engrained in the French services: an officer who obeys his lawful commander, or one whom he believes to be his lawful commander, cannot be termed a traitor or subsequently punished.

So whom would the French Forces recognise as their lawful commander? The Allies thought that the man for the job was General Henri Giraud, a very senior French officer who had been captured by the Germans early in the war, had twice escaped, and was now lying hidden in the South of France. He had a distinguished record in North Africa, had never collaborated with the Germans, and was something of a hero in the French Army. General Juin, who commanded the important garrison of Algiers, was ready to serve under him. That Giraud was an honourable man of considerable charm, but rather less intelligence, and very old fashioned in his ideas, I was to discover in due course.

On the night of 6 November he was picked up off the French coast by a British submarine and brought to Gibraltar. He was enthusiastic about 'Torch', so much so that it was with some difficulty that he was dissuaded from the notion that he should be the supreme commander of the whole show. On the 8th the Allied landings began. General Juin duly delivered Algiers, but at Casablanca neither the French nor the weather were co-operative, and German U-boats were hastening to the scene.

Nor was the reception of Giraud as friendly as had been hoped. All the high-ranking French commanders had been invited to Algiers, and many of them had come. And more or less by chance, Admiral Darlan was also in Algiers. They would not accept Giraud's authority. All power must derive from Marshal Pétain, head of the Vichy Government, and Giraud, having left France without his permission, could have none. Strangely enough, Giraud himself accepted this argument. Under great pressure from General Mark Clark, the American commander on the spot, the French brass-hats agreed to accept Darlan as their leader, and Darlan to order a general ceasefire of all French forces in North Africa, delivering Dakar into the bargain. The forces of Operation 'Torch' then had safe lines of communication to drive towards Tunisia,where German reinforcements were being hurriedly landed.

The Germans also occupied the whole of France, but failed to seize the French fleet in Toulon, where Admiral Laborde, though fanatically anti-British and refusing to bring his ships over to the Allies, scuttled them all in time.

Pétain, of course, repudiated Darlan and his defection. But many people felt he was acting under duress, and still to be the legitimate source of Darlan's legitimate authority. As Churchill was to remark, 'If Admiral Darlan had to shoot Marshal Pétain, he would no doubt do it in Marshal Pétain's name.'

De Gaulle's reaction to these events was swift and understandable. Churchill had only been able to tell him about 'Torch' on the night before the landings, and though he could offer more welcome news on Madagascar, which we had recaptured and were about to hand over to the Free French, the news had not gone down well. General Clark's agreement with a guilty man who had collaborated with the Germans shocked him even more. And the British press and public were upset and angry.

At a secret session of Parliament on 11 November Churchill loyally defended Eisenhower and Clark on military grounds, and by sheer weight of argument carried the House with him. But the undercurrent of disquiet continued.

This then was the situation on the evening of 22 December 1942, when I was sent for by the Prime Minister. I was then the Junior Minister at the Colonial Office, where I had been since the beginning of February. For most of that time my Minister had been Lord Cranborne, who, being in the Lords, left me a free hand in the Commons, and had put me in charge of the Economic Department. But for the past month the Minister had been Oliver Stanley. He was in the Commons, and my role was consequently curtailed. Although he was an old friend, I was not at all happy with my prospects, and had had serious thoughts of resigning. Fortunately I consulted Brendan Bracken; and he wisely advised me to wait.

Churchill asked me how far I had followed affairs in North Africa since the landings. I replied that I knew little more than I had read in the newspapers, and naturally was aware of the indignation caused by the Darlan–Clark agreement not only among General de Gaulle's organisation, with whom I had been working on colonial matters. Unfortunately I had not been able to attend the secret session. Churchill therefore began to rehearse the arguments he had used then, to give a full exposition of the military and political situations as they were now developing; the former was encouraging, the latter distressing and confusing. Although the Germans had occupied

Bizerta in Tunisia, there was a good chance of our armies pressing forward, so that within a few weeks the First (British) Army, under General Anderson, might recapture Bizerta and reach Tunis while the Eighth Army, under Montgomery, occupied Tripoli in Libya. And so the whole of North Africa would be ours.

But while these military considerations were supreme, and we recognised that their high command was American, we had a duty to express our opinions, especially in the political sphere. There was already an admirable Foreign Office official, Hal Mack, on Eisenhower's staff. But he had not sufficient rank or influence. The Cabinet was determined that it should now be represented at Eisenhower's headquarters by a ministerial colleague.

I soon realised that Churchill was not just giving me a private view of his political and strategic plans, but might be about to make me a participant in this drama. I tried to control my impatience as he came gradually to the point. There should be a minister at Allied Force Headquarters, now set up in Algiers. He would be of cabinet rank, though not a member of the War Cabinet. He would be entitled to report direct to the Prime Minister. His status would be roughly parallel to that of the Minister of State in Cairo. But there was an important difference. The Middle East was a purely British concern, and all executive power was in the hands of the British military and civil authorities. In North Africa, the command was American. The Headquarters were staffed equally by British and American officers, but the American general held the final responsibility, subject only to the Combined Chiefs of Staff in Washington. A Minister of State, therefore, although his rank would be similar to that of the Ministers now operating in Cairo (R. G. Casey) or in British West Africa (Lord Swinton), must depend on the influence that he could exert upon the Supreme Allied Commander. Although the debate in the House of Commons had done much to satisfy Parliamentary opinion, and criticism in and outside the House had been temporarily quietened, there was still an undercurrent of hostility and dismay. Moreover, although the command was American, the greater part of the armies, navies and air forces engaged were British. It was essential that the British Parliament and people should feel that they had more say in future developments. Here was a post of great potential significance. It would bring its occupant into the very centre of world events. Although it would entail secondment from the House of Commons, the chosen minister could still keep his seat. It would be an adventure of a high order. This post was at my disposition. It was for me to decide. I replied at once that there was no need to hesitate – I would accept it immediately and gratefully. Although the Prime Minister insisted that I should take a few hours to think it over, and send a formal reply the next day, the conversation proceeded on the assumption that the matter was settled.

Churchill then gave me a copy of his speech in the secret debate, which proved very valuable, for I had little knowledge of the background of this affair. He asked me when I would leave for Algiers. I replied, 'Tomorrow, or rather the day after tomorrow.' That seemed satisfactory. Would I go in uniform? I thought a moment and then replied, 'No, sir, I don't think I will go in uniform.' 'Why not?' he exclaimed. 'Are you ashamed of your uniform?' 'No, Prime Minister, but I think among all those generals, admirals and air marshals an infantry captain formerly in the Reserve, even of the Grenadier Guards, would not cut a very impressive figure.' Churchill calmed down and reflected. 'I see your point,' he said. 'You mean that between the baton and the bowler there is no middle course.' So it was arranged.

A private secretary was sent for and told that it was settled. But the Prime Minister was reminded that he had not yet cleared it with the Americans. No announcement could be made until President Roosevelt knew and agreed. However, there was no doubt at all in my mind that the Prime Minister intended to press his point to a conclusion.

On the morning of the 23rd I sent my formal acceptance to Downing Street and, as there must be some delay before the announcement, I went down to spend Christmas in the cottage in Sussex and to tell my wife the wonderful news. Before doing so, I informed John Wyndham, my private secretary, and asked him to come with me to Algiers. He at once accepted. On the afternoon of Christmas Eve, we heard on the wireless that Darlan had been assassinated. A wave of disappointment swept over me. I rang up John in London to find out what people were saying and to ask if any information could be obtained from the private office at No. 10. I feared that Darlan's elimination might so simplify the French situation that a new minister would not be needed. After a little reflection, I decided to do nothing and hope for the best. I had now become tremendously excited by the wonderful prospect, in a position where I would be completely on my own. Although neither I nor the Prime Minister had the slightest idea what I was going to do, I would do it with the utmost diligence and perseverance. Surely the cup could not be snatched from my lips at the last moment merely because a young man had assassinated Admiral Darlan. There must be plenty of other difficulties and confusions to be cleared up, even after the removal of the leading figure. There were.

My appointment as Minister Resident at Allied Headquarters in North-west Africa was cleared with the President and given out on the afternoon of 30 December. I was granted an audience by King George VI, the first time I had been received as a minister. I had done my best to find out something about the situation in Algiers and had had an hour's talk with the Deputy Head of the Foreign Office, Sir Orme Sargent, and had read through a large file of telegrams. But when I talked with the King, I had my first experience of the extraordinary diligence and accuracy with which successive occupants of the Throne make it their task to study all the details of the manifold problems which it is their duty to master.

And so on the night of 31 December, accompanied by John Wyndham, two typists, and two typewriters, prudently stolen from the Colonial Office, we set off on our Mission.

1943

January

Thursday, 7 January 1943

I suppose you will have been told by the Foreign Office that we arrived without misadventure. Anyway, you would have been told quick enough if we had fallen into the sea.

We got to Gibraltar about noon on Friday [1 January]. No incidents and a very smooth and comfortable journey. But it was an early start in the morning and a very rough and cold bed in a hut the night before.

The girls and John stood the journey well. Miss Campbell is a practised traveller and knows all the tricks – pockets full of chewing-gum and raisins. Miss Williams is more timid, but pretty and soon gets help from any soldier or airman, as required.[1]

We stayed the night at Gibraltar. Mason-MacFarlane[2] (the Governor) very friendly. The best thing about Gibraltar is a *cask* (mark you, a cask) of sherry standing always in the drawing-room and available at any time.

Lord Gort[3] was there on his way home for some leave. A very pleasant dinner in semi-viceregal surroundings – all the things we have forgotten in England – five or six courses, sherry, red and white wine, port, brandy, etc., etc.

We left Gibraltar at 9.30 on Saturday [2 January] and arrived at Algiers at about 12.30. Hal Mack (Foreign Office) and Consul-General to receive us.[4]

[1] John Wyndham (1920–72), later Lord Egremont, was my Private Secretary (as he had been at the Ministry of Supply and at the Colonial Office), a post he held once again when I became Foreign Secretary, 1955, and Prime Minister, 1957–63. Miss Campbell had been my secretary at the Colonial Office, Miss Williams was Wyndham's secretary.

[2] Lieutenant-General Noel Mason-MacFarlane (1889–1953), was Governor and C.-in-C., Gibraltar, 1942–4. He had been head of the British Military Mission to Moscow, 1941–2.

[3] Field Marshal Lord Gort, 6th Viscount (1886–1946) was Governor and C.-in-C., Gibraltar, 1941–2, and Malta, 1942–4, having been C.I.G.S., 1937–9, and C.-in-C. of the British Field Force which was evacuated at Dunkirk.

[4] Henry Mack (1894–1974), an Assistant Under-Secretary of State, was British Civil Liaison Officer to the Allied C.-in-C., General Eisenhower, 1942–3. The British Consul-General in Algiers, 1942–5, was John Carvell (1894–1978).

My first interview with General Eisenhower[5] was at 4 p.m. on Saturday afternoon. Considering that neither Washington nor London had informed him of my appointment (which one of his staff heard by chance on the radio) the interview was quite a success.

I will not write you the political stuff in this letter, because we have not got a proper bag arranged yet and this will be taken by some chap who happens to be going home. So I ought not to risk it falling into enemy hands.

The physical conditions in which we live are appalling. Yesterday (by great and generous help from a number of generals and others) I have got two rooms in a hotel as an office. They are in the same block as Mr Murphy's[6] office. This is very important, as he is my American counterpart and must be my partner, so I was determined to have my office 'located' right next to his. This took me till Wednesday to fix. There are no paper, no pens, pencils, typewriters, filing covers – and of course, no steel cabinets or tin boxes or anything. So all our documents have to be carted about with us wherever we go, which is a great bore, especially as the hotel is four miles off.

We have managed to get two telephones, but there is no method (such as we have) of the secretary taking the call. Everyone answers their own telephone, when there must be some etiquette about it. Then, of course, they are always busy and just say, 'Oh, I'll call you back', which, of course, they never do.

However, we have our typewriters, which makes everyone else *very* jealous. We have corporals to guard us, and we have a car – a fine Buick – with a corporal to drive. We also have a corporal on a motor-bike in front. And today they have produced a Union Jack and put it on the car. Thus pride defies security.

Roger Makins has not arrived. In his place, there came on Tuesday [5 January] a very nice young man (of about ten years' Foreign Office experience I should say) to help. His name is Dixon.[7] He knows a lot about Balkan politics. That should prove quite useful here, from what I can see.

We live in a hotel. Hot water from 7.30 to 8.30 a.m. only. Bed hard; bottom sheet (wet), no top sheet but coarse blanket. No fire or heating of any kind.

[5] General Dwight D. Eisenhower (1890–1969) was Allied C.-in-C., North African Theatre of Operations, 1942–4, Supreme Commander of the Allied Expeditionary Force in Western Europe, 1944–5, and of NATO forces in Europe, 1950–2. From 1953 to 1961, he was President of the United States.

[6] Robert Murphy (1894–1978), as President Roosevelt's Personal Representative in French North Africa and Chief Civil Affairs Officer on General Eisenhower's staff, was my opposite number at A.F.H.Q., until he became U.S. Political Adviser for Germany, S.H.A.E.F., in September 1944.

[7] Roger Makins (b. 1904), later 1st Baron Sherfield, became H.M. Ambassador to the United States, 1953–6, and Joint Permanent Under-Secretary of the Treasury, 1956–9. Pierson Dixon (1904–65), became Principal Private Secretary to the Foreign Secretary, 1943–8, U.K. Permanent Representative to the U.N., 1954–60, and H.M. Ambassador to France, 1960–4. He was known as Bob.

A naval mess takes pity on us and we lunch and dine with them. Nowhere to sit after dinner, except at dining-table or upstairs in one's room in heaviest overcoat available. *No* hot water for hot-water-bottle.

John has devoted himself solely to the task of trying to get us a house to live in. We hope to get a villa. We have seen one or two excellent ones. But how can they be obtained? By registering? How is that done? By the American Army authorities? What, for a British civilian minister! Well then, by the British Army authorities. What, for a civilian! Well, by the French authorities. Ah! that is better, but M. le Préfet is away – he is indisposed. The Préfecture only opens one hour a day – by bad luck always during an *alerte*. How can work be done during an *alerte*, with bombs and guns and so on?

However, John has – or thinks he has – overcome all these difficulties and obtained for us a rich and sumptuous villa belonging to a millionaire, who was also an Army contractor. He contracted so well that his boots were made of paper and thus the villa was built.

But in the house there are ten Jewish refugees, poor people, from the South of France. What is to be done? John has arranged it. He has squared the lady of the house. She will remain in a back part and in return she will eject nine members of her family. If we agree to this, she will leave us her housemaid and – unspeakable glory – her cook.

John is negotiating about this and hopes to settle today. Of course, there is a security problem. They may all be spies. So more corporals and military policemen and whatnot will have to be employed at the villa.

We shall have soldiers as batmen and to wait at table. The females will live (it is hoped) in oriental seclusion, as in a harem.

Moreover there is the *batterie de cuisine*. There is not a saucepan, teapot, kettle, kitchen knife or anything like it in North Africa. Our linen, our towels, scrubbing cloths, table-linen, blankets, pillow-cases, glass, silver, etc., where is that to come from? John has solved it. From the Fleet or the Merchant Navy. A huge list of articles has been seized from a [sunk] P. & O. liner and is waiting on the docks (pray Heaven it will not be bombed) to be taken to the villa when the final negotiations are complete. (Incidentally, there is only one villa. We are to have another smaller villa for the girls and any more staff that may arrive.)

Then there is the question of food. There is *no* food to be got, except in the black market, and there is a sort of self-denying ordinance (very rightly) that English and Americans should not compete with the inhabitants for what little food there is. So we must have rations. Yes, easily said, but not so easily done. Army rations or Navy rations? And who is to pay? On whose *vote* will it be borne? Will an M.P. ask a question at the Public Accounts Committee? All these questions John is coping with. He sees admirals and commodores and tells them what we want. We never see him (except at meals) and, while we are making slow progress with political questions, he is in sole charge of this much more vital aspect of our mission.

Meanwhile, owing to the frightful conditions, we have all got streaming colds. We have also been inoculated against typhoid, so we are not at our best. But we struggle on.

And (apart from our mess, when the Navy entertains us) I have lunched and dined with Admiral Cunningham[8] in his sumptuous villa (the Navy knows how to be comfortable) and several of the Americans – Mr Murphy, etc., and various Anglo-American messes of officers on the staff have been most kind in having me. So really life is very agreeable.

The lack of office amenities makes work trying and adds to the pressure, but we shall overcome them. John has temporarily left us to become Comptroller of the Household [i.e. at the villa], but Dixon is very good, and of course Hal Mack, who was already here, is a great standby.

I don't think there is any more paper available, so I shall have to stop. Nor do I suppose you will be able to read a word of this scribble. If you ask Geikie to type out all or any, he will do so and you could let anyone have it who you think would care to read it, but they must be reasonably discreet. (Also, Geikie may care to keep a copy in my records.)

I won't be able to write often, but will try to do so whenever there is a chance of a bag. So far, we have no news, no newspapers, no bag, no radio – we are isolated, remote, but undefeated as yet. If only we can get *chauffage* for the villa! Of course we can. The admiral is sending us some coal.

Hope all well at home. Give my love to all. Let Maurice and Katharine know I am alive, and tell Carol to look after herself and not worry. She will surely pass the next time. Tell Catherine to work hard next term and meanwhile enjoy herself; and tell Sarah to look after my dogs.[9] And look after yourself, do, and don't get too tired or bothered with the Land Girls.

Tuesday, 26 January 1943

Your account of Tanner's[10] wedding party is really magnificent. I wish I had been there. It must have been quite the event of the whole neighbourhood and will be talked about for a long time to come. Do write often in the way you have. I love having news about all that goes on. Let me know too what happens about the timber and anything else on the place.

[8] Admiral Sir Andrew Cunningham (1883–1963) was C.-in-C., Mediterranean, 1939–43.

[9] Maurice, Carol, Catherine, Sarah: my children. Katharine: Maurice's wife. Maurice was serving in the Sussex Yeomanry.

[10] Head gardener at Birch Grove, my house in Sussex. During the war it was occupied by a school and we lived at Pook's Cottage.

I received charming letters from both Catherine and Sarah written from Churchdale. I will try and write to them in due course. I am sorry to have to dictate all this, but I got back to find an immense amount of work to be done. As I say, you will now know where we have been.

We set off on Friday, 15 January, and flew in General Eisenhower's plane from here to Casablanca.[11] Casablanca is a large port. When it was attacked by the Americans the French battleship, the *Jean Bart*, was blown up in the fight. About two to three miles outside Casablanca is a curious kind of settlement [Anfa] consisting of rich villas belonging to Moroccan millionaires, centring round a three-storey hotel with about 50–100 bedrooms and appropriate dining-rooms and lounges. The dining-room is on top, and from it is a most wonderful view of the Atlantic on the one side and the hills and mountains of Morocco on the other. Eighteen of these villas were taken over at short notice by the American military authorities from the inhabitants. A wire fence of immense strength and solidity was constructed round the area covered by the villas and the hotel, and this formed a kind of Roman camp with a circuit of (I suppose) about a mile.

Arriving from the aeroplane at Casablanca, which incidentally we did after considerable emotions, since three out of the four engines went wrong in the course of the journey, we drove up to the camp. I have never seen so many sentries armed with such terrifying weapons. The rifle is almost forgotten here. There are machine-guns and tommy-guns and sawn-off shot-guns and all sorts of weapons of that kind. Every time you go in and out of the circle you have to produce a pass, and if you are one of the few civilians you are in danger all the time of being shot. On the other hand, once they recognise who you are, they are apt to turn the guard out and present arms to you. It is difficult to know quite which drill is going on.

In the villas were distributed the leading notabilities, and the main staffs were put up in the hotel. The very smart ate their meals in the villas, and the more ordinary in the hotel. The whole thing was rather like the *Normandie* or the *Queen Mary*. However, the arrangements were extremely well made. The whole thing was free, including most excellent food and quantities of drink. Even cigarettes, cigars, chewing-gum, sweets, of which the Americans are very fond, and soap, shaving-soap and razors – all these were freely distributed at the expense of the American and English taxpayer.

We arrived about lunch-time and went upstairs to lunch. Here we found all the notabilities, whose names you have now seen in the press.

[11] A conference attended by Roosevelt and Churchill and their Chiefs of Staff was to be held at Anfa near Casablanca. The main question to be resolved was whether to follow up the success of 'Torch' by invading Italy (as Churchill wished), or to reserve our forces for a Second Front in Northern France (Roosevelt's and Stalin's preference). My own chief concern was to advance the cause of French unity.

Admiral King, General Marshall, and all the American staffs, Admiral Sir Dudley Pound, General Brooke, Air Chief Marshal Portal, and so on.[12] In the course of time there also appeared General Alexander, Field Marshal Dill, Admiral Cunningham, Air Marshal Tedder, and indeed almost every conceivable personality in the armed forces of the American people and the British Crown of whom one has ever heard.[13] In addition, there were juniors – 'Pug' Ismay and all the Joint Planners,[14] and so on and so on. This together with great hosts of marines, Wrens, Waafs, typists, telegraph officers, etc. of all kinds. In the Bay stood the famous communication ship[15] which can send off as many as thirty wireless messages at the same time, and hosts of cypherers and so on.

The whole spirit of the camp was dominated by the knowledge that two men were there who rarely appeared in public, but whose presence behind the scenes was always felt. These were officially called Air Commodore Frankland, who lived in Villa 3, and Admiral Q, who lived in Villa 2. These titles, which were used universally throughout the period, covered, of course, as has now been revealed, the personalities of the Prime Minister and the President of the United States. All this took a great load off my mind, because the P.M. had told me about the meeting at Anfa Camp the night before I left England, and I had to know nothing about it for all this time. I christened the two personalities the Emperor of the East and the Emperor of the West, and indeed it was rather like a meeting of the later period of the Roman Empire.

The two Emperors met usually late at night and disported themselves and discussed matters with their own generals and with each other's generals. And there was a curious mixture of holiday and business in these extraordinarily oriental and fascinating surroundings.

Algiers is not really a very attractive place, because the climate is cold, and although the sun is hot during the day, the actual town is

[12] Admiral Ernest J. King (1878–1956) was C.-in-C., U.S. Fleet and Chief of Naval Operations, 1942–5. General George C. Marshall (1880–1959) was Chief of Staff, U.S. Army, 1939–45. (He was later the author of the Marshall Plan.) Admiral of the Fleet Sir Dudley Pound (1877–1943) was First Sea Lord and Chief of the Naval Staff, 1939–43. General Sir Alan Brooke (1883–1963), later 1st Viscount Alanbrooke, was C.I.G.S., 1941–6. Air Chief Marshal Sir Charles Portal (1893–1971) was Chief of the Air Staff, 1940–5.

[13] General Sir Harold Alexander (1891–1969) was soon to be appointed Deputy C.-in-C., North African Theatre of Operations. He had conducted the retreat at Dunkirk in 1940 after Gort's return to England, and had been G.O.C.-in-C., Southern Command, 1940–2, G.O.C., Burma, 1942, and C.-in-C., Middle East (at the time of the battle of Alamein), 1942–3. Field Marshal Sir John Dill (1881–1944) was C.I.G.S., 1940–1, then head of the British Joint Staff Mission in Washington. Air Chief Marshal Sir Arthur Tedder (1890–1967) was A.O.C.-in-C., Middle East, 1941–3.

[14] Lieutenant-General Sir Hastings Ismay (1887–1965) was Chief Staff Officer to the Minister of Defence (Churchill) and Deputy Secretary (Military) to the War Cabinet, 1940–5. The British and American Joint Planning Staffs served their respective Chiefs of Staff. Together they formed the Combined Planning Staff serving the Combined Chiefs of Staff.

[15] H.M.S. *Bulolo*, a converted liner.

disagreeable. But Morocco is superbly beautiful. Every conceivable flower, of which you would have known the names but I did not, was out. There were cactuses and plants of that kind of a vast size which would have made Nanny die with envy; bougainvillaea and all sorts of flowering shrubs in full bloom. And although the nights were cold, they were not so cold as in Algiers, and the sun by day was really wonderful.

The Emperor of the East's villa was guarded by marines, but otherwise things were fairly simple. His curious routine of spending the greater part of the day in bed and all the night up made it a little trying for his staff. I have never seen him in better form. He ate and drank enormously all the time, settled huge problems, played bagatelle and bezique by the hour, and generally enjoyed himself. The only other member of the Government present was Leathers,[16] and the P.M. had nobody except his secretaries, and so on.

The Emperor of the West's villa was difficult of access. If you approached it by night searchlights were thrown upon you, and a horde of what I believe are called G-men, mostly retired Chicago gangsters, drew revolvers and covered you. With difficulty you could get access, and then everything was easy. The court favourites, Averell Harriman and Harry Hopkins,[17] were in attendance, as well as the two sons who act as aides and, tragic as it seems, almost as male nurses to this extraordinary figure.[18] The President was particularly charming to me. There was a great deal of joking about me being the publisher both for him and for the Prime Minister. There was a lot of bezique, an enormous quantity of highballs, talk by the hour, and a general atmosphere of extraordinary goodwill.

As I say, the whole affair, which lasted for nearly a fortnight, was a mixture between a cruise, a summer school and a conference. The notice-boards gave the time of the meetings of the various staffs, rather like lectures, and when they got out of school at five o'clock or so, you would see field marshals and admirals going down to the beach for an hour to play with the pebbles and make sand-castles. Then at night came the meetings of the emperors and the staffs and great political discussions and debates. I thought the P.M. handled the situation with consummate skill. And as I was either at his house or the President's most of the night and had to do my own work by day, you can imagine it was fairly exhausting.

As you will probably have surmised from the announcement made, my work consisted of immensely complicated and rather unsuccessful

[16] 1st Baron Leathers (1883–1965) was Minister of War Transport, 1941–5.

[17] W. Averell Harriman (b. 1891) had been Roosevelt's special representative in London for the Lend–Lease negotiations in London. He was U.S. Ambassador to the Soviet Union, 1943–6, and to Britain, 1946. Harry Hopkins (1890–1946) was Roosevelt's personal assistant at foreign conferences.

[18] Roosevelt had been crippled by poliomyelitis since 1921. The two sons who attended him in Anfa were Elliott and Franklin Jr.

negotiations between the two generals [Giraud and de Gaulle][19]. It was decided at the beginning that a wedding should be arranged if possible. The President once said this must be a wedding even if it was a shot-gun wedding, and Murphy and I were responsible for making the necessary arrangements between the bride and bridegroom. The bride (General de G.) was very shy and could not be got to the camp at all until two days before the end. I never thought really that we would get them both to the church, and, as I warned both the emperors, the dowry required to make anything of it would be very large. However, as you will probably have seen from the films or the pictures, we got them there in the end, and, partly by chicanery and partly by pressure, forced them to shake hands in front of all the cameras. I hope the result will be of some use. Apart from chaff, I do think it will be the beginning, though only just the beginning, of the loosening out of a very complicated situation between the various French peoples.[20]

I have not time to tell you a long story of the negotiations, and anyway I suppose I should not do so.[21] I would like to try and give you the atmosphere of this extraordinary performance when men and generals in command of great armies and admirals of distant fleets came and went over thousands of miles and the whole affairs of the world present and future were being discussed. The only sad thing about it was that the Russians could not attend. If we had had the Red Emperor as well, it would have made the thing perfect. Perhaps at the next meeting, which will probably be in Iceland or somewhere like that, we shall see them all together.

I flew back here yesterday [to Algiers on 25 January] – a very long journey. The weather was bad, and we had to go right round by sea instead of coming across the mountains. And when I got back I found that arrangements had been made for us to move, and here we are in this amazing villa. I have never lived in such strange luxury. Everything is of marble or gold. All the pictures are Botticellis or Murillos (or copies of both). All the furniture is antique, or semi-antique. But the generous owners of it have done really everything possible to make us comfortable. Since I have a cold and am tired, I am sitting up, and working in a large and ornate bed. The

[19] General Henri Honoré Giraud (1879–1949) had been in command of the French Seventh Army when the German offensive in France opened in May 1940, and was taken prisoner but escaped in 1942. He became High Commissioner of French North and West Africa after Admiral Darlan's death.

[20] It took several days to persuade General de Gaulle to fly out from London. We failed to find a way of fusing the Free French and the Giraudists, largely because of de Gaulle's insistence that the Vichy leaders in North Africa should first be purged. Besides a good photograph, all we obtained was a communiqué stating the obvious: that Frenchmen should unite to fight beside the Allies against the Axis.

[21] At the Anfa Conference the Americans were eventually persuaded to accept our view that it would be premature to open a Second Front in France in 1943, and that we should attack Sicily instead.

It was also at this conference that Roosevelt stated the doctrine of unconditional surrender, which was later to cause some problems.

sheets, however, come from the P. & O., as do the blankets. The cutlery is from Gibraltar. Some of it was taken off Government House, some of it from P. & O. ships. And here in these strangely beautiful and bizarre surroundings we are to live our lives.

I think you could seriously think of coming out in a short time. You would love the sun and the flowers. I thought of flying back after not too long an interval on the excuse of reporting on the situation or something of the kind, and we might talk about your coming out. I really think it would do you good. You would love the country, and now that we are getting a complement of cars and so on, we shall be able to get out into the country. Our villa is almost out of the town, and you hardly see the town from it. You look out upon the blue waters of the Bay on the one side, and backwards to the hills and mountains on the other.

We are gradually getting our communication system better. It has been very bad up to date. But I think a bag will go now two or three times a week at least. So you should send your letters through the bag and tell other people to do so.

I expect you will be seeing Maurice, so I will not bother to write all this to him. In any case I do not think you should part with this letter, though you can show it to a few people if you would like to.

As I have still got this frightful cold, I am staying in bed this morning to try and check it.

I feel rather worried about the political situation. I do not think people quite understand it in England, and there will be great dangers ahead. Nevertheless it is something to have got the two generals together, and if we can gradually liberalise the régime here and get certain outstanding points dealt with – Jews, refugees, etc., – I think English public opinion will begin to quieten down.

I am sorry for this rambling letter, which I must now conclude.

Mr Dixon, who has been helping me here before Roger Makins could arrive, will take this letter home.

He will telephone you on arrival. He is very charming and if you are in London you might ask him to lunch and he will be able to give you our latest news.

February

With the Allied military successes in North Africa and most French territories rallying to either Giraud or de Gaulle, the time had come to tackle the anomalous position of the French fleet at Alexandria. When France had collapsed in 1940, we did everything possible to keep the French Navy out of enemy hands. In Alexandria, Admiral René Godfroy, commanding a squadron consisting of a battleship, four cruisers and a number of smaller ships, agreed with Admiral Cunningham to immobilise the ships – by discharging the fuel and repatriating some of the crews – in return for our undertaking to pay the remaining officers and men. I now had to try to persuade Admiral Godfroy to set aside this compromise and commit his squadron to the Free French forces.

Monday, 22 February 1943
from Maison-Carrée Hospital, Algiers

It seems to be extraordinarily difficult for me to get to Cairo. All the last ten days I have been waiting about for a situation to develop here which would contribute usefully to the problem of the French fleet at Alexandria. For one reason or another, there has been a good deal of coming and going – by telephone of course – between London, Algiers and Cairo to get the plan arranged in the best way.

I have always argued strongly against the tendency to rely too much upon Giraud for this purpose. In the first place, if we use him (as we have already done unsuccessfully) to send either an order or an appeal to Admiral Godfroy to rally his ships to the cause, we are clearly asking him to do so as head of a state. I mean just as a general he has no right to give orders to Godfroy. But if as head of a state, of what state? We and U.S.A. have only recognised Giraud as head of a provisional administration of French North Africa. That means Morocco, Algiers, Tunis. By what authority then can he give orders to a fleet at Alexandria? Only (and this is *very* delicate) by a more general authority over French interests as a whole which U.S.A. seem rather inclined (especially since de Gaulle's behaviour at Anfa) to concede him, but which H.M.G. is determined to deny him.

Anyway, Giraud has sent, not an order, but an appeal to Godfroy. I was against his doing so, but Cairo was very insistent that we should obtain it, and we did. I need hardly say that it had no effect whatever.

But I have hoped that it would be possible to get Admiral Michelier – who is the senior French naval officer not in German-controlled France – to take some part in this affair.[1] This was naturally not too easy, as it was after all only in November last that Admiral Michelier fought against the Allied landings at Casablanca.

Meanwhile, he has slowly been coming over to the opposition, first to a modified support and now, I think, to a really enthusiastic co-operation with the British Navy. This change of heart is largely due to Admiral Cunningham, who has managed him very well.

Anyway, after a lot of humming and hawing, Michelier (in association with Giraud but not exactly on his orders) has been got to take the step of sending his own chief of staff, Admiral Missoffe,[2] to Alexandria with a message to Godfroy, instructing him to bring over the Alexandria fleet.

This order he is to give him as a superior officer. (No politics: no Vichy: no theory of the *maréchal empêché* – just a naval affair.)

What exactly is to happen if Godfroy disobeys this order is still a little obscure. Anyway, regarding this as rather a triumph for Algiers diplomacy over that of Cairo, I started – or went to start – to Cairo on Sunday night, 21 February, with Admiral Missoffe, his flag-lieutenant, John Wyndham as the party.

We dined at the villa on Sunday night, where we had quite a large party. Willie Makins[3] (Roger's cousin) of the Welsh Guards, who was passing through, and a number of Treasury and Supply officials who were out to consult about North African Economic Board (N.A.E.B.)[4] affairs and the like.

We left the villa at 11.30. We made rendezvous with the admiral and flag-lieutenant and the two cars reached the aerodrome about 12.10. We went aboard the aeroplane – a Hudson similar to that in which we came from England – at about 1.15 on Monday morning, the 22nd.

I don't know why, but I mistrusted the whole thing from the first. The plane was not fitted for passengers – no seats – but that doesn't matter, and it is quite easy with rugs and flying-coats to make oneself happy enough on the floor. But there were no rugs; no arrangements for even minimum comfort; no officer at the airport to receive me. The crew were one rather casual gum-chewing Australian pilot, a Canadian navigator (a sergeant) and one or two others.

[1] Admiral Félix Michelier (1887–1966) commanded the French naval forces at Casablanca.

[2] Vice-Admiral Jacques Missoffe (1893–1982).

[3] Lieutenant-Colonel Sir William Makins (1903–69).

[4] The British and American N.A.E.B. had been set up by A.F.H.Q. in agreement with the French to restore the economic life of French North Africa. With the French Treasury, it formed the Joint Economic Committee.

We were asked to get well forward for the start and to move back *after* she was in the air. As the heaviest, therefore, I went right up into the cockpit (I think this is the name) and sat on a little seat next to the pilot. The navigator was in the nose, below us.

We taxied round in the usual way till we got to the far end of the runway. Then we started down it, gaining speed with the usual roar, as the throttle is opened out to full.

To my amazement, at this point, after rising a few feet off the ground, the pilot suddenly began to close the throttle to reduce speed to land again, and to put on the brakes. But he was, of course, too far along the runway to make this feasible. Sitting by his side I could see exactly what was happening and in a few seconds I had two rather clear impressions. (You know how ignorant I am about motoring and mechanics – these were not technical observations, but the impressions of a lay observer.)

First, I realised the immense pace at which we were going on the ground. It seemed ever so much faster than any motor car (whether we were just off or just on the ground at this point I am not sure, and I think there will be a Court of Enquiry to establish). But you know how when one is in a plane in the sky one gets *no* impression of speed. But racing along the ground (or a foot or two above it) I remember being conscious of tremendous speed.

The second feeling that I had instantaneously was of relief that the accident had come so soon. I felt so strongly that there was going to be an accident that I thought it was as well to get it over quickly. It really was very queer, and I think helped one to keep reasonably calm.

Of course, it was impossible for the pilot to stop the plane in the space allotted. In spite of his heavy braking, therefore, the plane ran on over the end of the runway into a field or bush or wall or something; gave a kind of stagger or drunken lurch, and then just settled down with a cracking sort of noise, like a child's toy motor or aeroplane that has been driven or flown into a wall.

The shock was not very great and none of us three in the cockpit were stunned. But immediately – just after one had time to realise that one had survived the crash – the flames began.

The pilot broke open the emergency exit on his left and disappeared through it. The navigator, who during the course of these proceedings had come out of the nozzle and was crouching near the pilot, did the same. Since this was clearly no occasion for a 'Casabianca' business, it was evident that the time had come for me to take what is technically called 'avoiding action'.

But middle-aged and rather portly publishers, encumbered by the weight of their own dignity and a large green Ulster overcoat, trying to spring through a smallish hole about the height of their head, this hole to be reached by scrambling over a confused mass of driving wheels, levers, and other mechanical devices of a jagged and impeding kind, if they are to achieve success in such an operation, must be inspired by a powerful and overwhelming motive. For lesser exertions, such as to enter Parliament, to struggle through years of political failure and frustration, lesser motives may serve. Ambition, patriotism, pride – all these can impel a man and finally bring him within the hallowed precincts of the Privy Council and the Cabinet.

But – to do what I did in the early hours of last Monday morning, only one motive in the world is sufficient – FEAR (not Fame) is the spur. I managed to get myself more or less through the hole but was not strong enough to make the final effort to get enough of myself through as to tip the scale and bring me down on to the top of the wing.

But the flames inspired me, and I remember finding myself out – out of this horrible burning prison – having gone through just that psychological moment when one wonders whether it's worth making a supreme effort or not. One is tempted to give it up and accept the inevitable and with it at least the negative pleasure of the cessation of struggle. And then, with one last spasm of the human determination to survive – I gave myself a great heave. I could smell then, and remember it distinctly, the scorching of (I think) my own hair (or perhaps hat).

And with this great heave I was on the wing, and from the wing I could slide, stumble or roll on to the ground.

Meanwhile, the admiral, the flag-lieutenant and John Wyndham – who had been in the back of the plane – as soon as she stopped, opened the door and walked out. A very rapid roll-call revealed that everyone was safe – all were out and the only thing to do was to walk away a bit further (for safety) and then look with melancholy satisfaction at our machine burning steadily, with flames darting here and there in the night, until soon the big petrol tanks were reached and up she went with a bang. I say 'melancholy satisfaction' – *melancholy* because there lay burning our hope of getting to Cairo and all our hopes there, *satisfaction* because if this aeroplane must burn, at least we were not inside it.

Meanwhile Roger Makins, who had come down to see us off at the aerodrome and had not fortunately driven away before the accident, appeared, together with the military police corporal who looks after my safety. He is a fine man, Corporal Nicholson. He takes a poor view of flying – anywhere on the ground, he will answer for me not being attacked – but in the air!

We walked or staggered away from the end of the aerodrome where the accident took place and finally, with the help of the corporal, I was got to a little first-aid hut.

Here, in the light, the situation was reviewed. John, Admiral Missoffe, Flags, and another member of the crew, were quite unhurt either by shock or burns. They were not much shaken when the plane stopped and merely opened the door and got out. The pilot (who got out quick) was unhurt. The navigator and I were burned – it was difficult at that stage to say how much. (I have since heard that the navigator is quite all right, but is burned in the face and head – slightly – and hopes to be out of hospital in a day or two.)

I had two small wounds on each leg, which were dressed. I think these were merely caused by catching against some bit of machinery in my efforts to get through that infernal hole.

I had no burns at all in any other part of my anatomy – hands, feet, arms, body or legs, except my face. I think my heavy green overcoat and my pig-skin gloves protected me wonderfully against the flames.

Immediately after getting out of the plane, while walking to the dressing station, I felt a terrible stinging in my face. But I knew it would really be all right because my spectacles were still on my face (which protected my eyes) and after all, in one's face it is only to one's eyes that one attaches (at my age at least) much importance.

After consultations at the dressing station, those who were quite unhurt decided to go back by car to Algiers (fortunately the cars had not left). I was given a first-aid treatment, viz., bandages soaked in soda, for my face, put on a stretcher, my leg wounds bound up, and taken in an ambulance to this hospital, where I now am.

By the time we reached hospital it was about 3 a.m., Monday. I will tell you frankly that, with some experience of pain – as men know it – I do not ever remember a worse pain that began on me then. Curiously enough, I suppose from excitement, the pain was not bad until I got into that ambulance.

Anyway, the hospital night (between 3 a.m. when I got into bed and 6 a.m when a hospital starts the day) was a very short one!

I was in a ward – and the old routine of orderlies, and sisters, and nurses, and ward-maids – all starting again. The mild flirtations between Sister A and Major X; the giggles of Nurse Y, the cockney pleasantries of Ward-Maid Q – it seemed as if thirty years had been lifted away, and one was back in the old No. 3 at Abbeville or Rouen.

About 9.30 a.m., a very nice R.A.M.C. officer came to examine me and then an older man, a surgeon.

At about 10.30 a.m. I was taken off to the operating theatre. I must say they have made a wonderful improvement in this part of the business since old days. I had an intravenous injection in the arm and without any fuss at all found myself back in my bed, this time in a very nice clean little room which has been assigned for me.

Tuesday, 23 February 1943

(Morning.) I got my story down to Monday morning, after the operation. I gather they opened up the various blisters, cleaned the cheek bones which were rather affected, and generally removed dirt, burnt hair, burnt moustache, etc., from my face. The reason it hurt me so much seems to be that the top skin was burned and therefore nerves exposed. But I have now (and had yesterday afternoon) very little pain at all, nothing but a sort of throbbing. Having cleaned me up, they have put a sort of mask over my head – made of bandages and plaster – with I suppose a dressing on the inside. There are slits for my eyes and my lips, but otherwise the mask entirely covers my head, like the members of the Ku Klux Klan or like those sanbenitos that you see in Spain. The only discomfort is that it is rather stuffy; but a very ingenious build-up of the mask enables me to breathe through my nostrils. My lips are still rather a bore, because they are very swollen, so that eating and drinking are very difficult. But I think the swelling is already better today. My eyes also ooze in rather an unpleasant way, but I think that will probably get better too. In every other way, I am fine.

Another doctor has just been in and tested me for a number of possible complaints, with excellent results. Apparently, when you are burned you lose a lot of fluid. This is the stuff that goes into the blisters. But it is really sound stuff and the blood-stream is no good without this nectar. It's the dash of bitters in the gin, as you might say. Well, this high-up medico fellow is as pleased as an old hen after laying an egg, because some absurd measuring machine with which he has been playing about here says that I have produced more fluid than I've lost – so everything is all right – except that the thing is so unlikely that I've no doubt the machine isn't working correctly. Anyway, today I am quite well. I have no headache and no concussion.

Yesterday afternoon Commandant [André] Beauffre, the adjutant to General Giraud, arrived to see me and to send me the general's condolences. Considering how rough I am with Giraud, he really has very good manners. Then Admiral Michelier and Admiral Missoffe arrived in person. I amused Michelier very much by telling him that it would soon be all over Algiers that I was a 'Cagoulard'. (The Cagoulards were the French right wing and Royalist Secret Society, which was supposed to be going for a revolution of the right. They were called 'Cagoulard' which means 'hooded' and everyone here is accused or accuses others of having been a Cagoulard.)

This amused Michelier a great deal and will make a good joke which will last quite a time. This is always so helpful to international relations – what one wants is a simple and lasting joke, that, like Royal jokes, can go on being repeated almost indefinitely without getting better or worse.

Roger Makins has been to see me this morning and we have got through some business. I can speak through my mask, but rather indistinctly, and I am not supposed to try to speak very much because of wrinkling my face when it ought to be smooth so that it can heal.

I don't think I shall leave here today, because it is better to be in bed here without a telephone and about half an hour by car from Algiers than to be back in the centre of things. I am really quite well, but I dare say I should get rather tired if I tried to do anything active. In any case,

I cannot very well go about in public without a face, so I shall stay here, at least for a day or two.

The admiral (Admiral of the Fleet, Sir A. B. Cunningham) has just been in. Everyone is tremendously excited. Nobody cares much about a poor old civilian minister; but an admiral of the fleet, with a white hat, and gold from his cuff to his elbow, and Flags with gold all over him, well, you can imagine how my stock has risen.

Incidentally the admiral has brought me some very good news of the battle here,[5] which has comforted me. He is a splendid man and absolutely first class and a most amusing and agreeable companion. He is, of course, not surprised at the failure of the R.A.F. to take anyone safely anywhere. 'For myself,' he says 'I generally travel American.' This, of course, is just naughtiness and to tease the air chief marshal [Tedder] and others.

I don't quite know what plans to make now. I shall get up for a bit this afternoon and see how I feel. Actually I feel sure I have no shock, except to the natural extent that such experiences are unusual in one's drab life and therefore are a little disturbing to the even course of middle age. But my lips are still rather painful, and I cannot therefore eat and drink with comfort or decency. But the extraordinary mask gives me a certain feeling of irresponsibility. No one in the world could know who it was beneath this turnip head. No one could apportion praise or blame to anything this phantom might say or do – so why worry?

If John comes to see me this afternoon, I will give him this letter to send in the next bag. It may be that it will not reach you for some time or together with other later or earlier letters. If you cannot read it, you must see what Geikie can do.

Meanwhile, here I am – idle, not discontented, rather bored, but very grateful to be alive and with a few days of rest anyway before me. I think so much of you all. The nurses are intrigued to know who is the Dorothy concerned – I suppose somehow revealed in the first night in the operating theatre. The orthodox explanation seemed to be likely to disappoint them, so I just say, 'Ah' through the hole in my mask and am put down as a gay fellow.

I was so delighted to get your long *typewritten* letter just before we left. I read it rather quickly just before dinner on Sunday – we have been working at the office till then and the bag came in about 7 p.m. I had meant to read it later more carefully, on the journey. Now I cannot find it, but I hope it may be in my pocket-book which I gave to John to take home when I was brought in here. What a tremendous excitement the aeroplane landing at Woodgate [near Birch Grove] must have been!

[5] During the previous week Rommel's forces had thrown back the First U.S. Armoured Division and captured Kasserine, Feriana and Sbeitla. But on the evening of 22 February Anglo-American troops forced him to withdraw behind the Mareth Line, leaving his rear exposed to the Eighth Army in the south of Tunisia.

How wonderful for you to have been there with Sarah! I couldn't quite make out whether the plane was ours or enemy – I assume ours.

We have lost, I am afraid, quite a lot of clothes. Actually, we had arranged to have one suitcase only, for lightness. This was John's. Then all the washing and shaving things, etc., were in the little zip-fastener bag which you lent me. Both bags, of course, are burned. I was travelling in an *old* grey tweed suit (which is saved) and had packed a quite nice slate-grey suit, which is burned. And of your six pairs of *new* socks, two are gone! Also one pair pyjamas, two shirts and four collars, about a dozen lovely handkerchiefs, my brigade tie, pair of new *brown* shoes – I was wearing the old black ones, now all I have. My hat has gone and, of course, all my washing things, including hair-brushes.

Nevertheless, I am not burnt (at least not to a frazzle) so I suppose one ought not to complain.

I have just discovered (to my great delight) that by using my tortoise-shell reading glasses I can make them stay on. I cannot use the others, as my ears are covered up by the mask, but the tortoise-shell ones will stay on against the plaster of the mask. Sister says it adds enormously to the effectiveness of the ensemble.

I must really stop all this nonsense now. It takes anyway from me all my love to you and the children. Except for the first part (about the fleet and so on) there is nothing confidential, so if the children are interested in my escape you can show it to them.

You can tell John's mother that he is *absolutely* unhurt. All he had to do was to open the door and walk out. But the fire prevented me from getting back [to the door].

Wednesday, 24 February 1943

(6 a.m. or so – put 6.30.) All hospitals are the same. Although I have now a little room to myself, I am woken up religiously and washed at 6 a.m. or thereabouts. I have no watch here. As it had on the end of the chain the key to my despatch case, I gave it to Makins after the accident. (By the way, the Government have now supplied me with a proper despatch case. I am so sorry you have had all the trouble to look for mine.)

We have just had an air-raid and a lot of firing. I did not hear any bombs fall. The guns like shooting off a lot of stuff, and I suppose it helps to keep up the raiding planes.

This is a French Army hospital. It is really not badly built at all – the wards are nice high rooms, the floors are tiled, the walls whitewashed. The lighting system is poor. In the room I have, [there is] no reading, only a centre light, by which I am now writing (it will be light about 7.30).

I have had a good night and slept since about 9.30 p.m. last night, with only one or two intervals. My face is still encased in my mask.

They are going to take off the dressing today and see how it is going. That means an anaesthetic – and its corollary, no breakfast.

I shall be glad to get rid of this mask because it is getting rather messy. I could see nothing at all of my face, of course, even if I had a looking-glass. But I walked along to the end of the ward next to my room and found one. As far as I can tell, my lips (which are all I can see) are better. My left eye is quite all right, but my right eye still oozes. I think it is from a blister just below the eye.

I don't know why I should give you all these gruesome details – it is just that morbidity which patients suffer from.

At first I thought I should quickly get out of here – but now I have almost given up hope. I feel the prison walls closing in. All the routine, the little jokes, the genial encouragement of the staff, and the sense of belonging to the place which gradually overwhelms one – Oh dear! I do wish I were home. I long to see you and the children. I shall stop wishing and try to go to sleep again.

The weather is still bad – or at least mixed. There was a heavy rainstorm in the night and it is rather cloudy this morning. If the sun comes out later, I hope to be allowed to sit out in a chair. The trouble is that there is rather a lot of dust if there is any wind.

I am to have a new mask at 10 a.m. – very exciting. But I have already told you, I think. Anyway, I'll stop now.

I am just out of the theatre and have woken up. John has come, so I give him this to seal and send off.

I have not heard yet what they have found.

. . .

They have done the dressing; I am back in bed, and have 'come to' successfully. I am to have some luncheon, after which I shall sleep. Then the surgeon will come and see me and I can (I hope) make some plans.

I expect to be driven back by car to the villa this afternoon. I can go comfortably to bed then (these Army beds are dreadfully hard) and I have the telephone. Also the food will be more agreeable, and short of seeing people (who might think my appearance a bit odd) I can carry on the greater part of my ordinary work.

I shall be glad to get back, for I am getting a little too old (and a little too convalescent!) for the routine of a military hospital. I do *not* like to go to sleep at 9 p.m. and be woken at 6 a.m. Nor do I like prunes and rice.

The surgeon (who seems quite excellent – one Captain Reeves, R.A.M.C.) has just been up. He is very pleased. He says that he has only just lifted the inner dressing and put it back. He says nearly all the blisters are finished. There is one on my left cheek-bone and one on my nose which are still troublesome. The cheek-bones are going on well where the burn was worst, and a completely new skin seems to be growing all over my face as it should do. He said it was very good for my age. I shall have another *outer* dressing done on either Friday or Saturday, and with any luck the whole thing may be removed by about Tuesday of next week. If so, that will not be too bad a job.

Of course, he can't be quite sure till he takes off the original dressing altogether, but I have no doubt that he is right.

It is really a great bore about this, because I particularly wanted to go to Cairo.[6] I am *most* excited about the French fleet. No telegram has come through yet but I would so like to get that fleet.

If no news comes, I may go down to Cairo on Saturday. Air Marshal Tedder (who seems a little concerned at my accident) will provide me with a Liberator which will be available by then. The only thing is that I shall look a bit odd arriving at the Minister of State's with my head in a bag. For if I go I shall still have my mask and then a pillow-case over it to keep out dust. Altogether it is an odd life we live here, but full of incident.

I have no more news of the battle here,[7] but the Germans seem to have been held yesterday or the day before in the most critical places. I feel sure the Americans will do well when they have had the experience. But (like our fellows two years ago) it's bound to take them time to learn. The great thing is that their higher command is flexible and *not* in any way conceited.

You told me about the crocuses in your last letter. Did they do as well as usual? I expect (after the war!) we shall have to renew them a bit – or perhaps dig them all up and split them up, and at the same time sow new grass in the drive and get rid of some of the weeds. I always like the white and purple ones that come out last. I can imagine them now.

Tell Sarah I have written to her by the last bag. I do hope they post our letters at the other end. I always feel that some old fool at the Foreign Office just leaves them in a drawer.

How is Sarah getting on? I hope she is quite happy at school now.

I forgot to ask – but how do you manage about petrol? It really is a bore for you. Do you manage to get an allowance for Stockton, etc? I should have thought you could have made use of me and said that you had:

(*a*) to come to London to do my private business,
(*b*) to go about the estate on estate business,
(*c*) to go to London on way to Stockton,

and so screw out a pint or two extra.

I'm afraid otherwise I shall have done you a great injury by going away and abandoning such a generous supply as we had.

[6] It was an especially good opportunity to go and see Admiral Godfroy, because I anticipated a pause in the political situation in French North Africa (see p. 28).

[7] The battle for the Kasserine Pass.

6 p.m. I have got back to the villa and am in a very magnificent bedroom. It seems quite like home after the hospital, and anyway the bed is comfortable.

I have been re-reading your letter of 14 February about the aeroplane. Of course, I see it was one of ours. I see you say you are looking forward to hearing. You should receive a letter in ink (in my hand) together with copy of my despatch to P.M.

I am very sorry to see that P.M. is laid up. God knows what we would do if anything happened to him. With all his faults, his is the lion heart. It is really wonderful to hear what soldiers, sailors and airmen (American and British) say about him.

I see the famous Churchill tank (the one there was all the trouble to improve)[8] has just been in action here and *done very well* in the critical battle yesterday and Monday. Our chaps (including Brigade of Guards) have done awfully well.

I have found a copy of Borrow's *Bible in Spain*. My word, what a good book! It is just the thing for bed – you can put it down and go on at any place.

Extracts from my despatch to the Prime Minister 12 February 1943

The exact degree of recognition of French sovereignty in this area has not been – and in my opinion ought not to be – precisely defined. There are three possible situations. First, the Allies might have taken over the full conduct of affairs; placed their own high military officers in charge of administration; and instructed the lesser French functionaries to operate under their own orders. That is one extreme. The Commander-in-Chief has (as I think, rightly) decided against it. Or, the Allied governments might recognise the French administration as a provisional government, with full sovereign rights over the territories in question. In that case, the position of the Allied forces would be not dissimilar to that which the British occupied *vis-à-vis* the French Government in the last war, when fighting in French territory. That, of course, is the position which the French administration would like to reach. In my view, it would be quite wrong to concede it. It would only have been justifiable if we had landed, as in 1914, on the invitation of a French government. The very contrary was the case. It could only be conceded at a much later stage, and many conditions precedent would be required, none of which are yet in sight.

There remains a kind of central position, illogical perhaps and difficult to define, somewhere in between that of a military occupation on the one hand and that of Allied forces operating on the territory of

[8] In November 1941 the Churchill tank was declared by the War Office to be unfit for operations unless sixteen modifications were carried out, most of them to the transmission and steering.

another Ally, on the other hand. That, as I conceive it, is the position which we wish to maintain. To preserve it requires careful and skilful handling. It is the relationship familiar to us in other parts of the world, between a local administration and a government which has – by tradition or by the trend of events – a recognised sphere of influence. It is perhaps comparable to our position in Iraq or (*mutatis, mutandis*) in Egypt. . . .

It will readily be understood that it is much easier to get what we want in the direct military sphere, than in the political or semi-political sphere. Wherever any of our demands upon the French can be justified as serving a military purpose, it is relatively easy to get satisfaction. But where we begin – as in the realm of internal politics, internees, radio and propaganda of all kinds – to encroach, without so clear a justification, upon French sovereignty, difficulties occur. We have to rely upon arguments based upon a more remote interest. We have to say that it is a military question that there should be political calm. We have to assert that the public opinion of the U.S.A. and Great Britain must be kept satisfied if the Governments are to obtain their enthusiastic support in the production and military fields. . . .

In order to understand the present internal situation in French North Africa, it is necessary first to establish the character and position of General Giraud. So far as his military attainments are concerned, I am informed that he is a general of the old school.

His experience is one of imprisonment and defeat. But these disagreeable accidents have in no way destroyed his confidence in his military knowledge. Those of our high officers who met and talked with him at Anfa will have formed their own view as to the value to be attached to his opinions on military affairs. But I feel sure that they will agree that – like those of many of the older generation of French soldiers – they are largely obsolete. They bear the same relation to modern strategy and tactics as did the ideas of the German and Austrian generals to the genius of Napoleon.

I am told that he is altogether neglectful of the science which is now called logistics. He does not seem to understand that modern armies cannot 'live upon the country'. And he appears, like M. Stalin, to regard the sea as a minor obstacle, across which troops and equipment can readily be flung, as if across a small stream.

I am afraid that this is true not only of General Giraud, but of the great majority of French officers. Before the war the command had fallen into the hands of old and rather second-rate generals. Promotion was intolerably slow. Battalion commanders were men of forty-five or more; generals of two to five stars were aged anything from sixty onwards. And the distressing longevity of marshals still continues.

Nevertheless, in spite of the overwhelming defeats of 1870 and 1940, and the very severe shaking of 1914–18, which they only survived through the amazing sacrifice of British armies and the genius of Foch and Clemenceau, their conceit is unbroken. They still regard themselves as the élite of the military world. The British are still only amateurs. But as we know from sporting analogies, there is no such unimaginative player of any game as the second-rate professional. And that is really what they are.

I fear very much that the French armies, unless they make a clean sweep in officer ranks and bring forward younger and more elastic-minded men, will never be of much more use in this war, even if they are re-equipped. The process of rearmament must take many months. But to train all ranks in the use of this armament will take longer still. And it will not be facilitated by the proud and obstinate complacency of the French Army, as it is now led. . . .

The result [of the French Army's obedience to the order of the High Command to resist the Allied landings] was that General Giraud lost his nerve. Instead of arresting Darlan (or indeed after arresting Darlan), he put himself under his orders. He began to shelter under the cover of Vichy and the doctrine of apostolic succession. The men had their *serment* to the marshal. So Giraud did the next best thing – he took office under Darlan. A story was told us by his Adjutant, Commandant Beauffre, that the real trouble was the loss of his uniform. This had been duly sent ahead but the package was mislaid. How to make a *coup de'état* in a bowler hat? What a problem! A new uniform had to be procured, of five-star general rank, and a precious day lost. In any event, General Giraud lost his nerve on these fatal nights after the disembarking of the Allied forces. *Hinc illae lacrimae*. From this event springs all the timidity, the wobbling, the whoring after the false gods of Vichy, the right-wing political flavour of the administration, the pathetic cry for 'order' (always the refuge of the weak man) and the hesitating, vacillating, double-faced policy which has lasted now since Darlan's elevation and assassination. . . .

Moreover, there are some disturbing incidents happening every day. For instance, decorations – Croix de Guerre with Palms – are given to brave French soldiers. For what? For resisting the landings. And how – by fighting English and American soldiers? Not even that – which (from one point of view) is a brave and meritorious act on the part of the individual soldier. No. For shooting two de Gaullist or pro-Ally irregulars who were helping to guide our troops.

Thursday, February 25 1943

(At the villa.) I have had a quiet day doing telegrams and so on and dictating to Miss Campbell from my bed. She seemed not to be too terrified by my appearance, which is now frightful, as my lips are just about to come off, revealing (I hope) a sort of Cupid's bow behind, that will be very attractive. Meanwhile, they are horrible. My head is still in the mask, but the doctor is coming here at 6 p.m. to put on another, which he thinks he can do without an anaesthetic. He will still leave on the first or bottom dressing, under which the skin is growing.

Air Marshal Welsh[9] came to see me today. He was very apologetic. Apparently the trouble was that the mechanic forgot to take the cover off the gadget on the end of the fuselage through which the air passes and operates the speedometer.

Apparently, [the pilot] could quite well have got this fixed by the navigator while in the air. Instead of that, he did this mad effort to land again and stop.

If I go to Cairo – which I hope still to do – I shall go in a Liberator and I have told them they must make it comfortable for me, as well as safe. I think they will do their best after this effort.

I have just got a number of newspapers, as late as 20 February. I gather the Government did rather poorly over the Beveridge debate – more by the badness of their speeches than of their policy.

Herbert Morrison must have done well, both for His Majesty's Government and himself. Is there any chance now of getting rid of Kingsley and Anderson – or at least Kingsley? Anderson's work is quite good, but he should be a civil servant, not a minister – just the opposite to Beveridge.[10]

Friday, 26 February 1943

I had lots of visitors yesterday, and managed with the help of Miss Campbell (who stayed up at the villa with her typewriter) to get through a full day's work with telegrams and papers.

Thank you so much for your telegram. You will no doubt have gathered from mine that I was all right, and I think several letters went by a bag last night.

My visitors included Colonel de Linarès,[11] who is *chef de cabinet* to Giraud. He is a charming fellow – escaped from France with, or at the same time as, Giraud. He has left in France his wife and eleven children – so we chaff him a lot about evading his responsibilities. Actually his views on politics are puerile. He is absolutely terrified of the Russians and of Bolshevism. But he does not have any idea of how to prevent revolution except that of putting revolutionaries into concentration camps.

Then I had General Bedell Smith,[12] Chief of Staff to Eisenhower. He

[9] Air Marshal Sir William Welsh (d. 1962) commanded the R.A.F. operating with Allied forces in North Africa, 1942–3.

[10] Herbert Morrison (1888–1965) had been my chief as Minister of Supply in 1940; he was Home Secretary, 1940–5, and member of the War Cabinet, 1942–5. Sir Kingsley Wood (1881–1943) was Chancellor of the Exchequer, 1940–3, and a member of the War Cabinet, 1940–2. Sir John Anderson (1882–1958), later 1st Viscount Waverley, was Lord President of the Council, 1940–3, Chancellor of the Exchequer, 1943–5. He was a member of the War Cabinet, 1940–5. Sir William Beveridge (1879–1963), Master of University College, Oxford, 1937–45, drew up the Beveridge Plan, the foundation of the Welfare State.

[11] Colonel (later General) François de Linarès (1897–1955).

[12] Major-General Walter Bedell Smith (1895–1961) was General Eisenhower's Chief of Staff, 1942–5.

is a most charming and excellent fellow, and I am very fond of him. He has helped me a great deal.

Did you know that in the American Army, when a man is wounded he gets (instead of a wound-stripe) some kind of decoration called a Purple Heart. Have you ever heard of anything so ridiculous? Bedell says he thinks he will get me a Purple Heart. I think that would be awfully chic.

Tedder is really a most interesting man. He has that rare quality of greatness (which you can't define but you sense). It consists partly of humour, immense common sense, and a power to concentrate on one or two simple points. But there is something more than any separate quality – you just feel it about some people the moment they come into a room. And Tedder is one of those people about whom you feel it.

We also had a conference in my bedroom about the future of N.A.E.B. (the supply organisation) with Lee (of the Treasury) and Marris (of Foreign Office, Washington) who are here on a mission to help us.[13]

Air Marshal Welsh also came in to pay his farewell visit, as he is going home quite soon. None of these people seem to mind my extraordinary appearance. The only part of it that is actually unpleasant which can be seen consists of my lips. Nothing else (except the eyes) can be seen, as I have a mask of bandages, etc., all over. (The doctor from the military hospital kindly comes out each day and puts on a clean outer mask.)

(Evening.) I have had a quiet day. Only one visitor, Commandant Poniatowski,[14] one of Giraud's Cabinet. I like him very well. He speaks fair English. I speak French to him and he speaks English to me; which is very silly, because we should get on much better the other way round. But it is good manners and gives us both practice.

The usual political intrigues are going on. But the battle is going better, which is a relief. I spent most of the morning dictating, and after Poniatowski left I had the day's telegrams and papers to go through.

We are not leaving now till *Sunday* night for Cairo. We shall have an air marshal with us, which is something of a safeguard or insurance, I hope! I am rather glad, because it will give my face another day. It is not now hurting, but itching terribly. I suppose it is the new skin growing. Everyone is really most kind here to me, and callers and messages are streaming in.

It looks as if the P.M. had been pretty bad.[15] I do hope he will be careful. After recent exhibitions of folly, both Tory and Socialist, in the House of Commons, one shudders to think what we would do without him.

[13] Frank Lee (1903–71), later Master of Corpus Christi College, Cambridge. Adam Denzil Marris (1906–1983) was Counsellor at the British Embassy in Washington, 1941–5.

[14] Commandant Poniatowski was General Giraud's military adviser.

[15] Tired by his travelling and by the sudden changes of temperature, Churchill had contracted pneumonia a few days after returning to London.

I forgot to say I had another visitor this morning in the shape of Mr McCloy,[16] American Assistant Secretary for War. He was very intelligent and interesting. His visit will be most useful. He seemed to me much more like a fellow member of the House of Commons or a minister in a British Cabinet than the ordinary American politician.

I was able to say some things to him about the situation here which I cannot get Murphy to understand.

Saturday, 27 February 1943

(2 p.m.) The doctor came this morning. He is very pleased with the progress of my face as a whole. He has changed the outer dressing and bandages and put me on a new mask. He has left the original dressings untouched. But he says the skin is growing well underneath.

My lips are less swollen, but with rather disgusting scabs which must not be removed until they come off naturally.

There is not much news. It is quite a warm, sunny day and I am sitting out on a balcony, outside my bedroom, overlooking the harbour and the bay.

This afternoon Colonel Pechkoff,[17] one of the Gaullist liaison mission, who has just arrived, is coming to see me.

I am, of course, able to dress. My bodily bruises are much better, although I am rather stiff still. And I am going out for a little walk this afternoon before Colonel Pechkoff comes.

I have spent this morning reading and dictating. Tonight we have a dinner party of eight. Mr McCloy is the guest of honour, and I have General Gale[18] (head of Q. [Quartermaster] side, British) and General [John] Whiteley (Deputy Chief of Staff, British) and some of the economic experts to meet him.

I propose to receive my guests before dinner. Then I shall go to my bedroom and have a tray. Then I will come down and join them after dinner. I think in this way I shall overcome anybody feeling sick at the sight of me.

During my walk – which was about half an hour or three-quarters – in a lane through the various villa and market gardens, I met a very nice French peasant woman. She gave me great bunches of jonquils to take home, as well as branches of broom or juniper – in very profuse flower (white flower with a dot of red at the base of the flower). But the children all ran away, thinking I was *le diable*. However, I found one or two less timid and gave them francs – which rallied the rest.

My Gaullist friends came at 3.30. They stayed till 5 p.m.

[16] John J. McCloy (b. 1895).

[17] Colonel Zinovi Pechkoff (1884–1970), a natural son of Maxim Gorky, was head of the Gaullist Mission to French West Africa, 1943, and delegate to China, 1943–5.

[18] Major-General Sir Humfrey Gale (1890–1971) was Deputy Chief of Staff and Chief Administrative Officer under General Eisenhower, 1942–5.

Then came General Bergeret.[19]

At 7 p.m. Admiral of the Fleet Sir A. B. Cunningham. At 8 p.m. my dinner party.

At 6.30 a.m. tomorrow (Sunday) I hope to leave the villa, and if all goes well leave the aerodrome at 7.15 for Cairo.

So now I will end this rather tedious letter and send as always – my love to you and all the children and all my friends at home. I have not written to your mother. Perhaps you could let her have some news of me some time.

Sunday, 28 February 1943

(In the air.) At last we have started. We had breakfast at 6 a.m. and drove to the airfield – the same field where we had our mishap exactly a week ago. Last time it was Sunday night – this time Sunday morning.

The same little hut – the same duty officer – but (since our poor Hudson is in ashes) a new machine and a different crew. This time we have a Liberator – a very large and very comfortable machine. There are seats fitted – which there were not in the Hudson.

I have been lent a really lovely flying-suit – which is very necessary as it is very cold and there is no heating in the machine. I have lovely leather breeches, with fur inside – a leather coat, with fur inside, and a hood. This is very nice as it covers my head, which is still in bandages. I have lovely fur-lined flying-boots.

Air Marshal Welsh sent these to me – I think as a peace offering. I have a good mind to keep them as a partial compensation for the loss of my own clothes.

We started at about 9 a.m. (Algiers time, which is an hour after your time); we shall lose an hour (or is it two hours?) by going east. If all goes well, we shall reach Cairo (or rather the aerodrome) in about ten flying hours – i.e. about 7 p.m. Algiers time and either 8 p.m. or 9 p.m. Cairo time.

It is now about noon – and I have just woken up from a very comfortable sleep.

John Wyndham and I are on the trip. The only other passenger is Philip Guedalla, who is coming out to do a book on the Air Force.[20]

I have left Roger Makins in charge of the shop. I rather want to be away in any case, because there will be a pause in the political situation in French North Africa now for two or three weeks. The Gaullist mission is beginning to collect; but Catroux[21] does not get back from

[19] General Jean Bergeret (1895–1956) had been Secretary of State for Air in the Vichy Government, 1940–2, resigned to become Inspector of Air Defences, rallied to General Giraud in November 1942 and became Deputy High Commissioner of North Africa.

[20] Philip Guedalla (1889–1944), an English historian, with the rank of Squadron-Leader travelled 20,000 miles to write *The Middle East, 1940–2: A Study in Air Power* (1944).

[21] General Georges Catroux (1877–1969) was head of the Gaullist Mission to the Middle East, 1943.

Syria till about 12 March. The internal political rows between the Giraudists are just coming to the boil. All this will take the first three weeks of March. Meanwhile (for your private ear) my colleague Murphy will intrigue with them all and tell them all a different story – and then, at the critical moment, when nobody can agree – the British Resident Minister, with the full support of the Commander-in-Chief (who hates the State Department) will come out with the solution which (if P.M. and President will agree) will either be accepted by all or *imposed* on all with all the authority of the great American and British nations.

That, at least, is my dream. It probably won't come off, but I think my way of handling it gives the best chance.

I hope to get rid of my mask and bandages in another three or four days, perhaps less. I shall be able to get a really first-class surgeon at Cairo, although I must say I had great confidence in the young man who looked after me here. I need hardly say that the nursing sister came from Forest Row and knew Dr Somerville and all about you and the children.

(3.30 p.m.) The only trouble with this aeroplane is that you cannot see out at all – that is from where the seats are. You can walk along to the stern – where the gunners are – there you can see – not very plainly. Anyway, there is nothing to see now except desert. The only fine scenery is going over the great mountain ranges of eastern Algeria and Tunisia. That was very fine – and in spite of the cold (for it is much colder in the stern) I had some peeps just to get the idea of the country.

I imagine we must have made a detour to avoid flying over the part where the Germans still are.

The plane is wonderfully steady – there is less movement than in a train. John produced a marvellous luncheon – hard-boiled eggs, cold chicken, cold duck, hot coffee, fruit, and brandy!

His ideas get more and more magnificent every day. He now wants to move into a larger and grander villa. Of course, we shall all be ruined, unless (as I hope) a little man we have now got out here from the Treasury can fix it. (He is a marvellous little chap called [A.] Harnett, and he is exactly like 'Kipps' to look at.)

I am still enjoying *The Bible in Spain* – just the book for a trip like this. I find I sleep an hour – read an hour – and so on.

I have had no news of Maurice and Katharine for some time. I do hope they are all right. I suppose Maurice has *not* moved to another job after all.

I expect I shall get some more letters when I get back. You have been marvellous about writing. The last one I have from you is the typewritten one – about the aeroplane landing at Woodgate.

We arrived in Cairo (or rather the aerodrome about thirty miles away) at 6.30 (Algiers time) or 7.30 (Egyptian time). We therefore did

1,830 miles in ten hours all in one hop. This was a lovely flight – absolutely steady the whole way and a beautiful night landing.

Drove to Casey's[22] house. It is a very beautiful house belonging to Mr Chester Beatty[23] and is about half an hour from Cairo. Dined and went to bed.

[22] R. G. Casey (1890–1976) was Minister of State, Resident in the Middle East, and member of the War Cabinet, 1942–3, having been Australian Minister to the United States, 1940–2.

[23] Alfred Chester Beatty (1875–1968) was a wealthy businessman and philanthropist.

March

Monday, 1 March 1943

I am waiting for the doctor to come and see what is to be done about my face. It seems to be healing up fairly well, but I am getting very tired of these stifling bandages. Perhaps I shall soon be able to do without them.

I will finish this letter now and try to get it off. Love to all.

Tuesday, 2 March 1943

I have sent you a letter from here which I hope will arrive in due course. I feel much better, having had a fairly quiet day yesterday. The doctor came in the morning and I arranged to go into Cairo at 2.30 in the afternoon to get my face attended to.

At 11.30 Admiral Missoffe came out here and we had a conference. Casey has been ill with fever, and only got up today; so it suited everyone to have the conference here. This lasted till about 1 p.m. We agreed on a general line and drafted our telegrams, to Algiers and London, accordingly.

Casey and I lunched on a sort of roof veranda together. The rest (being Mr [K.W.] Blaxter, a lady secretary, Mrs Casey and John) lunched downstairs.

After lunch I was driven to Cairo. It really is an odd place. This house and garden are a few yards from two enormous pyramids (the best two, I believe) and a bit further on is the old Sphinx one hears so much about.

Immediately under the pyramids are an hotel, a garage, a dance hall, a soldiers' camp, and a cinema – all very incongruous. The only thing is that these latter will disappear in a few years, and the old pyramids will go on.

The house is very 'millionairy' – wonderful rugs and parquet floors, and bathrooms, etc. The food and drink are marvellous. There is no war on here, anyway. In addition to my bedroom, I have a luxurious and well-appointed 'salon' adjoining it, full of silk chairs and chaises-longues and sofas and the like.

The Egyptian servants – in their long white robes – are charming and most efficient. I haven't had time to go round the large garden yet – what I can see from my room is charming – with bougainvillaea, beds of antirrhinums, and huge borders of delphiniums, as well as lots of other flowers all in full bloom.

Well, as I say, after luncheon I drove to the hospital. Sarah would be amused by all the funny people and animals we passed on the road. Most of the men wear long white robes and white turbans; some wear red fezzes instead of turbans. Along the road first you pass a flock of sheep, with lots of black and white lambs. Next comes a general, in a Humber; next a herd of goats, usually black – sometimes black and white – with lots of kids. Next perhaps an Egyptian or European magnate in a Rolls-Royce; then a lot of camels, with the men precariously perched on their backs; then a water-buffalo and calf, being led out into the pasture; then a cow or two and some calves. Altogether an extraordinary mixture of more or less biblical scenes and modern life.

At the hospital I had my face dressed and all the bandages put back. It took about an hour.

Then I went to the Minister of State's office in Cairo, and talked with various members of the staff for about two hours – then back to the villa.

Wednesday, 3 March 1943

(8 a.m.) Today is a lovely morning; there is a kind of veranda outside my room, where I have had my morning coffee. Now I am writing in my sitting-room.

Yesterday – feeling rather tired – I stayed in bed till about 11 a.m. Then I went to the hospital and – I am glad to say – the surgeon took off my bandages and mask. I have only left dressing on my chin and nose – all the rest is free. It's a *wonderful* feeling, after ten days of constriction.

My hair is burnt a good deal and has turned a curious kind of porridge colour. My beard was about an inch long (almost white) and has been shaved with extraordinary skill by the hospital barber. My forehead is pink – lovely new skin like a baby. My cheeks are rather mottled – there are one or two places not quite healed. Altogether, it is an odd effect.

I feel pretty well, except I think I am now feeling the effects of a slight concussion – that is, I have a headache each night, and a certain dizziness in the morning. No doubt this will wear off.

After lunch, slept. At 3.30 Mr Jackson – of the Middle East Supply Centre – came out to the villa to talk about various things.[1]

At about 5 p.m., John and I got a car (I need hardly add, a

[1] Commander Robert Jackson (b. 1911) was Director-General of the Middle East Supply Centre and Principal Assistant to the Minister Resident in the Middle East, 1942–5.

Rolls-Royce) and drove to the pyramids. I won't attempt to describe these, or the Sphinx. They are too well known. I thought them remarkable rather than beautiful.

We walked back in the evening light – a very pleasant walk and passing on the way all the animals – sheep, goats, water-buffalo, cows, camels, and all the people, young and old, coming in from the fields.

We had a quiet dinner – no guests – and I was in bed by 10.30 p.m. A very pleasant day.

Today we shall go into the town to do some shopping and to see various people. I have also to get my hair cut.

I have had a good talk with Casey and settled a good many points regarding our different interests. He is *very* pleasant – but not, I think, very clever. Mrs Casey is, though.

As I don't know when the bag will go, I think I will close this letter now. Please give my love to all. Tell Sarah I wish she could see all the donkeys here. Everyone seems to ride a donkey – and the bigger the man, the smaller the donkey.

Friday, 5 March 1943

Today is Friday, and I am writing this in the intervals between seeing people at the Minister's office in Cairo. I have been given a room and a secretary and altogether have been treated with the greatest kindness and consideration by my host.

For some reason, on Wednesday afternoon, I suddenly felt very ill and took to my bed. The doctor came (a very good man, I think, being a civilian doctor serving in the R.A.M.C.) and he made all kinds of tests, etc. He said there was nothing really wrong, but that I had what he called 'delayed shock' as a result of the accident. According to this medico it is very frequent that with burns the shock does not come on till later. Anyway, I retired to bed and spent all yesterday in bed until dinner time.

The Caseys are – I must say – the most kind and considerate hosts. Nobody could be nicer than Mrs Casey in looking after my comfort. The house is most comfortable and the servants (Egyptian) extremely good. The cooking is superb.

The rigours of the African campaign are not very great in Egypt. There is any amount of butter, milk, eggs, and so on. You can buy (at a price) anything you want to in the way of clothes, including crêpe-rubber-soled shoes and similar luxuries.

Last night there was a dinner party – Mr and Mrs Shone (British Minister), Air Marshal Sholto Douglas, an American general, Jumbo Wilson – the new Commander-in-Chief, Middle East – Lord Glenconner (who runs S.O.E. [Special Operations Executive] here) – quite an interesting party.[2] People dine very late here – 9 or 9.15. They

[2] Terence Shone (1894–1965) was British Minister, Cairo, 1940–4. Air Chief Marshal Sir Sholto Douglas (1893–1969) was A.O.C.-in-C., Middle East Command, 1943–4. General Sir Henry

start work pretty early in the morning, but the offices shut from noon till 5 p.m.

Today, I felt better and went into Cairo to the office. We had various conferences all the morning and afternoon (including one with C.-in-C.). I lunched with Lord Moyne[3] – who is Deputy Minister of State here – and returned last night from Beirut. He was as queer and as charming as ever.

I have conferences, etc., most of the afternoon and tonight I dine with the British Minister.

The weather has changed. It is a great swindle – being cold and rainy – a very unusual event in this country. Everyone is very put out about it.

We have not done any more sightseeing; but it is quite interesting just to watch the people in the streets. It is really the most extraordinary mixture of nationalities and civilisations. Owing to the enormous Allied expenditure here, the country has become incredibly prosperous, and the price-level has risen very high. But I think all the wealth goes to the pashas and their hangers-on. The fellahin look poor – ill-fed and ill-clothed. I have no doubt that there is terrible corruption right through the Egyptian administration.

I am not quite sure when we will leave here. My face is almost healed now – only the chin and nose are still bad, and my lips are still very swollen. I have had my hair cut and washed, but the peculiar colour as of burnt porridge remains.

I hope to go back to Algiers via Malta, if I can arrange it. I should like to see Malta, and it is more or less on the way.

Saturday, 6 March 1943

I went in a train!! I can't tell you how delightful it was – such a peaceful motion and such comfort.

I left Cairo at noon, with Admiral Harwood[4] – Commander-in-Chief, Eastern Mediterranean and Levant. We arrived at Alexandria at about 4 p.m. We travelled in an excellent Pullman car and had a very good lunch on the way. Egypt is certainly a place in which to escape from the rigours of the North African campaign. There is an apparently inexhaustible supply of the three chief needs of mankind, viz., food, drink and clothing.

We were met at the station by a most impressive ceremonial: the naval Provost-Marshal – accompanied by a guard of sailors and marines. These surrounded us (the admiral, the flag-lieutenant and myself) with a powerful posse of armed men and by sheer weight a

Maitland Wilson (1881–1964) was C.-in-C., Middle East, 1943–4. 2nd Baron Glenconner (1899–1983) was chief executive of S.O.E. in Cairo, 1942–3.

[3] 1st Baron Moyne (1880–1944) had been my chief at the Colonial Office in 1942. He was Deputy Minister of State, Cairo, 1942–4.

[4] Admiral Sir Henry Harwood (1888–1950) was C.in-C., Levant and Eastern Mediterranean, 1943.

passage was forced for us through the seething mass of humanity which filled the station and platforms to overflowing. It was a trifle embarrassing, but very successful, manoeuvre.

The train journey – at a modest pace – gave one a very good opportunity for seeing the delta and all its life. One could see the elaborate irrigation system; the wooden water-wheels, turned by buffaloes, pumping up water from the larger sluices into the smaller channels and thence to the fields themselves: wheels which have been operated in precisely the same manner for probably three or four thousand years or more. One saw the camels, the goats, the sheep, the luxuriant crops (four crops a year is quite normal), the pastoral and agricultural population – themselves not changed since biblical times. It is rather a restful and reassuring scene amidst all the madly rushing world of today.

My task at Alexandria was to see a certain Admiral Godfroy, who is the French Admiral in command of the important naval squadron which has been in the harbour since the [Franco-German] armistice.

I will not bother you with the details of the controversy which has been going on for some time about these ships. But it has involved us a good deal in French North Africa, and there have been many pitfalls into which Downing Street and Middle East have all but fallen into during their handling of the problem. Of course, we are all very anxious that Godfroy's squadron should rally to the war; but there have been important dangers to be avoided – including his scuttling the ships in the harbour, on the one hand, or our allowing Giraud to appeal to a sort of Vichy authority on the other, in order to impress Godfroy but naturally with dangerous reaction from de Gaulle.

My job was to give Godfroy a fair (but encouraging) picture of the recent developments in French North Africa with a view to impressing his duty upon him. It was to assist in this purpose that I was taking down Admiral Missoffe (Chief of Staff to Admiral Michelier at Dakar) on the unlucky journey which ended in the aeroplane disaster.

The interview, the dinner and the talk after the dinner lasted for about five hours (with intervals), and I did not therefore have much time for other pursuits at Alexandria.[5]

The Admiral (Harwood, I mean – the hero of the *Graf Spee* battle, you will remember) was very kind. I stayed in his house and left by the 9 a.m. train on Sunday for Cairo.

Sunday, 7 March 1943

I arrived back in Cairo by about 1.15 and got to the Casey's villa in

[5] Godfroy's main concern was about the status of Giraud's administration. I tried to convince him that we were respecting French sovereignty and treating the French as allies – my membership card of the Cercle Interallié d'Alger was evidence of the latter. By the end of the interview we were both suggesting suitable occasions for Force X to rally to Giraud. Over dinner our conversation was mainly about the past – partridge-shooting and the First World War.

time for a very agreeable luncheon party, which included his chief official, Sir Arthur Rucker, just back from Baghdad – with whom I had a long talk about mutual African problems after luncheon – Philip Guedalla, Wedgwood Benn, Lady Ranfurly,[6] and one or two others.

After luncheon, I motored into Cairo to the Minister of State's office, where I had some final interviews and discussions and some letters and memoranda to dictate.

A quiet dinner at the Caseys – who have been *quite extraordinarily* kind and thoughtful – early to bed.

Monday, 8 March 1943

We left the villa at 8 p.m. Our luggage is rather more than when we came. John and I have both bought suits of clothes – also some socks, shirts and shoes in Cairo – at huge expense! John (as comptroller) has also bought a lot of pots and pans and kitchen utensils which were unobtainable either from Army or naval stores, or from the shops in Algiers.

The aeroplane (a Lockheed Hudson – the same type as the one which was burnt up) left at 8.30 or so. A rather tedious flight over the desert and a rather tiring one. The plane was very full, both of parcels and personnel – and it was rather bumpy. We had one stop (El Adem) between Tobruk and Benghazi for refuelling. During the stop we ate an excellent lunch (provided by the Caseys) and then off again. The passage over the sea (Benghazi to Malta) was more agreeable flying. It was quite cold, but we had our flying suits. We arrived at Malta quite safely and landed without mishap at about 4.30 p.m.

We were met at the aerodrome by an A.D.C. and welcomed at the palace by the Deputy Governor – Admiral Leatham[7] – who is acting in Lord Gort's absence in England on sick leave. (I think I told you that we met Lord Gort in Gibraltar on 1 January on my way out to Algiers. He had been badly burnt in a fire here during the siege and has not got back yet.)

Tea; a walk in the garden; a walk in this charming little town of San Anton; a longer walk into the country – among the little walled fields (like the High Peak) and back at 6.30 for a rest before dinner. Dinner at 8. The Admiral and the staff, Admiral Talbot (Chief of Naval) Dockyards at the Admiralty, out here on an inspection), Admiral Bonham-Carter, the new Admiral in Charge at Malta[8] – quite a gaggle or pride or what you will of admirals. I confess I was so tired I could hardly keep awake at dinner or afterwards. (For some reason the flight was a very exhausting one.) Early to bed – a lovely bed, in a big, high,

[6] William Wedgwood Benn, 1st Viscount Stansgate (1877–1960) was Secretary of State for India, 1929–31, Vice-President of the Economic Section, A.C.C., 1943–4. Hermione, Lady Ranfurly was General Wilson's personal secretary.

[7] Admiral Sir Ralph Leatham (1886–1954) was Vice-Admiral, Malta, 1942–3.

[8] Vice-Admiral Sir Cecil Talbot (1884–1970) was Director of Dockyards at the Admiralty, 1937–46. Admiral Sir Stuart Bonham-Carter (1889–1972) was Vice-Admiral, Malta, 1943–4.

square room, with white nursery furniture and chintz chairs and curtains, rather reminiscent of a room in the citadel at Quebec.

Tuesday, 9 March 1943

I slept soundly from 10.30 to 8.30 this morning.

This house is really charming – it has got so much character. It is one of the *three* palaces which belonged originally to the Grand Masters and now are occupied by the Governors. This one – in the little township of San Anton – is a large, rambling, rather shapeless building, with a fine square tower in the middle, and with a host of rooms, passages, porticos, patios, and so on, all grouped round the central tower.

The rooms are large, lofty, and of good proportions. The pictures are frightful – but of that particular period of seventeenth-century badness which I have always found rather attractive; and, anyway, the frames are usually very beautiful. The furniture is of all kinds of styles and dates – splendid gesso side-tables, a lovely set of Hepplewhite chairs, good mahogany sofa, tables, huge Victorian mahogany wardrobes, and just good War Department hospital furniture. The whole makes a charming mixture, like an English country house.

The outside is very pleasing. Like every other building in Malta, the palace is built of the lovely local stone, which is soft when quarried and can be cut or carved like cheese – which hardens with exposure – and turns a lovely golden colour, rather like the old part of Chatsworth.

Like everything (literally *everything* in Malta – with the one exception of the brewery) it is of fine proportion and in the best Renaissance classical style.

(There are actually two or three Gothic houses which I have seen, in the style of the Venetian Gothic houses which you will remember. Of those, at least one was a modern imitation of the style. But broadly speaking, Malta is just a study in the best sort of Wren or Inigo Jones, only done fifty to one hundred years before.)

The gardens round the palace cover about twenty acres. The large, formal garden is public. There are also two or three smaller private gardens.

I wish I could describe to you the flowers and shrubs. You would like them very much. The gardens consist of large trees (some cypresses, some firs, some acacias, some sort of holm-oaks), which give rather a full appearance but are no doubt necessary for shade in the summer. There are stone walls (of the same stone) surrounding and dividing off the gardens into sections; below these walls, shrubs and creepers; in between them formal beds; a good deal of fountain and statue and fish-ponds and the like, all with exquisite workmanship and fine proportions.

As to shrubs and trees – the oranges are (alas) practically over. When they remain unpicked, the trees are a very pretty sight, covered with fruit. There are a great many hibiscus, still (I think almost perpetually) in flower. The red trumpet flower of this shrub is very pretty. There are lots of a huge white strongly scented flower, like a madonna lily hanging downwards; there are abutilons and figs and magnolias, and scores of others which I cannot recall or do not know the names of. There are lots of different heaths and brooms in flower (you remember our two large groups of *Erica mediterranea*, now destroyed by the schoolchildren at Birch Grove – this is common here and now in flower) and there are, of course, all kinds of pears, cherries, almonds and the like.

Of the flowers now out, I noticed cineraria (which in great groups are rather fine – planted under the trees), stocks, antirrhinums, sweet peas, madonna lilies (in great profusion), freesias (very strongly scented), single and double anemones and lots more. The roses are not quite blooming yet, except some of the ramblers. Then lots of creepers are blooming, jasmine and similar plants. Altogether the gardens, both here and in the other palaces to which we went yesterday, are really marvellous.

At 10 a.m. the Deputy Governor took me out on a sightseeing tour, which lasted till lunch. It was really most striking. This island, only about twenty-five miles by ten (the size roughly of Arran) has a population of a quarter of a million. Nobody quite knows the racial origin – some say Phoenician, some Arab. There is, of course, an admixture of Italian blood, etc. Never have I seen so many children and priests. The people are the most devout in Europe, so children and priests are the cause and the effect. The children are very pretty and look remarkably clean, well-dressed and well-fed, considering the very great hardships which the population has undergone. Even now the rations are considerably below our standard.

The island is very rocky – or rather consists of a great rock, with a shallow coating of soil. Indeed, it is said that there was originally no soil at all in Malta – that it has all been laboriously carried here from over the sea. In any case, it is carefully looked after and protected. It is the most valuable of all their possessions, and is nurtured and hoarded accordingly.

If (for instance) they are digging a quarry, this is the procedure. First, they take off all the earth and store it carefully away. The soil is about two feet or so – not more. Then they start digging the stone out. The quarry is usually square or at least rectangular; the stone is dug or rather cut by hand with axe or adze; it is lifted to the surface by a winch worked by a donkey; and so the quarry works. After twenty years or so, when the quarry is worked out, the soil is put back and then you have a beautiful walled garden (the stone sides of the quarry forming the walls), twenty, thirty or a hundred feet deep as the case may be. This walled garden (rather like the garden in the Keep at Farnham Castle) then becomes a splendid forcing house for early vegetables and so on. It is a wonderful sun-trap. Probably in the course of quarrying water has been struck – so there is your water laid on for you, as it were, before your market garden starts.

As they must have been cutting stone here on a very large scale for many centuries, there are by now many of these walled gardens, the product of the quarrying and agricultural habits of people whose interests are not divided, as in more sophisticated communities, but have remained interlocked.

Apart from the quarries, every field gives the appearance of a walled garden. In order to protect the soil from blowing away, they have built walls round every field or vegetable patch. These fields are usually very small – three or four acres would be a large one. Then, on the high sides and on the rocky coast of the island, the same patient effort over centuries has produced a host of little terraced gardens – just the same as you see in Tuscany or Umbria.

Of course, under present conditions the farmers are being asked to concentrate as much as possible on wheat, beans, potatoes, vegetables, etc. I think some of the orange groves have been abandoned for this purpose. And the aerodromes have unfortunately deprived agricultural and horticultural production of a good deal of valuable space.

Starting at 10 a.m., the Deputy Governor took me for a drive. We visited Rabat (the old Arabic word which means 'capital' city), a perfect gem of early and high Renaissance architecture – every house and door and balcony a thing of exquisite beauty. It stands high on a splendid hill – rather like Urbino or Assisi, but on a smaller scale, looking across a lovely little valley – with all the cultivated walled fields and terraces, and the mass of wild flowers – narcissus, iris, thyme, asphodel – a marvel of peace and reposeful age and dignity and grace.

From there to Mosta – where there is an enormous round church, with the third largest dome in the world – all dome and no church – practically as big a dome as St Peter's in Rome or St Paul's in London. From there to Dingli (absurd Pickwickian name, with memories of Mr Wardle and Mr Jingle and Mr Tupman and the cricket match, but in fact a charming little township).

Then to the great summer palace of the Grand Masters and Governors after them – a huge square tower, on a hill, with four long square towers, turned slightly inwards, flanking the main tower – with a glorious dry moat (a mass of flowers) and a lovely garden and orange grove. This palace is now (alas) a hospital, but it is the place I would live in if I were Governor. (The name of this exquisite place is – alas, I have forgotten.)[9]

At lunch – the party was added to by Mr [D.C.] Campbell (the civil Lieutenant-Governor) and his wife. Campbell (a first-class Colonial servant) was first in Tanganyika and then in Uganda. About fourteen months ago he was moved to Gibraltar. There Lord Gort liked him

[9] The Verdala Palace.

enormously, and soon after Gort got here he persuaded us to move Jackson (the Lieutenant-Governor who was here with Scobie)[10] and send him Campbell.

I had heard a good deal and dealt a good deal with Campbell when I was at the Colonial Office. I found him always a man of first-class value and efficiency, and I was very glad and rather intrigued to meet him. He proved to be a little man, with a strong Derry (not Belfast) brogue, married to a capital wife – half Hungarian and half Swedish.

Somehow, there is a curious incongruity about the man, who has served always in the primitive parts of Africa, dealing with the natives of Uganda and the like, being suddenly transferred from these huge spaces and unsophisticated native races to an old – incredibly old – confined island, where the architecture is superb and the people charming but of a very old civilisation, and the whole as opposite as possible to his previous official life. (Of course, a few months at Gibraltar may have served to make Malta seem, relatively, as large as Australia.)

Anyway, here he is – small, dapper, Protestant, with his Northern Ireland brogue and his wife, whose English is very uncertain, ruling with supreme skill a people, every one of whom is a devout Catholic and whose political life and affairs are dominated by the Church to the extent which would make Ireland, and even Quebec, seem modern and Erastian by comparison.

After luncheon a little rest. Then we set off again, this time for Valletta.

The Deputy Governor was holding a meeting of the Legislative Council at 3 p.m. which I attended. This Council takes the place of the old system of responsible government, which was abolished some years ago after tremendous rows in which that old rascal Lord Strickland[11] was the protagonist.

The new Council, of course, has an official majority and therefore is a very tame affair. Nevertheless it continues the form of a sort of parliament. The Governor is in the chair; the session starts with prayers; questions (from the unofficials) follow, and then bills, or estimates, according to a regular House of Commons sort of routine. I stayed for about half an hour or so.

The building in which the Council meets is the old Governor's palace,[12] in Valletta, now hardly ever used except for official entertaining. It is a magnificent Renaissance building. The armoury (the collection of armour is, I believe, even better than that which you

[10] Sir Edward Jackson (1886–1961) was Lieutenant-Governor, Malta, 1940–3. Major-General Sir Ronald Scobie (1893–1969) was G.O.C., Malta, 1942–3, C.G.S., Middle East, 1943.

[11] 1st Baron Strickland (1861–1940) was Malta's Prime Minister and Minister of Justice, 1927–32. He offended the Vatican shortly before a general election in 1930, and the bishops of Malta and Gozo issued a pastoral instructing their flocks not to vote for him or for his followers. The Colonial Office had to step in and suspend the constitution.

[12] The Magisterial Palace.

probably remember seeing at Madrid) is now stored away. But the room quite takes your breath away. It is of immense length – I should think about eighty yards long – and of quite lovely proportions.

The other rooms – ball-room, drawing-room, dining-room (the latter blown in by a bomb) are of great beauty, the furniture, tapestries and pictures have been stored away, but the impression of the whole is quite remarkable.

The staircase (partly but not completely destroyed) is of grey and white marble – a lovely turning stair, with very shallow steps and great dignity and originality.

After visiting the palace, we went to the Castille. This was the old palace maintained by the Kings of Spain during the periods of the Knights for their own ambassadors and visitors. It stands on a fortified rock overlooking the harbour. A very large bomb fell right into the middle of it and destroyed almost the whole of the interior (it was Military and Naval Headquarters). But by a miracle the lovely exterior was hardly damaged at all. It is a square building – of great beauty and simplicity of design – with lovely carving of shields and decoration on the façade – but not heavy or over-ornate.

After that, we went to the great cathedral which was the burial place of the Knights and Grand Master, and where each nation – Italy, France, Spain, etc., – maintained a chapel. It was built in 1577 – so the English chapel was very small, because no one quite knew which way Henry VIII was going – so they had an English chapel, but only a small one, as a sort of insurance.

The style, of course, is High Renaissance – a sort of Palladian miracle – but to my mind the inside is too ornate for really pleasurable effect. The stonework of the walls is all elaborately carved and gilded – the ceiling painted somewhat flamboyantly, and the floor inlaid with those coloured marbles of which southern Italians are inordinately fond, and in the making of which the Maltese craftsmen are remarkably proficient.

Wednesday, 10 March 1943

A busy morning; an exhibition of Commando tactics put on by the major-general [Scobie], who incidentally is an old friend since I dealt with him a good lot when I was at the Colonial Office.

This was a very good show; much good training went to it. I then went over all the various Army, Navy and Air Force Headquarters on the island and saw and talked to a great number of people. I was able to learn a great deal and make a number of useful contacts.

Luncheon was with Mr and Mrs Campbell (Campbell is really more or less responsible for the management of civil affairs).

He has a house of quite extraordinary beauty. It was built by one of the Grand Masters, in the best High Renaissance style. The rooms are lofty, yet well proportioned. Fortunately, largely through the efforts of Sir Harry Luke[13] (a former) and Jackson (the last Lieutenant-Governor before Campbell), the furniture is very good. Even the pictures are pretty good, which is rare. But the great beauty of the place is its garden. This consists of a stone terrace – as broad at least as the house is high, with two lovely lily ponds and two perfect well-heads. This is the rose garden. Below, a wall – below the wall, a large herbaceous border.

Then the orangery, divided by long stone walks, with occasional breaks for lily ponds – statues and the like.

Beyond this – surrounded again by a high wall – a great semicircle (about the size of that at Glemham[14] beyond the formal garden) in which is the kitchen garden.

The garden was a blaze of flowers – wallflowers, antirrhinums, *Echium* (a huge blue flower like a delphinium but growing like a tree lupin), anemones, French lavender, stocks, rosemary – all in flower at once. It is really a lovely spot.

After luncheon, I went round some of the aerodromes with the air vice-marshal.[15] At 4.15 a meeting of the Defence Committee – viz., the admiral at Malta [Bonham-Carter], the air vice-marshal, the general commanding the troops [Scobie], with Admiral Leatham in the chair. A very interesting discussion on many points, lasting till about 6.30. Dinner and early to bed.

Thursday, 11 March 1943

Left Malta at 6.30 a.m. in a Blenheim (very difficult to get into – you have to climb up on to the tip of the machine and drop into a sort of port-hole at the top).

Arrived Tripoli at about 8 a.m. After some waiting about at Tripoli (Castel Benito aerodrome) left in DC-3 (American transport plane) and after an uneventful journey arrived Algiers at 5 p.m. The trip through the desert is not very interesting – there is too much bunker and not enough fairway about the desert – but the part over the mountains, viz., from Biskra to Algiers, is much more interesting.

Sunday, 14 March 1943

Back in the routine, and a vast amount of work to catch up on. To add to our troubles, Prince Bernhard of the Netherlands[16] is staying with us. He left today.

I am just off to listen to Giraud's speech, which is the result of two-and-a-half months of work here. I do hope it will go well. I confess I am very satisfied with it.

[13] Sir Harry Luke (1884–1969) was Lieutenant-Governor, Malta, 1930–8.

[14] My sister-in-law Lady Blanche Cobbold's house at Woodbridge in Suffolk.

[15] Air Vice-Marshal Sir Keith Park (1892–1975) was A.O.C., Malta, 1942–3.

[16] Prince Bernhard (b. 1911) married Princess Juliana (later Queen of the Netherlands) in 1937. He was Chief Netherlands Liaison Officer with the British Forces and chief of the Netherlands Mission to the War Office.

Monday, 15 March 1943

Many thanks for your letters. It is very good news about Katharine[17] – I have had a very nice letter from her telling me her news. I do hope everything will be all right. But what is she to do in the flat without Nannie? I must say I am rather relieved that Mima is coming back. She ought to be able to find someone to look after her.

We live in the most extraordinary way here – entirely upon credit, but at a huge rate of expenditure. John is a man of large ideas and as we entertain daily to lunch and dinner I shudder to think what the final result will be. However, we have got a very good little Treasury clerk out here now – a sort of Shimwell[18] – and I hope he will assist in keeping down expenses and in claiming them all back from the Treasury.

I am very much amused by the accounts of Sarah's prowess with her gun. Give her my congratulations and best love. Perhaps one day she will shoot a grey squirrel, which will be useful as well as exciting.

Tuesday, 16 March 1943

After five days of wild excitement and intrigue, I think the political situation is now really clear. These were the steps:

Sunday. Giraud's speech (written by Monnet,[19] Bob Murphy and H.M.).

Monday. Invitation to de Gaulle through Cabinet. This is *correct*, as Catroux is head of liaison mission.

Tuesday. Resignations of Bergeret and Rigault.[20]

Wednesday. (To be announced.) At 12 noon all the necessary decrees, eight in number, to implement the New Deal.[21]

I hope the House of Commons will be pleased. The bag is just going – so I finish.

Friday, 19 March 1943

This has been rather a hectic week – and yesterday (Thursday) I retired to bed for one day. Perhaps John is right. I certainly felt very bad – with a sort of jumpiness and excitability which is not normal for me. I suppose it is really due to a mixture of causes. This climate is not a very good one. It varies from great heat to bitter cold, and it is rather nervy. Many people find it so. Then we have very long days and no

[17] She was expecting her first child. 'Mima', mentioned below, was her mother.

[18] William Shimwell (1895–1980) was Comptroller of the Household, Chatsworth House, 1921–50.

[19] Jean Monnet (1888–1979), economic adviser to General Giraud, had been a member of the British Supply Council in Washington, 1940–3. In 1946 he produced the Monnet Plan for European recovery.

[20] Jean Rigault had been involved in the secret talks with the Americans before the 'Torch' landings, but was strongly anti-British. He served under Darlan with responsibility for Political and External Affairs, and ran the newspaper *Le Jour*.

[21] All Vichy legislation subsequent to June 1940 was declared invalid; all racial discrimination between native Moslems and Jews was abolished, and the municipal assemblies and *conseils généraux* were re-established.

relaxation. We start about 9 a.m. and work till 7.30. At luncheon and dinner one is always being entertained or giving entertainment to others. Even Roger Makins is beginning to show signs of wear. And these mixed parties – English, American and now two kinds of French (for the de Gaulle mission is here) – are rather exhausting. I think, in future, I shall try to stay at least one day a week in bed and read a novel.

Then I dare say that this accident has some secondary results. But I hope they will gradually pass off.

The North African New Deal has at last begun. On Sunday we had Giraud's speech. The days immediately preceding it were days of the wildest rumours and the most fanciful intrigues. On the one side was M. Monnet (from Washington, who has been Vice-Chairman of the British Supply Council there for several years). He gained great influence over Giraud and was able, from the point of view of a detached Frenchman, to give him a picture of his duty which was on the same lines as that which we have been trying to paint, but had the advantage of French authority. On the same side, of course, was all the British and (I am glad to say) American influence. This is a great improvement over early days here. Then the Americans felt obliged to justify their original deal with Darlan, and this naturally made them unwilling to join in pressure on Giraud in the direction of a liberal and republican régime. But I think I have been able to change that – first, by associating myself with their decisions at the beginning and giving public support to Eisenhower in my first press conference here; secondly, by exploiting the friendship which the President and Prime Minister showed to us at Anfa and trying to impress on Murphy the support for these views which he would get from his Government.

We also have felt, during recent weeks, that some of the Frenchmen in positions here (especially the most intelligent like Peyrouton)[22] have begun to see which way the wind was bound to blow and have altered their attitude accordingly.

On the other side, of course, have been the reactionary forces which are very powerfully represented here. The trouble is that these people, although politically wrong, are much the nicest people here, both socially and to some extent morally. They are wrong-headed but (with some important exceptions) honest.

General Bergeret, who was really under General Giraud the chief administration officer, is of this type. He is quite charming to meet; I would trust his word and his personal probity absolutely. But his political views are a hundred years behind the times. A much more sinister influence was exerted by M. Rigault. He was actually no friend of General Bergeret's, and anyway a man of a very different type. He and Bergeret had been at daggers drawn for several weeks or months – a fact quite unknown to the superficial press critics here and at home

[22] Bernard-Marcel Peyrouton (1887–1983) was Governor-General of Algeria, 1943.

who ordinarily linked the two together. Rigault is a very low type in my opinion. He has a doubtful record; is said to be a drug addict; was a Cagoulard; is a mean, shifty, anti-British, shuffling creature, who reminds me always of a sharp solicitor in a second-rate line of business. But the difficulty about removing Rigault has always been that he did a great deal to help the Allies – and especially Murphy – in the various conspirations which led up to the landings. Poor Murphy has been so much attacked about the number of his pre-landing friends who have been let down, in one way or another, that he naturally shrank from demanding the sacrifice of Rigault.

Of the higher officials, Peyrouton (Algiers), Boisson (West Africa) and Noguès (Morocco),[23] none – except to some extent Peyrouton – were really consulted. They were more or less presented at the monthly meeting of the Council with General Giraud's decisions as a *fait accompli*. They reacted according to type. Peyrouton (who is what they call *homme très fin, très souple*) is now a moderate New Dealer. He is too intelligent to change his position too rapidly. He moves with dignity and grace. Noguès (who is a pure Vicar of Bray) changed sides with enthusiasm and fervour. Boisson (who is an able, hard, honest administrator) doesn't like it and says so – but I think will 'play ball' after reflection. Anyway, with the help of Monnet and with numerous suggestions from us, the speech was finally decided. We were given a text on Saturday at 5 p.m. Work on it continued till the early hours of Sunday morning. It was delivered at 6 p.m. on Sunday afternoon.

The scene was quite impressive. The hall was well filled (about 500–600) and the audience a meeting of Lorrainers and Alsatians. Murphy and I arrived together at 5 p.m. and were put in the front row of the platform, next to two empty seats – these being left for Giraud and Bergeret (with cards). There was a musical performance till about 5.45 when Giraud arrived, attended only by an A.D.C. The chair prepared for Bergeret was hastily removed – and by this, of course, I knew that his resignation had been given. Peyrouton and Boisson were on the platform. Noguès had already returned to Morocco.

Giraud's speech was delivered (after a preliminary presentation of bouquets and cakes by small children and their appropriate osculation) in a simple and soldierly style with no attempt at oratorical effect. The whole thing lasted under half an hour and was very well received by the audience.

After the meeting there was a Gaullist demonstration in the streets. I'm afraid Giraud was rather upset by this (or so he told me when I called on him the next day).

(Monday, 15 March 1943)

The next step was taken by the announcement of the resignations of

[23] General Pierre Boisson (1894–1948) was Governor-General of West Africa, 1940–3. General C. A. P. Noguès (1877–1971) was Resident-General and C.-in-C., Morocco, 1936–43.

Bergeret and Rigault. This was rather a sell for the newspaper critics who said the speech was all right, but action must follow, because of course we had the action all laid on.

(Tuesday, 16 March 1943)

The invitation to de Gaulle through Catroux was issued to the press.

This was quite correctly sent to Catroux in the first instance, as he is the head of the Gaullist mission here.

It was a sell for those critics who complained that the speech gave no specific invitation to de Gaulle, although of course it was implied in the speech.

(Wednesday, 17 March 1943)

Eight decrees were issued, together with explanatory memoranda. These decrees carry out the policy laid down in the speech. They range from simple repeal of existing laws (e.g. about the Jews) to rather complicated arrangements for gradual substitution of an alternative system (e.g. in the economic sphere) where it is obvious that there must be a transitional stage from one system to another.

On Wednesday I had a long interview with Peyrouton which amused me. He was evidently trying to find out whether H.M.G. were going to insist on his removal or not. I thought it rather fun to leave him uncertain.

On Thursday (as I told you) I retired to bed – although I got up in the afternoon for a walk in the country with John. I also dined alone with Monnet in the evening. But I did not go to the office.

(Friday, 19 March 1943)

Rather a hectic day. A meeting of the Political Council[24] in the morning – a huge luncheon party at Peyrouton's villa. Peyrouton has a lovely garden, and it is planted with cyclamen in enormous quantities, so as to appear to be growing wild under the trees, like bluebells. Meetings, etc., all the afternoon, and we gave a large dinner – French, American, English in the evening.

We have just heard that de Gaulle will be coming, probably next week.

Saturday, 20 March 1943

I went up with Makins to stay with General Alexander. I cannot tell you what a delightful change this was from the continual atmosphere of strife, incompetence and intrigue which surrounds us in Algiers. The only way to keep sane is to go out of the town at frequent intervals.

We left in the afternoon, by aeroplane, and arrived at an aerodrome

[24] The Political Council was chaired by General Eisenhower and included General Bedell Smith, Robert Murphy and myself.

after about two hours' flight, from which we drove to his Headquarters. This position is, of course, secret; but it was a most attractive spot – 3,500 feet up – and in beautiful country.

After a walk, we dined, talked and went early to bed. I had a very nice tent and slept (as in old days) in a sleeping-bag. I now have a roll of my own for these expeditions, which is very convenient.

It was *very* cold, but I had plenty of blankets and sweaters – so I was all right.

I was wakened by the sun streaming into my tent, at about 7 a.m. A wash, a shave, a walk – and breakfast at 8 a.m.

Sunday, 21 March 1943

At 9 a.m. we left the camp in a car; Alexander and I behind, aide-de-camp and driver in front, and a good selection of tommy-guns and rifles. We drove all day to different parts of the front, stopping at various H.Q. of corps and divisions. It was a very interesting experience. First, I saw a great deal of the country in which the fighting is taking place and got a real idea of the terrain – an extraordinary sequence of great mountains and mountain passes leading into extensive plains.

Next, it gave me the chance of an uninterrupted and very valuable talk with Alexander about this and future campaigns, and of the many complicated problems which arise.

Lastly, it enabled me to learn something of the character of this very remarkable man. He has quite extraordinary charm. He has made simplicity the rule of his life. The whole atmosphere of the camp is dominated by his personality – modest, calm, confident. His experience in this war has been remarkable. He was entrusted with the task of getting the remains of the British Army away at Dunkirk, and was the last man to leave the beaches. Then he went to Burma. He took over two divisions, one Burmese, one English. Both were surrounded by the enemy – the Burmese division surrendered, but he managed to extricate the English and form some kind of a static line. A week in England; then he was sent to succeed Auchinleck[25] in the Middle East. He found a dispirited army, seventy miles from Cairo, more ready to retire through the Delta than to fight. He moved his H.Q. from Cairo to tents in the desert. Ten days after he took over, the Germans attacked. The attack was held. Within a month he reorganised the army, and launched the Eighth Army in a battle which has taken it to the Mareth Line. He was next sent to this command here – in command of the First Army, the American Second Corps, and the Eighth Army – in other words he has been placed in charge of all active military operations on this front. On the day before he took over, came the

[25] General Sir Claude Auchinleck (1884–1981) was C.-in-C., Middle East, 1941–2, and C.-in-C., India, 1941 and 1943–7.

heavy German attack on the Americans and a very serious situation. He at once took charge and put things right.

On the Sunday – or rather on the Saturday night – began the great battle[26] which is now raging – with varying success. It is of vital importance. But I must say I have every confidence in Alexander bringing it off, if any man can. During Sunday, we drove over the country, saw a few officers, visited some charming Roman remains (in which Tunisia is very rich). He neither asked for nor received messages or news. When we got back in the late evening, he showed neither anxiety nor nervousness. After dinner, we listened to the P.M.'s broadcast speech. A few telegrams[27] were brought in – a few orders quietly given – and the rest of the evening we chatted about politics, sport, architecture, Roman history and the like.

Air Marshal Coningham[28] (who lives side by side with Alexander) also struck me as very good. They appear to work together in perfect harmony. They plan and concert all their operations as a single whole. Altogether it was a heartening and a refreshing experience.

We got back (by air) on *Monday, 22 March* to take up the daily round of telegrams, meetings, luncheons, dinners which constitute life in Algiers.

On *Thursday, 25 March*, there was a tremendous funeral ceremony in the cathedral. A certain Colonel Baril had been killed in an air accident.[29] He was a remarkable and quite charming man, with whom I had made great friends. He is a great loss to France and to us. It was through his work (largely) that the landings at Sidi Ferruch (near Algiers) and at Blida were practically unopposed, and he would have been a useful link in the de Gaulle–Giraud negotiations, since he had the respect and affection of both sides.

The funeral was a terrific ecclesiastical and civil ceremony – with speeches, march-past of troops, etc. The British detachment (Irish Guards) took everyone's breath away, so splendid was their bearing.

Friday, 26 March 1943

We are still awaiting Catroux, who is expected from Syria today or tomorrow. Then – I suppose – negotiations will begin. I have no doubt there will be some tricky and anxious moments, but I feel in my bones that we shall bring it off in the end. I think both sides are beginning to realise that the people of France will never forgive them if they go on squabbling while France is in agony.

I am sorry for this rather hurried letter, but we seem to have had

[26] The British Eighth Army had launched a frontal attack on the Axis forces behind the Mareth Line.

[27] One of these contained General Montgomery's first report of his attack on the Mareth Line.

[28] Air Vice-Marshal Sir Arthur Coningham (1895–1948) had formed the North-west African Tactical Air Force in February 1943.

[29] Colonel Baril, of the French North African Army, was on a mission to Syria when his aeroplane crashed near Beirut.

a very hectic week. The weather is not pleasant. There is a hot moist Sirocco blowing, and it makes one feel very slack. But the flowers and shrubs are blooming all the more – wisteria in full flower everywhere.

Saturday, 27 March 1943

John and I started off for a two-day jaunt. The weather was lovely – not too hot, but yet bright. We left Algiers by car (we have now got an excellent Buick) at about 8.30 a.m. Our destination was Sétif, about two hundred miles or so, and the road took us through some really wonderful mountain country. I do not think I have ever had a more enjoyable day through more beautiful scenery.

You cross a portion of what is called the Kabyle country. This includes the great range of the Djurdjura mountains, which rise to between 7,000 and 8,000 feet. You first go up (in a winding road) through the gorge of the Isser – at one point it narrows to only a few hundred feet between the rocks on either side. Further on, you pass through two quite extraordinary passes – called Les Portes de Fer – in the Biban range. Here the cliffs rise on each side like masonry. From time to time you pass Kabyle villages. These are built (like Tuscan or Umbrian towns) on the tops of hills. The houses are of stone, the roofs of red tiles. These Kabyle people are rather interesting. They are really the remnants of the original inhabitants – before the Romans or the Arabs or (of course) the French. They are said to be the tribes which owed allegiance to Jugurtha [King of Numidia] and after his defeat to the Romans in (I think) the first century B.C. They are Berbers by race – many quite fair, with fair hair and quite indistinguishable from Europeans. The women did not appear to be veiled. They fled to this mountainous tract, in the same way as the ancient Britons fled to Wales; and just as these withstood the Romans and then the Anglo-Saxon, Danish and other invasions, so the Berber inhabitants of Kabylia survived Romans and Arabs alike, maintaining themselves in their mountain villages. They were only finally subjugated by the French after prolonged struggles.

This territory, apart from its extraordinary charm and beauty, forces itself on our attention at the present time because of the many economic problems which it presents.

In peacetime, a very large proportion of the male population (which is about one-and-a-half millions in a very poor and barren country) ordinarily migrates to France, either permanently or for short periods, and as they are very intelligent (specially easily trained as mechanics) they earn good wages, a large proportion of which they send home. Owing to the war – and more especially since our arrival in North Africa has cut off all connection with France – these remittances no longer reach them. It is as if the Irishmen in the U.S.A. and Great Britain were to cease sending money home, and at the same time no

Irish labour was going over to England for the harvest, etc., and earning money in that way.

The population is therefore very poor, and the food and clothing position among the people has caused us all a lot of worry. So I was specially anxious to see the country and the people about whose affairs I had attended so many conferences.

We are trying to help them – the serious time is until the next harvest is in – partly by distribution of food and clothing and partly by recruiting the labour in works companies and battalions for road work and so on for military purposes.

I think they recognise the efforts to help them and all those I talked to seemed very friendly.

The extraordinary thing to me about this country is the entirely different view which one takes of mountains. (I suppose this is familiar to you, having been in Kenya.) But, to me, a valley is normally the rich, agricultural land, and when you climb up mountain gorges and passes, you expect to reach barren and useless peaks. But here it is just the opposite. The mountain gorges and passes through which we climbed are (like Jack and the Beanstalk) a road to high, fertile, well-cultivated plateaux – with ancient and modern cities. From a place called Mansoura (a Kabyle village) you climb up for a few miles and emerge through a pass on to a vast plain – called the Hauts Plateaux. The height is about 3,500 feet. The spring wheat is either just showing or (in some places) just about to be sown. The whole plateau is a flat cultivated wheat and grain country – and farmed mostly by French settlers or *colons*, owning large farms, which they work with Arab labour.

We reached Sétif (about seventy or eighty miles from Mansoura) at 4 o'clock. We had a picnic lunch and a bit of a walk on the way.

Sétif is a sort of market town, of quite a fair size, with some good modern buildings. It is of no great interest. *But*, about forty miles from Sétif is a really remarkable place, called Djemila, the ancient city of Cuicul.

After a short rest at Sétif, we started off for this place. The drive is through some delicious country – barren hillsides (for all the trees have been cut), but fertile little valleys. The light was extraordinarily beautiful – a sort of miraculous luminosity covering all the landscape as the sun began to decline. And – after the drive – suddenly there comes into sight, situated on a small hill, in a broad valley, with the great mountains beyond, the ruins of this extraordinary city.

The excavation was only undertaken about thirty years ago and had been going on slowly till the war. There is still a lot to do. There are really three separate towns. The first, at the lowest part of a long hill, was built in the time of Trajan. The forum is well preserved – with a beautiful little temple of Venus at one end, and with many of the columns standing. There are also the shops, with their counters (all of stone) and the places where the scales were hung. And there are the stone pans *in situ* for weighing out various measures – corn, olive oil, etc. Many of the columns are of a beautiful grey-blue marble – quarried at Philippeville (over 150 miles away) and brought here over the mountain passes. There are some beautiful fountains, a very well-preserved private house, and some well-preserved public baths in the old town, with the usual system of steam-heating through the double walls.

The second town is about the time of Septimius Severus. It has another forum, also very fine, and a magnificent temple of Jupiter, standing on a height above the forum, with some splendid columns and a fine doorway still standing. There are many colonnades and a splendid arch of Caracalla. There is also a magnificent theatre, the seats of which are practically intact, and the stage and stage buildings of which are well preserved also. The theatre held over 3,000 people seated. The site is splendid – looking out over the valley to the mountains.

Most of the mosaics from the houses and temples in these two old Roman towns have been taken away and put in a museum close by. The older mosaics are very good – especially a bathroom floor (with a lot of animals) and a drawing-room floor with the story of Bacchus. The later ones are coarse and poor work.

A little further up the hill there is the Christian town, of the fifth century. Here are two fine 'Basilicas' and a perfectly charming little round baptistery. There is a large bath for adult baptism and a small font for infant baptism.

Altogether the whole place is really wonderful, partly from its archaeological interest and partly from its magnificent position.

We motored back to Sétif, arriving back just after sunset, about 7.30 p.m. Here we dined with a general who is a friend and afterwards went to a concert given by the troops for the troops in the local theatre.

A long, but very enjoyable day. We slept in Sétif having brought our bedding rolls and blankets with us.

Sunday, 28 March 1943

We left at 8.30. We motored from Sétif to Bougie – a distance of seventy miles, and even more wonderful scenery than the day before. You drop down from 3,500 feet to sea level, and the pass or gorge of Chabet or Kerrata through which the road goes (cut in the rock) is an astonishing sight. You look sheer up to the crags, with eagles circling round, and sheer down to the river below. The narrowest part is a distance of about five miles. But all the road goes through fine mountain scenery. The last bit goes along the sea coast – the road rather like the Corniche.

We got back to Algiers at about 5.30 p.m.

Harold Balfour[30] (who is on his way through) came to dinner – also Air Chief Marshal Tedder.

Monday, 29 March 1943

The usual day at the office: meetings, papers, telegrams, etc. The new French Minister of Transport, M. René Mayer[31] (a professing Jew!) came to see me. I think he will be very efficient, and his appointment marks the extent of the political changes here.

Robert Sherwood,[32] the American dramatic writer, to dinner – with a lot of the propaganda boys.

Tuesday, 30 March 1943

General Catroux to see me. He seems very hopeful of an agreement [between himself and Giraud].

Lunch with the Princesse [Marie] de Ligne – in a villa some miles from the town – very French, very Faubourg St Germain – very agreeable, but rather dated.

In the afternoon, I went round two British hospitals with the chief medical general here – General Cavell. Tiring, but interesting.

A large dinner-party for the successor to General Bergeret, M. Couve de Murville[33] – young, intelligent, recently escaped from France. I think he will do well. Generals, commodores, air marshals, admirals, etc., to meet him.

Wednesday, 31 March 1943

Thank you so much for all your letters. They now seem to come weekly with great regularity. And how well you have learned to type. It would be a great advantage to you if I could do the same, for I'm afraid my writing is sometimes quite illegible.

The news is good. The battle of Mareth has been very severe, but I felt great confidence in Alexander and Montgomery and I gather that the air support was really tremendous.[34] If only we can get fine weather, the aerodromes will dry up and allow our air superiority to be used to the full.

[30] Captain Harold Balfour (b. 1897) was Parliamentary Under-Secretary of State for Air, 1938–44.

[31] René Mayer (1895–1972) was later Commissioner for Communications, 1943, Minister of Public Works and Transport, 1944, and Prime Minister, 1953.

[32] Robert Sherwood (1896–1955) was Director of Overseas Operations, Office of War Information. He wrote *The Petrified Forest*, 1934, *There Shall Be No Night*, 1940, and other plays.

[33] Maurice Couve de Murville (b. 1907) became a member of the F.N.C.L., 1943, and later a distinguished diplomat, and Prime Minister, 1968–9.

[34] The Eighth Army's first frontal attack had failed, so the commander, Lieutenant-General Sir Bernard Montgomery (1887–1976), sent American, New Zealand and French troops on a 200-mile southerly flanking movement. The Mareth Line was breached on 26 March and Mareth village captured on the 28th. The Western Desert Air Force had carried out a series of devastating attacks, destroying a large number of Axis tanks and transport vehicles, and on the 29th had flown 300 sorties in two-and-a-half hours, employing a new form of intense attack known as 'Tedder's carpet'.

If we can bring off a really resounding defeat of the Germans and Italians the moral effect here will be tremendous. For there are still many hesitant Frenchmen, oppressed with the sense of defeat and almost mesmerised by German power.

Meanwhile, there is everyday some improvement in things here – some rascal dismissed and good man put in his place.

I hope you had a good time in Stockton.[35] I'm afraid it is rather a bore having to go up, but they will be very glad to see you. I was going round a hospital here the other day, when I heard a cry of 'good old Mac' – a Durham Light Infantry man – from Garbutt Street (Stockton).

The political discussions between Giraud and Catroux are proceeding – some believe not so favourably. But there are bound to be ups and downs and a lot of hard bargaining, and I am determined to keep out of it (at least for the present) and make the French face their own responsibilities. We cannot always be in attendance on them, like nurses.

Mr [Ed] Murrow and Mr [Charles] Collingwood (American broadcasters) to lunch.

General Gairdner[36] (a great friend of all the Beresfords and a charming Irishman) to dinner.

The rest of the day the usual routine. We never seem to catch up, and we are still grossly under-staffed – only really Roger and I for the serious work and John Wyndham as sort of social A.D.C.

[35] My constituency, 1924–9 and 1931–45.

[36] Major-General (later General) Sir Charles Gairdner (b. 1898) was G.O.C., Eighth Armoured Division, 1943, and Chief of Staff, A.F.H.Q., 1943.

April

Thursday, 1 April 1943

The weather is absolutely lovely now. The villa gardens are full of flowers – great numbers of madonna lilies, growing in the open like daffodils; quantities of freesias, with their strong odour – pleasant enough in the open; montbretia (I don't know how you spell it) and on many of the houses wistaria in full bloom.

We went for a little walk last night before dinner in a valley behind our villa. It is quite cool in the evening and even cold at night. During the day it is like a nice June day at home. The weather seems to have settled at last, with clear blue sky and a drying sun; which will help us in the battle.

A long morning in a conference about the future administration of Tunisia, which we hope will soon be free from Germans and Italians. Lunch with M. de Vitasse (a French diplomatist) at the Club. I feel sorry for these poor French people although they are so ridiculous. They conceal their sorrows well. Families are divided; they get no news of sons and married daughters. Since November, of course, all communication with France has ceased. They do not even know whether their children are alive, or imprisoned, or transported to Germany as slaves. At the luncheon today were two French officers, recently escaped through Spain. One had been six weeks, the other two months in a Spanish prison. And I gather Spanish prisons are pretty tough.

Political internees and refugees were all mixed up with ordinary criminals. My friend's neighbour and companion in exercise in the prison yard was a Spaniard who had been convicted of shooting a man and eating his arms! I observed that doubtless he (the French colonel) kept his hands in his pockets. This seemed to amuse him greatly.

My neighbour at lunch is a lady of great sprightliness and charm – Comtesse [Yvonne] de Rose – a brunette, who fascinates us all here and is (in a society very lacking in women) the universal standby at all our parties. She is coy, espiègle, captivating – and not too clean. But there it is; *on fait de son mieux*.

Today is really hot; and M. Monnet is going to talk to me for an hour about the principles underlying the constitutional framework of the Third Republic.

We have just got a batch of English newspapers, from which I see that the Prime Minister's broadcast has very much fluttered the political dovecots. I listened to it – thought it pretty good. Of course, it was really an election address, and it would seem to have put the Labour Party in rather a quandary. The trouble of it is that no one really has any idea as to the future course of the war. One minute people rush to an extreme of pessimism – and think it will never end. The next they become so excited by a favourable battle that they regard it as more or less over. And the experts cannot give us any guidance. The better they are, the less willing I find them (I mean men like Cunningham, Tedder and Alexander) to express a view. Certainly there is no sign of any break in German morale on this front. They are fighting fiercely and valiantly.

Went for a walk before dinner 6.30–7.30. A pleasant change from this eternal office. After dinner, went to the private view of a pre-war French film called *L'Entente Cordiale*. The idea was that it might do as propaganda here – but it won't. It is silly and vulgar.

Friday, 2 April 1943

9 a.m. Saw General Eisenhower.
11 a.m. Political and Economic Council – weekly meeting.
1 p.m. Lunch. Deputy Chief of Staff [General Whiteley].
3–7 p.m. Continual stream of French callers:
(*a*) Giraudists
(*b*) Gaullists
(*c*) Neutrals
(*d*) Giraudists, with sympathy for de Gaulle
(*e*) Giraudists, without sympathy for de Gaulle
(*f*) Gaullists, with sympathy for Giraud
(*g*) Gaullists, without sympathy for Giraud.

I just sit and murmur from time to time – '*Oui, monsieur – comme vous dîtes, l'union française est indispensable*.'

In addition to all these activities, and throwing them all into still greater confusion, a row has developed (by telegram) between de Gaulle and Catroux. Catroux wants to be let alone to conduct a leisurely negotiation in this agreeable spring climate with his old friend Giraud. De Gaulle wants to quicken the pace and come out here at once. Catroux replies by threatening resignation. Everyone here got intensely excited – but I am convinced it is all a storm in a teacup. After several weeks or days of attitudinising and generally behaving like rather unbalanced children, they will reach an agreement amongst themselves and then look to the U.S.A. and Great Britain to show their recognition of how well the French are behaving by handsome wedding gifts.

Saturday, 3 April 1943

We are living in very strenuous and exciting atmosphere, which is gradually rising in temperature as de Gaulle's arrival is expected – or feared.

The cross-currents and eddies of intrigue are extraordinary. But I try to keep as clear from them as I can.

Today, owing to a number of problems I had to have two interviews with Eisenhower, who was as usual very friendly. His language is always refreshing – a most entertaining Middle Western slang, interposed with the oddest expletives.

We had a dinner party for Catroux – including an American general, Bob Murphy, Colonel de Linarès (of Giraud's Cabinet) and various others.

Sunday, 4 April 1943

Church at 10 a.m. As usual, filled with soldiers, both British and American, who sang the hymns very lustily.

After church – the office till 12.30. Then Roger, John and I went for a little motor trip. We drove out along the coast, through some very pretty country, and found a place for a picnic by the sea. We then drove on to a place where there is a very peculiar tomb, called Tombeau de la Chrétienne. It is in the shape of a huge beehive and stands on a hill about 700 or 800 feet up from the valley. The stones are large blocks (rather like the pyramids) beautifully cut and put together without mortar. Round the whole base runs a series of Ionic columns, about twenty feet in height – the tomb itself reaching I should say a height of a hundred feet or more. It is said to have been built by Juba, one of the old Berber kings, but no one seems to know much about it. I should say it was probably the second century B.C.

We drove back through another nice stretch of country and got home about 5 p.m. I forgot to say that we found a great many wild irises near the tomb and also wild snapdragon.

I dined with Jean Monnet alone. He kept me till after 11 p.m. talking about the situation.

Monday, 5 April 1943

A full day at the office, with a lot of telegrams to deal with. I am just leaving (7 p.m.) for a cocktail party given by Comtesse de Rose. Her husband was *chef de cabinet* to Lemaigre-Dubreuil and has gone out of office with him.[1] This will rather dash the ambitions of the Comtesse,

[1] Comte François de Tricornot de Rose (b. 1910) survived the setback and eventually became French Ambassador to Portugal, 1964–9. Jacques Lemaigre-Dubreuil (1894–1955), controller of the newspaper *Le Jour*, had been General Giraud's *chef de cabinet* and had taken part in the secret talks with the Americans before the 'Torch' landings. He was assassinated by Moroccan *colons* after the war.

who saw herself running a *salon* for her husband's political advancement. De Rose is joining the Army. But I expect the Comtesse will have a very gay time as a grass widow.

I dine with General Gale. He is such a nice man and most helpful to me in every way.

Tuesday, 6 April 1943

I have just got your letter of 24 March – finished on 29 March.

I think it is best not to send letters in bag addressed to other people. But I think it is all right for the family – I mean Arbell,[2] and your sisters, etc. In that case they should be enclosed in a letter addressed to *me* and should be open.

Thank you, I did get two parcels and clothes and I can manage quite well now with a few things I got in Cairo. Please do *not* send me the new shoes at present.

I was very much amused by your account of the Cobbold wedding.[3] Somebody told me that he is a very nice young man.

If only these Frenchmen would hurry up and settle their affairs, I might get home for Easter. But I must stay till this job is over.

It is lovely today – really hot, but not too hot.

It has been a day of alarms and excursions – not made easier by the arrival of Lord Gort from Malta. We had a large dinner for him, at the end of a very exhausting day. Sir Ronald Adam[4] (Adjutant-General), M. Jean Monnet, Air Marshal Wigglesworth,[5] and several others. But the whole afternoon and evening were thrown into confusion by the publication of de Gaulle's communiqué. This naturally caused great excitement among my American friends, especially Chief of Staff (Bedell Smith) and, to some extent, General Eisenhower. As usual, they were exacerbated rather than smoothed over by Murphy, who has the American anti-de Gaulle complex.

The true story was very simple. The Prime Minister informed me that de Gaulle had asked for a plane to go to North Africa, but before letting him go, he asked for the Commander-in-Chief's views. The Americans would have liked a blank refusal, on the formal ground that Catroux was carrying on the mission and therefore de Gaulle was not wanted till the negotiations had either got on further or broken down completely. I persuaded the Commander-in-Chief and Chief of Staff that such a course would draw down immense criticism on him and there was no object in putting his head out in this way. So we concocted a very polite and courteous telegram saying that as the battle was reaching its crisis this week and would occupy everyone's attention

[2] Arbell Mackintosh, my wife's niece, then driving for the Red Cross.

[3] My wife's niece Pamela Cobbold had married W. V. Hope-Johnstone on 27 March 1943.

[4] General Sir Ronald Forbes Adam (1885–1982), was Adjutant General to the Forces, 1941–6.

[5] Air Vice-Marshal Sir Philip Wigglesworth (1896–1975) was Deputy C.-in-C., Allied Air Forces, Mediterranean Air Command, 1943.

(including Giraud's) we would be very grateful if de Gaulle would postpone his trip for a few days.

The telegram (which I wrote) will certainly bear publication and I rather feel it ought to be published in fairness to Eisenhower.

It was rather a dirty trick of de Gaulle to publish the communiqué.[6] After all, the whole thing was a private exchange of telegrams. Anyway, I telegraphed immediately to the Prime Minister asking for strong support for Commander-in-Chief, and waited.

During my dinner party [that evening] I got a message from Catroux asking to see me.

Of course, Catroux is sore because he feels that the negotiations – having been entrusted to him – should be left in his hands. He was also very much afraid that de Gaulle's arrival would be the signal for demonstration and counter-demonstration, leading perhaps to riots and bloodshed, and certainly not calculated to help the battle in Tunisia.

Naturally, that was all along my chief reason for wanting to postpone de Gaulle's visit. But I had tried its effect this end without exciting C.-in-C. too much. Anyway, after much talk, Catroux agreed to return immediately to London. It is a far better place in which to have internal French rows than North Africa – at any rate till the Germans have been finally expelled.

Wednesday, 7 April 1943

A troubled morning; no news from London – the Americans very jumpy and almost openly saying that the Prime Minister will let down the C.-in-C. Luncheon at the Palais d'Été. The Field Marshal [Gort] and the General [Giraud] in terrific form – *anciens camarades, mes chers*, and all that. Guard of honour of Spahis, trumpets, a vast meal, and indeed everything the French love so much. Old Giraud is in crashing form. He had been to stay with Montgomery and was tremendously impressed with both the organisation and the men. He had also been to see General Anderson.[7]

A troubled afternoon – and then (as I knew all along) a very good private telegram for Ike from the Prime Minister and a good public communiqué from Downing Street. I also gathered that the English press, at least, was taking a more reasonable view, no doubt with official guidance. This telegram fortunately arrived before dinner, and I was able to give it to the C.-in-C.

General Eisenhower (Ike or C.-in-C.) very rightly never dines out.

[6] General de Gaulle wanted to visit North Africa for personal discussions with General Giraud, who was proposing for himself the double role of co-President and Commander-in-Chief of the Free French forces. De Gaulle's communiqué implied that General Eisenhower had prevented him from travelling to Algiers to effect a French union.

[7] Lieutenant-General Sir Kenneth Anderson (1891–1959) was commander of the First Army during the North African campaign, 1942–3.

But he broke his rule tonight, and it is regarded as a great honour. My party consisted of C.-in-C., Field Marshal Lord Gort, Admiral of the Fleet Sir A. B. Cunningham, and self. No aides, no staff. It was really a delightful evening and (owing to arrival of P.M.'s telegram half an hour before dinner) went off very well.

Thursday, 8 April 1943

A typical day here. I give my engagement book:

9 a.m. Commandant Poniatowski (French official).

9.30 a.m. Colonel de Linarès (of Giraud's Cabinet).

10 a.m. Morning meeting with Murphy (daily event).

10.30 a.m. North African Economic Board.

12 noon M. Hauck[8] (Free French Labour Adviser).

12.30 p.m. Deputy Chief of Staff [General Whiteley].

1.0 p.m. Lunch: Deputy Chief of Staff, Francis Rodd and young Duncannon who arrived today to join my staff.[9]

2.30 p.m. M. Muscatelli – a new Préfet of Algiers and districts. A friend of ours; subsequently in prison after Darlan murder;[10] now back in office as part of the New Deal.

4 p.m. M. Gentil[11] (French ambassador) going to London on mission to de Gaulle.

4.30 p.m. Count Grabski and another Pole.

5.30 p.m. M. Houet.

7.45 p.m. Dinner: M. St Hardouin[12] (Foreign Affairs), Murphy, M. Couve de Murville, Colonel de Linarès, General Bouscat.[13]

And so to bed – the end of a perfect day.

Friday, 9 April 1943

Things are beginning to disentangle themselves a little, and the atmosphere is clearer. Indeed, quite a few people are beginning to take a mild interest in the war!

I have just got a splendid letter from you – partly about the visit to Stockton and Thornaby (the Digging for Victory one) and partly about the flowers in the garden. I am so grateful to you for sending me all these details, which I just love to hear. These ridiculous Frenchmen

[8] Henri Hauck (b. 1902) was Director of Labour on the French National Committee, 1940–3.

[9] Major-General Francis Rodd, 2nd Baron Rennell (1895–1978) was General Alexander's Chief Civil Affairs Officer, 1943. Major Frederick Ponsonby, Viscount Duncannon (b. 1913), later 10th Earl of Bessborough, was G.S.O.2 (Liaison) in West and North Africa until 1944.

[10] Léon Muscatelli (b. 1899) was Prefect of Algiers, 1943.

[11] François Gentil (1886–1964) had been appointed Vichy ambassador to the Argentine in September 1942, but in January 1943 had left Buenos Aires to join the Free French.

[12] Jacques Tarbé de St Hardouin (d. 1956), General Giraud's Secretary for Foreign Affairs, had acted as a U.S. agent before the 'Torch' landings.

[13] General René Bouscat (1891–1970) was Chief of Staff to the Commander of the Free French Air Force.

have spoilt my hopes of an Easter at home, as I suppose I must now stay here to wait for the next act in this tragi-comedy.

Saturday, 10 April 1943

The crisis is temporarily over.[14] The Americans are slowly recovering their temper. It is extraordinary how sensitive they are, and however much I try to nurse them, they are always near to some emotional exhibition of nerves or temper. Of course, it's really due to a sort of inferiority complex, and it takes this form as with all people who are not sure of themselves. Fortunately, however much General Montgomery may infuriate them, General Alexander soothes them wonderfully. The truth is, that no sooner have they recovered from a fit of self-depreciation, than they become intolerably uppish again.

However, in spite of it all, I am really very fond of them – especially the soldiers.

Now that Catroux has gone home, we have a fairly quiet interval. The lesser lights chatter, and lunch, and dine, and intrigue. Meanwhile, the First and Eighth Armies move forward from victory to victory.[15] It is getting very exciting, and everyone is speculating on the end. I do long for a resounding defeat of the enemy. If we could kill, drown or capture the whole German Army, it would have an immense effect, even beyond its military importance.

I had to go to a frightful kind of party – a sort of cocktail party going on to a stand-up dinner. I believe it is officially called a *porto prolongé*. It nearly made me sick. It was given by a fallen minister, M. Lemaigre-Dubreuil. So we felt we must go. Everyone was there – Giraudists in place, Giraudists out of place, Giraudists expecting place, Gaullists, Americans, British and all the oddments. It was really frightful.

Sunday, 11 April 1943

Church at 10 a.m., packed as usual, and the men singing with great gusto.

After church at the office till lunch. Archbishop [Francis] Spellman (of New York) came to lunch. I found him very amusing and quite a character. He had been made very much of during his visit to England, with apparently excellent results. He told of his journey here; his projected tour – Malta – Cairo – South Africa – India – Burma – China, and so on. He also told us how he had lunched with the Prime Minister – been to Liverpool – gone to Belfast – stayed with the Duke of

[14] General Catroux had flown to London on 8 April.

[15] The battle at the Mareth Line had been completed on 7 April when an American patrol, part of the forces undertaking the 200-mile southerly flanking movement, met a patrol from General Montgomery's frontal-attacking forces. Barely pausing to regroup, the Eighth Army captured Sfax on 10 April, Sousse on the 12th, and on the 13th, pressing north towards Tunis, attacked the Axis stronghold at Enfidaville.

Abercorn[16] – and many other adventures. I said, 'Did you go to Southern Ireland, your Grace?' To which he replied, with something between a chuckle and a leer, 'Oh yes: I went for an odd day to Dublin. You see, I've got to go back to New York one day, you know!'

After lunch we took the car and drove into the mountains beyond Blida. It was the most lovely day, clear blue sky, warm but not too hot, like a perfect June day at home. The fields and vineyards are full of wild flowers. There is a lovely wild gladiolus – with a sort of red–purple flower – which grows everywhere. It is, of course, a smaller flower and has fewer blooms than the cultivated kind, but *en masse* it is very attractive.

The little purple wild iris are out everywhere – and also the large white.

We took the car up the mountain to a height of about 3,000 feet and then walked down – taking short cuts and old roads and scrambling down as best we could. It took us nearly one-and-a-half to two hours' walking and did us a lot of good. Being terribly out of condition, I got very hot. But I had brought a coat and so avoided catching cold on the way home.

I dined with Admiral Cunningham at his villa. As usual, it was a very merry party. Old Sir Walter Cowan[17] – the admiral of seventy-two who joined the Commandos and was eventually taken prisoner at Tobruk – was there. He has been released under some exchange system. He is very old and shaken but a very simple and charming old man. Also General Scobie (whom I knew at the Colonial Office, and has been at Malta as G.O.C. and is now Chief of Staff, Middle East) and my Yorkshire friend Air Vice-Marshal Wigglesworth – a great character, almost pure Thornaby.

Monday, 12 April 1943

The usual routine. A 'pride' of generals to luncheon: Lindsell[18] (Middle East), Scobie, Gale, Rennell. A long and dull day, with papers, memoranda, etc., and (thank goodness) no one to dinner.

Tuesday, 13 April 1943

9 a.m. Office.

10 a.m. Murphy.

11.30 a.m. Captain Moret (Free French Navy, but quarrelled with de Gaulle!).

12 noon. Count Grabski (Pole).

[16] 3rd Duke of Abercorn (1869–1953) was Governor of Northern Ireland, 1922–45.

[17] Admiral Sir Walter Cowan (1871–1956) served with Commando Forces, 1939–45, having retired from the Navy in 1931. He had been A.D.C. to Lord Kitchener in the South African War, 1901, and fought in the battle of Jutland, 1916.

[18] Lieutenant-General Sir Wilfrid Lindsell (1884–1973) was in charge of administration in the Middle East, 1942–3.

12.45 p.m. Lunch, Consul-General [Carvell], to meet M. Peyrouton.
Peyrouton made one good remark: '*On connait toujours la politique des militaires pars leurs moustaches. Giraud a la moustache très symbolique, comme le Lord Kitchener.*'

3–5.30 p.m. Long meetings on French West Africa, oil-seed supplies and on the wheat needs of Algeria in relation to hoarding in Morocco.

6 p.m. Visit to Giraud. Long discussion about Force X (Godfroy) at Alexandria – fairly satisfactory, but I'm afraid not enough for the P.M.!

7.45 p.m. Dinner (Cercle Inter-Allié) given by M. and Mme Schneider.[19] The St Hardouins (Secretary for Foreign Affairs with a Turkish wife!) and a French colonel. Not very exciting.

Wednesday, 14 April 1943

I spent all the morning at the villa, writing and dictating. The weather is vile – a strong wind from the sea and a moist clammy atmosphere. After luncheon, more talk about oil-seeds. Everyone's temper got very frayed. It really can be very trying here when the humidity is so great.

Thursday, 15 April 1943

One of the difficulties of working here is the extraordinarily low standard of efficiency in the middle ranks of the French civil administration, and (let it be said) of the American representatives on N.A.E.B. (North African Economic Board). After days of struggling with the oil-seed and palm-kernel situation, we produce – for a *démarche* to General Giraud to be made by Murphy and me – nothing but a perfectly unintelligible array of papers.

Like most other things, the only way is to do it oneself and with the help of a wet towel and lots of coffee, I succeeded last night in getting our demands on the French into four paragraphs.

Then – all the morning – I have to persuade my colleagues (including Murphy) that this is the right way to prepare a memorandum. They prefer to lose themselves in detail and the French are very quick to take advantage by fastening on a minor point and arguing for hours round it.

With all the other preoccupations here, I have not written to you very much about the supply side. What is so annoying is that if one was in *sole* charge one could easily make a team out of the English and American civil servants and businessmen here which would work efficiently. It is exactly what we did (with a little success) at the Ministry of Supply – what I did (with much more success) at the

[19] Charles Schneider (b. 1898) was manager of Société Schneider et Cie, armaments manufacturers.

Colonial Office, where I was on my own. But I'm afraid the task of trying to

(*a*) understand and simplify the problems,

(*b*) get Murphy to understand them,

(*c*) get the military authorities to understand them,

(*d*) get the French either to understand them or to play honestly in the team

– the task, now protracted over three-and-a-half months – is nearly driving me crazy. It is really causing one much more anxiety than the political side – because I feel that, while on the political aspect we have really achieved something, on the economic we are falling down.

Of course, it is not made any easier by the fact that it is (in theory) a purely American responsibility, and I can only work more or less on sufferance and with a great deal of diplomacy and tact.

However, we must do our best.

After a long morning, General Noguès, the Resident-General of Morocco, came to see me at twelve. The more I see of him, the less I like him. He is thoroughly discredited and dishonest, in my view. General Giraud would get rid of him at any moment, if only we could settle the de Gaulle union. We have been waiting for this, in the hope that Catroux or another from that side would take the job.

But now things are getting so bad in Morocco, that I really feel we should wait no longer. It is almost a unique experience to listen to a man for an hour, and not to believe one single word of all he says.

3 p.m. Interview with Bedell Smith, Chief of Staff to Eisenhower. As usual, agreeable – but there are a lot of difficulties to be overcome. Fortunately, Bedell and I agree on most things and have complete confidence in each other.

4 p.m. M. Cambon[20] – son of the old ambassador – sent here from London (rather against his will) by the Americans. He returns in a few days. He is pro-Giraud and anti-de Gaulle. He is old and rather talkative.

I am just finishing off this letter before the bag goes and I go back to dinner. The weather is still very unpleasant here and still very humid. Everything drips.

I have had a very characteristic letter from your mother which amused me. She is certainly well employed in planning for Chatsworth after the war. I was very sorry to hear that Rachel[21] had been so ill. She said that Carol and Catherine both looked very pretty.

Friday, 16 April 1943

I started from Algiers by plane at 9.15 a.m. together with Roger Makins and R. Herbert[22] (the chief British economic adviser). We flew

[20] Henri Cambon (1876–1960), son of Paul Cambon, ambassador to Britain during the First World War.

[21] My wife's sister, Lady Rachel Stuart.

[22] Roscoe Herbert (1895–1975) was chief British adviser to the N.A.E.B., 1942–3.

to Casablanca – where we stopped for lunch – and then on to Marrakesh. We got to Marrakesh at about 4.15 p.m. and arrived just at the moment that Lord Swinton[23] (who had come from Bathurst) was getting out of his aeroplane.

Since the purpose of my trip was to meet Swinton for two days' discussion on a number of points of common interest, the timing was rather remarkable! He had come 1,500 miles, and I about 800 miles, and we arrived together.

This (which, of course, was really a piece of luck) made a great impression on the French.

We had a guard of honour to receive us – partly white and partly black. General Noguès was very anxious to create a good impression on us – but nothing can persuade me (even guards of honour) that he is anything but a very slippery customer.

Swinton brought with him [F. J.] Pedler, an old Colonial Office friend, whom I had sent to Dakar just before I left the C.O. to protect British supply interests in French West Africa; also George Blaker (who was Casey's Private Secretary in Cairo and very kind to us then. He is on his way back to Cabinet Office in London via Algiers). Also [Folliott] Sandford, who is Swinton's chief official.

We were all entertained at a most wonderful villa belonging to an American lady and known as the Villa Taylor. It is a sort of Arabian Nights place – built round an open square with the usual fountain, etc. – and furnished in a sort of Arab–American Hollywood style.

Friday night we were given a great dinner by the general commanding the region in a much more genuine Arab palace. The Kaid (son of the ruling Pasha) was at the dinner, and a number of French notabilities. The usual guard of honour of Spahis – very handsome in their cloaks and swords.

Saturday, April 17 1943

After a conference which lasted till about 11 a.m. we all started off in two cars and drove about seventy miles into the foothills of the Atlas mountains. It is quite impossible to describe the glorious view which the great range presents as you approach it from the plain. All the great mountains are still snow-capped. The highest peaks must be at least ten to fifteen thousand feet. And in the foothills there is the usual extraordinary display of wild flowers of every conceivable kind.

Having arrived at a sort of col or *arête*, we got out and had a marvellous luncheon, sitting in the shade of some trees, with the great range in front of us.

Then we went on with our political and economic discussions till the agenda was more or less finished. I confess that I did not pay too much attention, but all the experts talked away busily, while I lay in

[23] 1st Viscount Swinton (1884–1972) was Minister Resident in West Africa, 1942–4.

the shade and admired the scenery and (I am ashamed to say) dozed a little.

We drove back to Marrakesh and, after a change of clothes, made a formal visit to the Kaid. This was the usual kind of Arab ceremony. A room of large dimensions with a large and ugly carpet and divans all round. Polite conversation, mint tea, almond milk, lemonade and sweetmeats. The servants and guard of honour were quite impressive.

Before dinner, we walked in the native town – crowds of Arabs, very dirty and smelly, and the usual markets, snake-charmers, etc., etc.

Sunday, 18 April 1943

Left the aerodrome at 8.15 a.m. Pedler and Blaker came back with us. Pedler is to be in Algiers for a few days to complete the supply negotiations.

Another guard of honour at the aerodrome. Swinton started off on his 1,500-mile journey in one direction, and we on our 800-mile trip in another.

At Casablanca (when we came down) something was wrong with the wireless, and there was a delay of two hours while they mended it. So we had lunch with the British Consul-General, Mr [William] Bond, who had come to the aerodrome to meet us.

Unfortunately, on landing at Oran to get petrol, there was a great storm of wind which suddenly got up. The weather reports from Algiers were also very bad, and the pilot decided not to go on. So we had to stay the night in Oran, in very uncomfortable circumstances.

Monday, 19 April 1943

This was my father's birthday. I expect Tanner had primroses as usual.

We set off about 8 a.m. and arrived safely at Algiers at about 11 a.m.

The usual round has started again. General Catroux has returned with fresh proposals[24] and the old atmosphere of intrigue and political excitement is thick upon us.

Tuesday, 20 April 1943

Meetings, interviews, discussions, telegrams. (And the *only* satisfactory thing so far, a reasonably good settlement of the French West African palm-kernels problem.)

I had M. Tron[25] (French Finance Secretary) and Mme Tron, and M. and Mme Schneider, and some Americans to dinner.

Hal Mack has turned up – for a short visit – in excellent form. I was

[24] These proposals repeated General de Gaulle's demand that there should be a single authority over all French officials in all French territories, including Metropolitan France. He also demanded that all Vichy 'capitulators and collaborators' be dismissed.

[25] Ludovic Charles Tron (1904–68) was General Giraud's Secretary of Finance, 1942–3, having been Director of Finance in Morocco since 1938.

delighted to see him and to hear that he had talked with you on the telephone.

Wednesday, 21 April 1943

9.30 a.m. Interview with Eisenhower.

10.30 a.m. Field Marshal Wavell[26] (on his way through Algiers).

11.30 a.m. Colonel [David] Stirling.

1 p.m. Colonel de Linarès to luncheon (Giraud's *chef de cabinet*).

3.30 p.m. M. Comert.[27]

5.30 p.m. Cinema. Showing of *Desert Victory* (with French captions). A magnificent film and excellent propaganda.

A large French crowd outside and much cheering for the British Minister. It was almost like election day at Stockton.

Thursday, 22 April 1943

Another long day – mostly talk. Giraud has gone to the front and everything is held up. He always goes to the front when he is in a fix.

Friday, 23 April 1943 (Good Friday)

More talk and more discussions and nothing to show. Old Giraud refuses to return till tomorrow and naturally will do no business on Easter Sunday – and so it drags on.

Meanwhile, the news from the front seems pretty good. But there will be fierce and bloody fighting before the Germans give in.[28]

As there is a bag going this afternoon I will close this very dull letter. I'm afraid I have not been in the writing mood and this long-drawn-out political crisis is beginning to get on my nerves.

My American colleague is very difficult to handle. He seems to be without any fixed purpose or plan and is affected by every changing mood of local opinion or Washington rumour. He is very pleasant, but without character or decision, and I am very much afraid I shall not be able to keep him up to the mark. In my view, Giraud should accept the proposals which Catroux has brought back and will accept them unless he thinks the Americans will support him in refusing. But time is on de Gaulle's side, and if Giraud misses the bus now he will be another Chamberlain. I propose to tell him so – very firmly – and if Murphy will play up to the extent even of *not* telling him the opposite, we shall bring it off.

[26] Field Marshal Sir Archibald Wavell (1883–1950) had been C.-in-C., Middle East, and defeated the Italians in North Africa, but failed to withstand Rommel's advances in June 1941. He then became C.-in-C., India, 1941–3.

[27] Pierre Comert (1880–1964) had started the daily newspaper *France* in London in 1940.

[28] The German positions at Enfidaville, well ensconced in hilly terrain, were proving a considerable obstacle.

Saturday, 24 April 1943

Rather an ordinary day. A good deal of business with the C.-in-C. and Chief of Staff. I dined with Francis Rodd (Rennell) who has turned up here as a major-general. Actually, he has been here for some time, and I have had a good deal to do with him. I cannot write about this affair, but it has now been going on for about two months and has caused me more trouble and anxiety than all the other work, even including French politicians and politics.[29] I am thankful to say that, largely owing to the good sense and loyalty of Eisenhower and Bedell Smith (Chief of Staff, American), I think we are going to emerge successfully. But the stupidity of London and Washington, from the highest quarters downwards, has been almost incredible. There are some people who seem to delight in complications and legalistic arguments. At the end of about two months' wrangling (which has put me in an extremely delicate position) I am delighted to say that there is every sign that both great capitals are about to propose (as a completely novel suggestion) the solution which the Chief of Staff and I agreed early in March. All that has been achieved is a great waste of time and straining of tempers. However, we have avoided a lot of pitfalls, and that is something. And another quite useful result is that my position with Eisenhower and Co. is strengthened, because I have stuck resolutely to my agreement with them, even under rather heavy fire from London.

Sunday, 25 April 1943 (Easter Sunday)

Went to church at 8 a.m. The little church was absolutely crowded with soldiers and sailors, English and American. I had meant to go to matins as well, to hear the hymn-singing (which is always spendid). But I have two guests at the moment – the Honourable [F.] Jones and his secretary. Hon. Jones is the New Zealand Minister of Defence. He is perfectly charming – simple and unaffected – the best type of trade union official.

They both arrived yesterday – but I managed to farm them out for dinner.

They were to have gone up to the front – to see General Freyberg[30] and the splendid New Zealand troops, but they did not get away owing to weather. I talked to them after breakfast and then went down to the office.

For luncheon, I managed to collect some generals and admirals. After luncheon, as we had a lot of work to do in the office, I sent them for a drive with John Wyndham. Dinner at Admiral Cunningham's – given for Hon. Jones.

[29] This was a dispute about AMGOT (Allied Military Government of Occupied Territory), which would administer Sicily and other enemy territory when it was conquered. London and Washington each wanted to be senior partner, while those of us on the spot wanted it to be a joint and equal operation.

[30] Lieutenant-General Sir Bernard Freyberg, (1889–1963), was G.O.C. New Zealand forces, 1939–45.

Monday, 26 April 1943

Political Council at 11 a.m. The situation *vis-à-vis* the Giraud–de Gaulle negotiations is becoming very difficult. My colleague Murphy is back at his old tricks and trying to impede the union, without quite consciously admitting (even to himself) that he is doing so. He has an incurable habit of seeing every kind of person and agreeing with them all in turn. The position of these negotiations is becoming very acute because Giraud is turning stubborn. I am convinced that this is because he believes that he can rely on American support. But it is a very short-sighted game – if the Americans are really playing it – and I think it comes from certain State Department people (Hull and Welles)[31] more than from the President. My only chance is to get the War Department people (Eisenhower, etc.) to disapprove and throw a little weight the other way. This is not too easy to do, especially in any overt way. Although Ike and Bedell Smith do not much like Murphy's methods, they have to go through the motions of standing together. But I still have hopes.

Meanwhile, Mr Jasper Knight[32] (of Unilevers and Ministry of Food) has come out with an urgent need for oil-seeds (palm-kernels, ground-nuts, etc.) to meet the rather serious oil and fat position which seems to be threatening. So far as this place is concerned, the whole thing is to make French West Africa (Boisson in charge) play the game and increase its production and give its surplus to United Kingdom. Not too easy! All the afternoon on oil-seeds!

At 6 p.m. I went to see Giraud. Murphy had seen him on Sunday evening, and of course I had only Murphy's account of the interview. But I had a cross-check through Catroux, who had seen Giraud also on Sunday (*after* Murphy) and whom I saw before I went 'to the Palace'.

I had an hour and a half with the old boy. He is a most difficult man to talk to, because he is really so nice and also so stately and stupid. I am sending you a copy, which you should treat like the other confidential documents. It will soon be time for a new instalment, by the way.

I came away from the interview rather depressed, because it seemed as if the union could not succeed. A long and exhausting day.

Note of conversation with General Giraud
26 April 1943

1. I saw General Giraud last night.

2. Either as a result of his tour of the front; of an attack of sunburn; or more likely of the stimulating doctrines of Messrs Monnet,

[31] Cordell Hull (1871–1955) was U.S. Secretary of State, 1933–44. Sumner Wells (1892–1961) was U.S. Under-Secretary of State, 1937–43.

[32] Jasper Knight (1909–72) was Finance Director, then Principal Assistant Secretary, Ministry of Food, 1939–45.

Boegner[33] and Murphy, which had been recently pumped into him like a drug, he was in a very firm, egotistical and even exultant mood.

3. He explained to me how he had made a complete tour of the front from north to south – three very busy days – and how gratified he had been to find that the ideas he had put forward for the conduct of the battle and for the operations which should succeed it had been acceptable to General Alexander and to the other generals. He had explained to them in detail his views on the operation which we call 'Husky'[34] but which the French appear to refer to quite unblushingly by the name of the country concerned. All his plans, he said, had found a ready acceptance by these British generals, with whom he seemed very pleased. I fear as usual that he misconstrues the natural good manners of English officers and their respect for age and experience. . . .

6. We then discussed the negotiations for French union between Catroux and himself. He brought out of a drawer and showed me the text of the reply which he was going to deliver to Catroux. He said there were certain points of fact which must be corrected. The memorandum of the National Committee stated that they were glad to see that Giraud regarded the Armistice as null and void. That was false: he had never said as much. He accepted the Armistice as a fact. He was not responsible for it, but he accepted it. 'The Armistice came to an end on 18 November 1942, when I, General Giraud, denounced it. I did so when I instructed my troops to fire upon the Germans in Tunisia.' I remarked that General de Gaulle had done the same thing three years before. But this was swept aside.

7. The National Committee remarks that it is certain of its support in France. Giraud observed that this was merely a statement of opinion and cannot be verified by fact. In fact, all the recent evidence he had from men coming from France was that whereas 85 per cent of the people were anti-German, proably more of them would be Giraudist than de Gaullist. I said anyway it was not worth making a point of disagreement on what was merely a matter of opinion.

8. We then came to the more important points of real difference.

(*a*) De Gaulle's conception of the central power is a civil power under which military officers would be employed. Giraud says that he wants two councils: a large council and a smaller council like our War Cabinet. In the latter he says the Commander-in-Chief must be. His argument is that in the present state it would be absurd for France to have something like a pre-war Cabinet; that the military problem is an all embracing problem; and that the Commander-in-Chief must be in charge of and consulted about economic and financial matters which have their reactions upon the military conduct of the war. He observed

[33] Etienne Boegner had been a member of General de Gaulle's mission to Washington in 1942, but was now siding with Giraud.

[34] The invasion of Sicily.

that the Prime Minister was Commander-in-Chief. I slightly demurred at this, but he said 'Oh, yes, it is so, for I know. He showed me all his maps at Anfa.' I said that he was Minister of Defence and if that was what Giraud meant by Commander-in-Chief, I agreed that he might well be in such a cabinet. In that case he would give orders to the appropriate naval and military commanders. Giraud clearly regarded the point in the French National Committee memorandum on this subject as aimed at him.

b) Giraud does not agree with de Gaulle about what is to be done in France after – and during – the war. He sticks to his conception of a military government under the Commander-in-Chief and of the *conseils Généraux*. The central power to be formed now should not impose its authority. I said it would not necessarily be the Commander-in-Chief who would act as Military Governor for the whole of France. There might be separate invading armies. However, this seemed to me to be a matter which could be arranged.

(*c*) Collaboration. Giraud said that there was a phrase in the French National Committee's memorandum which he could not accept. He could not agree that all men who had in any way acted with the Vichy Government could be dismissed under the term of collaborators with Germany. He drew a distinction between the traitors like Laval and the men who had done their best in the circumstances to accept the situation and maintain what resistance was possible to Germany. He instanced Boisson, who had kept the Germans out of French West Africa, and Peyrouton who had tried to arrest Laval. He could not abandon men such as these. I replied that there was of course a distinction to be drawn between individuals but probably this would be the subject of negotiations when it came to forming an administration.

9. He said he would give the written reply to Catroux tomorrow. I said, suppose it was agreed, as a matter of principle, that the Commander-in-Chief should be in the inner council, then presumably Giraud would wish to hold that position himself, and that in this event, he would give the position of *président de conseil* to de Gaulle. He said, no, that was impossible. De Gaulle was fifteen years younger, and was, moreover, a general only of the second grade. I replied that Mr Pitt was Prime Minister of England when only twenty-one years of age.

10. General Giraud then began to talk in a somewhat majestic manner, making the most of his high stature by standing up very straight and pointing to the sky, about the French Army. This is what he said.

11. He had 450,000 men, 120,000 of them French. He would find it very difficult to persuade the Army to accept de Gaulle at all, even as a member of the Cabinet. I observed that this did not surely apply to the younger members of the Army or to the civilians. He said he knew the Army, and as to the civilians their views were not important. This was

a war. He said that his army had held the line in Tunisia for several months before Anderson's First Army could get into position. It had held the line when the Americans had collapsed some weeks ago. He had, one way and another, 11,000 casualties. He clearly regards himself as responsible for the tactics and strategy of the present operations. I observed that our casualties had also been very heavy, and after the splendid news of victory there would come to many English homes painful news of personal loss. He agreed, but said he was more modest for France than was de Gaulle. France did not need a civil government with ministers and portfolios. He would not waste money on that. He would spend it on the war. But in other respects he was more ambitious. France was now being put in a position lower than China. They must be consulted in future regarding all the strategy and tactics of the war. I said that they would be more likely to realise his ambitions if they presented a united front. He agreed, but said he could not give in to de Gaulle who, after all, only had 12,000 men altogether. I said I thought he would make a great mistake if he allowed himself to be blamed for a breach between them, and that if it was put upon the basis of his personal ambitions it would not be understood. I said I was sure it was not the policy of the U.S. Government or the British Government to keep France weak by keeping her separated, but that such a policy might be followed by short-sighted men in the lower ranks, and I was sure he saw the dangers of it. He said he did. He reminded me that de Gaulle had told him at Anfa that although America and England would support France out of necessity he, de Gaulle, was the only man who could bring Russian support. He went on to say that he was very alarmed at de Gaulle's connection with the Communist party in France. He said that a certain Colonel Passy[35] was flirting with the Communists and ran a Communist organisation in France supported by war material dropped by English parachutes. I said I thought he was completely misinformed. De Gaulle had no longer any connection with the Communist movement in France.

12. Giraud then said that if de Gaulle accepted the reply, he would be delighted to see him at once. I observed that the written reply only seemed to touch on principles and not on the personal problem. The latter was an essential one. People all over the world, including France, were becoming bored with the battle of memoranda. They wanted union. I said it seemed to me that whether negotiations were successful or not, it was vital that he should have a meeting with de Gaulle. That after that meeting an agreed communiqué should be issued giving either, as I hope, news of a successful arrangement or the reasons why an agreement could not be reached. I said that if that were not done General Eisenhower, the British Government, and he, General Giraud

[35] André Devawrin, known as Colonel Passy, was director of General de Gaulle's secret service, the *Bureau central de renseignements et d'action*.

himself, would be accused of having played underhand politics. The only way was to have it out face to face. He agreed that this was necessary and he would see de Gaulle. His invitation still stood. At the same time he wished to finish the battle of Tunis first as he wanted to enter Tunis at the head of his troops.

13. I said that I still thought that if he demanded both positions – the *president de conseil* and Commander-in-Chief, that is in effect *Commandant-en-Chef, Civil et Militaire* – he would not be supported by public opinion in the world. I thought it my duty to tell him this. He asked me why we were so pro-de Gaullist in England. I said that de Gaulle had stood by us when we had not a friend in the world. He had held French Equatorial Africa; and if Boisson had done the same in North Africa we could have seen General Giraud in North Africa a year earlier. I said that English people had long memories and did not like abandoning the friends who had stood by them in the hour of need. He said he understood these feelings and respected them. But he had his own duty which he would perform. The danger was Communism, and he would not yield to it.

Tuesday, 27 April 1943

9.15 a.m. M. Lemaigre-Dubreuil to see me. A very unpleasant man. Since Giraud dismissed him he is very bitter. But he usually tells me something of interest.

10 a.m. Morning meeting with Murphy. Americans up – British down. Nothing openly said, but beneath the surface a certain tension.

11.15–1 p.m. Jasper Knight and others on oil-seeds.

1.15 p.m. Lunch with a charming American – Mr Short of OLLA (which is jargon for Lease–Lend Organisation).

4.30 p.m. Commandant Poniatowski (of Giraud's Cabinet). The old boy was apparently much impressed by my vehemence and appeal. The whole situation is changing. He is going to rewrite the memorandum to de Gaulle in a much more friendly form and he is suddenly back again on a genuine search for union. Really it is very queer. Anyway, I knew he was incapable of writing or rewriting either a memorandum or a letter, so I at once got hold of Monnet. He appeared at *6 p.m.* and confirmed Poniatowski's story. It seems that Giraud now intends

(*a*) to send a much more friendly memorandum in reply to de Gaulle's memorandum (nevertheless, since Monnet has written it, it will be very *long* and rather pedantic);

(*b*) to accompany the memorandum – to be sent by special messenger to London – with a letter – in friendly terms – asking de Gaulle to come to some quiet spot in North Africa (not Algiers) to talk things over. He says that the outstanding points ought to be overcome by personal meeting and he suggests a small meeting, three or four on each side;

(*c*) to inform Catroux that he will accept the principle of a War Cabinet of six or eight persons, he (Giraud) and de Gaulle to be Joint Presidents – to take the chair alternate days!

The question of Giraud's position as Commander-in-Chief is left over for discussion with de Gaulle.

In other words, Giraud has completely changed since last night!

I saw Catroux at 7.15 who confirmed the truth of all this, and showed me the note of his own talk with Giraud. He allowed me to send this news to P.M. and Anthony[36] only.

8 p.m. Dinner to Jasper Knight – English, American and French economic blokes to meet him. Very tiring.

10.30–12 midnight. Drafting and despatching telegrams to London reporting the last two hectic days of French politics. Roger Makins is an invaluable assistant, absolutely tireless, very scrupulous, and a splendid draftsman. He is really a great help. He has also a keen sense of humour.

As we were doing this, a 'Most Immediate' [telegram] from London, taking the other question (Anglo-American problem)[37] a further (and fairly satisfactory) stage. But it means another talk with Chief of Staff [General Bedell Smith] tomorrow.

Wednesday, 28 April 1943

9.15 a.m. Chief of Staff and Admiral Cunningham to help. The latter is a real stand-by; also he agreed a reply to London.

10.45 a.m. M. de Charbonnières[38] (one of Catroux's people) with the text of Giraud's note and request for passage by air to London for the courier.

11.30–1 p.m. Went with Jasper Knight to see Couve de Murville (Secretary-General or civil head of Giraud's administration) to try to finalise an oil-seed agreement. On the whole, successful.

1 p.m. Lunch with Catroux. I must stop now, and anyway this deserves separate treatment because it is, in its own way, a unique experience.

Catroux is a remarkable and interesting man. He is old – about sixty-three – *très fin, très souple*, and all that. A good diplomatist; a man of the world; with a very high standard of personal comfort; a French snob (princesses and all that) and yet a broad, tolerant, liberal view of life. He is a sort of French Whig. I find him very easy to deal with and very agreeable. He speaks beautiful French – witty, subtle,

[36] Anthony Eden (1897–1977) was Foreign Secretary, 1940–5.

[37] The AMGOT argument was coming to an end. Our broad scheme for the organisation under General Alexander as Military Governor and for the establishment of a liaison section at A.F.H.Q. (called the Military Government Section – later G5) was accepted. But there was to be no 'political Deputy Chief of Staff'. Instead, Murphy and I were to provide the political advice.

[38] Guy de Girard de Charbonnières (b. 1907) was a member of General de Gaulle's National Committee.

but not overstrained phraseology. Your grandfather Lansdowne[39] would have understood him perfectly.

Now a great event has taken place in the social life of Algiers. The famous Mme Catroux has arrived! She is what is called *femme formidable*. She was a beauty, and is now an interesting Edwardian survival. She is the nearest thing I have seen in French to Lady Willingdon.[40] Catroux – I need hardly say – has managed to get the best villa in Algiers for himself. He has guards of honour, Indo-Chinese servants, aides-de-camp, secretaries, and all the paraphernalia which the French adore. But Mme Catroux has pronounced the villa to be *effroyable*. She apologises for the bad food, the indifferent service, the poor display of silver, the *mauvais gout* of the furniture, the second-rate wine – in fact, all is exquisite. She bosses everyone; she is *mauvaise langue*; she knows that Eric Duncannon was practically engaged to the youngest Miss Churchill, that Billy Burlington wanted to marry Miss Kennedy,[41] that your father was a duke, and so on.

The luncheon was very *recherché* – exquisite food, exquisite women (mostly princesses) and a lot of bullying of the servants. Quite a relaxation.

3.30 p.m. Admiral Michelier, another admiral (Moreau)[42] and two other French naval officers arrived in my office. They seem to think that the Alexandria fleet of Admiral Godfroy is in the bag. I sincerely hope so, because the P.M. bullies me about it unmercifully with a constant flow of telegrams. I have given up answering them and am just trusting to luck.

4.30 p.m. Colonel (now General) Pechkoff. He is off to China. I am sorry, for he is an amusing character.

5 p.m. General Alexander, General Gairdner and General Lord Rennell. An hour's conference – very satisfactory. Alexander had flown down from the front for the day. The more I see of him, the more I like and admire him.

7 p.m. Murphy and I were summoned to 'the Palace' to receive from Giraud the text of the documents he is sending to de Gaulle. A long reading of these interminable memoranda, very stately and all that – but very dull.

8 p.m. Dinner with Monnet and the same talk as usual till 11 p.m. and so to bed.

[39] 5th Marquess of Lansdowne (1845–1927) was Governor-General of Canada, 1883–8, of India, 1888–93, Secretary of State for War, 1895–1900, and Foreign Secretary, 1900–5, and always very much a Whig.

[40] Marie, Marchioness of Willingdon (1875–1960), widow of the 1st Marquess, who had been a formidable figure in Canada, where her husband was Governor-General (1926–31), and in India where he was Viceroy (1931–6).

[41] Mary was the youngest Miss Churchill. William Cavendish, Earl of Burlington (1917–44) had become the Marquess of Hartington on the succession of his father to the Dukedom of Devonshire in 1938. He did marry Kathleen Kennedy (daughter of the U.S. Ambassador to London, Joseph P. Kennedy, and sister of the future President), in May 1944.

[42] Admiral Jacques Moreau (1884–1962) was Maritime Prefect, Algiers, 1942–3.

Thursday, 29 April 1943

I woke up early and wrote the first part of this letter. At 10 a.m. North African Economic Board (N.A.E.B.) fortnightly full meeting. Very dull. Two hours of American chatter before we reached any point.

At 12 noon, Brigadier Rabino[43] – the British finance expert at A.F.H.Q. Mostly on future finance problems.

At 1 p.m. Lunch with Commodore Morse,[44] the naval officer in charge of Algiers port, to meet the French admiral Leclerc,[45] who has done us very well here and whom we are trying to get appointed to Bizerta. He is a very nice man and very co-operative.

3 p.m. Rennell. A long conference.

5 p.m. Two Russians, who have come to look after Russian internees in the internment camps and to arrange their transport to Russia *via* England. Simple in principle, difficult in practice.

Now I am waiting for the last duty of the day, which is a very *pomposo* dinner in my honour. To be given by Admiral Michelier and the officers of the French Navy.

I wonder how you all spent Easter and if the church was nice. There must have been plenty of flowers, at any rate. I do so long to be home, even if only for a few days. This place is really intolerable, except when one is occupied. Fortunately, that is easy to arrange, but we are beginning to show signs of wear. Our household – Roger, John and I – are still on speaking terms, and that is something.

I have just heard that a bag may be going – so I will stop. The weather has been very bad lately and the bags therefore very uncertain. But I hope this will get back in reasonable time.

Friday, 30 April 1943

Friday morning, exhausted by the week's efforts, I stayed in bed and wrote or dictated. After lunch, I went for a drive with Francis Rodd partly to discuss some questions with him, partly to take the air. We drove up to the top of a mountain behind Blida about 4,500–5,000 feet. It was the road which we went partially up one Sunday and then walked down. This time, we went to the summit.

The weather has been quite horrible here for the last fortnight. Almost perpetual rain, mist, or hot steamy cloud sitting on Algiers. This has been very oppressive and made us all very bad-tempered.

But when we got about 3,000–4,000 feet up, we rose above all the clouds into the sunshine. It was really delightful. The place is called Chréa, and on the top there is a sort of settlement of small villas, rest homes, an hotel, and some admirable buildings for children – these are

[43] Brigadier F. A. Rabino was an Administrative Officer, Trading with the Enemy Department.

[44] Rear-Admiral Sir Anthony Morse (1892–1960) was Commodore, Algiers, 1942–3.

[45] Admiral Leclerc had been Senior Naval Officer in Casablanca at the time of the 'Torch' landings.

normally used in the summer for sending children and invalids – also, some private people send their own children or go out themselves during the hot months. The large children's holiday scheme covers about 500–600 in all, and is a municipal enterprise of the city of Algiers. The buildings and villas are in the chalet style – very simple and pleasant in appearance.

At this time of year the place was deserted, but I think the Allies are going to take over part of it as a rest place for flying officers and lightly wounded. It will certainly be splendid for that.

The top of the mountain in this area is well wooded, with fine pine trees – so there is plenty of shade. As for the flowers – they are really beyond belief. Carpets of blue and yellow wild pansies; violets; the little purple and the mauve wild iris and heaps and heaps of others of which, of course, I do not know the names. There was a great show (growing like bluebells in some parts) of what they tell me is a ranunculus of some kind – a large yellow flower, with stripes, the shape and size of our autumn crocus but more the colour of our ordinary yellow crocus.

I must say this was a pleasant afternoon, and quite delightful. (It followed an 'oil-seed' lunch for old Jasper Knight.)

We dined (Roger Makins and I) with Couve de Murville – a small and quite pleasant party, all French.

May

Saturday, 1 May 1943

A lot of telegraphing, backwards and forwards, from here to London about de Gaulle, etc. Hal Mack to luncheon. He remains very calm. At about 4 p.m. John and I left by car for a place called Tipasa – about an hour's drive westwards of Algiers. Still this low cloud and mist, but it was better when we got out of this town.

At Tipasa we had been told of a little French hotel which was quite clean and nice. We went for a walk and examined the ruins of a Roman city – forum, theatre, temples, etc. – on quite a large scale. This ruined city forms a sort of municipal garden – the excavations have not been very thorough and the whole is overgrown with plants and flowers – particularly the wild lavender, a very delicious soft grey, which grows in great profusion. Also all kinds of wild cistus (I think) mostly with white flowers – some mauve with a white stripe.

The little town (quite tiny) of Tipasa and the ruined city lie right on the sea, in a little cove, rather like Devon or Cornwall. The Roman city is on a point, or little promontory. A plain of about two to three miles to the west, leads to a great mountain range; on this day almost entirely in cloud. The colour of soil and stone is red – the cliffs are of a great red marble.

Dinner. Soup, omelette, potatoes – excellently served. Early to bed.

Sunday, 2 May 1943

A warm, muggy, soft day – like Ireland or the west coast of Scotland. Occasional sun – not much rain – we could not walk up the mountain, owing to weather. So we took the coast road, which we reached by first crossing the plain. Vineyards, corn, vegetables – then another little village in a delicious little bay – and then the road – a sort of Corniche road – sometimes rising to two or three hundred feet (when cut in the side of the cliff), sometimes returning to sea level.

Occasional little bays, with little farms (like highland farms) wherever the cliffs recede a little from the sea and there is room for cultivation.

The chief cultivation again seemed to be vines, corn and vegetables – together, in same place, with great orchards of fig-trees.

We started our walk at 9 a.m. and got back to the inn at 3.30 p.m., having covered about twenty miles.

When we got in, the good woman gave us an omelette and some excellent haricot beans. The car came for us, and we returned, exhausted, but in much better physical condition, to Algiers.

Monday, 3 May 1943

A confidential bag has come in, but no letters. We are still waiting – none too hopefully – for de Gaulle's answer. I feel sure he will insist on coming to Algiers at once, instead of the meeting proposed at Biskra or Marrakesh. He is really a most difficult man. My general is boring and old-fashioned, but at least a gentleman.

I saw Eisenhower this afternoon. He is in good form, but naturally anxious about the battle. I'm afraid the losses on both sides will be heavy. I really feel thankful that Maurice did not join the Grenadiers.

I hope all goes well with all the children. I'm afraid I hardly ever write to them, but you must explain that I cannot really manage more than your letters. I did manage to write to your mother by this bag.

Apparently, in spite of a sort of gentleman's agreement against any premature disclosure of the latest stage of the de Gaulle–Giraud negotiation, two statements were made on the wireless on 2 May, which Giraud's people claim must have come from Carlton Gardens.[1]

As usual, they began to run round in circles – concentric circles the centre of which is our office. All the old phrases – there will be an *équivoque* – it was accepted *en principe* – it is a breach of faith – *au point de vue morale – sur le plan politique – permettez!* ('you're a —— liar') and lots of fun of this kind. Eventually it was decided to publish a communiqué here, saying that Giraud had invited de Gaulle to meet him in a town in North Africa, and so on.

All this took a good time, and in the intervals I was drafting a telegram to London on another subject [Force X] which will probably lead to my dismissal! I cannot agree with the Government on a certain point and I expect a row, but probably they will give in!

Anyway, at last I get to my dinner [with Admiral Cunningham], which was very agreeable. Apart from the admiral and his staff, there was Admiral Vian[2] (just arrived), General Gale, and General Adam (the Adjutant-General) on his way home from India. I had seen him on his way out about a fortnight ago. He is very intelligent and agreeable. I knew both his brothers well – Eric Forbes Adam and Colin Forbes

[1] General de Gaulle's headquarters in London.

[2] Rear-Admiral Sir Philip Vian (1894–1968) was to command an assault force for the invasion of Sicily in July 1943.

Adam.[3] Colin, you remember, did the distressed area report for our north-eastern region many years ago.

After dinner, I stayed to do some business with Admiral Cunningham. In the course of it, he said, 'Minister, you must let me tell you something. You have made a striking success here, far greater than I thought possible. You have raised British prestige enormously. Do not worry about your trouble. I should certainly find it necessary to say that if you are not supported at home, I could not continue to command the Mediterranean fleet.' (This was half-serious and half-joking, but rather nice all the same.)

Anyway, like all the crises, it will probably end in a fizzle.

Tuesday, 4 May 1943

No news from London. We are waiting a telegram to say whether de Gaulle accepts or not. My bet is that he will say, 'Either I come to the city of Algiers or I won't come at all.'

He is a difficult kind of horse. He either starts down the course before the gate has been raised, or he won't start at all until the other horses are half-way round.

Two visiting Russians to lunch – rather amusing chaps. They have come nominally to see about the repatriation of about 120 Russians in internment here. But I can't help thinking they haven't only come for that. Consul-General Carvell (a charming man), Mrs Consul-General (whom John Wyndham fears and dislikes) and Miss Carvell (whom I think Mrs C. sees as the chatelaine of Petworth,[4] but not so John).

At last the weather has changed. It is a lovely day – not too hot, a clear blue sky, a slight breeze. This morning we heard of the capture of Mateur and we hope now for better news from the front. The weather has been so bad that we have not been able to make use of our superiority in the air. If we can only get fine weather in Tunisia for a few weeks, it will make a lot of difference.

I am hoping that the wretched French wrangle will soon end one way or another, so that I can get home. But my hopes have so often been dashed before, that I am not too optimistic.

I must say, though, that this life is quite agreeable. One meets a host of interesting people, and there is plenty to do. The only drawback is that it is all this *indirect* work (through other people, I mean, and without any *executive* authority) which can become very exasperating. One wants to shake them all and tell them not to behave like silly children.

Our Russian visitors proved to be quite agreeable. The younger of

[3] Eric Forbes Adam (1888–1925), a First Secretary in the Foreign Office, had died in Constantinople. Colin Forbes Adam (1889–1982) acted for the Commissioner of the Depressed Areas as District Commissioner for Durham and Tyneside, 1934–9.

[4] John Wyndham was to inherit Petworth House in Sussex on the death of his uncle, the 3rd Baron Leconfield, in 1952.

them did not think much of our villa, because (he said) a garden without a hard tennis court is no good to anyone. In Moscow, he said, he liked to play tennis, summer and winter, on a hard, covered court. We made suitable depreciatory and self-excusing noises.

After they had consumed the best part of a bottle of Bénédictine, however, they went away in great good humour.

Wednesday, 5 May 1943

She loves me: she loves me not. She loves me: she loves me not. She loves me: she loves me not. She loves . . . me: . . . she . . . loves . . . me . . . not!

Oh dear! today has been a bad day, and definitely by the end of it, one general does not love the other!

After the usual kind of morning, Catroux came to see me in the afternoon. De Gaulle's speech,[5] with its open attack on Giraud, has, of course, fairly put the cat among the pigeons. Catroux regards it as making his position as a negotiator almost impossible, and again talks of throwing up the sponge. But he won't.

At 7 p.m. a conference at the palace – Giraud, Monnet, Catroux, Murphy and I. I told them (after they had all talked a great deal and read out de Gaulle's speech in full) that they really couldn't break off a negotiation simply on the ground that one politician made an offensive speech about another. I told them that in my country this was the almost recognised procedure preliminary to forming a coalition government.

This chaff didn't go awfully well. It shocked Murphy (who of course didn't particularly want the union to come off anyway) but amused Monnet. I also told them that for a great country to remain divided because no one could decide whether the negotiation for a coalition should take place in London or Brighton seemed to me absurd. 'If you fear de Gaulle,' I said, 'and want to call the whole thing off, you must break on a question of principle. Make him accept your principles – especially the two you think vital, namely: (1) Cabinet government *not* personal government. (2) No attempt to form a government of post-war France, but the proper constitutional procedure according to laws of the Republic. If he accepts these points, let him come to Algiers. If he doesn't, don't let him come at all.'

The conference went on till 9 p.m. I just repeated the same thing every half-hour or so – which is my usual technique.

We had a large dinner, for which I was an hour late. M. and Mme de Vitasse (diplomat), Comtesse de Rose (our local Queen of the May), Major Lee (Eisenhower's A.D.C. – a nice Texan soldier) and Colonel [S. S.] Hill-Dillon, a charming Irishman, who hunts and knows all your Irish relations.

[5] Delivered on 4 May 1943.

After dinner, I composed a telegram to report the day's events (which is sent down by despatch rider to get off by midnight) and so to bed.

Thursday, 6 May 1943

9 a.m. Went to see Admiral Cunningham about some shipping questions. He was, as usual, in cracking form.

An idle morning. I read Macaulay, which I am still struggling through.

A *very smart* luncheon party at the villa (*déjeuner très intime*) and incredibly comic. The guests were Princesse de Ligne, Princesse Galitzine, General Giraud, his A.D.C., Captain Brownrigg, R.N.,[6] Eric Duncannon (now on my staff) Roger, John and I.

Old Giraud was really charming. He just loves princesses and swallowed down any amount of flattery and Bénédictine (of which we have somehow, by John's nefarious methods, acquired a store).

No politics; lots of reminiscence; magnificently and splendidly reactionary conversation, about the overpayment of wages and the impudence of the Arabs nowadays; about the hardships of life (no butter, no meat) and altogether great fun. I thought John would explode from time to time.

We had all Giraud's stories for the umpteenth time – about his escape, about his exploits as a major, a colonel, a général de brigade, a général de division, a général d'armée, and so on.

The poor princesses (who are really charming and very like your mother in some ways) fairly lapped up our good Navy butter and our lovely Navy white bread (the flour from the Malta convoy), and the Bénédictine just made it go. As the general left, he held up his hand and said, '*Du calme, mon cher ami, et du courage – surtout du calme.*' I somehow think I shall get de Gaulle to Algiers after all.

Friday, 7 May 1943

A day of waiting. I have at last a telegram from London by which I judge the struggle is still going on at that end. We are now led to expect a proper reply. I saw Catroux in the morning, and in the course of the day a host of French of all sides, ending with the last of them at 7.30. They are all very excited and each one has a different plan. But, of course, with the exception of the few that matter – like Catroux, Giraud and Monnet – they have no effect on the situation except to confuse it.

Another dinner tonight. The guests were M. Hauck (trade union leader, Free French) M. [Etienne] Boegner (violently anti-Free French), Mr Dolphin (British – U.K.C.C. [U.K. Commercial Corporation] – the Government buying agency), Captain Warburg

[6] Captain Thomas Brownrigg, R.N. (1902–67) was Deputy Chief of Staff to Admiral Sir Andrew Cunningham, 1942–3.

(American), Brigadier-General Hamblen (American, Q. side at A.F.H.Q.), M. Leroy Beaulieu (Giraudist French – Assistant to the Secretary-General) – a nice mixed bag.[7]

Saturday, 8 May 1943

We had a Council in the morning. The news from the front is wonderful and it is extraordinary to see the elation of everybody.[8] The French are quite worked up and most friendly.

12 noon. A talk with Catroux. Not much progress to report.

3 p.m. Monnet. Talk, talk, talk.

5 p.m. Quite an interesting ceremony – the handing over of the first great convoy of American equipment – tanks, guns, lorries, etc., to the French. The ceremony was performed by General Eisenhower who made an excellent speech – very generous to the British. Giraud replied.

Sunday, 9 May 1943

8.30 a.m. Went to a 'march past' of the new equipment. A great turn-out. The weather is now getting quite hot, so it is a good thing to have these performances early.

At 11.30 a.m. John, Monnet and I motored off to Tipasa along the coast. We had a delicious bathe in a little cove which we found. The sea was quite clear and not too cold. We bathed naked, but it was a deserted spot; and we sunbathed afterwards. Then we had a picnic lunch.

After lunch we drove on to a little town called Cherchell, where there is a dear little wooden town, and a lovely little harbour – also many fine ruins of a large Roman city.

We stayed the night in the hotel.

Monday, 10 May 1943

Rather a dull day. Ordinary routine. Mr [Hugh Stonhewer] Bird, the British Consul-General at Rabat, came to stay a few days – quite an interesting man.

A mixed sort of dinner in his honour.

Tuesday, 11 May 1943

Catroux came in the morning and stayed for two hours.

Wednesday and Thursday, 12 and 13 May 1943

The result of the campaign here has surpassed our most sanguine expectations. It has really been a triumph – for Alexander first, ably

[7] Captain Paul Warburg was adviser to Robert Murphy on Jewish affairs. The U.K.C.C. acted as agent of the Middle East Supply Corporation. Brigadier-General A. L. Hamblen (1894–1971). Paul Leroy-Beaulieu (b. 1902).

[8] Allied forces had captured Tunis on the previous day.

seconded by Tedder. The Germans appear to have been completely out-manoeuvred, and the final blows took them by surprise. Practically none have got away. Somehow, it's very satisfactory to get the Commander-in-Chief.[9] It seems (as in L'Attaque) to finish the game.

We are still waiting and talking – so far as the political game is concerned – with very little progress. It is now necessary for Giraud to write a reply to de Gaulle's last effusion. I went out on Wednesday afternoon (12th) to Tipasa with Monnet to talk it all over quietly. It was quite lovely out there – hot, but not too hot – and we walked in the old Roman city and bathed and talked. I came back on Thursday in time for lunch.

Howard Marshall (B.B.C.) and Bernstein (films) to lunch.[10] They had most interesting and exciting accounts of the advance on Tunis. Apparently the correspondents nowadays go with the leading troops, to get their news and film pictures.

A rather dull dinner at the villa – Mr Royce (new American head of N.A.E.B.), Mr Cuthbertson (the retiring one), Mr [Roscoe] Herbert (English head), M. Blondel.[11] Quite a heavy air-raid during dinner.

Friday, 14 May 1943

A dreary day: interviews and meetings most of the day. Quite an amusing dinner. M. Peyrouton (Governor-General of Algeria), M. Zimomi (his aide), Colonel Julius Holmes[12] (American, liaison section), M. René Mayer (Secretary for Transport – a very clever Jew, recently appointed) and a guest who has arrived to stay with us – the Turkish Ambassador in London, Mr Orbay. The latter is a most charming and interesting old boy – formerly an admiral in the Turkish Navy and very pro-English. His full name is His Excellency, Huseyin Rauf Orbay. He seems to have had a very adventurous life, having been in the 'Young Turk' revolution in 1907 and having acted as a collaborator with Mustafa Kemal (Atatürk) after the War.[13]

Saturday, 15 May 1943

As I had instructions to treat the Turkish Ambassador with the

[9] Rommel's successor, General Jürgen von Arnim (1891–1971), surrendered on 12 May 1943. In the course of the Tunisian campaign, the Allies had taken some 250,000 prisoners.

[10] Howard Marshall (1900–73) was B.B.C. Director of War Reporting and a war correspondent himself, 1943–5. Sidney Bernstein (b. 1899), later a television magnate, was Chief of the Film Section, A.F.H.Q., 1942–3.

[11] Alec B. Royce (1894–1968) was co-chairman of the N.A.E.B., 1943–4. Jules Blondel (1887–?) who joined Fighting France in September 1942, was later French Ambassador to Norway, 1945.

[12] Colonel (later Brigadier-General) Julius Holmes (1899–1968) was head of the Military Government Section newly set up at A.F.H.Q.

[13] Admiral Huseyin Rauf Orbay (1881–1964) was Turkish Ambassador to London, 1942–5. Mustafa Kemal (known as Kemal Atatürk) (1881–1938) was founder and first President of the Republic of Turkey. Admiral Orbay was Prime Minister of Atatürk's first revolutionary government in 1923.

greatest consideration, I devoted the morning to taking him round Algiers. We spent most of the time in the port, and visiting British warships, etc. It was great fun. Orbay proved to be a most delightful companion.

Lunch at the villa. Admiral Cunningham and Commodore Dick[14] to meet the Ambassador. After an afternoon at the office, I called on Giraud (who had just returned from Tunis) to discuss various things. I am at last beginning to hope that my visit to Alexandria will not have been in vain.[15]

8 p.m. Dinner with the admiral, to which I brought the Ambassador. The guests included Air Chief Marshal Tedder, who was in great form.

I heard from Giraud that the Germans have carried away his married daughter and all her children. She was living in Tunis, her husband being an officer in a North African regiment. They are really incredibly mean. The poor old man was terribly cut up about it.

Sunday, 16 May 1943

A lovely day. We took our Ambassador down to the airport and saw him off. He is on his way to Turkey.

Lunched with Monnet. We are still working on Giraud's answer to de Gaulle, but I am afraid that Giraud is less pliant than before. The Tunisian victory makes him feel he can stand on his own feet, and de Gaulle's insulting speeches and broadcasts have upset him.

We worked all the afternoon on the reply. It is not going to be too easy, but we will have another try. The trouble is, that even if you stack the cards and give de Gaulle four aces and a joker, he still throws in his hand and will not make a bet.

Henry Hopkinson,[16] who has been chief official to Minister of State, Cairo, for two years, came to stay. He is leaving now to take up position at Lisbon. A nice fellow – who looked after me well at Cairo.

Text of General Giraud's reply to General de Gaulle
Dated 17 May 1943
(Translation)

Thank you for your letter of 10 May which replies to my letter and my memorandum of 27 April.

This latest exchange of views convinces me that our preliminary discussions have come to an end, and that the hour of action and of our common responsibilities has come. Time presses; among other

[14] Commodore Royer Dick (b. 1897) was Chief of Staff, Mediterranean Station, 1942–4.

[15] In April it had been arranged that, while the British Treasury would continue to provide the funds for the Alexandria squadron, General Giraud would make the payment. On 15 May 1943, Admiral Godfroy at last rallied to Giraud, after the general had insisted that he would cut off the pay if he did not.

[16] Henry Hopkinson (b. 1902), later 1st Baron Colyton, was Counsellor and Political Adviser to the Minister Resident in the Middle East, 1941–3, Minister Plenipotentiary, Lisbon, 1943–4.

questions, the rapid fusion of all the French forces in a single army of victory is urgent.

I propose that we should pass to action and immediately bring about our union.

The method is simple and can be rapid.

It is sufficient for us to form immediately the Central Executive Committee, and at the same time to record our agreement on its essential bases, namely that its responsibility should be collective and that its life should be limited. Thus we shall conform to the tradition and to the laws of the Republic.

Thus established, the Executive Committee will meet immediately at Algiers.

The formation of the Executive Committee. The Committee is the Central Authority. It possesses the general direction of and the responsibility for all matters at present within the scope of the National Committee or of the High Command, Civil and Military, at Algiers. It will discuss *all the other questions* which have been the subject of our exchanges of views based on the notes which we have exchanged. In particular, it will organise the National Consultative Council and the Committee on Resistance, appoint the Commissioners, fix their functions, etc., etc.

The responsibility of the Executive Committee must be collective. All the essential decisions will be discussed and taken by the Executive Committee acting as a whole. In accordance with the proposal made by General Catroux, you and I will preside in turn; our responsibilities will be merged in the collective responsibility of the Executive Committee; with the Commissioner or Commissioners who may be responsible, we shall together sign the decrees or ordinances which may be discussed and decided in the Committee.

The duration and the functions of the Committee must be limited. In the action which we are now taking we are convinced that we are acting according to the wish of the French people. However, we must recognise that our authority derives from a situation of fact. We are not and cannot be the Government of France.

Immediately the Executive Committee begins its functions it should solemnly make known to the French people that it will hand over its powers to the provisional Government which, as soon as the country is liberated, will be constituted in France according to the law of 15 February 1872. The application of this law is contemplated when the legislative assemblies have ceased to function, which is the case today, and can be adapted by having recourse to other elected bodies on the advice of the National Consultative Council and of the Council of Legislation taking into account the changes brought about by the action of the enemy or by the development of the situation of labour in France (i.e. since the law of 1872 was passed).

If I have correctly represented the essential points of the opinions expressed by the National Committee and by myself on this subject, I beg you to give me the agreement on these points, which is essential for the establishment of our union. At the same time we can rapidly agree on the composition of the Committee. To begin with it will consist of two members proposed by you and two members proposed by me, making the first members of the Executive Committee six in all. I suggest that three places should be left vacant in order that the Executive Committee may fill them later.

Monday, 17 May 1943

An immense series of telegrams – all 'Immediate' or 'Most Immediate' – from London and Washington. It is very hot today, and I find it rather an effort to concentrate on all this. At any rate, they are on quite different problems from those which fill our minds, and this was a relief. I should be glad to finish with the French and get on to something else.

Tuesday, 18 May 1943

No letters from you. The bag is behaving very oddly – I don't know why.

A usual sort of morning. With the fine, hot weather, one wakes early. (Also, the night is made hideous by mosquitoes. We are trying to get nets, but they have not yet arrived.)

Lunch with Catroux, Monnet, Eric Duncannon, Princesse de Merode and others – a very ill-assorted party. Mme Catroux really is Lady Willingdon – with just a touch of Nancy Astor.

At 5.30 I went off with John and Monnet to Tipasa, to our little quiet hotel, our beautiful little secluded bay, and our Roman city. Walked and bathed before dinner.

Wednesday, 19 May 1943

Up at 7 a.m.; bathed; and breakfasted; took the car up a mountain road; walked with Monnet till noon; bathed; car back to the hotel; lunch. A very delightful morning and quite a useful one. Monnet is still the *éminence grise* here, and if I can persuade him of the wisdom of some plan or other, he can generally put it over Giraud in time.

(The sea is deliciously warm – not too warm, and clear and clean. We have no bathing dresses, but it does not matter as there is no one about except an occasional fisherman.)

Motored back to Algiers and arrived at the office about 3.30 p.m. I found a good deal to do and decided to leave for London with Catroux on Friday. I feel it to be absolutely essential to try to settle up the French dispute which has dragged on so long. I do not believe we shall ever improve much upon Giraud's last offer – (i.e. Cabinet, with collective responsibility, and joint premiership) and it seems that the best chance of getting de Gaulle to accept is for Catroux to take the offer back with him and threaten to resign and break up the French National Committee if de Gaulle is unreasonable. Of course, de Gaulle will not like the provision that this War Cabinet is to come to an end when France is liberated, when a provisional government is to be elected in accordance with the laws of the French Republic. At any rate, if he has some idea of making himself a sort of dictator, this will be a hindrance. But I do not see how he can openly refuse to bind himself to this clause, because to refuse is to disclose his Bonapartist tendencies (if he really has them).

Nevertheless, I do not think we shall really bring off the union without a great deal of pressure from H.M.G. on de Gaulle even to the point of threatening to denounce our agreements with him and cut off his enormous subsidies. And my real object in coming home [to London] is to try to persuade H.M.G. to take a firm stand.

Worked till 7.30 p.m. at the office, clearing up various things.

8 p.m. A small dinner-party – not very exciting – but including an old friend in Jim Putnam, one of the Managers of the Macmillan Company of New York. He is temporarily employed under the North African Economic Board. He has been at Dakar, and is now at Casablanca. He was in Algiers for a few days only. He is a most charming fellow. He normally acts as an Assistant to Latham (on the general literature side). His war work is now looking after palm-kernels and oil-seeds (of which he knows absolutely nothing).

(I am also rather amused at George Brett[17] having released Putnam for war work. He is charming, but can well be spared!!)

Thursday, 20 May 1943

A really splendid day. Left Algiers at 7 a.m. with Roger Makins, Murphy, Reber,[18] Monnet and some others. We arrived at Tunis aerodrome about 10 a.m. On reaching the aerodrome we found all the notabilities of North Africa either having just arrived or arriving by plane.

After the usual delays, a procession was formed, and we drove from the aerodrome, through the crowded streets of the town, to the spot selected for the saluting base.

The great naval and military and Air Force swells led the procession – but in closed cars. So Generals Eisenhower, Giraud, Alexander, Anderson, Patton,[19] etc. – Air Marshals Tedder, Coningham, Doolittle,[20] etc. – Admiral Cunningham – all these were scarcely

[17] George Platt Brett, Jr, had been President of the Macmillan Company of New York since 1936.

[18] Samuel Reber (1903–71) was assistant to Robert Murphy, 1943.

[19] Lieutenant-General George S. Patton (1885–1945) had commanded a corps in the 'Torch' landings, and was to command the U.S. Seventh Army for the invasion of Sicily, 1943–4.

[20] Major-General James Doolittle (b. 1896) was commander, U.S. Fifteenth Air Force, 1942–3, and North-west African Strategic Air Force, 1943–4.

recognised by the cheering crowd, and anyway were far too well trained to return their salutes except in the most formal way.

At the end of the procession, however, came the representatives of the civil power, and it was generally recognised that the honours of the day went to them. The reason was simple. At the end of the procession of closed cars and unseen generals, came an open 'command car' (a sort of superior jeep) and perched upon this, as in a Roman chariot, were Murphy and I. Immediately in front of us were the flags of our respective countries – the Stars and Stripes and the Union Jack – and (since we had the flags and were the only people who could actually be seen) I can tell you that our procession through the streets of Tunis was like driving through Stockton on polling day.

Encouraged by me, Murphy (although a career diplomatist and inexperienced in the art of popular elections) began to play his part nobly. Every street was packed; every window in every house was packed; every roof was packed. When the people saw our flags, they cheered and waved and threw flowers. We cheered and waved and kissed our hands to the ladies on the roofs and in the windows and on the street. It was a magnificent progress. Troops presenting arms; people cheering. It was much commented on. If ever I am forced out of English public life, I shall certainly put up for Mayor of Tunis.

At last we reached the saluting base. The minor personalities were put in smaller stands on each side of the main platform. Here were ranged the following, and in this pattern:

Guard of honour
GRENADIER GUARDS
ROAD

Churchill tank		Giraud	Eisenhower	Churchill tank
	Cunningham	Alexander	Tedder	
	Hewitt (U.S.)[21]	Catroux	Coningham	
		Macmillan	Murphy	

About 30,000 troops took part in the parade, which lasted over two hours. In addition, of course, there were troops lining the streets. The audience consisted of *all* the civil population (including Italians) and all the remaining troops. The atmosphere was extremely cheerful – like a jolly football crowd.

[21] Vice-Admiral H. Kent Hewitt (1887–1972) commanded U.S. Naval Forces in North-west African Waters (later called the U.S. Eighth Fleet), for the landings in Sicily and Salerno; he had commanded a fleet of 102 ships for the 'Torch' landings.

First came the French – Zouaves, Tirailleurs, Moroccan and Algerian native troops, Foreign Legion. The procession was led by a detachment of Spahis, making a brave show with their white horses, red cloaks, red leather saddles, and drawn swords. As they passed the saluting base, they rose in their saddles.

The great majority of the French were of course natives. The men are splendid – many with great beards and whiskers. But their equipment and clothing were pitiful – antiquated rifles, torn cloaks, slippers or bare feet. They had a tremendous reception from our own troops in the audience – especially the Moroccan Goums – who fought very well and very murderously.

I did not think much of most of the French officers. The few purely French battalions were also poor, in physique and general appearance. Nevertheless, the French detachment (led by their excellent General Koeltz[22] – an Alsatian) made a favourable impression, if only because one felt it a sort of resurrection of France, and because one realised what a brave show they had put up during all these months with such poor equipment and material.

After the French, two American regiments (representing the American Second Corps) led by a fine brass band. In contrast to the French, the American equipment and clothing are almost indecently rich. Every private soldier has a pair of lovely brown leather shoes with rubber soles. (Incidentally, you cannot march in rubber soles – I mean from the dramatic or review standpoint.) He also has a pair of leather gloves which would cost me a fiver in England; he has a wonderful kind of golfing jacket, a splendid helmet, lots of gadgets hung round, and is altogether a very expensive fellow who has cost his national treasury a lot of money.

The American troops have certainly learned a lot in this campaign – and their officers have learned how little they know about war. I am sure they *will* be very good but they still look like recruits, and even these detachments (presumably a picked lot) did not impress me. Of course, there are a very small proportion of Anglo-Saxon descent, and this fact strikes one forcibly when one sees a lot of them together. And they nearly all wear spectacles, of the most expensive kind!

However, they didn't march too badly, and they got a great cheer, and everyone seemed pleased, and there was no danger of an international incident.

By that time, about one hour or more had passed, and I thought we should perhaps have a small British detachment, and it would all be over.

But for once the British decided to put on a show which would take everyone by surprise. Except for a few detachments of the Eighth Army – your Derbyshire Yeomanry – Eleventh Hussars and some

[22] General L. M. Koeltz (1884–1970) commanded the French Nineteenth Corps (of the Algiers and Constantine Divisions under General Giraud) in Tunisia.

Gurkhas, it was a First Army affair. After months of waiting, and disappointment, and modesty, and playing down to the French, and carrying the burden of the American amateurishness, and getting fed up with the British public's infatuation with the Eighth Army, the First Army – which in November 1942 came to North Africa an inexperienced body of troops, most of whom had never seen a shot fired – determined to show us that it was worthy of being linked with the Eighth Army in a splendid partnership, which, under Alexander's magnificent generalship, had achieved one of the greatest victories in British history.

After the Americans had passed, there was a slight pause. Then, appearing from apparently nowhere a faint sound of pipes. Soon, came into view the massed pipers of Scots Guards, Irish Guards, and all the Highland Regiments available (I think these must have come partly from the Fifty-first Division, Eighth Army).

They marched in *slow* time, passed the saluting platform and neighbouring stands – the tune was 'Flowers of the Forest'. Then they *countermarched* (each line wheeling and passing through – you know the drill) and as they passed a point on the return, broke into quick time and marched away into the distance.

The effect was really very dramatic and made a splendid prologue.

Then began the long march of our men in splendid procession. It must have taken one-and-a-half hours.

Each division was led by the division general, his brigadiers, his staff.

Each battalion (a selection from battalions) was led by the colonel.

In a long file they came, formation after formation, regiment after regiment, unit after unit.

Unlike the French and Americans the British were in drill, not battle order, shorts, stockings and boots (shoes for officers), battle blouses or shirts with short sleeves – no helmets (forage caps and berets). The helmet gives a soldier the look of a robot, especially the German and American. With the forage cap or beret you can see his face – his jolly, honest, sunburnt, smiling, English, Scottish or Irish face – relaxed now, not worn or harassed as men look in battle – and confident and proud. All these brown faces, these brown bare arms and knees, these swinging striding outstepping men – all marched magnificently. Every unit seemed represented – Air Force, Brigade of Guards, Rifle Regiments, County Regiments, Pioneers, Engineers, Gunners. Honestly, they all marched like Guardsmen. A very good band (stationary – just *before* you reach the saluting place – an old parade trick) gets all the men marching at their best before they reach the saluting point.

Perhaps it is their shorts, and sleeveless shirts, but they all look so tall and well developed. And I like the modern generals, in shorts and shirts instead of boots and spurs – looking so young – some of the generals and colonels are really boys.

Part of the splendid appearance of the troops is really the reward for twenty years of education, health and housing progress. I am sure it has given them a better physique than the New York and Chicago slum and tenement boys, or the French, without games or sanitation.

Part is the good Army food and physical training. Part is discipline and pride in their achievements.

Anyway, taken as a whole, it was the finest thing of its kind, and the most impressive I have ever seen. These men – of this old country – were clearly the masters of the world and the heirs of the future.

After the Infantry, the guns, armoured cars and tanks, Derbyshire Yeomanry leading (Ian Walker[23] I saw in the distance). Guns and tanks polished and shining; the great trailers for the guns, the lorries, the cars – a magnificent and Roman progress. With our troops were General Leclerc's[24] regiment of Free French (who came from Lake Chad) and refused to march with the French, preferring English for companions. (Incidentally, the two kinds of French troops – Gaullists and Giraudists, now that there are no Germans to fight – will soon start a civil war amongst themselves, unless my mission to London is successful.)

At last, the parade ended. The generals inspected the Grenadier Guard of Honour – which was very good – and we moved off in our procession of cars, the American and British Ministers being again prominent in their elevated and public glory.

The notabilities then proceeded to the Resident-General's house or palace, where General Juin[25] (acting Resident-General) produced lunches for sixty to seventy guests at one long table.

I was between Juin and Catroux and had very pleasant conversation with both.

The *only* subject (almost embarrassingly so) of conversation among *all* the French and Americans was the British parade.

I must say that they were all very generous. Giraud said that when he had seen the Eighth Army at Sfax, he thought they must be unique. Now he had seen the First Army he realised that it was as good. He said that in his whole life he had never seen such a body of men. All that old Ike (Eisenhower) could do was to say ecstatically to me and others (and repeat it the next day) that he had never believed it possible to dream of having such an honour as to command an army like this. Really, it has been a grand day.

After luncheon, most of the generals, etc., went off for a courtesy

[23] Major Sir Ian Walker (b. 1902) of Okeover Hall, a Derbyshire neighbour of my wife's.

[24] General Philippe de Hauteclocque (1902–47), who adopted the name Leclerc to protect his family in Metropolitan France.

[25] General Alphonse Juin (1888–1967) had been captured by the Germans in 1940 and freed at the request of Marshal Pétain, who offered him the post of Minister of War; he became instead C.-in-C., North Africa, 1941–2, and commanded the Free French forces in Tunisia in May 1943.

call on the new Bey of Tunis, the late one having been deposed.[26] Whether by mistake or on purpose Murphy and I were driven in the wrong direction and never reached the palace at all till the ceremony was over (this has not prevented us being given a ridiculous star of tinsel with the sash in the M.C.C. colours, which will be fine for charades). However, we continued our progress in our glorified jeep, and were very well received with our flags to make us conspicuous.

In the event of any more trouble with the Bey, and popular election being substituted for the traditional system, we think we might run for joint Bey with good prospect of success.

We left by air at about 4.15 p.m. and got back to Algiers aerodrome about 7.15 p.m. (a long, tiring, but very splendid and memorable day).

Francis Rennell (back from London) to dinner and two air commodores (Sinclair and Cross) whom I had picked up at Tunis and promised to take to England with me.[27]

I had rather a lot of work to do with Francis, which was a bore but inevitable. At 11 p.m. Monnet came round (or rather came up to my little room – he had joined us at dinner) and so to bed about midnight.

Friday, 21 May 1943

Although it is rather absurd, I have whiled away the time in the long aeroplane journeys writing this letter. It will at any rate tell you about the parade; but I shall in fact bring the letter with me.

9 a.m. Called on Admiral Cunningham.
9.30 a.m. Deputy Chief of Staff.
10.30 a.m. Murphy.
11 a.m. Monnet.
11.15 a.m. Went to Palais d'Été to see Giraud.
12 noon Went to see Eisenhower.

He was, as usual, very friendly. He has given me a Flying Fortress – to take me to England and bring me back. 'Come back as soon as you can. I don't want to be without you.'

He fully agrees with the necessity to bring the present political situation to a close. The danger of incidents between the Free French and Giraudist troops is now increasingly great and (if the two generals do not get together quickly) the bitterness will increase.

I told him what I had done about de Larminat's (Free French) division.[28] But if de Larminat appeals to de Gaulle (as he will do), we shall have a really awkward situation.

[26] Muhammad al-Amin Bey had been installed in place of his nephew, who had ruled under German occupation, and whose loyalty was therefore suspect.

[27] Air Commodore Laurence Sinclair (b. 1908) commanded the Tactical Light Bomber Force in North Africa and Italy, 1943–4. Air Commodore Kenneth Cross (b. 1911), commanded No. 242 Group R.A.F., North-west African Tactical Air Force, 1943–4.

[28] General René de Larminat (1895–1962) commanded the First Free French Division, 1941–3, which had been fighting in Libya. His division was said to be recruiting in Tunis by offering inducements such as higher pay and advances in rank than the Giraudists could offer.

1.45 p.m. Left aerodrome. We have a very fine Flying Fortress with an experienced and battle-tried crew. The pilot has made fifty-four operational sorties. The party consists of Catroux and A.D.C., John Wyndham and I, Air Commodore Cross, Air Commodore Sinclair and two American colonels who asked for a lift. The crew is (I think) about ten in number.

We reached Gibraltar at 6.45 p.m. (Gib. time), a very quiet and smooth trip.

Bath and dinner at Government House. General Mason-MacFarlane as friendly and interesting as ever. We were booked to leave at midnight. But at about 9.30 p.m. the captain (Captain Johnson) of the Fortress sent up to say he could not leave as the landing weather in England was too bad.

Saturday, 22 May 1943

Left at 7 a.m. – a good take-off. Arrived safely at Portreath (Cornwall) at about 2.30 p.m. A very good and smooth flight. Lunched in the Mess – and then another great disappointment: no more flying (owing to a ridge of very bad weather across south England). Indeed we were nearly told to go back to Gibraltar when about two hours out from England. So, after telephoning to you and the children, there was nothing for it but to wait for the 8.06 p.m. from Redruth. Fortunately two sleepers were available at Plymouth for Catroux and me, and so we got to bed by 11 p.m.

It was rather absurd to write this letter – but I started it on the way down from Tunis and to go rambling on helped to while away the long hours from Gibraltar to England.

In any case – it finished the story for you. The rest I can tell you all myself. I am writing this at about 7 a.m. in the sleeping-car. The train is very late, and I am getting *more* and *more* impatient.

It will be so lovely to see you all – and it is grand to have *all* the family collected for me.

June

Friday, 4 June 1943

This is the end of a remarkable week.

I left Northolt on Thursday afternoon (27 May) with John Wyndham. I also brought with me on the Fortress General Catroux and General Bouscat. We left Portreath about 11 p.m. and reached Gibraltar about eight o'clock on Friday morning, the 28th, without any incident except that one out of the four engines broke down. On reaching Government House, after the necessary ablutions, I went in to breakfast, where I found all the Prime Minister's staff, together with General Marshall. They had arrived the night before from America. I went in to see the Prime Minister, who was in bed. He immediately attacked me about Force X and accused me of having disobeyed instructions, to which I retorted that at any rate he had got the fleet. 'No thanks to you,' says he. 'I don't know,' said I. 'You would have blamed me if the thing had gone wrong, so you must give me the credit when it has gone right.' He went on mumbling away about not carrying out his instructions to me. He then asked about the French, and I explained to him the situation. He told me all the difficulties which he had had in Washington – daily and almost hourly attacks by the President and other Americans on de Gaulle. This was what had led to the telegrams I had seen in London. Nevertheless, I think he seemed relieved that the negotiations were going better than he had expected. I took Catroux in to see him, and he was exceedingly polite to the general. We left Gibraltar about 11 a.m., arriving at Algiers about two o'clock.

Saturday, the 29th, was a very busy day. I called in to see the Commander-in-Chief and the Chief of Staff. I also went round to see Admiral Cunningham, and I spent a certain part of the morning with the Prime Minister, who was, as usual, at the admiral's villa. Lord Rennell came to lunch. At five o'clock M. Monnet came to see me to discuss the latest stage in the French negotiations. I dined at the admiral's – General Marshall and General Eisenhower were also there.

Sunday, the 30th, was the day of General de Gaulle's arrival. He was met by General Giraud at the French aerodrome, and from what we heard the first impressions were good. At 3.30 p.m. General Whiteley came to see me, and the rest of the afternoon was spent in various interviews. General Ismay and the Prime Minister's Private Secretaries dined with us.

On *Monday morning, the 31st*, I spent some time with the Prime Minister, he being still in bed. He told me that he had decided to ask Eden to come out, and he was expected to arrive that afternoon. He duly turned up at the aerodrome at 3.30 p.m., and I went to meet him. At six o'clock I heard from Monnet the first account of what had happened at the meeting in the morning. I attach a note of my conversation with Monnet (marked 'A').

General Eisenhower gave a dinner that evening to which he invited the Prime Minister, Eden, General Marshall, General Alexander, Air Chief Marshal Tedder, Murphy and others. I was there.

On *Tuesday, 1 June*, I saw General Giraud at 8.30 a.m. The attached note (marked 'B') gives the story of that interview.

At twelve o'clock Murphy and I made a formal call upon General de Gaulle. A copy of the record of our conversation is attached (marked 'C').

At 6 p.m. Catroux called to see me (note of conversation marked 'D').

Monnet came to dinner, and I explained to him how he had muddled the whole affair, and told him the proper way to call a meeting and circulate an agenda. He agreed that this should have been done on Monday and said he would see that it was done if possible. No meetings of the French took place during Tuesday, which was a day of anxiety and difficulty.

On Wednesday morning we heard the story of the resignation of M. Peyrouton. So far as I could piece the tale together, it appears to be this. Pressure was put on him by the Gaullists, or he was told that if he gave his resignation to General de Gaulle he would be looked after. At 9 p.m. on Tuesday, therefore, he delivered a letter sending in his resignation to General de Gaulle, a somewhat extraordinary procedure, since he owes his allegiance, if at all, to General Giraud. Apparently de Gaulle's reply was not quite satisfactory, or he did not see the price of his treachery forthcoming. He therefore delivered another letter at 1 a.m. on Wednesday morning, placing his resignation in the hands of Giraud. In the meanwhile, Giraud was infuriated by the whole affair – very naturally – and wrote an angry letter to General de Gaulle, accusing him of wishing to introduce a Nazi régime into France and asking him publicly to disavow any such designs before further discussions took place.

The events of Wednesday are pretty fully recounted in the attached records of conversations with General Giraud ('E'); General de Gaulle ('F'); and General Catroux ('G').

It was a day buzzing with rumours and great excitements, including the appointment of Admiral Muselier to keep order in view of a possible putsch by de Gaulle.

However, all this nonsense ended with the definite decision to forget about the folly of the previous two or three days and hold a meeting of the seven gentlemen concerned on the Thursday morning with the object of coming to some conclusion. Murphy and I had a press conference at seven o'clock, after which I went up to the admiral's to dine with the Prime Minister.

On *Thursday, 3 June*, we were all somewhat exhausted by recent events; and after a morning at the office, I took the Secretary of State out to Tipasa where we bathed and lunched. While we were having lunch we got a telephone message to say that the seven French stars had met and formed themselves into a definite constellation.[1] You will by now, of course, have read an account of all this and the decisions taken. The point is that at last an agreement has been reached and formally ratified in an official document. Noguès and Mendigal are to go, as well as Peyrouton, who will be replaced by Catroux. All this is very good, and at any rate we have reached some finality.

At 4.45 p.m. Massigli came to see me. My talk with him is recorded in documents 'H' and 'I'. After seeing some other people up till about seven o'clock, I returned to the villa, where we had a party for the Foreign Secretary. General Gale, Commodore Dick, General [Ben M.] Sawbridge (American), General [Everett S.] Hughes (American), Mr Reber and Air Vice-Marshal Wigglesworth were guests. This was a party of what one might call the 'second eleven'. After dinner we were sent for to 'No. 10', where we found General Eisenhower, Air Chief Marshal Tedder, Admiral Cunningham, General Montgomery. We passed a very interesting and delightful evening, and the conversation lasted well into the early hours of this morning. The Prime Minister seemed to be delighted at the turn in French affairs, and I think he has also reached a very satisfactory settlement of other questions with the Americans.[2]

I am dictating all this on Friday morning, the 4th. The P.M. and Eden have gone off to bathe at Tipasa. At 12.15 p.m. there is a press conference. And then will come the lunch to be given at the admiral's villa to the seven members of the new French Committee to meet the Prime Minister and the Foreign Secretary.

I am afraid this is rather a diary of a letter; but I thought you would like to have the records. I will try to write another letter in my own hand before the bag closes this evening.

The P.M. and Eden and the generals are expected to leave this afternoon for home.

[1] The French Committee for National Liberation.

[2] It had been agreed that mainland Italy would be attacked after the occupation of Sicily.

'A'

Record of conversation
Monday, 31 May 1943

1. At 6 p.m. yesterday I called on M. Monnet. He informed me what had taken place since General de Gaulle's arrival. He had had a long talk with General de Gaulle on the evening of Sunday, 30 May, from 11 p.m. till 2 a.m. the next morning. General de Gaulle's mood seemed to vary from comparative calm to extreme excitability. He was clearly very hostile both to the Americans and, to a somewhat less extent, to the British. In the course of conversation he observed that the Anglo-Saxon domination of Europe was a mounting threat, and that if it continued, France after the war would have to lean towards Germany and Russia. Monnet still finds it difficult to make up his mind as to whether the general is a dangerous demagogue or mad or both.

2. On Monday morning the following met together: General Giraud, General de Gaulle, General Georges,[3] M. Monnet, M. Massigli and M. Philip.[4] These six were supposed to be the first nominees to the Executive Committee. General Catroux was also present, having been invited apparently by General de Gaulle. The discussion opened by General Giraud asking de Gaulle to make a statement. De Gaulle made a long, rambling and violent attack on the whole management of North Africa, especially on the personalities. We must as quickly as possible get out of this *marasme*. It was an indispensable condition of working at all that the following should be removed: Boisson, Peyrouton, Noguès, Generals Mendigal and Prioux,[5] and Admiral Michelier. Giraud replied with a conciliatory speech, explaining the technical reasons and the difficulties of the colonial empire. Monnet spoke, and said that he thought the first thing to do was to form the Committee, but that if it would be of any assistance, he might say that, as far as he was concerned, when the Committee had been formed and started to consider personal questions, he (Monnet) would certainly be in favour of very radical changes in the Administration. He understood General Giraud's technical reasons but did not regard them as overwhelming. Broadly speaking – though not with regard to every individual mentioned – he would agree with de Gaulle; but the question should be studied by the Committee after it was formed. General Georges spoke warmly in support of these various officials, and said that as the

[3] General Alphonse Joseph Georges (1875–1951) had been commander of the North-east Front in France and Inspector-General of French Land Forces before his capture by the Germans in 1940. He escaped to become one of General Giraud's representatives on the F.C.N.L. as Commissioner without portfolio. He was an old friend of Churchill's.

[4] André Philip (1902–70) was Commissioner of the Interior, 1943–4, a post he had held in London on General de Gaulle's French National Committee.

[5] General René Prioux (1879–1953) had commanded the First French Army in 1940, and been prominent at Dunkirk. He was adjutant-general of French forces in Africa.

last person coming from France he could say that de Gaulle quite overstated his position there. He also discussed at some length the battle of 1940. Altogether, in Monnet's view, Georges made an unhappy and not a very helpful speech. Catroux followed on the same lines as Monnet in trying to build a bridge. Giraud replied shortly. Then de Gaulle said that the matter could not be taken any further and that he would see General Giraud privately at three o'clock that afternoon. A further meeting of the seven had been called for 5 p.m. but had been cancelled.

3. I am afraid I was rather rough with Monnet, and told him that he had behaved very foolishly in not calling attention to the fact that there was no motion before the quorum and in not moving that the seven individuals should constitute the Executive Committee charged with French interests, and asking someone to second it. Then they could have carried the motion at the end of the day after any number of hours' discussion. De Gaulle would have been forced into the position of voting for or against it.

'B'

Record of conversation
Tuesday, 1 June 1943

1. At 8.30 a.m. today I saw General Giraud. He began by congratulating me warmly on my appointment as Viceroy of India! – which had apparently been rumoured on some wireless transmission the previous evening. He said he felt he had had some part in this appointment, since no doubt the experience which I had been able to gain of *la question musulmane* in North Africa during the last five months had helped to get me the job.

2. I then read to him telegram Resmin 842 about Force X. He informed me that he already had been in communication with Admiral Cunningham over this matter, and that at the admiral's request had refrained from making any statement to the press or radio. I explained that I received the telegram late last night and had not been able to get in touch with the admiral but that I would discuss the matter with him. I certainly agreed that it would be wiser to say nothing.

3. Giraud observed that Vichy propaganda was made much less effective by the moderate and helpful way in which the problem had been handled, for which he said he had to thank me as having assisted him.

4. He then discussed the general situation. General Giraud gave me an account of yesterday's proceedings which tallied with that given me by Monnet. At three o'clock yesterday afternoon de Gaulle came to see him. He told him that he still could not work the Committee unless the prior dismissal of these officials was agreed upon. He took rather a

violent line. He also told Giraud that he did not propose to call on General Eisenhower. He was not acquainted with General Eisenhower. When he was master here, he (de Gaulle) would show the English and Americans where they stood. Giraud was very patient, I thought, this morning and very dignified.

5. I gave Giraud the same advice as I had given to Monnet, that at the next meeting a motion should be passed and either carried or defeated. I warned him that I thought de Gaulle was playing for position, but that I agreed that politically he was on a good wicket in demanding the resignation of some of these men. It would therefore be necessary immediately after the formation of the Committee to take steps to dismiss at least some of them. I rather encouraged Giraud to press ahead with the formation of the Committee and to bring the matter to an issue within the next few days.

'C'

Record of conversation
Tuesday, 1 June 1943

1. Mr Murphy and I called upon General de Gaulle this morning at twelve o'clock. After some preliminary sparring General de Gaulle expressed his views as to the character of the French administration. It should be, if not a government in name, as near to a government as possible in effect. The central Committee should consist of the necessary number of ministers or commissioners to carry out the work. There would therefore be the joint Presidents, a Minister of Finance, a Minister for the Colonies, a Minister for Transport, a Minister for Supply, a Minister for the Army, a Minister for the Navy, a Minister for the Air and a Minister for Foreign Affairs. There would also have to be a Minister for Justice and Education. It would probably also be desirable to have on the Committee a minister representing the interest of the Moslems. This should make ten or eleven in all, but it was essential if the work was to be done.

2. When asked by Mr Murphy whether the Executive Committee had formed itself, he said that that was not so. He had expressed his disappointment at the attitude taken in the discussion yesterday. He gave a different version from those we had already heard because he said that his disappointment was shared by Philip, Massigli and even Catroux. With regard to the proposed composition he expressed great surprise that General Georges had been brought out of France by the English for the purpose of putting him on this Committee. General Georges was an old gentleman, quite incapable of working as was needed today, and, moreover, associated with the defeat of France. Monnet was a good man, but more of an internationalist than a Frenchman and would be most useful on that side. In the course of

conversation he explained that he had made it a condition that the following should resign: Peyrouton, Boisson, Noguès, General Mendigal, General Prioux, Admiral Michelier. He wanted this done immediately. We said that this could be done after the Council was formed. But he said he was disappointed at the resistance to the resignation of these gentlemen, whether before or after the Council was formed, which was put up by General Giraud and General Georges. He admitted that the others did not take this view.

3. He said that many Frenchmen and others did not seem to realise that France was going through a period of revolution. An immense gulf was fixed between the period before the defeat and the present time. Just as the Royalist Army after 1789 was torn in conflict and divided loyalties, so had the French Army been. It must be renewed by the spirit of the revolution. It must be officered by the young and untried men. All these old generals must be got rid of.

4. At the same time, on being pressed, he seemed to think that the matter would be arranged, and certain discussions were now going on. He did not give any indication as to breaking off negotiations, and going back to London. But it was clear that he did not regard himself as committed, but spoke of himself as a separate power; and so the appearance of his villa was like the court of a visiting monarch. He further asked Mr Murphy to arrange for him to call upon General Eisenhower. He apologised for not having done so before because he had no Liaison Officer through whom these arrangements could be made. He also asked me to arrange for him to visit General Alexander and Air Chief Marshal Tedder.

5. He talked about the proper place for the French Administration. The central authority must be removed above the atmosphere of colonial politics. He therefore hoped it would be possible to find a town – Blida, Castiglione, or perhaps Constantine – to which they could go. In this atmosphere life would be simpler and more work could be done.

6. He repeated that his desire for the removal of the gentlemen he mentioned was not vengeance, but France expected new men for the new work that lay before her. She would not understand a government of old men associated with defeat. He had no intention of allowing himself to be imprisoned in an executive committee. He was quite quiet and rather pleasant throughout. His arguments clearly had considerable effect upon Mr Murphy. On leaving he took Mr Murphy by the arm and said: 'Why do you not understand me? Why do you always interfere with me? It is a mistake France will not understand, why your politics are contrary to me. I represent future France and it will be better for us all if you will support me.'

Murphy argued the point: but de Gaulle afterwards made the same accusation against Great Britain. I said that I thought my position had been recognised as a favourable one from his point of view while trying to keep a fair balance and not meddle too much with French affairs. He said he did not make these accusations against us personally, but our governments did not recognise the true character of the revolution which had taken place and must take place if the soul of France were to be saved.

7. One comes away, as always after conversation with de Gaulle, wondering whether he is a demagogue or a madman, but convinced that he is a more powerful character than any other Frenchman with whom one has yet been in contact.

8. My general conclusion is that negotiations will not be broken off, that de Gaulle will get his way as usual, and that a formula will be found which will give him what he wants while saving the face of some of the others.

'D'

Record of conversation
Tuesday, 1 June 1943

General Catroux called on me at six o'clock this evening. He gave me a similar account to that which I had already heard from Monnet and other sources regarding the events of yesterday. He took the story somewhat further.

The interview between Giraud and de Gaulle at three o'clock yesterday afternoon only lasted a quarter of an hour and was of a very unfriendly character. Catroux saw de Gaulle later in the afternoon and tried to persuade him that he was being foolish about the resignations because he would have a majority of the Committee on his side once the Committee was formed. De Gaulle doubted this. Catroux undertook to see Monnet, and came back later with a positive declaration of support from Monnet. De Gaulle would not decide that evening, but said perhaps the next morning. This morning Catroux saw Giraud at nine o'clock and found him very indignant but still prepared to carry through with the formation of the Committee. He then saw de Gaulle, who was unwilling to come to a decision until he had seen Murphy and me. Catroux said: Why? What had we to do with it? De Gaulle replied that he still would like to wait. He saw de Gaulle at lunch time and he still preferred to postpone his decision as to whether he would go through with the matter or not until tomorrow (Wednesday) morning.

Catroux finally decided that if de Gaulle does not definitely agree to the formation of a Committee, he and Massigli will jointly write to Giraud asking for an early meeting so that the Committee can be formed. Catroux maintains his customary patience and still hopes for a successful conclusion.

'E'

Record of conversation
Wednesday, 2 June 1943

Murphy and I called on General Giraud at 11.45 a.m. today on the general's invitation. He gave us a version of the events of Monday which corresponds more or less with what we had learned from other sources; he only added that the interview at three o'clock between himself and General de Gaulle had been brief and unfriendly.

On Tuesday no events took place and no meeting of the Committee was called, although Catroux had hoped to arrange it. Catroux telephoned to de Linarès at four o'clock on Tuesday afternoon to say that de Gaulle was not yet willing to have the meeting.

At nine o'clock on Tuesday night – information as to the hour and fact being supplied by Colonel de Linarès, no doubt through his secret agents – a letter was delivered from M. Peyrouton, Governor-General of Algeria, to General de Gaulle. Giraud read us the text of this letter. It was offering his resignation to de Gaulle in his capacity as President of the Executive Committee.

At 1 a.m. on Wednesday morning a letter in similar but not identical terms was addressed by Peyrouton to Giraud. There is some mystery about the difference in time.

At 1.20 a.m. a letter from de Gaulle to Giraud was delivered by an Officier d'Ordonnance, who handed it in at the iron gate of the Palais d'Été. On being asked whether it was urgent, he said, 'No, it could wait till the morning.' It was, however, immediately delivered, and it proved to be a letter from de Gaulle to Giraud informing him that he had received a letter of resignation from Peyrouton and that in the same letter Peyrouton had expressed his intention of asking for a position as captain in the Colonial Army. De Gaulle replied by accepting the resignation and saying that Peyrouton should regard himself as a mobilised officer and report to the Officer Commanding the French Army of the Levant (Larminat). He also informed Giraud that he proposed to ask [Maurice] Gonon, the present Secretary-General of Algeria, to carry on the functions of Governor-General meanwhile. General Giraud sent a reply to Peyrouton, the text of which was published in today's paper, as is the text of Peyrouton's letter of resignation to Giraud. The general did not give us the text of the letters which had passed between Peyrouton and de Gaulle or of the letter from de Gaulle to himself. Colonel de Linarès undertook to send us these texts later in the day.

By four in the morning General Giraud had completed the preparation of a letter of protest to de Gaulle which he despatched. In addition, he seems to have sent another communication to de Gaulle asking for a reply by four o'clock this afternoon. I was not quite clear what was the nature of this letter or to what proposition it is de Gaulle is asked to reply. I take it that it is connected with the meeting of the Committee.

While sympathising with the general about the way in which he has been treated, Murphy and I urged upon him the importance of handling the matter in a very correct way. It seemed to us that the correct thing to do was to hold a meeting of the persons concerned and elect a Committee; whether de Gaulle chose to attend or not was his affair.

Giraud observed that de Gaulle had said very hostile things to him about the English and the Americans. We replied that it was nevertheless necessary to proceed according to the agreement. Letters had been exchanged between Giraud and de Gaulle before de Gaulle came to Algiers and we strongly advised Giraud to act in accordance with these letters and to hold the meeting to elect the Committee. Just before we left a message was brought to Giraud to say that Catroux and Massigli proposed to break with de Gaulle.

After leaving Giraud, Murphy and I called in on Colonel de Linarès, who gave us a similar version and promised to supply us with a full dossier of the texts of all the documents which had passed this evening. We urged upon him the same considerations as we had impressed upon Giraud, and stressed the importance of preventing the general from writing letters without consultation with his advisers, and the extreme desirability of playing the cards well. Linarès confirmed that Catroux had broken, but was not quite sure about Massigli.

On leaving the palace we met outside a group of personalities, including General Béthouart,[6] just arrived from Washington, and General Georges. I had some talk with General Georges and impressed upon him the importance of the matter being handled correctly. General Georges said one could not rely on Catroux or Massigli. I rebuked him for this attitude, and said that if he advised Giraud in this direction he would soon put him in the position where he had no friends at all. Surely this was the time to rally all the moderate elements.

General Georges did not impress me very favourably this morning. He is obviously taking an extremely reactionary line. Murphy agrees with me in regretting his appointment.

I went from the palace with Murphy for a drink. Here we saw Gonon, who said that he thought Peyrouton had yielded to extreme pressure from the Gaullist party. He had been very unhappy during

[6] General Antoine Béthouart (1889–1982), then commanding land defences on the Moroccan coast, asked General Noguès not to oppose the 'Torch' landings. But he failed to arrest Noguès, as asked to do by Allied agents, and was himself arrested on a charge of treason, though he was released a few days later by the invading Americans. He was head of the French Military Mission to the United States, 1943.

recent weeks and it had probably been indicated to him that if he resigned quietly he would be looked after, but that if he was obstructive no one could answer for the consequences. I think he fears assassination. It is now said that Peyrouton has written to Giraud explaining that he wrote to both generals under the false impression that the Committee had been formed, and saying that he will accept Giraud's orders and remain in his position until a substitute can be found.

The time was then about 1.30 p.m., and on returning to the villa I found that de Gaulle had asked to see me, the interview being fixed for four o'clock this afternoon.

Murphy and I asked to see Catroux, and we are to see him at 5.30 p.m.

'F'

Record of conversation
Wednesday, 2 June 1943

General de Gaulle called to see me at four o'clock.

He told me that he could not understand the extraordinary atmosphere with which he was surrounded; the calling up of the Goums, the appointment of Admiral Muselier in charge of police and other measures, as if there was going to be a civil war. He laughed the whole thing off and said it was quite ridiculous. I told him that I thought the atmosphere of suspicion on both sides was very regrettable and even laughable, and I told him frankly that he was only saying about the Giraudists what they were saying about him.

He then discussed the Peyrouton incident, about which I said I thought Peyrouton was greatly at fault in sending his resignation to General de Gaulle when he knew the Committee had not been formed, and when he was the servant of General Giraud: and that I thought General de Gaulle was wrong in accepting it. He said he had accepted it because he was the head of the French National Committee and he took it that Peyrouton, by writing to him, acknowledged his authority. I said that was a bit thin, and what would he think of a man who had served him for five months and then sent in his resignation to the head of another party. De Gaulle replied: 'That is just the kind of man Peyrouton is! I have always told you all along he was a rascal.' In a word, he tried to laugh the whole incident off.

He then, however, informed me that he was going, in spite of everything, to make another attempt, and that a meeting of all the men concerned was to take place at 5.30 p.m. this evening to see whether they could end up by forming the Central Committee. I said that I was delighted to hear that. This gave me an opportunity for trying to make an appeal to him not to miss so great a moment in his own private history and the life of France. I asked if I might speak quite frankly to him: whether he would mind my speaking in English as it would be easier. He said he did not mind, he could understand.

I told him that I, like many other Englishmen, had fought in the last war and had been wounded on French soil on three occasions; I had lost many of my best and dearest friends in that struggle. We formed a friendship with France which had never been broken. In my country I was on the back bench in politics and was strongly opposed to the policy followed by the leaders of my party, Mr Baldwin and Mr Chamberlain. I had separated from them and joined Mr Churchill and others in the movement we made for rearmament in the years from 1937 onwards. I also told him that I thought probably his views on social matters were very like mine. In England it seemed that great advances could be made and had been made in recent years on social legislation. In my country, as in his, there were old men who looked backwards, rather than forwards to the future. We needed young men with young minds. Many people in my walk of life had quite realised that the future in our country would be wholly different. Great wealth would pass away. Property would be held in trust for the benefit of the people, but we hoped to see the transformation from one society to another without revolution or disturbance, and it depended in my country, as in his, on whether men of progressive opinions could work together and inspire the necessary changes. I told him that I had followed all that he had done with the greatest sympathy and admiration; that I realised his impatience on finding old men and old minds still in control; that I understood the difference between my country and his because we had not been subjected to great pressure; we had not suffered a great defeat and the sense of ignominy that followed that defeat. Nevertheless, I implored him to take courage; not to miss his opportunity to join honourably with Giraud in this national administration. I felt sure that as the weeks and months went by he could, without straining the law or acting in any way unconstitutionally, obtain for himself and those who were with him the reality of power. He could build up a strong machine for war which could also be available upon the reconstruction of France in peace, but that if he missed this opportunity he would merely condemn France to further divisions now and the prospect of civil war in the future. I ventured to make this appeal, not as a diplomat, as I am not a diplomat, but as one man to another, both of the same age and who have something of the same ideas.

The general listened to this harangue and said, whether he meant it or not (after asking if he might reply in French – which he did), that he would pay much attention to what I had said. He had always felt that I had always understood him and that he promised to weigh this very carefully before allowing a break to come. He found it terribly disappointing to find himself surrounded by such an antiquated point of view. I said that disappointments were made to be borne and obstacles to be overcome, and I had every confidence that he would play his role in an honourable manner.

On that he then left with every appearance of good feeling and friendliness.

I have since been informed by Monnet on the telephone that the meeting at 5.30 p.m. will not now take place. There was some doubt as to whether this was a meeting between the two generals or the whole seven. At any event Monnet tells me a meeting of the whole seven has been fixed with de Gaulle for ten o'clock a.m. tomorrow.

'G'

Record of conversation
Wednesday, 2 June 1943

Murphy and I called on General Catroux at 5.30 p.m. We found him sitting in his garden, cool and elegant as ever. Murphy complimented him on this, and said he was the most patient man in the world. Catroux replied that today he had not lived up to this reputation as he had lost his temper with de Gaulle. At this morning's meeting he reproached de Gaulle for his action over the Peyrouton incident. De Gaulle made an insulting reply, and Catroux said, 'The whole thing is insane; I can stand it no longer,' and walked out of the room. Since then he has not seen de Gaulle. He told us, however, that M. Philip had acted as an intermediary, and it has now been arranged that a meeting will be held at ten o'clock tomorrow morning. I impressed upon Catroux the importance of circulating a proper notice together with an agenda, and also of having ready a text of a resolution to be moved constituting the Comité Executif. Catroux said that he would inform both Philip and Giraud.

In further conversation Catroux said that de Gaulle had really proved a tragedy for France. Had it not been for his quarrels with the English, the Free French would have been entrusted with the North African affair. Then he (Catroux) would have found himself in Giraud's position, and he had more knowledge and a better position in Africa even than Giraud. All this had been ruined by de Gaulle's antics. Now there was a danger, even if the Committee were constituted successfully. He foresaw great difficulties ahead. Nevertheless, on being pressed by us both he said he would do everything he could to constitute it because of course he realised that this would mean the reality of French union even if later on de Gaulle became impossible and had to be removed.

Meanwhile he gave an amusing explanation of the Peyrouton incident. Peyrouton thought he could do a better deal with de Gaulle than with Giraud. It had been intimated to him that if he made his resignation to de Gaulle instead of Giraud the Gaullists would give him compensation either immediately or in a few months' time. He acted accordingly. But when de Gaulle's formal letter came back without any private intimation of the compensation to be paid, Peyrouton went off on another line and therefore wrote his letter to Giraud. This explains the four hours' delay. As Catroux said, it is not without an element of comicality that Peyrouton, accused by extreme Gaullists of being a traitor, has been offered a commission in the Gaullist Army of the Levant. Catroux, when asked who could replace Peyrouton as Governor of Algeria, said that he thought he might have to take the position himself and combine it with a seat on the Committee. I said that I thought it was important to be drafting the rules of the Committee tonight, so as to allow members to remain members of the Committee even if they were *en mission* or on other posts.

I suggested again to Catroux that General Georges might be sent as head of a military mission to London.

Finally, Catroux said, 'Well, I will go on, but it is very exhausting. I find myself between a madman and an ass.'

I observed that people should not write letters at four in the morning. Catroux agreed.

At any rate the day has ended better than might have been thought, that is, if the meeting really does take place tomorrow at 10.

'H'

Record of conversation
Thursday, 3 June 1943

1. M. Massigli has just left me – 5.30 p.m. He left with me the attached document, which is the statement of the new Committee which will be given out to the press.

2. An official note will be presented in London and Washington jointly by the Fighting French and Giraudist delegations to the Foreign Office and the State Department announcing the formation of the new Central Power and asking for recognition. This will probably be done tomorrow.

3. General Catroux has been appointed a member of the Committee with the special duty of being in charge of Moslem questions throughout the French Empire. Meanwhile he is to combine this office with the Governor-Generalship of Algeria. The resignation of General Noguès will be announced tomorrow, and his successor will also be announced. He will be M. [Gabriel] Puaux, who has served in colonial posts both in Syria and in Tunisia. He escaped from Tunis after the battle. General Mendigal, the present head of the Air Force, will be

replaced by General Bouscat, at present head of the Giraudist Mission in London. Other changes will be discussed and decided upon in due course.

4. M. Massigli told me for my private information that at the end of the meeting today General de Gaulle embraced General Giraud.

5. I should think it would be a good thing now to send out the invitations to tomorrow's luncheon party to the seven gentlemen concerned. You will notice that the list of names is given in alphabetical order.

Comité Français de la Libération Nationale

Les Généraux de Gaulle et Giraud comme Présidents, le Général Catroux, le Général Georges, MM. René Massigli, Jean Monnet et André Philip comme Membres, constituent le Comité Français de la Libération Nationale qui sera ultérieurement complété par l'adjonction d'autres Membres.

Le Comité ainsi constitué est le pouvoir central français.

Le Comité dirige l'effort français dans la guerre sous toutes ses formes et en tous lieux. En conséquence, il exerce la souveraineté française sur tous les territoires placés hors du pouvoir de l'ennemi; il assure la gestion et la défense de tous les intérêts français dans le monde; il assume l'autorité sur les territoires et les forces terrestres, navales et aériennes relevant jusqu'à présent soit du Comité National Français, soit du Commandement-en-Chef Civil et Militaire.

Toutes les mésures nécessaires pour réaliser la fusion des administrations dépendant de ces deux organismes seront prises sans délai par le Comité.

Conformément aux lettres échangées entre les Généraux Giraud et de Gaulle, le Comité remettra ses pouvoirs au Gouvernement provisoire qui sera constitué conformément aux lois de la République des que la libération du territoire métropolitain le permettra et au plus tard à la libération totale de la France.

Le Comité poursuivra, en étroite collaboration avec tous les alliées, la lutte commune, en vue de la libération intégrale des territoires français et des territoires alliés, jusqu'à la victoire totale sur toutes les puissances ennemies.

Le Comité s'engage solennellement a rétablir toutes les libertés françaises, les lois de la République et le régime républicain, en détruisant entièrement le régime d'arbitraire et de pouvoir personnel imposé aujourd'hui au pays. Le Comité est au service du peuple de France dont l'effort de guerre, la résistance et les épreuves, ainsi que la rénovation nécessaire exigent l'union de toutes les forces nationales.

Il appelle tous les Français à le suivre pour que la France réprenne, par la lutte et par la victoire, sa liberté, sa grandeur et sa place traditionnelle parmi les grandes puissances alliées, et qu'aux négociations de paix, elle puisse apporter sa contribution au Conseil des Nations Unies qui déterminera les conditions de l'Europe et du Monde après la guerre.

Alger, le 3 Juin, 1943

'I'

In the course of my conversation with M. Massigli today, he informed me that General de Gaulle was deeply moved by my conversation with him yesterday, and expressed very great pleasure at the sympathetic character of the arguments which I had addressed to him.

Note

Friday, 4 June 1943

1. Admiral Cunningham gave a luncheon party today to the members of the new French Committee for National Liberation. There were present the Prime Minister, the Foreign Secretary, the Resident Minister, C.I.G.S. (General Brooke), General Giraud, General de Gaulle, General Catroux, General Georges, M. Monnet, M. Massigli and M. Philip.

2. The party appeared to pass off very well. After lunch the Prime Minister made a short speech, without rising to his feet. He was himself deeply moved, and so were his audience. He referred to his first knowledge of the French Army and people thirty-five years ago, when he attended manoeuvres under General de la Croix. From that time onwards he had formed many friendships with French statesmen and soldiers. He had never wavered in his friendship and admiration for France, the French people and the civilisation which they had made. Nor had he wavered in his political support; even in bad times when some of his own countrymen seemed to be turning away, he had been loyal to the French connection. He had seen with the deepest sorrow the distressing years through which France had passed after she was overwhelmed by the brutal enemy; but he had seen with equal admiration her revival and renaissance. He believed that on this historic day, when all French people were united once more, prepared to take up in loyal co-operation with their Allies the struggle against the enemy, our hearts could well be glad even amongst so much sorrow. He pledged himself to continue to the full the loyal support which he had given. He pledged his Government and the people of Great Britain and the Empire, and he asked us all to rise to our feet and drink the toast of, 'La Belle France, La France Victorieuse'.

3. General Giraud made a short and very suitable reply, referring to the uplift in all French hearts which had been caused by the landings in North Africa and the successful conclusion of that campaign.

4. General de Gaulle then made a very well-phrased and really

moving little speech, chiefly about the Prime Minister's personal attributes. He referred to the three years during which he had seen the English people passing through terrible times. One judged individuals and people more by how they stood bad times than by their behaviour in times of prosperity. In prosperous times friends were easily come by, but in times of trouble one found the true value of individuals and of countries. He would never forget the inspiration the British people had given him.

5. The Foreign Secretary then made a short and very well-phrased speech, referring to the necessity of England and France holding together after the war for the reconstruction of the things in which they mutually believed – freedom, tolerance and the rights of the people to enjoy their own lives at their fullest development.

6. General Georges then made a few remarks, in which incidentally he referred to Joan of Arc, which caused some merriment, the Prime Minister exclaiming that it was not we but the Burgundians who were responsible.

7. The proceedings then ended. All the speeches were in French, the Prime Minister speaking in that vigorous French, drawing widely from both French and English vocabularies, in which he excels. The Foreign Secretary spoke in excellent and very idiomatic French. And the Frenchmen, of course, spoke their own language with their usual grace and clarity. After the luncheon the whole party were photographed together, and then finally a picture was taken of the Prime Minister and General Giraud and General de Gaulle. All this – both the entertainment and the photographs – was on rather a happier note than the famous photograph at Anfa. Something has been achieved in four months.

Saturday–Monday morning, 5–7 June 1943

On Saturday, we had a busy morning (Chief of Staff, Murphy, newspaper correspondents), farewell to Peyrouton, etc. But we got away about 2 p.m. and John and I left by car for a short trip.

We took our lunch with us, and stopped by the wayside in a little wood to eat it. The face of the country is now quite changed. The harvest is all ripe and mostly cut, so that (except for the green vines) all the earth is brown stubble – like a fine September day at home.

Most of the grass is also burnt up – and except for the late flowering jacaranda trees (a lovely flower – the colour of wistaria) there is little green and few wild flowers on the plain. When you get into the mountains, it is different, and if you get quite high you still get the various alpines in flower and both pansies and violets.

We motored across the hot plain (it is very hot now in the middle of the day) to Blida.

From there we motored up a steep and winding road to a place called Chréa – about 6,000–6,500 feet high – at the top of a mountain. Here there is a sort of French sporting and holiday settlement. Little chalets, like Swiss chalets, and a ski club and two or three simple hotels. The French came up in winter to ski and in summer to get out of the heat. They had some very good hostels for children and various institutions of that kind. Most of these have now been occupied by the military authorities for various purposes.

I was given a little chalet, and a batman and our driver (who is a soldier and a very good servant) helped to look after us. It was a most delightful rest after the heat and labours of Algiers. We stayed till early Monday morning – leaving at 6.30 a.m. and getting back to the villa at 8 a.m.

I really did enjoy the holiday. There was a military mess where we had our meals, and I had to give a lecture on Sunday night – but that was a small price to pay for all our pleasures.

By day the sun was very hot, and nobody wore any clothes to speak of, and all got horribly sunburnt. By night – especially Saturday night when there was a strong wind – it was really very cold, and I wore my fur-lined flying-jacket.

Sunset and sunrise were indescribably beautiful. Northwards from my chalet lay about forty miles of plain – and then the sea. Looking in every other direction, range upon range of high mountains – some wooded, some bare rock.

In the clear morning – before the heat haze – you could see sixty miles of mountains to the south. Beyond that (it is said) you can see the sandstorms in the great Southern Desert. It was really an indescribably lovely spot – a sort of Shangri-La.

Incidentally, nobody among the rank and file of the British Army wears any clothes in North Africa. It seems that people from cold northern climates have an urge to remove their clothes when at last they see the sun. (If you were here, you would be as red as a lobster.) The local inhabitants – Arabs, etc. – on the contrary protect themselves from the heat by wearing masses of garments.

It seems to be a point of honour of the troops to try to become the colour of a bronze statue, and since the First and Eighth Army boys are now in a wonderful state of physical health, they present a really splendid appearance. With their shiny bronzed bodies – no fat – taut muscles – and tremendously athletic, they are really a magnificent sight. They mostly wear only socks, boots or sandals, and shorts. It is the fashion to roll up their shorts as high as possible, and lower them as far as they think seemly below the waist.

I saw some troops bathing in the sea the other day and at first I thought that they had managed to get white bathing slips. But they were really bathing naked, only their buttocks were white and all the rest of them chocolate colour!

I don't know what the French girls and veiled Moslem women think of it. No doubt they just regard all the British as merely mad.

Monday, 7 June 1943

Back to work. I went to see General de Gaulle in the afternoon (at his request). I found him very friendly and in quite good spirits. There are a lot of problems still to solve, but I think they are making progress. The Americans are beginning to realise that although de Gaulle is often very tiresome, he is much the most intelligent of the French personalities. He is at least realistic and has a modern mind.

For dinner, General Mason-MacFarlane (Governor of Gibraltar), Admiral Sir Ralph Leatham (who was so kind to me at Malta and is on his way home from Alexandria), Colonel Terence Maxwell,[7] Colonel [Michael] Babington Smith, and one or two others.

Tuesday, 8 June 1943

A meeting of our Political Council at 11 a.m. There is a bit of a flurry about the question of Giraud and the position of Commander-in-Chief.[8] But I think they will settle it among themselves if we refrain from interfering.

12.15 p.m. An economic meeting – quite interesting.

Anstruther-Gray[9] (on his way back from home) to lunch. Quite a nice chap and a useful M.P. A very brave soldier, I am told.

The usual office routine in the afternoon. No excitements.

For dinner – M. Labarthe[10] (alas! a fallen minister), Count and Countess de Rose, the American Consul (Mr Wiley) and an American journalist, Miss [Helen] Kirkpatrick. Quite a good party.

Wednesday, 9 June 1943

Spent most of the morning (9.15 to 12) in conference with General Eisenhower, Admiral Cunningham and Air Chief Marshal Tedder about a number of questions.

In the afternoon General Béthouart called. He is a good man and was very helpful to us at the time of the November landings – in fact, so helpful that General Giraud thought it wiser to send him to an *exil doré* in Washington. He was head of the Giraudist Military Mission there. He will now, I hope, be head of a joint Military Mission, representing the new Committee.

Things are still very difficult here. There are so many people on each side (the small fry) who are trying to make trouble. The personal relations between Giraud and de Gaulle are not good. They are men of

[7] Colonel Terence Maxwell (b. 1905) was Deputy to Colonel Julius Holmes in the Military Government Section, A.F.H.Q., 1943–4.

[8] General Catroux had tried in vain to persuade General Giraud to relinquish either the co-Presidency or the Chief Command. General de Gaulle was now demanding that the office of Commissioner for National Defence should be created for himself, with the three Chiefs of Staff for the Services under him.

[9] Major William Anstruther-Gray (b. 1905), was Unionist M.P. for North Lanark, 1931–45.

[10] André Labarthe (1902–67), founding editor of the monthly revue *La France Libre* in 1940, had been appointed General Giraud's Secretary for Information on 9 May 1943.

such a completely different type that it could hardly be otherwise. Giraud is an old-fashioned, but charming colonel, who would grace the Turf Club. De Gaulle is a modern-minded, ambitious, conceited, but clever politician, who makes no pretensions to good manners and has a delight in violent and abusive attacks on individuals, particularly if they are of an older generation. Then, like Josiah Wedgwood[11] with us, he simply cannot understand why they take offence.

The rumblings of a storm are beginning to reach me, and the Americans are beginning to get all het up again. But nothing will prevent me going tonight to see Beatrice Lillie, Leslie Henson, Vivien Leigh,[12] etc., who are visiting Algiers.

Thursday, 10 June 1943

Diary of a Summer Day in Algiers

9.20 a.m. I went to see General Giraud and found him sitting alone. He handed me a letter which he said he had received five minutes before.

This was a letter of some three pages from General de Gaulle to General Giraud complaining that the so-called Central Committee was apparently poisoned by suspicion of himself, was harking back to Vichy ideas, and was trying to surround him (de Gaulle) with an atmosphere of 'putsch'. He was unable to make progress with his ideas, and the simplest proposition seemed to require interminable argument before any decision could be reached. In all the circumstances, therefore, he felt that he could not take the responsibility of continuing in such an organisation in view of the duty that he had towards France. He therefore tendered his resignation both as President and as member of the Committee.

General Georges then came in. He said that General de Gaulle's behaviour at the Committee was brutal and indecent. He (Georges) had the greatest difficulty in restraining himself. Even the smallest thing seemed to excite de Gaulle to a frenzy. For instance, whenever Marshal Pétain's name came up, as it must often do for the sake of illustrating an argument, he found that it caused the most violent reaction from General de Gaulle. He could not understand it.

Meanwhile General Giraud was sitting at his desk writing with his own hand a reply accepting the resignation and was proposing to send it off immediately. Both generals seemed to be delighted at the way things are working out and the possibility of getting rid of de Gaulle once and for all. They asked me what I thought of the position. I said

[11] Josiah Wedgwood (1872–1943) had been Liberal, then Labour, M.P. for Newcastle-under-Lyme, 1906–42.

[12] Beatrice Lillie (b. 1894), Leslie Henson (1891–1957) and Vivien Leigh (1913–67) were entertaining troops on an E.N.S.A.-sponsored tour.

that I was afraid my brain did not work so quickly as the brains of Frenchmen and that I would like to think about it. I would venture to advise that no action should be taken without careful consideration. I thought that the result of de Gaulle's resignation would be very grave. They rather pooh-poohed this; but I said, 'Well, it would not be so grave in three or four months' time when the Empire has been closely knit together under the new Commitee, when all the problem of the English agreements has been resolved.[13] But what will be the position now? To whom will the Governor of Madagascar and of French Equatorial Africa look? From whom will Larminat and Leclerc take their orders? And what will the Free French fleet and aviation do? It is too early to expect them to accept loyally the new Committee. If this resignation took place after three, or preferably six, months, things would have settled down, but I see in this the danger of very grave events and a complete break-up of the French Empire. It will be worse than if the union had not been made at all, that it should fail in eight days.'

All this seemed rather to impress the generals, and they thought they would think the matter over. I suggested that at least the Committee might meet. General Giraud then took up his pen again and started to write an order for it to meet at three o'clock the same afternoon. I suggested that they might take a little longer time to think. General Georges then suggested five o'clock. I said, 'Why not sleep on it?', again apologising for the slowness with which my intellect grasped these difficult affairs. General Georges went out of the room, and I took the opportunity to tell Giraud of General Lyon's approaching visit.[14] I thought it was the best thing to do in the circumstances. This news seemed to have a considerable effect upon the general.

A few minutes later General Georges reappeared, and soon Monnet came in. Monnet then argued on the same lines as I had, and had rather a row with Giraud about it. Monnet kept persisting that he was only interested in France, not in scoring off de Gaulle or any personalities, and the effect in the world would be that people would think that the French were really not capable of managing their own affairs and running a great empire. Meanwhile, Giraud showed great impatience at the non-arrival of Catroux, whom I assumed (rightly) to be with de Gaulle. The discussion went on in rather a vague form, Monnet and Giraud arguing, accompanied by a monologue from Georges on things in general. Finally Catroux arrived, and at this point I thought it best to retire and leave the four Frenchmen together. I arranged with Catroux to cancel my visit to him, which had been fixed for 11.30, and that he would come to see me immediately after the conference at the Palais d'Été had ended.

[13] Some of the newly appointed Commissioners were still in Britain, and arrangements had to be made for their conveyance to Algiers.

[14] 'General Lyon' was the code-name for King George VI.

I returned to the office at 11.30. I then went up with Makins and saw Murphy and Reber and explained what had happened from my point of view. Murphy told me that Giraud had sent the text of the letter by Poniatowski to General Eisenhower for information. I was glad to find that Murphy took a very quiet and reasonable view of the whole situation. He agreed that it would be quite lamentable to let the thing break up at this early stage. He also seemed to regard de Gaulle's action as having a certain amount of bluff in it. I thought it right at this conference to tell Murphy about General Lyon's visit.

At 12.30 Catroux arrived. I told him of General Lyon's visit, which I thought he ought to know about as Governor-General of Algeria. Catroux explained to us his general view of the position, which was that he had already told de Gaulle it would be madness and wickedness to allow the resignation to stand. He said that he had learned this from him late last night, that he had been with him this morning, and that he was making his best endeavour to get him to withdraw his resignation. He also told me that as the result of the conference at the Palais d'Été it had been arranged that the seven members of the Committee should meet at ten o'clock tomorrow morning to review the situation.

3 p.m. M. Puaux, the new Resident-General of Morocco, arrived. He seems a very reasonable man. He seemed to know nothing of this fresh crisis, and I naturally did not refer to it. He informed me that he was going to make a broad-bottomed administration in Morocco. He would keep the present Delegate-General for the time being at any rate – M. [Jacques] Meyrier. He would take [Léon] Marchal with him (Gaullist); and also Comte de Rose (Giraudist). I told him that he would be inflicting a great injury on Algerian society by removing the Comtesse, but that I was delighted to hear of François de Rose's appointment. I formed a good impression of M. Puaux – not outstanding, but obviously a sincere and respectable character.

At 3.30 General Georges came. I gave him the Prime Minister's message and said I would of course be glad to forward any letters through the bag that General Georges cared to write to him in a purely unofficial way. General Georges said he had already had that understanding with the Prime Minister. General Georges was exceedingly pleasant and is obviously a very sincere character, full of a genuine desire to serve. He is slightly naïve, I think. For instance, he said, 'I am an old man and want nothing. The fact of my age ought to help.' He talked a good deal about the Marshal [Pétain]. He expressed again the view that although everyone in France was 'Gaullist', that was merely a name for resistance. He felt convinced from what he had seen of de Gaulle that he was a Hitler in the making. He said that his behaviour in the Committee was always brutal and intolerable. Nevertheless, at the end of his talk, he expressed the view that it was necessary to keep the thing together at least for the present, and he said that he would certainly take that line. He talked throughout of 'we', by which he means Giraud and himself. He spoke rather depreciatingly of Catroux, whom he obviously suspects, and he does not think much of Monnet. He complained that on certain points in the Committee Monnet had actually taken the line contrary to Giraud. He said it was incredible that he should do so, having been nominated by Giraud. I gently tried to express the view that the members of the Committee should give their views sincerely on what they thought the merits of each case, and should not regard themselves as the nominees of one side or the other. This seemed to be a new idea to General Georges.

At five o'clock I saw General de Gaulle. I said the reason for my visit was to inform him, as I thought it right to do, of General Lyon's visit. I remarked that he was one of the only three Frenchmen who had been told, the others being Giraud and Catroux; and that at the luncheon on Sunday, to which he had been good enough to accept an invitation, he would be the guest of General Lyon. He expressed some surprise, but seemed to think it was a fine thing that General Lyon should visit the troops here. He then spoke about the delay in the arrival of Pleven, Diethelm,[15] etc. I told him that the official list had only reached us on 6 June, and that the telegram was sent off from Allied Headquarters for the American Command in London on 8 June asking that all those at Prestwick should be sent as soon as possible. Any delay was due first to the request not having been properly presented on behalf of the Committee, and secondly to the inevitable delays in the military machine.

De Gaulle smiled and said, 'Anyway, they haven't come, and all the people who dislike me seem to get here – Muselier,[16] Georges and many others. Why do you bring them here?'

I said that it wasn't I who brought them here, but I thought I would like to give him the facts about the party in England. I also told him that I understood that owing to some delay by the two Missions both in London and Washington, the note asking for recognition of the Committee had not been presented to the Foreign Office and the State Department until 8 June. There would therefore be an inevitable delay before an answer could be received. The Prime Minister's speech was merely a general review for the benefit of the House of Commons: the formal diplomatic reply would be made through the proper channels.[17]

De Gaulle then said that all this was interesting but might not

[15] René Pleven (b. 1901) was Commissioner for the Colonies, 1943–4; he was to become Prime Minister in 1950 and 1951. André Diethelm (1896–1954) was Commissioner for Production and Trade, 1943.

[16] Vice-Admiral Émile Muselier (1882–1965) was head of the Free French Naval Forces 1940–2.

[17] On 8 June 1943, the Prime Minister had said: 'Our dealings, financial and otherwise, will henceforward be with the Committee as a whole. There is a further and larger question, namely the degree of recognition of this Committee as representatives of France. This question requires consideration from the British and United States Governments, but if things go well, I should hope that a solution satisfactory to all parties may shortly be reached.'

interest him much longer. He did not think he could go on with the situation. He could not make progress. I expressed surprise at this, and asked what was the matter. He said, 'It is not a question of Giraudists and Gaullists; it is a question of old men or young men, old-fashioned men and modern-minded men. I want to make a modern army. Giraud wants to keep the old army that was beaten. I want to reform, and reform means getting rid of a great number of incompetent and outmoded officers. I am hampered at every point.'

I said that I thought he must be patient. The Committee had only lasted a week. It would take a little time before the thing settled down, but that if he would work patiently and adopt a rather more friendly attitude towards his colleagues, I felt sure he would get his way on every point on which it was right that he should do so.

He did not seem much in the mood to talk, but was very polite and friendly. He said, 'It is all very annoying. It is *embêtant*.'

I said that I was glad to find that although he had found many Englishmen *embêtant*, he now realised that many Frenchmen were *embêtant* as well. The fact was that one could not get all one's way in this world except by patience and sustained effort on consistent lines. I said I was always at his service, day or night, if he wished to see me. He thanked me very much and said, with a smile, 'If I am no longer in the Government, will General Lyon wish to invite me?' I replied that I felt sure that General Lyon would be glad to see a Frenchman who had done so much for England in the hour of her greatest need and had stood by us when we were alone. This seemed to please him very much. He accompanied me downstairs and saw me into my car.

As I was getting in, Palewski[18] came up and seemed rather agitated. I judged from his agitation that he thought he was on a losing wicket. He stopped me and said, 'You must sympathise with my difficulties'; and I said, 'You must give good advice to your chief; that is the way to serve him. You must serve your chief and your country, and you know the way to do it.' He said, could he come and see me some time? I said, at any time, I would always give him good and straightforward advice.

6 p.m. Wrote some telegrams. Told Murphy the day's events from my viewpoint. He told them from his. He mentioned that Monnet had rung up and seemed very cheerful and confident that the problem would be resolved.

7.15 p.m. Massigli called, and told us that three things were troublesome.

(1) The inexplicable non-arrival of Pleven, etc., from Scotland.

(2) The apparent confusion concerning Mr Churchill's speech.

(3) The fact that General de Gaulle, in offering the position of Commander-in-Chief to General Giraud, had been careful to explain that it had no functions and no purpose. This naturally did not

[18] Gaston Palewski (b. 1901) was General de Gaulle's *chef de cabinet*, 1942–6.

encourage General Giraud to accept it, and he is now insisting on being Commissioner for National Defence.

We did our best to comfort M. Massigli, who requires comforting from time to time.

M. Monnet tried to get in touch with us during this conversation. I hope to see him later in the day.

Thus ends a perfect summer day in Algiers.

The day extends to the night.

At 10 p.m. I called on Monnet, where I found him with MM. Philip and Massigli busily engaged in writing a paper for tomorrow's meeting on the question of military organisation. They all seemed to have reached a point of considerable exhaustion. At any rate it is a good thing they are collaborating in trying to reach a conclusion.

I left them about half-past-eleven still at work.

Friday, 11 June 1943

The day began stormily, with a lot of complicated telegrams reaching both my colleague and myself from the President and the Prime Minister. If Washington and London would trust more completely the men on the spot, we should get on better.

Extract from memorandum on the F.C.N.L.'s road to recognition 27 August 1943

In order to understand the events which followed [de Gaulle's resignation], it is necessary to digress on the nature of American policy toward French affairs. When the Allied operations against North Africa were planned, it was contemplated that the territory might have to be 'occupied' and some form of Allied administration set up. In practice this was unnecessary; the administration was carried on entirely by the French authorities, and although the Commander-in-Chief had extensive powers under the Clark–Darlan agreement, a great many of those powers were never in fact used and fell into desuetude.

But there is little doubt, in the light of the telegrams which he sent in the middle of June to Algiers, that the President was still thinking of North Africa in terms of an occupied country in which his representative, General Eisenhower, had something of the position of a Viceroy. As regards France, the official policy of the United States Government was that it desired to see a French union brought about. But there was a fatal dualism running through the American attitude, and another policy, which appeared to be that of the President, popped out from time to time. It was that the United States Government did not desire to see the constitution of a central French authority, but rather to deal separately with each province of the French Empire and ultimately with France itself. This policy had found expression in the documents, handed by the Americans to General Giraud at the Anfa conference, in which General Giraud was accepted as the representative of French interests in North and West Africa.

Moreover, the President, Mr Hull, many State Department officials and a great many American military officers had an antipathy to de Gaulle and his movement which amounted in some cases to a phobia. . . .

There were indications that while the official policy of the United States Government was the realisation of French union, the President had made up his mind to break de Gaulle if he possibly could do so, and that the final achievement of union in Algiers on 3 June had only forestalled Mr Roosevelt's intentions by a short head.

After rather a tiresome morning, we went to a luncheon given by de Gaulle to the English. The party included Roger Makins, Harold Caccia,[19] Eric Duncannon, General Gale, Air Vice-Marshal Wigglesworth. The latter (who is from Thornaby) was in cracking form.

After luncheon, I had a little talk with de Gaulle. He complained bitterly of his inability to get on, surrounded as he was by old diehards and incompetents. I told him once more not to be silly, but to give the thing a fair trial.

At 3 p.m. I went with Gale to a meeting at A.F.H.Q. to discuss in detail the plans for General Lyon's visit. (It was to deal with them in good time that I had arranged for Colonel Kavanagh[20] – one of the equerries – to be sent out in advance. He has been staying with us.)

After this, I had a long talk with General Eisenhower, who as usual was very sensible. He really has developed in an extraordinary way. He has a certain independence of thought which is very refreshing, and he is not afraid of taking responsibility for decisions – even when they do not exactly comply with his instructions from home!

During the course of the day all our effects have been moved to another villa – much larger and nicer one, which is nearer the centre of the town and incidentally the office. It was occupied by the Consul-General [Carvell] and we have long coveted it. We took the advantage of General Lyon's visit to borrow it for a fortnight. But I doubt whether we shall ever give it back! The new villa is in the same garden or *parc* as that allotted to General Lyon – which will be very convenient.

The weather has become very hot and stuffy. We dined at the Club (as the servants were moving from one house to another) and it was terribly oppressive. I was very tired and went home early to bed. The

[19] Harold Caccia (b. 1905) was seconded from the Foreign Office to serve on my staff, 1943.
[20] Colonel Sir Dermot McMorrough Kavanagh (1890-1958) was Crown Equerry, 1941–55.

others went to see Josephine Baker[21] in a charity performance. (She has returned from Morocco, where she had retired, and is old and far beyond any real ability to do her old turns, but retains – they say – a remarkable technique.)

Saturday, 12 June 1943

Arrived at airport at about 11.30. General Eisenhower, Admiral Cunningham, Air Chief Marshal Tedder and I were designated to meet General Lyon. (All this time secrecy was being preserved – so the King was General Lyon in all messages and telegrams and the visit was called Operation 'Loader'.)

The plane made a good landing at about 12.30. The only hitch was that they had intended to go *via* Gibraltar, but the weather was too bad. So they had to land and refuel, etc., at Fez instead – rather to the surprise of the Station Commander, who was in bed!

Eisenhower and Cunningham went off with H.M. Tedder and I waited for the next plane, which contained Archie Sinclair and P. J. Grigg.[22] Archie is to stay with Tedder, Grigg with me.

This party also arrived safely, but about an hour later, about 1.30 p.m. Archie leaped from the plane, with arms oustretched, and began to make a speech. He is very ridiculous but rather a dear. (Tedder imitates him excellently.)

P.J. is proving himself (rather unexpectedly) a very pleasant guest. His language is very rough, but he is intelligent and seems anxious not to give trouble.

Immediately after luncheon – which naturally did not end till late, as it is three-quarters of an hour from the airport to the town – I was sent for by H.M. to go through the programme. Unfortunately, he was very tired from the journey and had not slept at all. So I had a good deal of difficulty in getting him to agree to the various items, and thought it best merely to get definitely fixed the arrangements for Saturday, Sunday and Monday. The real trouble is that the courtiers are deplorable. Joey Legh[23] does his best, and, although looking quite half-witted, is not so. But Alec Hardinge[24] seems to me beyond the pale. He is idle, supercilious, without a spark of imagination or vitality. And his whole attitude to the visit makes one wonder why he advised the King to undertake it at all.

However, after a lot of cajoling and so forth, we got the first

[21] Josephine Baker (1906–75), the American Negro singer who became a great celebrity in France in the 1920s served with the Free French Forces as an ambulance driver and singer, for which she was awarded a Croix de Guerre.

[22] Sir Archibald Sinclair (1890–1970), was Secretary of State for Air, 1940–5, and Leader of the Parliamentary Liberal Party, 1935–45. Sir James Grigg (1890–1964) was Secretary of State for War, 1942–5.

[23] Lieutenant-Colonel Sir Piers Legh (1890–1955) was Equerry to King George VI, 1936–46.

[24] Alexander Hardinge (1894–1960), later 2nd Baron Hardinge of Penshurst, was Extra Equerry to King George VI, 1936–52, and Private Secretary, 1936–43.

two-and-a-half days agreed. Monday was the day set apart to visit the American Army. (I thought H.M. might as well get this done with.) This meant a longish day – two hours' flight to the spot – reviews, etc., and two hours' flight back.

At first the view was that H.M. had come to see his own armies, not the American. Alec seemed rather to favour that extraordinary idea! However, after a bit we persuaded them that they were wrong and that such an attitude would be an absolute disaster.

Actually, General Lyon was merely tired and feverish. I do blame Alec, because he just doesn't seem to live in the modern world at all. He would have been out of date in the 1900s, and King Edward would have sacked him as outmoded then.

However, everything was finally arranged, and, as always happens, the original programme ended up by being restored almost exactly as we had drawn it up.

8.15. Dinner with the King. Eisenhower, Cunningham, Secretary of State for War (Grigg) and self – together with appropriate courtiers, etc.

This went off very well indeed. The King had had a bathe and a sleep and was in excellent form. He was very good with Eisenhower, who was himself in excellent shape – interesting, amusing, not too shy or too much at ease – in fact, the real natural simple gentleman which he is.

After dinner, in the chief sitting-room of the villa, the little ceremony took place to which Eisenhower had looked forward with great and genuine pleasure. The King took the general a little apart (the rest of us stood in a group together) and presented him with the G.C.B. with a few very well-chosen phrases. General Eisenhower was very delighted, and we all shook hands with him and renewed our congratulations.

Sunday, 13 June 1943 (Whit Sunday)

Still no letters from home. I have only had one from you since my return and none from anyone else. I do so want to hear about Carol. It seems such a pity she cannot come out here to keep house for me.

Church in the Dockyard, with the Royal Navy. The admiral asked me and Grigg (who is staying with me) to attend. Punctually at 10.30 the King arrived. Church in a canteen or a store-room. A beautiful screen and altar; the band of the Royal Marines; about 500–750 sailors (all in white) and the officers very smart in their white uniforms and gold epaulettes, etc. It was a good service – good hymns – and good hearty singing.

At about 11.15 it was over, and we drove back to our villas. Of course, everyone in the town recognised the King, although he is still called General Lyon by us all in official messages, etc.

Lunch 1 p.m. in General Lyon's villa. Present: Giraud, de Gaulle,

Catroux, Murphy and myself. The King did very well and spoke in good French to both generals who were on his right and left. Opposite him, Catroux, with myself on his right and Murphy on his left – so general conversation was easy.

I think the generals enjoyed it – at any rate it all passed off agreeably.

After lunch, the King went to see a convalescent camp, about seven or eight miles out of the town, on the sea. I did not go, but I heard he had a tumultuous and most moving welcome from the soldiers. He then bathed, and had a military dinner. I had various British and American soldiers of the second grade to meet Grigg.

Monday, 14 June 1943

A fairly quiet morning and a lot of political rumours. I forgot to put in the queer way in which I spent yesterday (Sunday) afternoon. As we were leaving the Royal luncheon party, de Gaulle asked me how I was going to spend the afternoon. I said I would probably motor out to Tripasa and bathe. He asked if he might come with me and alone. I said, of course.

So I had three-and-a-half hours of driving, walking in the ruins, and continuous talk with this strange – attractive and yet impossible – character. We talked on every conceivable subject – politics, religion, philosophy, the classics, history (ancient and modern) and so on. All was more or less related to the things which fill his mind.

It is very difficult to know how to handle him. I do my best, and I know that he likes me and appreciated having somebody whom he trusts and with whom he can talk freely. I think I have persuaded him to stay in the Committee for the present and give the thing a chance. But I'm afraid he will always be impossible to work with. He is by nature an autocrat. Just like Louis XIV or Napoleon. He thinks in his heart that he should command and all others should obey him. It is not exactly 'Fascist' (an overworked word); it is authoritarian.

Anyway, I thought it encouraging that he should ask for this quiet outing, and he obviously enjoyed it. The only trouble was that while we were walking in the ruins we were recognised. The word went round and a little crowd collected in the village, which cheered him wildly and demanded a speech. This is very bad for him!

To go on with Monday, 14 June 1943

After a quiet morning, Archie Sinclair and Louis Greig and Air Vice-Marshal Dawson to lunch.[25] The latter is a man of extreme ability, who is responsible for all the wonderful repair organisation of the R.A.F., mostly developed by utilising and adding to whatever civilian

[25] Group-Captain Sir Louis Greig (1880–1953) was Personal Air Secretary to Sir Archibald Sinclair, 1940–6. Air Vice-Marshal Grahame Dawson (d. 1944) was R.A.F. Chief Maintenance Staff Officer, Middle East, 1941–4.

engineering plants existed between Beirut and Casablanca. He is really a most attractive and interesting personality.

In the afternoon, I had a long talk with André Philip (at his request). He is a good fellow, though rather excitable.

Grigg and I went out to General Alexander's camp (in a pine wood above the sea, about thirty miles by car) for dinner. The general was as delightful and interesting as ever. He is really a first-class man. The more I see of him, the more I like him. I am very flattered, because I have been elected a member of his Mess, to go and live or eat whenever I like both here and throughout the campaign. That is a high honour.

Tuesday, 15 June 1943

The usual office routine, enlivened by the usual rumours and counter-rumours.

12.30 p.m. I saw Alec Hardinge about further arrangements. He is gradually waking up a bit, but he is a dreadful stick.

Lord Trenchard[26] came to lunch. At 3.15, General Georges called. He was in a state of passionate emotion, because he had not been able to prevent Giraud going to meet de Gaulle at Catroux's house. That is Georges's idea of treason!

At 4 p.m. Monnet, also very excited, with several new *projects* and memoranda which he had written.

At 5.30 a film performance – a Russian film called *One Day of War*. The heat was intense, there being a sirocco. It was like sitting in a Russian bath, and when I got out of the theatre, my clothes were wringing wet.

The King gave a garden party at his villa this afternoon. About 170–80 officers and civilians, British and American were invited. The band of the Royal Marines played. I was very keen to get him to do this, and Joey Legh supported me gallantly. It was a *tremendous* success and H.M. did very well and was most gracious to everybody. The Americans were really delighted, and letters about it will reach every distant part of the U.S.A.

Billy Harlech[27] arrived about 8 p.m. from Cairo. He is staying with us. I thought he seemed rather exhausted, but otherwise well. It was very lucky seeing him and we had lots to talk about. In addition, we had for dinner Grigg, General McClure[28] (American), Sam Reber (Murphy's second man – very nice) and one or two others.

At 9.30 de Gaulle and Massigli came round to see me – at their request. I had Makins with me. Rather a formal little conversation took

[26] Marshal of the R.A.F. 1st Viscount Trenchard (1873–1956) had been Chief of the Air Staff, 1918–29.

[27] William Ormsby-Gore, 4th Baron Harlech (1885–1964), my daughter-in-law's father, was U.K. High Commissioner in the Union of South Africa and High Commissioner for Basutoland, Bechuanaland and Swaziland, 1941–4.

[28] Major-General Robert A. McClure (1897–1957) was Director, Political Warfare Branch, A.F.H.Q., 1942–3.

place, on the question of the French military reorganisation, which is now the great bone of contention.

The difficulty is that de Gaulle wants to be the Minister of Defence, with effective control over the forces, leaving the title of Commander-in-Chief to Giraud and not much else. The British and American Governments (the President leading, the P.M. following) object to de Gaulle having authority over the Army at the moment, because they have no real confidence in what he might do. Unfortunately, the Americans are (not Eisenhower) letting their views be known prematurely, and de Gaulle (if he gets a chance) will play the 'French sovereignty' card and 'interference by the Allies'. I would much rather get what we want – if we can – *through* the French, rather than by *imposing* it *on* the French. But it is a difficult hand for me to play.

Wednesday, 16 June 1943

The King's presence has been officially announced, so General Lyon is now revealed. He was to have left this morning on a trip to Tunisia, etc., but there was a severe thunderstorm and no flying. However, the storm has done good and the intolerably hot and sticky days we have had are temporarily over. It is much cooler, with a nice breeze.

At 11.30 I went to see Bedell Smith (with Murphy) to talk over the situation. We decided – in view of the French disorder and the instructions from home – that General Eisenhower had better see the two generals and talk to them frankly as one soldier to other soldiers. The meeting is to be asked for by a *démarche* from Murphy and me to Massigli. This was duly done.

A pretty hectic day – General Coles to lunch – long committee with him and others on the system of payment for French property requisitioned, with a view to a possible revision of the Darlan–Clark agreement. Various appointments all day, ending with General [Charles] Mast, the new Resident-General for Tunisia – a very good fellow, who helped us considerably at the November landings, was then put on the shelf, was nearly killed in a flying accident, and then (largely through our efforts with Giraud) appointed to his new job.

Thursday, 17 June 1943

Billy [Lord Harlech] went off in the morning to get his plane. Conference with Murphy and others at 11 a.m. The meeting between Eisenhower and the two generals has been arranged for Saturday morning. I am fearful of the result, but we cannot avoid it.

After luncheon, I went to see Bedell Smith to discuss the situation (also to discuss a very good telegram from the President about me, which will mean that I shall stay on here at Eisenhower's side and move with him in any future theatre of war.[29] This was the matter about

[29] After the invasions of Sicily and mainland Italy.

which I have been so concerned for a long time. But it is now settled. And although I think Washington does not much like the presence of a British Resident Minister at Allied H.Q., and hoped it would end with North Africa, the President has given in to the P.M. on this, largely at Eisenhower's own request. The Chief of Staff was very nice and said they could not do without me and would like me to be with them till we got to Berlin).

At 6 p.m. Murphy and I had the press representatives – at my villa – and we explained to them the present position, partly 'on the record' and partly 'off the record'. As always, with a few exceptions, they were very friendly – also very thirsty, which John resents!

7.30 p.m. Monnet – more talk, more discussions.

In the course of the afternoon – on instructions – I delivered a note to Massigli informing him officially that no further payments of any kind would be made to the French National Committee (the Gaullist organisation). Any payments necessary would be made to the new Committee, in its collective capacity. The effect of this (which I have been asking for for days) will be very salutary, especially to some of de Gaulle's hangers-on. It means that their personal interests are now tied up to the Unified French Empire. It is exactly (*mutatis mutandis*) the policy which I applied to Force X in Alexandria. When Godfroy's men could only get their pay from Giraud's treasury, they began to talk of coming over. As I telegraphed to the P.M. in thanking him for this decision, 'Where your treasure is, there shall your heart be also.'

Dinner – Sam Reber, Dick Crossman[30] (Political Warfare) and another P.W.E. [Political Warfare Executive] boy called Stephen. Pleasant talk about books and Greek philosophy! A nice change!

Friday, 18 June 1943

At 10 a.m. a meeting at the C.-in-C.'s office – General Bedell Smith (Chief of Staff), Murphy and I also present.

General Eisenhower showed me some further telegrams from the President, and I showed him mine from the P.M. General Eisenhower then said, 'What do you think I should do?' I said, that as he observed from my telegrams, my instructions were to give him absolute support in carrying out the President's instructions. He said, 'Oh yes. But, as a friend, what would you advise me to do?' I said that that was quite a different question, and that I thought we might interpret these instructions in our own way. Finally, he sent a very sensible reply to the President, which he dictated in front of us. He asked me to suggest amendments, and I made a few.

[30] R. H. S. Crossman (1907–74) was Deputy Director, Political Warfare, A.F.H.Q., 1943, and subsequently a Minister in the Labour Government, 1964–70.

Extract from memorandum on recognition of F.C.N.L.

On 17 June General Eisenhower received some violent telegrams from President Roosevelt, in which his intentions for the first time were clearly disclosed. The President said in effect that he regarded North Africa as an occupied country, that he had no wish to deal with a central French authority, and that he had come to the conclusion that he could not deal with de Gaulle at all. He therefore said that de Gaulle would not be permitted to direct himself, or to exercise control through partisans or any committee, the African French army in the field, or its supplies, training or operations. Secondly, he stated that Boisson[31] was to remain Governor of French West Africa and, if de Gaulle secured influence in that territory, he would be obliged to send an expeditionary force to Dakar. Thirdly, he directed that the Committee should be prevented from meeting further. This last demand was subsequently modified. However, after full consultation, I was instructed to support the President's desiderata. General Eisenhower informed Mr Roosevelt that he considered the difficulties of the situation in Algiers to have been magnified; that he hoped to settle the question of the command in a personal meeting with Giraud and de Gaulle; that the question of the administration of French West Africa was not at present an actual one, and he did not propose to bring it up.

[Diary continues] It was finally settled that we must intervene in this military dispute (Giraud claiming to be Commander-in-Chief and de Gaulle wanting to be Minister for War with full powers over the Army except actual operational command), but that we would try to make the tone of our intervention as delicate and as friendly as possible. The real trouble is that neither the President nor the P.M. has any confidence in de Gaulle. I am bound to say that in view of the immense commitments of our armies here, now and in the future, they cannot afford to take any risks. De Gaulle's temperament makes him very unreliable, and for the moment what we chiefly need is security and tranquillity. What worries me is the fear lest in the search for these (which our Governments are right to demand) we may only achieve insecurity and confusion.

However, we must do our best and try to get our objective by the velvet glove, even if it conceals the iron hand.

General Eisenhower has invited the two generals to meet him at his villa (this is thought more tactful than A.F.H.Q.) and will do his best with them.

In the afternoon, I had the usual succession of appointments – General Rabino (British Treasury) on the monetary situation in Tunisia; M. Marchal (ex-civil head of the Catroux mission) to take

[31] General Boisson had fought the British at Dakar in 1940, and had since collaborated diligently with the Germans. De Gaulle wished to have him removed.

leave before going to Morocco with M. Puaux, the new Resident-General; Mr [Victor] Schiff (a horrid little French Jew, who writes for the *Daily Herald*) to be cursed for sending silly messages and sowing discord between Britain and America; M. Monnet, to discuss and argue and deplore and hope – really for me to hold his hand; M. Massigli, to be given a message to say 'no more money from England for the Free French' (message already formally delivered) and to have an unexpectedly and significantly friendly reception of this news, for Massigli knows that it means de Gaulle cannot go back to London and must either support the Union or retire into private life; and finally to reach the villa at about 8.15 and just have time to jump into a cold bath and then a very pleasant dinner-party, with General Humfrey Gale, and two American friends of mine, General Terry Allen (still commanding the American First Division – whom I visited when they were at Tidworth) and his second-in-command, General Teddy [Theodore] Roosevelt.

Saturday, 19 June 1943

10 a.m. General Eisenhower saw Generals de Gaulle and Giraud at his villa. No one was present except his Chief of Staff (Bedell Smith) and the official interpreter.

Massigli, Murphy and I were sitting in another room in the villa, in case we were required. This plan was in order to emphasise the purely *military* character of the intervention. Since it was impossible (in view of Washington, supported by London) to avoid any intervention at all, I was very anxious to make it more acceptable to the French by insisting upon its military and probably short-term aspects. The real demand of the Allies may be boiled down to this:

(*a*) There is to be a Commander-in-Chief of French forces.

(*b*) The C.-in-C. is to be in effective control of these forces.

(*c*) Any reorganisation system must not take away the C.-in-C.'s effective control.

(*d*) The C.-inC. must be able to carry out the existing military agreements and give us the use of railways, deck and harbour facilities, etc.

(*e*) For the present, Giraud is to be C.-in-C.

All this – which on the face of it is an interference with French sovereignty – we justify on the ground of our enormous military commitments here and the impending operations. We really say 'Do not swop horses in this particular stream.' The question of army reorganisation in its more technical aspects does not come up, except that we say that changes in the higher commands should have the concurrence of the C.-in-C. during this period.

You can imagine that all this is gall and wormwood to de Gaulle. I think he has largely brought it on himself, by neglecting and even scorning to earn the confidence of the President and the P.M. Nor do I think he gives sufficient thought to the vast risks which we are running and will continue to run in this African enterprise and the great sacrifices we are making to maintain it.

The interview lasted about one-and-a-half hours. De Gaulle left first, evidently in a great rage – I think partly simulated (he is a good actor, and does his stuff well). Giraud left a few minutes later, dignified but flushed. Eisenhower seemed rather taken aback by de Gaulle's powerful personality (he had never seen him 'in action' before) but was otherwise unshaken.

After considerable discussion, it was decided to put the C.in-C.'s demands on the French into the form of a written memorandum, to be given to the two generals and circulated to all the members of the French Committee. This would at least avoid exaggeration and misunderstanding.

The problem was to draft the document, into a telegram to the F.O. and a personal telegram to the P.M., have lunch, and drive to the aerodrome so as to leave the ground at 2.15 p.m. However, all this (except the lunch, which was a bit scrappy) was successfully achieved and the following party left the ground in a Flying Fortress at approx. 2.30, on their way to Castel Benito, the airground for Tripoli:

(1) Admiral of the Fleet Sir A. B. Cunningham.
(2) Flag Lieutenant ? ('Flags').
(3) The British Resident Minister.
(4) Mr Roger Makins (Counsellor).

But I can write no more.

We left Maison Blanche at about 2.30 p.m. in the Flying Fortress. Admiral Cunningham, 'Flags', Roger and I were the party. I took Roger with me instead of John, because I thought he needed a change.

We had a wonderful flight – wind behind – and got to Castel Benito about 5.45. We drove into Tripoli – about three-quarters of an hour – and went to the Senior Naval Officer's house (or apartment) there, where we got a most welcome whisky and soda.

I had never been to Tripoli, and since the King's tour in the district of Eighth Army and other units was not over, we had time for a walk in the town and harbour.

It is strange to think that the Turkish Ambassador in London (who stayed with us here a few weeks ago) told me that he lived in Tripoli as a child, when his father was the Turkish Governor. There is a good deal of the Turkish town left – a fine mosque or two. But most of the buildings are modern Italian – rather 'White City-ish', but still a good general effect. Of course a good deal (but not excessive) damage has been done by our air attacks. The town itself is not too bad – most of the attacks were of course on the docks and harbour.

Here there is a sad sight – ships sunk by British air attacks; block-ships sunk (and now partially cleared) by the enemy before they left. These are generally filled with iron scrap and/or cement and take a bit of moving.

We went on board the cruiser (I had better not give her name) at about 7.30 p.m. The King and his staff went immediately in front of us.

At 8.30 (after bath, etc., I having an excellent cabin vacated for me by the commander) we dine in the commodore's cabin. The King, Alec Hardinge, Joey Legh, Admiral Cunningham, Commodore [William] Agnew and one or two others.

We sailed about 10 p.m. A lovely moonlit night, with an escort of destroyers.

The admiral kept teasing me that it was on my advice that the trip had been undertaken, since constitutionally the King can only take the advice of ministers. I kept telling him that this was my reason for coming, so that we should all sink or swim together!

Actually, I think that neither on the trip over (on Saturday night) nor on the return trip (on Sunday night) did any of the naval officers sleep at all. And I am sure they were all pretty relieved when the cruiser got back to Tripoli early on Monday morning.

Sunday, 20 June 1943 (Trinity Sunday)

I went on the bridge of the *Aurora* (I see the press have now given the name of the cruiser) at about 7.30 a.m. It was a lovely morning and a glorious sunrise. There was a nice cool N.W. breeze, and this lasted all day and made the temperature very agreeable.

At about 7.45 we passed the minesweepers, who had been busily at work to make all secure for us.

At 8.15 the King came on the bridge; a special little platform (like a pulpit of the old three-decker type or in some modern nonconformist churches) had been constructed for him, a little projecting from and higher than the bridge. Here he stood alone, in white naval uniform. As we steamed into the Grand Harbour [Valletta], a slow passage lasting at least three-quarters of an hour – all the cliffs and forts, filled with troops, sailors, airmen and civilians, thundered out a tremendous welcome. It was really a most moving sight. On the old castle of San Angelo (built by the brother of William the Conqueror and now a naval depôt) were rows of sailors and marines. On all the other vantage points were infantry, gunners, airmen, boy scouts, girl guides and the dense eager crowds of the civilian population. Whenever possible there was a choir or a band. Slowly we steamed into the inner harbour and found our berth – and still the cheers and flag-waving and tears of emotion and excitement.

A few minutes after we had anchored, the Governor (Lord Gort) came ashore in a launch, and at 9.30 the King landed, with all the customary ceremony of piping and saluting, and so on.

The admiral, Roger and I landed in another launch, after the King's party had got clear away. I expect you will have seen pictures or perhaps films of the reception which the King got from the people when he landed. We only saw parts of it; for we did not drive round but went off and had a pleasant day sightseeing. We only ran into the procession here and there. But we saw the start, and the whole great square in Valletta harbour packed solid with an applauding humanity. The King drove for two hours in the morning from town to town. In the afternoon he visited the aerodrome and drove through all that part of the island which he had not been through in the morning. We ran into the Royal progress on our way to Verdala Palace (where the luncheon took place) and in the afternoon at various other points. Flowers, flags, confetti – and all the people, usually led by their clergy, with religious banners and emblems outside each church and crowding every square.

Considering that they had only been told in the early morning, I don't know where they found the flags and how they had time to decorate the streets – but it was done.

The admiral (who had some work to do with the Vice-Admiral, Malta) collected us again and drove us in his car for luncheon to Verdala. Verdala is a magnificent tall rectangular palace, on a hill top, rising to a magnificent height – like a mixture between Hardwick and Lumley. The style is early Renaissance – about 1540 – and splendid it is. The rooms are vast and high, and there is a great sense of dignity and self-confidence (very different to our showy sham Algerian villas).

After luncheon, Roger and I got a car, and drove to various places. After an afternoon's sightseeing we went to the Lieutenant-Governor's house (the house with the lovely garden of which I think I wrote to you before) and so the afternoon and evening passed till dinner-time approached.

Dinner was at the vice-admiral's house. Roger and I were the only civilians – the rest naval officers, and a very pleasant, intelligent and hospitable lot they proved.

At about 9.30 p.m., the admiral guiding us, we went down to the Custom House jetty, found the launch and went aboard.

At about 9.45 the King went aboard – a huge crowd collected to see him off and a repetition of the morning's enthusiasm.

At 10 p.m. the *Aurora* sailed.

At 7 a.m. the next morning we reached Tripoli. It was a memorable and marvellous day. (Incidentally it was the first day since 1 January that I have spent entirely in the company of British people. Much as I like the Americans and Frenchmen, it is quite a relief.)

I do hope the pictures and account of the trip will do justice to its success and its profound moral effect.

Mussolini called the Mediterranean *Mare Nostrum* (Our Sea).

The King, in a cruiser with four destroyers, has crossed it twice in thirty-six hours, sailing proudly to Malta – island of many sieges and struggles, but with none so glorious in her history as that of 1941 and 1942.

Monday, 21 June 1943

8 a.m. Admiral Cunningham, 'Flags', Roger and I left the cruiser. By 9.15 we were in the air; we landed at Maison Blanche at 12.30. We were lunching in the villa by 1.30.

We got back to a pretty complicated situation. The General's (Eisenhower's) requirements had been put into a written memorandum sent on Sunday afternoon to the two generals. The full Committee met on Monday morning and, after taking note of the situation, adjourned after a three-hour debate until the next day.

This left the afternoon, evening and night for a real Algerian episode. I saw Philip, Monnet, and others of the Committee, including Massigli and Pleven.

Tuesday, 22 June 1943

By the morning, a formula had been found – which of course you have now seen in the press.[32] I think that it was the best that could be done in the circumstances. It meets the President's demand (supported by H.M.G.) that Giraud should remain effective C.-in-C. in French North Africa and French West Africa. It gives de Gaulle, at least nominally, an equal status, and although the mechanism of two Army, two naval and two air chiefs of staff is rather clumsy, it at least provides a single organisation through which the fusion of all French forces may ultimately come about.

Anyway, it will do for the time being. If it lasts three months, it will do. For in that time the conception of French union will have become too strong to be overthrown and the Committee itself will (I hope) have developed sufficiently for the civilian elements to be (as they are showing signs) able to stand up to the dictatorial methods of the generals. Most of Tuesday was taken up with various negotiations arising out of the formula and a number of other matters.

I am writing this very early, in the cool of the morning, after a delicious bath (in my now luxurious villa, where we are during General Lyon's visit) and while waiting for my morning tea.

We are really getting terribly spoilt here. We have *far* too much food and drink, and John seems to collect servants, like some people collect postage stamps. We now have collected a couple more Army cooks to work under our Grosvenor House chef. We have also collected two fascinating French housemaids, both young and pretty. I believe they are really Mrs Consul-General's servants, but they have stayed here to

[32] The F.C.N.L. had announced: 'Generals Giraud and de Gaulle are appointed Cs-in-C. of the French North and West African armies and the armies of other territories respectively. Generals Juin and de Larminat are appointed Chiefs of Staff of these commands.' All four generals were to be members of a Military Committee responsible for the unification of the French armed forces.

help us through during the Royal visit. There has apparently also been engaged an old and ugly one, to act as chaperone. Judging from what I see and hear, this is very necessary. Then we have a new Arab; and our own Arab (who was left at the late villa and is so unhappy there that he comes to us whenever he can, for Mrs Consul-General is a tartar).

Then we house and feed Corporal Nicholson, my police guard (who really doesn't guard me much, but does the marketing every day and returns with vegetables and fruit, bought in the market, and the naval rations from the docks).

Driver Pocklington (my personal chauffeur who drives my large Buick and looks after the flag which it flies. This flag is, I think, a pure invention of John's. It is *very* smart, if quite unauthorised, being the Royal Arms on a Brigade of Guards colours background).

Then there are two or three despatch riders and the chauffeurs of the other cars – we have now four, but are aiming at six. Who pays for this all, I cannot tell. John and Mr Harnett (our Treasury clerk) have long finance meetings and I gather they try to charge up everything to the Army or 'general expenditure in accordance with Operation Torch'. I only hope they will succeed, or my financial ruin will be complete. Then we have just taken a villa by the sea (for the senior staff) and a villa on a mountain (for the junior staff). So, altogether, we are getting into a very grand establishment.

I have written so much about all this that my pen has run away and I must stop without even beginning the diary. I will try to finish this letter today, because there is a bag going tonight.

Wednesday, 23 June 1943

Usual office morning and afternoon. We try to start early now, 8.30–9, as it gets so hot in the middle of the day. If possible, I do not go back to the office till 3 or 3.30 after lunch, and then go on till 8 p.m. or so.

8.15 p.m. Dinner at Admiral Cunningham's.

Guests: H. M. the King,
Eisenhower,
Alexander,
Tedder,

also one or two from admiral's staff. It passed off very well. The King was in excellent form and there was a lot of chaff and backchat between the various officers.

In the course of the evening, I heard that de Gaulle was now determined to force the issue on Boisson, Governor of French West Africa. (You probably know Boisson's history. He opposed us at Dakar in 1940. Since then, he kept French West Africa more or less to itself. To the Gaullists, he is a double-dyed traitor; to the English, mildly antipathetic owing to the memories of 1940; by the Americans greatly admired.)

The President, unfortunately, is equally determined to see Boisson kept in his position and therefore there is every reason to expect a new row. If we could overcome this fence, it might be the last for the next few weeks. Anyhow, I undertook to see Massigli early on the next morning to see if some compromise could be arranged. (I am in some difficulty, since I personally think the President's demands outrageous, but I am instructed to support them. Fortunately General Eisenhower shares my view and is trying to get some compromise out of the White House.)

This led to:

Thursday, 24 June 1943

'A typical Algiers day'.

9 a.m. I called on Massigli (Commissioner for Foreign Affairs). I found him in a very reasonable state of mind, anxious for an arrangement. I suggested that having just successfully got through the crisis over the Army commands, we might allow ourselves a little breathing-space, especially as it was so very hot.

Massigli replied that unfortunately the *affaire Boisson* was down on the agenda for Friday, but that he would certainly do his best to gain time. He thought he could probably get a majority of the Committee to be definitely *against* a dismissal. He would move that the matter be adjourned, and perhaps in the meantime Boisson would resign voluntarily.

9.30 a.m. Called on Tedder, partly because he likes to be kept informed of political gossip, and partly on a question of French aviation reforms.

10.15 a.m. Got to my office to find the boys much excited and amused. An A.D.C. of General Giraud's had just called to inform us officially that during the night General Giraud received a telegram from Boisson offering his resignation. He had immediately (without consulting de Gaulle or any member of the Committee) replied, accepting.

10.30 a.m.–12 noon. A long and interesting meeting of the North African Economic Board. Interesting questions, chiefly regarding 'stockpiling' in these territories for future needs. Properly handled, of course, French North Africa should be an *exporter* of grain, etc., once more.

12.30 p.m. General Eisenhower rang up to say that he had talked to General Giraud at the review of French troops held that morning for the King, and Giraud had told him about Boisson's resignation. Eisenhower replied that this seemed rather precipitate. Eisenhower asked me to find out the exact position.

1 p.m. Called to see Alec Hardinge and arrange to be excused from going to aerodrome to see the King off.

2.30 p.m. Called to say 'good-bye' to the King. He was very

pleasant. I think he has much enjoyed the trip and was obviously very exhausted. To come suddenly into this heat and travel about such great distances *is* very tiring. Also, everyone is suffering from a sort of mild dysentery.

2.45 p.m. Called on Giraud. The old boy was in capital form. He said that things were not going very well but that he had everything well in hand. He told me that Boisson had resigned, but that he (Giraud) had refused the resignation. I expressed some surprise, because I thought he had accepted it. 'Oh yes,' he said, 'but that is unimportant. Now I have refused it.' (I found myself, as in *Alice*, repeating to myself – important, unimportant, refused, accepted, accepted, refused, unimportant, important.)

Apparently, immediately the old boy got back from the review, after his few words with Eisenhower, he sent off another telegram to Boisson refusing to accept the resignation.

Poor Boisson must feel a little confused. All this is made the more strange because I cannot see that Boisson ought to send his resignation to Giraud at all. He ought to send it to the new Commissioner for the Colonies. In any case, Giraud has no right on his own either to accept or refuse it. I suspect that Giraud was afraid that Boisson had 'done a Peyrouton' and had sent his resignation to de Gaulle as well. So he thought he would get in quick with an acceptance.

3.30 p.m. Mr Tixier[33] (new Commissaire du Travail) called. A Gaullist. Not a bad little chap, but rather excitable.

4.15 p.m. Called in to see Eisenhower, who was, as usual, very agreeable. We both feel that if we can somehow get over this Boisson fence, we may at last be in the straight. (This is probably a mildly optimistic view, in view of past experience, but one must be an optimist here, or go mad.)

Back at office, telegrams, etc.

8 p.m. Dinner. Mr Berthoud (English visiting oil expert), Commodore Dick, Brigadier [Richard] Lewis, Colonel Dodds-Parker.[34]

Friday, 25 June 1943

More trouble. Admiral Cunningham is concerned about the proposed removal of the French admiral, Michelier, whom he has got well in hand. The trouble is that Michelier is politically disliked by the Americans, since he opposed their landing at Casablanca, and has the worst Pétainist and Vichyite traditions. He signed the Armistice. On the other hand, he has behaved very well lately, and I quite see our

[33] Adrien Tixier (1897–1946) became Minister of the Interior, 1944–6.

[34] Eric Berthoud (b. 1900) was seconded from the Ministry of Fuel and Power to the office of the Minister Resident in the Middle East, 1942–3. Lieutenant-Colonel Douglas Dodds-Parker (b. 1909) was Liaison Officer for S.O.E. Mediterranean with A.F.H.Q. and O.S.S. in Algiers and Caserta, 1943–4.

admiral's desire not to change horses now. It is all very complicated.

9.15–12 noon. I was occupied with various aspects of this, going between Eisenhower, Bedell Smith, Cunningham on one side, and Giraud's people on the other, to try to find a solution. I think that Admiral Cunningham will have to be content with a formal assurance from Giraud (in whose command the North African fleet is) that if Michelier is removed, all the arrangements made by him with us shall remain unchanged by his successor.

In between this, and lasting most of the afternoon as well, various jobs to be fixed with Lord Rennell, culminating in a conference with General Alexander at 7 p.m.

General Alexander stayed to dinner and was as charming as ever. Also present, Colonel de Linarès, General Miller (British), Admiral – I've forgotten who – (British), Captain Ritchie, R.N. ('Bartimeus' – a very interesting little chap), Sir Rupert Clarke (Alexander's Personal Assistant), and one or two more.[35]

After dinner, we sent for typists (Miss Campbell and Miss Williams) and worked on some stuff till midnight. Alexander then left, everything settled satisfactorily.

Saturday, 26 June 1943

I had a talk with Eisenhower at about 10.30, followed by a meeting of the Political and Economic Council at 11.

Archie Sinclair came to luncheon, together with Louis Greig. They were both very agreeable.

I got away from the office by 4 p.m., and drove to see my friends of the American First Division. They are not far from Algiers, on the sea. I had a most delicious bathe – the sea very refreshing after the boiling heat which there is here now. We had supper at about 7. Generals Terry Allen and Teddy Roosevelt and the officers of their staff.

Sunday, 27 June 1943

10 a.m. Church.

11 a.m. Murphy and I went to see Massigli to discuss the Boisson situation. I feel pretty sure we shall get over the fence now. But what a lot of faces I spend my time saving – and not French faces only, by any means!

Luncheon. I gave a large luncheon to the members of the Middle East Supply Centre (Cairo) who were visiting the North African Economic Board (Algiers). Altogether eleven of them came, and as our table holds only twelve, I had to send all my staff out for the day – for which they were duly grateful.

[35] Major-General Charles Miller (1894–1974) was Fifteenth Army Group's Major-General, Administration, 1943. Captain Lewis Ritchie, R.N. (1886–1967) wrote novels under the *nom-de-plume* of 'Bartimeus'. Major Sir Rupert Clarke (b. 1919) had been General Alexander's A.D.C. since 1942.

At about 3.30 I got away and drove to my favourite Tipasa. General Roosevelt joined me at about 5 p.m., and I took him to my own private rocky cove (only shown to the P.M. and Anthony) which lies under Chenoua mountain.

Here – instead of the sandy beach with miles of shallow water – you get straight into deep cool water. From a few feet above, you can see every detail of the bottom, so clear it is. Here only a few stray fishermen come, and you can bathe naked. You can lie on the blazing rocks, till your body can bear it no more; and then roll over into the healing water. This you can alternate as long as you like – a sort of perpetual rhythm of pleasure.

After our bathe, we walked in the ruined city; ate an excellent French omelette and he went to his camp, I to an early bed.

Monday, 28 June 1943

Walked early; got very hot; bathed with John Wyndham in our favourite place; drove back to the city, arriving at the villa for lunch. A lovely morning.

Of course, the penalty for this laziness was to be paid. I found a tremendous lot had accumulated and worked at the office till 8.30. A bag had come in, and with it a lot of official stuff, together with private letters. I was delighted to get a letter from you.

I will write separately about your letters and will try to finish this for a bag which looks like leaving.

Tuesday, 29 June 1943

Roger Makins left this morning for England. He will probably ring you up while he is there. I am sending him back to try to clear up various questions to which I can get no reply at present.

9.15 a.m. Visit to admiral [Cunningham]. Discussed Michelier's position.

10 a.m. Meeting with Murphy.

Rennell came to luncheon and we settled various matters.

3 p.m. Diethelm (Minister for Production, Gaullist). I had quite a satisfactory talk with him and formed a better impression of him than I had been led to suppose.

3.30 p.m. Christopher Stone[36] called.

4–5.30 p.m. Propaganda meeting. A lot of very ticklish problems. Went well on the whole.

6 p.m. Called on Giraud. I discussed with him (*a*) his proposed visit to America, (*b*) the Boisson affair, (*c*) Admiral Michelier's position, (*d*) the general situation. The old boy was as charming and as vague as ever. I like him more and more, but of course he is really out of his depth.

[36] Christopher Stone (1882–1965), author of novels and books on Eton and music.

7.30 p.m. Dinner with Bedell Smith. A very jolly party. Admiral Cunningham, Commodore Dick, Air Chief Marshal Tedder, Air Vice-Marshal Wigglesworth (my favourite; he said he was 'in a mucky sweat', as he came in late), General Bill Donovan (U.S. head of O.S.S. [Office of Strategic Services, forerunner of the C.I.A.]), General Spaatz (U.S. Air Force).[37] A lot of amusing and almost schoolboy chaff – this is the relaxation of these really great men. I find their company more and more agreeable, and I seem to have been adopted by them (in spite of being a civilian) as a comrade.

Wednesday, 30 June 1943

8.45 a.m. Went to see Bedell Smith at A.F.H.Q., to go over proposed reply to a Parliamentary Question by Anthony Eden tomorrow.[38]

9.30–12 noon. Office routine. We miss Roger, who dealt with all the telegrams very efficiently. Caccia is also away, as I have sent him on a visit to Tunis.

12 noon. Mr [G. H. G.] Norman – *Times* correspondent.

1.30 p.m. Luncheon at Catroux's villa. The party consisted of Catroux, Massigli, Monnet, Pleven, Murphy and M. [Pierre] Cournarie, Governor of French Cameroons. I had a very interesting talk with the latter after lunch in which I showed off all my old Colonial Office production repertory. He, of course, knew all about our West African Produce Board, as we had bought all the Cameroons production. He had flown here from the Cameroons in forty-eight hours!

3.15 p.m. Jackson – head of Middle East Supply Centre.

3.45 p.m. M. Philip – Minister of Interior.

5.30 p.m. Gala performance (and very hot too) of *In Which We Serve*.

The heat is getting very oppressive now. Fortunately, I sweat freely day and night at every pore. Although the result is not pretty, it is very healthy and a great relief.

I have just got back to the office after the film. I go to dine with (American) General Hughes (Theatre Commander!) and it will be very hot there too.

I have the impression that French affairs are settling down and that we are through the worst of our troubles. The atmosphere, as well as being hotter, seems calmer, and I feel happier about the future.

Having written this, I fully expect a first-class row tomorrow.

[37] Brigadier-General (later Major-General) William J. ('Wild Bill') Donovan (1883–1959) was Director of O.S.S., 1942–5. General Carl Spaatz (1891–1974) was Commanding General, North-west African Air Forces, 1943, and U.S. Strategic Air Forces in the Pacific, 1945–6, when he supervised the dropping of the atomic bombs.

[38] The question was answered by the Prime Minister, see note 1, p. 139.

July

Thursday, 1 July 1943

I had a pleasant dinner last night with General Hughes. He has a villa a little way out of the town, with a wonderful view of the mountains. We dined in shirt-sleeves, for it was very hot even at 1,000 feet above sea level. General Whiteley (British, Deputy Chief of Staff) and Mr Royce (new executive chairman of N.A.E.B., U.S.) were the other guests.

Thank you so much for your letters of 12 June and 18 June safely received. It is very nice indeed to hear the news from home. It is just six months since I came here. It has actually been an interesting time for me, but I confess that I often long to be home. Fortunately, the days are so full, that there is not much time to think about anything except the immediate daily round.

I wonder if you could send out to me an old pair of grey flannel trousers (with a stripe). They are at Birch Grove (I think), very old and dirty but will do for bathing etc. Also – a pair of shorts and two pairs of stockings (and garters), if you can find them.

The heat is getting pretty extreme – especially in the middle of the day – and the humidity makes it worse. For some reason, one is very hungry, which seems odd.

I wonder if you are having better weather now and bathing and sun-bathing. This is really the place for nudity, which I know you like. But (alas) this is only permitted to troops, not extended to diplomats!

There has been a water crisis the last few days, because the town main was burst. I understand that John had arranged with the mayor about mending it with the help of American or British engineers.

Poor Harold Caccia was nearly killed yesterday, in a forced landing on the way back from Tunis. Apparently, the crew forgot to fill up the petrol tank. However, he is quite unhurt – only a little shaken.

Love to all – and especially to you. I think of you all the time and wish you could be here to laugh at some very amusing things and people. I have read your letters through again and I am so glad to have your news. What a very active life you lead, and (I am afraid) without any of the amenities (like motor cars, servants, lashings of food and drink) which we enjoy here who suffer the rigours of the North African campaign.

9 a.m. Mr Herbert (economic adviser).

9.30 a.m. Brigadier Rabino (Treasury representative and my financial adviser), and a long, complicated discussion about the French monetary position.

The usual office day: Murphy, Major Macdonald (Intelligence), Commandant Beauffre (an old friend, who was in Giraud's military cabinet when I first came, then went into the battle and now is going with Giraud to America).

In the course of the day two events of interest – first, the French Committee's decision to appoint Cournarie instead of Boisson; secondly, the P.M.'s statement in the House about the Allied intervention[1] and the French situation generally. From the telegrams and radio, this seemed to pass off fairly well.

Dinner party at the villa – guests: Massigli, Monnet and Pleven (three members of the French administration), also Bedell Smith, Air Vice-Marshal Dawson, Caccia and John.

Friday, 2 July 1943

Murphy and I went to the airfield to see Giraud off. The old boy was in great form, like a schoolboy leaving for the holidays. What will happen in his absence, Heaven knows!

The rest of the day was the usual succession of interviews, telegrams, documents, etc., which are beginning to get rather tedious. The Deputy Consul-General [Richard Whittington], Colonel de Linarès, M. Maher (of *France Télé-Afrique*) – a journalist – etc., etc.

At 6.30 I could bear it no more and motored out for a swim at Sidi Ferruch. This made me rather late for a dinner at Murphy's, where I found Admiral Michelier (? in or out of office?), Admiral Cunningham, General Juin (Chief of Staff of Giraud's army), Commodore Dick and Royce. A very pleasant party, everyone just melting with the heat, but quite cheerful. I was next to Michelier, and of course did not dare ask him outright whether he was going to be dismissed or not. As he was pretty gloomy, I supposed he was.

Saturday, 3 July 1943

A long talk about the future with General Eisenhower – followed by more detailed discussion with Brigadier-General Holmes (U.S.A.), head of the new political section at A.F.H.Q. Many difficulties which

[1] Churchill said that the Allied intervention about the French C.-in-C. had been made for purely military reasons, and that there was no intention of giving Eisenhower full control over French civil administration.

had worried me a good deal about the future are being gradually cleared up.[2]

P. J. Grigg (Secretary of State for War) has reappeared. I spent most of the afternoon with him on the same subject.

5 p.m. Murphy. Discussed with him the results of my morning and afternoon's talk, as far as I could disclose it. I hope that we shall be able to settle up these questions which at present I can only refer to in a letter as ones which have caused me a lot of bother and have nothing to do with French questions.

6 p.m. Called on Massigli to make an official *démarche* from the Foreign Office on a very dull question. I found him in good heart, perhaps because he was going off to London the next day. These Frenchmen who have lived in London and Paris and other great capitals find Algiers pretty dull, I fancy.

Sunday, 4 July 1943

10 a.m. Church. We have now got quite a good choir, and the singing of the congregation is very enthusiastic. But the choir (being ambitious) are apt to choose some new-fangled and no doubt musically superior tune to the ordinary one. The congregation, however, firmly sings the well-known tune; the result is a bit queer.

11.30–12 noon. Fourth of July celebrations at A.F.H.Q. Bands, guns, etc. Ike made a very nice little speech. I told all my American friends that I was lineally descended (through my Grandmother Reid – my mother's mother) from one of the signatories of the Declaration. This was generally regarded as rather a score for me.

John, John Addis,[3] Harold Caccia, left at 1 p.m. by car. We motored out and bathed – picnic – motored on to Tipasa – bathed – dined – and motored home after dinner. A very nice change.

Monday, 5 July 1943

9 a.m. Called on Eisenhower. Bedell Smith came in.

9.45 a.m. Called on General Whiteley to go over in detail my talks of Saturday.

10 a.m. Eisenhower asked to see me again, and showed me with great pleasure a telegram which had just come from Washington saying that no difficulty would be made about Cournarie as Boisson's successor in French West Africa. So we have successfully 'gotten over' another fence – and one which seemed pretty formidable at first sight.

12 noon. Long and interesting talk with Mr McDavid[4] (Deputy Director of Sea Transport) whom I knew when I was at Colonial

[2] Relating to the organisation of AMGOT.

[3] John Addis (1914–83), an aide to Harold Caccia, was seconded to A.F.H.Q., 1942–4; he was later H.M. Ambassador to China, 1972–4.

[4] Herbert McDavid (1898–1966) was Deputy Director of Sea Transport, Ministry of War Transport, 1941–5.

Office. He is a very clever man and was responsible for all the shipping for the North African Expedition.

1.15 p.m. Colonel Maxwell (Deputy in Military Government Section, A.F.H.Q.) to lunch – a British officer, intelligent and honest, but without humour.

3 p.m. André Philip, Commissioner for Interior and Resistance in the new administration. He seemed in good form, but of course wants to go to London. At 7 p.m. after finishing, I took the car and (with John Addis) motored to Tipasa. We bathed and then dined about 9 p.m. The water was very warm; the atmosphere is better at Tipasa than in the city, but nevertheless it is very difficult to sleep at night.

I get the impression that things are beginning to settle down here. Perhaps it is the heat, perhaps it is the atmosphere of expectation.

I do not think the Committee will break down or the Union crash. One or other or both of the generals may resign or be driven out. But I think the central administration of the French Empire, once formed, will be difficult to destroy. If only we can keep it going another two or three months without serious internal dissensions or grave disputes with the Allies, I think it will be established. And its establishment and maintenance are the best hope that I can see for France, if civil war is to be avoided after the Germans have been expelled.

I only wish the U.S. and H.M.G. would give official recognition to the Committee. I do not seem able to get the true position understood at home – or rather, I think they do understand but are unwilling to press Washington. The Americans here (Eisenhower, Bedell Smith and Murphy) are absolutely sound now, and I find now that all I have to do is to follow in their footsteps, making polite noises of agreement with their ideas. But their conversion has not yet spread to Washington!

Tuesday, 6 July 1943

7 a.m. Bathed at Tipasa. Motored back to the villa.

8.15 a.m. A.F.H.Q. Saw Bedell Smith. Eisenhower is telegraphing today to Washington suggesting immediate recognition of the French Committee. Do I approve?

Really, this is an odd situation. I am very hopeful, although I fear there will still be some delay. But I am sure London will concur with whatever Washington decides.

1 p.m. General Gale, Eric Duncannon, and a very charming Mrs Twining to luncheon – she brought a letter from James Stuart.[5] She is a very pretty widow (twice a widow in this war) and has come out with Y.M.C.A. or something of the kind.

Eric Duncannon is very good at producing some female society. Mlle Andrieux (a cousin of his) and Comtesse de la Matte are the leading beauties.

[5] James Stuart (1897–1971), Government Chief Whip, 1941–5, and husband of my wife's sister Rachel.

3.30 p.m. M. [Henri] Bonnet (Commissioner for Information), quite a cultivated and agreeable man.

4.30 p.m. Mr Schwartz – American Jew, interested in refugees.

5 p.m. M. [Hubert] Guérin – new Permanent Secretary of the Commissioner for Foreign Affairs – under Massigli.

5.45 p.m. Conference with Murphy.

At 6.45 p.m. General Wilson (C.-in-C., Middle East) accompanied by Paddy Beaumont-Nesbitt.[6] A conference followed by dinner.

And so to bed! Before finishing, we had to send two 'Most Immediate' telegrams to the P.M. on the Eisenhower–Washington telegram about recognition, and one arising out of the conference with General Wilson. I need hardly say that Miss Campbell came up to scratch and did all the typing before midnight. The Consulate is kept specially open on these occasions, so that the cypherers can work through the night.

Wednesday, 7 July 1943

It is still very hot and very damp, and the mosquitoes and flies are the only things that are not quite torpid. We have got nets and this stops one being bothered at night. But I seem somehow to get bitten by various insects and swell up in a strange and disfiguring way.

There was an interesting conference at A.F.H.Q. this morning, following the discussions last week about future developments. Chief of Staff, Brigadier Holmes (American), Colonel Maxwell (British), Murphy, Reber, Caccia and H.M. This lasted from eleven to one.

1.30 p.m. [W.J.E.] Ringquist (who is now a major in the Military Government Corps and is stationed at Tripoli) came to lunch. He was here for a day or two on some liaison jobs. He has been in Kenya, Eritrea, Abyssinia, Cyrenaica and Tripolitania. He thinks it more amusing than Walford's office in Tinkle Street, Stockton-on-Tees. He was in great form and (I thought) very friendly and loyal. I think his experiences have improved him.

3 p.m. [Guillaume] Georges-Picot, new head of Giraud's Civil Cabinet.

4 p.m. Colonel de Linarès. He is going to London tomorrow. If you can get Hal Mack to give you his address try to see him. He is *charming*. He is a great friend of mine and Hal's. You might give them lunch or dinner if you are in London.

6.30 p.m. Monnet.

8 p.m. One of our dinners – guests: General Bouscat (Chief of Air Staff) – he has the wonderful pastime of acting for *both* Giraud's and de Gaulle's command; General [Paul] Devinck (Giraud's personal military Chief of Staff); Mr [Walter K.] Schwinn (American economic expert, a bore); Bigadier [Cecil S.] Sugden (British, Head of

[6] Major-General F. G. Beaumont-Nesbitt (1893–1971) was Senior Administrative Officer, Cairo.

Planning Operational); M. Diethelm (Minister or Commissioner for Production); M. Tixier (ditto for Labour). The last two were de Gaulle's nominees to the Committee. They are both doing pretty well and behaving reasonably, I think.

I am finishing this after dinner – which has lasted a long time and been very exhausting. Fortunately it is rather cooler tonight, but it is still very difficult to sleep until late.

Just before dinner a bag came in, with your letter (written in your own hand) of 28 June. I was delighted to get it.

Thursday, 8 July 1943

We had a baddish morning and really this sticky heat is getting me down. I feel very slack, and it is difficult to bring myself to work properly.

I had two important meetings in the morning:

(1) North African Economic Board. I think things are at last going better with all this work. Our English representatives are first class. They really carry the whole burden, and the Americans (who are generous people) now recognise it and do nothing but deplore the inefficiency of Washington and envy the efficiency of Whitehall. I wish some of the critics of British administration at home could hear them talk.

(2) A meeting for co-ordination of various secret services. Very interesting.

At luncheon, General Georges, M. Guérin (Foreign Affairs), Paddy Beaumont-Nesbitt (now a Major-General and over here from Middle East), General Gale, R. Crossman (of P.W.E.) and ourselves. Roger arrived at the end of lunch.

At three, I had to deal with our naval people, about the French naval reorganisation, which is still a subject of dispute. This is a very complicated situation, as everyone – including ourselves – is pulling different ways. I hope we shall sort it out in time.

We finished our work by six and then went off to bathe.

All the evening (which we had alone) we spent in talking to Roger [Makins] and hearing a thousand and one things from home. His visit has been very valuable, and my mind is a good deal clearer. It seems that most of my colleagues have put their confidence in my refusing to obey my instructions from the P.M. too literally, and in the chance that I should be able to straighten things out. I really think it is a bit mean of them. They might summon up enough courage to speak up in the Cabinet from time to time.

Friday, 9 July 1943

Hugh Fraser turned up this morning.[7] He seemed rather tired, but

[7] Major Hugh Fraser (b. 1918) served with the Lovat Scouts and the S.A.S., 1939–45; subsequently a Conservative M.P.

very well. We were able to give him a bed for the night, and he seemed quite happy just to dine quietly alone with our little party. I thought he had developed a great deal and improved. I feel sure he will go into politics if he gets through, and he ought to do well. It is curious how each generation in turn starts out with the sort of Young England idea. Disraeli left a great mark on England, and I am interested to find that the young men in the Tory party now read his novels and study his life with the same enthusiasm as we did thirty years ago.

Colonel Dodds-Parker, who runs one of the queer organisations here called S.O.E., came to luncheon. He is a very fine man – originally in the Sudan Service. He retired just before the war (at the age of about thirty-five) because he thought it a bore to spend the whole of one's life in the Sudan. He intends also to go into Parliament after the war.[8]

I love to hear the chaps of this period (and younger) discussing their political views and hopes. There is some pretty good material about if one can only give it a chance.

At 6 p.m. I went to see General de Gaulle. I began by telling him of the attack on Sicily which was due to start in the early hours of Saturday morning. I had no instructions to do this (and thought it wiser not to ask for any or to consult anyone) but I thought it would really be very discourteous to let the first news be given to the general from the radio or the newspaper. He seemed to appreciate being given this information and was of course much interested to know any details which I might be able to give him of its magnitude and ultimate objectives.

Apart from this, we talked about the French situation in general.

At 7 p.m. there was a meeting with Murphy, Sam Reber (his second man – very good and very charming), Makins, Colonel Julius Holmes, Colonel Maxwell (two of the newly formed Military Government Section of A.F.H.Q.) and self. This was dealing with various questions which may arise as a result of operations in Sicily, etc., and carrying our plans into greater degree of perfection on the administrative side. The general layout has been arranged some time back, and the necessary staff has been collected and trained under Francis Rennell. He will become Deputy Military Governor (under General Alexander) of any occupied territory and carry on the administration on lines similar to those in Eritrea, Cyrenaica, etc. – at least to begin with.

But you can well imagine all kinds of possibilities have to be considered and what system – whether Military Government by British and American officers, or a collaborationist Italian government (like Vichy) – ought to be used if by chance the whole country were to collapse.

[8] He became Conservative M.P. for Banbury.

Under the agreement recently made by the President and the P.M. my functions now extend to this sphere, so I have been trying to learn something about the problem during recent weeks. It is rather fun, for I am beginning to get very bored with the French and their affairs and very disgusted at the stupidities of London and Washington regarding them.

Saturday, 10 July 1943

D-Day – the day on which our hopes and fears have been pinned for weeks. I could not sleep very well – nor any of us, I found – for we were all thinking of the huge concourse of ships and their precious human freight. Actually, about 3,000 vessels of all kinds took part in this vast operation, converging on to the selected beaches, which each had to reach at the right moment and in the due sequence. Considering that this Armada started from Alexandria (in the east) and English ports (in the west), it was a pretty remarkable performance.

The weather conditions were not too good. There was a heavy swell and a 20–45 mile-an-hour north-westerly wind. This did not worry the landings in the south-east very much, but was very troublesome for the south and south-west beaches. In all this during the first days including the landings, I think only three merchantmen, one hospital ship (bombed with its full lights burning – a pure act of treachery), one American destroyer, and a few landing-craft were lost.

During Saturday morning, we had a further meeting of the Political [Military Government] Section and Murphy's party. About 11 a.m. we heard that the Canadian Division and one American Division had landed safely – otherwise no further news.

At 3 p.m. Harold Caccia and I took the air in a Hudson from the aerodrome at Maison Blanche. We arrived at the aerodrome at La Marsa (just outside Tunis) at 5.15 – a very rapid flight, with a following wind, high (about 8,000 feet) over the mountains.

We were met by John and one of my own cars which had left by road on the previous Tuesday. I sent John up, together with a Sergeant Brown, who does shorthand, typing and filing, to open up a residence and office in the Tunis area for me. I need hardly say that all this was done with the most admirable success.

We are living in part of the old Consular Residence. We have got one wing in operation – it consists of a large sitting-room, with a lovely domed roof – a large dining-room, which we use at present as a sort of hall – three or four bedrooms; bathroom; some servants' rooms for clerks, chauffeur, etc., and an office.

This wing is more or less self-contained and has its own entrance. In the middle of the house is a large central hall – about sixty feet by forty feet and about twenty feet in height. It is a really lovely room – with a fine marble floor, tiled walls and a splendid painted ceiling. Outside is a large covered terrace – about eighty feet by thirty feet – and the other wing leads off the hall. In this wing are three nice drawing-rooms. The ceiling of the terrace is very fine – rather faded – but of good Arab style. I think my wing is the oldest part of the house – probably in Arab times the women's quarters. The tiles on the walls of the dining-room are very beautiful. This also has a domed ceiling, with charming Arabesque traceries.

The history of the house is that it was given to Queen Victoria by the Bey of Tunis somewhere in the fifties, when of course the British influence in Tunisia was predominant. It was part of the gift that it should always be occupied by a representative of Her Majesty and her successors. It has been used as the Consular Residence ever since, except during the recent German occupation, and I was anxious to get it going again as soon as possible. The Germans used it (I think) as a Divisional H.Q. and (except for having stolen all the furniture) have done remarkably little damage. There is a nice library of English books which we have found, and these are very welcome. (I have found and re-read some of Disraeli's novels.)

John came up by car and got it all ready and scrounged or stole some furniture. We have some nice rugs which were sent by two leading Jews (M. Henri Smadja and M. Lévy Despas) in recognition for what I am supposed to have done for the Jews since I came to North Africa!

The other wing serves as ante-rooms for the officers' mess and the main hall (or terrace) for eating in. General Alexander has his H.Q. here (you had better not mention this at present) and I and my staff have been made members of the mess – so we don't have to arrange separate cooking, etc.

It is a most agreeable arrangement. The H.Q. live in tents in the garden and in neighbouring fields, and they only come into the house for meals and to read the papers, etc. I cannot tell you how nice the officers are to us – General Alexander and his chief officers are in Malta for the opening stage of the battle, but he is expected here shortly if all goes well.

We dined in the mess and speculated on the news. Very little has yet come through, but what has come sounds extraordinarily good.

Sunday, 11 July 1943

In looking through my description of the Consular Residence, I find it is not very clear. The whole effect from the outside is of a square white block (with some offices and outhouses at the back). The rooms are all really on the first floor – the ground floor being various offices and so on – outside the terrace there is a *perron*, with two sweeping curves of white steps, of marble. The whole is really rather like a white Chatsworth. The terrace which I described is really partly inside, not wholly outside the building – it is simply a long room outside the dining room, without an outer wall.

I am afraid I have drawn it very badly. But this is the sort of thing. There are no rooms above the *piano nobile* except lofts and attics.

Outside the *perron* is a white-walled garden, like that at Hardwick. You drive out through a gate in the middle.

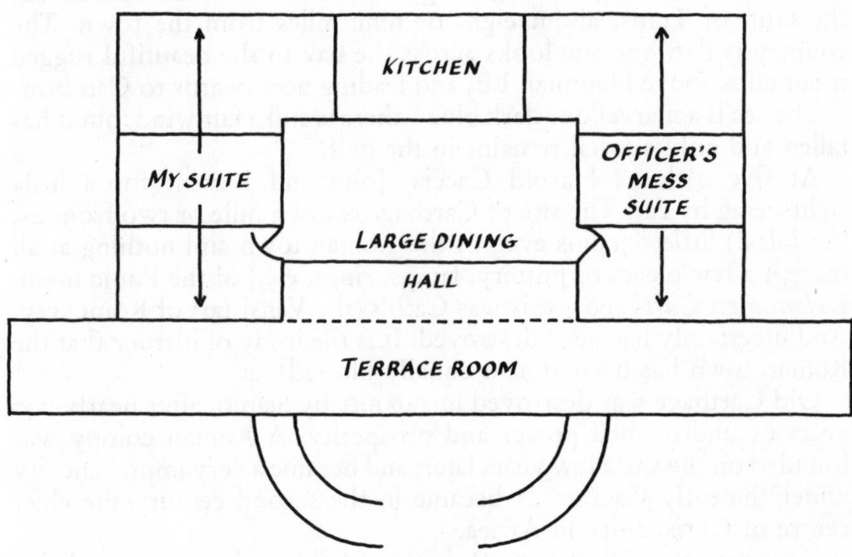

Behind the house is a garden (now very dried up and neglected); swimming-pools – also an orangery, and olive grove, and quite a large vegetable garden or home farm. This is where all the tents, etc., of General Alexander's H.Q. are. I suppose the whole outfit would amount to about 2,000 officers and men. The officers using the mess are the more senior on the personal staff, together with Air Marshal Coningham and some of his people. I suppose about twenty to thirty-five when they are all there. At present there are only about eight to ten – those left here while the general is in Malta.

10.30 a.m. Went to church. The congregation of soldiers and sailors packed the little church, a change for the few remnants of the English colony who survived the German occupation – viz., a few old ladies, pensioners, etc.

The clergyman preached a very good sermon and had a sensible short service – one lesson, four hymns, a few prayers, a sermon, all in forty-five minutes. That is certainly the right way for troops in hot weather. He seems a fine little chap. He was in hiding for six months during the occupation. The Germans apparently wanted him, because of the very useful intelligence work he had been doing for us during the last three years – since the Armistice. He managed to elude them, however, and at the same time look after various other prisoners or men in hiding (e.g. merchant seamen who had been torpedoed). His name is Dunbar.

After church we did some work – went for a short walk – lunched – slept. The Consul-General was away for the day, but the Vice-Consul came up to do some business with us.

La Marsa is a village (or township) which lies on the northern arm of the Gulf of Tunis, about eight or nine miles from the town. The country is flat, but one looks across the bay to the beautiful rugged mountains above Hamman Lif, and leading northwards to Cap Bon.

The sea is a marvellous dark blue – there is still a fair wind, but it has fallen and only a swell remains in the gulf.

At five o'clock, Harold Caccia, John and I went for a little sightseeing by car. The site of Carthage is just a mile or two from us, but (alas!) little remains even of the Roman town and nothing at all (except a few pieces of pottery, lamps, rings, etc.) of the Punic town. *Delenda est Carthago* – this was Cato's (the Vansittart of Rome) cry. And it certainly has been destroyed. It is the irony of history that the Roman town has been almost equally blotted out.

Old Carthage was destroyed in 146 B.C. by Scipio, after nearly 700 years of undisturbed power and prosperity. A Roman colony was founded on the site a few years later, and became a very important city under the early Caesars. It became in the second century the chief centre of Christianity in Africa.

If we have the fifth volume (I think) of Gibbon there is a wonderful account of the campaign of Belisarius in Africa under the Emperor Justinian. Carthage had been taken by the Vandals in the middle of the fourth century and was recaptured by Belisarius about a hundred years later. But finally, with the declining power of Rome, it was captured and overrun by the Arab invasion in about 700 A.D. and ruined by them for ever.

The only things remaining in this vast city which give me any conception of the importance are the Roman theatre, the Roman amphitheatre, part of an aqueduct, the stone bastions of the old harbours, and a mass of miscellaneous ruins of stone and rubble, dotted over a wide area, without beauty or meaning to the ordinary eye, however interesting to the trained archaeologist.

There is a rather attractive Monastery of the White Fathers (on the site of a former temple) which we visited. An English-speaking monk was produced, who spoke a delicious Irish brogue and seemed delighted to see us. He took a most patriotic, not to say sanguinary view of the war, and hoped to see all Germans and Italians properly 'destroyed'.

Nearby is an ugly little modern chapel, but romantic because it marks the spot where St Louis IX of France died in 1270, while leading a Crusade against Tunis.

After an hour or two's sightseeing, we returned to the residence. On the way back we had the thrill of seeing a great number of landing-craft returning to the harbour, first task in Sicily completed, and ready to sail again with the second wave of troops.

Monday, 12 July 1943

9.30 a.m. At Consulate. Talk with Consul-General [Gybbon-] Monypenny about Tunisian, particularly Arab, affairs.

10.30 a.m. Talk with American Consul-General Doolittle. I formed a very unfavourable impression of this man and his activities.

11–12 noon. Talk with the N.A.E.B. representatives. They are doing a good job in Tunisia, but there is a lot to put right. Curiously enough, the chief American representative is Jim Putnam, a director of the Macmillan Company of New York.

12 noon. Called on my old friend General Mast, now appointed Resident-General in Tunisia. He is a good man. I made friends with him in Algiers, and he is very pro-British and reliable.

At 1 p.m. I went with Harold Caccia to bathe at Air Chief Marshal Tedder's villa. A delightful beach – the water almost too warm.

2.30–4 p.m. Discussion with Tedder on certain French problems relating to our relations with the French Air Force.[9] Also discussion of politico-military problems of future developments. The news seems very good and everyone more than satisfied.

Tuesday, 13 July 1943

Morning at Consulate, finishing up various jobs and dealing with telegrams. When I am in Tunis important telegrams are sent to me here as well as to Algiers, so that I can keep my machine in full operation.

2 p.m. I was lent General Alexander's very comfortable aeroplane to take me back to Algiers. I looked forward to a very 'posh' trip – with a chair, writing-desk, etc. Unfortunately just as we started down the runway, one of the tyres burst. By good luck, however, we had not started to make any speed, so the pilot was able to keep the machine from turning over, which it would certainly have done if we had been going fast, or if it had happened when landing. We were only a little shaken – otherwise unhurt.

After about an hour's delay, Harold Caccia and I managed to get seats on the ordinary 'courier' plane. It was a very hot and bumpy journey, but we landed safely at Algiers about 6 p.m. well in time for a meeting at 7 p.m., which was the main object of my return. This was to draw up a suggested programme for General Eisenhower to send to Chiefs of Staff at Washington dealing with the political aspects of the new campaign.

[9] The French Air Force was being merged with the Free French Air Force.

Wednesday, 14 July 1943

The French national holiday, to celebrate the taking of the Bastille (incidentally, many of the rather reactionary personalities who have to take part in these celebrations would, I think, have taken a very poor view of this event).

8 a.m. A *défilé* through the town of small American and British detachments, followed by a number of the French units which have recently been re-equipped with American uniforms and *material*. Murphy and I were on the platform with the members of the French Committee (still unrecognised!). A large number of *hautes personnalités civiles et militaires* were also collected at the saluting point. In front General de Gaulle and (representing General Giraud) General Juin.

The procession was quite impressive. The up-to-date uniforms give a vastly improved appearance to the French troops, and the weapons of all kinds are, of course, of the latest and best design (they also had some old Valentine tanks, which we had given them). De Gaulle got great applause.

9 a.m. Went to see Chief of Staff (Bedell Smith). After talking it over with him, I decided to send another telegram to London recapitulating all the arguments for 'recognition'. It is really quite absurd to withhold it. It is merely silly and ungracious. And since it weakens the conception of a constitutional committee with collective responsibility (which it has been my whole purpose to achieve and which I succeeded in enacting), it merely plays into de Gaulle's hands.

If you take the worst view of de Gaulle (as the White House and State Department do) what could do more to elevate his position in French eyes than to try to snub him, and what could do more to weaken Giraud than to invite him to Washington? All history teaches the same lesson. The French are just as insular and proud a people as the English. And we preferred a Dutch king who was maladroit, and two Hanoverian kings who could not speak English, to the charm and attraction of all the Stuarts – and why? Because the Stuarts depended on France, for money, arms and political support. But of course the Americans do not read – or at any rate comprehend – history.

11 a.m. An immense meeting in the big square of the town. All political parties (now free to reform themselves and hold demonstrations) were represented, from the left to the right. The 'young Communists' were very prominent and (at least the female contingent) very elegant. They were charming *bourgeoises* who in Stockton would have probably been old-fashioned Liberals.

About 30,000 people present. Murphy sat on the right of the (unrecognised) de Gaulle. I sat on his (unrecognised) left. All the members of the Committee, except Giraud and Massigli (who is in London) and General Georges (who could not quite stomach such an affair).

De Gaulle made an excellent speech – well delivered, a good voice, enough humour, some epigrammatic points, a fine peroration – and all in twenty to twenty-five minutes. The crowd was rapturous – and Giraud (poor old dear) is in Washington.

After the usual afternoon at the office (the heat was stifling today in Algiers – much more humid than in Tunis) yet another ceremony. A tea, military, civil, diplomatic and so on to British, American and French given by de Gaulle at his villa. All the French were in high spirits and full of felicitations on the good news coming from Sicily. I begin to feel that there is not much disunion in the French ranks at bottom. I fear terribly that they may, in spite of all our efforts, be the cause of disunity in ours.

After this performance I went off to bathe at Colonel [Dodds-] Parker's beach and back for cold supper and early bed.

Thursday, 15 July 1943

Saw Bedell Smith early about Italian questions and agreed with him text of a further telegram.

The usual office morning. Luncheon at the villa. A Portuguese colonel – Postella by name. He appears to be more of a writer than a colonel and is very pro-British. I had a naval and military party to meet him. He was very talkative although quite interesting. My staff accused me of falling asleep by about 3.30 (at which hour he was still talking) but I deny the charge.

The news is scanty, but good. It really has been a remarkable achievement, and the co-operation between all the three services wonderfully close and successful. I think we have never in our history had three such commanders as Cunningham, Alexander and Tedder. And their subordinates are very fine quality also. And we are lucky also to have such a loyal and genuine spirit as General Eisenhower. The whole set-up is logically ridiculous, but it works – and that is the real test.

I went off at 5 p.m. with Bob Murphy for a bathe – and a talk. We went to a little cove (quite deserted) of which he knew. The wind was stormy, and the sea quite cold – which made it more refreshing. I had a very satisfactory talk, and I really feel now that I have got Murphy pretty well in hand. I try to give him all the credit, and he is delighted with a two-column article in the *Express*; very laudatory about him. The trouble is that General Eisenhower and General [Bedell] Smith don't really like him, and I have to be very careful about this.

Dinner with Sam Reber, and a cheerful party (including Murphy, Harold Caccia and General Holmes) to celebrate Sam's fortieth birthday.

The news is better and better. Sweepstakes are now being started, and we are all drawing for the date when Sicily will be ours.

Friday, 16 July 1943

General Alexander's plane has been mended and flown down to Algiers for me. He, Eisenhower (and for the first day Tedder) have been in Malta since the landings began, so as to be with C.-in-C. Mediterranean (Cunningham) who found it easier to command from there.

Tedder returned to Tunis last Sunday. Ike and Alex are expected at Tunis tomorrow.

The flight was without incident. We flew along the shore (over the sea) instead of over the mountains. This takes a little longer, but is much more pleasant and we had a smooth trip. We left Algiers at 9 a.m. and were in our house in Tunis by noon.

At 2.30, I went to see Eisenhower (who is in a small villa one mile away). He kept me for two hours talking. He was in great spirits, and I was glad to find his views about the future had considerably hardened along the lines which I wanted.

5 p.m. Commander [G.A.] Martelli (Intelligence and Propaganda) to see me. We discussed certain items of the propaganda campaign in Italy.

After this, I got a good number of London telegrams to attend to, and worked on them till dinner.

A pleasant dinner in the mess – the 'high-ups' (with the exception of Francis Rodd) are still away. After dinner I worked on 'Military Government in Sicily' problems with Francis (who is to be the head of the show and some of whose chaps have already got into place) and other questions arising out of possible future operations [in Italy].

In bed by 11 p.m. I am glad to be back in Tunis – I like this dignified Arab house; I like the climate (like hot July in England, with a nice breeze), I like this mess. Before going to bed I finished *Tancred*. I have also re-read *Coningsby* and *Sybil*.

Saturday, 17 July 1943

A busy day. General Alexander arrived about 7.30 a.m. and was in very good form at breakfast. Things seem to be going on pretty well, although it is too soon yet to be certain. Nevertheless, I get the feeling that the general is confident and satisfied. He is really a remarkable character – his simplicity, modesty and firmness make up a most charming and impressive whole. Like so many men of his responsibilities, he is dependent on a simple but complete faith in the certainty of victory and the guidance of Providence. He told me an interesting thing about the landings. When they were all in Malta – Eisenhower, Cunningham, Tedder and he – waiting up through Friday night and in the early hours of Saturday morning, they were all much disturbed by the quite unexpected (and for the time of year almost unprecedented) phenomenon of the gale. The wind varied from 20 to 45 miles an hour, and they worried terribly about the effect which this might be expected to have on the landings. In point of fact, it proved a double advantage. First, the enemy were certain no possible disembarkation could be attempted on such a night. One of the captured Italian generals described it as a 'pyjama night', i.e. they had thought this a perfectly safe night for a good sleep. Secondly, the sea, driven by the wind, carried the landing-craft safely over the many treacherous sand barriers which otherwise might have proved a serious impediment. 'So you see,' said the General, 'Providence was looking after us all the time and knew better than we did.'

At 10 a.m. I went to the Consulate, and received a deputation of the Maltese colony in Tunis on various questions – preservation of their national status as British subjects, arrangements for them to join the British Army (Pioneer Corps), and relief to the poor. There are altogether nearly 20,000 Maltese in Tunisia, mostly in the cities of Tunis and Sousse.

12 noon. Conference with General Alexander and some of his officers.

2.30 p.m. Conference at Eisenhower's villa. Eisenhower, Cunningham (who arrived by plane from Malta), Tedder, Alexander and their respective Chiefs of Staff. I attended the first part, which dealt with political as opposed to operational problems, and then left.

4.30 p.m. Admiral Cunningham and General Alexander came to my room in the Residence to discuss certain points arising out of the conference.

5 p.m. Alex drove me in his jeep (he driving) to see the Villa d'Erlanger (a most absurd and elaborate structure, costing umpteen million dollars in the imitation Arab style).

Then we went to another villa (lived in by General George Clark)[10] with a lovely beach where we all bathed. General McNaughton[11] (Canadian), General Eisenhower, General Gale (from Algiers) and others. A marvellous bathe, hot sun and almost equally hot sea.

Back for some work on telegrams: a telephone call to Roger Makins in Algiers; dinner; quiet read in my room; finishing this letter up to date, and then bed.

Sunday, 18 July 1943

This is a strange party. It is rather like a large country house. You come to meals and otherwise attend your own business. There is plenty of quiet amusement available – sightseeing, bathing or just agreeable conversation with the other guests. A cloudless sky, a dark and lovely sea, a slight breeze, a perfect August day, a cool night. No

[10] Major-General George Clark (1892–1948) was G.O.C. Lines of Communication, A.F.H.Q., 1942–3, and Chief Administrative Officer, A.F.H.Q., 1944.

[11] Lieutenant-General Andrew McNaughton (1887–1966) was G.O.C.-in-C., First Canadian Army, 1942–3, and Canadian Minister of National Defence, 1944–5.

fuss, no worry, no anxiety – and a great battle in progress. This is never referred to (except occasionally by some of the American officers on General Alex's staff) but is understood to be going on satisfactorily. We do not much like the wireless – except for some special message, *e.g.* the P.M.'s or the President's announcement. I am sure you are getting all sorts of news about the campaign – far more than I am. Except for serious matters which affect me 'professionally' so to speak, it is (in the mess) politely ignored. The conversation is the usual tone of educated (and there are some *very* well-educated) Englishmen – a little history, a little politics, a little banter, a little philosophy – all very lightly touched and very agreeable. It is a strange and fascinating experience. Very occasionally an officer comes in with a message to the 'Chief'. After pausing sufficiently for politeness the conversation in hand – the campaign of Belisarius, or the advantages of classical over Gothic architecture, or the right way to drive pheasants in flat country to show them well, or whatever it may be – General Alex will ask permission to open his message – read it – put into his pocket – continue the original discussion for a few more minutes and then, perhaps, if the message should call for any action, unobtrusively retire, as a man might leave his smoking-room or library after the ladies have gone to bed, to say a word to his butler, fetch a pipe or the like.

I have never enjoyed so much the English capacity for restraint and understatement.

This place is much nicer than Algiers. Algiers is like Marseilles or Toulon – a great hot town, crowded into the bay and sprawling up the hill; with large apartment houses, villas, etc., all jostling together; a political and now a sort of fashionable French society, over- and under-dressed women, politicians, journalists, businessmen, concession-hunters, hangers-on of all kinds and sexes, Tapers and Tadpoles and all the normal appurtenances of a capital.

Here we are eight or nine miles from Tunis. I like the great plain – quite brown and burnt now (the crops have been cut some weeks) and the grey and dusty olives, and the sea and lagoon on all sides of you, so that you seem surrounded by blue water, and the blue mountains rising dimly through the heat-haze across the gulf.

But the society is different – it is like an English school or university. It is almost exclusively male. A few odd W.A.A.C.s or A.T.S. seem to penetrate occasionally into this military monastery. If the environs of Algiers were a Lido, the sea-shores and beaches here are the Garden of Eden, without Eve. The ordinary costume for men at work is shorts, socks and shoes. When they are playing or bathing on the beaches their costume is either a sort of white triangle, so constructed as to preserve modesty but to allow the buttocks to be burnt the same chocolate colour as the rest of their bodies, or nothing at all. The sea is almost too warm, but the sun is not really too hot, as there is usually a pleasant breeze. And all along the beaches, when work is over are these naked figures, ranging from white (the newly arrived) to pink (those who brown that way) to pure bronze – with a really fine physique and bearing, either waiting as reserves for the next wave or as base details to fill casualties, or working at the base as clerks, drivers, teachers and so on.

The more I see of this Army the more I wonder what they will make of England after the war. Will they all be soothed in the syrup of Beveridge? Will they be victims of that Pied Piper [Herbert] Morrison? Will Dick Acland and Priestley[12] cash in on their vague aspirations and sentiments? Or will they be able (as we failed to do twenty-five years ago) to construct a virile creed, firmly based on the glories of the future Empire? It is all very strange and makes me feel very old. These men are and look so young – and yet sometimes seem so prematurely experienced (especially the officers) in hardship and danger and responsibility.

10.30 a.m. Church. By some strange piece of second sight the parson (Rev. Dunbar) has seen in me the kind of man who likes to read the Lesson. This I do. There is only one – Romans 8: 29–39.

12 noon. Bathed at General George Clark's villa. The sea is so warm as really to be like a warm bath. A large party of high officers and others – General Eisenhower, General Barré,[13] Mme Barré, General Gale, General Miller, etc., etc.

A most lovely French lady – called Mme Laleur – with the prettiest figure and ravishing legs and practically no clothes, together with other similarly attired beauties, kept turning up.

An excellent luncheon (General Clark has a very good French chef). I was next to old Baronne d'Erlanger[14] (the owner of the 'Hever' villa about which I have already written).

After luncheon – sleep – more bathing – sleep again – bathe again – a thoroughly degenerate and enervating day – but rather fun.

From about 6 to 8 we did at last do a little work on telegrams, etc. Dinner in the mess.

Monday, 19 July 1943

The news is still good, although progress is naturally slowing down as the Germans get together and collect new forces. No one still makes much reference to the battle, but I am allowed into the War Room and so can see what is happening. The atmosphere remains one of quiet and competent efficiency, which makes for confidence and calm. I worked in my room all the morning, on various papers and telegrams. The

[12] Sir Richard Acland (b. 1906), Liberal M.P. for Barnstaple, 1935–45, and J. B. Priestley (b. 1894), the novelist, had in June 1942 founded Common Wealth, a new political party which came to nothing.

[13] General Georges Barré (1886–1970), commanding French forces in Tunisia in November 1942, was the first Vichy commander to commit his forces to battle against the Axis.

[14] Baronne Catherine d'Erlanger, widow of Baron Emile.

Sergeant-Clerk (Brown) is not quite such a fast worker as Miss Campbell, but he is nevertheless very reliable.

2 p.m. M. Lévy Despas – a leading Tunisian Jew (the Simon Marks of Tunisia) who runs the African 'Monoprix' – came to see me. I have known him some little time and like him.

5.30–7.30 p.m. Greatly daring we have given a party. The guests were the British civilian community, plus the leading Maltese. About forty in all. Mrs Monypenny (the Consul-General's wife), an attractive, bustling, efficient woman, assisted us nobly. John also surpassed himself and produced food and drink in the most extraordinary way. We had all the staff of the Consulate, Vice-Consuls, cyphering clerks (female), etc., the Parson and Mrs Dunbar, the Maltese priest, etc., etc.

Billy Scott (who is on the staff here) came to help, and Hugh Fraser and Tony Warre blew in during the affair.[15]

Meat sandwiches, tongue, paté, Spam, etc., constituted the food – vermouth, vin rosé, muscat, lemonade the drink. The heat was terrific (a sirocco blowing up from the south). My rooms looked very nice, and we also used the garden. General Alexander looked in for a few moments, which pleased them.

8 p.m. Dinner with General George Clark. Generals Eisenhower, Alexander, Gale, Miller and about ten or twelve other officers of various ranks.

After dinner we had some very enjoyable singing – a concert party of Italian prisoners – mostly Sicilian and Neapolitan. They played concertinas and sang a number of duets, trios, choruses, etc., both sentimental and comic. They seemed very happy and contented.

The weather has suddenly turned very hot again with a warm south wind.

I like very much living at Tunis and would like to stay here. It is a very agreeable kind of life.

Tuesday, 20 July 1943

We started by car from Tunis at 8.30 a.m. We stopped at the Consulate to pick up some telegrams, and then drove through Zaghouan and Enfidaville to Kairouan.

The road took us past the mountains (which we left on the west) through the plain – about 120 miles or so in all. It was very interesting, because we went right through the battlefield, and all round were the grim relics of the campaign. Tanks, motor-lorries and aeroplanes lay upturned and useless, burnt-out hulks, by the side of the road and in the fields. And the sad little cemeteries – of German and British troops – were dotted at intervals along the road-side.

[15] Lieutenant-Colonel Lord William Montagu-Douglas-Scott (1896–1958), General Alexander's Military Secretary, was Unionist M.P. for Roxburgh and Selkirk, 1935–50. Major Anthony Warre (b. 1912) was married to my niece Arbell Mackintosh.

It was a terribly hot day, and there was no shade. There are a considerable number of olive groves (which afford a little shade to the troops – mostly Air Force – who camp among them). But for the most part the men who look after the large aerodromes live in the open – and a hard life it must be. It is better for them when they are nearer the sea, for they can at least get a bathe. But the inland airfields must be very trying.

However, they all look remarkably fit and healthy, and seem to despise the sun. No one wears a helmet (or any kind of head covering) and very few wear any but the scantiest clothes.

Kairouan (Caravan) is supposed to have been founded in 670 A.D. It is one of the holiest cities of Islam – and one of the hottest too, I should say. By the time we arrived (about 11.30) it was warming up well. By the time we left (about 2.30) it was a furnace.

Seven pilgrimages to Kairouan are supposed to equal one to Mecca. But I will rest content with one, and give the other six a miss.

The party consisted of Harold Caccia, John Wyndham and myself. Consul-General and Mrs Monypenny came in their own car.

The city is entirely Arab and entirely unspoilt by any European influences. It is surrounded by a brick wall, about twenty feet high, with towers and bastions, and a number of imposing gates.

A great part (almost all, indeed) of the city is out of bounds for troops, because of typhus and other diseases. It is a curious mixture of squalor and magnificence.

The native houses and shops are incredibly crowded and unbelievably filthy. We went into a number with our guide (the Chief Officer to the Kaid, to whom we were entrusted by the Kaid after a ceremonial reception).

I am bound to say that I found my natural courtesy sorely strained. The best thing that they could do with the place would be a prodigious slum-clearance.

But in spite of this (to me) rather unattractive dirt and misery, the whole thing is very picturesque, and I suppose not much worse than the Kasbahs (or native quarters) in the European cities like Algiers, Tunis, etc. Anyway, the whole gives one a very good impression of the real native life.

In addition to the slums (and the Kaid's palace) there are twenty-three large mosques, ninety small ones, and we were taken into two of these. (For some reason, Europeans are allowed in the mosques, the only city in North Africa, as far as I know, where this is the case.)

The Great Mosque is an enormous rectangular building. Outside is a vast square courtyard (which covers a cistern) surrounded by a double arcade of marble columns. These are very beautiful and are looted from an ancient Roman city nearby. There is rather a jolly minaret (which we had to climb) and the whole effect is rather pleasing – like a great quadrangle or court at Oxford or Cambridge.

The mosque itself is a large rectangle (about 130 by 240 feet) consisting of seventeen naves (or aisles) of eight arches each, resting on 296 magnificent columns (with various styles of capital) made of marble or porphyry. All these, again, are looted from the Roman city. There are also some magnificent red porphyry columns from Caesarea (in Algeria). The only really Arab work is the mosaics and the fine plaster-work on the walls – also the cedar-wood pulpit (said to come from Baghdad). The dome is supported by porphyry columns (Roman again), each nearly 40 feet high. The whole effect is magnificent and impressive, but of course it owes most of its beauty to Roman not Arab work.

We drove (with the Kalila – or Kaid's Minister) from the Great Mosque to the Mosque of the Barber. We passed on the way a magnificent stone cistern or bathing pool of a great size. It was built (he said) by a sultan. (It may really have been Roman.) In any case, it was a very fine bathing-pool and in the middle was a sort of throne or seat of stone. On this, he told us, the sultan used to sit with his friends and courtiers and delight in watching the ladies of his court bathing. It all seemed to me rather improbable, as the cistern was obviously a reservoir in a country where a reservoir is the first essential if you have been so foolish as to allow the splendid Roman aqueducts (bringing water from the mountains to the plains), with which Tunisia is splendidly equipped, to fall into disrepair.

The Kalila told me another, and better, story. Beneath the deep waters of the cistern lies a buried treasure. This is how the treasure can be obtained. If a man can slaugher one thousand sheep in one day with his own hand; make of the thousand muttons *couscous* and cook it himself in the same day; and in the same day also spin the wool of the one thousand fleeces into thread and weave them into burnouses – all in the same day – then he can get the treasure.

Alternatively, if he can find a woman who has never betrayed her husband either in deed or thought *(ou en fait ou en intention)* then he can get the treasure.

The Mosque of the Barber is really a gem. It is the burying place of the Prophet's companion Abu Zama el Belui – the Barber, so called – with him are buried three hairs from the Prophet's beard, which he carried about with him when living, one under his tongue, one next his heart and one on his right arm. (How the Barber did this without a life of some discomfort and even complication is rather obscure.)

Anyway, it's a lovely little mosque, where you see the Arab work at its best. You enter a charming little vestibule, with Andalusian tiles and the famous lace-like plaster arabesques. Then you pass into a little cloister, similarly decorated, the arches supported by slender marble columns.

Then a broad court, surrounded by arcades of white marble columns and splendidly domed with glazed faience and plaster-work. From this court you can enter the tomb or shrine of the Barber (or Companion) himself. This is curious, rather than beautiful. The Kairouan rugs are old and good, but I am not sure that I like ostrich eggshells hanging in large numbers from the ceiling as a form of decoration.

Nevertheless, the whole effect of this mosque – with its courts and vestibules and shrine, its delicate plaster tracery, and its lovely tiles, and its stained-glass – is certainly the most attractive thing I have seen yet in this style.

After bidding goodbye to our Arab friend we went to the mess of the Town Major (Major Adye) who is an old Algiers friend. Here we ate the picnic luncheon which we had brought with us and got some excellent and refreshing tea.

2.30–4.30 p.m. Motored from Kairouan to Sousse. Here I met the British Vice-Consul, Mr Caruana. We had a deputation of Maltese (there is a colony of some 400-odd adults at Sousse) and I made a speech to them in French.

Harold Caccia was rude enough to say that a gramophone record of this speech would sell better even than 'Monty on the Empire'. I thought it rather moving. It was rather amusing to be repeating at Sousse for Maltese the ordinary Stockton technique. There were the usual complaints – unfair distribution of relief, harsh treatment from the French authorities, lack of petrol, shortage of clothes, etc., etc.

I think our visit did good. We can help these people quite a bit. Of course, the 20,000 Maltese at Tunis I had already been dealing with.

If the drive to Kairouan from Tunis had been hot, the drive from Kairouan to Sousse was a scorching oven. A fierce sirocco started up about the middle of the day. We arrived quite exhausted, but M. Caruana refreshed us with lemonade and French conversation. Also his wife and daughter helped to entertain us.

Sousse has been much destroyed. Instead of a population of some 30,000, only about 3,000 remain. The harbour, docks, etc., are entirely taken over by the military and naval authorities. So the people are having a rough time, and are largely dependent on Anglo-American relief which is organised through the North African Economic Board. The only trouble is (as usual) the attempt of the French authorities to have the relief distributed through them. This we seem to have agreed to (in a weak moment) and of course it has meant favouritism, if not corruption. When I get back I will have it altered if I can.

We left Sousse about 6 or 6.30. By 8 p.m. we reached Hammamet. There we bathed and dined at a French inn (quite good omelette and good wine). The Air Force officers and men filled the sea, and I have never been so glad to get into the water. It was quite delightful.

After dinner, we motored home and went to bed at our house in La Marsa. (General Alexander came in for a talk about 10 p.m. until 11.30 or so.)

Wednesday, 21 July 1943

7 a.m. Bathed with General Alexander. I enjoy these morning bathes with him. He drives me in his jeep to a neighbouring beach, and it is a chance for a little talk with him before breakfast and the day's work absorbs him.

8.30 a.m. Left in General Alexander's plane (with comfortable seats!) for Algiers. Arrived at 11.15 or so and got up to the villa by noon. Here Roger came with all the Algiers news, telegrams, papers, etc.

(When I am in Tunis *all* telegrams on Italy are sent to me there and *all important* telegrams on French affairs repeated to me there. Telephonic communication is quite good, especially early and late, so I can really function pretty well in either place.)

There is still a refusal by the President to recognise the French National Committee. But the P.M. has sent a really wonderful telegram to him urging him to do so. I am told by [J.K.] Rooker (who has come out this week as Counseller on the *French* side) that he did seven drafts of it before sending it. It is witty, convincing, pleading, loyal – all at once. I feel it must have an effect. Also, the successful start of the Sicilian campaign will tend to increase the P.M.'s prestige. For it is he alone who has stood for the Mediterranean policy, and stage by stage has carried the Americans along with him, in spite of fierce technical – especially naval – resistance.

I had also a very nice personal telegram from him, explaining his position and difficulties and approving my actions. I hear from Murphy that the State Department are beginning to waver. Eisenhower and Murphy continue to plug in telegrams about this (I got Ike to send another from Tunis) and I think the cumulative effect will gradually wear down the prejudice of the President and Cordell Hull.

This afternoon and evening were pretty full, as you can imagine, and the day was not made any less so by our unexpectedly finding Mr Casey (Minister of State, Cairo) and Louis Spears[16] in our villa (as guests) on our return.

We managed to fix up various appointments for them and finally we had a little dinner, including Bob Murphy to meet them.

Thursday, 22 July 1943

The making of plans yesterday and today has been much complicated by a boil on Casey's behind. Fortunately it was lanced or burst in the course of the morning.

9 a.m. I saw Herbert (N.A.E.B.), and arranged with him a plan for improving relief distribution in Tunisia.

[16] Major-General Sir Edward Louis Spears (1886–1974) was Minister to Syria and the Lebanon, 1942–4. He had been head of the British Mission to General de Gaulle in 1940, and enabled the general to escape from France, but had now turned violently against him.

9.30 a.m. Saw General Bedell Smith and afterwards General Eisenhower. They are returning to Tunis tomorrow.

After rather a rushed morning we all collected for luncheon at the villa. Spears had been to see General Georges and Casey had seen Catroux. Both these visits will do infinite harm, as both of these colleagues are passionately anti-de Gaulle and have been pouring poison into the P.M.'s ear in London for the last month. I wish, however, that they would rest content with the mischief which they do either in the metropolitan see or in their dioceses. They need not poach in mine.

We had arranged to leave for Tunis again at 3.30 in General Alexander's machine, which was waiting for me at Algiers. I also agreed to take Spears and Casey with me, so that they could see General Alex. Unfortunately, at 3 p.m. the captain of the ship rang up to say that the hydraulic mechanism for raising and lowering the wheels was faulty – he could not risk the journey.

After great argument and confusion, in which all those great and pompous men gave different and conflicting advice, we went down to the aerodrome and got seats in the daily courier plane (if you can call them seats), which left at 4.15.

This (which I have already described to you) is rather a bad journey, because you have to come down at Telergma aerodrome (for Constantine passengers) and thus waste a lot of time and get very hot and cross.

Actually, we had a frightful trip. It was the bumpiest I have ever known and I was told afterwards that we dropped 2,000 feet in one of the worst moments. We ran into two conflicting summer thunderstorms and got fairly tossed about between them. I don't think there was really any risk, but it was very uncomfortable. One passenger and one crew (who were unwise enough not to use the straps) got rather badly hurt.

We arrived about 8 p.m. and drove to La Marsa, where we dined. After dinner, General Alex, Spears, Casey came to my part of the house and we chatted (about everything except the battle in Sicily!) till midnight.

Friday, 23 July 1943

I bathed with General Alex at 7 a.m. After breakfast desultory conversation with Casey and Spears, then two hours wasted on the aerodrome (from 11 to 1) waiting to see them off.

The only interesting part of the morning was at 10 a.m. when I was invited to attend General Alexander's morning conference in the War Room, with all the maps and the latest news of the campaign.

After lunch, Caccia and I worked on various telegrams, saw the propaganda people and prepared some minutes for General Alexander's guidance.

Bathed again in the evening; the water was almost too warm, but it was better than outside, with a fierce sirocco.

I also called on Baronne d'Erlanger who inhabits part of the remarkable Villa d'Erlanger, the rest having been handed over to General Spaatz, the American Air Commander.

General Mast (the French Resident-General at Tunis), an old friend, came to dinner at the mess. He clearly fell an easy victim to General Alexander's charm.

Saturday, 24 July 1943

7 a.m. Bathed with General Alexander.

10 a.m. Conference in War Room.

11–12 noon. General Bedell Smith came to my part of the house for a talk. He is always very easy to get on with and has been a good friend. He is a little perturbed at the extremely British character of General Alexander's staff and feels that Alex does not yet quite understand the Anglo-American set-up and its delicacy. I promised to talk to the general, but I told Smith frankly that he really must supply some better American officers to General Alexander if he wanted them taken seriously. The man who had been sent as sort of deputy to General Alexander was stupid, wooden, rather Anglophobe and ignorant. Bedell Smith took this quite well.

We afterwards discussed Tunisian politics and my desire to see the American Consul-General [Doolittle] at Tunis removed, as a source of trouble to the French and of disunity among the Allies.

After luncheon I went off and saw General Eisenhower who had just arrived at his advanced Tunis camp. He was in excellent form. Both he and Smith have a real affection and admiration for Alexander, but they find his reticence and modesty a little difficult to understand. Fortunately, after a bad beginning in the Tunisian campaign they have both got very fond of Montgomery. Of course, he is a much easier man for them to understand and appreciate.

I dined with my Jew friend, M. Lévy Despas, in a charming little villa at Sidi-Bou-Saïd. General George Clark (British) and Colonel 'Judge' Clark[17] (American) were there. We consumed a large quantity of excellent champagne – the first almost I have seen in this country – which he somehow concealed from the Germans.

Sunday, 25 July 1943

7 a.m. Bathed with General Alex.

8.30 a.m. Harold Caccia and I went in the car for a trip to see the old Roman city of Dougga. The distance was about seventy miles, and you go through the Tunisian plain (strewn with relics of the battle) to Tebourba and then to Testour. You pass the ruins of Ain Tounga

[17] Lieutenant-Colonel William Clark (1891–1957) who had been a U.S. Appeal Court Judge.

(ancient Thignica) where there is a magnificent citadel built by Justinian (in the sixth century A.D.) and a few much older remains of Antoninian temples, etc. (second century). It is splendidly placed, on the defile where the plain rises to the mountains.

Dougga (Roman Thugga) stands on hill (rather like an Umbrian city) overlooking the fertile plain. It must have been a truly magnificent city, and the remains cover a very large area – several square miles.

The theatre (with the whole of the temple scenery on the stage intact – a thing I have never seen elsewhere) is absolutely first class – in a very good state of preservation. The forum is fine, with a splendid temple of the Capitol, many of the columns of which are standing – all white and greenish marble monoliths, thirty to forty feet high.

The mausoleum would have been equally fine if a British Consul had not taken part of it away in the forties and given it to the British Museum. There are many other temples, houses, markets – a good aqueduct – and so on. The only fly in the ointment is that the Arabs have constructed a sort of straggly series of villages among the ruins (using the old stones) and all their filth and dirt and smell pervades the place.

We had a picnic lunch and got back (very hot) to our house by about 4 p.m.

At 5 p.m. Commander Martelli (propaganda and leaflets) came in and I worked with him for about an hour. Then a number of other visitors turned up, Major [John] Profumo, M.P., and the inevitable Randolph Churchill![18] Randolph had landed in Sicily with a commando, but seems to have got bored with the place and come back (for a drink, I suppose).

Dinner (very formal) with General Mast at the Residence. I was next to rather a pleasant French woman – Mme de la Tour du Pin. She was really almost English and not as silly as most of them are here. The husband was the usual little French aristocrat.[19]

On getting back from the dinner I was reading in my room when Commander Martelli rang up (about 11.30 p.m.) with the news of Mussolini's resignation. We found nobody up in the mess, except Billy Scott, and had a good deal of difficulty in making the radio work. But we got the midnight news (from somewhere – B.B.C. Overseas or something) which confirmed the fact but gave us no details. I wondered whether it was worth while waking up General Alexander but decided against it. I felt it would infringe the good manners of their mess, where (at least in company) the war is not allowed to impinge on conversation and social amenities. So I went – very cheerfully – to bed

[18] Major Randolph Churchill (1911–68), journalist and only son of the Prime Minister, was Conservative M.P. for Preston, 1940–5; he was serving on special operations.

[19] M. de la Tour du Pin had been First Secretary at the Madrid Embassy until he decided to turn against the Vichy Government in November 1942.

to lie under my mosquito net, sweating freely in the oppressive heat of the night.

All we knew at the time was that Mussolini had resigned and that King Victor Emmanuel III, the old king who had reigned since 1900, had appointed Field Marshal Pietro Badoglio, an almost equally old former Viceroy of Ethiopia, to be Prime Minister in his place. It was only later that we discovered that Mussolini had been deposed as a result of two separate plots. Hitler had told him on 19 July that Germany did not propose to defend Italy south of the Po – though in the event she did, most stubbornly – but would leave her to the mercy of the Allies. In this crisis Mussolini summoned the Fascist Grand Council at the insistence of Count Grandi. They talked for ten hours and resolved that Mussolini should hand over command to the King. As soon as he did so the King, who had been operating a separate conspiracy with the help of Marshal Badoglio and the Duca d'Acquarone, arrested him.

Monday, 26 July 1943

7 a.m. Bathed with General Alexander. I told him about Mussolini – he seemed pleased.

8 a.m. General Eisenhower rang up and asked me to come over at once to his villa. He was in a great state of excitement and full of plans and ideas for exploiting the Italian situation. He asked me to write an appreciation; a draft propaganda direction; a draft telegram for the Combined Chiefs of Staff on this question and to have them ready for the meeting at 10 a.m.

10.15 a.m. Meeting at Tunis in a small villa occupied by the H.Q. of Air Chief Marshal Tedder. Present: General Eisenhower, Sir A. B. Cunningham, Admiral of the Fleet, General Alexander, Sir A. Tedder, General Bedell Smith and all the leading naval, military and air staffs.

Fortunately, the admiral was late in arriving, so I had my job done in time. After a short general review of the operational situation, I produced my documents. After discussion, these were generally approved, subject to some amendments and suggestions. I then went out, got a typist, redrafted the documents and everything was approved and despatched by noon.

While it was inevitable that our military reaction to the fall of Mussolini would take time – Alexander estimated that Sicily would be reduced by the end of August and that landings on the Italian mainland might begin in late September – it was vital that our political reaction should be prompt. We must encourage the new Italian Government to make peace, and be ready for them when they offered to do so. Two proposals were put forward. The first was that General Eisenhower should send a broadcast message to the Italian people emphasising that in requiring 'unconditional surrender' we did not mean to impose dishonourable terms upon them. (This he did on 29 July.) Secondly we needed to know exactly what those terms were. At this stage the only terms consisted of a draft of some forty clauses compiled by an Allied committee in London and awaiting approval from the United States. It took no account of the fact that an Italian government wishing to capitulate might not be able to do so without reckoning with the Germans.

I had to draft telegrams on both points to London and Washington; and on the following day a telegram was sent to the Combined Chiefs of Staff suggesting ten simple conditions that should be imposed if the Italian Government should ask for an armistice before we invaded the mainland. These came to be known as the 'short terms'.

[Diary continues] The meeting ended about 1 p.m. After luncheon, Admiral Cunningham and some of his officers, Harold Caccia and I flew back to Algiers, arriving about 6 p.m. after another very bumpy journey – but not so bad as last time. I had just time before we left to get off a telegram to Winston describing the meeting and commenting on the various telegrams.

General Eisenhower returned to Algiers in his own plane immediately after the meeting.

6–8 p.m. Went through various telegrams and questions which had arisen in my absence with Roger Makins.

8 p.m. Dinner at General Eisenhower's to meet Mr Secretary Stimson,[20] the American Secretary of the War Department. I was put next to Ike. Murphy and various American officers completed the party.

Mr Stimson is an old darling (seventy-eight years) but I should not say a man at the height of his powers. Whatever they may have once been, they are faded now. Nevertheless, he was very charming to me and seemed very happy and contented. Anyway he was fast asleep by 9.45. I am bound to say that at the end of a longish day I was quite ready for bed too.

Tuesday, 27 July 1943

9 a.m. Saw General Eisenhower and discussed the general situation and telegrams passing between the two Governments and himself.

11 a.m. Meeting with Murphy and General Holmes (Military Government Section).

There are a lot of Italian problems to settle in detail. Somehow, in spite of all the planning work, all sorts of new and unthought-of questions are bound to arise.

20 Henry L. Stimson (1867–1950) was U.S. Secretary of War, 1940–5. He had held the same office under President Taft, 1911–13, and was Secretary of State, 1929–33.

My new Counsellor, Mr Rooker, and Dick Crossman (Political Warfare – propaganda) to lunch.

2 p.m. I was called away from luncheon for a further conference with Eisenhower.

3 p.m. Mr [Eric] Biddle and two colleagues from Washington. They are called 'Office of Budget Bureau' or something of the kind. I found it difficult to find out what exactly they were here for, and I think they had the same confusion of mind.

There are a lot of these wandering emissaries from Washington. It is as well to treat them with great courtesy and consideration.

4 p.m. I called on Giraud. I'm afraid that his visits to Washington and London have had a disastrous effect upon him. His natural, if naïve, conceit has been enormously increased. He thinks (perhaps with some justice) that the Americans have promised their material to him personally. He has, however, quite misunderstood the President's and Cordell Hull's game. His vanity is such that he really believes that they are interested in him as a statesman and general. Of course, they are only interested in him as a convenient instrument to (*a*) injure de Gaulle (*b*) break up the French union.

At 5.30 Massigli came. He was in quite good heart in spite of all the difficulties and obviously pleased by the courtesy and friendliness of his reception in London. Although he naturally deplores the delay in recognising the French National Committee, he quite understands the British position.

Of course the game which the White House and the State Department are playing is obvious. They hope by delaying recognition to excite a nervosity and lack of confidence of the Committee in itself. Then they hope that Giraud will (as a result of the promises or half-promises made to him in Washington) take such a stiff line on military questions as to provoke a dissolution of the Committee.

When that happens, the non-recognition of the Committee will have been a bull point for them and they can go back to supporting Giraud as Lord of French North Africa and a willing tool of the American Government. If the President knew how much this policy is disliked and even despised by the American Army here, I think he would get a rude shock.

Wednesday, 28 July 1943

A very long and difficult day. I was at the office from 8 a.m. to 8 p.m. A series of telegrams pouring in and out. We are now trying to keep two balls in the air at once – France and Italy. Each is in a critical position.

Fortunately, I have got a bit better help now. I have got the office organised as follows.

Makins (general). Then on France, I have now as Counsellor, Mr

Rooker (a nice oldish man who was with Charles Peake[21] and knows and handles de Gaulle well), assisted by Eric Duncannon. On Italy I have Harold Caccia. For general work, and especially liaison on all matters with Allied H.Q., I have John Addis. And then for everything else the 'Admirable Crichton' – John Wyndham.

I have also now a Press Attaché, caled [Tom] Dupree.

The most interesting interview of the day was with André Philip, who is Commissioner for the Interior and for French Resistance. He is just back from a visit to London.

At 6.30 I saw a strange American admiral, called Glassford,[22] who informed me that he had been appointed 'Proconsul of French West Africa'. It is a strange world.

Thursday, 29 July 1943

One of our best days. Two 'Most Immediate' telegrams (on Italy) in the course of the night – which means that one is woken up to read them and having done so, one goes back to bed, as there is obviously no action that can be taken at 3 a.m.

I spent from 9 to 12 going backwards and forwards between my own office and A.F.H.Q., and in conversation with General Eisenhower and Bedell Smith. The poor General Eisenhower is getting pretty harassed. Telegrams ('Private', 'Personal' and 'Most Immediate') pour in upon him from the following sources:

(*i*) Combined Chiefs of Staff (Washington) – his official masters.

(*ii*) General Marshall. Chief of U.S. Army – his immediate superior.

(*iii*) The President.

(*iv*) The Secretary of State.

(*v*) Our Prime Minister (direct).

(*vi*) Our Prime Minister (through me).

(*vii*) The Foreign Secretary (through me).

All these instructions are naturally contradictory and conflicting. So Bedell and I have a sort of parlour game in sorting them out and then sending back replies saying what *we* think ought to happen. As this rarely, if ever, coincides with any of the courses proposed by (*i*), (*ii*), (*iii*), (*iv*), (*v*), (*vi*) or (*vii*), lots of fun ensues. But it gets a bit wearing, especially with this heat.

At noon we had a meeting with the propaganda boys,[23] to try and tie up policy and propaganda regarding Italy. Fortunately, we have in this

[21] Charles Peake (1897–1958) was British representative to the French National Committee in London, 1942–4.

[22] Vice-Admiral Alex Glassford, Jr (1886–1958) was the personal representative of President Roosevelt, with the rank of Minister, to French West Africa, 1943, and commanded U.S. Naval Forces, Mediterranean, 1945.

[23] Propaganda in all its forms was handled jointly by the American Psychological Warfare Branch (P.W.B.) and the British Political Warfare Executive (P.W.E.).

field two admirable men – intelligent, humorous and loyal. These are Jackson[24] (American) and Dick Crossman (British).

After luncheon, we had a *French* interval. The Committee met again this morning for a second session to discuss military re-organisation, but made no progress. Giraud put up a plan yesterday which left him:

(*a*) Joint Prime Minister.

(*b*) Commander-in-Chief of all troops, navies and air forces, both in North Africa and elsewhere (i.e. absorption of de Gaulle's forces).

No place at all for de Gaulle (except a rather shadowy consultation on a 'Planning Committee'). He seems to have told the Committee that in Washington he had been promised equipment as an individual, *not* as President of the Committee. This plan was unanimously rejected by the Committee.

In order to reach agreement, de Gaulle today made three proposals, each of which Giraud turned down:

(*i*) Giraud to be C.-in-C., de Gaulle to be Minister of Defence, each also to be joint President. A small *war* cabinet to adjudicate any differences.

(*ii*) Giraud to be C.-in-C. (and joint President), a civilian to be Minister of Defence.

(*iii*) Giraud to be Minister of Defence and C.-in-C. but to resign from joint Presidency.

Apparently Giraud is now threatening to resign from the Committee, apparently relying on the Americans to support him as a sort of dictator.

I do not take all this too tragically, for we have been through it all so often and we usually reach a temporary solution. This time I feel that Murphy and I should not intervene at all for the present.

5.15 p.m. Monnet came in, on a fishing expedition. What would happen if Giraud resigned? What would happen if the Committee were to 'dissolve'? He caught nothing.

5.30 p.m. A fresh complication about propaganda to Italy. Went up with Crossman to A.F.H.Q. to see Bedell Smith and settle it.

I stayed with Bedell till about 7 p.m., then came back down the hill to my own office to finish some telegrams.

8 p.m. A frightful man called Bennett came to dinner – I think under the impression that he had been asked. He was rather tipsy and very ill-mannered, but nevertheless intelligent.

I sent Bennett away early and then got down to some drafting. It is so hard to get a telegram (especially to P.M.) which can describe the atmosphere. Facts and figures are easy; but the sort of general psychological situation whether on French or Italian problems, is hard to define in a few sentences.

[24] C. D. Jackson (1902–64) was Deputy Director of P.W.B., A.F.H.Q., 1943, and S.H.A.E.F., 1944–5. He had been Senior Vice-President of Time Inc. since 1931, and U.S. Ambassador to Turkey, 1942–3.

However, things may begin to move rapidly now. I believe that if the King and Badoglio do *not* within a few days ask for an armistice, we can get up a real revolution in Italy against them. But it would suit us much better *not* to be stimulators of revolution, which we shall only have to suppress later. We should prefer that the King, etc., yielded to (*a*) our threats and (*b*) popular agitation, so that we could have a more or less organised government with which to make an armistice now, and through which administration can be carried on later. We have neither the personnel nor the inclination to undertake the government of Italy. We only want to destroy Italian armies, etc., and use Italian soil to carry on the war against Germany. Of course, the immobilisation of Italian forces would have enormous results especially in southern France and the Balkans. But unless the telegraphing stops soon, even if they ask for an armistice, we shan't have the terms ready!

I am so delighted with your letter dated 15 July. Alas! I have not yet got to Sicily, as you will have seen by my letters. General Alexander invited me to come when I could, but I must keep close to Ike for the moment, as he needs a bit of nursing. Also, we are in the early stage of a new French crisis.

I am so glad you got to Eton and saw a number of old friends. It is such a bore in this war, because one never sees anybody. And I was also interested in your other various social activities. Your General Worthington[25] seems a friendly character. I am glad you met Paget.[26] I saw him out here, and formed a good opinion of him.

Your party at No. 10 must have been quite amusing. I am afraid I am bound to have a final row with Winston sooner or later, but for the present it has not materialised.

And what a lot of work you have done with the rugs and so on at Birch Grove. I am sure it would be a good thing to repack the furniture when it can be done. You could then get out some of the things which you may need now or which might be useful.

What a dreadful business about the East Grinstead Cinema. It is quite extraordinary how these places always seem to get hit.

I am much impressed by all your work with the Land Army. It is really a most trying and exhausting job, but you must feel it is worth while. It is one of those jobs which gets no recognition and where a sense of virtue must be its own reward.

I don't know why I write this, but I feel most of my letters are terribly egotistical. So I feel I must tell you how much I think about you all. I do hope Maurice is well and that K's baby will appear all right.

I suppose Mima [Lady Harlech] will be looking after Katharine. I do

25 Major-General Frederick Worthington (1889–1967) was G.O.C. Armoured Division, 1942–5.

26 General Sir Bernard Paget (1887–1961) was C.-in-C., Middle East, 1943–6. Until June 1943 he had commanded the Twenty-first Army Group preparing for the invasion of Normandy.

hope she will have a proper doctor and attention. These Cecils are so vague about these sort of things. There must *not* be any question of saving money. Please do what you can about it. I am beginning to get quite excited and rather anxious.

Sarah seems to take an interest also in the event, and is keen to get the New Forest foal broken in time for Maurice and Katharine's children.

We are now experiencing the worst months of the year. Every day is dull and cloudy, with a sort of steamy heat, like a Russian bath. Sometimes the sun comes out, and it is really better when it does. But most of the time there is this curious leaden haze. People get rather cross about trifles and I am afraid it is particularly bad for women. Miss Campbell remains pretty serene, but Miss Williams falls passionately in and out of love, and we are concerned about the 'love life' of various members of the staff. We are now getting to be quite a little team – this is the list (John Wyndham and I were the original members and proud of it):

H.M.
Roger Makins (Head of Mission)
Harold Caccia (Italy)
Rooker (France)

Tom Dupree (Press)

John Addis
Eric Duncannon

John Wyndham

Then we have the great Mr Harnett (of the Treasury). He started as a sort of 'Shimwell' – but the heat and the absence of Mrs H. have got him down and he is now rather helpless. We can and are curing the second difficulty (she is coming out on a convoy). But I'm afraid we can do nothing about the first. I observe, however, that he has got himself from the naval shop a white suit and now looks like a cross between a steward and a barber.

Miss Campbell and Miss Williams remain excellent workers. The Sergeant-Archivist is in love with Miss Williams, and since this passion seized him has neglected his work. Fortunately, this is done by a large, plain, red-faced and red-armed girl who has arrived recently and is very good. I suppose she will soon be a spoilt beauty in Algiers, where there is a definite shortage and therefore a correspondingly enhanced value put upon feminine society.

With the exception of a few Military Police, I think this completes the office staff. As you will see, it has quite a little life of its own.

But I must turn to graver themes more worthy of a Resident Minister!

Friday, 30 July 1943

A busy day. The two balls are both in the air, France and Italy. It is getting rather confusing, as there is so much to do about both at the moment.

We have been having the usual three- or four-day French crisis, and this time I have tried not to intervene personally and have persuaded Murphy to do the same. Of course, now that I have a more adequate staff, I have been able to keep in touch without always coming out into the open myself; and this is really a more satisfactory method of operating at this stage.

There have been any number of schemes proposed for the solution of the military problem. Everyone is agreed that the last compromise – the divided command – is absurd and unworkable. *But* it did serve its purpose. It met the Allied demands as put forward in the so-called 'Eisenhower intervention' – itself a very watered-down version of the actual 'instructions', coming from the White House and No. 10. Of course, I should never have carried out my instructions. I should have resigned. But Ike could not do that, and he was splendid about doing a good deal of Nelson blind-eye stuff.

In addition, the divided command preserved French unity and prevented a definite split.

Everyone knew that the Allied demands were largely based on the natural feelings of nervousness in the days before the great Sicilian expedition set sail. Had anything gone wrong (and really, the actual chances in favour were not put by the best authorities at more than 'evens' or a little better) we should have had a very awkward situation to face.

Anyway, the position is now quite different, and I have let it be known to the French (on my own authority) that any reasonable solution which they can make on their own will be accepted by us. Of course the Americans may turn sour, but not (I think) for long. I get the impression that the President's French policy is getting very unpopular in the States. And, of course, the successful launching of the attack on Sicily and the fall of Mussolini have enormously strengthened the P.M.'s authority *vis-à-vis* the President. I feel sure that the P.M. will now be able to play his hand much more confidently.

So far as Italy is concerned, you will probably have observed the game. We have given the Italians a little respite from bombing. We sent from the H.Q. quite a 'soft' message. We said, 'Well done, King. Well done, people. You have got rid of Mussolini and Fascism. That's grand. Come now and do the necessary.'

If (as I think probable) Badoglio tries to stall, and we get no overture, direct or indirect, we should (after a very short interval) turn on the tough stuff – we should say 'Well: a week's gone by. What is the King doing? What is Badoglio up to? Get on or get out. You have been idle, so we must be busy. We shall bomb Genoa, Naples, Bologna, Milan, Turin, Rome. And it will *not* be our fault. It will be the fault of the *King* and *Badoglio*.'[27]

I think we shall be able to carry out this combination of political warfare propaganda (through radio and leaflet) and actual bombing operations. As usual, one of the difficulties is the feverish and excited interference from London and Washington.

11 a.m. Political and Economic Council. Admiral Cunningham, General [Bedell] Smith and the usual others. Quite a good meeting and a number of decisions taken.

1 p.m. Luncheon at villa. Had the members and the officers of the Council to luncheon.

3 p.m. Colonel Jung. A nice French medical colonel, who has received an English decoration and wants to thank H.M. the King for it.

3.10 p.m. Comte de Rose. Back from Morocco. Fortunately, he has gone to work in Morocco, but he has left the fascinating Comtesse here.

3.20 p.m. M. Schumer (a French bore).

3.45 p.m. M. Picard[28] (Under-Secretary to Monnet – intelligent).

4 p.m. M. Boegner[29] (a French Protestant clergyman – an indescribable bore).

4.15 p.m. General Valin[30] (head of Free French Air Force). He is a charming man, gay, moderate, a loyal but not a partisan Gaullist, a good element in every sense. He is now working very well with General Bouscat (Giraudist) in order to make a fusion of the two Air Forces. These and other interviews kept me till about 7 p.m. when I went back, rather exhausted, to the villa.

8 p.m. Dinner at villa. Guests:

M. Abadie (Commissaire de Justice). One of the Committee – originally appointed by Giraud – a well-known Algerian surgeon. A nice but intellectually conceited man – a good liberal and very much like one of our home liberals.

Mme Abadie. Fat and very provincial – rather a dear.

Comtesse de la Marsa. The Kodak girl – Eric's new flame – too smart to talk.

Colonel Dan Gilmer (American). Very nice and naïve.

[27] General Eisenhower made a second broadcast to Italy on 31 July: 'Italians, we send you a solemn warning. . . . The breathing space is over. Be prepared. Soon the air offensive will begin again in earnest, by day and by night . . . and when the bombs fall, remember that the blood of every Italian stricken by them is on the hands of the men in Rome, who in Italy's hour of decision temporised instead of acting for honour, peace and freedom.'

[28] J. A. R. Picard (b. 1907) was Secretary-General of the Commissariat for Armament, Supplies and Reconstruction, 1943.

[29] Marc Boegner (1881–1970) was Honorary President of the Protestant Federation of France, and a member of the French National Committee, 1941–3.

[30] General Martial Valin (1898–1980) had been C.-in-C. of the Free French Air Force since 1941.

General Valin. Charming.

Colonel [D.J.] Keswick. Brother of the younger man who used to come to Chatsworth.

Eric Duncannon.

And the staff who live in (Roger, Harold Caccia and John). It was rather a heavy evening, only relieved by the American colonel suddenly observing to Mme Abadie, 'Est-ce que vous êtes procuresse? Je veux procurer une jeune dame pour des leçons.' Mme Abadie looked a bit surprised, but replied eventually, 'Oh, non. Il fait beaucoup trop chaud.' It transpired that the gallant colonel wanted lessons in the French language.

The news is good tonight. I understand that the French National Committee have now reached a complete agreement about the military organisation, that de Gaulle has been very conciliatory and that the settlement will be announced tomorrow. I have this from several sources.

Saturday, 31 July 1943

A very hot day – great humidity and much sweating.

10 .m. Captain [Cuthbert] Bowlby, R.N. (son of my old tutor Henry Bowlby).

11 a.m. Chief of Staff. A lot more London and Washington telegrams on Italy. Good news on France, and another effort to get the President to recognise. Everyone agrees that the compromise (or plan) announced today is a very good one and that de Gaulle has taken a wise decision.[31] In the long run he stands to gain, because Giraud will concentrate more and more on *military* questions, leaving the *political* questions in de Gaulle's hands. At last he is beginning to learn a little patience.

I do not see how the President can hold out now.

12 noon. Took the chair at a large meeting of the Psychological Warfare boys. I think their Italian stuff is going well. But we cannot expect, in my view, any result until the Sicilian battle is successfully over.

Lunch on a P. & O. liner in the port, given to the North African Shipping Board and the Eastern Mediterranean Shipping Control (who are on a visit here). A very good lunch and good fun.

5.30 p.m. Saw Massigli. He is desperately anxious for recognition, and thinks they now deserve it. So do I, and told him so.

[31] The F.C.N.L. issued two decrees. The first provided that 'General Giraud will preside in the National Committee when all matters concerning national defence are under discussion, and ensure their execution, while General de Gaulle will preside over all discussions of the Committee concerning other matters and general policy and ensure their execution.' The second appointed General Giraud C.-in-C. of all French armed forces, and stipulated that 'while exercising operational duties he will cease to exercise the functions of President of the Committee'. He was to be subject to the directives of the F.C.N.L. and of a newly constituted Committee of National Defence.

6–7.30 p.m. Cocktail party at the villa given by me to all the Mediterranean Shipping people and various others. Naval officers were distinguished and plentiful. A good party and somehow plenty of drink – the cook surpassed himself with the necessary sandwiches, etc., and the whole was voted a great success. The heat was intense.

August

Sunday, 1 August 1943

I was absolutely exhausted and stayed in bed, or lying on a sofa in a darkened room all day. It did me good.

Monday, 2 August 1943

I felt much better and was at the office as usual by 8.30. A fairly busy morning, and an anxious day – as the battle for Sicily, on which so much depends, began early this morning.

A fairly busy morning, in the course of which I saw M. Lévy Despas and Mr McDavid (Sea Transport).

Lunch at the villa. Guests: Admiral Vian (of Narvik), Admiral Morse (in charge of Algiers port); Captain [Thomas] Halsey, R.N., Captain Woodhouse, R.N. (captains of the *King George V* and the *Howe* respectively), Mr Murphy, Mr McDavid. A very nice party.

We finished work by 7 p.m., and motored out to bathe, getting back for a late supper. The sea was quite cool and more refreshing than usual, owing to a certain amount of wind. But the sirocco still blows.

Tuesday, 3 August 1943

8.45 a.m. At A.F.H.Q.; a word with General Eisenhower just back from Malta. No news at all yet of the battle. I liked Monty's 'Order of the day'.[1]

11 a.m. M. Roi – assistant to M. Diethelm (Minister of Production), not very attractive, but clever.

11.15 a.m. M. Guérin (Under-Secretary for Foreign Affairs). He handed me a memorandum demanding the right of the French Committee to be represented in fixing armistice terms for Italy and on any commission of control which the Allies might set up.

I am much interested (and a little amused) by this development. One of the chief arguments which I and my colleagues have used with the French urging them to settle their internal difficulties has been the

[1] 'Together with our American Allies we knocked Mussolini off his perch. We will now drive the Germans from Sicily. Into battle with stout hearts!'

rapidly changing world events. We have told them that they must get on or they will miss the bus. Apparently our argument has gone home only too well!

12.15 p.m. Roger Makins and I went on board H.M.S. *Howe* – a magnificent battleship. We were taken all round and given lunch afterwards. Very enjoyable.

2.30–5.30 p.m. Office: telegrams: London and Washington all worked up again: more telegrams – but no news of any sort yet of the battle. All depends on that. If we can only get a real success, I think things may move quickly. Propaganda can be a splendid means of exploiting victory, but it must follow not precede victory.

5.30–7.30 p.m. The heat was very tiresome today, more damp than ever. So I knocked off work early and went off to bathe. It was quite delightful. We go and bathe at a little place about twenty-five minutes in the car – quiet, secluded, and a house to wash one's feet in afterwards. Our hosts are some charming officers (British).

Dinner – given by Mr C. D. Jackson (editor of *Time* and/or *Life*) who is now on Psychological Warfare here – i.e. propaganda. He is a clever and amusing fellow, easy to get on with and generous-minded. The dinner was to meet Mr Elmer Davis – the American Brendan Bracken – of O.W.I. (Office of War Information).[2]

Davis struck me as a shrewd politician, full of native wit. He is very important to the President, because he comes from Indiana – a border state – and one which may go sometimes Democrat, sometimes Republican.

Wednesday, 4 August 1943

Still no news of the battle, other than the P.M.'s statement in the House, and a rather laconic communiqué.[3]

There is still a lot of unnecessary telegraphing between A.F.H.Q., London and Washington and I spent rather a difficult couple of hours with the C.-in-C. and Chief of Staff. Ike is beginning to get rather rattled by their constant pressure of telegraphic advice on every conceivable point. Also, the sirocco is still on, and we are all getting a lot on edge, so that incidents unimportant in themselves are magnified – mountains out of molehills.

General Mason-MacFarlane (Gibraltar) came to luncheon. A very intelligent and agreeable man.

6–8 p.m. We had a party for all the civilians in Algiers (British). To my astonishment, those now amount to over a hundred – people

[2] Elmer Davis (1890–1958) was Director, Office of War Information, 1942–5. Brendan Bracken (1901–58), a publisher, was Minister of Information, 1941–5, and one of the ministers responsible for P.W.E.

[3] A general offensive had begun in Sicily on 1 August. Two days later Churchill told the House that Centuripe, Regalbuto and Troina had been captured and the military communiqué reported 'very satisfactory progress'.

working in the Consulate, in the various economic missions, Red Cross, Y.W.C.A., etc., etc.

Among them was Sister Ridley[4] – your old friend. We had a Marine band off the battleship *Howe*, and altogether the party was a great success.

Thursday, 5 August 1943

We have just heard of the capture of Catania. This is a great success and should help considerably.

After another rather difficult morning with Ike, I agreed – at his suggestion – to leave for England tomorrow, to settle up a number of points.[5] I hope I shall succeed, but I am not very happy about it all.

Luncheon. M. André Gide (the French novelist), M. Palewski (de Gaulle's *chef de cabinet*) and Noël Coward.[6] A great success – Noël Coward sang us his new song, 'Don't let's be beastly to the Germans'. He told me he had seen you fairly lately.

The usual afternoon – various visitors – followed by a long-standing promise to speak to an American officers' club, at 8 p.m. My subject was 'The British Commonwealth and Colonial Empire'. A very daring one! A good audience and lots of good questions.

I finish this day now – a very long and hot one.

Friday, 6 August 1943

Yesterday morning, after a long conversation on a number of rather difficult problems relating to Italy and the future, Ike said to me – 'I wish you could get the P.M. to see my point of view – or, at least, I wish I could get a really clear idea of what he wants.'

Unfortunately, there have been a number of minor incidents which have caused irritation (quite naturally) on both sides. The P.M. thinks that Ike is too fond of 'propaganda' and makes too many 'statements' and 'proclamations to the Italians'. On the other hand, we have the great propaganda machine here, with the most powerful broadcasting apparatus in the world, and it seems a pity not to use it.[7]

General Alexander, in particular, is very keen on this weapon, and attributes the weak resistance of the *Italians* in Sicily to the excellence of A.F.H.Q. leaflet and broadcasting work.

Then the B.B.C. has been guilty of some frightful 'gaffes', which have upset the Americans terribly. They said the other day that the

[4] The nurse we had employed when Maurice was born.

[5] These concerned 'the short terms'.

[6] André Gide (1869–1951) lived in North Africa, 1942–5. Noël Coward (1899–1973) was entertaining the troops, and was said also to have been involved in some kind of intelligence work.

[7] The Inter-Allied High Command had broadcast to Italy on 2 August: 'Eight days have passed and still the Badoglio Government temporises. We warn you again: our Air Force will strike at you from the air and soon our land forces will be fighting on the mainland. . . . We have waited; we have warned you. We have no choice.'

Seventh Army had 'Nothing to do except walk through Sicily, eating melons and drinking wine'. This caused (as you can imagine) a terrific 'shimozzle'.

There are also a lot of much more serious problems still unsolved as to the future administration of Italy (supposing she surrenders).

So I volunteered to go back and have a talk at home. Ike jumped at this, and my journey was arranged yesterday afternoon (Winston may be much annoyed, but I felt I must do what the C.-in-C. asked).

9.30 a.m. Left by courier plane from Algiers for Marrakesh. John Wyndham came with me – no seats, only 'knifeboards'. A good trip as far as Oran (where we stopped for thirty minutes) but rather bumpy afterwards.

We got to Marrakesh at about 4 p.m., only to find that there was no 'ship' in (owing, I suppose, to bad weather somewhere) and we should have to wait the night.

There was a formidable sirocco blowing. The sandstorms made the landing quite difficult, as the airfield was quite hidden. The temperature was a hundred or more, even in the shade.

After the usual parleyings, we got into a very crowded lorry and got to this excellent hotel, Mamounia, where we found a modern and reasonably cool building.

We have had to share a bedroom, since the hotel is crammed with Americans. Marrakesh is now the great American junction for traffic to England, to West Africa, and to the U.S.A. (both northern and southern routes).

We dined sumptuously and went early to bed.

Saturday, 7 August 1943

Very hot. John has been to the airfield, and we are all set to start about 8 p.m. tonight. I am writing this after lunch, and shall now sleep in my bedroom (which is cooler than most other places). The wind has stopped, and it is just hot – but not that sense of hot air being blown at you which was so painful yesterday.

Left Marrakesh at 11 p.m., arrived Prestwick 9.30 a.m.

Sunday, 8 August 1943

Arrived Prestwick 9.30 a.m. A Lockheed met me and took us to Hendon, where Maurice and Katharine were there to meet me.

By the time I reached London, Churchill had already left by sea for Canada, where he was to meet Roosevelt and the Combined Chiefs of Staff at a conference in Quebec. I had long talks with Eden, who agreed that if the Quebec conference led to the recognition of the F.C.N.L. an Ambassador should be appointed to take over my French responsibilities as soon as possible.

We were also able to settle the 'short terms' for Eisenhower to use in negotiating with the Italians. The 'long terms' had still to be settled by the British and American Governments, and would be sent later.

Meanwhile, in the fortnight preceding my return to Algiers on 15 August, the Italian Government had been active. The armistice negotiations could not be mentioned in my journals at the time, but only referred to as Operation 'A'. So I set out the whole armistice story, shortly after it came to an end, in a separate memorandum. This first extract describes what happened while I was still in London.

Marshal Badoglio did not, during the first three weeks of his Government, make any direct approach to the Allied Governments for an armistice. What he did was gradually to establish the authority of his Government and to eradicate by degrees those aspects of Fascism which were particularly objectionable to Allied opinion. At the same time he did what he could to curb the impatience of the Italian people for peace by harping upon the impossibility of Italy accepting unconditional surrender. The Italian Government also put out a number of feelers. Their purpose seems to have been partly to gain time by explaining the difficulties of the Italian position and thus to obtain a mitigation of the force of Allied air attacks, and partly to confirm that the Allied intention to extract an unconditional surrender was not to be moved. To these ends the Marquess d'Aieta, the new Counsellor of the Italian Legation, spoke to H.M. Ambassador at Lisbon [Sir Ronald Campbell] on 3 August, and on the 6th Signor [Alberto] Berio, a Counsellor in the Italian Ministry of Foreign Affairs, told much the same story to the British Consul-General [A.D.F. Gascoigne] at Tangier. The main difference in these parallel approaches was that the Marquess d'Aieta at no time made any mention of peace terms, while Signor Berio said that he was ready and authorised to negotiate with any British representative in Tangier or with a representative of General Eisenhower. In addition the Greek President of the Council had told H.M. Ambassador on 6 August that the Nuncio at Berne had made two approaches to the Greek Minister requesting Greek mediation between the Allies and Italy for the negotiation of a separate peace. To complete the picture it should also be said that a Signor Busseti called on His Majesty's Consul-General at Barcelona in the first days of August claiming to be the bearer of a formal communication from various political parties of the Left. There is, I understand, good reason to doubt his credentials, but none to impugn the gist of his message which was to the effect that if recognition were given to these political parties they intended to take all possible measures against the Germans who occupied Italy and to act in concert with the Allies to this end.

So far as we know, no answer was given on behalf of the British and American Governments to any of these approaches except to that of

Signor Berio, to whom Mr Gascoigne was authorised to give the following answer on 13 August:

> Marshal Badoglio must understand that we cannot negotiate but require unconditional surrender, which means that the Italian Government should place themselves in the hands of the Allied Governments who will then state their terms. These will provide for an honourable capitulation.

Mr Gascoigne was asked at the same time to remind Signor Berio that the Prime Minister and the President had already stated that we desired that in due course Italy should occupy a respected place in the new Europe when peace has been re-established, and that General Eisenhower had announced that Italian prisoners taken in Tunisia and Sicily would be released provided all Allied prisoners in Italian hands were released. Signor Berio expressed considerable disappointment at this message, and though he said he would forward it immediately to Rome, he did not seem to be very sanguine of the results. In saying this, he little knew of what other arrangements the Italian Government had already made for negotiation with the Allies, and it may be convenient at this moment to allow him to fade out of the picture.

Sunday, 15 August 1943

I finally arrived at Algiers at 6.30 p.m. today after a most tiresome and fatiguing journey.

On leaving Hendon at about 1.30 p.m. on Friday, we only succeeded in getting as far as Lyneham aerodrome (near Swindon). Here we waited till about 10.30 p.m., when it was definitely decided to be impossible to fly either to Fez or Gibraltar. We slept in cubicles at Lyneham, and at 10.30 on Saturday we flew on to Portreath in Cornwall. Here we lunched and lounged away an afternoon and evening as best we could. Among the passengers was Sir Eric Speed, the Joint Permanent Secretary of the War Office – a very delightful and intelligent companion. We had a good walk in the afternoon, which did us good.

At 11 p.m. there still seemed difficulty about getting off – as Gibraltar was doubtful, and Fez (although safe) said to be closed for operational reasons. However, after some telephoning to the Air Ministry, we managed to get started.

The machine (which took us all the way from Hendon) was a most uncomfortable one, without seats and with nine passengers. After a rather cramped night on the floor, we arrived safely at Gibraltar at about 9.30 a.m. on Sunday.

Bath, breakfast, a sleep and then luncheon with the comforts of Government House and the attention of that most charming of hosts –

General Mason-MacFarlane – helped us to recover. The luncheon was superb – hot roast beef, Yorkshire pudding, roast potatoes, beer and lots of port wine. The temperature was about eighty degrees in the shade!

Fortified in this way, we set forth again about 2.30 and reached Algiers after rather a bumpy journey about 6.30. I don't know why we took so long. The pilot, instead of following the sea route, insisted on crossing into Africa and I think lost his way. No one was sick; I think Sir Eric was a trifle squeamish.

Monday, 16 August 1943

As usual, when one has been away for a week or more, there is a lot to pick up.

I sat up late last night reading files and also spent all this morning at the same job. Nothing very much has happened in my absence – but I feel my visit to London has been worth while. I have got a much clearer idea about certain problems and it does one good to see the people at home.

On the French side of my mission, there is nothing more to be done. The ball is not in our court. If the Quebec conference leads to the official recognition of the French Committee by the U.S.A. and H.M.G. – then that is the end of one definite phase in history. I feel that my work will have been accomplished, and although I shall have to be the first accredited representative to the French Committee, I shall wait impatiently for my successor to arrive. I would like to hand over (subject, perhaps, to a very general control) to a regular diplomat. Then I can concentrate upon *Italian* affairs.

As regards these, there are countless problems ahead. It is very difficult to plan the political and administrative side, when the military future is so uncertain. And – as in French matters – there is clearly a divergence of policy between the Americans and ourselves. This is, at present, not of immediate importance, because the events are still ahead of us. But I have been able to learn from my talks in London what (I think) my colleagues want, and once again I think we shall have to put it over the American Government in Washington by winning over the Americans here.

Broadly speaking, the difference is this. The Americans favour an Allied Military Government of Italy (AMGOT) even if and when the whole or the greater part of the country falls into our hands. We, being more realistic, would prefer to change over as soon as practicable from what might be called *direct* government (AMGOT) to *indirect* control – just as we did here when we recognised the authority first of Darlan and then of Giraud. In the early stages – especially while military operations continue – you must have *direct* government. But, in my view, as soon as the greater part of Italy falls to us, we ought to try to find some kind of central Italian government which we could guide and control, but which would relieve us of the almost impossible task of direct administration in each locality. Merely from the point of view of personnel, I do not believe an efficient team can be recruited on the scale required.

Actually, there are also some differences of view in the pre-armistice stage. But these have largely been removed, and anyway in this case the divergence has not been between the two Governments, but between the A.F.H.Q. view (Eisenhower, supported by the three British Commanders-in-Chief and his civilian advisers) and London and Washington. However, these differences have been overcome to a great extent – largely, I think, because the P.M. really leans to our view.

In any case, while the State Department and the Foreign Office have been working on a set of armistice terms since March, which runs to forty-two clauses and almost as many pages, the text of which is still not agreed and is not in the C.-in-C.'s hands, we have succeeded (Ike and I) in getting eleven points, which can be put on one sheet of paper, authorised by the two Governments for use if the occasion arises. (Incidentally, we got our knuckles rapped over this, but we got our way.)

Monday afternoon, I saw various visitors – General McClure (Publicity [P.W.B.]) and Colonel Hazeltine (the same), also Mr Biddle (of the U.S. Treasury) to say goodbye. Sir Eric Speed and General Julius Holmes (American, Military Government Section at A.F.H.Q.) came to dinner.

Tuesday, 17 August 1943

I saw General Eisenhower this morning and had a long and very pleasant talk with him. (He was away yesterday and only returned late last night.) I told him of all my talks in London and that although I had unfortunately missed the P.M. I had discussed fully with Eden the general's difficulties and grievances.

Fortunately Anthony had done his job well, and the P.M. had sent a very genial and soothing telegram to Ike, so that he was in radiant humour. It is extraordinary how sensitive he is (and all Americans the same), and it is terribly difficult to get even the P.M. to realise this fully. We then talked of future operations and of all my political discussions in London.

12 noon. General Holmes came to see me, for further talks on political government in Italy.

At 3 p.m. M. Massigli (French Commissioner for Foreign Affairs) came to see me.

At 3.45 I was summoned to see the C.-in-C. again, who had some important news. This took up the rest of the afternoon. I will keep a special record of the matter (which I will call 'A') and send it later on [see pp. 184–7].

Dined with Royce (American), the chief of N.A.E.B. Monnet was at the dinner; also General Hughes (American, Theater Commander). The talk was largely on supply questions.

Wednesday, 18 August 1943

Almost the whole day taken up with 'A' affairs. A very busy day.

Thursday, 19 August 1943

9 a.m. Herbert to see me (British head of N.A.E.B.).

10 a.m. N.A.E.B. meeting – nothing very important.

11 a.m. M. St Hardouin to say goodbye. He acted as Secretary for Foreign Affairs under Giraud. He is now replaced by Massigli. He is to be French representative to Turkey. As his wife is a Turk, this will presumably be agreeable to him.

11.30 a.m. Mr [Conrad] Gill – recently sent out by the British Council. A very wet and silly professor at a provincial university – just another useless mouth to be fed in North Africa – not worth the shipping-space.

12 noon. M. [Maurice] Dejean. A very keen, interesting, and attractive man. Formerly de Gaulle's secretary for Foreign Affairs (before Massigli arrived). He is now returning to London as representative of the French Committee with the Allied Governments in London. Dejean is very pro-English and very sensible. He told me he had observed a marked improvement in de Gaulle's behaviour recently. He seems to be losing that sense of inferiority which (in London) drove him to say and do many foolish things.

2.30 p.m. With General Eisenhower on 'A' matters.

3.30 p.m. Rooker (our new counsellor).

4.30 p.m. Brigadier Rabino (our financial expert). There are some extremely complicated financial negotiations going on with the French. These are to replace the Churchill–de Gaulle agreement and fit them into the new central structure. This involves calculations of what is nominally owed to us by the Free French, less the value of services or assets brought in by them. Then, for the future, we have to arrange what will be on a lease–lend and reverse lease–lend basis between us and the new Committee and what transactions (non-military in the ordinary sense) will be on a cash basis.

Fortunately, Brigadier Rabino is not really a soldier, but a perfectly good Levantine, formerly manager of the Paris branch of the Westminster Bank.

5 p.m. M. de Sangroniz, the new Spanish representative, called. He is fat, genial, shrewd and (I should think) completely unscrupulous. He was Minister for Foreign Affairs to Franco at one time. Then he fell into some disfavour, since he disapproves of the Falange and is a monarchist. So he went into an *exil doré* in some South American embassy, and is now on his way to this post. He amused me; it is clear that he knows which side is going to win, and I should not be surprised

to see some changes in Spain. Franco may well find himself either put on the shelf or with his claws clipped to suit a monarchist and conservative, rather than a Falangist and Fascist system.

I dined with Dr Abadie – Minister of Health, Justice, etc. He is Algerian by birth, the son of a settler. His ordinary avocation is that of a surgeon. Madame is fat, bourgeois, and quite nice. The guests included M. Pleven (Colonies), Admiral Lemonnier[8] – the new Chief of Staff (a nice, but ineffective little man) – and Mme Catroux. The latter behaved outrageously, arriving late and leaving early, just to show everybody that she belonged to smart society and her hosts did not.

Friday, 20 August 1943

A busy day.

10 a.m. Meeting with Murphy.

11 a.m. Office meeting. This is a new idea. Now that we have grown from a staff of one to a party of eight (not counting clerks, typists, etc.) I thought we would have a weekly meeting so as to make quite sure we were all in touch and working together.

PRESENT:	R. Makins	Chief of Staff
	K. Rooker	Counsellor
	H. Caccia	Italian affairs
	Eric Duncannon	Attaché
	John Addis	Second Secretary
	John Wyndham	Private Secretary
	Tom Dupree	Press

I think it will be quite a good plan, and the first meeting went off well.

Most of the day was spent otherwise on 'A'. I saw in the course of it Tedder, Eisenhower, Bedell Smith, and after dinner Admiral Cunningham, who returned to Algiers from Malta today. Brigadier [Kenneth] Strong (Head of Intelligence at A.F.H.Q., British) came to dinner.

Extract from Operation 'A' memorandum
15–20 August 1943
The First Dove

1. On the afternoon of 17 August General Eisenhower sent for me to show me the text of certain telegrams which Sir Samuel Hoare had sent to the Foreign Office on 15 August describing a conversation which he had had with General Castellano, Chief of Staff to General Ambrosio,

[8] Vice-Admiral André Lemonnier (1896–1963) was French Chief of Naval Staff, 1943–9.

and Signor Montanari of the Italian Foreign Office,[9] who as cover were travelling as members of an Italian Delegation which was passing through Madrid on its way to Lisbon. The purpose of the Delegation, which had a block visa, was to accompany a party of Chilean consuls and diplomats who were to be exchanged at Lisbon for the Italian diplomats and consuls who had been forced to leave Chile as a result of that country's decision to break off relations with Italy. General Castellano is a small, dark and insignificant-looking man in the middle forties and is said to be a Sicilian of Jewish extraction; but whatever his appearance or antecedents, there can be no question of his intelligence. Nor did his credentials seem in doubt, for he had in his possession a signed letter of introduction to His Majesty's Ambassador at Madrid from His Majesty's Minister at the Holy See[10] describing him as a representative of the Government of Italy. Further his bona fides were confirmed in a telegram of 17 August from Sir D'Arcy Osborne stating that he had obtained a signed statement from Marshal Badoglio that the general was authorised to speak for him. From the telegrams which General Eisenhower had received it was clear that instructions would come during the night from the President and the Prime Minister, who were then together in Quebec, laying down what steps were to be taken.

2. These instructions duly arrived, and at ten o'clock on the morning of 18 August the Commander-in-Chief showed me a telegram from the Combined Chiefs of Staff requesting him to send two officers of his Staff to Lisbon immediately to establish contact with General Castellano. He was also instructed to arrange a method of communication with the Italian General Staff during the coming weeks. The Commander-in-Chief decided to send his Chief of Staff, General W. B. Smith, and the Head of his Intelligence Section, Brigadier Strong. Arrangements were accordingly put in hand to try to get them off by aeroplane at 2 p.m. on the same day. The rest of a hot morning was spent in an atmosphere of amateur charades. Somehow the Mediterranean Air Command had to produce a British civilian aircraft to take the two officers from Gibraltar to Lisbon: somehow civilian clothes had to be obtained: somehow civilian papers had to be provided, for it was felt that if these two officers were to arrive openly in Lisbon the international press and the German Secret Service would be on to them in a moment. Fortunately both officers had common surnames and by juggling with the christian names and with the photographs, passable papers were provided before lunch time. Even so, there was a contretemps about General Smith, as my American colleague took the

[9] Sir Samuel Hoare (1880–1959) was Ambassador to Spain on Special Mission, 1943–4; he had been Home Secretary, 1937–9. The Italians were Brigadier-General Giuseppe Castellano (1893–1977), General Vittorio Ambrosio (1879–1958), head of the Italian Joint Staff, and Franco Montanari (b. 1905).

[10] Sir D'Arcy Osborne (1884–1964), was Minister to the Holy See, 1936–47.

view that he would do better to use the American diplomatic passport which had been given to him for his journey from London to Algiers last year, despite the facts that it referred to him as 'Bedell Smith', by which name he is well known, and that it gave as his next-of-kin the Adjutant General of the War Department, Washington, a strange relative for a civilian. Actually I heard afterwards that the Governor of Gibraltar had provided General Smith with a British civilian passport and had overcome all difficulties about obtaining the necessary Portuguese visas both for the General and for Brigadier Strong. So in the end it was left to the British to play the part of Clarksons for this act, and if we were amateurs at disguise, at least we apparently succeeded in fooling the Germans. In addition the Commander-in-Chief appealed to us to help about the channel of communication, and once again it was through British means that this essential wireless service was successfully established and maintained throughout the coming weeks.

3. On the evening of 20 August General Smith and Brigadier Strong returned after having had an all-night session with the Italian Delegation in the British Embassy at Lisbon. At the beginning of the meeting General Smith had said that he understood that General Castellano had come to signify the acceptance by the Italian Government of unconditional surrender. At this General Castellano bowed, and General Smith then proceeded to give him the terms of the military armistice. It soon became apparent, as had already been made plain to Sir Samuel Hoare in Madrid, that the Italians were not so much concerned with the exact terms of the armistice as with their preoccupation to obtain our maximum assistance to turn the Germans out of Italy. Indeed they desired nothing better than to become our allies for the purpose. In this it will be noted that Marshal Badoglio's approach exactly coincided with the views expressed by the left-wing parties in the communication made to His Majesty's Consul-General at Barcelona. As we had been forewarned of this in Madrid, General Smith had in his possession a form of words for the occasion. While not committing ourselves to any promise to the Italians, the formula pointed out that the better they behaved and the more they impeded the Germans, the more it would be put to their credit for the future. In brief the Italians were out for the best *combinazione* which they could get. On their side they hoped that this would put them in a better position for the ultimate peace, and we knew it. On our side we wanted to get their help particularly to obtain an unopposed landing and sabotage and delay of German communications in the very difficult operations which lay ahead of us, and they guessed it. The rest of a long night was taken up with discussion of details of intelligence and communication. General Castellano was not due to leave Lisbon for Rome by train with the home-coming party of Italian diplomats and consuls from Chile until 22 August and he could not travel separately

without obtaining special visas and travel facilities and thus drawing attention to himself and running the risk of giving away his cover. As a result he could not hope to arrive in Rome before 25 August, and as proved the case he might be delayed by one or more days. He was therefore given until midnight of 30–31 August to convey by the special wireless arrangements which were being made between the Italian General Staff and Algiers whether the Italian Government accepted the military terms of the armistice. It should be noted here that there is evidence for thinking that our readiness to grant the Italian authorities this comparatively long period of ten days to make up their minds may have given them the impression that the date of our landing in force on the Italian mainland would be later than had actually been planned, and that this false impression influenced their judgment on more than one occasion in the remaining days.

Saturday, 21 August 1943

I left Maison Blanche aerodrome at 8 a.m. with Harold Caccia. We were given a B17 (Flying Fortress) operational (and therefore without seats) and made a good flight in three hours and fifteen minutes to an aerodrome near Syracuse in Sicily. It was a lovely day and really a most enjoyable flight. It was rather fun coming over the sea, past Pantellaria and Lampedusa and to land in Europe. Since we were driven out of Greece until 10 July this year, no British troops have fought in Europe. After thirty-eight days fighting, the whole island of Sicily was in our hands, and it was quite a thrill to land on European soil.

We arrived at General Alexander's H.Q. about noon. As usual, his H.Q. staff is in tents – this time in walled fields, consisting of olive and almond trees and the corn-stubble between the trees. The almond harvest is now on – delicious they are too. Elsewhere (for instance where the mess tent is placed) are vineyards, with the grapes just ripening.

Alex himself lives in his usual two caravans – one his office, the other his private quarters. I explained to him the whole situation about 'A' which interested him very much.

Luncheon is in the open – a table under a huge ilex – and about a dozen officers or so of his own staff. Of course, these are always coming and going; as they go to Algiers for consultation with A.F.H.Q., and to the various H.Q. which are under General Alex's command – Seventh and Eighth Armies, etc. [The forces under General Alexander's command were known as the Fifteenth Army Group.]

Harold Caccia and I are in the guest-house – called The White House. This is a delicious little farmhouse, which Alex first took over for his own use, when he arrived in Sicily. It was too small for a H.Q. later on, and it is kept as a guest place for favoured guests. There is another camp, called Fairfield, for those less honoured or less welcome.

This farm consists of two good sitting-rooms and a large kitchen. It has all been cleaned (whitewashed, etc.) and makes a most delightful little place. Behind the house is a vineyard; and round it a delightful kitchen garden; and the estate consists of orange, olive, almond groves – tomatoes, grain, etc., being planted between the trees.

Outside the farm, there are the usual outhouses (in a sort of square) and a huge old olive to sit under (with large fig trees as well), which complete the picture. Every morning and evening the donkey works away by going round and round pushing a pole. This works a sort of 'sandy-andy' which lifts the water from a deep well into a little reservoir or tank, from which it overflows into the elaborate system of irrigation with little ditches and channels which was described by Theocritus and Virgil and no doubt dates from the very earliest times. It is a pleasant, soothing sound – a sort of click of the machine, followed by the swish of the water.

Our sleeping quarters are tents in the vineyard behind the farm, with camp beds on which are spread the sleeping-rolls which we brought with us.

After luncheon, I went on with further discussions with the general on both 'A' and other subjects. He was, as usual, both charming and intelligent. He has the great quality of seeing the point. We wrote a few telegrams and then I left him and drove to my farm (in a jeep) about two miles from the general's main camp.

After a very pleasant siesta (we had made an early start from the villa in Algiers and flying always makes one a little tired), the general called for me in his jeep about 4.30. We then went sightseeing (Baedeker in hand) and very delightful it was (if a trifle hot). We drove into Syracuse and went first to see the Cathedral – fortunately undamaged. It was built in the seventh century A.D. round a Greek temple of the fifth century B.C. All the great Doric columns of the temple were incorporated into the church. This temple must have been very fine, and the old side colonnades have been filled in to form aisle walls, but without damaging the columns themselves, about twenty of which survive in good preservation. Externally twelve columns, with capitals, architrave and triglyphs, are preserved. And there are two fine columns of the old temple entrance at what is now the western door of the Cathedral.

The Cathedral square or piazza is very delightful, with some good baroque buildings – a style of which I am very fond and is most attractively seen all over this and other Sicilian towns.

From the Cathedral, we drove to the Greek theatre. This is one of the most perfect theatres of the best period surviving anywhere. It is of the fifth century B.C., hewn out of the limestone rock – facing the great harbour – a really wonderful place. It is said that Aeschylus produced the *Persae* (the play about the Battle of Salamis) here in 472. It would have gone very well, because the Greeks in Sicily had also won a great victory over the Carthaginians in the Battle of Himera in about 480. So the Greeks had repulsed the 'barbarians' of both the east and west within ten years.

Behind the theatre are the famous stone quarries where the unhappy Athenian prisoners of war (survivors of the ill-fated Sicilian expedition) were incarcerated. We used to read about this at school in Thucydides – and wonderfully the tale is told.

Nearby is a good Roman amphitheatre (150 yards by 130 yards) of the Augustan period.

Once more trouble and misery have descended on the unhappy population, and the theatre, amphitheatre and quarries are now the squalid refuge of many bombed-out families or of those who still live in terror of the occasional German air-raids.

The AMGOT (Allied Military Government of Occupied Territory), about which I expect you will hear a great deal (mostly untrue) during coming weeks, does its best – and considering how short a time it is since the battle finished, it is wonderful what progress has been made.

All the Italians seem very friendly. General Alex has taken a lot of trouble, especially with the clergy, who are very powerful in Sicily. The Carabinieri are running all the traffic and other normal police duties. In a word, things are beginning to settle down. But, of course, there are immense difficulties. The roads are almost impassable and all require repair. Bridges (road and railway) are destroyed – either by our attacks or by the enemy before leaving – electric installations are injured; coal is very short; light and power are wanting, etc., etc.

After our sightseeing, the general and I went bathing. We found a most delicious rocky cove, where the water was deep and deliciously warm. It is also so buoyant, that you can really stand up in it without sinking (if you take a deep breath). I suppose the absence of tide and the evaporation with the hot sun makes the salt content very high.

Supper at eight – in the open – and early to bed.

Sunday, 22 August 1943

Early service at 8 a.m. – in the open – quite a large attendance, including the general. After breakfast, Francis Rodd arrived (by plane from Palermo, where his H.Q. are) and a general conference all the morning on AMGOT affairs.

Alex was present, and I thought again extraordinarily patient, intelligent and sympathetic.

After luncheon, Rodd and I drafted a lot of stuff for his approval. Our day's work was over by 4 p.m., and about 5 p.m. Alex came to The White House in his jeep to take me out bathing.

These two days the heat has been intense – drier than Africa but hotter. The advantage of a camp is that one can dress more comfortably. I have purchased some white short-sleeved naval shirts, which are very comfortable – also some thin army khaki trousers.

We bathed in a different place this evening – a sandy beach. A large number of troops were in and out of the sea. Everyone bathes completely naked here, and every sort of coloured body – from bronze, through brown and red, to white – can be seen. As usual, the men present a rather comical appearance, because their loins and buttocks are still more or less white (where their shorts protect them) although their bodies are sometimes as black as niggers' torsos.

A little reading; and then supper. Bed at 10 p.m.

I very much enjoy my visits to Alex. In this case there was quite a lot of work to get through – but instead of the rather heavy-handed and extremely talkative American methods there is a delightful atmosphere of quiet efficiency. I find all the staff here (with very few exceptions) the same. And Francis (with occasional lapses into a 'prima donna' mood) is really awfully good at his job. He is quick, intelligent and persistent. His chief fault is that he is sometimes impulsive and makes decisions almost too rapidly.

It was lovely being home, even for a day with you all. I have had no letter from you since I got back from England – which I hope means that you are having a well-earned holiday somewhere away from home. It seems a very unfair division of labour which leaves you in this war all the grind of daily life and family troubles, in squalor and penury, and allows me to live in considerable state and luxury, with a good deal of 'tourism' thrown in.

I had a very nice letter from Sarah, dated 16 August and written from Maurice's flat. She seems to be enjoying herself there and I hope she is useful in the home and kitchen.

I suppose Katharine's baby will be appearing soon. Will you arrange to send a telegram to me through the Foreign Office as to the sex of the child and the health of the mother?

I have a feeling (and a great hope) that it will be a boy. Do you remember all the excitement about Maurice? I remember dragging Moyra[11] into it somehow, and generally living in a world of panic and excitement. No other baby had ever been born before. I except Maurice will feel like that, so you will have to support him. My father was in India; I remember sending him the proud cable and how his Indian servant brought him flowers and congratulations. If it had been a girl, it would apparently have been a matter for condolence.

Monday, 23 August 1943

Flew back from Sicily to Algiers. Three hours and fifteen minutes, this time in a Mitchell bomber. An operational machine, with very little room – but there is a sort of ledge in which one can squat or

[11] Lady Moyra Cavendish, my wife's aunt.

half-recline with reasonable comfort. A lovely morning – the sea a glorious blue and a few white billowing clouds to set off light and shade.

The usual sort of day on arrival – chiefly taken up with discussions in the afternoon on the Italian questions.

Dinner with Massigli. Quite an interesting party, including [Roger] Garreau, French representative in Russia, Queuille[12] (Senator, formerly Minister of Agriculture in successive French Governments; bourgeois, respectable, *bon papa*, in running for Presidency – typical of much that is worthy and solid in French life), Monnet (becoming rather bored and discontented in Algiers). He likes metropolitan towns, Paris, London, Washington – and several others. Dinner was very late (starting about 9) and as we had got up at 6 a.m. I had the greatest difficulty in keeping awake after dinner.

Tuesday, 24 August 1943

Saw C.-in-C. in morning.

10 a.m. Conference with Murphy, General Holmes, Colonel Maxwell, Makins and Caccia – on Italian affairs.

12 noon. Herbert (economic affairs).

3 p.m. Admiral Muselier. He has quarrelled equally with de Gaulle and Giraud. He thinks he is in danger of arrest.

4–6 p.m. Further conferences with the same as in the morning. A lot of tiresome telegram drafting and rather an inconsequential argument. My own desire was to do nothing on this particular topic, and I think I have so confused everybody's mind that I shall get my way.

6.30 p.m. Bathed.

8 p.m. General McCreery[13] to dinner. He has just returned from England.

Wednesday, 25 August 1943

Saw Chief of Staff at 9.30. Bedell Smith was in rare form, and kept me for one-and-a-half hours on all kinds of topics – the Quebec decisions, so far as we know them; the immediate future in Italy [for the extract from the Operation 'A' memorandum relating to 25–30 August 1943, see p. 196]; the more distant plans; problem of an Anglo-American army and command and so on.

I always find Bedell Smith interesting, and he is straightforward and fair-minded as well.

12 noon. Meeting of same as yesterday on Italian developments. I think one is beginning to see clearer.

[12] Henri Queuille (1884–1970) held ministerial office on thirty occasions between 1920 and 1953, and was three times Prime Minister of France, the first time in 1948–9.

[13] Lieutenant-General Sir Richard McCreery (1898–1967), who had been General Alexander's Chief of Staff, 1943, was on his way to Tripoli to assume command of Tenth Corps (forming part of the U.S. Fifth Army) in preparation for the Salerno landings.

1.15 p.m. Stephens (Correspondent of *Daily Herald*), Commander [G.W.F.] Fitz-George, R.N., and a major from the Middle East (name unknown) to luncheon.

2.30 p.m. Conference at A.F.H.Q. Present: Bedell Smith, Murphy, General Holmes and H.M.

This was final meeting on many questions connected with Operation 'A'. More or less complete agreement was reached amongst ourselves.

4 p.m. Sir Eric Speed (War Office). A lot of troublesome little points.

4.30 p.m. A businessman sent out here to help Herbert (N.A.E.B.). Has resigned in a huff after a few weeks. He is a type I have not seen since some of the worst of the Ministry of Supply chaps – vain, egotistical and without a spark of patriotism. He told me that he earned £10,000 a year and expected to be put in charge of practically everything here the day he arrived. I am sending him home (by *ship*) at the end of the week, and I told him that I hoped Bevin would conscript him for an aircraft factory and give him not more than £5 a week.

As it has got very hot again, I thoroughly enjoyed the interview. Poor Herbert (a typical quiet, painstaking and unexpectedly able civil servant) is torn between pride and disgust because the gentleman called him 'a ruthless bastard'. On the one hand Herbert is offended; on the other he feels a real 'he-man' now, and is correspondingly elated.

5.30 p.m. R. Crossman (British author: propaganda expert). A very able chap and working splendidly. The Americans (rather unexpectedly) like him, although he is a Communist or extreme Socialist (which usually terrifies them).

6.30 p.m. Great excitement in the office. We have just received a number of telegrams about the recognition of the French Committee.

I think they are pretty satisfactory, although the American terms may not be any too cordial and the French may feel rather hurt.

A conference between Murphy and his boys and our own team as to how to handle things was not much use, because although we had the text of our recognition, the Americans had not yet received theirs. All we knew was that it differed.

8 p.m. Dinner with Admiral Cunningham. Eight admirals, Commodore Dick and 'Flags'. I felt like Daniel in the lions' den. I have been formally elected an honorary member of the Admirals' Club.

Thursday, 26 August 1943

All the morning at C.-in-C.'s office (Admiral Cunningham also there) on Operation 'A'. The confusion and folly which is going on from London, Washington and Quebec is really very distressing.

I have sent some pretty good telegrams home and expect instant dismissal.

2.45 p.m. Murphy and I called on Massigli and left with him the texts – British and American. He was a little disappointed at the wording, but took a very statesmanlike line. I felt sure he would play up.

The text of the British recognition, which was conditional on the F.C.N.L.'s acceptance (a) *of the principle of collective responsibility and* (b) *of the Committee's temporary character (that is, until the French people could choose a provisional government after the liberation of Metropolitan France), stated:*

> *His Majesty's Government in the United Kingdom recognise forthwith the French Committee of National Liberation as administering those French overseas territories which acknowledge its authority and as having assumed the functions of the former French National Committee in respect of territories in the Levant. His Majesty's Government in the United Kingdom also recognise the committee as the body qualified to ensure the conduct of the French effort in the war within the framework of inter-allied co-operation.*
>
> *They take note with sympathy of the desire of the committee to be regarded as the body qualified to ensure the administration and defence of all French interests.*

The American version, which was different from the British largely in the less friendly tone it adopted, declared:

> *In view of the paramount importance of the common war effort, the relationship with the French Committee of National Liberation must continue to be subject to the military requirements of the Allied commanders. . . .*
>
> *The Government of the United States recognises the French Committee of National Liberation as administering those territories which acknowledge its authority.*
>
> *This statement does not constitute recognition of a government of France or of the French Empire by the Government of the United States. It does constitute recognition of the French Committee of National Liberation as functioning within specific limitations during the war.*

Massigli's response was that the texts should not be examined under a magnifying glass as if they were a contract before a notary; they should be regarded as living, not legal, documents.

[Diary continues] 3.30 p.m. Mr Miller (N.A.E.B. representative in Tunis). Things are improving since the change made as a result of my visit, especially by getting rid of the American Consul there.

4 p.m. Murphy and I called on de Gaulle. Quite unexpectedly, he

made no complaints about the terms of the 'recognition' but seemed genuinely delighted and was really most friendly.

4.30 p.m. We called on Giraud. He did not take more than a polite interest in recognition, but told us about war strategy, as far as the invasion of Austria and the occupation of Vienna.

5 p.m. M. Pleven. He was rather critical about recognition. I argued as best I could and I think made some impression, especially when I told him what de Gaulle had said.

6–7 p.m. Press conference. Attended by British, American and French press. N. Bonnet, Minister of Information, in the chair. Massigli did very well, and much to my delight, found himself in the position of defending the British and American texts, explaining away the differences, skating over the weaknesses – all in the best style of a skilled H. of C. debater answering supplementaries. He really did awfully well and Murphy and I had very little to do except come in at the end and supplement it.

I made a joke – which went all right – and a sentimental appeal – which seemed to go also – and I think we have done the trick, at least so far as what goes out from here is concerned.

8 p.m. Dinner at the villa. General Giraud (and his A.D.C. – Panitowski), General Alexander (and his American A.D.C. – Ramsay), Murphy and our staff. Alex is staying the night – he is as charming, gracious, interesting and helpful as ever. Giraud was in terrific form – he likes Alexander enormously, since he treats him with courtesy and respect.

Fortunately, he left early – and enabled me to have an hour after dinner to discuss the latest developments in Operation 'A' with him [Alex].

Friday, 27 August 1943

9 a.m. Saw Bedell Smith. Operation 'A' is becoming a sort of Phillips Oppenheim affair![14] One of its minor troubles is that we receive a great number of telegrams marked 'Most Immediate'. The drill on these is that as soon as they are deciphered they are brought up, whatever the hour of the night may be. Last night we had three. The night before we had two. Poor Harold Caccia says that what with 'gippy tummy' (from which he has been suffering) and 'Most Immediates' he does not get any sleep at all.

The French press is *very good* indeed this morning on recognition – no criticism at all. This is very encouraging. I had some extremely nice messages coming in all the morning to the office from many Frenchmen – of some of whom I had never even heard – thanking my country and me personally for what has been done. I suppose they are partly 'blarney' – but I think some are really sincere.

[14] E. Phillips Oppenheim (1866–1947), author of 150 thrillers.

11 a.m. Office meeting.

1 p.m. Lunch with Giraud. A great affair. Admiral Cunningham and I the chief guests.

4 p.m. Meeting in Murphy's room on Operation 'A'.

5.45 p.m. Massigli called. In good heart. I congratulated him on his press conference, and said he ought to be a politician for good, not a civil servant. He is *very* pleased with himself.

8 p.m. Dinner at the villa. General and Madame la Générale Catroux; Sir Hugh Lloyd[15] (R.A.F.), Admiral Hewitt (U.S. Navy), Comtesse de Vogüe, Eric Duncannon (Madame la G. is a great snob!) and one or two others.

A successful, but trying party. Catroux, as usual, was charming.

Saturday, 28 August 1943

All morning on Operation 'A'. The plot is thickening, and the sub-plots and counter-plots and cross-plots increasing. London has gone quite mad!

4 p.m. Meeting of propaganda boys (with Murphy). Problem: how to tell them what to do without disclosing any secrets. Unanswerable – unanswered.

5 p.m. Mr [Frank] Gillard (B.B.C.) A nice fellow and very ready to take some hints. I tried to impress on him that the *only* news to which the American troops can listen is the B.B.C. so it really *does* matter what it says.

Hugh Fraser has turned up and is staying tonight and tomorrow. He likes to come to me for a bath, a bed, and some good food and drink – and I am glad to have him, for he has great charm.

Most of the evening and half the night in comings and goings on 'A'. I got to bed about 2 a.m.

Sunday, 29 August 1943

8 a.m. went round to Bedell Smith (whom I found at breakfast) with some of the early morning 'Most Immediates'. He showed me his batch of messages. I still think ours are sillier than his. After this I rested at the villa till 12.15, when I had to go (with Murphy) to make a communication to Guérin (Massigli's second-in-command) on 'A'. Roger Makins at last persuaded me to conform to my instructions (which I thought ridiculous) by proving to me that equally foolish communications were being made elsewhere by the Foreign Office and British Ambassadors all over the world.

3 p.m.–12 midnight. Motored out to a place where I often bathe (about half an hour from Algiers) and spent whole time on 'A'.

Back very exhausted.

[15] Air Vice-Marshal Sir Hugh Lloyd (b. 1895) was commander of Allied Coastal Air Forces, Mediterranean, 1943–4.

Monday, 30 August 1943

A very busy day – all on 'A'. Motored out again at 3.30 and returned about 7 p.m.

8 p.m. Dinner at villa. M. and Mme Guianchain,[16] Admiral Lemonnier (new Chief of Staff of French Navy), M. Lapie (French Colonial Office), Captain Wharton, R.N., Hon. Mrs Thorold (absolutely like her name – one of Lady Limerick's 'stooges') and so on.[17] Quite a success, but *very* tiring at the end of all this racket.

Extract from Operation 'A' memorandum
25–30 August 1943
The Second Dove

1. By 25 August the Italian Government had apparently become anxious at the delay in the return of General Castellano and decided to send a second delegation to Lisbon by air, consisting of General Zanussi, Principal Assistant to General Roatta,[18] and Signor Lansa di Trabia. In order to establish the bona fides of this party with the Allied authorities, they took with them General Carton de Wiart,[19] who had been held a prisoner in Italy since 1941. On the next day General Carton de Wiart called on His Majesty's Ambassador, who told him in broad terms the result of General Castellano's visit to Lisbon and said that unless instructed by London to do so, he saw no point in receiving General Zanussi as this might introduce unnecessary complications. General Carton de Wiart undertook to pass this on to General Zanussi at a secret meeting arranged for that night in a flat of a member of the staff of His Majesty's Embassy, when he would be told to remain in Lisbon until it was certain that there was no message for him.

2. Meanwhile, however, the President and the Prime Minister had agreed on the text of a comprehensive instrument of surrender of forty-two terms, and Lisbon were accordingly instructed by London to communicate this comprehensive text to General Zanussi with the explanation that it embodied both the short terms given to General Castellano and the political, economic and financial terms which General Castellano was warned to expect. On the morning of 27 August His Majesty's Ambassador carried out these instructions and

[16] Pierre Guianchain was the proprietor of the Hotel Saint-George just outside Algiers, used as his H.Q. by General Eisenhower.

[17] Pierre Lapie (b. 1901) was Governor of Chad, 1940–2. Captain Eric Wharton, R.N., was a member of the Naval Mission to Algiers. Mrs Phyllis Thorold, only daughter of 2nd Baron Ampthill, was working with the British Red Cross, whose vice-chairman was Angela, Countess of Limerick.

[18] Brigadier-General Giacomo Zanussi (1894–1966). Lieutenant-General Mario Roatta (1887–1968) was Chief of the Italian General Staff, 1941 and June–November 1943.

[19] Lieutenant-General Adrian Carton de Wiart, V.C. (1880–1963), had been shot down in April 1941 while on a British Military Mission to Yugoslavia. As a result of wounds in the First World War he had no left hand and wore an eyepatch, and was therefore a dangerously conspicuous choice by the Italians for this secret mission.

said that as the document was a long one, General Zanussi could take it away and study it, and that they could meet again during the afternoon. At that later meeting General Zanussi said that he understood he had no alternative but to place the conditions in the hands of his Government with the least possible delay. Speaking unofficially, however, he said that he viewed with regret and alarm the decision to force Italy to make a public surrender, and at one stage suggested that whereas the Italian Government might have no difficulty in accepting the short military conditions handed to General Castellano, they might have more difficulty in accepting the comprehensive instrument. He consequently urged that the time-table arranged between General Smith and General Castellano should be retarded so as to give his Government time to have received and studied the comprehensive conditions. He also said that further German troops had been coming into Italy since General Castellano had left Rome and that their total was now fifteen–sixteen divisions, though not all of them were up to full strength. Before the close of the meeting General Zanussi had agreed to the arrangements to get him back to Italy by an aeroplane leaving early the following morning from Lisbon to Gibraltar and thence via Sicily to Rome.

3. Meanwhile in Algiers A.F.H.Q. had also been receiving news from independent sources that the strength of the German forces in Italy was daily increasing. All the Commanders concerned, both British and American, were united in the opinion that the military difficulties involved in the proposed landing operations in the Naples area were so great that the value of an armistice concluded and announced before the landing could not be exaggerated, and I had therefore telegraphed on 26 August to London urging that if the introduction of the comprehensive terms of surrender caused such difficulties as to preclude the signature of an armistice, we should be content with obtaining an immediate signature for the shorter military terms communicated to General Castellano. On the 27th our anxieties were partially relieved at the receipt of a telegram from the Deputy Prime Minister saying that if the Italian emissary was only authorised to accept the short terms because his Government did not know of the comprehensive document when giving him his instructions, His Majesty's Government agreed that if military exigencies absolutely required it, he should be asked to sign the shorter document, thus bringing the armistice into effect, on the clear understanding, however, that this should be regarded merely as the military terms of the armistice and that it should be replaced later by the comprehensive document. Carefully handled, this formula could be made to serve. Further, on 28 August after a full conference at A.F.H.Q. at which Admiral Cunningham, Mr Murphy and myself were present, the Commander-in-Chief decided to send a telegram to the Combined Chiefs of Staff for the President and Prime Minister asking for

discretion to sign the short terms as a matter of military necessity. At the same time I was asked to send a telegram to H.M. Minister at the Vatican *via* London to ensure that the original arrangements made with General Castellano for conveying Italian acceptance of the military armistice by wireless should be rigidly adhered to. This was done partly to avoid any confusion and partly because General Zanussi had, unlike General Castallano, failed to bring any written introduction from the British or Italian authorities. Finally, arrangements were made for General Zanussi to be flown from Gibraltar to Algiers rather than to Sicily, and to be taken to a camp some miles out of the town where it was hoped his presence could be kept secret.

4. The necessity for maintaining the secrecy of these negotiations was of their essence, and we, as no doubt His Majesty's Ambassador at Lisbon, were in constant apprehension of some leakage. For instance to house General Zanussi in the Algiers area without his presence becoming known to servants or batmen and through them to an ever widening circle is not easy. A.F.H.Q. turned to the British in their difficulty, and the same British organisation as had provided wireless communication once again fulfilled their task with tact and success. With these anxieties on our hands, I was naturally dismayed on the evening of 28 August to receive a telegram from the Foreign Office requesting me to communicate to the French Committee of Liberation an abstract of the comprehensive surrender terms and invite them to be present at the signature. Similar communications had been or were to be made to a number of other Governments and it was with pardonable misgiving that I and my American colleague made a joint communication at noon on 29 August to the French Committee. We were at pains to point out that no question of signature had yet arisen and that our communication must be regarded as of the utmost secrecy.

5. In the afternoon of that day the Chief of Staff invited my American colleague and myself to visit General Zanussi with him to determine what the next step should be. We found General Zanussi a short, well-covered and talkative man of middle age, who made up for his absence of written credentials by the apparent sincerity with which he entered into all plans for compounding with the Allies as soon as possible. After some discussion, he decided to write a letter to General Ambrosio recommending that an immediate decision should be taken to accept the short military terms and that General Castellano should go to Sicily as had been contemplated in the arrangements made with him in Lisbon in the event of the Italians accepting our conditions. As a precaution it was arranged that this letter should be taken to Rome the following day not by General Zanussi himself, but by his companion, Signor Lanza di Trabia. The comprehensive terms of surrender were also removed from General Zanussi until after his companion's departure in order to ensure that their arrival in Rome should not be used by the Italians as a pretext for procrastination.

6. 30 August was a day of suspense, for at midnight the time limit arranged with General Castellano ran out. But the Commander-in-Chief was encouraged to receive early in the morning a telegram from the President acknowledging his cable of 28 August and saying that he was authorised 'to proceed with the military terms, obtain signature and then transmit the comprehensive document to the Italian representatives'. Thereupon tentative arrangements were nevertheless put in hand for the Chief of Staff, Mr Murphy and myself as well as General Zanussi, to leave for Sicily early the following morning. These arrangements were confirmed when late in the day we heard that General Castellano intended to arrive in Sicily on 31 August, as had been planned in Lisbon.

Tuesday, 30 August 1943

Breakfast 5 a.m.! Left airport with Bedell Smith and Murphy (I brought John Wyndham to look after me) at 6 a.m.

Arrived Sicily 10.30 – a slower machine.

I will write up the events of the day and give them to you one day with the rest of Operation'A' [for the extract from the Operation 'A' memorandum relating to 31 August to 3 September 1943, see p. 201].

The only thing I can say in favour of today was that we managed a good bathe and a nice dinner with Alex (General Alexander is gradually getting his charm over to the Americans, although they still find him a little odd – something quite out of their experience).

It is not quite so hot, and there are not quite so many flies. Four women (Y.M.C.A. or Red Cross or something) are reported to have turned up. But the rule is still to bathe naked – and will be as long as General Alex is in command.

I have a nice tent, with electric light and a telephone!

September

Wednesday, 1 September 1943

Went with Murphy to Palermo for the day – partly to see AMGOT H.Q. at work and partly to do some sightseeing. We got a plane at 9 a.m. and arrived at 10 a.m. I will not describe the sightseeing because you can read about Palermo in any book. We had time to see Capella Palatina and the church at Monreale (a mountain just outside Palermo). They are both exquisite – twelfth century – a curious mixture of Gothic and Saracenic art, with the most wonderful mosaics I have seen (except at Revenna). They are real gems.

We lunched at Francis Rennell's magnificent villa (where we found Con Benson,[1] looking very ill as he has had a bad go of malaria).

We saw Colonel Poletti (Deputy-Governor of New York State) sitting in a still more magnificent palazzo, and ruling Palermo as if it were New York (you learn a lot at Tammany Hall!),[2] and we called on the Cardinal Archbishop. Quite a day. I was very favourably impressed by the work AMGOT is doing. It has really been a great piece of organisation, in view of the difficulties, and the critics at home have no idea at all of how great they are. Back at 7 p.m. (our aeroplane stood by for us) and went over (with Bedell Smith) to dine at Alex's mess.

I am staying this time in an American camp here. It is just a sort of advanced post for General Eisenhower (who is actually in Algiers) and for guests and visitors.

Thursday, 2 September 1943

A very exciting day, which will be described later [see p. 201]. Thank God we got a bathe at 6 p.m. all right. Otherwise all day in the camp.

I am writing this at about 10 p.m. in my tent – I have in this way

[1] Group-Captain Constantine Benson (d. 1960) was chief of the Allied Military Government Section, Eighth Army, 1943–5.

[2] Lieutenant-Colonel Charles Poletti (b. 1903) was chief of the Allied Military Government Section, U.S. Seventh Army, 1943–5. He soon prompted a song at a local theatrical revue: '*Charlie Poletti, Charlie Poletti, meno ciarle e più spaghetti*' – 'less talk and more spaghetti'.

managed to get this letter diary up to date. I was afraid I should have to let it go, and I fear it is not very interesting. But I am keeping notes for the full story to be worked up later on.

I have absolutely decided on my course. I purposely left Makins and Caccia behind, they are both Foreign Office officials, and it is necessary to forget all that. I have taken my decision, and I do not at all mind what happens. But it is equally important to take negative as positive decisions, and there are some telegrams[3] from my colleagues in London which are going to remain in my red box and will *not* be shown to Bedell Smith or General Alexander until (I hope) the die is cast. General Alexander is a very good and reliable man – and I am quite sure that his military judgment is sound and balanced.

We spent all the day at the camp – but Murphy, John and I managed to escape for a bathe – the water was deliciously warm. It is now about 11.30 p.m., and as I have nothing more that I can tell you, I will go to sleep.

Friday, 3 September 1943

All day at the camp. Except for motoring over a few miles to lunch at General Alexander's camp, we have not left it – even for a swim. I am writing this at 10 p.m. We have been *completely* successful.

This is the anniversary of the declaration of war – four weary years. It has been in our minds all day.

The landing on the toe of Italy took place this morning. General Alexander has just shown me the latest reports, which look satisfactory. But, of course, the Germans will not bother much about this manoeuvre – their strength lies elsewhere in the country – particularly in the north and round Rome.

We seem to have been ages in this camp. Actually, it is the end of the fourth day. It is a delightful spot – a twenty- or thirty-acre olive grove – old trees and some carob trees also.

The whole enclosed by a stone wall. The olives are planted a good distance apart – and the rows also are fairly wide – like great avenues. This allows for the cultivation of the area in the normal way, and a corn crop has just been cut off it, leaving the fresh stubble.

The tents are quite comfortable – electric light and telephone. The American camp commandant must (I think) have run an hotel in civil life. The food is excellent – especially breakfast.

Extract from Operation 'A' memorandum
31 August–3 September 1943
The First Dove's Return

1. We reached Fairfield Advanced Camp, placed in an olive grove near Syracuse, in Sicily, at eleven o'clock on the morning of 31 August

[3] Pressing me to obtain Italian agreement to the 'long terms'.

to find that General Castellano had already arrived with Signor Montanari. A long discussion took place lasting until 4 p.m. at which neither Mr Murphy nor I were present. But we later heard that the Italian position had changed considerably since General Castellano had met General Smith in Lisbon, and even since our talks with General Zanussi at Algiers. This was due to the substantial increase of German reinforcements in Italy, there now being some nineteen German divisions on the mainland, with more troops pouring across the Alps. At the end of the discussion it was decided to allow the whole party except General Castellano to return to Rome where they would do their best, in view of what they had learned of Allied power and intentions, to persuade their Government to accept the short terms of the military armistice. The comprehensive document was wisely kept in reserve, since it was felt that its introduction at this stage might only lead to further delays which were not in the military interests of the Allies. At the same time it was clear from the talks that, although the Italian Government might clutch at any pretext to obtain delay, the main point that interested them was not the terms of this or that document but the relative power of Allied and German forces. In the evening a conference was held in General Alexander's caravan to consider if any special military action could be taken to hearten the Italians. After some discussion it was decided to recommend to the Allied Commander-in-Chief that an American airborne division should be used to land near Rome and thus bolster up the morale of the four Italian divisions in the neighbourhood. It was also recommended that this decision should be communicated to the Italians by the special radio communication between Algiers and the Italian High Command. The next day a telegram was received from General Eisenhower approving the plan and saying that a message had accordingly been sent to the Italians.

2. Otherwise 1 September passed without incident in Sicily, waiting for some message from the party that had left Rome the previous evening. But it was not everywhere so uneventful. When passing through Lisbon, General Zanussi had deposited in the safe keeping of the Italian Minister, Signor Prunas,[4] two packets containing various useful information about the Germans in Italy, such as their order of battle. Signor Prunas was an ardent believer in the necessity of Italy making her peace with the Allies and General Zanussi had arranged with him that these packets should only be given up to the person who delivered a personal note of hand from himself. While in Algiers he had suggested to A.F.H.Q. that these packets might be of interest and A.F.H.Q. had asked me whether I could trust any of my staff with the mission of obtaining them. With this purpose in view, Mr Dupree

[4] Renato Prunas (1892–1951) was Secretary-General of the Italian Ministry of Foreign Affairs until 1946.

arrived in Lisbon on 1 September with the ostensible purpose of seeing the Press Attaché on urgent Ministry of Information business. Actually, after consulting H.M. Ambassador and taking various precautions in an endeavour to cover his tracks, he presented himself at the Italian Legation at 8 p.m. in the guise of a Spaniard. After two minutes' wait during which he was the object of the curious attention of a host of secretaries, he was ushered into the Italian Minister's room where he received the two packages from the trembling hands of Signor Prunas.

3. The day also ended well in Sicily, for at 10 p.m. news came from Rome to say that 'The answer is in the affirmative'. On the morning of 2 September the Italian Delegation duly arrived at Termini Airport near Palermo and were brought to Fairfield Camp. However, on being asked whether they were now ready to sign the armistice, they unexpectedly replied that they had no authority to do so. The Italian Government had accepted the plan for the landing of the airborne division near Rome and desired them to carry on military talks. On hearing what had happened, I sent a message to warn General Alexander and to suggest that the moment had come when some display of firmness on our side was essential. General Alexander soon arrived in full dress, booted and spurred for the occasion. In a short and formal interview he expressed his amazement at the behaviour of the Italian Delegation. They had been sent back to Rome for the express purpose of getting their Government's acceptance of the armistice. They should have returned with full authority. They had better seek that authority immediately. He then left the tent where the discussions were taking place and a formal message was passed to General Smith for the information of those present that he had returned to his headquarters. General Alexander's intervention had the desired effect. The Italian Delegation drafted this message from General Castellano to Marshal Badoglio:

> Part I. The Commander-in-Chief, Allied Forces, will not discuss any military matters whatever unless a document of acceptance of the armistice conditions is signed. As operations against the Peninsula will begin very shortly with landings, this signature is extremely urgent.
>
> Part II. The Allied Commander-in-Chief would accept the signature of General Castellano if authorised by the Italian Government. Please send this authorization within the day by this means and give urgently to Minister Osborne [H.M. Minister at the Holy See] a declaration that I have been so authorised.
>
> Part III. The Commander-in-Chief will operate with the arrangements already explained by me and with sufficient forces to ensure the degree of safety that we desire. I am personally convinced that the operative intentions of the Allies are such as to ensure the

needs which we discussed in the conference on the morning of 2 September.

We heard subsequently that this message reached Rome at nine o'clock that evening.

4. While we were going through these anxieties over whether the Italian Government would be prepared to sign and announce the military clauses of the armistice at the most favourable moment to the Allied cause (that is, just before our intended landing on Naples), arrangements were being put in motion for the attendance of representatives of the Governments of the Dominions and other United Nations at what was hoped would be the official ceremony for the signature of the comprehensive terms of surrender of which they had been warned. As to this, I had already pointed out in a telegram of 30 August that for my part I should be very surprised if there was any chance of getting the long terms settled and signed by a responsible Italian authority before our intended attack in the Naples area. I had also emphasised that we should be lucky to get the short military terms settled by that date, for the task that faced us was to embark upon the conquest of a country with inferior forces opposed by ever increasing German armaments, and at the same time to impose upon the country we were invading unconditional surrender. It would therefore be most embarrassing if a number of representatives were to arrive in order to witness a ceremony when there was a strong chance of neither the bride nor the bridegroom being present. Nevertheless I was told in reply that all the considerations I put forward had been weighed but that it had been decided for overriding political reasons that the Dominions and Allied Governments interested should be associated at any signature, and I was therefore asked to do all I could to facilitate the reception of the delegates which any of these Governments might wish to send. To this end the South African, Australian, Canadian, Yugoslav and Greek Governments in fact nominated representatives.

5. One of these, the South African representative, General Theron,[5] had arrived on the scene in Algiers. General Eisenhower decided to take him to Sicily early on 3 September and thus put him in a most profitable position as compared to the other Allies concerned. Fortunately, General Theron was a man of good sense. He quickly understood that there was no immediate question of a signature of the comprehensive terms and that if the Italian Delegation received authority to sign the short terms his presence as the only representative of the Dominions and United Nations might lead to complications. It was therefore agreed that he had not been there! For the rest, the day was one of ups and downs. In the morning a telegram was received from Marshal Badoglio acknowledging General Castellano's message

[5] Major-General François Henri Theron (1891–1967) was commander of South African forces in the Middle East.

of the previous day and saying that 'the affirmative reply given on 1 September contained implicit acceptance of the armistice terms'. This telegram did not make any mention of the request for a declaration to be given to the British Minister at the Vatican, and we were further perplexed by a later signal from Rome cancelling the telegram without any explanation. As appeared later, the reason may have been that the three parts of General Castellano's telegram of 2 September had not all been correctly decyphered and considered in Rome. Whatever the reason, it was not till about 4 p.m. that the revised reply came to us. It said:

> General Castellano is authorised by the Italian Government to sign acceptance of the armistice conditions. The declaration which you asked for [i.e. from H.M. Minister at the Vatican] will be delivered today.

After receipt of this message the remaining formalities were quickly completed, and at 4.30 p.m. the military armistice was signed by General Smith for General Eisenhower and by General Castellano for Marshal Badoglio, in the presence of Signor Montanari, Brigadier Strong, Commodore Dick, Mr Murphy and myself. Thereupon, in accordance with the instructions which General Eisenhower had received on 30 August, the full surrender terms were transmitted to General Castellano.

Saturday, 4 September 1943

Returned to Algiers with Murphy, Bedell Smith, Commodore Dick, Brigadier Strong and others. John came with me. We left about 2.30 and arrived at about 7 p.m.

The morning was spent in conferences. General Alexander came over from his camp. The news of the landings in south Italy which began yesterday seems good. Of course no serious German opposition has yet been encountered. The Italian population were friendly and welcomed our troops most warmly.

As you can imagine, there was a good deal to do with Roger and Harold Caccia, and I am just finishing this off before going to sleep. I find these air journeys of 600–700 miles back and forward rather tiring. I expect we shall leave again tomorrow or Monday.

Sunday, 5 September 1943

I woke early this morning – the result of camp life. But it was rather delicious lying in a real bed and having a hot bath. Even a week without such luxuries makes one appreciate them.

After bath and shaving, I got into bed again for my breakfast and while waiting for it, lay half dozing thinking of you and the children and Birch Grove – and all the things I love best. I do wish you could have had a summer here, in this land of sun and nudity – the things you like so much. But you would have been like a lobster yourself.

Dearest Dorothy – I do think so much about you always.

We have had rather a heavy day in the office. I found that even in an absence of five days a number of rather important things had come up which Makins felt he must keep for me to settle. Also, my colleagues in London have sent me a number of rather foolish telegrams, to which I have concocted answers. I have more or less arranged to come back on General Alexander's staff when I am thrown out of my job!

But more sense is coming from Washington now, and when the P.M. returns fresh he will be able to communicate some of it to the Cabinet in London.

It's extraordinary how warlike the ex-conscientious objectors (like Morrison) and the critics of under forty (who can talk in Parliament but seem too proud to fight) can become at the safe distance of several thousand miles. I wish some of them would come and try landing on a defended and mined beach out of a barge, in which one has been three or four days at sea (and sick half that time) in the middle of the night!

Monday, 6 September 1943

9 a.m. Chief of Staff.

10 a.m. Air Vice-Marshal Wigglesworth (recovering from an air accident – so I went to see him on his sofa).

The usual day of interviews and conferences, including a long one at 5–7.30 at A.F.H.Q. on propaganda, news release, censorship, etc.

A minor trouble has occurred about our paper *Union Jack*, which we were printing in Constantine and want now to print in Algiers (for base troops) and Catania (Sicily) for forward troops. The editor is Captain Cudlipp (Hugh Cudlipp of the *Daily Mirror*[6] – who used to write those tremendous leading articles at the time of Munich). In order to smooth it out, I had to see M. Bonnet (the French Brendan Bracken). He was quite reasonable, and we reached a settlement without much difficulty.

Dined with Admiral Cunningham – a party of generals this time, including the Quartermaster-General from the War Office. They all played that football game where you turn a piece of wood to make your men kick (a game the children had) and this kept everyone happy till nearly midnight.

Tuesday, 7 September 1943

I have decided to stay in Algiers for the moment as there is a lot which I can only do from here. Very critical days are approaching, and it is extremely difficult to work things properly because all the commanders are necessarily scattered. The distances are very great and

[6] Captain Hugh Cudlipp (b. 1913) was editor of the *Sunday Pictorial*, 1937–40, and later chairman of Daily Mirror Newspapers Ltd.

communications are the great problem. If one stays here, one is sure of quick communication. If one goes to one of the advanced H.Q., one is nearer some of the commanders but one has great telegraphic delays. Anyway, I have some French business to keep me a day or two, apart from anything else.

10 a.m. General Gale.

10.30 a.m. The newly appointed Mayor of Algiers. He is not at all my idea of a mayor, but he was very polite and very declamatory in excellent French. He is, of course, a strong Gaullist.

11 a.m. Commodore [F. E. P.] Hutton, the successor to Admiral Morse as Commodore Algiers. He is responsible for the port of Algiers and any other Algerian ports which are in our control. I am responsible for trying to look after merchant seamen, and prevent them getting drunk and breaking up the town – a heavy task. But our hostels and clubs and Y.M.C.A. activities are now going fairly well and have made a lot of improvement.

A mass of excited telegrams – usually contradictory – continue to arrive from London and Washington. We do our best.

We had a heavy afternoon and early evening; a little supper with Murphy (Norman Davis, American Red Cross, was there) and a conference with Chief of Staff at 9 p.m. till about 10.30 p.m.

Wednesday, 8 September 1943

I am writing this at 7.30 a.m. in my bedroom. This is the day! I will write no more until midnight.

This has been an extraordinary day – the culminating point of Operation 'A' (or Armistice) of which one day I will give you a real account.

I can only say that it has been like the most absurdly improbable detective story that ever was written.

Extract from Operation 'A' memorandum
Suspense and Climax
4–9 September 1943

1. There remained only five days to complete such work as was possible for the co-ordination of military plans. The most important of these was for the landing of an Allied airborne division in the Rome area, which for its success would depend upon certain airfields being held by the Italians and upon transport being provided for these troops to move rapidly into Rome. Arrangements had also to be made for the announcement and publication of the armistice at an agreed time. Immediately after dinner on 3 September military talks began and lasted through the night. The next day, 4 September, a request was sent for a Military Mission to come over from Italy. The proposal was that General Castellano should head the Mission and that he should have at

his disposal an interpreter, three other Army officers including one specialist in German matters, one senior Naval and one senior Air representative. In addition, representatives of the Information Services in Algiers, who had been sent for the previous evening, had a prolonged conference with General Alexander and the Italian Delegation. As a result, it was decided that Marshal Badoglio and General Eisenhower should simultaneously announce the conclusion of the armistice on the wireless at 6.30 p.m. local time, on the day, to be called X Day, of the landing of the airborne division in the Rome area, and that the day should be made known to the Italians by the B.B.C. Italian Service broadcasting two short talks on the subject of Nazi activity in the Argentine between 11.30 a.m. and 12.45 p.m. G.M.T.

2. After these military and propaganda discussions, arrangements were made for one member of the Italian Delegation to return to Rome to clinch the proposals that had been worked out. The days passed. On the night of 7 September General Taylor,[7] the Commanding Officer of the airborne division, went by corvette to Italy and made his way to Rome with complete authority in respect of airborne operations. At the same time, two propaganda experts went to join the airborne division in Sicily in order that they might arrive at the outset in Rome and make contact with the Italian Ministry of Information. The Germans appeared to have no knowledge of what was brewing. At least they made no move against the Badoglio Government. But they may have had some instinct that it would be as well for German forces in the vicinity of Rome to move nearer the capital so as to be able more easily to overawe the Italian Government.

3. This move nearly proved the undoing of most of the work of the last month. At eleven o'clock on the morning of 8 September, which was the day on which the airborne division was due to attack, the Chief of Staff called me urgently to A.F.H.Q. to show me a message just received from Marshal Badoglio through our special wireless means. It said:

> Owing to changes in the situation which has seriously deteriorated and the presence of German forces in the Rome area the announcement of the armistice is no longer possible since the capital would be occupied and the Italian Government taken over forcibly by the Germans. The operation (concerning the airborne division) no longer possible as I lack the forces to guarantee the airfields. (signed) Badoglio.

In a further wireless message General Taylor said that the following further reasons had been given him why the airborne operation was impossible.

[7] Brigadier-General Maxwell Taylor (b. 1901) was Chief of Staff to Artillery Commander, U.S. Eighty-second Airborne Division, 1943, Chief of Staff to Acting Deputy-President of the Allied Control Commission in Italy, 1943–4.

Irreplaceable lack of gasolene and munitions and new German dispositions. The summary of the situation as stated by the Italian authorities was that the Germans have 12,000 troops in the Tiber area and the Panzer Grenadier Division increased by attachments to 24,000. The Germans have stopped supplies of gasolene and munitions so that the Italian divisions are virtually immobilised and have munitions only for a few hours of combat. Shortages make impossible success of the full defence of Rome and the provision of logistical aid promised to the airborne troops. The latter are not wanted at present as their arrival would bring an immediate attack on Rome.

4. These messages had been relayed from Algiers to General Eisenhower, who was in conference at Bizerta with the three British Allied Commanders. After a short dicussion, General Smith decided to send an urgent telegram to General Eisenhower saying that we strongly felt that the plans for the day should be gone through with notwithstanding the Italians' attempt to run out. A similar message was sent to the combined Chiefs of Staff. At 2 p.m. I again saw General Bedell Smith, who told me that he had already heard from General Eisenhower that he and the three British Commanders fully agreed with our view that our arrangements for announcing the armistice should carry on. But the proposal to send the airborne division had had to be abandoned. General Eisenhower had also sent a strong and even threatening message to General Badoglio demanding that the Italians should carry out their signed undertaking and announce the armistice as had been arranged. This is it:

Part I. I intend to broadcast the existence of an armistice at the hour originally planned. If you or any part of your armed forces fail to co-operate as previously agreed, I will publish to the world a full record of this affair. Today is X Day and I expect you to do your part.

Part II. I do not accept your message of this morning postponing the armistice. Your accredited representative has signed an agreement with me, and the sole hope of Italy is bound up in your adherence to that agreement. On your earnest representation the airborne operations are temporarily suspended.

Part III. You have sufficient troops near Rome to secure the temporary safety of the city, but I require full information on which to plan earliest the airborne operations. Send General Taylor to Bizerta at once by aeroplane. Notify in advance time of arrival.

Part IV. Plans have been made on the assumption that you were acting in good faith and we have been prepared to carry out future operations on that basis. Failure now on your part to carry out the full obligations of the signed agreement will have most serious consequences for your country. No future action of yours could then restore any confidence whatever in your good faith and consequently the disillusion of your Government and nation would ensue.

5. About five o'clock I heard that a telegram had been received from the Prime Minister and the President which by giving General Eisenhower full authority to go ahead without regard to the Italians, confirmed the arrangements which had been put in hand. Among the most important of these was a plan to ensure that Marshal Badoglio's announcement in Italian of the armistice to the Italian people should be broadcast at all costs. To this end the Information Services in Algiers had made a record of the Italian text which was in our possession in case the Marshal failed himself to go on the air in Rome.

6. At 6.30 I went to the Headquarters of the Information Services in Algiers to listen to the Algiers broadcast and to find out whether anything was picked up from Rome. I was told at once that Rome had been off the air since six o'clock. So we listened to the record of General Eisenhower's voice which came badly at the first reading, but better at the second. A declaration by Marshal Badoglio was then broadcast from Algiers. The text of this declaration had been given to General Castellano by the Marshal as the declaration he intended to make.

7. It then only remained to be seen whether Marshal Badoglio would at any later time speak his own part himself and it was with considerable relief that we heard that at 7.45 p.m. Rome radio had in fact broadcast the announcement of the armistice by the Marshal in exactly the terms which had been agreed upon. The explanation he later gave us for his delay was that he had missed the reception of the agreed wireless signal, i.e. the two short talks on Nazi activity in the Argentine, and that Part IV of General Eisenhower's telegram had been delayed en route. He said that he would have made his proclamation as requested without any pressure being necessary and that the pledge he had given was sufficient. But he added that excessive haste had found our preparations incomplete. Nevertheless, we could derive some satisfaction from what had been achieved in the last anxious weeks. The hazards of the enterprise which was before us were still great. When our troops landed in the early hours of the next morning, 9 September, in the Naples area they would be faced on the Italian mainland by formidable German forces. But subsequent events had proved how solid were the advantages to be gained. The surrender of the Italian fleet, the practicability of widespread landings in Calabria and Apulia, the disorganisation of the German supply lines, and the morale, as well as the material results of the defection of an ally – all this seems now to us to be ample compensation for the excitements and anxieties of recent weeks.

I had also to let the French know what was happening. At 5.30 p.m. Mr Murphy and I had seen Massigli and told him the news of the military armistice. As I rather expected this filled him with dismay – not, of course, about the result, but because the French Committee had not been informed. I felt rather impatient at his attitude, but it was clear that he meant to try and help, so I told him as much as I could of the story to underline the importance of secrecy from the military point of view. I also told him quite frankly about the day's happenings and the possibility that the whole thing would fall down.

At 6 p.m. Murphy and I went from Massigli to de Gaulle. He received the information with more self-control than Massigli, and with a certain sardonic humour he congratulated us that the war between our countries and Italy was at an end. He considered that France was still at war with Italy as he was not party to the armistice. When I observed that military secrecy and necessity should appeal to him as a soldier, he said, 'I am not a soldier.' I was tempted to ask why he dressed himself up in those peculiar clothes which surely no one would choose to wear unless military necessity imposed them upon him. As we left de Gaulle, we saw Massigli coming in, looking very frightened.

[Diary continues] However, the announcement was made at 6.30 and 7.45 p.m. Badoglio came on the Rome radio. At 10 p.m. a press conference. At 11 p.m. I had an hour with Massigli – the crazy French much hurt in their feelings because we had not consulted them. Poor dears, their inferiority complex is dreadful. I told him firmly that if the Committee were foolish enough to lodge any protest, my countrymen would form a very poor view of the French. We had brought off a military stroke – to save lives and make at least more favourable the chances of a very hazardous operation – and for that *secrecy* was absolutely necessary.

Finally, a sort of party at Murphy's and home at midnight.

That's the end of this letter which goes with all my love to you all.

Thursday, 9 September 1943

I am afraid my last letter ended on rather a confused, but I hope not hysterical, note. We have had rather an exciting time during the last few weeks, culminating in the extraordinary armistice – the biggest bluff in history! I will try to send you a proper story later on.

Of course, you have long ago seen all the news and there is no good in my repeating it here. I am afraid that our people at home will think that it means the end of the war in Italy. Of course, it really means the beginning – but under more favourable conditions than seemed possible a month or two ago.

The Germans have large forces in Italy, to which they have recently been adding considerably. Italy is therefore really assuming the proportions of a 'Second Front'. I have a strong feeling that the Germans mean to shorten their line very much in Russia, perhaps even abandoning all the Crimea and the Ukraine. This would give them many extra divisions for the western war.

After all these excitements, I was rather tired and spent most of the day in bed – at least till the early afternoon.

4 p.m. Propaganda meeting.

5 p.m. Massigli round again to see me and Bob Murphy.

He is very excited still but we did our best to comfort him. If we can think of some gesture to please the French, it would be a good thing. They are really as touchy as a divorced woman about their 'reputation' and their 'position in European society'.

If they could get a ticket for the Great Powers Enclosure they would be happy.

6 p.m. Went out to bathe. It is still very hot and sticky in Algiers and an evening bathe is very refreshing.

Friday, 10 September 1943

The first news is pretty good – the landings have been made successfully and the Italian Navy look like coming over without difficulty.[8] This is, of course, of great strategical importance, because it will release the battle fleet for the eastern war.

9.30 a.m. Chief of Staff.

10.30 a.m. Herbert (British economic adviser).

12 noon. Rabino (British financial adviser).

1 p.m. Lunch villa. Count Grabski (Polish Consul). Mr Gill (British Council), Lieutenant Lloyd[9] (author of *How Green Was My Valley* – now in Welsh Guards).

2.45 p.m. Massigli again – recovering slowly.

5 p.m. Meeting on future organisation of North African Economic Board. It has been decided to turn this into a purely civilian organisation, under the two Ministers, instead of under the Commander-in-Chief. General Gale and General Hughes[10] at the meeting, and everything was agreed.

6 p.m. Bathed.

8.15 p.m. Dinner with Chief of Staff (Bedell Smith) followed by a cinema performance. The film was *Goodbye, Mr Chips*.

[8] Allied troops landed at Salerno, thirty miles south of Naples, on the night of 8–9 September. This was, in Churchill's words, 'the most daring amphibious operation we have yet launched'. It was at the limit of range of fighter air cover and was bitterly contested by the Germans. Not till 16 September was the bridgehead consolidated, and the battle northwards to Naples could continue. Taranto was taken without difficulty on the 9th, and the Italian naval vessels in the harbour there came over to the Allies.

[9] Lieutenant Richard Lloyd (1907–83) wrote under the *nom-de-plume* of Richard Llewellyn.

[10] Major-General I. T. P. Hughes (1897–1962) was head of Allied Military Liaison, Cairo, 1943–4.

General 'Boy' Browning[11] was at the dinner and came to the villa after the film for a drink and a talk. He is a charming man and a very good soldier.

I have had Harold Caccia at Tunis during recent days, in case he could be of use to General Alexander or Admiral A. B. Cunningham. He returned today, with quite interesting news of things at advanced H.Q. I have been torn between going up to Tunis (John Wyndham is there, and I have my old rooms ready at the Consular Residence) and staying at Algiers, where (so long as the Chief of Staff is here) a great deal of the centre of power remains and great harm can be done unless one is careful. However, tonight things are beginning to work out and we decided to go up.

Saturday, 11 September 1943

Left aerodrome 7.30 a.m. Party consisted of General Bedell Smith, Murphy, one or two H.Q. officers and myself.

Reached Bizerta about 10 a.m. Motored to General Alex's H.Q. (Command Post only – his main H.Q. being still in Sicily).

The admiral soon arrived (he also has advanced H.Q. in Bizerta). Very pleased with himself. Then General Eisenhower (from Tunis, where he has an advanced post) and Air Chief Marshal Tedder, whose H.Q. are now at Tunis also.

The Commanders-in-Chief have a daily conference during the present operations. Murphy and I were present, and the proceedings were full of interest, combined with a good deal of *badinage* between the services.

1 p.m. Flew with General Smith and Murphy to Tunis (about 100 kilometres by road).

1.30 p.m. Lunch at General Eisenhower's H.Q.

3 p.m. General Eisenhower held press conference – just why, I don't know, but he loves a press conference. I must say I am always in agonies of apprehension as to what he may say.

After the conference the Americans had a ceremony and presented medals to each other.

5 p.m. I had taken the precaution of sending John and a car up to Tunis some days ago. This makes me more independent. Motored back to Bizerta (about two hours – a very hot and dusty road – with convoys all the time and therefore a slow road).

Dined and stayed the night with General Alex. He is at last driven into a house (or rather barracks) in a town instead of his caravan in a desert, a mountain, a vineyard or an olive grove.

We had a good talk on the general [political] situation, which is still very obscure.

[11] Lieutenant-General Frederick Browning (1896–1965) commanded the First Airborne Division, 1941–3, and was to be Deputy Commander at Arnhem.

Sunday, 12 September 1943

Left for Tunis by car about 8.30. Drove to Consulate, on the way to the Consular Residence at La Marsa (outside Tunis) to pick up telegrams. (When I am away I arrange for all important telegrams sent from London to be 'repeated' to Tunis. We have a staff of cypher clerks there, so that I get these telegrams just as soon as if I were in Algiers. One can in this way arrange to have telegrams 'repeated' to anywhere where there is a British Consul with the right cypher.)

I found a good deal had come in – including a very nice one from the P.M. This (*a*) gave me some very good news for the French and (*b*) a pleasant personal message.

Lunched with Consul-General and Mrs Monypenny. Mrs M. is a very pretty, middle-class, efficient Glasgow woman. She has excellent taste, a good cuisine, and a power of ordering everybody about for her own convenience which (if her husband could but rise to it) would make her a kind of second Lady Willingdon.

She has furnished the large Consular Residence with charming and appropriate furniture, all 'requisitioned'. There are excellent modern beds – wireless sets, linen, cutlery, etc., also 'requisitioned' – her own silver and glass (brought by car from Tangier) and so on. My bedroom is transformed; a new bathroom has been fitted; I have my old sitting-room. John and Mrs M. form a sort of mutual admiration society (they both have the same qualities) and conspire as to what or whom they can plunder next.

3 p.m. Called on Massigli, who is staying with General Mast (Resident-General of Tunisia) for a few days with my message from the P.M. He was delighted and relieved beyond measure.

Some more telegrams on my return, which kept me busy till 5 p.m., when I went to General Eisenhower's H.Q. for a chat.

6–7 p.m. Bathed. The sea here is really like a warm bath – almost too warm. It is a good deal hotter in Tunisia than in Algiers – but I find it a drier and less oppressive heat.

Dined at General Eisenhower's H.Q. General Whiteley (Deputy Chief of Staff, A.F.H.Q.), Bob Murphy, and General Mason-MacFarlane who had just arrived by plane. I will explain about him when I come to tomorrow. Now I shall go to bed.

Monday, 13 September 1943

I am writing this at the end of quite an eventful day, at least quite an occasion for me, for I have not managed to get quite such a sense of the 'campaign' before.

We are in the Hotel Bologna, Taranto. The party consists of General Mason-MacFarlane, General Max Taylor (U.S.), Bob Murphy and self. At the C.-in-C.'s Conference at Bizerta on Saturday it was decided to form a mission of some kind to try to get into touch with Badoglio and the Italian Government, believed to be in Brindisi.

Murphy and I were asked to go. After discussion, it was decided to make it a 'service' or 'military' mission, with us as 'advisers'. I thought this wisest, because I have no guidance at all as to the line H.M.G. or the U.S. Government want to take towards the Italian Government. We made a 'military armistice' and it's best (I think) to have a nominally 'military' mission (of course, we ought to be able to do our stuff under them just the same).

Mason-MacFarlane was whistled up from Gibraltar (I arranged the necessary with Colonial Office, War Office and the King) and arrived duly yesterday.

General Max Taylor (American Airborne Division), charming, intelligent and Italian-speaking, was added. Vice-Admiral Power (commanding at Taranto) was told to make any preliminary contacts possible.[12]

We started from El Alouina aerodrome (Tunis) at 9 a.m. in a Fortress – the four of us and Bombardier Casey (Mason-Mac's batman) who (I feel) is going to be the real leader of the mission.

The pilot of the Flying Fortress asked us where we wanted to go. We said either Brindisi or Taranto. He said, 'Aren't those in Italy?' We said, 'Yes.' He said, 'I think the Germans have got the aerodromes there.' We said, 'No. We sent a brigade into Taranto on Saturday (or perhaps Friday) and we think they have got Taranto.' He said, 'Yes – but the aerodrome is at a place called Grottaglie, about twenty kilometres from Taranto, and how do you know who has got this?' We said, 'Well, we can go and see. We try this first, and then Brindisi.'

We took off about 9.15 a.m. and flew past Sicily, leaving Messina and the Straits on our left, and about 12.45 we saw Taranto. We thought we saw a couple of cruisers and a destroyer. So the pilot sheared off then, for fear they would shoot us down. We were told not to use any wireless, for fear of enemy detection. He did try the wireless when we got near the aerodrome – but no reply. We circled several times round, flying very low. A number of Italian fighters were standing around, undamaged, and some damaged Italian and German machines. The aerodrome itself had been a good deal bombed, but the holes had clearly been filled in pretty well.

We landed – a very good landing – the crew stood to the guns – and we got out, rather timidly, wondering what would occur.

A large number of Italian Air Force came running up and excited conversation ensued. We felt rather like the discoverers of a new continent – with the aborigines gesticulating and gabbling in a strange tongue.

General Taylor has done 'Italian in Twenty Lessons' and was jolly

[12] Vice-Admiral Arthur Power (1889–1960), having been Vice-Admiral, Malta, since May 1943, was naval commander of the expedition which captured Taranto.

good. My old Venetian facility came back to me, and I kept saying alternately *Buon giorno* and *Fuori tedeschi* (which ought to mean 'Turn out the Germans').

I need hardly say that Casey made himself understood the best. As far as I could make out, he demanded the surrender of the aerodrome, which appeared to be readily conceded.

(Actually to our great chagrin, we found that a British officer in a Hurricane had in fact landed at noon – one hour ahead of us – so we were robbed of the glory of the first capture – rather like the discovery of the North Pole, etc. But we had anyway the thrill of thinking ourselves the captors, and he had gone away without planting a flag or anything, so I am prepared to dispute his claim.)

After these preliminaries, we found ourselves in possession of an excellent airfield, some partially destroyed buildings, the embarrassingly loyal attentions of a large number of Italian Air Force, including the Orderly Officer in a purple sash, no transport of any kind, and great difficulty in making a field telephone work. (We were also not quite certain whom to ring up. It seemed hardly correct to ring up the exchange at different towns and say, 'Excuse me – but can you tell me whether your town is in the possession of the Allies or the Germans?'). We also had (by a most unusual mistake of the Americans) no food or drink. However, after prodigious conversational and telephonic efforts a colonel was produced who had both a car and some gasoline. Casey and the crew were left in charge of the Fortress. Four of us crowded into a rather small Fiat, and drove to Taranto. We got there about 5 p.m.

On the theory (which I believe to be sound) on which I have now learned to work, we asked for Navy House. Here we found (as I expected) an admiral, a captain, several commanders and junior officers – a system of communication, an officers' mess, a commandeered hotel (with bedrooms and real beds) and a clear picture of the situation.

The Germans retired the day before yesterday and are now about fifteen miles away. We got originally one brigade and now have another ashore. These have advanced and have a screen round the town. The road to Brindisi is clear of Germans (at least, Admiral Power left by car and has *not* returned, so it's probably all right!). We are not sure of Bari, but hope to take it tonight. The Italian fleet had left like lambs.

We decided to wait for Admiral Power, and he finally turned up about 6.30. He gave us an admirable account of his contact with first Badoglio and then the Minister of Marine. He did not see any other ministers. He believed the King to be there, but did not ask. He could not form any judgment as to whether the Government as a whole was functioning or capable of doing so.

We dined in the mess and went for a little walk in the bright moonlight. This seems rather an attractive town. Most of the population have gone, but the remainder seem friendly. They will all be back in a few days (at least, to judge by Sicily).

Bed early – and this letter. No more till tomorrow.

Tuesday, 14 September 1943

Admiral Power came at 9 a.m. for further conversation. Left Taranto at 9.45, arriving Brindisi at about 11 a.m.

The four of us – General Mason-MacFarlane, General Max Taylor, Murphy and I were taken to the Admiralty buildings, where what remains of the Italian Government and authority are at present housed. These offices are in a fine medieval castle – greatly extended and added to in later times – surrounded by a moat. On one side the castle overlooks the harbour, with a wide view of the port as a whole.

The sailors – it appeared to be almost entirely a naval establishment – were clean and smart. The saluting was good and a very reasonably drilled guard turned out for our reception.

We were at once taken into a small room and introduced to General Ambrosio, the head of the Joint Staff (Army, Navy and Air). General MacFarlane explained in general terms the purpose of the mission. We were next taken to see Marshal Badoglio. After him the King. After this, we were taken to a naval mess for luncheon.

I sat next to Marshal Badoglio, and on my other side General Roatta, Chief of the Army Staff.

After luncheon, Murphy and I went to the Hotel Internationale, where two excellent rooms were provided for us.

We rested till about four, when we were visited by General Zanussi, the general whom we had already met in Algiers and in Sicily in the course of the armistice negotiations.

At 5 p.m. Murphy and I called on Badoglio again. He was alone. He speaks reasonably good French.

We drove back to Taranto and arrived about 7.30 – after one or two minor adventures with the car, including running over a dog.

The countryside is flat – very well farmed – olives, figs, vines – and the usual cereal cultivation in between the olives. The grape harvest is now in full swing, the peasants bringing their grapes in huge wine tubs to the presses.

All the transport is horse- or mule-drawn. It is very hot, especially at night.

Wednesday, 15 September 1943

Went round to AMGOT H.Q. in the old Fascist H.Q. at Taranto. Here we found about six British and American officers (headed by an American, from the South, one Major Wilson).

They were struggling manfully with their enormous problems – the chief of which is the refusal of the banks to take the Allied money. This we will deal with at once.

Drove to Brindisi – found rooms in the hotel. We saw General Zanussi again at about twelve, and he and General Roatta lunched with Murphy and me in my room.

At 5 p.m. we saw the King.

At 6 p.m. we saw Badoglio again (General MacFarlane was with us); General Ambrosio and Duca d'Acquarone[13] also present. These are just bald statements of the day so far. I will send you a copy of the memorandum of impressions and conversations later on [see Report on Mission to Italy on p. 219]. We have no typists, no transport (except a car which we pinched off an Italian colonel and the driver of which – we call him Wilfred – is loyal to us and seems to stick with us), very little food, and no help of any kind.

At Brindisi there are no British troops or sailors, except a few officers (about six in all) attached to the mission. So you see, we still continue to live on 'bluff'.

Dinner at hotel and early to bed, after a nice walk in the town after dinner, in the comparative cool of the evening.

The heat is quite as great as in Tunisia – and the nights are stickier. We have very little news and are at present handicapped by lack of efficient communications. These are being arranged.

We have decided to go back (Murphy and I) tomorrow with a first report, if we can get an aeroplane.

Marshal Badoglio has given the necessary order for the banks in Taranto and elsewhere to accept Allied lira notes (those specially printed by us for the campaign) as of equal value to Italian lira notes. So that is one question settled.

Thursday, 16 September 1943

The early part of the morning was occupied with talks with General MacFarlane as to certain subjects on which we shall report immediately on returning to Africa [see p. 219]. At 11 a.m. the general, Bob Murphy and I (accompanied by Air Commodore Foster,[14] R.A.F., who arrived yesterday) called on the Prince.[15] Prince Umberto speaks excellent English and has easy and agreeable manners. I thought he got through what must have been rather an ordeal with grace and dignity. He observed that he had purely by chance planned to come to Rome on the day the armistice appeared. Marshal Richthofen[16] came to see him about an hour before the announcement, and this had not been

[13] Pietro, Duca d'Acquarone (1890–1948), a former general, was Minister of the Royal Household, 1938–44.

[14] Air Commodore Robert Foster (1898–1973), Air Forces representative at Staff H.Q. of Force 141, was a member of our mission.

[15] Prince Umberto, Prince of Piedmont (1904–83), heir to the throne of Italy.

[16] Field Marshal Wolfram Freiherr von Richthofen (1895–1945) was commander of Luftflotte 2.

an easy conversation! The Prince is I suppose only about forty, but his hair is thinning and he has that look of a young man no longer young, but still being regarded as young, which is no doubt the fate of all heirs apparent.

I am told he had been rather dissipated and has preferred the beds of the maids-of-honour to that of the Princess. Nevertheless, since he is of good appearance and physique, and cannot be held responsible for his father's decisions (or indecisions) during the last twenty years, one feels there would be an advantage in the King's abdicating in his favour.

Formal interviews like this are not much use, except for a general impression. They must be followed up by more personal contacts if one is to learn anything from them.

At 11.30, the same party (less the air commodore) went again to see Badoglio. General Ambrosio was present during the first part of the interview; Duca d'Acquarone and the Prefect of Taranto, one Innocenti, during the second part. The first talk covered some of the old ground, about the status of the Government and the country *vis-à-vis* the Allies.

The second was on economic and financial matters. The Marshal professed complete ignorance of these; but M. Innocenti was certainly ill-named. I thought him very slick.

At about 12.30 we went back to our hotel. At 2 p.m. we left for the aerodrome and started back about 2.45 for Tunis in a Mitchell bomber (rather crowded in the cockpit and uncomfortable for a long journey) but very fast (up to 220–50 miles per hour).

When we got over Sicily the pilot thought he had not enough petrol to make Africa. So we came down at an aerodrome not far from Mount Etna (on the plain) and asked for some. However we could get none and after considerable delay, we flew on to another, near Gela, where we got it. By this time, it was getting late. However, we left at 6.30 and got to Tunis just as the sun was setting at 7.30 p.m.

After bath, and dinner with the Consul-General and Mrs Monypenny and John, I settled down to work, and my report was written and typed ready for the morning by 1.30 a.m. when we went to bed.

The Sergeant-Clerk did very well and sat up to finish the job most readily.

Extracts from Report on Mission to Italy 14–17 September 1943

This is the picture, as I see it:

A. *Dramatis Personae*

The King. Seventy-four years old. Physically infirm, nervous, shaky, but courteous, with a certain modesty and simplicity of character which is attractive. He takes an objective, even humorously disinterested view of mankind and their follies. 'Things are not difficult,' he said, 'only men.'

I do not think he would be capable of initiating any policy, except under extreme pressure, e.g. Mussolini's march on Rome and the Communist threat, which led to his decision of 1920; the hopeless state of the Fascist régime which led to his decision of 25 July 1943; the German threat to Rome, which led to his decision to leave on 9 September 1943.

I would imagine his interests to be his family, his dynasty and his country, in that order. I think under pressure, he would be inclined to take any decision which could be shown to him as serving those interests.

THE PRINCE. A middle-aged youth. Speaks good English. Pleasant and attractive manner. Good physique. I would not say a strong character but presumably not an objectionable one and of course much less committed than the King by the mistakes of twenty years.

MARSHAL BADOGLIO. Seventy-two years old. Honest, broad-minded, humorous. I should judge of peasant origin, with the horse common sense and natural shrewdness of the peasant. A loyal servant of his King and country, without ambitions. He states a case with clarity, in a few words. He is a little like General Georges but with more restraint and dignity. He is a soldier and clearly without much political sense, believing that he has the popular support at the moment and that it can all be concentrated in a military movement without a political side. In this he is a little like Giraud but with more modesty and less egotism.

GENERAL AMBROSIO. Chief of Combined Staffs (Navy, Army, Air). A neat, efficient, but not very impressive mind, at least to the layman. Gamelin,[17] at his age, I should have judged to be about Ambrosio's twin.

GENERAL ROSSI.[18] Ambrosio's deputy. I saw little of him. From General Mason-MacFarlane's account he seems one of the ablest of them if you could get him really firmly on your side. Rather an obscure character.

GENERAL ROATTA. A good linguist; a travelled and intelligent conversationalist, with tendencies to be a bore. The perfect Military Attaché. I would say that his brains were more developed and effective than his guts. Nor would I trust his loyalty to any cause that should show remote signs of becoming a lost one. A natural coward; he can be bullied if necessary.

[17] General Maurice Gamelin (1872–1958), the French C.-in-C. at the fall of France, was much criticised for being an intellectual who was too remote from the actual conduct of the war and uninterested in its technicalities.

[18] General Enrico Rossi had been commander of the Italian Sixth Army Corps and Chief of Staff of the Italian Army.

GENERAL ZANUSSI. 'Stooge' to Roatta. The impression formed at Algiers remains. He does not carry many guns, but I really believe he would fire them off. He is an enthusiast. He believes in the general point of view which the Allies represent. His position in this rather dreary military hierarchy is low. It would pay us to get it raised. He should make an excellent liaison officer with us for S.O.E. and O.S.S. work.

ADMIRAL DE COURTEN.[19] (Minister for Marine.) Hardly came into my life. He lunched well; seemed a friendly and sensible man, and has clearly loyally carried out his duties under the armistice. (If he keeps back anything, e.g., one submarine, four destroyers, some corvettes, and a modern cruiser called *Scipio Africanus*, which I saw at Brindisi, it is no doubt to protect the person of his King.)

DUCA D'ACQUARONE. (Minister of the Royal Household). He is a combination of Keeper of the Privy Purse and Principal Private Secretary. I should say his advice to the King would be of importance. I cannot tell his relation with Prince Umberto. Aristocratic, intelligent, and I should say, opportunist. In default of any civil ministers having left Rome with the King, he has been Commissioner for Civil Supply and for Finance.

(General Calvi di Bergolo,[20] the son-in-law of the King, has remained in Rome, and now commands the troops there and apparently gave the order for cease-fire as a result of the negotiations conducted by Guariglia.[21]

B. *The Position of the Government*

The Brindisi Party can hardly be dignified by the name of Government. It consists only of the King and his family, an aged Marshal as Head of the Administration, and a sprinkling of generals and courtiers. There are no civilian ministers (with the exception of the Duca d'Acquarone, elevated from a court appointment to a portfolio). Nevertheless they contend that the civilian ministers left in Rome are not disloyal to but merely separated from the Head of the Government by *force majeure*. I am not without some doubt on this point. I should have thought that at least Signor Guariglia (Foreign Minister) would have accompanied the party.

It may also be significant that the King's son-in-law (General Calvi di Bergolo) stayed in Rome and was party to the arrangement made with the German commanders.

These doubts were confirmed by the Duca d'Acquarone. He said

[19] Rear-Admiral Raffaele de Courten (b. 1888) continued as Minister for Marine under four Prime Ministers, until 1946.

[20] General Count Carlo Calvi di Bergolo (b. 1887) had married Princess Jolanda of Savoy in 1923.

[21] Barone Raffaele Guariglia (b. 1889), a former Italian Ambassador, was Minister for Foreign Affairs, 1943–4.

that there had been much dissension and disputes in the Ministry over the armistice decision. It may be that half the Government was left in Rome as a form of reinsurance.

In any event, the Government, from the military and civil point of view, is not much more than a name. Its importance is that it has unchallenged claim to legality. Except for the Fascist Republican Party now being organised in Germany by Mussolini and his gang, no other Government has so far claimed authority.

From the military point of view, the Government can only lay its hands on a few divisions in territory free from the Germans. It is not even in touch with the commanders of the other divisions, and cannot be so until some wireless communication can be got (with help of S.O.E.).

From a civil aspect, whatever sentimental support it may command, its writ does not run except in those parts of the territory which are:
(*a*) not in effective German occupation,
(*b*) not under Allied Military Government. Brindisi, perhaps Bari, the provinces in the south evacuated by (*b*) are the limits of its territorial, as apart from its moral, authority.

The characters of the men we have seen so far inspire sympathy rather than confidence. They are old and unimaginative. The King is (of his own motion, at any rate) ineffective; the Marshal has courage and a high sense of duty but he is long past his prime. The rest are men of ordinary parts, somewhat mediocre professional soldiers. They hate the Germans, but they fear them equally. All their divisions, in Italy and the Balkans, are 'surrounded' by a smaller number of German troops. There is an atmosphere of well-bred defeatism.

C. *The Problem*

The chief question which faces the Allies is the status to be given to this Government and to Italy as a whole. A decision on this vital point of policy will govern all executive action, whether in the military, political or propaganda sphere. It was excellently posed by the Marshal to us on the evening of 15 September.

'The Italian Government', says the Marshal, 'has signed an armistice. It was necessary for Italy to do so. The Government have tried loyally to carry out the terms of the armistice. The Navy has been surrendered and whatever orders the Government have been given which have been in their power to execute, have been carried out. But to the Italian people and armed forces, an armistice connotes a cessation of war. That is what they expect. Nevertheless, in the spirit of the message from President Roosevelt and the Prime Minister, the Government of Italy stands not for peace, but for war against the Germans. How will the people and the Army understand that this is their duty, unless some status of ally or quasi-ally can be given to Italy? How can the enthusiasm for military and para-military effort (particularly the latter) be created, if Italy has no better position than the signature of severe armistice terms?'

'Therefore', asks the Marshal, 'can we be regarded as an ally, not merely till the Germans are cleared out of Italy, but till the end of the war?'

'Shall we, as we should like to do, in order to make clear the position to our people, *declare war on Germany*?'...

The long terms were 'transmitted' to General Castellano after signature on 3 September. But since General C. has *not* returned to Italy, the Government do not know about them, except by hearsay. They cannot be said to have been effectively communicated to the Italian Government.

Are we to carry out our original instructions and demand signature? Where is this to be done?

Are the long terms to be modified? They are really quite inappropriate to present situation.

But if they are to be modified, will we look ridiculous *vis-à-vis* the United Nations Governments who have been informed? ...

D. *A Possible Plan*

There is a danger of our merely sliding into a *de facto* recognition of a position where the armistice becomes obsolescent. Would it not be better to devise a formula, short of alliance, but better than armistice?

In such a formula we might agree to provisional recognition of Government as co-belligerent subject to certain conditions.

Friday, 17 September 1943

9 a.m. Left for Bizerta by car. It is rather a dreary drive, although the scenery has a certain charm. You cross the flat plain – the mountains forming a ring in the background; here and there are flocks of goats, sheep and camels quietly feeding among the wreckage of tanks, motor-cars, aerpolanes (now largely cleared up into various salvage heaps) or great dumps of ammunition boxes, with every sort of shell and bullet.

It is a hot and dusty road, and rather tiring, because of the great convoys of lorries continually passing along it in both directions.

11 a.m. Commander-in-Chief's conference. Eisenhower was away, so General Alexander was in the chair. These conferences generally consist of General Eisenhower, his Chief of Staff, General Bedell Smith, and the three British C.-in-C.s – Admiral Cunningham, Air Chief Marshal Tedder, General Alexander, and their staffs. Murphy and I attended the conference, and (by arrangement with Murphy) I presented my report as an agreed report between him and me.

It was agreed that two telegrams should be prepared, one for General Eisenhower to send to Combined Chiefs of Staff, and one for me to send (together with a summary of my report) to P.M. Everyone was agreed on the general policy to be followed in Italy, and the meeting went very well in every way.

After luncheon (in General Alex's mess) we had a further meeting with General Alexander, General Holmes (Military Government Section of A.F.H.Q.), General [Bedell] Smith, Murphy and myself. Makins (who came up to Tunis yesterday to meet me) was also there. Francis Rennell had been sent for, but did not arrive from Sicily in time.

At this conference we decided to send Lord Rennell and General Holmes to Brindisi to work out a *modus vivendi* for the area in which the Italian Government found itself, something in between the full AMGOT system and Italian self-government. This was to fill the gap before we got a definite ruling on policy from London and Washington.

We motored back to Tunis (a hot and dusty two-hour drive) from 3 to 5. Here we found Francis Rodd.

Murphy and I sat down to draft General Eisenhower's telegram (which was approved and sent off that night) and I finished mine to the P.M. and got it off. Rennell and Holmes came to dinner at the Consular Residence, and we went through all the points and satisfactorily settled up the details. They were to leave the next morning and return to report by Wednesday.

Saturday, 18 September 1943

Roger and I drove over to Bizerta for the conference. (We had sent John down to Algiers to get off the long telegram through our Consulate there, where we have more cypherers than in Tunis.) Lunched with Alex after the conference.

At 3 p.m. we went to see the admiral [Cunningham] at his H.Q. (on a ship in the harbour at Bizerta). At 6.30 to see Tedder in his H.Q. at Tunis. The long drives are very tiring. After seeing Tedder, we had an excellent bathe, at the sandy beach to which General Alexander introduced me during the time I was here with him before. I usually bathe there at 7 a.m. and did so both today and yesterday. It is a lovely beach and fairly deserted, so one can bathe naked. I have only once seen a woman there (an A.T. or W.A.A.F. or something of the kind) and as she was also bathing naked everything seemed to be in order.

Sunday, 19 September 1943

Left La Marsa aerodrome at 8.30 a.m. by fast courier, and arrived at Algiers at 11 a.m. A very good flight, over the sea, and very smooth.

We went straight to the office, and although Roger had brought up a good deal of stuff which I dealt with at Tunis, I found a lot more had come in – sufficient to keep me employed at the office till dinner-time.

Harry Bourdillon (whom I knew in Colonial Office days – he used to help me with the French side of the West African Produce Board) came to dinner. He now acts as secretary to a thing in London called the Morton Committee. It is presided over by Desmond Morton[22] and deals with economic affairs in Africa generally. As the result of the recognition of the French Committee for National Liberation, we have got to reorganise all our economic arrangements here. We have to develop a system for dealing with the French Government on the economic affairs of *all* the French Empire (including Syria, Madagascar and so on) and reconstruct N.A.E.B., as a civilian organisation and no longer under General Eisenhower, to deal with the special problems of the French North African territories. Young Bourdillon is very intelligent, and I was very glad to see him again. We talked till midnight and then went to bed – rather weary.

Monday, 20 September 1943

A very hectic day. Italy, France – France, Italy – a series of problems and telegrams pouring in from London and Washington. Propaganda in Italy meetings; propaganda in France meetings; a French row about Corsica; a French row about our being too kind to the Italians; de Gaulle and Giraud have quarrelled; they have made it up; they want to see me; I refuse to see them, saying I am busy on important matters and leaving again in a few hours – and so on. A *splendid* telegram from P.M. *endorsing our policy* completely, with which General Smith was absolutely delighted. *No* telegram from Washington, which infuriates him. Quite a day.

On 8 September, as soon as the news of the Italian armistice became known, uprisings took place all over Corsica, some 15,000 men having been secretly armed by the Allies. On 11 September, Patriots seized control of Ajaccio. General Giraud at once asked A.F.H.Q. if he could send two French destroyers with French commandos to help the Resistance movement. A.F.H.Q. gave him permission, but the next day he lost his nerve and called the expedition off. On the 13th he changed his mind again and despatched the destroyers with a French general appointed by himself to administer the island under an état de siège, *and accompanied by a Prefect-designate of Ajaccio. The troops landed successfully, and many of the 40,000 Italian soldiers on the island were reported to have joined the French to fight the Germans. By 20 September most of west Corsica was in French hands.*

But Giraud had entirely failed to inform General de Gaulle or the F.C.N.L. of any of his actions. So he received a very hostile reception at the meeting of the Committee on 18 September, and was accused of going beyond his military sphere into the political. However, the Committee managed to present a united front to the world, and issued a

[22] Major Desmond Morton (1891–1971) was the Prime Minister's Personal Assistant, 1940–6.

proclamation congratulating the Corsican Patriots on their achievement and by implication asserting its authority over liberated Corsica.

Tuesday, 21 September 1943

After a meeting with the Chief of Staff at 9 a.m. and one with Murphy and the propaganda boys at 10 a.m., I managed to get two hours fairly free to deal with the economic re-organisation. Herbert and Bourdillon were most helpful. They came to luncheon, and we were able to agree on a complete scheme (to which I had already obtained previous American approval so far as they were concerned). We got the telegram drafted, and I got it in final form and sent off before going to bed. A great relief.

In the afternoon, Murphy and I called on Massigli and did our best to cheer him up. The French internal dispute (which is nothing but the old jealousy between de Gaulle and Giraud) will (I feel sure) end up as nothing but a storm in a Corsican tea-cup. They cannot really afford to break up the Committee, with world affairs moving so rapidly.

Dr Abadie called (Minister for Education) about getting more schools handed back from military occupation. He is a sweet little man, very grateful for what we have already done and very reasonable in every way.

At 6 p.m. I hoped to get away but another Frenchman, Chataigneau,[23] turned up, this time from Beirut, with letters of introduction from Spears. He seemed very friendly, so I took him up to the villa and filled him up with gin and vermouth, which delighted him.

7.30 p.m. Dinner at General Gale's. A large military party, followed by us all having to go to the Opera, for a charity performance given by the Royal Artillery band. Eric Duncannon came with me to a box, which I had to purchase for three nights! In the interval, Madame la Générale Catroux 'received' in her box, like a queen; after this, I slipped away, for there was at least two hours' work waiting to be done at the villa – a perfect flood of 'Most Immediates' having arrived.

Got to bed by midnight – everything more or less done.

Wednesday, 22 September 1943

Breakfast 6.15 a.m. Arrived aerodrome 7.30 and left for Tunis, with General Smith, Murphy, Reber, Roger and a pride of generals. A *very* rough journey – one of the worst I remember. We arrived at 10.30 at La Marsa in rather a shattered condition. However Mrs Monypenny produced iced beer in great quantities – which was very welcome.

The conference lasted from 11 to 1.30. Lunch in the mess; further meeting with Chief of Staff 2.30–4 p.m. Roger, Murphy and Reber returned to Algiers. At General Smith's request, I stayed on and

[23] Yves Chataigneau (1891–1969) was Free French Delegate to the Levant, 1943–4, and later Governor-General of Algeria, 1944–8.

worked on some telegrams to Washington, London, and General Mason-MacFarlane at Brindisi, which took me till about 6 p.m.

6.30 p.m. Francis Rennell came, and we went off to bathe. Dinner at Consular Residence. John arrived at 8 p.m. (an hour late, which alarmed me very much as there was a fierce sirocco and dust storms and I feared an accident) to find his brother Mark[24] (whom Mrs Monypenny had found in Tunis). There was great amusement at the very phlegmatic meeting of the brothers.

Thursday, 23 September 1943

Being somewhat exhausted, I have decided to stay here till Saturday, when the Chief of Staff and I will return to Algiers together.

An idle morning till about 10 a.m., when I went to see General Eisenhower and General Smith. The heat is intense and the more so because the sun is hidden by steamy clouds. The sirocco is still blowing and there is sand everywhere.

After luncheon, Mr Miller of the Tunis branch of the N.A.E.B. came to see me. I had two fascinating hours on olive oil and phosphates. In many ways, supply is more satisfying than politics. Something is sometimes actually achieved. The great feature of the Tunisian method of collecting olives is the 'combing' instead of shaking the trees. The Arabs are taught to 'comb' the trees with combs made of ram's horns and/or goat's horns. Cloths are spread below the trees, and thus the full crop is collected, instead of a large part being lost in the ground. After immense efforts, Miller has obtained 500,000 yards of material for these cloths (stolen, in the best Beaverbrook style, from the warehouses of the American relief department) and in this way we hope to double last year's crop. Moreover, by the olives being less bruised the percentage of acidity is much reduced, and thus, when the oil is extracted, no chemical is needed to counteract the acidity. In this way, the nutritive fatty content is much increased.

There is also the problem of getting *small* supplies (100 tons or so) of *first-class* quality. This is necessary for pharmaceutical purposes – especially injection. We have, with great difficulty, found some good stuff and when I fly back to Algiers on Saturday I shall take two sample bottles. These will be flown to England, and if the samples are up to standard, we shall take the 100 tons offered and ship them in containers (air-sealed) first to Bône (in an empty collier) and thence to England (in a returning transport).

At 6.30 we bathed at our favourite beach – no one there, except a few prowling Arabs – so we could bathe naked.

Dinner at the Residence. General Theodore Roosevelt turned up unexpectedly and stayed to dinner.

It was so hot at night that it was difficult to sleep. There is a

[24] Captain Mark Wyndham (b. 1921) served in the 12th Royal Lancers in the Middle East, 1941–3, and Italy, 1943–5.

shower-bath here, but the water is tepid. However, it is quite nice to have one now and then in the night.

A number of 'Most Immediates' arrived in the night, which made a diversion. Fortunately Stalin is being very sensible. He is all for the King of Italy (and the Pope [Pius XII] if necessary) as long as they will help to fight the Germans. He is much more realistic than our *New Statesman*, *News Chronicle*, etc.

Friday, 24 September 1943

Slept late – till nearly 8.30, after a restless night. Dealt with my telegrams in the morning. It is a very good thing I stayed up here, as there has been a lot to arrange with the Chief of Staff – largely detail, but none the less important. We are trying to get the King of Italy to broadcast. He is too old to let him speak direct into the microphone, and anyway we want to be sure of the speech. We have now managed to get a recording set to Brindisi and the records should get back here by air today or tomorrow. There has been a tremendous 'howdedoo' about this. The Italian Ambassadors at Madrid and Lisbon won't do their stuff about Italian naval and merchant ships in Spanish and Portuguese ports without it. (We have already got MS letters from Badoglio flown to Madrid and Lisbon.) Old Sam Hoare keeps on telegraphing in his ridiculously pompous style.

At 12.45 I went over to the Air Chief Marshal's camp (Tedder). We bathed – lunched – and gossiped till about 3 p.m. He likes to be kept in the know politically, just as Alexander and Admiral Cunningham do. So I do my best to supply what is called a 'felt want'.

I have just got back and am finishing this before trying for a little sleep. There is still a hot sirocco – like being in an oven – and it is not easy to find a cool spot. But the large room here (in the Consular Residence) is not too bad, and there is a ridiculous gilt Louis XV sofa (requisitioned from somewhere) on which I shall do my best.

After six we went and bathed at our usual beach – myself, John and Mark Wyndham, and a strange Derbyshire youth called Chandos-Pole, in the Grenadiers, who has somehow become attached as liaison officer to General Mast, the French Resident-General in Tunisia.

After dinner, we four went and dined at the Cercle Inter-Allié (the old Casino of Tunis) of which apparently I am a founder member. The food was bad, the wine good.

Saturday, 25 September 1943

Very hot; storms are brewing. I did some work in the morning and settled some things with the Chief of Staff. We are still awaiting a telegram from Washington before starting off again for Italy. But I decided that I must get back to Algiers, at least for one day, as there were ugly rumours reaching me (by telephone and telegram from

Roger) of fresh and perhaps this time irreconcilable dissensions among the French.

I got a seat on the 2 p.m. courier, which (in principle) should have got me to Algiers about 5 to 5.30 (with one stop at Telergma, near Le Kef).

The weather looked threatening, and there was a lot of arguing about whether the plane should go. We actually started about 2.45. After rather a bumpy trip, we reached the first stop all right. On leaving Telergma at about 4.30, we ran into terrible weather over the high mountains. After one or two spectacular drops, any of which we fully expected to impale us on a peak, the pilot succeeded in turning back out of the storm and running through a valley towards the sea. He then followed the coastline the whole way back to Algiers – flying a few hundred feet above the water. Visibility was practically nil and the ceiling very low. He could only go a slowish speed and hope for the best. We finally reached Maison Blanche aerodrome (he managed to recognise it after flying beyond it the first time) and landed about 7.30.

On arriving at the villa, I found Mr Ben Smith (Under-Secretary, Ministry of Aircraft Production) staying with me. A dinner-party in his honour followed, with a suitable number of sailors, soldiers and airmen. Finally, when all had gone and retired to bed, I could start on the accumulated boxes of papers and hear the Algiers news. I went, tired and rather disheartened, to bed at about 2 a.m.

Sunday, 26 September 1943

Our worst day I ever remember in Algiers since I came. I suppose I was tired to start with – by the end of the day I was cross, rattled and hardly approachable.

8–9 a.m. Mr Ben Smith at breakfast. Pleasant, but rather heavy going.

9 a.m. Went to Murphy's house to discuss the French situation with him. At 10 a.m. we adjourned to the Chief of Staff's. While we were talking, a telegram arrived from the P.M., instructing me to tell de Gaulle that 'any alteration in the system of co-Presidents (de Gaulle and Giraud) would overthrow the basis on which the French Committee had been recognised and would have the most serious results'.[25] He also told me to say the same to 'all the members of the Committee who are my friends'.

This put me in a great difficulty. I had already arranged to see de Gaulle at 11 a.m. If I were to deliver the message, he would, of course, get very excited over another 'Allied intervention in French affairs' and the chances of a settlement would be much reduced. Or, alternatively, we would be put in a rather ridiculous situation, with

[25] General de Gaulle had prepared three new decrees which would enable the Committee to appoint a civilian Commissioner of War (or Defence) to whom General Giraud would be responsible, de Gaulle's own powers remaining undiminished.

no real remedy except to withdraw recognition and undo the work of nine months.

If, however, I were *not* to carry out the P.M.'s instructions and suppress the message, and the affair were to go wrong, I should be told that it was all my fault for disobeying my orders and that the delivery of the 'intervention' would have saved the situation. What I ultimately did you will see by the enclosures [see below and p. 231].

11 a.m. Interview with de Gaulle.

Record of conversation with General de Gaulle
26 September 1943

1. I saw General de Gaulle this morning, he having asked to see me. We talked in general terms on the war, the position in Italy, and other matters. He seemed to be in a very cheerful and rather mischievous mood. When I approached the problems now confronting the French Committee, it was clear to me that he was anxiously seeking an intervention by the Allies as an excuse for a patriotic rallying. I therefore merely told him that in my personal opinion any break-up in the Committee leading to General Giraud's resignation would be very unfortunate. He said that he did not see that there was anything for it but to accept the collective responsibility of the Committee and stand by its decisions. The arguments in favour of the proposed decrees were from a practical point of view overwhelming. He did not want to see two Governments either now or when they entered France.

2. As it appeared to me from a tactical point of view that it would be unwise to give him any direct message from the British Government, I did not do so, but contented myself with once more preaching moderation. I reminded him that I had been a good friend of his all along and that my advice had proved sound. I hoped that he would take it again. It was essential to preserve the unity of General Giraud and himself. At this he rather ungraciously observed that there was no suggestion in the decrees to abolish the co-Presidency from a juridical point of view. It would of course cease from a practical point of view.

[Diary continues] 12 noon. Office. Excited telegram from the P.M. about some broadcast at Bari in which the King of Italy was referred to as King of Albania and Emperor of Ethiopia!! (Of course, it turned out to be merely a proclamation about currency and the rate of exchange, of which our mission had written the text but omitted to see the headings. So the printer had just put in the usual style, out of habit, I suppose.)

1.15 p.m. A large luncheon, party of young Guardsmen, off a ship.

2.30 p.m. Murphy and Reber came round for a talk about two Italians who had turned up and might be useful. We arranged to see them later in the day.

3–3.30 p.m. Herbert, Bourdillon on economic affairs, North Africa.

3.30 p.m. Murphy and I saw Massigli.

Record of conversation with M. Massigli
26 September 1943

Massigli told us frankly the whole story of the crisis, which, as he said, was based upon two things. First Giraud's very egotistical handling of the Corsican situation: secondly, the lack of confidence and good faith between Giraud and de Gaulle. He told us that the Committee discussed the matter of reorganising the Army and the Command on Tuesday in Giraud's absence. At that time it was suggested that texts of the decrees should be prepared so that they could be discussed when Giraud returned. At yesterday's (Saturday) meeting these texts were discussed. The drafters were René Mayer and Couve [de Murville]. Giraud expressed great resentment and said that he would not accept the situation but preferred to resign. With regard to the Commissioner for Defence, the name suggested is that of M. Queuille – a moderate man. Massigli saw Giraud at noon today and urged him strongly to accept, especially since the decree did not alter the co-Presidency and the arguments for a Ministry of War were really overwhelming. He also urged strongly on Giraud the good character of M. Queuille, who would be perfectly harmless to him. Massigli was not too optimistic about the outcome, but expressed privately the hope that it would be allowed to be settled as a French affair. Murphy drew from him the observation that intervention would be disastrous. Nevertheless, Massigli realises that the resignation of Giraud would produce an international crisis, clearly bad for France and the Allies. He will work as hard as he can to prevent it.

[Diary continues] 4–6 p.m. At office, doing telegrams, reports, etc. Chief of Staff came round about five to discuss the French crisis further.

6.30 p.m. Interview with General Georges.

7 p.m. Interview with General Giraud.

Record of conversations with Generals Georges and Giraud
26 September 1943

1. I saw General Georges at 6.30 today. He explained to me in much the same terms as M. Massigli the events of the last week culminating in the passing of the three decrees. General Georges took the view that these decrees were part of a plot the purpose of which was to reduce General Giraud's position from that of equality with General de Gaulle to something much inferior. He said that General Giraud intended to stand upon the decrees of 4 August. He saw no reason why the arrangements for the conduct of the Army should be changed.

They had never really been given a chance to work, partly owing to the non-arrival of General Legentilhomme.[26]

2. I pressed him as to whether he thought some accommodation could be reached, but he seemed to think that this was not likely. At the same time he expressed most strongly the view that it would be undesirable for me or Murphy to intervene at this stage. He thought it would only be a weapon in the hands of General de Gaulle.

3. I subsequently saw General Giraud, who expressed the same views. He said that he had been very patient and had agreed to many modifications, but that the firm basis upon which the whole Committee depended was the agreement between himself and de Gaulle in the original letters that passed between them. He was not prepared to do anything which would overthrow this. If he were defeated in the Committee tomorrow and the Committee insisted on retaining the decrees, he would resign. After his resignation he would inform the Allies and France of the reasons which had actuated him.

4. He attributed the difficulties largely to General de Gaulle's jealousy of his success in Corsica. He had taken great risks there and they had proved successful.

5. Giraud was in a very determined mood and did not respond to my suggestions that the matter might be accommodated at least by an adjournment. At the same time, when I asked him what he would like me to do, he took the same view as General Georges, that it would be most unwise for us to be trapped into making any intervention at this stage. He thought it would be used by de Gaulle with great effect against him. For that reason he was not at all sorry that he had not been able to see General Eisenhower.

[Diary continues] 7.30 p.m. The two Italian professors at my villa (Pazzi and Agnino). They are supposed to represent the coalition of the five anti-Fascist parties. They talked, without drawing breath, till 9 p.m. when I turned them out.

9 p.m. General Gueterbock (British) to dinner. He has been sent out by the War Office (without, as far as I can see, [consulting] any other Government department) to 'plan' an Armistice Commission. I'm afraid I got very cross with him before he finally left about 11 p.m.

11–1.30 a.m. Telegrams and replies. Another very animated telegram from the P.M. I replied, 'I find it rather difficult at the same time to look after all these details in Brindisi, to perform my duties at General Eisenhower's advanced H.Q. at Tunis, and to deal with a French crisis at Algiers. But I do my best.'

At last, at the end of a really dreadful day I got to bed. I leave early tomorrow for Tunis – from there to Brindisi. And I really have no idea

[26] General Paul Legentilhomme (1884–1975) was High Commissioner for the French Indian Ocean possessions and Governor-General of Madagascar, 1942–3, and Deputy Commissioner for National Defence since July 1943.

what will be the French situation when I return. However, one must hope for the best.

Monday, 27 September 1943

Left the villa at 6.45, leaving Maison Blanche airfield at 7.30. I took with me a little chap who has been sent to my staff. He speaks and writes Italian perfectly, but unfortunately does no shorthand. In every outward respect, he is like a small frightened rabbit.

Murphy (with his typist–secretary), Chief of Staff, with his A.D.C., completed the party.

We reached Tunis about 10 a.m. John Wyndham met me (with my Tunis car) and we went to General Eisenhower's H.Q. for a talk.

Our task is to prepare the way for a full meeting to take place as soon as possible in Malta between the Italians (Badoglio, etc.) and General Eisenhower and the other high Allied commanders. The idea is to settle up as much as we can, especially the signature of the full armistice terms (which I kept in my red box together with the telegrams about them, when we signed the short military armistice in Sicily on 3 September). This will not be too easy, because the long terms use the phrase 'unconditional surrender' which we studiously avoided before.

Left Tunis 12 noon. Arrived Brindisi without incident at about 3.30. The weather in Africa had changed, after a violent storm on Sunday. In Italy it is still very hot and stuffy.

We drove to the hotel and found General Mason-MacFarlane there. Brindisi has changed a lot since Murphy and I 'captured' it a week or two ago. Then there were neither soldiers nor sailors (except Italians). The hotel was still being run by its proprietors, and there was very little to consume (except exellent wine). Now the harbour and docks are full of Allied ships unloading great quantities of men and munitions and the streets are full of our troops. The Hotel Internationale has been taken over by the Military Mission (with Allied rations), and there is quite a little staff operating. It is extraordinary how rapidly all this is done.

I see the British press complains that we work too slowly! I wish the critics could come out here.

At 5 p.m. we went to see Badoglio (I enclose record of conversation).

Robert D. Murphy's record of conversation with Marshal Badoglio 27 September 1943

1. Macmillan and I accompanied General Smith and General MacFarlane on a visit to Marshal Badoglio at 5 p.m. today. By agreement with and under direction of the Commander-in-Chief, General MacFarlane presented to Marshal Badoglio two copies of the

long armistice terms. He recalled to the Marshal that the military armistice [the short terms] referred, in article 12, to the political, economic and financial conditions which will be imposed and said that the signature of the present long terms, which included all these conditions, was the principal item on the agenda of the Malta meeting scheduled for 29 September.

2. MacFarlane called the Marshal's attention to the amended preamble and said that the signature to the present document was required by the Allies for two reasons: (1) to satisfy Allied public opinion; and (2) to avoid the possibility of misunderstandings about points of detail at some later date. It was, however, to be understood that General Eisenhower had authority to make such modifications in the application of the terms as he thought fit. Moreover, some of the terms had already been rendered out of date by the process of events and the application as a whole would be carried out in the spirit of the declaration by the President and the Prime Minister.

3. Marshal Badoglio agreed to discuss the text immediately with the King and to meet with General MacFarlane and General Smith, as well as ourselves, at 10.30 a.m., 28 September.

4. There followed a discussion of the other points on the agenda of the Malta meeting. Particular reference was made to the question of an Italian declaration of war against Germany. General Smith emphasised a military feature, namely, that Italian personnel who might be captured by German forces risked treatment as *francs-tireurs* and the danger of being shot instead of being accorded privileges customarily granted prisoners of war.

5. We emphasised the importance of a declaration of war if our public opinions were to support the considerable concessions from the strict armistice terms which it was proposed to make, such as the modification of the Allied Military Government, the return to the Badoglio administration of Sicily, and the decision to support the King and his Government. Both of these points were understood by the Marshal.

6. Badoglio seemed to be content with the status of a co-belligerent, if that could be obtainable. He did not emphasise unduly a desire to be regarded strictly as an ally.

7. A suggestion was made by General Smith that, for propaganda purposes and for the purpose of inciting the Italians to the maximum war effort, the Italian Government might blur the edges of co-belligerency in speaking to their own people of the promised land of alliance, but that the technical, legal status must remain that of co-belligerency. He mentioned that there was no indignity in this because that was the technical relationship between the United States and Great Britain and France and Italy during the last war. He also pointed out that, for example, today the United States had no military alliance with Great Britain or the Soviet Union.

8. Here again Badoglio said that he would discuss the matter with the King and be prepared tomorrow morning to give us an answer. Our strong impression was that there was no need to make any concession on this point. We have the distinct feeling that the status of co-belligerency will be acceptable to the Italians.

9. The Marshal indicated that the other desiderata of the Allied Governments, such as the broadening of the basis of his Government and similar matters, could only be effectively dealt with after the King and his Government returned to Rome. He accepted it, in principle, as desirable.

10. With regard to the expression: 'It is understood that the right of the Italian people to choose their own system of government after the war', mentioned in the text of the armistice terms, Marshal Badoglio wished to see this altered to: 'It should be understood that free elections will be held after the war.' In other words, he did not wish to pledge the King and the Government to throw open the question of the monarchy by their own act. We must consider whether the form of words can be interpreted to mean merely that the Allies do not in any way by their actions now commit themselves to maintain the monarchy. Marshal Badoglio ventured the opinion also that the Italian people are not adapted to a Republican form of government and feels that the retention of the monarchy is essential to stability and unity of the country.

11. It was obvious throughout our conversation with the Marshal that in his own mind, and apparently in the minds of his associates, and this is confirmed by General MacFarlane, almost everything hinged on the return of the administration to Rome.

12. After the conclusion of the main discussion, General MacFarlane asked whether the King would assent to the introduction of certain words into the text of the broadcast speech already registered by him on a disc which would introduce the name of the Soviet Union by the side of those of Great Britain and the United States. Badoglio said that he would mention this to the King and obtain his consent. It was understood that it would not be necessary to have the King repeat the whole broadcast but merely to assent to the introduction of the desired phrase by the necessary mechanical means. Personally, Badoglio seemed to find no objection to the idea.

13. The meeting ended by the Marshal observing that tomorrow would be his seventy-second birthday.

[Diary continues] We dined at the hotel. The conditions of living are not good, because there is practically no water. The Germans have cut the great Apulian aqueduct on which all the water for southern Italy depends. At the same time, more and more troops are arriving, and more and more refugees are crowding into all the towns. The sanitary conditions are bad, and the health situation will soon become critical.

Fortunately, there are already at work excellent teams of experts, and the engineers hope to mend all the damage in another two weeks!

There are a lot of mosquitoes. I always take a net about with me and so hope to escape malaria.

I am a little tired with all this flying, especially after the heavy day yesterday at Algiers. I do wish we could get an aeroplane with a seat! My legs get very stiff, and my old wound has ached a good deal. But I shall be better tomorrow.

Tuesday, 28 September 1943

Went at 10.30 for further talk with Badoglio and his merry boys. (The record is enclosed.)

Record of conversation with Marshal Badoglio

1. Marshal Badoglio stated that he had studied the text of the long-terms document which had been appropriately referred to the King, and that he was now prepared to discuss it with us.

2. General MacFarlane explained that a necessary preliminary to the agenda which he had already given notice of to the Marshal was the signature of the long-terms document, of which we had left him a copy yesterday. The Marshal then went through the document of the long terms clause by clause. It became apparent that there were two points to which the Marshal took strong objections: (*a*) the title: 'Instrument of Surrender'; and (*b*) clause 1(*a*): 'Italian forces hereby surrender unconditionally'.

Both of these, he said, would have the most lamentable effect upon the Italians' morale and their capacity to continue the fight against Germany and he strongly urged that they be amended.

With regard to the other clauses he pointed out, over a considerable number, that the Italian Government were not in a physical position to carry them out literally. In addition, two verbal amendments were suggested in the finance clauses by Colonel Jung, both of which we accepted at once as improvements of drafting. At this point the Allied representatives withdrew and conferred together.

3. It was decided that we must insist upon the signature of the terms without amendment since these were the instructions of our Governments, and that even General Eisenhower was not in a position to take any other course.

4. After conference was resumed General MacFarlane and General Smith saw the Marshal and General Ambrosio and Colonel Jung alone. After considerable discussion it was agreed that the signature should take place, but that to assist the Italian side two steps would be recommended to General Eisenhower: (*a*) the writing of a letter by General Eisenhower to Marshal Badoglio which would set his mind at rest with regard to the point of physical incapacity to carry out the

terms and which would also explain that some of the terms were, in fact, superseded by the developments since 3 September, etc.; and (*b*) that General Eisenhower would verbally put before his Government the strong wishes of the Italians to amend the title and omit clause 1(*a*), and at the same time would transmit his strong recommendation that no publicity whatever should be given to the long-term clauses as a whole and more particularly to the unconditional surrender clause.

5. Immediately after the meeting, the Allied team, meeting together, drafted such a letter, which was in effect signed without amendment by General Eisenhower and given to the Marshal at the meeting on 29 September. A copy is attached [see p. 243].

6. Immediately before departure we reminded Marshal Badoglio of the enquiry made on the preceding day, whether the King would be disposed to include in his forthcoming broadcast, of which a phonographic disc has already been prepared, a specific reference to the Soviet Union. Marshal Badoglio replied in the affirmative and authorised in the King's name an amendment conforming to our suggestion.

7. We also left with him an *aide-mémoire*, regarding the return to Italy, under the authorisation of Marshal Badoglio, of Professor Pazzi and Professor Agnino.

[Diary continues] After the meeting, we lunched at the hotel, and took off (the same party) at about 2.30. We made a good trip as far as Cassibile airfield (near Syracuse) where we stopped to refuel. Unfortunately, on leaving Sicily to go back to Tunis, we ran into very bad weather. We got about half way across the sea, when the pilot decided to turn back. We managed to land in Sicily, but it was a forced landing and we could not make Cassibile again. We came down at rather a melancholy spot near Licata.

Here we were taken care of by an American air squadron to the best of their ability. They gave us a good meal and some blankets and we slept on the airfield until the next day dawned.

(N.B. I expect you will have seen in the papers all the fuss about the King's proclamation in which he is styled 'King of Albania and Emperor of Ethiopia'. It was a proclamation which we arranged about currency during our last visit, when we four were the only non-Italians in Brindisi, and it was a printer's error! The King and Badoglio were full of apologies!)

Wednesday, 29 September 1943

Left Licata at crack of dawn and flew to Malta. Here we found a lovely warm (not too hot) clear and sunny day. (The record of the Malta proceedings is enclosed.)

Record of conversation on H.M.S. Nelson *at Malta, 29 September 1943*

1. Marshal Badoglio opened the conversation with a statement on several points which he said he had in mind:

(*a*) His desire to see the formation of a Government on a broad, liberal basis.

(*b*) A declaration of war by the Italian Government against Germany on the return of the Government to Rome.

(*c*) In the interval, he emphasised, the Italians are in a *de facto* state of war and fighting against the Germans in Corsica, Dalmatia, etc.

(*d*) He stated that as soon as it would be possible to move Italian troops from Sardinia, he would be able to put eight Italian divisions at the disposal of the Allies.

(*e*) He expressed the fear that Italian prisoners taken by the Germans might be liable to treatment as *francs-tireurs* and, as such, to summary execution.

2. General Eisenhower stated that in his opinion the effort which the Italians are at present making is ample proof of their intention to co-operate, but that in view of (*e*) above, it would appear necessary that Marshal Badoglio's Government, which, after all, is the only legal Italian Government, declare war immediately.

3. Marshal Badoglio replied that he had already considered that point of view, but that the power of the Government at the moment extended over only a small part of Italy, which rendered a declaration of war in these circumstances extremely difficult.

4. General Eisenhower, however, pointed out that to the contrary the other exiled Governments, occupying not an inch of their national territory, have declared war against Germany. He expressed a desire to have the Badoglio administration undertake the administration of Sicily and other liberated areas, but it was not clear to him how such an arrangement can be made unless a declaration of war is undertaken.

5. Marshal Badoglio promised to refer this question to the King who, he said, in any event must decide. Under Italian law only the King can declare war. Badoglio therefore stated that he would reserve his answer until he could consult with the King.

6. General Eisenhower stated that everything Marshal Badoglio does to wage war actively against Germany will raise his Government by that much in the esteem of the United Nations. He pointed out that for three long years Italy has been an enemy of the United Nations and there has been built up a mass psychology which is not as willing to accept the Italians as soldiers in the field as it might be. Therefore, General Eisenhower stated, it is Marshal Badoglio's duty today to do so just as quickly as possible. He enquired if Marshal Badoglio would so advise the King.

7. Marshal Badoglio replied that he understood General Eisen-

hower's point of view and would present it exactly to the King as stated because his point of view corresponds to that of General Eisenhower.

8. General Eisenhower enquired whether it is Marshal Badoglio's purpose to seek anti-Fascists and invite them to participate in his Government.

9. Marshal Badoglio replied that the choice of members of the Government will be made by the King – he himself is only a soldier, he stated, knowing very little of politics.

10. General Eisenhower expressed his sympathy as a soldier but stated that the Italian Government must assume an anti-Fascist complexion if it is to fight with the Allies.

11. In the letter [see below] which he will give him, General Eisenhower will so state, but Fascism is one of those things we are fighting which we regard with deadly enmity.

12. Marshal Badoglio indicated that he understood all of this.

13. General Eisenhower reiterated that the extent he would be permitted by his Governments to co-operate with the Italians will depend upon this point.

14. Marshal Badoglio said that the fight will be (*a*) against Fascism, (*b*) against Germany, in that order.

15. Marshal Badoglio read a letter from the King asking for the participation of Count Dino Grandi,[27] stating in effect that Grandi made the initial attack against Mussolini and really is responsible for Mussolini's downfall. Grandi's presence in the Government would ruin the status of the Republican Fascist Government.

16. General Eisenhower said he would refer this question to his Governments. In his personal opinion, however, Grandi had been so closely associated for so long a period of time in the minds of our public opinion with Fascism that now for him to be included in the Italian Government would be subject to adverse misinterpretation.

17. Marshal Badoglio said that Fascism fell with the dissolution of the Grand Council. The leader of the attack was Grandi. If Grandi should today fall into the hands of the Fascists, he would be torn to pieces by them.

18. General Mason-MacFarlane at this moment pointed out that it would be necessary to make use of some men who in the past have been associated with Fascism, owing to the twenty years that have passed.

19. Marshal Badoglio then read another portion of the King's letter to the effect that Grandi would be able to create a schism among the Fascists and his presence in the Italian Government as Minister of Foreign Affairs would be a factor of tremendous importance in the war against Fascism and in injuring the Republican Fascist Government.

20. General Eisenhower replied that as soldier to soldier he fully understood all of this, but he could not overlook the fact that public

[27] Count Dino Grandi (b. 1895) took part in the March on Rome in 1922, was Ambassador to London, 1932–9, and Minister of Justice and chairman of the Fascist Grand Council, 1939–43.

opinion in Allied countries had crystallised on this subject and, as he had stated before, on a matter of this importance it would be necessary for him to consult his Governments.

21. Marshal Badoglio then said that the King's idea is to invite the chiefs of the different parties – that is, the political parties – in Italy as they are now constituted, with especial reference to the most influential people. In his opinion the King has today the best knowledge of available men in Italy. The King would name these men, Marshal Badoglio said, because while the Marshal is competent to choose generals, he is not able to choose politicians. He assured General Eisenhower that he would give a liberal character to the Government. If he discovers that any one of the Ministers does not follow the policy line laid down, he will be obliged to leave.

22. General Eisenhower said that he would refer the matter to his Governments. The President and the Prime Minister have indicated an outline of things which are necessary for collaboration. He said that it would be advisable that if the King takes additional people into his Government, he submit their names *a priori* informally through General Mason-MacFarlane's mission, and that this kind of co-operation would facilitate matters.

23. General Eisenhower then explained that he had no desire to interfere in internal Italian affairs, but that he could not overlook our Allied public opinion.

24. Marshal Badoglio said that he had every intention to avoid any possible friction between the Italian Government and the Allies and he is certain that he will come to a general accord.

25. General Eisenhower said that he could count on our understanding.

26. At this point General Eisenhower informed Marshal Badoglio of the message from Washington regarding the American desire to have Count Sforza[28] visit Brindisi in the near future.

27. Marshal Badoglio said that he knew Count Sforza well and recalled having been with him at the signing of the Treaty of Rapallo. He said, however, that the King does not regard Sforza with sympathy because of a declaration against the monarchy made by Sforza some time ago. Marshal Badoglio recognised, he said, that Sforza is doing useful work in the United States and he fully appreciates it. Marshal Badoglio stated that he would make a further effort to persuade the King of the advisability of permitting Sforza to visit Brindisi.

28. General Eisenhower stressed that our Governments attached great importance to Sforza's return to Italy and that it would have an excellent effect in our taking Italy into the Allied fold.

29. Marshal Badoglio stated that he hopes that by now General Eisenhower considers him a complete collaborator and that he would

[28] Count Carlo Sforza (1873–1952) had been Italy's Minister of Foreign Affairs, 1920–1, Ambassador to France, 1922, and a notable exile throughout Mussolini's régime.

be grateful if General Eisenhower would tell him something about the Italian campaign and what the Allied goal might be – just an idea of the plan of the campaign.

30. General Eisenhower replied that we are building up to drive the Germans out of Italy. The first move is to drive the Germans out of southern Italy – then out of Rome. He said that he had not as yet consulted General Alexander regarding certain details of the plan, but that personally he considered that German departure from Rome is something of the not too distant future.

31. Marshal Badoglio suggested that if Italian troops are necessary, there are troops in Sardinia (two divisions of infantry and one paratroop division). Marshal Badoglio hopes that some Italian troops would be allowed to participate in the entrance into Rome. General Alexander said that complete plans of the Italian campaign had been prepared but that participation of the Italian troops would depend upon an Italian declaration of war.

32. General Eisenhower offered the suggestion that if Italy declares war and co-operates with the Allies, he personally would promise that a token participation of Italian troops would be approved for entry into Rome.

33. Marshal Badoglio said that he understood perfectly that when military plans are made it is difficult to change them. In connection with his suggestion regarding the entry of Italian troops into Rome, he has in mind: (*a*) the effect it would have on the Republican Fascist Government in the north; and (*b*) he is certain that the Germans will do in Rome what they have done in Naples, that is, rob, loot and kill. He pointed out that Rome is not only the capital of Italy, but that there was a distinct obligation resting on the Italian Government to defend the Vatican. For that reason Badoglio asked that Italian troops participate. They would come from Sardinia to Fiumicino and would be in Rome in one day – the Nimbo paratroop division.

34. General Eisenhower said that General Alexander would consider the use of the Italian paratroop division in every way. He said that we have heard lots of good about that division. There is no difficulty about that point.

35. Marshal Badoglio said that German resistance at Salerno is due to Kesselring, who stands for resistance all along the line. In his opinion, he said, and you must excuse me, the Allies always give the impression of helping Kesselring's plans. He offered a suggestion that the Spezia–Rimini line has one weak spot, which is near Rimini. Marshal Badoglio spoke of his knowledge of Italy which justified his assurance in offering strategic suggestions and apologised with a smile for the characteristic love of old men to offer advice to younger men.

36. General Eisenhower made the suggestion that speaking as a soldier it is apparent that Italian troops have been through three years of a discouraging war. He suggested that as we go along and have

Italian troops participate with us, it is regarded as of the highest importance that Marshal Badoglio select the very best Italian divisions and concentrate the equipment of others if necessary so that these divisions will be well equipped and well supplied when the battle starts. He further suggested that Marshal Badoglio take other troops of lesser value and use them on lines of communication, labour battalions, work on the docks, etc. He added that as the United Nations' armies expand he could not promise to undertake to equip all Italian divisions. We shall help, of course, he added, with the enormous amount of Italian equipment now in our hands as the result of the Tunisian and Sicilian campaigns.

37. Marshal Badoglio replied that he agreed and, in fact, was already in the process of taking the action recommended.

38. General Eisenhower requested that General Mason-MacFarlane be kept advised of whatever progress might be made along these lines so that at the proper time the necessary inspection could be made.

39. Marshal Badoglio pointed out that at the present moment he is the head of the Italian Government and that these matters would be ironed out by the respective staffs. Marshal Badoglio would be grateful, he said, if we could pass on to him whatever enemy intelligence might be available and keep him informed of the Allied build-up.

40. General Eisenhower informed Marshal Badoglio that General Alexander's headquarters will shortly be moved to Italy (Bari) during the first week of October, and would provide liaison with Marshal Badoglio's staff.

41. Marshal Badoglio said that he would be very happy to provide General Alexander with any facilities necessary.

42. General Alexander promised to provide Marshal Badoglio with such enemy intelligence as might be available and said he would be able to give him a vast amount of detailed information regarding the position of enemy units now in Italy.

43. General Eisenhower said that he would direct his staff to the effect that the only publicity regarding today's meeting would be that limited to discussion of details of military operations against Germany and that no reference would be made to the signing of any document. General Eisenhower requested that Marshal Badoglio adopt a similar policy.

44. Marshal Badoglio agreed.

45. General Eisenhower added the request that Marshal Badoglio endeavour to galvanise the Italian military action against Germany and to expedite as much as lay in his power a declaration of war against Germany.

46. Marshal Badoglio pointed out that one of his chief difficulties lies in the field of propaganda. Only the Bari radio station is available to him.

47. General Eisenhower requested Marshal Badoglio to present him with an estimate of his needs in this respect and said that the Allies would do their best to co-operate with the Marshal, using the experts available in the theatre.

48. Marshal Badoglio asked he be permitted to contact Marshal Messe, now a prisoner of war in England.[29] Messe was formerly Aide to the King and in Marshal Badoglio's opinion could effectively go on the air at the B.B.C. in England. Marshal Badoglio suggested the use of outside radios as being most listened to and respected by the Italian population.

49. General Eisenhower asked Marshal Badoglio to send whatever material he desired to Marshal Messe for broadcasts and promised to send the suggestions to London through the proper channels.

50. General Eisenhower expressed his thanks to Marshal Badoglio and said that he hoped that great good would come from the meeting. Marshal Badoglio in reciprocating referred to the situation prevailing in 1918 when the Italians, he said, gave the decisive blow to the Germans. He also said that at that time there were with the Italian Army three British divisions and one American regiment, all of whom co-operated closely in the German defeat.

51. The meeting was adjourned at about 12.15 p.m.

Copy of letter from General Eisenhower to Marshal Badoglio 29 September 1943

My dear Marshal Badoglio,

The terms of the armistice to which we have just appended our signatures are supplementary to the short military armistice signed by your representative and mine on 3 September 1943. They are based upon the situation obtaining prior to the cessation of hostilities. Developments since that time have altered considerably the status of Italy, which has become in effect a co-operator with the United Nations.

It is fully recognised by the Governments on whose behalf I am acting that these terms are in some respects superseded by subsequent events and that several of the clauses have become obsolescent or have already been put into execution. We also recognise that it is not at this time in the power of the Italian Government to carry out certain of the terms. Failure to do so because of existing conditions will not be regarded as a breach of good faith on the part of Italy. However, this document represents the requirements with which the Italian Government can be expected to comply when in a position to do so.

It is to be understood that the terms both of this document and of the

[29] Marshal Giovanni Messe (1883–1968) had been captured in May 1943 while commanding the First Italian Army in Tunisia.

short military armistice of 3 September may be modified from time to time if military necessity or the extent of co-operation by the Italian Government indicates this as desirable.

Sincerely,
Dwight D. Eisenhower,
General, United States Army,
Commander-in-Chief, Allied Forces

[Diary continues] After the conference we had an excellent lunch (Italians excluded!) on H.M.S. *Nelson*. (The Italians retired to one of their own cruisers in Malta harbour!)

At about 2.30 (after a short C.-in-C.s conference) we left by plane and reached Tunis about 5.30 or 6.

We went to Advanced H.Q. and wrote up the minutes and dictated the necessary telegrams.

I spent the night at the Consular Residence.

Just before leaving Brindisi (yesterday) I got a telegram from Roger to say that the Algiers crisis looked (after all) like running its normal course. Everyone had quarrelled, everyone had resigned, and everyone had become reconciled in the course of Monday.[30] Giraud claims the victory; de Gaulle has won it. The only thing that matters is that the Americans should not get excited about it in Washington. I can easily keep them quiet at this end. So I ended the day in Tunis with an early bed and a much more contented mind than on Sunday. Both grave problems seem settled. The Italians signed the armistice terms satisfactorily and the French seem to have calmed down. But I was also very tired and was glad to get into a proper bed and sleep.

The weather is much cooler – like nice June days – and correspondingly less exhausting. John was at Tunis and looks after me most attentively. Now I must stop.

Thursday, 30 September 1943

Left Tunis by air 8.30 with Murphy and General Smith. Arrived Algiers about 11.45 – a good trip, following the sea *not* the mountains. This makes it much more comfortable although a little longer.

I went straight to the office, and plunged into a welter of paper. I had also to get off all my Italian telegrams and report to London.

In the afternoon, I had to go to hear this famous broadcast of the King of Italy. After all, the record is hopeless. He splutters and shuts his teeth and the impression is very painful. After a lot of argument, we decided to play the first paragraph only in the King's voice and have the rest read out.

[30] At a meeting on 27 September 1943, the F.C.N.L. had appointed General Legentilhomme as Commissioner of National Defence, and had issued a decree which divided the French forces into two categories, one at the disposal of the C.-in-C. for operations and the other under the direct authority of the Commissioner of National Defence.

Anyway, it is a poor speech and will not be liked in London. Let us hope it will encourage the Italians.

We finished work at about 8 p.m. Fortunately no guests to dinner – so early to bed.

October

Friday, 1 October 1943

Still no telegram. I am getting anxious about Katharine. I do hope she is all right.

A long day at the office – French economics and politics and Italian ditto. Murphy has been taken ill – I'm afraid malaria. I only hope I shall not develop it. He must have got bitten in Brindisi.

Gibson Graham[1] (North African Shipping Board) comes to dinner and I must leave off. He is a first-class man. He is just back from a visit to England and I shall hear with interest his account.

What do people say about the Government changes? Dick Law has done well – I'm so glad Bobbety is back at the Dominions.[2] They will all be pleased, especially the Masseys.[3]

And what about Beaverbrook?[4] I sent him a telegram and have had a characteristic reply.

I have just heard that Naples is in our hands. I think Allied H.Q. will be moving to Italy in five or six weeks if all goes well. Then I shall be:

(*a*) Resident Minister at Allied H.Q. (? Naples).
(*b*) Ambassador to French (Algiers).
(*c*) British Representative on Mediterranean Commision (?).[5]

They will *really have* to give me an aeroplane, or I shall resign. I cannot put up with the flying without a comfortable seat any longer.

[1] John Gibson Graham (1896–1964) was the representative of the Ministry of War Transport in the Mediterranean, 1942–5.

[2] Richard Law (1901–80), later 1st Baron Coleraine, who was a Parliamentary Under-Secretary at the Foriegn Office, 1941–3, was appointed Minister of State, 1943–5. Viscount Cranborne (known as Bobbety) (1893–1972), later 5th Marquess of Salisbury, became Secretary of State for Dominion Affairs, 1943–5, having held that office 1940–2.

[3] Vincent Massey (1887–1967) was Canadian High Commissioner in London, 1935–46.

[4] Lord Beaverbrook (1879–1964), owner of the *Daily Express*, *Sunday Express* and *Evening Standard*, became Lord Privy Seal, 1943–5. He had been my chief as Minister of Supply, 1941–2.

[5] When Stalin was told of the Italian peace feelers in August, he suggested the creation of an Inter-Allied Commission in the Mediterranean. On 21 September Churchill announced that it had been established and that I was the British representative.

Saturday, 2 October 1943

Admiral Sir Algernon Willis has taken over temporarily from Admiral of the Fleet Sir A. B. Cunningham.[6] He came to see me early this morning for a talk.

He seems *very* intelligent – a thin, scholarly face and very pleasant.

I also saw Oliver Leese[7] (going home for a little leave) and Paddy Beaumont-Nesbitt (over from Cairo).

An ordinary office morning – nothing very exciting. The weather is now quite delightful – sunny and clear, but not too hot.

Lunched with Catroux. Madame la Générale was in superb form. I think she is the most overwhelming person I know and she reminds me more of Lady Willingdon each time I see her. For some reason, she approves of me – at least for the moment.

General Legentilhomme (who has just been appointed Commissioner for War) was there. He is a nice little man – very pro-English. I'm afraid he is not a very powerful character.

After luncheon, various visitors at the office till about 5 p.m. I suddenly felt quite exhausted and went home to the villa to bed. I took some aspirin and some pills and after a little soup, etc., at 7 p.m. went to sleep.

Sunday, 3 October 1943

Woke at 7.30 – having slept for about ten hours. I feel much better, but rather weak. I think all this flying about (in such uncomfortable aeroplanes!) and trying to see so many people and deal with so many things at once has tired me. But I shall be all right if I stay in bed today.

Fortunately, Field Marshal Smuts,[8] who was supposed to arrive yesterday, does not come till this evening. I am arranging for him to go to the villa of the Admiral of the Fleet (Cunningham) where he will be more comfortable than here.

Admiral Cunningham is away and Admiral Sir Algernon Willis is acting for him. I shall *not* go to dinner, but send Makins.

I will have all tomorrow morning to talk to Smuts, as he does not leave till 2.30 for England. He is going to stay there more or less permanently, as a member of the War Cabinet. This is most fortunate for us all. He has all the qualities which will make him an admirable addition to the P.M. And it will be very good for Winston to have a colleague older than himself, whom he cannot browbeat!

[6] Admiral of the Fleet Sir Andrew Cunningham was temporarily in England. In mid-October he became First Sea Lord. His cousin Admiral Sir John Cunningham (1885–1962) succeeded him as C.-in-C. Mediterranean, and was himself succeeded as C.-in-C. Levant by Vice-Admiral Sir Algernon Willis (1889–1976), who held the appointment until December 1943.

[7] Lieutenant-General Sir Oliver Leese (1894–1978) was commander of 30th Corps, 1942–3, and took over command of the Eighth Army from General Montgomery, 1944.

[8] Field Marshal Jan Christian Smuts (1870–1950) was the South African Prime Minister and Minister of External Affairs and of Defence, 1939–48, and G.O.C. Union Defence Forces in the Field, 1940–9. He had been a member of the Imperial War Cabinet in 1917 and 1918.

9 a.m. Admiral Willis called. He came up to my bedroom and we had a chat about Smuts and other things. I like this admiral. He is very intelligent.

9.30 a.m. Sam Reber and Harold Caccia. Dealt with some Italian telegrams. I am sending Harold to Brindisi to the MacFarlane Mission. Sam Reber will go with him (representing Murphy). They leave on Tuesday and should be able to help to keep things straight then. It is terribly difficult to look after points of detail at this distance.

10 a.m. Miss Campbell came. I dictated till about 11 a.m., when Massigli came. He was very pleasant, and we had a long talk about the whole European situation and the future. The only thing was that he stayed for one-and-a-half hours, and I got rather sleepy. It is extraordinary how difficult it is to get a day's rest even in bed.

However, I managed to sleep most of the afternoon.

We have just heard that Smuts cannot arrive today after all. I hope we shall see him tomorrow.

I got up about 6 p.m. feeling much better, though still rather tired. I managed to finish two reports for London – rather letters. I do not like formal 'despatches' (such as ambassadors write and my staff try to compose for me). I am not an ambassador, and am not the servant of Mr Eden, or the P.M., or anyone else. But the Foreign Office tradition is strong. However, I have reached a compromise. When they feel the urge to compose a regular despatch in 'officialese' is too strong for them, they may yield to the temptation. It can begin with 'Sir, I have the honour' and end with 'Sir, I have the honour to be . . .' and so on. But it must be signed by one of them *for* the Minister.

I will *not* sign these documents, and it must be clear to my colleagues in London or any future student of Foreign Office papers that they are *not* my composition.

I don't know why I ramble on like this. I wish I were at home and could see you and the children. One gets intolerably lonely and depressed here if one stops work for a minute. So tomorrow I shall abandon my rest cure, which if it may benefit my body only makes my mind disturbed and melancholy.

Monday, 4 October 1943

I went down, with a great concourse of notabilities, to the airfield at Maison Blanche to meet Field Marshal Smuts.

He arrived about 11.45, and I motored him back in my car to the villa, where we had arranged a luncheon party for him at 1 p.m.

He seemed extremely well and gay – full of the desire to receive and impart information. He wanted to know all about my various jobs – the situation at A.F.H.Q. and the great experiment of an Allied H.Q. and Allied armies; the French problem; and the position in Italy. I did my best, and both in the car and in my room at the villa the talk went on. I found him charming, easy to talk with and listen to, full of fantasy, learning and humour.

Our party for luncheon included Smuts's Chief of Staff, General Gale, Admiral Willis, General Hughes (Deputy Theater Commander), Reber (Murphy being laid up with a chill) and various others – fourteen in all.

The luncheon was very successful – a good deal of general conversation – Smuts held the table and chaffed the American and British soldiers unmercifully, but in great good humour. At 2 p.m. he had to start for the aerodrome, since the plane must leave not later than 2.30 in order to reach Rabat before dark.

'Why don't you come too?' cried the old man. 'We can go on with our talk, and leave these gentlemen to their drink!'

'All right,' said I, 'I will,' and rushed upstairs – found a bag, got a shirt, toothbrush, etc., told John to do the same.

Smuts left, and we shouted that we would catch up his car at the aerodrome. So with a great scramble, we did – and got on board – left at 2.35 – not later.

The Ascalon (one of the York – indeed the first of the York – class) is a very comfortable passenger-body built on the fabric and engines of a Lancaster bomber. She is fast – noisy – and rather draughty – but otherwise very comfortable, with five beds or bunks, a saloon with six or seven chairs, a kitchen, etc., etc.

As we were only five in all – Smuts – his Chief of Staff – and his son, John and I, it was a very pleasant trip.

At Rabat, we were met by the Consul-General, Stonehewer-Bird (and a very queer bird too). The Field Marshal insisted on visiting the sights of the town before it got quite dark. So we drove rapidly round the native and European quarters. It's a very fine city – well placed and well constructed. The palace of the Sultan of Morocco – his main residence – occupies a great part of the native city. There was an immense concourse of people in an open space near the palace. A huge crowd coming and going, complete families. We were told that these were the people paying their annual tribute (which they do at the end of Ramadan). It struck me that we might organise something of the kind for income and surtax payers. It would be very picturesque. We might all assemble outside Brick House on a particular day with drums and cheque books.

Tuesday, 5 October – Friday, 8 October 1943

As you know, I was in England during these rather hectic days. From one point of view, I think I accomplished something. The Foreign Office and the War Office are beginning to see some sense both over Italy and France. But they do strike me as very tired and very unimaginative. They write their long memoranda and make their paper plans, but they do not seem to be able to visualise the reality – that is, what countries are like after battles and occupying armies and bombardments and dictatorships.

My luncheon with the P.M. on Thursday was quite successful. Oliver Lyttelton was the only other. Winston was in good form, but would not talk about any of my problems. He was only interested (for the moment) in Cos, Leros, Rhodes and the other islands of the Dodecanese.[9]

He struck me as having aged a good deal physically. But the vigour and originality of his mind are extraordinary.

Saturday, 9 October 1943

We arrived at Lisbon about 8 a.m. and left again about 10.30. We were taken from the aerodrome into the town for breakfast and had a little walk in this very attractive place.

I did so enjoy my morning at home yesterday. It was so lovely to be back and Catherine and Sarah were so nice and seemed well and happy. I'm afraid I was very unforthcoming, but I was very tired.

We got to Rabat about 1.30 p.m. Much to my disgust the aeroplane which had been promised by the Air Ministry in London was not forthcoming and no telegram of any sort had been sent. However, after a lot of fuss, I found a Marauder (medium bomber). These two boys (a New Zealander and a Canadian) undertook to fly us to Gibraltar. We left at 3.30 and got to Gibraltar in about an hour and twenty minutes.

We went up to Government House and spent the evening there.

Actually, I felt very ill (as I had done for some days), I think when I was with you at Birch Grove. I had some kind of fever, and at Gibraltar I felt like death.

Sunday, 10 October 1943

Started from Gibraltar in our Marauder at 7.30 a.m. John and I can just fit in, and it is really quite comfortable. Anyway, it is fast. The boys who drive it seem to have no difficulty in getting it up off the ground and controlling it when it is in the air. But they seem a little uncertain about landing it and argue a good deal amongst themselves as to the appropriate levers to pull or push.

However, we got to Algiers and landed without mishap. There was however the usual mistake about a car to meet us, and it was nearly 12 noon before we reached the villa.

The first thing I did was to go upstairs and take my temperature – it was just over 102°.

I found in the villa the following, who had arrived from England about two hours ahead of us:

[9] These islands were needed to provide air bases to attack Roumanian oil refineries and other Axis targets. When the Italian forces on Rhodes could not be persuaded to attack the smaller German garrison, British forces occupied Cos, Leros and Samos on 21 September. But the Germans recaptured Cos with its airfield on 7 October, the day of my meeting with Churchill.

Anthony Eden
Mr Strang (F.O.)
Mr Harvey (F.O., Private Secretary to Anthony)
Mr Lawford (F.O.)
Sir John Dashwood![10]
General Ismay
Bob Dixon (F.O.)

and a host of others – colonels, captains, officials, etc.

There soon also joined the party Admiral Sir A. B. Cunningham (who arrived from England last night) and Commodore Dick.

In this pandemonium, they were all making separate and impossible plans. They would stay here; they would leave at once for Tunis; General Eisenhower would be at Tunis: no, General Eisenhower was in Italy; yes, but he would be returning to Tunis; well, they would go to Cairo and stop on the way at Tripoli, and so on and so on. It soon emerged (when the officer in charge was given a chance to speak):

(*a*) that the tyre of the York required repair;
(*b*) that there was no flying round Tunis owing to weather;
(*c*) that it would not be possible to land at Tripoli owing to weather;
(*d*) that the bad weather was moving east, and if they wanted to make sure of Cairo, they had better leave very early tomorrow and get ahead of it.

Nobody seemed to pay much attention. Anthony, Ismay and the admiral discussed the situation in the Aegean, especially Cos, Leros and Rhodes:[11] Massigli (who had been asked to lunch) arrived and talked to me: finally we sat down to luncheon – fourteen at the big table and six at a sort of children's table which John had provided.

Massigli was very pleasant, and Anthony handled him very well. I got Massigli to give a dinner for Anthony to meet de Gaulle (but excused myself, as *souffrant*). After luncheon, I went to bed, and took several aspirins and thought no more about my guests.

Monday, 11 October 1943

Stayed in bed. I heard from John that my visitors had left – all but Bob Dixon who is staying on with us for a time. They asked for luncheon for twenty-four to be put up (the request was made at 6 p.m. yesterday) and it was ready for them when they left at 7 a.m. today. John is angry, but triumphant.

I felt very bad all day, with persistent diarrhoea and much headache. However, in the middle of the day your telegram arrived. I cannot tell you how much I was pleased. It is really splendid. Curiously enough it

[10] William Strang (1893–1978), Oliver Harvey (1893–1968), Valentine Lawford (b. 1911), Sir John Dashwood, 10th Bart (1896–1966) served in the Foreign Office, 1940–5.

[11] Cos had just been retaken by the Germans, Leros fell to them later in the month, Samos in November. Rhodes was being bombed by Allied aircraft.

was the same with Maurice, do you remember? Father was in India.

We are just going to celebrate our centenary.[12] So young Alexander is just in time for it.

In the evening Roger produced a very clever specialist to see me, called Colonel Richardson.[13]

Tuesday, 12 October 1943

In bed all day. The pains in the stomach are better and the temperature down. It was down yesterday by day, but went up at night. Apparently I have *not* got malaria (for which he took the blood test) and I have not any other organic disease. Colonel Richardson tested me thoroughly for everything possible. I have got a sort of inflammation of the stomach due to a germ and I have not thrown it off owing to being (according to this chap) in a condition of extreme exhaustion, approaching prostration. I think they all exaggerate a bit – the doctor to be on the safe side, Roger because he likes running the office and thinks I obstruct, John because he is really quite fond of me. So I am nursed and coddled like an old grandfather.

Actually, I managed to see Bob Murphy, Ed Wilson (U.S. representative on Mediterranean Commission), Mr [Esler] Dening (Foreign Office adviser to Lord Louis Mountbatten – on his way to Delhi), Mr Stone (Canadian External Affairs). I have asked the last two to stay here. I also had two hours (4–6) with Mr Herbert – our economic adviser. This is the part these Foreign Office chaps always neglect when I am away. There are a lot of things to be put right, and the chief thing which threatens us is the prospect of real locust plagues all over Africa, largely as the result of the French having neglected the precautions which we arranged for them to take this spring. We gave them all the necessary equipment for a big poisoning campaign, and that ass Giraud called up into the Army all the skilled scientific personnel! However, there is still time to save the situation if we act quickly. There is an international locust control – organised before the war – the expert of which is a Russian called [Boris] Uvarov (whom I saw here in March). Each territory must play its part or it lets down the rest – a familiar French role!

After Herbert went, I was very tired.

Wednesday, 13 October 1943

The medicine which Colonel Richardson has given me to cure my poisoned tummy has, unfortunately, a very lowering effect, and I feel like bursting into tears at any moment. It's sulphur and something else [sulphonamide] and certainly seems efficacious. My temperature is also down. But I don't feel up to any effort.

[12] The first book published by Macmillan appeared in November 1843.

[13] Lieutenant-Colonel John Richardson was my doctor for many years after the war, and was President of the General Medical Council, 1973–80.

The only effort I was required to make was to receive the new Russian Ambassador to the French, M. Bogomolov.[14] He has arrived here with twenty-five assistants – but like everyone else he has just got a room in the Aletti Hotel and eats in the American mess. As his standards of living are pretty high, he seems rather annoyed about it.

He has no car yet – so I sent John in ours to fetch him here. He asked John if he had been at Eton. Yes, replies John. Ah! says Bogomolov, a splendid school – a fine tradition – a splendid school, and went on muttering this all the way from the hotel to the villa.

Bogomolov is heavy – large-limbed with loose clothes – fat white hands, fat white face (continually putting his head down and rolling up his eyes) and talks or rather lectures at considerable length. (He was a professor of Marxist philosophy.)

He was very gracious – a little royal even. He talked a little about my stomach and at great length about his own, which requires constant attention and the rarest foods. These last are not found in the American mess or the Aletti, and he is rather put out about it. I had no difficulty with him – he stayed about three-quarters of an hour, and I dozed pretty comfortably through it. He left to see Murphy.

The only thing I told him was about the Italian declaration of war. He asked only one question on this. 'Did the Marshal Stalin know?' I showed him the Three-Power declaration, signed by Stalin, and all was well.[15]

At 5.45 I got up and dressed. There was a conference at 6 p.m. which I had to attend. (I forgot to say that I had already been out once at 12 noon, to see General Eisenhower. But I went straight back to bed.) They kindly held it in my house – Murphy, Reber, General Julius Holmes, General Whiteley (Deputy Chief of Staff), Roger Makins, Bob Dixon and H.M. It lasted from 6 to 8 p.m., and I was quite exhausted at the end. But I think we got what we wanted – that is, immediate steps to set up a skeleton Control Commission[16] in Brindisi to advise and organise the Italian Government and the early liquidation of AMGOT in Sicily, Calabria, etc., returning these territories *as soon as can be arranged* to the authority of Italian Crown and Government, properly advised by the Control Commission. It is a *huge* task, and we must set about it without delay. The position is very difficult and confusing, and I am disappointed at a rather weak attitude at A.F.H.Q. However, we pushed them about a bit and made progress. I went to bed, with (I'm afraid) a return of my stomach pain.

[14] Alexander Efremovich Bogomolov (1900–69) had been sent to London as Soviet Representative to the French National Council in 1941.

[15] 'The Governments of Great Britain, the United States and the Soviet Union acknowledge the position of the Royal Italian Government as stated by Marshal Badoglio and accept the active co-operation of the Italian nation and armed forces as a co-belligerent in the war against Germany.'

[16] An Armistice Control Commission, as specified in the 'long terms'.

Thursday, 14 October 1943

This has been a very good day, and I am making progress. I did *absolutely nothing* all the morning but lie in bed and snooze. The pain has gone and although I think the medicine is very weakening, it seems to be overcoming the trouble. The diarrhoea has stopped and I feel better, though quite washed out. Colonel Richardson seems to have frightened Roger about me, although admitting that my physique was excellent. But he said no one could work at such a pace, and so on. I don't really think it's the work, so much as the combination of heat and uncomfortable flying arrangements which I have had all the summer.

The weather is now quite lovely – like Indian summer days. Warm, not hot: cool nights and mornings – sun, with fleecy clouds – clear, limpid air, without excessive humidity.

At 12 noon, I got up and went (with John) for a little drive and walked for a little time in a wood – just an elderly, grandfatherly, invalidish morning. It was charming, and I felt all the better.

I have had no solids to eat since Sunday, but today was allowed an omelette for my luncheon. It was a beautiful work of art, by our loyal chef, Blom, of Grosvenor House Hotel.

Admiral Cunningham came to lunch – bringing with him Admiral Power, who is in command at Taranto – a splendid man.

We had a very useful conference after lunch (the two admirals, Bob Dixon and self) on the whole position. There are a lot of problems regarding the use of the Italian Navy not unlike those which we successfully overcame with Force X at Alexandria. The truth is that this 'co-belligerency' status is rather tightrope walking (especially with the French, Greeks and Yugoslavs clamouring for vengeance). But I am sure it is the right thing for the prosecution of the war against Germany. And I believe it is also the best thing for post-war peace and reconciliation.

After the conference – i.e. about 3.30 – I went to bed and am writing this now. I shall soon sleep and I have (so far as I know) nothing more to do today. Everything I can get *en train* is in motion, and I must wait a few days for the next steps. I particularly want to get well enough to go to Brindisi as soon as possible.

I cannot get over my pleasure about the baby. Do write me details – weight, eyes, hair, etc. Please tell me all the details. I hope everything is all right and no great trouble to Katharine as the result of her falls. I have a feeling that he will be just like Maurice. I suppose Nanny is greatly excited and all the children too. I must have a photograph of the christening.

Can you think of a present for Katharine? I feel I should give her something for my first grandson. Perhaps you will begin to shed some jewellery upon her! Honestly – I am so happy about it. I feel a new interest in everything and that so many things become more worth while – planting trees for instance and publishing books!

Friday, 15 October 1943

I am better – but very weak. I think this is largely the result of the medicine, which I am now to leave off.

The weather is really lovely now. I lie in my bed and look across the bay – the sea a deep blue, the sun bright, the sky clear – it is just perfect.

My day passed less peacefully than I had hoped. Roger is being very good about sparing me as much paper as possible, but people are insistent.

At 10.30 I had to get up to see Ed Wilson – who is to succeed Murphy as American Ambassador to the French. Then General Julius Holmes brought General Joyce[17] round to see me. He is an aged and very pleasant American general who is to replace Mason-MacFarlane as head of the Military Mission in Brindisi. He will act (provisionally) as head of the Allied Control Commission in Italy. His qualifications appear to be absolutely nil.

After this, we had a further conference about Italian matters, arising out of the decisions taken at the last one. The Chief of Staff (Bedell Smith) is still in Washington, so General Jock Whiteley (Deputy Chief) acts in his place. He is very friendly and helpful, of moderate abilities.

After luncheon, I went back to bed. Averell Harriman came to see me at about 6 p.m. He is here for a day, on his way to Moscow, where he is to be the new American Ambassador.

Record of conversation with Mr Averell Harriman
15 October 1943

> Harriman told me that he had seen Giraud, who expressed the most violently anti-Russian sentiments, and de Gaulle, who expressed the most violently pro-Russian sentiments. He had also seen Massigli, who held the middle view.
>
> Harriman's view of the Russians is that it is no good trying to blarney them. The thing is to tell the truth and stand up to them.

[Diary continues] I like Averell, having made friends with him at the Casablanca conference, where we shared a house. He is amusing, human, intelligent, and one can talk freely to him.

At 7.30 p.m. I got up and went to General Eisenhower's house to see Cordell Hull (American Secretary of State). He arrived a few hours before. He had come by cruiser to Casablanca and then by air from Casablanca here. It was the first time in his life that he had been in an

[17] Major-General Kenyon A. Joyce (1879–1960) was Acting Deputy-President, A.C.C., 1943–4.

aeroplane. He was very pleased with his adventure and determined to press on. So in spite of his doctor, he was going on at 10.30 tonight to Cairo! He is on his way to Russia for the conference.

These Americans travel in great style and in great numbers. Averell Harriman has two C54 machines – huge four-engined transport, each capable of holding thirty to forty people. Hull has another two.

I don't know why American statesmen are always so old. Secretary Stimson (Secretary for War) who came through here is over eighty. Hull is seventy-four. He is exactly like the portraits of all Americans of the Civil War period – a fine Southern gentleman. His views on internal politics are reactionary and on foreign politics based on the sort of vague Liberalism of the 'eighties' tinctured with personal prejudice. Nevertheless, he is obviously a 'character' and his fine head and striking appearance distinguish him in strong contrast from the sort of vague American face that most of them have. That is one of the difficulties I find with Americans – they all look exactly alike to me – like Japanese or Chinese. In uniform they naturally all look the same (I suppose our officers do) but in plain clothes also they are all exactly like dentists.

Record of conversation with Mr Cordell Hull
15 October 1943

I was ushered into the presence with due solemnity – Rob Murphy flitting about like a Monsignor in a Papal Palace, several doctors and others in attendance, including a little tubby man who looked like the anaesthetist, but who, I believe, was in the American State Department.

Mr Hull was sitting in a kind of semi-darkness, and after the introductions he observed in his high voice that he had heard a great deal about me. I said I hoped he had not heard ill about me. He said on the contrary that he thought I had done a good job. I said that we had tried to devise a policy at this headquarters which would be the Allied Headquarters policy in support of General Eisenhower. He said he quite understood that, and had been pleased at the co-operation between Bob Murphy and myself.

He said he was very tired but he had liked his experience in an aeroplane and was proposing to go on tonight. We talked a little about the Southern states of America, the relative advantages and disadvantages of Tennessee and Kentucky. When I told him that my mother's people had eventually migrated from Kentucky into Indiana, he shook his head sadly.

[Diary continues] Ike had asked me to stay to dinner, but I already had a dinner-party laid on – a farewell party for Admiral Cunningham, who now leaves us for good to take up his post as First Sea Lord.

This was a very good party. Admiral Cunningham, Admiral Sir John Cunningham (who is taking over as C.-in-C. Med. – at least temporarily), Air Chief Marshal Tedder, Air Vice-Marshal Wigglesworth, Mr Gibson Graham (head of North African Shipping Board), Commodore Dick, Captain Shaw (Paymaster-Captain – secretary to the admiral – who has been a splendid friend to us), Lieutenant-General Sir Humfrey Gale, General Whiteley, Roger Makins, Bob Dixon (who is here for a few days on visit from the F.O.), Admiral Hewitt (U.S. Navy) and self (fourteen in all). I proposed the admiral's health; he made a speech in reply, and we were all very merry.

Saturday, 16 October, 1943

Last night's dissipations have not done me much harm, I think. I ate a little fish (especially prepared for me by the chef) and left the six or seven courses of our gargantuan meal to the others. But I still feel very weak. I am writing this in bed, and I shall stay there at least till luncheon.

I keep thinking about my grandson. *Please* send me full description and, when possible, photograph. How does Aunt Sarah feel? I suppose immensely proud. Has the baby blue or brown eyes? And are they really going to call it Alexander?

I stayed in bed all the morning – papers are sent up to me in a box from the office and returned by a messenger.

I got up for luncheon – Herbert (N.A.E.B.), Mr Swiggett (!) of the British Supply Council in Washington (actually an American banker), Mr Goschalk (British economist – working on North African food questions). Quite an interesting party.

After luncheon, I returned to bed. Colonel Maxwell (Military Government Section, A.F.H.Q.) came in about four – otherwise no visitors.

At seven I got up and went to a meeting at Murphy's house on Italian affairs, followed by a dinner at which Mr Henry Morgenthau (Secretary to the American Treasury) was present. I thought him a pleasant enough man. He is supposed to be charged with getting the real 'low down' on the situation at Allied H.Q. I'm afraid this stimulated me to a lot of fooling and we even managed to make Morgenthau (who is a very serious man) laugh a bit. But I think he is puzzled.

He had a frightful little Jew – the worst type – called Dr White[18] with him, whose insulting attitude to the British annoyed the local Americans intensely. I teased him a good deal, and he got very cross and very silly. But I believe he is a clever man as a Treasury official.

I think both the British and the American visitors are a little taken

[18] Harry Dexter White (1892–1948) was Morgenthau's Assistant, 1943–5. Indicted in 1948 before the House of Representatives Committee on Un-American Activities on a charge of subversive and pro-Communist activities, he died shortly after testifying.

aback by the Anglo-American solidarity here. There was a two hours' meeting of N.A.E.B. for Morgenthau's benefit (I did not attend, but Roger represented me). Apparently the twin heads of each department (we have British and Americans as chairman or vice-chairman of each section) played up splendidly and would not allow Dr White or Morgenthau to make any sort of rift between them. I was very glad it went off well, because N.A.E.B. has enormously improved lately both in spirit and in performance.

Sunday, 17 October 1943

Church in morning.

11.30 a.m. Count Sforza was produced at my villa, for Murphy and me to talk to. He arrived from England yesterday. He talked for one-and-a-half hours without drawing breath. (I cannot picture what his conversation with the P.M. was like!) He said some witty, some interesting, and many revealing things. But I should like to see more of him before making up my mind. He goes to Brindisi today.

2.15 p.m. A great ceremony to say 'goodbye' to Admiral Cunningham. British and American guards of honour (naval and military) on the airfield and a great American brass band – playing 'Auld Lang Syne'. All the notabilities of Allied H.Q. and many French officers were collected. He actually took off at 2.30 sharp.

4.30 p.m. Visited an old boy called Sir Henry Craik in hospital. He is over sixty – returning from India, where he has been acting as political adviser to the Viceroy. He was formerly Governor of the Punjab.

His father – old Sir Henry Craik – was a great friend of the Macmillans and his uncle – Mr Craik – was once a partner (fortunately bought out!).[19] This poor fellow got desperately ill with broncho-pneumonia on a ship coming home and was put out in Algiers. He is in the military hospital of which my doctor (Colonel Richardson) is the physician and I think he owes his life to Colonel Richardson. He is now convalescent and we are trying to ship him home by air as soon as a suitable plane can be made available.

5.30 p.m. Sir John Cunningham – who is acting as C.-in-C. Mediterranean – called at the villa. He stayed about an hour. He wanted to find out the general political and politico-military position here. He has been previously admiral in the Levant. (He was the admiral in charge of the very unsuccessful operation at Dakar. He is nonetheless a keen admirer of de Gaulle, while Sir A. B. Cunningham loathed him!)

6.30–8 p.m. Francis Rennell has arrived from General Alex's H.Q. in Italy. We had a conference on the extremely tangled situation there, after which I went to bed, very tired.

It is quite extraordinary, but this disease has pulled me down to an

[19] George Lillie Craik (d. 1908) became a partner in Macmillan & Co. in 1865.

extent I did not believe possible. I realise now why Roger and this doctor have been fussing so over me. I feel suddenly like an old man – and have very little strength even to do the simplest thing – like walking or dressing. My mind does not function at all except for a few hours, and I really am very concerned. But Colonel Richardson assures me that I shall recover slowly. He has now stopped the sulphur cure, as the poison seems to be overcome, and given me a tonic instead – so perhaps I shall feel better. But he attributes my weakness not wholly to his medicine (which is perhaps natural in him) but to many years of overwork and overstrain, which he said would anyway have led to a collapse.

I thought that this was all the usual doctor's boloney, but I must say I have felt a little alarmed the last few days. I suppose really one goes on thinking one is young up to a certain point, when one suddenly realises that the resilience of youth is no longer there.

All this seems rather a wail, and I have no doubt I shall be quite all right in a week or two.

I hope you are keeping well. I thought you looked very well, and very youthful and very pretty the other day. I am anxiously awaiting some news of my grandson. No doubt I shall get a letter in a few days. I got telegrams of congratulation from a number of people, for which I was very grateful.

Monday, 18 October 1943

I spent a fairly easy morning, but had a conference with General Eisenhower and Murphy (attended also by our new American diplomat – Mr Ed Wilson) and managed to persuade the general to put forward to the Combined Chiefs of Staff as his own idea the scheme for Allied association with the Italian Control Commission[20] which I settled when I was in London, and of which both P.M. and Anthony approved. The literary part of this now fairly familiar procedure is always rather entertaining. I write a memorandum in normal English embodying the plan. Then the Chief of Staff (or in his absence, some other 'stooge') translates this into American and produces it for the general's approval.

He then generally introduces a few obscurities and some more words like 'activated' or 'from my standpoint', and the thing is then sent off.

The object of all this is, of course, to conceal the origin of the proposal, which would be painfully clear if a message were to arrive in Washington written in the clear and limpid prose affected by yours truly.

This sounds rather depreciatory of General Eisenhower, but really is not so. Although completely ignorant of Europe and wholly

[20] This was the Advisory Council for Italy, about to be set up at the Moscow talks.

uneducated (in any normal sense of the word), he has two great qualities which make him much easier to deal with than many superficially better-endowed American or British generals. First, he will always listen to and try to grasp the point of an argument. Second, he is absolutely fair-minded and, if he has prejudices, never allows them to sway his final judgment. Compared with the wooden heads and desiccated hearts of many British soldiers I see here, he is a jewel of broadmindedness and wisdom.

After the meeting, I dropped in for a chat with Admiral Sir John Cunningham. He is a very different type from his cousin. He is the intellectual sailor – I should say less character but more mental powers than A.B.C. It will be interesting to see how he gets on in this queer world at A.F.H.Q.

Lunched with M. and Mme Seydet, First Secretary to Belgian Legation. He is a nice little man, and his wife a pretty little woman – rather English in appearance. M. Menthon (one of the new Commissioners and lately head of one of the resistance groups in France) was there;[21] also M. de Charbonnières (a silly fellow – once monarchist, now extreme Gaullist) and some others.

After luncheon, I went to the office – for the first time since I left for England a fortnight ago. I did not work late and on getting back to the villa, went to bed.

Francis Rennell had arrived in the course of the afternoon from Bari. He goes to London tomorrow.

9 p.m. M. Monnet (member of the Committee of Liberation) came in. He stayed about an hour. He is going to Washington to air his views on the problems of (*a*) administration of, (*b*) relief of France, *after* the Germans have been ejected.

After he had gone, Francis came in and chatted about Italy, and all the related problems, till nearly 1 a.m.

Tuesday, 19 October 1943

Stayed in bed most of the morning and had papers sent up from the office.

Luncheon at 1.15. The chief guests were M. Bogomolov (the Soviet Ambassador to the French), M. Cerny (Czechoslovak Minister to the French), Admiral Sir John Cunningham, Mr [Selden] Chapin (second to Mr Ed Wilson, American representative on the Mediterranean Commission, which has not yet held a meeting!), Colonel Richardson (my brilliant young doctor), Colonel McChrystal (U.S. public relations [P.W.B.]), Colonel Higgins (A.F.H.Q. Liaison Section), and some others – fourteen in all. Bogomolov was in great spirits and insisted on drinking toasts with each course. The chef surpassed

[21] Comte François de Menthon (b. 1900) formerly a director of the Resistance movement *combat*, had just become Commissioner of Justice.

himself and gave us a sort of pre-war luncheon – too much for my poor 'inside'.

After luncheon I drove to one of the hospitals to see Sir Henry Craik. We shall get him off by air in a day or two, I hope.

I got back from the office at about 7 p.m. and went to bed.

Wednesday, 20 October 1943

8.30 a.m. Oliver Stanley, accompanied by Thornley (who used to be Bobbety's Private Secretary at Colonial Office) and Admiral Bromley (who had been on a jaunt to Cairo), arrived from Cairo on his way back from his trip to West and East Africa.[22] He [Stanley] stayed till about noon, when he went back to the airport (I drove with him) to go to Gibraltar. He was to leave there after a day or two for home.

I had a long talk with him. He seems to me much improved in health (he is fatter and less harassed-looking) and much less bitter and defeatist in his attitude to life. Whether this is the result of his return to high office or the death of Maureen or both I cannot judge. Although I know he was absolutely devoted to Maureen, I think he must have found her rather fatiguing.

I do not think Oliver will ever be anything but a Stanley. He will never run great risks or take bold decisions. Nevertheless he can be (and is) a very useful member of the rather thin Conservative team. He is a good administrator and a *very* practised Parliamentarian.

After luncheon, the usual office routine. At 7.15 General Joyce, General Eisenhower's selection (or rather the War Department's selection) as acting head of the proposed Allied Commission in Italy, came to see me. He stayed to dinner (we were alone: only Roger and John; Harold Caccia and Bob Dixon are in Brindisi, the former permanently and the latter on a visit before going back to London) and left about 10.30. So we had quite enough to form some judgment of his character and capabilities. But I will leave this for a further letter.

Thursday, 21 October 1943

A normal morning; lots of telegrams in, and with our depleted staff (Harold Caccia away) poor Roger has a very heavy time. I am hoping to hear from General Alexander about going to see him at Bari, but I cannot get away from here for a few days.

De Gaulle and Sir John Cunningham came to luncheon – a small, intimate party – only Roger, John and de Gaulle's A.D.C. I think de Gaulle enjoyed it. He talked pleasantly and frankly. He improves all the time; as he obtains power, so his sense of responsibility increases. He is still shy, sensitive, and very prone to take offence. But he *has* a

[22] Oliver Stanley (1896–1950) was Colonial Secretary, 1942–5, Colin Thornley (1907–1983) was his Private Secretary, Rear-Admiral Sir Arthur Bromley (1876–1961) was his Ceremonial and Reception Secretary.

sense of humour (rather puckish) and he can relax in company where he is at ease.

He stayed till past three o'clock. After luncheon he and I and the admiral were left by the others and de Gaulle spoke freely and naturally. I was glad of the chance, as I have not seen him for some time – I have rather avoided doing so. But I still feel anxious to hand over to a British Ambassador as soon as I can. It would be better for me to leave now, from both the French point of view and my own.

I think the fact that de Gaulle's talk with Mr Cordell Hull went off well is most fortunate. He did not speak so bitterly against the Americans as he generally tries to do – unless one stops him.

Colonel Tom Campbell (U.S.) and Mr [John] Fisher (Vice-Consul at Casablanca, British) to dinner. Quite an interesting evening. Colonel Campbell (of the Montana Agricultural Company) is an agricultural engineer. He was employed by the Russian Government in 1929 onwards. He was the organiser of their use and production of tractors and mechanised agricultural machinery of all kinds. He was the architect of the great government farms, to one of which, Gigant [in Rostov], I remember going in 1932. He has, during the war, been working on the Alaska highway, Persian railways, extension of Burma road and similar jobs, as well as the development of rapid aerodrome construction, with the use of the 'bull-dozer' and other powerful machines of the kind.

He has just been to China and India and is on his way home from this trip. He came to see me on his way out (some months ago) with a letter of introduction from Philip Swinton, and I was very glad to see him again.

Fisher is an intelligent, if quiet, young man, who was in the Eastern Consular service, and was at Bangkok. He, with others, was interned by the Japanese; after some months he was released (or exchanged) as having diplomatic status.

Even a fairly short career in those parts has given him a slightly Oriental appearance. But he has the poise and self-control which one associates with the Burman or Siamese and in these hustling, bustling days carries a certain charm. (Actually, all Consuls seem to maintain this detachment from reality, because, as far as I can see, none of them has anything at all to do: once upon a time they used to do something about merchant seamen and bills of lading, but now the Ministry of War Transport representative in every port takes care of these.)

Friday, 22 October 1943

Finished our office work by 12 noon (chiefly telegrams and receiving various journalists. Oh, my! if the people who read the papers could realise the ignorance and stupidity and vanity of those who write them!).

Roger, Bob Dixon and I went to luncheon at Tipasa. It was a

glorious day – hot in the sun, but not too hot – with lovely light and shade and fleecy white clouds and the blue sea – idyllic Indian summer weather – with that touch of melancholy which autumn brings all over the world.

The rain which we have had has turned the ground from brown to green – from burnt land to a sea of wild flowers of every kind – heathers and brooms in flower as well – wild cyclamen and scillas all over the place – a feast of beauty.

I did not bathe (as I am a little afraid still of my inside) but the others did. We lunched and walked in the ruins of the Roman city and idled, till the time came to leave and return to work.

6 p.m. Colonel Archdale – from War Office – to discuss the formation of a regular Military Mission to the French, which is necessary and should be arranged in due course. It will, however, be a delicate matter to agree, without hurting the feelings of A.F.H.Q., and particularly the Chief of Staff and General Eisenhower. As usual, I have been told to fix this up by London without delay, although I have explained the difficulties to them both by telegram and personally when I was at home. However, I expect I can get it through in due course.

7 p.m. Went to Murphy's villa to a conference with Mr Morgenthau (American Secretary to the Treasury) and his stooge, Dr White. The former is a pleasant enough Jew; the latter a very tiresome Armenian. Mr Morgenthau talked for half an hour; Dr White for another half an hour, and both made (I thought) very heavy weather over comparatively simple financial and economic questions. A further conference tomorrow.

8 p.m. Dinner at the villa. General Mason-MacFarlane (head of Military Mission to Italian Government), General Joyce (U.S., prospective head of the Allied Control Commission), General Whiteley (British, Deputy Chief of Staff, A.F.H.Q.), General Julius Holmes (Military Government Section), Colonel Maxwell, Bob Murphy, Sam Reber, Roger Makins, Bob Dixon and others.

After dinner a long and complicated discussion about the future of AMGOT, about the Control Commission, about Allied policy towards Italy and so on. The trouble with these discussions is that everyone seems (probably naturally) to be influenced by their own positions, present and prospective, in the organisation. However, made some progress.

Saturday, 23 October 1943

9.45 a.m. Conference with Morgenthau. I attended with my financial adviser, Brigadier Rabino (a very clever man – in civil life manager of the Westminster Bank in Paris), and Colonel Dunlop (finance officer to British forces). All the hares started last night were pursued and finally killed, and what had looked like rather a threatening inter-Allied situation was successfully 'liquidated'.

11 a.m. General Mast (Resident-General in Tunisia and an old friend) called. He is very much concerned by the Communist party in Tunisia, which is working hard among the Arabs and stirring up disaffection. He complains that he cannot get support from the French Committee in Algiers for strong measures against the Communists because de Gaulle is always flirting with Russia and the Communists.

But poor Mast is rather a 'fusser', and apt to exaggerate on this topic. I told him he ought to get Stalin to intervene and tell the Communists to be quiet as they are interfering with the war. He brightened up at this idea, and I will put him in touch with M. Bogomolov (the new Russian Ambassador), who has already (I am told) taken this line with the Arabs in Algeria who tried to enlist his sympathy.

12 noon. M. Puaux (Resident-General in Morocco). He had no particular complaints and seemed to be pretty confident about his position. I think he is a good man – honourable and with some character. Anyway, he is a vast improvement on General Noguès, who was a crook and a traitor.

12.45 p.m. A farewell (and very friendly) talk with Morgenthau. He has responded quite well to treatment. I am not so sure about Dr White.

After lunch, I went to bed and did not go back to the office till about 5 p.m. I am still feeling rather weak.

No one to dinner and early to bed.

Sunday, 24 October 1943

Left Algiers (Maison Blanche aerodrome) by air for Tunis. Sir John Cunningham, Commodore Dick, Murphy, Roger Makins, Sam Reber and I.

We got to La Marsa for the periodic meeting which General Eisenhower holds with the three British commanders (Cunningham, Alexander, Tedder). This time we all stayed at the American guest-house at Sidi Bou Said (above Carthage).

After luncheon, Alex and I went for a motor drive over the battlefields round Medjez el Bad and Tunis. He explained all the final phases and the importance of the various features (Longstop Hill, Grenadier Hill, etc.)

It was most interesting and gave one a great insight into his methods and the essential clarity of his thought.

We got back about 6.30. General Mason-MacFarlane arrived for dinner and we talked over the Italian situation till bedtime.

It was a lovely day – warm in the sun, but not hot – a sort of perfect 'Indian summer' day.

Monday, 25 October 1943

General Alexander, his Chief of Staff, Murphy, Roger, Sam Reber and I left for Bari in General Alex's plane (very comfortable – with seats!). We got to Bari in three-and-a-half hours – a perfect flying day, and drove to General Alex's H.Q., which are not far from Bari, in a pleasant little village on the sea.

After luncheon, the civilian party (four) drove into Bari, where we saw the AMGOT officers, the propaganda people, and the officers in charge of the broadcasting station.

In spite of some mistakes, I think these men have done a good job. They have got a local paper going; thrown out the Fascist editor; got the broadcasting station operating (under our supervision) and also got rid of any well-known Fascists in charge. There are all sorts of problems – about newsprint; about money (for employees' wages); about power and technical needs of the station; about programmes, and difficulty of communication with Algiers on these – and so on. I particularly like Major Ian Greenlees[23] (a journalist), whom I sent to Bari on our first visit to Brindisi and who seems to have occupied the station alone and operated it ever since.

Dinner at General Alex's mess – as always very pleasant – and talk with him afterwards. He is always charming and his rather whimsical humour and detachment and self-control have quite won over Murphy.

Tuesday, 26 October 1943

Roger and Sam Reber went over to Brindisi (about two hours' drive) to see Mason-MacFarlane, General Maxwell Taylor (second-in-command of the Military Mission) and Harold Caccia – whom I had sent to Brindisi some time ago. Murphy and I flew to Foggia, where we found some friends to show us round. (American General Spaatz kindly took us in his B17 or Flying Fortress.)

We had a good tour of the town, which has been very much destroyed but nevertheless contains some fine buildings in good condition – notably the Prefecture and the Fascist H.Q.

The bombing of the aerodromes and railways by our air forces has been incredibly effective and remarkably accurate. It gives one an extraordinary idea of what this long-range bombing can do, especially when you get more or less command of the air, as we have got in Italy.

The aerodromes are very good – gravel, soil and grass – and very large. When the Air Force really gets going from here, it will be very powerful. But, of course, it takes a little time to develop its strength and to move over all the vast quantities of men, machines and material which are required.

We left Foggia about 2 p.m. and drove to the very pretty fishing town of Manfredonia. One gets a very good impression of the country by car which one does not obtain by air. So we drove back to Bari, instead of going by plane, arriving just about dusk.

[23] Major Ian Greenlees (b. 1913) became Director of the British Institute, Florence, 1958–81.

The country is really lovely. Part of it is under cereal cultivation, in broad and apparently fertile plains. Then you come to great olive groves, extending over hundreds and even thousands of acres. The towns and villages are pleasant enough: no remarkable architecture, but usually a pleasing baroque church and occasionally a very old Romanesque church – going back to the twelfth or thirteenth century. Sometimes there are vineyards, between the olives or in separate closely planted enclosures.

On getting back from Bari (about 6 p.m.) we went to our guest-house. This is a comfortable little villa, quite near General Alex's. It is in a village some miles from Bari. General Alex has his own little house and his H.Q. in another larger building and his camp in the surrounding fields.

Soon after our return, General MacFarlane and Reber and Caccia turned up. They were in rather an excited mood (which is not unusual with them).

The political situation seems rather complicated, but I think they all worry unduly about this. All situations have been complicated ever since I arrived at A.F.Q.H. on 1 January. But it is no use worrying. One must also laugh.

The difficulty arises from our desire to see a more liberal and broad-based Italian government. But such party leaders as we can find at this stage are not very impressive. The more well-known figures are in Rome, Turin or Milan. Moreover, some of them refuse to serve under Badoglio, others refuse to serve under the King. Some demand a civilian prime minister; others demand, if not a republic, at least an abdication by the King, a renunciation of his rights by the Prince of Piedmont, and a succession by the young Prince of Naples[24] (six or eight years old and in Switzerland) with a regency.

There is a further complication that under the Italian constitution the Regent ought to be the next-of-kin. This means the new Duca d'Aosta,[25] who is regarded as quite impossible.

Sforza is running an intrigue to force the abdication of the King, to get Badoglio to act as Regent (in spite of the strict law) and to become Prime Minister himself. Badoglio is too loyal, as a soldier, to the person of the King to take the lead in such a scheme. But I think he might accept it if somebody else produced the crisis, and I am not sure how far he is working a *combinazione* with Sforza with this in view.

Meanwhile, there is the fear that if the Germans evacuate Rome, during the interval before the Allied armies arrive, a revolutionary government may come into being (rather like the Commune in Paris in 1871). In order to obviate this, Badoglio wants to send a message to these politicians in Rome through our Secret Service channels, appealing to them to hold their hands. In order to strengthen this

[24] Prince Vittorio Emanuele, Prince of Naples (b. 1937), son of Prince Umberto.

[25] Prince Aimone, Duca d'Aosta (1900–48).

argument he asked General Mason-MacFarlane to give him the authority to say that the Allies gave full support to Badoglio and the King and insisted on their retention of power. To my horror, the 'bull in a china-shop' (General Mason-MacFarlane) gave him this assurance *and in writing*. (Imagine the effect when this document is given to the British and American press!)

After some discussion, in which I had to take a very firm line with the general, it was agreed that this document should be recovered, and that any message sent to the Romans by our means should be most carefully censored and amended by us.

Dined at General Alexander's mess. General MacFarlane also dined. The others (Makins, Reber, Caccia and some junior officers of General Alex's) dined at our villa.

Air Marshal Coningham was at dinner and (as always) in good form.

Wednesday, 27 October 1943

Murphy and I (together with Reber and Caccia) set off for Brindisi at 8 a.m. General MacFarlane had left after dinner last night.

Murphy and I had an interview with Badoglio at 10.30. We found him rather pathetically aged and weakened. He is very unhappy about the armistice terms and the amendments which he hopes to get from the Allies. Here there is a very complicated and confused position, because once again the generals (who should never be allowed in diplomacy) have made a mess of it. They have actually given old Badoglio a written statement to say that the amendments he asked for at Malta will be granted by the Allies. In fact, this is *not* the case. However, this is a worry for the future, and we were able to field this particular ball today.

Later on, in the course of conversation, we were able to get Badoglio talking about the Rome group and the internal political situation. Murphy said that he understood that MacFarlane had given him a document as a sort of *aide-mémoire*, and we should be glad to see it in order to study it. Somehow or another we got possession of the document and managed to leave the room without returning it. It is now in the fire and reduced to ashes. So you see, sleight of hand is now a necessary additional accomplishment for Resident Ministers.

After that we went on a courtesy call to the King. We then motored back to Bari (a sandwich lunch in the car) arriving there about 2.30.

It was all arranged for us to leave by aeroplane at 3 p.m. for Naples – about forty-five minutes' flight. Unfortunately, the weather over the mountains was too bad, and we could not go. The only thing to do was to go by car. So we took (without permission, I'm afraid) General Alexander's lovely new Buick and left at 3 p.m. to drive to Naples by road (Murphy, Makins and I).

This proved to be a wonderful trip – at least while daylight lasted. First over the great rolling plain – all under cultivation – to Altamura and Gravina. Then the road goes up and up – through Irsina and Tolve, to Potenza – which we reached by about 7 p.m. The towns are on the tops of mountains – and the road goes winding up, with corkscrew turns and hairpin bends to each town and village, placed there on its rocky eminence for protection since medieval times. Then the road plunges down again into the valley and then winds up to the next town. Potenza is about 2,000 feet up, and the passes are often 4,000 feet or more.

At Potenza we had dinner – excellent soup, an omelette and *very* good wine. Prices are still low in the country districts, where there are no British and American troops. We drank three bottles of wine, and there were four of us (the corporal drove the car and dined). The bill was 6*s*.

We started off again about 8 p.m. and drove on in the dark – no moon – up hills and down valleys, till at last we reached the Salerno plain. We drove through the absolutely desolated village of Battipaglia – the scene of desperate and heroic struggles – through Salerno, Nocera, Torre Annunzianta, Torre del Greco – and finally to Naples, where we arrived at 12.30 a.m.

As we drove through the winding coast road in the darkness (past Herculaneum and Pompeii) we could see on our right the glow (like a huge cigar) of Vesuvius. And, of course, from Salerno onwards, the road was one dense block of lorries, guns, tanks, cars – all going up from the beaches to the front. Every house in every village reminding me of Poperinghe or Ypres. What the Allies have not destroyed by bombardment, the Germans have destroyed by demolition.

When we got to the outskirts of Naples, we got completely lost. The town is large, devastated, every road requires a detour. All the way along we had to overcome the problem of diversions to avoid blown bridges – all the way really from Bari to Naples. Now in the town there were endless detours where houses had been blown across the street or great holes in the road itself prevented progress. Poor General Alex's Buick rattled and shook ominously, unaccustomed to such treatment (it is not the car he uses himself – an open Ford V8 – but his car for visitors!).

Our destination lay at a spot some twenty miles out of Naples (I will not give the name)[26] and it was not till 3 a.m. that we finally arrived, exhausted but triumphant. At last! a cup of coffee, a biscuit, and a camp-bed in a tent, which seemed like the softest feather bed, so welcome was it.

Thursday, 28 October 1943

Breakfasted at 8 a.m. *à l'américaine*. We are at the H.Q. of General [Mark] Wayne Clark, commanding the Fifth Army. General Clark

[26] It was Caserta.

(the American Eagle, as Winston calls him) is far the most intelligent American soldier I know. He made the Darlan–Clark agreement (he was second-in-command to Eisenhower in the 'Torch' operation in November 1942) and subsequently took command of an American army for training in North Africa. The Salerno landings were his first big operation. (He was not in the Tunisian campaign after the first landings, or in Sicily.) He has an English Corps in his Army.

After breakfast, we motored into Naples and had the opportunity of seeing by daylight the scene of our wanderings in the dark. The destruction is bad – but a lot of fine buildings remain intact, and the life of the town seems to be recovering.

We drove to the Prefecture – now AMGOT H.Q., and spent the morning there in discussions with the various AMGOT officers. I am bound to say that I think they have done a very fine job. They found a town of 650,000 inhabitants (normally one million – the rest had fled), little food, no transport, no electric light or power (these were destroyed by the Germans), no sewage, houses much destroyed, roads impassable.

They have already – in three weeks – got essentials working. There is power for the flour mills and light for essential services (there is still no domestic lighting). The sewage is working; the unsafe houses are being demolished; the streets are reasonably clear. The Germans destroyed the large telephone exchange but passed over two small subsidiary ones, so there are now 3,000 civilian numbers working. No one has starved; there is as yet no serious epidemic; a single newspaper is being printed. The only trouble is that the news of these successes has gone round and the population are trekking back again, so that the full million will probably soon be on our hands. There have been a lot of particularly grim problems – hundreds of corpses to be buried. And there have been lots of German booby-traps and time bombs which have caused many casualties.

In the afternoon, we saw the Psychological Warfare Branch – who have also done good work. They are settling down better than they did in North Africa – or rather they are more experienced. And on the whole they are abstaining from private political intrigues.

We went back to the camp for dinner with General Clark. Among his guests were General [Brehon] Somervell (Q.M.G. at Washington) and several of his officers. I thought him very intelligent. I had met him at the Anfa Conference at Casablanca in February.

Friday, 29 October 1943

Drove to Sorrento – round the Bay of Naples. The road is very slow owing to various obstructions and heavy traffic. It was a lovely sunny day, after rather a cold and wet night.

We got to the little town about 12.30 and lunched at a restaurant where we had a tolerable meal of soup and spaghetti. At 2 p.m. we went to see Croce.[27] The Senator–philosopher talked to us for one hour and thirty minutes without drawing breath. He did not say very much except that he was a liberal and a monarchist, but that he thought the King must go, a Regency be set up. He also said that he did not regard economic questions of the highest political importance but only secondary. He is very rich.

On the way back, we stopped in Naples and saw Sforza. He had just arrived from Bari. [He appeared to go for a moment or two into a trance and then, in spite of a sore throat and a heavy cold, poured out a continual stream of words in his peculiar English. Except on one occasion when Murphy managed to interject a question, the Count spoke without stopping for one hour and a quarter.][28] He said the same as Croce, but with a lot of embellishments and much Court scandal. He thought the Prince of Piedmont must be passed over.

At dinner, we found General Alexander on a visit to General Clark and had a very agreeable evening. General Alexander told us that Roatta had been to see him (Roatta is an Italian general of bad repute whom we are going to dismiss). Roatta forgot himself in discussing the Russian situation. 'It is very bad, very bad indeed. Why, I doubt if the Germans will even be able to stand on the Bug. It is really very bad.'

I suppose it is just as confusing for the Italians as for us to remember which side they are on.

General Alexander was in great form – he is usually very quiet, but with an attractive and whimsical humour. Tonight, he was ragging like a schoolboy.

Saturday, 30 October 1943

Left Naples by air at 9.45 a.m.

Arrived Tunis at 1 p.m.

Left Tunis at 2 p.m.

Arrived Algiers at 4.30 a.m.

A very tiring journey in a transport plane – carrying mail and about sixteen passengers. Only those tin seats, like the knife-boards in Upper Chapel. I lay on the floor and felt rather ill and exhausted. It was also cold. We found Bob Dixon (who has been in charge of the office in Makins's absence) in good form. An enormous mass of paper, including all the telegrams from Anthony at Moscow to the P.M. which are repeated to me here. These seemed very encouraging. We worked on them till midnight.

A lot of letters from home. I am so delighted with them. They include your two of the 15th and 24th (the latter has come very quickly and assured me greatly with its account of the Land Army difficulties).

[27] Benedetto Croce (1866–1952), appointed a Senator of the Kingdom of Italy in 1910 for services to literature, was Minister of Education, 1920–1. He came to symbolise opposition to Fascism.

[28] Inserted from another record.

I also had a long and very happy letter from Maurice and one from Moucher.[29] It looks as if the baby was strong and healthy. It is an extraordinary pleasure to me to think about Maurice as a father. From his own point of view, I am sure it will be very good. We are indeed lucky to have him so happily married and a father.

As for my grandson, he has certainly made a timely appearance and I can well imagine the proprietary interest taken in the child by all at St Martin's Street [the offices of Macmillan & Co.].

Of course you were right about Withy Wood. Do let us preserve the large oaks as long as we possibly can. It looks as if they might escape altogether. By the way, now that they have escaped, do you think you could get Mr Gilson to get some of the *ivy* cut? It is injuring a lot of those fine oaks sadly. A week or two devoted by Bates, etc., to cutting the ivy in this wood would make a lot of difference. (As I understand the final settlement, the smaller trees are to be taken but the big ones left and the trees will only be cut round the sides of the square, in accordance with the little coloured plan which you sent me some time ago.)

I was very much amused by Catherine's letter. She has developed an amusing, if rather sarcastic style – quite in the traditional family vein.

Maurice tells me that he thinks Carol is much better and much happier and from what you say in your letter it seems she is more philosophic and less agitated. Where actually *is* she living now? You tell me that the flat idea is abandoned – no doubt a good thing. Please give her my love and tell her that I think so much about her and her work.

Perhaps when Maurice and Katharine are settled in Richmond, she will be able to see something of them and their friends.

I gather from what you tell me of Sarah's shooting that you have got some cartridges. If the gun is no good, please get *Hellis* (or Purdey) to put it right. I very much want her to have a proper gun. *Please* arrange this. If you cannot get it put right, *Hellis* will get you a good second-hand one. I do hope this can be arranged.

Well, I have read all these letters over and over again – and very pleased I am with them. Now I had better return to my story.

Sunday, 31 October 1943

Stayed in bed and read all my letters.

10.30 a.m. Called on General Bedell Smith. He told me all about his visit to Washington – a curious and interesting story. He also told me a lot which I already knew about decisions regarding both future operations and future commands, but which I naturally accepted as news. In any case, it was useful to have some surmises confirmed and also to see the picture from the American angle.

[29] Mary, Duchess of Devonshire (b. 1895), my wife's sister-in-law.

Morning at the office – no church, alas! – for there was a lot to catch up in paperwork, etc.

After luncheon I retired to bed and slept till four.

4.30 p.m. Meeting on Italian affairs in Murphy's house. General Holmes, General Joyce (who is to succeed Mason-MacFarlane and act as head of Allied Control Commission), C. D. Jackson (Publicity – a very good man, and very amusing – editor of *Time*), General McClure.

The position is getting very complicated in Italy, but not (to my mind) alarming – except for the amateurishness and naïveté of military diplomacy.

6 p.m. Meeting about some troubles between the British and French censorship authorities, particularly about radio news put out over the Algiers radio by the French. We have an arrangement by which the line on Radio France, Algiers, is shared between us and the French. Unfortunately, the French are apt to devote part of their time to amusing (but very scurrilous) lampoons on the British and Americans – particularly the latter. The climax was reached when the announcer said that the Second Front in Europe could not be launched until every American soldier had been accommodated with a travelling shower-bath!

November

Monday, 1 November 1943

11–12 noon. Italy again. Apparently Badoglio has failed to get any recruits [for a broad-based government] in Naples and has returned to Brindisi very discouraged. We talked it over (Murphy, Bedell Smith and I) and the others accepted the draft of a telegram of instructions to MacFarlane which I had prepared before the meeting.

The chief thing at this stage is strict *non-intervention*. They must work something out for themselves if they can. All we need insist upon is that King or republic, dictatorship or broad-based government – the terms of the armistice must be loyally observed. (Of course, we can have our own plan for what we want to happen, but we should *not* rush things at the moment.) We are in Italy in the relative position in which we were in North Africa when I first came. At such a stage, the *military* operations must take precedence. The *political* operations should be planned and follow on with the right timing.

3 p.m. Meeting with Murphy, Holmes and Joyce. General Kenyon Joyce may be what they call 'very high quality' and may have hunted with the 'Pytchley' or the 'Quorn' or what not – but he nearly drives me mad by the manner and the matter of his conversation. He speaks with that irritating deliberation affected by some Americans. And when at last he gets to the end of a sentence, the sentiments are dull, reactionary, full of that stupid self-satisfaction which is common with the old military types (British and American). He is really a sort of Yankee Colonel Blimp. Ike said he knew I should like him because he was very 'high class'! Bedell said he knew I should hate him because he was very stupid!

4 p.m. My dear friend Colonel (now General) Pechkoff called to see me – he is just back from China. He was as smart and intelligent as ever. (You will remember that he is a natural son of Maxim Gorky.)

At 7 p.m. M. Bogomolov (Soviet Ambassador) came to see me at the villa. He was in his usual form – a kind of rather engaging contempt for all mankind, especially Frenchmen.

Record of conversation with M. Bogomolov
1 November 1943

I asked him his impressions of Algiers since he had been here. He said he thought the position very complicated and he had not formed a very high opinion of French efficiency or powers of organisation. He had seen most of the leading members of the Committee and was not impressed by them. He told me that he had been informed by the French that it was because of Russian intervention that the French were to be excluded from membership of the Political Committee which is now to meet in London. He said that the French had told him that they had had this information from the Foreign Office. He did not believe it to be true, but gave it as an example of the continual French attempt to play one of the Great Powers off against the other. Moreover, he said that as he had means of reading all their letters – a fact which it was contrary to diplomatic usage to reveal – he was not concerned about Anglo-Russian relations, but merely gave it as an example of French perfidy.

Tuesday, 2 November 1943

A routine day. We are handicapped by many uncertainties, and cannot arrange our usual entertaining, which is rather a pity as the French think it so important. But I am waiting for Anthony from day to day and I do not know when I must leave again for Italy.

11 a.m. Went to see General Eisenhower, to tell him the latest Italian news. Badoglio has returned to Brindisi and told the King that he cannot form an enlarged government. The King has asked our permission to go himself to Naples. We have decided to allow it,[1] but to tell Mason-MacFarlane *not* to go with him himself, but to send an officer as an act of courtesy and to look after him. I do *not* want the Allied Governments to be associated *at this stage* with the dispute, either *for* or *against* the King. (Incidentally I have *no* guidance whatever from London as to H.M.G.'s views about abdication or anything else. General Eisenhower also has no idea of Washington's opinions, but distrusts Murphy. Murphy – with a sort of inverted Darlan complex – wants us to intervene and dismiss the King. But that is *quite wrong* at this stage. If they can solve their problem without *direct* interference by us it will be infinitely better both for us *and* for them, now and in the future.)

12 noon. Massigli called at the villa to see me – naturally full of complaints, chiefly about the Moscow decisions.[2] I tried, as usual, to chaff him out of his doldrums.

[1] The King's reception as he drove through Naples was unenthusiastic.

[2] The French were upset that decisions about their own future had been taken in Moscow in their absence. In particular they had not been included in the European Advisory Commission set up to advise on administering liberated Europe, and naturally felt that they should administer France, and not AMGOT. (They were eventually asked to join the Commission in November 1944.)

4 p.m. Sir John Cunningham to discuss various problems regarding the Italian fleet. I like our new admiral very much. He is clever and well-informed.

5 p.m. Herbert. Economic affairs in North Africa, chiefly locusts. It is almost impossible to get the French to work with the energy required. The trouble is that your own locusts destroy someone else's crops, thousands of miles away. So the French, with their curiously insular selfishness, find it difficult to take interest. However, I believe in certain stages locusts eat the young corn in their home of origin, so we try to make the most of this argument. I like Herbert. He is a very good and hard-working official, and has learned a great deal. Unfortunately, he has soon to go back to the Ministry of Supply. We worked on till about 8 p.m., and as Roger and John were out to dinner, I went to bed.

Wednesday, 3 November 1943

I took an easy morning and stayed in bed till 12 noon, writing this letter to bring it up to date and dictating some private letters to Miss Campbell. I am going to try to take these occasional hours in bed. I feel sure they help. I feel actually much better – in spite of the rather racketing time in Italy – but have not *quite* got back the resilience which I used to have. Perhaps I am getting older! or perhaps it is a sort of mystical feebleness that descends upon grandfathers!

The day did *not* prove so restful a day after all. At 12 noon Murphy, General Holmes, Roger and Bob invaded the villa full of excitement about the telegrams arriving from Brindisi.

However, they calmed down after a bit, and I managed to persuade them that what *we* should do was to send a clear and objective picture of the situation to London and Washington and to let them decide the great issues.[3] I do not see why great dynastic changes – for good or ill – should be made by a couple of generals, British and American, of low rank and limited political experience. This was finally agreed, and a telegram drafted for General Eisenhower to send to Washington to the Combined Chiefs of Staff setting out the position. Murphy was to be free to send his comments to the President and I would do the same to the Prime Minister.

The problem *may* be solved by the Italians themselves – without intervention from us. On the one hand, the various political leaders who should join a National Government may agree to waive the dynastic issue, at least for the time being. On the other hand, the King and the Prince may abdicate in favour of the child of six – the Prince of Naples. In either of these events, there is nothing for us to decide.

But I think it more likely that the politicians will maintain their refusal to serve, and that the King will decline to abdicate. He will

[3] Murphy had become very keen that the King should abdicate.

appeal to Badoglio, as a loyal servant of the Crown, to carry on as at present – *without* a broad government. Badoglio will say that he can only do this if the Allies support him in spite of his inability to get recruits to his Government of the kind we should like.

The arguments are rather balanced. From the point of view of our declared war aims and public opinion at home and in U.S.A., it would be good politics to get rid of the King. (I think I might even win the next election at Stockton as the man who drove Fascism out of North Africa and dethroned King Victor Emmanuel in Italy!)

On the other hand, the military situation is developing only slowly and we have a long tough fight ahead. The Italian Navy is co-operating well and efficiently on sea and on shore, in docks and workshops. The Army, if not fighting, is *working* for us. Practically all the [Italian] embassies abroad have rallied to the King. This also applies to merchant seamen. We are not sure what would be the effect on all these people of an abdication which was *not* voluntary but enforced.

Here, at any rate, is the problem. You may amuse yourself by trying to decide what telegram of instruction you would send me if you were P.M.! (Of course, he has received from us a great background of facts which I have not been able to send you.)

M. Pleven (Colonies) came to lunch. He was as charming as ever. To my mind he and Massigli are much the nicest of the French Ministers. I met Pleven first at Hever [Castle], just after I had gone to the Colonial Office. We worked together a good deal over the West African Produce Control Board, of which I made the Free French members. I think he was grateful for the assistance which I gave him in those days, and (although he got rather excited by political events from time to time) he has remained a staunch friend.

3 p.m. After luncheon we went to the first meeting of the new Assemblée Consultative Provisoire. This is a sort of parliament which has been set up, to try to give some democratic colour to the system here and serve as an outlet for public opinion.

Since, of course, no real elections can be held, the members (about eighty) are partly elected by the municipal and county councils here in North Africa, partly ex-deputies and ex-senators who have escaped from France, and partly nominated by the various resistance movements in Metropolitan France. Some of the last category have not yet arrived. As you can imagine, their escape is not easy and depends on the various underground methods which we and the French have developed for this work.

The meeting of this assembly was held in the meeting place usually used by the Algerian Council. It is arranged in a semi-circle, like the French Chamber, with the President like a judge, on a sort of elevated platform.

There was a diplomatic gallery, in which I sat, with Bogomolov and Murphy and all the other representatives.

After this performance, we went back to the office and worked at various telegrams till dinner. I also saw Miller (the N.A.E.B. official who has done such good work on the Tunisian olive crop). Early to bed.

I must end this letter now and catch a bag. Please give my love to *all* the children and do *not* forget about Sarah's gun. I hope Maurice will come and shoot some pheasants. I see *no* chance of getting home now for several months. So tell him to organise a shoot.

Thursday, 4 November 1943

For the moment, French politics are in a lull – before the next storm, I have no doubt. We are chiefly interested in Italian affairs, and all the complications of getting the Control Commission into operation. Also, we have to get an amendment signed to the long armistice terms and one to the [Italian] naval agreement made by Sir Andrew Cunningham.

The problem of treating people at the same time as a defeated enemy and as 'co-belligerent' is quite a big one. The Russians, the Greeks and the French want to divide up the Italian fleet as spoil. We want to make it work for us, doing both convoy and repair work in the docks.

10.30 a.m. N.A.E.B. meeting. One or two interesting items. One of the new problems is to what extent, if at all, 'private' trade is to be restarted. At present all our dealings with the French (and *vice versa*) are bloc transactions between Governments.

12 noon. Meeting with Murphy. Italian affairs – drafting telegrams of instruction, to Mason-MacFarlane, etc. Murphy is still very anti-King. But the President has agreed with the P.M. not to rush things at present.

1.15 p.m. Lunch with M. and Mme Schneider. He is a nice fellow (very interested in flying). He is the sort of 'Vickers' of France, Schneiders and Creusots and all that, and one of what they used to call 'the two hundred families', who were supposed to control the finance and industry of the country. She is pretty, efficient, and really interested in Red Cross work, where she quarrels violently with Mme Catroux. Massigli was at lunch, still rather tearful about the Moscow decisions. Comtesse [Madeleine] de Montgomery – amusing, smart, rather English in appearance – *une belle laide* – subjects hunting, shooting, stalking, the Portlands, the Sutherlands, the Londonderrys. Also Mme [Elizabeth] de Breteuil – American by birth – just arrived from New York. An excellent luncheon, amusing conversation, a good display of jewellery, hairdressing and clothes, with a remarkable and even rather touching outward vivacity covering deep wounds. Most of them have husbands or children whose present fate is unknown to them.

How they all *hate* North Africa and Algiers and *long* for France and Paris! After luncheon, I picked up Bob Dixon (who is still with us awaiting Anthony and his party from Moscow) and we went for a drive in the country – along the coast road west of the city, then up to the Tombeau de la Chrétienne – a strange monumental bee-hive erection (of very early Iberian times) which I think I described before. Then across the valley to Blida, and then home. It had rained a good deal in the morning, but it was a fine sunny afternoon and the mountains were magnificently revealed, with glorious colours and a much more luminous and attractive light than the hard summer sunshine.

6 p.m. Back to office. Long talk with Norman Smith. He is a civil servant from Ministry of Fuel. He has been on N.A.E.B. for a long time and dealt with North African coal requirements. Now he has (for some mysterious reason) become a Brigadier and is going to Italy to deal with Italian coal and fuel problems. He is a *very* efficient man.

On getting back from the office at about 8 p.m. I went to bed, as is now my practice whenever I can! I think it helps a lot and I feel much better, although I am not quite as strong as before. I have also developed (since the rainy season has now begun and the dampness in the air is terrible all the time – rain or fine) severe rheumatism in my left arm and hand. Fortunately my right hand is not so bad. My hip aches more than ever for many years. My good Dr Richardson has gone to England. When he returns, I shall get him to give me a cure.

Friday, 5 November 1943

9.15 a.m. I looked in to see General Eisenhower. He seemed quite cheerful, though a bit worried by the many uncertainties of the situation here, political and military. However, Mr Secretary Hull has been safely speeded home, and everyone is much relieved. Murphy is definitely to stay on for the campaign, as American representative at Allied Headquarters, with the rank of Ambassador. A Mr Ed Wilson is to be American Ambassador to the French.

10 a.m. Called on Giraud. I will not describe the conversation here but will enclose a record.

Record of conversation with General Giraud
5 November 1943

1. We began by discussing the military situation in Italy, from which he had recently returned. He regarded the capture of Isernia this morning as an important success. Nevertheless he was very critical of the faulty strategy which we were employing. It was not right to make frontal attacks upon the enemy positions. We should make use of our sea and air power by making a continual series of landings to turn the front. He had himself offered to lay on an attack from Corsica to land north of Rome. He had the troops. All he needed was to be supplied with the ships. He was thinking of flying up to see General Eisenhower

to put this proposal before him. Nevertheless, in spite of his criticisms of our strategy, especially of sending away ships and landing-craft from the area at this time, he was playing his part. He had promised to provide two divisions to the Fifth Army. This was now to be raised to three, together with a regiment of cavalry. They would be under the command of General Juin as Commander of the Expedition, and General Larminat as Commander of a Corps.

2. I then gave him the Prime Minister's message,[4] at which he expressed great gratification and to which he said he would send a formal reply. This led on to a discussion, half playful, of the Prime Minister's many promises which, according to the general, were not on every occasion fulfilled. I asked him what he had in mind. He agreed that the Spitfires which had been promised him at Anfa had been forthcoming, but said that he had also been promised a Lancaster bomber. It was not quite clear to me whether this referred to a machine for General Giraud's personal use or a number for operational purposes, but I did not think it necessary to press the point. Also Admiral Cunningham had promised him some fast vedettes to escort his ships which were bringing refugees from Spain to North Africa. At present they took a circuitous route, and he would prefer them to go direct from Cartagena in south-eastern Spain to Oran. He would also like to have a sloop or something of the kind so that he might sail about the Mediterranean. He was fond of the sea and would like to make his trips by sea.

3. From this we passed to the further disappointment of Moscow. He told me that when he came down to his breakfast, which he took with General Chambe,[5] M. Georges-Picot and his brother – all solid and serious men – they greeted him with the cry, 'Have you seen the newspaper?' When he had read the headlines his heart was broken. He thought France could not be treated in this way. After all her sufferings she needed more sympathetic handling. I replied on the same lines, pointing out that the Committee was not a government and that it never claimed to be. Secondly, from a practical point of view, France could not at the moment claim to be a Great Power in the sense of being able to dispose of great armed forces, although we all hoped she would one day take her place again. Her recovery must be 'progressive'. I was tempted to say *politique de perroquet*, but refrained. He agreed, but said of course things had changed. In France the Vichy Government was nothing but a ghost. It had the support of nobody. It was dead. In spite of the faults of individuals and the follies of many small men, the Committee at Algiers was in fact the only possible government of France. It should be treated as a government.

[4] Churchill promised that representatives of the F.C.N.L. should be involved in all discussions on European reconstruction.

[5] General René Chambe (b. 1889), of the French Air Force, had been General Giraud's Minister of Information and *chef de cabinet*.

4. He passed then in a wide sweep to the future of the war. He thought it was approaching its end. Hence the anxiety of the French to be in on the discussions for the future. He personally hoped that there would be battles in France, and that the Germans would not retire without a conflict in that country. That would be healthier because the French Army would regain its prestige and authority. As for the future, he said nothing should prevent the Russians from having the Baltic states of Lithuania, Latvia and Esthonia, and possibly Bessarabia. He thought they would have to have Poland up to the Curzon Line. Poland should be compensated by being given East Prussia and the German population should be moved. Germany should be split into three. One part of it with Vienna as its capital should form a Danubian Confederacy into which should fall Hungary, Roumania and Bohemia. The latter was of quite a different character and should be separated from the Czechs. There should also be a Northern Confederacy grouped round Prussia. Thirdly there should be a Rhineland Confederacy based upon the Valley of the Rhine. In this way the Germans would have a proper field for their activities and ambitions and the mistakes of 1918, by which they were made to feel hopeless, would not be repeated. General Giraud viewed the future with anxiety. He thought the peace of 1918 not so good as that which had followed the Congress of Vienna. I said that it may have been easier then. 'Ah, yes,' he replied. 'No press and no democratic institutions.' With his usual charming smile, the interview concluded, the general conducting me to the door.

[Diary continues] 12 noon. Meeting with Murphy. It is clear that the King of Italy is going to win the first round. I think he will out-manoeuvre Sforza.

Francis Rodd (Rennell) turned up from England. There is a terrific battle about his position, that of Mason-MacFarlane, and now General Kenyon Joyce. Francis (who is a great prima donna and a prime intriguer) has been to England and come back determined to resign from AMGOT altogether if he cannot become head of the Commission. The point is that we plan to have two systems in Italy. (*i*) AMGOT. This will be *direct* military rule. The King's writ will not run. General Alexander will continue as *Military Governor* and all legal and administrative action will be in his name. (*ii*) Allied Control Commission. In this territory, the King and the Royal Government will govern – at least nominally. It will be *indirect* control by the Commission, at first very strict and with a large number of officers, both at the centre and in the provinces to see that things are properly done.

AMGOT will be the territory immediately behind the armies.

Control Commission territory will be all the rest of liberated Italy.

As the armies advance, adjustments will be made from time to time, having regard, of course, to convenient provincial boundaries.

At present *all* liberated Italy (except the four provinces immediately contiguous to Brindisi, where the King is) is AMGOT territory, under General Alexander as Military Governor and General Lord Rennell as his deputy.

The plan, however, is progressively to hand back Sicily, Calabria, etc., as (*a*) the Commission gets organised, (*b*) the Italian Government gets into some sort of shape.

Now you will observe from all this that Commission is the waxing, AMGOT the waning star. The first will be more amusing than the second. One can dabble in politics and king-making and the like in the first. In the second, one has to slog along with dull administration. *Hinc illae lacrimae* – and hence British General Lord Rennell and American General Kenyon Joyce and all sorts of other people plot and conspire to worry – but fortunately amuse – me![6]

General Alexander was coming to stay with me in Algiers today. Unfortunately, I have just had a message that he has had to land at Bône and owing to the weather being so bad between Bône and Algiers, he has gone back to Italy.

Mr [R. E.] Stedman (minerals expert on N.A.E.B. – an excellent man), Brigadier Norman Smith (coal) and Francis Rennell to lunch.

The usual office in the afternoon – telegrams and paper keep pouring in.

At 5.30 I went to see de Gaulle. I enclose the record. I thoroughly enjoyed my talk with him.

Record of conversation with General de Gaulle
5 November 1943

1. I gave him the Prime Minister's message. He said he had already been informed by General Giraud of the Prime Minister's wishes.

2. I then mentioned the meeting of the Assembly and congratulated him on his speech, more particularly those parts of it dealing with the social problems of France. He expressed gratification at my interest, and proceeded to propound the theory that it would be necessary for France to make many changes in her social structure. France, like England, had to develop a system somewhere between the extremes of Communism and capitalism in its old sense. He had been reading the Beveridge Report, which he regarded as very striking. He knew there was controversy about its details, but he was impressed by the fact of its production in war-time and the great interest in reconstruction questions shown in Great Britain. I said that I agreed entirely with him, and thought that France and England together had the same problems and the same functions in the post-war world. I suggested

[6] Lord Rennell was offered the post of Deputy Vice-President of the Economic and Administrative Section of the Allied Control Commission, but turned it down and returned to England.

that some liaison might be made between those studying these matters in our country and in his. Possibly part of his Mission could get into touch with some of our Government authorities studying these questions. Or private arrangements might be made between a team of British economists and students and their French counterparts. If he would like to pursue the idea, I would be most happy to give what assistance I could. The general seemed interested in this, and talked for some time on these and similar problems.

3. He then went on to speak of the Assembly. He thought there were some good men in it, though many inexperienced men. He had suggested that one of the Commissions of the Assembly should be devoted to the study of social and reconstruction problems. I asked him what he was going to do about Pierre Cot.[7] He said he could not object to his coming here although he did not think much of him. He had refused to take him into his movement in London and had advised him to go to America. He was bound to say that Cot had kept quiet there, and if he behaved well here, he thought he might make something of his political life, but he would have to undergo the process of what he called *renouvellement*.

4. He then chatted about his reminiscences of Pétain, the general's early life and first contacts with him, his quarrels with Pétain, and so forth. He said Pétain was a man eaten up with ambition. Being essentially a small man, his only hope of obtaining a leading place would be in the disaster of his country. He had to make his country small in order to make himself great. I asked what he thought would happen to Laval and all the remaining collaborationists. Would they take refuge in Germany? 'Not at all,' he said with a smile. 'They will take refuge in England. You need not be afraid that Pétain will be shot. You will give him a villa in the south of England.' . . .

5. There was no mention at all during the conversation of the Moscow Conference or of French fears about its decisions. I thought it better not to raise the subject. The general was in a most agreeable and friendly mood and I was very much impressed by the study which he has clearly given to post-war economic and social problems. It was one of the most pleasant and interesting conversations which I have ever had with him.

[Diary continues] A pleasant dinner at home. General Jock Whiteley came in; Francis Rennell was in good form.

Saturday, 6 November 1943

Office all the morning – nothing of outstanding interest. The Italian affair is going on, satisfactorily from our point of view. We hold no brief for the King and Badoglio, but at the present time they can be

[7] Pierre Cot (1895–1977) was French Minister of Air, 1933–4, 1936–8, and of Commerce, 1938. He was a professor of law and a Communist sympathiser.

useful to us and do what we tell them. I think the attempt to form a 'liberal' government will fail for the present. Sforza – a vain and ambitious man – will refuse to serve unless the King abdicates. The King will refuse to abdicate. Badoglio will resign. The King will refuse the resignation. *All the other politicians in Italy* – especially in Rome, led by Bonomi,[8] etc. – will support the King and send messages by the various routes open to say so. Their reason will be *not* that they really support the King, but they don't want Sforza and the Naples gang to get all the jobs. So it will be decided that Badoglio shall carry on – with a government of functionaries and technicians, *not* politicians – until we get to Rome. It will be agreed that this is all without prejudice to the question of the King and the dynasty, which will be left open at least till Rome is liberated.

The press reaction in England and America will be bad, but it is more important for us to help the soldiers in a very difficult campaign. I think we will dismiss Roatta at this time. I have been saving him up for the moment when the attempt to form a 'liberal' government fails. Then we will throw him to the press and political wolves, and gobbling him up will last them for a week or two. After that, having breakfasted off Roatta, they might be given Ambrosio for dinner.

In the afternoon, we went to an immense party given on board the *Richelieu*, the French battleship which we battered very heavily on 8 November 1942 at Dakar, and which has now been repaired and refitted in America. She is a very fine ship – but as it was a frightful day – pouring with rain – we did not see much of her.

I dined at an Army mess – General Whiteley, Colonel Jimmy Gault, General Lewis and seven or eight others. Also a Brigadier Crockett. He has brought out a brace and a half of Italian generals, whom we are going to give back to them. One is Field Marshal Meise. I think we have chosen some quite responsible ones, so that they can take the place of Roatta and/or Ambrosio.

Sunday, 7 November 1943

10 a.m. Church. Absolutely packed, as usual, with troops, who sang with great gusto.

After church, office till luncheon. A spate of telegrams from all quarters. The Moscow result seems satisfactory, and the scheme for altering the character of the Mediterranean Commission (which I came to London to explain) seems to have been successfully put over by Anthony.[9]

[8] Ivanoe Bonomi (1873–1951) was head of the anti-Fascist C.L.N.; he had been Italian Prime Minister, 1921–2.

[9] The Advisory Council for Italy was to include 'High Commissioners' from France, Greece and Yugoslavia, and it would deal with day-to-day civil matters and Allied policy regarding Italy. Moreover it would take over the Allied Control Commission as soon as the Supreme Allied Commander felt able to relinquish the presidency.

Meanwhile the Mediterranean Commission (the body proposed by Stalin in August 1943) was

4–6 p.m. Party given by M. Bogomolov. He has now got a huge and very vulgar house. The usual party – tit-bits of food, vodka, posters of various kinds of Russian humour, war photographs, crowds of French, Americans, British – as well as the *corps diplomatique*, which is now beginning to assemble here but – alas! – no caviare! Much disappointment was expressed and some resentment by the guests.

Bogomolov is *all over* the British. It was rather like the old Londonderry House parties. The crowd was put in a big saloon or shepherded out on to the terrace. The inner circle – de Gaulle, Giraud, Murphy, General and Madame Catroux and I – were given *better* food and *better* drink in a small room from which the vulgar mass was rigidly excluded.

6 p.m. Went to evensong. Even more crowded than this morning. One of the hymns was 'All things bright and beautiful' which was sung with *great* fervour. The chaplain tells me that troops like occasionally to have children's hymns. It makes them think of home.

8–10.45 p.m. A frightful party, given by M. Lemaigre-Dubreuil, in his wonderful but uncomfortable Arab house (or rather houses). A sort of *couscous* dinner. You sit on the floor, and eat what you can get hold of.

After that, an Arab orchestra – or rather two gloomy old men hitting a drum with irritating monotony and one old fellow playing a sort of flute.

The party was to celebrate the landings, and was supposed to be for those who had taken part in the preparations. But it was a bad party. The difficulty about celebrating the landings is that no one quite knows whether it should be for the French a day of national rejoicing or of national mourning. After all, they did oppose our arrival and a considerable number of casualties took place on both sides. However, in spite of the somewhat equivocal position, there are to be celebrations. On the whole, the Giraudists will support the various ceremonies and the Gaullists will probably boycott them.

Meanwhile there is a new French crisis boiling up,[10] and it is hard to see quite what is going to happen. Fortunately, I feel that the President is gradually getting bored with French politics, so perhaps he will not react too strongly.

Monday, 8 November 1943

10.15 a.m. Went to see Chief of Staff – a good talk about a number of points – the French, Italians and Mediterranean command questions. Also one or two things which I am trying to get through. One of them has succeeded – namely, to allow those diplomats who are to be part of

to be transferred from Algiers to London, where it would become the European Advisory (or London) Commission and concern itself with questions of European administration after liberation.

[10] This concerned proposals to reconstitute the F.C.N.L.

the permanent embassy to the French to send for or bring out their wives. Up to now, this has been forbidden by A.F.H.Q. But North Africa is not really now a theatre of war, and in any case the city of Algiers is in effect the capital of France for the time being.

11 a.m. Murphy and I paraded at the 1914–1918 war memorial to watch Giraud *déposer une gerbe* (lay a wreath). De Gaulle did not appear.

12 noon. Meeting with Murphy and General Holmes to prepare telegram for General Eisenhower to send to General MacFarlane on Italian crisis. After a good deal of discussion, a text was prepared on lines which I know the P.M. wanted (I have now at last received a pretty clear indication of his view).

After luncheon, I went to rest for a bit. Then to the office for the usual series of interviews, etc., including Mr [C. B.] Lumby (the new *Times* correspondent) who seems a sensible and pleasant fellow; Gaston Palewski (de Gaulle's *chef de cabinet*) whom I have known for a long time but cannot bring myself to like.

Palewski gave me an indication of the way things were going. I felt I must warn him that if he forced changes on the Giraudists too brutally, there would be a strong reaction from P.M. and President.

An early dinner, followed by a very exhausting evening. From 8.45 to 12 midnight a concert of military bands. An American band; the Royal Artillery String Band (very good); and the Foreign Legion Band. Each of these separately gave a programme which would last me an evening. One after the other was a bit overpowering.

After the concert we all went to a supper party at General Gale's. A number of French ladies and French officers who had helped to organise the concert came. Bed at 2 a.m.! Dreadful dissipation!

Tuesday, 9 November 1943

8.15 a.m. Meeting with Chief of Staff. To discuss a revision of the telegram of instructions to Brindisi on which we agreed yesterday. General Eisenhower wished to strengthen the telegram in the direction which I knew the P.M. wanted, so I had nothing to do but sit quiet.

We finished the draft finally by about 10 a.m., and after that I had a long talk with General Eisenhower alone. He was in good form and very friendly as always. The trouble is that he is rather elusive nowadays, and rather tired. But when one can get him quietly, he is always interesting and sensible, if somewhat incoherent. At least he speaks a strange language of his own, which one has to learn to understand correctly.

11 a.m. I went to see General Georges. The French storm has blown up and is now raging fiercely. I think de Gaulle will get his way, but Giraud seems to feel that he has been roughly treated. Georges is *much* more intelligent than Giraud and does his best to help him.

12.30 p.m. Meeting with Murphy and Holmes. I had drafted a

propaganda line for radio and press guidance to deal with the situation in the British and American press which will arise when it becomes known that Badoglio has failed to form a 'political' government on a wide basis and intends nevertheless to carry on. I'm afraid there is bound to be trouble, and the left-wing attacks on the King and Badoglio will begin. (If I ever stand for Parliament again I don't see how I shall survive Darlan, Giraud, Badoglio and Victor Emmanuel!)

The draft was agreed, with some minor changes, and will go to London and Washington.

After luncheon, to which we had some British officers, I went down to the airport to meet Anthony Eden and his party. Some had gone direct from Cairo to London, but we had Strang, Oliver Harvey, Sir John Dashwood, Lawford, Steel[11] and some others – eleven in all. John was disgusted by their incompetence. They all jabbered at once and lost most of their luggage and papers. However, we got them safely up to the villa in due course.

Anthony went off to see a battalion in the neighbourhood where he had some friends and did not reappear till 7 p.m.

Then we had Sir John Cunningham in to discuss some naval problems as they affect our relations with the Italian Navy, and at 7.30 Massigli – full of French grievances and the French political crisis. I've calmed the latter down with fair words and sherry and finally sat down to dinner about 8.30. General Gale and General Sir Ronald Adam (Adjutant General) came as well, so we had quite a party. At 10 p.m. we all went off to the airport, and of course found that Lawford (the junior Private Secretary) had left behind at the villa the bag with all the Moscow papers and the draft of Anthony's speech. So we had to telephone up for a car to be sent out with these, and waited another forty minutes on the cold and damp aerodrome. At last we got them off, and so ended a heavy day.

Anthony seemed very pleased with his Russian mission. The plan which I had got General Eisenhower to put up for the Allied Advisory Council to the Control Commission in Italy (on which the Russians and French are to sit) apparently helped him very much in getting agreement to the much more important and significant European commission (British–American–Russian) which is now to sit in London. The fact that the Russians accepted these today, which will deal with war and post-war questions in Europe as a whole, including Germany, is very encouraging. Anthony seemed satisfied that the Russians meant to carry on the war until the defeat of Germany, and would not abandon the struggle or make a separate peace. At the same time, they have suffered terribly, both in losses of men and material. They are therefore *desperately* anxious to finish the war as soon as

[11] Christopher ('Kit') Steel (1903–73) was First Secretary at the office of the Minister Resident in the Middle East, 1942–4, and was then posted to my office.

possible. Meanwhile, all questions are judged by them on this basis. He also thought that their short-term policy at all events would be co-operative, not isolationist, because the destruction of their towns and mechanical plant has been on such a prodigious scale that they will require help from Britain and America in the process of reconstruction.

Wednesday, 10 November 1943

A real Algiers day. The French crisis in full swing. I will just give the day's schedule.

10 a.m. Talk with Murphy and General Smith on French situation. Today's papers (following last night's broadcast news) carry the account of the reconstruction of the Committee and the elimination of Giraud, Georges, Couve de Murville – all Giraudists.

11 a.m. Interview with Georges.

11.30 a.m. Further talk with General Smith and Murphy. They were rather alarmed, but not unduly so. Things have changed a lot in the last few months, and the Americans frankly recognise now that they backed a loser in Giraud.

1.30 p.m. Lunch with General Catroux. The luncheon was given after the baptism of the infant son of the young and pretty Princesse de Merode. Mme Catroux, the Princess, General Catroux (Godfather), Mme Schneider (Godmother), the priest and myself. A very flattering invitation for an Englishman! Champagne toasts, etc., etc.

After lunch, Catroux gave me his version of the crisis and the incredible stupidity which Giraud had shown.

4 p.m. Polish Ambassador called – nominally to pay his respects on appointment, really to fish for my views on the French situation.

4.30 p.m. Mr Tyler (Psychological Warfare Branch) asking for a director for radio and press propaganda on the French development.

5 p.m. General Georges again. The crisis is over! Giraud has withdrawn his resignation as C.-in-C. and everything is settled.

6 p.m. Herbert. A most complicated problem on the production of Madagascar, which is falling behind our expectations. We drafted a memorandum and covering letter to Pleven. The French are trying to develop inter-colonial trade instead of making the surplus products of any one colony available to the Combined Boards, for distribution by that machinery among the United Nations. (I'm afraid they are better 'takers' than 'givers'.)

7 p.m. General MacFarlane – on his way back from Italy, after handing over his job on the Allied *Mission* in Brindisi to General Joyce (U.S.) who is to be the first head of the Allied *Control Commission* which starts officially today.

8 p.m. Dinner party at the villa.

M. and Mme Tixier (Commissioner for Social Affairs).

General and Mme Bouscat (Chief of Staff, French Air Force).

M. and Mme Louis Joxe (Secretary to the Committee of National Liberation).

Mlle de Miribel (Free French representative in Canada – young and pretty).[12]

General MacFarlane.

General Timberlake (U.S.).

Mr Ed Wilson (American Ambassador-designate to French).

Roger and I.

11.15 p.m. Went round to see General de Gaulle and to hear his account of the political crisis and the future.

A good day.

The details of this crisis are explained in The Blast of War:

General Georges came to see me on the morning of 10 November. He gave me an unexpectedly objective picture, for he too was beginning to lose patience with Giraud, much as he distrusted de Gaulle.

This was his story. On 6 November François de Menthon, speaking in the Assembly, urged the reconstitution of the Committee to include fewer generals and technicians and more politicians, and made a strong attack upon Giraud. When the Committee met, the general answered with great dignity in a speech which deeply moved the majority of the Commissioners. He appealed to his record. He had fought in the last war, had been gravely wounded and had been taken prisoner. He had fought in this war and had escaped from Germany to continue the fight. He had served to the best of his ability during the past year since the landing in North Africa. He had been condemned to death by Vichy. His wife was languishing in a prison in Lyons. His children had been taken off a few weeks ago to Germany where they were prisoners. He knew that many others had suffered equally; but perhaps there were some among those who prided themselves on having been followers of Fighting France who had not made any personal sacrifices of a proportionate kind. Georges went on to say that had the vote been taken at that point, the Commission would have voted for Giraud. However, the debate proceeded; and it was decided that it was right that there should be a reorganisation of the Committee. General Georges offered his resignation and so did the other Commissioners. Since under the existing decrees the Committee was the only body empowered to accept resignations or make additions to itself, it was obviously impossible for the whole fifteen of them to engage on the task of Cabinet-making. It was therefore the general feeling that there should be a small sub-committee for this purpose, and General de Gaulle, René Pleven, Adrien Tixier and René Mayer were entrusted

12 Elisabeth de Miribel (b. 1915), supporter of General de Gaulle since 1941, was attaché to the Cabinet of the Provisional Government, 1944, and became a Carmelite nun after the war.

with the task. This resulted in a decree which in effect laid down that the Commander-in-Chief must become subordinate to the Government. Giraud thought that the intention was that he should remain co-President until he left to take command of the armies in the field. But this was clearly not the legal meaning of the decree and Giraud ought never to have agreed to it without clarifying this important point.

There was nothing now to be done except to try to find a reasonable solution. Catroux, with whom I lunched on the same day, gave me roughly the same account. But there were certain differences. He stated that at the meeting of the Committee two motions were carried: (1) that all the Commissioners, including Giraud and even de Gaulle, should place their resignations in the hands of the Cabinet-making sub-committee; (2) that the 'pouvoir militaire' should be definitely separated from the 'pouvoir civil'. Giraud accepted both these motions without demur.

Unfortunately, Giraud had not told the Committee that he hoped within a few weeks to take up his command and thereby, under the decree of 2 October, automatically vacate the co-presidency. However, on receipt of Giraud's letter of resignation, it was decided to send a delegation to see him. This in fact was done. When Murphy and I saw General Georges in the afternoon he told us that in his opinion the crisis was over. The deputation, led by Catroux and consisting of Tixier, Pleven, Mayer and some others, had assured Giraud that they had not wished to attack his position in any way; there had clearly been misunderstandings, and they thought the General had agreed to the propositions in full knowledge of their effect. A number of concessions were made regarding Giraud's position as Commander-in-Chief and it was agreed that a letter should be sent to him by all the members of the Committee, asking him to remain in that post. Georges took all this much more lightly than on previous occasions, and as he left us he said: 'So ends our monthly crisis. The only difference is that this one came ten days too soon; they usually take place in the week after the 20th of each month.' He said that he himself would be glad to resign.

After dinner I saw General de Gaulle. He clearly regarded this affair as of minor importance. In any event, far too much emphasis was being laid on Algiers and not enough on France. In reality the French crisis had begun in 1789 and had lasted until the outbreak of war with varying temporary systems but no permanent solution. It was his duty to bring about such a degree of national unity as would make possible a solution of the social and economic problems of France, without disorder on the one hand or extreme policies on the other. It was for that reason that he was so anxious about the position of the Communists and how best to handle them. Once again I ended the day feeling that de Gaulle stood head and shoulders above all his colleagues in the breadth of his conceptions for the long term. Meanwhile, he was clearly the victor in the short-term struggle for power. Giraud, while remaining for the time being Commander-in-Chief, left the Committee. At the same time Georges resigned or was expelled.

Thursday, 11 November 1943

Murphy, John Wyndham and I (with General Holmes) left at 8.30. We dropped off General Holmes at Brindisi and reached Bari at about 4 p.m. We drove out to General Alexander's H.Q., where we are his guests.

Reber and Harold Caccia, whom we had left as our representatives at Brindisi, came to meet us. General talk till dinner, where we were guests of General Alexander's.

As usual, he was very charming and friendly and anxious to hear all the political news. Lord Gort is also staying here. We are all in the same little guest-house as we were in before. Early to bed.

Friday, 12 November 1943

9–11 a.m. Talk with Reber and Caccia. There are a lot of troublesome questions to be got over. These two are very sensible and seem to have calmed down and taken hold. But, of course, they want to get news and guidance and they much welcome a visit. I have still no separate communications (other than through A.F.H.Q.) which makes things more difficult. I am trying to get a British Consul to Brindisi and then I shall be able to telegraph to Caccia in F.O. cyphers without my telegrams being common property.

11.15 a.m. Flew to Brindisi (half-hour flying instead of two hours' motoring). Saw General Joyce. Lunched with him and discussed various problems till 3.45. I am afraid the general is rather a 'stuffed shirt'. On the other hand, I don't think he will do anything in particular, and that suits us for the time being.

We have still to get an amending protocol signed (amending the long armistice terms) and also a naval treaty. There is great trouble about the latter, because we are really trying to combine two fundamentally contradictory policies. On the one hand we want to get the Italian Navy, naval bases, dockyards and workshops to co-operate with us; on the other we want to take physical possession of their ships, give some to the Russians, some to the Greeks, some to the French, some to the Yugoslavs and some to ourselves, leaving at the end of the war a weak or non-existent Italian Navy in the Mediterranean. It will require a more subtle mind than I fear General Joyce has to achieve these two purposes.

At 4 p.m. we left the airport at Brindisi and flew back to Bari, arriving just before dark.

Dinner with General Alexander and much interesting talk. The Adjutant General (General Adam) told us the London gossip. I gather

P. J. Grigg's position as Secretary of State for War is becoming rather shaky.[13]

Saturday, 13 November 1943

Left Bari airfield at 9 a.m. Went straight, without coming down for food or fuel, to Algiers. We arrived about 3 p.m.

I need hardly say that I found a French crisis in full swing – this time one in which we were seriously involved. Murphy also found waiting him a number of telegrams on the same subject – viz., the situation in Beirut (and the Lebanon as a whole). At 5 p.m. we therefore met for a conference and at 6.45 p.m. and 7 p.m. we went to see Massigli. Murphy first presented his stiff note. I followed at 7 p.m. with an oral communication (our written notes having been delivered by Makins yesterday on my behalf).

The whole of the affair seems to have blown up very suddenly – although (to tell the truth) we have seen the cloud on the horizon for some time. I have not yet seen the British press. The French press have, of course, minimised the whole affair.

Apparently there have been faults on both sides (between ourselves, knowing Louis Spears, I would say *great* faults on both sides). As you probably know, the French are committed to the policy of abolishing the Mandate and setting up an independent Lebanese government, retaining for themselves – by treaty – only the same kind of position as we have kept in Iraq or Egypt. In 1936 such a treaty was agreed with the Lebanese, but the French Government fell, and it was never ratified. In 1941, when we conquered Syria and the Lebanon and drove out the Vichy forces, the Free French troops fought with us and we restored the Free French administration. At that time, Catroux made the most solemn declarations and did indeed begin to take steps (very slowly and deliberately) to implement them. Since he left Syria, I think that his successor has been 'stalling' a good deal. However, the elections which Catroux had arranged for the Lebanese Parliament did in fact take place. These caused considerable friction, because Helleu[14] (Catroux's successor) violently accused Spears of taking part in the elections in order to secure the success of pro-British and anti-French candidates. Spears with equal vigour denied this, and accused Helleu of spending large sums in bribery and using all sorts of terrorist measures to get French partisans in at the polls.

Eventually, the elections took place. The French candidates were defeated heavily, and a government was formed with Ministers very hostile to the French – pledged to secure the independence of the Lebanon as soon as possible.

Helleu came back to Algiers for instructions, and I was told to bring

[13] Grigg held his post until 1945.

[14] Jean Helleu was French Ambassador to Turkey, 1941–2, before joining Fighting France; he succeeded General Catroux as Delegate-General in the Levant in June 1943.

as much pressure as possible on the French Committee to secure his return with a liberal policy.

The whole thing has been enormously complicated by a legal wrangle in which both the Lebanese and the French have argued with equal pedantry and folly. The argument has turned on the juridical position of the French Committee. Are they legal successors to the French rights and duties, including the Mandate? Can they, not being the legal Government of France, negotiate and ratify a treaty? Can the Mandate be brought to an end, with the League of Nations in abeyance? And so on, and so forth.

Anyway, Helleu went back. When in Cairo, he heard that the Lebanese Parliament was in session and prepared to pass a Bill revising the constitutional situation and declaring complete independence. Very naturally, he appealed to them to adjourn the debate until he could get to Beirut to explain the policy which had been agreed in Algiers and to negotiate.[15] Very improperly, the Government refused this. The debate was held, and the amending Bill was passed [on 8 November] through all its stages.

Helleu retaliated by arresting the [President and] ministers in the early hours of the morning, and closing the Parliament.

From this have started various incidents – riots, shootings, excesses by Senegalese troops, etc., etc. Minimised by the French in a most unblushing way, and exaggerated by Spears in unending streams of telegrams to the Foreign Office repeated to me.

I do not know what will happen. I have no very clear instructions from London, and I am woken up in the middle of the night by this constant outpouring of 'Most Immediates' from Beirut, Cairo and London.

After my interview with Massigli – which was not very satisfactory – I went to a troubled rest surrounded by files and telegrams knee-deep in my bedroom.

Sunday, 14 November 1943

10 a.m. Church.

11 a.m. Office. A very hectic morning. Telegrams streaming in.

Lunch in bed.

3–6 p.m. Office.

6–7 p.m. Church.

8 p.m. Bed.

I am very tired and plagued now with rheumatism. It is specially bad in my neck, left shoulder and arm and both my hands. I suppose it is the damp.

At 10 p.m. another communication had to be made to Massigli. But I

[15] Helleu was returning to Beirut with liberal instructions from the Committee which 'could lead to the fulfilment in a very short time of the 1936 Treaty, whereby the States of the Levant are to receive all the attributes of sovereignty'.

could not be bothered to do more than send up a written *aide-mémoire* by John's hand.

The only peaceful time of the day was two hours in church. I am afraid I went more for rest than religious consolation – as always, the services were very bright and the men sang the hymns with cheerful enthusiasm.

Monday, 15 November 1943

After rather a rushed morning, with meetings with Admiral Sir John Cunningham, General Smith and Murphy, I left for the aerodrome at 12 noon, John Wyndham accompanying me, a faithful Sancho Panza to my Quixote journey.

I am getting very used to aeroplane travel by now, whether for short or long distances; and I have developed a technique. John has got me a 'Li-Lo' and whenever there is room I lie on the floor, with pillows and rugs. My limbs are so stiff and my joints so creaky that this is a great comfort.

John and I left Maison Blanche at 1.15. A special aeroplane (a C47 or Dakota) had been provided by the Chief of Staff, so we were very comfortable. We arrived at Gibraltar about 4 p.m. and were met by the Governor's A.D.C. and looked after with the usual hospitality which one gets on the Rock.

Considerable confusion reigned, owing to bad flying weather between England and Gibraltar, and the non-arrival of a number of expected machines – or rather their failure to start.

However, telegrams kept appearing in swift succession, and at 6.30 p.m. I received instructions to leave Gibraltar at once by launch.

So John and I repacked our bags, collected our coats and papers, and with the Governor (Mason-MacFarlane) and a number of admirals we set out. A few miles outside the harbour we were put aboard the *Renown*, and greeted by her owner – or so he seemed – who was finding this an agreeable method of cruising.

The Governor and admirals, after paying their respects, withdrew – and H.M.S. *Renown* went on her way.

The party consisted of the P.M., his daughter Mary, Randolph, Sir A. B. Cunningham (my old friend – now First Sea Lord), Lord Moran[16] (the doctor), General 'Pug' Ismay, Major [Desmond] Morton and some others. The Air and Army Chiefs of Staffs and various other notabilities were not in the party, but proceeding by air.

The P.M. was in excellent form and asked a great deal about the French situation. He is still violently anti-de Gaulle but as always, if you maintain a point with energy, he is prepared to listen. I think he really fears de Gaulle's 'xenophobia' – and there is no denying that this is very strong. But I feel that new forces are showing themselves, even

[16] Lord Moran (1882–1977) was Churchill's personal doctor, and took advantage of his position to compile detailed politico-medical diaries.

in the Algiers Committee, which are very healthy. The new arrivals from France, both to the Committee and to the Assembly representing the Resistance movement, are by no means slavish or adulatory supporters of de Gaulle. They represent all sorts and types – aristocrats, bourgeois, workmen and peasants. But the 'resistance' has (temporarily at any rate) bound them together in a fierce spiritual unity – not to be neglected.

We managed to get to bed at a reasonably early hour – 1.30 a.m. Last night, they told me, he sat up till 5 a.m.

Tuesday, 16 November 1943

P.M. sent for me about 9 a.m. (he was having breakfast in his cabin) and talked till about 12.30.

It was really a fascinating performance. The greater part was a rehearsal of what he is to say at the Military Conference;[17] and he is *terribly* worried and excited about this. He naturally feels that the Mediterranean position has not been exploited with vigour and flexibility.

This, as you probably realise, is due to the extreme rigidity of the Combined Chiefs of Staff system, and of our American allies generally. It is, of course, infuriating for Winston, who feels that all through the war he is fighting like a man with his hands tied behind his back. And yet no one but he (and that only with extraordinary patience and skill) could have enticed the Americans into the European war at all.

I feel that he regards this coming conference as the real turning-point and the hardest job he has encountered.

The rest of his talk was on:

(1) France.

(2) The Lebanon.

I told him the situation about both. He is naturally very incensed at Giraud's disappearance from the political field, since he regards the 'co-presidency' as the basis on which British and American recognition were granted. But he knew in his heart that it was only a temporary expedient. I tried to explain my view of the new forces which were rising up, not in de Gaulle's hands and to some extent challenging his authority. This interested the P.M. enormously. What he fears is a sort of de Gaulle dictatorship, hostile to Britain and mischievous if not dangerous. This led on naturally to the Lebanon. I told him that I regarded this as rather a test case. If we handled the affair with some tact, as well as energy, we would get the support:

(*a*) of Catroux,

(*b*) of Massigli,

(*c*) of quite half if not two-thirds of the Committee, and we could put de Gaulle in a minority of three or four.

[17] To begin in Cairo on 22 November to discuss the prosecution of the war against Japan.

1. The author with General Alexander, Casablanca, January 1943 *(Imperial War Museum)*

2. Casablanca Conference – Churchill with his Chiefs of Staff, January 1943. Seated left to right: Portal, Pound, Churchill, Dill, Brooke. Standing (centre five): Alexander, Mountbatten, Ismay, Leathers, the author *(Imperial War Museum)*

3. Giraud and de Gaulle, Casablanca, 24 January 1943 *(Imperial War Museum)*

9 & 10. Press Conference, Algiers, 4 June 1943 *(Imperial War Museum)*

8. The author with Churchill, Algiers, 4 June 1943 *(Imperial War Museum)*

6. Taking the Salute on St Joan of Arc's Day, Algiers, 9 May 1943. Left to right: Peyrouton, Giraud, Catroux, the author, Morse, Couve de Murville
(The Macmillan Family Archives)

7. Victory Parade, Tunis, 20 May 1943 *(Imperial War Museum)*

4. The author with Anthony Eden, Algiers, 1943 *(Imperial War Museum)*

5. At the Palais d'Eté, Algiers, 7 April 1943. Left to right: Gort, Giraud, the author *(The Macmillan Family Archives)*

11. Cunningham's luncheon party for the French Committee, 4 June 1943. Left to right (sitting): Catroux, de Gaulle, Churchill, Giraud, Eden. Left to right (standing): Monnet, Philip, the author, Georges, Brooke, Cunningham, Massigli *(Imperial War Museum)*

12. King George VI with Eisenhower, Algiers, 12 June 1943 *(Imperial War Museum)*

13. King George VI visits Malta, 20 June 1943
(Imperial War Museum)

14. Badoglio reads the Italian declaration of war, 13 October 1943
(Imperial War Museum)

But this required avoidance of ultimatums, except if absolutely necessary. I am afraid I also said that I thought as long as *Spears* was in Beirut there would be open and bitter warfare between us and the French. P.M. did not much like this.

We arrived Algiers about 1 p.m. General Bedell Smith, Major-General Whiteley, Admiral Sir John Cunningham and a few others came on board.

After luncheon, P.M. insisted on sending for General Georges (who has lately been turned off the Committee) 'in order to mark his displeasure'. He asked me if I agreed. 'Now give your opinion frankly. You always do, I know, and I very seldom agree with it!' So I said I thought it would be a most deplorable error on his part. 'Very well then, I will do it. I will see him at 6 p.m.' I do not really think it much matters, and he certainly had decided anyway, but I thought I would keep my end up before so large a company.

Somebody rashly remarked that the Services were better co-ordinated in this war than in the last. The Chiefs of Staff system was a good one. 'Not at all,' said Winston. 'Not at all. It leads to weak and faltering decisions – or rather indecisions. Why, you may take the most gallant sailor, the most intrepid airman, or the most audacious soldier, put them at a table together – what do you get? *The sum total of their fears!*' (This with frightful sibilant emphasis.)

Murphy and Ed Wilson came out. (I forgot to say that Ambassador Winant[18] was in the *Renown* party, having come from England with the P.M.) Eventually, we all went ashore about 4 p.m. – a little exhausted, but stimulated.

6 p.m. Went with M. Bogomolov and Murphy to see Massigli. This was to give a formal invitation to the French Committee to appoint a representative on the new Allied Council on Italian affairs.

Wednesday, 17 November 1943

The Lebanon crisis is running absolutely full out. Meanwhile, it worries me greatly; because I feel that Spears is out for trouble and personal glory, and Casey is so weak as to be completely in his pocket.

I saw Massigli at noon. He was very anxious, but I pressed him to take decisions in time and not wait too long. Catroux is always a little leisurely, and of course he hates Spears so much that he may be led to commit an error of judgment.

After luncheon, the usual office – at 5.30 [André] le Troquer came in – the new Minister of War. He struck me as a straightforward, if rather silly little man.

6.30 p.m. Commander Cohon to see me.

[18] J. G. Winant (1889–1947) was U.S. Ambassador to Britain, 1941–6, and U.S. representative on the European Advisory Commission, 1943–7.

Thursday, 18 November 1943

10.30 a.m. Saw General Bedell Smith on the Lebanon. I told him of the decisions which I knew were going to be taken to present an ultimatum (or at least a time-limit) on the French in respect of our demands – these are (1) the recall of Helleu; (2) the release of the President and Ministers.

We discussed possible French reaction if by chance they were to take a very rash line, and the troops situation here. I do not myself fear any folly on their part, but I felt the general should know what was going on.

11.30 a.m. Norwegian Minister called – fishing for news.

12 noon. Mr Balensi, new Economic Control, Algeria. I had a long and quite interesting talk with him. He is *par origine, Israëlite*. He had therefore been got rid of from his post in the Algerian administration during the bad times. He has just been reinstated.

12.45 p.m. Lunch at Borg Polignac – Princesse de Ligne, Princesse Galitzine, Admiral Godfroy. The latter is my old friend from Alexandria; he is living in retirement with the old Princesses. He finally came over (you remember Force X at Alexandria) and brought his fleet to French West or North African ports. He at once resigned and lives quietly here. The other day General de Gaulle came to luncheon (which surprises me rather) and the admiral wisely went for a long walk. I suppose sooner or later the 'hue and cry' will be after him, and they will have him in prison.

He was as charming, as wrong-headed, as hopelessly 'Jacobite' as ever. But it is nevertheless pleasant to spend an hour or two in this rather old-fashioned company – good food (I do not know how got), good talk, good manners, good taste. And, of course, just a survival, a period piece. Poor Princesse Galitzine. Her happiest memory of all she treasures is *petits-chevaux* at Monte Carlo with the old Duchess of Manchester!

Major Desmond Morton (the P.M.'s Personal Assistant) is staying with me. He is a pleasant and intelligent man, and it is quite useful for me to have him at this time.

This afternoon was just one long farce – or tragedy. I have been told that a time-limit will be given to the French tomorrow by Casey in Beirut. This will expire Sunday morning! Rather short, I would think.

I have *not* been told to present it here, but to wait till Casey does so to Catroux. I have, however, let Eric Duncannon put out a 'calculated indiscretion' which may do no harm.

Bob Murphy and Ed Wilson to dinner to meet Major Morton.

Friday, 19 November 1943

I am afraid this diary is getting hopelessly scrappy, but I have not a moment to write it up. To add to everything, the weather is filthy. It is cold (and the central heating has burst in our villa); it rains continuously. My hands are practically unusable. And Beirut, Cairo and London bombard us with telegrams by day and night – all of which are marked 'Most Immediate' (which means you are woken up at any hour) and most of which are either unnecessary, foolish, obscure or undecipherable – the last are the best!

With the P.M. away, and Attlee[19] in charge, it is just as bad as the Italian armistice time. The Cabinet just 'dither' and make feeble and rather pawky little noises. Meanwhile, while they jibber, the Spears–Macmillan battle is raging hard. Spears is determined (as I see it) to elevate himself and to degrade the French. I will get *all* that H.M.G. requires from the French if I am given a chance. But I want to get it in such a way as preserves and does not destroy the work of nearly a year here and that carries with us the reasonable Frenchmen who are our friends. Spears wants a Fashoda; and I do not.

9 a.m. M. [Henri] Laugier, new Rector of Algiers University, called. He had nothing to say, but said it very nicely and even eloquently. He is a lover of the British.

10 a.m. Saw General Eisenhower and explained the latest phases of the Lebanese crisis.

12 noon. Office meeting. I have now (once a week or so) a meeting of all the staff. It is still not a very big one, for the work we do, but it is just too big for all to meet every day, so I have started these little meetings to preserve contact all through.

1.30 p.m. I lunched with Massigli. A pleasant party, with Jacquinot (new Minister for the Navy – a resistance man), d'Astier de la Vigerie (brother of the general and brother of the one who was so long in prison here as the suspected organiser of the Darlan murder).[20]

D'Astier is new Minister of Interior. He also has just come out of France one or two moons ago. Also, a professor of Juridical Law at the University of Toulouse called [André] Hauriou. He has just come also, and he is acting as *rapporteur* of the Foreign Affairs Committee of the new Assembly.

After lunch Massigli gave me the latest news. He will, he hopes, carry the recall of Helleu through the Committee.

4 p.m. Group-Captain [J.M.J.C.J.I.] Rock de Besombes to see me. He said he was English (which seems odd, with such a name) and had come to be my Air Attaché (which seems odder still). However, I said I thought that it would be all right. He is really an advance guard of a sort of military mission which I have been fending off for months.

[19] Clement Attlee (1883–1967), leader of the Labour Party, was Prime Minister, 1942–5, and Lord President of the Council, 1943–5.

[20] Louis Jacquinot (b. 1898) was Commissioner for the Navy, 1943–4. Baron Emmanuel d'Astier de la Vigerie (1900–69), a journalist and member of the Assembly, was Commissioner for the Interior, 1943–5. His brothers were the Air Force general François (1886–1956) and Assembly member Henri (1897–1952), who had helped the Americans before the 'Torch' landings, only to be imprisoned until October 1943 under suspicion of complicity in the murder of Darlan.

6 p.m. All the Consulate Staff (or quite a lot) to the villa. I had formally to present the medal of the M.B.E. to the Vice-Consul, Mr [Gawin] Wild. A great drinking of sherry, cocktails, etc.

Meanwhile, Colonel Ralston[21] (Canadian Minister of Defence) arrived to stay. He had a Colonel Dye (Canadian Army) with him. He seemed a little startled, because he arrived from the aerodrome just as the presentation was starting. But he is a jolly old boy, and joined in the drinking all right. Jock Whiteley, Brigadier Macdonald (Canadian) and a number of other officers to dinner to meet Colonel Ralston.

The telegrams kept pouring in – and what with my guests and my dinner-party and the need to work at night, we are getting a little strained. Also, the cold is frightful. We have got a wood fire in the big sitting-room, but no other room has a fireplace. The Engineers mended our boiler for the central heating this morning, but it apparently burst almost immediately again!

Saturday, 20 November 1943

9.15 a.m. Massigli called. In conformity with my instructions I had to give him the text of the *aide-mémoire* which Casey had given to Catroux and which amounts to an ultimatum. We demand:

(*a*) immediate recall of Helleu,

(*b*) immediate release of the imprisoned President and Ministers.

If this is not done by Sunday (10 a.m.) we shall declare British martial law and occupy Lebanon with British troops. (I have now got the time altered to Monday, on the ground of difficulty of telegraphy from Beirut to Algiers, especially for French.)

Massigli asked me to help him by *not* delivering the document till *after* the meeting of the Committee. He hopes to get the matter agreed *without* the use of the ultimatum.

12 noon. A deputation of Communist Deputies. They wished to congratulate Great Britain on things in general and the war in particular. A queer world!

1.15 p.m. Luncheon at villa, in honour of Morton. Pleven (Colonies), Diethelm (Production), also Joyce (American head of N.A.E.B.), Herbert (British head of N.A.E.B.).

At 4 p.m. Massigli called. He told me he had carried the recall of Helleu, and in principle the release of the Ministers, with de Gaulle and two others only against him.

He did not circulate the Casey note until this afternoon.

After he left, I went to the office and there was a lot of telegraphy to do – to London, to Cairo and to Beirut.

I dined quietly, but went at 9.30 to see Murphy so as to tell him the latest developments.

[21] Colonel James Ralston (1881–1948) was Canadian Minister of National Defence, 1926–30 and 1940–4. He was in North Africa to inspect the Canadian Corps which had arrived in October to gain experience for the invasion of France.

Sunday, 21 November 1943

All night the telegrams came in – at least enough to make it seem a continuous flow. As a result, I had to send a formal letter to Massigli on a *new* point – that is, the *status* of the Ministers *after* release.

I stayed in bed most of the morning, feeling very tired and anxious.

3.15 p.m. Massigli called. He gave me the text of the communiqué to be issued at 5 p.m. by the French, publicly. He also would send me later a formal letter of protest from the French Committee. (This is *not* important.)

The French decision is rather clever. It makes it *appear* to be done by them *on their own*, or on Catroux's advice. It recalls Helleu: it liberates *and* restores to his functions the President of the Lebanon republic: it liberates only (and leaves the point of their status obscure) the Ministers. But it does *appear* at least a voluntary decision and does save some face.

I telegraphed all this (and the text of the formal letter) all round. I know there will be further trouble about the *reinstatement* of the Ministers, but it is a great thing to get this far.

General Gale came to dinner.

Monday, 22 November 1943

As a result of the night's telegrams, another letter had to be sent to Massigli this morning. I did this from bed and also worked on telegrams for Foreign Office, etc.

11.30 a.m. Conference with Colonel McChrystal (P.W.B.) at the office about handling the news of the Lebanese crisis from this end.

I have telegraphed to Foreign Office saying what we are doing about this. We are *not* allowing any mention of any ultimatum – this on military grounds, since troop movements are necessarily involved.

12 noon. Saw Murphy. Discussed the new Italian [Advisory] Council – also alteration of Darlan–Clark agreement.

3 p.m. Went to meeting of Assembly. Two quite good speeches – the whole rather formal, but I should think would soon get more lively.

7 p.m. Went with Murphy to see Massigli. We gave him an *aide-mémoire* saying that Allied H.Q. and the two Governments recognised that the Clark–Darlan agreement (made between General Clark and Admiral Darlan after the landings) was out of date and that we were ready to sit down with the French Committee and make a new agreement as regards our military needs in North Africa. Massigli was pleased as this will help him at this time. We have agreed a public statement.

10 p.m. Called to see Massigli at his villa. He was *very* depressed. The time-limit has (he knows now) been extended to *Wednesday, 10 a.m.* But is it really to be enforced about the one point now outstanding – namely the automatic reinstatement of the Ministers in

office? Nevertheless he admitted that he had now received a telegram from Catroux *strongly* recommending this course, and indeed proposing to do so *on his own responsibility* unless the Committee actually forbid it.

He asked me whether our ultimatum still applied on this point. I said I did not know, but would it not be better for him not to have an answer until as late as possible? I therefore arranged with him to write him a letter, which would be sent to him during the Cabinet meeting tomorrow.

If he could carry his colleagues to adopt Catroux's proposal and reinstate the Ministers by argument, he would do so. If asked whether there was a British ultimatum on this point, he would say he did not know (my letter not having yet arrived).

Tuesday, 23 November 1943

As agreed, my letter to Massigli was sent down to him at about 11.30 a.m. They must of course be told H.M.G.'s decision, but I should much prefer to see Massigli get his way without reference to it. It will be better for us and for him in the future.

I stayed in bed, and worked from there, feeling very tired.

1.15 p.m. Three journalists (*News Chronicle*, U.P. and Columbia Broadcasting) to luncheon and various others, including Tom Dupree, our press attaché.

At luncheon, Massigli telephoned to say he had carried the Committee, and the order to reinstate the Lebanese Ministers would be given at once. Would I be sure to send off the necessary telegram at once, so as to avoid the danger of some mistake tomorrow morning? I gathered that he had *not* had to use my *aide-mémoire*, but carried it on Catroux's telegram.

3 p.m. Belgian Ambassador [Count R. de Vichenet] called. A very boring old man.

4 p.m. Went to the Assembly, to hear continuation of the debate on foreign affairs. Rather dull speeches.

7 p.m. Saw Massigli at his office. He seemed pleased but tired. He had won by a good majority – only de Gaulle, Pleven and Diethelm against him. But it had been a most painful scene.

De Gaulle had been in a terrible mood, and had been very rude to him. Massigli offered his resignation twice during the meeting, but it was refused by acclamation.

The ruse we had concocted worked out well. As soon as the session began (10 a.m.) de Gaulle had said, 'Another British ultimatum, I suppose.' 'I know nothing of this,' said Massigli. 'We are to discuss a telegram from Catroux' (which he then produced).

Massigli is tired and very anxious, but really rather triumphant. If only we could get rid of Spears, we might make a new start in the Levant.

Lord Stansgate (*alias* Wedgwood Benn) turned up to stay. He is to hold a post on the Italian Control Commission[22] – a queer choice, but I suppose we wanted a 'Labour' man in somewhere.

I'm afraid we spent rather a hectic evening alternately discussing French and Italian affairs.

I must stop now, and go to sleep. I have managed to get something more or less up to date, and we leave for Cairo at 7 a.m. tomorrow.

I'm afraid this is very scrappy but it has been a terribly confused period.

Wednesday, 24 November 1943

I left Algiers aerodrome (Maison Blanche) at 7.30 a.m. John Wyndham came with me, and Bob Murphy also. Air Vice-Marshal Dawson had kindly procured for me a Liberator (which is normally used for transporting urgent repair materials but in which three quite comfortable chairs had been provided). We had to make rather an early start from the villa, as one must allow about ninety minutes for the drive.

The weather has been terrible in Algiers for the last few weeks – cold and wet. The rain has been coming down in torrents and the roads and airfields are correspondingly saturated with water. I felt rather tired, and the Lebanese affair was really very exhausting. However, we got through the immediate crisis with very reasonable success, since we have got what we wanted without making things too difficult for the French Committee. I have felt real admiration for Massigli, and it has been interesting to see the newer members of the Cabinet making themselves felt. De Gaulle has a lot to learn and I hope the experience will do him good.

I do not know yet how the British press has reacted, as I have not got papers later than 16 November. Nor do I know what people will say about Duff Cooper's appointment.[23] It is, of course, what I have always wanted since the Committee was recognised. I have been through too many 'shy-making' experiences with these Frenchmen, in their unregenerate 'Balkan' days, to be of much more use to them. They will regard the appointment of a British Ambassador, with a duke's daughter as a wife who appears on the scene instead of lurking at home(!), as a compliment. They suffer from such an inferiority complex that it will do them good to be treated as a French Government in fact, if not in law. And I understand that Duff means to retire from politics (he has of course left the Ministry) and hopes to be the British Ambassador in Paris in due course.

The only fear I had was that owing to the Lebanese trouble the

[22] Vice-President of the Economic and Administrative Section.

[23] Alfred Duff Cooper (1890–1954), later 1st Viscount Norwich, was to succeed me as H.M. Representative with the F.C.N.L., 1943–4, and was Ambassador to France, 1944–7; he had been Chancellor of the Duchy of Lancaster, 1941–3.

announcement of Duff's appointment and that of his American colleague might be postponed. However, this was not done, and this was wise. It gave the French more confidence in what I was telling them – viz., that we had no desire to humiliate them. We simply wished, in their interests as well as in our own, a proper solution of the political problems in the Levant.

We had a good flight to Cairo, arriving about 5.30 (Cairo time). It was very cold for the first part of the trip, partly because these operational machines are not lined (like the regular transport planes) so the cold air comes through the joints and up from the floor; partly also because the weather was stormy over the mountains and we flew to a good height (17,000 feet or so) to get over them and the tempests in safety. But it was *very* shady and comfortable, and it was grand to have a chair.

I forgot to say that Desmond Morton (who has been staying with me in Algiers since the 16th) was of the party. I found him a most agreeable guest, and he was also useful during the Levant crisis, for he knows the P.M.'s mind very well and how he will react to a particular way of putting a point or an argument.

We drove from the airfield to the Casey villa (as it is called – it is really Mr Chester Beatty's and has been lent by him to Oliver Lyttelton and Dick Casey successively). It was in this villa that I stayed – in great comfort – with the Caseys when I went to Cairo in March, after my aeroplane accident.

Casey villa is, for the time being, No. 10 Downing Street. We were greeted by the now familiar faces of the entourage. Lord Moran (the doctor), Martin (the excellent Private Secretary), Brown (Second Secretary),[24] and of course the naval officer who runs the map-room, the detectives, the typists, the marines, Sawyers (the valet), and all the circus.

I was at once summoned into the presence – Winston was (as usual) in bed, surrounded by red boxes and smoking the inevitable cigar. He seemed in much better form than when I had last seen him (a week or so ago). He had wisely stayed on the *Renown* and had avoided any sightseeing or tour of the Italian front. He had got rid of his cold.

He listened with unusual patience to my story of the Lebanese crisis from our point of view in Algiers. He seemed impressed by my arguments that de Gaulle had been diverted from extreme courses by his own people and that this method was much more effective than British and American pressure – especially if openly used – which merely played into de Gaulle's hands and enabled him to appeal successfully to French pride and sensitiveness.

He kept me about an hour, in very friendly mood.

[24] John Martin (b. 1904) was Private Secretary to the Prime Minister, 1940–5. Captain Francis Brown (1915–67) was seconded to the Treasury as Assistant Private Secretary to the Prime Minister, 1941–4.

After leaving the Casey villa, I drove into Cairo, where I am staying. My host is one [E. F. W.] Besly, the legal counsellor of the Embassy, whom I knew at Oxford. He is a very nice and intelligent fellow. He used to live in 'digs' with Gilbert Talbot and Walter Monckton.[25] His wife is harmless (as women go). But the house is ugly and rather full of little ornaments – silver and china, etc. – which John and I played some havoc with. We dined quietly with the Beslys.

At 10 p.m. I went to the British Embassy for a talk with Alec Cadogan[26] on current French affairs – more especially the Levant crisis.

Thursday, 25 November 1943

Drove into the conference area in the morning. This consists of the Mena House hotel (just on the verge of the desert – close to the pyramids), the Casey villa, the American Minister's villa (called the Kirk[27] villa) and a number of other small and large villas in the neighbourhood. As at Anfa, the whole area is surrounded by barbed-wire fences, guards, guns, tanks, etc. Owing to the leakage in the *Daily Mail* and elsewhere, the security arrangements are fantastic. It is impossible to move anywhere near the 'great' without passing two or three barriers and showing innumerable 'passes'. The military conferences, etc., take place in the hotel (as at Anfa) – the secretariat and the officers (other than the highest who are in villas) are lodged there. I have been allotted a small bedroom (as an office). It is all very well done – complete military telephone system – typists and secretaries available – etc., etc.

At 12 noon there was a 'photograph'. This was at the Kirk villa (where the President is lodged) and took place in the garden. Fortunately, the weather is splendid. It is dry and warm – apparently it hardly ever rains at all here – but the heat is not great – rather like a really fine summer day at home – seventy to seventy-five in the shade. After the filthy weather we have been having at Algiers, this dry, warm weather is delightful. I feel much better than for a long time.

The photographs consisted of various groups. First, the GREAT, i.e. the President, the P.M., the Generalissimo and Mrs Chiang.[28] Next, the STAFFS.

Here there was an indescribable scene – all the American and British officers of whom one had ever heard. I suppose you will see the

[25] Gilbert Talbot had been killed in action at Hooge in 1915. Sir Walter Monckton (1891–1965) had been Director-General of Propaganda and Information Services in Cairo, 1941–2, and Minister of State, 1942.

[26] Sir Alexander Cadogan (1884–1968) was Permanent Under-Secretary of State at the Foreign Office, 1938–46.

[27] Alexander C. Kirk (1888–1979) was U.S. minister to Egypt and Saudi Arabia, 1941–3, and Ambassador to Greece, 1943–4; he became U.S. representative on the Advisory Council for Italy, U.S. Adviser to SACMED, and Ambassador to Italy in the course of 1944.

[28] Generalissimo Chiang Kai-Shek (1887–1975) was head of the Nationalist Government of China, 1928–49.

pictures published in due course, so I need not weary you with names. But while we were standing about in the garden of the villa waiting it was really like a sort of mad garden party in a newsreel produced of *Alice in Wonderland*. There were, of course, the Chiefs of Staff – General Marshal, Admiral King, General Brooke, Air Marshal Portal, Admiral A. B. Cunningham – with Field Marshal Dill, General Somervell (U.S.), and so on thrown in. Then the Commanders, Eisenhower, Admiral John Cunningham, Tedder, General Wilson (G.O.C., Middle East) (Alexander was away, being ill). Then suddenly in walk Lord Louis Mountbatten, General Stilwell[29] (U.S.) and General Carton de Wiart – all from the Indian theatre of war. In addition, all the well-known figures in the minor ranks – 'Pug' Ismay, Admiral Leahy[30] (President's aide), etc., etc.

After the 'great' (President, P.M., etc.) had been photographed with their military and naval staffs we had them with the civilians. In this photograph were Harry Hopkins (President's Personal Adviser), Averell Harriman (U.S. Ambassador to Russia), Ambassador Winant, Murphy, Kirk (U.S. Minister in Egypt), etc, etc. Also Anthony Eden, Sir Alec Cadogan, Lord Leathers, Lord Killearn[31] (formerly Lampson – British Ambassador in Egypt), Casey (Minister of State), and myself.

It really was a most extraordinary performance and (I suppose) a useful one.

Madame Chiang excited great interest among the British – rather less, I think, among the Americans, who have by this time seen and heard quite enough of her. She is a pretty little creature, but somewhat marred by having trouble with her eyes. She was wearing some very strange kind of glasses. I gather she gives herself great airs and behaves like an Empress – which did not go down very well in the U.S.A. during her recent trip.

After the photograph, lunch at Casey villa. Only P.M. and Anthony. Some interesting talk about French and Near East, and some sharp tiffs. Winston is getting more and more dogmatic (at least outwardly) and rather repetitive. One forgets, of course, that he is really an old man – but a wonderful old man he is too.

Actually, if one stands up to him in argument I do not think he resents it. And it is amusing to watch how he will take a point and reproduce it as his own a day or two later. He misses very little, although he does not always appear to listen.

After luncheon (which lasted till about 3.30) I went back into Cairo. Conference at 5 p.m. with Anthony on a number of questions at the

[29] Admiral Lord Louis Mountbatten (1900–79) was Supreme Allied Commander, South-East Asia, 1943–6. General Joseph W. Stilwell (1883–1946) was Chief of Staff to Generalissimo Chiang, 1942–4.

[30] Admiral William D. Leahy (1875–1959) was U.S. Ambassador to France, 1940, Chief of Staff to the U.S. President and member of the Joint Chiefs of Staff, 1942–9.

[31] Sir Miles Lampson, 1st Baron Killearn (1880–1964) was Ambassador to Egypt and High Commissioner for the Sudan, 1936–46.

Embassy. After the conference, I went to Casey's office and continued talks – particularly on Lebanon and Syria.

It is difficult to take a balanced view of these things, but I cannot help feeling that Spears has forced his policy too far and too unscrupulously. It is quite possible to be firm with the French without being offensive to them. He is a clever man; but the trouble is that he has the qualities neither of the British nor of the French.

Casey, who is intelligent but ill-educated, just has not got the experience. He is absolutely honest, patriotic and devoted. But he is weak.

All this, of course, means that he is completely in Spears's pocket.

Friday, 26 November 1943

Drove out to Mena House hotel in the morning. Conferences with various people in my room there – e.g. General Kirby (War Office, Civil Affairs), General Gubbins[32] (S.O.E.), Colonel Maxwell (AMGOT) and others.

Drove back to Cairo and met Anthony at the British Embassy about noon. Here we finally settled a policy towards France and the Levant, with necessary instructions to all concerned. I had a bit of a struggle, but Anthony was very helpful, and I think the policy finally agreed for submission to the P.M. is very reasonable.

We must make it clear both to the French *and* to the Syrians and Lebanese that we have no desire to see French interests in the Levant overthrown. We have no wish either to eject or (still less) to supplant the French. We wish the pledges for Levantine independence given quite clearly in 1941 to be carried out. This would mean a position for the French similar to that which we enjoy in Iraq or Egypt. Both these countries are now completely independent. We maintain no longer High Commissioners there, but Ambassadors. But we have special treaties freely negotiated, which guarantee to us the special rights which our past and present connections with these countries justify.

As for the immediate method of obtaining this, both the Syrians and (especially) the Lebanese must be deflated. They must be told that they cannot rely on us to help them eject the French, only to get a fair arrangement as outlined. Equally, the French must be told that in this liberal and progressive policy lies their only hope and that they must take this course or their Near East interests must inevitably go under in the end.

We agree, therefore, to get the French and Lebanese (and Syrians) to discuss and negotiate. We will not interfere, unless we are asked to come in as arbitrators by both parties. All this, of course, is all right on paper, but difficult to bring about in practice. I particularly doubt whether Louis Spears will or can address himself to the uncongenial

[32] Major-General Stanley Kirby (1895–1968) was Director of Civil Affairs, War Office, 1943–4. Major-General Colin Gubbins (1896–1976) was executive director of S.O.E., 1943–6.

task of 'deflating' the Lebanese. I cannot help thinking that being a popular hero in the Levant has rather gone to his head. I cannot believe he was ever so cheered and applauded in Carlisle![33]

Lunch at the Embassy. Lord Killearn, Lady Killearn (formerly Miss Castellani, daughter of the Italian doctor),[34] Lord Moran (English doctor – Sir Charles Wilson) Ambassador Winant, Mr Wong (one of the Celestials), Alec Cadogan, Anthony Eden, and a host of others.

It is so long since I was in a civilised house that I have almost forgotten what such a thing is like. The Embassy has lovely plate – some particularly beautiful seventeenth- and early eighteenth-century silver seal-boxes – and excellent service – Egyptians in very charming red and gold costumes. The A.D.C.s are charming, but inefficient, as A.D.C.s always are. It was quite like old times.

(When I think of you in the dreadful conditions in which you live at Pooks, without even water, I am ashamed. Really some day we must open up our own house, even if only for a short time, and live in a more or less decent way. If the war ends we could perhaps live at the big house for a few months, and give some parties for Carol and Catherine and a dance too!)

After luncheon, Murphy turned up for a talk. I introduced him to the various English notabilities. I then motored back to the conference area (Mena House) where I had some further appointments. Back to Cairo at 7 p.m. for a talk with General Maitland Wilson (Jumbo), G.O.C., Middle East. He is a shrewd, kindly, intelligent man. He gave me a very interesting account of the situation in the Lebanon which corresponded to what I had heard. He thought Spears's account exaggerated and went so far as to say that as long as Casey and Spears were in charge nothing would ever be solved. The French hatred for Spears was unbelievable.

7.30 p.m. Cocktail party at Casey's flat. (He has a flat in Cairo in addition to his villa near the pyramids which is now occupied by the P.M.)

Dinner at the Mohammed Ali Club. Our hosts were Mr and Mrs Besly. Mrs Shone (sister of Mrs Victor Mallet) was there.[35] Shone is Minister at Cairo. An excellent dinner. This is the best club in Cairo and the most select, with the most recherché food and wine. The Pashas use it, and play baccarat, poker, etc., here, in the best eighteenth-century style, staking against each other the enormous sums which (now that Egypt is free!) they can wring from the poor.

Saturday, 27 November 1943

Drove to Mena hotel. Talked most of the morning with Desmond

[33] Spears's constituency, 1931–45.

[34] Jacqueline, Lady Killearn, was the daughter of Dr Aldo Castellani.

[35] Sophie Shone's sister Christiana married Victor Mallett (1893–1969) who was H.M. Minister at Stockholm, 1940–5.

Morton (who is staying on here, the P.M. and the President having left this morning for Teheran). Everything seems still very uncertain about the arrangements for the Mediterranean command. I do not really know whether I shall stay on much longer or not. Apparently, Winston seems quite pleased with my work. But at the same time, he does not like opposition as much as he did, and I may have made trouble over this last incident, since Louis Spears is an old friend, and Winston is very loyal (too loyal, sometimes) to old friends.

However, I shall know more of the plans in a week or so, when the Emperors return from Teheran and the conference deals with matters nearer home.[36]

Above all, the question of the command, both in northern Europe and in the Mediterranean, *must* be settled without more delay.

Luncheon with American Minister (Kirk), a magnificent meal in a magnificent palace, the property of a magnificent Egyptian princess. But very dull company – mostly American civilians working in Middle East Supply Centre and a travelling circus of American oil 'executives'.

After luncheon, John and I went to do some shopping. We did find a *very* good bookshop, where there was a good stock of books of all kinds. We also bought some shoes, these are *very* expensive and do not last. But there it is!

After this, I rested in my bed for a bit – had a quiet dinner (alone) at the Turf Club, and then returned to the Beslys' house for a little more rest, preparatory to driving out to the aerodrome, which we did at

1 a.m., Sunday, 28 November 1943

We arrived (John and I) at the aerodrome – Cairo West – at about 2 a.m. (it is a longish drive – about thirty miles from Cairo). Murphy turned up a bit later, and after the usual weighing in and palavering about the seats (which is part of the nuisance of going by the 'courier' plane, instead of having a plane of one's own) we were 'airborne' about 3 a.m.

I was unable to keep Air Vice-Marshal Dawson's Liberator, which was wanted for other work, or to obtain another plane for my personal use. The 'courier' was the usual Dakota (C47 or DC3), slow but sure. We were twenty-three people (every tin bucket-seat occupied save one) and lots of mail and luggage. I am bound to say that it was *very* uncomfortable. I managed, however, in spite of the extreme discomfort of the seat (or lack of anything which one can dignify by such a name) to doze off for a bit. John (being of the right age) slept like a log.

We reached Benghazi about 7.30 a.m. or 8. Here we got a rapid breakfast, and then all got back into our seats and came down next at Tripoli – about 12 noon. The thought of another four or five hours in

[36] Roosevelt and Churchill travelled to Teheran for meetings with Stalin from 28 November to 1 December 1943. The Cairo conference resumed on 4 December and ended on the 6th.

the same crowded conditions was, I am bound to say, rather depressing. But, by good luck, Sir John Cunningham saw me walking disconsolately on the aerodrome, took us all into his plane (he had two other passengers only) and I finished the journey sleeping luxuriously in the admiral's deck-chair.

We arrived at Algiers at 5.30 p.m. rather exhausted. We had rough weather, and bad winds between Tripoli and Algiers, and I was thankful for the admiral's kindness which allowed me to sleep peacefully through it all, in relative comfort and luxury. On reaching the villa, a hot bath was very welcome and a quiet evening reading telegrams and newspapers; a large number of both had arrived during my absence.

Monday, 29 November 1943

Rather a long day. Started at 9 a.m. in the office, and proceeded without much incident with the usual routine – papers, telegrams, letters, visitors.

The chief question to be dealt with however, was that of forming the Advisory Council for Italy in conformity with the Moscow decisions. M. Vyshinsky[37] (Deputy Commissar for Foreign Affairs) had arrived in Algiers, with the usual Russian staff of about thirty, including one admiral and two generals. After some discussion with Murphy, we decided to have a luncheon (to be given by Murphy) and then an informal talk as to the procedure we should follow. This was duly arranged, and at 1.15 the party met in Murphy's villa. The party included Ed Wilson, Roger Makins, Seldon Chapin (stooge to Ed Wilson), General Julius Holmes. The French were represented by Massigli and Guérin (his Under-Secretary).

The Russian party consisted of Vyshinsky, Bogomolov and one or two civilian stooges.

After luncheon, we had a longish and very easy talk about procedure, etc., which we settled without much difficulty. There were one or two points on which the Russians were rather pedantic, and I detected a tendency to develop the Council from *advisory* to *executive* duties. But nothing with any real bite in it came up in these preliminary talks.

Vyshinsky is a strange personality. Outwardly he is genial, with red, fat face and white hair, the image of every Conservative mayor or chairman of constituency (he is *very* like the late lamented Mr Tyson Hodgson). The eyes, however, are blue, spectacled – and hard. And behind the geniality and bluff heartiness, I think (even if one did not know his record), one detects a certain toughness (again not unlike T. H.). But all the same it is difficult to visualise in him the cruel persecutor of the Russian terror – the scourge of prisoners, the torturer

[37] Andrei Yanuarievich Vyshinsky (1883–1954) was Soviet Deputy Minister for Foreign Affairs, 1940–9; he had been chief prosecutor at Stalin's notorious purge trials in 1934–8.

of witnesses, the gloating, merciless, bloody figure of which we read six or seven years ago.

The talk after luncheon was protracted, but by anecdotes as much as by serious discussion. It was agreed to have the first formal meeting constituting the Council tomorrow afternoon. We also agreed on various procedures – rotating chairmen, common secretariat, alternate members, etc., etc., as well as the text of a press communiqué to be issued.

4.30 p.m. Herbert – a number of N.A.E.B. questions to be settled as well as the further stages of the negotiations with the French on (1) a financial agreement, (2) a lease–lend agreement. These have been dragging on a long time, and I am most anxious (if I possibly can) to complete them before handing over to Duff Cooper.

6 p.m. Went with Murphy to see General Bedell Smith. The Darlan–Clark agreement is to be revised, and we made some progress on details. We also discussed the Advisory Council for Italy and the problems involved in its formation and handling.

I had to go back to the office from A.F.H.Q. and ultimately finished up about 8 p.m. I then went home, had a little dinner, and so to bed.

Tuesday, 30 November 1943

Stayed in bed all the morning, reading Richardson's *Pamela* and dozing.

1.15 p.m. A remarkable luncheon party given by Bogomolov at his newly acquired and magnificent villa.

Guest of honour: Vyshinsky.
Guests: Murphy,
Massigli,
and self.

Also – the Belgian, Dutch, Czech and Norwegian Ministers. *Not* repeat *not* the Pole!

Bogomolov is obviously *very* small beer compared to Vyshinsky, of whom he obviously stands in awe.

The luncheon was a miracle in Algiers. Caviare, smoked salmon, Russian bacon, tunny, sturgeon, and all the appanages of these delicacies in profusion. Vodka poured, like water, from carafe. Every two minutes Vyshinsky would leap to his feet and give a toast. 'To France and de Gaulle – Winston Churchill – Roosevelt – Democratic Liberties (*sic*)', etc., etc.

Then we all joined in this toast game. Every toast meant more vodka. More vodka meant more caviare and smoked salmon and so on.

The ordinary courses started to arrive by about two o'clock, and we finally staggered away about half-past three, exhausted but enthused with Sovietic ardour.

4.30 p.m. First formal meeting of the Allied Advisory Council. As a courtesy to the French, we voted Massigli to the Chair. The Chief of Staff welcomed the members on behalf of General Eisenhower; General Holmes gave a short account of the formation of AMGOT, the new conception of the Control Commission and so on. A few questions were asked – no difficulties were made – a few formal resolutions were voted – and that was all.

Then the press and the photographers got to work and I hope you may soon see the results.

After this meeting, Mr Ed Wilson and I (this time in my old capacity of Ambassador to the French) had an interview with Massigli. We are trying to get the French Government to part with some wheat stocks which they are holding. We will repay them later, but we want to save the shipping just at the moment. We need the wheat for Italy, where there is danger of great hardship and even famine.

John Astor[38] suddenly turned up here, dressed as a war correspondent! He came to dinner and was quite charming and gave me lots of news. It was a *really* nice change.

[38] Major John Astor (b. 1918) was a counter-intelligence officer; he became Conservative M.P. for Sutton, 1951–9.

December

Wednesday, 1 December 1943

Stayed in bed till 11 a.m. After that went to office for a little business.

M. Mendès-France[1] to lunch. He is the new Finance Minister in succession to Couve de Murville. He has just come from England, where he has for the last two years been an observer in a French Air Squadron under Bomber Command. He was their youngest Deputy in the French Chamber at one time and was Under-Secretary for Finance in the last Blum[2] Government. I thought him agreeable, intelligent, with a good political sense and apparently very pro-British. I spoke up strongly for his predecessor Couve (who has been rather unfairly attacked here). I hope he will be sent to England as Financial Adviser on Viénot's[3] staff. He would do well in that capacity as our Treasury people like and trust him.

Also to lunch – Major Gosling (Treasury), Mr Godfrey (second to Herbert), Mr Searight (Oil). He came with letter of introduction from Rachel Stuart.

3.30 p.m. Pierre Cot called to see me. I did not like him.

4.15 p.m. Called at the Algerian Government Building to see Catroux, returned yesterday from the Lebanon. I had an interesting talk with him.

6 p.m. M. Gouin,[4] the President or Speaker of their Provisional Assembly, called to see me. Gouin (no relation, I fear, to our Sir Lomer Gouin[5]) is a typical French 'Socialist' – very bourgeois, very talkative, very conceited and very ordinary. There are many Labour members of whom he reminded me. He had nothing really to say and took an unconscionable time in saying it.

[1] Pierre Mendès-France (1907–82) was Commissioner for Finance, 1943–4; he became Prime Minister and Minister of Foreign Affairs, 1954–5.

[2] Léon Blum (1872–1950), interned by the Germans, 1940–5, was French Prime Minister, 1936–7, 1938 and 1946–7.

[3] Pierre Viénot (1898–1945) was F.C.N.L. representative in London, 1943–4.

[4] Félix Gouin (1884–1977) was President of the Assembly in Algiers and Paris, 1943–5, and President of the Provisional Government, 1946.

[5] Sir Lomer Gouin (1861–1929) was Prime Minister and Attorney-General of Quebec, 1905–20.

7.30 p.m. Massigli called at the villa. He presented a formal note of protest of the F.C.N.L. at the way we had treated them over the Lebanese affair. It was six typewritten pages. I said, 'Tell me, I am not a diplomat, what do I do with this? Must I read it?' 'No,' said Massigli, 'you need not read it. You must send it, though, to your Government.' 'Fine,' I said, 'I will. Will you have a drink?' 'Sherry,' says Massigli, 'unless you've got gin.' 'Certainly I have gin – a little vermouth?' 'Please.'

So now you know the proper way of presenting and receiving diplomatic notes. (As a matter of fact, I am rather pleased, because Massigli has always understood that I have tried to help him, and this easy manner is a sign of confidence and good fellowship.)

Hugh Fraser has come to stay a few days. Unluckily John has gone back to Cairo, where I return shortly.

A quiet evening, reading and writing.

Thursday, 2 December 1943

Left Algiers (aerodrome Maison Blanche) at 8 a.m. with Murphy and Vyshinsky. Massigli comes tomorrow.

Murphy has two staff with him. *I* have brought Roger Makins (more to give him a change than for any other reason) and a young man who has lately joined me, Aubrey Halford.[6] He speaks Italian and (though we keep it dark) Russian.

Vyshinsky has five soldiers – eight civilians.

I am now writing this in the aeroplane – between Bizerta and Catania, where we shall (I hope) stop for petrol and a little food. The plane is hot and crowded; and since it is *very* bumpy somebody will soon be sick. I do hope it will be Vyshinsky. (He has never before in his life left Russia. So we are showing him as much *sea* as possible, in order that he may fully understand the difficulties of amphibious operations.)

We got to Catania about 12.30 and stopped for lunch in an American mess at the aerodrome. What curious food Americans eat. I can never get quite used to it. Today we had, all on one plate:

(*a*) Cold minced meat.
(*b*) Hot rice pudding.
(*c*) Hot cabbage.
(*d*) Boiled peas and beans.

There was also most excellent white bread and splendid cold butter. The Russians liked the food and ate enormously.

Arrived at Brindisi aerodrome about 4 p.m., where we were met by Harold Caccia, Sam Reber (Vice-President and Deputy Vice-President respectively of the Political Section of the Control Commission). (How

[6] Aubrey Halford (b. 1914) was Second Secretary on my staff, 1943–4, British member of the Secretariat of the Advisory Council for Italy, 1944, and Political Adviser to the Allied Commission in Italy, 1944–5.

extraordinary is the military mind! They have constructed in the War Department in Washington and the War Office in London this fantastically elaborate and top-heavy machine, with Chiefs of Staff, sections, sub-sections, sub-commissions and staffed either by second-rate professional soldiers – too stupid to be employed in any operational capacity – or quite good civilians, expert in finance, shipping, coal, etc., which they insist on dressing up as brigadiers, colonels, etc. Then the whole is put down to govern a few square miles and (at present) under twelve million people on a strictly military organisational basis – with returns in duplicate, and the incredibly complicated and hopelessly obsolete internal mechanisms of the two War Departments hopelessly intermingled!)

After wash, refreshment, we were formally received by General Joyce (Deputy President of the Control Commission). The General was in his most stately form but gracious in the sort of 'fine old American gentleman' style. After a short interchange of speeches, we were informed that business would begin tomorrow morning at 9 a.m., when he and his chief officers would be glad to see the members of the Advisory Council and their staffs and give what explanations were required.

I thought Vyshinsky took rather a poor view of this proposal. I think it would have suited him better to have started after dinner and worked all night. I believe, for instance, his chief Molotov never gets up till 1 p.m. and begins his daily work at 3 p.m. However, General Joyce had spoken.

A good dinner at the Deputy President's table in the mess in the hotel. Things have certainly changed in this hotel since the first days I came with Murphy and General MacFarlane just after the armistice. The hotel is right on the quayside – then almost deserted, now a busy scene, with ships unloading day and night – especially night! After gossiping for a bit with Harold and Sam and others, went early to bed – curiously enough in the room I had on my first visit, now occupied by Lord Stansgate (Wedgwood Benn) who had providentially gone to Palermo, where a large part of the Commission is being organised.

In spite of the roar of derricks and shouting of workmen, I slept fairly well.

Friday, 3 December 1943

A lovely bright morning, cold but invigorating. One feels *much* better here than in Algiers, and I am less stiff. But my hands are still very swollen, which is a great bore.

7–8 a.m. Went for a walk into the outskirts of the town, and in some country lanes. I think it is really lack of exercise from which I normally suffer.

At 9 a.m. we all collected into a room (formerly the bar) and after a short preliminary statement by General Joyce (of a very imperfect nature) the heads of the various sections gave the Advisory Council a report on the prospective organisation and duties of his section. On the whole, these were well done. Harold Caccia had the most difficult task, since the Russians are more interested in politics than in finance or food supplies.

Vyshinsky wanted to know how many Fascists had been tried and how many had been shot. The best that Harold could do was to murmur something about nearly 1,500 in prison – but Vyshinsky obviously thought this a very poor result of three months' work.

These explanations, of which American Colonel Foley on finance (he is really a Treasury official), General Taylor (U.S.) on the Army, Navy and Air Force, in which he gave an account of the really excellent and even specially courageous work of the two latter – while from the Army we are getting a lot of practical help (this I think impressed us all), and Captain Ellery Stone, U.S.N.R. (really chairman of Mackay Radio) were the best,[7] took up the whole morning till lunch (we had a five minutes' break at eleven, like schoolboys).

Massigli and the French party had meanwhile arrived, so the Advisory Council was complete.

Of course the proceedings are intolerably lengthened by the necessity for translating everything into Russian for Vyshinksy. (As he understands English and French quite well, especially the latter, this is really a pose or a precaution based on inherent suspicion.)

After luncheon, we had a formal meeting of the Council, at which we considered two specific questions. These were as follows:

(1) The Russians, basing themselves on article 37 of the long armistice terms with Italy, which were shown to and approved by them before signature at Malta, claim that they have the right to appoint officers as members of the Control Commission.

These you will remember were the *long* armistice terms which I would have nothing to do with in Sicily, in spite of feverish protests from the Cabinet (P.M. being in Quebec).

There we eventually signed on twelve simple clauses, which meant what they said, and, instead of being the result of six months' midnight oil in various Government departments, were written originally by Eisenhower, slightly amended by me (there were only eight clauses in our draft) and finally appeared in a twelve-clause edition for emergency use. And we used them, thereby winning a fleet for nothing, and making the invasion of Italy at least a sporting chance instead of a very hazardous and almost hopeless undertaking.

Well, these *long* terms were eventually signed at Malta and they are

[7] Edward H. Foley (b. 1905) was joint direct of the Finance Subcommission, A.C.C., 1943–4. General Maxwell Taylor was now Chief of Staff to General Joyce. Captain Ellery W. Stone (1894–1981) was Vice-President of the Commission's Communications Section until January 1944, Deputy Chief Commissioner, 1944, and Chief Commissioner, 1944–7. He was Vice-President of Mackay Radio and Telegraph Company, 1931–7.

so badly drafted that almost every clause (especially this one 37) is ambiguous.

Anyway, the Russians say that they must be represented on the Control Commission, not merely on the Advisory Council, and have produced some military officers (in our party yesterday) as their nominations.

On this the French at once made the same claim.

As a result of interminable talk, we agreed on a formula – viz., that the problem should be reported by us (in Council) *jointly* to General Eisenhower and by *each* of us separately to our Governments, asking for a reply as soon as possible.

I think myself that the French and Russians will realise that it is quite impossible for an executive body to function if it is completely polyglot and I think they (and certainly the French) will be content with three or four places each (out of the thousand), more as a matter of prestige than anything else. At any rate, I have recommended H.M.G. to accept a compromise on these lines.

(2) The second item was to answer a question referred to the new Council by General Eisenhower for their advice.

I do not know whether you realise the present situation in Italy, so far as the Italian Government AMGOT and the Control Commission are concerned. It is rather complicated.

When you invade another country, you are supposed to follow certain rules for its internal administration, and these are laid down in an International Hague Convention.

There are two courses. Either the *sovereignty* of the invaded country and government is suspended, or the local government is allowed to carry on.

In the first case, the commander of the invading army administers the country *directly* with officers responsible to him. The authority and sovereignty of the local government are suspended, and all authority flows from the Commander-in-Chief. What we have called AMGOT (Allied Military Government of Occupied Territory) is simply an Anglo-American variant of a common form. We have administered Sicily and the rest of the territory *not* in German hands on the mainland in this way. But we have made one exception. When (after the armistice) the King and Badoglio fled to Brindisi, we thought we must leave a sort of 'enclave' under the royal sovereignty, so that the Italians could have a little kingdom (however small) in which the Italian state legally continued. The 'enclave' consists of the four provinces of Bari, Lecce, Taranto and Brindisi.

Here, of course, we sent in AMGOT officers to supervise. But in this territory they acted *not* in the name of General Alexander (as Military Governor) giving *direct* orders and decrees. But they acted *indirectly*, supervising (and removing, by asking the Italians to do so, any undesirables) local Italian officials.

The Control Commission is being got ready to extend this system, and it has been our plan that all Italian territory, including Sicily and Sardinia (except a narrow strip in the immediate rear of the armies which will remain under AMGOT), shall revert to the Italian Government, advised and supervised by the Commission.

In other words, we are going to operate *indirect* government (however strict) instead of *direct* government. Perhaps an analogy would be the difference between native India and British India.

Now I have realised (especially from the British left-wing press – *Chronicle*, *Herald*, *New Statesman*, *Tribune*, etc.) that H.M.G., and especially I, are widely attacked as the men who are supporting Badoglio and the King.

Murphy and Macmillan (it is said) are the men who supported Darlan and Giraud in North Africa, and now the same sinister, reactionary and semi-Fascist forces are at work in Italy. If you have read all my letters since 1 January you will be able to judge how far this charge is justified. However, the point is that it is widely believed.

Now if we transfer (as for many technical as well as other reasons we must do) AMGOT territory (where General Alexander is Military Governor) to Control Commission territory (where the King and Badoglio at least nominally rule), this attack will be increased in intensity.

So the idea has arisen of getting General Eisenhower to ask the new Advisory Council if this new body, fortified with French and Russian membership, supports the return of the territory to the King and Badoglio. I think it will be rather a sell for our extreme left, and I shall find myself instead of in the bad company of Murphy, in a noble comradeship with Vyshinsky.

All this afternoon we argued about this, and at the end both Vyshinsky and Massigli agreed to recommend the transfer on two conditions:

(*a*) That only non-Fascist and pro-Allied officials should be employed.

(*b*) That we should not be committed indefinitely to the King and Badoglio but only up to the capture of Rome.

As both these conditions are what we want, I accepted at once. But if I thought the question settled I was wrong. Vyshinsky said he must refer the matter to Moscow and Massigli said the same about Algiers. (Of course, I might have known that Vyshinsky will never agree to anything without reference to Moscow. He has two Ogpu chaps who watch him all the time, and I suppose he has to watch his step.) However, both said they would recommend strongly that the decision be in favour of transfer, so we can only wait now for the reply.

At dinner Vyshinsky was in great form and we had a tremendous argument about politics. Vyshinsky was very upset about Mosley and could not understand why we had not shot him.

He also produced two gems (which I must save for a Stockton audience!).

'Democracy is like wine. It is all right if taken in moderation.'

'Free speech is all right, so long as it does not interfere with the policy of the Government.'

After dinner we talked for a bit and then went to pack our things. The French and Russians are to have a personally conducted tour round southern Italy before our next meeting. I think this will do them good. Vyshinsky has never been out of Russia in his life, so it is all rather new to him.

Saturday, 4 December 1943

Left Brindisi at 5 a.m. Murphy, Makins and I had the aeroplane to ourselves, so we made a comfortable trip. I slept well on my 'Li-Lo' with plenty of rugs.

Arrived Cairo 4.30 p.m. Drove to Lord Moyne's house, which (in Lord Moyne's absence) John Wyndham has more or less requisitioned. (I sent John back to Cairo while we were in Italy.) Bathed, shaved, and changed into clean clothes. I am writing this just before dinner.

Sunday 5 December 1943 (3.15 a.m.)

After dinner last night – about 11 p.m. – just as I was off to bed, the summons came. Would I go round at once to the Kirk villa.

By the time a car had been produced and so on, it was about 11.30–45 before I got there. I found Anthony outside in the lobby, very excited about what I had done with Vyshinsky. Apparently they had hoped that he would come to Cairo, but, of course, neither he nor I had received any telegram about it. I knew Vyshinsky to be sleeping the night at Bari and leaving the next morning for a trip by car to Naples. These great men may have very profound ideas about broad principles (I mean Anthony and co.) but they are strangely incompetent about details. They knew that I was in Cairo by 6 p.m. and yet they wait till nearly 11.30 before asking from me the information they want. Their principal assistants also seem to have very little knowledge of how telegraphic communication actually works or of what distances are in these parts. However, I left John to get all the messages sent off by various possible routes, which, of course, he achieved in a very short time with complete success.

The reason for trying to get Vyshinsky along is that Molotov seems to have suggested it in Teheran. Vyshinsky is one of the most senior of the Russian Foreign Office people, and as the *Turks* are here, I think they want Vyshinsky to join with the Russian Ambassador in Ankara and ourselves in bullying the Turks a bit.

Knatchbull-Hugessen[8] was also with Anthony and Alec Cadogan.

[8] Sir Hughe Knatchbull-Hugessen (1886–1971) was Ambassador to Turkey, 1939–44.

After explaining to them how to contact Vyshinsky, what was the mileage between Bari and Cairo, etc., etc., and leaving John to get it all fixed, I went into the drawing-room, where I found the President and Winston sitting on a sofa.

'My dear Harold,' the President exclaimed, 'why haven't you been to see me before' – and the famous smile and charm were turned on for which all men fall. There is something at once attractive and pathetic in this man – the great torso, the huge and splendid head, the magnificent frame, immobile, anchored to a sofa or a chair, carried from room to room, just able to seem to stand when held firmly up, while the poor withered legs and feet, like those of a cloth doll, are nothing but a mockery.

The President and the P.M. were both in good form, the former specially so.

The President is still very critical of de Gaulle and the French. He fears that the French will not recover, and for that reason must not be allowed, willingly or unwillingly, to let down the world a second time. Therefore Indo-China should *not* be returned to them; Dakar (in French West Africa) should be under American protection; Bizerta under British, and so on. There is no need to abolish French sovereignty in these places; the French flag can fly, 'But if Great Britain and America are to police the world, they must have the right to select the police stations. Dakar can be a French-owned station, with an American sergeant; Bizerta the same.'

This, I reminded him, goes back to a conversation which we had at Anfa in February, when he developed the same idea.

After a general conversation on various themes – ranging round the world like an elementary lesson in geography – the P.M. and I left about 1 a.m.

I then went with Winston to his villa where we talked of France (he still opposes in argument but accepts in reality a great part of my views), British politics; Russia; the next election; the Mediterranean war, etc. etc. He made a good remark about the Mosley debate. He had enquired by telegram whether any Ministers had abstained or voted wrong. The results were disappointing to him. 'I have made it clear that, as regards the present Government, all resignations will be gratefully received!'

'Does that mean,' said Randolph, 'that anyone can join who wants to?' 'No,' replied P.M., with a grin, 'but you can join the queue.'

I left about 3 a.m. and got back to Cairo and to bed by 3.45 a.m. Slept late.

Meeting with Casey at 12 noon. General discussion of Lebanon question. Casey seems to be taking a more moderate view, probably because Louis Spears is not here. He comes, I believe, tomorrow.

1.30 p.m. Lunch at Casey villa. P.M. is lunching out with the President.

I gather the Turks are being very sticky. Really this is a most extraordinary affair, Chinese, Russian, Turkish, Greek, Yugoslav, Italian, French – all these questions are bobbing about for settlement, like those little celluloid balls in shooting galleries at the seaside. It is a fantasy and a miracle – and more and more, in spite of everything, Winston begins to dominate the scene.

All the staff were at lunch, and afterwards we had General Gubbins (S.O.E.) and a lot of talk about the future organisation of the Mediterranean command. I think that undoubtedly it will be decided to unite the Mediterranean command under *one* allied commander – that is, Cairo and Algiers will be amalgamated. Who this commander will be is not so clear – whether Eisenhower or Alexander. Nor is it certain whether Casey or Macmillan will be liquidated. But clearly if there is one commander, there must also be one Resident Minister (with an American colleague).

I am not (frankly) very much worrying one way or the other. I should like the job (which should be very interesting) and it would be fun to get into new fields like Greece, Yugoslavia, etc. On the other hand, if I am not selected I shall be able to come home, and presumably Winston will give me something there.

So I am taking no particular part in the 'intrigue', but will keep out of it. I hear that Winston is trying to get Casey to accept the Governorship of Bengal.

After lunch – which was very protracted – Roger Makins came out, and we went for a walk round the pyramids, Sphinx, etc. What with Arabs, Egyptians, soldiers on camels, donkey-boys, A.T.S., W.R.N.S., etc., etc., it is a lively but rather 'bank-holiday' kind of scene.

A quiet evening in Lord Moyne's house (where we are all living). I have a wonderful bathroom made of marble, with a sort of swimming-bath in the middle. It is very 'posh' and quite frightful. I suppose if one had a lot of naked ladies bathing in it, it would be better. As it is all surrounded by glass and gold, I should say that is what it is designed for. As it is, I find myself in grave danger of slipping and breaking my bones – you have to walk down several steps into the bath, and it is most perilous.

Monday, 6 December 1943

Stayed in bed most of the morning. The bed is very comfortable, and it was quite a treat to rest, and doze and read.

12 noon. Meeting with Spears and Casey. Louis has turned up from Beirut in great fighting form. I enjoyed it.

Lunch at Mohammed Ali Club. Given by Casey. Mrs Casey (charming and intelligent as always), Mr and Mrs MacVeagh (an American publisher, Ambassador to Greece and Yugoslavia), General 'Pug' Ismay, Rex Leeper (British Ambassador to Greece), Stevenson

(British Ambassador to Yugoslavia) Mrs Vic Oliver (Sarah Churchill),[9] Louis Spears, and one or two others. To tickle your poor neglected English palates, and distend, if only in imagination, your poor famished English stomachs – I will give you the menu:

Cocktails.
Soup.
Curried prawns and rice.
Veal, potatoes, salad, etc.
A dish of peas.
Ice: chocolate sauce.
Cheese.
Oranges, bananas, nuts, dates, figs, etc.
Turkish delight.

White wine, red wine, brandy, cigars. Indeed, the Fleshpots of Egypt!

3.30 p.m. Meeting with Leeper and Stevenson on Greece and Yugoslavia as it affects
(*a*) Italy,
(*b*) Mediterranean generally.

We went over the ground of the organisation which will be required if the P.M.'s plans for the new Mediterranean combined command are approved.

A quiet evening. I went to bed from 6 to 8. Then a pleasant dinner, with Desmond Morton (P.M.'s secretary) and Sir William Croft (Casey's Chief of Staff).

Young Julian Amery,[10] who seems to be staying in Moyne's house, was in to dinner. He has much improved.

Tuesday, 7 December 1943

A morning at the office of the Minister of State (where I have a room) with various telegrams in and out. Quite a lot of stuff has reached us from Algiers, and Roger and I spent the morning sorting it out.

Louis Spears was in during part of the morning. There is to be a full meeting later in the day.

Sir Alec Cadogan to lunch at our house. He is remarkably calm considering all his worries – a real tower of common-sense English strength.

3.30 p.m. Meeting at British Embassy.

[9] Lincoln MacVeagh (1890–1972) was U.S. Ambassador to Greece and Yugoslavia, 1943, and to Greece, 1944. Reginald Leeper (1888–1968) was H.M. Ambassador to Greece, 1943–6. Ralph Stevenson (1895–1977) was Ambassador to Yugoslavia, 1943–6. The Prime Minister's daughter Sarah (1914–82), an actress and writer, had married the comedian Vic Oliver (1898–1964) in 1936.

[10] Julian Amery (b. 1919), who married my daughter Catherine in 1950, became Liaison Officer to the Albanian Resistance movement, and served on General Carton de Wiart's staff, 1944; Conservative M.P. for Preston North, 1950–66, and for Brighton Pavilion since 1969.

Present, Eden, Cadogan, Lord Killearn (Lampson), Casey, Spears, Sir William Croft, Lascelles (Spears's man), Roger Makins and I.

The meeting lasted about one-and-a-half hours and was (from my point of view) quite satisfactory. Louis always overstates his case and therefore there is no need (in an intelligent audience) to answer him, for he answers himself.

I think the final decision – which was to damp down the Lebanese a bit and induce them to reach an arrangement which would secure to the French a position rather like ours in Iraq – was the right one. I know (from his talks with me) that this is also the P.M.'s view. But I very much fear that Spears will not carry it out in the spirit (or even in the letter) unless he gets a very straight talk from Winston. This I am trying to arrange.

7 p.m. Saw P.M. He was in bed. He is tired, but triumphant since at the last moment his policy – his strategical policy – has triumphed. The Far East adventure is postponed, and all will be concentrated (as far as may be) on the Mediterranean and north European campaigns. If reasonable material is made available again for the former we may make some progress even during the winter.

This involves, among other things, amalgamation of the North African and the Middle Eastern Commands, so that the Mediterranean (Italy, Dalmatia, Balkans, Greece, Aegean islands and Turkey) is regarded as a single strategic problem.

P.M. explained all these ideas to me. The unification of the command is settled. An individual has not been chosen, but in any case it will be a British officer. Eisenhower is to go to England, to take the Supreme Command there. (This is a good plan; he can get all the technical help he needs more easily in England, and he has lately been rather going to seed here.) Bedell Smith may (*a*) go with Ike, which Eisenhower naturally wants, (*b*) remain here as Deputy Commander-in-Chief.

P.M. asked me what I thought of all this and about any views I might have on the organisation of the command. I asked about the political side, and he told me that Casey is to go and his place not be filled – so I suppose my area would be extended to the whole Mediterranean.

P.M. told me that he had not decided who was to succeed Eisenhower. He said that General Wilson was strongly recommended by C.I.G.S. I am afraid I strongly disagreed, and we had an hour's talk before he got up for dinner. I had intended to leave tonight for Algiers (or possibly Palermo), but P.M. made me promise to stay.

Wednesday, 8 December 1943

Message early this morning from P.M. that I am to see the C.I.G.S. and say to him everything that I had said to P.M. last night – also produce a paper with my views.

Morning at Minister of State's Office and at Embassy. There were a lot of minor (but to us important) points, and the chance of getting some of them settled in Cairo by Casey's people, and others of getting Secretary of State and Alec Cadogan (who alone can settle them in London) was not to be missed. Since (if the new arrangements come off) I shall have Greece and Yugoslavia on my plate, I am trying to find out what I can from the experts here. From what I can see the muddles and internal hatreds are worse than in North Africa.

4 p.m. After a search all day I tracked down General Brooke (C.I.G.S.) and had an hour's talk with him. He is clearly an able man, and has a lucid and flexible mind. But I still do *not* agree with him. The Navy and Air Force are pushing General Wilson, because they have never understood or liked General Alexander. But I think the public will not understand it, and I feel certain that General Wilson is too *old* and too *set* to undertake the Cromwellian reforms which are necessary if Algiers and Cairo are to be made to work. After all, Wilson has had the command in Cairo for nearly a year, and the Augean stables are still uncleaned

(Of course, I have to tread very carefully in all this, for if the Wilson appointment is made – as I believe it will be – I do not want to start on the wrong foot with him. And I am sure I *can* work with him – only, Alex is a younger man and I know him now so well, that I should prefer General Alexander. But Wilson is a good man too, and I naturally do not want him to think that I am working against this choice. But since Winston asked me, I felt I must give him my views. The argument of C.I.G.S., of course, is that A's talents, which are mainly tactical, would be wasted in the sort of proconsular job of Supreme Commander in the Mediterranean.)

6.30 p.m. Saw P.M. again. He was in bed. We talked over this for a bit, and then I had my memorandum typed in his office and got ready for him to study at leisure. I also discussed with him his proposed visit to Algiers. He seems very anxious to make a speech attacking de Gaulle! (This is Randolph's idea, who wants a 'secret session' of the Assembly.) Of course Winston plays about with these ideas – partly to tease more serious-minded ambassadors than I shall ever be – and then, in the end, does exactly the right thing in exactly the right way.

After my papers (on the Mediterranean command and the French visit) were ready, more talk till about 8.30.

9.15 p.m. Dinner at Mohammed Ali Club, with Mr and Mrs Shone (he is Minister here – second to the Ambassador, she is Mrs Victor Mallet's sister, curiously like old Lady Mallet – viz. intelligent but fatiguing).

11 p.m. Went along to the Embassy. Found a large party, including P.M., C.I.G.S., and a lot of young officers, including Julian Amery, young Jellicoe[11] and others. Winston was in great form and holding forth to a circle of these young men.

[11] George, 2nd Earl Jellicoe (b. 1918), who was the officer dropped into Rhodes in September

Thursday, 9 December 1943

12.30 a.m. Drove to airfield and found our aeroplane, all the arrangements having been admirably made by John.

Left about 2 a.m. A very comfortable trip – the 'Li-Lo' on the floor, my flying jacket, and plenty of army blankets – real luxury for once, with only three passengers instead of twenty!

Arrived Tripoli about 9 a.m. and had some breakfast. Arrived Tunis about 12.30. We went to the Consular Residence where we were entertained with the excellent food and high spirits of the Consul-General's wife, Mrs Monypenny.

2 p.m. Left for Algiers – arriving about 4.30 p.m. Here we found that the worst had happened. Anthony Eden had left Cairo the same night as we had, meaning to go direct to England (stopping just to fuel at Gibraltar), but the plane developed engine trouble, and they came down at about 11 a.m. this morning in Algiers.

I have, therefore, staying in the house, Anthony, Alec Cadogan, Ambassador Winant, Douglas Straight, Gladwyn Jebb[12] – as well as various servants and detectives. (Apparently detectives sleep *on* the billiard table, servants *under* it.) However, we got through the evening somehow.

Friday, 10 December 1943

Anthony and the Ambassador and the rest of the party got off at 1 p.m. I waited anxiously for their return (as the weather still seems very bad) but luckily they were safely airborne about 2 p.m. I have still Gladwyn Jebb (who has been taken ill).

The afternoon and evening were spent (as you can imagine) in trying to catch up with all that had happened here and reading a good deal of accumulated stuff. However, Reilly[13] (who acts as head of Chancery) and Halford (who does Italian affairs) are both excellent and they *reduce* what I must see to the minimum and *present* it in a clear form. (Halford is going to be particularly useful, as he speaks Italian and Russian as well as Arabic.)

6–7 p.m. Had a talk with Bedell Smith about the changes. He tells me that he has become 'an international incident'. Ike wants him to go to England; Winston wants him to stay here as Deputy.

Dined with General Catroux. We had expected the arrival of Ibn Saud's two sons,[14] who had been on a visit to the U.S.A. and England.

1943 in the unsuccessful attempt to persuade the Italian garrison to join the Allies, served in the Coldstream Guards and First S.A.S. Regiment, 1939–45.

[12] H. M. Gladwyn Jebb (b. 1900), later 1st Baron Gladwyn, as Counsellor in the Foreign Office attended the great conferences including those at Quebec, Cairo and Teheran.

[13] Patrick Reilly (b. 1909) served as First Secretary in Algiers, 1943–4; he was H.M. Ambassador to the Soviet Union, 1957–60, and to France, 1965–8.

[14] King Abdulaziz II Ibn Saud (*c.* 1880–1953) had unified the two kingdoms of Hijaz and Nejd to form the Kingdom of Saudi Arabia in 1932; he was reputed to have had 300 sons. The two

But they were delayed by the weather. So the formal dinner was postponed, and the party reduced to the general, Madame la Générale Catroux and Massigli. It was rather amusing. The chief relaxation was poking fun at General de Gaulle!

Saturday, 11 December 1943

I have got my doctor back from England (Colonel Richardson). He came to see me this morning and is giving me some treatment for my hands. Fortunately, the right hand is much better.

11 a.m. Mr Ed Wilson (Murphy's successor as American Ambassador to the French) to see me. A lot of new trouble has broken out about the use of the French Army, the rights of the Allied C.-in-C., a new attack on General Giraud, etc., etc. It is tiresome, but I think not tragic. Anyway, I must patch it up till Duff arrives!

11.45 a.m. Herbert (N.A.E.B.) and Gridley.[15] Herbert is going home and Gridley (temporary civil servant – in private life director of William Cory) is taking over. This reminds me that Lord Leathers (chairman of Cory's) arrived also yesterday, among the other travellers from Cairo. I find him very interesting and agreeable.

12.15 p.m. A little Yugoslav, called Altmayer – a friend of the two Amerys (father[16] and son). I did not like him at all.

12.30 p.m. Alec Royce (American head of N.A.E.B.). He is going back for a short trip to Washington, to try to straighten out some difficulties. I hope he will come back. He has been straightforward and easy to work with.

Lunch (about 2.30–3.45) given by me for the Arab princes. We only heard of their pending arrival about noon so the servants did well to produce lunch for fourteen persons at short notice. We had Prince Faisal (the eldest) and Prince Khalid – two of the thirty-four sons of King Ibn Saud. Also, their Minister in London and one or two other notables. I secured M. Meyrier (of the Moroccan Government) and M. de Vitasse (*Chef de protocol*) and some others. It was a dreary meal, for me at any rate. Precedence made it necessary for me to have the two Princes – of whom one spoke no known language, the other a few words of broken English. Nothing but lemonade to drink and no smoking!

What made it worse, was the prospect of doing it all over again at night – *chez* Catroux.

4 p.m. Vyshinsky called. He had enjoyed the trip to Italy (which had unfortunately been interrupted by the hurried journey to Cairo), and would like another trip arranged. He had no answer from Moscow to

visiting us were Prince Faisal (1905–75), King from 1964 until his assassination, and Prince Khalid (1913–82), who succeeded him.

[15] J. C. Gridley (1904–68) was joint chairman of the North African Joint Economic Mission, 1943–4.

[16] L. S. Amery (1873–1955) was Secretary of State for India and for Burma, 1940–5.

the telegrams he had sent, but expected answers soon. We arranged another meeting of the Council for Monday or Tuesday. He had nothing much to say, but was very jolly as usual.

5 p.m. Long talk with Chief of Staff about the latest French military troubles. (Duff must come soon, or I may not be able to patch it up after all!) Back to the office, on various things till 8 p.m.

8.30 p.m. Desmond Morton has turned up and will stay some days. Gladwyn Jebb is better. Roger and I left our guests and went to dine at Catroux. The same Princes, the same French officials, the same barley water and the same lack of cigarettes and cigars. We got away by 10.15 and then we motored out to Herbert's villa at Cheragas (about eight or ten miles) where he was throwing a farewell party to all the boys and girls of N.A.E.B. (English side only, as it is a tiny house really). It was a very successful party (rather like those in the station ward) and Miss Campbell enjoyed herself no end. (Miss Williams – *la femme fatale* as we called her in the end – has now left, having broken many military hearts, married and single.) We left about 12.30 a.m. (after Musical Chairs, Oranges and Lemons) and got home about 1 a.m. I was interested in your last letter about the snobbishness and class disdain of the English. I think that somehow when they get abroad, this is broken down by the bond of contempt for and antipathy to foreigners.

Sunday, 12 December 1943

I have been lazy and stayed in bed – actually finishing my letter to you. I have *not* been to church, but perhaps shall get to evensong. The *external* cure for my hands is very messy; the internal is just orange juice, etc. I think it is just that when one gets to be fifty, one uses up vitamins more rapidly than one makes them.

John has just telephoned from the office that C.-in-C. Med., Admiral Sir John Cunningham ('dismal Jimmy', as the P.M. calls him), is coming at noon. So I will stop now, and doze for another half hour before he comes.

I hope you have safely received by now my letters. I have read all your recent letters through again with great pleasure. You give a most vivid account of rural and political life in England. And I do so like getting the family news.

By the time you get this, Christmas will be far behind. I hope it was not too hectic for you. It is very sad to be away from home at Christmas. I cannot help recalling all those very great gatherings at Chatsworth, and your father's pleasure with the little children, even after his illness had made him difficult with their elders.

I broke off the diary in a hurry. Although the morning was peaceful (I stayed in bed till noon), things began to happen after luncheon. A long meeting with Sir John Cunningham and others about the arrangements for the proposed visit of the P.M. to Algiers and his return home.

As you can imagine, the movements of these great personages are a source of immense anxieties to the military, naval and air commanders. I do not believe they always realise the extent to which they dislocate operations and especially naval operations. These battleships have to be protected with a considerable force of destroyers, and of course air cover has to be available.

The rest of the day was spent in the usual way. I managed to snatch an hour off to go to evensong. I am now getting more and more immersed in Italian stuff and I feel quite helpless to deal with it at this distance, with poor communications and with (at present) no method of getting private information from Harold Caccia in Brindisi, since there is no means of telegraphing except through Army channels, and this is, of course, seen by many eyes. If only Duff would come out and I could hand over my French side, it would be easier. But Duff cannot come because we cannot get a villa for him. I have told him to send out his secretary and let him try. But the military will not give up their residences, and, until A.F.H.Q. moves out of Algiers, I must keep mine. So there is a regular impasse.

Monday, 13 December 1943

After breakfast a call from Tunis. The P.M. is laid up with a bad chill. Will I arrange with A.F.H.Q. to have a portable X-ray apparatus sent up at once, in order to ascertain the state of the lung. They fear pneumonia? Would I and Desmond Morton come up ourselves as soon as possible?

After a terrific morning of telegraphing and telephoning and finding out whether the frightful weather will allow flying, we discover there is a perfectly good apparatus at a hospital in Tunis.

The P.M. is in a house called The White House at La Marsa (near Tunis). This was formerly occupied by General George Clark (I used to go there in the summer) and is now General Eisenhower's. It is nice in summer, with large rooms and terraces. It is right on the sea. But it will be cold now and rather bleak.

At 2.30 Morton and I left by air. The weather was very bad, pouring rain and cloud everywhere. By taking the sea route we managed to get through. We arrived about 5.30 p.m.

We drove to the Consular Residence and arranged to stay there in what I call my wing. It is furnished with ugly, requisitioned furniture and is damp and cold. But it serves.

We then motored to The White House. We found there Sarah Churchill (Mrs Oliver), Lord Moran, John Martin and Francis Brown (secretaries), Tommy Thompson[17] (naval, A.D.C.) etc. They seemed very fussed about the P.M.'s condition.

[17] Commander C. R. Thompson (1894–1966) was Personal Assistant to the Minister of Defence (Churchill), 1940–5.

He insisted on seeing me, but seemed weak and drowsy. I escaped as soon as I could, as I felt sure he was seeing too many people.

Tuesday, 14 December 1943

P.M. is definitely worse, and has got pneumonia, and they fear pleurisy. General Wilson arrived. He is definitely to get the Mediterranean command (*not* Alex, which I deplore).

The P.M. asked me to discuss with the general the organisation of the command and write him a report.

In spite of his temperature (101°) he dealt with this in the evening and wrote a long telegram to the Cabinet about it.

A rather dreary day of waiting. Moran seems very worried. He is telegraphing all over the place for specialists. He has started to administer M. & B.[18]

Wednesday, 15 December 1943

P.M. is worse. His pulse is very irregular. Brigadier Bedford[19] (a heart specialist) has at last arrived from Cairo. He seems sensible and gives us comfort. He is giving digitalis to try to calm the heart.

Later in the afternoon Randolph arrived. His presence will do no good, as he will talk to his father about French politics!

At last a Colonel Buttle[20] – the great M. & B. specialist – arrived from Italy. He is an expert on how to give the stuff. He seems clever, determined, rather gauche and rude – just the chap we need. I had a long talk with him and begged him to be firm and *forbid* telegrams or visitors.

At 6 p.m. the P.M. had a heart attack – what is called 'fibrillation'. It was not very severe, but has alarmed them all. More digitalis is being given.

General Wilson has left. I have had good talks with him, and I hope I shall get on with him. But he is old (sixty-four), and although shrewd and intelligent, has not the broad and generous sympathies which make General Alexander such a good man to deal with.

Lord Moran tells me that he thought the P.M. was going to die last night. He thinks him a little better as regards the pneumonia, but is worried about his heart.

Thursday, 16 December 1943

P.M. much better today. His pulse is steadier, and the lung is clearing a little. The experts seem to think he is through the crisis. Desmond Morton and I decided to leave, as there is nothing much we

[18] Sulphonamide tablets manufactured by May & Baker.

[19] Brigadier D. E. Bedford (1898–1978), Brigadier Consultant Physician, was later President of the British Cardiac Society.

[20] Lieutenant-Colonel G. A. H. Buttle (b. 1899), now Emeritus Professor at St Bartholomew's Hospital Medical School, was adviser in blood transfusion, R.A.M.C., 1940–5.

can do here, and the work (judging from telegrams and telephone calls) is piling up in Algiers.

I saw P.M. before going. He was cheerful, though rather weak.

We left at 2 p.m. and arrived Algiers just before 5 p.m.

Tonight we had a farewell dinner for Brigadier Rabino (my financial adviser) and Mr Herbert (my economic adviser and British head of N.A.E.B.). They are both going home to England. It is rather a bore, as they are both first-class men, and we have still not completed the lease–lend agreement or the financial agreement. These have been under negotiation for many months and I should much like to finish them before leaving. They both have adequate successors, but of course they are new men, and I hate parting with those I know.

We had a party of sixteen – British and American. Murphy came. I proposed the health of our guests. Lots of speeches, including an excellent one by Murphy. Really this Anglo-American show *has* worked, especially in the civilian and economic sphere. It was quite an inspiring evening. The speakers were very kind about me – but of course I was the host!

Friday, 17 December 1943

A usual morning at the office. Saw Herbert, Rabino, M. Rozen (French financial expert). At 4.30 I called on de Gaulle, to tell him about the P.M. He was frigidly correct. He knows that P.M. dislikes him and cannot forget this.

At 5.15 I had a meeting at the villa of a number of military and other departments to discuss the problems arising out of the combination of the North African and Eastern Mediterranean command. An interesting discussion and quite a useful piece of work accomplished. But I see immense difficulties ahead.

We had a large luncheon party today of British and American journalists. It went off quite well.

Saturday, 18 December 1943

The news about the P.M. seems good. I judge that he is recovering, because telegrams are beginning to arrive – some rather disturbing!!

9.30 a.m. Called on M. Mendès-France – Commissioner for Finance. He was as amiable and pro-English as ever. I like the man. At any rate he has been an observer in a bombing aeroplane in the last three years, and that is more than can be said of most Chancellors of the Exchequer.[21] He seems sincerely anxious to complete the financial agreement. It is now only held up by the problem of the Levant States. These want to join the *sterling* area. Naturally the French want them to stay in the *franc* bloc.

11 a.m. Called on General Whiteley. The problem of the French

[21] Inserted from another record.

divisions and the Eisenhower letter to Giraud was discussed.[22] It is all a very stupid business – really Giraud's fault. I think we can straighten it out, but it is going to be a job, because de Gaulle will be difficult and some of the military are anxious to pick a quarrel with him.

11.30 a.m. Admiral Cunningham. The problem of the P.M.'s return. Also, some French trawlers, especially the decision to retire Admirals Godfroy (of Force X – Alexandria) and Michelier. I cannot help agreeing with the French Admiralty decision. They have not been severely punished considering their past actions. Admiral Godfroy is old. Admiral Michelier has also reached retiring age.

12 noon. Called on Vyshinsky, to discuss plans for the next meeting of the Italian Council and its next visit to Italy. (I think we shall reach a compromise on the Russian claim to participate in the *Commission* as opposed to the Council. I am recommending that they and the French have one high-ranking liaison officer with General Joyce – the Deputy President.)

1.15 p.m. A large and rather dull luncheon party. John has raked in all the odds and ends – all the letters of introduction and so on.

3 p.m. Went to a very dull show. The University of Algiers conferring an honorary degree on Professor [H. A. R.] Gibb, Professor of Arabic at Oxford. Interminable speeches, including one by M. René Capitant (Commissioner for Education) of three-quarters of an hour on educational reform after the war in Metropolitan France. De Gaulle made a short and effective speech.

5 p.m. Went to Admiralty Buildings to see M. Jacquinot (Commissioner for Marine), a very sensible man and a useful visit.

Record of conversation with M. Jacquinot 19 December 1943

I went to see M. Jacquinot at Navy House at 5.30 this afternoon. I was received with naval honours, including some trumpeting. M. Jacquinot seemed very pleased at my coming to see his establishment and introduced me to a number of the naval officers. I had an hour's talk with him; the Chief of Staff, Admiral Lemonnier, was present.

1. He spoke to me quite frankly about the problem of *épuration*. He wanted to assure me that he saw things from a moderate point of view. Although he was naturally subject to considerable political pressure, he only cared about the efficiency of the Navy and he recognised that he had in this a delicate path to tread.

2. For instance, he had not yet given any definite instructions for the removal of the portrait of Marshal Pétain from the French ships in spite of strong pressure to do so. He was trusting to the growth of a new spirit in the French Navy and that sufficient officers from the mixed

[22] At issue was the relative degree of control exercised over the French divisions by A.F.H.Q. on the one hand and the F.C.N.L. on the other.

navies in the recommissioned ships would make their weight felt. He showed me with some amusement a list showing the portrait position. They are being taken down one by one, but he has not used any disciplinary action. At the same time he had to make some examples, and he was so much pressed from the Committee and other political quarters that the decisions regarding Godfroy and Michelier were necessary. He knows that Godfroy has no political ambitions and will never make trouble. Michelier might be more difficult. If Godfroy cared to go and live quietly in England with his English relations and was acceptable to us, he felt sure that no difficulty would be made here. Having thus struck the two chiefs in this very mild way (they have merely been retired with minor control over their movements), he hopes that he will not have to take any further steps.

[Diary continues] 6.30 p.m. Dr Richardson to see me – my good doctor – about my hands. I think they are rather better.

7.30 p.m. Massigli called at the villa. He is anxious about the way things are going. The forces against de Gaulle (more extreme) are joining, and the known hostility to him of the President and the P.M. does not make things easier.

Sunday, 19 December 1943

9–12.30 p.m. Dictated from bed to Miss Campbell. I am trying to prepare another of my periodical reports. The last ended with 'recognition' of the Committee in August. I want this to be my swan-song!

A luncheon party – mostly young British and American officers. Lord Dalrymple[23] (Scots Guards), Mr Searight (a friend of your sister Rachel), Mr Gill (Engineer on N.A.E.B.), etc., etc.

3–5 p.m. Went for a drive to Blida and into the mountains with Roger and Desmond Morton. We had a bit of a walk in the mountains. It was a lovely sunny day, and the air did me good.

6 p.m. Evensong.

7–8.30 p.m. Telegrams, etc., at the office. Dined with Murphy.

Monday, 20 December 1943

A fairly easy morning at the office. Said goodbye to Murphy, who has gone for a month's leave to America. He certainly deserves it.

At 11.45 we motored out to Tipasa (Desmond Morton, Roger and I). We had a nice walk among the ruins of the Roman city and a good luncheon at the inn. It was a lovely day – hot sun, like spring. Some shrubs and wildflowers are beginning to bloom.

4.30 p.m. Meeting on *Italian* affairs. General Holmes, Colonel

[23] Lieutenant-Colonel Viscount Dalrymple (b. 1906), later 13th Earl of Stair, commanded 1st Scots Guards, 1942–3.

Maxwell, Roger, [G. Frederick] Reinhardt (Murphy's deputy), Halford and I. We are getting into a terrible mess. We cannot move the Commission from Brindisi because we cannot find quarters for it *and* the Italian Government in the Naples area. We are still trying, but the only possible places are (curiously) Vatican property and we are *not* allowed to requisition them. We have to get the Archbishop to ask the Pope. As you can imagine, the machinery for this is incredibly complicated, and gives wonderful opportunity for every kind of stalling and delay.

The food position is getting very alarming. And the political position is degenerating. Naples is restless. How I wish the Army could make progress and get to Rome. But I fear the weather is vile and there will be delay. It is really a frightful country in which to fight.

A quiet evening. Duff Cooper's 'stooge', Major Fane,[24] has arrived and is staying with us. He and John go out 'house-hunting', but with little success.

Tuesday, 21 December 1943

We are just about to enter upon another first-class row. Duff Cooper ought to be carrying the baby instead of me, but nobody can yet produce a house. I do not think the French are trying, and the soldiers and sailors stick to theirs like limpets.

The P.M. is recovering – rather too rapidly! Stimulated by Randolph, and having nothing else in particular to do, he is getting himself into a state of irritation with the French, which is bad for his health, and looks like leading to much trouble.

The French Committee have been terribly pressed from various angles, on the question of *épuration* or the 'purge'. The Gaullists are determined to prosecute people like Boisson, ex-Governor-General of French West Africa and Admiral Derrien (second in command to Admiral Esteva, who fought us in Bizerta from November 1942 to the summer of 1943).[25] The Resistance movement people are equally determined to attack ex-Vichy Ministers, like Pucheu, Peyrouton and Flandin.[26] The former is admittedly a black criminal. Peyrouton (who was Governor-General of Algeria – brought by the State Department) is just a moderate kind of rascal, and I do not think ever was a very serious traitor. Flandin (who is a great friend of Randolph) is a crook, but I think too clever to be hanged.

Yielding to this pressure, the Committee has decided to try these

[24] Major Freddie Fane, former secretary of the Travellers' Club in Paris, was Duff Cooper's Comptroller of Household.

[25] Admiral Louis Derrien (d. 1946) had been the Naval Prefect in Bizerta. Admiral Jean-Pierre Esteva (1880–1951) was Resident-General in Tunisia, 1940–3.

[26] Pierre Pucheu (1899–1944) was Vichy Minister of the Interior, 1941–2. Pierre-Etienne Flandin (1899–1958) was Prime Minister of France, 1934–5, and Vichy Minister of Foreign Affairs, 1940–1.

people for treason. (Châtel[27] – who was Governor-General, Algeria, when I came here, and General Noguès, who was Resident-General in Morocco, have prudently escaped to Portugal or Spain.) The two admirals Godfroy (of Alexandria) and Michelier (who opposed us in Casablanca but subsequently came round) have been dealt with by the simple process of placing them on the retired list; no further action has been taken against them except to prevent them from 'residing in dockyard towns' (i.e. Bizerta or Casablanca) – not a very serious inhibition. We are therefore left with:

Pucheu,
Derrien,
Boisson,
Peyrouton,
Flandin,

and one or two minor people, e.g. Tixier-Vignancour (Minister for Information in the Vichy Government) and one Albert, a Deputy.[28]

All these people are in the territory and have now been arrested and are awaiting trial.

As a matter of fact, with perhaps the exception of Pucheu – a proved traitor, who was the direct cause of the deaths of literally hundreds and perhaps thousands of Frenchmen by handing them over to the Germans in Paris – and (it may be) Admiral Derrien, I do not think that there is any intention of pushing things to an extreme. But, of course, if we interfere, we shall probably produce a more violent reaction.

However, after a morning in which nothing very unusual took place, a telephone call from the P.M. at luncheon threw everything into confusion. (I was having a party in honour of Professor Gibb, the Arabic scholar.) Randolph had of course been feeding his father with a lot of reports, partly founded on some small foundation of fact, mostly invented. The P.M. was in a most excited mood, roaring like an excited bull down the telephone – which incidentally is listened to by many British and American telephone operators at different stages of the line as well as all the professional French 'listeners-in'. He has certainly made a remarkable recovery.

At 4.30 Wilson (American Ambassador) and I went to see Massigli at his office. He handed us the French draft for a regular agreement between the French Committee and the Allies regarding the use and control of the French forces which we and the Americans have re-equipped. It was quite a good draft and I see no reason why we should not get a settlement without much trouble.

[27] Yves Châtel (1885–1945) was Peyrouton's predecessor as Governor-General of Algeria, 1941–3.

[28] Jean-Louis Tixier-Vignancour (b. 1907) was Minister for Information for only a few weeks, 1940–1. D. F. A. Albert (b. 1911) voted for the delegation of power to Pétain in July 1940, then retired from active politics.

I took the occasion to talk to Massigli about the arrests. I told him how serious a view we should take of any 'persecution'. He was obviously worried, but said that he was afraid it was too late to stop the action taken. He personally had been against the arrest of Flandin but had been overborne.

I see great trouble ahead. However, of the two current crises:

(*i*) use of French troops – row between Giraud and de Gaulle, involving Eisenhower;

(*ii*) arrest of Peyrouton, Flandin, Boisson, involving President, who is a friend of P. and B., and P.M., who is a friend of F.;

(*i*) is going on well; the fever is abating and the patient should be up and about in a day or two;

(*ii*) temperature still rising; crisis not expected for a day or two; fever increasing.

Rather a pleasant dinner. M. and Mme Offroy (he is the Edward Bridges of the French Cabinet),[29] M. and Mme Gaudin (Treasury official – very good friend of ours), Desmond Morton, and several others, including Reinhardt (Murphy's assistant).

Wednesday, 22 December 1943

A very full morning. The P.M. is beginning to ring up and telegraph from Tunis almost hourly. Randolph is stimulating him and I am sure it is bad for him.

He was in such a passion on the telephone today that I thought he was going to have an apoplectic fit.

At 11 a.m. I saw General Whiteley (Deputy Chief of Staff). We discussed the draft of a counter-proposal which we might render to General de Gaulle's formula about the use of French troops under allied command.

Colonel Terence Maxwell to lunch. Discussion of the future arrangements for Italy in view of the amalgamation of the Mediterranean command.

4 p.m. Saw Ed Wilson and told him the latest news of the P.M. We arranged to see Massigli jointly this evening.

6 p.m. Interview with Massigli.[30]

At 8 p.m. we had rather an interesting dinner. Generals Neame and O'Connor and Air Vice-Marshal Boyd,[31] lately escaped from Italy,

[29] Raymond Offroy (b. 1909) was Under-Secretary of the F.C.N.L., 1943, and of the French Provisional Government, 1944. Sir Edward Bridges (1892–1969) was Secretary to the Cabinet, 1938–46.

[30] Massigli said that as most of the potential witnesses were still in France there would probably not be enough evidence to bring Flandin and the others to trial. I urged that they should be given a proper trial only after France was liberated. In the meantime they could be held and evidence collected.

[31] Lieutenant-General Philip Neame (1888–1978), had been G.O.C.-in-C. and Military Governor, Cyrenaica, and Lieutenant-General Sir Richard O'Connor (1889–1981) had been

came to dinner (together with General Jock Whiteley and [General] Dick Lewis) on their way back. They had the most interesting adventures, having made seven attempts to get away from the place where they were before the eighth effort was successful. They spoke in the highest terms of the assistance which they had received (often at considerable risk) from the Italians, both in towns and country districts. I naturally did not like to press them too much about their experiences and impressions, but it was really a very interesting occasion, which we tried to make as festive as possible.

They have been between two and three years as prisoners of war; and of course this leaves its mark. O'Connor was supposed to have been one of our best generals, especially as regards tank warfare. It will be interesting to see whether they will be able to command troops in the field again, or whether they will only be fit for administrative posts.

The air marshal really had a grievance. His pilot landed him in Sicily two or three years ago by mistake for Malta, having got confused with these Mediterranean islands. (I feel sorry for the pilot officer during the next three years.)

Thursday, 23 December 1943

The most extraordinary telegram has arrived from the President to Eisenhower. It says:

> Please inform the French Committee as follows: 'In view of the assistance given to the Allied Armies during the campaign in Africa by Boisson, Peyrouton and Flandin, you are directed to take no action against these individuals at the present time.'

This telegram (to Eisenhower, *not* to the American Ambassador) has fairly put the cat among the pigeons. Wilson is furious; Eisenhower is in Italy; I am certainly rather concerned.

At 10.30 a.m. conference with Ed Wilson. He will *telephone* to the State Department this afternoon to say:

(*a*) that he cannot accept the position of Eisenhower receiving orders without his (Wilson) being informed;

(*b*) that he protests against this method of handling the affair, which is obviously intended to cause a final breach.

After a tiresome morning (in which I had to see the Greek Minister about Greece's place on the Allied Advisory Committee for Italy), I got hold of Massigli at 1 p.m. and told him that we had a very difficult situation to handle. Wilson was with me.

At 4.15 Wilson and I saw Bedell Smith just back from Italy. He took

G.O.C.-in-C. British troops in Egypt, when they were captured in April 1941 by an Afrika Korps unit behind British lines. Air Vice-Marshal Owen Tudor Boyd (1889–1944) had been A.O.C. in the Middle East at the time of his capture in November 1940. O'Connor did hold active command after his escape.

a very gloomy view of the position but agreed to defer action until the 26th or 27th. I had had another telephone conversation with the P.M. who seemed rather alarmed at the avalanche which he had started. I do not think he expected the President to react quite so violently or quite so rapidly.

The President hates de Gaulle and the French Committee. He would seize on any excuse to overthrow them and restore Giraud.

The P.M.'s sentiments are more complex. He feels about de Gaulle like a man who has quarrelled with his son. He will cut him off with a shilling. But (in his heart) he would kill the fatted calf if only the prodigal would confess his faults and take his orders obediently in future.

This crisis is now in full swing. Telegrams (and, alas! telephone calls) are coming in at all hours of day and night (P.M. even rang up Chief of Staff when I was in his room this afternoon and said, 'Keep Harold up to the mark. He is much too pro-French. He will not carry out my policy or my wishes. I rely on *you*!')

This makes life interesting but exhausting. It is really getting beyond a joke, and much as I love Winston, I cannot stand much more. I telegraphed to Anthony to tell him what is happening, but so far without effect. Meanwhile Duff keeps discreetly away until a suitable villa can be found for him and Diana. If he is not careful, he will never come, as we shall have broken off relations with the French and there will be no Ambassador, only a Resident Minister! That will be rather a sell for him, especially after resigning the Duchy.

Friday, 24 December 1943

No more news of the French crisis, except a call from Tunis in the morning. My telegrams (except personal ones to Anthony) are repeated to the P.M. He reacts strangely but today a little more reasonably! He is certainly getting better, though!!

11 a.m.–1 p.m. Meeting of the Italian Council. It was my turn to take the chair. Murphy being away, his second man, Reinhardt, took his place. Fortunately, he is an intelligent and well-trained official from the State Department. (Incidentally, Murphy's successor, Ed Wilson, is proving very good and very co-operative. He is much more orderly in mind than Murphy and with a better brain. I like him very much. He, of course, deals *only* with French affairs and will be Duff's colleague.)

We had a review of the political and economic position in Italy. Both are bad. When I can throw off France, I must really devote myself to Italy.

We also had some rather troublesome problems on which we were all agreed, except the American representative who had no instructions. The two points were:

(*a*) Russian and French symbolic membership – one liaison officer each – on the Control Commission, as opposed to the Council. I very much fear that the President will agree to the Russian, but in his present mood, refuse the French.

(*b*) The admission of the Yugoslav and Greek members to the Council. Here again we are all agreed, but nothing has come from Washington. The difficulty about the present state of these two *Governments* should not (I think) stand in the way of the representation of the *countries*.

4.15 p.m. General de Lattre came to see me. He made a good impression.[32]

5 p.m. Vincent Auriol.[33]

6 p.m. Ferrière.[34]

Record of conversation with M. Ferrière
24 December 1943

1. I should judge M. Ferrière before the war to have been either a journalist or a commercial traveller of the higher grade. As a man I was not very attracted by him – he has a large, white, fat face, and is rather too well dressed for these days. He clearly had a very high opinion of himself and seemed to live in an atmosphere of continual surprise that this opinion was not universally shared. Nevertheless, he is clearly a man of intelligence and courage.

2. His chief point with regard to the *épuration* problem seemed to be this. In his view what the Government should have done was to have arrested twenty, thirty, or perhaps even forty of the leading persons charged with Vichyism, etc., and with the maximum of publicity. They should have done it in the Russian way, good and strong. They should at the same time have announced that that was the end of *épuration* – no petty persecution of grocers in Constantine and minor officials in Philippeville. One swoop, and that should be all. To the French they could say that these men were being kept in prison. In fact they should be put in agreeable and comfortable surroundings in a town in the southern part of Algeria or Morocco.

3. M. Ferrière went on to express his views about General de Gaulle. He shared the common opinion that he was absolutely essential to the French people and that only under his leadership could that degree of unity be maintained which was essential both at this stage of the war and for the first period after the peace. He was under no illusions about

[32] General (posthumously Marshal of France) Jean de Lattre de Tassigny (1889–1952), who had been imprisoned by the Vichy régime, told me at this meeting that he believed both de Gaulle and Giraud to be essential at this stage of France's history.

[33] Vincent Auriol (1884–1966) was Minister of Finance, 1936–7, and of Justice, 1937, and became President of the French Republic, 1947–54. He had himself been arrested by Peyrouton, and he told me that unless the trials went ahead there was a danger of civil war in France.

[34] René Cerf, who took the name Ferrière when working for the Resistance movement *Combat*, was head of the representatives of the Resistance groups in the Assembly.

his difficult temperament and *orgueil*. At the same time he observed that the bad relations between the Prime Minister and General de Gaulle were becoming known in France. They were much deplored because the Prime Minister was the national hero of France. Nevertheless people were beginning to say that Mr Churchill was much too big a man ever to quarrel with General de Gaulle merely because of the latter's bad manners. Perhaps, therefore, *perfide Albion* had been creeping in again. Perhaps the British had been trying to take advantage of France's weakness to detach portions of her Empire, and in that case if General de Gaulle was quarrelling with the British and the Americans, perhaps he was not such a tiresome fellow after all. Perhaps he was a good French patriot. This is the kind of propaganda that some French make and the Germans of course encourage. M. Ferrière thought that what was needed now was to turn over a new page and to try to reconstitute those relations of confidence and good faith between Allies that ought to exist. Could I take the lead? Would the Prime Minister be generous and big enough, in spite of all the annoying difficulties to which he had been subjected by General de Gaulle, to make a gesture of reconciliation?

[Diary continues] 7 p.m. Mr Gridley – Herbert's successor. There are still further points about the lease–lend agreement (all the fault of London) and about the financial agreement. The latter is held up because of the uncertainty of the settlement which M. Catroux will be able to make with the Levant States. Otherwise it is agreed.

I shall be very disappointed if I cannot sign these agreements before I hand over to Duff, as we have worked hard and long on them.

At 8 p.m. we had a party for all our British civilian staff – my office and N.A.E.B. We managed it very well. A stand-up dinner (very good) and dancing.

At 9.30 p.m. I slipped away to see General Georges [who was in tremendous form and in full-dress uniform waiting to go to Midnight Mass][35] but soon got back to join the festivities, which lasted till quite late. I went to bed at midnight. My waltzing was, I believe, much admired.

Saturday, 25 December 1943 (Christmas Day)

8 a.m. Church – crowded, of course, with troops.

9.30 a.m. Left villa and drove to aerodrome.

10.15 a.m. Took off (after a search for the plane) in a nice little plane – Cessna – one pilot, two other seats.

1.30 p.m. Reached El Aouina aerodrome at Tunis, after a good but rather slow flight. We did not make more than 120 miles an hour. Drove to the P.M.'s villa, and found them all just having sat down to a

[35] Inserted from another record.

magnificent Christmas dinner – with soup, turkey, plum pudding – and champagne!

The old boy presided at the festive gathering (having just had a two-hour military conference in his bedroom) clothed in a padded silk Chinese dressing-gown decorated with blue and gold dragons – a most extraordinary sight. The guests included Mrs Churchill, Randolph and Sarah of his family; John Martin, Francis Brown, John Colville,[36] Tommy Thompson of his staff; Lord Moran, Dr Bedform and another doctor; Generals Wilson (new C.-in-C.), Alexander, Gale, Jock Whiteley, Hollis and Davy;[37] Admiral Sir John Cunningham; Air Chief Marshal Sir Arthur and Lady Tedder; Desmond Morton (who came with me from Algiers) and various others. (Eisenhower and Bedell Smith attended the conference but flew back to Algiers before luncheon.) It was indeed an odd way of spending Christmas. In the best Russian style (and looking in his strange costume rather like a figure in a Russian ballet) the P.M. proposed a series of toasts with a short speech in each case. (In spite of looking rather grumpily at me, he proposed mine in most eulogistic terms.)

After luncheon (which ended nearer to 4 p.m. than 3 p.m.) I managed to escape with Alex for a short walk (and delightful talk).

At about 5.30, just before the P.M. went to sleep, he sent for me. He was obviously *very* tired, as he had worked all the time since luncheon, dictating a résumé of the military decisions taken in the morning and on a telegram embodying them to his colleagues and the President.

He only kept me for a few minutes. He was very sleepy, and I left him, thereby earning a good word from poor Mrs Churchill, who does her best to make him spare himself.

I discovered from conversation with some of the staff and from Lord Moran that, as I thought, Randolph was the cause of all the trouble. They were much alarmed at the P.M.'s excitement and when he telephoned to me he was really beside himself and had a slight heart trouble afterwards. It is really too bad of the boy to worry his father. But Winston is pathetically devoted to him (as he is to all his family) and will not rebuke him as he should. Perhaps all fathers are the same!

At 8 p.m. or thereabouts there was a buffet dinner. All the officers of the battalion of Coldstream Guards who are providing the guard were invited as well as various other personalities. The P.M. (who also saw General Mast and Mme Mast before dinner) appeared after he had had his own dinner in bed. He was in capital form.

At about 11 p.m. he retired to his bedroom again and sent for me. He

[36] John Colville (b. 1915) was Assistant Private Secretary to Prime Ministers Chamberlain, 1939–40, Churchill, 1940–1 and 1943–5, and Attlee, 1945, and Joint Principal Private Secretary to Churchill, 1951–5.

[37] General Leslie Hollis (1897–1963), was Senior Assistant Secretary in the office of the War Cabinet, 1939–46. Major-General George Davy (b. 1898) was Director of Military Operations, G.H.Q. Middle East, 1942–4, Deputy Assistant Chief of Staff (Ops), A.F.H.Q., 1944, and commanded Land Forces, Adriatic, 1944–5.

was obviously rather embarrassed and really almost pathetically so. He actually asked for my views and gave me ten minutes free run to explain the present French situation as I saw it. Then he said, 'Well – perhaps you are right. But I do not agree with you. Perhaps I will see de Gaulle. Anyway you have done very well.'

Then he took my hand in his in a most fatherly way and said, 'Come and see me again before I leave Africa, and we'll talk it over.'

He is really a remarkable man. Although he can be so tiresome and pig-headed, there is no one like him. His devotion to work and duty is quite extraordinary. He was pleased with the military conference (of which he told me the decisions [including the approximate date for the invasion of Normandy]) and I think this put all the other worries out of his head. I have no doubt (and this the doctors confirm) that the secondary results of M. & B. are rather obscure. I am told he was very difficult and even passionate during his recovery last time.

Sunday, 26 December 1943

Left Tunis at 8.30 (alone, since Desmond Morton stayed with the P.M.) in the same aeroplane. Arrived Algiers at 11.30 and came up to the villa for a bath, etc.

Lunched with Ed Wilson. A telegram has come from the President, who has backed down completely. No ultimatum. It is left to the diplomats to try to deal with the problem of the political trials. A great triumph!

M. Tixier and M. de Menthon – both Commissioners – (the latter for Justice and the cause of all the trouble!) to luncheon, with various other French and Americans. De Menthon is a professor of law – very sincere, very legalistic, very drama-minded, very fanatical – and correspondingly dangerous. He is one of the Resistance people, not long out of France.

At 3 p.m. I went up with Wilson to see Bedell Smith. He was much relieved at the turn of affairs. Jock Whiteley joined us, and we rehearsed the drill for tomorrow's meeting with de Gaulle about the use of French troops.

I afterwards saw Eisenhower – he was quite charming. He wants me to go to England with him.

6–8 p.m. Conference with General Wilson, General Bedell Smith and General Gale on questions of organisation for the new Mediterranean command. I see immense problems ahead; but I like General Wilson, who seems wise and understanding. (They call him Jumbo. I hope he is wise. He is certainly ponderous.)

8.15 p.m. An enormous dinner party at the villa. M. and Mme Bogomolov, M. Vyshinsky, M. Massigli, Mr Ed Wilson, Comtesse de Montgomerie, General Julius Holmes, M. Jacquinot (Commissioner for the Navy), C. D. Jackson (O.W.I. or Political Warfare), a very amusing and excellent American, just returned from London, Major

Fane (Duff's secretary), Aubrey Halford (of my staff), Roger Makins – fourteen or sixteen in all (I forget which). M. Bogomolov had given me a present of vodka and caviare, which helped to start the party off. We had toasts *à la Russe*; the guests stayed till after midnight, and the party was generally regarded as a success.

Monday, 27 December 1943

Stayed in bed till 11 a.m. reading telegrams and dictating to my dear Miss Campbell.

11.30 a.m.–1 p.m. Meeting at de Gaulle's office. Present: (for the French) de Gaulle, Giraud, Massigli; (for the Allies) General Bedell Smith, Ed Wilson and H.M. A very successful meeting indeed. General Smith did awfully well and took de Gaulle completely into his confidence. This clearly pleased our Joan of Arc enormously, and I think we shall get an agreement. (At present we have only the rather shadowy arrangement made at Anfa between the President and General Giraud. We want a proper agreement, made by the French Committee, to place their re-equipped forces under the orders of the Combined Chiefs of Staff. They naturally want to make some conditions, which I think we can accept. No doubt London and Washington will raise objections, but if we can get what we think reasonable we shall sign up without asking them.)

After luncheon, I was very tired and went to bed. I read your letter (of 15 December) which was *most* welcome. It *is* so nice to get all the news. I have telegraphed about Gosses.[38] Of course, the children must have it, if they would like it. It will be lovely for us and I am so glad they should even think it possible to reside near us!

I had a lovely afternoon and evening in bed, with only a little work (Roger Makins and C. D. Jackson came at six and talked an hour about the reorganisation of propaganda or political warfare under this new command). I read a very good Trollope called *The Belton Estate* (new to me) and finished another one (also new) called *Cousin Henry* – which I had bought and read cursorily in Cairo.

Tuesday, 28 December 1943

Stayed in bed till 12 noon. I am better but still tired, and rather homesick. Lots of papers and letters have arrived. A letter from Sarah and one from Moucher [Duchess of Devonshire]. So I had a lovely idle morning (with Miss Campbell for an hour only).

At 12 noon I had to see poor Mme Flandin. I did my best to comfort her. I feel sure that he will not be shot (whether or not he ought to be is another question), and I think (now that we can handle the matter in a reasonable way), we shall be able to reach some arrangement which will not be too bad.

[38] A farm near Birch Grove.

Lunched with Massigli alone. We had an excellent and useful talk. He recognises that the present atmosphere of suspicion between de Gaulle and the President and the P.M. *must* be rectified. I told him that if we could get the military question settled and the problem of the political trials out of the way, I would see the P.M. and try to make a new start. Massigli confirmed my impression of de Gaulle's pleasure at the tone of yesterday's meeting.

3.30 p.m. Mr [Herbert L.] Matthews of *The New York Times*. He is just back from Italy – very critical of everything. How easy it is to criticise. (I have done it for many years in the House of Commons, so I know.)

4.15 p.m. René Mayer – Minister of Transport. He called to wish me a happy New Year and to thank me for my year's work – rather nice. We have just completed a *shipping* agreement (war and immediate post-war) which Lord Leathers has approved and Mayer hopes to get through the Committee in a few days.

5 p.m. Tixier (Minister, or rather Commissioner, for Labour and Social Questions). He has just returned from the International Labour Organisation meeting in London. He was less explosive than usual. He said that British opinion was much upset by the political arrests. I told him to say this to his colleagues.

6 p.m. Went with Ed Wilson to see Massigli. He gave us the draft of the proposed military agreement. It will need some amendments, but it is a good start.

7 p.m. Went to see Vyshinsky. He was in a very bad temper, because he was to have gone with his party, some French, and some of my staff to Italy today but, after keeping them two hours on the aerodrome, the plane refused to start. I asked whether this ever happened in Russia and he replied 'never'. (I cannot believe this.) I chaffed him a bit and told him some of my experiences and he cheered up. But he insisted on the Council making a formal and written protest to the Chief of Staff.

I went home after this to bed, and I have thereby rested some more and brought this letter up to date.

Wednesday, 29 December 1943

Morning in bed. You see I am trying to take more care of myself, as the doctor seems to think I should rest when I can. Miss Campbell and I did some dictating and read the morning's telegrams.

12 noon. Conference with Major-General Kenneth Strong (British), head of Intelligence at A.F.H.Q., on the reorganisation which will be required for the united Mediterranean command. Very satisfactory progress, Strong being a clever man, and without that animosity towards civilians which so many British officers seem to feel.

After lunch, went for a walk.

3.45 p.m. Conference with General Whiteley and Mr Ed Wilson on the proposed formula for agreement with the French Committee on the use of French troops. (This follows our encouraging and successful meeting with de Gaulle, Giraud and Massigli on Monday.) We were able to accept Massigli's draft, with one of two amendments, which we must get the French to agree.

5 p.m. M. Frenay[39] (Commissioner for Prisoners of War, etc.). A useful talk. I think we can help them with their parcels.

5.30 p.m. Gridley. We are still waiting for London to approve certain last-minute amendments to the lease–lend and financial agreements. Agreed telegram to London.

6 p.m. M. Chatelus, of the French paper *TAM* – an interview for publication on my year's work, etc. I shall (if he keeps his word) see the proof before it goes to press.

7 p.m. General Oliver Leese. He has arrived to take over command of the Eighth Army from Montgomery.

7.30 p.m. Saw Massigli (with Ed Wilson). He approved our amendments.

8.15 p.m. Dined with Humfrey Gale – lots of generals, British and American, including Oliver Leese. A very pleasant evening.

Thursday, 30 December 1943

I am anxious to get a British decoration for General Mast (Resident-General in Tunisia) and I hope I shall succeed. He helped us with the landings last November (at great personal risk) and has been a loyal friend to us ever since.

9.30 a.m. Went with Vyshinsky to airfield. The Advisory Council are off on another trip to Italy. I cannot go myself till Duff arrives, and I thought I had better 'do the polite' to the Commissar. Fortunately everything went well this time.

11 a.m. Mme Flandin. I have nothing yet to tell her but I am hopeful.

12 noon. Talk with General Whiteley about reorganisation problems. Quite useful.

12.30 p.m. Drove out for picnic lunch, taking with me General Julius Holmes. We talked over AMGOT, Control Commission, and his own future. He is a clever man, but has not always been easy to deal with – sometimes he has been a real thorn in our side, not from dislike of the British but because he has honestly disagreed with our French policy.

Back at the office at three. Massigli's letter has come, so de Gaulle must have agreed the amendments.

Colonel Maxwell called at 4 p.m. on some Italian problems, partly AMGOT, partly Control Commission. I fear great trouble ahead here and long to get into real action on it myself. The soldiers are making a real hash of it.

[39] Henri Frenay (b. 1905), who had been a founder of Secret Army and so of the Resistance, was Commissioner for Prisoners and Deportees, 1943–4, and Minister for Prisoners, Deportees and Refugees, 1944–5.

5 p.m. Miss Tamera – an American journalist (*New York Herald-Tribune*).

Ordinary office routine till about 7.30. Dinner 8 p.m. with Admiral Sir John Cunningham – a very pleasant dinner – only General Eisenhower, Commodore Dick and one or two aides.

Friday, 31 December 1943

I hope you have had a fairly enjoyable Christmas. It was very sad not to get home.

This morning I had a conference (10 a.m.) with General Eisenhower and Ed Wilson. It was very satisfactory. The two questions of the use of French troops and the political arrests have progressed considerably. The first is finally settled (following the conference on 27 December) by an exchange of letters between Massigli and Wilson (American Ambassador) and myself. The form has been approved as completely satisfactory by General Eisenhower and A.F.H.Q. *We* gain the complete control of available French forces under the Allied C.-in-C., and subject to the Combined Chiefs of Staff. The Committee gains the substitute of a governmental agreement, between itself and the Governments of U.K. and U.S.A. for the rather shadowy and (to French ideas) unworthy arrangements between the President and General Giraud. So everyone is pleased – or ought to be.

We have also made some advance over the problem of the political arrests. De Gaulle has given us a formal assurance:

(*a*) that they will be kept in a proper villa, with ordinary comforts and opportunity for exercise, pending the preliminary investigation;
(*b*) that the actual trial will be postponed till *after* the liberation of France – i.e. until a legal and constitutional government takes the place of the Committee.

General Eisenhower is telegraphing to the President strongly urging him to accept these assurances. Wilson is doing the same to Hull. I am recommending to Eden and Churchill that we should now let the matter drop. I fear that the P.M. will react a bit, but if the President accepts the points I shall be surprised if P.M. (after a few angry growls at me) does not do the same.

So that's that. The usual feeling of flatness follows so many emotions.

The rest of the morning was spent in sending off the necessary telegrams and preparing the necessary documents to implement the military agreement.

1.15 p.m. Lunch with Ed Wilson, General Catroux and Mme la Générale; M. Meyrier (Under-Secretary Foreign Affairs) and Mme Meyrier; C. D. Jackson; Massigli; and one or two others.

After the other guests had gone, stayed and talked with Massigli till 3.30.

4 p.m. Bogomolov. He is a fussy, legalistic fellow. He was much worried about the minutes of the last Italian Council and wanted explanations, which I gave him – very patiently.

I have telegraphed to the P.M. (who is at Marrakesh) about current French affairs. Perhaps I shall go down and see him *after* Duff arrives. I would like him to use the opportunity of being in North Africa to try to get a meeting with de Gaulle and perhaps a reconciliation. (The danger, of course, is that a meeting will only lead to a fresh row.)

6 p.m. Went to see M. Jacquinot at the Admiralty Buildings. He is Commissioner for the Navy. A very nice fellow. The admiral (French) in charge of the dockyard (Admiral Gervaise Laford) had been suddenly dismissed. As this had been done without warning to C.-in-C. Med. (Sir John Cunningham) our people were naturally rather annoyed.

Went back to office. Sent off some more telegrams – about Giraud's position, which is becoming very difficult, and about Civil Affairs for France. All this is a very complicated affair, and I am anxious that advantage should be taken of General Eisenhower's visit to Washington to get some light into that darkness.

Went to bed for dinner – read *Old Mortality*. The boys (Roger, Pat Reilly, John, etc.) went to a New Year dance, but I was too tired to face it.

All the staff of the office and villa – secretaries, drivers, cooks, etc. – went off to some show. Miss Campbell (who drinks whisky pretty generously on these festive occasions) was (I am told) the life and soul of the party. I gave them my cars and I heard strange noises between 1.30 and 2 a.m. as the party ended up with bacon and eggs (I have no doubt) in our kitchen.

All the sirens and hooters were sounded in the harbour. All the Americans fired off their tommy guns; the merchant seamen cracked off their Oerlikons with tracer shell – in fact the New Year was ushered in as though it had been an air-raid.

I wonder who was with you or where you were at this hour. Was it a fine night or a wet one? And were the children (or any of them) with you? Do write about this when you write again.

1944

January

Saturday, 1 January 1944

9.30 a.m. General [Charles] Moorhead (from Cairo), who is taking over the Adjutant General's job here, to see me. A useful talk. He struck me as a bit wooden, but I chaffed him, and he seemed to loosen up a bit. These British administrative generals, whose only experience of the world is a military mess at Aldershot or Poona, are a curiously narrow-minded lot. They seem to go all over the world without observing anything in it – except their fellow-officers and their wives (whether their own or their fellow-officers') and the various Services clubs in London, Cairo, Bombay, etc., but they are honourable, hard-working, sober, clean about the house and so on. At the end of their careers, they are just fit to be secretaries of golf clubs. War, of course, is their great moment. In their hearts (if they were honest with themselves) they must pray for its prolongation.

11 a.m. Reception by de Gaulle of the Diplomatic Corps. Very correct, very formal. I led with the congratulations as the *doyen*. Followed by biscuits, and rather nasty stuff called *porto*.

The weather has been very bad lately – pouring rain and storms, including one day violent hailstorms. My rheumatism is much better in all my body except my hands. Fortunately, the right hand is less affected than the left, so I can write without too much difficulty. The rest of today was spent in the office, clearing up a lot of things. I had to see Gridley, about lease–lend, etc. Also, Captain Wharton, R.N., the Naval Liaison Officer, about the dismissal of Admiral Gervaise Laford and the general position of the French Navy.

After dinner, the telephone began to ring. Unfortunately 'Colonel Warden' [Churchill] had discovered that he can get on from Marrakesh in a few moments by some special line. Of course the French tap the line at any and every point they want to over the whole vast distance. But undue discretion was never one of the P.M.'s faults.

He has decided to accept the proposal which I have made to him many times, and especially lately, that he should see de Gaulle and have a real talk with him and try to reach some basis of understanding and agreement. But in his impetuous way, I have to get de Gaulle to go at twenty-four hours' notice. A telegram (which I have not yet received) was despatched this morning telling me to give the invitation and make the necessary arrangements for de Gaulle's visit. This telephone call at 11 p.m. was the first I had heard of the matter, and I had in fact gone to bed. A rather difficult and complicated conversation followed.

Sunday, 2 January 1944

8 a.m. The resonant voice of Colonel Warden started to boom from 600 miles distance. I had explained last night that de Gaulle had President Beneš[1] with him and all sorts of ceremonies, etc., arranged. 'Bring them both; I would like to see them both. It will be very agreeable. Arrange it at once, there's a good boy', etc., etc.

Actually after a certain amount of back-chat – chiefly about 'vegetables' (the code or security name we invented last night for Beneš – or Beans!) a plan of some kind got itself sorted out.

10.15 a.m. I went to see de Gaulle and gave him the P.M.'s urgent invitation. He received it without much apparent enthusiasm, as I expected; and added that he was very busy and could not of course alter his plans at such short notice. Moreover, the P.M. had lately gone out of his way to insult him and thwart him. He had circulated libels against him to the British and American press (this is unfortunately true – but six months ago!) and so on. I, of course, told de Gaulle that all this was beside the point; that here was a splendid opportunity to get things on a better basis and that he *must* accept. He finally said that he would think it over.

At 12.30 I saw President Beneš, who said he would like to step off at Marrakesh on his way back to England. So this was arranged. He is to leave on Tuesday morning – spend the afternoon and evening with Winston, and leave for England about midnight.

I had not seen Beneš for a long time – not since the days of Munich and after, when we had Gosses Farm full of Czech refugees. We also published a book for him about that time. He was very pleasant, but he has always struck me as rather a conceited man. However, with the dogged, if unattractive, determination of the Czechs, he seems to get what he wants. His people are the Lowlanders of Europe.

The weather is very nasty here now. Cold and great storms of rain. There are occasional sunny intervals, but it is damp all the time. Fortunately, John's efforts have made the house very comfortable. We have good central heating and heaps of hot water.

At 1 p.m. I dropped in to see Massigli and told him that he really must get de Gaulle to accept the P.M.'s invitation. He, of course, agreed.

A heavy afternoon at the office, finishing off a lot of odd jobs.

[1] Dr Eduard Beneš (1884–1948) was President of the Czech Republic, 1935–8 and 1940–8, and President of the Czech National Committee, 1939–40.

P.M. has tried to prevent Duff Cooper coming out, but I think he has failed, and he should be here tomorrow. It will be a great relief to me.

5 p.m. We all had to go off to a diplomatic tea for Beneš – a very dull affair.

6 p.m. Interview for *France-Afrique* (the French Reuters). The giving-up direct control of French affairs corresponds almost exactly with the anniversary of my arrival here – so it's a good theme for the interview.

Dinner-party at the villa – C. D. Jackson, John Gordon[2] (editor, *Sunday Express* – a *dreadful* man), Gaskill, Colonel Douglas Dodds-Parker (S.O.E.), Tom Dupree, etc., etc. Quite fun – we kept it up till very late.

Monday, 3 January 1944

A military review for Beneš – rather a long-drawn-out and boring affair, although I always like Spahis (with their red cloaks and white horses and trumpeters and kettle-drums). They are such a relief after the drab uniforms and endless trucks, tanks, etc., of modern armies.

1.15 p.m. Luncheon for Beneš given by Massigli. Quite a pleasant party. I was put on the right of Beneš (who was opposite Massigli) and Bogomolov on his left. (This seems to have had some queer significance, but I do not quite know what).

4.30 p.m. Tea for Beneš. Present: H.M., Duff Cooper (who arrived safely this morning), Ed Wilson, Makins.

After Beneš left, I talked with Duff. He seemed *very* pleased to have arrived at last. We covered a great deal of ground and I think he will very soon pick up the threads. He is *very* intelligent, of course, and very sympathetic towards France and the French people. I feel sure he will be a success.

Unfortunately, the villa is not in good order. It was only evacuated yesterday by the French officers who had been billeted there and is of course in a mess. Moreover, there is no hot water, as the boiler is burst. Nor can any cooking be done – I suppose for the same reason. However, the Royal Engineers are at work, and I have no doubt will get things in order in due course. Meanwhile, the Duff Coopers, the Kingsley Rookes[3] (Mrs K.R. is terrific!) the Pat Reillys (who have one room in the town and one single bed), the Duprees (Mrs has arrived and seems very nice, less formidable than Mrs Reilly who has Buxton blood *and* shows it!) all have their meals with us.

John Wyndham wrings his hands in despair and says it is intolerable – *and* very expensive.

[2] John Gordon (1890–1974) had become editor of the *Sunday Express* in 1928. G. A. Gaskill (b. 1913) was Algiers correspondent of *The American Magazine*.

[3] Major-General Kingsley Rookes was Deputy Chief of Staff, A.F.H.Q., having been head of G3.

The Cooper villa is in the Moorish style – part of it is actually an old Arab house. This method of architecture (small windows, tiles everywhere – floor and walls – and little mysterious dark courts) is all very well in summer, to which it is well adapted. It is less pleasant in winter, since it excludes all light without preserving heat. (It is all right with good central heating.)

Diana took one look at it, and exclaimed, 'My God! It's like a brothel!'

Actually it's a very nicely situated house, and can be *made* a pleasant enough one. And there is a really lovely garden – neglected but with lovely bushes and shrubs which would really delight you. Since one can now get all the labour one wants in the shape of Italian prisoners, anyone who cares about gardening could make it really lovely without much difficulty.

The new Ambassadorial party was rather heavy weather at dinner. I went off at 9.15 p.m. to see de Gaulle.

Winston had been ringing me up all day, in a great state of anxiety and emotion. He told me to cancel the invitation to de Gaulle, since he could not be kept waiting. It was monstrously undignified; I was weakly pandering to the French, etc., etc.

I, of course, told Winston that I would see de Gaulle and cancel the invitation as soon as I could, but that I could not command the exact time for an interview. I would see him by hook or crook today. But all these junketings for Beneš had made it hard to get a time arranged.

Naturally, P.M. did not really wish to cancel the visit. He only wanted to preserve his dignity and give vent to his feelings on the telephone (to which, of course, the French listen intently all day). He showed his disappointment when I agreed to cancel the invitation, and at the end of each of his calls (three today before dinner) ended by saying he would leave it to me.

To my surprise (and relief) de Gaulle was in capital humour. Before I could say anything, he said he accepted with pleasure. It only remained to fix a date to suit for P.M. and himself. I undertook to telephone this message and then he kept me for an hour's talk – about France, Russia, Czechoslovakia, Europe in general – not of much intrinsic importance, but in a very expansive and friendly tone throughout. He is certainly a queer man.

On getting back to the villa, I found Diana and Duff both rather exhausted and slightly intoxicated. (I do not think I shall ever live in London again. It is too depressing. I had not heard the sort of talk and jokes and so on for so long that I had forgotten how banal is the conversation of the smart.)

I rang up Winston and gave him de Gaulle's message. He received it with a gasp of surprise, relief and some disgust into the bargain. But I rang off before he could say much.

Tuesday, 4 January 1944

I formally handed over my functions to Duff Cooper. I paid a farewell visit to Massigli – who was really charming and said more nice things about what I had done for them than I deserve. However, it was pleasant enough to hear them!

I lunched with Jacquinot, at Admiralty House. He is Commissioner for the Navy and a good fellow. He had a large party of admirals, captains, commanders, etc., and made a very moving speech about me and my services to France. (When I thought about my visit to Alexandria, and all the trouble about Admiral Godfroy and Force X, I could not help being rather amused.)

After luncheon, I went back to the villa – about 3.30 – and went to bed. I stayed in bed until

5 p.m. Wednesday, 5 January 1944

Except for reading *Old Mortality* (which I have now finished) I did very little but doze and snooze. It was very peaceful. I avoided all contact with the world – Duff Coopers and all. I thought about you all and Birch Grove, and Gosses Farm and my grandson. After all my troubles with the French, it was satisfactory to end with a success (I was very anxious that de Gaulle should accept P.M.'s invitation *and in time*) and I felt very tired. I really need a rest.

Dr Richardson came to see me. He has given me a tonic and some different ointment for my hands. These are really no better – rather worse, I think, and very painful. He overhauled me thoroughly and said I was all right, but in need of a month's rest at home. Yes, but how can I manage it? I must see what I can arrange when I see Winston next. If I am really to take on this job at H.Q. there is a lot to do to get things started right.

6–8 p.m. An *enormous* cocktail party at the villa – a farewell to me and a greeting for Duff and Diana. French, foreign diplomats, American and British soldiers – they just flocked in by hundreds. The servants organised it very well, and quantities of food and drink were consumed. (I am afraid the 'allowance' I receive will be rather strained. We must economise for a bit to make up.) It was voted the most successful party of all time. And if a party attains success which is hot and crowded – where no one goes early and more and more people arrive – I have no doubt our party can claim to have both deserved and achieved it.

Exhausted, I returned to bed.

Thursday, 6 January 1944

Roger and I left the villa at 6.45 a.m. We got an aeroplane which took us to Tunis (with some difficulty) through frightful weather. We were trying to get on to Palermo, but the pilot refused to fly any further, and no other plane appeared to want to go.

After a lot of talk and arguing and waiting at the aerodrome, we left. We went to the Consular Residence and there spent the rest of the day. It was cold, stormy, a tremendous gale blowing, with sleet and hail. There was one warm room, which I occupied and read Jane Austen's *Lady Susan* and *The Watsons* (which I have never read before and a copy of which I found in the house). They are slight pieces – not published by Miss Austen herself, who doubtless thought them unworthy. But although slight, they reveal the masterly touch in an inimitable way.

Friday, 7 January 1944

Left for airfield at 7 a.m. There was some mistake, and we were not put on the first courier plane. We finally left about ten, and arrived at Palermo about 11.30 a.m.

Here we were met by a charming young American officer (Captain LaFarge[4] – an architect and keen antiquarian) who looked after us well. The weather was still cold and stormy – no sun or warmth anywhere.

We found at the Hotel Excelsior (cold – without hot water – partly destroyed by bombing – lacking glass in the windows and plaster or wallpaper on the walls) part of AMGOT (and Allied Control Commission) for Sicily. Also, M. Vyshinsky, and five of his nine Russian 'stooges' who go about with him, including the formidable and sub-human Lett detective, whose pockets bulge with revolvers and grenades.

We went immediately to the H.Q. of AMGOT to make some plans. We lunched at the hotel; M. Vyshinsky and some of his party had returned a day earlier than had been expected from Sardinia; the rest would come tomorrow, including Reinhardt (Murphy's representative) and young Aubrey Halford, of my staff. Halford has been some few months with us now. He is very intelligent, with a scholarly and accurate mind. He speaks Italian and Russian, the first very well and the second moderately.

In the afternoon, I took Roger to see Monreale and the Chapel in the Royal Palace at Palermo (which I had seen when I had a one-day visit to Palermo from Syracuse last year). It was well worth seeing once more these glorious buildings; Norman architecture at its best, influenced by Arab and Moorish design and workmanship themselves drawn largely from Byzantine tradition.

The mosaics are still covered up to a large extent. Those visible are very impressive.

At 5 p.m. we went to see Colonel Poletti (American–Italian) Deputy-Governor of New York State. Tammany personified. He is the 'boss' of Sicily, and just loves it. The Sicilians seem to enjoy it up to

[4] Captain Louis B. LaFarge (b. 1900), later Monuments Officer, French Country Section, S.H.A.E.F.

a point. I think they feel rather proud that one of themselves should have 'made good' in America.

We discussed with him the effect of the transfer of Region 1 (Sicily) to the Royal authority, still delayed. All this handing over from AMGOT to Allied Control Commission (i.e. from the *direct* military control of the Allies to *indirect* control of Allied Commission acting through a legal Italian Government) was planned for November; then December, and is still delayed. This is partly due to the incompetence of some of the people at A.F.H.Q. (Algiers) but much more to the incredible stupidity, lack of imagination, and really insane legalistic confusion of State Department and War Department in Washington, and Foreign Office and War Office in London. They have so entangled the wretched people on the spot with documents, plans, charts of administration, etc., that they have made their job impossible. [Sir Frederick] Bovenschen (Under-Secretary at War Office) is one of the chief culprits. His heavy German mind goes turning out regulations, memoranda and plans like a sausage-machine. He has produced 1,400 officers and a total organisation of some 4,000 persons in order to administer that part of Italy in our hands. (500 British officials are the total employed in the whole of India!) The whole thing therefore wants a complete overhaul.

6 p.m. Talk with Vyshinsky. He has been here about eight days or so. I had to miss the earlier part of the tour. Vyshinsky was interesting. He thinks there is little in what he has yet seen in Italy on which to base any strong Italian Government. He thinks we must wait till something emerges, perhaps in the meantime allowing local and municipal elections and start the re-education of the people in self-government in this way. (All this is rather amusing in a way. Free press, free speech, free elections – for everyone else. I don't think there is much sign of them in Russia.)

I forgot to say that I had two visitors before I left Algiers. I was in bed, but they came up to see me. One was Colonel [J. A.] Prescott (Lieutenant-Colonel of the Grenadiers). If you see Arthur Penn[5] ask him why he allowed the Lieutenant-Colonel of the Regiment to come out instead of coming himself.

My other visitor was Maurice's C.O. – called Mackintosh (I think). He was charming and very intelligent. I gathered that in private life he ran a family business in Scotland. I was *very* much taken with him. He was awfully nice about Maurice, of whom he clearly had a very high opinion. Please tell Maurice that his Colonel called, and how much I liked him.

Saturday, 8 January 1944

Flew from Palermo to Naples. Our party now consists of seven

[5] Arthur Penn (1886–1960) was Regimental Adjutant, Grenadier Guards, 1941–5, and Acting Private Secretary to Queen Elizabeth, 1940–6.

Russians (Vyshinsky goes about with a great team of secretaries, 'contact men', detectives, interpreters, etc.), three Frenchmen, three Americans (Fred Reinhardt takes Murphy's place, while he is on leave in America) and three British (Roger Makins, Aubrey Halford and myself).

We lunched at Naples, in an hotel which had been taken over as an officers' mess. The place was squalid and dirty (like everything in Naples). It was also bitterly cold. Naples is still in a terrible condition. There has been great destruction of the houses, so that there must be many homeless people and much over-crowding. There is only a minimum subsistence ration of food (125 grammes a day of bread). There is of course only bread and vegetables – and fruit. But the price inflation has naturally followed the occupation, and vegetables and fruit are beyond the means of the poor. The Germans destroyed or carried off 92 per cent of the whole stock of sheep and cattle and 86 per cent of the poultry. There is a great and flourishing 'black' market – part of it purely speculative and part of it the result of workless and houseless people who tramp twenty miles into the countryside, buy as many potatoes or what-not as they can carry, troop twenty miles back again, and naturally and reasonably re-sell at a price that covers all their laborious effort. There is a very bad clothing situation – no boots or shoes or underwear. There is very little soap. With all this, typhus is naturally beginning – the first outbreak was not as serious as feared. But there are now thirty or forty fresh cases every day. At the same time, venereal diseases are rampant. One medical officer told me that he thought it would be more difficult to find an unaffected woman in Naples than a sufferer from one of these complaints.

After luncheon, we made plans for the next days and then drove to our billets. These proved to be a long way – about two-and-a-half to three hours by car – the roads are frightful; pot-holes everywhere; bridges all blown and replaced by narrow emergency structures. And the traffic, as you can imagine, is ceaseless. One huge line of tank-carriers, bridging machines; tanks; lorries; trucks of all kinds; commando cars, sedans and jeeps. Added to and interspersed among those are the hundreds of carts, traps, horse-drawn wagons, bicycles, etc., of the people – who all seem to be refugees flying towards Naples or refugees flying from Naples – all carrying all their large families and household goods with them.

However, repairs are going on all the time. The *autostrada*, which was out of action last time I was here, is now in partial operation. We drove out on this road towards Salerno – just short of which place we turned off to the right and got on to a wonderful 'corniche' road, going all along the coast, with startling and fascinating twists and curves, past vineyards, olive and orange groves, all in terraced sides of these steep mountains; and past houses, churches, villages, of immense antiquity, marvellously built on perilous hill-tops.

The weather had cleared – it was very cold, but the rain had stopped. There was an almost full moon, giving a picturesque and even weird lighting to this romantic scenery.

We finally reached Ravello (about 1,500 feet) where we were distributed, some to the local hotel (taken over as a rest home for Army officers), some to neighbouring villas. Our lot fell to go to the Villa Cimbrone (belonging to Lord Grimthorpe). From the Piazza to Ravello you must walk to the villa (fifteen minutes or so). The luggage is carried by local boys, glad to earn even some Allied Military Government lire.

Harold Caccia and Sam Reber (U.S.) had met us at Naples, and in this villa was also Fred Reinhardt. We found Lord Grimthorpe's nephew – Wing-Commander [Count Manfred] Czernin – the son of the late Austrian Ambassador to the Vatican. His mother was a sister of Lord Grimthorpe's and this villa seems to have been his home to a large extent. Czernin has had a very fine record as an airman and has the Distinguished Flying Cross. He is being rested now and has a job on the Allied Control Commission. There were one or two other British officers staying there, just out of hospital and having a rest.

The villa is large and well furnished – with lots of books. In spring or summer it must be delightful – or even in winter, in peace-time. But it was *frightfully* cold and there was no light or hot water. (Hot baths somehow were organised later, which was a comfort.)

And of course these villas, without carpets (tiled floors) and without coal fires, are not really intended for winter occupation. However, everyone was very cheerful, and there were quite good Army rations and *excellent* wine (made on the place) of which we partook generously.

Sunday, 9 January 1944

Left for Naples at 8 a.m. and drove into Naples. A horrid wet day. From 11 a.m. to about 5.30 p.m. we listened to representatives of the various political parties (the six parties) who are all grouped in the so-called Maples Committee of Liberation.

These parties range from the right to the extreme left (and include the Communists). As you can imagine, with Italian (translated into Russian and French and English) or bad Italian–French (translated into Russian) these discussions were tedious and exhausting. I was in the chair, and I found it very hard work indeed. (Massigli, who should have been chairman at this meeting – we take it in turn – did not arrive till the late afternoon.)

The Italians talked mostly in an excited fashion, with an irritating Neapolitan twang, but with some fascinating Neapolitan gestures, many of which were new to me. (One of the most interesting consists in clasping your hands together under your throat and then suddenly shooting out your arms like a swimmer.)

After this long day, we got home to the villa by about 8.30. Really, six hours' driving a day is too much.

Monday, 10 January 1944

Drove to Naples. Arrived at 11.30. Spent till luncheon (at 12.30 in the same cold and dirty inn) making various arrangements and holding the first part of our formal Council meeting (Massigli in the chair). This went very smoothly, except that we have not yet been able to get a settlement of the Russian and French 'token' membership of the Allied Control Commission. The President agrees to the Russian but *not* the French. I agreed with my American colleague that it would be very awkward to reveal this and that it would be better to say that we had no reply, pending a further effort to persuade the U.S. Government. This of course had the effect of making Vyshinsky *very* angry about the delay.[6]

1.30–5.30 p.m. Further meeting of the Council. General Joyce (Deputy President of A.C.C.) appeared to give evidence. (He is being *replaced* by General Mason-MacFarlane – rather a Box and Cox affair – who was his *predecessor*. The excuse is the change of command, but really General Eisenhower realised that Joyce, although a perfect darling, is not the man for the job.) After him, Marshal Badoglio and some of his so-called Government – viz., Reale (Interior), Jung (Finance)[7] and two others.

I thought the Marshal did well. He was rather annoyed at seeing the French there, and especially Massigli in the chair. This gave him a little fire and he seemed less depressed and deflated than when I last saw him.

After the discussion with the Italian Government, the Council heard the views and cross-examined in some detail some of the A.M.G. officers most concerned with the Naples area. (I had arranged this, as all kinds of statements had been made by the six parties' representatives, many of them prejudiced, and some definitely untrue, to which I thought the Council should have an answer.)

Vyshinsky naturally took the opportunity to submit the Allied officers to a good-humoured but merciless cross-examination. One saw, for the first time, the gimlet eye of the State prosecutor replace the Pickwickian benevolent beam. I re-examined after him, and Vyshinsky quite enjoyed the duel. The officers were grateful to me, and it really was quite an interesting and exciting end to the day.

Everything, of course, takes terribly long with all the language

[6] Eventually Vyshinsky proposed a compromise – that the Soviet Union and France should participate in the Control Commission as consultative members – and this was accepted.

[7] Badoglio had had difficulty in finding men of sufficient calibre to serve in his government, and therefore made some of them Under-Secretaries rather than full ministers. Vito Reale (1883–?) was Under-Secretary of the Interior, 1943–4. Guido Young (1876–1949), who had been Minister of Finance, 1932–5, was Under-Secretary of Finance, 1943–4.

difficulty, and by the time we got back to the Villa Cimbrone (after a long wait on a road-block) it was about 9 p.m. We dined and went to bed very soon after.

Tuesday, 11 January 1944

I have had a nice telegram from Anthony Eden, which has been sent on here. I quote it:

> Many thanks for your telegrams Nos. 24 and 32 [these dealt with de Gaulle's unwillingness to accept the P.M.'s invitation] and congratulations on your handling of yet another delicate situation.
>
> Now that Duff is taking over from you, I take this opportunity of expressing to you my warmest congratulations on your handling of French affairs over these many difficult months. Your tact, wisdom and patience have surmounted many formidable obstacles and have made a big contribution to the cause of Anglo-French friendship which we have so much at heart. You have every reason to be more than satisfied with your work and I am personally very grateful to you.

That is very handsome.

Today we managed to avoid driving into Naples. We slept late. After breakfast we pottered round the old town of Ravello and the vineyards and gardens of this very lovely villa.

At 10.30, however, another meeting was held, which I had arranged. This was of British and Americans who were actually engaged on Italian problems on the spot. It was a purely informal meeting, to see if we could reach some agreement as to what should be done to bring some order out of the present chaos.

I managed to keep the Russians and French happy by sending them on an all-day expedition (seven hours' motoring) to see Sforza and Croce. As Murphy and I had already seen these gentlemen twice (and as I know their gramaphone record the moment it is turned on) I did not wish to see them. And the French and Russians readily agreed that a formal visit of the whole Council to Croce (who cannot easily move from Sorrento) would be undignified.

So we were able to have our own meeting undisturbed. With the interval for luncheon, it lasted from 10.30 to about 4.30. After that we had to draft the agreement arrived at, and as there is no electric power reaching this area in sufficient quantity, we had to work by the light of candles and paraffin lamps. However, it was all done by dinner-time.

This was a tiring day, for I naturally had to preside at the conference, and there were many diverse interests and views. However, it really proved a great success, and we got in the end complete agreement of all present.

These included:

Reber (U.S.) Caccia	Political Section, A.C.C.
Lord Stansgate (Wedgwood Benn) Professor Grady[8] (U.S.)	Economic and Administrative Section, A.C.C.
Brigadier M. Lush[9] (U.K.)	Commanding AMGOT (*via* Lord Rennell)
Colonel Spofford[10] (U.S.)	Deputy Chief of Staff, A.C.C.
Brigadier-General M. Taylor (U.S.)	Second-in-Command [Chief of Staff], A.C.C.
Fred Reinhardt (Murphy's deputy)	

Roger kept the record and drafted the summary of agreement reached. (There are of course here neither stenographers nor typewriters, so we all worked at copying them out in the old Roman style – one reading, the rest copying from dictation, like slaves.)

A little walk before dinner. Then early to bed. (I got a lamp of my own and retired to bed with a copy of Miss Austen's *Emma* which I stole from the Consul's library at Tunis.)

Wednesday, 12 January 1944

Left Ravello at 7 a.m. Drove to Naples airport.

I am writing this in the aeroplane, where sixteen others and I are sitting on the knife-board seats and will be very cramped and exhausted by the five-to-six-hour flight to Algiers.

While travelling, I have been re-reading your letter dated 26 December, in which you tell me all the accounts of Christmas at home. I was so pleased with this letter and can see it all so well from your description. You seem to have been very assiduous in your church-going.

I was also interested to hear about the plans for West Derbyshire.[11] I shall be very surprised if Bill gets a 'walk-over'. The party truce seems

[8] H. F. Grady (1882–1957) was Professor of International Trade at the University of California, 1928–37, Deputy Vice-President, Economic and Administrative Section, and Vice-President, Economic Section, A.C.C., 1943–4.

[9] Brigadier Maurice Lush (b. 1896) was Executive Commissioner and Vice-President (later Chief of Staff), A.C.C., 1943–6.

[10] Lieutenant-Colonel C. M. Spofford was Chief of Staff, AMGOT, 1943, Deputy Chief of Staff, Allied Control Commission, 1943–4, and Assistant Chief of Staff, G5, A.F.H.Q., 1944–5.

[11] Lieutenant-Colonel Henry Hunloke (1906–78), my wife's brother-in-law, had caused a by-election in West Derbyshire by resigning from that traditional Cavendish seat. His nephew, Lord Hartington (Bill), heir to the Duke of Devonshire, stood in his place. He was to be soundly beaten by Charles White.

to be wearing rather thin. On the other hand, he will not have an official Liberal or Labour against him, and if he manages it properly he should get a fair number of the orthodox Liberal and Labour votes – or at least, abstentions. But of course Charley White is a good 'Common Wealth' name and I should think Dick Acland would back him with money. Really Henry ought to be spanked. He has behaved in a perfectly ridiculous way. So far as I can see, he has no excuse. He does not seem to be anything except bored with his wife and family. He has not even the excuse of coveting somebody else's.

We got in to Algiers aerodrome about 3.30 – a very good flight, direct from Naples to Algiers, without stopping at Tunis. John Wyndham was at the airfield with my car and lots of gossip. Duff and Diana have gone to Marrakesh. They covet my house and are trying to steal it. But we are standing firm. I have already surrendered my office. De Gaulle went to Marrakesh today; we do not yet know the result. P.M. wants me to go for dinner and sleep tomorrow (750 miles!).

And – most amusing news of all – Maud[12] has arrived. I feel sure she will defend my house against Diana. Your father would turn in his grave if he thought we had ceded it to a Manners.

Bath; tea; a look at the billiard-room (from which the billiard-table has been removed) which is now my office. John has arranged it very nicely. We had no door between it and the other sitting-room (which was good for parties but very annoying for sitting in either). The Army Pioneers have filled up the gap with a wooden (or lath and plaster) partition and a jib door.

At 6 p.m. I went to see General Wilson. I found there General Mason-MacFarlane, who greeted me with enthusiasm.

We plunged into Italian problems at once, and the talk lasted till eight.

General Bedell Smith (who leaves us to go to London with Eisenhower about the 20th) came in and was very helpful. General Holmes and Colonel Maxwell, who if not entirely the culprits are not without blame for much of the trouble, were present, which made it a little awkward. But I think I got my case over without offending them.[13]

Fortunately, Mason-Mac had reached about similar conclusions on most of the questions independently.

8.15 p.m. Dinner. Maud came down to dinner, bearing with her a splendid letter from you dated 5 January. I had not time to read it properly till I went to bed.

It is splendid having Maud here, and I think she will fit in all right to our bachelor household. At any rate, she can help to withstand the

[12] Lady Maud Baillie (1896–1975), my wife's elder sister, had been Controller, A.T.S., since 1942; her husband Brigadier G. E. M. Baillie had been killed on active service in June 1941.

[13] Holmes and Maxwell wanted their Military Government Section to take responsibility for giving the Commander-in-Chief political advice. But this would have been usurping my and Murphy's role.

Cooper attack. General Wilson told me that Winston has got excited about Duff's home and all the Army is being turned on to improve it. So far, they have destroyed the kitchen range and boiler and the central heating apparatus. Perhaps they will do better. I'm afraid my friend General Gale (who always has helped us in all our troubles) is rather annoyed with the Ambassadorial attitude. He is also a friend of Maud's. But (alas) he may be going to England with Eisenhower.

Early to bed; with a mass of papers, telegrams, etc., to read and answer. We managed to get five telegrams reporting on various aspects of the Italian situation written in the aeroplane. So we had only to get them typed to send them off tonight.

Thursday, 13 January 1944

9 a.m. General Mason-MacFarlane called for a short talk. The legal documents have now arrived (drafted in London and Washington) which are to carry out the proposed transfer of all territory *south* of a certain line (together with Sicily and Sardinia) to the Italian Government.

Unfortunately, in stating the necessary reservations which we have to make as to *our* rights in this territory (which we must of course preserve for the purposes of war) they (advised no doubt by the lawyers) have made the document so stiff, that it seems to go back on what we have already told Badoglio and to take away with one hand what it gives with the other. (All this nonsense, incidentally, arises from the famous *long* terms which I refused to use in the Sicilian orchard. If we had stuck to those terms of 3 September we should have been all right, because we carefully inserted a simple general clause, allowing us to do what we liked when we liked and as we liked for war purposes.)

General Mason-MacFarlane and I arranged to see General Wilson, the new Chief of Staff (General Gammell[14]) and the old Chief of Staff (General Bedell Smith), at 11 a.m.

As you can imagine, there was plenty to do between 9.30 and 11, and also after the meeting. For I had to be at the airfield at 1 p.m. to get the 1.30 courier plane to Marrakesh.

C. D. Jackson came at ten. There is trouble about the Political Warfare set up for the new Mediterranean command. I think we shall settle this, if London does not make trouble.

11 a.m. The meeting was duly held. It was decided to send a telegram of protest to Combined Chiefs of Staff. This General Wilson would send. I would telegraph to Eden and speak to P.M. if I could get the chance. Colonel Maxwell was present and I took him away after the meeting to my house to draft the necessary telegrams.

I have not yet had time to know what General Wilson's literary style

[14] Lieutenant-General James Gammell (1892–1975) had succeeded General Bedell Smith as Chief of Staff to S.A.C. on 8 January 1944 when General Wilson succeeded General Eisenhower.

is likely to be. So I made his telegram sedate in tone and mine more lively.

1 p.m. Arrived at airfield with John and some sandwiches. The courier was held up at Tunis and instead of arriving at Algiers at 1.30 it arrived at 5.45. Four-and-three-quarter hours sitting in a car! What a waste of time!

Fortunately I had brought a good many papers with me to work at. I am now writing this in the plane. It is about 8 p.m., and we ought to get in by 11 p.m. I am afraid this business of 'dine and sleep' is going to prove rather a bore. But it will give me another argument for a plane of my own. This one is cold, crowded – no seats, except the usual metal 'bucket' seats – no chance of even a snooze.

I have got *Emma*, and your last two letters, and some state papers, and some newspapers – so the time will no doubt pass away without too much tedium.

We arrived finally at Marrakesh at 10.30 p.m. and went at once to the Villa Taylor, where Winston had been staying since 27 December. We found them still at dinner – Winston, Mrs Churchill, Sarah, Max Beaverbrook and the staff. The Duff Coopers had arrived a day or two before.

P.M. was in a most mellow mood. The de Gaulle visit had taken place the day before and had gone off satisfactorily. This morning there had been a military review, at which de Gaulle and P.M. had taken the salute. Winston had been much moved by the enthusiasm of his reception.

He was very amusing about King Victor Emmanuel and Badoglio. He is all for keeping them at present. 'When I want to lift a pot of hot coffee, I prefer to keep the handle.'

He gave me a memorandum from the Cabinet about my own position and functions and asked me to comment on it. This I did, by getting up at 7 a.m. the next morning and getting hold of one of the typists just before they moved off.

Friday, 14 January 1944

I stayed at the Mamounia Hotel (near the villa). Called at 7 and got to the Villa Taylor at 8 a.m. I got my minute to P.M. copied out and sent in. At 8.30 I went in to see him. He was still in a very mellow and cheerful mood. There was only one point of disagreement and that was because he did not quite understand it.

The Cabinet memorandum, which proposed that as well as being High Commissioner of Italy I should also be responsible for Greece, Yugoslavia, Bulgaria, Hungary and Roumania (but not Turkey), stated that the Minister Resident in the Middle East would in certain matters 'act as Mr Macmillan's representative'. My minute asked if that meant as my agent and in accordance with my instructions. My minute concluded:

> If you think these suggestions reasonable I will accept the new position and do my best, but I must make one condition. The state of my health and trouble with old wounds makes it impossible for me to go through again the physical efforts of 1943. The doctors are urging me to take a long holiday. As High Commissioner for Italy I must go there from Algiers, five or six hours, or from Tunis, three or four hours, at least once and often twice a week. I am not in condition to support long journeys in crowded aeroplanes without seats and with long waits (as yesterday) at airfields. Under these conditions no work can be done properly. I would like a C47 for the use of Murphy and myself, fitted with a few simple seats and a desk.

[Diary continues] Attlee and Eden had written an *immensely* long and rather pompous paper about my functions, *vis-à-vis* other authorities in the Mediterranean and the new Resident Minister in Cairo. Winston was rather bored with it all and seemed inclined to accept a simpler structure. He asked me if I would prefer to go to Cairo. I said, 'No.' He asked me if I would like office at home. I said, 'Not yet.' He said 'Well, in spite of our tiffs, we have got on well together. You have done very well, very well indeed.' When he read the bit about the aeroplane, he was much upset and said that I ought to have asked before! I should certainly have it. (I did not think it worth reminding him that I *had* asked and been turned down by the Air Ministry.) Altogether, he was very charming and appreciative.

At noon, he and all his party left. I did not go to the airfield but said 'goodbye' at the house. He was bound for Gibraltar, whence he will return to England by ship.

The weather is quite lovely – very warm in the sun. We moved (Duff Coopers, John and I) into the villa. There is a wonderful view of the great range of snow-capped Atlas Mountains, springing out of the great plain. Sunrise and sunset are lovely – with the light on the snow.

John and I walked in the Kasbah (or native town) in the afternoon. It is curious and picturesque. I always have a feeling that the brass trays came from Birmingham and the leather bags from Wolverhampton – but perhaps I am too sceptical. There is a mass of the kind of things people buy on foreign trips – and then wonder what on earth to do with at home. They end in bazaars or as wedding presents.

Saturday, 15 January 1944

Duff, Diana, John Wyndham and I left at 7.30 a.m. A lovely sunrise; the mountains were quite beautiful as the day broke.

We had rather a bad trip. We waited an hour or more to start; came down at Oran, spent more time there and did not reach Algiers till about 3 p.m.

I found a good deal to do. My office is now in the villa and is really nicer than the old office in the town.

Maud came in before dinner. She seems very well and is really enjoying herself. She seems to know most of the soldiers here already. After dinner she and I 'gossiped'. It was nice to hear all the family news.

I loved your letter, which she brought out. I am looking forward to seeing a photograph of Alexander. Perhaps there will be some of the christening.

Sunday, 16 January 1944

Went to early service. Maud also came with me. Fortunately, the church is only a few minutes from our villa. After breakfast, worked at an accumulation of papers till about noon. I also wrote a number of letters, chiefly to the recipients of Honours. Have any Stocktonians got anything? I suppose you would see by the local press. By the way, if you read the north-eastern papers, you might send me any news of interest. I cannot make up my mind whether I shall ever be able to face a Stockton election again. It's a sort of nightmare. Probably, in the end I shall decide to go through with it. By the way, do you know what has been decided about Sussex? Admiral Beamish[15] will *not* stand, I imagine. Someone told me one Lucas-Tooth[16] has been chosen, which seems rather absurd. I also wonder whether Ralph Clarke[17] will really go on or not. Perhaps you could make some discreet soundings. Of course, if I stay in politics and remain a Minister, I must have a seat where I can get elected. I wonder what the chances would be at Stockton. I imagine they only think I am neglecting my war duty by paying no attention to them. And, of course, very few of the new electorate will have heard of us. I suppose there will be inevitably a swing to the left. Curiously enough, I think what the people still want is a 'Middle Way' – such as Allan Young[18] and I worked out and fought on in 1935.

At about 12.30, John and I went out for a drive in the hills, taking our luncheon with us. We also took Tom Dupree and his wife. There has been a delicious spell of weather – fine and warm.

6 p.m. Colonel Maxwell. Some problems about plans for Greece and Yugoslavia if and when the Germans leave!

[15] Rear-Admiral Tufton Beamish (1874–1951) did stand, and was Unionist M.P. for Lewes, 1924–31 and 1936–45.

[16] Sir Hugh Lucas-Tooth (b. 1903) was Conservative M.P. for the Isle of Ely, 1924–9, and for Hendon South, 1945–70.

[17] Colonel Ralph Clarke (1892–1970) was Unionist M.P. for East Grinstead, 1936–55.

[18] Allan Young had been an assistant to Sir Oswald Mosley, but broke with him on account of his Fascism. He worked with me on conservative reform and helped with my book, *The Middle Way* (1938).

6.30 p.m. General Bedell Smith to say goodbye. He has given me a nice photograph of himself.

7 p.m. General Gale. The problem of Duff's villa. Duff has written me a charming note, protesting his innocence of any plot to dispossess me. But General Gale sees no other solution, yet would hate me to adopt it. (Of course Duff and Diana have not been very clever with the military. The minute which Duff wrote to the P.M. has got back to them and they are incensed.) John Wyndham got much more out of them for me by kindness!

8 p.m. General Stawell[19] (Special Operations, Middle East) and Kit Steel (F.O. from Middle East) to dinner and talk on various problems connected with integrating the command. (Steel arrived from Cairo this morning and is staying with us.)

As an instance of the strange working of the mind of the Foreign Office in London – Roger Makins was woken up in the middle of the night in Algiers with a 'Most Immediate' telegram for an agreement to be entered into without delay with Marshal Badoglio on some matter or other.

Roger replied to this with some humour as follows:

> Badoglio is in Brindisi; Harold Caccia is in Salerno; General Mason-MacFarlane is in Sardinia; the Minister is at Marrakesh; Halford is in bed. With due regard to these difficulties as to personnel and location, I will carry out your instructions with the utmost rapidity.

Monday, 17 January 1944

9 a.m. Goodbye to Tedder.

9.45. a.m. Talk with new Chief of Staff (General Gammell) on one or two points.

10.15 a.m. Farewell visit to de Gaulle. He was in a very good mood, delighted with his visit to P.M. at Marrakesh. He thanked me most generously and even emotionally for all I had done for France.

12.15 p.m. Vyshinsky to see me. An interesting talk on Italian affairs. He thinks Badoglio and Sforza the only two men who count that he has seen. The rest are provincial men of small stature. He was more favourably impressed by Sforza than he expected. He thinks some local elections and free press might perhaps start in Sicily.

He thinks the King will have to abdicate eventually but not in a hurry. I told him Winston's phrase about keeping the handle if you have to lift a hot coffee-pot. This delighted him.

Vyshinsky and his interpreter (Professor Golunski) stayed to

[19] Major-General William Stawell (b. 1895) was in charge of subversive operations in the Mediterranean Theatre of Operations (S.O.M.T.O.), 1943–5.

luncheon. We also had M. and Mme Bogolomov, and the Duff Coopers.

3 p.m. Called on General Devers,[20] Deputy to General Wilson. A very good type of Middle Westerner. He made a most favourable impression on me. I feel sure he will be friendly and co-operative.

4 p.m. Saw General Wilson. Discussed Italy; the question of letting him see my Foreign Office telegrams (these will be *selected* by me, whether incoming or outgoing!) and other points. He was most friendly. I cannot yet sum him up. He has been well named in that he has clearly wisdom and shrewdness. (He has almost got cunning.) But how quick or receptive his mind may be I cannot tell.

5 p.m. Conference. Chief of Staff, General Rookes (in U.S. Operations), General Whiteley (Deputy Chief of Staff), General Bill Donovan (U.S. head of O.S.S. or Strategic Services), General Strong (U.K. Intelligence), General Stawell, Kit Steel. The subject was Tito[21] – quite a subject!

7.45 p.m. I dined with Mme Baril at the Cercle – a pleasant party enough – all French.

Tuesday, 18 January 1944

Left Algiers 10 a.m. General Devers gave me – very kindly – a lift in his plane. John Wyndham came with me. We reached Naples about 3.30. I drove to AMGOT H.Q. at Naples and thence to the Parco Hotel, where I found General Mason-MacFarlane, Harold Caccia and Sam Reber.

General Mason-MacFarlane seems in complete agreement for the schemes for reorganising AMGOT and Allied Control Commission. He is already making progress.

At 5.30 or so we drove out to Caserta, where we found General Alexander. He had just moved into a part of the enormous palace. Everything was in disorder, and he seemed (as usual) to have been fobbed off with the worst quarters. (I have a bedroom and sitting-room – or office – reserved for me in the A.F.H.Q. wing, and these are most comfortably arranged.)

General Alexander had a table, and two red plush chairs. He was, as usual, imperturbable and charming.

We went through our plans with him, and he agreed everything. He asked some excellent questions; made me one or two good suggestions; and was *very* quick to see the points. General Mason-MacFarlane had to go back to dine in Naples. I dined with Alex alone (except for two or three aides) in his mess. We had some

[20] Lieutenant-General Jacob L. Devers (1887–1979) succeeded General Alexander as Deputy Allied C.-in-C., and became Deputy SACMED and Commanding General, N.A.T.O.U.S.A., 1944.

[21] Marshal Josip Broz Tito (1892–1980) had been leader of the partisan Resistance movement since 1941; he was President of Yugoslavia, 1945–80.

delightful talk afterwards – on Italy, the organisation of the command, the post-war settlements, etc., etc. I left at 10 p.m. (the hour he always goes to bed) and I got back to Naples just after 11 p.m.

Wednesday, 19 January 1944

Breakfast 8 a.m. (unless you get down by then you get none!). All the morning with Harold and Sam on a large number of points – the chief being the problems of policy when we get to Rome. (The battle seems to be going well and there are great hopes.)[22] Then I saw Mason again and went through some further points. We shall take advantage of Jumbo Wilson's visit (he is expected today) to get everything tied up if we can. The trouble will be at home and in Washington. But I hope we can put a good many reforms into effect *without* consulting them.

After luncheon, John and I went to Caserta. We saw our rooms – which I shall probably *not* occupy on this visit, and which will be useful as a stand-by.

Talks with General Gammell – mostly on Tito and Yugoslavia.

I am *frightfully* handicapped by not having my own private communications from here to London. I have to use Army channels, and that restricts one a lot. (I have actually one other secret channel, but I cannot use it regularly.) Next time I come I will try to bring my own cyphers and cypher clerks.

Returned to Naples – arriving about six. Settled telegram to Roger Makins (which I can get specially sent) for repetition by him to London. Rome is going to be the big problem if we get there.

I have left the Advisory Council in Algiers. They are a cross I have to bear. But I want to get Anglo-American policy agreed (and agreed on the right basis) *before* undertaking the job of carrying the Council. (Murphy's absence is rather a blessing in some ways, as I can act quicker without him.) I shall go back to Algiers in a day or two and meet the Council on Monday.

Early dinner and early to bed. I have had a lovely *hot* bath (rare luxury) and the bed is warm and clean. The hotel is taken over by the Army and quite well run. I am just finishing writing and shall read for a little before going to sleep. John shares the room with me. He is a restless moaning sleeper, like Maurice.

Thursday, 20 January 1944

Lovely weather – warm in the sun, which is shining brightly, cold in the shade. No wind. This hotel is heated and there is hot water and a bath.

8.30–10.30 p.m. Worked with Mason-MacFarlane on the final draft of the new plans for A.M.G. and A.C.C. We have scratched up a very slow sergeant-typist.

[22] General Alexander had launched an attack across the Garigliano on 16 January and the Anzio landings were to take place on the 22nd.

Called to see Major-General Brian Robertson (son of the old Field Marshal)[23] – a very intelligent and efficient officer. He does not suffer fools gladly, and this has led to some difficulty with A.C.C. while it was under the genial but perfectly incompetent management of General K. Joyce. General Robertson seemed delighted at the prospect of the new scheme, and I am hopeful that in due course *so far as organisation is concerned*, we shall be on the road to solving some of our problems.

General Mason-MacFarlane, under the new system, will be head of both AMGOT and A.C.C. – direct and indirect rule – and the H.Q. staffs will be amalgamated. Obviously such things as the supply to civilians of food, housing, clothing, drugs and soap *is the same problem* whether it is in the area just behind the front line under AMGOT or the rest of Italy, under the Italian Government guided and directed by A.C.C. In any event the Army must be co-ordinated with the other two, because all *bids* for supplies of all kinds must be made through Army channels. The Army have the harbour, docks, cranes, lorries, trains, etc.

After luncheon, I motored out to Caserta. I put the new plans both for organisation and personnel to General Alexander and General Wilson, together with drafts of the Army orders to be issued by the two generals in respect of what is within their power to do, and a *draft telegram* for General Wilson to send to the Combined Chiefs of Staff in respect of things which need their prior approval. Everything was agreed.

Alex was very calm. The battle has made a good start, but the most dangerous operations are yet to come. The more I see of General Alexander the more I like and admire him.

I find General Wilson and his Chief of Staff, General Gammell, very pleasant and easy to deal with. 'Jumbo' Wilson is shrewd and cunning.

I got back to Naples about 8 – rather late for 6.30–7.30 dinner, but got something to eat all right. The day was lovely – fine and warm.

Friday, 21 January 1944

9 a.m. Saw General A. W. Pence (Peninsula Base Section, U.S.) about accommodation for the Advisory Council on Italy. We make little progress with this haunting problem, and I must be able to get the Russians and French over next week or they will be very suspicious.

Motored out to Caserta with General MacFarlane. We had a long talk with General Gammell and General Rookes to tie up various loose ends on the reorganisation scheme which was *generally* approved yesterday. This was a successful meeting.

I also arranged to send Harold Caccia and S. Reber into Rome (if

[23] Major-General (later General) Sir Brian Robertson (1896–1974) was Deputy C.A.O. (under Genral Gale), A.F.H.Q. Advanced Administrative Echelon, 1943–5. His father Field Marshal Sir William Robertson (1860–1933) was C.I.G.S., 1915–18.

evacuated by the Germans) with General Crane (the proposed Military Governor). There will be a lot of difficult and delicate diplomatic problems – regarding neutral ambassadors and ministers, enemy embassies and the protecting power, and of course the Vatican – on which the military will need guidance.

Everything was satisfactorily arranged, and we got back to Naples for a late lunch.

In the afternoon, John and I took a holiday. We got a car and drove with Arthur Forbes[24] to Pompeii. I had never been there and much enjoyed the visit. It is all too well known for me to describe to you, and in any case we had a very hurried look round. It was a lovely day and I enjoyed the outing.

The R.A.F. and the American Air Force have not improved Pompeii, but they have not done very serious damage.

We have really finished our work for this trip, and I hope to go back to Algiers tomorrow. The weather is fine, which is a blessing and should help operations.

The outflanking expedition by sea lands tonight.[25] There is a slight haze and a very calm sea. It is difficult to sleep for thinking of them as they crawl up the coast in the landing-craft. I got up several times and looked out over the Bay of Naples – all quiet, no lights, no German aircraft – a peaceful, still night, with a haze over the water, and the stars shining brightly above.

Saturday, 22 January 1944

John and I left at 10 a.m. We got an aircraft to ourselves this time – no seats, but my 'Li-Lo' makes me very comfortable.

We also brought an American officer and Lord Forbes.

Arrived at the villa about 4 p.m. A good trip.

Just before leaving, we had the first news of the landings, which sounded very good. By some miracle the thing was a complete surprise. How they can have failed to see the great convoys moving slowly up the coast all yesterday (they left 4 a.m. Friday morning) and going only about five knots, I cannot imagine.

On arrival at Algiers, I found a vast accumulation of papers. This kept me busy till dinner. I wish my friends at home would stop bothering about the publication of Croce's books and think more of the frightful problems of keeping the Italian people alive in some kind of decency!

Maud was at dinner – looking very smart and well. I gather she is having a *great* success here, and I think she is enjoying it. All the generals and colonels are asking her to parties. I think Anglo-American rivalry (if it existed here) is over. There are two schools – for

[24] Wing-Commander Viscount Forbes (b. 1915), later 9th Earl of Granard, had been Air Attaché to the Minister Resident in the Middle East since 1942.

[25] The landings behind enemy lines at Anzio.

Lady Diana or for Lady Maud – and this division wipes out or supersedes national controversies. I think that twenty years ago there would have been a walk-over for Lady Diana, perhaps.

Sunday, 23 January 1944

Went to church 8 a.m. Worked till luncheon – a lovely day and too fine to be indoors. I am getting very old and unfit, for I have scarcely had even a walk for a year.

Commodore Dick brought his successor as Chief of Naval Staff, Mediterranean, to luncheon. His name is Admiral J. G. L. Dundas – a charming and obviously very intelligent officer, whom I had met at Alexandria last year (he was then with Admiral Harwood) over the negotiation about Admiral Godfroy's fleet (Force X). I had a little walk after luncheon and then went back to my papers. There is a lot to do, because I am back again to Italy on Tuesday.

Dined with Humfrey Gale. Maud also came. We had a film after dinner. The life of generals at A.F.H.Q. is getting very like the life that millionaires used to live in pre-war England!

Monday, 24 January 1944

A quiet day; papers, etc., all the morning. I think we shall be in Italy for a week or more, so I shall take a larger staff.

Duff came to see me about a Franco-Italian problem – that is, the possibility of reopening certain trade mutually beneficial; for instance, the French need sulphur from Sicily and can use Sardinian coal. Italy, on the other hand, needs phosphates and Corsican pit-props for the Sardinian coal-mines.

The news of the battle seems good, although we have very little detail. The landings were unexpectedly successful and the weather is still good. We are all very hopeful, though we dare not hope too much. We know from experience that the critical time is three or four days after a landing, when the counter-attack comes.

3.15 p.m. Meeting of Allied Advisory Council for Italy. M. Vyshinsky was in the chair. There was more 'body' in this meeting than in any we have had before and a number of fairly controversial points which had been referred to us by the C.-in-C. Massigli presented a formal document, starting with a demand for the immediate abdication of the King, and going on to ask for Italian warships, merchant ships, aircraft, etc., to be distributed to the French as compensation for Italy's attack in 1940!

I was very indignant and Vyshinsky supported me strongly. Poor Massigli as good as admitted to me afterwards that the precious document had been put in on the orders of the French Committee, and he seemed rather ashamed.

Vyshinsky proposed that we should discuss the problem of the King 'at the meeting *after* the next one' – which we hope may be after the capture of Rome. As H.M.G. are very anxious (and I agree) to keep the *status quo* for the present, this suited me and was agreed to.

6 p.m. Called on General Gammell, the new Chief of Staff, and settled a few minor points with him.

6.30 p.m. Colonel Maxwell called. A number of Italian questions. The Allied Governments have accepted completely our view about the 'transfer' document, so I hope this will now go through. It is a great 'climb down' after all the pages of stuff which they write in London and Washington. But they never face the realities. The real problem is to get an Italian Government to accept the responsibility of even trying to govern southern Italy in present conditions, dependent as they are on us for food, transport, fuel and clothing. If Badoglio is too hard-pressed he will throw in his hand, and this will be very embarrassing for us.

We had also some talk about planning for Greece – if and when the Germans leave. This means a lot of problems – food, clothing, etc. – and also implies some central Greek authority to work with. I have not really had time to study Greek affairs – now that it comes into my field, I must begin to educate myself.

8 p.m. Duff and Diana to dinner. Also Mlle Eve Curie,[26] a charming French girl, daughter of the scientist. Diana still casts envious eyes at my villa!

Tuesday, 25 January 1944

10 a.m. Left by air. We had our own plane (but only tin seats) and a large party, including five Russians, three Americans and seven British. I thought it wise to suggest to Vyshinsky that the Council should be available in Italy at this time, and he jumped at it. I also brought a team of my own which I may leave in Italy. These consisted of Aubrey Halford, a clerk – a poor little creature, who can type and speak Italian, but has no great qualities besides – and two cypher clerks. The latter will enable me to do in Italy as I have always done in Algiers – viz., send and receive telegrams in Foreign Office cyphers and *not* through military channels where they are freely distributed to all and sundry.

We got to Naples at 3.15, after a very good steady flight.

We are *all* accommodated at the Parco Hotel (where we were last week), except John Wyndham and me. We are at Advanced A.F.H.Q. in the vast palace of Caserta (about which I wrote before; Murphy, Roger and I were in it for a night or two). I have also got my Grenadier Sergeant (Leyland) who is our butler at Algiers. He is very good and makes it more comfortable, by being a good valet and almost nurse. (Now that I am so obviously 'breaking up' my staff are becoming very solicitous of my welfare.)

[26] Eve Curie (b. 1904), younger daughter of Pierre and Marie Curie (the discoverers of radium), was a lieutenant in the Women's Auxiliary Forces, Free French Army, and Personal Assistant to General de Lattre de Tassigny, 1943–4.

The only trouble is that it is a good hour's drive from Naples to Caserta. I have business at each end, and this will be tiring. The road is very bumpy and full of 'pot-holes', and as it is the highway from the port of Naples to the front, you can imagine what the stream of traffic is like, ceaseless night and day.

4–5.30 p.m. Talk with Caccia and Reber in the hotel.

5.45 p.m. Drove with General MacFarlane to Caserta. Here we were to find General Alex, but he was still out and did not finally return till about 9.15. We dined at his little mess outside the palace. We were able to accomplish our business – chiefly the signing of the formal documents for the transfer of territory.

Alex was tired, but quite cheerful. The weather has not been quite so kind lately. The wind has been very strong and made it difficult to land the stores, etc., that are required. What they need is an 'off-shore' wind. If it is blowing from the sea it forces the ships forward, as they become lighter with the landing of their cargoes, and therefore there is a risk of them 'broaching' – that is getting stuck on the sand and thus becoming losses. It is really rather wonderful what they manage to do. There is only a tiny little harbour at Anzio (fortunately undamaged); all the rest of the stuff is carried over the beaches, even from big Liberty ships as well as from regular landing-craft.

I was naturally able to discuss many points in the reorganisation of A.C.C. and A.M.G. while waiting for General Alex. I think Mason-MacFarlane will make a good job of it. It is really very lucky for me that Murphy is on holiday in America. His *remplaçant* is quite intelligent and very junior. So I have really been able to take control and arrange everything with Mason-MacFarlane. Generals Wilson and Alexander seem quite prepared to accept whatever we agree upon.

Wednesday, 26 January 1944

10 a.m. Left Caserta for Naples.

11 a.m. Meeting of Council to hear General MacFarlane, who gave us an account of the organisational changes in A.M.G. and A.C.C. This was useful. I did not want the Council to interfere in making the changes, but I wanted them to be kept in the picture.

Reber also gave an account of the political situation.

The meeting was a success, and kept the Council quite happy for a couple of hours.

I left for Caserta at 2.15 and got there by about 3.15. I had a meeting with General Strong (D.M.I. [Director of Military Intelligence]) about the organisation of political and military intelligence in the new Mediterranean command and came to a complete and I think satisfactory agreement with him.

4 p.m. Saw General Wilson. He kept me an hour – covering a wide field. He was very pleasant. He is intelligent and even a little cunning. I do not think he will make many serious mistakes.

5 p.m. General Gubbins (S.O.E.): the usual problems of (*a*) co-operating with O.S.S. – the American organisation for subversive activities and clandestine warfare – and (*b*) Greek internecine squabbles and wrangles.

6 p.m. Left Caserta – by car.

7 p.m. Arrived Naples. Conference with Mason-MacFarlane on a few further points of 'personnel' in his show.

7.30 p.m. Dinner with Mason-MacFarlane. He has got himself a villa in Naples, and this was his house-warming, a pleasant party. Grady, Stansgate (Wedgwood Benn), Sam Reber, Harold Caccia, Colonel Spofford (U.S.) and one or two others.

10.15 p.m. Left for Caserta.

11.15 p.m. Arrived – tired and ready for bed.

Thursday, 27 January 1944

We rise early here – about 7.30 and breakfast at 8. After breakfast I wrote some telegrams. I have no shorthand typist here, which is a bore. I cannot very well have Miss Campbell here, and I have come to rely on her very much. However, I got them all done by 11 a.m. when I had to see Admiral Sir John Cunningham about the Bari conference.

I have, of course, decided *not* to interfere with the congress of the six parties and have telegraphed to the Cabinet to tell them so. I got a very absurd message, just as I was leaving Algiers for Italy, saying that the Cabinet wanted the congress postponed. I traced their alarm to a signal sent by Admiral McGrigor[27] (at Taranto) to C.-in-C. Mediterranean and unfortunately repeated to the Admiralty. The gallant flag officer at Taranto thought that the congress would perhaps lead the Italian Navy to:

(*a*) mutiny;

(*b*) scuttle their ships.

It was not quite clear whether they would adopt this course because:

(*a*) they were monarchists, and wished to protest against the views expressed at the congress;

(*b*) were Republican, and wished to show their sympathy for the said views.

Anyway, Admiral McGrigor's signal caused distress in London and a very foolish message to me from my colleagues. This congress was to have been in Naples. The military authorities refused permission at the time, but said it could take place in Bari at the end of January. It will be a 'ticket' meeting, and I have no doubt uncommonly dull. Croce will open, with at least one-and-a-half hours of his melancholy stuff, and I do not believe that there will be any serious disturbances.[28]

27 Rear-Admiral Sir Rhoderick McGrigor (1893–1959) was Flag Officer, Taranto and Adriatic, 1943–4.

28 Ninety delegates, from all the Italian democratic parties, met on 28–29 January and voted for the abdication of the King, an all-party government and a Constitutional Assembly as soon as peace was restored.

I am afraid I told Sir John that although I was quite prepared to accept the view that the Italian fleet would mutiny, I did *not* believe that this would be as a result of the congress at Bari, but rather due to the natural propensity of all fleets to mutiny. This seemed to satisfy him.

12 noon. The Advisory Council and their staffs were brought to Caserta from Naples. General Wilson received them, and spoke on the military and political situation for about three-quarters of an hour, with question and answer. He did very well, and Vyshinsky was obviously pleased and flattered. Luncheon afterwards for the party – twelve in all – in the general's mess.

After luncheon, a real holiday. No more work till 5 p.m. (when I had an hour's conference with General Wilson on various telegrams, etc.) and a lovely walk in the grounds of this fantastic place.

The house (built about 1760) is larger, I believe, than Versailles. There are four great courts, 3,000 or more rooms and so on. The garden leads up the hillside and is filled with fountains, statues, watercourses, etc. The canal pond is used by General [Mark] Wayne Clark (Fifth Army H.Q. are also here for the time being) to land a Moth aeroplane on (fitted with floats). The cascade (obviously the model for the Bachelor Duke's work at Chatsworth), the artificial rocks, the hillside, and today the warm sun – all made a delightful afternoon's pleasure. I have scarcely walked since last spring, but I managed a couple of hours without undue exhaustion.

5–6 p.m. General Wilson. Chiefly (*a*) Yugoslav questions, and (*b*) organisation of political warfare throughout the command.

6–8 p.m. Read and almost finished *Pride and Prejudice*.

8–10 p.m. Dined at Alex's mess. Alex was in capital form – a delightful evening.

Friday, 28 January 1944

Worked in my office in Caserta on various telegrams and papers. I am now getting my communication system into some kind of order and can *receive* telegrams from Algiers (and from London *through* Algiers) in my own cyphers. I can also *send* cyphered telegrams to Algiers and to London direct.

11.30 a.m. Conference with General Wilson on various points. I find him very agreeable and intelligent.

2 p.m. Motored into Naples for a meeting at 3 p.m. of the Advisory Council (informal) – we heard explanations of their work from Lord Stansgate and Mr Grady (Economic Section). This went off well, and I think impressed the Russians as to the value of the reforms.

4.30–6 p.m. Conference with General MacFarlane on a number of questions, chiefly the legal instruments for the transfer of territory and the problem of the prisoners of war.[29]

[29] Some 450,000 Italian prisoners of war were being held by the Allies, most of them being employed as agricultural labourers. Under the Geneva Convention of 1929 they could not be

I got back to Caserta about seven and dined very pleasantly with General Alex. General Wilson was a guest and a most jolly and even uproarious meeting – General Cannon (U.S.) and General Lemnitzer[30] (U.S.) were there and lots of good talk and good stories.

Saturday, 29 January 1944

A memorable day. Alex took me out all day in his open touring car (a Ford V8 which has been cut down to make an open body). It is a well-known car, painted for the desert, which has come all the way from El Alamein and has now been decorated officially with the African Star.

We went to see the French Corps (where we found General Juin in charge and General Giraud on a visit), to the American Second Corps (old friends of mine – including as it does the American First Division), and then round different parts of the line. We climbed up a hill from which we could watch the battle for Monte Cassino. General Alex was as calm, detached, and attractive as usual. He has the most effective way of giving not exactly orders but suggestions to his commanders. These are put forward with modesty and simplicity. But they are always so clear and lucid that they carry conviction. It is a most interesting (and extremely effective) method.

The rest of the drive he likes to talk of other things – politics, ancient art (especially Roman antiquities), country life. He hates war.

We got back about 6.30 and, after a bath, dined quietly together.

I really enjoyed this day. It was most inspiring in a quiet and unobtrusive fashion.

Sunday, 30 January 1944

Motored into Naples, arriving at 10 a.m. for a conference with Mason-MacFarlane, Caccia and Reber. I have now borrowed General Wilson's car (he has returned to Algiers) which is better than the old command cars or jeeps which I have been using.

The conference lasted till luncheon. John and I (with Harold Caccia) then left by car for the Villa Cimbrone – Lord Grimthorpe's villa near Ravello. This is about a three-hour drive from Naples (with the roads as they are) through Pompeii, Cava, almost to Salerno and then by a wonderful winding corniche road, out in the mountain-side, sometimes climbing a thousand feet or more, sometimes going down to the sea again. It was a lovely warm and sunny afternoon – very different from our last visit. The almond trees (in the more sheltered places) are beginning to flower. The hillsides are one mass of little terraces in the

forced to work on anything directly connected with the war. And so long as Italy's status was that of a co-belligerent they remained legally prisoners of war even if they volunteered to serve the Allied cause. Though encouraged to do so, few of them did.

[30] Major-General John K. Cannon (1892–1955) was Commanding General, U.S. Twelfth Air Force and Mediterranean Allied Tactical Air Force, 1943–5. Major-General Lyman L. Lemnitzer (b. 1899) was Deputy Chief of Staff to General Alexander, 1943–5.

rock (it is all limestone) mostly devoted to lemons, with some vines and vegetables. These in peace-time are the best lemons in the world. They commanded the best prices at Covent Garden. Now the poor people cannot sell them. We have managed to get some tonnages shipped away, but very little, and the lemons will rot away unused. The problem of the rapid turn-round of the ships with military stores makes export almost impossible at present. It may improve later, as it has done in North Africa – but for the time being everything must of course be made available for the battle, and as soon as ships have unloaded their supplies for the troops, they turn right back again for more without waiting to load exports.

Lord Grimthorpe, Count Manfred Czernin (his anglicised nephew – in the R.A.F.), Harold Caccia, Reinhardt (Murphy's *remplaçant*), Con Benson (who is in A.M.G., as well as Lord G).

I was very tired and slept from 10 p.m. till late the next morning. Anyway, there is no electric current, so one cannot read in bed!

Monday, 31 January 1944

Lazed all the morning. I found a copy of *Sense and Sensibility*, which I read and finished by the evening.

In the afternoon some of us (Con Benson, Caccia, Colonel Grafftey-Smith,[31] A.M.G. (really Bank of England) and I) walked down the mountain to Amalfi. It is about one-and-a-half-hours down a precipitous path – a most delightful walk and a lovely day. It was really hot in the sun.

Amalfi is a charming little old town, at the entrance of a deep ravine, with a pretty little fishing bay and great rocks and mountains all round. There is a charming early thirteenth-century cathedral – in the Lombardo-Norman style – some very good bronze doors, from Constantinople – and a dear little cloister (thirteenth century). For some reason, I have only heard of Amalfi because I think Beaumont and Fletcher or Marlowe or one of those poets wrote a play called *The Duchess of Amalfi* – which I have never read.

[31] Colonel (later Brigadier) Anthony Grafftey-Smith (1903–60), who had been Deputy Chief Cashier at the Bank of England, was Controller of Finance, AMGOT, 1943–4, and Chief Financial Officer, A.C., 1944–5.

February

Tuesday, 1 February 1944

Left Ravello at 6.45 a.m. Got to Naples just after 9 and had an hour with General MacFarlane clearing up some final points.

General Wilson kindly sent his aeroplane, and we had a most comfortable trip back to Algiers – with seats! We are off the aluminium standard at last! (These are the bucket seats in the ordinary C47s.)

We found a lot of work to be done at Algiers – and also two women in our house – Joyce Grenfell[1] and Miss [Viola] Tunnard (her accompanist). They are singing to hospitals and so on, and they appear to be more comfortable in our house than in the hotel.

Wednesday, 2 February 1944

I stayed in bed most of the morning, being very exhausted. My hands are worse again, and this wretched eczema is beginning in other parts of my body.

12.30 p.m. Vyshinsky came to talk to me. He is going back to Moscow – partly on Italy, but I fancy mostly on this reorganisation of the sixteen Soviet republics and their foreign relations.[2] He was very pleasant, as usual, and talked in a most interesting way about Russia and the new developments. I hope he will come back to us, but I have doubts.

Reinhardt came to luncheon.

3 p.m. Colonel Maxwell and a lot of Italian stuff. Badoglio has refused to sign the prisoners-of-war agreement, and I do not blame him. We have really asked too much of him – and, as usual, all done in Washington *without* consulting anyone here.

7 p.m. General Wilson called – to meet my staff. He was rather staggered to find it consisting of Roger, John Addis and John

[1] Joyce Grenfell (1910–79), singer and entertainer, was visiting troops in hospitals throughout the Middle East.

[2] It was announced on 1 February 1944 that the Commissariats of Defence and of Foreign Affairs would change from All-Union to Union–Republican Commissariats, suggesting that each of the sixteen Soviet republics would now control its own army and its own diplomatic representation.

Wyndham! He is accustomed to Cairo standards and the Minister of State's office there.

5.30 p.m. Called to see General Gammell.

7 p.m. Harman and Barnes[3] (successors to Crossman and Jackson as heads of Political Warfare). A large reorganisation is necessary with the new Mediterranean command.

8.15 p.m. Dinner with General Wilson, to meet some Russian generals. Agreeable, but rather heavy going.

Thursday, 3 February 1944

I stayed in bed again, doing my papers and dozing. I did not get up till it was time to go to a meeting of the new Political Committee which we have formed. This met at four. General Wilson, General Devers (U.S. Deputy C.-in-C.) General Gammell, General Rookes (Deputy to Chief of Staff), Reinhardt, Roger and H.M. A very successful beginning was made with many problems. General Wilson is an excellent chairman.

6 p.m. Colonel Maxwell. Trouble about the documents for the handover of Italian territory to the Italian Government. But I think we can straighten this out *without* reference to Washington.

7 p.m. My doctor, Colonel Richardson, called and stayed to dinner. He insists that I should go home for a rest. Perhaps I will try to do so, but it is very difficult as things are.

Friday, 4 February 1944

A fairly normal morning. Duff and Diana to luncheon, also Virginia Cowles.[4] Miss Grenfell and Miss Tunnard and an American colonel whose name escapes me.

3–5 p.m. Conference at General Wilson's office with him and General Paget. An immense discussion on the relations between Middle East and A.F.H.Q., covering almost every subject. At the end General Wilson thought I should go home to see the P.M., and I am going to telegraph to him tomorrow, following the telegrams I am sending on the points to be settled.

5 p.m. Gridley (N.A.E.B.); economic co-ordination in the Mediterranean area. What a subject! I consented to write a project which I finished by about 2 a.m. the next morning.

6.30 p.m. Colonel Maxwell – also on economics in the area (which in my view have nothing to do with him!).

7.30 p.m. Went again to see Generals Wilson and Paget to clear my telegrams with them (resulting from the conference today).

[3] Terence Harman, formerly of the J. Walter Thompson advertising agency, had been Regional Director, P.W.E., for the Low Countries. Russell Barnes (b. 1897) had been U.S. Press Officer at the Cairo and Teheran conferences.

[4] Virginia Cowles (1910–1983) was a newspaper correspondent, 1937–41 and 1943–5, and Special Assistant to the U.S. Ambassador to London, 1942–3.

Saturday, 5 February 1944

An easy morning – bed and papers to read.

12.30 p.m. General George Clark (who has succeeded to Humfrey Gale) came for a talk and stayed to luncheon. (I forgot to tell you that when I got back from Italy I found Maud had left for a tour – she is going to Bône, Bougie, Constantine, Tunis and then, I think, Naples.)

My old friend General Pechkoff to luncheon. He is just off to China again, where he is now head of the French Mission.

I had decided to telegraph to Winston and had already done so when I got your letter of 29 January. I hope he will agree to my suggestion, which was to go back for a fortnight to get this X-ray cure for my hands. I can have a bit of a rest and also be available for discussion of certain questions.

6 p.m. Massigli called. He was on a fishing expedition about the British attitude on Italy.

Sunday, 7 February 1944

Rather a hectic morning. The State Department have suddenly gone mad and sent the most extraordinary instructions to Reinhardt, who is acting in Murphy's place. Fortunately he is a loyal and sensible fellow, with a good deal of courage, and brings these telegrams to me before doing anything. The State Department (who will be much more difficult now that General Wilson has replaced General Eisenhower – since the latter had always the powerful protection of the War Department) have told Reinhardt (*a*) to tell Massigli that they agree with the French note and that they think the King should be 'removed' at once and a new Government be formed (apparently on a purely revolutionary basis and without any legal sanction) and (*b*) to tell the same thing to Sforza.

It would be difficult to imagine any diplomacy more crude or more futile. The French will immediately publish this *démarche* all over the world, of course emphasising the fact that they are in agreement with Washington and *against* London in the matter. Sforza – who we are trying to get to agree (after the usual Italian bargaining) to some compromise – will at once be so puffed up with conceit as to raise his price.

Fortunately, I was able to persuade Reinhardt *not* to carry out either of these instructions, but to waste time by sending over to consult Reber. Meanwhile, I must telegraph F.O. and get Winston to take it all up with the President direct and get Reinhardt's instructions changed.

Roger, Joyce Grenfell, Miss Tunnard and I went out for a picnic – 12.45 – 4 p.m. It was a lovely day and we picked great quantities of wild flowers – iris, jonquils, crocus, scilla, etc.

Meetings with Reinhardt, General Wilson, etc., between 4 and 6 p.m.

The Italian affair is gong to prove rather troublesome, but I hope we shall get some sense into the State Department.

I keep reading your letter of the 29th. I have telegraphed you to say that I will let you know my plans. I will certainly come home if P.M. gives me leave to do so. General Gammell to supper.

Monday, 8 February 1944

The usual morning. John and I went out for a drive, taking sandwiches, instead of lunching in. It was a lovely sunny day.

5 p.m. General Wilson. A talk on the reorganisation of the Military Government Section of A.F.H.Q. and my functions etc. He was very sensible and helpful.

I gave a dinner for General Wilson. Generals Devers (U.S. Deputy C.-in-C.), George Clark, Rookes, Vanier[5] (Canadian Minister to the French), also Reinhardt, Admiral Hewitt (U.S.), Captain Miller, R.N., Air Marshal Bowhill[6] (from England) and one or two others. It was quite a success – speeches on all sides. It was intended as a sort of welcome to Wilson, and American and British were well balanced.

Tuesday, 9 February 1944

10.30 a.m. Captain Cuthbert Bowlby, R.N. Lunch with the Duff Coopers, to celebrate the formal signing of the Mutual Aid and the Financial Agreement between us and the French on which I had worked so long. It was nice of Duff to ask me. All the usual French – including Massigli, René Mayer (Transport), Mendès France (Finance).

I also dined with Duff. General and Mme de Gaulle and a large party. His villa is now very nice, and he has a very fine 'set-up'. While we have been on the 'pewter' standard for so long he is on the 'silver' standard, with fine Ambassadorial plate and china. We had a successful meeting of the Political Committee at four.

Wednesday, 10 February 1944

11 a.m. Colonel Maxwell (drafting telegrams as a result of yesterday's meeting).

12–1 p.m. Meeting with General Wilson. Quite a large agenda – Italy, France, Yugoslavia, Bulgaria. General Wilson has agreed to a telegram to the Combined Chiefs of Staff asking for *no* political action while the battle rages in Italy. This should help to keep things quiet.

3 p.m. Maxwell again.

5 p.m. General Vanier (Canadian Minister). He is very charming, but it was not much more than a pleasant talk.

[5] General Georges Vanier (1888–1967) was Canadian Representative to the F.C.N.L., 1943–4, and Ambassador to France, 1944–53.

[6] Air Marshal Sir Frederick Bowhill (1880–1960) was A.O.C. Transport Command, 1943–5.

6 p.m. General Wilson called round to see me for some final discussions before I leave for England.

8 p.m. Lady Diana to dinner – also Peter Loxley (of the F.O.).

Thursday, 11 February 1944

Yesterday was my fiftieth birthday. It is terrible to reflect on all the follies and mistakes of so many years – so much attempted, so little achieved.

After rather a hectic morning, with all sorts of last-minute discussions and decisions, we left for the airfield at bout 12.15. My friend Air Vice-Marshal Dawson – the most intelligent man I know out here, who has set up all the R.A.F. repair shops from Tel Aviv to Dakar – has loaned me one of his Liberators. (It is one which the Americans gave him as useless, and he has repaired.) It will be cold (the plane is not heated) but it will be a good crew, and we shall have every chance of arriving.

We got to Gibraltar at about 4.30 p.m. A lovely day, like a warm June day in England.

Major-General [Frederick] Hyland is Acting Governor, and entertained us well. Lieutenant-General Martel,[7] who has for nine months been head of our Military Mission in Russia, was there – on his way back. He is relinquishing the appointment. He was interesting about the Russians. He thinks we are too weak with them, and that they respond better to firmness. He also said that they have twice as many divisions as the Germans – that the Germans use no air force at all on the Russian front (it is all kept to deal with our air attacks on Germany), and that if the Russians were not still fundamentally incompetent, they would have wiped the floor with the Germans months ago – a refreshing view.

Friday, 12 February 1944

We left at 1.15 a.m., arriving Lyneham at about 9 a.m. After breakfast and various ceremonies, we started by car for London about 10.30 a.m. and arrived at Claridge's at 1 p.m.

[7] Lieutenant-General Sir Giffard Le Quesne Martel (1889–1958), an expert on military mechanisation, had been commander of the Royal Armoured Corps in 1940.

March

Thursday, 9 March 1944

It seems funny to be back again in Algiers, writing another of my interminable letters. I enjoyed my four weeks at home enormously, although I am bound to admit that they were far from restful. However, a good deal was accomplished – I hope and pray for the best. The trouble is that I shall be travelling again soon, so that I shall miss your first letters.

Arrived safely at Maison Blanche aerodrome, Algiers at about 9 a.m. We started from Lyneham about 11.30 p.m. the night before, so it was a good flight. We came direct, without stopping at Gibraltar. The air vice-marshal's Liberator goes all right and boasts a splendid crew, but it is uncommonly cold. Even with my flying-suit (coat and trousers) and several rugs, I nearly froze. After the usual greetings – Roger and the others – we settled down to work. I do not feel that I have achieved much in London – beyond, perhaps, a better understanding of the P.M.'s mind and the many problems which confront him from every side. This is certainly going to be a very difficult and perhaps perilous year. But that is all the more reason for sticking to the ship. Quite frankly, I think my new job here is unworkable. I have a sort of nominal control over huge territories, but this is too remote to be effective. Italy, North Africa, Balkans, Roumania, Bulgaria, Hungary, it is all very much a paper affair, without much reality – the sort of make-believe job which I particularly dislike. On the other hand, I suppose one may be some use, to General Wilson, the American alliance and the P.M. I must wait and see how it works out.

It is quite clear to me that two things have resulted from the change of command here. First, General Wilson – although a shrewd, clever, humorous and rather cunning man – has not the capacity to make himself liked by the Americans here to the same extent that General Eisenhower was able to attract British sympathy and support. Secondly, the very fact that we have a British and not an American general in command paradoxically enough weakens instead of strengthening our political position. When General Eisenhower was here, if I could persuade him to recommend to the Combined Chiefs of Staff in Washington a course which I knew was what H.M.G. wanted, I knew that it would go through. The State Department would not venture to intervene against the recommendations of an American general. Or if they did, General Marshall and the War Department would come out in full cry and hunt the State Department to the death. Now all that is changed. The State Department is opposing our policy in Italy as well as elsewhere. And the War Department will naturally not rush to defend a British general.

I spent all the afternoon with General Wilson, General Gammell (Chief of Staff) and [Air Marshal] Sir John Slessor (Deputy Air Officer Commanding-in-Chief). There was a lot of ground to cover. After general discussion, I had to explain to Wilson alone all the trouble he had got himself into with the P.M. This arose from the poor general trying to be too honest, and sending all kinds of messages to the Combined Chiefs of Staff (whose servant he is) on Italian politics and military plans without first ascertaining that they coincided with the wishes of H.M.G.!

The whole situation is really rather difficult. Fortunately it is also quite comical.

Maud has returned from a very good trip – to all the North African ports and cities and also Naples and Bari. She seems very well. She fortunately saw Michael[1] – who has got chicken-pox!

Friday, 10 March 1944

A fairly heavy morning. Lunched with Duff Cooper and spent most of the afternoon with him. The Pucheu trial is the sole subject of interest and debate in Algiers. It has certainly been very badly conducted by the prosecution. Not only was the evidence badly prepared, it was also badly presented by General [Pierre] Weiss. This officer is apparently an object of universal contempt – he is among all other things an open and blatant pederast, surrounded by 'pansy' officers – he opened himself to devastating attacks from the dock.

Pucheu put up a very fine performance. He is clearly a clever, but unscrupulous man. Rough justice will, I think, be done if he is shot. But it will have a bad effect on de Gaulle's reputation and on the Committee generally. I think de Gaulle would like to pardon him, but will be afraid of the Resistance movements. To them Pucheu is a double-dyed traitor.[2]

4.30–6 p.m. Reinhardt (who is still delegating for Murphy) came to talk to me about Italy. Reinhardt is clever and loyal – I like him very much. He does not conceal from us the information which he gets from Washington, and the divergence between what the President would like and the Prime Minister insists upon. But, quite apart from

[1] Michael Baillie (b. 1897) was a lieutenant in the Scots Guards.

[2] Pucheu was shot on 20 March.

the internal problems of Italy, we have just had a telegram indicating that the Russians are contemplating a move to appoint an ambassador in Naples and accept an Italian representative in Moscow.

I have reported this at once to London and asked for instructions. But the Russians are lying low and telling us nothing.

7 p.m. I went to see Bogomolov. I dined alone with him (only Mme Bogomolov, in a very smart black silk dress and white silk shirt – also diamond earrings). I could get nothing out of Bogomolov. He is a furtive and unpleasant man – not an open and genial rascal, like Vyshinsky. I threw several flies at him, but he rose to none.

Saturday, 11 March 1944

The Russian rumours are confirmed by Mason-MacFarlane. But I can get no instructions. I suppose they do not like an open row with Moscow, but I wish we could be told to give some definite orders to the Italians.

10.30 a.m. Messrs Harman (British) and Russell Barnes (U.S.) – the Psychological Warfare (or Political Warfare) chiefs. They are in a great state of alarm because General Devers (American deputy to Wilson and commander of American troops in the 'theater') has cut their establishment by 50 per cent. After a lot of talk (although I secretly rather sympathise with Devers) I agreed to write a paper for the Allied C.-in-C. asking for a review of the situation.

11.30 a.m. General Wilson called to see me, to discuss:

(*a*) Russian intrigues in Italy – including their request for an air base at Bari. The excuse for this is to allow them to fly to and from their mission to Tito.

(*b*) The effect of the Pucheu trial on the French forces. I do not myself think there will be much reaction.

If they begin to try sailors and soldiers it will be another matter. Even then, there is a pretty strong case against Admiral Derrien – who helped the Germans at Bizerta.

6 p.m. M. Guérin (of the French Foreign Office) called – chiefly to pay his respects on behalf of M. Massigli (who is away in Rabat).

Sunday, 12 March 1944

A very nice day. Maud, Roger and I went for a long drive and walk combined. We started at 11 a.m. and got back at 6 p.m. I think Maud enjoyed it very much. She certainly found a wonderful number of wild flowers. I took her to Cherchel (an old Roman city) and to Tipasa (an old favourite).

Monday, 13 March 1944

The telegrams are now pouring in about the Russian move in Italy. General Wilson came in the morning to discuss it. At 12.45 Bogomolov came to tell me of the Russian decision. I solemnly expressed surprise – pained surprise – but said that I could not believe that Moscow was acting independently and had no doubt arranged it all with London and Washington but had forgotten to tell him so! Bogomolov (keeping as always his eyes on the ground or squinting sideways) said he had no information.

There is nothing that I can do. I asked Bogomolov if there was to be any announcement in the press. He would give me no guarantee. Of course they have been very clever and have bullied the Italians into announcing it first and will publish their own communiqué a day later.

1.15 p.m. Cadbury (food expert – whom I used to know in connection with cocoa on my West African Produce Board) and Gridley (British head of N.A.E.B.) to lunch. Also an American economist – Lieutenant-Commander Darlington.

A meeting followed in my house, with these three and Generals George Clark and Dick Lewis (A.F.H.Q. Supply) to discuss the co-ordination of supply and production and the economic structure generally in the Mediterranean area. A very long meeting and a very difficult subject. But we made some progress.

6 p.m. Duff Cooper and General Wilson called together, for further talk (*a*) on the French situation as a result of the trial; (*b*) an agreement to be signed – supplementary to the one which Eisenhower and I made with de Gaulle for the Mediterranean theatre – regarding the use of French Army and Navy in all theatres. This will present some – but I think not insuperable – difficulties.

General Gepp (War Office), Mr Dean (F.O.) to dinner.[3] Also Colonel Phillimore.[4] They have come out about the Italian prisoners-of-war agreement.

Tuesday, 14 March 1944

An idle morning. John and I drove out a few miles and then had a good walk for nearly two hours. It did me good.

I have no letters or telegram from you, but I could hardly expect that yet. The trouble is that I am leaving on Thursday for Italy and then to Cairo.

1.30 p.m. Lunched alone with Massigli. He was charming (as ever) and not so excited as usual. We talked over Italian affairs and I told him about the Russians. The French are naturally very anti-Italian and correspondingly suspicious of anything affecting the status of the Italian Government.

4 p.m. Political conference. General Wilson, General Gammell, Admiral Dundas (representing C.-in-C. Med.), Sir John Slessor (Air),

[3] Major-General Cyril Gepp (1879–1964) was Director of Prisoners of War, War Office, 1941–5. Patrick Dean (b. 1909) was Assistant Legal Adviser, Foreign Office, 1939–45.

[4] Lieutenant-Colonel Henry Phillimore (1910–74) was Assistant Adjutant General, 1943–5, Junior Counsel at the Nuremberg trials, 1945–6, Judge of the High Court of Justice, 1959–68, Lord Justice of Appeal, 1968–74.

Kit Steel (from Cairo), Reinhardt (representing Murphy) and H.M. Roger Makins and Reinhardt did the minutes. Arthur Forbes (who has somehow got himself partly on to my staff and partly on to Slessor's) helped.

A very good meeting – covering a great range. Bulgaria, Roumania, Tito, P.W.B. (Harman and Barnes), French trials, etc., etc.

Most important of all, I have now persuaded Wilson and Gammell to organise a proper secretariat (on more or less Defence Ministry lines – as run by General Ismay for the P.M.). We have got Colonel Lascelles from Cairo (who has been secretary of Defence Committee there) and he will start with us on 1 April. I will put my John Addis with the secretariat, which will also have representatives of the American Minister (Murphy's office), the Navy, the Air, etc. If we can get this properly established, we shall get some order into this, at present, very haphazard and amateurish show.

7 p.m. After this long conference, I had to receive M. Smilganić, representative of the Royal Yugoslav Government on the Italian Advisory Committee. M. Smilganić is a bore and a long-winded bore.

Wednesday, 15 March 1944

9 a.m. General Gammell and Colonel Lascelles (from Cairo) called to fix up the final details for the War Secretariat. Lascelles goes to London today, to have a little leave and get some staff.

11.30 a.m. Advisory Council for Italy – a truly formidable affair and the first meeting we have had when there has been a sense of reality. It was my turn to act as chairman, and I insisted on calling the meeting. Both Reinhardt and I had pretty stiff instructions and some nasty questions to ask Bogomolov. We beat him up for one-and-a-half hours and got at least some satisfaction. At first he said that he had no instructions and could not discuss the Russian diplomatic arrangements with Italy. Then – under pressure – he gave us his own view. He pretended (which is quite untrue) that the initiative came from the Italians. Then he said it was a very small affair (like the housemaid's baby – illegitimate but small) and that there would be no interchange of accredited ambassadors or ministers, but only agents. It was quite good sport, but will of course have no effect. Bogomolov came *alone* to the meeting. This was significant, as they usually bring six or seven attendants and interpreters. He also asked that no record of what he had said should be put in the minutes. I suppose he is afraid of being shot for disobeying his orders, which were obviously to say nothing at all. Reinhardt and I said indignantly that we must insist on the minutes recording what we had said. He had the usual right to correct the draft minutes as regards what he said. In order to impress further on him what we said, we undertook to give him the same afternoon an *aide-mémoire* in writing, which he could telegraph to Moscow.

After all this, we thoroughly enjoyed our luncheon.

Most of the afternoon was spent writing despatches and telegrams, and accounts of this morning's doings.

General Budget Lloyd and Tim Nugent turned up for luncheon. They were in great form.

I expect you will remember Mrs G. coming to see me at Stockton. She telephoned and wrote to me again before I left London. Apparently that silly fat husband of hers has fallen in love with a French nurse. He is thoroughly entangled, and I have got to disentangle him. It's a great bore – because he was a *very* bad agent and I should prefer to see him settle down in Algiers than return to Stockton, if I only thought of my own interest. But I suppose I must try to do something. I feel sorry for her and the three children.

Anyway I saw his chief tonight – a very nice officer called Brigadier [A. T.] de Rhé-Philipe. And we are trying to take some action – perhaps to get him posted elsewhere.

Quite a nice dinner-party tonight – Maud, Diana Cooper, General and Mrs Vanier, Air Marshal Sir John Slessor, Steel, General Catroux. I had not seen Catroux for some time. I thought him much aged and in low spirits (which is odd, considering that Mme la Générale is away in Italy) but he was as charming as ever.

Thursday, 16 March 1944

Roger, John, Reinhardt and I left for Naples by plane at 10 a.m. We also took Maud with us. She was going to stay with General Robertson. We were to stay at the villa which has been allocated to me, as British member of the Advisory Council. I shall give it over to Sir Noel Charles[5] when he comes out to take this job and to be permanently stationed as High Commissioner in Italy. The P.M. is annoyed with Mason-MacFarlane – whom he thinks weak. The F.O., of course, want their own man (Charles is a professional diplomat). I do not mind, as I think anyway my job is an impossible one and the more ambassadors, etc., I have to manage the merrier. I already have Duff Cooper, [Ralph] Stevenson (Yugoslavia), Leeper (Greece), Steel (F.O. chap for Roumania, Bulgaria, etc.). Now I shall have Charles (for Italy). Nevertheless, I expect there will still be something to do, because all the generals hate the Foreign Office men and distrust them profoundly. So I have no doubt there will be quite an amusing task in reconciling them and getting some reasonable decisions made.

We had a good flight, except that our radio went wrong and we had to put in at Tunis on the way and wait an hour there.

The R.A.F. have been stimulated by a terrific telegram from the P.M. and have produced a good machine (a Lockheed Lodestar) with six comfortable seats.

We got to Naples at about 5.30 p.m. and went straight to General

[5] Sir Noel Charles (1891–1975) was High Commissioner in Italy with the rank of Ambassador, 1944–7.

MacFarlane's H.Q. A long conference (Harold Caccia, Reber, Makins, Captain Ellery Stone (U.S.) etc.) followed by dinner and more talk at General Mason-MacFarlane's villa. Bed at 11 p.m.; rather a tiring day.

Friday, 17 March 1944

Our villa is quite pleasant – clean, not much furniture but nothing too ugly – with bath and hot water. Mr Garnett[6] (a consul, whom I sent over with two cypher clerks some weeks ago) has done a good job. We have good Italian servants, good cooking, and good wine.

Harold Caccia spent the whole morning with me, pouring out his views and his woes. He is in good form, however – much better than he was at Brindisi, where the foul conditions and bad weather rather got him down.

In the afternoon, I saw Mr Grady's man (the American in charge of supply and economic questions in the Control Commission – Grady himself has gone on a visit to Washington) and had also a long talk with Captain Stone (MacFarlane's second-in-command).

The economic situation is gradually improving, in spite of immense difficulties. Sicily is almost normal, prices falling steadily as the Allied troops move away. The Control Commission have got a hundred lorries out of the Army for transport of food in southern Italy; and as the bridges gradually get mended and the roads improved, transportation (which is the key to the food problem) becomes available and helps to deal with black market prices.

People do not realise that one of the main reasons for the black market is lack of transport. Peasants trudge twenty or thirty miles with their produce to the towns, and it is not unnatural that they should sell their produce to the black market operators at a price which recoups them for their toil and sweat, instead of in the ordinary market at the controlled price.

The other support of the black market is the stealing of Allied goods from the docks and warehouses. This has reached alarming proportions lately in the Naples area, and suggests that some British and/or American officers are in the racket in a big way. We have got a Scotland Yard chap on the job, and one or two minor offenders have been caught. I do not think the authorities are quite to the bottom of the trouble, but they hope for a big clean-up of both Allied and Italian rogues in a short time.

Of course, you always get some loss at docks through pilfering and petty thieving. Badly disciplined troops make ineffective guards. But the percentage of loss has recently been running at such a high figure as to suggest deliberate and large-scale swindling. Also, of course, individual soldiers will sell their tinned milk, cigarettes, chocolate ration, etc. And all this comes on to the black market. And the

[6] Bernard Garnett (b. 1913), who had been Vice-Consul, Algiers, since May 1943, reopened the Consulate at Naples.

purchasing power to pay these high prices is also provided by the troops, who buy silk stockings, watches, jewellery, as well as less desirable pleasures at inflated rates. Altogether the economics of invading armies are very complicated! It is interesting to see the North African experiences repeated.

Apart from these questions, I am afraid there is a good deal of difference of opinion here between the American view of the Italian political situation and that so strongly held by the P.M. I think myself that the truth lies somewhere between these extremes. But I am much distressed to see a worsening of Anglo-American relations generally (since Eisenhower left) and I am also not very hopeful of getting any new idea into the P.M.'s mind at present.

4.30 p.m. Conference on the new prisoners-of-war agreement and how to present it to Italians.

6–7 p.m. Talk with General Mason-MacFarlane. He is very pleasant to me always, but his political judgment is (I think) not too good. He is too earnest and too restless.

We all dined in a sort of officers' club – a large party of young men and others. I was the sort of old buffer among them all, but they were very kind to me – particularly an American colonel who told splendid Southern stories.

Saturday, 18 March 1944

Sam Reber talked to me most of the morning. He likes getting things off his chest. I appreciate and admire his intelligence and his good faith. And he is a good friend to us also. He is in a difficult position, knowing the views of the State Department and the President do not really agree with those of the F.O. and the P.M.

After seeing Sam, I had an interesting talk with a Mr [T. A. E.] Nalder (Ministry of Food). He did good work in Malta for us during the siege and I knew him in North Africa. He will be very-useful in Italy. He has been loaned to A.C.C. for a few months.

Brigadier Maurice Lush (originally of AMGOT, now running the AMGOT areas under MacFarlane) and Colonel Charles Poletti (who is running the city of Naples) to lunch at the villa.

I think I have already described these two. Lush is a splendid example of a good colonial administrator (Sudan Civil Service) with a good record in the last war. Poletti (who was at Palermo with AMGOT) is Deputy Governor of New York State. He is pure Sicilian, pure American, and pure Tammany Hall. A most amusing luncheon!

I spent the afternoon trying to summarise my impressions with a view to sending a report to P.M. [see pp. 394–6].

It is no good trying to do it by telegram, because it is impossible in a short space to introduce any new idea to him with sufficient tact to prevent his exploding.

I am not quite sure what I shall do, but it is a help to get something down on paper. I wrote it out with my own hand, as I have not my invaluable Miss Campbell.

5 p.m. Admiral Morse (an old friend from Algiers, where he commanded the port) came to call. He has been in charge of the port of Naples since the start. He has done a fine job. There are now *more* berths working than before the war, although the Germans destroyed all but two. Naples last month did a bigger traffic than the port of New York!

5.30 p.m. Left the villa – motored to Caserta, where I found General Wilson (arrived from Algiers). He showed me a number of recent telegrams, including the President–P.M. series (latest on Italy).

There were also brought to me some rather odd telegrams from the P.M.

After a talk with Wilson, I went to dine with General Alex whom I found as charming and as friendly as ever. After dinner, we went to sit in his train and 'gossiped' for a long time about Italy, Russia, England and so on. I think he likes a talk with somebody outside the purely military world in which he lives. He is certainly always anxious to see me and pressing me to return.

We motored back to Naples, getting back about 11.30 p.m. Vesuvius (of which we get a splendid view from our villa – across the Bay of Naples) was in full eruption, great flames shooting out, and hot lava running in two red-hot streams down the mountain side. It was clearly a fairly large eruption, and I kept getting up during the night to watch it.[7] All the sea was glowing red in the reflection of the lava and flames from the cone of the volcano.

Sunday, 19 March 1974

Roger, John Wyndham and I left by car. We motored to General Oliver Leese's H.Q. He is the new commander of the Eighth Army. He is a very nice fellow, a big, burly, efficient solid Guardsman. It was a beautiful spring day and the sun and the snow-covered mountains made it a very lovely drive. We passed through the town of Venafro and found further on the general's advanced H.Q. – being a tent or two, a hut or two, and some caravans in an olive grove.

General Anderson (who used to command our First Army in Tunisia) was there. (He is on a visit here. I like him very much and always got on with him in North Africa, but he has many enemies and is now relegated to Eastern Command.)

Oliver Leese was interested in the Polish problem (he has two Polish divisions in his Army) and I had some stuff to tell him about the

[7] It was the most severe volcanic eruption of Mount Vesuvius since 1906. A third stream of molten lava, almost a quarter of a mile wide and thirty feet high, flowed north-west and engulfed two villages.

present situation – which as you know is pretty unsatisfactory.[8] I shall probably come back again later and let General Anders[9] (the Polish general) talk to me, which will at least take some burden off General Leese.

After lunch, we listened to the Irish Guards band. Then we took two 'jeeps' and went up the valley to look at the Monte Cassino battle. We got up to a point about five or six miles from the mountain, and got a very good view of the battle. It is tough going for our men, through horribly difficult country. But they are doing splendidly, so far as morale and determination go, against a very tough enemy. The Germans are fighting with extraordinary courage and desperate determination also.

We finally got back to Naples about eight o'clock in the evening, after a splendid day. I love to get nearer to the armies and drive along the crowded roads and see the troops. If I resign my present job, I think I shall try to become a war correspondent.

Sam Reber and Harold came to dinner. They left early and we wrote telegrams and memoranda till midnight – occasionally stopping to have a look at Vesuvius, which is still erupting with some energy.

Monday, 20 March 1944

Left Naples at 8 a.m. by air. We are travelling (Roger, John and I) this time with General Wilson. He has only his personal assistant, Colonel Mark Chapman-Walker, with him. It is a comfortable aeroplane – a C47 with seats – and we have sent ours back to Algiers with some of General Wilson's people. We stopped at Malta for half an hour to refuel and get the weather. We took about two-and-a-half hours from Naples to Malta, flying past Stromboli and Mount Etna – the latter splendid in its mantle of snow.

Lord Gort came to the airfield and we had a pleasant chat with him. I am just finishing writing up these pages – it is 1.30 and we hope to be in Cairo tonight. One certainly gets around in this queer life which I lead.

I have finished *David Copperfield*, which I brought back from England with me. It is a noble and wonderful book – I think my favourite Dickens. I read *Pickwick* while at home. I am now embarked on Boswell's *Life of Johnson* – just the thing for air travel.

We arrived at Cairo at about 6 p.m. (our time) and 7 p.m. Cairo time – rather a long journey but a very comfortable aeroplane made it less tiring than it might have been. We were met, and General Wilson went to stay with General Paget, while Roger, John and I were taken to the Mena House Villa, near the pyramids. This extremely luxurious

[8] There was already serious animosity between the Russian and Polish Governments about the question of Poland's post-war frontier; and the Poles feared for their independence.

[9] Lieutenant-General Wladyslaw Anders (1892–1970), commander of the two Polish divisions in the Eighth Army, was commanding a calvalry brigade when Germany attacked Poland in 1939; he was interned in Lubianka jail by the Russians until 1941.

residence belongs to the millionaire Chester Beatty. Casey occupied it as Minister of State, and I stayed here a year ago when I came from Algiers about Force X (that time I had my face in bandages). Then the P.M. had it during the Cairo conference. Now Lord Moyne has taken it and uses it as a guest-house. He has another large house in Cairo itself.

After bath, etc., dinner. Lord Moyne, Sir W. Croft (his chief official), Colonel Curran (Secretary to Middle East Defence Committee). We talked over a large number of questions, preparatory to formal meetings tomorrow. I confess to have been very sleepy at the end and glad to get into my comfortable bed at midnight.

Tuesday, 21 March 1944

Left Mena House at 8.45 a.m. and attended a meeting at G.H.Q. at 9.15. Generals Paget, Wilson and various other generals, admirals, air vice-marshals, etc. Lord Moyne was also there. It was a great array of talent and quite an interesting review of the general position in the Middle East theatre.

11 a.m. Commander Jackson – an old friend, who runs the Middle East Supply Centre – called to see me. I have been given a room in Lord Moyne's office. We had a very useful talk on Balkan relief questions, which have got to be planned in Cairo, but under my general supervision and General Wilson's authority. How I am to carry this out is a bit of a problem!

12 noon. Brigadier Smith-Dorrien[10] – on Balkan relief plans from the Army point of view.

12.30 p.m. Mr Leeper – British Ambassador to the Greek Government.

Lunch with Lord Moyne, followed by the Cairo siesta.

4.30 p.m. Mr Broad[11] – Counsellor to the British Embassy to the Yugoslav Government. As the Yugoslav King and Prime Minister have gone to London and as the Royal Government is anyway a shadowy sort of affair, with scarcely any authority except perhaps in old Serbia, Mr Broad – a clever, amusing man – finds himself in a somewhat delicate position.

I think I shall try to get Broad moved to my staff and, either from Bari or Algiers, to give me information on Yugoslavia. Since the operational control of all efforts to help Tito is coming directly under A.F.H.Q. instead of under Cairo, I must be in a position to give political guidance to General Wilson. So, if I can get Broad, it will be a help.

5.30–7.30 p.m. Very interesting meeting at G.H.Q. on present

[10] Brigadier Peter Smith-Dorrien (1907–46) was Chief Political Adviser to B.M.L. in Cairo, 1943–4, and to General Scobie in Greece, 1944–5, and was later killed in the bomb explosion at the King David Hotel, Jerusalem.

[11] Philip Broad (1903–66) was Political Adviser to A.F.H.Q. at Bari, 1944–6.

position in Roumania, Hungary and Bulgaria. A number of communications from our agents there, as well as a direct one from Antonescu.[12] The appropriate replies – in most cases bombing attacks – were agreed.

We also discussed the whole organisation as between Generals Wilson and Paget and Lord Moyne and myself, and came to a working arrangement which I hope will succeed. There are great difficulties owing to the distance, and I think it will mean frequent personal visits between the two H.Q.s.

8.30 p.m. Dinner with General Paget. A galaxy of generals, admirals, air marshals, etc., etc.

Wednesday, 22 March 1944

10 a.m. Further meeting at G.H.Q.

12–1.30 p.m. Telegrams from London and replies to be composed. A new crisis is brewing up in Italy.

1.30 p.m. I have a small luncheon – Mr Leeper (British Ambassador to the Greeks), Mr MacVeagh (American Ambassador to the Greeks and the Yugoslavs), Mr Broad (Counsellor to British Ambassador to Yugoslavs) and Roger.

Mr MacVeagh is a charming American – oldish, good-looking, old-fashioned (with a turn-down collar and a black tie) and cultivated. Incidentally, he was a publisher until ten years ago, being managing director of a firm called Holt.

6 p.m. Owen (Ministry of Economic Warfare) to discuss new arrangements arising out of the Mediterranean command. Like all the rest, they are terribly frightened that they will be rooted out of Cairo.

8 p.m. Dinner with Shone, Minister at Cairo. A very pleasant men's party – mostly diplomatic – one or two soldiers.

Thursday, 23 March 1944

10.30 a.m. Generals Hughes and Smith-Dorrien, together with Mr Leeper, on Balkan relief planning. This is supposed to come under me now, and is a terribly difficult problem. We worked out a fairly satisfactory organisational scheme. Commander Jackson (of Middle East Supply Centre – an excellent man) also came to the conference. Day-to-day work will be done by a committee in Cairo – higher direction from Algiers.

I have finished my memorandum on Italy for the P.M. and Anthony and sent it off by bag [see p. 394].

11.15 a.m. Paddy Beaumont-Nesbitt (now a major general) to see me. He is to be the chief liaison officer for the Mediterranean. As there are French, Greeks, Belgians, Poles, Italians, Brazilians, to be dealt

[12] Marshal Ion Antonescu (1882–1946), Roumanian dictator, 1940–4, had signed the Axis pact but since the battle of Stalingrad in 1943 had been anxious to withdraw.

with (to name the first that occur to me) this is quite an important job and needs very careful co-ordination with my office.

I have just received a message that Murphy is *not* returning here. This is unofficial, but I have always thought we should not see him again. He is said to have got himself a job as liaison between the State Department and the White House. I can imagine no worse choice. He is a pleasant enough creature and amenable to kind and firm treatment. But he has neither principles nor judgment.

12 noon. General [Montagu] Brocas Burrows to see me, on his way to Russia, where he is to be head of the British Military Mission in succession to General Martel. I have known him since Eton and Oxford in a desultory kind of way. He is (for an athlete of distinction) not unintelligent. And at least he can speak Russian. He was Military Attaché in Rome till 1940 and had some interesting facts and superficial views to impart to me.

1.15 p.m. Luncheon at the British Embassy with Lord Killearn – a very small party and an interesting talk with a man of considerable personality – strong, unscrupulous and entertaining. He has served our interests well in Egypt and plays the Government against the King and the King against the Government very satisfactorily. Meanwhile King and Government and all the Pasha class get richer and richer, while the people got poorer and poorer. In no country in the world (I should say) are the extremes of wealth and poverty, luxury and misery, so great.

5 p.m. Brigadier Jeffries (Political Warfare) and Mr Murray.[13] The same reorganisation problem and the same clam-like determination to stick to Cairo and their jobs.

5.30 p.m. A final meeting of the 'big-wigs' to tie up all the conclusions reached. Lord Moyne in the chair, charming and ineffective as ever; General Wilson, humorous and sly; General Paget, espicopal and sound; Admiral Rawlings,[14] a talkative and enthusiastic representative of the silent service; Air Marshal Slessor, concise, firm, hitting every nail on the head – the most impressive of the lot.

At 8.30 we all went to a great farewell dinner given by Lord Moyne. Just before dinner some very urgent telegrams arrived for me, so I had to deal with them and be late. Italy (Mason-MacFarlane's weakness and Bogomolov's intrigues) is on the boil again and I have a message from the Secretary of State asking me to go there at once. It will really be a relief when Sir Noel Charles arrives – at present I have no one there whom I can trust. MacFarlane is not, of course, under my orders (being head of the Anglo-American and military organisation), and Harold Caccia (although a diplomat) is actually part of MacFarlane's machine.

[13] Brigadier W. F. Jeffries (1891–1969) was head of Intelligence, P.W.E. Cairo, 1943–4, and C.A.O., P.W.B., 1944–5. Ralph Murray (1908–1983) was a former B.B.C. official attached to P.W.E.; he was H.M. Ambassador to Greece, 1962–7.

[14] Vice-Admiral Bernard Rawlings (1889–1962), was F.O.L.E.M., 1943–4.

Note on the Italian situation

The unilateral diplomatic action by the Soviet Government has certainly increased our difficulties in Italy. Although for the time being it may appear to strengthen the hand of the King and Badoglio, yet the very fact that the Junta's[15] cohesion has been weakened, will in the long run favour the radical and subversive elements. . . .

If facilities for the Soviet Air Force in Italy are granted – and if the gradual permeation of Italy by Russian influence continues, the parties of the left are bound to gain from the increasingly strong position which the Russians are building up, based on a combination of admiration, respect and fear. The Italians have already been given mysteriously to understand that there are more plums in the Russian cake for them. What these are can only be conjectured, but they may include a recognition of alliance instead of co-belligerence or a guarantee of Italy's eastern frontiers.

At the same time, the bad faith shown by the Russians, equally aggravating to British and American opinion, should serve to consolidate the Anglo-American alliance. It has been apparent that this has been – as regards Italian policy – in danger of drifting apart. Intelligent observers, like Mr Reber of the State Department, are aware of it. I think our reply should certainly not be to follow the Russian example, by appointing ambassadors in Italy and accepting Italian agents in London and Washington. On the contrary, we should increase the emphasis on the Allied Control Commission as the only instrument upon which we are prepared to rely in our dealings with the Italian Government. We should not, I submit, retire from or seek to abolish the Advisory Council. But I think we should see to it that the British and American representatives on the Advisory Council are absolutely loyal to each other and to the head of the Allied Control Commission. They should stand in the same relation to General Mason-MacFarlane as Murphy and I have been first to General Eisenhower, and now to General Wilson. Their primary duty is to advise the Deputy President and strengthen his position. Anything that tends to weaken his authority is playing straight into Russian hands. I think it is desirable that Sir Noel Charles should not come until his American counterpart is ready to arrive or has at least been appointed. The Americans are already very sensitive as to their position in the Mediterranean since the departure of General Eisenhower. The Russian game is, I am convinced, to try to drive a wedge between us and the Americans. And we must take account of the many minor causes for irritation and difficulty between our forces which inevitably result from a protracted campaign under present conditions.

If, however, Charles and a suitable American colleague arrive more

[15] The executive committee of representatives of the six democratic parties which was established after the Bari congress in January 1944.

or less simultaneously; if their instructions are to act as sort of resident High Commissioners to advise and assist General MacFarlane; if they can work together and obtain both each other's confidence and the general's, then I think they can play a most useful role in checking a certain tendency to exaggeration and restlessness which I observe here in dealing with purely political, as opposed to administrative, problems. They can gradually take over, by their joint action, the work of the present political section (Messrs Caccia and Reber), who should only stay long enough after their arrival to make the transfer practicable.

But their purpose must be to build up, not undermine, the position of the Deputy President of the Allied Control Commission. They must do so both in reality and in appearance. The importance of the military character of the ultimate controlling authority must be emphasised, deriving from General Alexander and General Wilson, and representing the conquering power of the British and American Armies. It is this conception which makes the only realistic and satisfactory reply to the Soviet manoeuvres and intrigues. . . .

My memorandum then went on to discuss Churchill's policy, put forward to the House of Commons on 22 February, of 'No change until Rome'. But the gulf between the Junta and the King had narrowed. The King had suggested he should announce his intention to retire from public life after the capture of Rome, and to appoint his son Lieutenant-General of the Realm until such time, after the war, when a constitutional assembly could be convened and the whole question of the monarchy settled. This plan would probably be acceptable to Sforza and to the parties of the centre and right, and possibly to those of the left. The way would then be open for a coalition government. I therefore suggested that we should bring the two sides together and leave them to negotiate.

Note on the Italian situation

The advantages of a settlement now are clear. First, it would give us some internal stability until the end of the war and the calling of the National Convention. Secondly, it would dispose in the comparative calm of present political conditions a problem which we shall have to face sooner or later. Thirdly, it would probably result in a more favourable arrangement for the monarchy than may be obtainable later, especially when the weight of opinion of the northern industrial cities begins to make itself felt. Fourthly, it would ease Anglo-American relations in this affair. Fifthly, if we can settle matters now, before the full force of Soviet influence and intrigue has reached its zenith, it will be an advantage. For although Bogomolov and General Solodovnik[16] and the large Russian delegation are in constant

[16] General Solodovnik was the Soviet representative on the Allied Control Commission for Italy.

collaboration with the Communist organisations here (which they finance and largely control) yet, for the moment, their apparently cynical support of the King and Badoglio has temporarily strengthened the latter and somewhat baffled all but the more hard-bitten and disciplined members of the Communist party in Italy.

Finally if we maintain our attitude of no political change or development before Rome, we shall be giving greater latitude of manoeuvre to the Russians. They will certainly continue to seek advantage at our expense by representing us as repressing the free development of political life in Italy.

It is therefore perhaps, in the somewhat changed circumstances resulting from the Russian *démarche*, worth considering the advisability of making a reply to the Junta and to the King on the lines which I have suggested.

The King could be told that we see no objection to his plan as the basis of a solution of the political controversy, and the Parties could be told that we understand that the King is ready to discuss a plan of his own with them and that we see no objection to such a discussion.

But we should emphasize that this must be a purely Italian affair; that the responsibility for reaching a solution rests primarily on Italian shoulders; and that meanwhile we can tolerate nothing that impedes the administration of southern Italy and the conduct of the war.

Friday, 24 March 1944

12.30 a.m. Left 'Cairo West' in General Wilson's plane.

8 a.m. Arrived Tripoli and breakfasted.

It is now about twelve noon and I am writing this in the plane. We have just passed Tunis – so we are well on our way. It is rather 'bumpy' but the seats are comfortable and it is very luxurious in comparison to many of my trips.

I expect I shall have letters from England when I get to Algiers. Anyway, I shall try to answer everything this afternoon. I fear I must be off again tomorrow morning.

3 p.m. We have just arrived at the villa, have landed safely.

PS. I met a young man called Hughes Onslow in Cairo who had just arrived who told me he had seen Maurice and Katharine a day or two ago looking very well.

[*Enclosure*] *Italy*

What strikes me from recent telegrams, including General Wilson's, is the degree to which the Junta have climbed down. No more talk of Sforza and Croce's baby, the Regency, no more refusal to accept Umberto, and no real demand for forcible abdication of the King. The Allies are relied on to use moral persuasion. This is really a great advance, and I think means that the politicians south of the line are very anxious to get everything settled and themselves clearly in office before competitors arise from Rome.

And what if the King refuses to abdicate and the Crown Prince declines to delegate Royal powers? It is not at all clear how far this point has been considered in Naples.

23 February 1944 H.M.

Copy sent to Foreign Secretary and Sir Orme Sargent[17] on 23.2.1944.

I succeeded in seeing a good many people here during the evening, and I called upon General Wilson after dinner to explain to him the latest position regarding the Russian–Italian developments.

Saturday, 25 March 1944

Left in the Commander-in-Chief's aeroplane for Italy, taking with me Roger Makins and John Wyndham. Mr Harman (P.W.B.) and another of his officials also came with us. We reached Naples after rather a rough trip at about 3.30 in the afternoon. The last 100 miles flying was very curious. We dropped from 7,000 feet to about 100 feet and were just over the water underneath a thick cloud of smoke which was blowing out to sea from Vesuvius. The last 100 miles was almost completely obscured by this immense pall – a very strange phenomenon. The volcano had in fact somewhat reduced its activities, that is to say, there were no longer so many flames or rocks being thrown into the air, but there was an immense belching-forth of smoke of a thick oily character like a factory chimney in the North of England. The smoke practically obscures the whole Bay of Naples. In fact the wind has been very strong away from the town so that most of the ash has fallen on the villages either south of the volcano or right away as far as Sorrento. When the wind one day changed to the west some of the ash was carried as far as Bari right across the Apennines on the Adriatic coast.

On arrival I went at once to see General MacFarlane. I found him as usual rather low, and Sam Reber, who has become a regular Mrs Gummidge, added to the general sense of depression. I really do not know what is to be done about these people. I tried to chaff them, but they do not take it very well. Reber is of course in a difficult position as the American Government more or less seem to have lost interest and he is the only American official. Murphy has not yet returned,[18] Ambassador Wilson is absent, and no American of high diplomatic rank seems to be yet available for Italy. When Noel Charles comes this position will become very awkward, and I am glad to hear that on my recommendation H.M.G. are postponing Noel Charles's official

[17] Sir Orme Sargent (1884–1962) was Deputy Under-Secretary of State at the Foreign Office; he was Permanent Under-Secretary, 1946–9.

[18] Murphy had decided that he would after all resume his duties in the Mediterranean.

appointment until the announcement of some corresponding American diplomat with ambassadorial rank can be made.

MacFarlane informed me that he had seen Badoglio and told him verbally that he was to enter into no new arrangements with the Russians or any other country without the permission of the Control Commission, but when I pressed him I felt not too happy about the terms of this communication. From my own experience I know how easy it is for Englishmen to avoid the unpleasant task of making difficult communications and leave the foreign listener in some doubt as to the real importance which we attach to what we are told to say. I therefore persuaded MacFarlane to follow up his verbal interview with a very stiff formal note. There was, however, some difficulty in doing this as Reber protested that the Americans had had no instructions. Fortunately, in the course of the evening or early the next morning the instructions arrived, I am bound to say through Foreign Office sources telegraphed to my office in Algiers, but that is just because the State Department are always so slow in sending their messages. In any case MacFarlane sent the communication, which was a great relief to my mind.

Sunday, 26 March 1944

I called to see Bogomolov; it was really a very amusing interview.[19] There is something so comical about these Soviet professors sitting amongst the exaggeratedly Neapolitan furniture of the eighteenth century – little gilt chairs, imitation Louis Seize, with embroidered covers and cushions and lots of little miniatures in china in a rather delicately decorated lady's boudoir. Bogomolov is a professor of philosophy turned diplomat. He is not altogether unattractive but he has none of Vyshinsky's charm. Bogomolov is naturally shifty: Vyshinsky naturally frank. Vyshinsky would laugh with you and stand you a good dinner and drink vodka with you, and then pull out a revolver and shoot you quietly through the back of the head. Bogomolov would entertain you to a series of rather dreary repasts where you would be slowly poisoned in indifferent French wine.

Joyce Grenfell and her pianist friend came to lunch. They are just finishing with Italy and going off to Cairo, thence to Baghdad and India. After lunch I went for a walk by myself for a couple of hours which did me a lot of good.

At 5 p.m. Harold Caccia and Sam Reber came up. Sam had been to see Badoglio and had come back very cheerful. Badoglio protested that he knew of no fresh arrangements suggested by the Russians or anyone else, but he argued a good deal about the prisoners-of-war agreement. I think we shall find it difficult to get this through, especially if those

[19] About the exchange of diplomatic agents. Bogolomov tried to play the whole thing down, and said that the Soviet representative would be under the orders of Vyshinsky as member of the Advisory Council.

who represent the other side argue with so little enthusiasm in favour of it. Actually it is a very fair arrangement which will immensely benefit the Italian men themselves.

At seven o'clock I left by car for Caserta and dined there with General Alexander, who was, I thought, in very good form. Naturally the Cassino battle has been a disappointment to some extent, but General Alexander thrives on disappointments.[20] He is never downcast but is merely led by temporary failure to study more deeply and carefully the means of obtaining success in the future. He is an extraordinarily balanced character, drawing its strength from a combination of modesty, disinterestedness, a remarkable grasp of main principles, and a deep religious faith. Each time I see him I find him more attractive.

Monday, 27 March 1944

After a rather desultory morning dealing with ordinary telegrams, etc., I drove with General MacFarlane to Salerno and got there about 12.45. Here we found a luncheon party consisting of General MacFarlane, Captain Ellery Stone, U.S.N.R. (MacFarlane's second-in-command), Reber, Caccia, Marshal Badoglio and Signor Prunas, Permanent Head of the Italian Foreign Office. It was really a very ridiculous scene, because such is the skill of Italians that they have reduced these poor English and American soldiers and diplomats to a state of intellectual subjection. Badoglio himself, who looks a stupid old man, a sort of Giraud or Georges, is in fact an extremely clever and intelligent diplomatist. He seems to twist our people round his little finger. He made a remarkably able speech, which was received with the same kind of cheerful approbation as Mrs Weller and her friends gave to the orations of Mr Stiggins. I felt very much like Mr Weller Senior in having to apply the check, feeling that I was behaving rather like a cad in counter-attacking. However, I think it was a good thing, and when I got back that night General MacFarlane told me that he had every hope that the Marshal would sign the prisoners-of-war agreement. Roger takes a less optimistic view. He thinks that if I had stayed another day or two we could have got it through.

I arrived back at my house at Naples about 5.30 and the rest of the evening was taken up in talking to Mr Dean of the Foreign Office Legal Department, who has come out to try and get the prisoners-of-war agreement settled, and composing telegrams home. Harold Caccia and Dean stayed to dinner.

Tuesday, 28 March 1944

Left our villa at 6 a.m. We motored to the Pomigliano airfield about

20 The Anzio beachhead had difficulty in getting established. A German counter-attack on 16–19 February was repulsed, but both sides had settled down to a siege. Cassino was still in enemy hands, and the Gustav Line not seriously breached.

twelve miles out of Naples, and took off at 7 a.m. making a great sweep round Vesuvius which was still belching smoke. We rose to a very great height and flew back without stopping to Algiers at an average height of about 8,000 feet. This made the journey very comfortable and steady, though I think it is rather tiring and one feels a little light-headed on arrival. We got to the airfield at Algiers at 12.30 and arrived here at one o'clock.

3 p.m. Commander-in-Chief's meeting. Present: General Wilson, General Devers, Air Marshal Slessor, etc., etc. A very successful meeting. We discussed P.W.B. organisation in the Mediterranean area. This was followed by the latest account of the Roumanian situation;[21] and I gave an account of what I had done in Italy.

Later in the evening I went to see Duff Cooper. He seemed very much concerned about the President's attitude towards the French National Committee in France. I see there are rumours of Anthony resigning from the Foreign Office. I do not suppose this is on account of the French business. No doubt he feels he cannot do both the F.O. and the House of Commons. Nevertheless the President's decision must be a great blow to him.[22] I am afraid Winston is relapsing into one of his difficult moods about French affairs, judging at any rate from what Duff tells me about his telegrams.

A quiet dinner and early to bed.

Wednesday, 29 March 1944

Worked in bed in the morning.

At 12 noon I called to see General Wilson to go through a number of questions. The two chief were the attitude of the French Government [the F.C.N.L.] to the proposed arrangement for the control of French forces, and secondly, some problems regarding the American Army command here which are of an extremely delicate character.[23] General Wilson seems to find it helpful to consult me, and I think I can be of service to him in these matters from my experience.

1.15 p.m. Luncheon party here. I am afraid Maud was the only woman. Admiral Cunningham, C.-in-C. Mediterranean, General Timberlake (American Air) and a variety of notabilities, making twelve in all. Sir Tony Rumbold[24] is a great addition to our party here. He is very intelligent and very charming. I like him very much.

[21] Roumania had been occupied by the Germans in October 1940, and had been fighting against Russia. But she was increasingly disaffected with the Axis, and resistance groups were asking for military assistance. General Wilson replied that he could offer only air support. Meanwhile the Russians were trying to persuade Antonescu to bring Roumania over to the Allies.

[22] Eden was also Leader of the House of Commons, 1942–5. President Roosevelt had refused to recognise the F.C.N.L.'s authority in Metropolitan France, and this was hampering the negotiations for a new agreement on the control of French forces.

[23] General Mark Clark's removal as commander of the U.S. Fifth Army was contemplated, and it was important that this should not appear to be British in inspiration. In the event, he remained commander until December 1944.

[24] Sir Anthony Rumbold (1911–1983) was Second Secretary on my staff, 1944.

At four o'clock General Vanier came in to see me. He is the Canadian Minister.

4.30–6 p.m. Conference with General Lewis about the economic reorganisation of the Mediterranean area.

At 6 p.m. I called to see Massigli regarding the agenda for the next meeting of the Advisory Council. Massigli, however, was quite unwilling to discuss Italy, and plunged into an official but nonetheless bitter attack upon the President of the United States. I am afraid the Americans are muddling their French policy and dragging us behind them. I quite see the difficulty of H.M.G. standing up at this delicate moment, but I am afraid it is going to make a very bitter feeling against us in France. The trouble is that this does not really hurt the Americans after the war, but with the growing power of Russia I feel that we must depend upon France and other Central European countries to work with us.

Sir Noel Charles has arrived. He seems a merry little man, intelligent, lowbrow, tough, rich. His father was a distinguished heart specialist who was made a baronet. He was Minister in Rome before the war and has just come back from being Ambassador in Brazil. The announcement of his appointment has not yet been made, so I must keep him here in cold storage learning something about it, which he seems very ready and quick to do.

Dined with Admiral Sir John Cunningham, and took Sir Noel Charles along with me. A very pleasant dinner. Sir John is exceedingly intelligent, but lacks the fire and buoyancy of Sir Andrew. The Prime Minister calls him 'Dismal Jimmy' and not without cause!

Thursday, 30 March 1944

I worked in bed in the morning with my papers. Went out for a drive from eleven till one which included an hour's walking. I am trying to get a little more exercise whenever there is a chance. After lunch worked again till 4.30, when General Wilson came to tea with me alone.

The Balkans seem to be dying away so far as we are concerned. I do not believe there is much that we can do except to stand in the pavilion and cheer the Russians' innings. However, as you can imagine, the Foreign Office and the Cairo people are quite happy making much ado about nothing.

6–8 p.m. Conference with General George Clark (Chief Administrative Officer), General Lewis and Roger Makins on economic and supply reorganisation. The problem is still Italy and it is not only technical but personal. However, I think we are making progress.

Friday, 31 March 1944

I started for the aerodrome with General Gammell, Tony Rumbold and John Wyndham. We were also taking Reinhardt with us. When we got to the airfield the pilot took a gloomy view of the situation, and after a conference we decided to give up the attempt. This is annoying because it is a lovely day here, but apparently there was a very bad piece of weather between here and Naples, and also round the landing ground at Naples.

On returning to Algiers I found your telegram about Carol:[25] so it was perhaps lucky that I did not go, for I should not have been able to answer until tomorrow at least. I will write all about this in a separate letter. As we had no day planned out for us, we found ourselves rather at a loss, and so I got hold of Maud and we motored into the mountains at Chréa, where we had a picnic lunch and a good walk, getting back at half-past five. We hope to get off to Italy tomorrow, Saturday, 1 April.

[25] Announcing that Carol was about to marry Julian Faber, then a major in the Welsh Guards.

April

Saturday, 1 April 1944

I hope you will get my letter quickly – the one enclosing a note to Carol. It will (I fear) not reach you till after the wedding. I think about her all the time. I am sure she will make a wonderful wife to any man – because she has so much loyalty. She is impulsive and very sensitive. I always think she is a mixture of you and of my father. She often reminds me of him – especially his shy and sensitive side, which made him suffer so from vulgarity or loudness whenever he encountered them.

I feel somehow that Julian has qualities deeper than appear on the surface. Anyhow, he gave me that impression when he came to see me. He will not offend her taste – for he is quiet and dignified and has a certain reserve of manner which I liked. Perhaps he will develop ambition; I hope so, for I feel she could play a useful part in the world when she settles down – a new world in which her real understanding of and sympathy for the mass of the people should be used.

Do you suppose he would like to go into the Foreign Office after the war, or the Diplomatic Service? I am told that they will be recruiting a lot of people, because their ranks are now very depleted and they will need a larger staff after the war with so many international organisations to deal with and man. Please write me about all the wedding and Catherine and Sarah and Nanny and what everyone says and does. I suppose you will have got my cable and given Carol my message. I simply cannot imagine how you can possibly do any of the arrangements in the time.

I left Algiers this morning at 7.30 a.m. General Gammell (Chief of Staff, A.F.H.Q.), Tony Rumbold, Reinhardt, John Wyndham and one or two others. A very comfortable and successful flight, arriving at Naples at 12.15 – a following wind and a very good time.

Caccia and Reber came up to see us at the villa. Then Sir John Slessor (Deputy Air Officer Commanding Mediterranean) at the office, and of course Mason-MacFarlane.

At 5 p.m. a meeting of the Allied Advisory Council for Italy. This was rather a difficult and inconclusive meeting, but I enjoyed it. It was made particularly ridiculous because we met in an enormously lofty Fascist-constructed council chamber. With its marble floor and walls and great height, and with no carpet or curtains, no one could hear a single word. And as we spoke in about four languages, it was worse than the Tower of Babel.

I suppose all these international organisations have some value; they certainly give one a good laugh. Everybody is excessively courteous to everyone else, and not a single word is said that is not transparently false, since everyone is in fact carrying on his own intrigue *outside* the Council altogether.

Bogomolov was in capital form. I am beginning rather to enjoy him. He is a very able and quite unscrupulous man.

After the Council, I had a conference with Mason-MacFarlane. He is very 'girlish' and self-centred to an extraordinary degree. But – oh my! – isn't he twisted round Badoglio's finger by that wicked old Marshal!!

Dean (legal department of F.O.) and Phillimore (ditto of War Office) to dinner. The prisoners-of-war agreement (which everyone thought was in the bag after my talk with Badoglio on Monday) has slipped through our fingers again. According to these two, it is due to the weakness of Mason-MacFarlane, Harold Caccia and Reber. I have written a note to Mason-MacFarlane and urged him to make a final and *firm* effort. He is to see Badoglio tomorrow.

Palm Sunday, 2 April 1944

Went to English Church in Naples. A very full church (all troops) and a nice service, with plenty of hymns and good sermon from an Army chaplain.

After church, Tony Rumbold, John and I went for a drive (taking sandwich lunch) and as we could get along the road which goes up Vesuvius we got to the observatory and some miles or so beyond – after that the road is engulfed in the latest lava stream. The volcano has returned to normal – smoking away quite like an old man puffing a cigar – but the clouds of dust still cover the slopes like snow, and the streams of molten lava are still smoking. It is an extraordinary scene of desolation.

5 p.m. Bogomolov called. A very pleasant, fencing kind of talk. Bogomolov does not think Italy or Fascism of much importance. Italy has no coal, no petrol, no iron. Germany is quite another thing. Fascism was always largely play-acting. Nazism is genuine – and is merely the old militarism in a new guise.

6 p.m. Meeting with Generals MacFarlane and Gammell. Not much progress. Mason-MacFarlane very much on the defensive.

I motored out to Caserta and dined with General Alex, whom I found in excellent form. There was a good deal to discuss, some of it delicate and difficult.[1] But, as usual, he was very quick to take any points and most grateful for any advice. He is really a very easy man to deal with – and yet he stands up for his own view. But he has none of the ordinary inhibitions of the professional soldier.

Monday, 3 April 1944

Drove with General Alexander to a parade of the Fifth Battalion, Grenadier Guards. General Alexander presented a V.C. to a young Grenadier officer named Sidney.[2] This boy is Lord Gort's son-in-law, and Gort had come over from Malta for the occasion. There was a great gathering of Grenadier officers and others and I saw a lot of old friends. The parade was splendid – a magnificent 'present arms' and the men as steady as a rock during the inspection. Afterwards, there was a very good little speech by Alex and then a march past. It was a moving and inspiring sight – but, oh, they are just children and look as if they ought to be playing cricket, not this stern and cruel game of war.

After the parade, I motored back to Naples and lunched there – Harold Caccia and Sam Reber came.

I had to go back to Caserta again for a talk with Air Marshal Slessor, and got there by 6.30. All this motoring is very tiring because of the very bad condition of the surface and the crowded road. It is almost unbelievable – the permanent line of lorries, trucks, guns, tanks, jeeps, sedans, coming and going.

Dined with Alex and went afterwards with him to the train. We had an excellent talk, and I think both the points about which I was anxious will be safeguarded. He will get General Wilson to make sure that all the plans for the new operations are sent to the Combined Chiefs of Staff at Washington *before* Alex leaves for England. (This will make it quite clear that the P.M. has *not* interfered and will protect Alex from that being said.) Secondly, if there is to be any question of removing General [Mark] Wayne Clark – that again will be put forward by General Devers (the American Deputy Commander-in-Chief) to Washington *before* Alex leaves. (This in the same way will avoid the story getting round that this has been done in London.)

We talked of many things – both of war and peace. As always I found it a pleasant evening, with a man of a very receptive and attractive mind.

Tuesday, 4 April 1944

Motored into Naples – arriving about 10 a.m. The Italians have finally refused to sign the prisoners-of-war agreement. There is

[1] General Alexander was about to visit London and we were concerned lest the question of General Mark Clark's replacement and the plans for military operations at Cassino should appear to have been settled in London.

[2] William Philip Sidney (b. 1909), later 1st Viscount de L'Isle and Dudley, later a Conservative politician and Governor-General of Australia, 1961–5.

nothing more that I can do. I am advising London to go right ahead with organising the Italian prisoners into pioneer battalions and to put them on to work which is technically forbidden by the [Geneva] Convention. After all, there is nothing which Badoglio can do, except lodge a protest with the protecting power – Switzerland. I do not believe he will do this,[3] especially as he has already agreed to those in North Africa being employed on such work (the Badoglio–Eisenhower verbal agreement). After all, there may easily be in his mind a distinction between the *positive* act of signing an agreement (which may be unpopular in Italy and used against him by his enemies) and the *negative* act of acquiescing in our organising those Italian prisoners of war who volunteer into units to work for us.

I have just received your telegram saying that you all feel that the wedding ought to be postponed. Of course I have no idea what it is all about and must await your letter in patience. I can well understand that it was absolutely impossible to arrange everything in the space of three days! It always seemed to me rather an ambitious plan. But I do hope Carol is not in a terrible 'flap' and making herself unhappy. It is really a shame to leave you to deal with all these problems. It is so much easier to do my work here and much less harassing! Mr Gladstone (or was it Dr Johnson?) said that 'No man ever lay awake at night over a public disaster'. It is certainly true that private problems are much more disturbing.

Perhaps I shall get another telegram from you saying what is happening, or at least a letter when I return to Algiers.

12 noon. Tony Rumbold, John and I left by car with a sandwich lunch. We got to Pompeii and spent an hour there and then drove on to Salerno. Here is the 'seat' of the Italian Government and of part of the Control Commission. I had an interesting hour's talk with Prunas. He is Permanent Under-Secretary of State for Foreign Affairs (or the Alec Cadogan of the Italian Ministry). He is very intelligent and quite sensible in his views – with a greater sense of realities than the Marshal. But he is also insinuating and needs watching. He has a face like a weasel. He is of course quite ready to play the Russians off against us and the Americans and to try to get advantages for Italy by threatening us with Communism and the Soviet danger. I am afraid he is a good deal too clever for some of our friends here. At the same time, he is interesting and I think genuinely 'pro-British' – in the sense that he understands the folly of Italy ever allowing herself to be estranged from Great Britain. Prunas realises that Italy's geographical position makes it necessary for her to seek England's friendship so long as we remain the dominant naval power in the Mediterranean. That is a greater reality than memories of Lord John Russell and Lord Palmerston or the reception of Mazzini and Garibaldi by the Liberals

[3] No such protest was lodged.

of London. It was only when we seemed to be losing that superiority that Mussolini was able to persuade Italians to take the plunge. And it certainly seemed a fairly good bet (from the Italian point of view) after the fall of France.

I learned a good deal from Prunas who talked very volubly and did not seem to need much of an answer.

We then drove to Lord Grimthorpe's villa – Villa Cimbrone – which I have already described. It is a lovely drive and it was a most beautiful evening.

Wednesday, 5 April 1944

A completely idle day – ambling in the garden, reading and sleeping in the sun. I found a volume of Warde Fowler's *Life of Julius Caesar* (in the Heroes of Nations series) which I read. An old-fashioned and not very effective book. I also found Stendhal's *La Chartreuse de Parme.*

Just before dinner, Ian Walker and Bertie Clowes came in – they are at a rest camp near by. They were in capital form and we had a good gossip.

Thursday, 6 April 1944

A new French crisis has blown up – the telegrams were brought to me yesterday evening at Villa Cimbrone. But I did not think I could do much about it. It may amuse you to read the two which I have received and my reply – so I enclose them.

The French telegrams

I

From: Supreme Allied Commander-in-Chief
To: Combined Chiefs of Staff, British Chiefs of Staff, Eisenhower, etc.

4 April 1944

1. Action of French Committee of National Liberation in passing and publishing ordinance [on 4 April] without consultation with Giraud arrogating to President C.N.L. final authority in matters relating to organisation and employment of French Armed Forces has led Giraud to declare his firm decision to resign office and retire to private residence in United Kingdom. He has signalled Juin urgently to come Algiers for conference between 1200 and 1500 hours tomorrow, 5 April, with announced intention of counselling continuation in battle in Italy and collaboration with Allies.

2. Devers, on my request, saw Giraud at 1930 hours in effort to persuade him defer decision at least until after seeing Juin but Giraud indicated decision was irrevocable. He did, however, agree to withhold

telegram to Eisenhower asking assistance in securing approval of British Chiefs of Staff to his residence in United Kingdom until after seeing Juin.

3. Indications are that action of C.N.L. dictated in part by dissatisfaction at degree of political recognition accorded and partly by dissatisfaction with the terms of FAN 343 [Roosevelt's refusal to recognise F.C.N.L. authority in Metropolitan France] which in their view failed to take sufficient account of French sovereignty as represented by C.N.L.

4. I do not anticipate any immediate serious repercussions since I depend upon Giraud loyally to use his influence in favour of continuation of the present collaboration. Devers and I are conferring with Duff Cooper and Chapin tomorrow morning and I will keep you advised of developments.

II

From: Supreme Allied Commander-in-Chief
To: Combined Chiefs of Staff, etc.

5 April 1944

In conversation with Ambassador Duff Cooper, Giraud maintained his determination to resign but agreed to withhold action pending conference with Juin and Political Adviser Murphy who returned from U.S. this afternoon, 5 April.

Juin, who arrived here for conference with Giraud, is reported to have view that despite fact Giraud's departure would lose to Army a stabilising influence, there would be no appreciable loss of morale and no diminution of war effort. Appears to feel that a Chief of Staff over a General Staff within the framework of the ordinance of the Committee of National Liberation would prove a satisfactory institution for the conduct of operations.

III

From: Resident Minister, Naples
To: Resident Minister, Algiers

6 April 1944.

Personal for Makins.

1. Giraud has been an unconscionable time dying. Let him die.

2. But stick to JUIN. His views seem very sensible, and I believe he knows the Army well.

3. I am sure Ambassador Cooper will take it all calmly. I do not know what Ambassador Murphy will say, but let General Wilson know that in my view Giraud's departure will be no real loss.

4. Please show this to Ambassador Cooper.

IV

From: Resident Minister, Algiers
To: Resident Minister, Naples
8 April 1944

Private and Personal for Macmillan from Makins.

Ambassador Cooper is taking the affair so calmly that he has gone to the desert whence his staff are feverishly trying to extricate him.

[Diary continues] Giraud has deserved his fate. I do not quite understand the exact circumstances, but I have no doubt that de Gaulle's decree is really an answer to the President's attitude about the position of the French Committee in Metropolitan France. With all the President's immense virtues, he has a curious blind spot about France and especially about de Gaulle. This is the old story of the American recognition of Vichy – the evil influence of Admiral Leahy – and the series of gradual defeats which Americans have suffered in their French policy. Now their favourite Giraud meets his final decline – and, to add insult to benefits received, asks permission to reside in England!

Of course another object which de Gaulle has in view is to put an end – once and for all – to the conception that Giraud – as Commander-in-Chief – has a kind of extra-constitutional position and has private agreements with the Allies which are not within the purview of the F.C.N.L. This started last February at Anfa. It has finally perished fourteen months later.

We left Villa Cimbrone (at Ravello) at 9.30 and arrived at our Naples villa at noon. M. [Georgios] Kapsambelis (Greek) came to see me. He is the second Greek delegate ([Athanasios] Politis is the head) on the Italian Advisory Council. A nice man – of course he talked for an hour, not about Italy but about Greece.

3.30 p.m. Sir Noel Charles arrived from Algiers, his appointment having been gazetted – chirpy, friendly and imperturbable.

4.30 p.m. John and I started off on a visit to General Oliver Leese (Eighth Army) at his forward H.Q. near Venafro. A very rough and tiring drive, arriving finally at about 7 p.m. We are in an olive grove, under a high mountain, with an excellent mess, consisting of one of those iron huts. A fine stone fireplace has been built by some mason in the Army, and a cheerful wood fire warms the room.

Major Verney is Personal Assistant. The A.D.C.s are nice friendly boys; the G2 (Ops)[4] one Bruce – who is a friend of Maurice. He seemed an able boy, having been out nearly three years and got the M.C.

We dined at 8 p.m. – an excellent dinner, and then I went to talk to the general in his caravan.

[4] G2 [=G.S.O.2] (Ops) is the General Staff Officer, Grade 2 (i.e. a major), dealing with operations.

Apart from actual business (such as Polish politics, which very much conern the general, who has two Polish divisions in his army; and the problem of a new editor for the *Eighth Army News*) I think all these generals like to talk about general world affairs. They are naturally rather out of touch – with little contact with what is going on – and I feel it is a service one can render to go and see them, as well as a very enjoyable experience for oneself.

I had a nice caravan for myself – very comfortable. I read Dr Johnson for a bit, and thought about Carol and wondered when I shall hear more news. It seems so far away and I hate leaving all the troubles and difficulties to you.

Good Friday, 7 April 1944

John and I left at 8.30 sharp and got back to our villa in Naples by 11 a.m. Here we had a sort of general conference – Charles, Caccia, Rumbold and I.

At 4.30 Murphy came round, having just arrived from U.S.A. I had not seen him since 20 December when he left Algiers. We never knew when or whether he was coming back – but he has turned up at last – looking ten years younger and in capital form.

I gather that all is not too well at the White House. The President (like the P.M.) found the winter trip to Cairo and Teheran very exhausting. He came back thoroughly tired out, and has not really been well since.

Unfortunately Harry Hopkins – on whom the President depends greatly – has been seriously ill, with two dangerous internal operations from which (if he recovers at all) he will be incapacitated for some time to come.

Old Cordell Hull is still powerful – chiefly because of his position with Conservative elements in the Democratic party. But he is not one of the President's 'cronies'. So often important affairs are settled by one or the other – almost without personal contact – or left unsettled between them. Murphy was offered the job of 'liaison officer' between the State Department and the White House. I gather that he managed to postpone the decision for the time being. His first reason was a wise unwillingness to appear to be taking Harry Hopkins' job from him while he was away (for this work of trying to arrange matters between the President's office and the State Department was rather Harry's speciality). His second was a natural unwillingness – as a 'career' diplomat – to commit himself so intimately to an administration which has not very long to run.

I got a good deal of information from Bob on both French and Italian affairs. The President is still very 'anti-de Gaulle' but he will gradually yield to realities. On Italy, he is very keen to have something to show politically before the Presidential election.

He would like an abdication of Victor Emmanuel and so on. But he –

however reluctantly – agreed to Winston's formula of waiting till the capture of Rome. I can see that it will help relations very much if we can get some move on in Italy before that – and I think we can.

6.30 p.m. M. Smilganić, the Yugoslavian member of the Advisory Council, called. He talked for an hour about the situation in Yugoslavia. He (unlike his chief man, Krek[5] – who is a rabid Serb) seems to hold moderate views and I gather would like some arrangement – at least for war purposes – between the Royal Government and Tito.

7.30 p.m. M. Guérin (French representative, substitute for Massigli).

He told me that the French are appointing Couve de Murville – an old friend and a good man – as their permanent representative on the Council. Guérin will, however, preside at tomorrow's meeting of the Council which is being regarded as adjourned from that of 1 April.

After dinner, Noel Charles and I talked over the situation, and what I had learnt from Murphy. I drafted a telegram to the P.M. and sent it off 'Most Immediate'. I am enclosing the text [see below]. I do not know whether we shall get a reply in time, but if not we shall have to take a chance. Noel Charles had stayed a night at Chequers before coming out and therefore was able to advise from that angle. I think I know more or less what he wants. But I should like to help Murphy also. If we can push the King along a bit, it will do no harm to anyone.

Outgoing telegram

From: Resident Minister, Naples
To: Foreign Office, London

7 April 1944

Following for Prime Minister. Personal.

1. Please see my telegram No. 55 to the Foreign Office. It is probable that a new Italian Government will be formed on an all-party basis without any interference on our part and without prejudice being caused to the position of the monarchy. I hope you will think this a satisfactory development since it appears to meet the immediate objectives of all three Allied Governments, British, American and Russian. There are however two points of which it is in our interest to make certain. The first is that the new Government should accept the obligations of both sets of armistice terms and the various other undertakings entered into between the present Government and the Allies. The second is that Sforza should not be either Prime Minister or Foreign Secretary; the chances of his being made Prime Minister are small since Badoglio will presumably continue in this office, but there

[5] Dr Miho Krek, a leading Slovene statesman and former Deputy Premier.

is quite a possibility that he may be offered the post of Foreign Secretary; it is the only post for which he has any technical qualifications and there is no other post which is obviously suited to him.

2. We are having a meeting of the Advisory Council tomorrow afternoon and if you agree we would like to get the Council to adopt a resolution for transmission to the C.-in-C. as follows:

(*a*) welcoming the developments leading to the formation of a broad-based government;

(*b*) stating it to be in the Allied interest that Badoglio should continue in such a Government to hold the offices of Prime Minister and Foreign Secretary;

(*c*) emphasising that the new Government must be made to declare its willingness to assume all the obligations of the old Government;

(*d*) insisting that whatever arrangement is entered into between the new Government and the King must be regarded as binding until such time as the whole Italian people can be consulted on the institutional issue at the end of the war. If MacFarlane were armed with instructions from the Supreme Allied Commander based on advice of this kind he should be able to ensure that our interests were fully protected.

3. I have not yet seen Murphy but will have a chance of doing so tomorrow morning before the meeting. Unless he has come with positive instructions to back Sforza to the limit, I hope to be able to persuade him to support a resolution of this kind. There should be no difficulty with the other delegates.

4. I should be grateful to learn whether you agree to this proposal which Sir Noel Charles and I have concerted.

[Diary continues] Read Boswell and went to sleep thinking of you and Carol. I fear I shall hear no more till I get back to Algiers.

Saturday, 8 April 1944

11.30 a.m. Meeting in General Mason-MacFarlane's room to discuss the situation. Murphy, Reinhardt, Reber, H.M., Noel Charles and Caccia.

It was quite clear that the Americans were very anxious indeed for something to be done which would help their internal political situation.

They would really like the abdication of the King right away. But of course they know that the President is more or less bound by the 'wait till Rome' formula. On the other hand, I think the whole situation has been largely changed by the Communist move. Under orders from Moscow, they have let it be known that they will enter a Government *without* raising the question of the King and the monarchy. (This is of course a very clever move on their part, since they at the same time can say they are only 'out for the war' and consolidate their position and power for later needs!) But this Communist position makes the liberal and moderate parties very uncomfortable. On the one hand, they long to enter the Government and would hate to see the Communists and Socialists collar all the best jobs and all the power; on the other hand, they have made so many speeches and uttered such brave words, that a lot of the latter would need to be eaten if they were to come along and join Badoglio. It is, therefore, in my view necessary for a sufficient gesture to be made by the King – whether abdication, or a Regency, or a promise of a Regency – for the other parties to enter on coalition government immediately, without too much loss of 'face'.

This is the usual problem, and should (I think) be treated as the central one. The effects on British and American opinion are important, but secondary.

If we can obtain a 'broad-based democratic government' by a comparatively modest move by the King, we are not entitled to demand a drastic one merely to please American voters. On the other hand, I should much like to get something which will please our allies and help the President to be re-elected.

After a lot of talk, we adjourned for luncheon – which was at the American villa.

After luncheon (after some talk on the way with Charles) I reached a decision as to what we would do. I am glad to say that Charles agreed, and it was most useful to have his help.

There are under discussion at the moment two 'plans'. One – the King's plan – was suggested to General MacFarlane by the King on 21 February. It was duly reported to London and Washington, and has been discussed, but no answer has been given. The plan was put to the King, I believe, by an Italian politician called De Nicola.[6] It has become more or less known in political circles – but there is some indication that the King is now disposed to 'back out' of it. It has, of course, never been publicly put forward, and he could not be held to be committed.

Under this plan, the King would announce *now* his intention of appointing Prince Umberto as 'Lieutenant-General of the Realm' or Regent *after* the taking of Rome.

There are certain points to be tied up, even under this plan. For instance, the King appointed a Lieutenant-General of the Realm in the last war (when he was at the front). It must therefore be made clear that the appointment is final and irrevocable. What is to happen if the capture of Rome is long delayed? – and so forth.

The second plan is a variation of this, as to both time and content. It is suggested by some of the parties' leaders that this plan would be satisfactory and enable them to join the Government, if the King were to *make* the appointment now, instead of waiting to implement it. Others again are arguing that the Prince should not have *full*, but only honorific powers, and should delegate his powers to yet another body.

[6] Enrico De Nicola (1877–1959) became the first President of the Republic of Italy in 1946.

But, broadly speaking – since H.M.G. would certainly not agree to a 'watering' away of all the Royal authority – the question looks like becoming Plan A (the King's original suggestion) – to announce *now* the intention to make the appointment later or Plan B (which all this morning's meeting seem to prefer, that is the Americans and General MacFarlane and Caccia).

Anyway, I decided to plump for Plan B and agree to give my support to it. I asked Murphy – in return – to support a resolution which I was going to move at the Council meeting, and he agreed. I told Murphy I was acting without instructions and he was duly appreciative.

4 p.m. Meeting of the Council. General MacFarlane gave a twenty minutes' résumé or exposé of the political situation. While he was speaking P.M.'s reply to my telegram of last night was given me. This (telegram enclosed) was encouraging, as it gives me support and a certain latitude regarding the various plans for the monarch's position.

P.M.'s reply

From Prime Minister to Mr Macmillan at Naples
Personal and Secret of 8.4.44

I am very glad to receive your news. You have evidently handled the situation with remarkable skill. I approve your proposed course of action. I do not mind very much whether the King retires now or waits till Rome is taken so long as Umberto is created Lieutenant and Badoglio remains at the Head of the Government. Do all you can to keep Sforza out of any office of real power.

[Diary continues] After the general had finished, there was a desultory discussion. Bogomolov was not anxious to be drawn. Finally, I moved my resolution. Murphy supported it, as did everyone else except Bogomolov, who said he had no instructions.

Guérin was not sure about the phraseology of the second resolution – and made some reservation for the Minutes.

In spite of all this I insisted on its being voted on, and told Bogomolov that he could *abstain* from voting, and ask for instructions as to whether his Government would agree. But he could not *delay* the matter, since it was urgent that General Wilson – whom we are supposed to advise – should be guided as to his attitude during the present political crisis in Italy. Finally, Bogomolov agreed and the resolution was put and carried unanimously – with the Russians abstaining and a French verbal reservation!

All very puerile, but it enables me to get a telegram to Wilson and formal instructions to MacFarlane to tell Badoglio of our attitude. This will in fact be welcomed by Badoglio, since it will strengthen his hand against extremist's both before and after his new Government is formed. We went back to the villa after the meeting and sent off the necessary telegrams to Algiers and London.

Sunday, 9 April 1944

Church at 8 a.m. Halford came with me. I met after church an old friend, Major-General [Ronald] Penney. He used to be General Alexander's signal officer and now commands the First Infantry Division – which has fought admirably on the Anzio bridgehead.

At 10.15 we had a conference – Mason-MacFarlane, Murphy, Charles, etc. MacFarlane was anxious that Murphy and I should take on the job of seeing the King ourselves and also Badoglio – with a view to getting the King's *immediate* retirement (Plan B) if possible. I will not go into great detail as I am composing a short separate 'piece' on the events of these days, which I will send you [see pp. 416 and 417].

12 noon. M. Politis (Greek member of Advisory Council). He talked for over an hour on Greek, *not* Italian affairs. Politis is quite interesting and shrewd. I think he gave me a useful picture of the Greek tangle.

The situation has got very bad. The Greek P.M. Tsouderos[7] has resigned. Sophocles Venizelos[8] was designated as his successor, but there has been some hitch; meanwhile the EAM (and the ELAS partisans depending on EAM)[9] became more and more intransigent.[10] They are partly Communists and partly bandits, not as well organised as Tito's followers and I think losing rather than gaining ground in Greece. We are trying to get the King[11] (1) to make a more specific declaration of his readiness to abide by a plebiscite after the war, (2) perhaps to promise *not* to come into line until *after* a plebiscite favourable to the monarchy – i.e. not to come and canvass! (3) to form a broad-based government now much more to the *left* than the present, and including representatives of both the 'Conservative' partisans (EDES)[12] and the Communist partisans (ELAS).

After luncheon, John and I went for a long walk. We returned wet through from a thunderstorm.

[7] Emmanuel Tsouderos (1882–1956) had been Prime Minister since 1941.

[8] Sophocles Venizelos (1894–1964), the son of former Prime Minister Eleutherios Venizelos, was twice Prime Minister again in 1950.

[9] EAM (*Ethnikòn Apeleŭtherotikòn Métopon* or National Liberation Front) was the political movement and ELAS (*Ethnikòs Laikòs Apeleŭtherotikòs Stratòs* or National Popular Liberation Army) the paramilitary one.

[10] On 4 April a group of Greek officers had called on Tsouderos, Prime Minister of the Greek Government-in-exile, which had been in Cairo since the spring of 1943, and demanded his resignation. On the following day he resigned; and on the 6th EAM supporters mutinied, demanding a broad-based government, and took over Greek warships in Alexandria. The First Greek Brigade, encamped thirty miles outside Alexandria, likewise refused to obey orders. Not until the 13th did Venizelos manage to form a Provisional Government and become Prime Minister.

[11] George II (1890–1947), King of the Hellenes, 1922–4 and 1935–47.

[12] *Ethnikòs Dimokratikòs Ellinikòs Sýndesmos*, the National Republican Greek League.

Charles and I dined with Bogomolov.

Caviare – Hors d'oeuvres (vodka)
Soup
Macaroni
Fish
Chicken
Lamb
Neapolitan ices and cake
Cheese
Fruit

and various wines, coffee, liqueurs. When the proletariat of Naples are living on the bare minimum necessary to live, this seems in rather poor taste. In order to demonstrate this (and because I was not in any case hungry) I stopped after the macaroni.

Monday, 10 April 1944

Drove from Naples to Ravello. General MacFarlane, Murphy, Charles and I saw the King at 11.

Extract from memorandum on the King of Italy

Old age has not deprived this monarch of any of his subtlety in negotiation and ingenuity of mind. He immediately greeted us with the question as to whether there was any news of the battle and when we hoped to take Rome and drive the Germans out of Italy. As he is kept well informed of military events, this manoeuvre was well designed to have a somewhat damping effect upon us. I took the opportunity to introduce Sir Noel Charles as my successor and to say that I had waited upon the King because I had not had an occasion for seeing him since my visit to England. Mr Murphy said that he had come straight from a long visit to the United States and close touch with the President. By arrangement Mr Murphy then developed his theme, which he did with considerable force and skill. He told the King quite frankly the view of American opinion about himself as an individual and his conduct of Italian affairs during recent years. He said that as the King was bound up in the American mind with Fascism for twenty years and with the guilt of having declared war against his old friends, it would be better for the preservation of the monarchy if the King would declare his intention to abdicate at once, or at least retire immediately in favour of the Prince by appointing him Lieutenant-General. He urged this theme forcibly but with dignity and without exaggeration. I supported it in what I thought was appropriate language. To have to say hard things to a man many years one's senior is never a pleasant situation, and it is all the more distasteful to one brought up in monarchical principles to have to say them to a personage who has for forty years exercised Royal authority.

The King affected to be very much surprised. He thought that we had merely come on a courtesy visit. He showed great alarm and some indignation. In a rambling manner, which I think was more put on than genuine, he spoke to us of the losses of his subjects caused by our bombing of Rome and a number of other rather irrelevant topics. We subsequently heard that he had been perfectly well informed of the object of our visit and was merely trying to gain time. He said he must consult on such a matter with his Ministers, but in point of fact he has never discussed this except with his immediate entourage and his trusted friend, the Master of the Royal Household, the Duca d'Acquarone. After this interview, which was fortunately not protracted, we retired to the Villa Cimbrone some quarter of a mile away to await events. A message was brought to us about lunch time to say that the King must ask for forty-eight hours to make up his mind. In view of the fact that the Junta was meeting on Wednesday, the 12th, we said that that was too long. He must make a decision within twenty-four hours. This was agreed to. Later in the afternoon General MacFarlane, who had gone down to Salerno to see Badoglio, sent [a] note, in which he stated that the Marshal thought the King ought to accept immediate retirement.

In the afternoon I walked to Amalfi and along the coast about two hours and a half. It was a lovely spring day.

All the rest of the day was taken up with conferences and argument. Harold Caccia and Reber joined the party at the Villa Cimbrone.

I read Kipling *The Day's Work* in the old [Macmillan] edition de luxe, which I found in this excellent library.

Tuesday, 11 April 1944

Lovely weather – a few rain-storms – the fruit-trees are in full bloom, apples, plums, almonds, etc.

11.30 a.m. Prunas.

12 noon. Duca d'Acquarone.

3.30 p.m. Marshal Badoglio.

6 p.m. Prunas.

10 p.m. Prunas.

A regular right-down royal day!

In between I read *Plain Tales from the Hills* in the same edition.

Further extract from memorandum on the King of Italy

He was in a state of some emotion. He gave us an account of Marshal Badoglio's views completely contrary to that which General MacFarlane had indicated. From General MacFarlane's note I understood clearly that Marshal Badoglio was in favour of the immediate handing over of powers to the Prince. Prunas denied this completely. We therefore asked him to arrange for Marshal Badoglio to see us in the course of the afternoon.

At twelve o'clock the Duca d'Acquarone arrived and said that the King had given thought to what we had told him and that he was prepared now to bind himself by making an immediate announcement. Although his plan had been put forward to a number of politicians, he did not consider himself necessarily bound by it because it had not been accepted either by those politicians or by the Allied Governments. Nevertheless he would now make a definite statement and he produced the text, which ran as follows:

> 'I have decided to appoint my son, the Prince of Piedmont, Lieutenant-General of the Realm. The formal transfer of power will take place on the day on which the Allied troops enter Rome.'

He said that if we were prepared to accept this formula the King would see us at four o'clock in the afternoon, accompanied by Marshal Badoglio, and bind himself formally to abide by it. Mr Murphy strongly protested against this decision and fought with all his energy for an immediate transfer. He also observed that the text of the announcement was very jejune and in the King's interest should be somewhat amplified. I contented myself with giving as much support to Mr Murphy as was consistent with my undertaking without getting too much personally involved in the dispute. Mr Murphy then retired to produce his suggested text.

At 3.30 Marshal Badoglio arrived and, as indicated by Prunas, argued strongly in favour of the King's original plan. The points which he made seemed to me sensible. He said that his only interest was to preserve the monarchy, and the King also was thinking not of himself but of his dynasty. It was a mistake in politics, especially when dealing with Italians, to make great concessions at any moment. They were soon forgotten and no thanks were given. It would be better to dribble them out one by one. He himself felt very doubtful as to whether in any event the monarchy could be saved. When the people of the industrial north were able to express themselves and when a constitutional assembly was held after the war, he was afraid that the people would turn against the House of Savoy.

The only hope was to use the interval while the war lasted to satisfy the crowd with a series of concessions. By this scheme something would be done now. He believed the politicians would enter a broad-based government. Then when we got to Rome the Prince would actually take over. This would give the opportunity of summoning a new government. A fresh interest and emotion would be caused. Finally, there was always the card to play that the King might at some moment decide to abdicate definitely in favour of his son. He was therefore in favour of the policy of small concessions doled out little by little.

Again Mr Murphy argued strongly, naturally more from the point of view of American public opinion than from the Italian aspect. I think I was successful in giving him sufficient support to carry out my share of the bargain. I reminded Badoglio of the other argument that the King might by making a generous gesture now obtain more credit and give a better chance to the Prince. Signor Prunas was also present at this interview but took little part in it.

We retired for a few moments to confer, and I persuaded Mr Murphy to take the following line: That we should ask Badoglio to see the King and tell him that we still felt that it would be in his own interest to take the plunge but that we would not bring any pressure upon him as representing the Allied Governments. We were there to advise him, not to force him. We were not Prussians. We were not exercising our power as representing the conquering armies. We were giving what seemed to us the best advice. If he refused it, if it proved impossible to form a government, if he then had to make a further concession in order to obtain a government which would rob him of the advantage of having made a voluntary gesture, then he must take the risk. We would leave it to him to decide. Badoglio then left to take this message to the King.

At six o'clock Prunas returned, apologising for Badoglio's inability to do so as the Marshal was tired and not well. He told us that the King had listened to the arguments and had now put forward another suggestion, that is to say, that a sounding should be taken as to whether a government could be formed on his original plan, and if in two or three days it was found to be impossible to obtain ministers on this basis, then he would reconsider the whole position.

We told Prunas straight away that this was the worst plan of all and we could not possibly accept it. It would have the grave disadvantage of delay, the King was bound to nothing (he seemed now to be trying to evade even the concession he had made), and he did not definitely pledge himself to accept the more drastic version in the event of failure to form a government. We therefore said that we must ask him to stand by the original plan. Prunas said that he would inform the King accordingly. We said that we must have the decision that night and that he must return at ten o'clock with the text of the proposed declaration which was to be put on the radio and given to the press the next morning.

At ten o'clock Prunas returned saying that the King would accept and bringing with him a draft of the declaration. In my view this was not strong enough. Without attempting to alter the inoperative paragraphs, which I think had been drafted by the King and the Duca d'Acquarone, I insisted on the insertion in paragraph 3 of the words 'I have decided to withdraw from public affairs', and on the inclusion of the last paragraph, 'This decision is final and irrevocable.' Prunas said that he could not accept this without authority but that he thought the King would approve.

Wednesday, 12 April 1944

Left Villa Cimbrone about 10 a.m.[13] After lunch, at 3 p.m., Murphy and I held a press conference. There was a very large number of correspondents. We did our best to 'write up' the King's public declaration and the chances of a new government. A press conference is rather like a political meeting, and the questions are the important part. I have had more experience than Murphy. One has to ride off or joke off the awkward questions!

After the conference, Charles and I went to see the Villa Rosebery (now inhabited by an air marshal) which we covet!

6 p.m. Bogomolov called. We fully expected trouble (since we had acted without the Russians) but butter would not melt in his mouth![14]

At 7 p.m. my old friend Couve de Murville, who has just been made permanent French representative on the Advisory Council for Italy, called to see me. We discussed French affairs!

Harold Caccia came to dinner.

Thursday, 13 April 1944

Left Naples by air – in a Lockheed Hudson (with seats!) specially provided for me and my party. Murphy, Reinhardt, etc., came too. Since the P.M.'s orders, the Air Force treats me with much consideration.

We arrived safely about 4.30 p.m. and at once plunged into a whirl of papers, telegrams, memoranda, etc., on French, Greek, Yugoslavian, Roumanian and other affairs!

In order to read these at leisure, I retired to bed.

8.30 p.m. Dined with de Gaulle. He was very pleasant. He seemed quite satisfied with Cordell Hull's latest declaration on the French Committee's position in Metropolitan France.[15]

After Giraud, I think he genuinely deplored his refusal to accept the honorific post of Inspector-General.[16] But he was quite firm in his

[13] Before we left the villa, we learned from Prunas that the King had approved the additional words, and his announcement was duly broadcast.

[14] He told me that the resolution I had moved at the meeting of the Allied Advisory Council on 8 April (about the formation of a broad-based Italian government) had been approved by Moscow.

[15] On 9 April 1944 Cordell Hull said, 'In accordance with this understanding [that the F.C.N.L. wished as soon as possible to allow the French people to choose a government] the Committee will have every opportunity to undertake civil administration in Metropolitan France, and our co-operation and help in every practical way in making it successful.'

[16] On 8 April the F.C.N.L. had issued a decree appointing Giraud Inspector-General of the French Army in place of his former post of C.-in-C. On 10 April Giraud had refused it, partly because the new post was honorific and did not exist in time of war.

determination to remove him from active command. I am bound to say that I think he is right.

After dinner, I called round to see Duff Cooper and told him of my conversation with de Gaulle.

When I got back, I found your letter of 5 April which explained to me much which had been rather obscure from your telegram about the postponement of Carol's wedding. I do hope things will work out all right. I must wait for more letters.

Friday, 14 April 1944

12 noon. The Political Committee. General Wilson, General Gammell (Chief of Staff), Admiral Dundas – acting for C.-in-C. Mediterranean, Air Marshal Slessor, Murphy and self – with the usual advisers, civil and military, on the different items. A very businesslike meeting, ranging from French problems (Giraud, etc.) to Italian, Roumanian and Greek. The Greek mutinies in the Army and Navy are still in full swing. It is hoped to starve them into reason. The whole Greek position is very obscure. I should much like to pay a visit to Cairo to see for myself.

1.15 p.m. Lunch – M. and Mme Schneider. Maud, Roger and I went together. The other guests were a young French princess – fat and ugly – (niece of the Comte de Paris) and the Czech Minister [Cerny].

Worked all the afternoon at the villa. General Wilson came to see me at 6 p.m. to discuss:

(*a*) Giraud. We both agreed that we should make no effort to intervene. The P.M. has been sending some rather troublesome telegrams to Duff, but he has 'batted them back' stoutly.

(*b*) Greece. We both are concerned at the lack of progress and agreed on the text of a telegram for me to send to the P.M.

7 p.m. A ridiculous figure – one of the great bores of St James's Street – [Lieutenant-Colonel Count John] de Salis called. He thinks he has the right kind of qualifications to be Governor of Rome. A queer delusion, which is unfortunately shared by General Wilson, who is a friend of de Salis. (I have not yet checked this with General Wilson himself.)

8 p.m. Dined with Duff Cooper. Diana is away. Mme de Breteuil, Miss Virginia Cowles (American news correspondent), Bloggs Baldwin,[17] M. and Mme de Lesseps (the latter English and very pretty, I found next to me). A pleasant evening – with some private talk with Duff afterwards. Giraud seems to have behaved very stupidly – quite true to form all through.

Saturday, 15 April 1944

Stayed in bed all morning, reading through mass of papers which have accumulated while I have been away.

[17] A. W. Baldwin (1904–76), later 3rd Earl, was second son of the Prime Minister, and a pilot officer, 1941–5.

Fred Pedler – an old friend of Colonial Office days – who left the C.O. for Africa two days before me (31 December 1942) and has been in Dakar ever since (on supply problems in French West Africa), came to see me at 10.30. He is on his way home to England. He has been promoted to a good position in the C.O. He richly deserves it, being intelligent, hard-working and tough.

1.15 p.m. A rather dull luncheon. Lucas (*Daily Express*), [Henry] Brandon (*Sunday Times*), Major Sebag-Montefiore and a number of others with letters of introduction. 'A polishing-off party' John calls it. I drove out in the evening to see my doctor, Colonel Richardson, at the Ninety-fifth Hospital. He is laid up with a poisoned leg, which will not heal.

Sunday, 16 April 1944

I have got your letter of 6 April about your visit to Hever and to Chatsworth. I loved getting it. It gave me such a clear picture of a lovely spring day at Chatsworth and of all your memories. Alas! I fear I cannot write now what I would like to – but I read and re-read your letter and could see Dorothy Cavendish – first a little girl I never knew with pig-tails – then Canada – and then the young woman and always that love of trees and woods and streams which I (poor fool) dared to imprison in the stucco and railings of Chester Square. Dear, dear Dorothy – please forgive me.

8 a.m. Went to church. Maud left about 11.30. She is off to Cairo! With a number of generals!

I took Pedler for a drive and picnic. A lovely morning and afternoon, but after we got back rain and wind made a hideous moaning dreary cold kind of a night. At dinner came your telegram about Carol.

Monday, 17 April 1944

10.30 a.m. Interview with some press men – on Italian developments.

12 noon. M. Krek, Yugoslavian member of Advisory Council for Italy. He talked for an hour about Yugoslavia – from the point of view of a Royalist, a Catholic and a Slovene. He says we are selling out civilisation in the Balkans by backing Tito – who, he declares, is a Trotskyite bandit of the worst type. He left a mass of papers to prove this point.

Luncheon. Brigadier Fitzroy Maclean, Colonel Deakin (the two founders of our work with Tito), Colonel Douglas Dodds-Parker (S.O.E.), Mr Broad (now Counsellor to Stevenson, who is Ambassador to the Royal Yugoslav Government but on his way to Bari, where he will be my representative on Yugoslav questions with the military H.Q. at Bari), Jim Bowker (my new F.O. Balkan expert) and Roger to lunch.[18] A very interesting afternoon, going through all the problems before us. Fitzroy Maclean is just out of Yugoslavia and will be here some days. He will then (probably) go to England to see the P.M. He has brought with him Colonel [Vlatko] Velebit (of Tito's army) for military discussions. In theory the talks are confined to them, but in fact they raise political problems at every stage.

6 p.m. Sir Clifford Heathcote-Smith, British representative on the Inter-Governmental Refugee Council. A soft, smooth man. I don't quite know what he is supposed to do – nor does he.

7 p.m. Colonel Spofford (American) to discuss (*a*) reorganisation of Military Government Section – which used to be run by Holmes and Terry Maxwell,[19] (*b*) economic problems of Mediterranean as a whole. A very useful talk – Spofford is a clever man – a company lawyer in New York – and we made considerable progress. He stayed on to dinner. Also to dinner – Reinhardt (U.S.), Colonel Lascelles (head of new secretariat at A.F.H.Q.), Broad. A pleasant and interesting evening with good talk.

Tuesday, 18 April 1944

Stayed in bed till noon. I was incensed to read a foolish and quite untrue communication to the press by Vyshinsky about recent Italian developments. So I sent the telegram enclosed to the F.O.

Vyshinsky and Italian developments

From Minister to Foreign Office, dated 18.4.44

1. Monsieur Vyshinsky's statement to the Tass Agency gives a very one-sided picture of the Italian developments. With regard to the latter part of his speech where he refers to the resolution passed by the Advisory Council on 8 April and quotes part of the text, this resolution was proposed by me and seconded by Murphy; Bogomolov refused to vote for it on the ground that he had no instructions. He also struggled for a considerable time to get a postponement.

2. George III, after a long period of illness, is said to have held the belief that he had been present at and won the Battle of Waterloo. It seems that some similar delusion would be the most charitable excuse for claiming the authorship of a resolution which one has neither composed, proposed, seconded or supported and to which the only contribution one has made is to abstain from voting.

[18] Brigadier (later Major-General) Fitzroy Maclean (b. 1911) commanded the British Military Mission to the Yugoslav partisans, 1943–5, and was Conservative M.P. for Lancaster, 1941–59. Colonel William Deakin (b. 1913) led the first Military Mission to Tito in May 1943, and was Warden of St Anthony's College, Oxford, 1950–68. James Bowker (b. 1901) served as Counsellor on my staff, April–June 1944.

[19] Since the debate about its future in January 1944 (see p. 359), M.G.S. had grown as its responsibilities in Italy increased, and in May 1944 it became a full staff section – G5 – of A.F.H.Q. Maxwell remained on the staff, but Holmes had accompanied General Eisenhower to serve at S.H.A.E.F.

3. I really think in justice to ourselves that a discreet indiscretion might be arranged through your Press Department.

[Diary continues] Murphy came to see me for a talk on a wide number of subjects. He is in a very pleasant and helpful mood.

Lord Gort arrived – to stay two nights with me. He is a charming guest, always so modest and friendly. I have arranged a good programme for him. It does him good to escape occasionally from Malta.

4 p.m. Meeting of Political Committee (General Wilson in the chair). This was a short meeting – not more than an hour – and quite businesslike. The new secretariat is making progress.

5 p.m. I went with Lord Gort to see General Giraud at the Palais d'Éte. Poor Giraud has been badly advised all through and has maintained his refusal to accept the post of Inspector-General. This is almost his last day in the Palais d'Été – of which, after Darlan's assassination on 24 December, he took possession. Giraud was then complete master of the situation – *Commandant-en-Chef Civil et Militaire*.

He is very forgiving to me, considering everything, and bears no rancour. I think the truth is that he is too stupid to have understood the British role in all their diplomatic story. Duff Cooper came, and General Wilson also to this little party. General Georges – witty, cynical, and strong-minded – completed the circle.

Giraud behaved with the dignity which makes one forgive all his failings. There was no reference in all the talk and cross-talk (for an hour) to any recent event. It was just the interchange of reminiscences about the last war and the first year of this war – such as you would hear in the United Services or the Naval and Military Club.

We had a great guard of Spahis – swords, red cloaks, white horses and much music to see us in and out of the palace.

I think Giraud really appreciated the visit, and it was pleasant to feel that this sad little ceremony had something of dignity and personal quality at the end.

A large dinner at the villa to meet Lord Gort. General Wilson, Admiral Hewitt (U.S.), Air Marshal Slessor, General Barr (U.S.), General Rookes (U.S.), Admiral Troubridge[20] (who was at Summer Fields [school] with me), Bob Murphy, Brigadier Maclean (from Yugoslavia) were the chief guests.

Wednesday, 19 April 1944

My father's birthday. I got your telegram about the wedding.[21] It

[20] Lieutenant-General D. G. Barr (1895–1970) was Chief of Staff, N.A.T.O.U.S.A. and Sixth Army Group, 1944–5. Rear-Admiral Thomas Troubridge (1895–1949) had commanded Force B in the invasion of Sicily, and the Northern Assault Force for the Anzio landings; he was now helping to plan the invasion of Elba.

[21] Carol's marriage to Julian Faber had been rearranged for 20 April.

really seems strange, and I can hardly believe it. All those years have gone by so quickly – and I suppose even Sarah will be grown up soon. I do wish we had some more children – very small. Dear Carol – I hope you will give her my letter now. I sent a reply to your telegram. I do hope you will be able to get out here *very* soon.

Maud is still in Cairo – but I have left your note for her.

General Alexander arrived from England at about 9 a.m. He is staying with General Wilson. With Lord Gort and his A.D.C. (Captain Woodford) and with Jim Bowker and Tony Rumbold, I have no more room.

However, Alex came round to the villa at about 10 a.m. and chatted with me till noon, when he had an appointment with His Jumbonic Majesty – as we now call General Wilson.

After lunch, I took him for a drive to Tipasa. He was enchanted and enchanting. I find him more and more attractive. Except for a short account of Winston's health, we managed to keep almost exclusively off the war or anything to do with it!

5 p.m. I had an appointment with General Wilson to settle a few matters. He was, as usual, very pleasant. He has a foolish habit, however, of sending off telegrams from time to time, without consulting me, to P.M. And in these he is apt to air his views of political problems. In fact, the old boy just signs the telegrams which are written by his rather strange personal entourage – his son, General Davy, Lady Ranfurly and Lady Ranfurly's sister.

The P.M. invariably sends him a 'rocket' back and tells him to 'confine his observations to military matters' and asking whether I have been consulted. The poor general always promises to do better next time, always forgets – or rather signs a day or two later any of the concoctions of this 'private office' which are put before him. (This is perhaps a little exaggerated but it gives you the general picture!)

Alex remained in my villa – reading a book and talking to Roger – until 7.45 p.m. when we drove him back to General Wilson's villa. After all, he is supposed to be staying with him!

6 p.m. Duncan Sandys, M.P.[22] (who succeeded me at Ministry of Supply) came in. He gave me an account of the 'secret session' debate on tanks, which I was glad to have.

I also saw Gridley (British, of N.A.E.B.) and Mr Johnstone (U.S., also of N.A.E.B.). Johnstone is going back to Washington to try to get some of the difficulties, which have latterly arisen, properly sorted out.

I dined with Duff Cooper. Guests: Lord Gort, General Catroux, General de Lattre de Tassigny, General Bethouart (new Chief of Staff to French Army), Colonel Douglas Dodds-Parker (S.O.E.), Admiral

[22] Duncan Sandys (b. 1908), later Baron Duncan-Sandys, was Parliamentary Secretary, Ministry of Supply, 1943–4, Minister of Works, 1944–5, and held various ministries, 1951–64.

Troubridge, General Willoughby Norrie[23] (head of a useless military mission to the French which has just arrived – a palpable bit of W.O. jobbery) and some others. I sat between de Lattre and Bethouart and thoroughly enjoyed my evening, since they are both witty, intelligent and charming men. (But de Lattre protests too much.) I had a chat with Catroux after dinner.

Thursday, 20 April 1944

9 a.m. General Alexander has persuaded me to go with him to Italy – so here I am writing in the aeroplane once more. John is with me. It will be nice to be with him and to see something of the Army. I will be twenty miles from Sir Noel Charles and will *not* interfere with him. But I expect he will want some news and perhaps guidance. The Italian situation (politically) seems to be developing normally.[24]

Murphy and his boys are also going over for a meeting of the Advisory Council tomorrow. Since Ambassador Kirk has not arrived yet from Egypt, Bob is still the U.S. member of Council. He urged me to 'be around' as I think he would like me to be available if anything cropped up.

General Wilson is coming over on Saturday.

All these are just excuses to salve my conscience. I am afraid poor Roger is rather shocked and thinks I have got so restless that I shall never sit still in one place again. But I know that it is best to take one's chances whenever possible. Anyway I am sending Roger home on Saturday – so perhaps you will see him. Meanwhile, Jim Bowker and Tony Rumbold will be in charge – and they are both very capable chaps.

It is a lovely day – deep-blue sea, light-blue sky, a few white wisps of cloud. The machine is absolutely steady. It is now 12.30, and I have finished *Oliver Twist*. (*Handley Cross* lasted me well, but I have finished it.) I am still only half way through Boswell's *Life of Johnson* – but John has taken it from me. It is very pleasant – and the slight sense of truancy (for this is almost entirely a joy-ride) adds to the pleasure.

We arrived at 2 a.m. – at an aerodrome about one hour's drive from General Alex's H.Q. The rest of the day was spent – so far as I was concerned – in sauntering, reading, writing and dining.

I rang up Sir Noel Charles (twenty miles away in Naples) to get the news. I think Italy will be brought safely to bed of a 'democratic government' – of which I am the putative father, and Mason-MacFarlane and Charles the midwives. But the labour has been long and painful.

[23] Lieutenant-General Willoughby Norrie (1893–1977), later 1st Baron and Governor-General of New Zealand, 1952–7.

[24] The Junta met on 17 April and announced that the King's declaration had removed all obstacles to a democratic War Cabinet. Badoglio and his Cabinet resigned, and the Marshal was at once invited by the King to form a new broad-based government. He had been locked in negotiations ever since.

I have been trying all day to imagine what it has been like at home. It seems ridiculous that Carol should be being married today. How you could possibly arrange it in the time, I do not understand. I hope Catherine and Sarah and Nanny and Gibbs have all played their parts successfully. It does seem impossible for me to imagine it – especially at this distance. I do hope she will be happy and Julian turn out to have at least 'humour and geniality'. I suppose they had really meant to marry all along, and were just seized with a fit of nerves at the last moment. I cannot imagine where she will live or on what! But if she is happy, that is all that matters.

Friday, 21 April 1944

Yesterday was Carol's, today our wedding day, twenty-four years ago.

I spent a very pleasant and quite idle day. John and I are living on the train; no one else but General Alex and his A.D.C. It is *very* comfortable indeed.

In the morning after going with the general to the 'War Room' for the morning review of the position by the various air, naval and Army officers, I went for a long walk with John. Above the palace of Caserta is a long formal garden; a lengthy canal pond; above that a cascade; above again a rock from which the water pours. It is exactly the same as Chatsworth, only about five or six times as large. Well, above the rock are delicious woods and valleys and a fine limestone hill. The woods were absolutely crammed with huge wild anemones – like ours but twice as big – and a mass of wild cyclamen. These were really very pretty, and reminded me of the two or three you tried to grow in the pond garden at Birch Grove.

It is obvious that they like limestone, for I think you said they grew at Holker. Here, they are just like bluebells in Sussex.

The mess is in a house in the village. We walked till lunch-time, and I was really quite tired. It is tiresome to realise that one cannot walk now without some effort – at least up mountains, etc.

A very lazy afternoon reading and writing. I rang up Harold Caccia who told me that the birth was now expected at any moment. At 6 p.m. he rang up to say that an infant Government had definitely come into the world and was expected to live.

The P.M. will be pleased because Badoglio remains P.M. and Foreign Secretary; Sforza is only one of five (!) Ministers without portfolio; and Croce also. Moreover, the Interior is a Christian Democrat (moderate), *not* a Communist. All this conforms to what Winston (and we) wanted.

Sir Noel Charles came to dinner. I asked Alex to have him, so as to make his acquaintance. It went off very well, and I think they will work well together.

Saturday, 22 April 1944

The mornings are lovely here. I woke at 6.30 (4.30 by the sun) just at daybreak. After rather a perfunctory toilet (there is a *hot* bath, but it is better to have it in the evening, I think) I went for a walk, among cornfields and vineyards. It was cool – even chilly. There was rain in the night.

I hope to hear something from you when I get back to Algiers. General Alex told me that he had seen the announcement of the engagement and wedding in *The Times* on the day he left London. I suppose that was Monday 17th. I long to hear all about it.

10 a.m.–3 p.m. Went out with Alex. We drove in an open car – which is very nice for seeing (and being seen) but is rather tiring. We went up to the southern part of the line – to the river Garigliano. We visited various troops and H.Q. including the French. General Juin was not at his H.Q., but his Chief of Staff, General Carpentier,[25] was there, who impressed me as a keen and efficient officer. We also visited Mme Catroux's advanced dressing station (about two to three miles from the line). Unfortunately, she also was away.

The line was very quiet; a little desultory shelling of roads.

The French here show up much better than in Algiers. Here they are keen and well on the way to recover their confidence. We ate our sandwiches by the side of the road. The country is really lovely – great valleys and mountains. But it makes offensive warfare very difficult.

6 p.m. Motored into Naples, for a talk with Sir Noel Charles. The new Government seems quite satisfactory from our point of view.

8 p.m. Dined with Mason-MacFarlane. For some reason, he was like a bear with a sore head. He sulked all through dinner, never speaking a word. He remained the same till about 10 p.m., when he came out with his grievance. Apparently all it amounts to is that his work is not sufficiently recognised, and no one is kind to him! He is really a nice man and clever, but frightfully temperamental and a regular prima donna. I am afraid I lost my temper with him in the end and told him that he was behaving in a ridiculous way.

Sunday, 23 April 1944

I have a note from Roger (in Algiers) saying that he hopes to leave for England today. I particularly want him to get some leave – or at least change.

Alex and I went off at about 10.30. We went to Eighth Army H.Q. where we found Oliver Leese and a number of his corps and divisional commanders, including an old friend, Dick McCreery. We lunched with Eighth Army; drove round some of the ground and got back to our H.Q. at about 5 p.m. – a very pleasant day. The weather was fine,

[25] General Marcel-Maurice Carpentier (b. 1895) was Chief of Staff to General Juin, 1943–4, and to General de Lattre de Tassigny, 1944.

but very windy. This makes motoring in an open car very fatiguing.

Bob Murphy and Mason-MacFarlane came to dinner. Bob was in very good form. Mason-MacFarlane was full of apologies for his behaviour last night. These were graciously accepted.

Monday, 24 April 1944

Started off with General Alex at about 10 a.m. Returned at 7.30 p.m. The gale was very strong and on the high ground really most trying. The general insists on using his open car, without a windscreen. The dust is very bad, and of course the roads absolutely crowded. We went through some lovely mountainous country. The more one sees of this peninsula the less suitable it appears for modern military operations. It is really wonderful how much we have done already, when you consider the extraordinarily strong natural defensive positions.

We lunched with General Anders, Commanding the Polish Corps. I thought him very attractive – a keen soldier and a powerful political controversialist. Fortunately, for the time being the former interest is uppermost in his mind. But naturally memories of Poland, fear for his fate, and equal hatred of Russians and Germans are never far removed from his thoughts.

We saw an exercise, some way from the line, by one of their battalions. It consisted of an attack on a hill, covered by smoke-screen for mortar and machine-gun fire. It was most realistic, live ammunition was used throughout.

After the exercise, we were given tea at battalion H.Q. It consisted of 'zakouski' – various *hors d'œuvres* – and scrambled eggs, with red wine and tea. We had then some songs and recitations – a very good show indeed, with most talented playing of mandolins and accordions.

We arrived at General Anders's H.Q. just at noon. The trumpeters played a curious and appealing call, which ends suddenly – broken off in the middle of a musical phrase. We were told that this is always played at noon. It commemorates a trumpeter who was calling the people of Cracow to muster against the Tartars. As he was playing, an arrow pierced his throat. Ever since, for six or seven hundred years, this call is played at noon, in memory of the Poles' long struggle against barbarism and urging them still to fight in the same cause. It always ends on this broken note.

This Polish Corps has had an extraordinary history. It is almost entirely recruited from the Polish population *east* of the 'Curzon Line'[26] – Vilna and such places. Therefore they were imprisoned in Russian internment camps in 1939 (subsequent to the Stalin–Ribbentrop pact – and the defeat of Poland by Germany). After

[26] The Curzon Line (the eastern frontier of Poland proposed in 1920 by the British Foreign Secretary, Lord Curzon, as the basis of an armistice agreement between Poland and the Soviet Union) was the border which Stalin had been offering the Poles since the Teheran conference in 1943.

Germany attacked Russia, we pleaded with the Russians to let them free. After incredible adventures they walked (like the Greeks in Xenophon's *Anabasis*) all the way eastwards, till they finally reached Persia and Palestine. Now they have re-entered Europe in Italy.

One of the officers told us that when they were in Turkestan they gave a concert in the market place of some town. The people asked for the trumpeters of Lukistan (Poland) of whose musical powers they had heard. So they played every conceivable tune. But the people asked if they knew no more – so at last they played the noon-day call. This was recognised by the delighted crowd who knew the legend of the Tartar's arrow. They had a story that only when this trumpet call was played by a trumpeter of Lukistan in Turkestan itself, would peace and freedom come to all the people of the world. *Prosit omen!*

I dined with General Wilson (who has a small house here) and went through some papers with him, but I was too sleepy from the wind to make much sense.

Tuesday, 25 April 1944

Went into Naples for talks with Mason-MacFarlane and Noel Charles – also an S.O.E. officer who had just come out of Albania. It was very hot. No wind. A real summer day.

Dined quietly with General Alex.

Wednesday, 26 April 1944

I left Naples at 8.30 with General Wilson. We had a very bad trip and did not reach Algiers till 2.30.

I found (after an absence of a week) an *immense* batch of files to be read.

At six I went to a cocktail party given by Bogomolov – caviare and vodka for the swells in the small room – meat-rolls and red wine for the masses in the large room (rather like Londonderry House in the old days).

6.45 p.m. Harold Nicolson,[27] who is here on a lecture tour, came round and we had a good gossip.

8.15 p.m. Left for the aerodrome to meet Field Marshal Smuts, who arrived about 8.45 p.m. from Cairo. After seeing him to General Wilson's house I left him and went to bed.

General Alex was supposed to have arrived also from Naples, but could not get beyond Tunis owing to the weather.

Thursday, 27 April 1944

9.30 a.m. Colonel Ralph Clarke, M.P., called to see me. He is giving up the Army, having commanded his Regiment for four years, and returning to his constituency and the House of Commons.

[27] Harold Nicolson (1886–1968), author, journalist and former diplomat, was National Labour M.P. for West Leicester, 1935–45.

10–12 noon. Meeting at A.F.H.Q., General Wilson in the chair. The purpose was to explain to Field Marshal Smuts the whole military and political situation in the Mediterranean.[28] Rather characteristically General Alexander (who had arrived at my house from Tunis at about 10.30) did not appear. A rather dull affair, except for brilliant intervention from time to time by Smuts.

12 noon. Sir Francis Rugman – ex-financial adviser to the Sudan Government. He is now to be financial adviser to the Allied Military Organisation which is to undertake Balkan relief. This is (as regards the politics and economics) nominally under me. An interesting preliminary talk, but not sufficient time, so I told him to come back later.

12.30 p.m. Brigadier Salisbury-Jones[29] of the British Military Mission in South Africa – a courtesy call, to give me news of and a message from Billy Harlech.

Lunch at General Wilson's – a large party for Field Marshal Smuts. General Alexander was there. After luncheon, I had about twenty minutes alone with Smuts, and Alex the same. This was the only useful part of the day. The Field Marshal was very friendly and very interesting. I wish he could have stayed here another day.

We drove down to the aerodrome and saw the Marshal off, getting back about 5. I then retired to work in bed!

6 p.m. Sir Francis Rugman again. A long and useful talk this time.

8.15 p.m. A funny little dinner-party. The young men were out, and we were just General Jumbo Wilson, General Alex, Maud and Jim Bowker. A very amusing evening, everyone in very good and characteristic form – Jumbo with his splendid heavy guffaws of laughter and Alex with his rather delicate mischievous twinkle. Alex took a great fancy to Maud and has asked her to stay with him in Italy and will send his plane for her!

Friday, 28 April 1944

10.30 a.m. Political meeting at A.F.H.Q. General Wilson in the chair. A very good and business-like meeting (General Alex returned this morning to Naples).

Lunch. Mr Gridley (economic adviser and British head of N.A.E.B.) to lunch. At 3 p.m. I attended the last meeting of N.A.E.B. Murphy and I appeared as 'founder members'. It will reappear as N.A.J.E.M. The significance of this is that N.A.E.B. (North African Economic Board) was attached to A.F.H.Q. and had nominal allegiance to General Eisenhower. It was therefore part of the

[28] The Greek mutinies had been suppressed by force on 23–24 April. EAM and EDES agreed to send representatives to Cairo to discuss joining in an all-party government. Nevertheless Venizelos resigned on the 26th.

[29] Brigadier Guy Salisbury-Jones (b. 1896) was head of the British Military Mission to South Africa, 1941–4.

'occupation' period. N.A.J.E.M. (North African Joint Economic Mission) will be the economic advisers of the British and American Ambassadors sitting together. It belongs to the new conception of our relations with the French Committee. This is in exact accordance with the plan which I had arranged months ago and is quite right. The delay has been simply American procrastination. But it means that I fade out, and Duff is *not* interested in economics!

5.30 p.m. Longuin (*New York Post*).

6 p.m. Brandon (*Sunday Times*).

6.30 p.m. Sir Clifford Heathcote-Smith (refugees).

Your telegram has arrived! or rather one from Bob Dixon about you – Hurrah, Hurrah! It is splendid and we are all much excited.[30] It will be such fun, and I am sure will do you good. (It seems absurd to write all this in a letter which I shall now *not* send.)

Saturday, 29 April 1944

Your letter about the wedding has arrived. Also a very charming one from our Moucher. It sounds a lovely wedding and the flowers must have been very nice. I am so glad that Macmillan & Co. was well represented.

Worked at papers all morning.

12 noon. Belgian Ambassador – all about nothing.

1.15 p.m. General [G. S.] Hatton, Captain Smith, Colonel ? (U.S.) to lunch. These were a delegation from Middle East about Balkan affairs.

3 p.m. Brazilian Minister (da Cunha), a very charming man. The Brazilians are beginning to get some of their troops and air squadrons available.[31]

The rest of the day I spent in reading and writing.

I must really get out for a walk or I shall perish from want of exercise. A quiet dinner. I have finished Boswell now – also read an excellent book by Miss Sackville-West called *The Eagle and the Dove* – it is a brilliant piece of writing. I have started *Pendennis*, which will keep me happy for a bit.

Sunday, 30 April 1944

Went to early church. I rather hoped to get a telegram about your arrival. Bob Dixon had said that you would be leaving either 29th or 30th. Perhaps we shall get something in the course of the day.

A very quiet day. I lunched with General Wilson, who left for England in the afternoon. The French have accepted our views on two important points at issue – viz., the choice of command when French

[30] She was coming out to join me in Algiers in a day or two.

[31] U-boat attacks on Brazilian shipping had provoked Brazil into declaring war on Germany and Italy on 22 August 1942. A Brazilian Expeditionary Force arrived in Italy in the summer of 1944.

troops are detached for a special objective and the question of forming a new Corps H.Q. in Italy for de Larminat. S.A.C. (General Wilson) was able to comfort General de Lattre on the first point by accepting a suggestion made at the conference on Friday that a French staff officer should sit at A.F.H.Q., see the signals sent to the French detachment, O.K. them, or refer to de Lattre if he thought necessary.

On the second point General de Larminat will go himself to Italy with a few officers and be at General Juin's disposal and learn what he can of modern methods. But no second French Corps will be set up.

At about 6 p.m. we got a telegram to say that you were definitely leaving tonight. That is splendid.

Fred Lawson (Lord Burnham)[32] and Harold Nicolson to dinner – also the Duprees. Fred Lawson has come out as the result of my telegram to P. J. Grigg to straighten out the editorship and conduct of *Eighth Army News* and other Army papers. He is a very sensible fellow.

[32] Major-General E. F. Lawson, 4th Baron Burnham (1890–1963), was Director of Public Relations in the War Office and Senior Military Adviser to the Ministry of Information, 1942–5.

May

Monday, 1 May 1944

I have just heard that you are expected about noon. I have papers and a meeting, but am sending John to the aerodrome.

So this series of letters will end, in the most agreeable way possible, by your coming yourself.

Dorothy arrived safely at about 4.30 at the villa. The aeroplane had been signalled for 12 noon, so I did not go to meet her, but sent John Wyndham instead. She seemed very cheerful on arrival, but very tired.

Dinner for Sir Keith Murdoch,[1] Australian newspaper magnate (recommended to my attention by Brendan Bracken), Sir John Cunningham, General Gammell, Lady Ranfurly, and some others. A very pleasant party and Sir Keith Murdoch (who stayed on for a talk) seemed pleased.

Tuesday, 2 May 1944

Fortunately, things are pretty quiet – an immense amount of reading to get through, but (alas!) little effective action. This gives me time to see more of Dorothy than if she had been here a year ago. The chief things at the moment on which I am working are:

(*a*) long-term Italian policy,
(*b*) Italian economic policy,
(*c*) short-term Yugoslavia questions.

In the afternoon, Dorothy and I went for a drive and a walk in the forest. There is so much to talk about!

Wednesday, 3 May 1944

Colonel Spofford (Military Government Section), General Gammell, Air Marshal Slessor.

We had a pleasant luncheon party – Mrs Vanier (Canadian Minister's wife), General George Clark (Chief Administrative Officer),

[1] Sir Keith Murdoch (1886–1952), father of Rupert Murdoch, was chairman and managing director of The Herald and Weekly Times Ltd.

Mr and Mrs Adrian Holman (Duff Cooper's new Counsellor), Etienne de Rosières (de Gaulle's A.D.C.), Fred Reinhardt (Bob Murphy has gone to Marrakesh), etc.

In the late afternoon, we went to Tipasa; walked in the ruins; dined at L'Hôtel du Rivage. M. and Mme Vallin (hotel-keeper) surpassed themselves by producing both omelette and lobsters to celebrate the occasion.

Dorothy loved Tipasa. It was a beautiful, clear, sunny day – the lights and colour were most beautiful and the old city in its garden of myrtle and figs and greenery as romantic as ever.

Thursday, 4 May 1944

All the morning wrestling with the problems of the Yugoslavian Navy and naval forces – a most intricate jigsaw of rivalries and complications. After an hour with C.-in-C. Mediterranean I drafted a telegram to show him later.

We went (Dorothy, Anthony Rumbold, Jim Bowker and I) for a picnic luncheon to Rivet (in the foothills beyond Maison Carrée). Back by 4 p.m. A very nice place for a short drive into the country, only half an hour by car.

Dinner with Sir John Cunningham. The Duff Coopers, Admiral Troubridge, Captain Laing (Assistant Chief of Staff), etc., etc. Admirable food – excellent drink – and the Navy at their best!

We went through our Yugoslavian problems after dinner and I arranged for Captain Laing, R.N., to call the next morning.

Friday, 5 May 1944

A quiet morning – papers and telegrams. Captain Laing came at noon – and we agreed the draft. M. Schneider came for advice. He has had to give up his work on Air France, since Communist Grenier[2] has taken control of the Air Ministry.

The weather is very nice – hot but clear and not sticky. In the afternoon, Dorothy, John Wyndham and I went to bathe with Colonel Douglas Dodds-Parker. I never thought last year I should bathe on that beach in May 1944. The time has sped by, but A.F.H.Q. has not moved!

Dinner with Duff Coopers. Diana in great form. Miss Virginia Cowles, Bloggs Baldwin, [John] Curle (Duff's new Third Secretary).

Saturday, 6 May 1944

I have worked fairly hard at my Yugoslavian detailed troubles but am more pleased with having completed my Italian 'Saving' telegram[3] on general policy.

[2] Fernand Grenier (b. 1901), imprisoned by the Germans, 1940–1, was Commissioner (later Minister) of Air, 1943–4.

[3] A telegram of low priority, despatched only when the wire is free from more urgent traffic.

Tony Rumbold (who 'drafts' excellently) has been a great help. I have also prepared another 'follow-up' telegram which I will send tomorrow. It is quite clear that Charles shares my view that this time *we* should take the lead and not leave it to the Russians.

I am also working at a paper on the Italian economic situation. I have demanded a meeting here – which is now fixed for Tuesday.

But (alas) the weather has changed. It is hot and clammy; there is a sirocco.

9 a.m. John Addis (agenda, etc., for Tuesday's meeting).

10 a.m. Gridley and Gosling (of N.A.J.E.M.) came to help me with my Italian economic paper. It is not their business really, but they are good chaps and anxious to be of use.

We had a luncheon party – quite good. Admiral Hewitt (U.S. Navy), Major-General Lewis (G4 or Q [Supply, A.F.H.Q. staff section]); Mr [Hervé J.] L'Heureux (U.S. Diplomatic Corps!), Miss Virginia Cowles, Air Marshal Slessor. I think Dorothy is enjoying this new world – a little more spacious than Pooks Cottage. I think it is good for her.

There was rather a lot of work all the afternoon, with telegrams and my paper. So we only got out for a short walk together. But it was quite a pleasant little stroll in a valley behind the town. No dinner; writing, reading and the sirocco.

Sunday, 7 May 1944

I slept very badly – got to sleep in the early hours at last and overslept myself – so missed church. It was hot and sticky all night and a warm south wind blowing up from the desert.

10.45 a.m. Finished my economic paper (Italian) second draft.

Dorothy, John Wyndham, Eric Duncannon and I went to Chréa for the day. Although the drive over the plain to Blida was intolerably hot, yet when we got up the mountain the wind was tempered by the height (nearly 5,000 feet).

We had a delicious picnic on a grassy slope, covered with yellow and purple pansies – slept and walked till 5 p.m.

An *enormous* cloud of locusts, which I supposed had been carried by the sirocco from the desert to the plain, came over the mountain as the wind suddenly changed. I have never seen locusts (except the tail end of some at Marrakesh when I went to meet Lord Swinton). This cloud was absolutely terrific in size – height, length and breadth. The locusts kept being blown in all directions by the high wind – and settling on the ground and trees and everywhere. The cypress trees suddenly began to look brown instead of green. It was really an extraordinary and rather unpleasant sight.

Monday, 8 May 1944

A normal day. Mr Dening (Adviser to Lord Louis Mountbatten) to stay. Scott-Bailey (on censorship), Dodds-Parker (on S.O.E.) and so on.

Tuesday, 9 May 1944

11 a.m. Murphy.

12 noon. M.G.S. Meeting on the situation created regarding southern France by the cutting off of the Eisenhower–Koenig conversations.[4]

4 p.m. Political Committee.

5.30 p.m. Meeting on Italian economic situation.

8 p.m. Large dinner-party. Guests: Mr and Mrs Chapin, M. and Mme de Lesseps, M. and Mme Teyssot, M. and Mme Schneider, Mr Dening, Eric Duncannon and others of the staff. Mme Teyssot is pretty and very nice. Teyssot is A.D.C. to de Gaulle. The Schneiders are very old friends, from the first days.

Wednesday, 10 May 1944

Usual morning. The paper-work is getting frightful. And yet so little seems to be achieved. I had a long talk with Murphy and found that he agreed largely with my views on Italy. He is going to make the same kind of recommendations to the State Department.

The Economic meeting yesterday was not discouraging, and the paper which I circulated was quite well received. I am getting E. M. H. Lloyd[5] (from Middle East) to go to Italy and advise, and I hope something will follow. General Clark was quite helpful – at least he understands the problem.

Luncheon party. Guests: M. and Mme Guianchain (proprietor of Hôtel Saint-George and leading bookseller), John de Salis, Mr Dening, Captain Raphael (A.D.C. to Duff Cooper), Mr and Mrs Rooker, Colonel John Wrightson (Sir Guy's son), Captain Wharton, R.N. (Naval Liaison).

I dined with General Rookes. A large party, including General Wilson, Admiral Hewitt and all the leading naval, military and air figures. Too long a dinner. Too long a cinema. We did not get away till after 1 a.m.!

Thursday, 11 May 1944

A morning at the villa with a mass of paper.

General Wilson came at 12 noon. He gave me a full account of all that had happened during his visit to England. I gathered that he was pleased (and rather relieved) at his reception. The P.M. was all smiles.

[4] General Marie-Pierre Koenig (1898–1970) was Military Delegate to the F.C.N.L., 1944, and commander of the French Forces of the Interior and Military Governor of Paris, 1944–5. His conversations with Eisenhower, temporarily halted, were about the status of French Forces in Metropolitan France.

[5] E. M. H. Lloyd (1889–1968) was Economic Adviser to the Minister Resident in the Middle East, 1942–4.

Luncheon party: Duff Coopers; Massigli; Catroux; Gaston Palewski and Mme Baril. Rather a good party, which went well. All these people are very pleased to see Dorothy, and I am trying to work through all the old friends here who have been (on the whole) very generous and tolerant to me.

Friday, 12 May 1944

Meeting on *Austrian* planning (Spofford, Maxwell, Murphy, etc). In the end I and Murphy agreed to telegraph to F.O. and State Department making specific recommendations on procedure. The difficulty is that the Russians are not easy to bring to any agreed view of *German* affairs. But we hope to get them to treat *Austria* on a different basis, on the lines of the Moscow declaration.[6]

Went for a good walk with Dorothy in the evening. The weather is still heavy and dull.

Saturday, 13 May 1944

The first news of Alexander's battle is coming in. It seems a good start.[7]

10.45 a.m. Eric Linklater[8] called. I had heard from Daniel [Macmillan] that he was coming. He was charming and whimsical – looking very odd in shorts and khaki shirt (a major!). He is to write the history of the Tunisian and Italian campaigns.

Colonel Maxwell called. He is now getting very excited about Austrian planning.

Dorothy and I lunched with Catroux. Only the Comtesse de Montgomerie. I had a long talk with Catroux after luncheon. He is still very unhappy about Spears in the Lebanon. Apart from that he feels that de Gaulle is improving, although still liable to be badly advised and impulsive. The unfortunate effect of cutting off cypher communications with London is upsetting. Catroux feels that de Gaulle ought to go himself to London. I promised to pass that idea to Duff Cooper.

Dorothy and I motored to Tipasa. We had a very nice drive and a good walk. We dined and stayed the night at the inn.

Sunday, 14 May 1944

Motored back to Algiers in time for lunch. General Wilson and General Gubbins (S.O.E.) to luncheon. S.A.C. [Supreme Allied Commander] is off to Italy tomorrow.

After luncheon, Gubbins and I (with Dorothy) motored out to Dodds-Parker's place. Here we found Slessor, Gammell and General

[6] The Conference of Foreign Ministers at Moscow in October 1943 had agreed that Austria should be restored to independence, while taking account of her military support for Hitler.

[7] The Eighth Army had been moved secretly from the Adriatic coast to the Cassino front and, joining the Fifth Army, had launched an attack on the Gustav Line at 11 p.m. on 11 May.

[8] Eric Linklater (1899–1974), Macmillan author, served in the Directorate of Public Relations, War Office, 1941–5. His book, *The Campaign in Italy 1943–5*, was published in 1951.

Caffey[9] (U.S.). Dorothy bathed and we conferred. The chief subject was the organisation of an Adriatic command (for work in Dalmatia and with Tito). We agreed the paper, for Wilson to send to London.

Cinema at General [George] Clark's at 8.45.

I found a mass of paper on my return. I did not finish till about 1 a.m.

Monday, 15 May 1944

9.30 a.m. S.A.C.'s meeting. A large agenda – French, Yugoslavian, Italian (prisoners of war), etc.

Mr E. M. H. Lloyd arrived last night. I am sending him to Italy (having borrowed him from Lord Moyne). He will be a great help on Italian economic problems. He left in S.A.C.'s aeroplane after luncheon.

Dorothy and I went out again to Tipasa to dine and sleep.

Tuesday, 16 May 1944

10 a.m. Murphy. We discussed General de Gaulle's pronouncement on the Darlan–Clark agreement. This appeared to amount to unilateral denunciation. Murphy was quite reasonable and we agreed that it would be better to take no notice of this Parliamentary intervention. We would continue to operate under the terms of the Darlan–Clark agreement and to negotiate with the French for its amendment. If the French continue to come to the Joint Committee which was studying revision, they would be tacitly admitting the validity of the agreement.

About the vote of the Assembly asking the Committee to rename itself 'Provisional Government of France', we agreed that this was not our affair. Duff Cooper joined our conference and was most helpful.

Luncheon party:

General Moorhead (D.A.G. [Deputy Adjutant General]).

General [Leslie] Nicholls (Chief Signals Officer).

Mr [L.] Hitchen (Sulphur Control, Ministry of Supply – just back from Sicily).

General Caffey (U.S.) (G3, Special Operations [A.F.H.Q. staff section]).

Air Commodore [Leonard] Pankhurst (Chief of Staff to Slessor).

Mr Curle (Third Secretary, British Mission to French Committee).

A pleasant and successful party.

4 p.m. Political meeting at A.F.H.Q. General Gammell presided (in General Wilson's absence). A large agenda. The chief difficulty was a proposal from the State Department to declare Rome an 'open city'. The British Chiefs of Staff and F.O. had sent a waffling telegram (F.O. particularly feeble) and I had a good deal of trouble in persuading my

[9] Major-General Eugene M. Caffey (1895–1961) commanded the First Engineer Special Brigade, 1943–5.

colleagues that our chief interest was not so much the desire to *attack* Rome while in German hands, but to *use* the city when we had captured it. We must be very careful not to *tie* our hands. Eventually I got the meeting adjourned.

5.30 p.m. General Gubbins.

7 p.m. Colonel Crichton[10] (a lawyer) to tell me about the meaning of the expression 'open city'. I was amused to find that it had no legal meaning and was *not* used in the Hague Convention of 1907.

7.30 p.m. Colonel Maxwell – relations between A.F.H.Q. and S.H.A.E.F.[11] (i.e., Wilson and Eisenhower) on French civil affairs.

Worked till late on a mass of papers.

Wednesday, 17 May 1944

11 a.m. Political Committee. Murphy was *most* conciliatory. He conceded my point of substance and we accepted his draft. Rome will be at our service!

Luncheon party:
Mme Bogomolov (wife of Russian Ambassador).
M. Guérin (French Foreign Office).
M. da Cunha (Brazilian Minister).
Count R. de Vichenet (Belgian Ambassador).
General [Daniel] Noce (U.S.) (Assistant Chief of Staff).
M. Cerny (Czech Minister).
General Beaumont-Nesbitt (Liaison Section, A.F.H.Q.).

A good party.

3 p.m. Went to see my doctor, Colonel Richardson, who is still laid up with a bad leg. I fear he will have to go home.

4 p.m. Murphy, Spofford, Maxwell – various M.G.S. (now G5) questions.

5 p.m. Brigadier Forestier-Walker – Yugoslav relief (A.M.L. [Allied Military Liaison]).

Roger Makins has returned – looking much better and full of news.

Dorothy and I dined with Mme Baril. The Duff Coopers, Maud, General [Clément] Blanc, M. Frenay (of the Committee). Frenay is a charming man, young, enthusiastic, and with a fine record in the Resistance movement.

Thursday, 18 May 1944

A morning with papers and talking to Roger. A lot to hear and a lot to do.

Dorothy, Maud and I went to lunch with the Princesses (de Ligne and Galitzine) at the Borg Polignac. They were as charming and

[10] Colonel Robertson Crichton (b. 1912) was a judge of the High Court of Justice, 1967–77.
[11] Supreme Headquarters Allied Expeditionary Force, for the invasion of France.

interesting as ever. Their garden is being completely destroyed by locusts, which is a pity, as it is really beautiful. M. Genlis (ex-Ambassador and *very* wet) and Count de Tocqueville[12] (grandson or great-grandson of the historian).

4 p.m. Meeting with Bob [Murphy]. We drafted a letter for Wilson to send to de Gaulle about the use of French manpower.

Bob is in good form. He told me a good deal about Stettinius[13] and his visit to London. Apparently Stettinius formed a very good impression and was delighted by the frankness with which we discussed matters over a wide range.

Duncan Sandys to stay – on his way back from Italy.

A special communiqué announces the capture of Cassino by the British and of the Monastery by the Poles (another diplomatic success for Alex). Also, the Gustav Line is broken; the battle is now for the Adolf Hitler Line.[14] (General Gammell tells me that the enemy are beginning to abandon this name in their own communiqués and propaganda – a hopeful sign!)

The weather is lovely now. Hot and sunny, but not too hot.

I have finished *Pendennis*. Also a novel called *Hotel Berlin* [*Grand Hotel*] by Vicki Baum. I prefer Thackeray.

The locusts are flying everywhere about the town. They are repellent.

Friday, 19 May 1944

10 a.m. General Gammell called. He gave me the latest battle news, which is excellent.[15] Then a long talk about organisation for the Balkans. Roger Makins was present and I think we made some progress.

A day of paper. Dorothy and I got a walk (for an hour) in the forest.

A dinner-party:

M. Chatelus (Director of *TAM* – a weekly French review).

Mme Chatelus (she is a very gifted and charming lady. She makes some charming tiles which adorn many houses here, including our villa).

Mr Harry Woodruff (Murphy's staff).

Mr and Mrs Whittington (British Consul).

Mr Eric Linklater.

Mlle de Miribel (fanatical Gaullist, French M. of I.)

Major Derek Walker (M.G.S.).

[12] Count Jean Clerel de Tocqueville (1896–1974), great-nephew of the historian, was Inspector (later Inspector-General) of Finances in North Africa, 1941–50.

[13] Edward R. Stettinius, Jr (1900–49) was U.S. Under-Secretary of State (in succession to Sumner Welles), 1943–4, and, having deputised for Cordell Hull during the latter's illness, took over as Secretary of State in November 1944.

[14] Five to twenty miles behind the Gustav Line.

[15] The battle for the Adolf Hitler Line had begun.

A nice party. They stayed rather late and this means a lot of work. I was up till late with papers.

Saturday, 20 May 1944

A very hot day – sirocco. General Wilson arrived back from Italy last night. Everything seems to be going on well.

9.30 a.m. Meeting of Political and Economic Committee. The chief business was the French action in calling up too many men, both European and native, from the farms and the workshops. This is going to have a deplorable effect on the agricultural and mining programme. The phosphate mines only require about 350 Europeans. The target (five million tons in 1945) is of the utmost importance.

A letter was sent (drafted by Murphy and me) by Wilson to de Gaulle – I hope it will do some good.

The French have also got into great difficulties with their wheat and cereal situation generally. Five days' supply in Tunisia, a week's in Algeria – and the harvest not yet in. They have twice been wrong in their calculation already this year. They have borrowed over 30,000 tons from us already (and they ought to be an *exporting* and not an *importing* country in French North Africa). It is really most aggravating. It is a pity they pay so little real attention to the French Empire about which they talk so much.

I suppose the truth is that the Metropolitan French (and especially the Government) are thinking about nothing but France. It is as if an exiled British Government were sitting at Nairobi. The English settlers would hate them as bitterly as the *colons* hate the whole set-up here. The *colons* are as anxious to be 'liberated' from the French as the French are to be liberated from the Germans!

On the top of the miscalculations and muddle have come the locusts. It is *vital* to have the bran ready for the poisoning campaign when the hoppers hatch out in a month to six weeks from now. We finally agreed to lend them some more wheat, on the condition that they got a good bran extraction from their present and this new stock. For the rest, they must tighten their belts and live on vegetables till the harvest. We also decided to tell them the Allied plans for feeding France. Then, if they are really hoarding or stockpiling here for Metropolitan France, they may be prepared to produce these hidden quantities, knowing in detail our generous plans for France when liberated.

4 p.m. Dorothy and I went to the dock to meet the *Gripsholm*, come from Barcelona with British and some American repatriated prisoners. Generals Wilson, [George] Clark, etc., Duff and Diana. We found the men in remarkably good heart, considering their grievous wounds and long imprisonment. A number of Teesside and Tyneside lads – one Stocktonian. They were really wonderful to talk to. One Stocktonian sergeant said, 'The Germans are getting very timid now, sir; very timid

indeed!' (I could not quite discover how they showed this; presumably a less harsh treatment of our prisoners.)

6 p.m. Murphy, Makins, Russell Barnes (P.W.B.) – a general conference of censorship, staff, policy and various questions.

Sunday, 21 May 1944

Dorothy and I started at 9.30 (after church at 8) for a two-day trip. I think I have described most of the country and places in letters. It was *wonderful* weather (cloud and sun – not too hot, not cold, a nice breeze – perfect for motoring). We went east from Algiers – through Tizi-Ouzou to Djidjelli (where we stayed the night), a most wonderfully changing and picturesque drive – through the Kabyle Mountains to Bougie and then on by the Corniche Road, along the sea.

Monday, 22 May 1944

Left Djidjelli 7.45 a.m. Drove to Sétif (through the Chabet Pass and Kerrata – a most wonderful and awe-inspiring canyon). Got to Djemila and its old Roman city. Left again about three, and drove back through the rich grain-bearing plateau, through the desert country near the pass of the iron gates, down to another plateau, down again through the Gorge of the Isser to a sort of rolling valley rather like the Border country – and back to Algiers, where we arrived at 9.30 p.m. Two heavenly days.

Tuesday, 23 May 1944

The news is still good. The critical moment, however, has now arrived – the vital moves in Alexander's tactical game. The forces on the Anzio bridgehead attacked this morning; at the same time the Eighth Army attacked the Hitler Line across the Liri valley – the strongly defended and prepared line, which is only a real line in the valley area. Meanwhile, while the centre is being attacked, French forces will try to turn one end, and Polish the other flank.

A vast box of papers – which I managed to get through by the end of a long day. I saw General Wilson at 10.30 and arranged to go with him to Italy tomorrow.

12 noon. Captain Bowlby, R.N. about plans for the Balkans. Roger has made a redraft of my Balkan paper and edited it for circulation to the Political Committee (an Anglo-American body). I shall now produce a more interesting version, restricted to British circulation.

Lunch with Massigli. Dorothy looked very well and very pretty. Comtesse de Montgomerie, Mme de Breteuil, M. [Emmanuel] d'Astier de la Vigerie (Minister of the Interior), M. Chataigneau (lately from Beirut) and one or two others.

Worked all the afternoon on papers. At 6 p.m. Colonel Spofford to discuss economic and food problems in Italy. The meeting is now fixed for Monday, and we shall have:

(*a*) The A.C.C.'s views on monetary and economic policy – with Lloyd's help.

(*b*) The report of the Supply Mission for Combined Civil Affairs Committee of Combined Chiefs of Staff.

As they all disagree, it should be a good show. I hope some good will come of it.

7.30 p.m. Looked in to Duff and Diana's garden party – obviously a great success. A cold *mistral* came on and heavy rain during the night.

1–23 May 1944

This has been a period without any violent crisis, although a good many day-to-day questions have been dealt with in the ordinary course of business. Three major questions continue to occupy my mind and a certain amount of progress has been made.

The first two relate to Italy. I have been convinced for some time that England cannot continue with a purely negative policy on Italian affairs. We cannot merely drift along in the Micawberish hope that something will turn up. It seems to me that we should definitely make up our minds as to whether we intend to allow the grievances and emotions of recent years to colour our Italian policy and urge us into courses dictated by passions rather than reason, or whether we are going to consider calmly our own interests and the broader needs of Western civilisation. I strongly feel that we should have a positive policy based upon the desire to rescue the Italian people and help them to preserve their general social, economic and religious life, and thus prevent them, perhaps, from falling into the hands either of the extreme Communist movement on the one hand or of Fascist reaction on the other. The second might easily come after the war if the people feel that the liberal Government has failed to deliver the goods. This general policy was worked out by me in telegrams No. 141 'Saving' of 2 May, and No. 648 of 7 May, to the Foreign Office.

I have felt that the Foreign Office was taking a dangerously blind view, and one of my main objects in sending Roger Makins home – apart from the need that he had for a change – was that he should try to put forward our views more forcibly to Sir Orme Sargent. I gather that this has not been altogether without success, and that they are working at the possibility of making peace on the lines that I suggested. Knowing that Sir Orme Sargent is permanently overworked, and knowing the obstruction that I think the Foreign Secretary would himself offer to this course, I think we shall have to continue to press hard in order to get any results. I propose during this weekend at Naples to have a round-table conference on the purely political aspects with Sir Noel Charles, Murphy and Kirk (the new American member of the Advisory Council), and as a result to send some more pressing telegrams home.

The second problem concerns the Italian economic situation.

Reading the many telegrams which have been passing between the C.C.S., M.G.S., A.M.G. and A.C.C., I felt that this matter was not being tackled with any real grip. I therefore made a number of suggestions and circulated some notes to General Clark, Colonel Spofford and others. Commander Southard,[16] an American economist of some repute, has been quite helpful, but I think my most useful achievement has been to obtain from Lord Moyne the services of Mr E. M. H. Lloyd, who is now in Naples helping the A.C.C. to produce their report on economic and especially monetary questions. A full conference begins in Naples on Monday, 29 May, on the draft report of A.C.C. At the same time, it so happens that a Supply Mission from the C.A.A.C., that is, the Civil Affairs Advisory Committee responsible to the C.C.S., has been in Naples for two months. I met the British member of it, Mr Nalder, in Naples when he first came out. He is a man who helped us over Malta one time when I was at the Colonial Office. They have now completed their report. In some respects their recommendations are going to run counter to those of the monetary experts. This will have to be straightened out. Whatever the final result may be, at least we can say that during the past month a determined drive has been made to alleviate as far as possible a difficult and intractable problem. Of course these two aspects of the Italian policy are bound up together. Inflation will result in the destruction of the middle classes and the fall of a government based upon moderate support. At the same time, the weakness of the Government and the lack of an effective administrative machine make it very difficult to apply remedies based upon economic policy followed in England, a policy which has only been made possible by the combination of a highly disciplined and patriotic people and a very effective administrative machine.

During this period the greater part of our time seems to have been taken up with Balkan affairs, ranging from the romantic and dramatic Tito right through the whole gamut. An incredible number of telegrams arrive on minor issues, but no single thread of major policy seems to have emerged. The Prime Minister's present policy is that in the period of the war he will support any movement which will fight the Germans. He will therefore support Tito in Yugoslavia, who is a Communist, Communist bands in Albania, but in Greece he is trying to support the claims of the King and of a moderate and liberal Government on the grounds that EAM do not really fight the Germans. The difficulty is that with modern communications as rapid as they are, and the universal listening to the radio, it is difficult to be a Communist in Yugoslavia and a Royalist in Greece. A great deal will turn, I think, on the outcome of the conference of Greek politicians at Beirut. If this goes well and a coalition government is formed under

[16] Lieutenant-Commander F. A. Southard, Jr (b. 1907) was Financial Adviser, A.F.H.Q., 1943–5, and Professor of Economics at Cornell University, 1931–48.

M. Papandreou[17] it will certainly have a great effect in other parts of the Balkans and do a good deal towards stabilising things.

Meanwhile, although these territories are nominally under the command of General Wilson, I am much disturbed at the lack of any planning or even any directive from the Combined Chiefs of Staff to get on with planning Allied policy in this part of the world. So far as British policy is concerned, I have had no guidance or directive of any kind. To clear my mind I wrote a paper which I showed to one or two people including Colonel Dodds-Parker, and Makins has now produced a redraft of it suitable for circulation to the Political Committee, including the Americans. I am afraid it is going to be rather a complicated business, because we shall have to operate two sets of enquiries at once: first, the broad lines of the functions which A.F.H.Q. is to fulfil on the assumption (as yet unconfirmed) that the Americans are prepared to take their part in Balkan affairs; and secondly, a more detailed set of plans purely British in character and intended to secure and defend purely British interests. I do not mean that British and American interests conflict in any way; the difficulty is, however, to get them into any clear position. They either wish to revert to isolation combined with suspicion of British imperialism, or to intervene in a pathetic desire to solve in a few months by the most childish and amateurish methods problems which have baffled statesmen for many centuries. Somewhere between these two extremes we have got to guide them, both for their own advantage and ours and for that of the future peace of the world.

These three weeks, therefore, although they have shown, I am afraid, very little tangible results, have not, I think, been altogether useless; and on our return from Italy next week we should be in a position to pursue some of these matters more effectively.

Wednesday, 24 May 1944

Left Maison Blanche with General Wilson in his plane at 2 p.m.[18] After rather a slow journey we arrived at Caserta aerodrome about 7.30. I dined that night with General Alexander, whom I found in good heart. There have been many ups and downs in this battle, but the general progress although somewhat slow was satisfactory.

Thursday, 25 May 1944

9 a.m. Went to the morning meeting with General Alexander. Did a certain amount of business with General Wilson and Air Marshal Slessor after the meeting.

10.30 a.m. Left with General Alexander and drove with him to

[17] Giorgios Papandreou (1888–1968) had accepted the premiership on 27 April 1944, after the resignation of Venizelos, and the pan-Hellenic conference in the Lebanon had been called to discuss the composition of his Cabinet. Papandreou was Prime Minister, 1944–5 and 1963–5.

[18] My wife remained in Algiers.

Cassino. We spent most of the morning looking at the ruins and going over the battlefield of S. Angelo. The capture of this key point on the enemy side of the Rapido river was clearly a remarkable feat of arms. We lunched with General Leese of the Eighth Army at his Forward Headquarters not far from Cassino. He seemed in very good heart. The Canadian Corps was beginning to move, and although inexperienced, he thought it would give a good account of itself. We motored back to Caserta in the evening and I dined with General Alexander. Maud Baillie has turned up at the villa. Mr Vellacott[19] was also staying there.

Friday, 26 May 1944

We held a full meeting at ten o'clock to discuss procedure for Rome. General MacFarlane, General Robertson (representing General Alexander), General [Harry H.] Johnson (American Fifth Army and Governor-Designate of Rome), Mr Vellacott and various other officials were present. General agreement was reached on procedure.

(*a*) There will be no formal entry into Rome. General Alexander is very anxious that the capture of Rome should be treated militarily on its true basis. The battle is for the purpose of destroying the German Army, and any triumphs should be delayed until that object is completed.

(*b*) General Johnson will act as Governor on behalf of General Clark of the American Fifth Army. He will be accompanied by S Force, who will carry out all their duly appointed tasks, and the AMGOT officials will also work under him. At the end of the first phase AMGOT will take over and the second phase will begin.

(*c*) The position of the Italian Government was discussed. It was clear to me that General MacFarlane has already largely put himself under an obligation to Badoglio and the Prince. I do not like it at all.

At 11.30 we left for Bari – General Wilson and I in one car; Roger Makins and Lieutenant Schultz in another. It was a most beautiful drive through Benevento over the mountains. We had a picnic lunch on the way. General Wilson was in excellent form and discussed many matters, including the Balkans and the proposed reorganisation of the Mediterranean command.

I was put up in General [Eric] Nares's flat in Bari. This flat, which is in the most vulgar style of modern Fascist art, is nevertheless very luxurious. General Wilson was also staying there, and we were provided with an admirable dinner including all the latest luxuries. Mr Broad of the Foreign Office, who is my representative at Bari, was at the dinner.

[19] Lieutenant-Colonel Paul Vellacott (1891–1954) was Director of Political Warfare, Middle East, 1942–4, and Master of Peterhouse, Cambridge, 1939–54.

Saturday, 27 May 1944

We had a very full day looking into the whole organisation of Special Operations (Mediterranean) in the Bari district. The course of our tour took us from Monopoli to Brindisi, Ostuni, Mola and back again to Bari. The day finished with a dinner with General Twining[20] and the officers of the Fifteenth American Air Force, followed by the inevitable film during the course of which both General Wilson and I fell asleep.

Sunday, 28 May 1944

An equally full day, ending up by a tour of the port, from which we drove immediately to Bari aerodrome and returned to Caserta by air, arriving there just after four o'clock. I went with the general to his room where we dealt with a number of telegrams covering a large range of subjects – the French Army, Tito, and so on.

Apart from the tour, while I was at Bari came the news of the German attack upon Tito's headquarters. It appears that the attempt to capture him and Randolph[21] – which would be the greater prize it would be difficult to say – failed by a hair's breadth, the Marshal having escaped to the hills some two hours previously. Thinking the Prime Minister would be worrying I sent him a telegram. The draft of a telegram to be sent to Marshal Tito arrived from the Prime Minister.[22] We thought it might be a little inappropriate as it was clearly drafted before the news of the attack, and I therefore sent him another telegram. He subsequently asked that his original telegram should be delivered as soon as it was possible to do so.

Another matter which had to be dealt with at Bari was a telegram from Sir Alexander Cadogan about [the recall of] Mr Bowker. I hope he will not be unduly annoyed by the reply which I sent.

Another question which we had to settle was the matter of the Special Operations Committee. The Foreign Office for some reason were fussing because General Stawell was chairman of it instead of Mr Broad, not realising that it is far better for Broad to be a member as he will also have to have an American counterpart.

A message reached me from Lord Moyne on the subject of looking after Roumania and Bulgaria, and I have made a reply which I hope will at least settle the matter.[23]

[20] General Nathan F. Twining (b. 1897) was Commanding General, Fifteenth Air Force in Italy and of Allied Strategic Air Forces in the Mediterranean, 1944–5.

[21] Fitzroy Maclean had invited Randolph Churchill to lead a Military Mission to Tito.

[22] This ended: 'Give my love to Randolph should he come into your sphere. Maclean will be coming back soon. I wish I could come myself, but am too old and heavy to jump in a parachute.'

[23] It was later agreed that Roumania and Bulgaria should remain under the political direction of Lord Moyne.

Monday, 29 May 1944

Went to General Alexander's morning meeting. It is always interesting to attend these conferences where the daily progress at sea, on land and in the air is given by the experts, first from the British point of view and then from the German. It is extraordinary how the fog of war has been largely dispelled by the skill in picking up enemy radio. All his movements are much more open to us now than in the old days. The Germans are fighting well and skilfully, but I am very confident that General Alexander will be successful. His calm and complete confidence are extremely impressive.

After the conference I motored down to Naples, where I lunched with Sir Noel Charles and discussed with him two points which are chiefly worrying me.

The first is regarding the arrangements made for the Italian Government to be taken to Rome together with the Prince. I am quite sure that there is a real danger in this. Although Charles did not quite share my view, I sent my telegram No. 97 to the Foreign Office (attached). Charles rang me up later in the day to say he thought he ought to send a telegram, which he did – see No. 99 (attached).

Telegrams 97 and 99

From: Naples
To: Resident Minister, Algiers

No. 97 31.5.44

Addressed to Foreign Office telegram No. 178, repeated to Resident Minister, Algiers.

My telegram No. 1 Citizen.

Following from Mr Macmillan. Begins.

High Commissioner has shown me his telegrams 164, 166 and your reply 273.

2. We have discussed this matter further with particular reference to plan of taking the Prince and Badoglio and some of the party leaders to Rome a few days after the occupation. I do not know how far you are aware of the implications of this proposal. General MacFarlane proposes to let Prince and Badoglio and party leaders go to Rome only for (grp. undec.) of one day in order to make contact with party leaders and to bring them back the same night with or without representatives of other parties.

3. There are arguments both for and against this proposal. The Marshal and the Prince no doubt feel that having left Rome as safeguard they would like to show themselves there at the earliest moment and it is strongly contended that the visit is necessary in order to maintain the prestige and authority of the Badoglio Government.

4. On the other hand this chase after political recruits may in the

long run injure rather than assist their prestige. It may be a question of who shall come to Canossa. Moreover I do not wish Italian politicians to try any tricks and I fear the use that may be made even of a short visit and in spite of safeguards, by press propaganda and Italian manoeuvring. We do not want a political crisis staged in Rome nor an attempt to re-open closed questions such as the monarchy and armistice terms. And it may not be desirable to give the Crown Prince and Badoglio a chance to represent themselves as 'entering' Rome before we are ready for this.

5. Perhaps you would consider this point and send your views to Sir N. Charles. I hope you will also arrange for the necessary instructions to be sent to General MacFarlane through General Wilson. If any change of plan is to be effected the matter is urgent as General MacFarlane has already broached his proposal with Badoglio.

From: Sir N. Charles, Naples
To: Resident Minister, Algiers

No. 99

Addressed to Foreign Office telegram No. 181, repeated to Resident Minister, Algiers.

My telegram No. 178.

I fully appreciate points raised by Mr Macmillan especially in the first part of para 4. I think however it would be dangerous at this stage to make change in plan arranged with the Marshal.

2. I feel it is essential for the reasons given in para 3 for the Marshal and Crown Prince to go to Rome without delay. As regards party leaders it would be most difficult and well-nigh impossible to furnish explanation acceptable to them (Croce, Sforza, Rodino and Togliatti[24]) for cancellation of visit to Rome where they are expected. They would lose face with their parties whose wrath would turn on the Allies. They have already been trying to send their agents ahead of them and permission has been refused.

3. I have not mentioned the subject of this telegram to my U.S. colleague, who has not yet received any views about original plan from his Government.

4. Political crisis must be avoided at all costs whether here or in Rome. The Marshal and the Prince should have strict warnings to avoid all occasions which the volatile Romans could seize upon to make a political demonstration. Political leaders are to have twenty-four hours to make their contacts with their colleagues and according to Secretary-General of Italian Foreign Office [Prunas] there is a fair chance that the new Cabinet will be formed in essentials.

5. The situation is naturally very delicate. Application of restraint

[24] Ugo Rodino (b. 1904) was leader of the Christian Democrats and Palmiro Togliatti (1893–1964) was leader of the P.C.I.

on leaders may give rise to conjecture and afford scope for those who want to fish in troubled water.

6. Considerations which may well count most with the Romans are food and order. If the former can be rushed into the city and the population can be relieved of its fear of starvation, Marshal Badoglio, Prince Umberto and members of a Government which enjoys the support of the Allies can look forward to a favourable, if not a good, reception provided that they behave with reasonable tact and there is no untoward incident.

[Diary continues] I spent the afternoon at the Allied Control Commission talking to various people and drafting a telegram on the second point which is worrying me; that is, the general development of our Italian policy. I hope it will have a good effect at home. With the approaching fall of Rome it is really very important that we should begin to develop our Italian policy on sensible lines. If we don't we shall miss the boat.

Motored back in the evening and dined at General Alexander's mess.

Tuesday, 30 May 1944

Attended the morning conference as usual. People's nerves are beginning to get just a little on edge. Air Marshal Slessor seems to think that General Alexander is missing his chances and does not fail to say so. General Wilson is extremely tactful at these meetings and I much admire his handling of them.

Immediately after the meeting I motored down to the A.C.C., where we had a full day's conference. This conference took place in a very crowded and hot room. It was difficult to hear. It was nevertheless extremely interesting, and on the whole I was much impressed by the progress which has been made by the A.C.C.–A.M.G. organisation since the time we instituted the reform early in February. General MacFarlane, although an incautious politician, is an extremely fine administrator. He has done a wonderful job in pulling this organisation together and getting it to work.

Wednesday, 31 May 1944

The whole of this day was taken up with meetings of the Economic Committee. Captain Ellergy Stone, U.S.N.R. (a radio manufacturer disguised as a captain in the American Navy) presided. Colonel Foley, U.S. Treasury, Colonel Upjohn, K.C.,[25] Colonel Grafftey-Smith, Bank of England, Mr E. M. H. Lloyd, financial adviser in the Middle East, Colonel Spofford, G5, A.F.H.Q., Bob Murphy and myself were present. The meetings were very successful, and I was impressed by the work that has been done. Lloyd's arrival has been, of course, an

[25] Colonel Gerald Upjohn, K.C. (1903–71), was Chief Legal Adviser, A.C.C., 1943–4, and Vice-President of the Civil Affairs (Administrative) Section, 1944–5.

absolute godsend and the ginger that I tried to apply some weeks ago could not have been effective without his coming. He has been both tactful and intelligent and, of course, drafted the greater part of the reports. All the matter is in my financial file. I am very hopeful that we shall be able to do two things:

(1) Agree on the immediate raising of the bread ration from 200 to 300 grammes a day. This will have the effect of persuading the farmers to bring their harvest in instead of hoarding it, as they will fear the black-market price will fall when increased supplies become available at the proper price.

(2) By allowing the wage-earners to purchase their needs at the legal price instead of at the fantastic black-market price, prevent the rise in wages which would otherwise be necessary and which would certainly be the beginning of a vast inflation spiral.

All the other recommendations on savings, taxation, conversion, blocking of accounts, etc., are on sound lines. They will take longer to carry out, but they must be pressed forward with energy if a spiral of inflation is to be avoided.

General Wilson has left today and he is sending his plane back to take me to Algiers on Saturday.

June

Thursday, 1 June 1944

Saw Mason-MacFarlane in the morning. He has at last insisted on the King carrying out his decision to retire from the throne and appoint his son Regent. It appears that the Little Man is still trying to wriggle out of his engagement. I have also persuaded MacFarlane not to allow him to go to Rome and not even to go to Naples. I told MacFarlane that if the King makes any nonsense he should put him in an aeroplane and send him to Kenya.

A further meeting of the Economic Committee was held this morning, chiefly to draft a telegram which General Wilson is to send on the increase of the bread ration. There will of course be trouble with the Combined Chiefs of Staff, but they will be wrong if they oppose it. I had hoped to be able to persuade General Wilson to make the increase on his own responsibility.

Lunched with Brigadier Lush and a party in a delightful villa.

After lunch I went back to further conferences on economic questions and also a conference with Murphy.

A quiet evening. I moved from General Alexander's headquarters to stay with General MacFarlane. He has a very finely placed villa right on the bay. Sat out in the lovely sun and enjoyed the sea. Inside the villa is hideous beyond belief. It was once lent to Herr and Frau Goering and seemed suitably furnished for what I should imagine would be their taste.

Friday, 2 June 1944

Being somewhat exhausted by the week's efforts, I loafed in the morning. I have now finished the first two volumes of Gibbon, and very good they are. I also read a book which although one of the most famous books, I had never read before – Munthe's autobiography [*The Story of San Michele*]. I did not like it very much.

I lunched with Ambassador Kirk, Murphy and Charles. The party was only for the four of us, and took place in one of Kirk's vast palaces. The talk was supposed to be on future policy in Italy, but I did not think it very satisfactory. Kirk and Murphy rambled, and Charles seemed rather out of his depth. I am not at all hopeful. I think the Italians are much too clever for all the people on the spot with whom they find themselves in contact. In the afternoon I went to do a rare thing for me – a little shopping. I bought some tiny presents for the children.

Spent a quiet evening – very delightful.

Saturday, 3 June 1944

9 a.m. Went to A.C.C. for a final talk with MacFarlane. Having explained to him in great detail my Italian policy, I found to my surprise that he is more or less in favour of it. He was in a very genial mood and much easier to talk to than usual. I believe that like all military men he is best taken early in the morning.

Commander Jackson has arrived from the Middle East together with an expert on the collection of crops called Murray. I had telegraphed to Lord Moyne asking him to send them over to help us because our need was great, and he responded at once. I put in my telegram 'Come over to Apulia and help us.' I hope he got the allusion.[1]

After settling all the final details with regard to the report of the Economic Committee, MacFarlane motored me to the aerodrome where we found General Wilson's admirable plane. Murphy, Offie,[2] Colonel Spofford, Roger and I returned in it and reached Algiers about 3.30. I found Dorothy in good heart, a large number of letters from England having arrived. All the children seem well.

I found also an enormous mass of paper which kept me up till the early hours of the morning.

Sunday, 4 June 1944 (Trinity Sunday)

Woken up in the middle of the night by a 'Most Immediate' saying that Tito had had to leave Yugoslavia and was now at Bari. I think it is of great importance that he should leave Italian soil as soon as possible, and after consultation with General Wilson we sent a message to say so.

After a meeting at 9.30 in the morning we also decided to send Maclean immediately to Bari. The proposal is that the Marshal should go to the island of Vis, which has already been taken from the Germans by joint action of British Commandos and partisan troops. He will then be on Yugoslavian soil and not a refugee. Broad seems to think that he will be able to control the movements of his partisans more effectively from Vis than if he goes on the mainland, but I am not sure what the psychological effect will be. In some ways it may be helpful because it should increase our hold over him. Incidentally we have a telegram from one of the British Liaison Officers with the partisans

[1] See Acts 16:9.
[2] Carmel Offie (b. 1909) was assistant to Ambassador Kirk.

saying that the British bombing of the German attack is very successful and has immensely raised our standing.

The news of the battle is very good this morning. The Eighth Army has joined the First and they are advancing right through the gap between the Alban Hills and Palestrina.

After working at my papers, this afternoon I went out alone with Dorothy for a bathe and picnic, returning at five o'clock to hear the news that Rome was entered by our troops this morning. In this connection I have received a delightful telegram from the Foreign Office suggesting that General Wilson or General Alexander might like to issue a proclamation. They seem to have a genius for missing the bus.

I go this evening to a Fourth of June dinner. I sent General Alexander a telegram running as follows:

> Many congratulations on the successful development of your battle and all good wishes for its exploitation.
>
> It was moreover thoughtful of you as an old Harrovian to capture Rome on the Fourth of June.[3]

Monday, 5 June 1944

A long talk with Murphy in the morning. It is clear that Washington and London are not as close as they were. The honeymoon stage between the President and the Prime Minister is over, and the normal difficulties and divergences, inseparable from staid married life, are beginning to develop. This all has its effect upon the Americans in this theatre. Although my personal relations with Bob are as good as ever, I feel that the points of difference in policy (as directed by Washington) are harder to overcome.

On French affairs, the President remains quite intransigent. Bob complained to me about Duff Cooper's failure to inform him or Chapin (the U.S. Chargé d'Affaires) of the British invitation to de Gaulle to go to London. It was the first time in twenty months that there had not been complete confidence between American and British diplomats in Algiers, etc., etc. I did my best to explain it away, as due to the rush of business, but I do regret the incident very much.

In the same way, Bob has put in an official protest (under instructions from the State Department) about the setting up of a Balkan affairs committee in Cairo, without American approval. (MacVeagh has done the same to Lord Moyne.) Nevertheless, although Washington is trying to pull out of the Balkans and has now definitely decided *not* to be associated with any military expedition or 'civil affairs' activity in any Balkan country, confining their interest to relief, Bob is himself getting more and more interested. He is forming

[3] General Alexander replied, 'Thank you. What is the Fourth of June?'

ideas of his own. Of course (under O.S.S. inspiration) he inclines to Mihailović, and cannot follow the P.M.'s pro-Tito policy.[4] But it is a great thing to get him interested. I have always felt that we should try to bring the Americans into Balkan affairs. And I feel equally sure that the way to do it is through A.F.H.Q. (which was started by Americans and has a genuine Allied tradition) rather than through the Middle East. Cairo is suspect – it is somehow connected in their minds with imperialism, Kipling and all that.

Dorothy and I lunched with Bob. Bonnet (Minister for Information), [Somerville P.] Tuck (new U.S. Minister to Cairo) and others. A very pleasant party.

General Wilson called at six. We went through some items for tomorrow's meeting. We agreed to settle the Balkan question 'out of court'.

Rome is taken. I have sent a telegram to Alex.

The whole world will be thrilled with the news. But knowing Alex's plans, I am much more interested in Part II of the battle. He has a real chance of destroying the German Army during the coming weeks.

General Alexander's plan was to move eastwards across the rivers Po and Piave, seize Trieste and the Istrian Peninsula, and march through the Ljubljana Gap towards Vienna. Germany would have to move an enormous number of troops from the west; and her forces in the Balkans could be cut off. It would also have the political advantage of limiting the Soviet advance into western Europe.

But Alexander had already had to give up divisions for Operation 'Overlord', the invasion of northern France which began on 6 June, and now faced further depletion in support of Operation 'Anvil' – the invasion of southern France due to take place in August 1944. I gave details of these in a later memorandum, from which the following extract is taken.

In order to make 'Anvil' a success, three American divisions have already been taken from General Alexander and put into training for amphibious operations at Salerno. One further American division will follow. Four French divisions will be taken from him, making a total of at least eight divisions in all. At the same time nearly 70 per cent of the Air Force operating in support of the battle of Italy will be removed. The strict instructions of the Combined Chiefs of Staff up to the present are to halt upon the Pisa–Rimini Line, make no attempt to force the Apennines and leave the Apennine positions, the Valley of the Po and the famous strategic strength of the 'quadrilateral' in

[4] Dragoljub Mihailović (1893–1946) was head of the Chetniks, the Royalist Serbian underground army, and Minister of War in the Government-in-exile, 1942–4. There was evidence that his forces had collaborated with the Germans and the Italians to further his war against Tito's partisans.

German hands: in other words to call off the Italian campaign at the very height of its success.

[Diary continues] Motored out to Tipasa, where Dorothy had gone earlier in the day. Dined and slept at the inn there.

Tuesday, 6 June 1944

Motored early to Algiers, where I heard the news of the landings in France. 'Overlord' is launched at last.

Talk with Murphy, and agreed with him about the course to be taken on his 'protest' about the Balkan affairs committee in Cairo at today's meeting. He, Generals Wilson and Devers and I will discuss it alone *after* the meeting.

3 p.m. General Gammell called about P.W.B. A small, but potentially dangerous problem. If we agree to Vellacott's demand that P.W.B. should be taken out of INC.[5] and put under his sole authority (thereby by-passing General McChrystal, head of INC.) we shall offend the Americans at a critical moment. It is *all-important* to get them to agree to General Alexander's strategy and not to risk any little trouble here. If we do not agree, Vellacott will resign and London will be offended. I have advised the latter alternative; London cannot hurt us.

3.45 p.m. Saw S.A.C. about Vellacott before the meeting. He was inclined to agree with me, although he is rather attached to Vellacott from Cairo days.

4–6 p.m. Political Meeting – a varied text of subjects, Yugoslavia, Greece, France, Italy, etc.

We settled the Balkan question 'out of court' (so far as lies in our power) and I drafted the necessary telegrams, which I will perfect tomorrow.

Motored to Tipasa. Lovely weather. Dorothy had stayed there and enjoyed the sea and the sun.

Wednesday, 7 June 1944

Stayed at Tipasa all the morning – lazing in the sun and reading *Coningsby*. Motored to Algiers in time for lunch.

3 p.m. Vellacott. I listened patiently and explained the American point of view. He was very sensible. Got Gammell along, and he will see Devers and try to settle the matter.

4 p.m. Mr Stuart (P.W.B.) on ill effects of indiscriminate bombing in Serbia, especially Belgrade. I will discuss with Slessor.

5 p.m. M. Djoudvić – Yugoslav Minister to the French – a boring and inconsequential talker.

The first news from France about the landings is beginning to come

[5] INC. was the Information and Censorship Section, which (among other activities) controlled the Italian press.

in. The start seems good. The Italian campaign is going very well, but I fear the 'professional' diplomats are going to muddle the political side. A silly telegram from F.O. on my proposals for a provisional peace. I drafted and sent off a reply.

Proposals for provisional peace

From: Foreign Office, London
To: Resident Minister, Algiers

Resmin 1211

Addressed to Resident Minister, Algiers telegram No. 1211, repeated to Naples and Washington.

Naples telegram No. 1 Citizen.

I fear there is some misunderstanding about the proposals set out in my telegram 4515 to Washington.

2. It was never my idea to conclude or to start negotiating any preliminary peace treaty with Italy, with the capture of Rome as a starting point. The idea was merely to inform the Italian Government now that we would be prepared to replace the armistice régime by a preliminary peace treaty once we were satisfied that the military position admitted of it and that the Italian Government had sufficient authority to speak on behalf of the whole of the Italian people and not merely that part of it at present under their administration. Despite the views of Generals Wilson and Alexander I am not convinced that the situation at present is such as to justify embarking on these negotiations. After all we only hold a third of Italy at present. Nor do I feel that any Italian Government at this stage can justifiably be said to speak on behalf of the whole of the Italian people. The industrial north has yet to speak.

3. The whole question needs very careful consideration and as you will have seen from Washington telegram 2906 the State Department require further elucidation before they are able to express any opinion on the matter. It would of course be impossible for us to make proposal to Italian Government for conclusion of peace treaty without prior consultation with the Soviet Government who are co-signatories of the armistice.

Extract from my reply to Foreign Office

3. I take it that your idea is merely to tell Badoglio now that you will be prepared to negotiate a peace at an unspecified time in the future. Sir Noel Charles will be able to say what the effect of such a communication would be on Badoglio. I foresee that it will be a very disheartening one and that as well as risking the success of the negotiations when they do take place you would in the meantime only

weaken Badoglio's position. To tell him that you would be prepared to negotiate when the Italian Government had sufficient authority to speak on behalf of the whole Italian people would be to invite an enquiry as to the criterion by which the Italian Government is judged to have such authority. Without a definite answer on this point he would suspect you of meaning that you wanted to wait until the whole of Italy was liberated. Moreover, when 'the industrial north speaks', it is quite likely to speak in much more truculent tones and be less inclined than Badoglio might be at an earlier date to accept the unpleasant parts of the peace. In any case the Italian Government's moral authority for the preliminary peace would be far greater than for the armistice. Then it consisted of a fugitive King and Prime Minister, two Germanophil generals, and a rather crooked courtier, huddled together in a fortress in Brindisi.

4. So far as the military position is concerned, I have discussed this in some detail with Generals Wilson and Alexander. We are now pursuing the German Army. The only question in doubt is whether they will be wholly destroyed or whether they will be able to stand upon the Pisa–Rimini line. There does not seem much chance of their obtaining reinforcements at present.

5. I fully realise the importance of the issue and that the U.S. Government will need time and further elucidation before they can express an opinion. I also agree that it would be impossible to say anything to the Italian Government without the prior agreement of the Soviet Government.

Thursday, 8 June 1944

The usual morning with papers, telegrams, etc. I am not too happy about the Greek position. At 3 p.m. Brigadier Benfield[6] (from Cairo) who explained to me M. Papandreou's scheme. He wishes to form a Greek National Army by *normal* means – viz., calling up men and appointing regular officers. This involves asking the Greek partisans and irregulars to dissolve themselves. I do not believe they will agree to this.

I discussed later with S.A.C., who shares my views. He thinks the irregulars should be made the basis of the National Army, and gradually weaned from extremism by infiltration of moderate elements. EAM is more likely to agree. Will Papandreou? We decided to draft telegrams on the matter to Cairo and London respectively.

We also discussed the question of getting Marshal Tito over from the island of Vis (where he now is) to Caserta some time next week. General Wilson will propose this to the P.M. in a personal message.

General and Mrs Vanier (Canadian Minister) called – bringing with

[6] Brigadier K. V. Barker-Benfield (1892–1969), commander of S.O.E. in Cairo, was in charge of Special Operations, Greece, 1944, and commanded Crete Force, 1944–5.

them M. Closon[7] (French Resistance), an interesting but rather discouraging talk.

The President shows no sign of moving from his position and I do not see what de Gaulle or London can do.

Friday, 9 June 1944

10 a.m. Air Vice-Marshal [William] Elliot called. He is on his way to Bari to command the new Balkan Air Force. He will also co-ordinate the Army and Navy and the S.O.E. efforts. Broad will advise him on my behalf; [Carl F.] Norden on Murphy's.

He will do the job well. He has experience of inter-service work, having been in Whitehall on Ministry of Defence Planning staff for several years. I have known him some time and like him. His sphere will be Yugoslavia, Albania, Hungary.

Office all morning (I am now using Duff Cooper's room, as he is in London). I did a telegram to Leeper, suggesting he should get the Russians to bring his Greek Communists into line.

Luncheon party. Consul-General and Mrs Carvell, General Sawbridge (U.S.), Colonel [John] Anstey (S.O.E.), Colonel Fourget (Canadian), M. and Mme Offroy (he is Secretary to the French Cabinet) and some others.

After luncheon Holman (who is acting for Duff Cooper, who is in England with de Gaulle) showed me his telegrams from London and told me of his talks with Massigli. The prospects are not bright.

Dorothy is planning a trip to Tunis with Mme Baril for the end of next week. It should be very interesting for her. I expect to go again to Naples and Bari.

General Alexander has sent General Wilson an appreciation of the strategic situation. It is certainly (for him) very optimistic. But I fear that the Combined Chiefs of Staff are hankering after 'Anvil' (South of France) and will try to stop the full exploitation of the battle. This must be prevented at all costs (even of Vellacott and de Gaulle!) Poor P.M.! He is in a quandary – the President is so helpful on some things and so difficult on others.[8]

I have just seen two telegrams from MacFarlane. It seems to be working out as I foretold. As the result of the Rome meeting (to which I objected) and no doubt due to Sforza intrigues, Badoglio has fallen and the Prince has asked Bonomi (Liberal, ex-P.M., seventy years old) to form a government.[9]

Mason-MacFarlane has warned the Prince that we insist on the declaration of the late Government about (*a*) the institutional question

[7] Louis-Francis Closon (b. 1910) was Delegate of the F.C.N.L. in occupied territory, 1943–4.

[8] To please Stalin, who wanted Allied offensives to take place as far west as possible, Roosevelt was opposed to the advance on Vienna and in favour of 'Anvil'.

[9] Mason-MacFarlane went to Rome, but took neither Charles nor Kirk with him, and failed to warn their governments, so the first that Churchill learned of the changes was from the morning papers. He was furious that Badoglio had been supplanted.

[i.e. the monarchy] (*b*) the armistice and other obligations. But I have no doubt that we are only at the beginning of the story. The armistice (long terms) has not been published; and I should not be surprised if the new Government try to argue about them. It may even be a put-up job, with Badoglio consenting.

Alternatively, I feel we have let down Badoglio (if he is playing the game with us). All this comes of letting the Italian Government rush off to Rome instead of making the Roman politicians come to Salerno.

I cannot help being rather amused, because I warned MacFarlane and Charles. When they rejected my advice, I warned the F.O. They preferred Charles's views. Incidentally, Mason-MacFarlane has, of course, been obliged to let the Government party stay on in Rome. Will he ever get them out again?

6.30 p.m. Air Vice-Marshal Nutting[10] called. He is very disturbed (as is General Nichols, the Chief Signal Officer) about the backwardness of Cable & Wireless compared to the American companies. This is an old subject here. I have agreed to take it up with London, and have written to Harry Crookshank (Postmaster-General) accordingly.

Dinner with Czech Minister, M. Cerny, M. and Mme Tixier, René Pleven, M. and Mme Schneider and others, including an amusing Pole.

Saturday, 10 June 1944

The Italian crisis is in full swing. The Prime Minister, the Foreign Secretary, General MacFarlane, Charles – all are involved in one splendid turmoil of confusion.

Brigadier [C. D.] Armstong came to lunch. Brigadier Armstrong was the British Liaison Officer with General Mihailović and has just been brought out successfully. I was not very impressed with him. He seemed to have got on badly with General Mihailović, whom he had not seen for several months. As usual, he prefaced his observations by telling me that he was a simple soldier and did not understand politics. In that case I do not understand why he was chosen for a job which is so largely political.

At 4.30 General Wilson called. He told me he had had a telegram from the Prime Minister in typical language suggesting that King Peter[11] should land at Vis and take possession of his Kingdom. He, Mr Stevenson, the Ban of Croatia,[12] and other members of the party were all leaving London tonight on their way to Malta. They would then go on to Vis. The Prime Minister seemed to be under the impression that the York could land at Vis and that the island was more or less in British hands. After some discussion we sent telegrams to Gibraltar,

[10] Air Vice-Marshal Charles Nutting (1889–1964) was Telecommunications Adviser to the Minister Resident in the Middle East, 1942–4.

[11] Peter II (1923–70), King of Yugoslavia, 1934–45 (under a Regency until 1941).

[12] Dr Ivan Subašić, a prominent member of the Croation Peasant Party and Ban, or Governor, of Croatia in 1939, had been in the United States. King Peter had invited him on 1 June to form a government, and he was on his way to negotiate with Tito's representatives.

Malta and Rabat to try to stop the aeroplane and ask Stevenson to see us on his way.

Most of the evening was taken up in a series of hurried consultations both on Italy and on Yugoslavia. There was also clearly a breakdown of the negotiations in Greece,[13] and at S.A.C.'s request I sent Mr Leeper some views on the reorganisation of the Greek Army.

We had a dinner party at the villa, at which the following were present in addition to Dorothy, Wyndham and myself: Lady Diana Cooper, General Devers, Mr Baldwin, Mr and Mrs Renchard,[14] Mr Gibson Graham, M. Jacquinot, M. Pleven, Mr E. M. H. Lloyd, Mr and Mrs Reilly, Comtesse Madeleine de Montgomerie and Colonel Chapman-Walker.

Before dinner M. Schneider came to see me. I am afraid he has been very badly treated. I should not be surprised if he were not even in danger of arrest. I wish I could get him to England, but I am afraid it is now impossible. I told him I would let him know as soon as there was any chance of communications with England reopening.

Major Jasper Rootham also came to see me. He had come out with Brigadier Armstrong, but being a well-trained civil servant by origin (he had once been one of Mr Neville Chamberlain's Private Secretaries), he seemed to have managed better than Brigadier Armstrong. He gave me a very interesting account of the situation. He had maintained touch with General Mihailović himself until the end.

Sunday, 11 June 1944

This was a hectic day.

At eleven o'clock in the morning I was told that the York had arrived at the airfield. I rushed off with Makins to meet them, missed them, and found that the party had been sent to General Wilson's villa. There were eight of them altogether. The King, the Ban, Ralph Stevenson, Colonel Bailey[15] and the King's A.D.C. were brought up from the airfield, the rest being left behind. We motored back at full speed to the general's villa, where we found them fairly contented. The general had gone up to Chréa for the day. I brought the party to my villa and gave them lunch, and then we had a talk with Stevenson on the plans to be adopted. General Wilson turned up at three o'clock and we had a full discussion at which the King was present. It was decided that the King should stay in Malta until the right opportunity arose, and that if possible Stevenson and the Ban, after a short visit to Bari for the purpose of seeing Captain [Živko] Topalović, General Mihailović's

[13] EAM and Communist delegates at the discussions on the composition of Papandreou's Cabinet had failed to obtain consent from their followers to join the Government, from which they were therefore excluded.

[14] George W. Renchard (b. 1907) was U.S. Consul, Algiers, March–September 1944.

[15] Colonel S. W. Bailey was Brigadier Armstrong's second-in-command on the Mission to Mihailović.

Political Adviser, and various other Yugoslav notabilities, should proceed to Vis. If Tito was willing to come out to see General Wilson at Caserta, the whole party would return and the King would or would not be produced at a suitable moment from Malta according to Tito's mood.

I saw the King off at the airfield and got back to the villa about 5.30. I spent most of the rest of the evening getting off the necessary telegrams.

Monday, 12 June 1944

I saw Mr Murphy in the morning to explain to him the Yugoslav situation.

At eleven o'clock Mr Russell Barnes called, very concerned over the resignation of Mr Vellacott and the general situation of P.W.B. Russell Barnes is an American – a nice man, but with little experience, and I should think unable to run the P.W.B. machine. Nevertheless I am sure it has been right to let the Americans have their way. Mr Vellacott's introduction would have been a source of irritation. It is not worth while when there are so many more important things at stake.

At 11.30 Mr Gibson Graham called to see me about one or two matters connected with the Mediterranean Shipping Board.

At 12.15 General Beaumont-Nesbitt came. The War Office are still trying to send out a fully fledged Mission to the French Government unattached to A.F.H.Q. They temporarily abandoned this a few weeks ago, but are now coming back to the charge. I advised him to repel it as much as he could, which he promised to do. I sent off the necessary telegrams.

All the afternoon was taken up with the Italian crisis.[16] The situation is becoming more and more complicated. I am afraid that poor General MacFarlane has got us into a mess. Although I think he was intrinsically right – the Bonomi Government is probably an improvement on the Badoglio – the management of the affair has been weak.

At 7.30 Massigli came to see me. I found him in a state of considerable emotion over the Anglo-American-French situation.[17] I told him that, of course, I could not see him officially as the matter was not in my hands, but he seemed anxious to talk as a friend. I arranged with Holman before seeing him, and as the result of the meeting (and with Miss Campbell's co-operation), drafted a telegram to London which was sent off the following morning after some amendments by

[16] Churchill was still hostile to the new Italian government, and General Wilson, in accordance with the long armistice terms, was withholding consent to its formal assumption of power until it gave guarantees of co-operation with the Allies.

[17] Roosevelt had reacted strongly to the F.C.N.L.'s decision to call itself the Provisional Government of France (see above, p. 439) and had forbidden these words to be used (see below, p. 464). Hence Massigli's emotion.

Holman. I hope it may be of some use. It was a personal telegram to Duff Cooper.

Tuesday, 13 June 1944

At 10.30 I saw Murphy. We discussed all our problems – Italy, Yugoslavia, France. The State Department protested against MacFarlane's statement that the Allied Governments do not like Sforza. The American Government like Sforza very much, and still more do the guileless politicians at Brooklands City. New York State is the key state of the election, and Sforza claims to swing millions of votes.

Dorothy and I lunched with Bogomolov and Mme Bogomolov. They have the strangest parties. We were the only guests. He was in – for him – a merry mood. Madame was very pleased with her collection of antique china which she found in London, and some old jewellery. She also found a book of drawings of the old Russian times at the beginning of the nineteenth century, on hand-made paper, beautifully engraved. Algiers is not very chic; the Cercle is badly run, and so on.

I called on Sir John Slessor at 3.45 (just before the political meeting) to clear up one or two points. Then the usual political meeting with General Wilson in the chair. We decided to leave over the Italian question and discuss it after the meeting. The other items were got through fairly simply. The State Department raised an objection to General Alexander putting some of his staff in Rome. But as this is essential if we are to get to Caserta, Murphy accepted this on a temporary basis. There was an unfortunate discussion about P.W.B. in view of the President's directive that the words 'Provisional Government of France' are never to be used. This makes it impossible even to quote French statements and has stopped the leaflet campaign in France and the French use of United Nations Radio, and has other disadvantages. Nevertheless I felt that we had better support the Americans at the moment until General Wilson receives specific instructions from the C.C.S. He is after all as much an officer of the American Government as of the British.

7 p.m. Mr Murray of P.W.B. called. He wanted to return to England as the result of Vellacott's resignation, but I prevented him from doing so.

Wednesday, 14 June 1944

General Wilson, Murphy and I decided to summon General MacFarlane, and he is due to arrive in the afternoon.

I went round to S.A.C.'s Headquarters at 11.30, where we had a discussion on the War Office reaction to the general's wish to take over the Middle East. They are not prepared, unfortunately, to play to the full. I gather the compromise is that the War Office stores in the Middle East should be under the War Office direct command, but

General Wilson will have the right to draw from them. However, it seems that the War Office is to be the final arbiter.

12 noon. General Beaumont-Nesbitt came to see me with his preliminary plan for Allied Missions to the Balkans in the event of a German withdrawal – 'Rankin C' conditions.[18] We thought his plan was much too elaborate and decided it should be redrawn with regard to one specific country, Roumania, which may be the first that we shall have to deal with.

Lunch at home. M. and Mme Tixier came. Tixier talked till 3.30 very bitterly about the French situation. Roger Makins made a note of the conversation.

3.30 p.m. Meeting with General Wilson to discuss the Italian position. General MacFarlane was present. He gave an account of his action which was interesting, but I am afraid not convincing, so far as method was concerned. I feel sorry, because he is an able administrator though a naïve politician. He is also, I am afraid, not at all in good health. We decided we should take no action officially and General Wilson was content with the telegram which I had already sent to the F.O.[19] I think the Prime Minister will climb down, because I don't think there is anything that can be done, nor would it be really wise to do it.

8 p.m. Farewell dinner to Jim Bowker. I shall miss him very much. It is a great shame that they are taking him away from me, and there seems no chance of a substitute. However, Anthony Rumbold is to do the Balkan work and Wyndham will go into the Chancery and do the Italian.

11 p.m. Three 'Most Immediates' arrived from London, one from the Prime Minister and two from the Foreign Office. I think it looks as if the crisis is to be solved. The Italian Advisory Council will meet. I had seen Bogomolov earlier in the day and asked him to go to Italy at once if possible, and he consented to go on Saturday. The Foreign Office appear to have adopted my suggestion that the Allied Governments should use the Advisory Council as the excuse for the delay and ask for specific statements in writing that all the members of the new Government have seen the obligations entered into by the late Government – short terms, long terms, etc., etc. – and are prepared to acept them; also a statement in writing that the institutional question will not be raised without the permission of the Allies.

Thursday, 15 June 1944

Papers and telegrams in the morning.

[18] Operation 'Rankin' was a contingency plan for the rapid occupation of Germany in the event of a Nazi capitulation followed by only light resistance. 'Rankin C' described the plan if resistance collapsed completely.

[19] I wrote: 'It is clear from General MacFarlane's account that, as I had expected, the moment Badoglio decided to go to Rome he was outmanoeuvred by his new and prospective colleagues.' I added that Murphy and I felt that the date could not now be put back.

11 a.m. Mr Harman of P.W.B. came to see me. Obviously great confusion exists. We must try to get on to this when we get back.

12 noon. General MacFarlane came. He was very nice, but I am afraid he is very tired. He seemed relieved when I showed him the latest telegrams from the Foreign Office.

We are leaving for Naples at 2 p.m. today.

Farewell dinner for Mr Bowker
Wednesday, 14 June

Mr Macmillan
Lady Dorothy Macmillan
Mr Bowker
Comtesse de Rose
Vicomtesse de Dampierre
Mrs Dupree
Mr Reinhardt
Mr Makins
Colonel Chapman-Walker
Major Strachan
Major Henderson
Mr Dupree
Sir Anthony Rumbold
Mr Wyndham

Left Algiers 2 p.m. As we 'taxied' to the runway, the tyre on the back wheel of the plane burst. This delayed us about three-quarters of an hour.

A very comfortable flight in General Wilson's luxurious plane; Murphy, Mason-MacFarlane, Roger, Offie, and Mark Chapman-Walker.

Mason-Macfarlane had been to see me before luncheon. He was still in a very unrepentant but nervous mood. He obviously thinks he has done very well over the Italian crisis. I am afraid he had made a complete mess of it. Moreover, once you break down the dam, you never know what will happen. Stalin is supporting Churchill. He has telegraphed to say that he will instruct Bogomolov to do what we like – restore Badoglio if we wish. But the President has begun to be very cautious. Kirk is of course very pro-Italian and is no doubt telegraphing accordingly from Naples. Murphy is much firmer – but agrees with me that it is too late to reverse engines. Moreover, there is the Presidential election and the Italian vote.

Mason-MacFarlane also told me that he had not been at all well for a long time. As the result of his accidents and falls (he has a broken neck) he is threatened with arthritis in an acute form. As soon as he feels he can leave things fairly quiet, he will apply for a medical board and go on sick leave.

I discussed this with General Wilson later in the day, to whom General MacFarlane had told the same thing.

Friday, 16 June 1944

He accordingly sent a telegram to the Secretary of State for War. I did the same to the P.M. The best course would be for Mason-MacFarlane to go home on sick leave, and then announce his resignation on grounds of health after a short interval (and a medical board). I am sure this is in his interests, since P.M. is so angry about his behaviour that he will insist on his removal.

Murphy and I are in two charming rooms in the Hunting Lodge, General Wilson's residence above the palace of Caserta. It is a delightful old house, in the hills above the great cascade, with a pleasant view over the valley, a nice garden and orchard and some fine trees. Roger and the others are in tents in the garden.

Went into Naples in the morning and saw Charles. He is puzzled and rather frightened by the P.M.'s violence. I'm afraid he has a lot to learn about politics.

Broad (from Bari) and Randolph Churchill came to luncheon. After luncheon, Broad, S.A.C., Roger and I discussed the timetable and general handling of the Yugoslavian affair. The Ban (Subašić) and Stevenson have been to Bari, had some useful talks, especially with Mihailović's representative, Captain Topalović, and gone on to Vis. King Peter is in Malta.

When this was over, I had to put up with an hour of Randolph. He was very indignant with me at giving orders for him to be taken out of Yugoslavia (or rather persuading General Wilson to do so). He has a certain charm, but his manners are dreadful, and his flow of talk insufferable. He always manages to have a row or make a scene wherever he goes. Of course I did not want him captured and perhaps tortured by the Germans, partly for the P.M.'s sake and partly because I felt sure he knew too much – including perhaps the date of the Second Front in France. Anyway, he has not had a bad time since he came out. He has been to Rome, interviewed the Pope, spent £200 at Rome (which he tried to borrow from me) and generally enjoyed himself. It was finally arranged that he should go to England on leave and then return as a British Liaison Officer to Bosnia.

A quiet dinner and early to bed.

Saturday, 17 June 1944

Down to Naples in the morning. Charles has received further instructions from the F.O. Of course, we have had to climb down, partly owing to the President's attitude and partly owing to the circumstances. However, I think the Council will probably agree to recommend two 'face-saving' conditions: (*i*) a written statement from Bonomi that he accepts the short and long armistice terms and all other engagements of the Italian Government *and* that all the members of the Government are personally acquainted with them and accept them, (*ii*) that the question of the monarchy will *not* be raised again.

Later in the afternoon, we heard (Mason-MacFarlane came up himself at 7 p.m.) that the Advisory Council had adopted the British resolution. We told him that S.A.C. would now authorise the Government to take office, *after* complying with the conditions.

12.45 p.m. Went to meet General Alexander at the aerodrome. He came with Generals Harding,[20] Robertson and Joe Cannon (U.S. Air Force). Alex is in tremendous form and looks ten years younger. His armies are advancing splendidly and he has had a resounding success.

After luncheon, Alex and the others went to a conference with S.A.C. The great problem of strategy now has to be settled. Alex gave me a copy of his appreciation. He wants to strike east – but I fear the C.C.S. will insist on a movement west. The problem of the future of Alex and his armies is a grave one. It seems a terrible pity to entrust a difficult operation in south-west France to untried French and American generals, and to leave unused or break up the armies in Italy, which are now a great fighting instrument, confident in themselves and their commanders.

A lazy afternoon. I read – and finished – *Orlando* by Virginia Woolf. A strange, clever, intriguing book.

The afternoon and evening were very quiet, except for some telephone messages from Bari about the conversations in Vis, which seem to be going well.

Mason-MacFarlane came up before dinner, as described above.

Sunday, 18 June 1944

A violent thunderstorm disturbed the night. The lightning seemed to be almost in the house and set the telephones ringing.

I drafted for General Wilson before breakfast:

(*a*) Reply to M. Politis, president *à tour du rôle* of the Advisory Council – accepting their recommendation, etc., and introducing some phrases at the end reaffirming our armistice rights [i.e. to allow the effective prosecution of the war].

(*b*) Draft telegram to C.C.S. (FAN 715).

Murphy accepted these drafts and General Wilson also.

I also did a telegram to the P.M., which I hope will give him some comfort!

Went into the office at Caserta. Discussed the Yugoslav position with S.A.C. Some progress has been made, and Tito and the Ban of

[20] Lieutenant-General John Harding (b. 1896) was Chief of Staff, Fifteenth Army Group (later A.A.I.), 1944–5, and Commander Thirteenth Corps in Italy in 1945.

Croatia (King Peter's new P.M.) have agreed a joint communiqué.

Unfortunately bad flying weather is going to delay the programme by at least one day.

Lunched at the Hunting Lodge.

2.30–10.30 p.m. An enormously long drive with General Wilson to Campobasso to Fifth Corps H.Q. General Allfrey[21] was there – also Bertie Clowes.

It was a stormy day. But the light and shade in the valleys and hills was very beautiful. The car we started in broke a spring; a second followed behind and we had no great disaster with it, beyond flooding the engine with water on the way back and further delays.

Monday, 19 June 1944

A lazy morning – I read *Scenes from Clerical Life*.

Fitzroy Maclean turned up in the evening. He seemed quite pleased with the Yugoslav conference. The provisional arrangement between Subašić and Tito seems a real advance. Tito is not anxious to come to Caserta or see the King at present, and I think he is probably right.

It is impossible yet to say what will be the effect on the old Serbian loyalists. But it should not be forgotten that Tito has a great muster of Serb supporters, and in the cities the 'proletariat' is probably Communist or with Communist leanings.

7.45 p.m. Immense dinner given by General [Ira C.] Eaker (U.S. Air Force). Generals Wilson, Marshall (U.S. C. of S.), Arnold[22] (U.S. Air Force), Alexander, Air Marshal Slessor, and a large number of other distinguished officers. At a previous conference General Alexander's plan – for advancing to the Piave river and threatening an attack through the Ljubljana Pass, directed on Vienna – had been discussed, as a rival or alternative to 'Anvil' (southern France). Generals Marshall and Arnold did not react as unfavourably as had been expected. But it is thought that Eisenhower will not like it.

After dinner, I had a talk with Alex. He was very anxious for me to go back home with General Gammell and see the Prime Minister. I then went to see General Wilson, and later (at 10.45 p.m.) after obtaining his approval – strong support would perhaps be fair – returned to Alex. I found him on his train and we talked the whole thing over for an hour – he explaining the strategical and tactical aspects with his usual simplicity but with quite a new vigour. He showed me his personal telegrams to the P.M. couched in strong, even eloquent language.

I leave for England tomorrow.

21 Lieutenant-General Charles Allfrey (1895–1964) commanded Fifth Corps, 1942–4, and was G.O.C. British troops in Egypt, 1944–8.

22 Lieutenant-General Henry H. Arnold (1886–1950), who had been taught to fly by the Wright brothers in 1911, was Chief of the U.S. Air Staff throughout the war.

General Alexander's telegram to P.M.
18 June, 1944

Thank you so much for your telegram. As I see it, Kesselring's[23] Tenth and Fourteenth Armies are a beaten force, but not yet eliminated from the field. They have suffered grievous losses in men and material as the following German intercept will show [quote]. The location of the German divisions are known to me, but to summarise [quote] We have now taken close on 30,000 P.o.Ws and there may be many thousands more who have taken to the mountains, which may be written off as of any combat value to the Germans.

It is clear that the Germans intend to try and hold the Apennine position with the equivalent in fighting value of ten to twelve divisions, a front of 180 miles. Against this, I can, provided I have left to me intact my present forces, amass such a powerful force of fresh divisions, tanks, guns and artillery as will split the German Army in half and eliminate the German forces in Italy. I shall then have nothing to prevent me marching on Vienna unless the Germans send against us at least ten or more fresh divisions and if this should be the German course of action, I understand it is just what is required to help 'Overlord'. I believe we have here and now an opportunity of delivering such a defeat on the German Army as will have unpredictable results and such a chance must not be missed at this stage of the war.

Tuesday, 20 June 1944

8 a.m. Left Naples, in General Eaker's Fortress. General Gammell, Captain Barnaby (U.S.) and John.

We stopped for an hour at Algiers. Dorothy had left for Tunis, where she went for a week's trip by car. She was accompanied by Mme Baril, and was to stay with General Mast at La Marsa.

I managed to catch her on the telephone and then left for Casablanca. We dined at Casablanca in a very comfortable villa at Anfa run by the Americans. This recalled all the Anfa conference of February 1943, my first real introduction into international affairs on the grand scale.

We left at 9.30 p.m., but had to come back after three-quarters of an hour with a faulty plug to one of the four engines. However, after an hour's delay we got off and arrived safely in England on

Wednesday, 21 June 1944

After luncheon, I went to my rooms at the Cabinet Office. I arranged to see Anthony Eden at 4 p.m.

He was naturally rather surprised – and as I learnt afterwards 'put

[23] Field Marshal Albrecht Kesselring (1885–1960) was C.-in-C. South-west and Army Group 'C', 1943–5.

out' – at my unheralded return. I think I must have arrived almost as quickly as the telegram.

I explained to him the military situation. We also discussed:

Italy

Balkans – especially the control of Roumania, Bulgaria and Greece and some other matters.

On Italy, it is clear to me that the F.O. has been thoroughly 'beaten up' by the P.M. over the change of the Italian Government. Poor Anthony – he has a difficult life. He has the leadership of the House of Commons, the Foreign Secretaryship (with P.M., Moyne and myself, as well as Hull, the President, the American and British Chiefs of Staff all acting as rival Foreign Secretaries) and, of course, the interminable talks and late hours which the P.M. delights in. No wonder he seems a little jaded.

He did not seem at all to like my suggestions about the 'control' of Balkan affairs. Indeed, he was quite agitated about the matter. I explained – or tried to – that we already had Yugoslavia and Albania at A.F.H.Q. and that it was *Lord Moyne's* own suggestion that he should hand over the rest. But he was very obstinate.

6–9.15 p.m. with P.M – recorded in special note:

Note of meeting with the Prime Minister

The Prime Minister received me at six. He was in bed in the Annexe. He began by saying 'I think I will tell you that the Foreign Office are rather annoyed at your coming without permission.' I said that I had sent a telegram. Of course I had left at short notice. He went on to say: 'I must also tell you that I am very pleased you have come. You are not a servant of the Foreign Office. You are my servant and colleague and you must do whatever you like.' This seemed a very auspicious start. In the course of a long discussion covering a wide field I think I was able to get the P.M. to see the picture as we saw it in the Mediterranean. He read a large number of papers and telegrams, had moments of contemplation and others of active talk; but I could see that he had not been seized up to date of the importance of General Wilson's telegram. He had been much impressed by General Alexander's personal telegram to him, but he seemed to be a little uncertain as to what move to make.

Eden came in about eight o'clock and took part in the talk. The Prime Minister had suggested a meeting of the British Chiefs that night, but on consideration we thought it better to give them a little more time to see General Gammell and to make their own study. This meeting was therefore put off till the following day.

[Diary continues] 10 p.m. After a sandwich at Pratt's, went to see Moucher at her hotel and heard all the family news.

The 'flying bombs' or 'doodlebugs' went on intermittently all night, but the continual 'alerts' and 'all clears' woke me up more than the bombs. I stayed at Claridge's.

Thursday, 22 June 1944

10.30 a.m. Office. Papers and telegrams – chiefly on Italy.

12 noon. Bruce Lockhart.[24] The 'Vellacott' affair has caused a terrible commotion at home. Brendan Bracken and Anthony have almost had a reconciliation by a common attack on me! Bruce Lockhart was much more understanding, for he knows – and has suffered from – Vellacott.

I suggested that Sherwood should come out. If Vellacott is to be restored [as head of a new Italian–Balkan section of P.W.B.] it must be on *American* initiation. It is wiser to place the ball firmly in their court.

1.15 p.m. Lunch with Harry Crookshank at the Guards Club. A lot of pleasant gossip. I heard about the tragic death of Ivan Cobbold and Olive Penn when the Guards Chapel was destroyed by a flying bomb last Sunday.

Went to F.O. and had a short talk with Sargent. He has got rather an impracticable scheme for reforming the A.C.C., and dividing 'political' from 'administrative' problems. This seems to me rather unrealistic as you can't divide them. No real reform is possible until the preliminary peace treaty with Italy is negotiated, but there is *no* progress here. I got the impression that the F.O. and H.M.G. do not really approve of the idea, although Sargent does.

5.30 p.m. Looked into House of Commons (smoking room only!). Owing to flying bombs it is back at Church House.

6.30 p.m. Went to Macmillan & Co. and saw Daniel. He seemed pretty well. After talking over (and settling) a number of matters we went for dinner to the Beafsteak.

10.30 p.m. – 2 a.m. Meeting with P.M., Eden and British Chiefs of Staff – described in separate paper:

Note of meeting

There were present: Admiral of the Fleet Sir Andrew Cunningham, the C.I.G.S., Field Marshal Brooke, Chief of Air Staff, Air Marshal Portal and Mr Eden. Generals Ismay and Hollis were in attendance. The Prime Minister opened the subject in a very ingenious way, not committing himself definitely either for or against 'Anvil' or for or against 'Armpit' [Alexander's plan]. He asked me to put forward the plan as I understood it, and more generally General Alexander's enthusiasm and confidence. This I tried to do. It was clear that the Chief of the Air Staff was very much attracted, chiefly by the argument

[24] Sir Robert Bruce Lockhart (1887–1970), who had been British Agent in Moscow during the Revolution, was Director-General of P.W.E., 1941–5.

against breaking up the Air Force and using it in two theatres. The C.I.G.S. seemed more uncertain, and the First Sea Lord took little part in the discussion. After the meeting broke up the P.M. kept me till about 2 a.m. He is clearly getting very worked up and interested in the immense strategic and political possibilities of 'Armpit'.

Friday, 23 June 1944

11 a.m. Sir Orme Sargent. Some progress on Italy. I think I convinced him that his scheme must be modified. Bovenschen (War Office) at the meeting.

12 noon. Eden. I renounced my Balkan aspirations, while warning him of the weakness of the present system.

He is *not* however at all interested in Balkan *relief* (including Greece) and gives us a free hand to do what we like about General [I. T. P.] Hughes's (A.M.L.) organisation, now situated in Cairo.

Lunch with Wyndham Portal[25] at Claridge's. He was, as usual, full of gossip. Oliver Lyttelton's 'gaffe' about America[26] and the 'flying bombs' seem the chief subjects of interest.

I rang up all the children. I learned from Katharine (who is at Brogyntyn) that Maurice is now in France.

2.45 p.m. Sherwood (American head of O.W.I. in Europe). He was very pleasant and sensible. I urged him to come out to A.F.H.Q. as soon as he could.

3.30 p.m. Lord Wolmer [Minister of Economic Warfare]. We discussed the use of S.O.E. in the period immediately following the war. I found that he had received (presumably from Colonel Dodds-Parker) my paper on the Balkans and was enthusiastically in favour of the ideas. But we are up against much resistance, active and passive.

4.30 p.m. Bridges. He confirmed that the P.M. was very glad I had come back for a talk with him.

5 p.m. Lady Margaret Alexander called at my office. I gave her the latest news of the general.

5.30 p.m. General Gammell. He gave me the story of his talks with the British Chiefs on 'The Grand Design'.

Went to S.H.A.E.F. H.Q. (with Sir William Strang) to dine.

A lot of old friends – General Humfrey Gale in tremendous form. I was much pleased and even touched at my welcome. He had arranged the inevitable concert – Royal Artillery String Band. This was very enjoyable, but made me very late in getting home.

We were pursued by 'flying bombs' from Bushey Park to Claridge's, and my poor old chauffeur was much alarmed.

[25] Lord Portal (1885–1949) was Minister of Works and Planning, 1942–4.

[26] In a speech on 20 June to the American Chambers of Commerce he said that America had not been forced into the war by Pearl Harbor, but had provoked the Japanese by their aid to the Allies.

Saturday, 24 June 1944

10.30 a.m. Sir Alexander Cadogan. More talk about Italy and the Balkans.

11 a.m. Jebb. The old question of the publication of the armistice terms. I rather weakly agreed.

11.30 a.m. Motored to S.H.A.E.F. H.Q. (at Bushey Park) and lunched with Bedell Smith. He was very pleasant, but obviously suspicious about my return. However, we got off military questions, on to de Gaulle, etc. Eisenhower and Bedell are obviously anxious for a settlement and have (as usual) taken some risks of Presidential displeasure. From the President's letter to Eisenhower (which Bedell Smith showed me – a rare act of friendship) I gather this was incurred. We talked over some possible plan of compromise at great length. I promised to do my best with the P.M. (which I did on Sunday).

Charles Peake was at lunch.

I drove back to London – picked up Daniel and Catherine and motored to Pooks. Here we found Carol and Sarah – also Nanny and Gibbs. A lovely day and a most happy evening. Sarah has been doing a lot of horse-coping in the absence of us both. She went to Hunstanton and bought a horse. She has also got Catherine's mare in foal (an Arab sire) and has persuaded poor Mr Gibson (my land agent) to pay the cost of both these enterprises.

Sunday, 25 June 1944

11 a.m. Motored to Chequers (day with P.M. described separately). Got back late to Pooks.

Note on day at Chequers

I spent the day at Chequers, and it was on this day that the Prime Minister finally produced C.O.S. (44) 571 (0).[27] He was immensely pleased with this document, which was printed by the late evening. It is indeed a most powerful statement of his case. He was anxious for it to be before the British Chiefs on Monday so that they could put their views to the American Chiefs. He was very exhausted by its composition, and sitting in the drawing-room about six o'clock said, 'I am an old and weary man. I feel exhausted.' Mrs Churchill said, 'But think what Hitler and Mussolini feel like!' To which Winston replied, 'Ah, but at least Mussolini has had the satisfaction of murdering his son-in-law.' This repartee so pleased him that he went for a walk and appeared to revive.

Monday, 26 June 1944

Left Pooks early by car with Daniel and Catherine. We had intended to leave tonight but our work is not yet completed.

[27] A memorandum to the Chiefs of staff on Operation 'Armpit'.

10 a.m. Sir Gilbert Laithwaite (deputy to Edward Bridges).

10.30 a.m. Desmond Morton – as usual in wonderful form. Apparently P.M. was very hard on the F.O. over the Italian affair. According to Desmond, my stock is high.

12 noon. Jebb. German armistice terms this time! What has this to do with me?

12.30 p.m. Lockhart – to confirm arrangements for 'liquidating' the Vellacott affair made with Sherwood.

1.15 p.m. Lunched with Arthur Penn and Bobbety Cranborne. A talk with the latter after luncheon, when I gave him my proposed 'compromise' on the de Gaulle affair. He seemed to like it and said he would discuss with Anthony. My idea is that the Committee should move from Algiers to France (as soon as practicable); broaden its base; summon the 'notabilities' of France to form a sort of consultative assembly (to be merged with that now in Algiers) and solemnly reaffirm the constitutional procedure already approved in Algiers for elections, etc., in due course, together with a sort of French 'Declaration of Rights'. On this, recognition of Provisional Government of France by U.S. Government and H.M.G. to follow.

3–4.30 p.m. With P.M. More talk about the plan and other matters – especially Yugoslavia. Randolph appeared, slim but truculent. He irritates his father, who adores him.

5–6 p.m. Office – telegrams, papers, etc.

6.30 p.m. Called on George Hall,[28] at F.O. A charming man.

8.30 p.m. Dined with Max Beaverbrook at Brook House. A very amusing evening – Camrose, Alexander[29] (First Lord and *very* pompous), Brendan Bracken and Randolph. Also plenty of champagne.

Tuesday, 27 June 1944

Motored down very early to Pooks Cottage to say goodbye to Sarah and Carol. Then a fairly quiet hour in the Cabinet Office before lunch.

Lunched with W. S. Morrison.[30] He has had a terribly difficult job with Town and Country Planning. His final scheme seems a reasonable compromise between the extreme 'Letchworthers' and the extreme defenders of the rights of property. Like all compromises, however, it will not enthuse anybody.

2.45 p.m. General Gammell. I explained to him my failure with Eden on the Balkans.

[28] George Hall (1881–1965) was Parliamentary Under-Secretary of State at the Foreign Office, 1943–5.

[29] William Berry, 1st Viscount Camrose (1879–1954) was Editor-in-Chief of the *Daily Telegraph*, 1928–54. A. V. Alexander (1885–1965) was First Lord of the Admiralty, 1929–31, 1940–5 and 1945–6.

[30] W. S. Morrison (1893–1961), later 1st Viscount Dunrossil, was Minister of Town and Country Planning, 1943–5.

4 p.m. Eden. A further talk on the Balkans. He is still adamant, and seems to think I want to be Foreign Secretary everywhere. I quite see his point of view; I told him, frankly, that if I were Foreign Secretary I would secure the immediate liquidation of all Ministers Resident wherever and whoever they might be.

Dined quietly at Pratt's and went early to bed. Our return was postponed due to weather.

Wednesday, 28 June 1944

11 a.m.–1 p.m. At House of Commons. Saw a number of people, who all seemed very friendly.

5 p.m. Eden (Cadogan and Sargent present). We discussed the revised scheme of A.C.C. I am not very sure about it, but perhaps we can make it work.

After the Cabinet, went to see P.M. to say good-bye. He told me the latest position about 'Anvil' (described in separate paper):

Note on Operation 'Anvil'

By evening it was found that the American Chiefs' reply had come. It was not only a brusque but even an offensive refusal to accept the British plan. It so enraged the P.M. that he thought of replying to the President in very strong terms; but after consideration it was decided that the British Chiefs should reply formally that they could not change the advice that they were giving to His Majesty's Government to whom they had the duty of giving the best professional opinion which they could form. Meanwhile, when I saw the Prime Minister after the Cabinet between eight and nine, he had rewritten his paper and he gave me an uncorrected proof. He thanked me for my comments, which I had written at his request, on his first paper. He decided to telegraph his revised paper to the President with an appeal for further consideration. He is still exceedingly anxious on every ground to continue the Italian battle at least to cross the Pisa–Rimini Line, to seize the Po Valley and, if further exploitation towards Trieste is not possible this summer, at least to have this possibility open for next spring. I left him anxious and a little harassed, and I also strongly got the impression that, in view of the heavy contribution of the American forces to the European campaign and the general situation, we should have to give in if Eisenhower and Marshall insisted upon 'Anvil'. We can fight up to a point, we can leave on record for history to judge the reasoned statement of our views, and the historian will also see that the Americans have never answered any argument, never attempted to discuss or debate the points, but have merely given a flat negative and a somewhat Shylock-like insistence upon what they conceive to be their bargain. Fortunately on this issue there is no international feeling involved so far as sacrifice is concerned, for

'Anvil' will be an operation purely American and French in which there will be no British except a few naval units.

[Diary continues] After looking in at a dinner of the 'Young Tories' ([Harold] Nicolson [Quintin] Hogg, [Viscount] Hinchingbrooke, [Peter] Thorneycroft, etc), left for the airport.

Thursday, 29 June 1944

Arrived about 11 a.m. after a good trip. As usual after an absence, there was a mass of paper to get through.

At 5 p.m. General Wilson called, and I gave him a full account of all that had passed in London. At 6.30 we went out to bathe. Very refreshing after a night in the air! It is quite lovely here now, hot but not too hot. It was nice to be able to give Dorothy the latest accounts of the children.

8.15 p.m. Bob Murphy to dinner. I told him my news and he seemed in very good heart. He is really an excellent colleague.

Friday, 30 June 1944

A terrific day from 8.30 a.m. till nearly midnight. Partly paper, partly interviews.

Steel (F.O. Adviser at Cairo) is here. He is very disappointed about the Balkan decision and wants to go to London to explain the real position as he sees it.

General Wilson called 5 p.m. for a further talk.

Lord Rothschild[31] to dinner – a clever and amusing man.

[31] Lieutenant-Colonel Victor Rothschild, 3rd Baron (b. 1909) was serving in Military Intelligence.

July

Saturday, 1 July 1944

Left 8 a.m. in General Wilson's aeroplane. John Wyndham, General Gammell and one or two others.

We arrived at Viterbo main [aerodrome] about 1.30 p.m. – a good trip. From there, we got into 'cubs'[1] and after a short flight (ten–fifteen minutes) were landed at General Alexander's Advanced H.Q. on the east of Lake Bolsena. It is a most agreeable, even delectable, spot. The weather was lovely – hot by day and cool by night. Alexander is back in his famous caravan, poised on a hill, amidst olives and oaks, overlooking the lake.

The guest camp is a little way off – very comfortable tents. The ante-room and mess are in tents.

I found the general in his usual imperturbable good humour. We had a long talk on the whole situation. I gave him the P.M.'s papers. But I was forced to admit that I was not very hopeful and that I felt sure he would have to reconcile himself to 'Anvil', involving the loss to his forces of three American and four French divisions and seventy per cent of his air.

He was already making plans to see what he could still achieve in this event.

After tea, we went for a trip on the lake in a motor boat – a sort of 'duck' [amphibious vehicle], whose real purpose is to haul pontoons.

We landed on one of the little islands (about four miles across the lake) and walked over it. There was a pleasant old monastery converted into a residence – belonging to some Italian duchess or other. The guardian received us kindly, as also did some French officers who were using the place as a rest-camp. Wine and sandwiches were produced, and general interchange of courtesies.

After dinner, we had some further talk on the military situation.

[1] Taylorcraft Cubs, light two-seater aeroplanes used for reconnaissance.

Gammell had spent the afternoon going over the ground with General Harding (Alexander's Chief of Staff).

Sunday, 2 July 1944

The military spent all the morning at work. I lazed, read *The Woodlanders* and enjoyed the sunshine and the view.

After luncheon, General Alexander and I drove to Orvieto – a very pretty drive. We spent an hour in the splendid Cathedral – fortunately quite undamaged. The curious Gothic west front does not appeal to me. But the bronze statues (especially the lion, eagle, etc. – the four evangelists) by Orcagna are very fine.

The splendid Romanesque nave – interior and exterior is very impressive. And fortunately the frescoes in the south aisle are in quite uninjured condition. The roof is by Fra Angelico and most attractive. The Signorellis (Last Judgment, etc.) are superb.

We drove back to the camp and went for another boating expedition. A telegram has now arrived saying that 'Anvil' is on and 'Armpit' off – or rather that all priority is to be for 'Anvil'. The P.M. also telegraphed asking General Alexander to return at once.

We went through again all the possible methods of securing at least the minimum results of the Italian campaign. If we can get one division from the Middle East (perhaps two), scrape together some extra 'air' (say from Coastal Command – the submarines in the Mediterranean being very few), collect another two Italian divisions to hold a quiet part of the line (for this purpose the military subcommission of A.C.C. would be abolished and General Alexander should have *direct* relations with the Italian military authorities), take any odd troops from Malta and Gibraltar (replacing with Home Guard) and generally scrape M.E. for all 'service' troops – then General Alexander thinks he may still be able to:

(1) Force the Apennines and carry the Pisa–Rimini Line.
(2) Cross the Po and seize the 'quadrilateral'.
(3) Perhaps advance to or beyond the Piave.

Then, if things in France should not go too well, we have a splendid and menacing position which we can exploit next spring.

Monday, 3 July 1944

Left by 'cub' from the camp to Viterbo main at 7.30. From there to Rome by DC3. From there by the Prime Minister's York to Algiers. General Alexander, General Harding, two A.D.C.s and self. Gammell returned by Caserta, as he wished to see General Devers, who is there. He took John Wyndham, who is making my arrangements for the move to Caserta.

We got to Algiers about 2.30 p.m. General Alexander left for England at 4.30 p.m. Good luck to him!

Tuesday, 4 July 1944

9.15 a.m. Colonel C. M. Woodhouse, British Liaison Officer in Greece. An interesting and intelligent young man.

The usual papers all day – Italy, Yugoslavia (Tito's visit to Caserta is being planned for next week).

A very hot day.

4 p.m. Political Committee, A.F.H.Q. A large, but not very exciting agenda. We decided to let the Italian Government return to Rome (probably by 1 August) and to return the provinces south of Rome to their authority. (This requires the formal approval of the Advisory Council.)

Poor Sir Noel Charles continues to send a large number of rather agitated and ungrammatical telegrams. Presumably because the F.O. has been so beaten up by the P.M., he is to have an extra counsellor, Henry Hopkinson from Lisbon. I used to do the French and Italian work alone, with Makins, Reilly and John – with Aubrey Halford at a later stage.

Now we have two Ambassadors, four counsellors, two first secretaries, two second, two third and various A.D.C.'s and attachés. It is really rather comic.

An enormous party at Bob Murphy's for 'Independence Day', to which Dorothy and I went.

Colonel Woodhouse and Fred Reinhardt to dinner.

Wednesday, 5 July 1944

10.30 a.m. A.F.H.Q. meeting on Albania.

1.15 p.m. Gave lunch in honour of Mr Lyn-Jones, who has been British coal expert here since the landings. A nice party which went off well.

4 p.m. Meeting with Murphy and General McChrystal on *Greek* censorship – the makings of another row with Middle East.

9.30 p.m.–3 a.m. We gave a very successful dance. A lovely night. About 250 came – mostly young and some very pretty. It was said to be the best party given yet in Algiers, and served as a sort of 'farewell party'.

A large selection of people – including Duff, Diana, Randolph Churchill (on his way back to Yugoslavia), Virginia Cowles, Mrs Hemingway,[2] etc., etc. We did *not* ask the Ministers and Ambassadors, except those who were thought to be 'dancing men'. I have no doubt but that we shall have made a lot of enemies!

The household was magnificent and produced vast quantities of food and wine. The band consisted of the refugee band of a Vienna

[2] Martha Gellhorn (b. 1908), war correspondent for *Collier's Weekly*, was married to Ernest Hemingway, 1940–5.

night-club, enlisted into the British Pioneer Corps. They were very good and played some excellent waltzes.

Thursday, 6 July 1944

Morning at the office – a good many telegrams. The usual Yugoslav, Italian and Albanian problems.

Greece is going sour on Ambassador Leeper, I am afraid. And I should not wonder if Yugoslavia does the same on us. The P.M. is trying to go too fast and not leaving enough to the Ban (Subašić) and Tito themselves. I learned with the Giraud–de Gaulle affair *not* to interfere *too* much and not to appear *too* interested in the result.

12.30 p.m. Randolph Churchill called. He was more subdued and less exuberant than usual. He returns to Yugoslavia on Saturday. His only complaint was about A.F.H.Q. censorship and P.R.O. I sent him to see General McChrystal.

Meeting of new Economic Sub-committee of Political Committee; General Clark in the chair. Quite a businesslike meeting. We agreed a number of subjects for study.

The most amusing item was to answer a telegram from C.C.S. to General Wilson personally for having taken the decision to increase the bread ration in Italy without obtaining permission from C.C.S.

A formal reply was agreed and I am sending a telegram personally to S. of S. for War [Grigg]. I read this to the Committee who seemed amused.

The Italian Bread Ration

From: Resident Minister, Algiers
To: Foreign Office, London

Personal for the Secretary of State for War from Macmillan.

Please see GWAR Cable from C.C.S. to SACMED No. W60096 of 4 July about the increase of the bread ration in Italy. One must assume that when a telegram is sent personally from the Combined Chiefs of Staff to the Supreme Allied Commander Mediterranean it has a true title to the high authority it claims.

2. But in fact I feel sure that it emanates from a much humbler quarter. I will not bore you with the details of the bread ration problem in Italy. But I feel it right to let you know, in view of this pompous criticism of General Wilson, that Mr Murphy and I investigated the matter personally with great care, that we obtained the assistance of the best economic experts, not only locally but borrowed from the Middle East, notably Mr E. M. H. Lloyd, and that all the British and all the American experts on the spot were agreed upon the urgent need of increasing the ration not on humanitarian grounds but in order to ensure the maximum delivery of the harvest. It was an anti-hoarding

and anti-inflation measure. To succeed the decision had necessarily to be rapid; and our experience of the organisation operating under the title Combined Chiefs of Staff in economic affairs is that it is portentously slow. For example, proposals which we sent them earlier in the year on inflation were returned to us without the change of a comma or a word of comment on 9 April, after three months' delay. I therefore urged General Wilson most strongly, and was supported by my American colleague, Mr Murphy, that on this occasion he should take speedy action.

3. The Combined Chiefs of Staff are concerned lest this decision should lead to the necessity for a rate of imports higher than would have been necessary without it. We claim that it will have the opposite effect, but in any case it was made clear by General Wilson that should our hopes be disappointed and hoarding by the farmers and consequent black marketing continue, he would not hesitate to decrease the official ration later in the year.

4. The hypotheses upon which the Combined Chiefs of Staff are working are wrong and the deductions false. I hope that in the circumstances you will feel that General Wilson deserves praise not censure for a bold and timely action which all economists with experience of the problems created by modern war will approve.

5. If the Prime Minister should notice the telegram in question, perhaps you would show him my comments.

[Diary continues] 5 p.m. Saw S.A.C. Turkey, Yugoslavia, Italy, 'Anvil' – a useful talk. I showed him my telegram to Grigg in his defence, with which General Wilson seemed pleased.

Motored out to Tipasa. Dined with Jean Monnet (back a day or two ago from U.S.A.) in our old haunt. Dorothy came with me. M. and Mme Bonnet (Minister for Information) were of the party. Walked in the old Roman city in the moonlight.

I had some private talk with Monnet that night, and also the next morning.

Friday, 7 July 1944

After which Dorothy and I motored back to Algiers.

11 a.m. Brigadier Jeffries. He came with Harman (P.W.B.) to discuss the Vellacott situation. After all the fuss, Vellacott is sick in Egypt and wants to go direct home, which S.A.C. has approved.

We agreed that Brigadier Jeffries should at once accept Brigadier McChrystal's offer – to become Chief Military Officer in P.W.B.

12 noon. Bogomolov. He had two points: (1) Russian request to get three ships from us with which to send Russian stores to Bari for the Yugoslav partisans. As the ships are to be British, the air protection British and the stores American, we had already (as result of Tuesday's Political Committee) telegraphed to C.C.S. asking that this should be

turned down. I did not tell him this! (2) He wanted to get ten Poles out of the British Pioneer Corps who, he says, want to be Soviet citizens. This, of course, is just to annoy the Poles!

All afternoon at office.

6 p.m. Sherry party for Miss Davidson (one of my clerks) who is to marry a Corporal Yardley tomorrow. A cheque for £50 was presented to her from my staff and that of the Ambassador.

7 p.m. Randolph at the villa to say goodbye.

A quiet dinner – only Dorothy and Roger. Worked after dinner and early to bed.

Saturday, 8 July 1944

10.45 a.m. Miss Davidson's wedding at the English church followed by a reception at the villa. A very enthusiastic affair.

Went out to bathe with Dorothy. A high wind and great breakers made it very exhilarating.

4–7 p.m. Worked in office.

7.15 p.m. Went to cocktail party given by charming young Mr Renchard (of the American Embassy) and gushing young Mrs Renchard. She is very attractive, very anxious to succeed in her first post, and altogether a very pleasing young thing, who has already learned how the middle-aged (like me) appreciate flattery and attention.

They have taken the remarkable Arab house which M. Lemaigre-Dubreuil made (for a short time during Giraud's ascendency) the centre of reactionary intrigue. He has now fled to Spain – to escape arrest.

8.15 p.m. Dined with M. Diethelm, Commissioner for War. The beautiful Madame de Lesseps (Sussex-born) acts as hostess, her husband being Diethelm's *chef de cabinet*.

Sunday, 9 July 1944

Dorothy and I went to church at ten. A nice service as usual, but a poor sermon.

A little work till luncheon – nothing vastly exciting.

At 5 p.m. Dorothy and I motored to Mrs Rooker, where we found that remarkable lady in great form in her remarkable house.

Went on to bathe at Dodds-Parker's beach and then to Tipasa for dinner. A lovely day.

Monday, 10 July 1944

10 a.m. Political Committee. A number of interesting items. We rather rushed through in order to let General Wilson get away. He left for Caserta at about 1.30. General Alexander turned up from London at about 11 a.m. He told us the result of his work there and seemed very satisfied as to the support which the P.M. and C.I.G.S. are giving him.

We hope to get at least the equivalent amount of three British divisions – which will make four or five Italian *fighting* divisions. These can help – at least in quiet places of the line.

We may also get some extra troops by combining the Middle East. The most difficult gap to fill will be in the air. General Alexander came to my villa for refreshment and I motored down to the airfield with him.

4 p.m. Major Ellis with draft telegram for Sir Frederick Bovenschen about the American desire to hand over civilian relief expenditure in Italy to civilian agencies and no longer carry this on War Department funds. This raises two separate problems: (1) system of control, (2) system of accounting. Both present certain difficulties from the British point of view.

5 p.m. Governor Cochrane – U.S. representative of U.N.R.R.A. [United Nations Relief and Rehabilitation Administration] at A.F.H.Q. A dear old boy.

8.30 p.m. Dined alone with Massigli. A long and interesting talk on post-war problems. Massigli feels the necessity for England to take the lead in the formation of a Western European bloc.

Tuesday, 11 July 1944

9.30 a.m. Mr Camozzi, representative of Cable & Wireless in Western Mediterranean. He did not impress me. He should have been pensioned by the company long ago.

1 p.m. Left for Caserta by air. Roger Makins came with me. We stayed with General Wilson at the Hunting Lodge.

Discussion on Tito at A.F.H.Q.[3]

Wednesday, 12 July 1944

Apart from Tito, a long talk with General Wilson and Noel Charles (who came to lunch) on various Italian problems:

(*a*) Increase of Italian Army.

(*b*) Publication of long armistice terms.

(*c*) Residence of King Victor Emmanuel at Naples.

Charles is still very apt to give in to any Royal request.

We heard this morning that King George would be coming on a visit to the troops in Italy next week. In view of this, I sent later in the day a firm telegram to Charles about (*c*).

Thursday, 13 July 1944

Most of the day on Tito, etc. John Wyndham and I drove to see the villa at Naples which we are to have – Villa Carradori. It will be very

[3] We had learned on 11 July that Tito no longer planned to visit Caserta to meet General Wilson. Subašić's new Government was being hampered by the old Serb Party, and the Yugoslav Ambassador in the United States, but on the 12th Brigadier Maclean arrived and told us that Tito was sending General Velebit to London with two nominees for Subašić's Government.

nice. We shall also have a small house at Caserta (the one I used to go to when it was guest house for General Alexander's guests) and some fine offices in the palace.

The move over is going to be incredibly complicated. But John (who is here as advance guard) is being as competent as usual, and Ralph Anstruther[4] will look after the rear echelon.

General George Clark came to stay the night at the Hunting Lodge.

Friday, 14 July 1944

10 a.m. General Wilson and I flew to Viterbo main and from there motored to General Alexander's Advanced H.Q. on Lake Bolsena. A lovely day – hot but not unbearably so. We arrived at about 12 noon. After an hour's talk on various military and political questions, luncheon and more talk. We got back to Caserta about 5 p.m.

General Sosnkowski[5] to dinner. He made a splendidly Polish observation. When General Wilson asked him what sort of country it was between Vilna and Grodno (meaning open or enclosed, etc.) he replied at once, 'Why, Polish country, of course!'

Saturday, 15 July 1944

A completely Yugoslavian – and very busy – day. M. Subašić, Ban of Croatia and New Yugoslav P.M., to dinner. He was in capital form. Not for nothing did we christen him 'George Robey'.

Extract from memorandum on Marshal Tito

The jovial Ban came to dinner on Saturday night. He was in excellent form, all his good humour restored, full of enthusiasm and hope and with many stories of the battles of the last war and of the struggles and trials of this. His general idea is to return to London, bring what influence he can upon the old Serb Party, chiefly mobilising the King and the Court, then perhaps pay a visit to Moscow and, with the blessing of Stalin and the merit of having made a pilgrimage to the Holy Places of Marxism, suggest another meeting with Tito. This he thinks will ease Tito's position, who is clearly suspect by the extremists in his own party and might be fatally injured by the reproach of having sold out to the moderates and the King.

Sunday, 16 July 1944

A morning at Caserta, with telegrams, etc.[6]

Left about 3 p.m. with General Wilson. Arrived Algiers 7.15 – a very good flight. Now that Corsica is in our hands and we have progressed

[4] Captain Sir Ralph Anstruther (b. 1921), my Private Secretary.

[5] General Kasimierz Sosnkowski (b. 1885) was Vice-President and Minister of State under General Sikorski.

[6] Tito now said he wanted to visit Italy to meet General Wilson.

further in Italy, we take a more direct route, passing the southern end of Sardinia.

Dorothy and I dined with Murphy, to meet Mr Bullitt,[7] of whom I formed a favourable view.

Monday, 17 July 1944

11 a.m. Meeting with Gridley, Mr Dort[8] (U.S. State Department), Major Ellis and one or two others. A preliminary talk on the Italian relief problem. I think the Americans are beginning to realise that the question is more complicated than they had imagined.

12 noon. Sherwood (O.W.I.) and the perennial question of Vellacott and his successor.

1.15 p.m. Vice-Admiral Geoffrey Miles, new Flag Officer, Western Mediterranean, to lunch.

3 p.m. Economic Subcommittee. The A.C.C.'s report on 'Anti-Inflation Measures for Italy'. A long but rather inconclusive discussion. General Lewis acted for General Clark in the latter's absence. Lewis is a clever man, but too clever to be a good chairman.

Steel to dinner – on his way back to Cairo.

Tuesday, 18 July 1944

A morning at the villa with papers, telegrams, etc.

4.30 p.m. The French 'Provisional Government' called to say 'goodbye' to me. Owing to a Cabinet meeting, they could not come to our farewell party, so they came before. De Gaulle was too busy but sent Mme de Gaulle.

I thought this rather a touching attention of the Committee. Catroux made a little speech, and I replied in French.

5.30–8.30 p.m. Cocktail party at the villa. About 450–500 people came – all the diplomatic corps, French of all kinds, British and American soldiers, sailors and airmen. Dorothy was in great form and it seemed a great success – marred only (or perhaps enhanced) by one of the waiters getting drunk and nearly knocking down M. de Lesseps.

Wednesday, 19 July 1944

Morning at office. Dorothy and I lunched with M. and Mme Tixier. Monnet and R. Mayer also there.

Bathed and had picnic dinner with Dorothy in evening. Very hot, but the lovely bathing makes up for a lot.

I hope the P.M. and Anthony will not be too much angered by my reply to their telegram of censure of our Yugoslavian performance!

[7] William C. Bullitt (1891–1967) was U.S. Ambassador to France, 1936–9; he then joined the First French Army, holding staff appointments.

[8] Dallas W. Dort (b. 1908) was Adviser, Liberated Areas Directorate, State Department, January–October 1944.

15. Conference of Chiefs of Staff, Sidi Bou Said, 24 October 1943. Left to right: Sholto Douglas, the author, Bedell Smith, Murphy *(Imperial War Museum)*

16. Cairo Conference, November 1943. Left to right (seated): Chiang Kai-Shek, Roosevelt, Churchill, Madame Chiang. Left to right (standing): Cadogan, unidentified, Eden, Steinhardt, Winant, the author, Dr Wong Chung-Hui, Casey, Killearn, Kirk, Harriman, Douglas, two unidentified, Hopkins *(Imperial War Museum)*

17. Christmas Day, Algiers, 1943. Eisenhower, Alexander, Churchill *(Popperfoto)*

18. Duff Cooper with the author, 1944 *(Imperial War Museum)*

27. Archbishop Damaskinos with Winston Churchill, Athens, 26 December 1944 *(Imperial War Museum)*

28. Athens Conference, 26 December 1944. Left to right: Eden, Churchill, Damaskinos, Alexander, the author *(Imperial War Museum)*

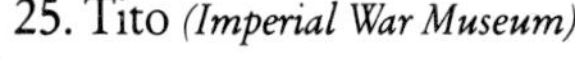

23. John Wyndham *(Private Collection)*

24. General Sir Henry Maitland Wilson *(Imperial War Museum)*

25. Tito *(Imperial War Museum)*

26. George Papandreou *(Associated Press)*

22. The bombing of Monte Cassino, 15 March 1944 *(Imperial War Museum)*

19. King Victor Emmanuel III
(Popperfoto)

20. Prince Umberto, May 1944
(Imperial War Museum)

21. Count Sforza with Benedetto Croce, January 1944 *(Imperial War Museum)*

29. The Liberation of Modena, 23 April 1945 *(Imperial War Museum)*

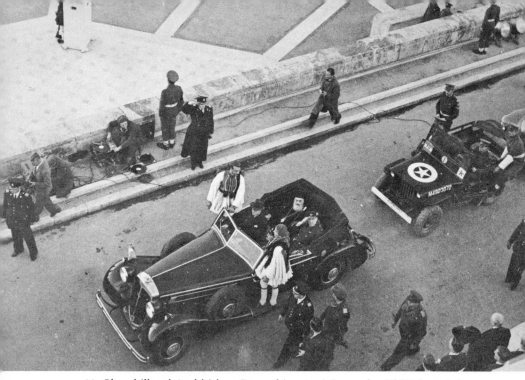

30. Churchill and Archbishop Damaskinos arriving at the Old Palace, Athens, 14 February 1945 *(Imperial War Museum)*

31. Churchill in Athens, 14 February 1945. Left to right: Sarah Churchill, Alexander, Churchill, Scobie, the author *(Imperial War Museum)*

Yugoslav Telegrams

From: Foreign Office, London
To: Resident Minister, Algiers

No. 1565

MOST IMMEDIATE

Your telegram No. 15 from Caserta.

We did not agree with your solution and do not commend your action. We should have preferred that the Yugoslav P.M. and party should have waited at Caserta for Tito to come round as we felt confident he would. Now, however, those who might have taken part in the politico-military talks have dispersed.

2. In the circumstances the Prime Minister and I think that Tito can well be kept waiting at least forty-eight hours for General Wilson's answer on the line you suggest. The Yugoslav P.M. has again arrived and this will give us a chance of hearing what he has to say. This, I feel, seems all the more politic since, according to para 5 of your telegram No. 13 from Caserta, military conversations are not now of such importance. While we sympathise with Tito's difficulties a little waiting will do him no harm.

From: Resident Minister, Algiers
To: Foreign Office, London

Your telegram No. 1565.

I find it difficult to reconcile the severe, not to say wounding censure in the first sentence of your telegram with the tenor of the remaining portion. It seems to me that like Balaam you started out to curse but remained to bless.

2. Your plan seems to differ from ours only in one respect, that we allowed the Ban and his Ministers to return to London. I believe when you have seen the Ban and considered Ambassador Stevenson's report you may take rather a different view. In any case one cannot keep a Ban on ice at Caserta indefinitely.

Thursday, 20 July 1944

The preparations for leaving have made the villa uninhabitable. Everything is in great confusion. The ship with most of our belongings is stranded at Bougie. Heaven knows when it will reach Naples. We have no cars and no servants.

Went with Dorothy to bathe and picnic lunch at Captain Fitz-George of the British Naval Liaison. An extraordinary scene – all the 'lovelies' or 'pin-ups' of Algiers – French, British and American – displaying themselves practically naked on the rocks and in the sea. The men trust to the charms of their 'torsos' to captivate the ladies.

Cocktails, wine, sandwiches and altogether *très mondain*. We said goodbye all over again to our French friends.

4.30 p.m. Meeting with Murphy and P.W.B. on text of General Wilson's declaration to the French people for 'Anvil'.

5.30 p.m. Went for a farewell talk to Duff's villa. He is really a charming friend and is doing awfully well as Ambassador. His staff are not so good as he is.

6.30–8 p.m. Cocktail party at General Wilson's villa. More goodbyes to everybody!

Dined alone at the villa with Dorothy on sandwiches and wine.

Friday, 21 July 1944

9.30 a.m. Mr Bullitt called – a long but rather interrupted talk on post-war Europe. Our last possessions are being packed.

11 a.m. Bob Murphy – to pick up the approved (and much improved) text of General Wilson's declaration. S.A.C. writes better English than P.W.B. and materially improved the draft himself.

11.30 a.m. General Wilson – a number of points:

(*a*) Turkey.

(*b*) King George's visit.

(*c*) Balkan affairs.

12 noon. Brazilian Ambassador (da Cunhà). Like everyone else, he wants to go as diplomatic representative to Rome. I stalled – we must wait for reply from C.C.S. on the Polish case.

12.30 p.m. General Vanier – Canadian Minister to the French – for a little farewell gossip.

Dorothy and I had a sandwich lunch before leaving.

Meanwhile, Roger Makins, Ralph Anstruther, clerks, typists, drivers, servants, cooks (including M. Blom who weighs eighteen stone), hens (they laid two eggs on the trip), cats, etc., left in a specially arranged Dakota – fourteen persons and a quantity of luggage to be distributed between the villas at Naples and Caserta.

Dorothy and I came in S.A.C.'s plane, with the general, Lady Ranfurly, Mark Chapman-Walker and an almost equal quantity of luggage and livestock, including a parrot.

We got to Marcianise aerodrome (near Caserta) about 6.30. Indescribable confusion followed. General Wilson came to stay in my villa at Naples and brought his A.D.C., his Sudanese servant and his Anaamite servant – but not his kit, which was lost.

The others (except John and Ralph who came to villa Carradori) went to Caserta. All the lorries and most of the cars broke down (including General Wilson's) and everyone got very hot and rather cross. It was very enjoyable. The villa at Naples is staffed with Italian servants (about eight or nine in number) and their friends and relations (almost eighty or ninety in total).

Our English servants had gone to Caserta, except one sergeant and one batman.

Dorothy and I and General Wilson dined at the magnificent Villa Emma with C.-in-C. Med. – Sir John Cunningham.

So ends – definitely and finally – my official residence at Algiers. A.F.H.Q. at Algiers closed yesterday – and opened today in Caserta. The Resident Minister's office has done the same – Tony Rumbold in charge today.

I have been in Algiers for nineteen months, off and on. I leave it without much regret, but grateful for an experience which has been the most interesting, even exciting, of my life.

We now continue the story in Italy – perhaps not for very long, if the rumours of disturbances in Germany and an attempt on Hitler's life are at all true.[9]

Saturday, 22 July 1944

9.30 a.m. Conference at my villa. S.A.C., General G. Clark, and General Gammell.

The King's visit; the reform of A.C.C.; a proposed new Balkan relief committee and various other questions. The Turkish situation is still obscure. The military feeling is rather against encouraging her to break off relations with Germany, if the only result is to make a call on our resources which cannot be met without detracting from 'Anvil' (southern France) or 'Diadem' (Italy).

After luncheon, Dorothy and I motored to Caserta. There is terrible confusion in our offices (which are magnificent but noisy) and in our villa there (which is a sort of small suburban house, divided into flats by its owners). Back to Naples in evening.

Sunday, 23 July 1944

8 a.m. To Caserta.

10 a.m. Meeting with S.A.C. and other military commanders. The chief point on which I had to take part was on Yugoslavia. It seems to me that we should no longer try *ourselves* to settle various matters about the old Royal Yugoslav forces and the new partisan forces. We should try to encourage the discussion of all these questions direct between M. Subašić and General Velebit (Tito's representative) in London. If this can be done, it will help co-operation and a habit of settling things reasonably amongst themselves, instead of for ever getting us to intervene.

Solomon is all very well; but his judgments were for Jews.

12 noon. S.A.C., General Devers, Murphy, Gammell. Bob Sherwood attended. Rather unexpectedly he reported very favourably on the P.W.B. organisation in the command and proposed Russell

[9] Count von Stauffenberg's attempt to blow up Hitler at Rastenburg had failed on 20 July.

Barnes (U.S.) as permanent head (vice Vellacott, retired hurt) and Harman (British) as deputy.

I am afraid I still have the feeling that Barnes is not up to the job. But the Americans have got the equipment, and have spent most of the money, and we need their help. As I explained in a telegram to London, the constituent groups are more important than the centre.

We have British officers in charge of all these (except the French branch which *after* 'Anvil' is secure will come under Eisenhower). Rome, Bari and Cairo are all controlled by us. If we were to insist on a British head at the centre, we should have to give up Rome, Bari and Cairo. And I therefore thought it necessary to agree to Barnes.

Miss Campbell has a dreadful cold and seems altogether run down. So I took her down to Naples. She can stay quietly in the villa there for a few days.

4.30 p.m. Arrived at Pomigliano aerodrome. S.A.C., C.-in-C. Med., Slessor's representative, he being ill, and I met the King, who arrived very punctually at the time arranged – 5.15.

Eric Miéville and Mouse Fielden[10] were with him. Old Joey Legh (with his weak tummy and his fleas) we already have. Drove to Villa Emma, where the King is staying.

8.30 p.m. Dinner C.-in-C. Med. Wilson and I the only guests. A very agreeable party. The monarch seemed in excellent form. I had a little difficulty in explaining to him that if Umberto or the King sent him a message or asked to see him, he should send no reply without putting the responsibility for such a reply on one of his Ministers. Sir Noel Charles and Sir D'Arcy Osborne dined at my villa, with Dorothy. Also Roger Makins, Harold Caccia, etc. The King expressed a desire to see them and they were sent for. As the Villa Emma is only five minutes by car from Villa Carradori, we expected them at once. But there was a long delay, at which His Majesty seemed vexed. It was finally discovered that they had arrived at the Villa Emma but had been sent about their business by Admiral Dundas (Chief of Staff), who thought they were ubiquitous press correspondents! They finally arrived – Charles a little the worse for drink – and a very merry evening continued till quite late.

Monday, 24 July 1944

General Wilson (who stayed last night at Villa Carradori with me, his own not yet being ready) went off early in the morning to join the King. I went to Caserta, and found my Ambassador guests in the Villa Vittoria – quite cheerful in spite of the physical hardships.

At 1 p.m. we went over to the great reception and banqueting hall in the centre of the palace. These are really splendid and were splendidly

[10] Sir Eric Miéville (1896–1971) was Assistant Private Secretary to King George VI, 1937–45. Wing-Commander Edward Fielden (1903–76) was Captain of the King's Flight, 1936–52, and Equerry to the King, 1937–46.

decorated for the occasion of a luncheon for the King, to meet over a hundred officers of all services, nations, etc. as well as civilians. Our party (which 'fell in' on me as the right-hand marker) consisted of Charles, Osborne, Makins, Caccia, Rumbold, Broad (from Bari) and Wyndham.

The King walked all round the circle shaking hands, each guest being presented by his 'section leader', since, of course, S.A.C. could not know them all. I think the Americans and French were impressed. It was a splendid setting for the luncheon (there is nothing in Buckingham Palace or Windsor on so grand a scale) and carried out with simplicity and dignity.

I was between Wilson and General de Lattre de Tassigny, who was as agreeable as ever, and a trifle less excitable.

General Juin was invited, but did not appear. Did the French sabotage the invitation?

After the luncheon, we returned to the first large saloon in which we had gathered. While the band played outside (as it had done during the whole proceedings very well) a number of people were brought up for the King to talk to – if from the Forces, by S.A.C.; if civilians, by me. At about 3 p.m. or so, His Majesty left and was airborne at 3.30 at Marcianise. He will now be in General Alexander's hands for several days.

8.15 p.m. Osborne, Charles, Caccia and Makins to dinner. Why do diplomats never discuss anything except houses, furniture, motor-cars, food, wine and money?

Tuesday, 25 July 1944

8.30–10 a.m. Worked on various papers at villa. Miss Campbell is very suspicious of being 'cosseted' – so I give her some work.

10 a.m. Went with Dorothy and Ralph Anstruther. We drove to Pompeii, where we spent from eleven to one. It was really delightful to have so much time and to be able to see it all at leisure. Although it is not '*fine*' (like Dougga or Djemila or El Djem, or any of the North African and Spanish relics of Roman grandeur), yet it gives an intimate picture of provincial Roman life.

We had a picnic lunch, and motored round Vesuvius, through Acerra to Caserta.

4 p.m. Political Committee Meeting. The main items were Greece and Yugoslavia. Should we make an agreement with the Greek Government before entering Greece or not? (In other words, should the new Greek Government be really recognised as effective or should we wait on events? The usual Anglo-American disputes!)

On Yugoslavia, the Russians want to give to Tito two of the twelve Dakotas which we allowed them to put at Bari. This seems rather an impertinence, considering that the Dakotas are lend–lease articles which Russia obtained from America! Diplomatic bribery with gifts you have received yourself! It is rather like passing on wedding presents.

7.30 p.m. Back at Naples. A quiet evening – Miss Campbell, Ralph Anstruther and Dorothy.

Wednesday, 26 July 1944

My room at Caserta is at last ready, with rugs, and some pictures from the palace – Marat, Mme Mère, Joachim Bonaparte in a sea battle, etc., etc. They make splendid funiture and to some extent help the acoustics. My room is forty-five feet long – twenty-four-feet wide, with a big window as well. It is magnificent!

Arrived with Miss Campbell about 10 a.m. Papers and telegrams till lunch. Mark Chapman-Walker and Arthur Forbes to lunch at Villa Vittoria, the latter from S.H.A.E.F. and full of gossip. England is bored with the war, and the politicians are playing for position with increasing ardour and impudence.

11 a.m. Russell Barnes called. He really *is* slow. But he is amenable and harmless.

4–6 p.m. Conference with S.A.C. Chief Administrative Officer (General [George] Clark) and General Hughes (of A.M.L.) about Balkan relief. If it can be done, we are all anxious to get General Hughes's organisation moved here – probably to Naples. We feel that American co-operation would be easier, and interferences by Moyne, Paget and co., less dangerous. As usual, the Greeks are the bone of contention. It is odd how people seem to want impossible assignments and quarrel to get insoluble problems entrusted to them.

6.30 p.m. Left for Naples with Miss Campbell, after calling at Villa Vittoria to see Roger Makins, who is sick.

Thursday, 27 July 1944

10 a.m. Mr Harman – of P.W.E. – a very lachrymose gentleman and of course made more so by the fall of Vellacott and the appointment of Barnes (U.S.).

All the people concerned with propaganda and publicity and political warfare are a neurotic, feminine type, and quarrel with each other a great deal. They are much more difficult to handle than anyone else in A.F.H.Q., or indeed in the theatre generally.

Dorothy and I lunched with S.A.C. at the Hunting Lodge. After luncheon, we were taken on a personally conducted tour round the palace of Caserta by the Italian curator. There are really some lovely rooms in it – and the general air of faded grandeur is set off by the busy life of the A.F.H.Q. officers and men who occupy them as offices. Altogether a strange contrast between the old Bourbon kings and a modern army. Even the Napoleonic occupation cannot have been so startling a change.

Friday, 28 July 1944

Motored early into Caserta from Naples. A morning at the office with the usual alarms and excursions – chiefly now about Turkey.

11 a.m. Bullitt called. He is still full of Russian fears.

12.30 p.m. D., Roger Makins and I left by car for Rome. We had a wonderful drive – by Highway 7 – across the Pontine Marshes, etc. We left the main road towards the end, and came in over the Alban hills (the road skirts Lake Albano) past Castel Gandolfo.

It was a glorious day – not too hot – and a lovely evening. We arrived rather tired – about 6.30. Dorothy went to the British Embassy, which Sir Noel and Lady Charles have just opened up. Roger and I went to the Grand Hotel, where I was given a magnificent suite of rooms – with everything except hot water.

Saturday, 29 July 1944

9 a.m. Saw General [Langley] Browning, head of Military Subcommission. We discussed the re-equipping of four Italian divisions, to make five in all, with British equipment. Although plans are going ahead well here, we are still awaiting formal approval of C.C.S.

The question of the retention or abolition of the office of *Comando Supremo* (now held by Marshal Messe) was also discussed. I told the general that I would support the maintenance of the Commander-in-Chief (although in my view an obsolete system of organisation – as the Duke of Cambridge and General Giraud have shown) on political grounds as an element of conservatism and as freeing the services from possibly dangerous political control, so long as I could be assured that Messe would *not* in fact interfere with the reorganisation of the Army on modern lines.

10.30 a.m. Brigadier Lush – at A.C.C. H.Q. They have at last got a splendid building – the Ministry of Confederations – in which they can all work together in decent conditions. Very different from first Brindisi, and then Naples and Salerno.

A god talk, chiefly on the necessary administrative changes to suit new conditions and on the problem of Italian production. This is now a subject of great contention between Allied Armies in Italy (Army) and A.C.C.; nor has it been made easier by the personal equation as between General Robertson and Mr Grady. Perhaps Grady's return to America may help. I am seeing his successor, Colonel O'Dwyer[11] (political attorney from New York!) tomorrow.

12 noon. [B. A.] Workman (once of Messrs Longman – publishers – now of Ministry of Production). He is doing an inspection here and will be helpful.

[11] William O'Dwyer (1890–1964) was Vice-President of the Economic Section, A.C.C., 1944, and Mayor of New York City, 1945–50.

1.30 p.m. Dorothy, Roger and I went to lunch at his rooms in the Vatican with D'Arcy Osborne. He was charming – and so were his tiny suite of rooms. Not a bad prison, in which this attractive and rather whimsical man has been for four years incarcerated. His only sorrow is that close association with the Vatican and its atmosphere of petty intrigue has been a disillusionment!

3 p.m. Ellery Stone (Acting Chief Commissioner [having succeeded General Mason-MacFarlane in June 1944]). He was very pleasant, but very hot on the production question. Fortunately, I had got General Alex to invite him to dinner at his H.Q. to meet the King. He was just leaving and full of excitement.

5 p.m. Meeting at the Embassy – Charles, Harold Caccia, Henry Hopkinson, Roger and self. A useful talk on a number of outstanding questions. (I am a little concerned at a sort of half-baked connection established between some P.W.B. officers and the German delegation to the Vatican. Since I think the Germans cleverer than the P.W.B. boys, I have ordered the contact to cease, until (if desirable at all) it can be placed in more skilful hands – e.g. Dudley Clarke or one of C's people.[12])

8.30 p.m. Large dinner at Embassy – including Kirk and Myron Taylor (U.S. Ambassador to Vatican – old, rich and charming).

Sunday, 30 July 1944

9 a.m. (At hotel) Colonel Tod, British head of Industrial Subcommission – a genial, intelligent, vulgar man – a company promoter in private life. I should say that his talk was his best selling asset, but he is no fool and doing quite a good job.

10 a.m. Colonel Upjohn, K.C. – a good man.

11 a.m. More talk with Lush.

12.30 p.m. Went for picnic with a large party, Lady Charles, D'Arcy Osborne, etc., etc. Sir Noel and Dorothy got stopped (the roads being cleared for the King's car going from Highway 7 to Highway 5) and *they had the lunch!*

6 p.m. Archbishop Griffin (of Westminster) called. A charming and obviously *very* intelligent man.

7–8 p.m. Colonel O'Dwyer – new Vice-President of the Economic Section of A.C.C. I found him refreshing. I prefer this type to the Grady sort.

8.30 p.m. Dinner quietly at the Embassy.

Monday, 31 July 1944

Left Rome by car at 7 a.m. We motored back *via* Frosinone and Cassino – Highway 6 – a wonderful experience – one could see the whole battlefield and reconstruct its various stages.

[12] Brigadier Dudley Clarke (1899–1974) was head of 'A' Force, which carried out plans to deceive the enemy in the Middle East and the Mediterranean. 'C's people' were the Secret Service.

The destruction of some villages and towns is completed. Others are uninjured. This modern war concentrates fire more than in 1914–18 and the variations of devastation are correspondingly great.

Arrived at San Angelo (between Venafro and Caserta) at 12.30. We were lucky to find the way. I had been invited to attend the review by the Canadian Corps. While we were crossing the hill to Venafro, we saw a large plane – escorted by fighters – come down near Venafro. We followed the King's party to the parade ground – half an hour's drive. Troops were drawn up along the roads and gave the King a splendid reception.

The parade itself was very fine – an old-fashioned drill parade. His Majesty presented a V.C.[13] Roger and Dorothy went on to Naples. I lunched with the Canadian officers and the King and S.A.C.

After luncheon, we drove back to Cassino (about six or seven of us in all) where General Alex met us and explained the whole battle. This was a great treat, and His Majesty seemed very pleased. He was in excellent form and most genial. After picnic tea motored back to Naples – arriving at my villa at about 7.30 p.m. A long and tiring day.

8.30 p.m. Dined at Villa Emma. Only the King, Joey Legh, C.-in-C. Med., Dorothy and self. The King in excellent form and pleased to say nice things about me to Dorothy.

[13] To Major J. K. Mahony, a former newspaperman from Vancouver, for gallantry during the Canadian Corps' thrust through the Gustav and Hitler Lines.

August

Tuesday, 1 August 1944

Went at 9.45 to Villa Emma, with a number of telegrams, etc., for the King to see on Greek, Yugoslav, Turkish and Italian affairs.

He was ready at 10 a.m. and kept me for just over an hour. He was in excellent form and (as usual) I was impressed by his retentive memory and his detailed knowledge of what is going on.

When he is talking quietly, his judgment is good and sensible. (When excited by company, he is sometimes rather wild in his talk.)

He was immensely amused by an incident which took place early this morning. The King of Italy (as we discovered a day or two ago and as I had informed the King yesterday) came to Naples about ten days ago without asking anybody's leave and set himself up in the Villa Rosebery.

Unfortunately I forgot to inform C.-in-C. Med. and the picket boat (which patrolled all night outside the Villa Emma) arrested a suspicious-looking couple who were fishing from a small boat just off the villa, in the early hours (about 5.30 or 6 a.m.). These proved to be the King and Queen of Italy. They (or rather the Queen) protested vigorously and the noise woke up the King of England who put his head out of the window and called for silence!

(A regular *Rose and the Ring* scene.)

Finally, the Queen of Italy produced an enormous visiting card (of *Alice in Wonderland* proportions) and gave it to the naval lieutenant.

The young officer's report (with the card) amused the King enormously and he kept the card as a souvenir.

But really this only shows how right I have been about the King of Italy's residence. It is lucky he was not shot out of hand. Anyway, I have now insisted that he should leave Naples at once and return to Ravello or Brindisi.

4 p.m. Political Meeting – Turkey, Greece, Italian rearmament, and the usual Yugoslav questions.

Tito is now to come here on the 6th and Churchill on the 8th. What a circus I live in!

A lot of work kept me at Caserta, but I got back by 8.30. Changed, a hurried dinner, and then went to Villa Emma to see a film about Nelson and Lady Hamilton. His Majesty very happy.

Wednesday, 2 August 1944

Went at 10 a.m. to Villa Emma. The King gave a M.V.O. to Mark Chapman-Walker (at my suggestion). He is a good fellow; he has served General Wilson for several years and is very co-operative with my office.

Admiral Hewitt (U.S.) and General Devers (U.S.) got their K.C.B.s or K.B.E.s or whatever they were and seemed highly delighted.

12 noon. S.A.C., Slessor, C.-in-C. Med. and I saw the King off at Pomigliano aerodrome. His Majesty in the highest spirits till the end. It has been a really happy and successful visit.

2.30 p.m. Brigadier Norman Smith (a coal-dealer in uniform). I knew him in N.A.E.B. days. A very clever man.

3 p.m. Workman. A good report on his visit.

4 p.m. Robinson[1] (M.P. for Blackpool). He wants to be Governor of the Bahamas! What an ambition!

5 p.m. General George Clark – a number of problems, chiefly connected with A.C.C., especially the industrial problem. I promised to write him a note of my views.

Papers and telegrams keep flooding in. A long talk with Slessor (a very clever man) about Turkey and sending in our R.A.F. Radar experts – ? in mufti, or uniform?

Finally, a visit to S.A.C. about a telegram from the F.O. asking him to see de Gaulle about reinforcements for the Leclerc division now in England. Fortunately, de Gaulle (who was here today) could not be found. He is leaving for Algiers early tomorrow and Duff Cooper will have to undertake the job.

At last, back in Naples by 9 p.m., with a heap of papers in the box on which I worked till 11.30 p.m.

Thursday, 3 August 1944

Stayed at villa in Naples in the morning. Miss Campbell came down, and I got through a lot of dictation. She really is a wonderful worker. Everything was ready for me in the afternoon.

1.15 p.m. Dorothy and I lunched with Admiral Morse. A very pleasant party in a lovely villa. Admiral [John] Mansfield (of the *Orion*), Captain [Kenneth] Collins, R.N., and others.

4 p.m. Talked with S.A.C. on Greece. He will prepare a military plan and I a political, which we can discuss with Churchill when he comes. We decided to bring General Hughes (Allied Military Liaison) who does planning for the Balkans to Naples as soon as possible.

[1] Wing-Commander Roland Robinson (b. 1907). He was Governor and C.-in-C. of Bermuda, 1964–72.

Worked at various papers till 7 p.m. Went down for dinner, taking Roger and Hermione Ranfurly to Naples for the night.

Saturday, 5 August 1944

Dorothy, Ralph Anstruther and I left Capodichino aerodrome at 10 a.m. in General Wilson's reserve plane – a very comfortable Dakota. We arrived at Viterbo main at eleven and at General Alexander's Advanced H.Q. on Lake Bolsena at noon. I found the general as agreeable as ever – a little tired, and of course a little disappointed. The interference of 'Anvil' (now renamed 'Dragoon') with 'Diadem'[2] has been very great in terms of material It has taken several American divisions from Fifth Army as well as a lot of service troops and equipment. It has deprived A.A.I. of seventy per cent of the Air Force. But it has also affected morale – both the remaining Americans and the Eighth Army feel that something has gone out of the campaign. And this a little was reflected even in General Alex's resilient and controlled temperament.

We discussed future plans – relation of A.C.C. and A.F.H.Q.; the possible occupation of Austria, etc., etc. A useful preliminary to some serious planning which must now be done.

After luncheon, General Alexander left by air for Fifth Army H.Q. Dorothy and I, with Ruper Clarke's assistance, did a little boating on the lake. We left Viterbo at five and were back at Capodichino at six. A very pleasant, peaceful and useful day. Dorothy enjoyed it very much, I think.

Lady Ranfurly is living with us at the Naples villa – she is a very pleasant guest.

Sunday, 6 August 1944

10 a.m. Brigadier Jeffries – (British) Chief Administrative Officer to P.W.B. The usual troubles, but the brigadier seems quite a sensible man. Apparently Russell Barnes is quite useless but does no active harm apart from Brigadier McChrystal (the head of INC., a branch of which P.W.B. constitutes). Meanwhile, I have a telegram from London showing that Sherwood (head of O.W.I.) has told quite a different story in London and here. He told General Wilson (in a written report) that everything was fine with P.W.B. and recommended (*a*) the retention of INC. with McChrystal, (*b*) the retention of Russell Barnes as head of P.W.B. He has told Lockhart (in London) that he made the report under pressure from Murphy and General Devers and that McChrystal and Barnes are no good!

What a laugh!

12.30 p.m. Dorothy and I went to luncheon on H.M.S. *Orion* with Admiral Mansfield. A very nice party and we were 'piped' on board in rare style.

[2] The military campaign in Italy, which was intended to benefit 'Overlord' by engaging German divisions which would otherwise be sent to France.

3.30 p.m. Admiral Morse took us on his lately Prince Umberto's launch to Ischia where the British Navy have taken possession. A lovely trip and a lovely spot on arrival. We went to a charming house (belonging to the German Ambassador to Madrid – it is extroardinary how property changes hands in war!) which Morse took over last autumn when he arrived. We bathed (the sea round certain rocks is *boiling* hot, from the underground sulphur springs) and drank delicious Ischian wine. The admiral, Flag-Lieutenant Long, Baron Corst and his wife (formerly Miss Diana Wingfield), Colonel Clarkson (American port engineer, who has done, with Morse, a wonderful job at Naples).

A lovely sail back to Naples – the sun setting. All the party to supper – also John Addis.

Monday, 7 August 1944

Tito duly arrived last night. He had a military talk with S.A.C. and has gone to see General Alex – by plane. Either he was genuinely frightened, or he wanted to stay in Rome, or he was sick because he had eaten and drunk too much of S.A.C.'s lavish entertainment – in any case, he absolutely refused to get into the aeroplane to come back. He has gone to Rome (? to see Bogomolov) and will not return till tomorrow.

Meanwhile, a telegram from P.M. announces that he will now leave England Saturday the 12th, arriving here evening of 13th. S.A.C. has to go to Corsica (in conection with 'Anvil', or 'Dragoon') and I shall be left with:

(*a*) the P.M.,
(*b*) Prime Minister Subašić and Mr Stevenson,
(*c*) Tito.

Tito has got to be kept here awaiting (*a*) but must be kept in the dark about the arrival of (*b*).

There is moreover a fresh problem. British Chiefs of Staff (impelled by Churchill) are now suggesting switching 'Anvil' from southern France (Marseilles, Toulon, etc.) to Brest, St Nazaire, etc. U.S. Chiefs are strongly opposed and want to stick to the original plan. I have no doubt that (once again) British Chiefs will be overborne.

A long and tiring day at the office – a hot sirocco and dust storms. I had several talks with Wilson in the course of the day, whom I found as usual calm and philosophic. Apart from other (more pressing) questions, I told him about Sherwood and the P.W.B. difficulties.

Dinner-party for Archbishop Griffin of Westminster. Lord and Lady Ranfurly, Father Clarke (R.C. Chaplain), Major-General [Henry] Whitty (R.C.), Bob Murphy, Roger Makins, Ralph Anstruther, Colonel Higgins (Liaison Section), Dorothy and self. A pleasant enough evening. The Archbishop very pleasant, but he does not strike me as a great character, intellectually or morally. They should have appointed Ronnie Knox.[3]

Tuesday, 8 August 1944

Letters from Carol – very welcome. I am afraid Dorothy will have to go back and deal with many family matters.

9.30 a.m. S.A.C. Latest Tito developments.

1.15 p.m. Air Marshal Slessor to luncheon at the Villa Vittoria (in Caserta).

Wednesday, 9 August 1944

11 a.m. Meeting of the Economic Subcommittee. A very interesting discussion on various Italian problems, chiefly the method of organisation of external Italian trade.

1 p.m. Marshal Tito came to lunch at the villa in Caserta. He was accompanied by two of his staff officers and Mme Hume who acts as interpreter, and also by Brigadier Fitzroy Maclean. I told the latter that I was not prepared to have Marshal Tito's personal bodyguard standing in my dining-room during lunch. I thought Brigadier Maclean might explain to the Marshal that this was not the custom among gentlemen in our country. A firm position proved successful. The bodyguard stood in the passage. We shall gradually reduce them to standing outside the house. I had a very interesting discussion with the Marshal of whom I formed on the whole a favourable impression. He is quiet, well-behaved, interesting and seemed reasonable. I think he is very much on his best behaviour. It is difficult to form an estimate of his quality. He obviously has character and power of command. He is shorter, stockier, and even fatter than I expected, but he has a certain dignity which is impressive.

4.30 p.m. A talk with General Gammell about the perpetual P.W.B. troubles. London are being very pressing and very tiresome. I am hoping to get a compromise by taking P.W.B. away from the direct control of General McChrystal and putting it under the Chief of Staff himself.

5–6.30 p.m. Political Committee. A varied and quite useful agenda.

6.30–7 p.m. A talk with General Wilson, chiefly on the Prime Minister's visit.

Thursday, 10 August 1944

The usual rather hectic day at the office with papers, telegrams, etc. General Maclean took up a great deal of the afternoon in making the necessary arrangements for Marshal Tito's entertainment. The Americans cannot resist any social figure, and in spite of their natural leanings to General Mihailović have taken Tito to their bosom. An

[3] Monsignor Ronald Knox (1888–1957), the Catholic writer, an old friend ever since my Oxford days.

immense dinner was given by General Eaker in his camp, with bands playing and drink flowing freely. The Marshal seemed duly impressed by the wealth and magnificence of the American display.

Friday, 11 August 1944

8.15–12 noon. A very interesting tour of the local hemp industry organised by the Hemp Controller, Mr Backhouse. General R. Lewis accompanied me. We were shown the various processes of hemp collecting, drying, carding, spinning, etc. We were then taken to the rope-making and other specialised factories. I was interested to see that a lot of the specialised machinery came from Coombe Barbour of Belfast, a firm I used to deal with in the Ministry of Supply days. Backhouse has clearly done a great job. He has over 8,000 men in the factories drawing regular pay and seeming reasonably happy. His production is very good. For instance, the whole Mediterranean naval-rope needs have been met since Backhouse took over.

12.15 p.m. I met Marshal Tito at Navy House. He was to go out on a trip to Ischia, and I caught him just before he left. I gave him a message to say that the Prime Minister was arriving tonight – two days earlier than had been expected and would see him tomorrow. I also informed him that Dr Subašić would be coming with some of his advisers for discussions with the Marshal. Tito took this quite well and seemed quite happy about these arrangements. It is clear that he is looking forward with great pleasure to seeing Mr Churchill.

Dorothy and I lunched with Mr Gibson Graham, who lives in a charming flat. Lunch was out of doors – excellent food and very pleasant company. General de Rhé-Philipe, Movements Control, was there, and one or two others.

In the afternoon I motored out to the aerodrome to await the Prime Minister's arrival. He arrived at 5.15 about an hour after schedule. It was a very hot and thundery afternoon, and we were very glad when he finally arrived. We drove in to Naples and I stayed to dine with him that night. I had arranged to dine with Murphy, who gave a large party in honour of Tito. Dorothy went in my place. I thought the P.M. looked very tired. We had rather desultory conversation after dinner on Italy and other matters. He was rather cross and not very helpful.

Saturday, 12 August 1944

Waited about at the Villa Rivalta, where the Prime Minister is staying, most of the morning. Marshal Tito arrived at noon and a conference took place between the Prime Minister and Tito. The only other persons present were Bob Dixon, who took notes of the proceedings, and two interpreters. I gather that the talk went fairly well, but had not really broached the realities. There was a luncheon after the conference at which I was present. At the end of the luncheon the Prime Minister proposed the toast of Marshal Tito. General

Velebit acted as interpreter. Marshal Tito then replied with a very happy speech interpreted by General Maclean.

I then went back to the office to do a little work, and did not get back to Naples in time for dinner. I went in to see the P.M. after dinner. We had some discussion about the Italian set-up, which he did not seem to understand. He pressed me very hard to take on the Chief Commissionership of the Allied Control Commission, a post which is clearly unsuitable to a Cabinet Minister. However, I thought it better to let the conversation go fairly easily and not press him about any particular points. At his request I am sending him two notes, one on Italy and one on the Mediterranean command in general.

Sunday, 13 August 1944

Further conferences with Tito, Subašić, Ralph Stevenson, etc., took up most of the day. The P.M. went out in a motor-launch in the afternoon and bathed, which gave him great pleasure. Later in the evening he met Marshal Tito and Subašić jointly and the conference seems to have gone pretty well. Dorothy and I dined with him that night. He was in excellent humour, very pleased with the Battle of Normandy. Most of the evening was taken up in the Map Room where the progress of the battle was explained in great detail.

Monday, 14 August 1944

The Prime Minister left for Corsica in the afternoon so as to be present at the landings in the South of France – Operation 'Anvil', renamed 'Dragoon', due for tomorrow morning.

Tuesday, 15 August 1944

8.30 a.m. Bob Dixon, Ralph Anstruther and I left by plane for Rome. We were given a B25 – very fast – made the journey in about forty-five minutes. We spent most of the morning in discussions with Sir Noel Charles on the Italian position. I found Charles as charming as ever, but no more intelligent.

I have now discovered that Bob Dixon's real job in coming out here is to wind up the post of Resident Minister, Mediterranean.[4] I have charged him with this to which he has rather shamefacedly admitted. If only Anthony had told me straight out that he wanted to get rid of me I would willingly have resigned. Indeed I have told both him and the P.M. that I am ready to wind up the show at any moment. But I do resent being got out by the back door, and I have told Bob Dixon so. I shall now fight for my position to the bitter end.

A pleasant lunch in the Embassy – Lady Charles, Captain Stone (Acting Chief Commissioner of A.C.C.) and Charles's large staff.

4 p.m. I held a press conference. I found the press in a great state of

[4] Dixon was now the Foreign Secretary's Principal Private Secretary.

indignation because of the secrecy maintained about the Prime Minister's visit. I did my best to calm them down. After the conference Bob, Ralph and I went for a very pleasant drive. He [Dixon] knows Rome well and was an excellent cicerone. A most delightful evening, beautiful light, a really wonderful experience.

I rested before dinner. A large party – Sir John Dashwood, Couve de Murville, M. Guérin and others.

Wednesday, 16 August 1944

Left Rome by air at 8.30 arriving at Marcianise aerodrome, Caserta, about 9.15.

A long, hot, weary day. Miss Campbell had to rewrite I don't know how many times my memorandum on the Mediterranean command which reached finality just before it was time to leave for Naples.

I dined with the P.M., who had returned from the South of France. He did not much enjoy his trip. The trouble was he did not see enough shooting and fighting. However, he seemed to be in a merry mood and was very pleasant to Dorothy. We had one tiff, but I answered him back. I am sure this is the right way to treat him. He then becomes very amenable and pleasant. If you let him go on, he tramples on you.

My reading has been very poor lately. I finished *The Woodlanders*, *The Trumpet Major* and *A Pair of Blue Eyes*. The first two are excellent; the third a very poor book – I had forgotten how bad. I am now engaged in re-reading Rebecca West's *Black Lamb and Grey Falcon*. It is far more interesting to me now that I have been engaged on Yugoslavian affairs for some months.

Thursday, 17 August 1944

Exhausted by all the efforts of recent days, and in view of the very hot weather, I stayed quietly in the villa in Naples and idled all day. Bob Dixon and Roger came down in the afternoon and we argued in a detached kind of way about the situation. Poor Bob Dixon is getting more and more embarrassed. I feel sorry for him – he is such a quiet and charming fellow.

A telegram has come offering Murphy the job of American Adviser for the German Control Commission. He proposed to accept. It also suggests that Kirk should act both as American High Commissioner for Italy and as Political Adviser at A.F.H.Q. I am going to suggest to General Wilson that this is not possible. If he is to be Adviser at A.F.H.Q. he must come and live with us.

Friday, 18 August 1944

Murphy seems rather sad at leaving us, but I have told him that in his own interests he had far better get out of this organisation which shows every sign of decay. As a career diplomat the job he is being offered is a very high tribute to him.

4.30 p.m. We had S.A.C.'s Political Meeting at which a number of minor problems were dealt with. Afterwards I had a long talk with Slessor and C.-in-C. Med. about the future. Both of them are very depressed at the way things are going. What between the ambitions and the obstinacy of the Middle East and the vacillations of the Americans, it looks as if A.F.H.Q. is going to fade out. I am sure this is not in our interest.

General Béthouart, Consul-General [Harold] Swan (a ridiculous and minute little man who arrived this afternoon) and Colonel Sutton of P.W.B. came to dinner. The last is a very sly fellow who does not look you in the face. There is something to me very unpleasant about all the P.W.B. business. I have never seen any except C. D. Jackson and Dick Crossman who were either reasonable or honest. Colonel William Makins also came to dinner. He is a very old friend, and I was delighted to see him again.

Saturday, 19 August 1944

10 a.m. General Stawell, Colonel Dodds-Parker, and another officer came to see me – the usual talk about the future of S.O.E. Many words: no results.

11 a.m. I was asked to attend a meeting of British officers presided over by General Gammell to prepare an agenda for the C.I.G.S. and the Chief of the Air Staff (Alan Brooke and Portal), who are coming to Rome in a day or two. The draft agenda prepared was a very poor document. Slessor, however, was very helpful and I think at the end we shall have something fairly good to start with. I was very much pleased at being asked to attend. Often these generals are very cagey, but they seem now to depend very much on my advice.

1 p.m. Randolph Churchill arrived and came to lunch. The clans are beginning to gather at Rome. Ambassador Leeper comes this evening; Papandreou tomorrow; Lord Moyne, General Paget, etc., etc., all crowding in. I do not expect that much will result. But it may be not without some entertainment value.

4 p.m. Brigadier Eve, A.M.L., Greece, called to see me on the whole question of Greek planning.

8 p.m. Randolph and Ambassador Leeper to dinner – they were staying in my house. Tubby Clayton[5] also came to dinner. He is a dear old man. I had not seen him for years. Dorothy had discovered that he was about in Naples and got hold of him. He has spent the whole of the war travelling on oil tankers administering to the men. It is really rather remarkable for an old clergyman of sixty.

Sunday, 20 August 1944

Morning at the office.

[5] Rev. P. T. B. 'Tubby' Clayton (1885–1972) had founded Toc H. [Talbot House], a famous mission to the forces during the First World War.

Lunch at the Villa Vittoria. Murphy came to lunch. He has now definitely decided to accept the new post for Germany. It is very sad that he will be leaving us. By and large he has been an excellent colleague and a cheerful and genial friend. His Irish characteristics have made him sometimes a little difficult to deal with, but he has been to me personally I think loyal and helpful.

2.45 p.m. Left Caserta in two cars. The party consisted of Roger Makins, John Wyndham, Miss Campbell, another secretary and myself.

6.30 p.m. Arrived Rome. We are in very comfortable rooms in the Grand Hotel.

8.30 p.m. Dined at the Embassy. A small party. Very agreeable, as always. Bob Dixon was there, and Rowan.[6] The Prime Minister arrives tomorrow.

Monday, 21 August 1944

I have very comfortable rooms in the Grand Hotel; a bedroom, with bath, etc., and a sitting-room (which serves as my office). There is also a sitting-room on the floor above, which serves as Roger's office. It is obviously a great advantage to have two secretaries, as there will be a lot of drafting and minute-writing to do, as well as lots of telephone calls.

John Wyndham is as efficient as ever. He uses my sitting-room and has a bedroom next door to me. He gets on so well with everyone that I get a great deal done.

9.30–12 noon. Worked in my room on different papers. I then went to the Embassy, where I found the C.I.G.S. (Field Marshal Brooke) and the C.A.S. (Portal). They were both very friendly and had approved altogether of the plan which we had prepared on Saturday. There was a military meeting on Sunday at Caserta. Both C.I.G.S. and C.A.S. see the necessity of dealing with the Balkans as a whole and support the idea of transferring Greek questions and the Greek command *directly* to A.F.H.Q. from Cairo.

The P.M. arrived for lunch – in excellent form.

Lunched at the Embassy. After lunch he discussed the Greek questions with C.I.G.S. and C.A.S. and S.A.C. I was not present, but I heard that he approved the Greek plan. At a meeting with General Gammell at 5 p.m. I heard the result and General Wilson was very elated. Unfortunately the aeroplane bringing General Paget (Middle East) and Lord Moyne broke down, so they were not present at the discussion.

At 6 p.m. the P.M. saw M. Papandreou (Greek P.M.) alone. I heard later from Leeper that he suggested that the Greek Government should move at once to Italy. Papandreou accepted enthusiastically, the more

[6] Leslie Rowan (1908–72) was one of the Private Secretaries to the Prime Minister, 1941–7.

so as he wants to keep the five EAM ministers (who have at last agreed to join) away from the poisonous atmosphere of intrigue which reigns at Cairo.

All previous Greek Governments in exile have been broken in the bar of Shepheard's Hotel [in Cairo].

The Government will come to Salerno; Leeper will come with them (and presumably MacVeagh – the American Ambassador to Greece). The H.Q. of A.M.L. Balkans will come to Naples, together with as much of General Hughes's relief organisation and of U.N.R.R.A. as is necessary.

One airborne brigade will be ready to move from Bari to Athens and two other brigades (either from Middle East or from Italy according to the *general* state of the war when the Germans in Greece surrender or retire).

General Scobie (an excellent choice) will act as corps commander or force commander, with one division for law and order and to take the surrender of the Germans or to chase out the stragglers; the other to carry out the relief work as planned.

6.30 p.m. I called on Captain Stone, Acting Chief Commissioner. The chief problems are still power and transport. I promised to take up the question with S.A.C. of stopping any further Allied bombing of public utility plant in Italy. The destruction of the Pescara dam has deprived central Italy of ninety-eight per cent of the power. There is no certainty that the Germans will have time to destroy all the hydro-electric installations in north Italy before they go – especially if they have to go fast or if a general collapse takes place.

8.30 p.m. Dinner at the Embassy. P.M., M. Papandreou, Lord Moyne (arrived in the late afternoon) and a large party of Greeks, officials, etc. I sat next to Papandreou, who looks like Paderewski[7] and talks excellent French.

Further telegrams were prepared on Greece. I fear Anthony may not like the decision. Poor Bob Dixon seems rather alarmed. And of course the President may raise objections. But the P.M. is determined to have his way and has rather bounced everybody by informing Papandreou of the move (though *not* of the plans for sending a military police force).

Nevertheless the new EAM position will help the President, and I am sure that we can work a lot of things with them through A.F.H.Q. which we could not hope to do through Cairo.

Left about 1 a.m. Winston in very good heart. He made a speech proposing Papandreou's health at the dinner, to which Papandreou replied.

I cannot help being amused by Bob Dixon's predicament. He came out with orders to abolish me. In the first day's work he has given me

[7] Ignace Jan Paderewski (1860–1941), classical pianist and Polish politician, was a striking figure with masses of white hair.

Greece. Tomorrow he has got at least to get me out of Italy! Roger is triumphant.

Tuesday, 22 August 1944

Randolph (who was at the dinner last night) started a ridiculous hare about the regulations governing food brought into Rome.

Only ten kilos can be kept for personal consumption by anyone who fetches food from the countryside by cart or car, the rest must be sold on the market. Of course this is to help to get the food to the poor and to prevent the black market. The P.M. took this up and I am sorry to say both Noel Charles and D'Arcy Osborne supported the chase. I argued resolutely on the other side. So this morning I have had to chase round A.C.C. and get a minute prepared for the P.M. As I fully expected, the case in favour of the regulation is overwhelming!

Talked with Gammell on the Greek settlement. General Paget is naturally rather sore, but the P.M. is seeing him this morning. He is a fine fellow and I am sure will appreciate the strong arguments for the transfer.

Roger attended a meeting of generals, etc. (with Leeper) to work out details.

12 noon. Meeting at Embassy with Moyne, Steel, Leeper and Roger on Greece. Moyne very charming, as ever. But rather a strained atmosphere!

1.30 p.m. Lunch at Embassy. P.M., Bonomi (Italian P.M.), Badoglio and a few others.

Winston had three-quarters of an hour with Bonomi before lunch and after lunch a little chat with Badoglio. The Marshal greeted me with enthusiasm and we 'reminisced' about the early days at Brindisi. I do *not* think, however, that Badoglio has relinquished all political ambitions (these *grands chefs* never do!). But for the moment he is backing Bonomi and is assisting in the coalescing of the parties of the right and centre.

2.30–7 p.m. A wide-ranging discussion on Italy. The heat was intense, but the P.M. never flagged. The 'whisky' interval (at about 5 p.m.) helped.

Winston gave a really remarkable demonstration of his powers. The party consisted of:

P.M.
H.M.
Noel Charles
Roger Makins
Henry Hopkinson
Bob Dixon.

I was sorry that Harold Caccia was not there, but somehow he got missed out. He really knew much more about Italy than anyone else!

Winston was like a dog worrying at a bone. But his peculiar method does succeed in eliciting the truth – and throwing over all those sort of bureaucratic Foreign Office proposals which sound all right but are quite obviously unworkable.

Bob Dixon struggled manfully with his brief. His task is to elevate Charles and liquidate your humble. But Winston would have none of it. When Charles cried out piteously, 'But what am I to do?' he replied, 'What do Ambassadors ever do?' He was very scornful of the title 'High Commissioner' when he realised that Charles had *no* executive functions and that his diplomatic functions were confined to being Ambassador to a shadow government.

He wants *me* to be head of the Control Commission and run the new policy. He will *not* have a [preliminary peace] treaty, but he wants a steady process of relaxation of control. This, he says, is the task of the politician not the diplomat.

We finally broke up at 7 p.m. – all but Winston completely exhausted.

8.30 p.m. Dinner at Embassy. Noel and Lady Charles, P.M., Myron Taylor, Brigadiers Lush and Low, Captain Stone.

After dinner, telegrams were drafted to London summarising the afternoon's discussion. Bed at 1 a.m.

Wednesday, 23 August 1944

A busy day for P.M.

11 a.m. His Holiness the Pope.

12 noon. Press conference.

1.30 p.m. Prince of Piedmont (Lieutenant-General of the Realm) to luncheon.

3.30–4.30 p.m. Italian Government.

He thus saw in one day all forms of power – spiritual, regal, governmental – and the fourth estate of the realm.

His versatility is extraordinary and he was clearly very pleased with it all. It was a good idea to see *all* the members of the Government and thus overcome an incipient attack here and at home based on his only seeing the political 'right' (Bonomi and Badoglio).

At 5 p.m. Leeper and I (with John Wyndham and Miss Campbell) left by car for Naples – arriving about 8.30 p.m.

Thursday, 24 August 1944

7.50 a.m. Dorothy left by air for home (via Casablanca). It is very sad to lose her. I think she has enjoyed her time and she has certainly given a great deal of pleasure to others. Her simplicity and charm have endeared her to all.

Leeper to lunch at Caserta. All sorts of Greek plans under discussion.

3 p.m. Gammell.

3.45 p.m. S.A.C. on the Roumanian news.[8] We ought to be organising a mission. I telegraphed to the F.O. – but I expect they will turn down our ideas. Anyway, it is good news. The 'satellites' seem to be 'on the run'. It is amusing that Roumania declares herself 'co-belligerent'. The Italians will be furious!

(I never thought that when I suggested the phrase 'co-belligerent' to Eisenhower in Tunis last September that it would become so famous an expression!)

All sorts of Greek plans under discussion.

Friday, 25 August 1944

Being very exhausted, I took a morning off and stayed in Naples – reading Rebecca West's great book on Yugoslavia.

3 p.m. Met Deputy P.M. (Attlee) and Under-Secretary for Foreign Affairs (George Hall) at Marcianise aerodrome. Took them to Caserta to talk with S.A.C. Attlee's 'tummy' was troublesome; George Hall was also rather tired. We sent them into Naples.

5 p.m. Meeting in S.A.C.'s room. Gammell, Slessor, Clark, Roger and H.M. Greece, Russians arriving in great numbers to A.C.C., Russian misdemeanours in Yugoslavia and Greece, message from Mihailović and other questions.

The meeting lasted a long time and I did not get to Naples till after eight. I found Diana Cooper and Bloggs Baldwin had arrived to stay the night.

Dinner-party. Attlee, George Hall, Bob Murphy, Slessor, Gammell, Roger, Diana Cooper, Bloggs Baldwin and various 'stooges' – quite a good party.[9]

Saturday, 26 August 1944

P.M.'s movements very uncertain. He went back to General Alexander's H.Q. from Rome to watch a battle. He is expected here today or tomorrow.

Morning at office.

Lunch with S.A.C. at Hunting Lodge. Attlee, George Hall, General Clark, Paddy [Beaumont-] Nesbitt and [Major-General George] Lammie (No. 3 District).

After lunch Attlee and Hall came to my office. We had an hour's talk on the problems of the command – especially Italy. A touching reunion took place between George Hall and Miss Campbell – she having been his private secretary at the Colonial Office, where he preceded me.

[8] Following the successes of Russian forces in Roumania, the Antonescu régime was overthrown and an armistice signed with the Soviet Union, the United States and Great Britain.

[9] The liberation of Paris had just been completed.

I finished my paper (or redraft of Dixon's paper) on Italy. I will give copy to P.M. and to Dixon.

P.M. postponed his return till tomorrow. Dined at Villa Rivalta. Attlee, George Hall and the usual high officers. A dullish evening.

Sunday, 27 August 1944

Rested all the morning in the garden, with occasional colloquies with Dixon. Roger came down in the afternoon.

Dinner at Rivalta – the whole circus back in great form. P.M. was very pleased with the President's reply about Greece, agreeing to all his proposals, including the use of American aeroplanes to carry British troops to Athens and to the immediate move of the Greek Government from Cairo to Naples.

I left my Italian memo. He will read it in the aeroplane tomorrow.

General Wilson, Admiral Cunningham, Air Marshal Slessor, etc., etc. I think they were grateful to me for leaving early (about 11.30) and allowing them to escape.

P. J. Grigg (S. of S. for War) has turned up. The tourist season is in full swing!

Monday, 28 August 1944

Went to Pomigliano aerodrome to see the P.M. off. He was in excellent spirits, especially with the latest news from the battle fronts and the sudden events in Roumania.[10]

An officer of the Roumanian Air Force arrived here last night. It is suggested that we should fly a team in at once – a plan which the P.M. liked very much. But I expect Anthony Eden and the F.O. will be too scared of the Russians!

After luncheon, left for Rome, by car. Ralph Anstruther came with me. We drove by Route 7 (Pontine Marshes) arriving about 6.30. We have been given some excellent rooms in the Grand Hotel.

Dined with P. J. Grigg, General [Ronald] Weeks, Ralph Beaumont, M.P. (Grigg's P.P.S.), Colonel Geddes. An interesting talk on Italy, A.A.I. and A.F.H.Q., and various other matters. Grigg was as offensive, profane and intelligent as he always is.

Tuesday, 29 August 1944

9 a.m. Went round to Embassy to see Attlee. A rather desultory conversation. He really is *not* an inspiring man.

Among the many other crosses which we have to bear is a party of British and American trade union leaders who have arrived in Italy. The British pair are [Tom] O'Brien and William Lawther – the latter a Durham miner, the former a Catholic from Lancashire.

[10] Roumania had declared war on Germany on 25 August.

The Americans are Baldanzi and Antonini.[11] They speak excellent Italian and very bad English. They have already caused some excitement by giving press interviews on the day of their arrival, imputing the worst charges against A.C.C. and all its officials and alleging that the British are trying to turn Italy into a colony.

Charles and Kirk tried to persuade Scott-Bailey (censorship A.F.H.Q.) to stop the article. But he very wisely refused. It would have reached New York in due course, and the papers would have had a splendid headline 'British General Tries to Gag American Labour!'

Anyway, these four, with a Belgian colleague, arrived at the Embassy at about 10.30 to arrange their plans. They demand a great deal – three stenographers, four motor cars, two interpreters and two guides for three or four weeks!

But they are very powerful and must be cajoled and conciliated – more especially as the Italian vote may easily swing both Pennsylvania and New York States and thus the whole Presidential election, owing to the large number of members of the Electoral College which these states return. The meeting at the Embassy went off quite well. After it was over, I went with Ralph to an admirable exhibition of pictures in the Palazzo Venezia – including some splendid masterpieces. Only forty or fifty pictures in all and beautifully shown.

The della Francesca Flagellation (from Urbino) and the Madonna and Child, Saints and Angels with Duke Federigo (from the Brera). A splendid Memling (Deposition) from Prince Doria's collection (which I had never seen). The Tempest (of Giorgione) from Venice; a fine Correggio (Danaë) and the lovely Raphael from Milan of the Marriage of the Virgin.

1.15 p.m. Lunch at the hotel. P. J. Grigg, General Weeks, George Clark, Gammell, etc. P.J. was very rude to me about the censorship, and it was quite embarrassing. I do not wonder that he gets a bit peeved, because Winston and Anthony settle A.C.C. and other Italian affairs without reference to the War Office, and poor P. J. is supposed to be responsible to the House of Commons for the Control Commission.

3.30 p.m. Saw Captain Stone – Acting Chief Commissioner. A useful talk. He seemed very pleased with Winston's 'address to the Italian people'.[12]

6.30 p.m. Cocktail party for the trade union delegation. They *all* drank too much, but seemed to enjoy themselves.

After dinner, who should I see at the Grand Hotel but Andrew

[11] George Baldanzi (1907–72) of the Textile Workers' Union of America was representative of the C.I.O. Luigi Antonini (1883–1968) of the International Ladies' Garment Workers' Union was representative of the A.F.L.

[12] Delivered on 28 August. Churchill said, 'I believe that the British nation will be happy to see the day when Italy, once again free and progressive, takes her place among the peace-loving nations.'

Cavendish,[13] looking very well. He told me the tragic news about Charlie Lansdowne and Ned Fitzmaurice.[14] It is really too awful.

Wednesday, 30 August 1944

Left Rome by car about eight. Came by Route 6 (Cassino) and arrived for lunch at Caserta.

In the evening, Murphy gave a great farewell party at the Villa Lauro. Generals Wilson and Eaker and Air Marshal Slessor, etc. A very pleasant party but too long. At 11 p.m. we had a film – very bad, banal and boring – which lasted till 1 a.m.

Poor General Wilson – who had been in France for two days – was quite exhausted.

Thursday, 31 August 1944

11 a.m. General [L. G.] Phillips (Signals, War Office) and General Nichols (Chief Signal Officer A.F.H.Q.). Further iniquities of Cable & Wireless. I showed them my correspondence with Harry Crookshank for which they were grateful. But I fear that nothing will be done. The vested interests are too strong. There ought of course to be an imperial communications system, owned by the Government of U.K. Dominions and colonies and operated as an imperial service. But the old chairman and board of Cable & Wireless stand in the way, and the Government are too fearful of Conservative pressure or too indolent to get a move on.

12.30 p.m. General Hughes (A.M.L. H.Q., Balkans) and Mr E. M. H. Lloyd met for a talk in my room. Under the new Greek arrangements Hughes and his organisation will be at Naples. Lloyd, who has just accepted the post of Economic Adviser to U.N.R.R.A. in the Mediterranean, will also be coming in due course.

3 p.m. Owen (Ministry of Economic Warfare). I want some of his people for missions to Roumania, Bulgaria, Hungary, etc.

4 p.m. Colonel Sutton (P.W.E). I showed him the proposed reorganisation of P.W.B., which he seemed to think would satisfy London.

5 p.m. General Wilson. We discussed a number of points chiefly connected with our proposed missions to Roumania and Bulgaria. Owing to the weakness, timidity and delays of the F.O., we have lost our chances in Roumania; the Americans, on the other hand, have gone right in, and incidentally saved eight hundred of their aviators who were prisoners of war there.

[13] Lord Andrew Cavendish (b. 1920), later 11th Duke of Devonshire, was my wife's nephew, and was serving in the Coldstream Guards.

[14] Captain Charles Fitzmaurice, 7th Marquess of Lansdowne (1917–44), and his brother, Lieutenant Lord Edward Fitzmaurice (1922–44), both second cousins of Lord Andrew Cavendish, had just been killed in action, Lansdowne in Italy on 20 August, and Fitzmaurice in Normandy on the 11th.

6.30–11 p.m. Cocktail party, followed by dinner in Murphy's camp. A very jolly, impromptu affair. I made a speech (which was quite good, I think) and everyone seemed very pleased with themselves and each other. But all rather exhausting!

September

Friday, 1 September 1944

Splendid news still from all theatres of war. How long can the Germans last? The optimists here feel it will be over by November.

11 a.m.–1 p.m. General Wilson's Political Committee. A very long and very *varied* agenda. A useful meeting.

Today and yesterday have been intolerably oppressive – a sticky heat which is very tiring. Roger is rather under the weather, but took a morning off.

John and Anthony Rumbold came to Naples villa for a quiet evening. I slept at the Caserta villa last night. It is comfortable but rather squalid.

Saturday, 2 September 1944

Left Naples 8 a.m. and got to Marcianise aerodrome (near Caserta) to see Bob Murphy off. He left at 9 a.m. for Washington. From there he goes to London – and then (I suppose) to Berlin.

The news is still wonderfully good from every front. It seems almost too good to believe. After so long and dreary and apparently endless a period of war, it is hard to attune one's mind to even the possibility of peace.

12.30 p.m. The trade union delegates turned up from Rome and arrived at my office in Caserta. It was a sweltering hot day – Mr Will Lawther, sweating and in braces; Mr O'Brien perspiring in an Oxford accent; Messrs Antonini and Baldanzi and the Belgian Secretary of the International Congress of Trade Unions – five in all, with [Richard] Nosworthy (of the British Embassy) and others in attendance.

General Rookes gave a luncheon for them; I gave a dinner for them – and altogether the representatives of the people, having been 'wined and dined' to a prodigious degree, were gracefully ready to admit that they had really nothing to complain of in their reception.

They are staying some days in Naples and some kind of a programme is being arranged for them. General Wilson will see them on Monday.

Sunday, 3 September 1944

The most confusing situation is developing in Roumania and Bulgaria. The telegrams keep pouring in, and (more to our immediate concern) the arrangements for moving the Greek Government here and for preparing the British force to enter Greece (by sea and air) are going ahead. There are all kinds of problems about proclamations, political warfare directions, legal position of the British forces, money for the troops (the present Greek currency is in a condition of runaway inflation and a loaf of bread cost 60 million drachmae!) about which office is appealed to by A.F.H.Q. for advice.

The Americans (especially Colonel Spofford of G5) are being very reasonable and helpful, as I knew they would be when the operation was transferred from the control of Cairo to that of Caserta.

1 p.m. Tony Rumbold and I left for Bari by car. We arrived after rather a tiring drive, through a heavy thunderstorm in the mountains, about 7 p.m. We stayed with Philip Broad in his bizarre Fascist *nouveau art* flat – noisy but comfortable.

Monday, 4 September 1944

A long conference with Broad and Deakin (the other members of his staff are one Haldary Porter and a Major P. Walker). A lot of problems about those Yugoslavs who ought to be sent back and those who ought not – culminating in the case of Knezević and Todorović (lately military attachés in Washington) who are being returned by Washington but are regarded here as undesirable. I had rather weakly agreed to Murphy's proposal some time ago, without realising that these were dangerous and extreme Pan-Serbs and that their return would injure the King and Subašić even more than Tito.

I must try to get this undone in Caserta or at least the men held here for the time being.

I am much struck with Broad's efficiency and character and with Deakin's broad grasp of the political situation in Yugoslavia and the underlying motives and aspirations of the partisan movement. But he is not blind to the great merits of the Serbs and is not himself so prejudiced as I feel Fitzroy Maclean to be.

Luncheon at Broad's flat. Mr Norden (U.S. State Department) and Mr Joyce (O.S.S.) to lunch. Rested in afternoon.

Our conferences continued from about 6 p.m. to dinner. Air Marshal Slessor, Air Vice-Marshal Elliot (O.C. Balkan Air Force) and others to dinner including Colonel [John] Macnamara, M.P. (who is Chief of Staff to Brigadier D'Arcy here – land forces Balkans). A very nice party. Colonel Young (U.S. Air Force) and one or two other officers.

Tuesday, 5 September 1944

Further conference with Broad, etc. There is no doubt that the only hope which Subašić has is to come out here as quickly as possible after operations cease. Tito may or may not accept him or stick to the spirit of his agreement. But if Subašić remains an émigré government in London *after* the Germans have left Yugoslavia, he is lost.

3 p.m. Left Bari by Fairchild aeroplane (a little fellow – one engine – three seats). A lovely day and we soared magnificently in our Lilliputian machine over the Apennines to a height of 6,000 feet. I am not quite sure that I should have liked the trip on a stormy day. We arrived at Marcianise (near Caserta) at about 5 p.m.

Dined with General Wilson in Naples. P. J. Grigg, Sir Harold and Lady MacMichael[1] (returning from Palestine), Admiral Morse, General George Clark, Air Marshal Slessor, etc.

After dinner the news reached us that Russia had declared war on Bulgaria! And poor Lord Moyne in Cairo is struggling to sign an armistice with the Bulgarian delegates!

A long conference on the Greek expedition. P.J. in good form and giving useful advice, only occasionally lapsing into the peculiar language of the gutter which he often affects.

Wednesday, 6 September 1944

11 a.m. Economic Subcommittee. Rather inconclusive, as most of the papers were circulated too late. But a useful talk on A.C.C. We will meet again in Rome on Friday – and get some of the A.C.C. to attend. I am still very worried about A.C.C. The Americans treat it as an instrument to win the Presidential election. The British send *very* inferior personnel. It is a hard struggle.

1.15 p.m. Ambassador Kirk (Murphy's successor) and General Wilson to lunch in our small house in Caserta.

2.30 p.m. A most curious interview with Prince Cantacuzene, just arrived by plane from Bucharest.

3.30 p.m. Political Committee. After a difficult struggle, I got agreement to keep Knezević and Todorović here till London and Washington could be further consulted.

Kirk was quite helpful but I could see that the American War Department had sent instructions to General Rookes (Deputy Chief of Staff), and it was one of the most awkward affairs we have had recently.

The other points went off easily.

A lot more telegrams and discussions – Greece and Yugoslavia are now the chief worries.

Leeper and Mrs Leeper have arrived and are staying at my Naples villa.

L. S. Amery has arrived also – to visit the Indian troops. He looks terribly aged. He came to dinner and much pleasant talk followed.

[1] Sir Harold MacMichael (1882–1969) was High Commissioner for Palestine and Trans-Jordan, 1938–44.

Thursday, 7 September 1944

11.30 a.m. Air Vice-Marshal Elliot (A.O.C. Balkan Air Force) to see me. He was concerned with:

(1) the American desire to back Knezević and Todorović to Mihailović.

(2) a protest which Tito had sent to the British and American mission for transmission to their Governments regarding the taking out of Yugoslavs from Mihailović and the continued contact with M.

I explained to the air vice-marshal the decision which we had come to at the last Political Committee in regard to (1). And I thought that in regard to (2), if instances could be found where the Americans had broken their undertaking that *their* mission to Mihailović would be purely for the purpose of rescuing American airmen from Serbia, it would really help me to maintain the ban on the return of Knezević and Todorović.

3.30 p.m. Leeper arrived from Cairo and I took him to see General Wilson. Unfortunately General Wilson has rather a prejudice against Ambassador Leeper. And I think Leeper has not much liking for the general. However, the meeting went off fairly well and we discussed various ways of trying to keep the Greek Government harmlessly amused during their residence in the Bay of Naples.

4 p.m. M. Gavrilović – [Foreign] Minister in M. Subašić's Government. I liked him very much. He seemed straightforward and intelligent. We discussed the various arrangements for the amalgamation of the Royal Yugoslav Army with Tito's forces, and for the reorganisation of the Air Force and the Navy in accordance with the Tito–Subašić agreement. I urged him *very* strongly not to try to form a special unit from loyal Yugoslav soldiers who were unwilling to join the Army of Liberation. This would seem to Tito a breach of the understanding and as he only expected to find under 1000 men in this category, it was not worth the risk. Gavrilović agreed and telegraphed accordingly to Subašić. We also discussed the probable situation when the Germans come to leave. I urged (as I have done on H.M.G.) that Subašić should immediately arrive in Yugoslavia and try to come to an arrangement with Tito. He might fail. But if he remained the head of an émigré government *after* the Germans collapse, he would just wither away. Gavrilović also agreed to the proposition.

5 p.m. Meeting in my room to straighten out the various proclamations, etc., in connection with operation 'Manna' (return of Greek Government to Greece supported by British troops). Present, Generals Gammell, Scobie (O.C. Force 140), Mr Leeper, Mr Barnes (P.W.B.), Mr Offie. General agreement was reached, but I have got to get General Wilson to *alter* his speech – a delicate task!

Mr and Mrs Leeper are staying in the Naples villa. Brigadier Jeffries

(P.W.B.) and Colonel [C. E.] Temperley (A.C.C. Regional head of southern Italy) came. The latter struck me as highly competent.

Friday, 8 September 1944

Started for Rome at 9 a.m. by air from Marcianise (Generals G. Clark, Lewis, Colonel Spofford, Mr Offie, etc.). When we got nearly to Rome we had to turn back owing to a severe thunderstorm and the news that the Littorio airfield was under water.

11.30 a.m. We held (without the A.C.C. members) the meeting of the Economic Subcommittee which we had intended to hold in Rome. A large number of items (chiefly Italian) made it necessary to meet again at four and continue till late.

I succeeded at last in rousing Generals Clark and Lewis (who are the administrative generals concerned) regarding the condition of food in Rome and regarding the general problem of Italian rehabilitation. A very interesting and useful discussion took place and we decided to draft a telegram for General Wilson to the C.C.S. to call attention to the situation and to ask for a wider direction than the present restricted one in order that he may deal with the more pressing needs.

Saturday, 9 September 1944

A very heavy day at the office.

11.15 a.m. I did my best to persuade S.A.C. to alter his Greek speech. I think he will agree. A lot of talk about 'Manna'. I have persuaded S.A.C. to let me go on the cruiser *Orion* with Admiral Mansfield and General Scobie. The F.O. will be furious!

Leeper came in during the day for further discussion on currency, censorship and other Greek problems. I like him well enough, but he is terribly vague and donnish. He is clever, but in a negative sort of way.

General Gammell, Miss Gammell (daughter – an A.T.) and Hermione Ranfurly to dinner.

Sunday, 10 September 1944

A complete holiday. Hermione Ranfurly and Mark Chapman-Walker had borrowed Admiral Morse's launch for the day and they invited me to come [to Capri]. I brought with me Ralph Anstruther and Michael Baillie (who is at a camp at Benevento, after an attack of dysentery, waiting to go up the line). It was a glorious day – hot, but not too hot. We did all the right things – bathed in the Blue Grotto, went up the funicular from the harbour to the little town [Anacapri], bought souvenirs and so on. We got back pleasantly tired at sunset.

Michael is a charming boy and seemed to enjoy himself and the society of Miss Gammell (who was also of the party).

I have finished Rebecca West's two volumes. It is much more interesting for me to read them now, when I have learnt something of

Yugoslavia. She writes brilliantly – and if she is prejudiced, it only makes the book more stimulating.

I have also read Sumner Welles's book on foreign policy [*The Time For Decision*], which I thought very superficial.

Monday, 11 September 1944

Left Naples early – another very heavy day. I saw General Wilson in the morning. The Bulgarian situation is *very* unsatisfactory, even alarming. I fear the F.O. have 'missed the bus' again. If they had allowed us to handle it, instead of Cairo, I believe we could have got the armistice signed *before* the Russian intervention. Had the Bulgarian delegates come here, I would have treated them as we did the Italians in Sicily. After all, we have the strategic Air Force in our hands and we could have bombed Sofia or threatened to do so unless (*a*) the authority to sign and (*b*) acceptance of the terms had been immediately forthcoming. But while a pedantic argument about terms and clauses was going on between London and Washington, the Russians seized the initiative. I fear our prestige in the Balkans will suffer correspondingly. Already the Greeks are restive, and the Communist members of the Papandreou Government may easily resign. They are arguing that Greece should be looking to the rising sun of the Kremlin, not the setting orb of Downing Street.

2.30 p.m. Mr Radford[2] – formerly of the British School at Rome – now of P.W.B. A queer little fish.

3.0 p.m. Mr Waterhouse[3] – of Mr Leeper's staff – also by trade an antiquarian.

3.30 p.m. Major Greenlees – formerly of British Council in Italy – now P.W.B. He wants to restart the British Council.

4.30–6.30 p.m. S.A.C.'s military meeting (C.-in-C. Med., A.O.C.-in-C. [Tedder] and all the various military, naval and air staff). A full account of 'Manna' was presented from all the Services' points of view. I was asked some political points. It was a very interesting meeting, admirably conducted, each officer who spoke being clear, succinct and well informed. But I felt very doubtful of the feasibility of the plan except in the event of the German surrender. The First Lord (A. V. Alexander) was present.

8.30–12 midnight. A great naval dinner at the Villa Emma in honour of the First Lord. Wilson, Gammell and Clark were the soldiers present; Slessor represented the air. I found myself next to A. V. Alexander and on the other side Ronald Hardy,[4] my Sussex neighbour! A small world.

[2] Ralegh Radford (b. 1900) was Director of the British School at Rome, 1936–9.

[3] Ellis Waterhouse (b. 1905) was Librarian at the British School at Rome, 1933–6.

[4] Lieutenant-Commander Ronald Hardy (1900–54), who lived in Horsted Keynes, was Flag Lieutenant to the Board of Admiralty, 1940–5.

Tuesday, 12 September 1944

11 a.m. Ambassador Leeper came to see General Wilson, quite a successful talk, but I am worried about the Greek situation. So far as I can see there is little chance of our getting to Athens (for the operation is not really 'on' if the approaches are defended). At the same time, the Russians are approaching Sofia and may advance into Thrace. The Germans are leaving the islands and the Peloponnese, and if there is a gap, unfilled by a legitimate Greek government, EAM/ELAS will undoutedly seize the authority and another Communist (or brigand) government will be installed in the Balkans. Where will British prestige be then?

Worked all through the day till 7 p.m. (sandwiches in my room). A mass of Greek, Yugoslav and especially Italian papers – in readiness for Thursday's meetings in Rome.

Wednesday, 13 September 1944

10 a.m. M. Papandreou (Greek P.M.), Leeper, General Wilson, General Scobie. A useful meeting. I tried to bring it to a head by writing the conclusions (during my luncheon of sandwiches in my room) and circulating them to all concerned. My conclusions were more clear and decided than the actual conversation warranted, but they may (?) produce results.

11 a.m. – 1 p.m. S.A.C.'s Political Committee. A useful meeting – mostly Italian. A telegram was agreed for S.A.C. to send to C.C.S. *demanding* some clearer and less restricted formula for partial 'rehabilitation' in Italy. Ambassador Kirk was helpful.

2.45 p.m. Mrs McCormick[5] (American columnist) to see me. She seems friendly, intelligent and sensible – a great tribute to any journalist!

After completing various jobs – including a telegram to Winston in Quebec[6] on Italian civilian needs – and one to London emphasising the need for Dr Subašić to be ready to come to Yugoslavia at short notice (he *must* appear as soon as the Germans leave if his Government is to have a chance). Left by car for Rome. Anthony Rumbold and Ralph came with me.

Arrived about 7.30. We had comfortable rooms at the Grand Hotel. Harold Caccia met us. Henry Hopkinson (of Noel Charles's staff) dined with us.

Thursday, 14 September 1944

A meeting at 9 a.m. in Captain Stone's room (Acting Chief

[5] Anne O'Hare McCormick (d. 1954) wrote a column called 'Abroad' for the *New York Times*, 1937–54.

[6] Churchill and Roosevelt were in Quebec discussing both the continuation of lend–lease and the short-lived Morgenthau Plan for the 'pastoralisation' of Germany and the dismemberment of her industrial economy.

Commissioner). The chief problem was how to deal with the desire of the Italian Government to institute a roving enquiry into the events of 8, 9, 10 September 1943 which led to the occupation of Rome by the Germans.

These were, of course, the days immediately following the armistice and were marked by the flight of the King and Badoglio and the miserable collapse of the Italian Army.

No doubt the main purpose of the investigation is to attack the King and Badoglio and thereby weaken the Crown. It will also serve to select particular scapegoats for a general poltroonery displayed by the Italians as a whole.

The arguments against the A.C.C. allowing this Commission to function are obvious. On the other hand, with one or two exceptions the members of the proposed tribunal appear to be safe and respectable men and would perhaps produce a noncommittal report. Moreover, there is something to be said for getting the whole thing over now, instead of postponing it to a time nearer the reopening of the 'institutional' question [i.e. the monarchy] and a holding of popular elections.

After a considerable discussion it was decided to allow proceedings against any individual person against whom a *prima facie* case could be made but *not* to allow a general roving enquiry. I am not quite sure that we have done right but since both Stone and Kirk were strongly in favour of this solution, I accepted it. Noel Charles was not present, but was represented by Henry Hopkinson.

11.30 a.m. Meeting of the Allied Resources Board. General Robertson (A.A.I.) handed over the chair to General Clark (A.F.H.Q.), who now becomes responsible head. Stone will act as co-chairman.

2.30–7.30 p.m. A series of meetings on the economic position of Italy. Some of these meetings consisted of nearly sixty people, some of five or six. General Clark was in the chair. Unfortunately, he does not know much about it all, but he does his best.

I fired a vast number of questions at them, and I think they like to feel that I have given careful study to the many reports which come from A.C.C. Nevertheless, I feel alarmed at the general state of affairs. The Economic Section has never had a chance. First Grady came from America – stayed five weeks and then returned to the States and was absent nearly five months. He returned for a month, was quite useless, and then retired. After him came Brigadier-General O'Dwyer, a New York lawyer and a purely political appointment. He is a Democratic Leader in New York State. He has now gone back to U.S., presumably to campaign for the President. He was unexpectedly sensible, but of course fundamentally ignorant. His second, [Anthony G.] Antolini, is another political appointment. We have no British second-in-command of the Economic Section, though we have men on the various subcommissions. Some of these are fairly good, others distinctly poor.

I had a large bundle of notes and worked relentlessly through them all day, leaving them all exhausted by 7 p.m.

Friday, 15 September 1944

Left Rome by car, with Ralph Anstruther, at about 11 a.m. We took the journey quietly, and stopped at Orvieto. The Cathedral is quite undamaged. The Signorellis in the south transept and the Fra Angelico roof paintings in the same transept are very fine, especially the Signorellis. It is really a great experience to come again (from all the squalor and pettiness of our life here) into such a realm of beauty.

An excellent picnic lunch, of hard-boiled eggs and chicken sandwiches (provided by the Grand Hotel, Rome) and a lovely day increased our sense of happiness and contentment.

Reached Siena about 5 p.m. We spent half-an-hour in that lovely (and fortunately quite undamaged) city. We then motored to General Alexander's Advanced H.Q., some three miles from Siena.

As usual, the general has found a lovely spot, in a little wood, in rolling country, with farmland and vineyards all round. My billet is in a farmhouse (taken over as a guest house). The general is, as usual, in his caravan. The mess and ante-room are in tents. The customary air of quiet efficiency pervades the camp.

General Alexander looked, however, rather tired, even strained. He feels rather bitterly the neglect by the powers-that-be of his campaign and the lack of support which he has received. Even on the basis that everything was to be sacrificed to the operations in France, a more determined effort to rake up a little help would have meant a great deal to him. He has lost seven divisions (to 'Anvil') and seventy per cent of his Air Force. But a single airborne brigade, or a division from Middle East would have made all the difference. As it is, the Germans have twenty-six divisions against his twenty (which include Brazilians and Negroes) and have in the Gothic Line a naturally defensive position almost stronger than that at Cassino.

However, he still feels that he has a chance of achieving a breakthrough, in spite of all the disadvantages of his position.

Dined quietly in the mess. General Anders was there, and I had a long talk with him after dinner. He was very sensible, recognising the necessity of first defeating the German enemy. But he is naturally very bitter about the Russians and the tragedy of Warsaw. Nevertheless, he made it clear that he regarded Sosnkowski's declaration as foolish and ill-timed.[7] I have a feeling that Anders will take his place. He is on his way home to confer with the Polish Government.

[7] A popular uprising against the Germans in Warsaw had broken out in August. But Stalin not only refused to help the Poles but denied the Allies the facilities for doing so. General Sosnkowski, the Polish C.-in-C., issued an unauthorised Order of the Day on 1 September

Saturday, 16 September 1944

9 a.m. Morning conference and review of the battle position. Some advance by the Fifth Army on the Futa Pass front (Florence–Bologna road) and some by the Eighth Army on the Rimini front. But the Germans are fighting desperately and are reinforcing their left. General Leese has now nine German divisions against his seven. It is a race against time, among other things, since the weather will break soon and with the rivers in spate the mountain line will be impassable till the spring.

10 a.m. Left with General Alex in the famous open car. We motored to Florence, where we found Fifth Army H.Q. in the Carceri Gardens, by the racecourse. General [Mark] Wayne Clark was out, but General Alfred Gruenther explained the position. He is hopeful but clearly worried.

We motored on north of Florence to a village called La Trellia. Then we climbed to the top of a hill and on the top of the hill to the top of a high tower in a large house (owned by a certain Scaretti, who married a sister of Gladwyn Jebb of the F.O.).

From this tower one could see the whole great Apennine range stretched before one's eyes, and for two hours with glasses and maps we watched the fierce battle which was taking place.

The main effort of the Fifth Army troops was concentrated round the Futa Pass and an attack was in progress upon a certain Monte Catria (5,600 feet high) to the south-east. This proved partially successful, but the miracle to my mind is that any progress can be made at all in ground so wonderfully adapted to the defence.

The great use of smoke makes it difficult to follow a modern battle even from such a vantage point as ours. The smoke-screen is the infantryman's only hope of approaching such strongly held positions and apart from the smoke bombs and shells fired by supporting artillery, he uses his own mortars for this purpose. The American colonel in charge of the O.P. [observation post] (which was being made by the heavy corps artillery) explained to us the salient points of the battle. General Alex (with his usual diplomacy) accepted the lesson – but it was clear that he had every feature of the landscape already firmly in his mind and knew (by a kind of tactical instinct) on what points the ultimate fate of the operation would depend.

On our way home, we stopped in Florence. The Duomo, Baptistery, Giotto's tower, Palazzo Vecchio, Loggia di Lanzi, S. Maria Novella – all these stand quite uninjured. The bronze doors of the Baptistery are walled up (or removed) and pictures (like Sir J. Hawkwood) in the Duomo removed. And poor Florence is dusty and

complaining of the Allied failure to aid Warsaw. He was dismissed on the 25th and succeeded by General Komorowski ('General Bor'). Komorowski was captured by the Germans during the fall of Warsaw and was replaced as C.-in-C. by General Kopanski.

wounded – since all the bridges (except Ponte Vecchio) are destroyed and many houses by the river also. No Allied shell or bomb fell in the city (except on the marshalling yards outside). These were General Alex's orders. All the destruction is German.

He is very proud of the fact that so far in this campaign he has succeeded in saving Rome, Florence, Pisa, Siena, Assisi, Perugia, Urbino from any except minor damage and that wantonly inflicted by the enemy when retiring. The general has a reputation for his anxiety to spare the lives of his men. He is careful of the arts.

We got back late, after a most interesting but tiring day. Alex is not confident about the issue of the battle – there is little progress today on the Eighth Army front. But I thought him a trifle less anxious and he was quite merry at dinner. But (in spite of his great outward self-control) these continuous five years of command, almost always in conditions of great anxiety and usually with insufficient forces, have left their mark on him.

Sunday, 17 September 1944

Rested in the morning. Read Walt Whitman's *Leaves from American Life* – very vivid scraps and full of good descriptions both of man and nature.

After luncheon, drove to the aerodrome (some forty minutes) and arrived at Capodichino about 5 p.m. (General Alex sent me in his Dakota which will wait for me in Naples, since I have – rather rashly – promised to return.)

I found a Yugoslavian crisis, which Roger had dealt with very well. The P.M. wants to send messages to Tito; but as his messages were full of inaccuracies of fact, Roger and Jumbo have held them up. I think we shall probably have to send them and the best thing to do is to amend them without letting on at home.

I also found that Air Vice-Marshal Stevenson and Mr Le Rougetel[8] (the latter staying with us) have turned up. H.M.G. have at last agreed to send a mission to Roumania in spite of the delaying tactics of the Soviet Government and it is our job to 'launch' it. I like both the service and the political head. The first is a splendid-looking officer, brave and sensible; the second seems a cool and experienced diplomat, who has been in some tight places – Riga, Moscow, Bucharest – till 1941 – and seems under no illusions as to the difficulty of his task and the impediments which will be put in his way.

Monday, 18 September 1944

11 a.m. Talk with Le Rougetel.

12 noon. Talk with General Wilson. Greece is a great worry. The difficulty of launching 'Manna' and even what I call 'Quail' is resulting

[8] Air Vice-Marshal Donald Stevenson (1895–1964) was Commissioner, Roumania, 1944–7. J. H. Le Rougetel (1894–1975) was British Minister in Roumania, 1944–6.

in a grave danger of EAM seizing power whenever the Germans are leaving. Moreover, we fear that the Soviets will encourage the Bulgarians (who are to have northern Greece) to hand over to EAM. However, our plans are making a little progress. We have seized Kythera and the Greek Commission are on their way to the evacuated islands.

There is trouble in Rome. During the trial of the Fascist Caruso,[9] the mob rushed the court (or rather the taxi leaving or arriving at the court), and lynched the chief witness for the prosecution – a Fascist – torturing the wretch, who had turned King's Evidence. They no doubt feared that he would thus escape his proper punishment. There is naturally going to be trouble over this. We may be forced to place Rome under military government (it is now handed back to the Italian administration).

A mass of papers to read, so sandwich lunch at the office.

Immediately after lunch, a fresh problem – a telegram from P.M. saying he has settled with the President that I am to be head of the Italian Control Commission (in addition to my other duties!).

The other problem (of a personal kind) which worries me is that they want to give up Makins. After a lot of thought, I have telegraphed my agreement, but insisting on his having some leave first.

4 p.m. Leeper. The Greek Government are getting very restive. We discussed the plans for:

(*a*) hastening the despatch of the Greek Commissioners with small bodies of Greek or British troops to various points evacuated by the Germans;

(*b*) talks with General Zervas (*Andartes* [guerrillas]) and General Saraphis (EAM), should they arrive.[10]

4.30 p.m. Took Leeper to see S.A.C. for further discussions. After Leeper left, discussed P.M.'s telegram to me about Italian Control Commission. I decided to send delaying reply.

6 p.m. Air Vice-Marshal Stevenson, who is to be head of the Mission to Roumania, called. I formed a good opinion of him. He has had a good fighting record, has been director of operations at Air Ministry, and although he has no knowledge of the Balkans has clearly common sense and good judgment.

With Le Rougetel, we decided on the plan to be followed and the lines of the telegram to be sent to British Ambassador, Moscow.

I forgot to record that on Sunday night, in addition to the various problems awaiting me, I found Mr [J. H.] Hofmeyr (Finance Minister

[9] Pietro Caruso (1899–1944), as Chief Constable of Rome in the first half of 1944, had caused thousands of people to be arrested and sent to the Nazi concentration and labour camps. He was shot at dawn on 22 September.

[10] General Napoleon Zervas (1891–1957) was joint founder and effective leader of EDES (the nominal leader General Plastiras was living in France). General Stephanos Saraphis (1890–1957) was the leader of a small Resistance group until his capture by ELAS forces in March 1943, whereupon he was persuaded to accept the military leadership of ELAS.

of South Africa, Smuts's right-hand man and probable successor) staying in the Naples villa. General Theron and another officer were at Villa Rivalta (S.A.C.'s Naples villa).

Roger had arranged an excellent dinner-party – S.A.C., C.-in-C. Med., Slessor, Offie, Rookes. Oliver Lyttelton also turned up. A very pleasant evening, with good talk and plenty of good humour. The party broke up pretty late. Hofmeyr left the next morning for the front, as did Oliver Lyttelton.

Tuesday, 19 September 1944

I had drafted my proposed reply to P.M. last evening (Monday 18th) and after showing it to Generals Wilson and [George] Clark despatched the telegram, together with one to Anthony and another to the F.O. about Roger Makins.

The Greek guerilla generals have been delayed by weather, so we can do no more about this.

A new complication occurred just after luncheon. A telegram arrived from Cairo saying that the Greek Regent or Diadoch[11] was leaving Cairo tomorrow to see S.A.C., myself, Leeper and Papandreou.

I telephoned Leeper, saw S.A.C. at 3.30 p.m. and sent off a reply to stop him.

After this, went to see John Wyndham who is in No. 2 hospital, Caserta, with jaundice. He seems to be making a good recovery.

Wednesday, 20 September 1944

The Diadoch is coming! or perhaps it is a mistake. Anyway, we despatched a further 'Most Immediate' to hold him.

Political Committee at 11 a.m. Not a very long agenda, the news from A.A.I. front seems encouraging. It will be really wonderful if Alex brings it off.

Last night there was a violent storm and it rained hard all the morning. I had intended to leave at 3 p.m. (in Alex's plane) to return to his camp. But the weather was too bad and the pilot would not risk it.

Perhaps this was as well, since there was a lot to do and I was kept busy on Yugoslavian, Greek, Italian, and various odd questions till 8 p.m. I dined and slept at the Villa Vittoria (in Caserta).

Thursday, 21 September 1944

More trouble in Bulgaria. Two British S.O.E. officers from Greece have gone on their own to Sofia and seem to have entered (on behalf of General Wilson but without his knowledge!!) into negotiations with the Bulgarian Government about the evacuation of Greek territory. They seem to have put forward the idea that the Bulgars should police

[11] Prince Paul (1901–64), the King's brother, later King Paul I of the Hellenes, 1947–64.

the territory, so that it should not fall under either *Andarte* or EAM groups, until the legitimate Greek Government can arrive and take possession. This exceedingly naïve idea has naturally caused a howl from London, especially as the *News Chronicle* have got hold of the story!

I saw General Wilson at ten and cleared this and many other urgent points with him very rapidly. As usual, he was most friendly and co-operative. He is really a charming man to work with.

The weather is still bad, but the pilot thinks we might make it – so we have started off in General Alex's Dakota (very comfortable – with seats). We took the air about 11.30 and I am writing this now in the plane. We have a good cargo of wine and spirits for the general, to which my personal contribution is a ham!

Arrived at 1 p.m. Drove to Alex's camp, passing through Siena. The rain has passed, and a bright sun is shining through. The country is green and freshened; and the old city looks (since the dust is laid and the walls washed) quite spick and span. Arrived at the camp to find General Infante[12] (former divisional commander in Italian Army and now principal A.D.C. or secretary to the Lieutenant-General) exchanging reminiscences of the Western Desert with Alex.

The general seems in good spirits. After a very heavy day's fighting yesterday in which the Americans at the Futa Pass and the British on the right suffered heavy casualties (3,000 casualties in the Fifty-Sixth Division) good progress is being made. Rimini is taken and there is a good hope that the slogging match is drawing to an end and that the enemy will not be able to take much more punishment.

After a talk with Alex on a number of local questions, I went to the guest-house (the same farm as before) and slept and read *Cousin Henry* (a good Trollope) till dinner.

Oliver Lyttelton and his two sons (Antony in the Intelligence at Bari and Julian in the Third Battalion, Grenadiers)[13] are staying here. Oliver Lyttelton in great form at dinner. Our dear American flying general, Joe Cannon, is back at Alex's H.Q. with some of his Air Force from France and Corsica.

Friday, 22 September 1944

9 a.m. C.-in-C.'s conference. The battle is beginning to move, and the general seems more confident.

9.30 a.m. Left by 'whizzer'[14] with General Alex (each in our own) for the airfield where his DC3 is stationed.

We got to General Leese's H.Q. (Eighth Army) about 12 noon –

[12] General Adolfo Infante had been Prince Umberto's A.D.C. since February 1944, having commanded the Pinerolo Division in Thessaly, where he had agreed to fight the Germans, only for ELAS to seize all his division's arms.

[13] Captain Julian Lyttelton (1923–44) was killed in action in Italy in October.

[14] A small, fast bomber, the Bristol Buckingham, converted into a four-seater passenger plane.

after a very good flight in fine weather. General Leese's Divisional H.Q. are just over the Coriano ridge, a few miles this side of Rimini.

We all went off to luncheon with Canadian Corps H.Q. (General E. L. M. Burns). They were in excellent form and very pleased with their success all through this wonderful battle. Their armoured division, together with the New Zealand armour, is beginning to cross the Marecchia river (which runs through Rimini) and is advancing into the plain. The capture by British and Canadian infantry of the last dominating feature (the Fortunato hill) allowed the Greek brigade to enter Rimini and bring the Army into the plain. For a month they have battled across one mountain ridge after another. In view of the German superiority in numbers and greatly superior physical position – the almost inexpugnable high ground – it is a great feat of arms.

After luncheon, Alex, Oliver Leese and I drove to the 'Fortunato' feature (captured the day before yesterday) and watched the battle for the crossings of the river to the east; we already have bridgeheads at Rimini. We then drove (in jeeps) to Rimini. The town is rather badly damaged, but not irreparably. There are some lovely Renaissance buildings as well as some of earlier date. Naturally, since the place was only taken yesterday, it presents a pretty depressing appearance. But I feel sure it will 'clean up' better than it now appears.

One great difficulty with these partially destroyed buildings is to prevent further deterioration with the bad weather and rain approaching. But the Fine Arts Subcommission of A.C.C. are helping the Italians and have done splendid protective work.

The whole population of Rimini, with very few exceptions, had fled – mostly to San Marino, where there are 60,000 refugees.

The Greek brigade fought quite well outside Rimini (round the airfield) and actually entered the town and cleared it. But of course the 'Fortunato' feature was the key of the whole position.

We drove over the river and watched the armour going forward – they had got about a mile or one-and-a-half miles ahead. The Germans were shelling pretty heavily and putting up a very firm delaying action.

We got back to General Oliver Leese's H.Q. about four o'clock. Generla Alex left by 'whizzer' for the airfield where he had parked his Dakota.

A pleasant evening in Oliver Leese's camp – on a hill behind Rimini, with a splendid view of the battle. I found young Bruce (a friend of Maurice's), John Buchan's eldest boy (who has done very well with the Canadians) and several other friends. Oliver and I chatted in the evening and retired early to bed. I had a very comfortable caravan, with some excellent gilt furniture. This had been specially 'liberated' for the use of King George when he came.

Saturday, 23 September 1944

A wonderful day. General Leese and I left by jeep – he driving his own. We drove over the whole front – by various lateral roads – and at different distances from the actual front line. Everywhere everything was on the move, and everywhere the general is received with smiles and greetings. He is indeed a very popular figure, and I told him that he conducts the whole affair like an election campaign. It is a remarkable contrast with the last war. Then a general was a remote, Blimpish figure in white moustache, faultlessly tailored tunics, polished boots and spurs, emerging occasionally from a luxurious château, and escorted as a rule in his huge limousine Rolls by a troop of lancers. Now an Army commander is a youngish man, in shorts and open shirt, driving his own jeep, and waving and shouting his greetings to the troops as he edges his way past guns, tanks, trucks, tank-carriers, etc., in the crowded and muddy roads, which the enemy may actually be shelling as he drives along.

We drove to San Marino – now occupied by troops of an Indian Division and a Scottish Brigade. With all the traffic on the roads and the mines, etc., which had to be avoided and the broken bridges and corresponding detours, it was about 12.15 p.m. before we got to the little square on the top of the mountain.

This tiny republic is a somewhat absurd mixture of old and new. We were received by one of the co-regents – who wore white gloves and a very long swallow-tail coat (like a *maître d'hôtel*) – and by the cabinet. (We assumed that there was only one swallow-tail coat between the two co-regents and therefore that they can only function one at a time.)

After an interchange of courtesies, we were led up to the council chamber. The town hall is 1850 Gothic – rather like the hall at Balliol – and the product of one of San Marino's chief exports, viz., the sale of titles. This building, together with a great part of the medieval town that crowns the rock, was largely built by an American lady. This benefactress also put in a water supply. For these – especially the last service – she was suitably rewarded by the title of 'Duchessa d'Acqua-Viva'!

After a ceremonial wine-drinking and a few speeches, the co-regent began to open up on the question of compensation for damage by bombing, etc., within his state. Fortunately, at this moment, the pipes began to pipe vigorously in the square outside and allowed me to escape from this awkward problem under cover of their deafening sounds. Moreover, the Divisional Commander of the Indian Division turned up with plans for a counter-attack on a hill nearby, where a furious battle was raging some 2,000–3,000 yards away.

The whole scene was really fantastic. The 'waiter' co-regent in his swallow-tails; the general and I making polite conversation amid the din of the pipes and the guns; and the battle going on quite close to us. From our great height we could look down on the foothills and the river and watch the fight.

Finally, we escaped from San Marino officialdom and went off for a picnic lunch. We motored back (a long and dusty journey through crowded roads) and got back to the camp about 4.30 p.m. Among our trophies were some stamps (San Marino's most important export after titles) and a flag apiece.

Sunday, 24 September 1944

I have just heard about Bill Hartington's death in action. It is really a tragic thing – poor Eddy and Moucher. They loved the boy with more than ordinary affection and pride. It is a cruel blow.

9 a.m. Left the camp with General Leese and motored over the Gothic Line which was successfully pierced by his troops at the end of August. It was a very strong position in a broad valley, heavily wired and mined, and reinforced by very strong points, including tank turrets sunk in cement bases in commanding positions in the range of hills behind. It was only taken by a ruse. The attack was made without warning by six divisions on a narrow front. The Germans were holding the range of hills *in front* of the prepared line, and were really bustled out of the position before they had time to man the line properly. The marked lanes through the minefields remained open and our troops rushed them and bustled all the Germans out of the line in forty-eight hours – a splendid achievement.

Left at 11 a.m. by 'whizzer' for the main airfield, where I found General Wilson's aeroplane. Got to Marcianise (near Caserta) at 1 p.m.

As always a large number of problems have arisen in my absence and as always been admirably dealt with by Roger.

First, a Hungarian general has arrived here by air. Of course he wants to make a death-bed repentance and make an armistice with the British and Americans and avoid a Russian occupation. Of course, also, like the Roumanians and Bulgarians, they will fail.

Anyway, the Hungarian's credentials appeared to be rather shadowy. We have telegraphed to F.O. and asked for instructions and no doubt the usual triangular negotiations will begin between London, Washington and Moscow. Moscow will 'stall' until the Soviet troops are well into Hungary.[15]

The second problem was the visit of the Greek Crown Prince (or Diadoch).

The third was the perpetual Yugoslavian difficulty. The P.M. sent Tito an inaccurate protest, which I held up. Now he insists on it being forwarded and so does Anthony. I have done so, while altering the more glaring errors. Meanwhile Tito has mysteriously left Vis without a word to anyone. We think he has gone to see the Russian general commanding in Bulgaria. Anyway, we have forwarded the message but it cannot be delivered!

4.30 p.m. The Brazilian Minister of War called, with a gaggle of

[15] Soviet troops invaded Hungary on 6 October.

generals. Also my old friend da Cunha, who was Brazilian Minister at Algiers. A *visite de politesse* only.

6 p.m. Went up to Hunting Lodge to discuss plans for the Greek negotiations. General Zervas (*Andartes*) and General Saraphis (EAM/ELAS) have arrived.

8.30 p.m. A large dinner given by General Rookes (U.S.) for the Brazilians. Practically everyone (except Ambassador Kirk and me) got decorated with magnificent Brazilian orders.

Monday, 25 September 1944

A very busy day.

We have become a sort of 'launching site' for missions to countries which have surrendered. I am glad to say that the Roumanian party has at last got off (after one false start owing to weather). Now the Bulgarian mission is expected to collect here towards the end of the week. The only trouble is that they expect to be put up and given every comfort and are rather horrified to find the conditions under which we live here.

The Greek situation is developing. General Zervas (EDES) and Saraphis (ELAS) have arrived. Ambassador Leeper came up from Cava at 11.15 and tried to alter the programme. But although I share his fear and suspicion of the S.O.E. generals (like Brigadier Barker-Benfield) I had to take some risks, or we get the military unwilling to co-operate.

M. Papandreou turned up at 11.30, with four members of his Government. Mr [A. R.] Burn (of Leeper's Embassy, who works in our office) gave me the attached list of their names and distinguishing characteristic. This was most useful. The names were:

Papandreou (P.M.)
Svolos
Tsatsos
Porphyrogennis
Zevgos.

Greek Ministers here:

1. *Papandreou.*

2. [*Alexandros*] *Svolos*. Minister of Finance. History professor at Athens; ex-president of EAM's Political Committee of National Liberation; theoretical Marxist. Very widely read. Small, plump and amiable.

3. [*Themistocles*] *Tsatsos*. Minister of Justice (dark with moustache – a trifle like Laval?), aged about thirty-six. Scholar (Plotinus, etc.).

4. [*Miltiades*] *Porphyrogennis*. Minister of Labour. Communist. Lawyer, of middle-class origin, with considerable education and *savoir-faire*. Tall and grey-haired.

5. [*Ioannis*] *Zevgos* (current alias of Talayiarris). Communist, higher in hierarchy than Porphyrogennis. Small and debonair. The only 'proletarian' in the bunch. Said to be responding to treatment as a human being, but no doubt also on look-out for attempts to corrupt him.

Language. All except perhaps (5) speak French, and at least numbers 1, 2, 3 understand and read English. (5) may be isolated through talking only Greek.

A.R.B. 25.9.1944

During the morning, the military conversations have been taking place between General Scobie (with his staff and Barker-Benfield) and the guerilla leaders. At about 12 noon a purely Greek meeting between the guerilla leaders and the Cabinet Ministers took place. The soldiers (Zervas, who looks like a Greek priest or archimandrite, with a long black beard almost to his waist) went off to lunch with S.A.C. I took the politicians out to Villa Vittoria (Caserta). We can only seat eight in the little dining-room there, so we had the five Greek politicians, Leeper, Roger Makins and myself.

I thought the atmosphere rather sombre, so I gave a toast and a speech which Papandreou responded to. After a certain amount of drink, they began to cheer up, but there is clearly a good deal of anxiety as to the outcome.

After luncheon the Greek Ministers went off to their conference room in the palace for further talks with the guerilla generals. Before leaving, Papandreou had a talk alone with me in the garden. He seemed very anxious and was most keen that we should send the Government into Greece *at once*, even if it could not go to Athens. Any further delay would weaken its prestige, lead to a breakdown of the Lebanon agreement, and make it impossible for the ELAS/EAM members of his Government (even if they wished to) to play the game. The gap after the departure of the Germans would be filled. If the Government and the British troops were not there, the Communists would step in and build themselves too strong a position to allow of their subsequent ejection.

I told Papandreou I would think over this and discuss further with General Wilson.

3.30 p.m. Fitzroy Maclean. He gave me a short account of his recent visit to Serbia. He will come down tonight for further talk.

7.30 p.m. Conference with General Wilson and Ambassador Leeper. After the conference I drafted a telegram to Winston suggesting that we put the Greek Government into Patras or Araxos (on Gulf of Corinth) as soon as possible. I did the draft after the meeting – got Leeper's and S.A.C.'s approval and sent it 'Most Immediate' to London.

Fitzroy came down to Naples. We were alone and Fitzroy was in a good mood. He anticipates that when the European war is over Tito will proceed to hold an election or plebiscite on the Russian plan. (He does not think there will be much of a civil war, for Mihailović will be on the run and Tito's power, with a Russian Army at his side[16] and the splendid equipment which we have given him, will be very strong.)

This election will result in the one hundred per cent return of all the 'party' men and Government nominees. They will proceed to elect a constitutional assembly and so on, and the Federal Union of Yugoslavia will come into being based on the principles already enunciated by the National Committee of Liberaton.

The King will be ignored and also the Subašić Government. If Subašić and his friends arrive in Yugoslavia, they will not be shot. On the contrary, they will be asked to join the Government. They will probably accept – indeed, Maclean thinks that Subašić and Tito have already reached an agreement.

The question of recognition by the Great Powers of this *de facto* Government will then arise. Russia will give enthusiastic and immediate recognition. They will send an Ambassador and a large and impressive staff.

What will Great Britain and America do? If we hum and haw and recognise the King's Government (either with Subašić if he proves loyal to the King or with another if Subašić deserts to Tito) as *de jure* Government of Yugoslavia but compromise by sending an 'observer' or an 'emissary' to Belgrade, we shall miss our opportunity, throw away all the goodwill we have built up painfully over a long period, and of course push Tito into the arms of the Russian bear. He may not be too anxious for that suffocating embrace. But (if he is cold-shouldered by U.S. and Great Britain) he will have no alternative.

This is F.M.'s [Fitzroy Maclean] thesis. I am bound to say that I find it convincing. But of course the F.O. will never agree to a clear course. They will shilly-shally and finally 'miss the bus' in both directions.

Tuesday, 26 September 1944

11 a.m. Mr Leeper. He tells me that the Greeks, after their traditional tug of war, have agreed pretty well. I urged him, however, that we must have a proper *plenary* session and a proper document, signed by all parties, embodying both the political and military agreements.

As a matter of fact, I had already expressed my view as to this during the last day or two to General Wilson, and got his assent.

The rest of the morning therefore was spent in preparing the necessary documents and summoning the proper people. The meeting is to be at 3 p.m.

[16] The Russians had invaded Yugoslavia the previous day.

12.30 p.m. Colonel Dodds-Parker (S.O.E.) called – a farewell visit, as with the change in the situation, S.O.E. activities have become largely military or para-military in this theatre. I do not know what Dodds-Parker will do. He is an excellent fellow and I think would like to get into the House of Commons. He would certainly be a great addition to that body, as he is young, earnest and attractive. And he loves talking.

Sandwich lunch in the office.

2 p.m. Economic Subcommittee. General George Clark in the chair. The two subjects were (*a*) B.M.A. [British Military Administration] notes and their drachma exchange value, (*b*) the opening by the Italian Government of a lira account and undertaking the duty of 'procurement' for the Allied forces.

On (*a*) a telegram which I had drafted was accepted. It is obviously wiser to attempt no formal rate of exchange with the drachma in view of the runaway inflation going on, but to let the B.M.A. notes find their own value on the open market.

On (*b*) the discussion was inconclusive and a decision postponed.

3 p.m. Greek Plenary Session. General Wilson was in the chair and conducted the proceedings effectively and with dignity. After a lot of talk and argument about verbal expressions, our prepared drafts were substantially accepted. I did not think that the EAM/ELAS generals were enthusiastic, but their civil ministers played up quite well. Papandreou's manner was good and his authority is clearly considerable.

At 5 p.m. I had Brigadier Eve on a prepared directive to be sent by H.Q. of the Balkan relief organisation to the officers in the field. We agreed the text after some discussion.

6 p.m. I got Mr Offie (of Mr Kirk's office) up. Although the Greek Agreement has been done by the British side of A.F.H.Q. only (to spare American political susceptibilities) I have kept Kirk or his office informed. I gave Offie (and sent to General Rookes, Deputy Chief of Staff, U.S.) copies of the text which had just been signed. The Americans appear pleased by this attention.

7 p.m. Colonel Grafftey-Smith (Finance Officer, A.C.C.) for further talks on the lira account question.

8.30 p.m. Dinner in Naples by S.A.C. for the Canadian Minister of Defence – Mr Ralston. A dull party for a dull visitor.

Wednesday, 27 September 1944

11 a.m. Political Committee. The most important discussion concerned a proposed Civil Affairs Agreement with Yugoslavia governing the conditions under which Anglo-American relief will be distributed. This was drawn up on the general lines of the agreement now being negotiated with the Greek Government for a similar purpose. But of course there are great differences in the situation. If we

make an agreement with the Royal Yugoslav Government (Subašić), that would be correct, but useless, since Tito controls the country. If we make it with Tito it would be useful but incorrect, for we recognise the Royal Government. My solution is to get delegates from Subašić and Tito at Bari (they are coming out for discussions anyway) and after getting them to meet together, discuss the problem with them. If an agreement is reached, it should *not* be a governmental agreement, drafted and signed with the formality of a treaty, but a 'memorandum of agreement' between representatives of Royal Yugoslav Government, representatives of Marshal Tito and representatives of General Wilson. This was agreed, and I undertook to get the machinery in motion.

2.45 p.m. Meeting with General [I. T. P.] Hughes, Brigadier Eve, Mr Offie, Roger, to discuss mechanism for Yugoslav agreement. We decided on the general course which will be embodied in a directive to Broad and Norden (F.O. and State Department advisers at Bari) to come here on Friday for a discussion.

In the course of the afternoon I went to see John Wyndham still in hospital at Caserta No. 2 with jaundice. He seemed better and in good spirits.

Mr E. M. H. Lloyd turned up from Cairo and came to the Naples villa for the night. With him came Steel, who is Roger Makins's successor. I am terribly grieved at losing Roger, but I think it is the best thing for him. Prolonged association with me is doing him harm with the F.O.

Read *Doctor Thorne* (Trollope), a charming work.

Thursday, 28 September 1944

A quiet morning with papers and telegrams. The weather has broken, and the rain (which is very heavy) has made a lake of the palace grounds.

No news from London or reply from P.M. on:

(*a*) My position with A.C.C.

(*b*) Greece; plan to send Government to Peloponnese at once.

(*c*) Hungarian envoy.

I suppose they are all overwhelmed with work and the meeting of the House of Commons.

The Chief of Staff came to ask my view of a proposal (backed by General [George] Clark) that we should move A.F.H.Q. to Rome on 15 December or 1 January. The argument in favour is that the conditions of life are very hard on the troops in winter. Many thousands are in camps and huts. There are really no amusements or recreations available. Caserta is a tiny township, with one cinema, etc., and twenty miles from Naples.

On the other hand, I feel that there are great objections to having A.F.H.Q. in a foreign capital. (We had a lot of trouble from this at

Algiers.) Our territory covers far more than Italy. If we are at Naples, the Mediterranean command is a reality. If we are at Rome, we seem to emphasise the *Italian* aspect, and General Wilson will be continually harassed by members of the Italian Government and representatives of the Vatican. In any case, I strongly urged Gammell to make no proposal to the C.C.S. without *first* getting London's point of view. I feel the P.M. would probably object strongly.

11.30 a.m. Talk with S.A.C. Oliver Leese is leaving the Eighth Army for the Asia Army Group (General [Sir George] Giffard). This is a great loss. Dick McCreery will get the Army in his place. Fortunately, Alex likes him (he was his Chief of Staff in Tunisia).

General Wilson also told me that he was going to a meeting in Rome tomorrow to discuss with Mr Myron Taylor, Archbishop Spellman and other ecclesiastics and Ambassador Kirk charitable relief for Italy. This has certain dangers, and I have sent him a minute about it.

Sandwich luncheon in the office (I am ashamed to say that I read Trollope's *Doctor Thorne* for an hour. It was a great mental rest).

Mr [William] Houstoun-Boswall and General [Walter] Oxley arrived. They are the heads of the Bulgarian mission which we are to organise and launch from here. H.B. is a queer fish – looks very stupid (like a retired major in *Punch*) but I should think is quite intelligent. The major-general is quiet and I should say quite intelligent. He has lately been O.C. troops in Malta.

Long discussions on the conflicting orders which these two gentlemen have received. H.B. (and I have the same instructions) has been told to go in as soon as possible. The general has been told to await the 'all-clear' from the War Office and Sir Frederick Bovenschen. I at once sent a telegram to London on this point.

Friday, 29 September 1944

3 p.m. Meeting to 'launch' General Oxley and Mr Houstoun-Boswall to Bulgaria. The telegram to Russia was agreed. (Of course it was not ready – so I had to dictate it myself in front of them.)

4.30 p.m. Meeting on Yugoslavian relief. It is clear that we cannot have a regular agreement covering 'civil affairs' with the Tito administration and that it would be fatuous to have it (as the Combined Chiefs of Staff propose) with the Royal Yugoslav Government.

We agreed (Kirk, General Hughes, G5, etc., etc.) a formula by which Tito and Subašić's representatives would be asked to meet together and if an agreement was reached, it should be embodied in an informal memorandum of agreement to be initialled by S.A.C.'s representatives and those of the other two. A telegram was agreed to Balkan Air Force accordingly. (Unfortunately in view of a direct order from C.C.S. to deal with the Royal Yugoslav Government which came later in the day, we had to postpone things till we could telegraph to C.C.S. telling them how absurd their instructions were.)

Farewell party for Roger Makins 5.30–7.30 in the office. My room, with its Bonapartist pictures and magnificent sofas, looked very nice. The party was a great success, and a great tribute to the position which Roger has won for himself at A.F.H.Q. Over a hundred people came; the servants played up by producing quantities of food and drink and not getting too drunk themselves. (It was sad that John Wyndham was still in hospital – so that the oldest member of my staff was away.)

After the party, we went up to a select but delightful dinner given by General Wilson and his staff at 'The Kennels' – also in Roger's honour. Mark [Chapman-Walker] and Hermione [Ranfurly] surpassed themselves in the arrangements – a string band and a film were provided. Jumbo proposed Roger's health, which I supported. Roger briefly replied.

We motored back to Naples – arriving about midnight. Roger left early the next morning. It is naturally a great loss – even a great grief – to lose Roger. He has been a most loyal supporter in all my difficulties and a most agreeable companion and friend. I think it is a tribute to both of us that we have lived together for nearly two years like subalterns in a company mess without quarrelling (and Roger's temperament is more highly strung than mine). The inspiring thing about him is his standard of work. He is *never* satisfied with the second best. And this goes through the office and inspires the others.

It will be a great change. Kit Steel will, I think, be agreeable and efficient. But he has not that rapier-like brain combined with that almost monastic devotion to duty which makes Roger such a unique figure in the public service.

Saturday, 30 September 1944

11.30 a.m. Mr Leeper. The Greek problem grows more and more difficult. Now that the hour of action approaches, the Greek Government is of course beginning to lose its nerve. Leeper tells me that Papandreou does *not* want now to go to Patras or to anywhere in the Peloponnese. He argues that they cannot afford a failure; that there are insufficient British and no Greek troops; that the relief supplies which are projected will be disappointingly small and so on. Leeper (whose telegrams to the F.O. always seem to include a paragraph urgently recommending that he (Leeper) shall not go until everything is comfortably and quietly settled in Athens) either openly fosters or secretly shares these views. He was proposing to telegraph accordingly to London, but I persuaded him *not* to do so. We shall indeed appear foolish and vacillating in the eyes of the P.M. if one day we telegraph *urgently* for permission to send an expedition and introduce the Government into Patras; and the next day say that we have thought better of it and that we and the Greek Government are now taking counsel of our fears.

We went along to see Jumbo. The general of course supported me, and I think we have, at least temporarily, silenced the Ambassador.

12 noon. The Crown Prince of Greece. He called at General Wilson's office. Leeper and I were also present. I felt sorry for the Prince. He was obviously sincere and anxious to do his best for his brother and the dynasty. But I fear he suffers under the usual illusions of royalty. He believes that he has only to show himself in Greece for a 'landslide' to take place.

We tried to explain to him that if he were to go now to Greece, the carefully constructed Government of M. Papandreou would fall to the ground and the only beneficiaries would be EAM/ELAS who would take over the country.

A long and rather painful discussion followed. It was clear that the King does not regard himself as bound by his declaration that he would not go back to Greece without the consent of his Government. There was always something equivocal about this situation. It has even been maintained that the King's letter was so couched as to have an ambiguous meaning in Greek, although the English version seemed clear enough and satisfactory enough. Of one thing I am certain, that even Winston's popularity will not enable him to force a King upon Greece by British arms.

At the end of the meeting the Diadoch (or Crown Prince) and Leeper came to luncheon in my little Villa Vittoria at Caserta. This went off very well.

I had not been feeling well for several days. Today I realised that I had got a regular chill and sore throat. So after luncheon, I motored to Naples and went to bed.

October

Sunday, 1 October 1944

In bed all day. Felt very bad. I'm afraid I have some congestion in the lung. I got a doctor in the afternoon, who wanted to move to me the Ninety-second (Military) Hospital immediately. As, however, Sir Noel and Lady Charles were motoring down from Rome specially to see me and stay the night, I waited till 8.30 p.m. to be moved.

Noel came at 5 p.m. We had a long talk on Italian affairs. He was very nice, as usual, and, as usual, very incoherent.

He naturally wants to know what I am going to be – whether Chief Commissioner or not. He has only had a telegram similar in substance to that which the P.M. sent me on 18 September. So I showed him my replies and could only tell him that I was still waiting to hear. He really is a very pleasant fellow, and one is rather ashamed of teasing him – but it is irresistible. He should have stayed in South America.[1]

I got to the hospital about 9 p.m. – Ralph and the faithful Corporals Pocklington and Smith assisting. I felt like death, but got somehow into the frightful hospital bed, swallowed my sulphonamide tablets and settled down.

Monday, 2 October 1944

A very bad night. My throat and chest are very painful.

I finished *Doctor Thorne* yesterday. I have only *Pride and Prejudice* with me – so must not read too much, so as to make it last. Perhaps I can get some more books.

I really feel I ought to go home. I have had a letter from Dorothy and a very sad one from Moucher. It is really terrible for her – she was so *completely* devoted to Billy Hartington.

Kit Steel told me last night that the Diadoch wants to go to London. I told him to tell Jumbo that I saw no objection – especially if he didn't come back.

The hospital is rather bleak. But I have a room to myself. They are

[1] Charles had been Ambassador to Brazil, 1941–4.

giving me a drug called sulphonamide or something. It is supposed to clear the congestion from the lungs and throat by attacking the hostile bacteria. It has, however, rather a lowering effect. Miss Campbell came at 4 p.m. and I did about one hour's work with her.

Tuesday, 3 October 1944

A little better today; the infection is clearing.

Philip Broad (from Bari) arrived about noon and we settled various points. The Yugoslav negotiations about relief are to begin unless a direct order from C.C.S. arrives tomorrow to prevent it. (I think there is hardly time for this.)

Steel came on his way to Naples – in the evening. There was not very much for me to settle. But I must get out tomorrow, for the political meeting at A.F.H.Q.

I have read *Pride and Prejudice* and finished *Doctor Thorne*.

Wednesday, 4 October 1944

Felt much better. The cold wind and rain have stopped and a milder spell is beginning. I drove direct from the hospital to Caserta arriving about ten.

11 a.m.–1 p.m. Political Meeting.

The chief items were Italian and Greek. On the Italian side is the complicated question of the method of 'procurement' of the Armies' needs. For the last year, the Armies (British and American), and also the other services, have procured their needs (labour, materials, etc.) and paid for them direct with A.M.G. lire. It would be more correct (and more strictly in accordance with the armistice terms) if the Italian Government were made to do the procurement on our behalf and were to pay for the cost with their own lire – borrowing from us if they are physically short of currency, but from their own lire account. This would also let the Italian people and Government know what was their *true* contribution and their real budgetary deficit. At present this is concealed, because we pay for goods and services with our imported lire and give the Italians no account of the total.

The argument against the change is 'Let sleeping dogs lie'. We might easily set up a storm of abuse and trouble.

After a long discussion, it was decided to let Stone (Acting Chief Commissioner) sound the Italians and see their reaction and at the same time ask the view of the C.C.A.C. (Civil Affairs Committee of the Combined Chiefs of Staff).

The other Italian point was a variation of the old 'prisoner of war' theme. This time it is about the 30,000 Italian service troops which the Seventh Army are using in southern France. The Italian Government have made an enquiry. I rather objected to the proposed *written* reply. Since we are in fact breaking the letter (not, I think, the spirit) of the Geneva Convention, I thought an *oral* explanation would be safer.

The other major item was the question of the plans for relief supplies to Greece. Since the Rome decision by the P.M. to move the Greek Government and Ambassador Leeper to Italy, Greek affairs have been taken over by General Wilson from General Paget. It has been tacitly assumed that Lord Moyne's responsibilities have similarly passed to me.

I have lately been making a number of discreet (and indiscreet) enquiries into the state of preparation. And I am horrified to find a great deal of paperwork but very little reality. *Food* fortunately is all right – but only because it is to be drawn from general Army stocks and therefore even the Cairo planners could not help it being there. Drugs and medicines are the same – and I suspect for the same reason.

But when I ask about blankets, clothing, transport, nails and small tools for house-repair, soap, fertilisers, seeds, etc., etc., everything is 'on order' and 'expected in December'. (What would happen if the Germans left Greece too soon, the planners don't seem to have thought of.)

But 'on order' means that the order has been registered with the vast machinery of Washington (which I remember so well from Ministry of Supply and Colonial Office days) and 'expected in December' means that if there were any ships and the ships were allocated to the job and did leave America in October they would probably reach Alexandria in December.

I really do not know what these people have been doing in Cairo for two years. But I know that I shall now be made the scapegoat for a disgraceful failure (if it occurs) instead of Casey, Moyne and Paget.

I said all this very forcibly at the meeting and demanded a proper report. General Wilson was very good and supported me secretly, while pretending to be impartial.

After the meeting, luncheon at our little villa in Caserta and then back to work. A long afternoon. General Hughes (Greek Relief) came to talk to me, but I was not impressed. He is honest, very honest, but has no drive. (He is assistant to the Deputy Sergeant-at-Arms in the House of Commons – not an exacting post.) He is very charming.

Colonel (now General) Spofford (G5, American) who is a *really* clever man has promised to help.

One of the many absurdities is the position about clothing. The American Red Cross have 600,000 garments which they want to *give* to the Greeks. U.N.R.R.A. [United Nation Relief and Rehabilitation Association] says goods must be *sold* not *given*. So the American Red Cross are threatening to *give* them to the French, who (being sensible people) have contracted out of U.N.R.R.A. altogether.

I got hold of Governor Cochrane, U.N.R.R.A. representative at A.F.H.Q., and told him all this was nonsense and must be stopped. He seemed to agree but he also seemed totally ignorant of Greece and

U.N.R.R.A., and quite inarticulate. (One of F.D.R.'s political appointments – from the Conservative South, I would judge.)

Thursday, 5 October 1944

Ralph [Anstruther] and Tony [Rumbold] are in bed in the nursery (two beds side by side) at Naples. John has at last got out of hospital and is going to Rome to convalesce. The staff is now Kit Steel, and no one else! (And that Greek Embassy are so incompetent that you practically have to wipe their noses for them.)

Houstoun-Boswall (the major, we call him) is a refreshing contrast. He seems to be unlucky though about getting to Bulgaria, because the weather stopped them today. They will try tomorrow.

Frightful rain – the road was so flooded and the traffic so disorganised that it took us two-and-a-half hours to get from Naples to Caserta.

The Greeks are bad starters. They are now trying to get out of going to the Peloponnese.[2] Generals Wilson, Scobie and I discussed it today and we are sending for M. Papandreou and Leeper tomorrow. Leeper is awfully good with them, but more as a nurse than a leader.

Came back early and went to bed – to read and write. It is really the best way of getting through the papers, and one can at least keep warm. The palace is beginning to get very draughty as the winter comes on.

Duff Cooper has written to ask if I would like him to suggest my name for St George's. After thinking it over, I am going to accept. (Of course, it is more than likely that the Committee won't look at me. It would be sad to leave Stockton, but if I am really to go on in politics (and look after Macmillan & Co. to some extent!) I really cannot travel six hours up and down to Durham. Also, I am too old to risk not being in the next House, and I should imagine St George's would still be pretty safe.

Nothing more about the Italian Control Commission, except a curious wire from Anthony to say that he is discussing my appointment with the Secretary of State for War and doing his best. As if I wanted the job!

Friday, 6 October 1944

9 a.m. Colonel [W. D.] Keown-Boyd. He is to go to Thrace with the Greek Commissioner. He seemed rather a vague young man, in the Rifle Brigade, and naturally puzzled as to his duties in a very confused situation. The Bulgars allege that on instructions from the Russian Commander they are remaining in Thrace simply to form a protection to the Russian flank against a possible German threat from Salonika. The Greeks suspect a more sinister motive for the Bulgar refusal to evacuate the territory. In any case, the situation is very confused.

[2] British forces started landing in Greece on the previous night.

10 a.m. Talk with S.A.C. about the visit of the P.M. and Anthony Eden on their way to Moscow.[3]

3 p.m. Colonel Katzen, the chief technical officer of A.M.L. Balkans H.Q. Supply. I was not much impressed by this officer. He seemed to me rather glib.

I am still very uneasy about the supplies available for Greek relief.

4 p.m. Meeting between S.A.C., Leeper, M. Papandreou and self. Scobie was also present. It was agreed that Papandreou should undertake the trip to Patras and the date was definitely fixed for Wednesday, 11 October.

A lot of telegrams all day and paperwork of various kinds.

8 p.m. Dined with Ambassador Kirk at the Villa Lauro – an agreeable party.

Saturday, 7 October 1944

I saw General Wilson in the morning on the Greek situation. Things are not going too badly in the Peloponnese – but I fear we shall have trouble with Aris[4] – the EAM commander there – who is nothing but a sadistic thug.

1.15 p.m. General Alexander came to luncheon. After luncheon, we drove to Caserta Vecchia – on the hill behind the palace – a charming old village. We went to see the lovely old Norman church. The pillars in the nave are from a Roman temple. The general style is transitional between Romanesque and Gothic (the double circles crossing each other on the west front and tower are a splendid example of the period (1100 *circa*) and the emergence of the Gothic arch from the intersection of two Roman arches).

We talked to some Italians, and drank some of their sweet, unfermented wine, from the wine press. A very charming type of peasant – with sufficient returned emigrants to be able to converse in the American language.

4.30 p.m. Saw S.A.C. – various plans for tomorrow's visit.

7.30 p.m. Went in for a drink to Gibson Graham's charming little house in Naples. He is a very intelligent and attractive fellow – a nice party, sailors and G4 officers.

Sunday, 8 October 1944

A fantastic day. Got up at 5 a.m. and left the house in Naples – with Kit Steel and Ralph Anstruther – at 5.30 we drove to Pomigliano and waited on the airfield, until at last (about 7.15 a.m.) the party arrived, in a Liberator and two Yorks.

The Prime Minister, Foreign Secretary, Field Marshal Brooke (C.I.G.S.), Generals Ismay and Jacob, Messrs Dixon, Oliver Harvey,

[3] For a conference, accompanied by military advisers, with Stalin and Molotov. Averell Harriman represented the United States.

[4] Athanasis Klaras (known as Aris Veloukhiotis) (1905–45) was one of the leaders of ELAS.

Guy Millard, etc.[5] Lord Moran, Commander Tommy Thompson, Martin (P.M.'s Private Secretary) and all the usual circus.

We drove to Naples, where the party were distributed between S.A.C.'s villa and mine for baths and breakfast.

I drove from the airfield with Anthony – who was very pleasant, as usual, and rather *distrait*.

After breakfast a military talk took place (Generals Wilson, Alexander, etc.) with P.M. presiding, and at the same time Eden had a talk with M. Papandreou – who had been duly paraded by Leeper.

Then the P.M. came out and had a talk with Papandreou (Wilson, Leeper, Anthony Eden and I sitting round), which was entirely confined to a monologue by Winston in praise of monarchy in general and King George of Greece in particular. M. Papandreou looked very uncomfortable – but not more so than the rest of us.

When the homily was over, the party left for the airfield. They took off about 11 a.m.

In driving back with Anthony, I was able to discover that the visit [to Moscow] was:

(*a*) To try to find out the Russian military plans.

(*b*) To try to settle the Polish question.

(*c*) To try to unravel some of the Balkan tangles – especially the armistice with Bulgaria and the position in Thrace.

Anthony seemed very distressed at the obvious ill effect on Papandreou of Winston's royalist sermon. He asked me to do what I could to smooth things over.

I had only a word or two with Winston during the morning. He seemed surprised that the Italian Commission question was not yet resolved.

I gathered subsequently from Anthony that (*a*) the President had not informed the War Department or the State Department of the arrangement which he had made with Winston about myself, (*b*) that the War Office – especially P. J. Grigg – was opposing my appointment – or at least trying to seize the opportunity to get out of any responsibility for Italian civil affairs.

At his request I sent later in the afternoon two telegrams to Moscow, repeated to London.

After we got back from the aerodrome (about 12 noon) I dictated these to Miss Campbell (who was at the Naples villa). After luncheon, I went off to Cava, to see Ambassador Leeper. I arrived about 3.30 and discussed the situation with him. It was agreed that I should see Papandreou the next day at 12 noon.

The weather has been frightful for the last week – heavy, almost torrential rain, with occasional bright intervals. The road was very bad going home. A car in front of us skidded badly and overturned. In

[5] Major-General Ian Jacob (b. 1899) was Assistant Secretary (Military) to the War Cabinet, 1939–46. Guy Millard (b. 1917) was Assistant Private Secretary to the Foreign Secretary, 1941–5.

trying to extricate the passengers (who were actually unhurt) a door dropped on my right thumb which was badly bruised. No one else was hurt!

Monday, 9 October 1944

11 a.m. Mr Harden (Ministry of Production). Apparently there has been a terrific dispute going on in London about Italian civil affairs and a raging interdepartmental war – chiefly between the War Office and the F.O. This is still going on most bitterly, and has been accentuated by my proposed appointment.

12 noon. M. Papandreou.

Record of conversation with M. Papandreou
9 October 1944

1. At the suggestion of the Foreign Secretary I called on M. Papandreou at 12 noon today. For fifty minutes in idiomatic and fluent French he presented a general picture of the situation in the Eastern Mediterranean and the Balkans as he saw it. As the result of the military strategy followed by England and America, the European war is reaching its end under conditions which necessarily add to the insecurity of this area. The tradition of Anglo-Greek friendship is based upon the long amity between the two countries and cemented by mutual interest. It is a British interest that Greece should be a fortress guarding the Imperial route. It is a Greek interest that Greece should be fortified by British protection against Slav aggression. This is a historic position and still holds good. At present Roumania is almost entirely under the control of the Soviet Union. Nothing can prevent that, and M. Papandreou regards Roumania as henceforth a puppet state of Russia. Bulgaria has always found herself in a curious position. Owing to the patriotic rivalries of the Yugoslav and Bulgarian peasants the Slav union has been divided: for this reason the Communist movement in Bulgaria was never made effective. Nevertheless Bulgaria is now falling under Soviet control and the Greek Prime Minister is deeply suspicious of the way in which this power will be used in respect of Macedonia and Thrace. In Yugoslavia the policy we followed with Tito has always been a mystery to M. Papandreou. He believes that here again for ideological as well as for racial reasons the Slav Communist movement will prevail. Greece alone remains, and if Greece is lost, Britain's interests are gravely threatened. It is therefore not merely an act of justice in return for the heavy sacrifices of Greece in the early stages of the war, but an act of high policy for Great Britain to give Greece every support in her power.

2. M. Papandreou went on to say that we could not disguise from ourselves the fact that British prestige had fallen in spite of our great victories in the west and in Italy, while that of Russia had risen in the

Balkans generally. Moreover, in our desire to attack the Germans we had roused and armed most dangerous Communist forces in Greece itself. He did not regard Communism as a political party in the ordinary sense. He regarded it as a revolutionary movement. For the moment, because this suited Moscow, EAM were serving the Government, but he knew that the moment that it was thought more advantageous, the order would be given to leave the Government and make as much trouble as possible. The same policy, he observed, was being followed by the Communist movement in Italy.

3. At this point M. Papandreou remarked that he thought our policy towards Italy was wise and far-seeing. He wished Italy and Greece to be on good terms. He thought we were wise to deprive Italy of her African colonies so that the southern shores of the Mediterranean could never again be a source of danger to our Imperial communications; but at the same time to give as much economic and material support as possible to Italy proper in order to avoid despair and revolution.

4. M. Papandreou regarded four main questions as being of immediate importance.

First, Bulgaria should be made to evacuate Greek territory. If it were necessary, as was alleged, for Bulgarian troops to act as a flank guard to the Russian army, such a question should be regulated by a military arrangement with the Greek Government. But in any case, since the Bulgarians were acting under the orders of Russian generals, every effort should be made to induce the Soviet Government to instruct the Russian High Command to clear the Bulgarians out of Thrace as a matter of principle. If this failed, the prestige of the Greek Government would be terribly, even disastrously, weakened.

Secondly, to land as large a number of British troops in Greece as possible. It was, however, necessary to land them before the total evacuation of Greece by the Germans in order to give greater reason for their presence. While the Germans were still in Salonika, for instance, there would be every reason to continue to bring in British troops. He realised the difficulties, but he was terribly disappointed at the number of troops which appeared to be available.

The third point was the immediate formation of a Greek National Army. He had already put up this request to the Middle East and he understood from General Wilson that he had put forward a specific plan for consideration in London. It was vital to have a National Army partly to play some part, however modest, in the war against Germany so long as it lasted, and partly to maintain internal order. It was only when a National Army was created that he could proceed to disarm the guerillas. So long as the guerillas remained armed they would be a permanent threat. He only asked for small arms and uniforms. He realised that artillery and heavy weapons would be impossible to supply.

Finally, his fourth point related to the need for a special effort to make Greek relief effective and striking. It was by the relief that he hoped most effectively to support the prestige of the Government.

5. After he had finished his discourse, which was based upon a written memorandum, I asked him a few questions. I explained to him that military strategy had for its purpose the ending of the war as soon as possible and that it must be judged on that and that alone. We must take a long-term view and we must not jump too hastily to conclusions. Our immediate purpose was the defeat of Germany and for that we relied upon close collaboration with our Russian ally. The peace of the world in the generation to come would depend upon effective co-operation between the Anglo-Saxon world and the Soviet Union, and although we should not be blind to dangers, we should also not be panicky. No one could tell the precise policy that Russia would follow nor what her internal condition would be after the war. This did not mean that I did not agree with him as to the importance of Greece from all the points of view that he had mentioned.

6. With regard to the specific question, I said that I thought he had been fortunate in having had a talk with Mr Eden the previous day on the Thracian problem. He agreed, but thought that Mr Eden had been a little too optimistic and had rather airily waved aside M. Papandreou's fears. At the same time he assured me that nothing could have given him more pleasure than the opportunity he had had of discussing the whole matter personally with Mr Churchill and Mr Eden. With regard to the question of British troops I said he knew the efforts we were making and the plans we had, and as for the provision of uniforms and arms for the Greek Regular Army, I would certainly do my best and I felt sure that the British Government would do everything possible to help. With regard to supplies, while the Greek Government was in Cairo it was outside my theatre, but since their move I had taken a personal interest in the matter and I felt that M. Papandreou should not listen to too pessimistic stories about the position. It was true that there were inevitable delays, but the provision for Greece was much more advanced than that for any other liberated country and on a more generous scale. I felt that the problem during the first few months would not be a shortage of supplies themselves but difficulties of transport and port restriction.

7. M. Papandreou then brought up the question of the King. He said that compared with the great historic issues which we had been discussing the question of monarchy was really less important. The great divisions were not as between republican and monarchist, but as between revolutionary and evolutionary. It would therefore be tragic to divide the moderate forces on what was really an obsolete debate. At the same time, the situation was very delicate. He had listened with considerable concern to Mr Churchill's observations. He was still more worried by the fact that this was the only Greek question on

which Mr Churchill had spoken to him. I replied that this was no doubt due to the fact that he had discussed the many broader questions with the Foreign Secretary. It was also no doubt because Mr Churchill was discharging what he regarded as a moral obligation. M. Papandreou said he quite understood this. He placed Mr Churchill above all living statesmen: he thought him one of the really great men of the world, and he realised that in his sense of personal loyalty to the King he was true to traditions of honour which he rightly thought so important. I observed that the King was at any rate intending to remain in England and I thought this was probably due to Mr Churchill's advice. The other side of that advice was his sense of obligation to put forward the cause of the King to the Greek Prime Minister. M. Papandreou said he understood this, and seemed after reflection not to resent it. However, there remained a practical difficulty which had got to be solved. When the Government got to Athens certain changes of Ministers would have to be confirmed; certain decrees would have to be signed. How was this to be done if the King was in England? At the same time, if the King were to come to Greece the Government would immediately collapse and EAM would seize power by revolution. All the careful work of months would be brought to nought. M. Papandreou then proceeded to say that he was working on a plan for a Regency to be held by three people. He thought that this Regency Commission might have as its President M. 'X' (eighty-five years old), the revered head of the Liberal Party,[6] and that the other two members might be M. 'Y' and M. 'Z' who were personal friends of the King and therefore would be regarded as trustees of his interests. M. Papandreou was going to work out this proposal and before putting it to the King he would discuss it with Mr Leeper and would be guided by his advice as to whether he should put it to the King now or some weeks after the Government's return to Athens. I said that I thought that after the Government had got established it would have a much stronger moral position. It would also be clearer what the country really thought. The technical problems due to the absence of the King could perhaps be solved for the first few weeks by consulting the King through the Greek Ambassador in London. Then the Regency plan could be put to the King after the Government was solidly established; and M. Papandreou should consult Mr Leeper as to whether His Majesty's Government would be prepared to recommend the King to accept the plan. M. Papandreou said that this course seemed to him sensible and he would pursue it.

8. At the end of the conversation, which lasted for one-and-a-half hours, M. Papandreou reverted to his sense of deep obligation to the British Government and in particular to Mr Churchill, and he also paid

[6] Themistocles Sophoulis (1861–1949) was Prime Minister of Greece, 1924, 1946 and 1947–9; he succeeded Eleutherios Venizelos as leader of the Liberal Party in 1935 and was imprisoned by the Germans in 1944.

a high tribute to the patient and unflagging assistance which he had received from Mr Leeper.

[Diary continues] Lunch (sandwich) in the office – a mass of paper to be got through.

3.30 p.m. General Nadoy – the Hungarian emissary who came out to try to make an armistice some ten days or more ago. I had to tell him that negotiations were now *en train* in Moscow and that his mission was now of no value. He will go to Berne and stay there. He is a charming old boy, and took the news quite well.

4 p.m. General Hughes. He told me that my fears had proved correct and that the Balkan supply programme of ships due to arrive in November had been cancelled. The reason given was that the supplies were not available, although shipping was forthcoming. (Next month there will be available supplies and no ships!) I agreed to send a 'high level' telegram to London, and repeat to Foreign Secretary in Moscow.

5.15 p.m. Saw S.A.C. A number of questions, including Albanian policy and the latest Greek developments.

Henry Hopkinson came to stay the night at Naples. He is on his way to London. He is contemplating resignation from the F.O. in order to stand for the House of Commons. We discussed this at length. I think it is rather a pity that all the men of energy and talent should want to leave the Foreign Service.

Tuesday, 10 October 1944

11 a.m. S.A.C.'s Political Meeting – a long but not very exciting agenda. Ambassador Leeper came to lunch – also Commodore (just promoted!) Stone of A.C.C.

The D-Day for operation 'Manna' is now definitely fixed for 14 October. This means that I shall embark on H.M.S. *Orion* on Friday, 13th.

I saw General Wilson about 6 p.m. and went through different points with him. I left him a note on the question of Aris (the most dangerous of the EAM/ELAS brigands, whom most of the more moderate EAM people both fear and detest). He agreed the general plan.

There is real difficulty in getting any more British troops. The Fourth Indian Division is now suggested – but there may be objections to this.

I had a talk with Stone after luncheon – he is pleased with being made a commodore, but very much annoyed with the U.S. Government for its treatment of the Commission generally. He is a Republican – but apart from that, he is shocked at the flagrant use of the Commission for political purposes by the President. The Economic Section, in particular, to the head of which the Americans have the nominations, has been shamefully treated.

I told Stone confidentially the plans for my own position which had been discussed between the President and the Prime Minister and told him also of the present state of the negotiations. He seemed quite pleased with the idea, especially as it would confirm him as Chief Commissioner – a position in which he has now been acting for four months (since General Mason-MacFarlane left).

Dinner in Naples. Henry Hopkinson and Nosworthy stayed the night, having failed to get off to England this morning. Much talk about Italy. Nosworthy thinks that the Communist party are bound to get control, but doubts whether they will keep it.

Wednesday, 11 October 1944

A quiet morning. Brigadier-General Spofford (G5) and Fred Reinhardt to luncheon.

S.A.C. wants to put the Fourth Indian Division into Greece. I do not feel quite sure how this will go with the Greeks and have telegraphed to Leeper (who is on his way to embark at Taranto) for his views.

There are said to be 30,000 Russian prisoners of war working for the Germans in northern Italy. These men want to desert to us, but want a guarantee that they will *not* be sent back to Russia. This is a delicate point, and we telegraphed to F.O. for their views. I fear that they will object, but it seems a pity not to get them over somehow.

3.30 p.m. Mr Harman (P.W.B., British). He seems a nice man and much more settled. The great P.W.B. organisation is in process of going through, involving the liquidation of INC. (General McChrystal), and everyone seems much happier.

We discussed future programmes, in view of the rapidly changing situation in the Balkans.

Thursday, 12 October 1944

3 p.m. General Hughes (A.M.L., Balkans). At his request I sent a strong telegram to London (repeated Moscow) protesting against the delay in sending the supplies which were expected from America. The ships which we were expecting for November have been cancelled – apparently owing to the 'non-availability' of supply. I understand that the chief need in Greece and the Balkans generally will be for clothing. Statisticians have worked out that if the citizens of the U.S.A. would accept a standard of clothing for themselves three-and-a-half times as good as that enjoyed by the British, the present capacity of America could in one year produce sufficient to reclothe the whole of Europe. But the slogan naturally is 'no rationing in a Presidential [election] year'.

5.30 p.m. Mr Marris (British) and Messrs Mitchell and Jackson (American) arrived from Washington *via* London. They are members of the C.C.A.C. (Combined Civil Affairs Committee) which is a subcommittee of the C.C.S. (Combined Chiefs of Staff). These are apparently charged with putting into effect the 'New Deal' for Italy.[7] But they seemed singularly vague as to just what they wanted to do or the machinery required to accomplish their purpose. Marris is a *very* clever man (formerly in Messrs Lazard) and has obviously a great knowledge of Washington politics and the extremely complicated internal wrangles between various American departments (especially the War Department and the State Department). These disputes are even more bitterly contested than those between our Ministries.

After a long conference, lasting till after seven, Marris came down with me to Naples – also Steel and Tony Rumbold.

Friday, 13 October 1944

A busy morning. The Yugoslav situation seems more hopeful. Tito has invited Subašić to come out and discuss the future with him. I do *not* believe that this means that Tito intends to admit the claims of the Royal Yugoslav Government. To me it seems more likely that he will succeed in suborning Subašić from his loyalty to the King.

At twelve o'clock I went in to see General Wilson to say goodbye, before embarking. The news from Greece seems encouraging so far.

Messrs Marris, Mitchell and Jackson came to luncheon at the Caserta villa. We arranged their general programme, and I hope that they will still be in Italy when I get back from Greece.

At 5 p.m. I embarked from the admiral's steps, near the Castel dell'Ovo. The admiral's launch was sent for me. Ralph Anstruther and Sergeant Leyland came with me. General Scobie (the general in charge of the expedition) and his M.A. [Military Assistant] Major Greene embarked at the same time. We were received with appropriate honours by the Captain of the *Orion* – Captain [J. P.] Gornall – and the admiral in charge of the flotilla, Admiral Mansfield.

I have been given the admiral's cabin, which is very comfortable, and seem to be treated with almost embarrassing deference.

A very pleasant dinner on board – Brigadier R. J. Springhall (Brigadier General Staff) and various other officers completed the party. The admiral's secretary ([Commander M. A.] McMullen) is an admirable and most helpful fellow.

We cannot sail till *one* minute after midnight, as today is not only a Friday but the thirteenth of the month.

[7] The 'New Deal' for Italy derived from Roosevelt and Churchill's Hyde Park Declaration of 26 September. This recognised that Italy had 'worked her way' in the twelve months since the military armistice, and shown her desire to take a place among the democratic countries of the United Nations. The Italian Government was therefore to be given greater responsibility; the Allied Control Commission would become the Allied Commission; the British and American High Commissioners would become full Ambassadors. The presidency of the Commission was to go to a civilian in place of the Supreme Allied Commander. U.N.R.R.A. would send medical aid and other essential supplies, and steps would be taken to restore the Italian economy.

Saturday, 14 October 1944

Sailed at 0001 hours – and then to bed.

A quiet and very restful day at sea – fortunately pretty smooth, freshening a little towards evening. I stayed in bed most of the morning. I have got *Our Mutual Friend* – a nice, long, friendly book, which should last me the voyage.

Sunday, 15 October 1944

A memorable and eventful day. We reached the 'rendezvous' – outside Poros Bay at 7.30 a.m. That part of our expedition which had sailed from Alexandria duly joined us. We had brought only with us the *Sirius* and one or two destroyers. We were joined by the cruisers *Aurora*, *Ajax* and *Black Prince*– as well as various destroyers, landing-ships and minesweepers.

A further convoy of landing-craft, merchantmen, 'gantry-ships' – together with the Greek battleship *Averoff* – are behind.

Altogether, in the first group are nearly forty ships; in the second other seventy or eighty.

We proceed at a slow rate – about eight knots – the minesweepers leading. Behind the minesweepers, we had the cruisers, *Aurora* immediately behind us. The admiral on the bridge in charge of the whole expedition has a great responsibility. The captain and a mass of other officers and petty officers all busy with their appropriate tasks – a heavy overcast sky, with occasional rain storms, but a calm sea. (The general and I are invited to the bridge, and it is indeed a fascinating experience.)

About 9 or 9.30 the first serious hitch. We have seen a number of mines going up in front of us as the sweepers touched them off. Then a sweeper is blown up (a British ship). We can see her through our glasses – she is all over to the starboard, but still afloat. A great scurrying of motor launches and craft of various kind to help her. There are a number of casualties – but we are not told how many.

About 10.30 a Greek minesweeper strikes a mine and sinks – then another British sweeper is damaged. By that time we have proceeded – at a slow but steady rate – to about opposite the northern tip of Aegina. (It is incidentally rather lucky for us that the commandos had managed to clear the German gunners out of Aegina a day or two ago. There were some very strong coastal batteries (at the southern and northern ends of the island) which would have caused us terrible damage as we passed by – or halted – embroiled in the problems of the minefield.)

With the difficulties in which the minesweepers were placed and the very formidable character of the minefield, the admiral then decided on his plan. We reversed and returned a few miles to a point opposite Poros harbour. Here we waited until the sweepers could get ahead and widen the channel. The half-sinking sweeper, which was first hit, passed us – towed by M.L.s [motor-launches] – and I think got safely into Poros harbour. Another also got to safe anchorage. But a small water-ship (the *Petrouchka*) struck a mine very near to us – just off our starboard bow – and went down like a stone. Twelve men were saved, the other ten or fifteen were drowned.

Meanwhile, a number of mines which had been cut from their moorings began to float down the line, shot at by a great variety of weapons. It was rather like trying to shoot rabbits in thick bracken. The mine is hard to see and hard to hit. Sometimes they are penetrated and thus flooded. Sometimes they are exploded. One was successfully exploded very near to us by a 'pom-pom' – an excellent shot, which was received with appropriate applause.

Altogether about twenty to thirty mines were dealt with up till 2 p.m. when the admiral decided to resume our progress.

At a slow speed we proceeded on our way. A few more mines were cut adrift or exploded (forty-five to fifty are claimed for the whole day) and finally the leading section of the flotilla was brought safely and successfully to anchorage in Phaleron Bay – about five miles from shore – thirty to forty ships in all. The weather was improving slightly – great dark clouds being shot with the light of the setting sun. *Orion* cast anchor about 4.30 or 5. It was dark by 5.30 and just after dark the last ship was safely brought through and anchored in the allotted position.

We (the amateurs) kept away from the bridge (except for short visits) during the greater part of the day, since we felt that the admiral had a sufficiently difficult day without being troubled by us. But McMullen (his secretary) kept us informed all the time and we could see well enough from the quarter-deck.

The second part of the flotilla was halted for the night in Poros Bay.

Altogether it was a thrilling experience – it really gave one an idea of the problems confronting a navy today, and the skill of all concerned. Fortunately we were not troubled with enemy aircraft. One only approached us (a Ju.88) and was promptly shot down by Spitfires who had got themselves into Megara airfield yesterday.

After we had anchored a conference was held. It was decided (in spite of the telegraphed protests from one of the Greek ministers in *Averoff*) to make no attempt to land that night but to wait for the morning. But some officers who had got in with the motor-boat parties and commandos yesterday came aboard and gave us the news, which seemed pretty satisfactory. One battalion of the airborne brigade was well established – the others will arrive at Megara tomorrow and march in from there.

Although the ELAS propaganda is very strong, the city is quiet and British troops rapturously received by the mass of the population.

Monday, 16 October 1944

A quiet day. Neither General Scobie nor I went ashore. I was up early and spent the morning on deck looking at the Acropolis and all the famous scenery – Lycabettus, Hymettus, Pentelicon – through field-glasses and watching the landing-craft starting to put the troops ashore.

Various reports came in as to the state of the harbours and town. In the inner harbour of the Piraeus the German demolitions are very severe. In other places, they are not so bad. The power station was saved by ELAS troops, who beat off the German attack upon it. So there is light and power. The Marathon dam is not destroyed. Explosive charges are known to have been put in – but are said to have been removed by a mixture of courage and bribery thoroughly worthy of Odysseus. If there is no delayed-action explosion that means that the water supply is safe.

The Swedish relief has clearly worked wonders. There are some ships here now, which will help for another two months, at least to keep the people fed.

M. Papandreou and the Government have telegraphed their wishes. There is to be a formal entry on Wednesday. The P.M. will drive from the Piraeus with General Scobie to the Acropolis and so on. Meanwhile, a number of points have come up on which I have been able to help Scobie. But *of course* I shall keep right away from any ceremonies and so will Leeper – when he lands. The Greek Government must not appear to be under our political influence – from the point of view either of their public or of ours!

There are some difficulties developing with ELAN[8] (the naval side of ELAS) and the port authorities (Royal Greek Navy) whom the former will not acknowledge. But I think it can be sorted out. The great thing for us is to stick to the letter and the spirit of the Caserta agreement and always refer every difficulty to the superior officers of the various organisations – all of which are parties to that treaty.

A lovely evening – after a nice bright sunny day. The setting sun on the Acropolis is a wonderful and thrilling sight.

There has been a good deal of telegraphing to and fro about General Wilson's visit. It is not a matter of great importance, but we feel that if he comes *immediately* after the state entry of the Greek Government tomorrow, it will be a bit of an anti-climax.

Tuesday, 17 October 1944

A quiet morning, reading and writing. Ralph and [Major] Greene have gone ashore. General Scobie and I will do so 'incognito' this afternoon. We expect the Greek Government and Leeper to arrive this morning in *Averoff*, which has gone back to Poros to meet the ship in

[8] *Ethnikòn Laikòn Apeleútherotikòn Naútikòn*, the National Popular Liberation Navy.

which they are coming from Taranto. They will tranship into the old Greek battleship and come through the swept channel. Let us hope the Greek admiral will stick to the narrow path!

Several mines went up in Heracles harbour yesterday, but no damage. The sweeping goes on all the time, against the delayed-action magnetic mines.

I ought to have explained about our lifebelts. During the passage of the minefield on Sunday, we were all served out with the neatest of lifebelts. These are of blue silk and are worn like a 'cummerbund'. When you actually fall in the sea and *not* before you have come up – the first time – you blow it up with the little tube. You also have an electric bulb (which you fix to the lapel of your coat) and a battery (which you put in your breast pocket). These are impervious to water and the red light shows for many hours. In this way you may be picked up at night.

I did not actually wear mine, as did everyone else. It was carried by my marine orderly – an excellent fellow who never left me night or day. I felt sorry for him, having to stand about all the time, awaiting my slightest desire or whim. But he told me reassuringly that he would otherwise have been doing something much worse. Moreover, I managed to get rid of him from time to time, during which intervals he consumed tea and rested.

At 2 p.m. General Scobie and I went ashore – incognito; we were taken in a fine motor-gunboat and landed at Port Heracles. There we were met by an open car – the one in which General Scobie and M. Papandreou are to make their processional entry tomorrow. We drove from the Piraeus to Athens, through crowded streets, filled with cheering crowds, like an election day at home. Whenever a British uniform appeared, great enthusiasm and applause. The first British troops to arrive were literally carried into Athens. Even today, the excitement was hardly less. I did my part and encouraged General Scobie to do the same, bowing, waving, blowing kisses, etc., from the open car.

We made a short tour of the town – went up to the Acropolis and saw all the great monuments – Parthenon, Erechtheion, Temple of Wingless Victory – also the Theatre of Dionysus. (The last time I was here was with Maud, Arbell [Mackintosh] and Maurice, when we 'cruised Hellenically'.)

We went back to the ship and did some telegrams, etc. General Wilson wanted to come tomorrow, but we have persuaded him to postpone his visit.

A lovely evening again.

(We were rather disturbed during the night (and last night) by light depth-charges – or bombs – which are thrown out of the ship at intervals. These are against swimmers who might swim out to stick a limpet mine on the ship!!)

Wednesday, 18 October 1944

M. Papandreou and the Greek Government would not have landed yesterday, even had it been possible. For Constantinople was captured by the Turks on a Tuesday and although this happened in 1453, the fatal day is not forgotten, and its dreadful consequences are still at the base of all the Balkan tragedy.

I left the *Orion* (attended by Ralph) at 7 a.m. I picked up Mr Leeper (from the *Prince David* – ex-Channel steamer, plying in happy days of peace between Dover and Calais or Newhaven and Dieppe). We left in great style in a motor-gunboat, and very soon got to the landing-stage at Port Heracles. Here we found a car, which had been arranged for us, and drove into Athens.

We went first to the Grand Hotel – where a fine suite of rooms had been prepared for me – sitting-room, bathroom, bedroom, etc., with a fine balcony overlooking the square in which the Royal Palace stands (Constitution Square I think it is called).

We then went to see the British Embassy. Here we found the Swiss Chargé d'Affaires who was in process of handing over the property, for which he had been responsible since 1940, to one of Leeper's staff. The old Greek Chancery servant appeared and in a very emotional scene greeted me as the British Ambassador, shook me warmly by the hand, and burst into tears! When it was explained about Leeper, he repeated the process. It was really rather moving and the old chap's devotion and loyalty were really genuine.

After going round the house – which is really a very beautiful one, having been built by Venizelos for his personal use and subsequently acquired by H.M.G., we returned to the hotel.

From the balcony we watched a remarkable scene – not to be forgotten and full of interest. It had its solemn and its comic aspects.

A vast crowd collected during the morning, partly of unorganised spectators and partly of organised processions. The latter were entirely EAM (or KKE Communist)[9] with representatives of ELAS (the Communist guerillas) who were allowed to take part in small numbers. These processions had quantities of banners and other symbols, and were obviously well organised, under a single control. They were quite orderly and very cheerful. The banners commonly bracketed the names of Stalin, Roosevelt and Churchill. The whole crowd, whether Communist or bourgeois, seemed very pro-Ally and particularly pro-British.

At last, after a great interval taken up by very good-humoured singing and cheering and counter-cheering, at about 12 noon or a little after, M. Papandreou appeared at the balcony of a house on the side of

[9] *Kommounistikòn Kómma Elládos*, the Communist Party of Greece.

the square immediately facing the palace. On either side of him, looking rather sheepish and uncomfortable, were General Scobie and Admiral Mansfield.

(The earlier part of the morning had been taken up with a drive through the town and attendance at a *Te Deum* in the Cathedral which we did not see or take part in.)

The Greek Prime Minister was well received and made a long and impassioned speech. The organised EAM bands (which together made up about half the crowd) interrupted, but not offensively, from time to time by chanting their choruses – 'E – A – M – we – want – no – king,' etc., etc. These did not seem to disturb M. Papandreou unduly, but clearly caused some annoyance to the quiet part of the assembly. P. obviously tried to raise a universal enthusiasm by his references to the Dodecanese, Northern Epirus and other territorial claims. But apart from this, we judged that his speech was effective. The EAM bands were kept in check and clearly had no desire to insult Papandreou or his Government. They were merely stating their own claims. And beneath the surface one felt that the *immediate* crisis was over. Had there been any longer delay between the departure of the Germans and the arrival of the Greek Government; or had the Government arrived without the disembarkation of substantial numbers of British troops and Air Force at the same time, I think EAM would have seized power. This *coup d'état* would perhaps have not been bloody, but it would have been successful. Baulked of this, and perhaps because the order from Moscow had been given, EAM seemed ready to accept the situation fairly good-humouredly. Nevertheless, I foresee a very difficult time ahead for Papandreou and his colleagues.

The speech lasted nearly an hour, and after it was over the crowd began gradually to disperse.

Later in the day, Generals Gammell (Chief of Staff), [Terence] Airey (G2 [Intelligence section at A.F.H.Q.]), McChrystal (P.R.O. and censorship), with Brigadier Davy (from Patras – who has been operating in the Peloponnese with Land Forces Adriatic Detachments), turned up. A considerable conference took place on the situation, followed by a dinner in the hotel given by General Scobie, to which Admiral Mansfield, Leeper and I were invited.

My only contribution to the situation was:

(*a*) Unless Papandreou deals *at once* with the *currency* situation there will be a most serious crisis and a collapse of the Government.

(*b*) Unless some way can be found to disarm ELAS forces (and all other guerilla forces) in the territories evacuated by the Germans and to start a Greek National Army into which the better guerilla elements should be incorporated, there will be a most dangerous situation leading inevitably to civil war.

(*c*) Unless *relief* supplies can be rapidly landed and backed up by a better delivery programme than we have any assurance of to date, we shall cause a great disappointment to the population which will react *against* the legitimate Government.

All these propositions were agreed, but it is a job to get any real action taken to carry them out, especially in London and Washington! (The War Office and Treasury have been particularly remiss on the currency question.)

The Two Princesses

During the course of the evening – between 6 p.m. and 7 p.m. I made two 'Royal' calls. I sent Ralph to fix the times, and make the arrangements.

The first was on Princess Nicholas of Greece (Princess Helena), the mother of the Duchess of Kent. Although I understand that this old lady is regarded by us with some suspicion (she is said to have had Germanophil tendencies) I thought it a proper courtesy, in case she might be in difficulties or wish to send a message to her daughter.

She certainly seemed to be in no material difficulties. She inhabited a large and comfortable palace; and an excellent tea (which I did not want at that hour) was prepared. She also had a radio set, which she informed me she had been allowed to keep during the occupation.

The Princess is a lady of fine presence; she must have been a beauty. The eyes, dark and lustrous, are remarkable. She reminded me of any Edwardian *grande dame*. Her conversation, though making the conventional references to the faults of the Germans, was more concerned with the dangers of revolution and Communism. EAM is of course anathema: 'It must be stopped at once. It is the only chance. I know. It must be stopped.' One cannot help a feeling of sympathy for people like the Princess. They are survivors of an age which two wars have destroyed for ever – a period, highly cultivated and civilised, of European history when international society was indeed an agreeable system for those who by birth, or talents formed an international governing class with common ties, interests, pleasures and traditions.

After half-an-hour's conversation, easily and gracefully guided by the Princess, I took my leave. She gave me a short message which I undertook to send to the Duchess of Kent.

My next call was on a lady of a very different type and period.

No doubt because of her English birth and unequivocal loyalties, Princess Andrew of Greece was living in humble, not to say somewhat squalid, conditions. Her brother, Lord Louis Mountbatten, has been sending a number of telegrams to General Wilson asking urgently for news of her. This was the real reason of my call.

She is a rather blowsy, lumpish and very *Hausfrau* type. It would be hard to imagine anything more different from Princess Helen's character. I should imagine that there were no – or only the most formal – relations between the two Princesses. Hence the contrast between the palace and the flat.

Princess Andrew is not intelligent – and seemed very nervous and clumsy. She stayed in Greece and has been obviously working hard and sincerely on relief, for children especially, with the Swedish Relief Scheme and the Swiss Red Cross. She made very little complaint, but when I pressed her to know if there was anything we could do for her, she admitted that she and her companion (an old lady-in-waiting who must, I think, have been the governess) needed food. They had enough bread; but they had no 'stores' of any kind – sugar, tea, coffee, rice, or any tinned foods. (These are now going to be given to her by the Army – and the officer whom I had sent to call on her yesterday had been very good and some stores had arrived today.)

Apparently the boy is in our Navy – a Lieutenant or Sub-Lieutenant – and is doing very well.[10] The Princess was hoping he might be in the Mediterranean; but he has gone to the Far East.

This was a more agreeable interview and a more straightforward one than the last. But I rather enjoyed Princess Helen. She has the character! And a survival has always a certain charm – like our dowagers, who live on memory, and whose ruthless and unquestioning faith in their own creed (however narrow and selfish it may seem now to us) has in it something that commands respect and even admiration.

Thursday, 19 October 1944

Left Athens (Kalamaki airfield) 9.30. After stopping at Bari to drop off Brigadier Davy, arrived Marcianise (Caserta) at 2 p.m., after a *very* bad trip indeed and a most dangerous landing. I thought the machine would turn over and so did those watching from the ground. However, it was all right.

4 p.m. Meeting of S.A.C.'s conference. Report on Greece, etc., etc. I think we are going to get 30,000 battledress (jacket, trousers, shirts, socks, boots, etc.) for the Greek National Army. We shall take them from theatre stocks and hope for replacements!

Friday, 20 October 1944

A dull day, but very busy reading a great accumulation of paper and writing a number of minutes. Lots of letters from home – excellent ones from Dorothy and Maurice.

Saturday, 21 October 1944

Hal Mack has turned up, which is great fun. He is to be the political head of the Austrian Control Commission and has come out to start planning. He will go back to London in a few days with the soldiers

[10] Her son Lieutenant Philip Mountbatten, R.N. (b. 1921), later Duke of Edinburgh.

whom he has picked. He will do the job admirably, as he gets on so well with everybody, especially the military. He brought many messages from my friends at home, especially from Harry Crookshank, whom he knows well.

11 a.m. Meeting about U.N.R.R.A. Mr Kirk, General Hughes, Sir William Matthews (British head of U.N.R.R.A. at Cairo), Offie and self. It is clear that U.N.R.R.A. are getting into a great mess about Yugoslavia and the agreements to be made. After some discussion, I undertook to draft a telegram for General Hughes to send. This I did and another to the F.O. If we try to call off the *military* agreement which is now in process of negotiation and is practically settled with Tito *and* Subašić, we shall do infinite harm.

12.30 p.m. Commander Southard (G5). He is an American economist and *very* good and intelligent. The Greek currency crisis is – as I expected – at its peak. The final stage of inflation has been reached, when the value of the drachma has practically – indeed completely – disappeared. This means that all the shops put up their shutters, and buying and selling stops, with consequent hardship, misery and despair.

The suggestion comes from Athens to send 200,000 gold sovereigns. But of course these will just go down the drain in a few days. Southard and I agreed absolutely on the remedy and prepared a note, which General Clark (C.A.O.) approved. Commander Southard will fly this to London tomorrow and try to get War Office, Treasury, and Bank of England approval to our scheme, which is to issue B.M.A. notes as a *new* currency (like the temporary *Rentenmark*)[11] until the fresh *Greek* printed currency can be introduced.

1.15 p.m. Hal Mack and Sir William Matthews to lunch. The latter is rather heavy and a rough diamond – but I think intelligent and tough.

After luncheon, I motored out to Pomigliano airfield, where Winston and the Moscow party (less Anthony Eden, who stayed in Cairo) finally arrived about 4.30 p.m. I drove Oliver Harvey back with me, as he is to stay in our villa.

8.30 p.m. Dinner at General Wilson's villa – a large and very enjoyable party. General Wilson, C.-in-C. Med., Field Marshal Sir Alan Brooke, General Alexander, General Ismay, Lord Moran, Air Marshal Slessor, etc. etc. I was put on Winston's right. He gave a most interesting account of the Moscow visit and was obviously pleased with the reception which had been given him. The Russians were more forthcoming than they had ever been before. The fact that Stalin dined at the British Embassy (which is absolutely without precedent) made a great impression. He also came to the airfield to see them off.

The *military* discussions went very well. The Russians disclosed their plans very much more freely and seemed very ready to work in

[11] A currency token issued in 1923 to curb German inflation.

with us. (Poor General Brocas Burrows, head of our Military Mission, has had to go, though. He gave a lecture to some officers and N.C.O.s in Cairo in which he said the Russians were 'little better than savages'. This somehow got back to them – probably through Mr Gallacher, M.P.[12] – and Brocas Burrows has left for West Africa![13])

The *political* discussions were – as usual – slow and tortuous. Molotov is a very hard bargainer, and both he and Vyshinsky pedantic and legalistic. Some progress was made with the Polish problems, and Winston talked very straight to the Polish P.M. when he saw him alone. The Poles *must* accept the Curzon Line, and then get what other concessions they can.

On Yugoslavia, the talks resulted in a really useful declaration and there now seems a good chance that Tito and Subašić will come to terms. (But the F.O. and Winston *must* abandon the King.) On the Control Commissions for Bulgaria, Roumania and Hungary there was a lot of very stiff argument and we got the worst of it. Greece was satisfactory.[14] Altogether, the results were *well* worth the visit, and P.M. seemed more hopeful about the future than I have ever known him.

The chief change that they noticed in Moscow is that now *everyone* is in uniform. Molotov, Vyshinsky and all the other civilians and diplomats are in smart tunics and gold epaulettes. The price level is *very* high (purposely so) for anything but absolute necessities. There is a great monetary inflation and the most curious and ingenious methods are devised to try to mop up purchasing power. (One of them is to open second-hand *bric-à-brac* shops in all the towns at which the peasants buy antiques and sham-antiques for fabulous sums.)

P.M. talked to me a good deal about his plans for internal problems. He seemed annoyed by the Tory opposition to the Town and Country Planning Bill. He is certainly *not* going to give up! He is full of ideas for the General Election – with or without the comrades!

He has now sent off the telegram to the President about my being appointed head of the Italian (Control) Commission. The law officers have given their opinion that I can – and must – have a special certificate.[15]

We left about 1.30 a.m. – not too bad – after a really delightful evening – all smiles and no grumpiness or rows!

Sunday, 22 October 1944

Our visitors always seem to come and go on Sundays, and I never get

[12] William Gallacher (1881–1965) was Communist M.P. for Fife West, 1935–50.

[13] To become G.O.C.-in-C., West Africa Command, 1944–5.

[14] Stalin had agreed that until the post-war peace conference, Greece should be predominantly a British responsibility.

[15] Otherwise I could have been deemed to hold 'an office of profit under the Crown' and been disqualified from being an M.P.

to church. Up at 7.30. Left villa at 8.30 and finally saw our visitors off at about 9.30 on Pomigliano aerodrome.

After they had gone, I had some talk with General Alex about some of our problems here. I am more and more convinced that if we have to fight another campaign in this theatre, there must be *drastic* changes. There is really no room for A.F.H.Q. and A.A.I. (Generals Wilson and Alexander) and there needs a *tighter* and more efficient control at the centre. I promised Alex to think over things and see him again. Alex is in a specially difficult position. He likes Jumbo Wilson and is very unwilling to take any action which might be construed as a personal intrigue against him. And yet he realises that things *must* be changed. So am I fond of Jumbo and admire him. But there it is. The matter must be treated objectively and a plan of reorganisation prepared *without regard to or mention of personalities*. And I suppose I shall have to do it and get into trouble with the C.I.G.S. and the P.M.

Drove back to Naples. Hal Mack and D. Marris (British Embassy and C.C.A.C., Washington) to luncheon. Marris also to dinner. He gave me full account of his meetings in Rome with the Allied Commission.

Monday, 23 October 1944

10.15 a.m. Meeting with Marris, Mitchell (U.S.), Kirk, etc.

It took Marris and Tony Rumbold most of the rest of the day to prepare the minutes.

4.45 p.m. Went to see General Wilson – Greece, Albania, Yugoslavia. M. Topalović has sent us (through Sir Noel Charles) a message from Mihailović. Poor Gammell fell into the trap, but it was all right. Imagine the fury in London if we were to undo the whole of the Stalin–Churchill agreement on Yugoslavia and wreck the Tito–Subašić discussions by General Wilson accepting overtures from Mihailović at this stage! However, as Kirk has got the same message we had better go through the motions of considering it by putting on the agenda for the Political Meeting tomorrow.

Tuesday, 24 October 1944

Broad turned up from Bari. We agreed what I was to say to Eden about Yugoslavia, and Broad's own position if a British diplomatic mission is soon able to go to Belgrade.

We also agreed about Albania, and how to treat Hoxha.[16] Hoxha has incidentally declared the National Liberation Front the Government of Albania.

After Broad, Hal Mack came in to talk about his Austrian plans. This took up most of the morning.

Then a nice little luncheon party at the Caserta villa – Mack, Broad,

[16] Enver Hoxha (b. 1908) directed Albanian resistance to Italian rule from 1939 and founded the Communist Party of Albania in 1941. He has ruled the country ever since.

John de Salis, Mrs John Hichens (the widow of poor John – Hermione [Ranfurly] had written to tell me she was here as an A.T.)[17] and the staff.

4 p.m. S.A.C.'s meeting. We managed to kill the Mihailović business all right, although the Americans rather hanker after him still. I also got a proleptic agreement to the new supply plan for Italy and the action which we are to take to force Washington's hand.

I raised – having read about it in some report – the *extraordinary* action of P.W.B. in *filming* the Caruso and Azzolini[18] trials. When a man is being tried for his life, it seems an odd thing to bring arc-lamps and cinema cameras into the courtroom. The Italian judge protested – but P.W.B. overruled him! S.A.C. gave orders that such a thing should *never* be done again.

After the meeting, discussed with Marris and Mitchell their Italian supply drafts. They seemed to me rather complicated and I shall try to redraft tomorrow.

Before going down to Naples, went round to Caserta villa to see Broad (who failed to get back to Bari by plane and is staying the night there). Settled the final draft of the Albanian telegram and the Yugoslav note for Secretary of State.

Henry Hopkinson (on his way back from England) to dinner. He brought a letter from Dorothy with news of Carol and the children. Hal Mack to dinner also.

Wednesday, 25 October 1944

Being very exhausted, I stayed in bed till 11 a.m. Then drove to Naples. General Vasiliev[19] (Bogomolov's successor on the Advisory Council) called. He had nothing to say.

Had sandwich luncheon in the office. I redrafted the Italian supply stuff for tomorrow's meeting in Rome. There was a good deal of reading matter to get through, so I stayed late and went to Villa Vittoria (at Caserta) for the night. It is really very uncomfortable!

Thursday, 26 October 1944

Left Marcianise at 9.30 a.m. – with Lieutenant-General G. Clark, Offie, Rumbold, Colonel Lewis Harris (G5), Colonel Goodbody (G4).

The landing-ground at Littorio was too bad to land, so we had to land at Ciampino and drive twenty-five minutes into Rome in a jeep and a command car (the sedans having gone to the wrong airfield).

However, we arrived in time for the meeting, which took place in Kirk's house – Palazzo Barberini. In these sumptuous surroundings

[17] Mary Hichens (b. 1894). Her husband W. L. Hichens (1874–1940), who was chairman of Cammell Laird & Co, 1910–40, was killed by a Luftwaffe bomb on Westminster.

[18] Vincenzo Azzolini, former director of the Bank of Italy, was accused of having consigned to the Germans the Bank's gold reserves.

[19] Lieutenant-General Alexander Philippovich Vasiliev had been Soviet Military Attaché in Algiers.

we discussed the sordid problems of Italian supply and the Presidential promises. Commodore Stone, Brigadier Lush, Mr Antolini (American Deputy Head of Economic Section) were present. After a very good and sensible discussion, *all* my plans and drafts were approved. Now for action in London and Washington!

After luncheon with Kirk, we got back by air to Caserta about 4.30. More papers at Caserta and a change of plan. Secretary of State has telegraphed for me to go to Athens tomorrow. I must do so, and shall get a lift in Slessor's B25. Let us hope for fine weather this time.

Got back to Naples villa about 7 p.m. to find the house in total darkness. However, the Italian electrician at last got things going. I retired to bed (with a light supper and some papers – including the diary – to finish) about 8 p.m. I have finished *Our Mutual Friend* and am short of a good novel at the moment, so I am reading *Troilus and Cressida*, in a volume of Shakespeare's tragedies which I have found.

Friday, 27 October 1944

Left Marcianise (Caserta) airfield at 10 a.m. in Air Marshal Slessor's plane. The air marshal, his P.A. (Wing-Commander [J. S.] Orme), Kit Steel and I were the passengers. The plane is a Mitchell (B25) and fitted with fairly comfortable seats. It has the great advantage of being fast, cruising at about 220 miles per hour.

The weather was very bad. We got across Italy and the open sea fairly well, but just west of the Gulf of Corinth we ran into a very nasty front.

First the pilot tried to get *underneath* it, and flew a few hundred feet above the sea. This was not possible, and we shot up to 11,000 feet in an attempt to get *over* it. Fortunately I had my fur 'flying-coat' and a rug – as it got very cold. We could not however get over it without going *very* high – and as we had no oxygen, this was abandoned.

Then we tried to go *round* it, down we skidded across the Peloponnese to the south.

At last we decided to try to go *through* it (and turn back to Araxos or Brindisi if we failed to find a gap near Athens). Fortunately, just as we were near, a gap did appear. We sighted Aegina through the clouds; and in a rapid and skilful descent the pilot landed us successfully at Kalamaki airfield (a few miles east of Athens) at about 1.30.

We (Kit Steel and I) drove to the Embassy, where we found a large party at luncheon. Ambassador and Mrs Leeper, Lord Moyne and Colonel Curzon, Anthony Eden, Bob Dixon, Guy Millard and the Embassy staff.

The general atmosphere is very hectic. It is clear – as was indeed clear to us all in Caserta when Greek affairs moved from Cairo – that (*a*) Greek financial position is quite desperate, (*b*) Allied supplies have been planned on a hopelessly inadequate scale. Anthony is now trying to get a move on. But as Leeper pathetically remarked from time to time, he has been warning the F.O. about all this for over a year. The War Office insisted on the Military Liaison to take charge of supplies, and these personnel are as inadequate to the task as the stores.

In this situation, great confusion and excitement reigned. A meeting of all those in the house, together with General Wilson, Admiral Cunningham, General Scobie, Brigadiers Smith-Dorrien, Eve and [Thomas] King (of Military Liaison – the Ministry of War Transport man) and anyone else who happened to be passing, was in almost continuous service during the afternoon, evening and night. During this time, encouraged and abetted by Mr Lloyd – the economist – and Sir Francis Rugman – financial expert – we all discussed with no little heat a large number of subjects with which we were very imperfectly acquainted. Denny Marris (of the Embassy, Washington, and C.C.A.C.) joined in the fun.

We despatched an enormous number of telegrams calling for cruisers, coffee, gold sovereigns, oil seeds, aeroplanes and various other commodities which were believed to be useful in a monetary crisis. We had interminable discussions about the state of the port and different estimates from a large number of Army and Navy officers of the tonnage which would be cleared. We broke into the late Ambassador's (Palairet) cellar and refreshed ourselves with his champagne. Finally, about 2 a.m., we retired to our fevered couches, conscious of our splendid efforts and each other's shortcomings.

Saturday, 28 October 1944

Lord Moyne left early. He is going to send us Commander Jackson, of the M.E. Supply Centre – an excellent man. We are expecting Sir David Waley (of the Treasury) from London.

At 9.30 I walked round to the King George Hotel where I found Denny Marris and his American colleague, Mitchell. We went over the Italian ground at some length. A message has just arrived that the President of the U.S. has agreed to the P.M.'s proposal for my appointment as Acting-President of Allied Commission for Italy. The news is not to be broken to the American public until *after* the election – 10 November. This is rather amusing.

I told Mitchell, who seemed pleased. He was most helpful in discussing the many and tortuous supply problems which lie ahead.

After getting mixed up in a procession, I got back to the Embassy about 11.30. Anthony Eden was getting up, and I had a good talk with him till luncheon on a number of points.

Apart from the new arrangements for Yugoslavia which will follow a successful Subašić–Tito agreement, a proposed invitation to Hoxha in Albania to send out delegates to discuss relief (which will give us contact with this so-called Government without too much commitment) and a general talk about the Italian political and supply problems, Greek affairs were the main preoccupation.

I had come to the conclusion – during the confused and disorderly scenes yesterday, which were reminiscent of Lord Beaverbrook in his most improvising mood but without his touch of genius – that we must really set up some orderly and workable system.

It was clear that the military needed expert assistance. But this should be in the form of advice, not executive action, which ought to be taken through the proper military channels. (The only alternative would be to abolish the military control, and substitute a civilian for a military relief system. But this could hardly be done without asking U.N.R.R.A. to come in at once. And this they are not ready to do. Moreover, the military relief system is necessary at the opening stages if the docks are to be repaired by engineers and other experts. It also provides the 'cover' under which a force of British troops occupies Athens and prevents ELAS from staging a *coup d'état*.)

I therefore prepared a plan by which a committee of advisers should be set up to help Scobie. Acting under their advice he would give his orders to the major-generals and brigadiers. And the necessary action for expediting supplies would be pressed on A.F.H.Q. and follow the proper channels, both as to requisitioning and shipping.

Anthony agreed to my proposals, and the committee will be set up at once, if Generals Wilson and Scobie agree also.

The committee will consist of (1) Steel (representing me, as Resident Minister). This involves placing Greece quite clearly in my sphere, and no longer balanced uncertainly between me and Lord Moyne. (2) A finance expert, Waley, when he arrives; meanwhile Lloyd. (3) A supply man, Jackson, who comes tomorrow.

We will telegraph to State Department, asking them to nominate similar experts. Meanwhile Leeper will ask MacVeagh (the American Ambassador) if he will nominate temporarily any American available to act either as a member of the team or as an observer.

After luncheon, I got hold of Generals Wilson and Scobie. They both welcomed the plan. It will, I feel sure, help Scobie enormously – if only by canalising the expert advice through a proper channel and protecting him from the unsolicited and generally contradictory exhortations and suggestions of highly placed personages, including generals, admirals, Secretaries of State, ministers, etc.

Leeper also accepted the scheme most generously, although it means superseding the Embassy to some extent during the emergency. But he realises that he can best help in other ways – particularly by his influence with Papandreou and the Greek Ministers.

Unfortunately, Ambassador MacVeagh was too timid to act without instructions.

I proposed to Anthony – and he accepted – that Harold Caccia should leave the Italian Commission (where he has served for over a year with great success) and be my representative on the Committee. Steel will act till he arrives. This will involve replacing Caccia by Henry

Hopkinson (now Deputy High Commissioner and Assistant to Noel Charles). Charles will resist, but neither he nor Henry Hopkinson have much to do, and Charles will have to give in about it.

Various consultations took up most of the afternoon and evening. But by dinner-time everything was arranged and all the necessary telegrams had been sent off.

Ambassador and Mrs MacVeagh, Mitchell and Marris came to dinner. This was at my suggestion (as regards Mitchell). Anthony was very polite to him and this will help me in Washington.

Sunday, 29 October 1944

General Wilson left early. He agreed to send a telegram which I had drafted for him to the C.C.S. on Italian supply. This resulted from our meeting in Rome last Thursday.

10 a.m. Jackson arrived from Cairo. He will be a tower of strength. He brought with him a food expert, called Murray.

Consultations of various kinds took up the morning. In the afternoon I drove out with Anthony to Daphni (where there is a charming little Byzantine church) and Eleusis. The ruins at Eleusis are very fine. It was a lovely day, and the drive round the bay of Salamis was perfect. The colouring of hills and sea was superb. It was fun seeing where Xerxes had sat to watch the battle.

All day we have waited for Waley. At last he arrived (about 8 p.m.) landing with the help of flares specially arranged.

Waley's coming was rather like that of Sir Omicron Pie. All these provincial practitioners are all very well. At last the great London specialist had come – a guinea a mile and a big fee as well. He is a splendid little man, obviously a strong character, with a charming, even boyish, smile and sense of fun. He listened patiently (at a consultation which took place after dinner), approved the remedies so far applied, thought an operation urgent, thought the patient would probably die but nevertheless there would be no trouble about the death certificate – and sent us all to bed a little deflated but much impressed.

(Actually, I think he purposely teased us a little, but very gently and subtly.)

Anthony was rather restless, but will now get away tomorrow.

Monday, 30 October 1944

Anthony, Bob Dixon, Marris, Guy Millard and I left for Rome at about 10.30. We travelled in two Hudsons, as there was a good deal of luggage. A wonderful trip as far as Bari. We flew low over the Corinth Canal and up the gulf – then past Corfu and the Ionian islands. But crossing the Apennines we ran into a very bad, and even dangerous storm. We had no wireless, for some reason, and therefore no warning. We tried to dodge the storm and finally succeeded in crossing the mountains much more to the south than the direct route, emerging at Salerno Bay. From there we flew up to Rome by sea which is of course much safer – and in spite of driving rain and a very low ceiling managed to land outside Rome without much difficulty, in spite of the airfield being more or less under water. We arrived about 3.30.

Marris and I stayed at the Grand Hotel – Anthony and his party at the Embassy.

At 5.30 conference at Embassy. Broad (from Bari) had turned up, so we started with Yugoslavia and Albania. Then, with Charles and Hopkinson, went on to Italy and the problem of Caccia and Hopkinson. This had not been settled by 7 p.m., when various people invited by Charles turned up to meet Anthony, viz., Stone, Lush, Brigadier Low, etc. Dinner followed. Bonomi (Prime Minister) and Carandini[20] (Ambassador-designate in London). Carandini is a good man, whom I had met before. His wife is nice and homely. She told me she was going to have a baby in March and asked my advice. I didn't see that I could do much about it and said so. She then explained, blushingly, that she was not thinking of an abortion but of the difficulty of finding a nursery in London and getting milk (all this at the top of her voice).

Tuesday, 31 October 1944

The staff problem is settled. Caccia is to go to Athens as my representative. Hopkinson is to take Harold Caccia's place on the Commission, at least temporarily and will take Halford (now Acting First Secretary to Charles) to help him. (Halford is a clever young man, whom I had originally in Algiers and then placed in Italy.) George Clutton from F.O. and Garnett (from Consulate at Naples) will come to help Charles.

But whom am I to get to help Steel when Rumbold returns? Perhaps a chap named Russell,[21] a temporary civil servant, now at Cairo.

9.30 a.m. Called to see Stone. He is passionately anxious to become a rear-admiral, I cannot imagine for what reason, and talks of little else. I don't know what I can do about it. It rests with the U.S. Senate, and I do not feel that my intervention would go down very well.

10 a.m. Saw Lush. There is trouble about General Wilson's telegram, which G5 (meaning Brigadier-General Spofford) object to. Also more stuff from C.C.S. about changing the character of the Commission and introducing civilians instead of soldiers. He will come down to Naples today.

11 a.m. Went to Embassy to see Anthony and say goodbye. After settling the 'staff' and other problems, left by car with Marris and Miss

[20] Count Nicolo Carandini (b. 1895) was appointed Italian Ambassador to London, as part of the New Deal, having been one of Bonomi's Ministers without portfolio, July–October 1944.

[21] Major Alaric Russell (b. 1912) was seconded to my staff from the King's Royal Rifle Corps.

Cameron (Caccia's secretary) for Naples. Harold Caccia followed in his beloved jeep.

Arrived Naples about 4.30 – rather a slow trip, but we lunched on the way. (I had had my car sent up from Naples to meet me in Rome.)

5.30 p.m. Meeting in my room at Caserta. Ambassador Kirk, Marris, Spofford, Offie, Lush, Rumbold. After nearly two hours' discussion *all* the decisions taken in Rome last Thursday (in Brigadier-General Spofford's unavoidable absence in France) were confirmed. General Wilson's telegram was also agreed, and will now be despatched subject to some verbal amendments.

We got down to Naples for dinner by 8.30. I had a mass of papers to get through which had accumulated during my absence. I finally finished them about 2.30 a.m.

November

Wednesday, 1 November 1944

9.30 a.m. Kirk at Caserta. Also Lush and Stone. Discussion on civilians in Allied Commission and arrangements for drafting a preliminary reply to C.C.S.

10.30 a.m. Saw General Wilson, bringing Caccia with me. Harold Caccia is, of course, an old friend. He was with Jumbo during the Greek campaign in 1940.

12 noon. Left by plane for Athens. General Wilson lent me his comfortable machine. Harold Caccia, his Miss Cameron, my Miss Campbell, Ralph Anstruther, Keith Egglestone and Lomax (my batman). We arrived about 3.30 after a splendid trip. We found that some, though not much, progress had been made. It is still hard to get a really accurate picture of the port capacity and supply position. There are really too many brigadiers. Jackson had unfortunately to return to Cairo after forty-eight hours. But he will come back to Athens tomorrow. Waley is finding the Greeks very difficult to handle. But he is patient and skilful. Lloyd has gone down with bronchitis.

Apart from the economic situation, the political situation has not improved. EAM/ELAS are still quiet, but they really dominate the country. The most essential thing, after supply and monetary stabilisation, is to disarm the guerillas of both sides, EDES and ELAS.

Thursday, 2 November 1944

Worked in my bedroom in the morning on various papers and telegrams. I am beginning to disentangle some salient points. Oil (the only fat available), whether olive or cotton seed, is the crucial thing. And what olive oil there is in the country is either hoarded or sold at fantastic black market prices or difficult to transport. We arranged to despatch a Greek party to Kalamata (in Peloponnese) and to Mytilene to try to get some oil. They will be armed with sovereigns, coffee and sugar to buy it with.

On the monetary side, the wage structure must be reformed. At present, all *basic* wages are the same – for dock labourers or Cabinet

Ministers – since at twenty million million drachmae to the pound sterling, they are worth only a farthing or a penny respectively. An additional wage is calculated every three days based on the cost of living. But this takes into account the black market price of unobtainable commodities and hence reaches astronomical and unusual figures.

12.30 p.m. Called to see General Scobie. I found him cheerful but rather baffled.

After luncheon, Mr and Mrs Leeper took me for a drive. We went through some lovely country out to the Marathon Dam. This, on which all the water of Athens depends, was fortunately not destroyed by the Germans. It is a great structure, built in 1927–9.

5 p.m. General Hughes came to see me. I want him to take command of the M.L. side instead of his present post as 'inspector'. Although he is not brilliant he is very agreeable. He gets on with everybody, soldiers and civilians. And this is half the battle in a show like this.

Went to General Scobie's office where I found General [George] Clark (C.A.O. from Caserta) and various other generals and colonels. We had a useful discussion and settled various points.

Waley talks of leaving tomorrow. At my suggestion, he has produced a three-page memorandum setting out the plan of monetary stabilisation and all the things (wages, supplies, budget equilibrium, etc.) which are necessary to make it a success. It also sets down certain technical needs (such as legal proclamations, availability of new notes, propaganda, etc.) which the Greeks, in their passion for theoretical argument, are apt to overlook. This 'child's guide to stabilisation' will be most useful to us all. He has been through it at a meeting with Svolos (Finance Minister, EAM representative) and Zolotas (Acting Governor of Bank of Greece). They seemed to approve *en principe*.

Friday, 3 November 1944

8.30 a.m. Mr [L. A.] Hugh-Jones (one of the financial experts on U.N.R.R.A., who knows Greece well having acted as Deputy Commissioner) to see me. He is going to assist Waley. The question as to whether we (Waley and I) can return to Italy is settled for us by the weather – and a good thing too, as we really must bring things to a head. I spent the morning in composing a note on the whole situation in the form of a minute to the P.M. (Winston). This deals both with the economic problems and the problem of order – that is the political problem, which hinges on disarmament.

I finished this – and the wonderful Miss Campbell had it all typed by 11.30. Generals Scobie and Clark called to see the Ambassador at 12 noon, so that I could get agreement of all three by luncheon. (I have not attended personally the meetings of the Economic and Supply Committee. I thought it best to leave them alone. It seems to have got started quite well. Kit Steel took Harold Caccia with him to this morning's meeting, and I know H.C. will get his teeth into things right away.)

Waley made some amendments and suggestions to my memorandum after luncheon, and by the evening I had complete and revised copies.

Waley and I agreed this morning to send a message to Papandreou to say that we should like a meeting with himself, Svolos and [Xenophon] Zolotas to reach some conclusion. This duly took place in Papandreou's flat at five o'clock (in preparation for it the supply experts worked all the afternoon to get us the most authoritative picture. This proved to be far *better* than I had expected or hoped).

Papandreou took the chair at my request. On his right [Angelos] Angelopoulos (Under-Secretary of Finance – a young professor), Zolotas, Svolos (at the other end of the little dining-room table and opposite P.). I was on P.'s left, with Waley next to me and on Svolos' right. Harold Caccia came with us and took a note.

The interview lasted two hours and was most friendly and interesting, though rather discursive. At a Cabinet meeting earlier in the day, all Waley's suggestions (contained in the memorandum which he had shown to the Greeks yesterday) were approved, including the reform of the wages structure. But before coming to a definite decision, the Greeks asked for further help from us in two directions. They wanted an increase in supply, to give a more varied diet, especially in oil. They also wanted a loan.

At the end of a good deal of discussion, we were able to provide a fairly, indeed a very satisfactory picture, on the first point. I opened the discussion in reply to Svolos and dealt only with supply. But I began (rather firmly) in saying I would not ask H.M.G. to give any further assistance unless it was quite clear that they would carry out all the things necessary, not only to make the stabilisation but to preserve it. The most important of these were, naturally, the alteration of the system of calculating wages and a real attempt to achieve budgetary equilibrium by other than purely inflationary means. That is, they must cut down expenditure on salaries etc., they must tax, and they must – as soon as possible – start saving and internal loans.

All this was accepted, and Papandreou was clearly grateful that I pressed Svolos (his Communist or EAM Finance Minister) so hard. I then described all the efforts, starting with Mr Eden's visit last week and his summons of myself to Athens, which we were making to accelerate supply and raise the *quantity* above the standard already planned by M.L. We were trying to buy cotton from Egypt to restart industry. We had brought in special 'money-earning' supplies like coffee by warship. We were trying to obtain cotton oil seeds from Turkey. These had been bought pre-emptively by U.K.C.C. and U.S.C.C. [United Kingdom and United States Commercial Corporations] some time ago and we would do our best to obtain early release and shipment. We were sending the parties to Mytilene and Kalamata with sovereigns to buy olive oil.

I told them, finally, that the date on which we expected supplies to be distributed on a higher scale to the population of Athens would be 15 November, reaching a peak about 25 November.

I left Waley to deal with the question of loan or financial support. He was *extremely* good – spoke excellent French and was at once firm and agreeable. He went over the budget figures and sounded his warnings solemnly, but in a friendly and singularly attractive way. I was deeply impressed by his performance. He gives such a sense of probity, both of intellect and character, as to be very striking.

Finally, it was agreed that we should recommend to H.M.G. that the new drachma and B.M.A. notes would be interchangeable (thus giving the public confidence in the new drachma). B.M.A. notes up to £3 million would be made available. The figure would be an agreement between Governments and *not* revealed. Nor would the B.M.A. be exportable and themselves convertible into English sterling. Nevertheless, the Greeks felt that local interchangeability would give confidence.

Finally, on the understanding that the B.M.A. notes would be available (if agreed by H.M.G.) and that we could make a *public* statement on the *supply* programme similar to that which I had made, the Greeks suggested Thursday, 9 November as the day for the issue of the new drachma. After further talk, this was postponed one day – to 10 November. After much hand-shaking, the meeting broke up.

We walked back to the Embassy. I wrote a telegram to F.O. describing what had happened and asking for further help. Greece owes H.M.G. £46 million from 1940. It is really a 'war debt'. If we could now publicly announce that we are writing off this claim, it would add enormously to public confidence, especially since the Greek Government has £45 million sterling balances in London. This is 'blocked'. But it would nevertheless be regarded as ample cover to the new note issue.

8.30 p.m. Drove out to General Scobie's house. A pleasant dinner. General Clark, Brigadier Springhall and sundry other officers.

Saturday, 4 November 1944

Up early. After breakfast, while the others went to their various meetings, I first drafted text of memorandum on the supply situation to be given by General Scobie, on behalf of General Wilson, to the Greek authorities. This to be in a form suitable for publication. After that, while waiting for the figures, which were to be studied further at a meeting at 9.30 of the Committee, I wrote up the diary to date.

At eleven Harold Caccia and Waley came back from the meeting. They brought two officers, Colonel Katzen and Colonel Stockton – the first South African and the second American. These officers seem *much* more competent than the brigadiers whom they serve and really talked sense. The figures are really encouraging, and Waley seemed much relieved. They will help him with his jigsaw puzzle of *revenue* and of *wages*.

12 noon. Dashed off to see E. M. H. Lloyd. He is in bed, with slight bronchitis.

12.30 p.m. Left Embassy. Kit Steel, Keith [Egglestone], Ralph, Miss Campbell, Lomax and I completed the party. Waley is to stay and see the stabilisation through, like Mr Britling. General Wilson's aeroplane awaited us and we took the air at 1 p.m. (Greek time) or 12 noon (Italian time).

When we were well away, and looking forward to luncheon, we found that those idiot boys – Keith and Ralph – who have nothing to do except enjoy themselves, had left behind at the Embassy the excellent picnic basket which kind Mrs Leeper had prepared. Ralph is always doing this. He is really infuriating. But I am much too weak and instead of making a fuss have accepted the situation philosophically.

We are now sailing along over the Adriatic at 11,500 feet very steadily. I have finished the diary and can conscientiously sleep or read. I do not really like being quite so high. One feels the lack of air somewhat.

Arrived Marcianise about 4 p.m. (Naples time). Drove to Caserta and plunged into various papers, etc.

Got down to Naples about 8.15 – bathed and dinner at 9. Steel, Tony Rumbold, John, Ralph, all at Naples villa.

Sunday, 5 November 1944

Sunday after Sunday seems to go by, and I am either travelling, attending conferences, or so exhausted that I cannot get to church.

Left Naples 9.30, having had a fairly long lie.

10.30 a.m. Saw Generals Wilson and Gammell to go over various Greek questions. Heard from them the latest Tito and Russian moves. Things certainly seem to be much improved by the Moscow conference. '*Pourvu que ça dure.*'

12 noon. Generals Spofford (G5, U.S.) and [Percy L.] Sadler (M.L., U.S.) together with General Hughes (British).

A terrible 'how-de-do' has been started among the Americans by our performances in Greece. It is of course a delicate matter. The Americans participate for relief and rehabilitation but *not* for politics or military operations. Naturally, it is not too easy to draw the line, and they are equally offended by being asked in or left out.

Unfortunately, Box Dixon wrote a record of all the extraordinary performances on the nights of 26 and 27 October and gave it to S.A.C. He gave it to C.A.O. (General G. Clark) who gave it to General Spofford (G5, American). *Hinc illae lacrimae!* The Americans were up in arms. Not only had we held meetings at the British Embassy with Secretary of State, Lord Moyne, General Wilson, Admiral Cunningham and myself. But we also gave (or thought we had given) orders contrary to the C.C.S. directive which governs the *prices* at which relief stores are to be sold. In our effort to get some revenue for the Greek Government, we had broken the laws of the Medes and Persians (Washington-made).

I managed to laugh it off somehow, chiefly by explaining to them how foolish and excitable I thought our behaviour had been and calling their attention to the setting up of the Committee to advise General Scobie and the invitation to Washington to nominate American members. (Mr H. Hill,[1] an American financial expert, is now sitting in informally.)

1.15–4 p.m. Went for a picnic with John and Tony. We walked back from the hill behind Caserta to the office – a good hour's walk and my first exercise for months. A lovely autumn day, without a cloud in the sky.

It looks as if (due to the Moscow Conference) a Subašić–Tito agreement will go through. The only danger is that Winston will get up in arms about the proposal to appoint three Regents. He has a most remarkable fondness for kings. But really it would be a terrible error to sabotage the very hopeful development because of King Peter. I do not believe there is any chance of this poor boy regaining his throne whatever we may do. And it is far more important to avoid civil war in Yugoslavia and strengthen British influence there. Both these things we have a good chance of doing at the present time.

Stayed at Villa Vittoria, Caserta. Colonel Maclean and Julian Amery to dinner.

Monday, 6 November 1944

A pretty busy day. Offie, Kirk, Spofford – on the American side of the house. Kirk was very pleasant and not quite so elusive as usual.

I saw General Wilson in the morning, having just heard of Brigadier Barker-Benfield's performance. He seems to have arranged with Scobie (and says he has General Wilson's approval) to spend 250,000 pounds or 50,000 gold sovereigns as a month's pay to ELAS troops (not as a final payment on demobilisation). Of course, all this is quite irregular. It came to my notice last night, and I at once sent a written protest to Wilson. Poor Jumbo – he agrees to everything with anybody. My job is really acting as a kind of long-stop, otherwise these generals let a terrible lot of balls go by to the boundary.

Jumbo was very reasonable – as always – and as things seem to be getting rather sticky in Greece, I agreed to return tomorrow (Tuesday)

[1] Henry A. Hill (1896–1959) was manager of the American Express Office, Athens, 1921–41, and U.S. economic adviser to the Military Liaison Mission in Greece, 1943–5.

instead of waiting till later. The general will kindly lend me his plane.

Colonel McLean[2] (from Albania) and Julian Amery came to luncheon – also Offie. Julian has not changed – he is still rather bumptious, but is clever and ambitious. I liked the young colonel. He has been both with Kupi[3] (the conservative whom we have abandoned) and N.L.F. (the Communists whom we now support). They came last night at my invitation, and today at Kit Steel's. But I was very glad to see them again, and Offie got on well with them.

2.30 p.m. Colonel [Robert H.] McDowell – a charming American professor dressed in uniform. Round the innocent head of this sweet old man has raged a tremendous storm. He has been the O.S.S. mission to Mihailović. The President agreed in August (with Winston) to withdraw him. But for various reasons – because he could not be found or because he could not find all this team or because he wanted to see Father Sava – he has only just come out. Broad (at Bari), Air Vice-Marshal Elliot and all the real Tito fans (urged on by Brigadier [Fitzroy] Maclean) have ascribed the most sinister causes to this episode. But I feel sure that the dear colonel was not a very mysterious or dangerous force. He likes the Serbs, got interested in talking to them, does not think much of Mihailović and still less of the old government party in Belgrade. The colonel professes (in peace-time) Balkan history in some provincial university of U.S. I asked him if he had read Rebecca West's book. He looked surprised and said no. I tried one or two earlier writers on Balkan affairs (Seton-Watson, Buxton, etc.) but drew a blank. (Perhaps after all he is professor of something quite different.) In any case the colonel seemed to have very sensible views. The Serb peasants, according to him, are not particularly loyal to the King and certainly have no liking for the Belgrade people. But they are quite well off, with good land, and being strong individualists will oppose Communism, collectivisation, etc., to the end. The farming co-operative movement they want to run themselves, for their own benefit. They are also good Christians, and will oppose atheism as well as Communism (the two are practically synonymous to them).

Since the colonel believes these opinions to be shared by eighty to ninety per cent of *all* the people of Yugoslavia, he feels the tragedy involved in the quite unnecessary civil war now being (he says) prepared by the extreme elements on both sides – the Communist fanatics round Tito and the Royalist Serb-dominated fanatics stirring up trouble round Mihailović.

I said that perhaps the Tito–Subašić agreement would be the beginning of more moderate policies but the colonel pointed out that

[2] Lieutenant-Colonel N. L. D. (Billy) McLean (b. 1918) was head of the first Military Mission to Albania, 1942 and 1943, and Conservative M.P. for Inverness, 1954–64.

[3] Abaz Kupi, leader of the supporters of the exiled King Zog.

Subašić has no real following, even in Croatia. He is no Maček.[4] I could not but agree.

3.15 p.m. General Hughes. I hope he will now go to Greece and take on a definite executive post there. He is not a brilliant man, but he has charm, character and goodness.

We got down late to Naples. Tony Rumbold leaves us on Wednesday, so I shall not see him again. I am very sorry. He has worked admirably and is a most delightful companion.

Major [E. B.] Hoare (conducting the band of the Grenadier Guards), Colonel Lewis Harris (G5) and some other officers to dinner.

Tuesday, 7 November 1944

Left Marcianise airfield at 8.30 a.m. in General Wilson's most comfortable Dakota. I took John Wyndham with me instead of Ralph this time, as I thought it would make a change for him. Miss Campbell with her typewriters (two) and Sergeant Leyland with the luggage made up the party.

A most lovely flight – the deep-blue colour of the sea, the wonderful pink of the Greek islands and mainland, the high Pindus mountains and the extraordinary luminous atmosphere which distinguishes Greece from any country that I know, made it a flight through a scene of continuous beauty.

Arrived at Tatoi at 12.30 (Greek time – 11.30 Naples time), a splendid journey, only three hours.

We got to the Embassy for luncheon, where we found the hospitable Mr and Mrs Leeper – also Waley (rather depressed) and Caccia (buoyant).

The usual Greek confusion reigns. No one stays 'put' for long. Waley gets them to agree to a scheme at the end of a long day's talk. But during the night they have lots of new and bright ideas, and so by the next morning he is back where he started.

Nor has any progress been made on the side of public order. The plans for the demobilisation of the guerillas are under discussion (considerably confused by Brigadier Barker-Benfield's efforts) but no real steps are taken. A new National Guard is to spring into being on 20 November (like Athena from the head of Zeus). No one has ordered uniform or equipment for these 10–20,000 men (I suppose they expect it to appear in the same way from General Wilson's tummy).

After some rather desultory discussions with Harold and Leeper, we arranged a meeting for 9.30 p.m. – Scobie, Brigadier Nicholson[5] and Waley to attend. This did not go very well. Everyone seemed tired and a little peevish. Even the charming and imperturbable Waley. However, it was decided that I should see Papandreou tomorrow and

[4] Dr Vladimir Maček, leader of the Croat Peasant Party since 1928 and a close associate of Subašić, joined the Yugoslav Government as Vice-Premier, 1939–41.

[5] Brigadier J. G. Nicholson (1906–79) was B.G.S. (Plans), A.F.H.Q., 1944–5.

present him with a *written* document on the financial problem with a series of *precise* and *clear* decisions which must be taken.

Wednesday, 8 November 1944

The visit to Papandreou duly took place at 12 noon, in the Ministry of Foreign Affairs. P. was accompanied by Svolos (Finance Minister, EAM, but moderate), Zolotas (Governor of Bank). Waley and I had Caccia with us. For the first three-quarters of an hour we had (quite unexpectedly and unarranged) an incursion of M. Sandström (?) and various members of the Swedish Red Cross Committee who have been distributing relief during the German occupation. The Swedes have really only acted as agents – the food itself having been the gift partly of the U.S. and partly of the Canadian Governments. These activities, admirable and essential as they have been during the last two years, now present a serious if paradoxical problem. Under the arrangements made, all their food is practically given away – the small cost to those who can afford it is to cover distribution costs. All those who say they are indigent obtain their supplies free. Now, since the Greek Government have no revenue, and since they must have a revenue if they are to function and survive, we want the Swedish Red Cross supplies, like the military supplies, to be given to the Greek Government rather than the Greek people. The Government will sell at prices related to wages (all this is an essential part of the stabilisation scheme) and only *give* away supplies to those who are proved to be without work or money. (I fancy the Swedish administration has been very lax even about this distinction, the more so as there was only the small charge for distribution which distinguished the terms to those employed from the free distribution to the rest.)

But, says M. Sandström, I cannot do this without:

(*a*) authority of my Government,

(*b*) approval of the donors – U.S. and Canadian Governments,

(*c*) German acceptance that to give these supplies to the Greek Government (as opposed to the Greek people) will not be regarded as a breach of neutrality!

This last point (*c*) produced much protestation from us all and was refuted in a long and incredibly subtle argument by M. Svolos, worthy of the Councils of the early Church.

Finally, we got an agreement that the Swedes would agree to moderate prices being charged; we would telegraph the U.S. and Canadian Governments for approval; we would give him (S.) a sort of personal indemnity; the Germans could be left to protest if they liked and still had any 'kick' in them.

After the Swedes withdrew, the discussion began on an excellent memorandum, prepared by Waley. I took them through it (in bad French) clause by clause. There was much talk about the new *wage* level. We did our best to persuade them that paper cannot be eaten –

only supplies of food. But Svolos realised that these are arguments which Waley and the Treasury do not always succeed in putting over the British wage-earner!

Finally, everything was agreed, including the question of convertibility of the new drachma into B.M.A. currency, and the meeting broke up about 2.30 p.m. After lunch, I sent off the appropriate telegrams on the results achieved.

At 5.30 there was a meeting of a purely technical kind to put the final touches to decrees, proclamations, etc. It was expected to be quite short. Actually, it lasted from 5.30 p.m. to 10.30 p.m. I did not (fortunately) have to go, but Waley returned – quite exhausted.

Today the drachma has slumped worse than ever and there is almost a panic. It is feared that the shops will not be open tomorrow.

At 11 p.m. M. Zolotas came round to the Embassy. It is clear that the best thing to do is to announce in tomorrow's papers the date and general character of the stabilisation scheme. M. Svolos agrees and is to see M. Papandreou. Much talk, telephoning, gesticulating, etc. About 12.30 all is arranged and we retire hopefully to bed.

Thursday, 9 November 1944

The papers carry the announcement – including a reference to me as ὁ ὑπουργός διά τήν Μεσογείάν, ὁ κύριος Μαχμιλαν (which we take to mean Ruler throughout the Mediterranean). Waley and co, are οἱ λοίποι Ἄγγλοι καί Αμερίκανοι εμπειρογνώμονες (the rest of the British and American experts). This is a distinct score for me.

The announcement gives the exchange rate – one new drachma for 50 (or is it 5?) million million! 600 new drachma to the £ sterling – and convertibility into B.M.A.

Let us hope it will restore confidence! At present everyone sells gold in the morning and drachmae in the evening! The loss may perhaps be outweighed in the public mind by a sense of relief and the hope of stability in the future. But this depends, we know, on the Government obtaining a revenue by sales of supplies, taxation and/or borrowing internally. Under present conditions, the last two are very difficult. If they are driven once more to print notes every week to pay their employees and fail to draw in equivalent notes by one of these methods, a fresh inflation will occur in a few months' time, leading to a fresh collapse.

9.45 a.m. Went to see Papandreou. He was alone. I congratulated him on the final decision on the financial question and then went on to discuss the demobilisation of the guerillas and public order generally. He was sensible and in good heart. But I am afraid his staff is poor. There is no follow up to any decision. I got rather a shock on being told that Brigadier Barker-Benfield had been to see M. Papandreou and had promised him 50,000 gold sovereigns from British sources to give to the soldiers of ELAS and EDES on demobilisation!

11.30 a.m. A great procession. The three battalions of the so-called 'Mountain Brigade' marched through the streets. These are troops who left Greece in 1941 – they fought at Alamein. They have recently been in the Eighth Army in Italy, and captured Rimini a few weeks ago. (They are also the Brigade in which the mutiny took place in Egypt earlier in the year!)

These troops are naturally regarded by EAM/ELAS as 'reactionary'. They should certainly be a source of strength to Papandreou. They disembarked last night at the Piraeus (from Italy) and the march-past today was an occasion for immense enthusiasm. This time the National Front showed up strong. The streets and walls were painted blue (not red). The banners and songs were PE–ANite not EAMite – and the crowd was clearly more bourgeois and less working-class than that which I had seen in the organised demonstrations of 18 October.

John and I watched the procession from General Scobie's H.Q. He and M. Papandreou took the salute at a point a little way down the street.

After luncheon Cresswell, John and I went for a walk. We climbed Lycabettus (in spite of the German mines) and got a lovely view.

6 p.m. Meeting in Ambassador's room. Leeper, Waley, Caccia and I (civilians), Generals Gammell, Scobie, Hughes, Brigadier Nicholson (military). Also Commander Jackson, of M.E.S.C. a great supply expert, came in for the second part of the discussion.

This was a *most* successful meeting – ranging from problems of military security, number of troops required, etc. (especially in the light of a telegram from the P.M.), to a consideration of the whole structure of M.L. and the reorganisation of method and personnel made necessary by the actual conditions found in Greece. Although this was delicate ground, it was very successful and a large measure of agreement was reached, involving definite decisions to be taken immediately.

The meeting broke up just after eight. Gammell (C. of S., A.F.H.Q.) stayed to dinner.

Friday, 10 November 1944

Stayed in bed till noon – I had a good deal of dictating to do and the diary to write.

I have finished *The Works of Man* (which I found here) by [Lisle] March Phillipps – a very good book which I remember reading when I was at Oxford. I have found a most delicious book called Stanley's *Eastern Church* (1862) by the then Regius Professor of Ecclesiastical History at Oxford. It is fascinating – and (rare pleasure) admirably printed!

This was a real day off. John, Waley, Cresswell and I went off in two cars for a picnic. Waley had to return earlier, and in any case we somehow got separated. We drove up to Tatoi (where the Royal property was being fairly heavily eaten into by people cutting down the trees and a general ELAS occupation). It is a lovely spot – and a fine warm day added to the pleasure. From there we drove across country (some extraordinary roads!) through lovely mountain scenery, till we at last debouched on the plain of Marathon. This is both a historic and a beautiful spot in the mountains, the plain filled with fine old olive trees, and the sea. We stood upon the mound that celebrates the heroes of that great fight and mused (with excellent wine and sandwiches left over from the picnic) upon the mutability of human affairs.

On the way back, we stopped at an inn, and (I am ashamed to say) took to more drinking (κρασί – very strong and resinous – and ouzo – pure alcohol tinctured with aniseed). A splendid guitarist played and sang Samian songs; a mustachioed bandit (or muleteer) danced Cretan dances, while the old shepherds and farm labourers drank and ate at our expense. (The food was excellent – cold cabbages, chipped potatoes, mutton, chicken etc.!)

Saturday, 11 November 1944

D-Day for stabilisation! Also, of course, Armistice Day.

At 10.30 there was a parade – Unknown Warrior's Tomb – flowers – etc. The parade was put on by the British and was a very typical affair, slow and inappropriate hymns (e.g. 'Now the day is ended' at 11 a.m.), and rather moderate-looking chaplains in surplices, but always redeemed by the marvellous appearance of the Archbishop of Athens,[6] who was good enough to come. This splendid figure – well over six foot – in black robes, with a black hood draped over his Orthodox hat, and a long black ebony cane with a silver top, intoned a blessing in a fine musical baritone, with appropriate hierarchical gestures, dignified, traditional and immensely impressive.

After the service, a march-past. The British armoured cars (tanks are on their way but have not yet arrived) were much cheered by the crowd which was obviously the Nationalist Front people. EAM/ELAS boycotted the service.

Apparently the money reform has made a good start. There certainly seemed to be no undue excitement.

At 1.30 we all went to an enormous luncheon party given by M. Papandreou and the Greek Government to 'Sir Waley' and me. Sir Waley made a very good reply to Papandreou's speech proposing his health. I had also to 'say a few words'.

The luncheon must have gone a long way to 'unstabilise' the currency! It was obviously based on black-market food.

Dined on H.M.S. *Orion* with my old friend Admiral Mansfield – a very delightful evening.

[6] Archbishop Damaskinos (1891–1949) was elected Archbishop in 1938, only for his election to be voided by the dictator Metaxas; he went into exile but returned in 1941.

Sunday, 12 November 1944

Left at about 10 a.m. (Athens time) in General Wilson's aeroplane. Sir David Waley came with me. We got to Marcianise about 1 p.m. (Naples time) and went to the villa for luncheon.

After luncheon worked at the office – the usual mass of paper to be gone through. No very serious crisis!

Motored to Naples and dined there with Sir David Waley, who stayed the night at the Villa Carradori.

Monday, 13 November 1944

Morning in bed – papers, telegrams, etc. Sandwich luncheon at Caserta office.

4 p.m. General Spofford. I am most anxious for him to come to Washington with me. He seems genuinely pleased at my appointment as President of the Allied Commission, and I think will co-operate. He has some very interesting ideas about reforms and improvements.

5 p.m. S.A.C. I gave him a general account of the position in Greece.

Tuesday, 14 November 1944

9.30 a.m. General Airey. One of the major problems about Greek currency is the continual influx of money without any corresponding (or sufficient corresponding) increase in things to be bought. The operations of S.O.E., Force A, M.I.9, and I.S.L.D.[7] immensely increase this problem. We fixed a meeting for 3 p.m. (Generals Gammell, Airey and Stawell) which was held and reached quite sensible decisions.

2.30 p.m. General Lewis (G4). I have asked him to co-operate with Brigadier-General Spofford (G5) in preparing a scheme for the new 'channel of communications' consequent upon my Italian appointment.

5–7 p.m. I gave a party for A.F.H.Q. – British and American – soldiers, sailors, airmen and civilians. For this purpose we borrowed one of the splendid reception rooms in the palace. Two fine Aubusson carpets added much to the beauty of the room. About 500–600 came. Benevento gin and local wine somehow produced adequate cocktails – food by the Army Catering Corps. The band of the Grenadier Guards (which was in the district, and which was the real point of the party) supplied musical entertainment. When General Wilson entered the Guardsmen played the Rifle Brigade (Ninety-fifth) march, which delighted him. I think the party was a very great success. All the credit was due to Ralph Anstruther, who arranged it all while I was in Greece.

[7] Force A was responsible for strategic and tactical deception of the enemy in the Middle East and Mediterranean. M.I.9 was a branch of Military Intelligence concerned with escape and evasion. I.S.L.D. (Inter-Service Liaison Department) was an overseas cover for the Secret Intelligence Service (otherwise known as M.I.6).

Dined in S.A.C.'s Naples house. General Laycock[8] was there, on his way east.

Wednesday, 15 November 1944

10 a.m. Political meeting. Nothing very controversial, except the usual P.W.B. row. Also the difficult problem of the province of Venezia Giulia (when we get there, which will be *after* the Yugoslav partisans!).

Immediately after the meeting, conference with S.A.C. (British only, since the American interest in Greece is supposed to be confined to relief, without responsibility for order!) Some rather disquieting information from secret sources and from General Scobie, about the EAM/ELAS intention to force the issue and try a *coup d'état*. It was agreed that we should send stern orders to Scobie – reporting to our P.M. Accordingly Chief of Staff (Gammell) undertook to prepare the military orders and disposition. I was to do the telegram to P.M.

We met again at 3 p.m. and agreed the texts. Left by car at 3.30 p.m. for Rome, where we arrived safely at about 7.30. I took Ralph and Miss Campbell with me. Steel is in hospital with jaundice – so John Wyndham is in charge and alone! Anthony Rumbold has gone home, no replacement has arrived, so I am back to the old staff with which I set out for Algiers on 1 January 1942 – John and Miss Campbell. (Ralph is new, but only acts as a sort of A.D.C.)

I found an *immense* and very pre-war party at the Embassy, where I am staying. Twenty-four or twenty-eight to dinner – Princess Colonna (widow of the Mayor of Rome during Fascist times), Duchessa di Sermoneta, etc., etc. All very odd, and more 'allied' than 'co-belligerent' – but I think on the whole right and certainly inevitable for anyone like Charles (who knew them all when he was here in 1940). In any case, they are but children – some naughty, rude, cruel and disagreeable children – others charming children – but all children.

Thursday, 16 November 1944

8 a.m. Miss Campbell came to the Embassy (she is staying in the hotel) for some dictating.

9 a.m. Went to Allied Commission building – a large, modern, Fascist erection, formerly the Ministry of Corporations, where I was received by Commodore Stone. He is obviously very pleased with his appointment [as Chief Commissioner]. He seemed also ready to co-operate completely with me.

After an hour with him, I had talks with various other officials and settled the rooms which I and my staff are to have. I have a nice room

[8] Major-General Robert Laycock (1907–68) was Chief of Combined Operations, 1943–7.

next to the Chief Commissioner and the Chief of Staff [of A.C.] (Brigadier Lush). This (and various telegrams, papers, etc.) took till luncheon.

3 p.m. John de Salis. I am going to try to get him to find me a house or flat in Rome.

4 p.m. A lot of telephoning from John Wyndham from Caserta. Kit Steel seems definitely to have got jaundice. I shall get Broad over from Bari to act in my absence. I have telegraphed to him to come on Tuesday.

5 p.m. Called on Sir D'Arcy Osborne. He will arrange an audience with the Pope for Saturday, if he can. I have never wished for this before (because I rather dislike this sort of rubber-necking). But D'Arcy seemed to think it would be proper in view of my new appointment.

5 p.m. An hour with Sir Noel Charles. I think I will be able to get his full co-operation. He is charming, but a slow thinker.

Motored out to Brigadier Lush. Dined with him. He returned from London yesterday and explained to me the general view of the future of A.C. held by the War Office. It seems they hanker after a complete separation between A.C. and A.M.G. (indirect and direct government). This would be a most reactionary step. We had this position before the famous meeting in the Cimbrone villa last February, when we abolished this fatal dualism. Bed by midnight.

Friday, 17 November 1944

8.30 a.m. Miss Campbell at the Embassy. I did some dictating in my little sitting-room (which is very comfortable and has a wood fire) before going to the A.C. office.

10 a.m. Commander [G. R.] Holdsworth and General Stawell about plans to maintain the Italian partisans in the north of Italy through the winter. The problem – as usual – with those Committees of National Liberation and partisan movements, is to prevent them from becoming purely revolutionary and political rather than military. One idea of this scheme is to link the Committee of National Liberation for Northern Italy [C.L.N.A.I.] (which operates in Milan) directly with the Italian Government.

11.30 a.m. Colonel Poletti – ex-governor of Sicily, Naples, etc., under A.M.G. – now in Rome under A.C. The colonel liked direct government, but finds indirect government much less attractive. It was grand to hear this bright Sicilian or Neapolitan-born American expressing his contempt for the Italian people generally. Poletti is a true American, a 'hundred-per-center'.

Lunched with Kirk at the Barberini palace. It really is a *most* beautiful house. Kirk agrees about the changes in the political section of the committee and was most helpful.

3.30 p.m. Meeting with General Wilson (in his suite at the Grand

Hotel) and General Stawell. The procedure about the partisans in north Italy was generally agreed, subject to A.A.I. (General Alexander). We are also working on a plan for their care after liberation, to try to avoid the situation which has been allowed to develop in Greece.

4 p.m. Talk with Brigadier Lush about the A.C. structure and functions and possible changes.

5 p.m. Italian Under-Secretary of State for Foreign Affairs, Marchese Visconti Venosta. Rather a dreary old boy, but with considerable shrewdness.

6.30 p.m. Went to Palazzo Chigi, to call on the Prime Minister, Bonomi. (I had met him only once before, during Winston's visit.) He received me in one of the large and cold rooms of the palace. We sat together over an oil stove, like two old labourers in a street over a brazier.

Bonomi talked quite sensibly. He spoke of his intention to make some changes in the Government; to introduce a sort of inner cabinet (he has twenty Ministers, which is necessary to please the various interests, but too many for serious work). He wants to keep the Socialists and Communists in the Government at all costs, in order that they may share the burden of responsibility during this difficult winter. All this was quite sensible, but not very thrilling. I asked him why he and his colleagues objected to Allied Control, and why they wrote violent articles in the newspapers attacking us. He was very apologetic, but I told him that I quite understood the political side. What of the realities? Did he want us to withdraw from Sicily and southern Italy? What changes did he really want? If he would write down on one sheet of paper the changes or concessions he would like and let me have it by Monday, I would see what I could do. But I warned him only to put down things he genuinely wanted to see happen. This paper should be private and personal between him and me; therefore there was no need to put down things simply 'for the record'. It should be truthfully what he thought would benefit Italy; not a political manifesto. He promised to do this. I think he is quite a good man, with some subtlety and shrewdness, and more firmness perhaps than he is generally credited with.

Dined at British Embassy. Count and Countess Carandini to dinner – no one else. He leaves for London on Monday, where he is to be Italian representative, with rank of Ambassador. He is a *very* nice fellow – quite one of the best of them I have seen. He is modest, conscious of the difficulty of his task, and will (I think) do well in London.

Saturday, 18 November 1944

At 10 a.m. (after doing about one hour's work at my office, chiefly on the mass of Greek telegrams now literally crowding the ether) I went to Sir D'Arcy Osborne's office. We went together in my car to the Vatican, the private audience having been fixed for 10.30.

I will not attempt to describe the Vatican, or the details of the ceremonious reception which I imagine is the time-honoured tradition. It was a lovely sunny day; the colour of the stone (which is one of the main beauties of Rome) was wonderfully played upon and brought out by the strong light.

I drove through various squares, round the east end of Saint Peter's, into a large cortile. Here (at the entrance) we were met by a very resplendent gentleman in a sort of court dress. Preceded by the Pope's bearers in a crimson uniform (designed by Michelangelo), six in all, and led by our chamberlain, we advanced ceremoniously through a series of rooms and corridors, in each of which were various guards of honour, in a variety of uniforms and drawn from different categories of attendants on His Holiness. (I forgot to say that we had gone up in the lift to the first floor.) Room after room, marble floor, gilt and crimson walls, gilt furniture, and the usual variety of *objets d'art* (gifts to different popes). Finally, we were met by a little Monsignore (in magenta) in the room next to the Pope's library.

Here there was a pause – we could see from the window the old stone roof of the Vatican, and the great sweep of the colonnade that leads to the Cathedral.

After some minutes' delay, an ecclesiastic came out of the Pope's room and I was ushered in, Sir D'Arcy Osborne preceding me. He bowed (the inclination of the head that we use to the King), and I did the same. Sir D'Arcy introduced me, and left the room.

The Pope, in white soutane, with no decorations except a beautiful jewelled cross and ring, was sitting at a desk. He rose to greet me; shook hands; and put me in a chair near to him.

The Pope is small; well made; with very beautiful hands. The head is small (or seems so, perhaps because the nose is large and aquiline). The little white cap and the white cassock and cape make the face seem more sallow than natural, and the hands very pink and well manicured. I remarked particularly the nails.

He began to talk in English, but I had been warned that he speaks more fluently in French, so we soon changed into that language. In spite of the considerable experience which I have now had of recording conversations, I find it difficult to give a very accurate account of what he (or I) said. Many subjects were touched upon – in a quick, bird-like quiver from one to another. I think I cannot have listened with great attention, since I was thinking of so many other things – the Pope's appearance, voice, gestures; the room; the occasion; the long history of the papacy, and the queer chance that brought me into the Vatican – a long way from St Martin's Street and further still from Arran!

The Pope seemed depressed about the world, as well he may be. He spoke of Communism, infidelity, misery. He lived much in Germany, knew England, and of course Italy was his home. For all he grieved, especially Italy torn by faction and ruined by the disasters of war. He spoke of our Prime Minister with respect, almost awe. Of our King, with affection. Of the loss to the Church of England by Archbishop Temple's premature death.[9] But I found it difficult to say much or remember what I said. I think I murmured encouraging little sentences, as to a child. The Pope went on, sadly, from one point to another. The chief impression on my mind all the time was the extraordinary contrasts – the vast edifice of outward magnificence and beauty – St Peter's – the Vatican – the unending suites of rooms, the rich furniture and vast store-house of wealth and overwhelming quantity of 'stuff' (what a sale it would make!). And then a sense of timelessness – time means nothing here. Centuries come and go, but this is like living in a sort of fourth dimension. And at the centre of it all, past the papal guards, and the noble guards, and the Monsignori and the bishops and the cardinals and all the show of ages – sits the little saintly man, rather worried, obviously quite selfless and holy – at once a pathetic and a tremendous figure.

He gave me a little medal – and a sort of unofficial blessing. Later he sent round a count something or other with another and better medal, and a message of great goodwill.

After the Pope, S.A.C. A meeting in his room at the Grand Hotel. I got Kirk to come. Against the experts of G4 and G5, I forced through an acceptance of General Scobie's proposal that we should guarantee extra rations to the Greeks – this is really a political weapon to help Papandreou. The pedantic supply officials were rather shocked – not at the quantities, which are negligible, but at the principle. They do not like acting contrary to the rules – especially Washington rules. But I say, what is a *Supreme* Commander for except to break rules?

S.A.C. and Kirk went out to lunch. So I stayed in his rooms, wrote the minutes of the meeting and the telegram to A.F.H.Q. and Scobie giving S.A.C.'s orders. (I find that this is the best way to get what one wants. 'The hand that writes the minutes rules the world.')

After this, General Gammell arrived, hot from Naples and full of new Yugoslavia problems. Tito has been behaving rather rudely to us. He had drafted a telegram to the P.M. which I rewrote. I then left for the airfield.

Left Littorio airfield (Rome) at 3 p.m. A good flight over the Apennines, now crowned with snow. Arrived Iesi about four (a Hudson) and drove to Ancona, where I found General Alexander's train in a siding.

A very delightful evening as usual with Alex – a lot of talk and gossip. I settled one or two questions very quickly with him, and then gave him a rough report on my world – the Mediterranean. He likes to

[9] William Temple (1881–1944), Archbishop of Canterbury, 1942–4, had died at the end of October.

see the telegrams and hear the news. It is a great pity that we are all so separated in different parts of Italy.

Sunday, 19 November 1944

Left Ancona about 9 a.m. Flew back to Rome. There was some delay at the airfield owing to uncertainty as to whether Rome was suitable for landing. Again, a wonderful trip. The sun, and the snow, and the sharp limestone peaks, and the valleys below – these made a fine picture.

Reached the Embassy about noon, where I found the Ambassador about to leave for a little golf.

After luncheon worked for a bit, then Ralph and I motored out to Tivoli (rather badly damaged) and the Villa d'Este. This is a melancholy sight. Bombs, neglect and time have played rather havoc with house, gardens and fountain.

5–7.30 p.m. Miss Campbell came to my room at the Embassy. We got through quite a lot.

7.30 p.m. Went to a party at Ambassador Kirk's (at the Barberini) to meet an American, Ambassador W. S. Culbertson. Rather a dreary old man, on some vague mission here.

Dinner at Embassy. Brigadier Lush came at ten, and we had an hour going over the agenda for tomorrow.

Monday, 20 November 1944

Some more Greek telegrams have arrived. London wants me to prepare text of a statement if we have to intervene. I suggested this some days back in my telegram to P.M. – but I thought (with all their resources) they might have done it themselves!

So Miss Campbell arrived at 8 a.m. and we got it all dictated and typed. And telegraphed from the Embassy before going to the Allied Commission buildings.

9 a.m. Colonel Hancock[10] and other visitors till 11 a.m., when we had a full meeting. Chief Commissioner Stone, Chief of Staff (Lush), Upjohn, K.C. (Administrative or Civil Affairs Section) (very good), Antolini (American – economics), Grafftey-Smith (Finance), Generals Lewis and Spofford from Naples (A.F.H.Q.), Henry Hopkinson and Schott (U.S. Embassy). A very good meeting, covering a wide field. We went steadily on (with a short luncheon interval) till about 6.30 p.m. I have collected an immense folder of statistics and facts. I have now to digest them.

7 p.m. Count Galeazzi (from the Vatican) came with my better medal.

7.30 p.m. Nosworthy (Commercial Counsellor) and Hopkinson. (I had by now retired to bed.) Sandwiches and whisky.

[10] Deputy to Colonel Poletti.

9 p.m. Miss Campbell – dictated till
10 p.m. Brigadier Lush.
11 p.m. Lights out.

Tuesday, 21 November 1944

Left Ciampino airfield (with Ralph and Miss Campbell, also General Lewis) in a Mitchell. A very fast flight – I was in my office at Caserta by ten o'clock.

Papers, etc., all the morning. I went to see General Wilson at about 12.30. Statement on Greece, further message to P.M., etc.

Since Steel is laid up, I am getting Broad over from Bari to act in my absence. I have also recruited one [C. N. F.] Odgers (a major in the Rifle Brigade, who comes of a family of lawyers and wants to go into the F.O.).

Wednesday, 22 November 1944

Left Marcianise airfield (Caserta) at 8 a.m. in a Dakota. The party consisted of Major Talbot (of the Allied Commission), John Wyndham, Ralph Anstruther, Colonel Bastion, Secretary-General Staff A.F.H.Q. (lent to me for the trip) and Miss Campbell.

The pilot and crew seemed rather inexperienced and we were not surprised when we came down at Marseilles to ask for petrol and the way. The former was not forthcoming – at least not under two hours – and the news about the latter seemed far from reassuring. However we started off again about 1 p.m. and made for Paris. The weather got worse and worse – almost impenetrable fog, and at Dijon the officer in charge decided to give it up. We made a good landing, but our position was not very encouraging. Happily, Eddy Bastion proved a tower of strength, and by extraordinary exertions succeeded in producing from the American general in command of the district two motor cars and one truck – into which our luggage and ourselves were packed. We left about 4 p.m. in pouring rain, which continued steadily until we reached Paris at about 1 a.m. on the morning of

Thursday, 23 November 1944

Our guardian angel (in the shape of Colonel Bastion) arranged our accommodation by telephone from Dijon. We are all in an excellent hotel, Hôtel Raphaël, Avenue Kléber. This was obviously a very rich and respectable sort of Brown's – largely residential. It is now reserved for American generals, and therefore has hot water.

I was very tired with the long drive. At about 10 a.m. I got up and went to see Duff Cooper at the British Embassy. I found him in capital form, much enjoying the 'Empire' splendour of the apartments, as well as his great diplomatic success. It is quite clear that Duff has now really found (or returned) to his proper profession. But he has returned immensely strengthened and developed by his experience in politics.

At 12 noon I drove out to Versailles, to the H.Q. of S.H.A.E.F. There I found my old friend General Bedell Smith who is still Chief of Staff to General Eisenhower. He took me off to lunch alone with him in a charming little house which he has taken in the woods between Versailles and St Cloud.

Although the latter stages of the battle have not come up to their more optimistic expectations, it is obvious that S.H.A.E.F. are by no means reconciled yet to the war lasting all through 1945. Bedell still feels that the Germans may burn themselves up with constant counter-attacks, if we can keep up the pressure. But I am not sure whether this policy of attacking over so wide a front is going to prove successful. It is certainly not the 'Monty' method.

After luncheon (there still being no chance of flying to England today – the weather awful) I returned to the hotel and went to bed. Here I worked with Miss Campbell until nearly midnight. We produced together a long paper (about twenty to thirty pages) which embodied *all* my recommendations for Italian reforms. This delay has really helped me. There was no chance of getting this written *before* leaving and it would be difficult to settle down to write it *after* arrival.

My paper made the following recommendations:

(1) That the change of name from Allied Control Commission to Allied Commission should be given real meaning: the Commission should function as a mission of experts offering advice, except to the extent that the Allied military authorities might require to control specific functions or to take over particular properties.

(2) That we should stress that for military reasons (a) *the amount of Allied help would depend on how far the Italians made an effort to help themselves, and* (b) *it was essential that law and order be maintained.*

(3) That the Political Section should be abolished, since it was a left-over from the days when the King and Marshal Badoglio were the best Italy had to offer as a government.

(4) That we should formally allow communications between the Italian and other Governments, and that we should relinquish control over Italian legislation and (with certain military exceptions) Italian appointments on Italian territory.

(5) That the so-called Liaison Officers should be withdrawn from the Prefects' departments, where they were in fact discreetly exercising authority.

My paper concluded:

It will be seen from the foregoing that the task of those who have to plan for the needs of the Italian people is no easy one. It reminds one of those ingenious puzzles that torture young or old who fall beneath their spell, where it is necessary to entice four mercury balls in a small cardboard box to fall into their respective or appropriate holes. Two may easily be done at once, three often, but the whole four present a formidable test of patience and determination. In this case the four balls are availability of supply, finance, shipping and port acceptability. It has seldom been possible to obtain clearance on all these at once, and yet without some miracle of concurrent agreement, reasonable planning for the future becomes impossible.

It may also be urged that there is no reason to worry ourselves too much about the unhappy position in which the Italians find themselves. Their disasters are their own fault. But this policy, brutal and cynical, would at least have been practicable had it not been for the recent declarations formally made on behalf of the two Allied Governments. To turn now from the path of generosity there marked out is unthinkable. In addition, this more generous mood seems to me greatly in the interests of the United Kingdom, the people of the British Empire, and the world in general. Whatever may be the post-war policy towards Germany, we have accepted Italy into a position different from that of a beaten enemy, we have invented and, to some extent, benefited by the doctrine of co-belligerency, and, from the larger aspect, prosperity like peace is indivisible.

The problems that face Italy are serious enough. When we reach the north we shall find large populations as in Turin and Milan. It will test all our efforts to keep them alive. They will be the first large urban populations in our care situated inland and not upon the seaboard. Even to bring them food without railways or trucks will present a formidable problem to Allied Military Government. At present, slaves although they may be of German occupation, the factories are running and the people are largely employed. When they are 'liberated', the power will probably be destroyed, the factories largely dismantled, the machine-tools wrecked or taken to Germany, and the raw materials not available. It will need all the patience, courage and devotion that British and American administrators can give if we are to preserve Italy from total collapse to anarchy, revolution and despair. To fail to make the effort because of our grievances against Italy, however justified, would be *propter vitam vitas perdere causae* – to have won the war and lost the peace.

Friday, 24 November 1944

Left Paris at last and arrived Northolt about noon. Drove to Cabinet Offices, where I deposited my luggage, and then to Claridge's, where I found Dorothy, Sarah, Debo Cavendish.[11] It was delightful to be home after so long a delay.

After luncheon, went to Cabinet Office and made a few arrangements. But (perhaps sign of approaching peace) it is clear that I cannot do any work in London on Saturday or Sunday.

[11] Deborah Cavendish, Marchioness of Hartington (b. 1920), later Duchess of Devonshire.

Motored to Birch Grove – arriving for late dinner (Dorothy and Sarah went by train). Talked to Carol on the telephone.

Saturday, 25 November 1944

A very lovely winter day. Dorothy had arranged a shoot. We did Wheeler's, Brigham's and Hopgarden Shaw before lunch. After lunch, Stripes, Round Wood, and then Buttocks Bank up into Smalls and Smalls Wood back. The two drives after lunch were very good. We got sixty-five pheasants and a woodcock or two. I thoroughly enjoyed it, and so did Sarah. Catherine also turned up, and Carol.

Mr Witherington, Ronald Hardy, Rolenden and the usual local guns.

Went down to dine with Carol at her cottage and saw her lovely little baby. Carol, Nanny West and Gertrude produced a wonderful dinner. It was very sad that Julian [Faber] could not get leave.

Sunday, 26 November 1944

Church at Horsted Keynes – Carol walked up from her cottage. After church, *all* to lunch at Pooks, including the new granddaughter.

Rain again in the afternoon, but we pottered about happily enough.

Monday, 27 November 1944

At last my work can begin. General Wilson (who has been appointed to succeed Field Marshal Dill[12] in Washington) has arrived from Caserta and came in to see me in my room at Great George Street. I (of course) am delighted that the plan which I suggested to Anthony Eden has come off. And I think that 'Jumbo' is really rather pleased to hand over the Mediterranean command. He is going to be made a Field Marshal when he arrives in Washington – so that will help. Of course it will be delightful for me to have Alexander,[13] and I am overjoyed at his Field Marshal rank. Nevertheless, General Wilson has been a splendid man to work with – a loyal and honourable friend and a most staunch supporter. His native shrewdness has stood him in good stead and he has managed the Americans very successfully.

Lunch with Daniel [Macmillan] at The Beefsteak and had a talk with him afterwards on some business matters.

3.15 p.m. Really started work. An informal meeting with Sir Orme Sargent (and his boys) from the Foreign Office and Sir Frederick Bovenschen (and his boys) from the War Office. We started on my Italian proposals. I had circulated the long paper on Saturday (John arranged all this while I was shooting!) to all departments concerned, together with a short (one page) summary of the recommendations. We went through the *political* and *administrative* today, reserving *supply* and *finance* for another meeting.

[12] Dill had died on 4 November.

[13] Alexander was appointed Supreme Allied Commander, Mediterranean Theatre (SACMED).

We also dealt with other points affecting W.O. and F.O. in Greece, at A.F.H.Q., etc., most of which arose from Bovenschen's meticulous – not to say pedantic – care for constitutional procedure.

Tuesday, 28 November 1944

We are still only just getting under way. The only thing to do is to *avoid* Ministers (especially the *Prime Minister*) at all costs, until I have cleared my proposals at the *departmental level*. Meanwhile the situation in Italy is getting rather acute. The *Sforza* business has blown up in my absence and been badly handled. Poor old Charles will take the Prime Minister's instructions *au pied de la lettre* and I fear that the F.O. let these telegrams go out without the courage to control them.[14]

2.45 p.m. Saw John Murray[15] (at Albemarle Street) who is Treasurer of the St George's Conservative Association. Duff Cooper (in resigning – or rather announcing his intention not to stand again) suggested my name. Jack Murray was as pleasant and as deaf as ever. He wondered whether I would be 'true blue' enough for some of them. In any case, I have made it quite clear that I am not *asking* for anything. If they make me an offer, I will consider it.

4–6 p.m. With Sir Orme Sargent at the F.O. We went through my Italian proposals again – and then a large number of other matters. Really the P.M. should *not* have interfered so heavy-handedly about Sforza.

8 p.m. Dinner at 10 Downing Street – the eve of a new session. All Ministers in the Commons – an immense company. Winston in excellent form. The King's Speech was read before dinner (in accordance with custom) by the P.M. After dinner, Winston proposed the health of the Labour and Liberal Ministers in the Coalition, to which Bevin made a very good reply. The whole thing was rather sentimental, like a party of undergraduates at the end of their last university term, pledging themselves to friendship but knowing that their ways in life will inevitably part.

Wednesday, 29 November 1944

A great day of meetings and papers, leading up to the preparation of an agreed paper (if I can get it) for the Cabinet. I saw today Edward Bridges, Denny Marris (of C.C.A.C.), and two hours of Bovenschen. There was also in the morning a meeting of *Supply* and *Treasury* officials, similar to those already held with the Foreign Office and War Office chaps.

Dined with Daniel and Betty.

[14] Bonomi resigned on 26 November after weeks of disharmony in his Coalition Government. Two days later a new ministry was formed with Count Sforza as Foreign Minister. Charles duly told the new Government that this appointment was not acceptable.

[15] Sir John Murray (1884–1967), head of the publishing house of John Murray in Albemarle Street.

Thursday, 30 November 1944

Another long day of conferences. At 12.30 I went (with Colonel Bastion) to the American Embassy to see Winant, the U.S. Ambassador. He was friendly but inarticulate – as usual. His chief interest was to learn my lessons from the Control Commission in Italy for application in Germany.

In the day, I saw Moucher Devonshire, Sir Edward Grigg (lately appointed to succeed Lord Moyne in Cairo),[16] and also had a conference on propaganda in Italy with Sargent, Bruce Lockhart (P.W.E.) and Cyril Radcliffe[17] (M. of I.). There was general agreement to my proposed scheme.

Bob Murphy came to dine with me at the Turf. I took him afterwards to Pratt's where there was a large and mixed company. He seemed to enjoy it very much.

[16] Sir Edward Grigg (1879–1955), later 1st Baron Altrincham, was Minister Resident in the Middle East, 1944–5. Lord Moyne had been assassinated on 6 November 1944 by the Stern Gang.

[17] Cyril Radcliffe (1899–1977) was Director-General, Ministry of Information, 1941–5, and a Lord of Appeal in Ordinary, 1949–64.

December

Friday, 1 December 1944

10.30 a.m. Called at War Office to see P. J. Grigg. After a good talk I got him round to quite a sensible view. It is a pity he is so very rude and quarrelsome and hates the Foreign Office, the Americans and so many other people and institutions. For he is quick, intelligent, able and patriotic.

11.30 a.m. Meeting with Supply boys of Ministry of Production, etc., on *Greek* needs. Tommy Brand, Playfair (Treasury), etc.[1]

3 p.m. Hal Mack, imperturbable as ever.

I went to the House of Commons.[2] The Greek situation is not good.[3]

Saturday, 2 December 1944

Motored early to Birch Grove and had a day's shooting with the syndicate at Danehurst. A poor bag, but a nice day in the open. Admiral Beamish and Mrs B to dinner.

Sunday, 3 December 1944

A nice day at home. Carol and the baby came up to luncheon. Carol seemed well in herself and very happy. But she is rather white and finds feeding the baby rather a strain. Nanny West is very proud and happy.

[1] Thomas Brand (1900–65), later 4th Viscount Hampden, was chairman of the Supplies for Liberated Areas (Official) Committee, 1944–5. Edward Playfair (b. 1909) was then an Assistant Secretary at the Treasury.

[2] Eden told the House that Count Sforza had worked against the Bonomi Government and therefore his record 'is not one that gives us confidence'.

[3] The latest Greek crisis involved the organisation of the Greek Army. The EAM ministers drafted a decree under which the new National Army would consist half of regular forces: the Mountain Brigade, soldiers who had remained loyal after the Alexandria mutiny and had fought at Alamein and Rimini; the Sacred Battalion of Army officers; and an EDES unit. The whole of the other half was to consist of an ELAS Brigade. All guerilla forces were to be disbanded by 10 December. The provincial Gendarmerie was to be reorganised as a National Guard. The National Militia, an unofficial police force, was supposed already to have been disbanded.

But on 29 November, when Papandreou announced the terms of the decree and said that he expected it to be signed that day, the EAM ministers went back on their word, refused to sign, and insisted on the Mountain Brigade and the Sacred Battalion being disbanded. Papandreou naturally refused.

Monday, 4 December 1944

After great efforts my paper to the War Cabinet is now in draft. It is to come before a joint meeting of two *official* committees today – at 3 p.m. These are Bovenschen's committee and Brand's committee, one on control, etc., of liberated areas and the other on supply.

11 a.m. Saw Bobbety Cranborne.

1.30 p.m. Lunch with P.M. at Downing Street. Somebody had foolishly asked not only Harold Balfour (which would have been delightful) but also M. Paul-Boncour.[4] The latter, who has been described as 'sea-green, perhaps, but not incorruptible', speaks no English and is very deaf. It was a terrible party and P.M. got very cross and bored.

The whole supply and shipping question for Europe has been opened up by these Italian proposals. And the shipping position is desperate. Partly because the German war was expected to end by 31 December 1944, and partly because of the Germans holding on so long to the French ports, and partly by the large liberated areas to be looked after without the war ending. All the calculations have gone wrong, and there is an estimated shortage of at least five million tons during the first quarter of 1945. Moreover, the Americans are insisting on diverting more and more ships to the Pacific war. And the more successful their operations, the longer become their lines of communication and the greater becomes their demand for ships. It is a vicious circle.

7 p.m. Sir Frederick Bovenschen came to see me. He is really an indefatigable servant of the public, if a trifle pedantic and obstructive. He seems anyway very friendly to me and has worked hard. As a result, my draft paper, subject to a few minor amendments which I have accepted without hesitation, has now received the approval of all the members of those two large official committees, at the departmental level. The problem now is, what to do next? At 8.30, this problem unresolved, I went to dine with Lord Portal.

I found Wyndham [Portal] alone in his flat. He told me the whole story of his resignation and the appointment of Duncan Sandys.[5] He is clearly much hurt at the manner but, I could not help feeling, a little relieved by the fact of his retirement. Oliver Lyttelton came in about 10.30 and we had a good gossip on the political situation in general.

Tuesday, 5 December 1944

I gave a luncheon party at Claridge's for Count Carandini, the new Italian Ambassador in London. Richard Law, Eddy Devonshire,

[4] Balfour had been appointed Minister Resident in West Africa on 21 November 1944. Joseph Paul-Boncour (1873–1972) had been Prime Minister of France, 1932–3.

[5] Churchill had asked Lord Portal to resign so that his office (Minister of Works) could be held by a Minister in the House of Commons.

Major Talbot, Count Roberti, M. Migone, Ivor Thomas, M.P.[6] Anthony Rumbold, Mr [Michael] Williams (F.O.), Douglas Howard (F.O.), and Colonel Bastion (U.S.). I think it helped to give Carandini a start. He is a nice fellow and one of the best Italians I have met so far.

2.45 p.m. I gave a talk to the Conservative Foreign Affairs Committee. Quite a success from what I learned later.

4 p.m. Meeting at Foreign Office with Anthony. He was alone. He seemed rather harassed. The Italian position is bad. No government yet, and all this trouble about Sforza causing ill-feeling between London and Washington.[7] Meanwhile, the Greek situation looks very threatening.

5.30 p.m. Went to see the St George's Westminster Conservative Committee. I gave my position to them quite frankly – I sought nothing but would accept if asked.

6 p.m. Sargent at F.O. Settled a telegram about Badoglio, who is the latest victim (or threatened victim) of the Italian purge. I suggested that we should ask the Americans to *join* with us in intervening on military grounds. If they do not take their share of the responsibility, we should warn them that we shall *not* act alone and his blood will be on *both* our heads. If we do not do this quite firmly, there is the danger that they will trust us to act and then get them out of our joint hole.

6.30 p.m. Meeting of all Ministers (other than War Cabinet) at No. 10. This seems a periodic affair, and consists of a monologue by P.M. on a number of subjects.

The Greek news is really bad. It looks now like civil war. And another intervention by the P.M. in favour of Papandreou and against Sophoulis seems quite unnecessary.[8]

Wednesday, 6 December 1944

I was summoned to see the P.M. at the Annexe at 10.30. But Winston was so worried and harassed, that after waiting a short time, the appointment was cancelled.

10.45 a.m. Saw General – now Field Marshal – Alexander.

11 a.m. Bruce Lockhart.

11.15 a.m. Lord Beaverbrook. I called in to see him at Gwydyr House. Max was as mysterious as ever. He thinks the Greek affair will

[6] Count Guerino Roberti (b. 1903) was Minister Plenipotentiary at the Italian Embassy in London. Ivor (later Bulmer-) Thomas (b. 1905) was M.P. for Keighley – in the Labour interest, 1942–8, Conservative, 1949–50.

[7] Bonomi had replied to Eden by defending Sforza and denying that the Count had impeded his Government. Sforza made a similar declaration.

[8] The EAM Ministers had resigned and an EAM-organised protest meeting in Constitution Square in Athens on 3 December had ended in bloodshed, with shots being fired into the crowd either by the police or by a Communist *agent provocateur*. The Greek Civil War had begun.

Meanwhile Sophoulis had agreed, at Papandreou's suggestion, to try to form a government, since the left-wing Ministers seemed willing to serve under him. But Leeper and Scobie intervened to say that Churchill insisted that 'any change at present in the head of the Greek Government was impossible'.

lead to a lot of trouble. It is always difficult to know what Max is after; but I felt that his power was greater than last year. He seems to be getting his hands on the Conservative machine in some mysterious way.

12 noon. Called on Lord Leathers. For one hour he gave me a clear and well-marshalled *exposé* of the whole shipping situation. It was really a masterly performance.

Went to House of Commons in the afternoon for a short time.

6 p.m. Meeting with Brand and his party on civilian supplies for Italy and Greece, now interconnected with supplies for liberated Europe generally. My paper is now agreed and will be printed and circulated tonight as a Cabinet paper.

7.30 p.m. Dinner with the Tory Reform Group – Quintin Hogg, Hinchingbrooke, Nicolson, Thorneycroft, etc. A very pleasant evening.

Thursday, 7 December 1944

The Greek news is very bad, and so is the Italian. Greece has a revolution, and Italy is without a government. And in both cases we have drifted apart from our American ally[9] and a great part of British opinion is disturbed and hostile. Yet the facts in Greece are clear. If we yield now, we shall be committing the first act of appeasement in the liberated countries to the Fascism of the left – viz., the proletariat dictatorship of the left.

10 a.m. M. Massigli (now French Ambassador in London) came to see me. Partly for old time's sake, partly because he had heard that I was bound for Washington on supply problems. The case of France is particularly urgent. They have been given port capacity by S.H.A.E.F.; they have money to buy raw materials and the raw materials can be bought. But there are no ships.

11 a.m. Max Nicholson – the shipping expert – late Political and Economic Planning. He gave me a more detailed account of what was told me by Lord Leathers in general terms.

12.15 p.m. Meeting in Anthony Eden's room in House of Commons. Eden, Leathers, Lyttelton, Grigg, Law and self. Approval was given to my Cabinet paper and a note prepared to P.M. to that effect. This means my purely Italian and Greek work is cleared and I can start with my full directive. They also recommended that I should take up the whole case of supply to liberated areas in Washington.

1.30 p.m. Lunch at *Times*. I could not help reproving Barrington-Ward [the Editor] for the very unhelpful line which *The Times* is taking.

[9] The State Department announced on 6 December that the United States had no objection to Count Sforza. On the 7th Stettinius, now Secretary of State, criticised British policy in Greece and stressed the principle of 'allowing liberated countries to work out their problems of government without influence from outside'.

3.30 p.m. Anthony asked me to come over to F.O. to talk about further developments in Badoglio case. The State Department is friendly, but fears to recommend interference. I told A.E. that I thought we should stick to our points and not intervene alone. If we say this and they really believe it, I think we can shame the Americans into co-operating with us.

4.30 p.m. Went for a gossip with Leo Amery.

5 p.m. Met with R. Law at F.O. and drew up with him the minutes of this morning's Ministerial meeting and the recommendation to the P.M.

5.30 p.m. Mr Stopford[10] (of War Office) who is coming to Washington with me.

Friday, 8 December 1944

The Greek debate. I went to the House of Commons and heard Winston. His speech was a superb Parliamentary performance and its courage magnificent. It was not, however, a very *profound* speech – that is, I think it oversimplified the problem. Perhaps that was necessary, and in any case Anthony's brilliant 'wind-up' was complementary to the P.M.'s introduction and filled in many points of detail – especially about Greece. The framers of the amendment made a great tactical error in making it so wide. If they had narrowed it to Greece, the P.M. would not have been able to develop the general argument, and here Belgium, Holland, France, etc., were of great assistance to him in expounding his theme. The British press is bad so far, the American worse.[11]

Lunched at the House. Then went to St Martin's Street to talk some Macmillan & Co. business with Daniel.

5.30 p.m. Monnet – on the French supply claims. He is also bound for Washington.

6.30 p.m. Nicholson. More shipping details.

8 p.m. Dinner with Daniel at Garrick Club. At 10.30 I went (at P.M.'s request) to the Annexe where I found him alone. He had slept after the debate, dined about 9 p.m., and was in a very exhausted and rather petulant mood.

After some general talk on the debate, he made a sudden attack on me for 'deserting my post'. He almost hinted that my absence from Rome and Athens was poltroonery. Of course, he is old and worried. I

[10] Robert Stopford (1895–1978) was a financial adviser at the War Office, 1943–5, having served as a Financial Counsellor at the Embassy in Washington, 1940–3.

[11] The amendment regretted that the King's Speech of 29 November 'contains no assurance that H.M. forces will not be used to disarm the friends of democracy in Greece and other parts of Europe, or to suppress those popular movements which have valorously assisted in the defeat of the enemy and upon whose success we must rely for future friendly co-operation in Europe'.

Churchill replied that valorous action against the Germans did not entitle the popular movements to become masters of their countries: 'Democracy is no harlot to be picked up in the street by a man with a tommy-gun.'

told him firmly that I came to England on his orders; that I was now the President of the Allied Commission in Italy; that I had just received (as I had a few hours before) his approval of yesterday's meeting of Ministers and the decisions reached there, and finally that he had sent a few hours ago a telegram to the President saying that I would be in Washington in a day or two to discuss all these Italian questions and in addition the supply question of the Mediterranean and of liberated Europe generally.

He admitted all this, but still said that he felt instinctively that I should go back and help Alexander. I said that nothing would give me greater pleasure, and I would set out immediately. He must clear things with the President and send some other Minister to Washington.

He rambled on in rather a sad and depressed way. The debate had obviously tired him very much, and I think he realised the dangers inherent in the Greek policy on which we are now embarked. He has won the debate but not the battle of Athens.

Saturday, 9 December 1944

John Wyndham rang up very early to say that Field Marshal Alexander's plane had been delayed. So I can go with him on Sunday if it is so agreed.

10 a.m.–1 p.m. I spent an extraordinary morning, mostly in the Private Secretary's room in the F.O., with a vast amount of cross-telephoning between Anthony, Winston and myself. (Anthony was in the country, Winston still in London.) Winston repented in the early morning and rang Anthony to say I should go to Washington. Then Anthony thought I should go to Athens. Then I said I wanted to go to Athens, but still more wanted some orders. Finally it was decided that I should get a firm decision at 2.45. It was for Alexander and Athens. I am delighted. The supply problem in Washington is certainly insoluble. The political problem in Athens is probably insoluble also. But the second is human and exciting and in a field where I feel what talents I have will be more useful. Anticipating the decision, I had arranged for 3 p.m. a meeting of Sargent and some F.O. chaps, Bovenschen and some War Office chaps, so as to take all the necessary steps not to waste my work in London. After an hour's meeting, at which everything was agreed, John and I did all the telegrams ourselves and had them off by 7 p.m.

The *political* decisions about Italy will, I think, certainly commend themselves to the State Department. The difficulty here was likely to be in London, not Washington. All these I have cleared with the Cabinet and we have telegraphed the text of my paper to Halifax.[12] The supply question for the Mediterranean will perhaps be all right with

[12] 1st Earl Halifax (1881–1959) was Foreign Secretary, 1938–40, and Ambassador to the United States, 1941–6.

Marris (of C.C.A.C.) and Brigadier-General Spofford. The wider supply question will require a Minister to go specially. I am sending Colonel Bastion to Washington with a letter to Spofford and full account of what I have got my colleagues to agree.

Dorothy came up from Birch Grove. We dined together at Claridge's. We went afterwards to the Dorchester, and by gate-crashing a dance found Catherine looking very pretty.

Sunday, 10 December 1944

6 a.m.! Left by car for Lyneham. Miss Campbell, John and I filled two cars with ourselves, our luggage and our red boxes.

9.30 a.m. After a good breakfast at Lyneham we took off in a York. Rest of the party consisted of F. M. Alexander, Colonel Cunningham (his M.A.), General Brian Robertson, who will be the new C.A.O. at A.F.H.Q., and General Lewis, at present deputy to General George Clark, the present C.A.O.

Arrived at Caserta after a good flight about 4 p.m. Went up to see Generals Wilson and Gammell. We went over the whole Greek position.

About 6 p.m. I went to my office and despatched some business with Broad. It was desperately cold and I have a desperate cold – or really 'flu'. The aeroplane trip has not improved it.

The Badoglio position is still critical. We are suggesting to Winston that we should fly him to Malta. But I would much like at least to *inform* the Americans.

Dined with Alex at the Hunting Lodge. Jumbo Wilson was attending a farewell dinner given by the admiral in Naples. We managed to be excused on score of fatigue.

Monday, 11 December 1944

Went in to see Wilson at 9 a.m. to say goodbye. Left by Dakota from Marcianise at 9.30. Alex, Brigadier [Hugh] Mainwaring (B.G.S., A.A.I.), Rupert Clarke, John and I. I decided to leave Miss Campbell at Caserta. She seems very tired and one does not want to add to the Embassy's difficulties.

We arrived at Kalamaki aerodrome about 1.30 (Tatoi airfield is in the hands of the insurgents). After about an hour's delay, owing to the road between the airfield and the centre of the town being under shellfire from the insurgents, we left for General Scobie's H.Q. Alex was in one tank, I in another. (The room provided for middle-aged politicians is not great.) It was quite an interesting progress and I could see through the periscope what was going on. Actually, things were fairly quiet, and there seemed not more than a certain amount of sniping.

At General Scobie's H.Q. we went at once to the general's room. Here Alex (with his Brigadier Mainwaring) immediately made himself aware of the military situation. It was very striking to see how rapidly he seized the salient points. Actually, it could hardly be worse. We have really been taken by surprise and seem to have hoped, up to the last, that things would be settled. And I think we have underestimated the military skill, determination and power of the insurgent forces.

At present, the British forces (and the Embassy) are besieged and beleaguered in the small central area of Athens. We hold about five to ten out of fifty square miles of built-up area (Athens and Piraeus). The airfield at Tatoi is lost, and nearly 800 Air Force H.Q. and ground staff cut off in that suburb. Our airfield at Kalamaki is very insecure and the communications between it and the main body in Athens all under fire. We do *not* hold a port at all. We have lost the Piraeus, Port Heracles, etc. We are defending on the beaches at Phaleron Bay, but we have no real communication between the airfield and the beaches or between Athens and the beaches. In other words, we have no secure base anywhere from which to operate.

The rebels hold four-fifths of Athens and Piraeus. They hold all the hills round. They hold the harbours; they have captured one airfield, and threaten another.

We had dumps of food and ammunition in the town, but the majority of these we have lost. We have about five days' ammunition and about eight days' food at present rates. The rebels have control of the power station.

After discussion of the situation, we all went to the Embassy (about quarter of a mile from Constitution Square and Military H.Q.). There we found Ambassador Leeper – looking a little fatigued and very glad to see us. With him we discussed the political situation at some length.

It was then agreed that the F.M. should return to H.Q. and work out some detailed military problems. Leeper and I continued our political examination.

Alex returned for dinner. He told me of his general appreciation of the situation and his proposed plan. We therefore agreed that I should draft a telegram which we should send jointly to the P.M. This we did – he wrote in two military paragraphs and it was sent off late tonight.

I have had some talk about the command with Alex. I feel that we need a more up-to-date *fighting* officer to command whatever forces are put in, leaving Scobie (who is a splendid character, a loyal, honest and altogether high-minded Englishman) with the general authority.

It is clear that on the political side, we must make some step. Leeper seems to think that Archbishop Damaskinos should be used, so we have made the proposal.[13]

[13] This proposal was that the Archbishop should become Regent. 'In this way,' our telegram argued, 'a proper measure of responsibility can be restored to the head of the Greek state, and the most powerful cry against us, foreign intervention, effectively answered.' Alexander's paragraphs concerned reinforcements to clear the port of Piraeus and make possible the full relief of Athens. We also both recommended two additional measures to be taken once we had sufficient reinforcements. 'The first is once more to proclaim all those opposing us rebels, and at the same

Tuesday, 12 December 1944

Alex came round to the Embassy about ten. We settled the terms of the reply which General Scobie should make to Porphyrogennis, who is coming to see him from the insurgents. The terms are very moderate and reasonable (and correspond to our weak military position!). We ask them to withdraw from Attica (so far as the regular irregulars are concerned). Those in Athens to lay down their arms – and then steps for a settlement. Leeper wishes me to stay here, and Alex also. After luncheon, my throat and cough were so bad that I retired to bed where I remained the rest of the day.

Wednesday, 13 December 1944

I woke feeling much better. The life in the Embassy is indeed a strange one. About fifty people (including servants and guard) are sleeping and living in the house. Except for a little exercise in the small part of the garden which has a wall round it, no one is allowed out at all. Even to get to this, you have to risk the sniper's bullet. All the front rooms have been evacuated, and the beds are in the passages. The dormitories of typists and 'cypherenes' are excellently arranged by Mrs Leeper. I pass through these passages of beds to get to my room – which is on the side.

The rebels are about 200–300 yards away and hold all the territory immediately over the Ilyssus river. To go from the Embassy to H.Q. one should go in an armoured car or tank, or else drive as fast as possible in a 'thin-skinned' car through some back streets.

All meals are in common – in the hall or lounge of the house. Twenty-four to twenty-six sit down. Rations are Army rations on rather a reduced scale.

There is no heat (for there is no electric power to drive the oil-heating apparatus). There is no water (for the rebels have drained Hadrian's reservoir, on which we depended). There is no light (for the rebels have the power station).

We have fortunately filled all the baths; we have a lily-pond in the garden; and today we have found a disused well, which will probably give us at least water fit for cooking and some washing.

Mrs Leeper is a really splendid woman. She keeps all the Embassy staff, male and female, in a good temper, and with the slender resources available, she and the cook produce really remarkable results.

At present, until reinforcements arrive, we can only do sort of sporadic tactical offensive–defensive movements. There is a good deal of sniping and shelling going on. The Air Force have broken up a large formation in the Stadium area, which we thought was about to attack

time declare that all those found in civilian clothes opposing us with weapons are liable to be shot. The second is to give twenty-four hours' notice that certain areas held by the rebels are to be wholly evacuated by the civil population. This will enable us to use ships' fire, artillery and air bombing if necessary.'

us from the front. At our rear (half an hour's walk to the top) is the hill Lycabettus. The top is held by our troops; the lower slopes (immediately behind the Embassy) by the rebels. Then again we have a block of streets.

The job of cleaning up is very difficult, because all street fighting is difficult. Then many of the insurgents are in civilian clothes; others in British battledress, with British weapons (Oh, Dr Dalton. Oh, Lord Selborne, what things were done in your names!).[14]

Moreover, we have very little heavy stuff – a few twenty-five pounders, a few tanks, etc. And we do not wish to kill a lot of innocent inhabitants or destroy the greater part of Athens. The problem, therefore, is a really difficult one.

On the political side, it is also very confused. Until we get some reply on the proposal to make the regency, there is little we can do. And, in any case, we must get into a stronger *military* position before we can make much political progress. We must be able to negotiate from strength and not from weakness. Conciliation must follow military ascendancy, not precede it.

A very friendly and helpful reply has come from P.M. The War Cabinet entirely approved the telegram which Alex and I sent off on Monday night. But, since the King is obstinate, they suggest the Archbishop should be Prime Minister instead of Regent. This, of course, is not feasible, and we concocted a powerful reply, asking them to keep more pressure on the King.

Telegram Out

Most Immediate   Secret

Personal to Prime Minister from Macmillan.

Your telegram No. 441 [of 12 December].

Leeper and I are most grateful for your support and for your strenuous efforts with the King. But he does not seem to understand the gravity of the position or the splendid opportunity before him.

2. Greece is gripped in a vice of internal hatreds and on the brink of civil war. Athens, with its million and a quarter inhabitants, is without food, light or water. To leave the home even to search for a scrap of food involves risk from gun, mortar, machine-gun and rifle fire. The next enemy will inevitably be typhus and cholera. From all this misery the King has the possibility of relieving his people. There is no act which H.M. could possible perform today more calculated to strengthen in the future his royal cause. It would be universally regarded as that of a statesman and a patriot, since it would clearly be the greatest contribution which the King could make to his people at

[14] Dr Hugh Dalton (1887–1964) and Lord Selborne as Ministers of Economic Warfare had been responsible for supplying resistance movements.

this time. It is the general opinion here that if he fails to rise to this opportunity his chances of achieving his throne are lost for ever.

3. The King must remember that everyone is talking of this possibility of the Archiepiscopal regency as a way out. If he remains stubborn, two embarrassments will follow. He will still further endanger his cause by being regarded as the sole obstacle and H.M.G. and the British people generally will be accused of connivance with the King's selfish policy. The press of England and America will not be slow to make this point. We beg you to remember that the regency of the Archbishop is not the sudden idea of the British Embassy or the Minister, but the general hope and wish of the people.

4. Moreover, we have strong reason to believe that the Archbishop will not repeat not consent to act as Prime Minister. In that capacity he would not have that detachment from the ordinary political scene which his rank and profession require. And since he would only be one of that succession of figures, mostly shadowy, who filled the post, he could not give that guarantee of stability which is an essential part of any accommodation between the contending parties today. At the moment fear dominates the political scene. The parties of the left feel that if they are beaten now there may be bitter reprisals from the right. The parties of the right feel that the loss of this contest means terrorist dictatorship from the left. The Archbishop must be appointed to a post and for a period of time calculated to give confidence to all. Such a post should naturally be that of Regent. And the regency should remain until by plebiscite or free elections the people themselves are able to express their will.

5. We trust therefore that you will return to the charge. We should not abandon the only political measure we can see to get out of this impasse. Since it is a unique weapon, it must not be lightly used; for if it fails we are left only with a long and difficult military operation with all the embarrassments in the field of international politics of which you are only too well aware. We very much hope that we may get a further reply from you in the course of today.

6. Alexander left for Caserta yesterday. We have repeated your telegram and this to him.

I also sent some telegrams about *The Times* representative here (who is a disgracefully incompetent and foolish fellow) and on the press and Americans generally.

Osbert Lancaster[15] has arrived as Press Attaché. He will be a tower of strength and commonsense.

A very heavy attack was made on us last night. The rebels rushed the H.Q. of one of our armoured brigades and got in. The fighting is still going on there now. It is about 300 yards from the Embassy.

[15] Osbert Lancaster (b. 1908), the philhellene cartoonist, remained at Athens as Press Attaché until 1946.

Thursday, 14 December 1944

10 a.m. Papandreou came to see Leeper and me. We strongly urged him to recommend the regency. He promised me that he would do so. At the time I thought he was sincere. But I learned afterwards that he was either double-crossing us or was weak. Of course he and his Government are afraid that the Archbishop would change them, and they would lose their jobs.

At 10.30, the Archbishop came to see us at the Embassy. We went over the whole situation. I was impressed by the wide grasp of European politics, the good sense, humour and courage of this ecclesiastic. He is willing to accept the regency, but realises the difficulties. He shares our view that there must be no reprisals and no counter-revolution.

Slept all the afternoon. My cold is still very heavy and my chest inflamed.

6 p.m. Went to see Papandreou, to receive (as I was told by him in the morning) a telegram to send to the King recommending the regency. Instead, I got a complete 'sell-out'. He had executed an absolute *volte-face*. He said that *all* the leaders of the parties were against a regency. That it would be regarded as a sign of weakness; that Communism must be absolutely crushed, etc., etc. He produced two colleagues (populists or royalists) who took the same line. I returned very discouraged. Today's fighting has not gone too well for us. The rebels were eventually thrown out of the armoured brigade H.Q., but took a hundred prisoners or so – which is very bad. We expect another heavy attack tonight. The rebels are forming up both behind our house (on Lycabettus) and in front (in the area across the Ilyssus). In the latter area, the R.A.F. are trying to disperse them with machine-gun fire.

A mass of telegrams are being sent off by us to London. We have a telegram from them to say that Papandreou has advised the King *against* a regency! I am not sure of the date of this advice, nor is it easy to know if the King speaks the truth.

Friday, 15 December 1944

I have a telegram from Alex to say that he is appointing General [Sir John] Hawkesworth (Tenth Corps commander in Italy) in charge of operations in Athens and Piraeus. Scobie remains (or becomes) C.-in-C., Greece. This is good.

10.30 a.m. Scobie, Leeper and I called on Papandreou. We urged him strongly to recommend a regency to the King. We gave three grounds:

Firstly. That Greece must have a 'head of the state' at this crisis. They had at present the advantage neither of a monarchy nor of a republic. We all knew the King could not come to Greece. And there was not a President. Therefore we argued for a regency in principle. Again, when a truce had been arranged or the rebels in the immediate vicinity of

Athens captured or driven back, there would have to be negotiations for a peace settlement. These ought to be conducted under the presidency or chairmanship of a Greek, not a British Minister or general.

Secondly. The Archiepiscopal appointment would do much to satisfy American opinion.

Thirdly. It would help the position of H.M.G. Mr Churchill had carried the day by his prestige. But there was great and growing criticism at home, and this move would help H.M.G. enormously.

Papandreou said he was moved by what we said. He argued however now in favour of a regency of three persons not one. He suggested the Archbishop, General Plastiras[16] (ex-dictator and republican) and Mr [Philippos] Dragoumis (a much respected friend of the King – now Under-Secretary for Foreign Affairs). He said this solution would have the support of M. Sophoulis.

12 noon. Leeper and I saw Sophoulis. He said that he had been against a regency, but would now accept it. But he preferred one Regent, the Archbishop.

All this was duly reported by us to London, and the motives which we believed actuate these politicians. Sophoulis is very old, very sly, has a number of political leaders under his control, and wants (at eighty-four) desperately to become Prime Minister.

By about 6 p.m. we got Papandreou's message to the King (to be sent by our channels) and Sophoulis's. Papandreou recommends a regency, but three Regents; Sophoulis recommends a regency, but one Regent. (I have no doubt that each are sending other messages to the King through their own cyphers!) All this took most of the afternoon.

6 p.m. General Plastiras called. He has been in exile for about twelve years. He is a keen republican. He was a dictator, but resigned voluntarily (this makes him a 'good' dictator) and held elections, after which he left Greece. He was very much against the rebels, but otherwise did not disclose his hand. I think he wants to be the sort of 'return of Cromwell' and take Papandreou's place in due course.

After dinner, an emissary came from the Archbishop to say that everything had now been agreed between himself, Papandreou and Sophoulis. Papandreou and Sophoulis would recommend to the King one Regent (Archbishop), Plastiras would become Prime Minister, Papandreou and Sophoulis joint Deputy Prime Ministers.

About midnight came the emissary again. M. Sophoulis has now ratted on this arrangement. The Archiepiscopal emissary said, '*C'est dégoutant*'!

[16] General Nikolaos Plastiras (1883–1953) was leader of the revolutionary committee which forced the abdication of King Constantine in 1922. He imposed a brief dictatorship in 1933, and was to be Prime Minister of Greece, January–April 1945.

Saturday, 16 December 1944

9.30 a.m. M. Kanellopoulos[17] to see me. An intelligent little man, at present Minister of Finance (vice Svolos EAMite Minister, resigned). He says he favours the Archiepiscopal regency. But they all tell me that, and then send messages to London in the opposite sense.

10.30 a.m. Went to H.Q. Got through without a bullet. Saw Scobie and told him the present situation. The military situation should begin to improve, as Hawkesworth and the Fourth Division are arriving.

11 a.m. Had a talk with a number of press correspondents. I hope it will do some good.

12 noon. I called on the Archbishop – Balfour[18] (of the Embassy) came with me and interpreted. A very good interview. My opinion of His Beatitude is confirmed each time I see him. About the rebels, he wishes to be quite firm; but he wants no counter-revolution. I said that there was a proper distinction between the condonation of sin and its forgiveness. This pleased him.

2.30 p.m. The rebels have replied to Scobie in writing. The reply is not too bad. It accepts one condition and ignores the other. It then makes a number of points, all of which (except one about the Mountain Brigade) are relevant to the peace not to the truce.

3 p.m. Meeting in Ambassador's room to draft Scobie's reply. Ambassador, General Scobie, Colonel Astley (Public Relations Officer), Lancaster, Caccia, Smith-Dorrien and self. The general read out his draft – a most extraordinary document – the sending of which would have lost us any support we may have in U.K. or the world! There was an awkward pause: all looked at me! I pretended to have forgotten the text of our original statement. This was sent for and read out. Gradually, I got agreement to the reply which I had already drafted. So it was sent and duly repeated to London and to Caserta (for the Field Marshal).

All this occupied a good deal of time. Later in the evening the usual flow of politicians came round, Kartalis,[19] Tsatsos, [Ioannis] Francis and all the rest of them. Papandreou and Sophoulis and all the others are plotting away, and it is impossible to follow them as they turn round and about, like a hunted hare.

Sunday, 17 December 1944

A number of telegrams have arrived from London. It is clear that the politicians have double-crossed us (and each other) completely. They have told the King that they are opposed to the regency from the Greek

[17] Panaghiotis Kanellopoulos (b. 1902) had been Deputy Prime Minister and Minister of Defence (in Cairo), 1942–3, and was to be Prime Minister in November 1945 and April 1967.

[18] Major David Balfour (1903–83), former Orthodox priest and Confessor to the Greek royal family, was Second (later First) Secretary at the Embassy to the Greek Government, 1943–7.

[19] Georgios Kartalis (1908–1957), a wealthy intellectual fluent in English, French and German, was a Minister without portfolio.

point of view. But they feel they must accept it if it is true, as Macmillan and Leeper (especially Macmillan) tell them, that H.M.G. and Churchill will fall unless it is agreed. They have totally misrepresented my arguments; even the one which I used about public opinion at home, they have exaggerated out of all knowledge. Thus they have enabled the King to say to the P.M. and Anthony that his Greek advisers are against the regency and to make trouble between me and London by this false account of what I have said. Fortunately, Winston and Anthony have not believed them, but are naturally slightly puzzled. Anyway, on present form the King holds out. I have of course immediately telegraphed the true story to London. Later in the day, a very nice telegram came, personal from Winston to me.

Churchill's telegram

MOST IMMEDIATE
TOP SECRET, PERSONAL AND PRIVATE
Following from Prime Minister for Mr Macmillan

1. I have a great sympathy for you and Mr Leeper in the tangled and excited situation in which you are placed. . . .

2. You need not worry about my personal position or that of the Government being in danger. We can I think rely upon a ten to one vote in the House of Commons. I am confident I can explain matters in a broadcast to the country at any time. But even if these good and solid conditions did not exist here we should still do what we deem our duty. At the moment Greek question is somewhat obscured by Poland in which far graver issues are involved.

[Diary continues] 10.30 a.m. Tsatsos came in. He said it was now all arranged and Papandreou would telegraph a proper telegram to the King, urging the regency on proper grounds.

11.30 a.m. The Archbishop came to the Embassy (at his request) to see me and the Ambassador. He told us that Papandreou had shown him the text of a telegram which he proposed to send and which included a kind of 'confession of faith' or 'political declaration' which the Archbishop was to make. The object of this was (*a*) to make the Archbishop give a testimonial of the most fulsome kind in favour of the Government, (*b*) to tie the Archbishop's hand as to a future settlement. For instance, it made him say that no EAM supporter (whether he had taken part in the rebellion or not) should ever be employed in either the Army or civil service! His Beatitude wished to have our advice. I told him that the Government seemed to regard him not merely as a prelate of the Church, but as St Peter himself. He replied, 'No, it is not Heaven that they want, it is the earth.' Finally, we strongly advised him to insist on writing his own declaration in his own way. (The first clause was particularly tricky. It made the Archbishop declare himself a royalist. But it was so carefully phrased as only to be *capable* of bearing this interpretation.)

3 p.m. We had a very nice service in the Embassy. All the staff and the soldiers of the guard attended.

4 p.m. Major Mathews (interpreter) came with a message from the Archbishop to say it was all off. Papandreou would not accept his statement in its new form.

5 p.m. I went to see Scobie. I asked him (and he agreed) to go to Papandreou and tell him quite plainly that we were *not* (repeat *not*) prepared to become the tool of a right-wing reaction throughout Greece. We wished a settlement of conciliation and we would not allow ourselves to be dragged into a long war from one end of Greece to the other to exterminate the Communist party.

5.45 p.m. Papandreou expressed amazement at Scobie's communication, but according to the general seemed rather shaken by it.

6 p.m. Another Greek Cabinet meeting, to decide on the text of a telegram to the King.

After dinner, a new comedy (or tragi-comedy) began. Tsatsos came round about 10 p.m. with the draft telegram. I strongly objected to that part of it which purported to give the British view. It was untrue and misleading to the King. I told him to go back with this message to Papandreou. He returned about 11.30 p.m. with a message that he would accept my draft for this part of the telegram. So we sat down and wrote it. About midnight a message came from Papandreou to say he wanted to go immediately to London to see the King. We took no notice of this, and went on with our drafting. I also objected to the other part of the telegram. I said I thought it a very disingenuous document. About 1 a.m. Tsatsos (a good fellow, who agrees with us) suggested that as Papandreou was very overwrought and excited, we had better leave everything till the morning, when the Ambassador could see him and try to soothe him down.

Today has been a day like the others. A good deal of fighting and shooting all round us. We have now got some rocket-firing aeroplanes. I think myself that we are through the most critical period, and that at least we shall not now be overcome and either murdered or captured by the insurgents.

Monday, 18 December 1944

After all our exertions, we woke tired and cross. The siege (especially not going out) is beginning to tell on the nerves of all. I always make a point of walking (or driving) from here to H.Q. once or twice a day for this very reason. John Wyndham (whom I had sent to Caserta by air a few days ago) returned yesterday – with thirty-six eggs and some whisky! This has helped to brighten us.

10 a.m. Ambassador called on Papandreou at the [Hotel] Grande

Bretagne. He seems to have soothed him, but I fear he may himself have been deceived again. Anyway, Leeper now says that a satisfactory telegram will go to the King. We shall see.

I sent an account to F.O. of all yesterday's performances.

There is little to do now but wait. The military situation is definitely improving. I have read a number of books, including a short history of modern Greece, and more of Stanley on the Eastern Church. I read *The Egoist* while I was in England. I had not read it for years, and found it more readable than I had expected. I have some Meredith volumes here, so I will try another.

5 p.m. General Scobie asked to see me. He expects a further reply from the insurgents through Porphyrogennis (EAM ex-Minister). I told him to stick exactly to his published terms.

A dreary evening – cold and wet. There is no heating in the house and the cold is very tiresome – so are the draughts. I sit mostly in the chancery (half-basement) where John also sleeps. A bullet came through the window a day or two ago. We call this room 'Pratt's club', and now that we have gin and whisky, there is a little party there every evening before dinner, with some of the girls, which helps to cheer things up.

Tuesday, 19 December 1944

John brought me a good many Italian papers, and I have also telegrams from Broad (at Caserta). I worked at these in the morning. At about 10.30 John and I walked to H.Q. I saw some journalists – not too many at a time is the best way – and gave them my general view. The position militarily is improving, except for the Air Force H.Q. at Kephyssia, who have been surrounded and cut off for over a fortnight and may have to surrender – to the tune of some 700 – which will be very unfortunate. A tank rescue party is trying to get through to them, but it will not be easy.

After luncheon, wrote the diary and read some English newspapers, which have just arrived. I am horrified to see that I am expected to 'settle' this affair.

The Ambassador tells me that Tsatsos has been round to ask for the text of the British view for Papandreou's telegram which I wrote on Sunday night. So perhaps it will now go at last!

5 p.m. Called on Papandreou at the Grande Bretagne. I only wanted to be mildly polite to him, as I fancy he is offended with me – and I think suspicious of me. He was in a most dangerous mood of vague optimism and seems to think that we are prepared to spend any amount of effort to keep him afloat. He will not hear of compromise or conciliation, and talks of nothing but an out-and-out victory over the Communists. He may be right from his point of view and perhaps from the long-term view of Europe. But I don't think he has any idea of our military difficulties or of the dangers on his northern frontier.

We do not wish to start the Third World War against Russia until we have finished the Second World War against Germany – and certainly not to please M. Papandreou.

6 p.m. Called on Scobie. The general, who is a man of great charm and honesty of purpose, was as pleasant as ever. But if a good man, he is a fundamentally stupid man, which is a pity.

After dinner, and consulting with the Ambassador, I decided to go to Caserta tomorrow. I must see Alex and tell him how things are going.

A very angry telegram has reached me this evening from Winston. He is annoyed with me for having pressed the regency with arguments about the political position at home and Anglo-American relations, instead of confining myself to purely Greek considerations. Of course, the real reason is that he is anxious and is beginning to realise what a troublesome affair this is going to be. It may well threaten the present Government and delay the whole progress of the war. In spite of what he says, he will be very grateful if we can get him out of it. But the Greek politicians have double-crossed us over the only constructive plan which I can see – the regency – and H.M.G. have been lamentably weak with the King of Greece.

Wednesday, 20 December 1944

Left the Embassy about 9.15. Harold Caccia and Ed Warner[20] came with me. As before, we made the journey in tanks, since one gets sniped a good deal on the road.

I had Air Marshal Slessor's Mitchell available and this got me to Marcianise airfield (at Caserta) by 12.30 (Naples time). A splendid trip; fine, sunny weather. We went in a direct line, over mountains of Peloponnese, Gulf of Corinth, and then the Apennines – at about 10,000 feet all the way.

Lunched with Alex at the Hunting Lodge. After luncheon, a conference at A.F.H.Q. Present, Alex, Slessor, General Harding (Chief of Staff in succession to General Gammell), General Theron (representing F. M. Smuts) and Harold Caccia.

After a very comprehensive review of the tactical and strategical situation in the Mediterranean generally (including likely developments on the Italian front) we came to the political situation in Greece, which I did my best to expound. It was finally decided:

(*a*) That General Harding shall draft a telegram setting out the military situation for Alex to send to Winston. That the telegram should be ready for me to see tomorrow morning, before leaving for Greece.

(*b*) General Theron would telegraph to F. M. Smuts setting out the military situation broadly and the political in greater detail and

[20] Edward Warner (b. 1911) was Second (later First) Secretary at the Embassy to the Greek Government, 1943–5.

strongly urging Smuts to advise the King of Greece *in favour* of the regency. (Smuts has been appealed to by the King of Greece, who has telegraphed to him saying that Winston is putting great pressure on him to appoint the Regent. I was glad to hear this!) Smuts has a great influence with the King, partly because of a friendship made in Cairo, and partly because of the Indian summer idyll which the old F.M. is carrying on with the Crown Princess.[21]

(*c*) I should continue to press the regency on H.M.G. and on all Greek politicians whom I could influence locally.

We would have an early meeting in Athens, when present military operations had progressed a bit further.

I spent the rest of the day with Broad in my office at Caserta, going through a lot of neglected work – mostly Italian. Broad is a very competent fellow and is doing very well. I also saw Offie (who was very friendly). My Italian plans, on which I lavished so much effort, are going ahead at Washington, but (I fear) in a rather leisurely way. It is sad that I cannot be there to put some drive behind the job.

Motored to Naples and dined there. A hot bath before dinner was a most wonderful luxury after so long without washing.

Thursday, 21 December 1944

8 a.m. Left Naples. Finished some Italian work at Caserta, and wrote a letter for the bag for Anthony on the Greek affair.

9.45 a.m. Saw Alex and went through with him the text of his telegram to P.M. It will do a lot of good, and should put the situation in a more realistic perspective. Poor Winston! What with Greece, Poland and the German breakthrough on the Western Front,[22] this is going to be a grim Christmas.

Left about 10.30. Owing to very bad weather, we could not risk the flight over the Apennines. We went all the way round by the sea route, and got to Brindisi about 1.30 p.m. Here we filled up with petrol and got the weather report. After some discussion, we decided to risk it, and finally arrived safely at Kalamaki airfield, Athens, at about 4 p.m. (Naples time) or 5 p.m. (Athens time). There was some muddle about sending the armoured cars for us and after a long wait we finally reached the Embassy about 7 p.m. – a long and tiring day.

Nothing much seems to be happening and little progress, political or military. The sniping and gunfire go on all the time, with bursts of machine-gun fire. I gather we are progressing well in the Piraeus area. Round the Embassy, we are still much harassed by ELAS fire. We are just on the borders of an area which they hold strongly.

[21] Princess Frederika (1917–81), later Queen, wife of Crown Prince Paul.

[22] The Polish Prime Minister had resigned over the question of the Soviet–Polish frontier discussions, and a major offensive on 16 December had enabled German forces to advance into the Ardennes.

Friday, 22 December 1944

The long-awaited reply from the insurgents to General Scobie's statement on 16 December has not yet reached us. The story is that it has been a subject of fierce debate among them. At a meeting at noon, with Ambassador, Scobie, Caccia, Brigadier Smith-Dorrien and myself, we decided to send a message through the intermediary to make it clear that the British would (*a*) guarantee no reprisals and a political amnesty, (*b*) get a conference under way, if the truce conditions could be accepted. This was done through Major B., of I.S.L.D., who was sent for.

At 6 p.m. I went for a talk with Scobie. I walked from the Embassy to H.Q. The centre of the town was quieter and no sniping. The street just outside the Embassy is rather dangerous and bursts of machine-gun fire pour down it from time to time. I persuaded Scobie to let my telegram to Alex stand, and I hope he will come on Saturday (23 December).

At 8 p.m. the reply from the ELAS Central Committee arrived – a very woolly and inconclusive document. We discussed it at some length, but decided to wait before publishing it or making any rejoinder.

Saturday, 23 December 1944

9.30 a.m. Called on General Scobie. The military situation is improving, but progress is necessarily slow. I developed to the general the idea that the Field Marshal on arrival should reply by asking the ELAS Committee to come and see him. This seemed rather revolutionary to all at first sight (Leeper approves) and may still be a little premature. General Scobie was more receptive than I supposed likely. I have come to the conclusion that, like many military men, he agrees with anything put before him, if it is put with any delicacy and tact.

A message came during the morning that Alex has been unable to come by air, owing to the weather. He will come by destroyer, and is expected at 9 p.m. tomorrow night.

Lunch with Admiral [Charles] Turle, Senior Naval Officer in Athens, in a house off Constitution Square. Admiral Mansfield was there and a number of other naval officers of various ranks. Also Mr Kemp of Whitehall Securities, who manages the various public utilities in Athens for which W.S. have the concession. 'The Navy always travels first class' – the best food and drink I have had during the siege.

5 p.m. Papandreou to tea. He was not very sensible. His press interviews, which he thinks wonderful, are doing a lot of harm – as are those given by the rest of his colleagues. The Greek bourgeois class is determined to eliminate the Greek Communists, and will fight to the last British soldier to do so. And yet, there is a lot of truth in what

Papandreou says. The true doctrinaire Communist is irreconcilable and cannot be weaned away from his dreary faith, in which he believes with fanatical enthusiasm.

A quiet evening, reading and writing. There is very little I can do – a certain number of Italian and Yugoslav telegrams come through, but I cannot deal with them effectively here.

Sunday, 24 December 1944 (Christmas Eve)

A good deal of fighting during the night round our part of the town. I stayed in bed all the morning. I read *Miss MacKenzie* (a good Trollope) and finished a book of Somerset Maugham's stories – also a short history of Greece. (I find I keep reading bits of books – it must be the restlessness of the siege.)

The sniper who shoots down our street is being active, but he seems to be letting us alone in the garden. I got up only for lunch. The rest has done me good. We now hear that the destroyer is delayed, and Alex will not arrive at 9 p.m. tonight as was expected. No time is yet given.

After further talks with Leeper, we decided to ask the Archbishop to come to see us.

5 p.m. Archbishop came. I am much impressed with his shrewdness and moderation. What his knowledge of theology may be, I do not know; but he has a very complete knowledge of politics and a much wider point of view than the Greek politicians whom I have hitherto met. We went through with him the text of his Christmas allocution. He tells the insurgents that they must lay down their arms; at the same time he indicates that there must be a peace of reconciliation, not a truce followed by reprisals.

Just after dinner we got a mysterious telegram from Winston, asking us to see a telegram which he had sent to Alex. Unfortunately, a later message tells us that owing to the very bad weather at sea, Alex is still further delayed and not expected till tomorrow. So this leaves us very much perplexed.

11.30 p.m. We had a nice little service in the drawing-room of the beleaguered Embassy, nearly all the staff and the soldiers not on duty attended. Mrs Leeper had made some sweet little Christmas trees – out of nothing – and Mr Osbert Lancaster had cut out some silhouettes (St Joseph, the Virgin, the Holy Child in the Manger, the Kings and Shepherds) which, with a light behind them, made a charming decoration.

We had some carols at appropriate points in the Communion Service, which was over about 12.15 a.m. Thus began

Christmas Day, 1944

The guns are firing briskly – there is a night attack on a part of the town behind Lycabettus. I am afraid things are getting more bitter. ELAS are committing some terrible atrocities, and our troops – who started rather doubtful of the rights and wrongs – are now getting very angry. The letter censorship shows that this is almost universal – even among the Glasgow Communists, who are said to be well represented in the Paratroop Brigade.

11 a.m. Alex turned up at last. He had been unable to fly, owing to bad weather. He therefore motored (eight hours) to Taranto, where he got a destroyer. They had terrible weather and took forty-eight hours to get to Athens. After a military conference at H.Q. we went over to the Embassy. Here he revealed the mystery, by producing the telegram: 'Two friends of yours, of which I am one, are coming out to join you.' This, of course, means P.M. and Foreign Secretary.

Leeper and I discussed with Alex the plan which we had concocted – of summoning a conference 'generally representative of Greek political opinion', including ELAS delegates. The idea was to put the Archbishop in the chair. Now, of course, we must wait for the arrival of P.M. and F.S. Nevertheless, I am sure it is the right plan.

After luncheon, we all went to the airfield (Alex, Leeper and I), and at about 3 p.m. the plane arrived. It was bitterly cold – a terrible biting wind from the mountains. We persuaded Winston to stay in the aeroplane and there the conference took place. I had expected rather a difficult time – but Winston was in a most mellow, not to say chastened mood. After two hours (in which Alex was most helpful and Anthony also) the whole strategic, tactical and political problems were reviewed and general agreement reached. It was decided to proceed with our plan. We had a draft communiqué ready, and all we had to do was to make the necessary changes to substitute P.M. for Alex as the 'convener' of the conference – and, of course, to see both the Archbishop and Papandreou. Winston, Anthony and their party (which included Lord Moran and Bob Dixon) went off in an armoured vehicle to the Piraeus (most of which we have now recaptured) and from thence to the *Ajax*, to which Admiral Mansfield has now transferred his flag. Alex went with them. Leeper and I returned to the Embassy.

We mobilised the Archbishop (who was in bed) and Papandreou, and took them down in an armoured vehicle to the landing-stage. The Archbishop kept his dignity, and his black, silver-knobbed staff, throughout. We got them on board by about 7 p.m. Winston and Anthony saw them separately – and by about

8 p.m. everything was agreed. It was decided to call the conference for the next day at 4 p.m. and to keep it small, four or five to represent the various parties in and out of the Government and three or four delegates from ELAS.

9–2 a.m. Dinner and immense talk on the *Ajax*. Leeper went back before dinner, but I stayed and was made to explain, argue, discuss *and* listen! It was exhausting, but quite amusing. Winston seemed to like the Archbishop and to have got over his distrust of my recommendations. Anthony was very friendly – he has evidently had a rough time. The King of the Hellenes has been very obstinate and Winston unwilling to press him unduly.

Tuesday, 26 December 1944

11 a.m. The Archbishop came to the Embassy. We went over the names of the delegates and the draft of his opening speech – also the drill to be followed. We arranged the plan to be followed in the event of ELAS either accepting or refusing the invitation.

There was (as we expected) an immense amount of confabulation and intrigue about who should come. Sophoulis refused at first – partly to meet ELAS, partly to accept the limitation of the delegates. The Royalist branch of the Populist party would not accept Maximos[23] and wanted separate representation. Papandreou – who obviously disliked the whole thing and has begun to see the handwriting on the wall – tried to get several of his friends asked. Finally, the Ambassador sent *written* invitations to the selected delegates and we made it clear by various means that they must either accept without further argument or take the responsibility of publicly refusing Mr Churchill's invitation.

At 12.30 Anthony Eden arrived at the Embassy and various further points were discussed – including a draft of the P.M.'s speech. It was terribly cold and I am very much afraid that Winston may get a chill.

At 3 p.m. Winston arrived. We still have no definite news about ELAS. At 3.30 a message came asking for an hour's delay – to this we agreed. The Greek politicians are gathered at the Grande Bretagne; the ELAS delegates will be taken to H.Q.; we wait at the Embassy. The meeting is to be at the Greek Ministry of Foreign Affairs, but this is being kept as dark as possible on security grounds. We are already a little shaken by the discovery this morning of large quantities of dynamite under the Grande Bretagne. The communiqué was duly published last night on the B.B.C. It should have a good effect in England.

At 4.45 there was still no news of ELAS. So we sent a messenger to the Grande Bretagne to bring the Greek politicians to the meeting-place. The Archbishop came to the Embassy and we all started in two armoured vehicles just before 5 p.m. Mr MacVeagh (the American Ambassador), Colonel Popov,[24] and the French Minister were invited as 'observers' and all accepted. This is rather a *coup* for us and should help.

As there is no electric light (except with military generators) the conference room was lit by hurricane lights on a large oval table. The Archbishop took his seat in the middle. On his right were Winston (in

[23] Dimitrios Maximos (1873–1955) became Prime Minister of Greece in 1947.

[24] Colonel Gregori Popov was head of the Soviet Military Mission to Greece, 1944–5, having headed a similar mission to Tito's partisans.

the uniform of an air commodore) and next to him Anthony. On his left were Alex and I. The Greeks sat opposite. At one end of the oval were the four observers. At the other end, places were left for ELAS. Major Mathews interpreted, and one or two other officials and stenographers completed the party. It was very cold to start with, but with the heat of the lamps and the people it soon warmed up.

The Archbishop opened with a short speech of welcome – very dignified – very happily expressed. He called then on Mr Churchill to speak.

The P.M. had been speaking for about five minutes, when there was a loud knock on the door. The ELAS delegates had arrived!

We all stood up. Three men in English battledress came in. They bowed and we bowed. We took our seats, and the conference began again. The Archbishop repeated his speech. It was again translated. Then the P.M. began and spoke for about twenty to twenty-five minutes – of course it took longer, with the interpreting. His speech was very good – clear, firm and persuasive. He left no doubt in the minds of the ELAS on the one hand of our military power. On the other hand, he made it clear to the politicians that he did not mean us to be used for a reactionary policy. He wanted peace, amnesty and a continuation of the work of relief and economic rehabilitation. He made it clear that Stalin had agreed to British intervention. And he went a long way to suggest that Roosevelt had also agreed – as indeed he did in August, and if we could publish his telegram to Winston it would indeed make the Americans look foolish (the President has let us down badly, and Winston is very hurt about it). Anthony then said a few words, useful, conciliatory and short. The Field Marshal made a short, soldierly speech, in excellent style and taste: 'Instead of me putting my brigades into Greece, I should like to see Greek brigades coming to help me in Italy in the war against our common enemy.'

The Archbishop then asked for questions. After a pause, M. Kaphandaris[25] made a short speech welcoming the conference. Papandreou then spoke in the same vein. Then one of the ELAS rose – a man called [Dimitrios] Partsalides. He is the secretary of EAM – a professor, of extreme and fanatical Communist opinions. A nice-looking fellow, with a pleasant smile and beautiful white teeth, he spoke in a quiet and soothing voice as if butter would not melt in his mouth. The other two delegates are Siantos,[26] a nasty rat-faced man, the secretary of the Communist Party, and General [Emmanuel] Mandakas – a big, burly Cretan – nice-looking, rather English in appearance. Partsalides made a very courteous and smooth speech – welcomed Mr Churchill's action, claimed to represent the mass of the Greek people, and hoped for peace between Greece and Great Britain.

[25] Georgios Kaphandaris (1873–1946) had been Prime Minister of Greece in 1924.

[26] Georgios Siantos (d. 1947) was Acting Secretary-General of KKE during the confinement of Secretary-General Zakhariadis in Dachau concentration camp, 1941–5.

I thought it all very disingenuous, especially remembering the frightful atrocities these men are committing both on our troops and on harmless fellow-countrymen throughout Greece. Winston was much moved however.

After this, the question of representation was raised, I think by Sophoulis. Anthony explained that we had merely convened a number of representative people as a start and had thought better to keep it small. But, of course, the question was entirely one for the conference to settle, and they could co-opt anybody they wished. P.M. then got up and thanked the delegates for what they had said. The conference would now – having been initiated by us – pass entirely to Greek hands. 'We have begun the work. You must finish it!' We all then went out, P.M. leading. We shook hands with all the delegates, including ELAS, as we went round the table to the door. The foreign observers came out with us. The P.M. went straight to the ship. It was about 6.30 when we left.

I walked back to the Embassy with Harold Caccia. The guns were firing in a battle near the Stadium, and machine-guns and rifles cracking away. A strange performance!

I do not think the conference will result in an immediate settlement. But it will do good, at home, abroad and in Greece. It will, I think, in due course *lead* to settlement; but only if we can get the regency. *That is the essential starting point, because it will naturally lead to a change of government.*

Alex and I went down to the ship for dinner. Another long evening. We got home to the Embassy about 2 a.m. A lot of telegrams from 'Monty' about the battle in Belgium and various other subjects relieved the talk. But most of it was on Greek affairs. Fortunately, Winston has fallen for the Archbishop.

Wednesday, 27 December 1944

10 a.m. The Archbishop came to the Embassy and reported on the proceedings *after* we had left. Apparently they were very rowdy! They went on till about 10 p.m. and adjourned till today. Our own sources (listening outside!) had already given us this information. At one point General Plastiras was heard to shout at one of the Communists – 'Sit down, butcher!' Anthony arrived about 10.15 and so heard the Archbishop's account together with his conclusions and recommendations. Then he went off at 11 a.m. to the adjourned meeting.

Harold Caccia and I then spent an hour preparing a record of all that the Archbishop said. (This is included in a yellow paper marked 'A' which I am putting in a special folder, marked 'Greece 27 December' [see p. 621]).

Winston arrived from the ship about 1.15, and we all lunched at the Embassy. It was still bitterly cold, but we got some military stores which helped a bit. He was in good form and had been taken by Alex to an 'observation post' from which he could see the whole city and get an idea of the fighting. Of course this affair is a sort of 'super Sidney Street', and he quite enjoyed having the whole problem explained to him by a master of the military art.

3 p.m. Ambassador MacVeagh came for an interview. I was not present, but I think Winston told him some home truths.

3.45 p.m. There was a press conference, partly 'off' and partly 'on' the record. P.M. and F.S. were both good – P.M. did the talking, but Anthony's little explanations were excellent also.

4.30–6 p.m. The Archbishop arrived and told us the situation. The conference had adjourned at 4 p.m. There followed a long discussion with the Archbishop (this is all in paper marked 'B' in the same folder [see p. 623]). Meanwhile, the ELAS delegates asked to see Winston privately. On the Archbishop's *strong* recommendation he replied in a letter (marked 'C' [see p. 627]). Winston was very inclined to see them, but I persuaded him (and Anthony agreed) that if we were going to put our money on the Archbishop, we must let him play the hand as he thought best. Winston partly wanted to see them as a good journalist, and partly because he has an innocence which is very charming but sometimes dangerous. He believed he could win them over. But I felt he would much more probably be deceived and betrayed.

At 7 p.m. Winston, Anthony and Alex left for the ship. Those present at this interview [from 4.30 to 6 p.m.] were P.M., F.S., Leeper, Archbishop and myself. It was agreed that Leeper and I should send for Papandreou and *force* him to send an honest recommendation to the King in favour of the regency. I wrote a draft telegram for this purpose (marked 'D' [see p. 628]).

At 7.15. Papandreou came. He is a worthy man, but vain – and therefore shifty. He now realises that he made a mistake in not backing the Archbishop for regent without equivocation. And he probably knew that this telegram would prove his death-warrant.

It was a most unpleasant half-hour. But Papandreou promised us faithfully that he would send the required telegram to the King. He would not agree to send the actual text. But it would be the substance of the telegram *dans son style personnel*.

I dined at the Embassy. About 10.30 a minute (marked 'E' [see p. 628]) was brought up. We got in touch with the Archbishop – of course to find that he had already issued a communiqué covering these three points – and a fourth; viz., that Papandreou had this morning tendered his resignation. There are certainly no flies on the Regent-elect!

I got to the ship about 11.30 p.m. and left about 2 a.m. Winston is more and more delighted with the Archbishop, but is still worrying about his refusal to grant a private interview to the ELAS delegates.

'A'

Part 1 – Debate

10 a.m.

The Archbishop gave the following account of the proceedings at last night's conference after we had left (26 December). He began by asking the Greek delegates to address themselves to the problem of the future of Greece. They had not in fact responded to his appeal.

The Secretary of the Communist party, *Siantos* (the middle of the three), made a violent attack on the Government, whom he held responsible for the bloodshed. ELAS represented the whole of the people and they were prepared to fight on even for forty years for its liberties. *Plastiras* (Republican ex-dictator) then broke in with a fierce reply saying that the Communists had not liberated but destroyed Greece. After these two explosions the meeting calmed somewhat while *Kaphandaris* (Progressive Party) tried to take a middle line. He said that Greece was suffering from an unprecedented situation in history in that there was no one to act as head of the state to regulate their present differences. In his view a regent must be appointed. The *Communists* hastened to say that they not only accepted the idea but they ardently desired it. *Maximos* (Popular Party, anti-Venizelist[27]) said that he was in favour of a regency provided that it was acceptable to His Majesty's Government. *Sophoulis* (Liberal Party) said that he had not only agreed to it but had proposed a regency even before the Lebanon conference. He saw no further necessity for the discussions to continue and he said that in any case no conclusion could be reached that night as the political parties were not fully represented. He said he was cold and wanted to leave. *Plastiras* then burst in again to say, 'Yes, that is all right about the regency, but I want to ask some direct questions of the Communists.' There was then another explosion which provided *Sophoulis* with the opportunity of withdrawing unobserved.

When order was restored *Papandreou* made a long apologia for his Government. He detailed the repeated concessions which he had made to the Communists particularly about the demobilisation issue. For instance he revealed that in preparing lists of officers for the new Regular Army he had actually submitted the names to the headquarters of the Communist Party for approval. Out of 280 names submitted 270 were objected to. He recounted a number of similar concessions to the Communists which the Archbishop told us went twice as far as he would ever have gone himself. The *Communists* however persisted that they would never hand in their arms to the present Government or to the British. Nor would they hand in their

[27] Venizelists (Liberal, republican) were followers of Eleutherios Venizelos, Prime Minister of Greece, 1910–15, 1916–20, 1928–32 and 1933.

arms until the Mountain Brigade and the Sacred Regiment had first done so.

These speeches give a picture of the debate which, the Archbishop explained, was subject to great varieties of emotion. He thought it wiser to allow a considerable latitude in order that they might get all these feelings off their chests. The debate brought out that, while the EAM members formed a solid front, this was not true of the anti-Communist parties. Considerable differences were revealed amongst them, mostly based on the historic division between the Venizelists and the anti-Venizelist parties.

PART II – ARCHBISHOP'S CONCLUSIONS

The Archbishop's conclusions, some of which emerged as a result of questions by the Foreign Secretary and the Resident Minister:

1. He did not think the Conference would last after today.

2. The *Communists* wanted a way out in spite of their brave words but they would prefer to see the war ended. Nevertheless they would struggle hard to get themselves into a favourable political position, so as to be able to achieve their ends by other means.

3. The solution which they would prefer would be a Coalition Government formed on traditional lines containing representatives of all the various political parties and groups. The extreme left (*Communists*) by following a consistent and determined policy among their vacillating colleagues would gradually obtain domination over the political situation.

4. Apart from the extreme Communists many people genuinely share the fear of the left of a Royalist *coup d'état*, leading to dictatorship and reprisals. This explains the feeling against the Mountain Brigade, who were accused of being cavalier troops marching to cavalier songs harking back to the days of King Constantine.

5. *Papandreou*'s Government is dead. It only remains to be buried. *Papandreou* himself said yesterday that he did not wish to stand in the way and recognised the fact that he cannot carry on.

PART III – ARCHBISHOP'S RECOMMENDATIONS

1. A regency should be created because at such a time the functions of head of the state must be carried out if the crisis is to be solved. He spoke with some diffidence because of his own position.

2. The acting head of the state should try to create a small Government, representative not of each particular party, great or small, but rather of Greek public feeling in its broadest sense. He would choose reliable and responsible men from either the right, centre or the left. He gave instances of such figures. The only opinion excluded should be regular official Communist Party. Such a Government

would allay fears of reprisals and thus provide no handle to malicious propaganda. When asked whether the Communists would make a peace with such a Government he said, 'I do not exclude it.'

3. Asked who should be the head of the Government it was clear that he intended General *Plastiras* but wished this kept very quiet. *Plastiras* would be generally acceptable except perhaps to the Popular Party, but even they had proposed that he should become Commander-in-Chief.

4. At the suggestion of the Secretary of State the Archbishop said that he would try to obtain from the conference today recommendations about a regency and a new government. He thought that the only opposition to the proposal for a regency would come from the anti-Venizelists (i.e., the Popular Party, many of whom are Royalists).

5. At the suggestion of the Foreign Secretary the Archbishop agreed that he would try to keep the conference nominally in being and end the proceedings rather by adjournment than by dissolution.

PART IV – ARRANGEMENTS FOR THE SECOND MEETING

The second meeting of the conference was arranged for eleven o'clock on 27 December. In addition to yesterday's members the following were being invited:

M. Tsaldaris[28] (Popular Party, Royalist)
M. Rallis[29] (Popular Party, moderate)
M. Theotokis[30] (Nationalist right-wing group)
M. Mylonas[31] (Agrarian with Liberal leanings)
M. Sophianopoulos[32] (Agrarian with Socialist leanings)
M. Kanellopoulos (representing moderate left)
M. [Apostolos] Alexandris (representing centre group)

'*B*'

PART I – ARCHBISHOP'S ACCOUNT

The Archbishop gave the following account of the Second Conference which started at eleven o'clock in the morning [27 December] and finished at about 4 p.m.

He said that the meeting had been attended not only by those present yesterday, but by an additional number of representatives of political parties. The complete list was as follows:

1. Papandreou (Prime Minister)
2. Maximos (Popular Party)

[28] Constantine Tsaldaris (1884–1970) became Prime Minister of Greece in 1946.
[29] Pericles Rallis (1891–1945) was Minister of the Interior, 1935 and January–February 1945.
[30] Ioannis Theotokis (1880–1961) became Prime Minister of a caretaker Cabinet in 1950.
[31] Alexandros Mylonas (1881–1967), founder of the Agrarian Party, was Minister of the Navy, 1944, and of Finance, 1945–6.
[32] Ioannis Sophianopoulos (b. 1888) was Foreign Minister, 1945 and 1945–6.

3. Tsaldaris (Popular Party, Royalist)
4. Rallis (Popular Party, moderate)
5. Stephanopoulos[33] (Popular Party, moderate)
6. Alexandris (National Reform Party, centre group)
7. Theotokis (Popular National Party, a right-wing group)
8. Sophoulis (Liberal)
9. Gonatas[34] (Liberal)
10. Kaphandaris (Progressive)
11. Sophianopoulos (Agrarian, Socialist)
12. Mylonas (Agrarian with Liberal leanings)
13. Plastiras (Republican, ex-dictator)
14. Kanellopoulos (Union Party, moderate left)
15. Siantos (ELAS, Communist Party)
16. Partsalides (ELAS, General Secretary of EAM)

General Mandakas of ELAS Central Committee, who was one of the three delegates at the first conference, did not attend the second meeting.

For the benefit of the newcomers he gave a résumé of yesterday's proceedings and after explaining that the question of the regency had been raised, asked for the views of the conference. A lengthy discussion ensued as a result of which all present expressed themselves unanimously in favour of the establishment of a regency. All except members of the Popular Party were in favour of the regency being created at once, and the latter party only thought that the actual establishment of the regency should be deferred until ELAS had accepted General Scobie's terms for a truce.

When the meeting had concluded discussion of the question of the regency, the representatives of ELAS were questioned at length in order that their views on other matters should be made clear to all present. The Archbishop gave the following list of ELAS demands:

(*a*) Collaborators should be punished (ELAS had demanded that not only those who had collaborated with the Germans but also those who had served the Metaxas[35] dictatorship should be dealt with. In the Archbishop's opinion their argument for including those who had served Metaxas was weak.

(*b*) Civil service should be purged.

(*c*) The Gendarmerie should be dissolved and replaced by a National Guard recruited from age groups to be decided at a later date.

(*d*) Certain elements in the city police should be purged.

[33] Stephanos Stephanopoulos (1899–1982) was Prime Minister of Greece, 1965–6.

[34] General Stylianos Gonatas (1876–1966) was Prime Minister of Greece, 1922–4, after leading the coup against King Constantine I with General Plastiras, and founded EDES with General Zervas in 1941.

[35] General Ioannis Metaxas (1871–1941) was dictator of Greece (with the authority of King George II), 1936–41.

(*e*) The Army should be purged, not on a basis of professional qualifications but on political grounds.

(*f*) A new government should be formed in which the share of EAM/ELAS should be forty to fifty per cent. Their immediate demand was for the Ministries of Interior and Justice, and for the Under-Secretaries of War and Foreign Affairs. They would desire some other posts in addition.

(*g*) An immediate plebiscite should be held on the constitutional question. (The Archbishop explained that this would mean in the period while ELAS dominated the whole countryside.)

(*h*) In the month of April elections for a Chamber should be held.

After the above points had been elucidated, certain members said that they were not prepared for further discussion on such a basis. Indeed the whole feeling of the meeting was that such terms were unacceptable. In the Archbishop's personal opinion it would be a criminal act to agree to them; for that would hand over Greece to EAM/ELAS control despite the fact that the latter only represented a small percentage of Greek people.

The Archbishop thereupon adjourned the meeting, stating that he would call a further session when he thought fit. In doing so he said that he had made it clear that in his view a further meeting would not be worth while for the present. By this no doubt he meant until the question of the regency had been decided.

PART II – DISCUSSION WITH ARCHBISHOP

After describing what had happened at the second conference, the Archbishop proposed the following programme. In the first place a regency should be established and then a new government should be formed of persons of general confidence including left-wing representatives. These left-wing representatives should be men who were conscious of their responsibilities. Such a government would have a wide popular support, and would make the extreme left realise that they were up against strong opposition. Assuming that this was done and that in the meantime Attica was cleared the time might then have come to call a further conference with the reasonable chance of a settlement.

The Prime Minister explained that the question of a regency could not be settled by himself or His Majesty's Government. When he and the Foreign Secretary had discussed this question with the King he had shown himself strongly opposed. Although it had been pointed out to His Majesty that a regency was an effective manner of keeping alive the monarchical theory, the King had said that it was not of himself that he was thinking. He had received letters and telegrams from his supporters in Greece begging him not to abandon them. His Majesty's Government would endeavour once again to overcome the King's scruples. But if he were to refuse it was difficult to see what legal means could be found to achieve the object. A revolutionary procedure was always a possibility but had its weaknesses, especially if a long term would inevitably elapse before elections could be held. The Archbishop said that the King should not pay too much attention to the advice of his friends; His Majesty depended on His Majesty's Government and if His Majesty's Government showed him that they would not support his cause, he would agree to the regency. When the Archbishop was asked what he suggested should be done if the King continued to refuse, he replied that he had not faced this possibility, since he felt sure that the King would yield if pressed by H.M.G. If, however, the King should refuse it would be necessary for the Greeks themselves to find their own solution alone.

The question was then raised, how long a regency should last if it were established. It was finally agreed with the Archbishop that on return to London the Prime Minister and Foreign Secretary would urge the King to set up a regency for a year, or until a plebiscite could be held under normal conditions of liberty and tranquillity. The Prime Minister said that he would ask President Roosevelt to support H.M.G. in urging this course on the King. The Archbishop said that he was sure that whatever term the King saw fit to put to the length of the regency, it would raise no difficulty in Greece.

The Prime Minister pointed out that one of the factors which had led the King to refuse the regency was that hitherto he had received equivocal messages from individual Ministers. What was required was advice from the Greek Government as a whole. The Archbishop said that Papandreou at the second conference had announced that he would advise the King to establish a regency. It was consequently agreed that Mr Macmillan and Mr Leeper would see M. Papandreou immediately and urge him to send definite and unqualified advice on the point to the King. The Archbishop further said that he was going to state publicly that the conference had expressed itself unanimously in favour of a regency.

When asked whether he would accept the regency if offered, the Archbishop replied that he would and that the King could be informed that nobody would discharge this duty with more respect to the person of the King or to the monarchy than himself.

The conclusions were:

(*a*) On the return of the Prime Minister and Foreign Secretary to England the King would be asked to establish a regency. If he refused, alternative steps would have to be considered by which the Archbishop might exercise powers of Regent, e.g. under a mandate from the three great powers, or by the conference of Greeks or another body making a declaration, which H.M.G. would endorse, that they conferred the powers of Regent on the Archbishop; any of these steps would, of course, carry with them a transference of recognition.

(*b*) The Archbishop is meanwhile considering the Government to be formed. He indicated privately that his provisional choice for Prime Minister would be Plastiras and he thought that the other posts could easily be filled. He would keep us informed. The administration would be a small representative government of best men rather than of parties which would hand back powers to the political world as soon as conditions permitted.

(*c*) The new government would need from British sources foodstuffs and equipment for the formation of a National Army to keep the peace.

(*d*) Meanwhile British operations would continue in full vigour until ELAS accepted General Scobie's terms or the Athens area were freed. The Prime Minister made it clear that we could not commit ourselves to military operations after the clearing of Attica, although we could try to keep British forces here until the Greek National Army had been formed.

Before leaving, the Archbishop was asked whether he intended to include Communists in the Government. He replied with a decided negative. His calculation was that the establishment of a regency and formation of a small representative government would split the moderates from the extremists in EAM. Prime Minister then explained that he had had a message that two of the ELAS delegates to the Conference (Siantos and Partsalides) had asked to see him on the strength of a statement at the first conference that he was ready to be called in by the conference if required. The Archbishop was strongly against compliance and after some discussion the Prime Minister wrote a reply refusing this request on the grounds that as the conference was wholly Greek in character, it would not be desirable for him to be involved in what might seem to be negotiations apart from the conference at whose disposal as a whole he and his colleagues had placed themselves.

Finally the Prime Minister said that he would like an assurance from the Archbishop that in the event of his becoming Regent the safety of M. Papandreou personally and of those who had supported him should be guaranteed by any new government. The Archbishop said that he would give this guarantee absolutely and without question.

'C'

Letter from Mr Churchill to two ELAS leaders who asked to see him

27 December 1944

Gentlemen,

I have received your request that I should meet you both privately. Although personally I should have been willing to comply, I feel that the conference being wholly Greek in character does not make it desirable for me to be involved in what might seem to be negotiations apart from the conference, at whose disposal as a whole I and my colleagues have placed ourselves.

Let me add my fervent hope that the discussions which have taken place and the contacts which have been made will result in a speedy end to the melancholy conflict proceeding between men of one country.

'D'

Telegram sent by M. Papandreou to the King

As Prime Minister of Greece it is my duty to report to Your Majesty that at the conference today all present were unanimously in favour of the establishment of a regency. All except members of the Popular Party expressed themselves in favour of the regency being created at once. I myself agreed that an immediate regency was necessary. The members of the Popular Party thought, however, that the establishment of a regency should be deferred until ELAS had accepted General Scobie's terms for a truce.

In view of what happened today and in the interests of Greece as well as of the Royal House, I, as Prime Minister, formally tend to Your Majesty the advice that you should appoint a regency forthwith. It is further my advice that there should be a single Regent and that he should be the Archbishop of Athens.

'E'

Minute from Mr Eden to Mr Leeper

10, Downing Street
Whitehall

H.M.S. *Ajax* to British Embassy, Athens
EMERGENCY

Please pass urgently to Ambassador from Foreign Secretary. BEGINS:

1. Colonel Kent [Churchill] and I consider it important that the Archbishop should put out a statement tonight about today's proceedings at the conference.

2. Points to be brought out:

(*a*) The conference today was attended by representatives of all the political parties as well as ELAS.

(*b*) That large majority of meeting was in favour of a regency.

(*c*) The conference was not dissolved but was adjourned pending further summons from Archbishop.

3. We must leave it to the Archbishop to decide how to describe the way in which relations were left at the end of the conference between

EAM and the other delegates. We should however deprecate anything that closed the door to resumption of conference.

10 p.m.
27.12.44

(*Note on other side of minute*)

The Archbishop has, of course, already done these three things. He has also announced that Papandreou offered his resignation.

27.12.44
(10.30 p.m.)

Thursday, 28 December 1944

We had arranged to leave the airfield at 1 p.m. and return to Naples. This meant that when I rolled myself into my cold bed at 2 a.m. this morning, I looked forward to a quiet morning. At 10 a.m., however, Alex, Leeper and I were summoned to the cruiser. Alex had gone out to see some troops; but Leeper and I had to go. We found Winston still fussing about the ELAS delegates. He thought he would stay another day and summon a further meeting of the conference. He did not like the idea of going home without a peace, or at least a truce, arranged. I argued strongly in favour of his immediate return *to secure the regency*. This would be a service to Greece which only could be performed in London (since the King was the stumbling-block and the King was in London), and which only he (Winston) could carry to a successful conclusion.

Finally, to clinch the matter, it was decided to issue a communiqué – which would commit H.M.G. publicly to the regency. This was drafted and agreed (document 'F').

'F'

COMMUNIQUÉ TO BE HANDED TO THE PRESS
BY HIS MAJESTY'S AMBASSADOR

The Archbishop of Athens, in his capacity of chairman of the conference convened at Mr Churchill's desire on 26 December, called on Mr Churchill and Mr Eden yesterday evening. He gave the British Ministers an account of the proceedings of the first two days of the conference, and reported the overwhelming desire of those present for the immediate establishment of a regency as an essential prelude to the solution of the many other problems before the conference.

Mr Churchill and Mr Eden undertook, on behalf of His Majesty's Government, to recommend this course to the King of the Hellenes. The Archbishop has adjourned the conference for the time being. Mr Churchill and Mr Eden have left for London.

28 December 1944

[Diary continues] So at last we got away. We went from the ship to the airfield. John had already left with Rupert Clarke in the Field Marshal's aeroplane. I went with P.M., F.S., etc., in the P.M.'s plane, a new C54, much more comfortable than the York.

We got to Naples about 4.30 p.m. and I went straight to the Villa Carradori and to bed. I had a hot bath – a great pleasure, not having washed for so long. There were a lot of Washington telegrams about my proposals for Italy to be read – as well as various routine affairs. Broad is very efficient and has looked after things very well in my absence.

9 p.m. Dined with P.M., Alex, C.-in-C. Med., Slessor, etc., at the Villa Rivalta (Wilson's – now Alex's – guest villa near mine in Naples). We got away by 1 a.m. – a great feat.

Friday, 29 December 1944

Up at 6.30. Motored to Pomigliano airfield to see P.M. and party leave at 8 a.m. Motored from there with Alex to Caserta, where I got some breakfast in the Villa Vittoria. After dealing with some telegrams, left at 10.45, with John and Miss Campbell, for Rome.

3 p.m. Saw Stone (now Admiral Stone – Chief Commissioner) and Brigadier Lush (Chief of Staff). I have terribly neglected my Italian responsibilities – but not through my own fault. They were all very pleasant at the Commission offices and we worked on a number of problems till about 6.30 p.m.

I then went to the Villa Parisi (Via Nomentana – beyond the British Embassy and the Porta Pia). The house is largish – beautifully warm, with excellent bathrooms – and ugly beyond anybody's imagination. It is in a sort of pseudo-French style (like the dining-room at Cliveden parodied by a South American prostitute). But it will serve our needs and seemed a dream of luxury after the sufferings of cold at Athens.

Lush came to dinner. We worked on various points arising from the way my Italian plans are being handled at Washington. Miss Campbell came at 10 p.m. and I dictated telegrams, etc., to deal with the various points. The Americans are being very pedantic, and I fear that in my absence my ideas are not going to have a real chance of acceptance. Went to bed about midnight.

Saturday, 30 December 1944

Left at 7 a.m. for Ciampino airfield. There was a good deal of talk about the possibility of flying. Finally we took off in a Mitchell and got to Marcianise (Caserta) at 8.30. Drove to Villa Vittoria, where I breakfasted. I left John in Rome.

At 10.30 we had S.A.C.'s political meeting. It was the first one which I had attended with Alex in the chair. He was very businesslike and we got through a long agenda in an hour.

There has been a lot of trouble over an agreement between the

C.L.N.A.I. (or partisan movement) in northern Italy and A.F.H.Q. and the Italian Government. The F.O. has been tiresome and pedantic. I thought Alex was quite right in his decision and I have supported him and telegraphed the F.O. accordingly.

12.30 p.m. Left by car for Rome with Alex. We arrived about 4.30 p.m. He went off to his train and came back for dinner at 8 p.m. I went to bed (after a lovely hot bath) and worked in bed. Admiral Stone and Brigadier Lush to dinner – also Henry Hopkinson, who is doing very well in Harold Caccia's old post.

Alex left at 10 p.m. to go aboard his train. He is going up the line tonight to see General [Mark] Clark (Fifteenth Army Group) and also Eighth Army.

Sunday, 31 December 1944

I stayed in bed till 4 p.m. – being very exhausted with all the movement and excitement of recent days. Finished Trollope's *Miss MacKenzie* – wrote up the diary – and dozed.

At 5 p.m. went to see Sir Noel Charles. He has left the Embassy and moved into an apartment in the Palazzo Orsini. He was in bed and not at all well, having got an attack of arthritis in his right arm.

John and I dined alone and went early to bed – a reposeful end to 1944. What will 1945 bring?

We heard the news on the wireless yesterday that the King of the Hellenes had at last agreed to appoint the Archbishop as sole Regent. This is a great gain. In the first place, it is a move; and when a political situation has got into a 'jam', the great thing is to bring about some kind of movement. I hope very much that the new Government which the Archbishop will appoint will be able to break into the EAM position and detach the more moderate from the more extreme elements. This is the only way in which we can achieve our purpose. Even if we had the troops available to undertake operations throughout Greece (which, of course, is not the case) we could not by military power alone bring about the isolation and then the reduction of prestige of the extreme revolutionary Communists.

Secondly, it is the only contribution on the political, as distinct from the military, side which we can make. It was for this reason that Leeper and I urged it so strongly and with such painful iteration on London. Winston's visit has convinced him both of the necessity for a 'head of the state' and of the suitability of Archbishop Damaskinos for the post. Anthony was already convinced. It is now up to us to steer the Archbishop. I have so much to do in Rome that I cannot leave for a few days. But I must try to get back as soon as possible to Athens to help Leeper. Until we can clear up this Greek position it is like a running sore. It drains away both our military strength and our political prestige at home and abroad.

1945

January

Monday, 1 January 1945

I went early to bed last night and slept till 9.30 a.m. I must have slept for eleven hours. This, with most of yesterday in bed, has quite restored me. I felt very low on Saturday night, with a strong desire to burst into tears! It is extraordinary what sleep can do. It is the best of all restoratives.

I came to my office at the Commission's H.Q. at about 10.30. There was a good deal of preliminary work to do – but (being New Year's Day) it was a holiday and except for a few leading officials the office was deserted. Brigadier Lush came to see me, and I have got hold of a lot of papers and am sorting out my own Italian files.

The Americans – both locally and in Washington – have revived the idea of *dividing* Italy into a military and a political sphere. This, of course, is quite foolish and unworkable. I convinced the War Office and all the other Departments in London of its futility. And I believe I could perhaps have done the same in Washington if I could have got there. Meanwhile, after talking it over with Alex on Saturday, I have sent the necessary telegrams to London and Washington. And, hearing of an attempt to organise a 'political section or G5' at Fifteenth Army Group (the successor to Allied Armies in Italy) I telegraphed to Alex asking him to veto it, at least until the final directive arrives from Washington.

On the Italian side, there are a large number of questions still to be settled. The food ration, the Italian forces, the housing situation, the prisoners of war in Italy, and the use and misuse of the 'purge'. In addition, industrial reconstruction, local elections, the transport problem, and the partisan movement in northern Italy are pressing matters. I must look into them all and see how matters stand. As far as I can see, the team here is pretty good on the administrative, but very weak on the economic, side. They have been hampered by A.F.H.Q. and still more by Combined Chiefs of Staff and Combined Civil Affairs Committee at Washington.

I worked through the day – it was not necessary to get any lunch as I had a good breakfast at 9.45 – until about 4 p.m. Then – as the office was deserted and I had made a fair start – I went for a walk with John. It was a lovely day – cold and a bright sun in a cloudless sky.

I wonder how Christmas and the New Year have passed at home, with my wife, children and grandchildren! And how Maurice is keeping and how Katharine and her prospective baby. Soon – if all goes well – I shall have *three* grandchildren – a most inspiring if sometimes sobering thought!

As the *press* (who rule us) have been very mystified by my behaviour since my appointment as Acting President of the Allied Commission (and not without some cause) it has been decided to cultivate them a little. Reuter's man and the *Times* man are being asked to luncheon tomorrow. And a press conference is being laid on for Wednesday afternoon. After that, I feel I ought to return to Caserta for a day or two, and perhaps to Greece.

There are a number of French novels in the Villa Parisi. I read Anatole France's *L'Orme du mail* till dinner. Dined with Brigadier Lush, Colonel Grafftey-Smith, Major Talbot, etc. John de Salis came round after dinner to the Villa Parisi with John, who had been dining with him.

It is now exactly two years since I started on this strange politico-diplomatic enterprise in the Mediterranean. On 1 January at 1 a.m. John and Miss Campbell and I set off from Cornwall for Algiers. Other members of my staff have come and gone – Bob Dixon, Roger Makins (who gave me eighteen months of splendid help), Harold Caccia (who is still my representative in Athens), Jim Bowker (who was only with me for a month or two), Tony Rumbold, Kit Steel and Philip Broad. But the only survivors are the original party of three pioneers – John, Miss Campbell and I.

Tuesday, 2 January 1945

9 a.m. Went to my office in the Allied Commission. It is very well appointed, in a flash kind of way. The building is a Fascist one – the Ministry of Corporations. There is a curious irony in the fact that it is now the H.Q. of the Anglo-American authority.

Broad rang up with a message from Alex. Scobie and Leeper want to withdraw the truce terms and give ELAS an ultimatum. I am against this. We should leave things as they are and let the situation develop a little. Broad rang me back later to say that the F.M. agreed with my view. Instructions will be sent to Athens accordingly.

A lot of telegrams have arrived from Washington about my proposals for Italy. I cannot understand why the C.C.S. and the C.C.A.C. make such heavy weather about everything. Over-organisation is the curse of this war, and the Americans are far worse in this respect than we are.

I worked at the A.C. building all the morning on these and a number of other questions. All I can do – while waiting for the direction from Washington – is to go into a number of specific problems and ask for information. I feel rather as I did during my early days at the Colonial Office. There is in the A.C. a large and rather uncoordinated organisation, very nervous about criticism and rather uncreative. I must try to stimulate without unduly alarming it. I like Stone – he is a fine man, but rigid and nervous. Lush (Chief of Staff) has perhaps some faults, but he is energetic and keen on the work – and that is a great deal.

1.15 p.m. Luncheon party at the Villa Parisi. Messrs [C. J. S.] Sprigge (Reuters), Lumb (*Times*), Lucas (*Express*), More (*Daily Telegraph*) and Miss Elizabeth Mackenzie (*Chronicle*); also Major Fielden (P.R.O.) and John Wyndham. The party went very well.

4.30 p.m. Conference with Stone and Lush which lasted till about 6 p.m.

Dined quietly at the Villa Parisi with John and went early to bed.

Wednesday, 3 January 1945

9 a.m. Walked to A.C. office – a lovely, bright, cold, sunny morning.

11.15 a.m. M. Exindaris (Greek member of Advisory Council for Italy), a very wordy, critical, but not unintelligent man. He was very critical of M. Papandreou.

12 noon. Count Carandini, the new Italian Ambassador to London. He is back for a short visit of consultation with the new Italian Government. He is really an excellent man, and I like him greatly. He is far above the average Italian, in character and moral standing. He is very anxious for me to do something about the enlistment in the Army of the patriots who cross the lines. At present it seems that they are rather 'cold-shouldered'. I must look into this.

1.15 p.m. Another 'press' luncheon – Packard (U.P.), Norgaard (Associated Press), Chinigo (Internews) – all American agencies. Also Major Burgin [?] (U.S.), P.R.O. Quite an amusing party, and a lot of frank speaking. The guests did not leave till nearly 3.30, so I assume they enjoyed themselves.

5.30 p.m. Press conference. I gave them a piece 'on the record' and a good deal 'off the record' – we also had 'questions' which I tried to handle rather like a political meeting at Stockton. One of my luncheon guests, Mr Norgaard – a very earnest liberal – questioned me about British intentions regarding Italian colonies. He said that our unwillingness to regard Italy as an 'ally' (instead of a co-belligerent) was because if she became an ally we 'could not take colonies or territories off an ally – it isn't done'. I at once walked up to him with outstretched hand and shook his hand warmly, saying, 'Put it there, my friend. The Italian colonies in the West are safe.' This quite brought down the house.

7.15 p.m. Left by car, arriving Naples at 11.15 p.m. – a lovely drive – a clear, frosty, moonlit night.

Thursday, 4 January 1945

7.30 a.m. Left Naples, arriving Caserta at 8.30 a.m. Had a talk with Alex on Italian and Greek questions – as well as some matters regarding the organisation of A.F.H.Q. The F.M. was as charming and helpful as usual. He motored down to the Marcianise airfield with me, to see me off. Unfortunately, there was some delay as the Mitchell bomber which was to have taken me had some defect. Eventually a Hudson was produced, and I left about 11 a.m. (accompanied by Major Odgers).

Arrived Athens about 4.30 (Greek time) after a bad trip. We had to go all round by sea, as the weather did not allow the direct flight over the mountains. I got to the Embassy about 5 p.m. where I found the Ambassador looking rather worn and tired. He seemed very pleased to see me. We talked over the whole situation, which is gradually improving so far as Athens is concerned.

6.30 p.m. I walked round to H.Q. to see Scobie. I found him rather harassed.

After dinner, just as we were going to bed, General Scobie rang up to say that he was very worried about the situation at Patras (in the Peloponnese, on the Gulf of Corinth). Admiral Mansfield, who was lying off Patras in the *Orion*, and Brigadier Hunt, who was in command of a brigade there, reported that the position was deteriorating. The troops must either be withdrawn or reinforced. General Scobie was telegraphing to F.M. Alexander. Would I support his plea for reinforcements?

I replied that I could not telegraph Alex in support of Scobie's view without seeing his telegram. The general then said he would send Brigadier Firth round with the draft.

The brigadier in due course turned up at the Embassy with a pencil-draft telegram. It was a short, pitiful affair. After reading it I said that I thought the general had better come round and see me and the Ambassador.

At about 11.30 he arrived. After a lot of talk, I undertook to send Alex my own 'military and political appreciation'. I dictated the telegram, which General Scobie and the Ambassador approved, and I also sent a short one suggesting that Alex should come over himself to discuss both the question of Patras and the future policy. It is clear that we are now approaching the end of a phase in the Greek affair. Athens (and probably Attica) will soon be cleared of ELAS forces. We must consider the next steps. All this took till about 2 a.m., when we finally went to bed.

Friday, 5 January 1945

9 a.m. A number of 'Immediate' telegrams were brought to me from London and Washington regarding my Italian plans. I found them

rather difficult to follow, but eventually managed to produce some replies. It is very disappointing to me that they are arguing every point so pedantically. My proposals – as finally cleared in London – were simple and reasonable. But the Washington bureaucratic machine is transferring them into an incredibly complicated tangle.

10 a.m. It is said that the ELAS leaders want to come and talk about a truce, so we had a conference as to what we should say. It was agreed (and General Scobie was informed at 12 noon) that we should stick to our two terms and refer any other questions to the Greek Government. At 2.30 I went to see the Regent. I found him installed in a fine villa, with a guard of Evzones. He was very charming and entirely agreed that the Greek Government should (if the ELAS representatives came to see them) refuse to discuss any political points until the truce had been accepted.

Actually, it was all a waste of time, because the ELAS representatives failed to turn up.

4 p.m. F.M. Alexander arrived. He came straight to the Embassy. I explained to him what had happened last night and why I had asked him to come over. I also asked him to deal with General Scobie's staff. He was very understanding and seemed quite glad to have come at this stage. On Patras he had accepted my view, and ordered a brigade from Italy and an armoured regiment. But they can hardly arrive until the 11th, and there will be an awkward interval. On the staff question, he had brought Brigadier Hugh Mainwaring – an excellent and experienced officer – who will replace Brigadiers Firth and Springhall and become Chief of Staff to General Scobie. He will also immediately appoint General Hawkesworth as officer commanding all operations in Greece (not merely Athens) under General Scobie's general direction.

After our talk, Alex went off to H.Q. to see the situation for himself and consult with the officers there.

6 p.m. General Plastiras – the new Prime Minister – called at the Embassy. The Ambassador and I saw him. I was much struck with the increased vigour and energy which he showed. He was very sensible and seemed to understand that he must help us politically, just as we were helping him militarily.

Alex returned about 7 p.m. We dined at the Embassy (where Alex also is staying) and went to bed at a fairly reasonable hour.

Saturday, 6 January 1945

The military position is improving very rapidly. We have made great progress in Athens and the suburbs, and it looks as if the insurgents were retiring.

Harold Caccia, Brigadier Smith-Dorrien and I met in the morning. I am anxious to prepare the right plans for the next phase. What I have in mind is that the Greek Government should deal with *all* the questions which have been the subject of controversy (Mountain Brigade, Sacred

Battalion, Gendarmerie, police, purge of Quislings, amnesty, etc.) and thereby isolate the Communists altogether from the general body of EAM supporters. We discussed detailed plans of this. They depend to some extent on the military plans for the reorganisation of the Greek Army, which Alex and his staff are discussing this morning.

After luncheon, Alex, Rex Leeper and I went for a walk. The whole atmosphere of Athens is changed to an unbelievable degree. *All* the population are out walking and sunning themselves in areas in which it was dangerous even to be seen a few days ago. We walked down to the Stadium and through all the areas across the Ilyssus, which was strongly held by the insurgents last week and from which they used to snipe us in the Embassy. Alex was very generally recognised, and all the civilians bowed – by taking off their hats or waving to him. It is quite touching to see the extraordinary pleasure and delight of a people at what is generally called 'the second liberation'.

6–7.30 p.m. A long talk with M. [Georgios] Sideris, the new Minister of Finance. I thought him intelligent, if long-winded.

The F.M. has been doing a lot of thinking today. I arranged with him that we should do another joint telegram to P.M. and F.S. and I will sketch out the plan of it tonight. There will be a military and political appreciation and recommendations from us both on the whole problem.

Meanwhile, it occurred to me this afternoon that General Scobie's truce terms were now obsolete and that we should look very foolish if ELAS suddenly accepted them. They have been driven from Athens and will soon be out of Attica. And although the original truce terms were reasonable when they were first put out (11 December), and although we have stuck to them since then, they are quite out of date now. Among other things, they do not deal with prisoners and hostages. So I drafted a communiqué withdrawing the terms. Of course I know this will mean a lot of criticism in London, so I tried to draw up the notice with an eye to the great British public.

I consulted Osbert Lancaster (the press expert), and the Ambassador and Alex gave their approval. So this is done.

Sunday, 7 January 1945

Worked with Caccia on various telegrams. When all this is over, we shall be back with the financial and economic problems with which we were trying to deal when the revolution broke out. I want a good financial expert (and am asking the Treasury to send one) and I am also going to ask for Commander Jackson of Middle East Supply Centre to come up from Cairo for a bit to get things started.

Meanwhile, General Brian Robertson is over from A.F.H.Q. He is, I am glad to say, going to make a complete purge of the Q side of General Scobie's staff and particularly of the 'Relief and Rehabilitation' section. This is long overdue, and I am very pleased.

I began my draft of the joint telegram to London.

1 p.m. Luncheon with Ambassador and Mrs MacVeagh. If a weak diplomat, he is a charming, cultivated and scholarly man. He knows Greece very well, and is passionately interested in Greek history and antiquities. He and she are a very good type of the old New England American. I thoroughly enjoyed the luncheon; we never mentioned present-day Greece!

4 p.m. A conference of the British press. I tried to explain to them our reasons for withdrawing the present truce conditions. I hope they will not be too hostile. It is evident that most of them are ignorant of the true situation. Even if they send sensible reports home, most of the editors do not print them.

6–8 p.m. Worked on the long telegram, and agreed all the draft with Alex. This was sent off. After dinner, Scobie came round and we drew up the terms of a truce to *supersede* the old terms. He should use these if he is asked. Meanwhile, rather half-hearted attempts to get into touch with us are being made by ELAS. A man arrived on a *tricycle* at the American Embassy this afternoon, but his credentials seemed rather shadowy. The new truce will demand a line further forward, and will also require the disarming of ELAS forces east and south of this line – i.e. Boeotia, Attica and *all* the Peloponnese – also the Cyclades islands. This will allow us to strengthen our position in Salonika.

Monday, 8 January 1945

Left airfield 9.30 with F.M. We arrived at Marcianise at 1.15 (Naples time) and I went up to luncheon with him at the Hunting Lodge. A bad trip back – cloud and storms and again we had to come round by sea.

Worked at the office after luncheon; a fair number of papers on a variety of subjects. Broad is doing very well. He is most efficient and methodical and keeps everything well under control during my absence.

5 p.m. Colonel Henn[1] (G5) – in private life a Professor of Poetry and Fine Arts. He is a great improvement on his predecessor, as he clearly has a good brain.

6 p.m. General Robertson. (1) Reform of Greek and Balkan relief organisation. (2) Italian – especially food – problems. There is still no satisfactory decision on the 300-gramme ration. The Americans are trying to put the responsibility (without the necessary shipping) on to SACMED. (3) Organisational problems as between Allied Commission and Fifteenth Army Group. I like doing business with General Robertson, for he is a very clever man. General George Clark, his predecessor, was charming but less competent.

[1] Colonel T. R. Henn (1901–74), as Deputy Assistant Chief of Staff, G5, was responsible for works of art in the battle and liberated zones in Italy and later in France. He was to be President of St Catharine's College, Cambridge, 1957–61 and 1968–9.

Tuesday, 9 January 1945

Motored up from Naples. Went to see Alex about 9.45. The P.M. seems rather annoyed that we have withdrawn General Scobie's truce terms without consultation with London. But the 'tricyclist' episode proves that we were only just in time! We decided *not* to answer P.M.'s telegram.

11 a.m. General Robertson – a few points of detail only.

1 p.m. M. Sandström (of the Swedish Red Cross) whom I had met in Athens. He had returned to Sweden and is now on his way out again to Greece.

4.30 p.m. Messrs Barnes and Harman (of P.W.B.) came to see me. I am trying to abolish P.W.B. in respect of liberated Italy, and hand in their work to the Commission and the Embassies. On the whole, they are taking this idea well. Political warfare should be directed *against* the enemy – this is their proper job. In liberated territory they should hand on their functions.

5.30 p.m. Colonel Henn again. He makes sense.

Motored down to Naples. The lights won't work and there is no heating or hot water. So we went to bed at 10 p.m. to try to keep warm. The rain is very heavy – a cold, clammy atmosphere pervades the house.

Wednesday, 10 January 1945

Motored to Caserta and went to see Alex about 9.30 a.m. Messrs Scobie and Leeper are sending a number of excited telegrams, which tell their own story. Apparently a properly constituted delegation from ELAS has turned up – Zevgos, etc. Scobie asked (and Leeper supported) for authority to give them the truce terms which Alex and I drew up on 7 January and left with them in Athens. They telegraph *both* to London and to Caserta (which makes it more confusing). At 7.45 last night they seemed quite happy with these terms, but by 12 midnight (whether due to more reflection or more drink) they want to step them up, by putting back the line to include Lamia and Volos and also to include a withdrawal at Salonika. After talking it over, Alex and I decided to accept Salonika but *not* the advance northwards on to the mainland to Volos and Lamia, and telegraphed accordingly to London and Athens.

I think Leeper's telegram a little hysterical – perhaps the long tension of the siege is beginning to tell on him.

At 1.15, after finishing my work, I left for Rome by car. I reached the Allied Commission by 5 p.m. and at once saw Stone and Lush on a number of matters, ranging from the appointment of a new press officer, to the trial of General Roatta, the position of General Orlando,[2] and the relations of the Commission with the Fifteenth

[2] General Taddeo Orlando was Minister of War, April–June 1944, before becoming head of the Carabinieri.

Army Group. In the course of the evening, Broad telegraphed to say that there were some further rather excited telegrams from Athens. Scobie and Leeper seem to be going to give their (revised) version of the truce terms unless they hear to the contrary by 4.30 p.m. today. But they should receive our instructions before that.

Left Commission at 7.30 and came to my house, which if still as ugly as ever is warm and comfortable.

Lord Selborne, on his way to Naples, has been forced to land near Rome. I have just spoken to him on the telephone and hope to see him tomorrow. Meanwhile, a talk with Broad (about 11 p.m.) reveals *no* news from either Athens or London.

12 midnight. Went to bed – and there finished writing up the diary.

Thursday, 11 January 1945

On thinking over events in Greece, I can but feel that – in addition of course to the Communist plotters of KKE – the King of the Hellenes is the real villain of the piece. Far back at Cairo in the winter of 1943 he twisted and turned. Had he written a clear letter (and not an equivocal one) at that time saying that he would not return until called by a vote of the people, this powerful weapon of anti-monarchical propaganda would not have been available to the extremists. It must be remembered that Greece has always been about evenly divided between monarchists and republicans. The King has been head of a party – generally the pro-German party – not of the state. The Venizelist tradition is similarly republican – and pro-British.

But the tragic side of this division is that it disunites the bourgeois parties instead of letting them come together in opposition to Marxism and revolution. And it splits over an obsolete question. The issue of the second half of the twentieth century will not be monarchism *v.* republicanism, but a liberal and democratic way of life versus the 'proletariat dictatorship of the left' and the police state.

Again, if the King had given a frank pledge after the Lebanon conference, Papandreou's position – instead of being obscure and open to misrepresentation – would have been solid. This has always been Rex Leeper's view and he has been a consistent opponent of the King.

Even after Alex and I got to Athens on 11 December, had the King immediately accepted our joint recommendation, instead of wasting three precious weeks in futile bargaining and intriguing with Papandreou, I think the Archbishop might have stopped the fighting at that early stage. At least he would have, by his mere existence as Regent, prevented so large a rally of EAM/ELAS supporters to the extreme leadership of Siantos and the Communist Party. Instead of EAM 'breaking' up by all the more moderates leaving it at finding themselves (like Svolos) hopelessly between the two sides, something might have been done to fix up an arrangement. Whether in the long run this would have been better for Greece or not, I cannot tell. But it would certainly have saved us a lot of trouble.

Spent the morning at A.C. working on a number of Italian questions.

Lunch at Villa Parisi. Selborne, Admiral Palmer, Mr [J. Harland] Cleveland (U.S.) of the Economic Section; Mr [Angus] Malcolm, First Secretary at the British Embassy, Captain Quayle (British), M.A. to Admiral Stone.[3] Malcolm is the son of old Sir Ian Malcolm,[4] who has just died. He seems both agreeable and able.

4–6 p.m. Meeting between members of the Economic Section and various Italian Ministers. This is a new, and excellent, plan to improve co-operation. Colonel Dunsmore (U.S.) acted as chairman. My presence seemed to be welcomed. The subject today was the fertiliser programme, as to both imports and the possibility of Italian production. There was rather an amusing discussion about brass and copper 'scrap'. We should like a national campaign to collect this to make copper sulphate. The Italian Ministers thought that if the people had any idea given to them that it was valuable, they would hoard it or at least want a high price. I was rather indignant and explained our 'scrap' collection system in England. 'But that is just what Mussolini did! He even took their gold wedding rings from the peasants! That is Fascism!' However, M. Ruini[5] promises to set about it, and it will be interesting to see what comes of it.

8 p.m. Dinner with Ambassador Kirk, in great splendour.

Friday, 12 January 1945

9 a.m. At A.C. office. Major-General Dick Lewis (A.F.H.Q.) called to say goodbye. He is going to a job at the War Office.

The news of the terms of the Athens truce has at last arrived. It seems pretty good. I am very much relieved that it has gone through. This means that we are safely past another stage.

Stage one was the siege. Then, all we could do militarily was to take measures to avoid another Khartoum. Politically, all we could do was to get rid of the King – as an issue – and the Papandreou Government. This was the one achievement of Winston's visit. The second stage – the clearing finally of Athens and chasing the insurgents into open country – ends with the truce. We have now got to make a *military* and *political* plan for the third stage. We must try to turn the truce into a peace; and we must make the right military dispositions for the event of not being able to get a peace. I shall try to get the Field Marshal to go over with me in a day or two. Leeper and Scobie are not capable of

[3] Captain Anthony Quayle (b. 1913), the actor, had been a member of the S.O.E. Mission to Albania, 1944.

[4] Sir Ian Malcolm (1868–1944) was British Government Representative on the Suez Canal Board, 1919–39.

[5] Meuccio Ruini (1877–?) was Minister of Public Works and National Reconstruction, 1944–5.

framing a satisfactory plan. But if Alex and I continue the technique which we have devised of always making a *joint politico-military* plan and sending it in both our names to H.M.G., I think we can probably achieve something. Our difficulty will now of course be with the Greek Government. Even Leeper has become very bellicose. And Plastiras – the Greek Cromwell – wants to smash the rebels. But (as the Germans found) it is not so easy when they retire to the hills. Neither our military commitments in the war against Germany nor British public opinion will allow a fight to the finish. Fortunately, ELAS have retained the Greek hostages.[6] I am sorry for the people but otherwise delighted. It will prove a useful weapon for us. It damages ELAS politically at home; and it should enable us to persuade the Greek Government of the necessity for a general amnesty.

10 a.m. Marchese Lucifero[7] – Minister of the Household of Prince Umberto – called. I thought him sensible. He told us of his efforts to get a different society round the Prince from the old one of soldiers and aristocrats. He seems to be getting him to see republicans, professors and members of a variety of professions and types. This is not easy – for many will not come. But, from Lucifero's account, the Prince himself is most affable and co-operative. His handling of the recent political crisis has undoubtedly improved his position.

11 a.m. Brigadier Lush. The admiral has gone up to see General Mark Clark, Fifteenth Army Group. I have told him to be firm about any attempt to separate A.M.G. and A.C. This is the old heresy, and under American War Department influence and the personal ambitions of individuals here, it may be dangerous.

11.30 a.m. Ambassador Kirk and Henry Hopkinson (representing Sir Noel Charles, who is still laid up). The chief problems were:

(*a*) *General Orlando*, head of Carabinieri. The Yugoslav Government (or rather Tito's Government) have asked that he should be tried as a war criminal. What do we do? (An awkward problem of co-belligerents who have changed sides!)

(*b*) *General Roatta* is to be tried in a week, and the trial will perhaps reveal a lot of details surrounding the signing of the armistice in September 1943, as well as secret service papers covering 1934–9, probably very damaging to the U.S. and British Governments. It is even said that Roatta – who ran an excellent secret service which got all the telegrams to and from London and Washington, by suitable arrangements to obtain keys to the safes in Rome – has a document in which Chamberlain offers French colonies (e.g. Tunis) to Mussolini!

These are two quite nice little problems. But I shall not allow Alex to take any action on either unless I have the support of the U.S.

[6] ELAS had refused to release, as part of the truce, some 15,000–20,000 people of all ages whom they were holding as hostages many miles from their homes.

[7] Marchese Falcone Lucifero (b. 1898) was Minister of Agriculture in Badoglio's first Cabinet, 1943, and Minister of the Household during the lieutenancy and reign of Umberto, 1944–6.

Government. They backed out on the Badoglio trial, and on other matters, and left us with sole responsibility. I do not want any more Sforza incidents.

1.15 p.m. Lunch at Villa Parisi. Mr and Mrs Henry Hopkinson, Colonel Dunsmore, a journalist called Alastair Forbes, and one or two more of the A.C. staff.

4–6.30 p.m. An immense meeting, summoned by me, to decide on a plan for the surrender by Psychological Warfare Branch (P.W.B.) of all sorts of publicity functions to be performed in future – in Liberated Italy – by either the Allied Commission or the Embassies or both. This is a very complicated and tangled affair, covering Intelligence, newspapers, books, radio-control and a hundred other things. P.W.B. is an A.F.H.Q. organisation, and has been on bad terms with A.C. We had a large gathering, some from Naples, others from Rome. The lights went out and the little heat there is supposed to be faded out. But we got complete agreement on every particular, subject only to confirmation by C.C.S., F.O. and State Department. (No doubt they will upset the apple-cart successfully in due course!)

7 p.m. Went to see Sir D'Arcy Osborne who had wanted urgently to see me. I went to his house. He had nothing really to say, except that he was worried about Italy, Anglo-American relations, and the cold. But he is so charming that I enjoyed my visit, even at the end of a rather tiring day.

8.30 p.m. Lady Charles – in her wonderful apartment in the Palazzo Orsini – gave a large dinner-party. Palazzo Orsini was the property of the Caetani family, was built over the ruins of the Theatre of Marcellus – an old Roman theatre of the first century A.D. The Duchessa di Sermoneta owns it now, and has a very nice apartment in the palace – which is now subdivided into a number of separate houses. Owing to the illness of Sir Noel, I had to act as host. The style, food, service, footmen were pre-1914 rather than pre-1939 war. We sat down twenty. Lord Wolmer represented British aristocracy; Prince Doria,[8] Marchese Lucifero, and a number of others the Roman aristocracy; we had Einaudi,[9] the new Governor of the Bank of Italy, to represent the intelligentsia; we had a Communist minister (for Finance) whose name escapes me.[10] It was really terrific. I was so tired that I could eat nothing but a piece of dry toast, which much distressed Princess Doria, on my right. She is a very sensible Scottish hospital nurse, whom Prince Doria married in the last war. He is a remarkable man – a real medieval saint, of spotless reputation. Mussolini, of course, had him in prison. Before the Italians went to war, Prince Doria took advantage of his high rank to write a letter to the King imploring him *not* to go to war against

[8] Prince Filippo Doria-Pamphili had been Mayor of Rome since June 1944.

[9] Luigi Einaudi (1874–1961) was Governor of the Bank of Italy, 1945–8, and President of the Italian Republic, 1948–55.

[10] Professor Antonio Pesenti (b. 1910) was Minister for Finance, 1944–5.

England. It was an argued statement of the case, on grounds of sentiment and reason, tradition and practical necessity. He offered (he was not then actually in prison but only under a sort of 'surveillance') to help the King with his friends if he would stand firm against the régime on this one issue of war against England. The King of Italy did not reply to his noble cousin; he gave the letter to Mussolini. Doria was imprisoned. When the armistice was signed, the Prince and Princess and her daughter were in hiding. They never went out from September 1943 till the capture of Rome, June 1944, except by night. They were passed from one friendly home to another. Doria is rather a broken man now physically; but charming and really a splendid character. He is, of course, partly English – his mother or grandmother having been a Talbot. All this was told me by the bustling, lowland Scot – now Princess Doria – during dinner. I liked her. I think the story about King Victor is really dreadful. After all, he need only have burned the letter. I am now so glad that I bullied him at Ravello. 'You are putting me with my back to the wall' – he said to me, when Murphy and I were making him abdicate or at least retire. If I had known about this story I would have reminded him of it. Anyway it removes any qualm I had about the King. And I will not let him come back to Naples – to Lord Rosebery's villa – as he is now asking to do. He says he is cold at Ravello or wherever he is. Let him perish of cold. Even a Stuart king scarcely did such a dirty trick (except perhaps James II).

At last, when the last of the guests had gone, I got away and to bed.

Saturday, 13 January 1945

Before I went to Athens last time, I had drawn up a list of questions about which I wanted information from the appropriate officers of the Allied Commission, and I left John Wyndham to collect the necessary papers. Today, I saw the officials concerned on each topic. I had the head of the sections (there are two at present – Economic and Administration) and the head or heads of the particular subcommissions – e.g., transport, electricity, local government, etc., etc. Each subject was given half-an-hour, and it worked well. It gave me both information on the questions and a chance of forming some judgment on the capacity of the respective officers. We started at 9 a.m. and went on till 1 p.m. John had arranged the time-table very well and I got through eight periods of half-an-hour; or eight subjects and sets of people. I have about another twelve to do, which will be on my next visit.

Left office at 1.30 and went round (at his urgent request) to see Charles. He was in bed. He had nothing really to say, but he likes to know what I am doing. My own car had broken, so I borrowed an American car and left for Naples at 2.30. I got to Caserta about 6.30. There was a lot of snow and sleet, so it was a slow journey.

Saw some telegrams in the office, and went down to Naples. We had a dinner for Top Wolmer (Selborne), including C.-in.C. Med. (Admiral Cunningham) and various other generals and officers – mostly those connected with S.O.E. work, which Selborne's Ministry controls.

Sunday, 14 January 1945

I never seem to get to church now – except at Athens! I left Naples early; saw Alex at 9.30, and discussed with him the Greek situation. We agreed to go together to Athens the next day. A good deal of work at the office. I had all the minutes of yesterday's interviews to write up. I am sending them back to John, with instructions for action or more information, as the case may be. (This will have a good effect in Rome, and make them realise that even when I cannot be there, I am working at the problems.) There were also more telegrams from London and Washington about my Italian 'Directive'. The negotiations proceed at an oriental pace but fairly successfully. And there were some tiresome telegrams about Yugoslav affairs. What a bore these kings are! (In the case of King Peter, the nigger in the wood-pile is Princess Aspasia,[11] his mother-in-law.)

I lunched with Alex at the Hunting Lodge. After lunch, we went for a drive. We had a jeep to follow us and went up in the car to the observatory on Mount Vesuvius. Then we got into the jeep and went as far as one now can get up the road. The great stream of lava, which came from the old crater, is now cool. But another great stream, covered by some fifty feet of ash, is still hot, and smoke comes out in little jets over all this side of the mountain. There was a lot of snow; unfortunately, a grey, cold, sunless day.

Got back at four and worked at the office till 7.30, when I had to go to a cocktail party to bid farewell to Major-General Rookes (U.S.). He is a charming man, and has been with A.F.H.Q. since it began. I have always found him most fair and helpful. In Algiers, he was first head of G3, then Deputy Chief of Staff. He has done splendid work as an Allied officer. He is going to France and hopes to get a command in the field.

Finally, I got back to Naples and went to bed – exhausted.

Monday, 15 January 1945

Our flight has been cancelled, as although it is a lovely sunny day here, the weather in the Adriatic is very bad. I am rather distressed by the delay, but we hope it will only be for one day. Meanwhile, it gave me time to tidy up a few things. And – best of all – a bag has come in at last with a splendid letter from Dorothy, giving all the family news, including the birth of my new grandson! I really think they might have sent me a telegram; but I suppose everyone thought that someone else

[11] Princess Aspasia (1896–1972), widow of King Alexander I of Greece.

would do so. I have got a *Times*, with the account of the christening of Carol's baby at Horsted Keynes – on Christmas Eve. It is sad to be away, with such family events going on. But it is wonderful to get the long typewritten letters which D. sends me, full of all the details which I like to have.

Le Rougetel (our diplomatic representative at Bucharest) is staying with me on his way home to report. His account of the Russian management of the Control Commission in Roumania is interesting. The Russians seem determined to get everything they can out of the country. They have taken away a large part of the machinery of the oil wells (which incidentally belongs to British and American shareholders) and they are now deporting a large part of the population. They take men and women (children are left behind) to work in Russian coal-mines, etc. But as they put them into open cattle-trucks (with no heating) in the bitter winter weather, their action seems not only brutally cruel but very stupid – since few of them will ever arrive. (The population which they are drawing on is the 600,000 Roumanian citizens of German descent, who have been settled in Roumania for many generations, even centuries.)

4 p.m. Slessor – on the future of the Italian Air Force. The Air Marshal is a very clever and co-operative man. He is handling this problem sensibly. I have told him not to enter into any post-war commitments. The Italian Air Force *must* be reduced in size to the squadrons for which we are prepared to give planes now. All the rest should be made available to us as ground and maintenance staff, thus relieving our manpower problems.

Dined quietly, but sumptuously, at Naples – Le Rougetel having brought caviare from Bucharest. We have now closed the villa at Caserta. So Broad, Russell and Odgers all live at Naples. John Wyndham and Miss Campbell are permanently in Rome. I can just manage two houses on my allowance, but not three. And I want to reduce my use of soldier servants. The chef Blom has gone to Rome, where he should be happier than at Caserta.

Tuesday, 16 January 1945

Left Naples 8 p.m. We settled the line to be taken about the Roatta trial. Stone will be told to *ask* Bonomi to arrange that no evidence shall be admitted, either by prosecution or defence, which (*a*) involves Allied operations, (*b*) documents belonging or alleged to belong to any Allied Government. *But* he is not to *demand* this, without further authority from me or the F.M. Meanwhile, Broad will telegraph on my behalf to F.O. for a ruling as to whether we should *insist* on this; Offie will telegraph on Kirk's behalf in similar terms to the State Department. By this means, if we decide to act, I will get the Americans committed. I refuse to act unilaterally, although Kirk and Offie would like me to do so. But would they share the responsibility when the row comes, and Mr Drew Pearson[12] attacks us for interfering with Italian justice?

9.45 a.m. Left Marcianise airfield in Alex's plane. F.M., Rupert Clarke and myself. I took no one with me, because I have no one to spare. I am trying to get another officer in place of Ralph Anstruther.

Arrived about 3.30 (Athens time). A bad trip – very cloudy weather and rather bumpy. We went at once to the Embassy. Scobie and Leeper discussed the general situation with Alex and myself. Alex then went to G.H.Q. for military talks. I put forward my political plan to the Ambassador and Harold Caccia. I found them rather pessimistic about the chance of getting the Greek Government to accept so generous a programme. However, after considerable debate, my draft telegram was agreed, with some minor amendments.

About 7.30 Alex returned with Scobie and Brigadier Hugh Mainwaring (who is now definitely appointed B.G.S. to Scobie). The F.M. had redrafted his military contribution to the telegram. We had it all copied out before dinner.

After dinner (to which Scobie and Mainwaring stayed) we went carefully through the redraft and it was finally passed for despatch about 11.30 p.m.

Wednesday, 17 January 1945

Alex and I left the Embassy at 9.30. We went to see some troops in Athens, and then drove to Eleusis. Here we saw the H.Q. of the Fourth Division; we then drove on to Megara and as far as the eastern end of the Corinth Canal. Unfortunately, it was a very poor day; first drizzle and then heavy rain. The canal is blocked by a sunken ship at this end; the sides are also blown in at various points. It is said that it would take a year's work to restore it. We lunched off our sandwiches, and returned to Athens by 4 p.m. General Hawkesworth came with us. 'Ginger' H. has had command of the troops under General Scobie and has done an excellent piece of work. He is a first-class fighting officer.

On the way back we went to look at the ruins of the temples at Eleusis. Unfortunately, they are almost entirely destroyed, but one can realise their importance and magnificence from what remains.

5 p.m. The Field Marshal and I called upon the Archbishop–Regent. The object of our visit was to enlist his support for our plan. The F.M. began by giving a rather defeatist account of the military future. He emphasised the great difficulty of operating in the mountains if it were necessary to clear out the rebels by force. He also explained the need to reduce his military commitments in Greece to the minimum, in view of the need to send divisions to the Italian and perhaps to the Western Front. Of course the purpose was to deflate a little the Greek attitude. The Archbishop did not react very favourably; he seemed rather put

[12] Drew Pearson (1897–1969), American journalist, wrote a column called 'Daily Washington Merry-Go-Round', 1931–69.

out. Then I developed my political thesis. Here also I met with rather a frigid reception, especially regarding the 'amnesty'. Eventually, we found a formula on this, to *include* all those merely charged with taking up arms against the Government, but to *exclude* men charged with offences – murder, rape, looting and the like – which are punished in any respectable army by court-martial.

On the other points, we began to make some progress, especially on the question of the conference, or offer of a conference. He pointed out the very strong feeling roused by the taking of hostages among civilians, and the refusal to surrender them as part of the truce. He would not find it easy to persuade his Government to meet the ELAS people at all, without making the surrender of the hostages a prerequisite or *condition préalable* to the meeting. However, we went through all the questions which would have to be settled if the conference took place – the date, place, composition, chairmanship, etc. He agreed that Plastiras should *not* go, but that Sophianopoulos – a more flexible negotiator – (who is Minister of Foreign Affairs) should be the chief Government delegate.

We left at 6.30 – a long, difficult and rather fatiguing interview. I drafted a telegram home reporting the talk. After dinner, we discussed the situation and made various plans. We will repeat the 'softening' process on General Plastiras tomorrow.

Thursday, 18 January 1945

A lot of Italian telegrams, still about my wretched directive. I answered them before breakfast. There is also a further development in the Roatta case – rather satisfactory. Bonomi seems to think that the trial can take place without the awkward revelations which we feared.

At breakfast, more bad news. It is reported that General Gonatas, an old friend of Plastiras, is to be appointed by him as Governor of Macedonia. Gonatas is said to be an able and energetic man – one of the most competent in Greece. Unfortunately, he is also accused of being compromised with the 'Security Battalions'. These were raised and armed by the Germans (or with their approval). Actually, it was the only self-defence which the respectable people could put up against the ravages of ELAS. Now that we know more of the facts, we can see the other side. But at the moment, it would be a fatal move.

10.30–11.30 a.m. F.M. and I went to see General Plastiras. After the initial welcome, I left them to a purely military discussion. I remained at the Ministry of Foreign Affairs, to catch the Ambassador, who was interviewing Sophianopoulos. I had in my pocket a very stiff *aide-mémoire* to give to Plastiras, dealing with the Gonatas appointment, with General Plastiras's interview about the amnesty, and other points. But after talking with Leeper, we decided (really on Sophianopoulos's advice) to get Plastiras along to the Embassy after his talk with the F.M. Naturally, we are very anxious to clear up all these points, including the question of arrests going on in Athens, *before* the two-day debate in the H. of C.

At 12 noon General Plastiras arrived. The F.M.'s talk had clearly had an effect upon him. But I greatly fear that the general falls into the category of *un grand chef*. 'Give me an armoured column for three days and I will make an end of them' is rather his attitude. (This touch is pure Giraud!) This annoyed Alex, who tried to explain the difficulties of mechanised armies in mountain country; the lack of mules, mountain batteries, etc. But it was no good, it seems. However, he must have made an impression, for we found the general very reasonable and after an hour's talk (translated) he agreed to all our points. These were duly reported to London and should help Winston and Anthony. No Gonatas; a very reasonable formula for the amnesty; no more interviews, etc.

1.30 p.m. Alex and I motored out to the Marathon dam. It was a nasty day, but we could stretch our legs and get some air. On the way back we went to look at the R.A.F. H.Q. at Kephyssia, where nearly 700 men were taken prisoner by ELAS.

4 p.m. Meeting with Sophianopoulos. We went over the ground. Things are obviously improving. There seems to be a general acceptance of the need for a conference. We discussed at length the content of the Government proposals and the tactics for presenting them. One general view now is a conference of three a side and at Athens. We drafted a reply to be sent to ELAS in the Regent's name, if the latter approves.

This meeting (Sophianopoulos, Leeper, Caccia and H.M.) lasted till about 6.30. Arrangements, telegrams, minutes, etc., took till dinner. After dinner, we listened on the wireless to Winston. He seems to have made a very powerful speech and full of good humour. He has made good use of our material. In the course of the evening a personal telegram from him to me, thanking me for a phrase, 'Trotskyite deviation to the left', which I had used at Christmas and he had stored in his memory and found useful at Question Time.

A very late night, because I had to see Commander Jackson, of Middle East Supply Centre, who is helping with economic problems in Greece. Relief; the future of M.L. (Military Liaison) which is now responsible for relief; how to bring in U.N.R.R.A.; how to make U.N.R.R.A. reasonably efficient, etc. Finally, I decided to send Jackson to Caserta the next day with the F.M. He can have talks there and then go to London. I would like to detach Jackson from Cairo and make him my economic adviser. Jackson would like this. All these decisions involved teelgrams to London and Cairo (to Grigg personally) and we got to bed about 2 a.m.

Friday, 19 January 1945

9.30 a.m. F.M. left. I must stay till tomorrow, as there is still a good deal to tie up here and the Regent wants another talk with me.

10–11 a.m. An interview with some representatives of ELD.[13] They are Socialists, and have now (rather late in the day) broken with EAM and the KKE (or Communists) who dominate EAM. They seemed a very mild lot of little men and I talked to them paternally. Their chief worry is fear of being arrested. We are ourselves concerned by the arrests taking place in Athens by various Gendarmerie and police authorities. I promised to lay their case before the Regent. I also advised them to get into touch with Sir Walter Citrine,[14] who is on his way out here. Citrine and his delegation should be useful and help to get decent democratic trade unions and political organisations running on constitutional lines.

Worked on various Italian papers and telegrams till luncheon.

4 p.m. Leeper and Caccia on the programme for the conference. (The Regent and the Government have agreed to the reply to ELAS in accordance with our draft.)

5 p.m. Called on the Regent. I found him in cracking form. He is, of course, delighted with Winston's speech, especially by the references to himself. He rather apologised for his attitude on Wednesday the 17th when Alex and I had seen him. Since then he has been working on Plastiras and the Government in accordance with our wishes. We have seen some of the results. The offer has gone to ELAS and other decisions (e.g., about General Gonatas) taken in accordance with our advice. He has to persuade his Government; he has to 'knead' them (this, twisting his great hands in pantomime).

I thanked him, and went through the other points in our programme – disarmament, hostages, amnesty, etc., and he accepted them all. He would send the delegates to see me tonight, and begged me to return next week to see things through. This I promised to do.

6 p.m. The colonel in charge of police and security (British) and Caccia. I now got to the bottom of the trouble about the arrests. (I had previously left a memorandum on the subject with the Regent, embodying the complaints of my deputation.) There is still an *état de siège* (or martial law) in Athens. Therefore *both* military and civil police are operating and there is hopeless confusion – the Minister of Interior is not really master in his own household. All decisions to release men (even *after* examination by the seventy-five magistrates) have to be confirmed by the Greek military staff. After extracting a complete account of what is the real situation – as to what both the British and the various Greek authorities are doing – we decided that

[13] *Énosis Laikìs Dimokratías*, the Union of Popular Democracy.

[14] Sir Walter Citrine (1887–1983) was General Secretary of the Trades Union Congress, 1926–46.

Caccia and Brigadier Smith-Dorrien should draft a letter for General Scobie to send to General Plastiras recommending the ending of *état de siège* and reverting to the ordinary civil law. Then no one will be kept in detention for more than twenty-four hours except (*a*) by remand, after the police have established a *prima facie* case before a magistrate, (*b*) on warrant, with same conditions. We will also get the civil authorities to stop their wholesale arrests on mere suspicion.

7.15 p.m. Went to see General Scobie, who agreed to the proposals above. I chatted with him for a bit. He is a charming man, but *not* gifted with brains. He has been fortunate in having been sustained in the military sphere by the Field Marshal, who has supplied him with General Hawkesworth and Brigadier Mainwaring. The latter is a very able young officer, who carried through all the negotiations for the truce, and all the arrangements to make it effective, with remarkable skill. Scobie has also been sustained in the political field by the Ambassador, by Caccia and by myself. But I'm afraid he does not quite see it in this light.

7.45 p.m. Interview with [Sylvain] Mangeot (of Reuters) who has just come out and will help. I knew him in Algiers.

Mr Gerald Barry[15] also turned up (editor of the *News Chronicle*). We told him some home truths.

8.45 p.m. Dinner. F.O.L.E.M. [Flag Officer, Levant and Eastern Mediterranean] (otherwise Admiral [William] Tennant) and my old friend Admiral Mansfield. I was late for dinner and had to leave the table at

9.30 p.m. to see Sophianopoulos, Perikles Rallis and [Ioannis] Makropoulos – who are to be the three Government delegates. Sophianopoulos is the clever one – the others rather mute. We went over the whole ground and made much progress on the *content* of the Government programme. But on the tactics the Greeks are very insistent to know how far we will back them if the conference fails and force is the only way out. If they feel they have enough backing, they will take rather a tough line at the conference – which they believe is the only hope of success. I promised to think this over and let them know. The conference ended about 11.30 p.m.

Saturday, 20 January 1945

I was to have left at 9 a.m. But apparently (although it is beautifully fine here – the first sunny day we have had) the weather in Italy is very bad, and no airfields are serviceable.

Perhaps it was a good thing, as it enabled me to draft (with Leeper) a number of telegrams setting out our talks with Sophianopoulos and recommending a line to P.M. and Anthony.

[15] Gerald Barry (1898–1968) was editor of the *News Chronicle*, 1936–47, and Director-General of the Festival of Britain, 1948–51.

In my view, we should now make a *public* announcement that if the conference fails, we shall support the Greek Government with all our military power. We should add that the Government will put forward most conciliatory and generous proposals, to be framed in consultation with us. I think this method is the *only possible way* to give us any chance of converting the truce into a peace. Any weakness will merely make ELAS more intransigent.

After lunch, with the diary; read and dozed. This life is really very wearing. I am told that we shall get off tomorrow. I have six M.P.s (touring Italy) dining with me in Rome on 22 January. Incidentally, F.M. and I have invited them to extend their tour to Greece.

I have sent Scobie's letter to Plastiras about the *état de siège* to the Regent – or rather a copy. His Beatitude can do a bit more 'kneading'.

Anthony's speech has come over the wires. It seems pretty good and very firm. The division is good also.[16] I get the impression that the Labour Party at home are not so sure that Greece is really a good wicket to bat on after all. But (alas) a good division in the House of Commons does not solve my problems. It rather increases them, as it tends to make the Greeks too uppish and to question my argument for conciliation on the ground of public opinion at home. Fortunately, I think the Archbishop is too sensible to get thrown out of his stride by such considerations.

ELAS are getting frightened about the hostages. We have just heard from Mr Lambert, of the International Red Cross, that they have undertaken to set them free (? return them) with the exception of 'known criminals'. The exception may prove something of a boomerang. It will greatly strengthen our argument for only a modified amnesty, not to include those guilty of personal crimes.

4–6 p.m. Went for a very pleasant walk. The weather has improved. A cold wind, but a lovely clear blue sky and brilliant sun. I went to the Acropolis and on the way there and back pottered about old streets and found old bits of temples and market-places. This is really a most attractive city. It somehow gains by there being so comparatively little to see, and all of it so lovely.

A quiet evening. I read an interesting book which I found here called *Power – A New Social Analysis* by Bertrand Russell – published 1938. It is witty, pungent, philosophical, whimsical and bitter. I enjoyed it.

The Archbishop has sent me a signed photograph – very fine. Poor Gerald Barry went to interview him (*News Chronicle*) but was quite overwhelmed and forgot all his questions.

Sunday, 21 January 1945

Left Athens at 9.30, in a Mitchell. I brought with me Mr [Alexander]

[16] Winding up a two-day debate on the war (which was dominated by the crisis in Greece), Eden defended General Plastiras's reputation and Britain's activities in Greece. The Government won, by 340 votes to 7, a Vote of Censure moved by Sir Richard Acland.

Hutcheon (Inspector of Consulates), Colonel [S.] Prosser (of the Palestinian police, doing police work in Athens with the Army) and Colonel Katzen (Military Liaison – supply).

Arrived at Marcianise airfield, Caserta, at 12.15 p.m. (Naples time). Went up to the office to settle some matters with Broad. Then motored out to luncheon at the Hunting Lodge, where I found Alex and his usual staff (Generals Harding, Robertson, Lemnitzer). Alex seemed rather tired and had a slight cold. After lunch, talks with Robertson on (1) Italian food situation and the 300-gramme ration, for which 'authorisation' but *not* shipping has been provided by Control Chiefs of Staff. We also discussed Greece, Yugoslavia and Albania. General Robertson agrees with me as to the importance of getting the military unit and U.N.R.R.A. into the relief business as soon as possible. But, apart from the negotiation of formal agreements with the countries concerned and their *de jure* or *de facto* Governments, there are many prerequisites to the transfer – among them, giving U.N.R.R.A. (who are very badly staffed) some of the present military staff (whether by secondment or demobilisation) and getting a proper head; especially for U.N.R.R.A. Greece.

The last question we discussed was the problem of Italy's industrial plight – the economic section of Allied Commission and the relations between them and the Army authorities. General Robertson is ready for a 'New Deal' – recognising that up to now the co-operation has been poor. I outlined to him certain plans which I had been turning over in my mind, and found that he had been thinking on similar lines. It would really need a bold scheme to make a 'merger' between the Army and A.C. and set up some 'production board', with the best executives available, to undertake production on behalf of *all* users (like the Ministry of Supply); leave *allocation* to another body. This is really the best plan, if we can bring it off, because it separates the *production* of commodities (cement, steel, etc.) from the argument about who is to have them. At present the Army requisitions plants and then abandons them as it moves forward. But when A.C. and the Italians get them back, they have neither the transport nor the coal to work them properly.

After General Robertson I had a number of telegrams (chiefly to Washington on my still unfinished directive) and other minor items. I finally got clear by six o'clock and motored to Rome, arriving about 10.30 p.m. It was a very slow drive, through sleet and snow.

Monday, 22 January 1945

Although I sent my representatives and my full plans (agreed by H.M.G.) to Washington on 8 December, there is still no finality about the Italian 'New Deal'. All the political and supply questions have been agreed – after much debate – in practically the same sense and even words of my original draft. But the Americans have thrown two spanners into the machinery: (1) the proposal for a *peace* treaty with Italy, (2) a most complicated *financial* plan to alter the present arrangements. I spent most of the morning with Stone, Grafftey-Smith and Lawtor (U.S.) concerting a reply, giving A.C. views. By showing the F.O. telegrams and the British Treasury view very openly to Stone and Lawtor (as I used to with Bob Murphy) I find I get a most co-operative attitude from them. They much appreciate frankness, and are very critical of their own side in Washington for causing so many difficulties. I then had a private talk with Stone, on the general Italian situation and especially the patriot problem. Unless we are very careful, we shall get another EAM/ELAS situation in northern Italy. The operations of S.O.E. in arming nearly 100,000 so-called patriots will produce the same revolutionary situation, unless we can devise a system for taking them, immediately on the liberation of the territory, into either our or the Italian Army. Then, in return for pay and rations, we may be able to get hold of their weapons. The lesson of Greece is that nothing matters except 'disarmament'. The political questions are the excuse for retaining armed power.

1.35 p.m. A small luncheon party, including Gerald Palmer, M.P. for Winchester – a very agreeable and intelligent fellow. He has been serving in Italy as a subaltern, but is now regarded as too old for infantry work in the line. I have offered to take him to Greece with me.

3 p.m. My old friend of Algiers days, M. da Cunha (Brazilian Minister). He had nothing to say.

3.30 p.m. Mr Allbrough (U.S.) and another American, of the Agricultural Subcommission. They gave me a review of their work, in which they have many (and almost insuperable) difficulties. I found it difficult to appraise their value.

4.30 p.m. Major-General Browning (Army Subcommission) – a very interesting talk. I got a number of points to take up with the Field Marshal. B. has a plan for the patriots which must also be discussed at A.F.H.Q.

5.30–6.30 p.m. Mr [W. H.] Braine (of the Ministry of Labour). He is Labour Attaché at the Embassy, and I have now persuaded Mr Bevin[17] to allow him in addition to act as head of the Labour Subcommission. He is an *excellent* civil servant, of the best type, with sound and progressive views. I feel sure he will be able to help us a lot.

This was a very heavy day, as in addition to the interviews, there was a mass of paper work about A.C. which had accumulated.

8.15 p.m. Wing-Commander James, Major Studholme, Jack Lawson, R. Bernays, Captain Bellenger, J. D. Campbell – the six M.P.s touring Italy.[18] With them came Brigadier Partridge (conducting

[17] Ernest Bevin (1881–1951) was Minister of Labour and National Service, 1940–5, and Foreign Secretary, 1945–51.

[18] Wing-Commander Archibald James (1893–1980) was Unionist M.P. for Wellingborough, 1931–45. Major Henry Studholme (b. 1899) was Conservative M.P. for Tavistock, 1942–66. John Lawson (1881–1965) was Labour M.P. for Chester-le-Street, 1919–49, and Secretary of State for

officer) and also to the dinner General Browning, Brigadier Lush (Chief of Staff, A.C.), Colonel Bonham-Carter (Deputy, Regional Commission, Rome area), Colonel Young[19] (Public Safety Subcommission) and Brigadier Low (Deputy Military Commander, Rome). A very successful evening, followed by a sort of lecture by me on: (*a*) Italy, (*b*) Greece, with lots of questions and argument. I think everyone enjoyed it. Lawson is a particularly nice fellow – with a generous heart and mind. Bellenger is rather a 'smart-alec' and suffers from trying to be too clever.

After they had gone, I worked on an accumulation of papers till about 1 a.m.

Tuesday, 23 January 1945

9 a.m. Chief Commissioner (Stone) on a number of outstanding questions.

10 a.m. Went to see the Lieutenant-General of the Realm, Prince Umberto. I was received with modest, but suitable and not unimpressive ceremony at the Quirinal. I found the Prince rather nervous, but definitely improved since my last talk with him at Brindisi. He talked sensibly about his difficulties and without concealing the dangers to the monarchy and to Italy. The P.M.'s phrase 'we do not *need* Italy' has been printed here very widely (it was of course rebutting a charge of power politics in the Mediterranean).[20] The Prince said he was trying to counter this as much as possible.

After the 'audience' I was shown over part of the magnificent papal palace. The view of Rome from the terrace is very fine.

11.30 a.m. Commodore Warren, R.N. – who has just taken over the Naval Subcommission. I told him to *reduce* the size of the Italian Navy, and he seemed to agree. There is little work for them to justify 70,000 men drawing pay and rations.

12.15 p.m. Called on Mr Myron Taylor (U.S. Ambassador to the Vatican). He was in bed. He is a clever, but very talkative old man. He looks after American Relief in Italy – a charitable organisation – and naturally fights with us all, partly as an ally, partly as a competitor, in the battle for shipping. I did my best to reassure him and took notes of a few things I can do to help him.

The afternoon was filled with the usual interviews, telegrams and papers. As I am trying to get back to Greece tomorrow, it took me till 8 p.m. to get approximately finished. Philip Broad and Alaric Russell

War, 1945–6. Captain Robert Bernays (1902–45) was Liberal M.P. for Bristol North, 1931–45. Captain Frederick Bellenger (1894–1968) was Labour M.P. for Bassetlaw, 1935–68, and Secretary of State for War, 1946–7. J. D. Campbell (1898–1945) was Unionist M.P. for Antrim, 1943–5.

[19] Colonel Arthur Young (1907–79) was Assistant Director of the Public Safety Subcommission, A.C., 1943–5, and Commissioner of the City of London Police, 1950–71.

[20] In his speech opening the two-day debate in the House of Commons on 18–19 January, Churchill had said, 'We need Italy no more than we need Spain, because we have no designs which require the support of such powers.'

came up in the afternoon from Rome and we dined quietly at the Villa Parisi. Philip had brought up some things for me to deal with, but we got early to bed, in view of an early start next day.

Wednesday, 24 January 1945

Left the villa at 7.30 a.m. I had a Mitchell waiting, and took Philip Broad and Russell back with me. Left Ciampino airfield at 8.15 – arrived Marcianise at 9 a.m. Motored up to the palace, and saw Alex on a few matters, chiefly arising from my last two days at Rome. I had prepared short minutes for him, as I usually do. He motored back to the airfield with me, and as I was just about to take off again to Athens the 'Met' officer came along and told us it was too bad to go. There is apparently a very bad belt of weather all along the western Adriatic, stretching far south into the Mediterranean – so we cannot get round it. This is rather a bore, but it is no good taking a risk. I hope to get off early tomorrow.

I came back to my office in the palace, where I found quite a lot to do. But I do hate changing my plans.

The six M.P.s left Rome for Bari yesterday in two aircraft. I have just heard that one, holding Bernays and Campbell, is missing. There is still a chance that they landed at some out-of-the-way or deserted airfield, or even airstrip. They had a Dakota, which can land easily. But I fear they may have got into a storm over the Apennines. The weather was pretty bad coming from Rome this morning, but of course we went out to sea and had no mountains to cross. I do hope they will be found. It will be a tragedy if they have been lost – especially Bernays, who has lately married and got two young children. There is still a good chance, as they have not been lost for twenty-four hours yet and communications are bad.

Lunched with F.M. and his staff.

Gerald Palmer, M.P., and Colonel Deakin to dinner.

Thursday, 25 January 1945

In spite of a telegram from Caccia last night saying that the Greek Conference would not take place, since no agreement had yet been reached about the delegates, I decided to leave. Just before taking off (at about 9 a.m.) Leeper's telegrams on this question reached me. I am rather alarmed at the delay and the apparent stiffening of the Greek Government's attitude. They have a good hand now to play, if they do not overplay it. Moreover, I fear that H.M.G. (having acceded to my request to promise the Greek Government full support) may get too 'uppish' and try to squeeze us unduly. They naturally want us to use our troops to hunt down the ELAS forces and destroy them. We want a peace – if it is humanly possible to get it – in order to withdraw the greater part of our forces as rapidly as possible.

After landing at Brindisi, we finally arrived at Athens about 3 p.m. I brought Alaric Russell (who joined my staff recently) and Gerald Palmer with me.

The Ambassador explained to me the general situation and the Archbishop's last telegrams to EAM/ELAS. I am still not happy about it. The Archbishop has changed his ground twice. First he said he would accept five delegates from EAM. Then he reduced it to three, still from EAM. Now he demands three members of KKE – this on the ground that EAM has no reality and that the Communists really dominate the situation. This is, of course, true. And I think he is entitled to demand the attendance of principals, not 'stooges'. But it would have been better if he had taken this line immediately after the truce and stuck to it. Leeper does not share my apprehensions, but I think he does not realise the nervousness of British opinion and its intense desire to see the Greek problem solved. We do *not* believe it can be solved rapidly. All the more need to have a cast-iron case. If I had been here, I would not have allowed the last two telegrams of the Archbishop to go as phrased.

Meanwhile, there are a lot of M.L. (Relief) and U.N.R.R.A. problems to settle. The financial situation of the Greek Government is hopeless. They are paying out considerable sums and have no revenue. Hugh-Jones and Brigadier Palmer (successor to Brigadier King) came for a discussion after dinner, and we got through a good deal of business. Harold Caccia was present. I sent off a number of telegrams – chiefly asking for economic and financial advisers. I am much disappointed that Marris cannot be spared from Washington.

After they had left, Brigadier Smith-Dorrien came. There is still a lot to be done about the 'arrests' which continue in Athens and to clear the prisons. Although General Plastiras refused to abolish the *état de siège* (as I had asked) he has in fact got rid of one of its effects, by agreeing that the examining magistrates shall have executive and not merely advisory powers. So we are getting the prisons emptied and the cases dealt with pretty well. But the military still have the power of arrest. And we must have this tied up in the same way.

Got to bed about midnight.

Friday, 26 January 1945

Left Kalamari airfield (Athens) at about 10.30 (instead of 8.30, as planned; some difficulty with a battery). Harold Caccia, Gerald Palmer, Edward Warner (First Secretary here). We had an excellent flight in the Mitchell. I sat in front with the pilot. I must have now been a dozen times or more up and down this Gulf of Corinth. I have never seen it more beautiful than today. There was a splendid view of Mount Parnassus – snow-covered – and of the great mountains of the Peloponnese on the southern shore. Passing south of Itea, we could see the peaks that dominate Amphissa and Delphi more clearly than usual. It was a bright, frosty day.

We reached Araxos airfield – about an hour's drive to the west of Patras. The airfield had been opened up before the troubles, but abandoned later. We had only one brigade, as delicately placed in Patras as the other troops were in Athens. The perimeter (even after more or less military dispositions had been taken up) was very small and overlooked by the hills. The port area, however, was in our hands and the cruisers outside gave some sort of confidence to our troops.

From Araxos to Patras lies through a rich, flat (and at the time of year somewhat water-logged) plain. The soil seemed productive – wheat, oranges and lemons, vines (currants, raisins and wine). Of course a great deal has been looted by the insurgents.

We stopped to talk to some soldiers (British) and Greek (National Guard) who seemed quite cheerful. I saw some poultry and quite a lot of turkeys – but we were afterwards told that the greater part which had been hidden from or escaped the Germans, had been stolen by ELAS before they retired.

Mr Nichol (a retired officer, who served as Private Secretary to Sir Harold Macmichael in Palestine and was shot through the lung when Macmichael was attacked by the Stern gang) met us at the airfield. Considering that he must be nearer sixty than fifty, he has made a good recovery. He is now acting as a sort of honorary or temporary member of the Foreign Service, and is consul at Patras.

We went immediately to Military Liaison (M.L.) H.Q. This is the organisation responsible for distributing relief. It will be succeeded by U.N.R.R.A. – that is if U.N.R.R.A. ever gets going and has any money left after paying the salaries of its officials. Meanwhile, these British officers struggle manfully against terrible difficulties. The first problem of course is what to attempt in ELAS-held territory. Are we to distribute relief there? On the one hand, the people are in great need. On the other, it is almost certainly immediately seized by the insurgents. A sort of compromise has been reached. Where some barter can be done – that is to say, where a caique can go in with stores of bread, flour, sugar, etc., and return with olive oil – this is being started. Sometimes the caiques return with their cargo; sometimes they do not, and that area is written off.

Apart from that, all the usual problems that I have seen in the Mediterranean generally, as I have moved eastwards. North Africa, Italy, and now Greece, have presented very similar problems. After the military phase comes the frightful tangle of economic difficulties. The North African economy was not seriously or gravely wounded by the Vichy period and the short war following our invasion. The French were soon able, with our help, to repair the damage. Italy, and still more Greece, are faced with the almost complete destruction of resources necessary to life as it has been developed since the industrial revolution. And there is always the same puzzle. Either there is no power, or no machinery, or no raw material, or no labour, or no money (by which I mean, physical money – lire or drachmae). If by any chance all the necessary ingredients to production can be got together, at one time and in one place, it is a miracle. And if this miracle (which is not uncommonly performed) is not immediate and automatic, then the British military authorities are subject to violent criticism and attacks – locally, but much more cruelly at home, by the pundits of *The Times*, the *Manchester Guardian* and the *New Statesman*.

After seeing M.L. I saw the brigadier (Brigadier Hunt) who was in charge throughout the critical period. In Patras (as in Salonika), in spite of the battle of Athens, no attack was ever actually made. But that we did not suffer another or even more disastrous experience than at Athens, was probably due to the mixture of tact, firmness, bluff and fair play exhibited by this young British officer. We lunched with Brigadier [A. P.] Block (of the Forty-sixth Division), who has just taken over from Hunt. The major-general (a bluff and efficient-looking New Zealander called [Norman] Weir) arrived for lunch. A large mess in an old hotel – with the usual officers, looking very well and cheerful and a happy crowd.

After luncheon, I saw the Prefect or Mayor – his Greek title is Nomarch. He seemed sensible. For a Greek, he had some dignity and did not chatter. The brigadier and M.L. like him and want to help him. They fear that the Minister of the Interior will put in a friend and send their man – [Constantinos] Georgopoulos – to Pyrgos. It is true that the situation at Pyrgos is very bad. Owing to there being no proper road, although according to the truce Pyrgos should have been evacuated by midnight on the 24th, we have not been able to get more than a patrol. The Navy will help us to get there by sea. Pyrgos has a very rich agricultural population (as Greece goes) and ELAS seem to have carried off everything they could lay hands on – cars, sheep, poultry, etc. But Patras (with 70,000 or more inhabitants) is a more important centre than Pyrgos. So I promised to arrange for the retention of 'George' as Nomarch. (This was subsequently arranged in Athens by Brigadier Smith-Dorrien at my request.)

We left Patras at about 3 p.m. and drove back to Araxos. We got off and made a successful return trip, landing at Kalamaki about 5 p.m.

Sir Walter Citrine and his party were to have come to dinner. Actually, only Mr [John] Benstead (railway employees' union [N.U.R.]) turned up as the rest were exhausted by their labours. I am glad they have come. I think they will get something of a shock.

Saturday, 27 January 1945

This was a really wonderful day – one of the most enjoyable in my two years in the Mediterranean. We thought last night that it would be fun to go to Crete. We sent off a signal to the small British force there, and thought no more about it, except to hope that somebody might produce a car or a jeep. We would take our picnic lunch – see something of the island – talk to the British Liaison Officer (B.L.O.) and the M.L. (Relief) Officer and be off. Actually, we had a 'gala' day of unprecedented splendour and enthusiasm.

We left Kalamaki (Athens) at 9 a.m. It was a lovely, clear, frosty morning. I took with me Harold Caccia, Alaric Russell and Gerald Palmer. I sat with the pilot and got the most beautiful views as we sailed through a lovely and almost cloudless sky – just a few white fleecy clouds added, rather than detracted, making up the picture – the azure blue of the sky, the deep blue of the sea, and the white puffs of cloud. We passed by Sunium (with its lovely little temple on the point) and then the islands so well known by name in Greek history and mythology. We swung away east a little to avoid Melos, which the Germans still hold and from which one may get shot. We left behind us Naxos – and thought of poor abandoned Ariadne – and then, high in the sky, above a light, thin bank of vapoury cloud, the snow-capped and magnificent peaks of Mount Ida came into view.

The massif is really splendid – with fine, round, dome-like slopes, leading to the final crown of the mountain – so that the whole gives something of the appearance of a Byzantine church. Snow covered not only the top, but the lower slopes of the mountain, accentuating and giving statuesque form to its contours. East and west one could see the other two mountain ranges – that to the east dominating the area still in German hands.

After circling two or three times to have a good look at the airfield, we managed a safe landing at Heraklion. The field, or strip, lies a few miles from the town and harbour to the east, and is right on the sea coast. (Indeed, I thought at one time that we were going to overrun the strip and fall into the sea, like a golf ball on the twelfth green at Turnberry.)

In the course of our preliminary sweeps, I looked anxiously at the airfield to see if one at least of the two British officers believed to be in Crete on the operational side, or one of the two or three said to be on the relief side, would be there with a car. To my surprise – and alarm – there seemed to be a largish number of figures and quite a train of vehicles.

As I stepped out of the machine (or rather clumsily staggered down the sort of ladder that allows you to emerge from the belly of the machine) I was greeted by applause, and the sound of sharp military orders. Then I realised that our visit to Crete would be a memorable day!

First M. Pappaioannis (afterwards to be called P.). He is the Civil Governor of half Crete. Another man – of very poor type – is Civil Governor of the other half. P. fears that he will be superseded by this interloper. And P. is the father of his people – a Cretan figure on heroic lines – with white head, and three years in the mountains, and a great

Cretan chieftain, who has fought alongside and led his clansmen. He wears the black Cretan cap (a sort of glengarry), not indeed with those queer fringes hanging down over the forehead (like a Victorian aunt) but the bandage type, with one end tucked up to look like a Phrygian cap. And P. knows the people. P. has their confidence. P. will stop any nonsense with ELAS. There is little ELAS nonsense here, and what there is P. will deal with. He has already bumped off a few dangerous men and put others into the cooler. If P. remains Civil Governor of his half, or better still becomes Civil Governor of the whole, and if this little political or bureaucratic understrapper is sent packing, Crete will be safe in P.'s hands. The 10,000 Germans on the island (now in a kind of voluntary imprisonment) can be either left to starve or be liquidated as my noble excellency may decide, and the Cretans will be ready and proud to embark upon any war anywhere and against anybody whom my noble excellency may designate.

I do not say that all these points emerged in the few seconds between the time that P. received me on the airfield in his capacity of Civil Governor and his introducing me to the Military Governor, the head of the National Guard – being formed today – the Town Mayor, the head of EOK,[21] the loyal guerillas, the Greek naval officer in charge, Major [J.] Smith Hughes (the B.L.O. who has been working in Crete on and off for three years), and all the other notabilities. Nevertheless by the time we had inspected the guard of soldiers, and the guerilla guard, and one or two other odd guards, and got into the cars and driven to the town (say, ten minutes to a quarter of an hour) I think I had got P.'s general ideal. (I need hardly say that Mr P. *has* been confirmed as Civil Governor for *all* Crete and his rival has slunk away in disgrace. This was arranged in Athens on Monday, 28 January.)

The procession of cars was very impressive. They were of different sizes and makes and ages. Somehow or another they were all got to start. I had an open car, flying a splendid yellow flag with a cross and other ecclesiastical symbols. It had been lent by the Archbishop.

On arrival in the main square of Heraklion, we were taken into a sort of town hall or municipal offices. The streets were packed. The entire population seemed to be turned out. At different places on the road were stationed guards of honour – splendid-looking bandits, with beards and black Cretan caps and a most formidable appearance. Sometimes the newly formed National Guard, in more orthodox British uniforms; we stopped and inspected these. On getting into the town hall, through the cheering crowds and the flowers and kisses, I was duly presented to further leading citizens and officials, both laymen and clerics. The Mayor, the council, the clerk, the chief moneylender, the chairman of the hospital and so on. Also the Archbishop, and a number of clergy – the Archbishop in the usual

[21] *Ethniki Orgánosis Kritòn*, the National Organisation of Cretans.

black robe and head-dress and a splendid pectoral cross. After the presentations and a little polite conversation, a glass of brandy all round and a toast. More presentations, more brandy, and another toast. Meanwhile the crowd outside was growing and I suggested that I should go on to the balcony and make a speech. This was acclaimed as a most statesmanlike decision and we filed upstairs and out on to a sort of balcony, not unlike that which we used to have at Stockton for the declaration of the poll.

I spoke from the balcony to the crowd. It was all rather ridiculous, because although they naturally could not understand a word, I thought it polite to shout as loud as possible. The interpreter had not a very good voice. It would have been better the other way round. However, everyone was in a merry mood, and I got a few Greek sentences for the end – *Zeto he Krete! Zeto he Hellas!* [Long live Crete! Long live Greece!] – and so forth, which were generally regarded as a success. After the speech, which was followed by a most eloquent address by P., we came down into the streets, mounted our cars, and through a fresh storm of plaudits and flowers, set off for Knossos.

The last time I was here was in the spring of 1930 (or 1931) when I came on a 'Hellenic Cruise' with Maud, Arbell and Maurice. We were taken over the ruins, so admirably excavated and largely restored by Sir Arthur Evans. It was very interesting and the guide (a Greek) seemed very knowledgeable. An immense cortège of Cretans (mostly with tommy-guns and bandoliers) followed us round. We returned to Heraklion for luncheon. At this entertainment, there were about fifty guests. I sat between Mr P. and the Archbishop. Mr P. apologised profusely for the meagre fare, which was due to the short notice. However, we had *Hors d'oeuvres* – Macaroni – Lamb Cutlets and Vegetables – Pork and Potatoes – Caramel Pudding – Coffee, so we did not do too badly. We also had large quantities of excellent Cretan wine – rather like luncheon port, and of course 'Ouzo' (a sort of vodka) with black olives and biscuits, before the luncheon began. Not bad for a starving island, one part of which is still occupied by the Germans!

After luncheon, the procession reformed and we all went to the local hospital. We next visited the port, and finally reached the aerodrome about 4 p.m. Here further speeches and cheers and affectionate farewells took place. At last, we went aboard and flew back to Athens. It was really a wonderful day – quite unique, and made more remarkable by its spontaneity. I should have stated that at the luncheon we had a large number of speeches, going over the whole history of Crete and Greece for hundreds – even thousands – of years, and full of Byron, Canning, Gladstone, etc.

We returned to the Embassy. No news in particular. Sir Walter Citrine and his party seem to have formed the right impressions and are properly horrified by the massacres and the hostages. Sir W.C. was coming to dinner, but cried off. Mr Benstead came in his place; for the second night in succession. He was in grand form.

A reply has at last come from ELAS. They express considerable surprise at the Archbishop's change of front. Owing to some confusion, immediately after the truce he agreed to accept five delegates from EAM. This he subsequently (for practical reasons) changed to three. He then (during my absence in Italy) altered his position and demanded three representatives from KKE (all to be Communists). I was not at all happy about this, although the Ambassador did not share my fears. After dinner, we had an enormously long discussion (in which Brigadier Mainwaring joined us) and I still could not get my way. This worried me very much – even to the extent of keeping me awake. I had finally prepared a draft, which I thought might be acceptable to the Archbishop and meet my position to some extent. The Ambassador (with whom for the first time I found myself in some disagreement) more or less accepted it. The object was to insist only on Siantos (secretary of the Communist Party) coming, and to leave the other choice of delegates to the insurgents themselves.

Sunday, 28 January 1945

I got up early, and worked on some further drafts. After breakfast, the Ambassador and I discussed the proposed reply still further. At 10.30, we went to see the Regent. I found him more difficult than usual, no doubt because his Government is stiffening daily in its attitude. I had to warn him that we could not be asked to pull their chestnuts out of the fire for them except on our own terms. It was finally agreed that we should get away from EAM or ELAS or any of these Protean institutions altogether, and ask for three Communists, two of whom should be named – viz., Siantos and Partsalides. But P. is (although a Communist) also Secretary of what was (or is) EAM. Therefore, we are in fact inviting EAM. It is as if we were to ask the Secretary of the Labour Party and the Secretary of the T.U.C. – this should cover the 'Labour Movement' without any arguing about the precise composition or functions of these various bodies. The Archbishop agreed to draft a telegram on these lines and send it for us to see. It arrived in the course of the afternoon. We made a few further amendments, and sent it off to Trikkala, now the H.Q. of the insurgents.

A large number of complicated Italian telegrams have come in – mostly on finance. I carry my files about with me, so with the help of Russell I managed to get them answered before dinner.

The remaining M.P.s came to dinner at the Embassy – James, Studholme and Lawson. I fear there is now no hope for Bernays and Campbell. It is very sad. Bellenger returned home from Italy.

Monday, 29 January 1945

Having despatched the Regent's reply, there is an interval until we get some further news from the insurgents. I worked till about noon on various telegrams and papers (the latter chiefly dealing with specific questions raised at Patras and in Crete, which I wanted to clear up). I also saw Brigadier Smith-Dorrien (who is now doing excellent work) on the question of the arrests in Athens. We are gradually getting some sense into the Greek Government. But I fear that Plastiras is going to prove another Giraud.

I set out with Russell and Gerald Palmer by car for Thebes. We took sandwiches and had a lovely drive through most beautiful country. Crossing the mountain range which divides Attica from Boeotia, we got a splendid view of Mount Helicon. At Thebes, we found General [Dudley] Ward (commanding Seventh Division) – he seems as efficient as he is charming. He insisted on our going on to Chalkis (on the island of Euboea). He drove me in his open car and the others followed in our car. It was a lovely drive – the view from the pass before you drop down to the sea is glorious. At Chalkis we found a young brigadier, named [Stephen] Shoosmith, in charge. Although this is nominally in our territory under the truce, no representative of the Greek Government has yet appeared (as Prefect or Nomarch) and the brigadier appeared to be governing the place quite successfully, with a joint committee of insurgents and nationalists. (If only our officers could govern this country permanently, it might have a peaceful and happy existence.) I warned him that when the Greek Government official arrived, he would probably arrest all the EAMites. This seemed to sadden the brigadier, who was on excellent terms with them. He was organising the fishing, the fire brigade, the post office, the telephone system, and other services under his own beneficent and generally accepted benevolent autocracy. A queer world!

We were late getting back – most of the way (and a very perilous way) in the dark.

Dined with General Scobie to meet the M.P.s. A large number of officers of the three services and an immense dinner.

Tuesday, 30 January 1945

We are still waiting for a reply from EAM, ELAS, or whatever we are now to call them.

We therefore decided to see some more of Greece and started off about 9.30 for Salonika. Unfortunately, my aeroplane (the Mitchell) was out of action, but I borrowed a Wellington from the A.O.C. ([Air Commodore Geoffrey] Tuttle) which although very cold, seemed fast and serviceable. But the weather between Athens and the Gulf was very bad. We flew by the sea-route, about 250 miles; although we had a fast machine, we had also a fifty-mile gale against us. We took nearly two-and-a-half hours to arrive. When we actually got into the gulf of Salonika the weather had cleared. It was very cold; a piercing wind swept across the plain from the snowy mountains to the north.

We were met by Brigadier Lovett and Consul-General [Thomas] Rapp. Both the soldier and the diplomat have done very well through an exceedingly difficult period. The situation at Salonika has always been perilous, since we had only small forces against the formidable and well-equipped armies of ELAS. The ELAS general, [Euripides] Bakirdzis, is a buccaneer and adventurer. But we were able to maintain reasonable relations with him. He is a Regular Army officer, with a British D.S.O. won in the last war. By a combination of firmness and suavity, we avoided a crisis. Even during the battle of Athens, the ELAS troops at Salonika (as at Patras) remained quiet, although threatening, insolent and insufferably provocative. But the brigadier knew his weakness and the Consul knew his man. Interminable discussions, with long historical digressions, filled the day – and as each day went by without an actual attack, the British situation in Athens began to improve, with corresponding effects in Salonika.

From the airfield we drove to Rapp's house, where he and the brigadier gave us their accounts. We also discussed the future situation and the probable developments. The Government representative (or Governor-General), whom we saw later, is a weak character, [Georgios] Modis by name. But the only màn who could do the job and whom General Plastiras wished to appoint – that is, General Gonatas – is politically impossible at the present time. This is rather a serious difficulty. The economic situation at Salonika is, of course, desperate. The perimeter which we hold has a radius of some twenty miles. The city of 400,000 people lives entirely on charity. The greater part of the rich plain and of Macedonia as a whole (on which alone Salonika can live) is in enemy hands.

After lunch, we went for a little drive round the town, docks, etc. It is a most ugly sprawling modern town. The plain behind has a certain charm, no doubt, under certain conditions; but not with a fifty-mile north wind and the temperature below freezing point. A fine mountain, with a somewhat volcano-like summit, rises from the plain. I had told the pilot that we should start at 3.30, in order to be sure of getting back by daylight. We arrived punctually at the airfield. At about 3.45 the pilot and crew turned up, having been into the town. Since, however, they had taken no precautions to keep the engines warm, the icy wind and cold had done their work. For two hours, with every effort and coaxing, with new batteries and the like, the engine both of the port and starboard side refused to move. (There was no supplementary self-starter available.) At last, when we had quite given up hope, both engines started and we finally took off about 5.45. By this time, a large number of people, mostly brigadiers, had mounted the plane. We finally left with about ten passengers.

The trip back was quite eventful. Darkness came on rapidly. Our pilot (although a somewhat casual young man) was a most skilful 'night flyer'. He brought us successfully through storms and cloud-banks until (after much buffeting) we saw, to our relief, the lights of Athens. Then came the landing. Kalamaki airfield has no *electric* method of lighting the runway, only flares. In the gale, these blew out as soon as they were lit. Round and round the pilot flew, seeking a moment when his opportunity for landing coincided with at least a reasonable path of light showing him the runway. At last he succeeded, and we landed successfully about 8 p.m.

I found a message to go immediately to General Scobie's H.Q. There I was told (*a*) that ELAS had now sent a reply to the Regent's message; (*b*) that the Regent had sent a reply back for the military authorities to despatch. But Brigadier Hugh Mainwaring (Scobie's B.G.S.) had held it up pending my return. I at once gave orders that *on no account* was it to go.[22]

After dinner at the Embassy, Mainwaring came round and we discussed with the Ambassador and Harold Caccia the whole position. The proposed reply, sent to G.H.Q. for them to send to ELAS by military channels, was said to be that of the Regent. It became clear to me from Leeper's account of the afternoon's manoeuvres that it had *not* the sanction of the Regent, and that both the Regent and the Ambassador had been tricked by Sophianopoulos. In any case, after a very long and rather unsatisfactory talk, during which a large number of proposals were made and drafts prepared, we went rather gloomily to bed. I feel more and more depressed about the position. I feel sure that the Greek Government do not *now* want a conference or an agreement. They want a military victory by *our* troops over *their* rebels.

Wednesday, 31 January 1945

At eleven o'clock Leeper and I saw the Archbishop. Fortunately, by holding up yesterday's message, the ELAS delegation, consisting of Siantos, Partsalides, Tsirimokos, General Saraphis and two military experts, with three additional individuals, apparently chosen from EAM parties but *not* intended to be members of the conference, have left Trikkala and are on their way to Athens. It was decided that (*a*) all the delegation, including the disputed figure of Tsirimokos, should be allowed to proceed to Athens and taken to the villa prepared for them outside Athens, beyond the Kalamaki airfield; (*b*) the extra three would be stopped at Thebes.

The question of Tsirimokos could be approached separately. There

[22] It objected to Elias Tsirimokos being included (because he was not a Communist and would have given the delegation an excuse for claiming to be more broadly-based), and was designed to hold things up. It was agreed that General Saraphis, and his two assistants, could attend as military advisers.

were three possible solutions: (*a*) Tsirimokos would declare himself to be a Communist, (*b*) the conference would be reduced to four – two a side, (*c*) Theos[23] would be elected in place of Tsirimokos – Theos being a Communist.

All this nonsense is, of course, the result of two foolish and ill-considered telegrams sent by the Archbishop (or in his name) and agreed by Leeper in my absence in Italy. After the discussion of the *composition* of the conference, we went on to the Government programme. I am still most anxious about this.

4 p.m. Sophianopoulos to see Leeper and myself. Two hours' argument about the Government programme. There is going to be trouble about the dissolution of the Sacred Battalion and the Mountain Brigade. I keep telling the Greeks that if they get the disarmament of the irregular forces as the result of the conference, nothing else matters. But I think they enjoy these tedious and useless arguments even more than the French or the Italians. It is a sort of national sport. Sophianopoulos left just after six.

I then had a little peace. I read a novel called *Young Bess* by Margaret Irwin – quite a readable book, in the modern style of historical novel.

8 p.m. Leeper and I were asked to go to the Regent. We found there Plastiras and Sophianopoulos. An immense discussion: (*a*) on the composition of the conference; (*b*) on the programme. On the former, the delegation are on their way. We have given orders to the military only to let pass the six – Siantos, Partsalides, Tsirimokos and General Sapharis and his two experts. I took the line – very strongly – that we must do this and sort out the question of whether Tsirimokos was to be a member or not *after* they had reached Athens. After a lot of talk, this was agreed. They reached Thebes about 11 p.m., and I heard later reached Athens at 3 a.m. on

[23] Kostas Theos (d. 1958) was the Stalinist organiser of an underground labour movement.

February

Thursday, 1 February 1945

Another wasted day, full of coming and going. David Balfour (who is quite excellent, since he knows the Greeks and speaks their language perfectly) started the day by taking [Demetrios] Stratis and Ralameres to the villa where the Communist leaders are. They were to have given a written resignation on behalf of themselves as leaders of SKE[1] and ELD from EAM, unless agreement is speedily reached. The letter was all prepared, but the two heroes did *not* in fact deliver it. However, they assured us that they had done so verbally. It transpired that Siantos and Partsalides had come to Athens with the idea of reaching an arrangement. They will argue a lot about the amnesty and they will claim seats in the Government. But if we do not handle the membership of Tsirimokos with great circumspection, the conference will not meet. Siantos and Partsalides will go home, rather than accept a humiliating rebuff on this affair. It would of course be an act of real folly to allow the conference to break down – or not to meet – on this piffling issue.

12.30–2.30 p.m. Went on board the *Ajax*, to luncheon with my friend, Admiral Mansfield. It is always a pleasure to see this party of delightful officers.

4–12 midnight. The whole of this time (with the exception of an hour with Commander Jackson on U.N.R.R.A. and relief questions) was spent in a ridiculous and even farcical *va-et-vient*, between M. [Ioannis] Georgiakis (the Regent's *chef de cabinet*), Balfour (who had been with Tsirimokos at the Communist villa), and the Embassy. Tsirimokos asked leave to go to Athens to see his aged grandmother. This (after a great show of resistance by the British military, intended to disarm Communist suspicions) was ultimately agreed. He was taken to H.Q. under guard; then to his own house; then (secretly) to the Archbishop's residence. It seems that he has had a satisfactory talk with the Archbishop. He is still willing to resign from the conference,

[1] *Sosialistikòn Kómma Elládos*, the Socialist Party of Greece.

but fears that Siantos and Partsalides will make trouble. At the same time, he has definitely promised the Regent that he will oppose the Communist claims on two important issues. Finally, it was agreed (very late) that the Archbishop would have a further conference tomorrow with Tsirimokos and then convene a further meeting with Leeper, myself, Plastiras and Sophianopoulos.

The evening was made even more fantastic by a dance (for British officers, A.T.S., cypherers, nurses, etc.) going on at the Embassy, with a deafening band of the Fourth Hussars roaring through the hall.

Bed about 12.30 a.m.

Friday, 2 February 1945

Another fantastic day. The Greeks are really oriental in their methods. Time wasted, so long as it is wasted in talk, is time enjoyed. Nothing takes place at any ordinary hour and, above all, at the hour arranged.

We had expected to be summoned to the Regent's house at about 10.30, when he would have had his second talk with Tsirimokos. However (what with church ceremonies and so on – it being the Feast of the Purification or Candlemas), we did not get his request to attend till about 12 noon. We then had a very sticky discussion. Plastiras was ill; Sophianopoulos alone represented the Government. And for some reason he was absolutely intransigent on the question of admitting Tsirimokos. Tsirimokos has written the necessary letter to the Regent, saying that he did not wish to be an obstacle to the conference and offering to resign. But Tsirimokos (and the Regent) fear that on this Siantos and Partsalides will refuse to go ahead. The Regent has also arranged (or practically arranged) that Siantos and Partsalides should write him a letter saying that there has been a genuine misunderstanding over the composition of the conference; that they are quite willing to reduce it to two a side; but that this would mean returning to Trikkala to get approval of the change by their governing committee; and suggesting that perhaps, in order to save time and without prejudice to his rights, His Beatitude might be prepared to waive the objection.

The Regent very sensibly thought that these letters (which could if necessary be published and the general purport of which he would certainly make known) entirely protected his prestige and that of the Government. He also slyly reminded us that Tsirimokos was a considerable advantage to us, since he had given us prior information as to the line which his partners in crime were going to take and was prepared, at the appropriate moment, to betray them. Sophianopoulos, who threw some doubt on Tsirimokos's capacity for sustained treachery and feared that he might double-cross us and them, was adamant. The restriction of the conference to KKE or Communists on their side had become a matter of principle; the prestige of the

Government would be fatally injured it if were to yield, etc., etc. Leeper spoke, supporting the Archbishop's view. But Sophianopoulos would not be shaken. Ultimately, I spoke, urging that since it was the Regent who was the convenor of the conference, it was a question of his prestige, not the Government's. But (we were now about 2 p.m.) I thought that the unfortunate illness of General Plastiras had put M. Sophianopoulos into a difficult position. I suggested that the Regent should see the three delegates alone, and that if the other two agreed to the proposed procedure, M. Sophianopoulos's position would be eased. Sophianopoulos was very sulky and quite unexpectedly intransigent – I think he is frightened by recent attacks upon him in the right-wing press here. He has also committed himself to the foreign press that he would never agree to the presence of Tsirimokos. It therefore became necessary for me to make a rather firm – even severe – statement reminding the Regent and the Greek Government that the continued support of H.M.G. must depend on the Greek Government being prepared to take our advice on these questions. H.M.G. had made (through the Ambassador) a formal statement of the degree of military and other support which they would give. I referred them to the fourth paragraph of that *aide-mémoire*, in which the conditions on which this support would be forthcoming were clearly laid down.

The meeting then broke up. It was agreed that the Regent would see MM. Sophianopoulos, Pericles Rallis and Macropoulos (the three delegates) together. And as I shook hands with the Regent, he said a few words in Greek, which Balfour (our interpreter) was intended to overhear. They were, I thank you deeply. You may rely on me to bring the greatest pressure for the conference to meet.

We got back to the Embassy at 2.15 for lunch. From three to five I had a very pleasant walk with Harold Caccia – up to the Acropolis and so forth. It was a lovely warm, springlike day. The shops are full of jonquils, narcissi, anemones, and almond and peach blossom.

At 5.30 more messages from the Regent through M. Georgiakis. Everything is at last agreed. The conference will meet at 9 p.m. M. Sophianopoulos agreed under pressure, and in a flood of tears.

7 p.m. Sophianopoulos appeared at the Embassy, very spick and span and highly delighted with himself. You would have thought that no hitch of any kind, or argument, had occurred during the day. We went through his speech and wrote a summary of the Government proposals for him. One of the advantages of the row about personalities attending the conference is that everyone seems to have lost interest in the substance. Sophianopoulos accepted all our proposals, without a murmur, although many of them covered points which have been the subject of bitter dispute for weeks (e.g., the disbandment of the Sacred [Battalion] and the Mountain Brigade).

At 8.15 we had a small dinner in the Ambassador's room (Sophianopoulos, Leeper, Caccia and I). We gave him a bottle of champagne and sent him off at 9 p.m. The conference actually met at about 11 p.m., in a very fine house some miles from Athens [in Varkiza]. As soon as we heard that Sophianopoulos was 'up', one of our officers telephoned the news, and we released the summary (which we had written in English) to the foreign press.

Bed at 11.30 p.m. I read a very good monograph on Father Campion, by Evelyn Waugh – extremely well written.

Saturday, 3 February 1945

More Italian telegrams. Our directive [for implementation of the New Deal] (which I started on in November and had cleared in London on 8 December when I came here instead of going to Washington) has at last arrived – it is in terms hardly dissimilar from those which I originally proposed; but the waste of time in argument in Washington has really suited me. Otherwise I should have been accused of neglecting my *Allied* responsibilities in Italy in favour of my *British* duties in Greece.

Fortunately, the text of the *public* statement is not yet settled, and there must be forty-eight hours' delay in order to inform the members of the Advisory Council ahead of the publication. So I may *just* do it, if the Greek conference does not last too long! It will be a 'damned close-run thing'.

I dined last night alone with General Scobie, to discuss future organisation, military and diplomatic, in the event of either war or peace. Rather an inconclusive talk.

Apart from reporting progress, there was little to be done this morning. I finished my Italian and other papers about noon; and at 12.30 we all started out for a picnic. A large party (including Ambassador, Mrs Leeper, Miss Leeper, Harold Caccia, Gerald Palmer, Osbert Lancaster, etc.). We drove up to the Royal Palace (or summer residence) of Tatoi. The woods are (or were) beautiful. They have been terribly cut by the Germans, and now (with the shortage of fuel) the people are helping themselves as they like, cutting quite recklessly and without any plan. The poor people walk miles out from Athens in a continuous stream, with donkeys or hand-carts. They cut a load of fire-wood in the most haphazard way (generally as near the road as possible) and even in the private grounds of the King's house. They then haul or push the cart back to Athens to sell. Most of them are ill-clad and ill-shod – bare feet are more common than shoes or boots.

We had a delightful picnic in the woods below the Fort of Deceleia (which played a great role in the Peloponnesian War). The ground rises steeply from Athens to the mountains; and the views are lovely. It was a warm and sunny day. The woods in which we sat and walked were carpeted with thousands of little crocuses, yellow and blue.

We walked back to the palace – a horrible scene of dirt and

destruction. Every chair ripped of its coverings (no doubt for clothing), furniture smashed; the filth of a monkey-house in every room, and some unburied and putrifying corpses. Such was the result of an occupation by the noble army of ELAS, so beloved and admired by the *Times* and its editor (? its proprietor?). Harold speaks quite fluent Greek. We had a talk with the wife of one of the devoted old park-keepers. Her language about the rebels you can imagine.

Returned to Athens about 5 p.m. No news yet of the conference. Today is being kept as 'Christmas Day' by the troops and a holiday in the various British offices. This is to make up for Christmas Day spent in the battle of Athens. We gathered in the Chancery to drink local ouzo or retsina and to eat caviare – a present from Bucharest!

After dinner (about 10 p.m.) M. Georgiakis came in to tell us the news. The conference has gone badly. He told us the full story. Siantos absolutely refused to accept the Government's formula for the amnesty. He demanded its extension to all crimes – even murder, rape, looting or arson. (This, of course, is because he fears the break-up of the sort of Communist Ogpu or terror gangs, who dominate the towns and villages and on whose continuance his power depends. He would face the disarmament and disbandment of his regular forces, who are of a better type. He cannot tolerate the loss of the core of his revolutionary organisation.) M. Georgiakis (the Regent's *chef de cabinet*) was very despondent. He has always been very hopeful of a settlement and especially encouraged by the first evening's meeting. But he feels that the Regent cannot ask for further concessions than those proposed and would not be able to get a government to do so even if he tried. It looks therefore as if we have definitely failed. It was agreed that the Regent should again send for Tsirimokos the Trimmer tomorrow morning and that Leeper and I should see him later in the morning to decide on the next step.

Sunday, 4 February 1945

I could not sleep at all well – very unusual for me. About 3 a.m. I woke and worked for two hours on telegrams (a series) to Winston; first to tell the story up to date; secondly to comment on the situation; third to give a political and military appreciation; fourth to put forward a plan of action. I wrote these out and went to sleep.

At 7.30 I was called, and after a bath and shave, got back to bed and got Miss Manley [Leeper's secretary] up to take down the texts of my telegrams. The plan which I have is to ask the P.M. to let me see Siantos and threaten him with all the resources of H.M.G. if he does not yield. Of course, this must depend on my talk with the Regent. I got the first three telegrams despatched at once to P.M. (who is in the Crimea at the Three-Power conference)[2] as they are merely descriptive.

[2] Roosevelt and Churchill, with Stettinius, Eden and the Chiefs of Staff, met the Soviet leaders at Yalta from 4 to 11 February.

But it will save time to get them cyphered and sent off right away.

After doing this I received General Hughes in my bedroom. We discussed the position which would follow if U.N.R.R.A. takes over relief from the military authorities and we are still occupied in operations in Greece. I did another telegram to Winston. General Scobie and Brigadier Mainwaring came to see me, and agreed my military appreciation. All this was cleared by 10.30 a.m. and I then dozed till 11.30 a.m. or 12 noon. After dressing, in my Sunday clothes, I was ready to go to the Regent. Rex [Leeper] and I called on him at 12.30 p.m.

After His Beatitude had explained to us M. Tsirimokos's latest twist – he now seems prepared to abandon his associates on the amnesty question – we discussed my plan. The Regent was very grateful for our renewed offer of support. But after a long discussion it was agreed that a direct British intervention with Siantos and co. would be unwise – it would merely provide him with the opportunity of getting out of his difficulties by an attack on British attempt to settle Greek affairs, etc., etc., and so cover up the real issue. Moreover, it would mean delay till we could hear from Churchill, and delay would terribly weaken his own and the Government's position, already very delicate as regards Greek opinion on the subject of (*a*) the hostages, (*b*) the amnesty. Naturally, I agreed to accept the Regent's view, which incidentally relieved me of suggesting an extension of H.M.G.'s commitment. I therefore altered the *fourth* telegram which I had drafted and asked only for guidance as to whether (in the event of a final breakdown) we should denounce the truce and embark on restricted or extended military operations. I also suggested that we ought to have a meeting with Winston, Anthony, C.I.G.S., F.M. Alexander, etc., on their way back from the Crimea.

A few sandwiches, and by 2.45 p.m. Harold Caccia, Gerald Palmer and I were off for a short drive. It is essential to get some air and a walk if one is to stand this incessant talk, writing, intrigue and worry amid so much of human failings, folly and sinfulness.

We drove out beyond Kalamaki aerodrome, along the sea, to a delicious cove, where there is a hot sulphur spring in a sort of little lake. We walked up a stony mountainside to a saddle from which the clear blue sunlit sea could be seen extending into another bay, and the mountains beyond. The whole hill side was covered with crocuses, anemones – white, blue and crimson – wild aubrietia, cyclamens and thyme. You, dearest Dorothy, would have been in ecstasies of pleasure.

Back to the Embassy at six. A fresh trouble about some trials by court-martial (under this accursed martial law) which seem, and will be represented as, a breach of the Government's 'amnesty' policy. Of course the explanation is that the Government's plan is a proposal. Meanwhile the ordinary law takes its course. After a talk with

Georgiakis (invaluable man!) I persuaded the Ambassador to demand an immediate interview with General Plastiras and to request in the strongest terms a definite order *postponing* all these trials until a final decision about the conference is reached and future policy decided. Of course these incompetent Greeks ought to have arranged this. But it is impossible for any of them (with very few exceptions) to do anything reasonable or sensible. Poor Plastiras is getting more like poor Giraud every day: *Un grand chef*. I dictated an *aide-mémoire* for Rex to take with him. I did not feel like dinner (it was by now about 8.30) so after some caviare and retsina I went down to the Chancery to write the necessary telegrams reporting all this and await the Ambassador's return from his mission. I hope he will be very firm.

The Ambassador returned later after a successful visit to General Plastiras. But it is clear that the poor general is hopelessly confused about the matter. The truth is that as long as the military administration of justice continues, there is little chance of any sensible system being arranged.

Before going to bed, we heard that Tsirimokos (who had gone back to the Communist villa this evening) proposed to stay until tomorrow, presumably to persuade Siantos to make some concession to the Government view on the amnesty. The Government's reply was shown to us – to be sent down in writing. It repeats that the Greek Government cannot go any further than the Pericles Rallis proposals. But it says this in a conciliatory way, with no suggestion of breaking off the conference.

The Rallis draft amnesty decree

Article I: An amnesty is granted for purely political offences committed from 3 December 1944 to the (date of signature) 1945. From this amnesty are excepted *common* crimes connected with a political offence but not exclusively and imperatively necessary for its accomplishment.

A second article set out the machinery for handling disputes over the meaning of the first.

Monday, 5 February 1945

A very idle morning. I stayed in bed till about 10.30 – reading and writing. I am afraid even Harry Hopkins has got hold of the wrong end of the stick about Italy. But he talked sense about Greece. I was very sorry to miss Hopkins in Italy. It is quite untrue that British and American policy towards Italy are gulfs apart. The Americans talk more and actually do less to help than we do. They have not even yet produced the head of the Economic Section. A perfectly incredible suggestion – one General Immel – is now being put forward by the

War Department. He is a great stupid German from Wisconsin – with a square head and hair *à la brosse*. The only good he might do would be to frighten the Italians into thinking the Germans were back in Rome. He is supported by General Marshall! It would be far better to have Antolini back (the buyer for Macy's). All the mischief is being made (*a*) by some discontented American dismissed from A.C. for incompetence, (*b*) some anti-British press writers. I do not think we need take it too seriously; but it is tiresome when men as sensible as Harry Hopkins are taken in by this nonsense.

M. Teyberg – the charming Swedish Minister here who is looking after the Red Cross and the relief ships – invited me to go to luncheon on one of the ships. We had a very enjoyable party – Harold Caccia, Peter Smith-Dorrien, Admiral Mansfield, Captain John Cuthbert, R.N. (H.M.S. *Ajax*), Paymaster-Commander McMullen and M. Teyberg himself. We went in the admiral's launch. Luncheon began at 1.30 and ended about 4 p.m. I have never seen – let alone consumed – so much excellent food and drink.

On our return, a conference with General Scobie and Brigadier Mainwaring on future military plans in the event of either failure or more or less successful outcome of conference, and especially the plans for equipping the new Greek National Guard, out of which the mobile field Army must ultimately be formed. As a result, I sent telegram to Winston, asking him to speed up a decision on the equipment side.

We have now heard that Siantos answered the Greek Government's reply on the amnesty, asking Sophianopoulos to talk it over informally. Sophianopoulos refused (after consultation with Regent and ourselves) but sent the refusal in a very courteous letter. Late tonight we learn that Siantos has now *accepted* the amnesty formula in principle. He wishes the conference now to discuss the details, on which he requires certain further guarantees. So the conference is still alive! It is very interesting to see the line the Communists are taking. Probably they have decided not to break off on any point, at least till the Three-Power conference is over. They seem persuaded that Stalin will do something to help them. For my part, I feel sure that he will try to bargain Greece against Poland. If we could recognise the Lublin Government[3] (probably enlarged and made more respectable) he will sell the Greek Communists 'down the drain'. In view of the lull and the likelihood of a few days' comparative quiet in the Greek crisis, I decided to return to Italy tomorrow.

Tuesday, 6 February 1945

Left Athens 9 a.m. I arrived at Marcienise (Caserta) at 11.30 a.m.

[3] In July 1944, a Communist-organised Polish Committee of National Liberation had been set up inside Poland, claiming administrative powers in Poland and authority over the Polish Army in the Soviet Union. It declared the Polish Government in London illegal, exchanged envoys with the Soviet Government, and in August 1944 a Popular Assembly was convened in Lublin which invested the Committee with provisional legislative powers.

(10.30 a.m. Naples time). Philip Broad had gone for a couple of days to Florence – to the marriage of his sister. Alaric Russell met me. There was a certain amount of minor business to attend to. No further telegram on the public announcement of the 'New Deal' for Italy; but the full text of the directive has reached A.F.H.Q. and is being studied in A.C.

After a talk with General Robertson, on A.C. matters – the most important of which was the still unfilled post of head of the Economic Section – I had a message from General Harding, Chief of Staff. The Field Marshal is still away at the Three-Power conference. But it is clear to me that in order to make everything available for a tremendous effort to finish the German war, the Malta conference – where the Chiefs of Staff of Great Britain and U.S. held a meeting on their way to the Crimea – was extremely anxious to see a Greek agreement on almost any terms, in order to enable British divisions to be released. I lunched at the Hunting Lodge with the Chief of Staff and told him the state of affairs in Athens. I still feel that there is a good chance of an agreement – even if it is not a sincere one. The fact that Siantos was prepared to accept a formula on the amnesty which will sacrifice to justice some of his favourite 'thugs' in the so-called OPLA,[4] is very significant. Either because he has been tipped the wink that he will get no support from Moscow, or from a fear of wholesale desertions from the regular ELAS forces, he may feel it necessary to come to terms now and put the inner core of the movement underground. At any rate, my recent visit has allowed the conference to meet (by stopping the ridiculous attempt of the Greek Government, partially supported by the Embassy, to stop it on the question of the personalities who were to be members) and we have surmounted the most difficult fence – the amnesty.

I left Caserta for Rome at 3.30 p.m. in the Mitchell. Before leaving, I had a talk with General Spofford (G5) just arrived from Washington. He has done splendid work there and I look forward to hearing the full story from him at leisure. Reached A.C. offices about 4.30 and saw Admiral Stone (Chief Commissioner). He was just going to preside at a meeting to discuss the methods of giving effect to the new directive, so I had no long talk with him.

A great accumulation of papers on many Italian subjects kept me at the office till 8 p.m. Brigadier Lush (Chief Commissioner) came to dinner and we had a useful talk afterwards.

Wednesday, 7 February 1945

After my talk with General Harding yesterday, I sent a telegram to Leeper strongly urging the necessity of an agreement from the military point of view. A telegram arrived in the course of the day, giving an

[4] KKE's Gestapo (*Omádes Prostasías Laikoù Agónos*, or Units for the Protection of the People's Struggle).

account of Leeper's talk with the Regent yesterday morning. The Regent fears difficulties over the army. But these can perhaps be overcome by referring the knobbliest points to a technical subcommittee, to which the advice of the British Military Mission should be made available.

Admiral Stone is laid up with a cold. But I had a useful meeting (from ten to twelve) going through all the measures to be taken on the new directive with Brigadier Lush. Other appointments took me till luncheon, when General [Enoch] Brown (U.S.), head of the Rome military district, and Colonel Dunsmore (U.S.) of the Economic Section came. Gerald Palmer was also there. I have acquired a cheery American lieutenant, named John Atkinson, as my A.D.C. This serves to emphasise that, in Rome, I am an Allied officer!

3–4 p.m. Meeting on proposals for a new financial arrangement with the Italian Government. Although this was finally omitted from the main directive, the U.S. Government reserved the right to raise the question, which they have done in a long telegram to A.F.H.Q. Chief of Staff (Lush), Grafftey-Smith and Lawtor (U.S.). It was decided to call A.F.H.Q. representatives tomorrow for a meeting to draft a reply. Curiously enough, the Americans on A.C. are far more critical of Washington and the U.S. Treasury than the British!

Left the office at 7 p.m. Another telegram arrived from Greece giving rather a hopeful account of the conference. Also a telegram to say that Winston and Anthony Eden are expected in Athens on the 11th. I shall therefore return not later than the 10th, if I can do so without upsetting the time-table for making the announcements here to the press and the Italian Government about the new arrangements.

Had dinner in bed. Read Osbert Sitwell's *Letter to My Son* – which I greatly enjoyed. After that (I am ashamed to say) some detective stories by Dorothy Sayers – and then the diary and a box full of papers for tomorrow.

Thursday, 8 February 1945

I do not understand the flow of abuse and accusations against alleged British policy towards Italy which is coming from every American source. We are said to be contemplating the annexation of Sicily, as well as all the African colonies. And it is we (not the wastefulness of the War Department and the insatiable claims of the Pacific War) who are preventing the 300-gramme ration being extended north of the Garigliano. The only explanation I can think of is that the Americans are suffering from the 'morning after' their election débâcle.[5] Such absurd and impossible promises about Italy were made to get Roosevelt that vote at all costs, that they must now account for the failure to implement them. The easiest way is to 'blame' it on the British.

[5] Roosevelt had been elected for a fourth term on 7 November 1944.

A morning of visitors – including M. Prunas (Permanent Under-Secretary of [Italian] F.O.) whom I knew in old Brindisi and Salerno days. Prunas is a very lachrymose fellow, as wet as the sea. But he means well. He at last understands that on the material side we are doing all we can for Italy. But the limitations in this field make Prunas want us to do something in the moral sphere. This – as usual – is the claim to be an 'ally'. For my part, I wish that Winston had not turned down so finally the proposals for a 'preliminary peace', which I originally made in May of last year. The F.O. backed the idea at the time, and even put it to the State Department. Anthony made no fight, partly from deference to Winston, and partly from prejudice against the Italians. The Americans revised it in the Washington discussions of my directive, but the F.O. did not venture to do anything but oppose. Eventually, Winston and Anthony agreed on a counter-proposal for a 'preliminary peace' with Italy immediately at the end of the European War, instead of waiting for a general peace conference. Having gone so far, I think it would have been better to have gone the whole way, and if possible as a British initiative. Perhaps I shall try to take up this question later; there does not seem much chance of reopening it at the moment. But we ought to be ready with definite plans, because the German collapse may come at any moment – probably earlier than we now dare to hope.

I got some letters today from home, including one from Maurice, who seems to be well. He is very pleased with his second son [Joshua]. I also had an amusing letter from Roger Makins, who is remaining in Washington as Acting Minister for the present. After Mr Balfour's arrival from Moscow, Roger is to go to Cairo – in Terence Shone's place. I am not sure that he much likes the prospect, and it seems to me that he will be rather wasted. He ought to be in the F.O.

A long meeting, lasting most of the afternoon and evening, about the financial proposals which the American Treasury want to force down the throats of the A.C. and the Italian Government. In theory, the object is to restore more liberty to the Italians. They are to be responsible for the issue of lire, including making them available (instead of A.M. [Allied Military] lire) to the Allied Military Authorities (in accordance with article 23 of the *amnistia*). In practice, in the name of a concession, they will be forced to face overtly the very heavy burden of the huge issue of A.M. lire (already fifty milliards) and the issue of five milliards monthly for Allied expenses. Naturally, this is an obligation which they cannot avoid. But in the public mind, there is still a hope that dollar and sterling credits will be made available in part, if not in whole, to cover the note issue. And I do not feel that the Government is strong enough at the moment to stand the shock of disappointment. Admiral Stone, Colonel Grafftey-Smith (British) and Command Lawtor (U.S.), all of the Allied Commission, share this opinion. Commander Southard (an American economist) of A.F.H.Q.

takes the other view. Brigadier-General Spofford (U.S.) also of A.F.H.Q. is more or less neutral, but knows how strongly certain elements in the U.S. Treasury are pressing this point. After a very long discussion, and by some careful handling, we got a general agreement in favour of what I wanted, and it was decided to have a draft ready (to be drafted by the three experts) for tomorrow.

Sir David Waley – charming and most welcome visitor – has turned up. He arrived today in Naples and followed me to Rome. He will stay with me and go on to Athens when I go on the 10th. Meanwhile, he and I and all the party of the financial conference and numerous others, found ourselves somehow at dinner with Ambassador Kirk in his magnificent Palazzo Barberini.

Friday, 9 February 1945

Rather a petulant letter from P.J. [Grigg] (S. of S. for War). I promised to let him have a private letter every fortnight about things in Italy – especially Commission and A.M.G. I have naturally not been able to do this. However, I got a long one written and despatched today.

Last night (to be quite sure of getting the thing in the right form and balance) I did a draft of the reply to C.C.S. on the financial problem discussed yesterday. I got to the office at 8.30 a.m. and Miss Campbell got it typed and distributed to the drafting committee.

9.30–11.30 a.m. A long talk with Brigadier-General Spofford, who gave me the background of all the discussions at Washington. It is really a most extraordinary story of oriental diplomacy and occidental red tape. I'm afraid the Americans are very sore and suspicious about Italy. They complain that the Mediterranean is governed by the Field Marshal and me, and that they do not get a look in. And of course they say that my being Acting President of the Commission and Lush (a Britisher) Chief of Staff gives the British complete control. When Admiral Stone is quoted against this (after all, he *is* the Chief Commissioner and a man of strong character) they reply that he is (*a*) a Republican, and not a Democrat, (*b*) in the pockets of the British! They are also very sensitive about the Greek affair. If only we can pull off the *peace*, it will irritate their guilty consciences all the more. But one cannot be annoyed with them – they are really so charming and so naïve and (at heart) so kind and reasonable.

I sent Leeper some stiff telegrams during the last day or two, begging him to keep the conference going at all costs. I have today various telegrams – some hopeful, some less so. The amnesty question is settled. There has been trouble about the date for the removal of martial law. But no conference can break on that. Now they are on the disarmament problem and the new Greek National Army. As usual, Brigadier Hugh Mainwaring seems to have come to the rescue with a plan by which 'British technical experts' would carry the burden of unpopularity. I am therefore now pretty confident. Anyway, I hope to be in Athens again tomorrow.

11.30–12 noon. Mr Kirk, Nosworthy (acting for Charles, who is still laid up) and Stone – the usual Ambassadorial meeting which Stone holds twice a week and I attend if I am in Rome. I had just received a telegram saying that Mr Stettinius has now refused to agree the text of the public statement (which has been so laboriously negotiated in London and Washington) and does *not* wish any statement at all. His reason is that the concessions fall so far short of what U.S. Government would like for Italy that any statement will cause nothing but disappointment. As I knew that Kirk had inspired Harry Hopkins and Stettinius with their idea when they were in Italy on their way to the Crimea, I read out my telegram. Kirk seemed rather confused, and the admiral was indignant. It is all quite ridiculous; but Kirk (who has a purely destructive mind) tried to defend this position. He is a clever, but strange – even unnatural – man. A millionaire, a dilettante – and an intellectual snob. But he is kind, generous and occasionally amusing. He has a mind, but does not apply it to any creative purpose. He is an excellent diplomat.

12–1 p.m. Conference with Admiral Stone, Lush, Spofford and General Robertson – who had come up specially from Caserta at my request. In view of the failure to produce an American civilian as head of the Economic Section or a British civilian as deputy, we discussed a plan for temporarily, at least, getting two really good officers from A.F.H.Q. Robertson was very helpful and I believe we may succeed at last in getting a solution of this problem, which has dogged the steps of the Commission for a year. The Americans (who have the nomination) have sent professors or politicians or salesmen. None has stayed more than about six weeks, and most of the time the post has been vacant. Naturally, the military authorities have looked with contempt and disgust upon this side of A.C.'s activities. This has resulted in back-biting and non-cooperation over the whole internal industrial and production field. Now that General Robertson – a very clever man – has succeeded General Clark – not a very clever man – at A.F.H.Q. there is the opportunity for real progress.

1.15 p.m. Luncheon at villa. Sir David Waley, General Robertson, Randolph Churchill, Lush, Mr [Harold H.] Tittman (U.S. Chargé d'affaires at Vatican) and some other officers. I had a useful further talk with General Robertson after luncheon.

3.15–5 p.m. The drafting committee of the financial telegram met with Stone, Spofford and myself. Waley was invited to be present. I found that they had virtually accepted my text and all that was necessary was to get it correct in technical details. As usual, the final verbal agreement took a long time, but there was complete harmony as to the substance, and they all enjoyed themselves.

After polishing off a number of other papers – Italian patriots,

U.N.R.R.A. agreement with Italy, and so on – I got back to the villa by 7 p.m., had a bath and got into bed for a rest before dinner.

8.15 p.m. Dinner at villa – a party of twelve. Mr Kirk, Admiral Stone, Sir David Waley, Colonel Poletti, Colonel Fiske[6] (both U.S.), Colonel Grafftey-Smith (British), Mr Nosworthy (Counsellor, British Embassy), Brigadier Upjohn, Commander Lawtor (economist, American) – also John Wyndham, John Atkinson (my new American A.D.C.) and myself. In order to emphasise my position in Rome as an *Allied* officer (as President of Allied Commission) I have now an American A.D.C. and a flag on my car with A.C. colours (green and white) and 'President Allied Commission' in gold letters. Both these moves – an A.D.C. and the flag – are well regarded. Mr Atkinson is a charming officer – a lieutenant in the American Army. He had been in Rome before the war (as a press reporter) and seems both efficient and agreeable. Before dinner he made me go (about 6.30 p.m.) to a cocktail party given by United Press at the Grand Hotel. He thought this would be a good move, and I think he was right.

Our dinner party went off well – if staying late is a test. Bed by midnight. A tiring but quite useful day.

Saturday, 10 February 1945

My fifty-first birthday. I do not feel so old (except occasionally, when I feel seventy-one). Left Rome (Ciampino airfield) in 'my' Mitchell. I seem to have managed to purloin this machine and crew. I took with me Sir David Waley, Randolph and Miss Campbell. We left at 9.15 a.m. We stopped at Brindisi (to get the weather and some fuel). The report was not too good, but the pilot thought we could manage it.

Having refuelled makes it much safer, as if there should be difficulty in getting through a 'front' in the canal, we can always turn round and come back.

John Wyndham has got hold of a copy of George Trevelyan's *English Social History*, which looks very attractive and I started to read it on this trip. After Brindisi it got rather 'bumpy' and reading is not pleasant. When we got to the entrance to the Gulf of Corinth, the 'front' was too bad and we turned back. After some consideration, the pilot decided to try to get us to our destination by flying all round the Peloponnese. In spite of very bad weather, he succeeded in this. We flew out quite low above the sea and at last emerged into some better weather just as we were coming up past Aegina. We landed at Kalamaki at about 4.30 p.m.

I found the Embassy in good heart. The conference has practically foundered once or twice, but has scraped through. The questions (*a*) of disarmament, (*b*) formation of National Army, produced a deadlock among the Greeks. It was eventually solved (after about nine hours of

[6] Colonel Norman E. Fiske, a former U.S. Military Attaché in Italy, was Deputy Executive Commissioner, A.C.

argument) by the invaluable Brigadier Mainwaring. If peace is eventually concluded and these clauses are effectively carried out, there ought to be a very good level of actual disarmament. ELAS declared (*a*) the position of their various divisions, (*b*) their armament. Of course they understated (*b*). But the fact that they were prepared to talk with even this degree of frankness makes me hopeful.

The chief trouble is now about the application of martial law. This question is still for discussion.

Sunday, 11 February 1945

Little news from the conference. A message from the Regent told us that informal discussions would take place today on the question of martial law. The Ambassador, Sir David Waley and I discussed the financial situation. This – alas – is no better and may soon lead to another monetary crisis. We have as yet no British official to take the place of Hugh-Jones. Waley has come out to persuade the Ambassador to take Sir Quintin Hill. This is an appointment which I cannot help feeling is more to suit the Treasury than (necessarily) the needs of Greece. Sir Quintin Hill was head of Department of Trade, being originally a Board of Trade man. He was Deputy Secretary at the Ministry of Food, but French and Woolton threw him out.[7] He has been two years *en disponibilité*. However, since there seemed no other choice, the Ambassador finally agreed. After all, the quarrel may not have been his fault, and he may make a success in Greece. In any case, they should be flattered by his high rank.

At 11 a.m. we all went on a picnic. We drove to Sunium (through Laurion, where were the old Athenian silver, and are now the modern lead mines). It was a lovely day and the hills and valleys surprisingly beautiful in the sunlight. Miss Campbell came and thoroughly enjoyed it. The little temple on the cape is placed on a rock overlooking the sea – a very fine piece of architecture on a superb site. We got back about 4.30 – a really delightful expedition, which did us all good. Rex hardly ever can be dragged from his study; but he thoroughly enjoyed the day.

On return, I found some telegrams on Italian affairs. The F.O. are trying to get the whole subject of the directive, the public statement now objected to by Stettinius, and the possible provisional peace treaty discussed at the Three-Power conference. I see little chance of any final decision. But perhaps if Winston and Anthony come here we can discuss it.

I was just going off to dine with General Scobie (about 8 p.m.) when a message came from Georgiakis (the Regent's observer at the conference) that the situation was desperate. No agreement (after four hours' discussion and many suggestions) could be reached. He

[7] Sir Henry French (1883–1966) was Secretary, Ministry of Food, 1939–45. Sir Frederick Woolton (1883–1964), later 1st Earl, was Minister of Food, 1940–3.

suggested that we should come down at once and try to settle the final point. After a little consideration, we replied that we would do so, but only if it were the wish of both sides. After a short delay, the answer came inviting us to come on this clear understanding. A hasty dinner, and we started down to the villa (near the village of Varkiza) about 9 p.m. We were met by Georgiakis at a rendezvous on the way, who told us the situation. After trying to form a rapid plan, we finally arrived at the house about 9.45 p.m. and began what proved to be a fantastic and eventful night.

The conference took place in the large lounge–sitting-room of a millionaire's newly built villa. It stands a mile or two from the main road which leads to Kalamaki airfield and about ten miles from Athens. It is well situated and with the usual sort of millionaire's garden (statues, swimming pool, etc.) and luxuriously furnished. After ten days' use by the EAM/ELAS delegates, however, and by the conference as a whole, it was in a pretty squalid condition – cigarette-ends, orange-peel and every sort of litter covering the floor, and scattered over tables, chimney pieces, window-sills and so on.

The conference consisted of three Government delegates, MM. Sophianopoulos, Pericles Rallis and Macropoulos on one side of the table; Siantos, Partsalides and the now famous or infamous Tsirimokos on the other. Two secretaries and two shorthand clerks at one end; the Ambassador and I took our seats at the other (looking and feeling rather like the kings in *The Gondoliers*). Lots of other people crowded into the room – to the number of about twenty or thirty, but they were eventually ejected. The only other person present was the Regent's representative, M. Georgiakis. The Ambassador explained in a few words the reason for our coming, and asked each side to state their position on this last question of importance now outstanding.

Encouraged by this, M. Sophianopoulos made a long, but masterly speech, covering the whole course of the conference to date, and very conciliatory in tone. He explained that after ten days of incessant labour, with the assistance on various technical points of the British officers, notably Brigadier Mainwaring, complete agreement had been reached on the difficult questions of the amnesty; disarmament of irregular forces; formation of new National Army; the future of the Gendarmerie or police; the political liberation of the citizens, including the right of association in trade unions and of public meetings; the purging of collaborators from the public service and their punishment in suitable cases; the return of hostages and prisoners. One final question remained – the moment at which military law (or martial law) under *état de siège* would be lifted. The Government's view was that it should remain in force until 'pacification' had been effected. They were prepared to define this as 'when disarmament is complete'. They had now proposed a further concession – that instead of full martial law, a modified form known in the constitution of 1935 as *Kappa Delta*, should be applied. Article 5 of this gave the government power to suspend various rights normally laid down for citizens. Included in these guarantees of individual liberty was the provision that no man should be arrested without a warrant. The Government were prepared to abandon the right to waive the warrant procedure *after* disarmament, but not before.

M. Sophianopoulos's speech lasted from 10 p.m. to 11 p.m.; when he sat down, M. Siantos (secretary of KKE) rose. Siantos (whom I had seen, together with Partsalides) is a set-faced, sly, shifty-looking man, of middle height, in battledress, rather bald (with an irritating kind of tousled hair on the back of his head). He looked tired and exhausted – but I think this was partly affectation. He spoke as if all the weight of the world's cares were upon his shoulders – the weary Titan. He began very quietly – almost inaudibly – gradually working up to his various points of climax. His injured-innocence method was subtle and effective. You felt almost convinced by the end that there had been no civil war, no insurrection, no disorders even – except in a Pickwickian sense. There had been a certain confusion, due to misunderstanding. There had been no crimes – perhaps, and naturally enough in the circumstances, some regrettable incidents on both sides.

He began by thanking the British – their friends and allies – for their interest in the work of pacification. He was grateful for the presence here tonight of such distinguished representatives of Great Britain as the Resident Minister and the Ambassador. The conference had met and carried on its work in a spirit of mutual understanding. He and his friends had two main objects (which had been their purpose all through), the general disarmament of all irregulars on a fair basis, and the constitutional liberties of the Greek people! As regards disarmament, complete agreement had been reached and the agreement would be carried out sincerely and honestly. (I had that morning received from most secret sources the orders for trying to evade the terms – make secret dumps of the best weapons, handing over only inferior ones and so forth – which ELAS command had already sent out to the various divisions and formations! So much for sincerity!) On the question of constitutional liberties, Siantos and his friends felt very strongly. (You would have thought a Liberal professor, not a blood-stained and callous criminal was speaking.) Any form of martial law – even the modified system proposed by the Government – or any suspension of the normal processes of civil law cannot be reconciled with liberty. It cannot be justified even by the gravest internal situation. Nor was there any serious reason for such a revolutionary system. Disarmament has been agreed, and will be complete. ELAS will hand over *all* their arms, without exception (I thought of my own information and smiled benignly at the orator). He gravely feared that the clause in the amnesty allowing common law crime to be punishable would be abused – more particularly if men were to be arrested without warrant. It would be the instrument of a proscription under the guise of law. And in any event, he did not believe in anything except a few crimes, on both sides, in the heat of battle. (I thought of the mutilated bodies of men and women, of all ages, found at Peristeri and elsewhere.)[8] Siantos is going back to the mountains – to persuade his forces to accept the peace and to disarm, and the refugees who have come away from Athens to return to their homes. How can he do this, if they are to be in terror of illegal arrest, under a system of martial law, without the constitutional guarantees provided by the processes of civil law? Already there have been thousands of arrests in Athens (a good point). If arrests without a magistrate's warrant continue, either the refugees will stay in the mountains under terrible conditions, or if he persuades them to return and arrests *en masse* continue, there will be panic, not pacification. Nevertheless, in the interests of peace and a settlement, he and his friends have accepted the *Kappa Delta* law insofar as it allows (*i*) right of search of private houses, (*ii*) suspension of right of public meeting, (*iii*) postal censorship – all suspensions of constitutional rights. This one point – the right of arrest without warrant – remains. To that he cannot agree. He cannot sign a peace containing such a clause. Even if he were to sign, he could not get it accepted. He would be repudiated by his people.

He should also mention two other points still unsolved – the treatment of men in the civil police or Gendarmerie who might have joined ELAS and of civil servants who had done the same. But he felt that agreement should be possible on these two questions. On the sanctity of the magistrate's warrant he must stand firm.

This brought us to about 11.45 p.m. I asked for clarification of certain technical questions. It seemed that (*a*) EAM/ELAS agreed to suspension of three out of the four civilian liberties in article 5 of the Constitution. This should continue at the Government's discretion – probably till elections could be held. (*b*) On the fourth right – that is, freedom from arrest without magistrate's warrant – the Government proposed to continue the suspension till *after the completion of disarmament*; EAM proposed that the normal system should be restored immediately *after the signature of the peace*. Was this correct? Yes – agreed by both sides that this was the point.

How long, I asked, was disarmament to take under the agreement?

Fifteen days in principle, perhaps twenty days in practice. Was that so? Yes – agreed by both sides. Then there were fifteen to twenty days about which it was proposed to endanger all the work of the conference, and plunge Greece again into civil war?

Well, it seemed so (very Socratic). The Ambassador and I thought that it would be now a good thing to break off the formal meeting, and

[8] Some 1,500 bodies had been found in Peristeri, an Athens suburb, apparently murdered by ELAS.

for us to see the delegates of both sides separately. Would that be a good idea? Excellent.

About midnight, therefore, Leeper and I went into another room and the three Government delegates followed us. It was 2 a.m. before the full conference was resumed.

It soon became clear, from our talk with the Government side (Pericles Rallis, Minister of Interior, was chiefly concerned) that the fifteen to twenty days were really of importance. The Government wished to use that time to arrest a very large number of suspects. The rebels equally wished to evade arrest under martial law or its equivalent, relying on the complications and slowness of the civil law.

After we had talked to the Government delegates, who seemed very unwilling to make any further concession, we saw Siantos and his comrades. It was quite clear that they were thinking of the effect on the situation in Athens and the Piraeus, from which a large number of Communists had fled with the ELAS forces as they retired. Siantos knows very well that lots of these people have committed atrocious crimes. But he knows also that lots more will be arrested 'on suspicion' and by this means kept safely under lock and key for a long time. But these are the very people whom he relies on to rebuild the Communist cells (ὅπλα) in the great cities.

After we had seen both sides, we conferred with M. Georgiakis. A suggestion was made that the following would be a possible compromise – that the normal civil method of arrest by magistrate's warrant should be retained (*a*) in Athens and the Piraeus *immediately* after signature of the *peace*, (*b*) in the rest of Greece after the effective carrying out of the *disarmament* plan. The argument for this would be that the Government had been in effective occupation of Athens and the Piraeus for several weeks and had had time to organise normal methods, whereas in the other parts of Greece there were no magistrates, no prefects or mayors – in fact none of the apparatus of civil government. This compromise was put forward by M. Georgiakis to both sides (in separate rooms) as our *decision*. After some little time, he came back to tell us that it would 'do the trick'.

At about 2 a.m. (therefore) the full conference resumed. I explained the compromise plan as a suitable and reasonable settlement. Both sides showed proper surprise and delight at so novel, unexpected and reasonable a proposal. After a good deal of talk on various details of its application, it was finally agreed.

Then two more rather tiresome questions which had been left over, came up. First, the treatment of EAM/ELAS sympathisers in the police who had deserted their posts. The second was the future of civil servants or other functionaries who were in the same category. A very long discussion took place on these points, but in rather an unreal way, since both sides knew that the agreement would now be reached and that these questions would *not* be a cause of rupture. Finally, a rather complicated formula was agreed – I was not really much interested in the terms of it.

It was now about 3 a.m. and Siantos and co. thought it time to go to bed. But this would mean another meeting tomorrow and the danger of fresh issues. Moreover, the Government delegates did not conceal their fear that their colleagues might repudiate them for their action in accepting the 'compromise' on the right of arrest. A good deal of the agreements already reached was in draft. Could not, I said, M. Pericles Rallis and M. Tsirimokos (both lawyers) rapidly agree a text covering the questions dealt with tonight? After some talk, work was begun, but by about 4 a.m. it was clear, first, that no proper draft had really been made covering the agreements reached during the ten days of the conference and secondly, that the task was too great to be accomplished tonight; thirdly, that Siantos refused absolutely to sign the document until he had proper time to go through it. Nevertheless, with the possibility of Winston arriving today (or tomorrow) and the danger of a breakdown on some new points, I was determined not to leave the house without a signature. It was therefore decided to prepare a *summary* of the points agreed; a statement that *full* agreement of *all* points at issue had been reached by the conference; that a Greek text was being prepared but that owing to the late hour this could not be ready till later in the day; that it would be formally signed at 2 p.m. today; that the short document was signed in the presence of myself and the Ambassador. The document in question was prepared; a press communiqué agreed; and about 5 a.m. the final conference met again – three on each side, Leeper and I at one end, and the secretaries. The rest of the various onlookers who were sleeping or lying about the room were taken up and removed. After formal signature, M. Sophianopoulos made a short speech; M. Siantos also, and I said a few words of congratulation to both sets of negotiators and good wishes. (This was recorded in the formal record.)

At about 5.30 a.m. the Ambassador and I left the villa and returned to Athens. It was 6.30 a.m. when I got into bed.

Monday, 12 February 1945

9 a.m. I got up after an hour or two. I sent off the necessary telegrams to F.O., etc., giving the news of last night's work. Lancaster and some of the press then came, and I gave an interview to Reuter. We got a slight shock by hearing that Winston and Anthony were to arrive today, but this was subsequently cancelled. Randolph is still here, very friendly. He is editing a great statement to the press, which is giving him much pleasure!

The rest of the day was spent in trying to keep the plan arranged early this morning. Actually, in true Greek style, it was somewhat delayed. The formal document was not ready at 2 p.m. There was much argument about wording, and it was 7 p.m. before it was actually signed. However, there was no real danger, owing to the procedure which we had adopted. I think they were just enjoying themselves.

Siantos and his two colleagues saw the [Greek] Prime Minister, after signature, and then the Regent. The latter seems to have spoken to them in very severe terms.

8.30 p.m. Dined with Scobie. At last, and on an auspicious occasion.

Tuesday, 13 February 1945

A morning in bed. Telegrams, both Greek and Italian. At 12 noon, Mr Graham and Mr Hogarth (of the Ministry of War Transport). The Greek Government have asked us to return six coasters. We are ready to do so, but of course they have no organisation of any kind to manage them. The Greeks are admirable individualists and private traders. The system of state socialism, which war requires, is repugnant to them and they seem unable to work it at all.

12.45 p.m. Went for a very nice drive and picnic – along the sea-coast beyond the airfield. After luncheon, some returned, others walked on. I went with the walkers – an hour or two over a beautiful hill and then along a lovely bit of shore to the village of Varkiza. It was a warm sunny day – perfect spring weather. New flowers of every sort every day.

5–7.30 p.m. Read Trevelyan's *English Social History* – an admirable book.

After dinner, M. Georgiakis came round for a talk. After the political crisis, comes the economic. Unless something is done, another inflation threatens. Sir David Waley explained his views. The general conclusion was (*a*) that the Finance Minister, M. Sideris, was incompetent; (*b*) that M. Varvaressos,[9] now Governor of the Bank of Greece, was the only man capable of handling the situation. Could he become Deputy Prime Minister or Minister to co-ordinate all finance and economic questions, with fully authority? It was decided that (*a*) Georgiakis should sound the Regent; (*b*) Leeper and Waley should see the Regent tomorrow on the question.

Wednesday, 14 February 1945

We had been very disappointed yesterday by a telegram to say that Winston would *not* be coming, only Anthony. The Regent (who was informed) was very disappointed. So both Leeper and I telegraphed separately to Winston, urging him to come, if only for a few hours. We were correspondingly delighted to get a telegram, early this morning, announcing the arrival of the whole party at 4.30 p.m. today. We told the British military authorities immediately after breakfast and then the Regent. A general plan was worked out in the course of the

[9] Professor Kyriakos Varvaressos (1884–1957) was Finance Minister, 1932 and 1941–4, and Deputy Prime Minister and Minister of Supply, 1945.

morning, which proved very successful. The problem was to combine success with security. As always, a compromise is necessary.

After these meetings, I spent a rather hectic day (with Miss Campbell's help) in preparing all the agenda for the meetings which I hope to arrange for tomorrow. It is a good opportunity to get many things settled. With Anthony, Alex Cadogan, F.M. Alexander, Sir Edward Bridges, etc., we ought to be able to deal with many questions – both Greek and Italian. The Embassy here is (with the exception of Leeper and Balfour) perfectly useless. So I had to do all the Greek drafts myself (with the help of Harold Caccia) and the Italian and Yugoslav ones also.

At 2.30 we had a little meeting (with Scobie, Caccia, Smith-Dorrien, Waley, etc.) to go through the Greek papers, before the final copies were to be made.

At 3.15 we left for the airport. At 4.30, the party arrived. It was a *most* beautiful afternoon – an absolutely cloudless sky, with sea, mountains and city lit by the wonderful Greek lighting, that seems to have a quality of its own.

The great machine landed, their escorts of fighters circling round, and after various presentations, etc., we set off for Athens. P.M. and Ambassador in one car, Anthony and I in another, Field Marshal and Scobie in a third – and so on. We drove through the town to the Regent's house – which is between the British Embassy and the old palace and Constitution Square. The streets were packed, and the crowds most enthusiastic. After a few minutes of formalities, the procession reformed. This time the Regent and P.M. rode together in an *open* car, which drove at a snail's pace through a wildly enthusiastic mass of people. The Greek soldiers lining the streets could not control their emotions and I was rather alarmed lest in the commotion some rascal might try an assassination. However, at last we got through the (fortunately) short distance – a few hundred yards – from the regency to the palace, which we entered by a side door. Passing through, we then came out on to the terrace, overlooking Constitution Square. Here was an upturned sea of faces and a crowd of a size and character beyond anything I have seen. The estimates range from 20,000 to 70,000. I believe about 40,000 would be about right. The whole square (except for a space left empty in front of the 'Tomb of the Unknown Warrior' and thus making a gap between the front rank of the crowd and those on the terrace of some fifty yards) was packed. All the houses, windows and roofs, were black. The Grande Bretagne alone must have held hundreds. And the old palace behind us was full at every window and roof. The reception was remarkable not only for its enthusiasm, but for its orderliness. There was little of the organised chanting which we had before with 'E– A– M' or 'E– D– E– S'. Even the Royalists made no separate demonstration. It was a *democratic* crowd, applauding in the Archbishop and Churchill democratic leaders. And so the totalitarian technique of joint choruses and so on was obviously out of place. Having seen the crowd on the day of Papandreou's entry on 14 October, I was struck with the difference. In that crowd there were two bitterly hostile sections; there was a sense of challenge all through and a sense of tension. In this crowd, there was a sense of relief, as well as of triumph; a feeling of gratitude and pride, of a people who had been through a hard and gruelling test and gladly acknowledged and honoured those who they knew had brought them through – the Archbishop–Regent, representing Greek effort, and the British Prime Minister, representing in his person all that they admire in their ally – courage, fairness and determination.

Naturally, the visit following on his previous one, made it a dramatic occasion. Everyone had in mind Christmas Day – cold, dark and armoured cars or tanks. And now, peace signed; glorious warm sun (so that Athens was really 'violet-crowned' today), and a procession in open vehicles, like a football match or a race-meeting in peace-time. The contrast was, I have no doubt, in all men's minds.

The Archbishop spoke – a few, dignified words. Winston's reply – extempore – was excellent. (The time to translate each phrase was helpful.) After a few suitable ceremonies (and speeches by Plastiras and by Anthony Eden) and much loud music and cheering, we retired into the palace – Winston returning for one last cheer before leaving. In the palace, a few of us (Winston, Anthony, Leeper and I) went in with the leading Ministers (Plastiras, Sophianopoulos, Sideris, etc.) for a talk. This was held in the 'Cabinet Room' and although not very serious, allowed some useful things to be said. The Regent presided. After about three-quarters of an hour, we all left. The Regent in his own car, P.M. and Anthony together; Ambassador and I in the third. From the palace to the Embassy there were great throngs and much cheering.

A huge dinner at the Embassy followed (thirty-six people) which was quite amusing. I sat on Winston's right. He was in excellent form, having enjoyed the whole thing enormously, and been much touched by the scene. Both he and Anthony were very complimentary to the Ambassador and me. I think they have realised the political difficulties as well as the military.

The Crimean conference has put them all in a good humour. The whole atmosphere seems to have been very good; the Russians have shown more candour and friendliness than ever before.

At 10.30 the Regent came round for a private talk with P.M.; Anthony, Leeper and I were also present, as well as M. Georgiakis. The discussion was partly in a light and gay mood; partly serious. A great success.

At 12 midnight – the P.M. and all his party (Sarah, Randolph, Lord Moran, etc., etc.) left. He goes to Alexandria and then Cairo. Anthony and his party (Cadogan, Bridges, Dixon, Lawford, etc.) stay for tonight.

Thursday, 15 February 1945

10.30 a.m.–1.15 p.m. A very successful conference. The Greek agenda first; then Italian and Yugoslav. I had prepared an agenda, written a memorandum on each question (or got one written, e.g. Waley on the financial questions) and had the whole thing circulated last night to all taking part. We therefore had a more orderly talk than usual. Bob Dixon took a note of decisions, which was ready late afternoon. On most of the specific things we got a fairly good answer and decision. On general Italian policy, there is still much uncertainty. But I think I persuaded Anthony not to let his natural irritation with American exaggerations affect his judgment. Italy is a British interest, in the sense that we do not want to see an important Mediterranean power in dissolution or in a state of permanent revolution. We do not want to see Italy break up and/or 'go Communist'.

1.15 p.m. F.M. Alexander and I lunched with General Scobie. Afterwards, Alex and I went to Marathon in a jeep. The road was very bad (hence the jeep), but the country quite lovely. The victor of Alamein, etc., should (I felt) see Marathon. (The Persians were twenty-six miles from Athens, just as the Germans were seventy miles from Cairo.)

A quiet evening – some useful work with Harold [Caccia] and Peter Smith-Dorrien – chiefly on Greek organisation. Really, I think we have taken on a heavy task. The more one sees of the problem, the more difficult it seems. There is no civil service, and no governmental structure capable of functioning.

8.30 p.m. A vast dinner for Anthony Eden (to which the Ambassador, Field Marshal, General Scobie, Alec Cadogan, Bridges and I were bidden). We had *excellent* food and drink (lobster, lamb, ices, and Louis Roederer 1928), and much speech-making. I sat between General Plastiras (Prime Minister) and Pericles Rallis (Minister of Interior).

After dinner, and a certain amount of general conversation, Anthony, Leeper, Bridges, Waley, Cadogan and I were taken into a room for a talk with Plastiras, Sophianopoulos and Sideris on the economic and financial situation. Anthony started with a good little lecture (which we had prepared for him) urging them to help themselves – *not* lean entirely on us. All that we *could* give them, they were getting or would obtain. Begging for more would do no good. Many of their problems could only be solved by their own organisation and effort, etc., etc. All this went well enough, till Sideris replied, with a long, dreary, whining speech. This annoyed Anthony, who was rude. We were then all rather rude, and it was all very awkward (especially after the dinner). But it may do some good. They *must* take a hold on themselves, or they will drift into another crisis and no one can avoid it. The Regent was *not* present at this talk, but

Anthony went to say 'goodbye' to him and told hm what had happened. The Regent was highly delighted!

Friday, 16 February 1945

Left Athens 9 a.m. Miss Campbell – also Miss Manley (Ambassador's secretary) – for a holiday in Rome.

Arrived Marcianise 11 a.m. (Naples time), that is, three hours later. A good trip. Broad met me.

Morning at office – a good deal to see, not much to do. Broad is *very* efficient and gets the office routine done in an admirable way. I have appointed him 'deputy' to the Resident Minister, which pleases him.

General Robertson (C.A.O.) came to see me. *The 300-gramme bread ration* is at last agreed. There has been trouble about our plan for the Economic Section of the A.C. I must see General [Joseph T.] McNarney. At 2.30 I went to see him. He is 'Deputy Theatre Commander', i.e. deputy to Alex. I would not say that he knows much about soldiering. He is an office general. But he is shrewd, knows the War Department well, is liked by Marshall, and will not ever put a foot wrong. He is rather a cold fish – more like a solicitor than a soldier. With some air of mystery, he produced a telegram from McCloy[10] urging him to see me and get my approval of the appointment of General Immel (in civilian clothes) to the head of the Economic Section. Knowing how strongly this had been and would be opposed by Admiral Stone, I told General McNarney that I should like to discuss the matter with the Chief Commissioner. I tried to get some expression of opinion from the Deputy Theatre Commander; but he would not rise to any fly.

Dined and slept in Naples. Andrew Cavendish came for dinner and stayed the night.

Saturday, 17 February 1945

I have a letter from Sir John Murray about St George's, Westminster. I think this may go through. According to Murray, the Committee all want me, but were told by Ralph Assheton[11] that Winston objected. It seems that he does not approve of members leaving one seat for another. I discussed this with him at Athens, and he withdrew his objection. I have telegraphed to Murray accordingly.

I have also splendid letters from Dorothy and Catherine. Catherine is to work at the F.O. I hope she will enjoy it, and not do too much damage to the interests of His Majesty or the hearts of the young men.

11 a.m. General Nichols to say goodbye. He is going as chief signal officer to S.H.A.E.F.

11.45 a.m. General Robertson. I explained to him the situation

[10] John J. McCloy (b. 1895) was Assistant Secretary of War, 1941–5.

[11] Ralph Assheton (b. 1901), later 1st Baron Clitheroe, was chairman of the Conservative Party Organisation, 1944–6.

about Immel. He was much shocked. Apparently Immel is a really impossible man – of a very low type. What a bore it all is! It means, either to give in and let things get still worse in this vital part of the Commission's work, or else have another row with the Americans in which we (British) will be accused of interference and so on. Why can't they recommend a proper man?

12.45 p.m. Left for Rome by Mitchell.

1.30 p.m. Arrived Ciampino. John met me. Drove to A.C. and saw Lush and Stone. Discussed the Immel problem. They were both shocked and horrified. But *quoi faire?* It was clear to me that we must put up some reply for McNarney to send. It was finally decided (*a*) that I should draft this and give it to McNarney on Tuesday, after consultation with Stone, (*b*) that I should privately telegraph to F.M. 'Jumbo' Wilson [in Washington] (through Embassy channels) giving him something of Immel's character and history. The F.M. will remember, because General Airey (Intelligence) tried to get General Immel thrown out of Naples on security grounds, and Wilson had a lot of trouble about the case. We discussed other Italian matters – especially (1) Patriots, (2) Venezia Giulia.[12] On the first we have now a committee at A.F.H.Q., and I hope for an early report. On (2), the F.M. is going on Wednesday to see Tito. He may be able to negotiate a military zone, which will give us Trieste and the necessary communications, leaving a final settlement of the frontier till the peace treaty. But here again the State Department is taking a curious line. I think Kirk will say that we ought to put A.M.G. in *all* Venezia Giulia. If Tito is there first, this will in fact be impossible, and I think it is much more realistic to admit it.

4.30 a.m. Left A.C. Left Ciampino at five. Arrived Marcianise at 5.45 and back at my office by 6 p.m.

The P.M. has wired the President (at my suggestion) to say that if he wishes to see me, I am at his service. The President's ship will be at Algiers tomorrow. Kirk has been summoned down; presumably to talk on Italy.

6.15 p.m. Brigadier Hugh Mainwaring (from Athens).

6.45 p.m. General Spofford (G5). Apparently General McNarney has *not* told him about the Immel proposal.

Worked at Caserta till 8 p.m. when I went to dine with F.M. Alexander. Generals Harding, Robertson, Lemnitzer (U.S.) and poor General Anders.

Rather a distressing evening. General Anders (who was accompanied by his A.D.C., Prince Lubomirski,[13] whom I had met several

[12] Venezia Giulia, on the east side of the Adriatic (including Trieste and the Istrian peninsula), was acquired by Italy under the Treaty of St Germain in 1919, and as a result half a million Slovenes soon found themselves suffering Fascist oppression.

[13] Prince Eugeniusz Lubomirski (1896–1982) had been A.D.C. to General Anders since 1942 and continued as his private secretary after the war.

times before) was in a bitter, despairing mood. The dinner passed off with discussion of trivialities. After dinner Alex wisely let the general have a fling. (He had already had one-and-a-half hours in his office.) A rather painful discussion – or rather monologue – in which General Anders said that Poland was finished, betrayed by her allies. It was now merely a question of time before all Europe would succumb to Bolshevism, etc., etc. We tried a few general observations, of a comforting character. But it was not much good, except to keep the thing going, which good manners demanded. General Anders is a very fine man. He has been eight times wounded. He has been two years in a Russian prison. He has been with his Poles in that extraordinary march all round the world – Russia, Turkestan, Palestine, Egypt, Italy. I am very sorry indeed for him. But I cannot see what else we could do. And I feel sure that if General Sikorski had been alive, the Polish Government in London would never have been allowed to drift into the futile and fatuous position it now occupies.[14] General Anders leaves for London 'for consultation' tomorrow. His soldierly loyalty has made him do his best. But I fear that our two Polish divisions will be much disturbed. At the worst, they will disintegrate into a rabble of refugees. At the best, they will be kept enough together to hold a sector of line, without attacks or counter-attacks. I do not think they could now be used offensively. With three divisions in Greece, then two Polish divisions disaffected, one Negro division, one Brazilian division – our Italian forces are a very wasting asset. But they seem nevertheless to be fulfilling their allocated role.

Sunday, 18 February 1945

I have received no message, so I am spared a flight to Algiers. Being *quite* exhausted, I have stayed all day in bed – dozing, reading and writing. For some reason, I felt terribly bad this morning. I am rested this evening. I have been very active lately and forget that I am fifty-one years old. It seems absurd to be over fifty. I used to think such an age patriarchal.

Monday, 19 February 1945

A nice spring morning – a cool wind but lovely sun. I still feel very tired; I should really like several days' holiday, moving nowhere either by motorcar or aeroplane – at the same level, so to speak, all the time – and with nothing to read more modern than Jane Austen, or perhaps Trollope. Catherine's letter to me about how she has become a 'Foreign Office' girl is very amusing. I cannot see why she should have

[14] At the Yalta conference Britain and America had insisted that some members of the Polish Government-in-exile in London should be included in the Lublin Government. Although they would continue not to recognise that administration, this effort to make it more representative merely undermined the position of the government in London. General Wladyslaw Sikorski (1881–1943), Prime Minister of the Polish Government-in-exile and C.-in-C. of the Free Polish Forces, 1939–43, died in an aeroplane crash at Gibraltar.

less time off than Elizabeth Cavendish[15] at the Treasury. She will have to join a union and put things right. The St George's affair seems to be likely to come off, although the Committee have not formally met. I should be sorry to leave Stockton from a sentimental point of view – after all these years – but if I am to get on at all in Parliament, I must have some less distant constituency, and devote more of my time to politics (including reading and thinking) and less to the mere effort of getting elected.

No message has come to me from the President. It will be interesting to hear from Kirk part, and from Offie all, of the truth of what passed. If, on the other hand, Kirk has criticised our policy very much, it will not make things easier for me.

11 a.m. General Airey came to see me (head of G2 or Military Intelligence). Discussions on Venezia Giulia, Greece and General Immel. The record of this gentleman appears worse the more it is re-examined. I suppose he must have some political 'pull', because he is one of those coarse and flagrant Germans who are not usually very successful in America, where the subtler Irishman and Italian are more suited to democratic politics.

A telegram from the President. Unfortunately, the P.M.'s suggestion got there too late. Otherwise, he would have been delighted. So there we are; de Gaulle was asked in time, but refused.[16] I asked myself, would have been acceptable; but was too late. The President has had no luck with his Algiers invitations and visitors (incidentally, what an extraordinarily clumsy method the Americans followed in this invitation to de Gaulle. Algiers is, in law, part of Metropolitan France. It is as if the President had invited the King to meet him at Cowes!).

2.30–6.30 p.m. The usual succession of telegrams, papers and visitors. General Robertson, General Maclean, M.P., Randolph (turned up from Cairo) and various others. Dinner quietly in Naples – with a few consuls and travelling civil servants invited; agreeable chaps.

Tuesday, 20 February 1945

10.30 a.m. SACMED Political Meeting – a long meeting which lasted till 1 p.m. A large number of important questions were dealt with – notably, the winding up of P.W.B. in liberated Italy; relations with Albania, especially recognition (which U.S. and U.K. are *not* disposed to grant to General Hoxha) and relief, which they are ready to give subject to the usual conditions; the endless problems of Venezia Giulia and the Yugoslav claims to Fiume and Trieste; the methods of implementing the new Italian directive; the patriot problem in northern Italy; the withdrawing of cypher and the granting of bag

[15] Catherine's cousin, daughter of 10th Duke of Devonshire.

[16] Returning from Yalta, Roosevelt invited General de Gaulle (amongst others) to meet him in Algiers, but the general declined lest he should have to commit himself to decisions taken without French involvement.

facilities to Italian diplomats; the future of the Italian Air Force; and a number of other questions. The most important was that of Venezia Giulia, since the P.M. is to leave tomorrow on a visit to Tito. The F.O. (and the Field Marshal) want to negotiate a purely *military* arrangement, to be made direct between the two Marshals, fixing a military zone, east of which Allied troops will not go or set up A.M.G. This is the most realistic approach, and we would insist on Trieste as a necessary base for any operation or occupying forces in Austria. The Americans strongly objected. As 'trustees' for Italy (they said) we should insist on occupying all Venezia Giulia and setting up military government in accordance with the Italian armistice terms. This is all very well in theory; in practice it is difficult to see how we are going to eject Tito. However, in view of the American objections, I had to advise F.M. to ask instructions from the Combined Chiefs. This means that he must only 'sound' Tito on this trip and in the light of it make a recommendation on his return. This will mean a F.O.–State Dept. negotiation, and a decision as to whether to bring in Russia. Of course this matter (which may easily become urgent) ought to have been dealt with at the Crimean conference. But they either overlooked it or shirked it.

On the patriots, a subcommittee (as I had previously arranged with Alex) has been sitting and made an admirable report. A great deal of work has already been done and new plans – mainly by enlisting the patriots into the Italian army on favourable terms – are being made to try to avoid another ELAS situation.

After the meeting, I discussed the position of General Immel with General McNarney. He agreed to send off a strong telegram, in terms which I had drafted.

Luncheon with General McNarney – a very pleasant party – F.M. Alexander, Mr [Henry J.] Taylor (Scripps-Howard Press, just back from Greece), Offie and I.

3 p.m. Left by air for Rome. Half way there, something went wrong with one engine. The pilot returned – and landed successfully – at the airfield.

4 p.m. Left by *car* for Rome. My Roman car met us half way (at Terracina) and I changed cars. Arrived in Rome at 7.30 – a fast trip.

8 p.m. Dinner at my villa (Parisi). Present: Sir D'Arcy Osborne (British Minister at Vatican), Colonel Astley (P.R.O.), Brigadier [George] Parkinson (A.C. Health), Mr Taylor (A.C. Transport – American), Commodore Zeroli (A.C., American), Lord Ranfurly, Colonel E. T. De Wald (A.C. Fine Arts, American) and one or two others. My American A.D.C. (Lieutenant John Atkinson) arranges these things very well.

Wednesday, 21 February 1945

8.30–12.15 p.m. At Commission. Saw Stone, Lush, Ambassador

Kirk, Nosworthy (Noel Charles and Henry Hopkinson are both ill and Nosworthy is in charge) and several others.

Motored back to Caserta, arrving at 4 p.m., where I had an U.N.R.R.A. meeting. Commander Jackson (who has now joined U.N.R.R.A., to its great advantage), Sir William Matthews, Mr Hendrickson (U.S.).

Left Caserta at 6.30 and on getting to the villa found Eddy Devonshire and Andrew already there. I thought Eddy looked fairly well. He was, of course, delighted to see Andrew. Admiral Sir John Cunningham, General Robertson, Offie, Captain [Michael] Stanley (Oliver Stanley's son) and a few others to dinner.

Thursday, 22 February 1945

A quiet day. Apart from Generals Robertson and Spofford, no visitors. I was able to get through a lot of reading. Among other things, some interesting papers from Chief of Staff on post-war territorial arrangements in the Mediterranean – a pretty problem when we come to making peace with Italy.

Eddy left for Cairo early this morning. I think the change will do him good.

At 4 p.m. Jackson (now U.N.R.R.A.) who returned at 5.30 with his U.S. colleague Hendrickson. We drafted a telegram from myself to Law, about the organisation. It is necessary to remove Sir William Matthews (at Cairo) and generally simplify the machine, if it is ever to work. General Spofford came later in the evening. He is always easy and agreeable to deal with; but the Americans seem very nervous about the 'New Deal' in Italy and more particularly about what I may say at any press conference.

The news from Greece is not too good. Rex Leeper seems to be much worried about General Plastiras and his 'goings-on'. Of course he wants to get all his old Republican and Venizelist friends (mostly aged generals) back into office. He grows more like General Giraud every day.

Friday, 23 February 1945

Left by car (with Miss Campbell) from Caserta and got to Rome by lunch.

3 p.m. Talk with Admiral Stone about the plans for tomorrow, which now seem all laid on. There will be a meeting of the Advisory Council for Italy at 10.30. Stone will attend then and explain the main points of the new directive. At 4 p.m. he and I will call on Bonomi (P.M.) and De Gasperi[17] (Foreign Affairs) and go through the points

[17] Dr Alcide De Gasperi (1881–1954) was Foreign Minister, 1944–5 and 1951–3, and Prime Minister, 1945–53.

with them. At 5.30 I will have a press conference. We went through the various papers and settled a few outstanding points.

Dined with Brigadier Lush.

Saturday, 24 February 1945

Stayed in bed till luncheon, composing my speech for the press conference. This necessitated a great number of drafts and redrafts. It is rather a ticklish problem. If I play up the concessions too high, it may cause that disappointment in America (reflected from Italy) which the State Department fears. But if I use the soft pedal too much, I shall produce exactly that disappointment which I want to avoid. Anyway, I prepared a long rhetorical speech, as to a public meeting, trying to give a sketch of our relations with Italy over the last eighteen months. This is intended to show the progressive development, and to put any particular stage in its proper perspective. I hope it will succeed.

4.30 p.m. Stone and I paid our call upon Bonomi and De Gasperi. I went through the document in detail, explaining exactly the changes proposed. They asked a few points of detail (for instance, would they have cyphers as well as diplomatic pouches? – answer, No!) which Stone answered. I then did a kind of résumé of my speech for their benefit. They both seemed gratified (if a trifle alarmed) by the concessions. Like all people who cry out for freedom, they are a bit taken aback if it is given to them. However, in general, they appeared fairly satisfied. Like most Latin races, they are interested in the theoretical and juridical aspect; we eschew them, and go for the practical. They would like to be 'allies' not 'co-belligerents'. But they are very anxious about the withdrawal of our local officials, from 'Italian Government Italy'.[18] They fear the disimprovement in administration standards which will surely follow.

5.30 p.m. The press conference went off fairly well. Although there was no official 'hand-out', I agreed to give them all copies of my speech. This lasted about half-an-hour and seemed a success. All this was 'on the record'. Then (like a political meeting) we had 'questions'. Some of the answers are 'on', and others 'off', the record – and one has to be careful to specify carefully. One man asked if my reference to 'professional muckrakers' was pointed at Mr Herbert Matthews of *The New York Times* – who was present. I could only reply that it was pointed at those who made the insinuations which I denounced – viz., saying that British and American policy was divided and that the British wished to keep the Italians starved and enslaved. Like a political meeting, some left early and others stayed on chatting till about 7.30. I must await the reaction, but I have hopes that it will be quite good. The English press will not be very interested; it is the American press which matters.

[18] I.e. that part of Italy under the control of the Italian Government, as distinct from those parts controlled respectively by Kesselring and by A.C.

Sunday, 25 February 1945

Left at 9 a.m. (with my American A.D.C. – L*oo*tenant John Atkinson) and my Humber car, driven by Sergeant Pocklington. The weather was glorious – like a fine June day at home – clear and cloudless blue sky. I am starting a four-day tour, in which I shall be mainly (if not entirely) in the American Fifth Army region. One of Admiral Stone's defects is that he does not get into the field. He scarcely ever leaves Rome, except to go to Caserta. I feel that one ought to get out and see the chaps who are doing the real work – often under conditions of great difficulty, hardship and danger. Also, it will be a very nice trip, through the loveliest part of Italy!

Stopped at Orvieto (slightly out of the direct route) where I went again to see the Signorelli frescoes. They are truly magnificent. Orvieto is a charming town, beautifully situated.

Reached Siena at about 3 p.m. Saw the A.M.G. officer in charge and discussed a number of problems with him. Atkinson (who was formerly a press reporter) is a very useful assistant. He takes all the notes. I have yet to see how he will 'present' them. He is to write a draft report of the serious side of the trip – under various headings: personnel, problems of finance, industry, food, health, patriots, etc. Siena – in the bright sun – was as lovely as ever. There was an additional attraction in a most remarkable and comprehensive exhibition of Sienese painters – from the earliest to the latest – with extremely fine examples drawn both from Siena and elsewhere.

Left Siena about five and arrived at Florence about 6.30. I have a nice room in the Excelsior Hotel (and a sitting room) overlooking the Arno. Dined with British generals and senior officers of Fifteenth Army Group (A Mess) – a very agreeable evening.

Monday, 26 February 1945

A very long, but quite lovely day. We went to Pistoia, Lucca and Pisa. In each place we combined interviews with the various A.M.G. officers and sight-seeing. I had never been to Pistoia and Lucca. The latter is a *most* lovely walled town, hardly touched by war. Its towers are its great beauty – brick and stone mixed – some round, some square. At a distance, you recall Oxford. Major-General Grettinberg (U.S. Fourth Corps) entertained me to a terrific luncheon party – with string band – and full honours. Really the Americans are most charming and hospitable. I had not been to Pisa since 1920 (on our honeymoon). The south side of the city is terribly battered. But the Cathedral and the baptistery are quite unscathed. Unluckily, one of our shells fell on the Campo Santo, and the lead roof collapsed and fire and water have done a great deal of damage to the frescoes – especially the Benozzo Gozzolis. A most careful and scientific work of restoration and preservation is going on, guided by American and British experts from the great museums.

Dined with General Mark Clark (now commanding Fifteenth Army Group) – no one but the general and his Chief of Staff (Al Greunther). I had known both since Algiers days. The general was in good form and most friendly.

I think success has improved him. He is still vain, but conceals this weakness more skilfully than before. He is also very ambitious.

Tuesday, 27 February 1945

An early start and a long day. We drove to General [Lucian K.] Truscott's advanced H.Q. (he now commands the American Fifth Army). He received me and we had a pleasant talk in his hut. His troops have had a very rough winter in these cold and snow-clad mountains. But their health has been good and also their morale. His own camp is just short of the Futa Pass – at a considerable height. Truscott is an American and a good, old-fashioned type – rather a Cromwellian face and fine head.

He sent us on to the Second Corps Advanced H.Q., well beyond the Futa Pass – beyond Loiano. All this is on the road to Bologna. Here General [Geoffrey] Keyes – an excellent, elderly, pious (Catholic) and obviously much-loved general, gave us a tremendous welcome and a gargantuan luncheon, 'old-fashioned' cocktails and plenty of food and drink. After this, we staggered on in a jeep to the H.Q. of his advanced division in the line, and from there to an excellent O.P. [observation post]. From here, an excellent view could be obtained of the whole battlefield – and the peaks and ridges still to be overcome or by-passed before Bologna falls. Unfortunately, it was rather hazy; nevertheless, we got a good idea of the military problem. The various A.M.G. officers took us round the little ruined villages – such as Monghidoro – to which the inhabitants are now returning after the wave of battle. Many of these villages and townships are, of course, still under more or less daily artillery fire. I was on the whole well impressed by these A.M.G. officers. Some of them are British, the majority (being Fifth Army front) American. Relations seem very good. British policemen are among the best of our chaps. They seem to be born with a 'flair' for managing people, from the humblest beggars to the mayor and prefect of the province. The Americans are very good on their health side – anti-typhus and typhoid precautions and so forth.

We got back to Florence about 6.30 p.m., and at 8 p.m. Brigadier-General [E. E.] Hume (A.M.G. Fifth Army) gave a vast dinner in my honour – printed name-cards, etc. I was also made to sign the golden book in the Palazzo Vecchio, to the tune of silver trumpets, and various other slightly ridiculous ceremonies. Before setting out I was taken to a 'refugee centre' in Florence, which seemed to be doing good work. The nuns were running the school for infants and older children, and a good spirit prevailed. Italian doctors were in charge of the hospital. The site was an old barracks – rather primitive – but improving with our help. All the children of Florence were given a great Christmas party. It was financed by the troops – mostly American – who for weeks beforehand were asked to contribute their 'candy' and their money. All these are at least some alleviations to the bitterness of war. General Truscott came specially to the dinner and various other American and British officers. A great affair, on a lavish scale so far as food and drink go.

Wednesday, 28 February 1945

Left Florence at 8.30 a.m. Motored to Arezzo (along the valley of the Arno). Here we saw the local Army officers as usual. There are a good many special problems in the semi-industrialised valley of the Arno between Florence and Arezzo. The lignite mines are workable; but there are problems of equipment and finance which are somehow not yet solved. There is not, at present, much unemployment, because the Army can use men on road and bridge repair. But the railway from the south does not go beyond Arezzo; I doubt whether the Army will want to repair the line between Arezzo and Florence. They have easier means of supply from east and west (Ancona and Leghorn), and it would anyway be a very big job owing to the large number of important railway bridges which are utterly destroyed. Arezzo has been much bombed, shelled and dynamited – by the Allies and the Germans. From Arezzo, we went on to Perugia – a lovely drive. Major-General [C. A.] Heydeman (British), commanding the area, received me and lunched me. He seemed rather a character, in a red face and jodhpurs. From Perugia, I could not resist a detour to Assisi. It is quite unspoilt – absolutely remote and eternally beautiful. I spent an hour and a half there – the great church of San Francesco – with the upper church and the splendid Giottos and the lower church and its mysterious grandeur – all are intact. (The Hotel Subasio – where we stayed twenty-five years ago – is an Army rest hotel, for officers.) Santa Chiara – with its strange flying buttresses – and all the strength and brightness and attractiveness of that lovely town are there still for the delight of the world. After seeing so much destruction, it is a double pleasure to see such a gem unimpaired.

From Assisi to Terni – through lovely mountain country – like going from Bolton Abbey to Middlesbrough. Terni has one of the largest steel works in Italy (employing about 15,000 men). It was almost completely destroyed, but is now being patched up again. It was quite amusing to be back in the atmosphere of an industrial town – and somehow very strange. Major Ringquist (of Stockton-on-Tees – Treasurer of Constitutional Association) is an A.M.G. officer at Terni. He and his colleagues entertained me very hospitably. We went along to the works and found M. Gasperi – the managing director or works manager – who took us round. They have managed to get some blast furnaces going and also some sheet and strip mills. The Germans did a great deal of damage (more than the bombers) but with the help of the British Royal Engineers a remarkable work of reconstruction has been and is being accomplished. Already heavy steel castings (for destroyed hydro-electric plants) are being made. It was very nostalgic to see a night shift again at a rolling mill!

I left Terni about 8 p.m. and we reached Rome at 10 p.m. – rather tired, but having thoroughly enjoyed our four days' journeyings.

March

Thursday, 1 March 1945

Stone is laid up. Saw Brigadier Lush and worked at A.C. on various papers, etc., till 3 p.m. (sandwich lunch). I went out in the morning to see poor Noel Charles, who is still in hospital. I found Randolph Churchill in a neighbouring room in the hospital.

Flew to Caserta (Marcianise) in a beautiful new Mitchell.

I found a good deal at Caserta waiting for me. I had a talk with the F.M. Rex Leeper has sent me and him an appeal to go to Athens at once. It appears that the Plastiras Government is behaving rather stupidly. The forcing of Pericles Rallis out of office was a dangerous sign of a 'Right-wing' reaction.[1] All kinds of military appointments are being made, mostly of elderly Venizelist generals who were friends of Plastiras in 1922 and are unsuitable either politically or professionally. (The 'Venizelist' or 'Liberal' is now a reactionary in Greece, as in England.)

The F.M. seemed rather annoyed that the Ambassador should not be able to handle all this himself, and was very disinclined to accede to his appeal. We will discuss it further tomorrow.

Alex much enjoyed his visits to Marshal Tito and Tolbukhin.[2] He seems to have formed a very favourable opinion of Tito (rather too favourable, I thought). But it is also clear that he (Alex) has had a great personal success, and that even this tough Muscovite and Slav revolutionary fell victim to his charm.

The problem of Venezia Giulia remains. Alex tried to draw Tito on this (to the extent that he could in view of his last meeting), and it is clear that Tito intends, somehow or another, to get a good slice of this territory.

Left Caserta about 7.45, which made me rather late for dinner in

[1] Rallis resigned on 20 February in protest against the appointment of a Royalist officer as Under-Secretary of the Interior, in charge of the Gendarmerie and police – an infringement of the Varkiza agreement.

[2] Marshal Fyodor Ivanovich Tolbukhin (1894–1949) had captured Belgrade with the help of Tito's partisans in October 1944. He was now in Hungary, having besieged Budapest through the winter.

Naples at my villa. Hal Mack and Gibson Graham came to dinner, and we had a very pleasant evening of gossip and reminiscence.

Friday, 2 March 1945

10 a.m. F.M.'s Political Meeting – all the usual members. F.M. gave a very good account of his tour, especially of the two Marshals. Apparently the Russian Marshal was an old Tsarist officer. (He referred always to Petersburg, not Leningrad – as I am told Stalin also does nowadays.)

The greater part of the meeting was taken up with drafting a telegram to Combined Chiefs about Venezia Giulia. As always, in these big matters, the result was not very satisfactory.

I spent the rest of the day in the office (sandwich lunch) and got through a good deal. The main thing was to send a telegram of my own to F.O. about Venezia Giulia, setting out the position as clearly as possible and making a suggestion for a solution. I also saw Gibson Graham, and telegraphed as a result to the F.O. and Lord Leathers about the necessity for some alteration and relaxation in our system of shipping control, especially the small schooners and coasters of the Italians, Greeks, Yugoslavs, etc. It is really absurd that we (British) should go on chartering these ships at great expense and then send other ships (also at our expense) to supply these countries. We should release some of these ships to the Italian, Greek and Yugoslav owners and tell them to get on with the job. More telegrams from Leeper. The situation is obviously deteriorating. I have therefore decided to go tomorrow.

I dined with Alex. He told me that he had now definite instructions to go as 'deputy' to General Eisenhower. He will be leaving shortly. It is really rather hard on him to be a 'Deputy Commander', and it will be a most difficult task. It will require all his firmness as well as his tact if he is to achieve anything. Of course, he ought (on professional grounds) to have the command. But the disproportion between British and American troops makes this impossible. It is a great blow to me, for my association with Alex has always been so delightful. Apparently we are to have Air Marshal Tedder in his place. I do not know how the Army will like this. It should work well enough.

In the course of the day a bag arrived with a letter to me from Max Beaverbrook (written at P.M.'s obvious instigation) imploring me not to give up Stockton for St George's. He promises, however, that if I lose Stockton, whoever gets St George's will be made a peer to make room for me. I am really rather annoyed about all this fuss. But in view of this pressure and these promises, I could only telegraph my acceptance. It is really a dreadful prospect. I have scarcely been near Stockton for five years. I have no agent, no association and no funds! I asked Max to see Dorothy and explain the situation to her. It seems my fate to try to get away from Stockton, but never to achieve it.

Saturday, 3 March 1945

Left Marcianise 9 a.m. with Major Elliot (now on my staff) and Miss Campbell. The weather was very bad, and there was some doubt about starting. I had borrowed the Field Marshal's Dakota, as 'my' Mitchell was wanted by its owner, Air Marshal Slessor. I was offered a Hudson, but I am not enamoured of them, and Alex kindly lent me his slow, but very reliable plane. The crew are excellent, and with great skill they got us in safety to Athens in five hours, creeping along the sea coast, avoiding storms and so forth.

Rex came out to meet me, with Mrs Leeper. The rest of the afternoon and evening were spent in discussing the situation. I had formulated my own plan on the way over. I do not want to go, either with the Ambassador or the Field Marshal or both, and make a row with the Greek Government over a *particular* case – whether the appointment of incompetent generals, the choice of officers in contravention to the Varkiza agreement, the incompetence and nepotism in civil appointments or what not. This will really lead us nowhere. In any case, if these individual protests are to be made, it is the Ambassador's job to make the *démarche*, not mine or the F.M.'s. But I feel that Great Britain, having intervened in Greek affairs to so great an extent, has a moral responsibility which it must discharge. The only way to do this effectively, and without constant friction, is to have a working agreement, in writing, with the Greek Government. This agreement should set out the general principles of sound administration which it is proposed to follow and in particular refer to the Varkisa agreement. It will also provide for the machinery of collaboration between the British military, naval, air, police and other missions and the representation of the British authorities as liaison officers with the chief Greek civil ministries. If we could get this, we can 'intervene' at a low level, *before* some scandalous thing is done, instead of at an Ambassadorial level, *after* it is really too late and when the Greeks cannot withdraw without serious loss of 'face'.

Rex Leeper accepted this idea.

Sunday, 4 March 1945

Stayed in bed till lunchtime. Worked, with Miss Campbell's aid, on a draft agreement. I also had to do a long telegram to Sir John Anderson about some silly complaints which Morgenthau had made about the Allied Commission in Italy. These were founded on the tittle-tattle of an American official who had been in the Finance Subcommission but had been sent home. I had asked John [Wyndham] to provide me with some 'dirt' about this creature – one Tasker – and in the course of the day a splendid telegram arrived from Rome. John has surpassed himself. Brigadier Smith-Dorrien came in the morning, with some ideas for the Greek draft, excellently done. Also Jackson of U.N.R.R.A.

In the afternoon, Brigadier Hugh Mainwaring and Smith-Dorrien came round, and we worked on the various drafts till 6.30.

At this hour, Leeper and I went to see the Regent. We found him in capital form, after his successful visit to Salonika. We had a long conversation (one-and-three-quarter hours) in which we adumbrated delicately our idea. He took it very well and thought he might even get Plastiras to agree. He is anxious to keep Plastiras as Prime Minister for the present. A change now would upset public confidence. But he has no illusions about him. He laughed very much when I said that he reminded me of Giraud – all heart and no head.

After dinner the brigadiers, who had dined at the Embassy, produced a further draft on which they had been working while we were seeing the Regent. With a lot of hard work, we finally got a satisfactory text about midnight. I find that the only way to do these things is to make one draft after another, taking bits and pieces from different people's ideas, until we finally arrive at something presentable.

Monday, 5 March 1945

Worked all the morning on the draft agreement, making some final amendments. The Ambassador did a covering telegram to the F.O. explaining the need for this agreement, and I did a personal to Prime Minister. The three telegrams (the draft being one) are now on their way to London. I expect it will all have to go to the War Cabinet. If they agree, we might start on the negotiation this week-end. Perhaps this is too optimistic, as London is sure to raise some objections in detail, if not in principle.

Saw Jackson (of U.N.R.R.A.). He is making progress in cleansing a really Augean stable.

Wrote up the diary, and read Trevelyan's *Social History of England* – a useful morning. It rained hard all yesterday; but today it has cleared and the sun is out. We are to leave for a picnic lunch at 1 p.m.

Various U.N.R.R.A. discussions with Jackson. We still have found nobody for Greece, since Brigadier Palmer maintains his unwillingness to take on the job. Saw Sir William Matthews in the evening and broke to him, as nicely as I could, the news that he was to go home.

Tuesday, 6 March 1945

Left Athens at 9.30, in a Hudson. Mrs and Miss Leeper came with me. I have invited them to stay with me in Rome for a few days. I thought Mrs Leeper deserved a change, after all the pressure of the siege of Athens. And as she is very cultivated and an artistic person, she will enjoy it.

Arrived at Marcianise (Caserta) about 2.30 – after rather a bad trip, in that we had to go very high (over 12,000 feet) and, since the heating had gone wrong, it got frightfully cold. I felt quite exhausted.

I did a good deal of routine business with Philip Broad. Then saw F.M. at 5 p.m. I dined with him at the Hunting Lodge and stayed the night there, thus avoiding a tedious journey into Naples.

The new Chief of Staff, General [William] Morgan, has now taken over from General Harding. He seems both agreeable and efficient.

Wednesday, 7 March 1945

Left Caserta by car (with Miss Campbell) and got to Rome about 3 p.m. I spent the morning in various routine business. I hope the row between the State Department and the American Treasury – which reacts upon me – will calm down a little. I am afraid there are still a lot of people who want to make trouble between U.K. and U.S., or who harbour quite extraordinary suspicions of British foreign policy. This they believe to be extremely subtle, Machiavellian, even Jesuitical. If only they could realise (as I have learned in these last years) how amateurish, hand-to-mouth and incompetent a department the F.O. really is, they would be surprised indeed.

Saw General Spofford before starting for Rome and arranged with him the main lines for a reorganisation of the Economic Section. It will not be ideal, but I think it can be made to work. At 7 p.m., in Admiral Stone's house in Rome, we had the meeting to put it through. Stone, Lush, Spofford, Antolini (who is to be head of the Section) and General [Edward B.] MacKinley (who will, I hope, run it). It was the first time I had met MacKinley. He seemed to me very intelligent, and with seven-and-a-half years' experience in the War Department at Washington, he should be able to help us. The meeting lasted for two hours, and a great deal of useful ground was covered. The whole party came to dinner. Mrs and Miss Leeper (who motored directly from Caserta to Rome yesterday) were there. They are excellent guests. They amuse themselves all day with the sights of Rome, and are agreeable additions to our rather too exclusively male parties.

Thursday, 8 March 1945

The escape of General Roatta has made a great stir,[3] but the Government has survived. I think the Communists still feel it better to wait.

The whole day was taken up by a meeting of A.C. This included all the regional commissioners and their chief officials and the heads of various sections and subcommissions at H.Q. I had to make the opening speech, which I did with moderate success. I have not felt at all well today or yesterday. I think the great height at which we flew on Tuesday has affected me. I feel thoroughly 'done up'. The meetings

[3] Roatta escaped on 4 March from a Military Hospital (where he had been confined because of heart trouble).

(10–1 and 2.30–6) were interesting, but fatiguing. After the afternoon meeting, I have a cocktail party at the Grand Hotel, to which all those present at the meeting were invited and a great many other notabilities of Rome.

1–2.30 p.m. I attended a luncheon given in my honour by De Gasperi (Christian Democrat), Minister for Foreign Affairs. Reale (Communist) and Morelli (Liberal), his two Under-Secretaries, were also of the party, which included Croce (now very old and talkative, but with a great deal of wit and mischievous humour), Brosio (Liberal, Minister without portfolio), an earnest man, and various officials.[4] Croce was very amusing after luncheon in his chaff of the Communists and their philosophy.

After my cocktail party (i.e. about 8.30 p.m.) I went back to the villa and to bed.

Friday, 9 March 1945

Got to A.C. at 9 a.m. Found a complicated telegram from Max Beaverbrook about Stockton and St George's and a letter from George Gage, asking me to stand for Lewes! Between them all, they will get me in for nowhere. John Wyndham drafted an excellent reply for me to send. I have decided to leave it to P.M., Max and Ralph Assheton between them to decide what I am to do. I am perfectly ready to fight Stockton if it will help the Government as a whole. But if I am beaten, they must recognise an obligation not to leave me in the lurch.

The A.C. conference resumed at 9.30 and went on till 11 a.m. I then motored to Ciampino airfield and got into my Mitchell (now temporarily returned to me). Arrived Marcianise and went to the office, where I found Ralph Stevenson. He arrived in Naples last night, bound for Belgrade. He particularly wanted to see me and the Field Marshal before going on, and this was the main reason for my return to Caserta for a few hours. I gather that Stevenson is on excellent terms with his U.S. opposite number, Ambassador [Richard C.] Patterson. If they work closely together, they should be able to have some effect on Tito.

We all lunched with the F.M. and found there General [Xavier] de Savin, my French general on A.C., and an old friend.

I went down to the airfield with F.M. to see Stevenson and his party off (about 3 p.m.) and then returned to Caserta with Alex. He told me the news, received through O.S.S., of an indication of a desire of certain officers on Kesselring's staff (including his chief of staff) to treat for terms. Having some experience of these operations (remembering our Italian armistice) I advised the F.M. first to report to

[4] Eugenio Reale (b. 1905) was Under-Secretary for Foreign Affairs, 1944–6. Renato Morelli (b. 1905) was Under-Secretary, 1944–5. Manlio Brosio (1897–1980) became Minister of War, 1945–6, Italian Ambassador to the Soviet Union, 1947–51, to the United Kingdom, 1952–4, to the United States, 1955–61, and to France, 1961–4, and Secretary-General of NATO, 1964–71.

the P.M. and C.I.G.S., setting out clearly the course he prepared to pursue; secondly (*after* hearing that London agrees) to report news and plan of operation to C.C.S. If German officers want to do business, they must go into Switzerland; they must have a signed letter of authority from Marshal Kesselring; they must agree to come to A.F.H.Q.; and the discussions must be for a military surrender only – there can be nothing on the political or governmental level. Alex agreed and I drafted the telegram accordingly (very roughly) for the Chief of Staff to send. I then went back to the airfield (Alex came with me) and got back into my Mitchell, arriving at Rome about 5 p.m. I do not put much weight – or at least too much – on this contact with the Germans. First, O.S.S. (the American secret service) are always rather optimistic. They are not very experienced. Secondly, both the Germans named are S.S. men, and I should have thought it more likely that we should be approached by the old regular Army rather than the Hitler–Himmler crowd. Of course, it may be an attempt by individuals to save their skins.

Back in the office of A.C. at Rome. I saw Marchese Lucifero (the Prince's chief Private Secretary) and one or two others. Dinner at 8 p.m. with Colonel Fiske (U.S.) to meet the visiting regional commissioners.

Saturday, 10 March 1945

Morning at A.C. Mr Wade,[5] of British Treasury, came for a talk on all our Anglo-American troubles. Being a very clever, as well as a very charming, young man, he has observed that these exist not in Rome but in London and Washington.

Luncheon at villa. Mr [Stewart] Brown (the new Public Relations Officer of A.C., American), Brigadier Grafftey-Smith, Commander Southard (U.S.), Wade (British Treasury) – quite an interesting and useful little party. After luncheon, went to see Ambassador Kirk, where I found Ambassador Patterson, who is going to Belgrade. I particularly wanted to have a talk with Mr Patterson. He seemed sensible and co-operative, and obviously liked and admired Ralph Stevenson. We all drove to the airfield to see him off. I still do not feel right. I am quite exhausted and cannot throw off a sort of lethargy which has attacked me. So I went to bed about 8 p.m. (after finishing things up pretty well at A.C.), had some soup, took two aspirins and slept.

Sunday, 11 March 1945

Did not wake till about 10 a.m., having slept round the clock. The Leepers are perfect guests – out all day, sight-seeing, lunching, dining.

[5] H. W. R. Wade (b. 1918), Q.C. 1968, was a temporary Administrative Officer in the Treasury, 1940–6, and Professor of English Law, Oxford University, 1961–76. He has been Master of Gonville and Caius College, Cambridge, since 1976.

I am still waiting for a telegram from Rex (who has incidentally been given his K[nighthood]). I really do not much want to go over again, but must do so if he makes the request.

The news from the Western Front is very exciting. If we have really got this bridge across the Rhine, it may have startling results. One gets (at last) the feeling that German resistance must end soon.

11 a.m. Went to see Admiral Stone. He is still laid up, but seems on the whole better.

I returned to the villa. First Prunas (the Alec Cadogan of Italy), then Randolph. The latter was much exercised as to whether to have an operation on his knee or not. It will take six weeks and he fears that the war may be over and the election in full swing *before* he recovers!

After luncheon, the Leepers went for an expedition to Frascati and Tivoli. John and I drove to the Appian Way, and had a walk for an hour or so, which did us good. I have finished Trevelyan's *Social History* – an excellent work. I have read [A. L.] Rowse's book of essays [*The English Spirit*], which are readable enough. I am glad to see he has become a Macmillan author. I found today a copy of Tchekov's *The Bishop* – a volume of stories.

6 p.m. Went to see Noel Charles. He has got out of hospital and is now back in his beautiful apartment at the Palazzo Orsini. He seems better, but walks still with difficulty.

A pleasant little dinner at the villa – the Leepers, Sir D'Arcy Osborne, Field Marshal Alexander, John Wyndham, John Atkinson (my U.S. A.D.C.) and Major [J. D.] Chichester-Clark (Alex's A.D.C.). The F.M. was in very good spirits. He had heard from London and reported officially to C.C.S. his proposed action on the German approach. He seems to think we may really be able to do business – but not probably immediately. He was also pleased at a message from the P.M. The plan of sending him as Deputy Commander to Eisenhower is dropped. Alex is much relieved; it would have been a most difficult and awkward position.

A telegram from Leeper came in the course of the afternoon. I shall go to Athens tomorrow.

Monday, 12 March 1945

Left Rome with Mrs and Miss Leeper, in the new Mitchell. Left at 9.30; stopped at Marcianise, where Alaric Russell and Robert Cecil[6] were on the airfield. Robert arrived in Naples on Friday. He had brought me letters from London, but unfortunately had sent them on to Rome, and they missed me. Robert came on board and we started off again about 10.30 a.m., arriving at Athens at 1 p.m. (Naples) or 2 p.m. (Athens) time. It was a really lovely day – bright sun, scarcely a

[6] Robert Cecil (b. 1913) was my A.D.C. until becoming Second Secretary at H.M. Embassy, Washington, in April 1945.

cloud, snow-clad mountains, olive hills and dark-blue sea. We did not have to go too high – never above 7,000 feet.

Rex met us at the airfield. After talk at the Embassy till 5.30, we escaped to go up the Pnyx to see the sunset on the Parthenon – the view of the Acropolis from the Pnyx is the best, and with the rays of the setting sun shining obliquely on and illuminating the whole great monument, it is ravishingly beautiful.

7.30 p.m. M. Georgiakis (Regent's *chef de cabinet*) for a *tour d'horizon*. This was a particularly Greek performance. It appeared to involve a most complicated and original piece of juggling with all the pieces on the political board. It will need a little pondering.

9.30 p.m. Our pondering began and (with the help of Brigadier Smith-Dorrien) lasted till about midnight.

Tuesday, 13 March 1945

Another lovely day. The wind is from the north and cold – but the sun is shining gloriously from an absolutely clear sky. I feel much better; was up at 7.30 and had finished the diary to date and a draft paper on last night's talk before breakfast. Brigadier Smith-Dorrien and M. Georgiakis in the morning.

At 12 noon, at my own request, I called on General Plastiras. I think he expected a drubbing, and started off in a very reserved mood. However, I thought it wiser to keep him guessing, so we spent half an hour or so in polite talk about the British Army, the progress of the new Greek Army, etc., etc. The general said that he was absolutely convinced of the orderliness of the country and the complete faith of the people in him personally. In his view, there was no need for British troops to remain, excpet perhaps in Salonika. (Considering that a great part of Greece is still in ELAS hands, and that neither the British troops nor, of course, any Greek Government authority have arrived, in accordance with the plan, this is a splendid remark!) The general then went on with a few *Giraudesque* observations, but in a most friendly and agreeable tone. I ventured to press him a little about the formation of the National Army in strict accordance with the Varkiza agreement. He seemed to think the precise terms not important; but he hoped that some of the junior ELAS officers and N.C.O.s could be chosen. The selection boards were now sitting. There is no doubt that Plastiras is a nice man; he is vain and stupid, but really quite a dear. Earlier in the morning, General Scobie had been to see me. He and Plastiras are really very much alike. I gather that they do *not* get on too well together. General Scobie thinks General Plastiras stupid. General Plastiras regards General Scobie as bone-headed.

A picnic luncheon, on the shore beyond Eleusis.

6–7.30. An intolerably dreary discussion with M. Sideris [Finance Minister]. This conceited and prolix politician is more than usually insincere, ambitious and (I am told) not above suspicion financially.

The Archbishop–Georgiakis plan (to which Leeper and I had rather weakly assented) was to make him Vice-President of the Council (or Deputy P.M.) with a view to 'kicking him upstairs'. We should then bring in M. Varvaressos – the present Governor of the Bank of Greece – as Finance Minister *and* Minister for the co-ordination of economic affairs generally. At the same time, M. Sophianopoulos (to keep him sweet) would be made joint Vic-President. The only part of this programme which appealed to M. Sideris was that which promoted him to a higher position. It was clear that he had no intention of abandoning his present role, which is to interfere with everything (relying on his friendship with Plastiras) and everybody, and achieve nothing. Sideris is not an attractive man – he is like a great white slug, and talks with the ruthless persistence of a tap with a worn washer – a constant, irritating, inexhaustible drip.

After he had left – a short interval followed. Then Sophianopoulos (Foreign Secretary) from 8.15 (including dinner) till midnight. He made it quite clear that if Sideris got the deputy-premiership, he (Sophianopoulos) would resign. (Sid and Soph are *not* on good terms.) And he also made it clear that he thought Sideris (and Plastiras) reactionary and out-of-date, and that the whole Government's swing to the right was full of danger. I like Sophianopoulos (in a way) because, although he is personally ambitious, he is interested in ideas, as well as persons. He would like to *achieve results*, not merely become a minister or a prime minister. Sideris is a politician of the old style – his ambitions are on a lower level.

Altogether, quite an amusing, though a slightly exhausting and depressing, day.

Wednesday, 14 March 1945

A wonderful day – a real red-letter day. Left the Embassy at 8 a.m. We motored to Corinth, which we reached in about two hours. It was an absolutely halcyon day – blue sky, no wind, no clouds. The pale light-blues of the sea as we passed Eleusis and the Bay of Salamis were marvellous. The coast road to Corinth is very fine – the Mediterranean at its best. There was a slight haze during the morning, which passed off as the day went on. From Corinth, across a fine bit of plain, rising to the pass which divides Corinthian from Argolid territory. On entering the plain of Argos one is struck by the much richer character of soil and more prosperous agricultural community. This territory has not long passed out of ELAS hands, and the people were correspondingly enthusiastic on seeing our car, with the Union Jack of Freedom on the bonnet. Almost every peasant, men, women and children, saluted either by taking off and waving caps and bonnets, or by the 'thumbs up' gesture. There was certainly no mistaking the sympathies of the people. Argos is a pleasant modern town – with the acropolis and its Venetian citadel or fortress on a neighbouring rock.

From Argos the road goes to Nauplion, passing Tiryns on the way. We stopped to examine this remarkable ancient monument, dating from about 1400 B.C. or so – with its magnificent cyclopean architecture of vast unhewn stones. The keep and main gate are massive and impressive – and the centre of the city and the water store and all the rest of the remains are very wonderful. Tiryns must have been a great and strong city – worthy of Theseus and the heroic figures of those ancient times. After a picnic lunch in the ruins, surrounded by wild anemones of every colour, rosemary and thyme – we went on to Nauplion. This is a pleasant little sea town – rather damaged by both German and ELAS occupation – with the usual Venetian fortress crowning the rock. There is a pretty little island, with another Venetian castle, in the bay. From here on down to Mycenae. I will not try to describe these wonderful remains of a magnificent civilisation. We spent an hour or more in the acropolis and tombs where so many wonderful treasures were found. The dark red anemones flower with the greatest profusion among the great massive stones. The alabaster floor of Agamemnon's palace can still be traced – as well as the bath where he was struck down by Clytemnestra's adulterous hand. (I am bound to admit that she had a grievance about the sacrifice of Iphigenia and the bringing here of Cassandra – who must have been an impossible bore in any house.) The scene and setting of this splendid city is wonderful. And the beehive tomb of Agamemnon is one of the wonders of the world.

The drive back to Athens was as beautiful, in the evening light, as can be imagined. We got home at 6 p.m. Dined with General Scobie and Hugh Mainwaring. I gather that F.M. Alexander has been persuaded to leave us the Forty-sixth division in Greece for another fortnight – which is a great advantage to carrying through the military plan of reoccupation as arranged.

Thursday, 15 March 1945

I forgot to record the visit of three EAMite signatories of the Varkiza agreement last evening. MM. Siantos, Partsalides and Tsirimokos came at 7 p.m. to see me. Each spoke in turn and they also left with me a long document in Greek. Balfour translated; Cecil took a note. Although they have a number of detailed complaints against the Government regarding the strict carrying out of the agreement, I did *not* think that their case as a whole was very convincing. (At any rate, not so powerful as it would have been without the continual pressure of the Ambassador and myself upon the Greek government!) They alleged that the National Guard had not been fairly called up by age-groups, but retained some right-wing volunteers. They said that although they were free to print their newspapers, the newsboys who sold them were set on by the people! They said that the Fascists were arming in the towns for a counter-revolution. They said they did not like M. Sideris (I agree with them on this!) and so forth. They left a long memorandum, which I undertook to send to H.M.G. and to the Greek Government. Although they had a certain case, it was not really a very powerful one, considering that a civil war has only just ended and when one imagines what they would have done to the liberties of the Greek people had they been victorious. The whole thing led up to a request for an Allied Commission – British, American and Russian – to supervise the Greek Government. This is, of course, a bare-faced attempt to make trouble. A Commission to see to the freedom of election (the clause in the Varkiza agreement to which they referred) is, of course, quite another matter.

10.30 a.m. Brigadier Smith-Dorrien called. He is getting on well with the Ministries of Interior and Justice. As far as I can make out, the former is more or less run by our Major Mathews – a boy of twenty-four – whom Smith-Dorrien has planted inside the Ministry!

11.30 a.m. The Ambassador and I called upon the Regent. A long and useful talk. The Regent on the whole seemed relieved at our view that no immediate change should be made in the Government. He felt a great responsibility towards Great Britain, and he had been worried by his failure to influence the present Government in the way which both we wanted and he knew to be in the national interest. The fact was that Plastiras was a blockhead. He had the brains of an evzone (private soldier). But, since things were beginning to settle down, and since the military and civil reoccupation of the country was not yet complete, he agreed that it was wise to postpone a crisis. He would have a new Government ready – that is, in his own head. If and when, either because of some British interest (e.g. strong Parliamentary pressure against some specially foolish act of the Government) or because of some Greek interest (e.g. continued inability to handle the financial and economic position), a change became necessary, he would be prepared. We all felt that this was *not* a satisfactory position, but in present conditions it was probably the lesser of two evils.

1.15 p.m. General Plastiras was so delighted by my interview with him the other day (when I seemed to him to play the role of Balaam) that he has laid on an enormous luncheon in my honour – or really in his own – at the Grande Bretagne. All the Cabinet, the foreign ambassadors, the leading military personages, etc., etc. His purpose – and that of his entourage – was of course to strengthen the position of the Government. The gossip of Athens was expecting my arrival to foreshadow a British intervention in favour of a change in the Government. Now it appears that H.M.G. is not going to take so drastic a course; and Plastiras and his friends would like to make out that we are giving active and willing support, not merely tolerance *faute de mieux*. In spite of my being perfectly aware of this, I did not quite see how to refuse the invitation. But I prepared a speech, in which I tried to get across a note of warning. I think I succeeded in this. Our

Greeks are very quick. And I think they understood well enough my references to the need for 'scrupulous carrying out of the Varkiza agreement, in the letter and the spirit', as well as to the reformation of the Army 'without political or personal favouritism', and to the organisation of a civil service on similar lines. It was rather fun, and I think may have a little turned the tables on the plan of Plastiras's entourage. Plastiras himself is an honourable but stupid man. Nevertheless, I feel sure that it is right to leave things alone for the present.

5 p.m. Admiral [R. R.] Turner, senior British naval officer.

6 p.m. M. Mylonas (a leader of a small, inveterate left-wing party), a pleasant man, but not very impressive.

Friday, 16 March 1945

A lovely day – warm sun, with blue sky. Left at 10.30 a.m. with Robert Cecil and Mrs Leeper. A splendid drive to Thebes, Chalkis, and back over very rough roads behind Deceleia to Athens. A most interesting drive. The flowers are getting very lovely everywhere. I wish I knew something about them. Once again one felt the country coming to life. There is a certain amount of movement; quite a bit of Greek civil transport (old cars, mules, donkeys) and a fair traffic in wool, oil, vegetables, etc., beginning to start. It is all obviously on a small scale, but it is something.

Back at about 5.30.

6 p.m. Called on M. Sophoulis (the aged Liberal leader). He is not without capacity and a certain charm. But he is very 'dated' – a Gladstonian Liberal in a sense, and looking back to the great exploits of his master and guide, Venizelos, rather than forward. He did not seem very conscious of the depth and implications of the social and economic problems of Greece and of modern Europe.

8.15 p.m. Dinner with Sophianopoulos – *en toute intimité* – at his flat. The Ambassador, Varvaressos and I – with one or two others. An interesting evening. Sophianopoulos talked a great deal – egotistically and vulgarly, but intelligently.

Saturday, 17 March 1945

I had intended to stay over the week-end, in order to accept an invitation from Admiral Voulgaris to go (with the Embassy party) by destroyer to Admiral Kondouriotis's house on the island of Hydra and do a little cruising off the coast.[7] This – especially in this perfect weather – would have been a very pleasant holiday, and would also have allowed me to see something of Admiral Voulgaris, who has apparently been selected by the Regent and the Ambassador as a

[7] Admiral Petros Voulgaris (1884–1957), who had played an important role in suppressing the Alexandria mutiny in April 1944, was Prime Minister of Greece, April–October 1945. Admiral Paulos Kondouriotis (d. 1940) was President of Greece, 1924–9.

potential Prime Minister. However, news from Italy and a telegram from the Field Marshal made me feel that I should return. Accordingly, Robert Cecil and I left at 9.30, in Air Commodore Tuttle's Wellington, which he kindly lent me.

Arriving Caserta about lunch time, spent the afternoon and evening at the palace – going over a number of papers. An interesting talk with Alex. We are having some further 'feelers' from the Germans, and Generals Airey and Lemnitzer are now engaged in Berne in seeing if there is really any substance in these advances. So far, there is little real news. Another troublesome question has come up about COGENA ([Compagnia Genovese di Navigazione] the Italian shipping organisation) and an attack on its probity, involving also allegations against the Mediterranean Shipping Board, including Gibson Graham. All this arises from an enquiry started by the Allied Commission. I have no doubt myself of Gibson Graham's personal integrity. But I fear we cannot now avoid an enquiry on formal lines, and a lot of mud will be slung about, some of which will stick where it does not belong.

Sunday, 18 March 1945

Church in Naples early. Then to Caserta. I still have no message from Lord Beaverbrook about St George's and Stockton and I am really in a great quandary. I must make some reply to St George's – I have had their letter for over a week. A telegram from Dorothy makes me very uneasy. She would like me to come home (especially as Maurice is to have leave on the 24th), but if the Italian situation develops, I cannot of course get away. At 12.15 I went out for a drive with the Field Marshal. We took some sandwiches, and visited Pompeii and Herculaneum. I thoroughly enjoyed the afternoon.

On getting back to my villa in Naples, I found Eddy (Devonshire) on his way back from Bosnia. We managed to get hold of Andrew and fixed for him to go back to England with his father. (He was anyway in Naples, ready to sail back to England with some or all of his battalion.) This we succeeded in doing through Air Marshal Sir Guy Garrod (Slessor's successor) who was fortunately dining with us. Alex also came to dinner and we had altogether a very pleasant party.

Monday, 19 March 1945

An uneventful day; at Caserta – nothing very exciting. No news yet from Berne. Osbert Lancaster (from Athens) to dinner. Eddy and Andrew got off all right this morning.

Tuesday, 20 March 1945

The situation in Roumania is very bad. It seems pretty clear that the Russians are draining the country of all it possesses and will reduce the population to a position where absorption into the Soviet Union will be welcomed as the only way out. The present Government is a creation of Russia, and the outlook is very bad. The reactions in the U.K. and U.S. will be deplorable and (if Germany is not quickly finished off) it may lead to a serious crisis between the Yalta partners. The absorption of Roumania will be most unpalatable to British and American public opinion. Moreover, there seems no development of the Lublin Committee in Poland as was agreed. Roumania, following on Poland, will have a big repercussion in the West. I have been reading a very strange book by Arthur Koestler [*Darkness at Noon*]. I did not like it at all. But it is exceedingly well written. I have found Thackeray's *Book of Snobs* and *Travels in London*, which I am enjoying.

The 'Gibson Graham' affair was discussed again today. Gibson Graham (whom I like) has behaved with great sense and dignity, welcoming and indeed demanding a full enquiry. It is a great bore, though, as it will waste a lot of time and may have some unfortunate repercussions.

I am anxious to leave for Rome, but am kept here pending other developments. So I have sent for John and Miss Campbell, who are coming down by car this morning.

Picnic lunch with John on the hill above Caserta. John Wyndham came with me and we walked back. Not much news from Rome, but a lot of papers to be gone through. I dictated my informal letter to P. J. Grigg (which I send every fortnight or so, to keep him happy) and finished off the rest of the work before leaving for Naples.

Two interesting telegrams from Leeper. The Archbishop has now decided that he must reach a conclusion on one of two alternatives. Either (*a*) he must reform the Government, with a new prime minister, but on the same general lines – a government of political personages and on a more or less normal basis. In that event, nothing would be said about the date of a plebiscite or election, but a national council would be formed on the de Gaulle model. The elections would be postponed for a longish time – till the country is more or less settled. Or (*b*) he would form a small 'service' government, with few or no politicians, closely under his control. In that case, the plebiscite would be announced to take place in (say) three months, with elections soon after. There would be *no* national council.

In his second telegram Leeper advises the first alternative. I have telegraphed very strongly to London in the same sense. A plebiscite now would probably result in a vote for the King's return. But he would make a mess of it and there would be a rapid counter-revolution. From Greece's point of view, it is better to wait. From our point of view also, the early plebiscite and return of the King would be politically dangerous. A counter-revolution would place us in a terrible dilemma. I hope very much that London will follow our advice.

Major-General Beaumont-Nesbitt, Brigadier Lush and Colonel Perrara to dinner. The colonel is on the French Mission to A.F.H.Q. – an agreeable man.

Wednesday, 21 March 1945

Mr Ed Flynn,[8] one of the many 'personal representatives of the President', came to see me at Caserta this morning. I had heard a good deal about him, but had never previously met him. He is a very old friend of F.D.R.'s, having been his 'campaign manager' right back in the days of his first 'running' as Governor. He appears to be a sort of super-boss; and he is, withal, a man of fine presence and considerable charm. His manner reminds me somewhat of Robert Murphy's. He has the pleasant Irish smile. But he is, I should say, a much stronger character.

Flynn's views on Russia were interesting, and rather unexpected. He admired enormously the political machine which controls U.S.S.R. 'Those are "some" boys.' But he thinks, we are all apt to overestimate the supremacy of Stalin. He does not regard him (as it is now fashionable to do) as a sort of Bonaparte – First Consul, if not Emperor. In Flynn's view, a political machine is only as strong as the pillars which support it. The 'boss' must have first-class 'deputy bosses'. These must be strong, active, intelligent, hard. If not, the 'boss' will himself be endangered. Nor can he rely on a spiritual sanction (like the Pope) or a ritual and sanctified tradition (like an anointed King or Tsar).

In Flynn's view, the Politburo (or whatever it is called) is still very strong. And he thinks that the 'boys' were not too pleased by Stalin's concessions at Yalta. Many thought he went too far in conciliation over Poland, Roumania and liberated territories generally. And ever since he returned to Moscow the 'boys' have been 'stalling on the deal'. They have (with Molotov's active co-operation, Molotov being jealous of Stalin) done everything to prevent carrying out the agreement reached. And, in Flynn's view, Stalin does not venture to take any active steps, although he personally would like to carry out his word. Stalin, like Roosevelt and Churchill at these conferences, likes to pose as all-powerful. Although the forces controlling (and often opposing) the President and the Prime Minister are overt, they are not much stronger than those which secretly and privately exercise considerable power over Stalin. Flynn went from Yalta to Moscow. He is now going to Rome; then Paris, London and home. It is generally believed that he has some mission to negotiate a diplomatic agreement between Moscow and the Vatican. If he has, he did not tell me about it, or respond in any way to any fly thrown over him. But he is, of course, a very experienced old fish.

[8] Edward J. Flynn (1891–1953), leader of the Bronx Democrats.

Lunch with Offie. A large party, to meet Flynn, Ambassador Patterson, etc.

2.45 p.m. Saw Alex. Not much progress with the German negotiation. I am very sceptical about it. In any case, Kesselring's departure from the Italian front must necessarily slow things up.

4 p.m. Visited the A.M.G. H.Q. in Naples. This included the few A.C. officers for acting as liaison or specialists with the Italian Government in the Italian territory. Under the 'New Deal' all A.C. officers in this territory were to be withdrawn. But (at the request of the Italians themselves) we have agreed to leave about thirty to forty who will help with transport, roads and certain other activities. There are also being left another twenty to thirty who are helping with the oil-amassing campaign. These, however, will only stay till 15 April.

Naples Commune – the actual city – remains A.M.G. territory – under our direct control. This is thought to be necessary in view of the large commitments and installations which we have in the port. Some twenty to thirty officers are to be kept for this. After 15 April therefore, we shall have made our withdrawal from 'King's Italy' virtually complete. I spent two hours with Brigadier [John] Dunlop – an excellent officer, who will go into Venezia – and thoroughly enjoyed going round the building talking to the various officers concerned.

Thursday, 22 March 1945

Admiral Morse to breakfast. I had not seen him for a long time. An interesting talk about the dock situation and what the Italian workmen feel. I fear that they prefer English to Italian control!

At 10.30, the Political Meeting at A.F.H.Q. The chief item was a long examination of the proposed 'surrender instrument' for the Germans in Italy, and the Army, Navy and Air orders to be issued under it.

12 noon. Wade – a bright young man from the British Treasury. His talks in Rome have gone fairly well. He has got on well enough with the redoubtable Tasca[9] (now arrived from Washington) but does not rely much on Tasca's sincerity.

Friday, 23 March 1945

Stayed in bed in morning; lunched in the garden, and afterwards went with Philip Broad and Robert Cecil for a drive. We explored an extraordinary volcano just beyond Posillipo – I forget the Italian name. The guide called it *La Petite Vésuve*. We also went to Herculaneum. A day's rest and holiday, which did me good. The spring weather is now perfect: warm sun, but cool – almost cold – at night. We had an agreeable dinner for a certain General de Peyronnet.

[9] Angelo Tasca (b. 1892) left the Italian Communist Party (which he had joined at its foundation) in 1929 in protest against Stalin's rule in the Soviet Union.

The general is on his way to Belgrade. He proved to be the great-nephew of Mother's old friends (Lady Sligo and Mlle de Peyronnet). He told me that he had seen Isabel Browne quite lately at Mount Browne.[10] The Chief of Staff (Lieutenant-General Morgan), Colonel Perrara (French) and various others – twelve in all.

Saturday, 24 March 1945

Left Naples early – Robert Cecil with me. Stopped at Caserta for an hour or so and on to Rome.

Randolph Churchill came after luncheon to see me. Most of the evening was taken up with talks with Admiral Stone on a number of points – none very vital or very conclusive. The news is splendid and our hearts are high with hope.[11]

I have had a number of further communications from Lord Beaverbrook, and a long letter from Dorothy. After much debate, I have decided to refuse the St George's offer and stand again for Stockton. I am sending John Wyndham home to see various people concerned. He can also have some leave, which he has not had since he joined me in 1941. I fear my decision will cause a lot of trouble with St George's, especially after all their thoughtfulness, but I am sure it is the best thing to do. Poor Dorothy will have to undertake again those awful journeys to the North. But I feel that she will always be spiritually happier in Stockton or Thornaby than in Eaton Square!

Sunday, 25 March 1945 (Palm Sunday)

I did not, alas! get to church, as I should have liked. But I had such a lot of work to finish, that I stayed in bed all the morning, writing and dictating. I want to get all my letters – to Sir John Murray and the Secretary of St George's; to Mr Walford of Stockton; to the Prime Minister; to Lord Beaverbrook; to Ralph Assheton; to Lord Gage (who asked me to stand for Lewes); to Duff Cooper (who first suggested St George's); and, of course, to Dorothy – ready to go by the Rome bag. This closes Monday night or Tuesday morning. I have also done some necessary telegrams to Lord Beaverbrook and to Dorothy. I have heard from her that Maurice will be on leave this week. But I am afraid I cannot leave here. Anything may happen at any moment.

1.15 p.m. Lunch with General Theron (South African Army). A large party, stand-up lunch, fish and cold tongue balanced on a fork, etc., etc. All rather exhausting. The F.M. had come specially from Caserta. After luncheon, and a long wait, we went to a football match – Rugby – between a United Service team and a South African team. A good game – won by the South Africans, who were clearly better

[10] Lady Isabel Browne (1881–1947), granddaughter of Vicomte de Peyronnet, lived at Mount Browne in Surrey.

[11] A special communiqué was issued by S.H.A.E.F. at 1 p.m.: 'Allied forces are today crossing the Rhine on a wide front north of the Ruhr' – the biggest Allied operations since D-Day.

trained together. After the match, we all went off to an immense 'rout' at the Barberini Palace, given by Kirk. Dined with Philip Astley – who has a charming apartment. He has done a good job as Public Relations Officer.

Monday, 26 March 1945

At the office at 9 a.m.

10 a.m. Meeting at Mr Myron Taylor's office, on Italian relief. All the different agencies – American relief for Italy, U.N.R.R.A., Italian Red Cross, Vatican, A.C., etc., have this co-ordinating committee under Mr Taylor's chairmanship. The Italians have made a good effort, and I think it is a new precedent for the church to come in as a constituent part of a joint team.

11 a.m. Air Vice-Marshal [William] Bowen-Buscarlet – Air Sub-commission.

12 noon. Nosworthy – plaintive, as usual, about the position of the British Commercial Counsellor.

12.30 p.m. Commander Lawtor. I showed him the latest F.O. telegram on the financial issue. Although Lawtor is American, I can trust him implicitly. He helped me to concoct a reply, which will present the British point of view but help to please the U.S. Treasury and might be the foundation of a compromise. I think that anyway the situation has improved.

7.30 p.m. Called on Signor Bonomi (Prime Minister). My object was to discuss with him the plans for northern Italy when it falls into our hands. Although it will be under A.M.G. in the initial stages, I want to strengthen the hands of the Italian Government and 'play them up' in every possible way. There are many ways in which this can be done, and corresponding reduction in the danger of violent action by the Communist partisans. I proposed that a Government statement should be broadcast; that although in A.M.G. territory, victory meetings should be held in Milan, Genoa, Turin, Venice, etc., at which the Government members of all parties should speak. Then there was a question of re-forming the Government – both to include Socialists and Action Party, and to get some new figures from the north. I am also keen that the new Italian *gruppi* (or combat brigades) should lead the march in; and of course if they go in, there is no reason why the Prince should not visit them – and at the same time his subjects in the north of Italy. Bonomi was very pleasant and seemed very grateful – but (oh my!) he is as wet as the ocean. No wonder Mussolini kicked him out when he was P.M. twenty-two years ago.

8 p.m. An enormous dinner given by the Ambassador and Lady Charles in honour of Mrs Clare Boothe Luce, the American Congresswoman.[12] The dinner was in the Ambassador's splendid

[12] Clare Boothe Luce (b. 1903), a playwright, was Congresswoman for Connecticut, 1943–7, and U.S. Ambassador to Italy, 1953–7.

apartment in the Orsini Palace and was magnificently done. The guests were Ambassador Kirk, Mr and Mrs Myron Taylor, Major [B. B.] Stimson (the brilliant American surgeon who joined the British R.A.M.C. at the beginning of the war), Mr Brown (Public Relations) and many others. I sat between Mrs Luce and Mr Brown. The Ambassador was in good form, and all went very well. Mrs Luce, however, was obviously not (repeat not) liked by Mrs Myron Taylor. 'I wouldn't have her in my drawing-room in New York. Why should she keep me waiting here?' (Mrs Luce of course managed to be the last guest to arrive.) Mrs Luce is certainly not without charm. The men crowded round her after dinner like bees round a honey-pot. She 'turns it on' in rather a marked fashion. But that goes very well with the sex-starved soldiery.

Tuesday, 27 March 1945

9–11 a.m. At A.C. office. I then left for Civitavecchia accompanied by Colonel [M. D.] Sieff (son of Israel Sieff of Marks & Spencer) and John Atkinson. Colonel Sieff is in the Transport Subcommission of A.C. He is very intelligent (as one would expect) and has considerable charm. The port of Civitavecchia has now been handed over by the military to the Italian Government. A.C. is assisting them in its repair and reconstruction. The work is under the Italian authorities, and we have only two officers (one a port liaison officer on traffic and the other a Tyneside engineer on repair work). I was much impressed by the effort that is being made. The harbour was much damaged and its facilities (which had been excellent in the way of cranes, wheat elevators, etc.) altogether destroyed. There are now five berths working – the majority able to take Liberty ships and not merely coasters. The beautiful Michelangelo port has been damaged by shell-fire but not irreparably. Returned to Rome about 5 p.m.

5.30–7 p.m. Count Galeazzi – the head of the civil side of the Vatican city and an intimate friend of the Pope – called to see me at my villa and we had a long talk. Galeazzi is obviously a very clever man and is said to have more influence with the Pope than anyone. But the conversation was rather disappointing. We kept coming up to questions and then turning away from them. Perhaps the next conversation will be more fruitful.

7.30 p.m. Went round to see Noel Charles. We had a few points to settle.

The news from Germany is wonderful. It looks like the beginning of the end.[13]

Wednesday, 28 March 1945

10 a.m. Mr [E. E.] Hunt, head of Foreign Economic Administration

[13] The entire German defence line in the west was collapsing.

in Washington. I found him agreeable and on the surface, at any rate, co-operative.

10.30 a.m. Count Carandini, Italian Ambassador in London, called. He was full of enthusiasm about England and the generosity of his reception. He seems particularly to have enjoyed his visits to Oxford and Cambridge.

11.30 a.m. Admiral Stone. Routine business.

12.30 p.m. Henry Hopkinson (Political Adviser to A.C., lent to British Embassy).

12.45 p.m. Mr [N. J.] Abercrombie (Admiralty civil servant) on the recruitment of labour from Italy to work in the Far East. I think we shall get the 20,000 men we require.

1.15 p.m. Lunch with Sir D'Arcy Osborne in his delightful house. He is very charming and soothing.

3 p.m. Left by car for Caserta, arriving 6.15 p.m. After about an hour's work there, got down to Naples for dinner.

Thursday, 29 March 1945

10 a.m. Called on Air Marshal Sir Guy Garrod (Jack Slessor's successor) at Caserta. He was friendly and pleasant; but he is not quite the character that Jack was.

10.30 a.m. SACMED's Political Meeting. This was mostly taken up with going through again the terms for a possible German surrender in Italy. We also had (at the subsequent operational meeting) the problem of the German forces in Crete. There are still about 11,000 Germans and 5,000 Italians (16,000 in all). These may soon be starving and willing to surrender. The problem is to deal with them. After much argument, I suggested that they might surrender formally to a Greek general (which would give great pleasure to the Greeks), who could then delegate to a British officer and a suitable British force the task of disarming, feeding and finally shipping them off to the Middle East.

12.30 p.m. Mr Gibson Graham called. The A.C.–COGENA–Mediterranean Shipping Board row is in full swing! Everyone now accuses everyone else of corruption. Lunch with Alex. The news is more wonderful every day and we are correspondingly elated. Talk about northern Italy and various plans to increase the prestige of the Italian Government and Army. I still fear that we shall have trouble with the partisans.

3–4 p.m. Talk with General Robertson on a large number of points. He is an admirably, refreshingly efficient man. The rest of the day was spent in papers, telegrams, etc. – the usual routine.

Friday, 30 March 1945 (Good Friday)

Left Caserta early by car. Arrived Rome at 12.30. Lunch at the villa for Mrs Luce. I asked Lady Charles to come; the rest were fairly junior officers in A.C. – British and American. A great success. Mrs Luce captivated them all by her conversation and beauty.

Saturday, 31 March 1945

The news is good, so far as the 'operational black-out' allows one to guess. Worked all the morning at A.C.

After luncheon, drove to Ostia with Robert Cecil and John Atkinson and spent a pleasant time in the ancient city. The ruins are really remarkable. We stopped at the Church of San Paolo on the way. Although almost entirely modern it is very fine. (The mosaics over the apse alone remain from the old fifth-century basilica.)

Back at A.C. at 5.30. Worked till 7 p.m. Cocktail party given by Mr Brown for press.

7.30–10 p.m. E.N.S.A. entertainment in one of the theatres – not a bad show, and the troops very cheerful.

10 p.m. Commander Jackson (late M.E.S.C., now U.N.R.R.A.). A lot of trouble and many difficult problems. We have still *not* found the right head for the mission to Greece.

April

Sunday, 1 April 1945 (Easter Sunday)

7.30 a.m. Robert and I went to church. A very large congregation – soldiers, sailors, airmen. Many South Africans. Commander Jackson was in church and came back to breakfast with us. A long talk; a F.O. telegram; a minute – and by 11 a.m. the day's work finished!

Robert, John Atkinson and I went for a drive – round Lake Bracciano, and across country to Civitavecchia and back. We visited two great Odescalchi palaces – one at Bracciano, the other by the sea, near Civitavecchia. A lovely day – warm, not too hot, cloudless sky. We got back about 5 p.m. Harold Caccia and Alaric Russell had motored up from Naples, Harold having arrived yesterday from England. A great deal of discussion will be necessary, so I shall keep Harold here tomorrow.

Hendrickson (U.N.R.R.A.) and Jackson came to dinner. Harold and Alaric are staying at the villa. A very pleasant evening, with a lot of argument and good-natured Anglo-American banter.

Monday, 2 April 1945

Stayed in bed all morning and talked to Harold. It seems that the War Cabinet approved my paper on the 'get-up' in Athens and the staff necessary to assist the Ambassador in the duties which he (with Harold's help) will have to undertake when General Scobie leaves. The naval, air, military and police missions, as well as the co-ordination of economic and financial advice, will fall to the Ambassador. Caccia will have rank of Minister, and will 'co-ordinate' them all – rather as happens in the immensely larger but not dissimilar structure in Washington. The next problem is actually to get the staff. Towards this we are making fairly good progress. The most important are the financial, economic and military. All these are filled. General [Gerald] Smallwood, who is coming from Turkey where he has had a somewhat similar experience, is expected in a day or two as head of the Military Mission. After the question of staff and organisation, comes that of relations with the Americans. MacVeagh (the Ambassador) is very shy and rather *protocolaire*. But I hope we can persuade them to join with us in a joint economic and financial committee. To facilitate this, I shall propose the chairmanship of such a committee be entrusted to the head of the U.N.R.R.A. mission.

Ambassador Leeper has been sending some interesting telegrams on the general position (political and economic) in Greece. From the political point of view, we must really now formulate a proper plan. This must depend on the length of time during which we are prepared to leave at least two British divisions. I do not want to get into a position again where we have only one division – enough to get 'committed' but not enough to keep order effectively. We should either get out of Greece altogether or keep enough troops to maintain law and order. The key date will, of course, be that of the plebiscite and election. Gave a dinner party for Harold Caccia to meet his old friends on the Allied Commission, etc. Kirk, Stone, D'Arcy Osborne and seven or eight others.

Tuesday, 3 April 1945

A busy morning at A.C. – mostly routine affairs. Clare Luce to luncheon. She was very amusing, particularly on the American method of electioneering. Her visit to Italy certainly has had a good effect – for the time being. She expressed very pro-British views. I expect it will wear off and the old lion-twisting Adam (or Eve) reappear.

Left by car after luncheon for Naples. Dinner with C.-in-C. Med. to meet the Archbishop of York [Dr C. F. Garbett]. The guests were all naval officers. A pleasant evening; the Archbishop was agreeable and interesting. He is going to Greece later on, and he will be the guest of the Archbishop–Regent.

Wednesday, 4 April 1945

A very interesting morning – a tour of the docks under Admiral Morse's guidance, and lunch with him and his staff. They have certainly done a good job. I was much impressed by the way in which they have organised the Italian workmen on modern and humane lines.

Thursday, 5 April 1945

The wonderful news of the battle in Germany is giving us a great thrill. I have had a very nice message from Winston about my decision to go on at Stockton. But I have, of course, yet had no news from John Wyndham, except a short telegram to say that he has fixed things with Ralph Assheton and Sir John Murray. Poor Dorothy! She will be the chief sufferer! Those weary journeys to the North are still worse under the conditions of railway travel in England today.

10.30 a.m. S.A.C.'s Political Meeting. Not much business – no further instructions about Venezia Giulia. I fear we have a difficult problem ahead of us over the disputed territory.

Friday, 6 April 1945

Early to Caserta; nothing but routine telegrams and various messages from Rome. This attempt to do business in two places is very fatiguing and means dreadful duplication and waste of effort. But it cannot really be helped. Left Caserta at noon; returned to Naples to lunch with Mr Gibson Graham (Mediterranean Shipping Board). C.-in-C. Med and Lady Cunningham were there. After lunch left by car for Rome, arriving about 7.30 p.m. I found a good deal of paper-work to be got through; so I went to bed and finished about midnight. A fresh row is boiling up in Greece, but all Leeper's telegrams are not yet to hand.

Saturday, 7 April 1945

9 a.m. M. [Mauro] Scoccimarro – the Communist Minister for Liberated Italy. He wants to be allowed to enter the north 'immediately on liberation' in order to use his influence for goodwill and toleration all round. Fortunately, an exact plan has been drawn up, defining precisely the role of the Italian Government, and there was no need to do more than listen.

9.30 a.m. Marchese Lucifero (the Lieutenant-General's man). He is concerned at the danger of the Communists making trouble in the north. He is afraid that if the Government is reformed, the 'left' will take occasion to raise again the 'institutional question' and probably refuse to take the oath.

10.30 a.m.–1 p.m. A most useful meeting – Admiral Stone, Antolini (Economic Section), General Spofford (G5, A.F.H.Q.), General Robertson, Brigadier Anderson and myself. We settled a really good plan for reorganising the [Economic] Section and making available to it the services of the Army officers (under Anderson) who have been engaging in restoring and running those plants (especially at Terni) which the Army has requisitioned. These plants cover store, bricks, cement, etc., and the idea is to make a sort of merger of A.C. and the Army, at the same time formally de-requisitioning the plants. Each industry will have an advisory board (or control) composed of A.C. (with the specialist Army officers concerned), the Italian Government, and representatives of Italian management and labour. If we can really implement this plan it will be a great advance.

A very full afternoon, in which I saw Kirk, De Gasperi (Italian Foreign Secretary) and Charles. At the same time, it is clear from Leeper's telegrams that General Plastiras must go. The Royalists have published a most indiscreet letter – a real *Grand Chef*'s letter – which makes him out a sort of Quisling in 1940 and 1941. But I am sorry that this should be the occasion of his going and he may make trouble.

Sunday, 8 April 1945

7.30 a.m. Church.

9 a.m. Left by car for Caserta. Leeper has telegraphed asking me to go at once to Athens. So I shall fly over tomorrow. Spent an hour with Alex in the afternoon. He is 'all set' for an attack which I hope very much will succeed. It might lead the Germans to make a general retreat from Italy if it can be pressed home. Lord Ranfurly came down with me by car. He and Hermione came to spend the day at the villa in Naples and also stayed the night.

Monday, 9 April 1945

After an hour with telegrams and routine, left Marcianise about 10.30 in a Mitchell. Major Elliot and Miss Campbell came with me. We had a good flight – about three hours. After a short rest, Leeper and I discussed the situation. On the whole, I think he and the Regent have made the best of a bad job. It was always the Regent's intention to replace Plastiras by a more reasonable and tolerant figure, without that 'dictator' complex which makes Plastiras so difficult to handle.[1] But it is unfortunate that the 'letter' has led to the actual break. The Regent has done everything in his power to make the change appear to come on other grounds. And, of course, the fact that he was contemplating a 'service government' was pretty well known. Nevertheless, the Royalists have scored an apparent success, although I think they will be disappointed by the actual composition of the new Government. There is an additional complication due to the Americans having rather 'taken up' Plastiras. They have been showing him a lot of attention lately and sending over all kinds of people from U.S. on various excuses. Kind people say that the Americans liked Plastiras because he was a Republican. More suspicious folk say that they were trying to get concessions for post-war trade. This latter view is supported by the fact that they practically got Plastiras to sign a most favourable 'aviation' agreement, which would have given Pan-American Airways a powerful and predominant position. Fortunately, we heard of this and stopped it in time. But this would explain the American attitude, and especially Stettinius's observation at a press conference that the American Ambassador had not been consulted by the Regent on the change of government.

Later in the evening, Harold Caccia, Brigadier Smith-Dorrien, Brigadier Mainwaring and Sir Quintin Hill (financial adviser) came for conferences.

Tuesday, 10 April 1945

It was decided last night to inaugurate formally the new British system by which all the missions and advisers (British) will be

[1] Admiral Voulgaris replaced General Plastiras as Prime Minister on 7 April.

co-ordinated under the Ambassador instead of under General Scobie. This is the result of our talk in Athens in February (when Anthony and the 'Yalta' party were here) and a paper which I wrote for that conference. This paper has now been approved by the Cabinet and we are to put it into effect forthwith. General Scobie will be relieved by a corps commander whose work will be confined to commanding British troops in Greece. General Smallwood has now arrived to take control of the Military Mission and will be responsible for the equipment, maintenance and training of the Greek Army. Admiral Turner and Air Commodore Tuttle are already here. Sir Quintin Hill has come as financial adviser.

We duly held the meeting at 11.30 (this gave me time to write a speech) and it passed off well. I put General Scobie in the chair and sat on his right. I explained the new system and the background, and read them the relevant parts of the Cabinet's decision. Actually Harold Caccia (who now has the rank of Minister) will preside (not the Ambassador, except on special occasions). I ended with a suitable tribute to General Scobie (the only mistake I made was to give my notes afterwards to the Secretary to help him with the minutes, but to forget that at this point my notes ran 'Flowers for General Scobie'!)

2.30 p.m. A long meeting on the future of British propaganda in Greece. We have somehow to keep the Athens radio on right lines, to publish pamphlets and papers, and generally to keep our propaganda and intelligence going. We ended by agreement on various plans, which I undertook to put to A.F.H.Q. and London for agreement.

6–7.30 p.m. Meeting at Brigadier Smith-Dorrien's house, to discuss the establishment required for his 'Liaison Section'. These are really to be the chaps who will be under Caccia's orders. We shall plant them in the various Greek Ministries where they will try by advice (and pressure) to get something done. They have already done very good work.

8.30 p.m. Mr and Mrs Philip Noel-Baker[2] to dinner. They are reformed characters now about ELAS; but we chaffed them a good deal. (I expect they will 'lapse' when the British elections come!)

Wednesday, 11 April 1945

Worked all the morning on various minutes and telegrams arising out of yesterday's meetings. In addition, I did the draft of a telegram which I shall suggest to Alex (when I return) that we should send jointly to the P.M. and the F.S. on the next phase of our intervention in Greece. It is quite clear to me that the elections cannot in fact take place till October or November. Therefore we ought either to take our troops away *altogether* by August, or stay till January. I feel very strongly that we ought to try for the latter course. There will almost

[2] Philip Noel-Baker (1889–1982), Labour M.P. for Coventry, 1929–31, and Derby, 1936–50, was Parliamentary Secretary to Minister of War Transport, 1942–5.

certainly be renewed trouble *after* the elections; and I think we should see the thing through, now that we have put our hand to the task. Moreover, in the dark and confused state which I foresee in south-east Europe, I feel we should retain our strategic position in Greece.

Went for a picnic lunch. Back by three.

4–6.30 p.m. Meeting with Leeper, Caccia, Mainwaring, Hill, Smith-Dorrien, etc., on my draft. We also discussed the points which we should take up with the new Prime Minister, Admiral Voulgaris, after dinner.

7 p.m. Went to see General Scobie and say goodbye.

8.30 p.m.–1.15 a.m. The new Greek Prime Minister! Admiral Voulgaris is quite a character. His appearance reminds one of some gnome or dwarf. (He is certainly not 'Grumpy', but that merry one of the seven.) His little fat face is divided by a mouth which is really like that traditionally drawn by comic artists to denote pleasure – a long incision in his face, with the two ends turning upwards and reaching his ears. His appearance was made the more grotesque because he had the misfortune to break his ankle the other day, and was in plaster of paris. 'Cloppety, cloppety, clop' – he marched bravely in with sticks and smile in a resplendent Admiral's uniform and an excellent temper.

It was a small family dinner – made more agreeable by Sir Michael Palairet's champagne – justly produced on these occasions in the national interest. And then he talked – the good Levantine French, mixed with Parisian slang – which Greeks love so much. (They talk of abandoning French in the schools, and substituting English, but I do not believe it will really suit them. The sort of second-rate-ness of modern French life and the lure of Paris will be too much. Every Greek politician knows that he must spend some of his life in exile – as we have to be in opposition. Exile in London is no fun at all. Paris is the ideal place for political exiles.)

After dinner the more serious conference began in the Ambassador's room. Only the admiral, the Ambassador, Harold Caccia and I. Except that we got terribly sleepy (both Leeper and I actually fell asleep at different times), it was a success. The admiral is really a very attractive personality and very human. He is humorous, sly, cynical – and understands what suits him. Compared to Plastiras, he is a paragon. Plastiras was stupid, vain, pig-headed, romantic, living in the past. Voulgaris is clever, sensible, pliant, sceptical – and lives in and is determined to enjoy the present.

We had prepared a 'brief' of the points which we wished to impress upon him. On the whole, we got what we wanted. He readily agreed to the general system of co-operation which we are already working or in process of extending (Caccia, Smith-Dorrien and the thirty young officers who will be distributed among the Greek Ministries both at Athens and in the provinces). On economic questions, he was unable of course (or unwilling) to understand the elements of the financial problem, but he had a good grasp of the supply. (He grasped almost the entire contents of a bottle of whisky in the course of the evening.) But I had the impression that he really understood more than he pretended. 'The simple sailor' stuff is just a defence measure. On politics, he was intelligent, sensible, moderate, humorous and fair. He wants the elections as soon as possible, but recognises that practical difficulties will make it impossible till the autumn. For that reason, he rather favours the national council. He wants a centre, even a left-centre, policy. He adheres to Varkiza. But he was frank about the extent of the anti-KKE reaction and the violence of the feelings roused by the barbarities of the civil war. 'A revolution or a rebellion anyone can understand. But why unspeakable atrocities, more suitable to barbarians than to Greeks?'

At last – when there was no more whisky and Harold and Leeper were sound asleep and I dozing intermittently – the funny little man went (reluctantly) away. It was only 1.15 a.m., but the effect of bad French or talking through an interpreter (which he had) for about five hours on end is considerable and exhausting.

Thursday, 12 April 1945

Left Athens (in the Mitchell) at 9.30. Rather a 'bumpy' flight. A sandwich lunch at the office at Caserta, and the usual batch of accumulated business. Saw General Robertson (on Greek affairs and on Italian shipping), and the F.M. on Greek affairs. The F.M. has just begun his battle in Italy. It has made a good start; but of course our forces are very weak, and the Germans have some of their best divisions. I have had no news from England for some time; whether because of Easter or for some other reason I do not know. Philip Noel-Baker (on his return from Greece) stayed the night at the villa. Consul-General Swan and Mr Hogarth (Ministry of War Transport in Naples) came to dinner.

Friday, 13 April 1945

I felt tired today and did not go up to Caserta, but sat in the garden (the weather is perfect just now) reading, writing and dozing. A very pleasant day. I read *Three Plays* of Tchehov (I do not much like them – *The Cherry Orchard* is the best) and then (much more refreshing) Stevenson's *The Black Arrow*.

6.30 p.m. Went over to see C.-in-C. Med. (Admiral Cunningham) at Villa Emma. I wanted to talk to him about (*a*) Naval Mission to Greece, (*b*) the row between A.C. and MEDBO [Mediterranean Shipping Board]. Early to bed.

Saturday, 14 April 1945

The news came to us yesterday of President Roosevelt's death. I had, of course, heard of his deterioration in health, which everyone noticed at Yalta. Moreover, the publication of a photograph showing the President with Churchill and Stalin had caused a great impression, since the President appeared so weak and thin. Nevertheless his sudden death was a great shock – a very big loss both to U.S.A. and Great Britain.

10 a.m. Brigadier Jeffries (P.W.E.) on British propaganda activities in Greece and the staff required. There is going to be a big battle about this, as officers and equipment are wanted for northern Italy. But we cannot afford to neglect Greece.

Major Mathews (from Greece) on the question of Smith-Dorrien's establishment. I hope we can get this finally settled now.

General Robertson and Admiral Cunningham came to see me about the allegations of corruption in the Italian schooner business, affecting both Allied Commission and MEDBO officers – a very worrying and tiresome business. Lunched with the Field Marshal. General [Sir Edmond] Schreiber (Governor of Malta) was there. Also the Lieutenant-Colonel of the Welsh Guards, who spoke very well of Julian Faber – which gave me great pleasure. After luncheon, a talk with Chief of Staff and F.M. on the major Greek problem – when to withdraw the troops. Alex had not had time to study my draft properly, and we postponed decision till Tuesday. After finishing my work at Caserta, I left at 5 p.m. for Rome. I had my new Daimler car – an excellent machine – and arrived by 8 p.m.

A little dinner; Miss Campbell came round at 9.30 and we finished A.C. and other papers by 11 p.m. Bed at about midnight. The news [from the Western Front] is still excellent.

Sunday, 15 April 1945

Worked in bed from 8.30 till 10.30. Miss Campbell came for dictation. Got up and went to the American Church for a memorial service for the President. The church was full and the service impressive. The whole Italian Cabinet attended – also the Lieutenant-General (Prince Umberto). The service was rather too long, but well done. I then went to see Randolph Churchill in hospital.

1–4 p.m. We went out (Cecil, Atkinson and I) for a picnic in the Alban Hills.

4 p.m. Admiral Stone (Chief Commissioner) called to see me. He stayed about an hour and we got through a good deal of Italian business ranging from hemp to the eternal question of the partisans in the north. The real difficulty of the north is the number of uncertain factors. If we knew whether the Germans will fight back every inch of the ground or ultimately surrender *en masse*, it would be much easier to make our plans. I think that we may very likely see something between the two – that is, the Germans and Italian Fascist forces might be split into two or more groups and gradually forced to a position where the inner core would remain for a time and ultimately give in.

But we cannot be certain. It is quite likely that if the Germans decide to fight it out, it will be impossible to bring the matter to an issue without sending more troops to F.M. Alexander. He is trying now to fight a final battle without sufficient forces. By good tactical use of his overwhelming air strength, and by his superiority in gunpower and ammunition, he may be able to bring it off. But it will be a very remarkable achievement and we must be prepared for delay.

All these factors of uncertainty make it difficult to form a very clear plan on the 'irregular' and political side.

Moreover, we have made it rather difficult for ourselves by the large number of different people at A.F.H.Q. and A.C. who come into it and have to be consulted, but who approach the problem from very different angles.

I am writing a minute, setting out the questions to which we require an answer, and I shall have to get the Chief of Staff to ask for an objective paper, explaining clearly the plans we have made to meet various eventualities, and the extent to which they do not conflict with each other and have received the final approval of SACMED.

Another complication is that the American part of Austria[3] (from latest information) is more likely to be entered from Germany than from Italy. Therefore a large number of officers will be taken away from Italy for Austria to work with Dever's Sixth Army Group, approaching from the west, not the south. Since it was anticipated that the entry would ultimately be made from the south, these officers were destined to play a dual role, viz., work in forward Army and A.M.G. areas in Italy, and then gradually follow up the Army, and have their work in Italy well started. This change (which is operationally correct) is going to need a lot of sorting out. As for the patriots, I feel that the most important thing is to disarm them as quickly as possible and absorb volunteers, either singly or in groups, as rapidly as possible into the regular Italian Army. But (in view of the underground Communist propaganda, which by no means corresponds to the official and public statements of Togliatti[4] and Scoccimarro) this will not be easy. It is of great importance to give a generous and friendly gesture – good camps – good food – medals and praise generally, so as to make the process attractive and honourable –not furtive and mean. All this means a lot of organisation, and is hampered by the fact that we are *not* in northern Italy and the Germans are!

5.30 p.m. Miss Campbell – for dictation and typing on my talks with Admiral Stone.

6.30–7.30 p.m. Sir Noel Charles. A certain number of questions, none of great importance, but some of them rather ticklish and

[3] Austria, like Germany, was to be divided into separate zones of Allied occupation.

[4] Palmiro Togliatti (1893–1964), leader of the Italian Communist Party for forty years, had been a Minister without portfolio under Marshal Badoglio, 1944, and became Vice-Premier under De Gasperi.

requiring careful handling. After dinner, Miss Campbell came and we finished about 11 p.m.

Monday, 16 April 1945

9 a.m. Signor [Pietro] Longhi (non-party Chairman of C.L.N.A.I. [Il comitato di liberazione nazionale dell'Alta Italia] in Milan). He is a banker; fat, genial, good-tempered, educated at London University, and seems a sensible and patriotic fellow, without the usual swank, panache, blather and overweening vanity which seems the chief Italian characteristic. In fact, he struck me favourably. He was almost (but of course not quite) like an Englishman. He does not conceal his fears. But he thought it better to accept the position and try to moderate the extreme left than to refuse it. In any case, the Communists would like to get rid of him. He had some useful bits of advice as to how we might succeed in dealing with the so-called 'patriots' after liberation. The chief problem – as usual – will be disarmament. Longhi will *not* go on with politics, but go back to business. It seems a pity, and I told him so.

After he had gone, a talk on mine clearance, with various A.C. officials. We are making progress, but much remains to be done. I want to increase the number of Italian companies on the job from four to at least twelve.

11.30 a.m. Ambassadors Kirk and Charles, and Admiral Stone for naval conference. Nothing very startling.

The day went on with the usual series of talks and visitors – including M. Exindaris (Greek member of Advisory Council) on a fishing expedition for news; Mr Biddle, of U.S. Budget Control Commission (an old friend); a party at Kirk's for Admiral Glassford, and finally a dinner party at the villa for Colonel Humphrey Wyndham.[5]

Tuesday, 17 April 1945

10 a.m. Stone and Fiske. The great controversy about A.C./A.M.G. officers for Austria still rages, but I think a compromise will be reached. If we were to hand back Naples to the Italian Government we should save thirty to forty officers for use elsewhere – so this is a reserve available. And I think we could borrow some Eighth Army officers for the Fifth Army.

12 noon. Sir John Serrao (Legal Adviser to H.M. Ambassador). I had known him before – when we stayed with Ronald Graham.[6] He wants me to meet old Orlando.

12.30 p.m. Mr Hoffman – on International Petroleum Conference – the organisation to look after U.S./U.K. oil interests in Italy. The Fascists had seized these and we are trying to arrange for an equitable

[5] John's uncle.

[6] Sir Ronald Graham (1870–1949) had been Ambassador to Italy, 1921–33.

plan for the future, on which the Italian Government is 'stalling' with some success.

1 p.m. Left for Caserta by air from Ciampino airport. The R.A.F. supplied a Hudson (a two-engined machine); one engine failed, but we managed to land at Marcianise without turning over – a difficult feat. I saw the fire engines and ambulances coming out (which always alarms me). I had a message later from my staff that the air marshal's office were anxiously enquiring if I proposed to make a report. I replied that I did not want to make reports, but that I would like aeroplanes which would go and not crash from sheer old age. (These Hudsons are medieval – quite unfit to fly.)

3 p.m. Conference with Alex and General Morgan on Greece. It was decided that I should send my telegram on my own to H.M.G. (instead of the usual joint one from Alex and myself) and Alex would telegraph direct to C.I.G.S. on the military implications. The F.M. is as keen as I am to keep *two* divisions in Greece until *after* the plebiscite and elections. Alex also supported my wish to keep A.I.S. (the publicity, intelligence and propaganda organisation) in Greece for as long as possible. We will take the Austrian team for northern Italy in the first instance.

There was a good deal of work at the Caserta office – but *no* letters from home. The bags have been very irregular of late. Dined with Alex at the Hunting Lodge. A lovely warm evening and an excellent dinner, with caviare (from Yalta) and asparagus (from the Plain of Naples).

Wednesday, 18 April 1945

A normal office day. Got to Caserta about 9 a.m. and left at 6.30 p.m. Nothing of very great importance except a conference with General Robertson on Greek roads and railways and Italian coasters and schooner shipping.

Thursday, 19 April 1945 (Primrose day. My father's birthday)

10 a.m. General [R. F. H.] Nalder, Chief Signal Officer. He tells me that the American Ambassador at Athens (MacVeagh) is trying to eject Cable & Wireless from their offices (which they have had for seventeen years). Leeper is weakly advising C. & W. to give way. A strong telegram to Leeper, ending with 'What we have we hold'.

In the course of the morning an R.A.F. officer in Mediterranean Allied Air Forces came in. He has seen a signal from American Air Command to their Air Transport Command telling them to try to obtain permanent rights in airfields in Rome, Athens, Florence, Berlin, etc., etc. This confirms what we already know about Athens and suspected about Rome. (It is, of course, an absolutely *direct* breach of our agreement with the Americans.) I telegraphed the news home at once. Of course, I think it more than likely that the State Department have acted in good faith towards us, and do not know, and are not told, of these activities of the War Department.

Motored to Rome leaving Caserta at 1 p.m. The car (Daimler) developed some defect and we had to send for one from Rome. I reached the villa at Rome at 9 p.m. (eight hours on the road!).

Friday, 20 April 1945

Morning at A.C. offices, seeing Stone, Fiske and various others of the staff – also some telegrams from London and Athens.

Left Rome for airport, but was told 'No flying from Naples'. The R.A.F. had promised me the Mitchell, to take me from Rome to Florence (to lunch with General Mark Clark) and thence to Forli. In their usual offhand and casual way, they did not send the machine up the night before. Owing to early mists there was no flying out of Marcianise or into Ciampino. When flying *from* Rome onwards was allowed, of course my plane was not there. Finally at 3.45 p.m. (after four hours' waiting) an American colonel put us on an American routine Dakota to Florence. My party consists of Mr Stewart Brown (American) – the new Public Relations Officer of A.C., and my A.D.C. Lieutenant Atkinson. General Clark sent a car to meet us and gave me tea at his H.Q. I found him very anxious for the French threat in north-west Italy to be maintained and even increased. I told him that he could use my name with the F.M. so far as the political implications were concerned. The *further* the French intrusion (especially if they go right on beyond the Val d'Aosta into undisputed Italian territory) the less political danger. And anyway, we want to keep those German divisions there (especially the good Mountain Division) as long as we can. General Clark lent me his own aeroplane. We left Florence about 5.30, arriving Forli at 6.30. Here we were met by Air Commodore Con Benson (Chief A.M.G., Eighth Army) and some of his staff. Con was in very good form, although I thought he looked rather tired. After going to his camp at Eighth Army Main H.Q. and a short talk with him and some of his officers, I went with Con to dine with the Army Commander, General R. McCreery – an old friend who used to be General Alexander's Chief of Staff in Tunisia. He took over the Eighth Army from General Leese, when the latter went to Burma. Dick McCreery is the most charming man – and a very clever one in addition. He has always struck me as one of the ablest of the military officers whom I have seen out here.

After dinner, the general took me to his caravan. He explained to me the course of the battle up to date. It is really very satisfactory, and we are all hopeful of a really big result. The Poles and New Zealanders opened very well on the Eighth Army front.[7] The former claim to have killed 2,000 Germans. The latter have inflicted big losses also. And

[7] On the evening of 9 April the Eighth Army had launched an offensive on a ten-mile front along the Senio river, near Ravenna.

they have both been dealing with first-rate German divisions – paratroops and Panzers.

Saturday, 21 April 1945

A very full day – 9.30 a.m.–11 p.m. Con Benson had laid on an excellent programme of A.M.G. activities. We started from Forli (in the modern Municipio of which I had spent the night in Fascist luxury) and our trip covered Faenza, Imola (just captured – to the neighbourhood of which Eighth Army was moving today), Lugo, Ravenna, Classe, Cesena, Rimini, Riccione and Pesaro. Our tour covered meeting the provincial officers and discussing various problems with them (Colonel [Alfred C.] Bowman (U.S.), the Regional Commissioner, was our guide); seeing a repaired pumping station and the need of further repairs to control the drainage system of the valley; visiting an Italian mine-clearance squad at work; seeing institutions for the reception and care of civilian refugees; and a hundred and one other activities, great and small, carried out under Allied supervision and assistance. The military courts (where the chief offence seems to be 'being in illegal possession of Allied property') seem to work smoothly enough. In general, the areas seemed in pretty good shape. Now that the Army is on the move, they are all 'teed up' to go forward and take over from the enemy the northerly provinces of the region.

In addition to these professional activities (which were the excuse or reason for the trip), I was able, under the guidance of Major [N. T. K.] Newton (U.S.), Eighth Army archaeologist, to see something of Ravenna and Rimini. Rimini has been pretty badly destroyed – unfortunately the lovely so-called Temple of Malatesta has been much battered. It must have been a most lovely thing, and indeed enough of the exterior remains to enable one to realise its extraordinary beauty. It was originally a late thirteenth-century Gothic church. By order of Sigismondo Malatesta it was transformed by the genius of Alberti into a splendid Renaissance building.

Ravenna, more important artistically, has also been more fortunate. San Vitale, the Mausoleum of Galla Placidia, the Baptistery of the Orthodox, Sant'Apollinare Nuovo, the Baptistery of the Arians and Sant'Apollinare in Classe Fuori – all these are more or less intact and their magnificent series of mosaics preserved. I think I prefer the Mausoleum of Galla Placidia to all the rest. Unfortunately, we cannot get the true lighting effects, because the windows are still blocked (except one) for protection. I have never been before to Ravenna or realised the extraordinary effects which this Byzantine art could produce. You can get no idea of the mosaic from books, reproductions, or the debased use of it which one sees elsewhere. The Tomb of Theodoric is also undamaged, although a bomb actually hit it, exploding a few feet away. It is a really stupendous affair – with a monolithic cupola, thirty-five feet in diameter and weighing 300 tons!

This very strenuous but most interesting day ended in a dinner given in my honour at Riccione. Colonel Bowman was the host; about sixty or seventy officers were present; speeches and toasts and all the rest of it. It had not escaped my kind host that it was my Silver Wedding. (I suppose John Atkinson – my American A.D.C. – must have seen my telegram to Dorothy.) A very pleasant evening. I motored back from Riccione to Imola, where I slept in the Field Marshal's 'Caledon Camp' – near Eighth Army H.Q. I had a most comfortable caravan and a very good sleep.

Sunday, 22 April 1945

Started at 9.30 by jeep with General Sir Richard McCreery, commanding Eighth Army. Another strenuous but splendidly exciting day. I could not have chosen a better time for my visit. The battle is in full swing and going well. We went up to Fifty-sixth Division (General R. K. Arbuthnott) and from there to the Twenty-fourth Guards Brigade (Brigadier Erskine). They were about a thousand yards from the most forward positions. The Scots Guards and Coldstream were held up by a bridge (which the Buffs had tried to rush before it was destroyed). The Engineers would take six hours, and then the advance would continue. It was clear that everyone was in good heart, in spite of some heavy fighting. We returned to Eighth Army Advanced H.Q. for luncheon, where we found my old friend General Sir John Harding (who used to be Chief of Staff to Alex at A.F.H.Q. and now, much to his delight, has got a Corps – the Thirteenth). We spent the afternoon and evening seeing the New Zealand Division (tea with General Freyberg) and the Poles (more tea with General Anders). The Poles have fought splendidly and were in crashing form. Not a word about politics or the future of Poland; nothing but triumphant exposition of their operations. I hardly recognised General Anders, whom I had last seen in very gloomy mood at Caserta. '*Une très jolie petite bataille – nous avons tué plus que deux mille Boches – on les sent partout.*' Back about 7.30 and dinner with General McCreery in his mess.

Monday, 23 April 1945

Eighth Army lent me a car, military policeman, etc., and I drove into Bologna, with Mr Stewart Brown and Lieutenant Atkinson. At Bologna – which the Poles and the Americans had entered yesterday – we found considerable excitement but no confusion. Brigadier-General Hume (who corresponds in the Fifth Army to Con Benson in Eighth) had arrived at the splendid – and undamaged – Municipio (or town hall) and installed his A.M.G. officers there. The Fascist Black Brigade had finally shot two well-known Liberal leaders just before leaving. These were now lying in state in the Town Hall and a large (but orderly) crowd streaming by, with flowers and tears. One of the murdered men, known as Mario, was old, white hair, fine well-cut face – obviously a man of character. The coffins were open so that friends and admirers could see the faces of their leaders for the last time. They had been shot against the wall of the Municipio – the bloodstains were clear. Above the place where they had stood were already flowers and – pathetically – photographs of men and women of all ages who had been put to death during recent months by the Fascist Black Brigade. The *questore* [Chief Constable] – a Fascist – had failed to make his escape in time. He had been shot by the partisans next door to the last victims. You could see the brains spattered against the brick and the blood on the ground.

We spent the morning talking to the various A.M.G. officers and some Italians. The Committee of National Liberation came to see us and appeared fairly calm and reasonable. Provisional appointments to the posts of Prefect and Mayor have already been agreed and the town was in pretty good shape. Water – and a limited supply of electricity – are available. There seems a fair amount of food. The population is swollen by an influx of villagers from the battle area. It is probably now 600,000, instead of a normal 400,000–500,000.

After luncheon at a restaurant already taken over by A.M.G. (where Italian cooks are now serving American rations to Allied officers instead of Italian food to German officers), Brigadier-General Hume, Brown, Atkinson and I started out in two jeeps for Modena. The situation in this town, which lies about twenty miles north-west of Bologna, was not known. Hume had tried to get in yesterday, but was turned back by the firing which was fairly heavy. However, it was said that our tanks (American) had been through it this morning.

The drive was quite amusing, and even exciting. There was some traffic going forward and at each village the people turned out with flowers, etc. About five miles from the town, we passed an American infantry battalion, advancing in rather a gingerly fashion. We asked them what they were doing, and they said they were going to attack and occupy Modena in due course. (However, on our return, we found them resting in an orchard outside the town, so they may have thought better of it or had contradictory orders.)

We drove into the town. There was a little desultory sniping but not much more. Our arrival at the Municipio caused some excitement. There was a lot of shouting and embracing. The leader of the partisans kissed me on both cheeks on being told that I was the famous Harold Macmillano – said by the B.B.C. to be the ruler and father of the Italian people. I was presented with an armlet and taken into the Town Hall, to be formally enrolled. Either because all this caused rather a crowd, or because the hour of siesta was over, or because a procession of Fascists was being taken off to prison, things suddenly began to get rather hot. A two-hour duel began between the partisans (who were quite well armed) and a number of Germans and Fascists who had taken up some pretty good positions in various windows, etc.

However, our chaps behaved quite well, and began to shoot them up in quite a soldierly way. They got a machine-gun on to one particularly tiresome group of snipers (who commanded the main street) and did quite well with hand-grenades. I and my companions tried to take as little a part in all these operations as honour would allow; but naturally one had to pretend to do something. It was really quite an exciting little action while it lasted and quite spirited. Of course a lot of partisans fired off their pieces quite aimlessly and threw grenades just for fun. Indeed these gentlemen and their curious assortment of rifles, grenades, tommy-guns, etc., caused me more alarm than our opponents.

Finally, the thing rather died down. We had got our jeeps into a position under a covered alley near the main street. After a lot of hand-shaking and cheering, we got in and made a dash down the street. All went well – scarcely a shot fired – till we came to the barrier which we had passed without incident on entering. Some chap *outside* this barrier had been stirred into activity by the noise (or perhaps awakened from his afternoon sleep); anyway, he covered the exit fairly effectively. We jumped hastily from our jeeps, and got as near to the walls on each side – rather inglorious but wise. Some of our friends turned up, and eventually they got him from the window of a neighbouring house. We then left, as fast as possible, and without further incident. A very interesting episode. Brown and I, of course, are now claiming that we two civilians 'liberated' Modena!

Returned to Bologna, where my car and military police escort had prudently stayed. The crowds were gay but not violent. A few alleged Fascist girls had been shaved – but no worse. The A.M.G. officers made a fuss about this, which the partisans attributed to foolish boys, not to their legitimate followers. More talk on the situation. We are going to try to disband and disarm the 3,500 partisans in Bologna on Wednesday (the 25th). They are all to be paraded, and marched past General Clark. They will hand in their rifles and get a sort of certificate from Field Marshal Alexander. (This has already worked in some places further south, and I am told that in the black market these certificates command a good price – which is encouraging.) They are given a choice of joining the Italian Army (if of the right age) or going into special centres where we shall try to feed them and look after them until they can be employed by the Allies or returned to normal civil employment. The scheme is a good one on paper. I hope it will work out.

We left Bologna about 6.30 – Atkinson and I returned to Caledon Camp (near Imola), Brown returned to Forli.

Dinner at Eighth Army. F.M. Alexander had arrived – a very cheerful dinner, everyone in tremendous heart about the battle which continues to go well.

Tuesday, 24 April 1945

Left the camp at Imola at 7.30. Motored to Forli where I picked up Stewart Brown. Thence to the aerodrome. Left by Expeditor (belonging to General McCreery) and stopped at Fano. I had discovered that Michael Baillie was in hospital at Pesaro. I had arranged for a car to meet me at Fano and drove to Pesaro. He was in hospital all right, and I found him without difficulty. He was suffering from a return of malaria. In other respects, he seemed quite cheerful. Maud had written to me about him and seemed rather worried. But I shall be able to reassure her.

Left Fano eventually about 11.30 and got to Rome at 12.30. This trip has really been a *most* enjoyable one and everyone has been most kind and helpful.

1.15 p.m. Sir John Serrao brought old Orlando to luncheon – no other guests. I enjoyed the old man. He is eighty-four and reminds me a good deal of Lloyd George. He is a Sicilian (as L. G. a Welshman) and thus a little outside the ordinary Italian type and cast of thought. He has a great deal of humour and seemed very much alive. I thought him far better than poor Bonomi. We talked till 3.30. Orlando was pessimistic about the immediate future, but confident of the ultimate recovery of Italy. He does not think Communism will last in its Marxist form, but will have to adapt itself to the Italian genius or fail to maintain itself in the long run.

Afterwards I went to A.C. office, where I stayed till about 6.30. Being rather tired I then went to bed. Randolph Churchill came round.

8.15 p.m. Got up for dinner. Henry Hopkinson (Counsellor at British Embassy) came. We dined alone, and since he only returned today from England I got some useful information about the F.O. plans for Italy – or rather lack of plans.

Wednesday, 25 April 1945

Left Rome by air at 10 a.m.

Morning at Caserta. Hal Mack came to see me. He is to be British Diplomatic and Political Representative in Vienna. There was an important meeting at 3 p.m. F.M. Alexander, General McNarney, Chief of Staff, Hal Mack, [J.G.] Erhardt (Mack's U.S. colleague), Offie and myself to decide on the plans. The Russians have invited us to send a forward party of our missions, but they have *not* agreed the principles on which Vienna or Austria is to be divided between the (four) occupying powers.

Finally, a telegram to C.C.S. was agreed. I telegraphed privately to F.O.

A lot of varied jobs to be done. Greece is still a trouble, over P.W.B. radio, newsprint and U.N.R.R.A. London have turned down my suggestion of Grafftey-Smith (from Italy) and we are no further on.

A pleasant dinner at the Naples villa, with Hal Mack, Brigadier [John] Winterton (also for Austria), Offie and others.

Thursday, 26 April 1945

10.30 a.m. F.M.'s Political Meeting. Venezia Giulia was the most important item in a long agenda. We still have no instructions. After a long discussion, the draft prepared by Deputy Chief of Staff (Lemnitzer) suggesting occupation of all Venezia Giulia in default of instructions was turned down. I carried my proposal that the F.M. (if not instructed to do something more for *political* reasons) would content himself with trying to get Trieste and the Robertson (or Wilson) Line [of 1919]. This can be defended against Tito and/or Stalin as a *military* necessity to secure Allied communications into Austria.

Lunched with Mr Erhardt (U.S.) – a very agreeable party. After luncheon, I finished off a lot of routine work, seeing Brigadier Jeffries (on Greek publicity needs) and others. Left by car (with Miss Campbell) for Rome at 5 p.m. Dined alone and went to bed.

Friday, 27 April 1945

Morning in bed. Private letters; news of Stockton from Dorothy; a piece for A.C. bulletin and my trip in northern Italy, etc., etc. Brigadier Anderson (an excellent officer who is taking over the *production* side of the Economic Section) and Nosworthy (Commercial Counsellor at the Embassy) to luncheon.

The news gets better every day.[8] Our battle in Italy is a real triumph – the Germans *completely* defeated and nearly 70,000 prisoners to date.

3 p.m. Stone. Plans for Liberated Italy and other details.

4 p.m. Brigadier Lush who has just got back from England.

5 p.m. Ambassador Charles and Henry Hopkinson. I have arranged for Henry Hopkinson to go to Genoa and then to Milan with the advancing Army, to be a member of my staff and to send *objective* news of what is happening to me and to the Ambassador. Charles agreed the scheme and will share the information.

6 p.m. Hal Mack. Some administrative questions for Austria and lots of gin. I delight in Hal – always fresh and interesting and with a wonderful sense of humour.

Saturday, 28 April 1945

Motored to Terni, leaving Rome at 8.30 a.m. Pouring rain – the drought broken at last. I spent the whole day at the steel works, with the South African Engineer officers who have taken over direction of the plant and done a truly wonderful job. The rain, the smell, the rolling mills and the steel furnaces made me very homesick. It was just like Stockton or Middlesbrough! I lunched at the mess and finished the

[8] U.S. and Russian forces had met at Torgau in central Germany the previous day. And in Italy Genoa had been liberated and Allied forces were approaching Venice.

tour of this enormous works (including the power station) by 5 p.m. The power station was almost entirely wrecked by demolition. But the repaired plant at Terni has got two units going (heavy steel forgings, new turbines, etc.) and will have the two other units by end of May and end of June respectively. The plant is making Bailey bridges, tank parts, sheets, and a lot of civilian stuff. The power station is, of course, hydro-electric, run by a great waterfall nearly 600 feet high, where the 'Lake in the Grove' has been tapped above the Nera river. A most interesting and even inspiring day. Atkinson returned to Rome; Robert came up in another car, and we motored on to Assisi. We are staying in the Hotel Subasio, near San Francesco. The rain cleared off and it was quite a pleasant evening. Assisi was very beautiful, the sun coming out just before sunset. I stayed twice before at Subasio. In 1912 or 13 with Daniel [Macmillan], Sligger (Urquhart) and Humphrey Sumner.[9] Again in 1920 with Dorothy, on our honeymoon.

Sunday, 29 April 1945

A most peaceful day, ending with thrilling news. Being very tired, I slept till 9 a.m. Robert and I started in real English April weather at 10 a.m. for a walk to the little monastery (Eremo or Casceri) where St Francis lived on the slopes of Mount Subasio. It took about three hours (there and back) and although rather fatiguing it did me good. It was really wonderful to have a peaceful day in such lovely surroundings. We got very hot in the sunny intervals and cooled off by the rain showers.

In the afternoon we went to all the great churches – the upper and lower churches of San Francesco (the Giottos splendid and inspiring), Santa Chiara, San Rufino and so on. There were many flags, but no excitement.

In the evening, we heard the news that the partisans of Milan had seized and hanged Mussolini and other Fascists. Later, a telephone call from Caserta that the German military delegates (who arrived, as I knew, yesterday) had signed up a *military* surrender at A.F.H.Q. We had settled all the precise terms, and I rather wanted to be out of the way. It is important that the Russians should not suspect us of anything *political*, and I thought it discreet to be absent from Caserta. I am delighted, especially for Alex's sake, that his triumphant battle (there are now 100,000 prisoners) has been followed by the surrender of the armies opposed to him. It is a complete vindication of his strategical and tactical dispositions. The radio also gave us the account of Himmler's attempt to surrender to British and U.S. and the firm reply from Downing Street.[10] It seems really a very stupid thing for

[9] F. F. Urquhart (1868–1934), fellow and tutor of Balliol College, Oxford, 1896–1934. Humphrey Sumner (1893–1951) was fellow and tutor at Balliol (where we had been undergraduates together), 1925–44, and Warden of All Souls College, Oxford, 1945–51.

[10] On 24 April Himmler had offered to arrange Germany's unconditional surrender to Britain and the United States only – not Russia. He was told that Germany must surrender to all three powers.

Germans to think that they could 'get away' with such a transparent trick at this stage. According to the radio, Himmler said that Hitler was dying of 'cerebral haemorrhage', which seems very convenient for everyone concerned. After listening to all this (and getting some more telephone calls from Caserta and Rome) we walked in the square outside the great church and pondered in the quiet starry night on the mutability of human affairs. At any rate, I never expected to be at Assisi to hear the news of the end of the Mediterranean campaign and the last stages of the European war. It seems sometimes six weeks, six years, or six decades since the war began. And it is hard to 'take in' its end – or approaching end.

Hitler has lasted twenty years – with all his power for evil, his strength, his boasting. St Francis did not seem to have much power, but here in this lovely city one realises the immense strength and permanence of goodness – a rather comforting thought.

The night was lovely. After the unsettled weather of the last two or three days (rain was *much* needed by the farmers and anxiously prayed for) all the clouds had cleared away. It was a lovely starlit night. Later, when I had gone to bed, the moon rose – an almost full moon. All the valley was lit as if by artificial light. This morning:

Monday, 30 April 1945

An absolutely clear, cloudless sky – like a very fine June day in England. It is cool, but not cold, even at 7 a.m. summer time (5 a.m. by the sun). We left for Rome at 8 a.m. by car. No more news before leaving.

I had a luncheon party at my villa in Rome – Bonomi, De Gasperi (Foreign Affairs), Togliatti (Communist), Brosio (Liberal), Ruini (Socialist) and one or two others. Stone, Lush, Upjohn and some others from the Commission were there to help. The news is wonderful. I know, of course, that the German signatures to the Italian surrender agreement may be repudiated – but I doubt it. The Italians were quite cheerful, but of course apprehensive of each other. De Gasperi talked a lot about Trieste, etc., I could give him no news for certain. Togliatti is torn between loyalty to Moscow and to Italy. The former will prove the stronger; but of course it does not help the Communist Party in Italy. I had a talk with Bonomi. He improves on acquaintance, I think. He has considerable political flair. Whether he has the 'guts' to go through a difficult and semi-revolutionary period, I do not know. Perhaps after twenty-five years, his nerve has improved! Whenever I see him, I preach strength and determination to him. After all he has a wonderful position – no Parliament and no election. Nothing, except his own weakness, can lead to his fall.

After lunch, left by car for Caserta. Here I found the F.M. and General Morgan, rather excited and very pleased with themselves. The German delegates have got back to Bolzano, but no sure news of the acceptance has come through. There is one weak spot in our armour. Although the instrument of surrender was duly signed, negotiators said that they had (as they had) letters appointing them plenipotentiaries; at the end of the proceedings they explained that they had perhaps exceeded their powers and that higher authority must confirm their action. General Morgan said 'we accept that'. I hope and trust that this will not lead to trouble.

8 p.m. Brigadier Jeffries (P.W.B.) and Mr Paniguian[11] (P.W.E. for Athens) to dinner. Long discussion on propaganda in Greece, by radio, papers and books, and plans for financing these.

[11] H. A Paniguian (1903–73), later a director of J. Walter Thompson, the advertising agency.

May

Tuesday and Wednesday, 1 and 2 May 1945

These days have passed in such a hectic atmosphere and with so much excitement that one can only summarise the picture. Apart from all that is happening outside our Mediterranean theatre (such as Hitler's death!)[1] every hour has brought a change of news. I have been in hourly consultation with the F.M. and General Morgan (Chief of Staff). General McNarney (U.S.) has generally joined our talks and (in Kirk's absence in Rome) Offie. We had, on 1 May, communication with Wolff[2] in Bolzano, but no exact messages. We could not tell whether or not the agreement signed on Sunday would be honoured. Then, in the course of the 1st, we heard that Vietinghoff[3] (the German South-west Commander) had been dismissed. Then (from Wolff) that he (Wolff) and his friends were under arrest. Then, later in the day, that Kesselring had taken over, but wanted twenty-four or forty-eight hours before making up his mind. Then we were told that an air rescue should be arranged for Wolff – then this was cancelled. Finally, early on 2 May, we got a message that Kesselring and Wolff (after four hours' telephoning to each other) had reached an agreement and that the terms of the surrender would be carried out. But Kesselring still wanted twenty-four hours' delay before publication. To all these messages we always returned the same reply – that the signed agreement must be kept. Finally, in the course of the afternoon of the 2nd, we picked up radio messages *en clair* from German H.Q. at Bolzano giving the necessary orders to the various units for the surrender. On this we sent a final message to Wolff (and through him to Kesselring) that since these messages were being sent *en clair* we should make the public announcement at 6.30 p.m. We decided this at a meeting at 5 p.m. on the 2nd and the announcement was duly made. At 7.30 the P.M. spoke in the House of Commons.

All through these days we had to keep making appropriate replies to

[1] Besieged in his Berlin bunker, Hitler shot himself through the mouth after lunch on 1 May.
[2] General Karl Wolff (b. 1900) was the senior S.S. commander in Italy.
[3] General Heinrich von Vietinghoff (1887–1952) had succeeded Kesselring in October 1944.

the Germans; inform Combined Chief of Staff through Alexander's official telegrams; keep London informed through my channels – quite a job. And I was determined to get an announcement at a time when Winston could speak in the House!

The whole thing was rather reminiscent of the Italian surrender in September 1943. The great thing in surrender negotiations is never to let the other fellow have a loophole. Get his signature and hold him to it. This I was determined to do – and it has paid.

We have just finished listening to the P.M.'s House of Commons speech – the chief part of which was on the 9 p.m. B.B.C. I am so delighted with his tribute to Alex and the Army of Italy.[4] We have won after all – by a short head! Now for bed – after two very wearing days.

Thursday, 3 May 1945

Berlin has fallen – but we still were first![5] I confess to a certain anxiety about the actual carrying out of the surrender throughout this area. But so far the news is very reassuring. The orders are being given and complied with. Alex is, of course, very delighted and proud – and well he may be.

Friday, 4 May 1945

The German plan is now becoming pretty clear. It is to obtain *de facto* what they failed to obtain *de jure* – viz., a surrender to the British and Americans instead of to the Russians. They are now making and will go on making these piecemeal surrenders – holding the Eastern line with rearguards and trying to save their men, not their territory. They know that if Germans become prisoners of war to U.S. or British troops, they will be looked after, fed, cared for – and ultimately returned to Germany. But they greatly fear that if they fall into Russian hands they will never be seen or heard of again. Kesselring (through Wolff) has sent Alex a message asking to be put in touch with Eisenhower – a very interesting development.

Meanwhile a fresh headache is rapidly developing – Yugoslav armies are advancing into Venezia Giulia and Austria – in a fierce race with the Eighth Army.[6]

Saturday and Sunday, 5 and 6 May 1945

Continuous meetings over Venezia Giulia – things are moving very fast, and what with the labour of attending the meetings, writing my own telegrams to London, and helping to draft the A.F.H.Q.

[4] 'It brings to a conclusion the work of as gallant an army as ever marched, and brings to a pitch of fame the military reputation of a commander who has always enjoyed the fullest confidence of the House of Commons.'

[5] I.e. Berlin had fallen to the Russians, but Alexander was the first to obtain surrenders.

[6] Yugoslav troops had reached the centre of Trieste on 1 May, the day before the New Zealand Second Division arrived. Fiume fell to the Yugoslavs on 3 May. And on the 4th S.H.A.E.F. announced the surrender of the German Forces to Montgomery.

telegrams to Washington and London (C.C.S.) there is not much time left for writing up the diary. I have decided to stay here [in Naples]. Things in Rome are all right, and north Italy (except for Tito on the east and the French on the west)[7] is behaving better than I expected. I telephone twice a day to Stone and once a day to Ambassador Charles. But I must stay here to deal with Tito.

Unfortunately, the Americans began by taking a very pedantic attitude. They thought we must occupy and govern *all* Venezia Giulia. This is quite unrealistic. Last February, I think the F.M. when he visited Tito could easily have got a purely military agreement as to a line of demarcation between our forces and his. This would have given him Fiume and Pola, and us Trieste. Italian opinion would have been satisfied and things could have been kept quiet till some final peace settlement. I am not sure that this is now possible. Even now the Americans (through the State Department) demand the whole. But the War Department wants to use *no* American troops and the President is beginning to take fright. Unless we are very careful, it will be another Greece – with us carrying the baby, as usual. I am still anxious for an Alexander–Tito agreement on a *military* basis, without reference to political questions, such as sovereignty, etc. But I fear it may now be too late. As usual no instructions from U.S. and U.K. Governments – only vacillation or silence. Meanwhile, New Zealand troops hold the docks, the Yugoslavs the town of Trieste. The race is going on. We have given an *American* division the task of getting *Gorizia*. (This is a good plan, and the F.M. has managed to arrange it very cleverly.)

On 6 May, I went to early service at Naples, before coming up to Caserta for a meeting with F.M., Chief of Staff, General McNarney and Offie. (I have advised F.M. always to have the Americans well represented at our talks and sharing our decisions.) Except for these tiresome local troubles of ours, the news is wonderful. It cannot be long now. It seems almost impossible to imagine. We have much to be thankful for. I believe and trust that Maurice is all right. I long to hear for certain where he is.

Monday, 7 May 1945

9.30–11.30 a.m. More meetings, telegrams, etc. – all Venezia Giulia.

The race continues. No incidents at present, but we have had to abandon any attempt to set up Allied Military Government even in those areas where our troops are. The Yugoslavs are in control, with a civil and military organisation. (All very like Greece!)

11.30 a.m. Left by car for Rome. It was a very hot day and a tiring drive. I held a meeting at 3 p.m. at the Commission, with Stone, Lush, Grafftey-Smith. I had to go through with them a communication which I had been instructed to make to Bonomi on behalf of H.M.G.

[7] French forces had crossed from France into the French-speaking Val d'Aosta and were refusing to withdraw unless ordered to do so by the French Provisional Government.

on the subject of Italian purchases in U.K. as part of programme B (the 'rehabilitation of Italy' programme). All this arises from my discussions in London last November. The programme has all been agreed with the Italian authorities and forwarded to Combined Liberated Areas Committee in Washington. Owing to the much smaller amount of destruction of plant, etc., in north Italy than we all expected, some alterations and amendments will no doubt be necessary. But the orders are well in hand and the only question still unresolved is the British share of the financing. The A programme (disease and unrest) will be financed, of course, by U.S. and U.K. jointly in accordance with the proportions fixed in the overall agreement. But this additional programme is more complicated. The Americans will provide finance up to the amount of American troop pay actually spent in Italy (probably 100 million dollars or so). H.M.G. have now agreed to finance their contribution up to the sterling value of Italian imports already made or to be made. At the moment this only stands at about £2 million (8 million dollars) when various adjustments have been made. But if the scheme for recruiting Italian labour (up to 15,000 men) goes through, the value of their wages will count as an export from Italy. In three years it should reach £12 million.

At 6.30 I went to see Bonomi. I made him a written and an oral statement. I also, at H.M.G.'s request, invited him to send a purchasing agent to U.K. (with appropriate staff) to make the necessary contracts and generally supervise their execution. B. seemed quite pleased. Although the sum is not large, it is all that we can afford and it makes a beginning.

At 7.30 I went to see Ambassador Charles. He is very much perturbed about Trieste and the general developments. He feels that the Italian Government may fall over the affair. Dined quietly with John Wyndham and Robert Cecil. Worked till later after dinner on my papers and telegrams.

Tuesday, 8 May 1945

5 a.m. Left Rome by car for Caserta. Arrived at 7.30 a.m. (a record run). No traffic on the road and deliciously cool. It was dark when we started. The breaking of the day was very lovely. Breakfasted at the Villa Vittoria in Caserta, which has now been taken over by Alaric Russell and his wife.

8.30–9.30 a.m. Talk with General Morgan, who left immediately afterwards for Belgrade. We fixed the final terms of the military agreement which he would propose to Tito, and went through the arguments he should use.[8] After a good deal of doubt it now seems that

[8] Although Washington had specified that Allied Military Government should take over the whole of what had been Italy in 1939 and administer it until a peace conference could settle its future, much of Venezia Giulia was already occupied by Yugoslav partisans who would fight to

today is to be V.E.-Day [Victory in Europe Day]. We organised at short notice a little cocktail party at noon in my room in Caserta Palace. We invited all our staff, including servants from Naples, drivers, batmen, orderlies, etc., and all Kirk's staff. It seems almost impossible to imagine that it is all really over. If it were not for our new crisis over Venezia Giulia, things would seem very flat.

Lunched at Villa Vittoria, and listened to Churchill's announcement at 3 p.m. which gave the official news of the final German surrender.

At about 4 p.m., feeling quite exhausted for some reason, I drove to Naples and went to bed. Philip Broad and I listened to the King's broadcast at 9 p.m. A very quiet V.E.-Day! But a long one!

Wednesday, 9 May 1945

10 a.m. A service was held at Caserta – semi-religious in character, and half British and half American. I was on the platform, with F.M. and all the various Allied commanders. It was short and impressive. Alex made an excellent little address and looked very smart and dapper.

After this ceremony, a meeting of the leading people (Alex, McNarney, Offie and myself) to see General Morgan's telegram from Belgrade. Tito has turned down the F.M.'s offer. We drafted a telegram to Morgan telling him to be firm. We gather that Tito has a counter-proposal to make, but it will not probably be satisfactory.

I spent the afternoon at Naples, in the garden of the villa – dozing and meditating. I am very tired – and very worried about this Tito affair. I feel that we must be very careful. Neither British nor American troops will care for a new campaign in order to save Trieste for the 'Eyeties'. On the other hand, to give in completely may be a sort of Slav Munich. Nor do I know what advice to send to London. It is difficult to guess what will be Winston's mood. I do not want to excite or depress him. So far, we have only reported events and devoted the rest of our efforts to advising Alex so as to keep him on the right line and avoid any traps.

Hal Mack and General Winterton to dinner. We listened to the wireless account of V.E.-Day in London, etc., and a very curious affair in praise of Churchill – the latter in poor taste, I thought.

Thursday, 10 May 1945

10.30 a.m. S.A.C.'s Conference. An hour and a half on Venezia Giulia, without much progress. The chief object of these large and formal conferences is that of a Cabinet – to let everyone know what is

hold on to it. But Alexander needed his lines of communication, and had made an agreement with Tito that he should control Trieste and the routes through Gorizia and Trevisio to Austria. Tito, however, while allowing Alexander the use of Trieste and Pola, refused to cede control of these ports, now jointly occupied. So Alexander was now sending Morgan to Belgrade to try to obtain a purely military agreement, giving him control of the territory west of a suitable demarcation line.

happening and have his say. A long dispute between Ambassador Kirk and General McNarney was very illuminating. The State Department violently anti-Tito and demanding strong action; the War Department much more temperate and thinking of the Far East.

Tito's counter-proposal (which we now have in full) is reasonable in a way, but could not possibly be accepted by the Field Marshal, since it is founded on the political assumption that all territory east of the Isonzo is *de facto* and *de jure* under Yugoslav sovereignty. He offers, in exchange, free user rights of Trieste and the lines of communication and a kind of military condominium.[9] The rest of the area he claims, and will occupy and govern himself. We decided on (*a*) reply to Tito – saying that as he has raised the political issue, F.M. has no option but to refer the matter to his two Governments, (*b*) instructions to the planners for a full military appreciation of the force required to throw out the Yugoslavs.

General Morgan arrived back after lunch. He is obviously impressed by Tito's determination and character. Our Ambassador, Ralph Stevenson, on the other hand, thinks he is bluffing. He (and his U.S. colleague) has telegraphed recommending strong action and an ultimatum. I am more and more worried about it all. I have started to draft an appreciation and advice to P.M. But I am not satisfied with it. I gave it to Philip Broad to work on, but it came out longer, more confused and worse. Finally I took it down to Naples and worked on it late into the night. Unfortunately, I had to go to dinner with the French Military Mission. However, this was interesting, because Leon Blum (the French Socialist Prime Minister) was there, after three years of a French prison and two years of a German one. The last time I had met him was at a small dinner given at the Ritz Hotel, towards the end of May 1940, at which Spears was the host and Dalton and I the other guests. 'The Battle of the Bulge' was then on. I am bound to say that, considering his experiences, Blum was very sprightly and amusing.

Friday, 11 May 1945

Worked on a redraft of my telegram – which I have cut into two – a short summary of possible courses of action and comments separately. I showed them to Alex and General Morgan and sent them off with a few amendments suggested by them. Alex has sent the following to the Combined Chiefs of Staff – 'In the event of hostilities against Yugoslavia, I must know on what divisions I can rely. I would be glad if you would consult the U.S., U.K., New Zealand, South African, Indian, Brazilian, Polish and Italian Governments.' I think this should flutter the dovecotes in Washington!

Sandwich lunch in the office. News from Rome that the Bonomi Government may fall on Venezia Giulia. I spoke to Charles on the

[9] Thus the safety of Alexander's line of communication would continue to depend on Yugoslav good will.

telephone and sent him a telegram urging him to fortify Bonomi. If he plays his cards well, he can turn the tables on the Italian Communists. They are on the horns of a dilemma and they should be firmly impaled.[10]

The Tito problem is immensely difficult and I am *most* anxious about our British position. General McNarney has told us quite frankly that his orders are not to allow himself to be embroiled in the Yugoslavian row, and yet the State Department (and Stevenson, our Ambassador at Belgrade) want us to call Tito's bluff. I feel that we must be certain of physical as well as moral support from the U.S. if we are to take the risk. I certainly do not want to see another Greece.

Got down late to Naples, where I found Randolph. About 11 p.m., Mr Douglas Woodruff (editor of the *Tablet*) arrived and stayed till 1 a.m.!

Saturday, 12 May 1945

8 a.m. Left by Dakota with Philip Broad. We arrived at an airfield near Treviso, not far from Venice. We had a very good flight across the Apennines – it was a lovely day, very hot on the ground, but nice and cool in the air. We arrived at Treviso about 10.30 a.m., and were met by the Eighth Army commander, General McCreery. The general drove us to his H.Q. – a nice camp in the garden of a large country house. Here we had a conference, which included Chief of Staff, Eighth Army (Brigadier [Sir Henry] Floyd) and Con Benson (A.M.G., Eighth Army). It was clear to me that the general was rather worried, and a bit sore over his lack of information. So I thought it best to let him and the Chief of Staff and Benson explain all their problems and difficulties. Naturally, coming so soon after their victory, it is disappointing for them and their troops to find themselves in such a difficult and delicate situation. They are not allowed to exercise any authority by force of arms. So they have to sit by and watch the Yugoslavs set up a local government of their own, seize all the public buildings in the areas into which they have and are still infiltrating, and conscript villagers, requisition food and transport and the like. Not only are they in effective control of the territory east of the Isonzo (we have a brigade in the dock area of Trieste, the Yugoslavs control the town) but they have also made A.M.G. unworkable in certain areas west of the river. The British soldier can only lean up against them (like the London policeman) and there are many more of them than of us. After about one-and-a-half hours of questions, etc., I summed up the political and military situation; the problems confronting the Field Marshal and H.M.G. and the equivocal and uncertain attitude of the Americans. I had brought all the files, and showed them the most recent and relevant interchange of telegrams from different capitals in the world. I think

[10] The Communist leader Togliatti had declared his support for Tito's claims in Venezia Giulia.

this did a lot of good from the psychological point of view and put the general and his staff thoroughly 'in the picture'. The conference (in the shade of some trees) lasted from 11 a.m. till 1.30 p.m.

After luncheon, Philip Broad and I motored back to the airfield, and got into two 'whizzers'. We had a forty-five-to-fifty-minute flight to a strip near Monfalcone. Here we were met by our old friend General Harding (who used to be the Chief of Staff at A.F.H.Q. and is now commanding Thirteenth Corps). He has settled himself in a splendid castle belonging to a Höhenlohe – on the sea with a delightful garden and beautiful view. The chief feature of the garden and grounds at the moment was a wonderful display of blue irises.

General Harding explained to us the position of his troops. He is a very firm, confident and stalwart character, as well as a very clever professional soldier. To tell the truth, his morale seemed higher than that at Eighth Army H.Q. He does not like the position, since everywhere he and his troops are 'on sufferance'. But he thinks he can maintain this uneasy position for several weeks, if necessary, while negotiations proceed and decisions are taken on a governmental level. We left John Harding at about 6.30 and were back at Eighth Army airfield about 7.20.

We drove back to Caledon Camp – washed and changed our very stained and dusty clothes. I think today's visits have done good. Both Generals McCreery and Harding seemed very pleased at the opportunity of explaining their own position and difficulties. And I think they were glad to hear us explain the political background and all the issues involved, as well as our own problems at A.F.H.Q.

About 8 p.m. we drove into Venice – Brigadier Floyd (Chief of Staff, Eighth Army), Con Benson, Broad and I. We got there just in time to get some light. It was a great thrill to go down the Grand Canal – pass the Ca' d'Oro and the great Renaissance palaces – and stop opposite the Salute and the Custom House – all intact and all with the same calm, satisfied beauty, at once confident and nostalgic. We dined at the Grand Hotel. The food (British rations) was excellently cooked. The wine was very good. The waiters attended us as deftly and reverently as no doubt they had the German officers until a few weeks ago.

Sunday, 13 May 1945

Left the Camp at 8.30 for the airfield. Went by Dakota (Broad, Brigadier Floyd, Con Benson, one or two other Eighth Army officers and I) to Klagenfurt. This was a truly wonderful flight. It was an absolutely perfect day – very hot indeed on the ground; nice and cool at about 10,000 feet. The flight across the Alps was really magnificent. The Apennines seemed like modest hills in comparison with these tremendous mountains, with their great jagged peaks and cliffs, some still snow-clad.

We landed safely at Klagenfurt airfield about 10 a.m. The field is a grass one, small and rather bumpy, but the DC3 machines land well in such circumstances. We were met by General Charles Keightley (Fifth Corps) and some of his staff. This officer, whom I have met from time to time, is an admirable soldier and a very level-headed and sensible man. He is well suited for his difficult and embarrassing task.

I have never been in Austria, and had no real picture in my mind of what Klagenfurt and the district would be like. It is really a beautiful Alpine valley, of fair size, with lakes, etc., and Alpine fir plantations. The only access to the south lies through the great mountain passes and winding road which leads through Villach and Grazia. Hence since the only effective line of communication into this part of Austria lies through these towns and is best served by Trieste (rather than Venice) the problem of our occupation of an Austrian zone is intimately linked up with that of Venezia Giulia. Here again, the Yugoslavs (under Tito's orders) are a source of trouble and anxiety. They claim part, if not all, of the province of Carinthia. With the same idea as in Venezia Giulia – that possession is nine-tenths of the law – they have raced us into Austria. They actually reached Klagenfurt a few hours after us, so we could secure the best buildings and put sentries in them. We have, however, not enough men to occupy and guard every place. The Yugoslavs are bringing in considerable numbers – partly regulars and partly irregular forces – and repeating the Venezia Giulia tactics. We put up A.M.G. notices. They pull ours down and put up their own. They requisition and loot and arrest so-called Nazis and Fascists. We have to look on, more or less helplessly, since our present plan is *not* to use force and *not* to promote an incident.

Moreover, in addition to the Yugoslavs, to the order of 30,000 to 40,000, General Keightley has to deal with nearly 400,000 surrendered or surrendering Germans, not yet disarmed (except as to tanks and guns) who must be shepherded into some place or other, fed and given camps, etc. On his right flank Marshal Tolbukhin's armies have spread into what is supposed to be the British zone in Austria, including the important city and road centre of Graz. With the Russians are considerable Bulgar forces. Moreover, among the surrendered Germans are about 40,000 Cossacks and 'White' Russians, with their wives and children. To hand them over to the Russians is condemning them to slavery, torture and probably death. To refuse, is deeply to offend the Russians, and incidentally break the Yalta agreement. We have decided to hand them over (General Keightley is in touch and on good terms with the Russian general on his right), but I suggested that the Russians should at the same time give us any British prisoners or wounded who may be in his area. The formal procedure is that they should go back through Odessa (which I understand means great hardship). I hope we can persuade the local Russian to hand them over direct (we think he has 1,500–2,000) and save them all this suffering, in exchange for the scrupulous adherence to the agreement in handing back Russian subjects.

We have already found a good number (I think over 1,000) British prisoners (many of them sick and wounded) in the Klagenfurt area. I watched the ambulances bringing them in to the airfield. They are flown straight away in Dakotas to Naples or other hospitals or camps in southern Italy.

To add to the confusion, thousands of so-called Ustashi or Chetniks, mostly with wives and children, are fleeing in panic into this area in front of the advancing Yugoslavs. These expressions, Ustashi and Chetnik, cover anything from guerilla forces raised by the Germans from Slovenes and Croats and Serbs to fight Tito, and armed and maintained by the Germans – to people who, either because they are Roman Catholics or Conservative in politics, or for whatever cause are out of sympathy with revolutionary Communism and therefore labelled as Fascists or Nazis. (This is a very simple formula, which in a modified form is being tried, I observe, in English politics.)

We had a conference with the general and his officers covering much the same ground as those with Generals McCreery and Harding yesterday. He gave us his story and we gave him ours. I feel sure it was useful and helpful all round.

Left Klagenfurt about 12 noon; flew first to Eighth Army (at Treviso) where we were met by the commanding general, McCreery. A short chat; picked up some sandwiches, etc., and then Philip and I took off for Caserta. We arrived at Marcianise airfield about 3.30 p.m.

Drove to the office, where we found some interesting telegrams, particularly one from the President to the P.M. The Americans have suddenly hardened; the President will not be 'pushed about' any more. He proposes a stiff note to Tito, amounting almost, if not quite, to an ultimatum. This, of course, entirely alters the position from last Thursday (when General McNarney told us categorically that his orders were that American troops were not to be used in the Yugoslavian affair). I at once telegraphed to Churchill saying that the position seemed to me radically changed (I wonder for how long!) and that my telegrams of 11 May must be read in the light of the new American mood.

Drove up to F.M.'s Lodge at about 6.30 p.m., had a bath there and changed my clothes. A pleasant dinner; after dinner we listened to Churchill on radio. It was good, but I thought he seemed tired – as well he may be. Drove back to Naples, where I got to bed about 11 p.m.

Monday, 14 May 1945

The last two days were very tiring. So much flying, whizzing, motoring, jeeping and talking, combined with the great heat, are fatiguing. I stayed in bed or lounged in the garden all the day, with a little desultory reading and much dozing. It did me good.

Tuesday, 15 May 1945

Took the morning off, motoring up for luncheon at Caserta in the old villa (which the Russells still have). A lot of telegrams. The text of the Anglo-American notes to Tito (*a*) on Austria, (*b*) on Venezia Giulia, have been agreed. The former we presented first, and the Americans adhered to later. The latter is being jointly presented. There is nothing now to do but wait.

Wednesday, 16 May 1945

Rather a confusing day. Anthony Eden telegraphs from Washington the changing American moods. Apparently Alex's military appreciation, asking for considerable strength and emphasising the importance of consulting and studying the morale of our troops, has rather worried them. The F.M. had naturally to point out, that coming immediately after V.E.-Day and following months and years of praise of Tito by press and B.B.C., it was not just too easy to ask them suddenly to embark on operations on a considerable scale against Yugoslavia. Anthony also mentioned that Kirk and Offie had reported my views as hesitating. (What really happened was that Offie got hold of a memorandum which I prepared for one of the F.M.'s meetings giving four possible courses. This memorandum I used in preparing my long telegrams to London 853 and 854. Grew[11] must have picked out *one* of my alternatives and quoted it to Eden as my *recommendation*, which it was not. It was simply one of four courses, set out objectively. The Embassy at Washington, who had the telegram in full, ought to have been able to put this right.)

This change of American intention has naturally much upset Winston, who telegraphs sadly, if not indignantly, to Alexander.

So after discussion, the F.M. compiled a new signal to C.C.S. in which he sets out what he really meant by his reference to the morale of the troops. It is obvious that if you are going to ask them to do this new job *wholeheartedly*, you must tell them what it is all about. Your B.B.C. and press propaganda must be good. There must be no division at home (as over Greece) and there must be direct information from the Field Marshal through the chain of command. All this takes a little time. Moreover, during this time the troops in the area will get to know and dislike the Yugoslavs. They will see the so-called Yugoslav administration, thieving, raping and killing; and they will not like it.

I also sent telegrams to London and Washington explaining how my memorandum had been misunderstood and one passage quoted out of its context. I also made Offie telegraph to the State Department, setting the matter in the right perspective. Of course, all these are unrealities. If the Americans are undecided and get cold feet they will naturally try

[11] Joseph C. Grew (1880–1965) was U.S. Under-Secretary of State, 1944–5.

to cover themselves. And it is easier to put the blame on Alex or me than to shoulder it themselves. Meanwhile, the President says he cannot make war against the Yugoslavs unless they 'attack' our troops. But as they are in possession and keep moving in more forces, of course they will not 'attack' us. The point is that unless we can push them out by force, there is no way of ejecting them.

Most of the day was taken up with this going backwards and forwards from the Field Marshal's room to mine and composing telegrams on all these points.

As part of regular routine, I had a conference with General Robertson on various Italian questions, chiefly the industrial problems now that military programmes are not so important or can be reduced. Our Industrial Board Scheme is still undecided. The Italian Government is stalling, I think, and I fear also the Allied Commission.

Thursday, 17 May 1945

The usual full-dress political conference has been put off till tomorrow, in order to allow General Mark Clark, commanding Fifteenth Army Group, to attend. Hon. F. C. Sturrock, M.P. (Acting Minister of Defence, Union of S. Africa), and General Sir Pierre Van Ryneveld (Chief of General Staff, U.D.F. [Union Defence Forces]) called, introduced by my friend General Theron. It was only really a courtesy visit. They are doing a short tour of Italy, to see South African troops and installations. General Van Ryneveld reminded me of the day when I went back to England with F. M. Smuts at five minutes' notice, after luncheon in my villa at Algiers. This rapidity of decision seemed to have made a deep impression on him!

3.30 p.m. Left by car for Rome. Took the Daimler and got to Rome in three hours.

Gave a dinner in my villa. The guests were Sir Noel and Lady Charles, Major Stimson – the great woman surgeon – Admiral Stone, Harold Mack (awaiting to go to Austria and very jealous that I went there on Sunday!), Mr Taylor (U.S. head of Transport Subcommission, A.C.), Mr Stewart Brown (P.R.O., A.C., with whose help I liberated Modena), Sir Ronald Storrs,[12] who is lecturing in Italy, Major Quayle, Admiral Stone's Military Assistant, and my staff (twelve in all). It was a very successful party, though perhaps a long way for me to travel for the purpose. But I have been kept in Caserta a lot lately, and I was able to do some business both with Stone and with our Ambassador after dinner.

Friday, 18 May 1945

Left Rome by car at 6.30 a.m., arriving at my office in Caserta at 9.30 a.m. It was deliciously cool – the nicest time to travel. On arrival I

[12] Sir Ronald Storrs (1881–1955) was Military Governor of Jerusalem, 1917–20, Civil Governor of Jerusalem and Judaea, 1920–6, and lecturer for the Ministry of Information, 1940–5.

found a rather 'corrupt' telegram from Winston asking if I could come home 'for consultation'.

From the style I was not sure if it was meant for me or F.M. Alexander. I telegraphed for a clarification, adding that if P.M. wished me, I would leave the next day.

10.30 a.m. Political Meeting. Tito's reply has come – it is unsatisfactory. He merely repeats to the two Governments the counter-proposals which he made to General Morgan.

A long meeting, chiefly taken up with publicity, press and propaganda plans of all kinds for both the public at home and the troops on the spot.

A long day's work at the office, tidying up, etc., in case I go to England tomorrow. Alex walked round to my room about 6 p.m. and we discussed what I should say (or he, if he is to go) to the P.M. I think our ideas are becoming clarified.

Got down to Naples about 8.15 p.m. Gibson Graham (Mediterranean Shipping Board) to dinner, after a trip to Greece, France and England. He was in excellent form.

Saturday, 19 May 1945

I am to go to England today. Winston (in a characteristically courteous telegram) wants me to come, if the weather is good, and stay at Chequers. But to take no risks. I suppose the weather has been stormy at home. It seems hard to believe. We have had day after day of blue sky, cool nights, but very hot days – quite perfect.

I had already arranged for a plane to stand by (the B25 or Mitchell, with the excellent pilot Wright; which I used so often backwards and forwards to Greece at one time).

After a morning at Caserta, among some papers and an hour's talk with Alex on various last points, Robert Cecil and I took the air at twelve noon exactly.

Arrived Northolt about 5 p.m. and drove direct to Chequers. Winston appeared for dinner – Lord Cherwell[13] and Colville and I – a very small party. At dinner a lot of talk – chiefly on the political situation at home. The P.M. has written a letter to Attlee, suggesting that the Coalition should go on till *after* the Japanese war. If necessary, a referendum to take place on the question of continuing the life of Parliament. The letter was produced and read at dinner. One passage (about the carrying into effect of the various social reforms) was inserted at Attlee's suggestion. Bevin and Attlee think they will be able to 'get away' with this proposal at the Labour Party Conference. I do not believe it. The Labour Party are much more suspicious of Bevin than of Churchill.

After dinner, a short film, and then a lot of talk (till about 2 a.m.)

[13] F. A. Lindemann, 1st Viscount Cherwell (1886–1957), Churchill's scientific adviser and a member of the War Cabinet, was Paymaster-General, 1942–5 and 1951–3.

about Tito. I did my best to explain to P.M. the whole position, as we saw it at A.F.H.Q., and all the various problems which we had to face locally. He was very much encouraged by Truman's[14] forthright attitude. It takes rather a long time now to talk with P.M. He thinks and talks of so many things at once. But I find that if one ploughs steadily on, what one says sinks in. It is stored somewhere at the back of that immense head, and reproduced at the appropriate moment.

Sunday, 20 May 1945

A quiet morning. General and Lady Auchinleck to luncheon. He did not strike me as very intelligent. P.M. pulled his leg gently. The conversation was mostly reminiscences of India in Winston's youth. More talk of Tito after luncheon. I still think it will be settled with firmness and patience.

Motored to Birch Grove, arriving about tea-time. My Catherine, Carol, Sarah, my granddaughter – all at Pooks.

Monday, 21 May 1945

All day till about 5 p.m. at Pooks and Gosses – a very exciting day, my first introduction to Alexander and Joshua Macmillan. They seem splendid babies – I liked Alexander's quiet and happy temperament.

Mima and Billy Harlech came down for the day to see Katharine. It was very nice seeing them after so long. I left about five and went back to Chequers.

Dinner at Chequers – same party plus Randolph. It is really great fun finding oneself alone with Winston at this critical moment. The Labour concerns have forced Attlee's hand. P.M.'s proposal to continue the Coalition has been rejected. Of course they want an October election; but it is quite impossible to go on till then, with a Government in effect in dissolution. Winston was hurt at the unnecessarily waspish and even offensive tone of Attlee's reply. It arrived during dinner. Archie Sinclair made a characteristically weak reply. He could not deal with this over Whitsun because he must consult his Liberal friends.

Most of the evening was spent in drafts and redrafts for the P.M.'s reply to Attlee, at which we all tried our hand. Incidentally P.M. wants me to take the Air Ministry, with a seat in the Cabinet.

Tuesday, 22 May 1945

Saw Winston before leaving. He suggested Ministry of Labour, but I think I have been too much out of politics for this job. But I left it to him. He has been extraordinarily kind and considerate throughout.

Left Northolt with Robert Cecil, at 11 a.m. Arrived at Caserta about 4 p.m. – a very good and rapid flight.

[14] Harry S. Truman (1884–1972) had become U.S. President on Roosevelt's death.

Spent the evening with the Field Marshal, and slept at the Hunting Lodge.

Wednesday, 23 May 1945

A very heavy day, making all sorts of preparations for my return. I am to go back on Saturday, but as the appointments are not yet out, I can only take F.M. into my confidence. There is a lot to do; I must make dignified and appropriate farewells after nearly two-and-a-half years at A.F.H.Q.

A long meeting on Venezia Giulia in the afternoon, and appropriate telegrams to C.C.S. were drafted, in accord with the Americans.

My staff are playing up well, and are arranging various entertainments. I have really been most fortunate in having such good chaps.

Thursday, 24 May 1945

10.30 a.m. Political Meeting – mostly Venezia Giulia, and the French behaviour in the Val d'Aosta.[15]

1 p.m. Kirk gave a farewell luncheon to me at the American Camp. Offie really organised it. Everyone was there – F.M., C.-in-C. Med. and Air Marshal Garrod on the British side; General McNarney, Admiral Glassford, General Cannon on the American. That is, all the Commanders-in-Chief of the three services and their deputies. General Morgan, C. of S., and General Lemnitzer (Deputy C. of S.), Broad, Offie, etc. They drank my health (after a speech by Kirk) and I replied. My speech, which tried to be both light and serious in due proportions, seemed to please them.

5. 30 p.m. Cocktail party to all my staff, including cypherers, typists, clerks, etc., in our rooms in the palace. Sergeant-Major Brown proposed my health in a very good speech.

6–8 p.m. Cocktail party to all in A.F.H.Q., Navy, MEDBO, P.W.B., Consulate, Kirk's office, etc. About 250 came. The Field Marshal came early and stayed to the end, giving thereby great pleasure to all. I slept the night with the Russells at the Villa Vittoria in Caserta.

Friday, 25 May 1945

8 a.m. Left by air for Rome. After a bath, etc., at the villa, started on my last, and rather hectic day in Rome.

11 a.m. Audience with His Holiness. The same splendid ritual of a private audience. I had a long and rather moving talk with the Pope. He was very gracious and very grateful for all we had tried to do in Italy.

He is, of course, much concerned and saddened; the future seems dark. But one cannot help being impressed by his saintliness and goodness of heart. Poor, solitary figure!

[15] Under pressure from Truman, General de Gaulle eventually agreed to a phased withdrawal in June 1945.

1 p.m. Luncheon in my honour by Admiral Stone (Lush, Antolini, Grafftey-Smith and all the rest). More speeches.

3 p.m. Audience with Prince Umberto, to say goodbye. He was gracious and friendly. I think he has also developed during these months.

4.30 p.m. Called on Bonomi. A shrewd and I would say honest politician. He doubts whether he will survive the present crisis, but he does not despair. Undoubtedly, the Trieste affair is a setback to the Communists in Italy.[16]

6–8 p.m. Cocktail party to members of the Embassies, A.C., etc. (no Italians). D'Arcy Osborne, Charles, Kirk and Myron Taylor all came – a great success.

8.30 p.m. Dinner with Kirk.

9.30 p.m. Left by car for Naples.

Saturday, 26 May 1945

The Cabinet appointments are out, and I am to be Secretary of State for Air. How odd!

Left at 10 a.m. from Marcianise airfield, in the Field Marshal's Dakota. John Wyndham, Robert Cecil and Broad (who returns tomorrow). Miss Campbell is going to stay in Italy and take some leave. If the election goes right she will return to me.

A very good send-off – the Field Marshal and lots of officers, British and American, were at the airfield. It has been a great rush, but I think I have forgotten nobody. John and Robert have been excellent – tips to servants, photographs, etc. etc.

As we got in much last farewells and cap-waving. It is the end of a chapter – Mediterranean merry-go-round or from Darlan to Tito.

Arrived in England about 5 p.m.

[16] Togliatti had declared his support for Tito's claims in Venezia Giulia. This problem was not resolved until long after I had left Italy. The 1947 treaty gave most of the city of Gorizia to Italy and the bulk of Venezia Giulia to Yugoslavia. But in Trieste itself no border could be agreed, and it remained 'provisionally' divided until a final settlement was made in 1954.

Index